Merriam-Webster's
Vocabulary Builder

韦氏 英汉双解 扩词手册

〔美〕玛丽·伍德·科诺格（Mary Wood Cornog） 著

臧红宝 冯春波 崔建强 王芳 译

北京大学出版社
PEKING UNIVERSITY PRESS

著作权合同登记号　图字:01-2020-4595

图书在版编目(CIP)数据

韦氏英汉双解扩词手册 /（美）玛丽·伍德·科诺格著；臧红宝等译. —北京：北京大学出版社，2021.10
ISBN 978-7-301-32286-4

Ⅰ. ①韦… Ⅱ. ①玛… ②臧… Ⅲ. ①英语－词汇－手册 Ⅳ. ①H313-62

中国版本图书馆CIP数据核字(2021)第146630号

书　　　名：	韦氏英汉双解扩词手册
	WEI SHI YING-HAN SHUANGJIE KUOCI SHOUCE
著作责任者：	〔美〕玛丽·伍德·科诺格（Mary Wood Cornog）著　臧红宝　等译
组 稿 编 辑：	王林冲
责 任 编 辑：	刘文静
标 准 书 号：	ISBN 978-7-301-32286-4
出 版 发 行：	北京大学出版社
地　　　址：	北京市海淀区成府路205号 100871
网　　　址：	http://www.pup.cn　新浪微博:@北京大学出版社
电 子 信 箱：	liuwenjing008@163.com
电　　　话：	邮购部 010-62752015　发行部 010-62750672
	编辑部 010-62754382
印　　刷　者：	北京盛通印刷股份有限公司
经　　销　者：	新华书店
	710毫米×1000毫米　16开本　48.25印张　2529千字
	2021年10月第1版　2021年10月第1次印刷
定　　　价：	128.00元

未经许可，不得以任何方式复制或抄袭本书之部分或全部内容。
版权所有，侵权必究
举报电话: 010-62752024　电子信箱: fd@pup.pku.edu.cn
图书如有印装质量问题，请与出版部联系，电话 010-62756370

A GENUINE MERRIAM-WEBSTER
正宗梅里亚姆-韦伯斯特声明

The name Webster alone is no guarantee of excellence. It is used by a number of publishers and may serve mainly to mislead an unwary buyer.

Webster 这个标识本身并不能保证优秀。许多出版商使用这个标识,可能会误导未留心的读者购买。

Merriam-Webster™ is the name you should look for when you consider the purchase of dictionaries or other fine reference books. It carries the reputation of a company that has been publishing since 1831 and is your assurance of quality and authority.

Merriam-Webster™ 是你在考虑购买词典及其他优秀工具书时应该认准的标识。它承载着一个从 1831 年以来就从事出版的公司的声誉,也是质量和权威的保证。

INTRODUCTION
to the Second Edition
第二版序言

Merriam-Webster's Vocabulary Builder is designed to achieve two goals: (1) to add a large number of words to your permanent working vocabulary, and (2) to teach the most useful of the classical word-building roots to help you continue expanding your vocabulary in the future.

编纂《韦氏英汉双解扩词手册》(*Merriam-Webster's Vocabulary Builder*)的目标有二:其一,大量扩充读者的永久性工作词汇量;其二,传授最有用的经典构词词根,帮助读者今后持续扩充词汇量。

To achieve these goals, *Merriam-Webster's Vocabulary Builder* employs an original approach that takes into account how people learn and remember. Some vocabulary builders simply present their words in alphabetical order; some provide little or no discussion of the words and how to use them; and a few even fail to show the kinds of sentences in which the words usually appear. But memorizing a series of random and unrelated things can be difficult and time-consuming. The fact is that we tend to remember words easily and naturally when they appear in some meaningful context, when they've been shown to be useful and therefore worth remembering, and when they've been properly explained to us. Knowing precisely how to use a word is just as important as knowing what it means.

为达成上述目标,本书根据人类的学习与记忆规律,创新了编纂方法。同类书籍中,有的只是按照字母顺序列出单词,有的极少甚至没有诠释单词及其用法,还有个别甚至连常用的例句都没举出。然而,记忆毫无关联的、随机的东西难度大而且耗时长。事实上,单词应该被放在有意义的情景中,让其价值得到体现,从而值得去记,还要被诠释得当才好。只有这样,记单词才轻松自然。懂得如何正确使用单词和了解这个单词的意义同等重要。

Greek and Latin have been the sources of most of the words in the English language (the third principal source being the family of Germanic languages). All these words were added to the language long after the fall of the Roman empire, and more continue to be added to this day, with most new words—especially those in the sciences—still making use of Greek and Latin roots. A knowledge of Greek and Latin roots will not only help you remember the meanings of the words in this book but will help you guess at the meanings of new words that you run into elsewhere. Remember what a root means and you'll have at least a fighting chance of understanding a word in which it appears.

英语单词多源自希腊语和拉丁语(第三个主要来源是日耳曼语系)。这些单词都是在罗马帝国衰落很久以后才进入英语中的,至今还不断有新词进来,多数新单词——尤其是科技词语——仍使用希腊语和拉丁语词根。掌握希腊语和拉丁语词根既有助于记住本书中单词的词义,又有助于猜测在别处所见生词的词义。若能记住某个词根的含义,就有可能破解该词根所在单词的词义。

The roots in this book are only a fraction of those that exist, but they include almost all the roots that have produced the largest number of common English words. All these roots (sometimes called *stems*) formed parts of Greek and Latin words. Some are shown in more than one form (for example, CRAC/CRAT), which means that they changed form in the original language, just as *buy* and *bought* are forms of the same English word.

本书所列词根,为数虽然不多,但却将最能产生常用英语单词的词根几乎都收入囊中。这些词根(有时又称"词干")是希腊语和拉丁语单词的构件。有些词根的形式不止一个(比如 CRAC/CRAT),这意味着在源语中它们的形式就有所改变,这种情形在英语中也一样,比如 *buy* 和 *bought* 就是同一个单词的两种形式。

Each of the more than 250 roots in this book is followed by four words based on the root. Each group of eight words (two roots) is followed by two quizzes. Every fifth group of words is a special eight-word section which may contain words based on classical mythology or history, words borrowed directly from Greek or Latin, or other special categories of terms. Each set of 40 words makes up a unit. Thus, the 30 units in the book discuss in detail a total of 1,200 words. In addition, the brief paragraphs discussing each word include in italics many words closely related to the main words. So mastering a single word (for example, *compel*) can increase your vocabulary by several words (in this case, *compelling*, *compulsion*, and *compulsive*).

本书介绍了250余个词根,每个词根后面有4个基于该词根的单词。8个单词为一组(两个词根),每组后面有两个小测验。第5组是一个特殊八词组,这些单词可能来自古典神话或历史,可能直接从希腊语或拉丁语中借用,也可能是其他特殊类别词汇。40个单词为一个单元,全书30个单元,详细诠释了总计1,200个单词。此外,在用来阐释单词的小段落中,还有很多与这些主要单词密切相关的词语,用斜体标明。因此,掌握一个单词(比如 *compel*),就相当于在读者的词汇量中新增好几个单词(比如 *compelling*、*compulsion* 以及 *compulsive*)。

The words presented here aren't all on the same level of difficulty—some are quite simple and some are truly challenging—but the great majority are words that could be encountered on the SAT and similar standardized tests. Most of them are in the vocabularies of well-educated Americans, including professionals such as scientists, lawyers, professors, and doctors. Even the words you feel familiar with may only have a place in your recognition vocabulary—that is, the words you recognize when you see or hear them but don't actually use in your own speech and writing.

本书所列单词的难度级别并非整齐划一——有的相当简单,有的真的好难——但绝大多数都能在学术能力评估测试(SAT)以及类似的标准化考试中见到。书中这些单词大多出现在受过良好教育的美国人(包括科学家、律师、教授和医生等专业人士)的词汇表里。还有一些读者感觉上很熟悉的单词,也许只能算是读者的认知词汇——也就是说,能读懂、能听懂,但并未实际用来说和写。

第二版序言

Each main word is followed by its most common pronunciation. Any pronunciation symbols unfamiliar to you can be learned easily by referring to the Pronunciation Symbols table on page vii.

每个主要单词的后面先列出最常见的发音。如有不熟悉的音标符号,参考文前第 7 页的音标符号表就可以轻松学会。

The definition comes next. We've tried to provide only the most common senses or meanings of each word, in simple and straightforward language, and no more than two definitions of any word are given. (A more complete range of definitions can be found in a college dictionary such as *Merriam-Webster's Collegiate Dictionary*.)

然后列出该词的定义。本书只提供最常见的定义,用语简单、直接,每个词的定义不超过两个。(更全面的定义参见《韦氏大学词典》*Merriam-Webster's Collegiate Dictionary*。)

An example sentence marked with a bullet (•) follows the definition. This sentence by itself can indicate a great deal about the word, including the kind of sentence in which it often appears. It can also serve as a memory aid; when you meet the word in the future, you may recall the example sentence more easily than the definition.

定义之后是例句,用圆点(•)标明。例句本身所诠释的内容很丰富,其中包括该词经常出现在哪类句子中。此外,例句也可以用来辅助记忆,以后见到这个单词,回想例句比回想定义来得更要容易。

An explanatory paragraph rounds out each entry. The paragraph may do a number of things: It may tell you what else you need to know in order to use the word intelligently and correctly, when the definition and example sentence aren't enough. It may tell you more about the word's roots and its history. It may discuss additional meanings or provide additional example sentences. It may demonstrate the use of closely related words. And it may provide an informative or entertaining glimpse into a subject related to the word. The intention is to make you as comfortable as possible with each word in turn and to enable you to start using it immediately, without fear of embarrassment.

例句后面有一个小段落,用来进一步解释该词条。这个小段落可能会告诉读者,除了定义和例句之外,还需要了解别的什么知识才能用好、用对这个单词;也可能会告诉读者更多关于这个词的词根及其历史的信息;也可能阐释更多的词义,提供更多的例句;也可能解释与这个单词关系密切的词语的用法;还可能聊一聊与这个单词有关的某个话题,既增长见识,又愉悦身心。其目的是让读者树立对每个单词的信心,能够马上开始使用,无窘迫之虞。

The quizzes following each eight-word group, along with the review quizzes at the end of each unit, will test your memory. Many of them ask you to fill in a blank in a sentence. Others require you to identify *synonyms* (words with the same or very similar meaning) or *antonyms* (words with the opposite meaning). Perhaps most difficult are the *analogies*, which ask that you choose the word that will make the relationship between the last two words the same as the relationship between the first two. Thus, you may be asked to complete the analogy "calculate: count:: expend: ____" (which can be read as "*Calculate* is to *count* as *expend* is to ____") by choosing one of four words: *stretch*, *speculate*, *pay*, and *explode*. Since *calculate* and *count* are nearly synonyms, you will choose a near synonym for *expend*, so the correct answer is *pay*.

每组后面有两个小测验,每单元后另有复习题,用以检验读者的记忆能力。多数题是句子填空,也有同义词(意义相同或相似的词)、反义词(意义相反的词)辨析。最难的可能是类推题,要求读者选择一个词,使题目中前两词之间的关系与后两词之间的关系相同。比如,从 *stretch*、*speculate*、*pay* 和 *explode* 四个词中选一个,完成类推题"calculate : count :: expend : ____"(这个题可读作"calculate 之于 count 就像 expend 之于____")。因为 calculate 和 count 是同义词,所以正确答案是 *expend* 的同义词 *pay*。

Studies have shown that the only way a new word will remain alive in your vocabulary is if it's regularly reinforced through use and through reading. Learn the word here and look and listen for it elsewhere; you'll probably find yourself running into it frequently, just as when you've bought a new car you soon realize how many other people own the same model.

研究表明,想让新单词在读者的词汇表中活跃起来,唯一的方法是在使用和阅读中不断加以强化。在此处学会一个单词,到别处看一看、听一听,也许会发现自己能经常碰到这个词。这就好像是买了一辆新车,很快发现其他很多人也有同一款车。

Carry this book in your shoulder bag or leave it on your night table. Whenever you find yourself with a few minutes to spare, open it to the beginning of a brief root group. (There's no real need to read the units in any particular order, since each unit is entirely self-contained. However, studying the book straight through from the beginning will ensure that you make maximum use of it.) Pick a single word or a four-word group or an eight-word section; study it, test yourself, and then try making up new sentences for each word. Be sure to pronounce every new word aloud at least once, along with its definition.

把这本书放到背包里,或者放到床头柜上。什么时候有了几分钟闲暇,就打开它,翻到某组词的开头。(本书各单元完全独立,没有必要按某种顺序阅读。不过,直接从头开始,效益将会最大化。)读者可以挑一个单词,也可以挑一个四个单词的组或八个单词的组,学习,自测,尝试造句。一定要大声朗读每个单词,大声朗读单词的定义。

Start using the words immediately. As soon as you feel confident with a word, start trying to work it into your writing wherever appropriate—your papers and reports, your diary and your poetry. An old saying goes, "Use it three times and it's yours." That may be, but don't stop at three. Make the words part of your *working* vocabulary, the words that you can not only recognize when you see or hear them but that you can comfortably call on whenever you need them. Astonish your friends, amaze your relatives, astound *yourself* (while trying not to be too much of a show-off)—and have fun!

马上开始使用这些单词吧。一旦建立了对某个词的信心,就开始尝试把它用在写作中——论文、报告、日记、诗歌——哪儿合适就用在哪里。老话说得好:"使用三次,就是你的了。"这话也许对,但不能止于三次。一定要把它们变成自己工作词汇的一部分,不仅看得懂、听得懂,而且无论何时有需要,都能轻松回想起来。到时候,你会语惊四座的,亲戚、朋友,甚至自己都会大吃一惊(不要太炫耀啊)——偷着乐吧!

第二版序言

Acknowledgments：The first edition of this book, written by Mary Wood Cornog, also benefited from the contributions of numerous members of the Merriam-Webster staff, including Michael G. Belanger, Brett P. Palmer, Stephen J. Perrault, and Mark A. Stevens. This new edition was edited by Mark A. Stevens, with assistance from C. Roger Davis and with the support and encouragement of Merriam-Webster's president and publisher, John M. Morse.

致谢:感谢本书第一版的作者玛丽·伍德·科诺格,也感谢梅里亚姆-韦伯斯特公司的众多员工,包括迈克尔·G.贝朗格、布雷特·P.帕尔默、斯蒂芬·J.佩罗、马克·A.史蒂文斯等,感谢他们所做的贡献。感谢本书新版的编辑马克·A.史蒂文斯,也感谢C.罗杰·戴维斯的协助,还要感谢公司总裁兼发行人约翰·M.莫尔斯,感谢他给予的支持和鼓励。

PRONUNCIATION SYMBOLS
音标符号

ə—banana, collide, abut

ˈə, ˌə—humdrum, abut

ᵊ—immediately preceding \l\, \n\, \m\, \ŋ\, as in battle, mitten, eaten, and sometimes open \ˈō-pᵊm\, lock and key \-ᵊŋ-\

ər—further, merger, bird

a—mat, map, mad, gag, snap, patch

ā—day, fade, date, aorta, drape, cape

ä—bother, cot

är—car, heart, bazaar, bizarre

au̇—now, loud, out

b—baby, rib

ch—chin, nature \ˈnā-chər\

d—did, adder

e—bet, bed, peck

er—bare, fair, wear, millionaire

ē—easy, mealy

f—fifty, cuff

g—go, big, gift

h—hat, ahead

i—tip, banish, active

ir—near, deer, mere, pier

ī—site, side, buy, tripe

j—job, gem, edge, join, judge

k—kin, cook, ache

l—lily, pool

m—murmur, dim, nymph

n—no, own

ⁿ—indicates that a precceding vowel or diphthong is pronounced with the nasal passages open, as in French un bon vin blanc \oeⁿ-bōⁿ-vaⁿ-bläⁿ\

ŋ—sing \ˈsiŋ\, singer \ˈsiŋ-ər\, finger \ˈfiŋ-gər\, ink\ˈiŋk\

ō—bone, know, beau

ȯ—saw, all, gnaw, caught

ȯi—coin, destroy

ȯr—boar, port, door, shore

p—pepper, lip

r—red, rarity

s—source, less

sh—as in shy, mission, machine, special

t—tie, attack, late, later, latter

th—as in thin, ether

t̲h̲—then, either, this

ü—rule, youth, union \ˈyün-yən\, few \ˈfyü\

u̇—pull, wood, book

u̇r—boor, tour, insure

v—vivid, give

w—we away

y—yard, young, cue \ˈkyü\, mute \ˈmyüt\, union\ˈyün-yən

z—zone, raise

zh—as in vision, azure \ˈa-zhər\

\—backslash used in pairs to mark the beginning and end of a transcription: \ˈpen\

ˈ—mark precceding a syllable with primary (strongest) stress: \ˈpen-mən-ˌship\

ˌ—mark preceding a syllable with secondary (medium) stress: \ˈpen-mən-ˌship\

-—mark of syllable division

CONTENTS
目 录

UNIT 1 ··· 1

UNIT 2 ··· 24

UNIT 3 ··· 47

UNIT 4 ··· 73

UNIT 5 ··· 96

UNIT 6 ··· 120

UNIT 7 ··· 143

UNIT 8 ··· 168

UNIT 9 ··· 194

UNIT 10 ·· 217

UNIT 11 ·· 241

UNIT 12 ·· 264

UNIT 13 ·· 290

UNIT 14 ·· 314

UNIT 15	340
UNIT 16	366
UNIT 17	392
UNIT 18	416
UNIT 19	441
UNIT 20	466
UNIT 21	491
UNIT 22	517
UNIT 23	542
UNIT 24	566
UNIT 25	590
UNIT 26	616
UNIT 27	641
UNIT 28	667
UNIT 29	693
UNIT 30	719
ANSWERS	745
INDEX	752

UNIT 1

BENE is Latin for "well." A *benefit* is a good result or effect. Something *beneficial* produces good results or effects. The Latin root can be heard in other languages as well: "Good!" or "Fine!" in Spanish is "Bueno!"; in French, it's "Bon!"; and in Italian, just say "Bene!"

BENE 是拉丁语,表示"好的"。benefit(好处)是好的结果或效果。something beneficial(有益的事物)产生良好的结果或效果。这个拉丁语词根也可以在其他语言中听到:"好的!"在西班牙语中是"Bueno!",在法语中是"Bon!",在意大利语中就是"Bene!"。

benediction \ˌbe-nə-ˈdik-shən\ A prayer that asks for God's blessing, especially a prayer that concludes a worship service. 祝福,祈祷文

• The moment the bishop had finished his benediction, she squeezed quickly out of her row and darted out the cathedral's side entrance. 主教刚做完祝福,她就快速挤出人群,冲出教堂的侧门。

In *benediction*, the *bene* root is joined by another Latin root, *dictio*, "speaking" (see DICT, p.294), so the word's meaning becomes something like "well-wishing." Perhaps the best-known benediction is the so-called Aaronic Benediction from the Bible, which begins, "May the Lord bless you and keep you." An important section of the Catholic Mass was traditionally known as the *Benedictus*, after its first word (meaning "blessed"). It was St. Benedict who organized the first Christian monasteries; many Christians have been baptized Benedict in his honor, and 16 popes have taken it as their papal name.

在 benediction 一词中,词根 bene 与另一个拉丁词根 dictio("说")(参见 DICT,第 294 页)相结合,因此这个词的意思是"祝福"。最有名的祝福也许是《圣经》中所称的亚伦祝福,其开头为"愿主赐福与你,保佑你"。天主教弥撒有一个重要的部分,传统上称 Beneditus(颂歌),得名于它的第一个词(意思是"有福的")。组建第一批基督教修道院的人正是 St. Benedict(圣本笃,又译:圣本尼迪克特)。很多基督教徒被授以 Benedict 教名,以表敬意。共有 16 位教皇将它作为自己的教皇名。

BENE

benefactor \be-nə-ˌfak-tər\ Someone who helps another person or group, especially by giving money. 捐赠者，赞助者，施主

• An anonymous benefactor had given $15 million to establish an ecological institute at the university. 一位匿名捐赠者捐了 1500 万美元，在这所大学建造一个生态研究所。

A *benefactor* may be involved in almost any field. One may endow a scholarship fund; another may give money to expand a library; still another may leave a generous sum to a hospital in her will. The famous *benefactions* of John D. Rockefeller included the gifts that established the University of Chicago, the Rockefeller Foundation, and Rockefeller University. Many benefactors have reported that giving away their money turned out to be the most rewarding thing they ever did.

benefactor(捐赠者)涉及几乎所有领域。有人赠予奖学金，有人捐钱扩建图书馆，还有人立遗嘱给医院留下一大笔钱。约翰·D.洛克菲勒的著名 benefaction 有价值(的捐赠)包括建立芝加哥大学、洛克菲勒基金会和洛克菲勒大学。许多捐赠者表示，捐钱是他们所做过的最有价值的事情。

beneficiary \ˌbe-nə-ˈfi-shē-ˌer-ē\ A person or organization that benefits or is expected to benefit from something, especially one that receives money or property when someone dies. 受益者，受益机构

• Living in a trailer in near-poverty, she received word in the mail that her father had died, naming her as the sole beneficiary of his life-insurance policy. 她住在一辆拖车里，生活几近贫困。她在邮件中得知父亲去世了，指定她为人寿保险单的唯一受益人。

Beneficiary is often used in connection with life insurance, but it shows up in many other contexts as well. A college may be the beneficiary of a private donation. Your uncle's will may make a church his sole beneficiary, in which case all his money and property will go to it when he dies. A "third-party beneficiary" of a contract is a person (often a child) who the people signing the contract (which is usually an insurance policy or an employee-benefit plan) want to benefit from it. In a more general way, a small business may be a beneficiary of changes to the tax code, or a restaurant may be the beneficiary when the one across the street closes down and its whole lunch crowd starts coming in.

beneficiary 常与人寿保险一起使用，但也出现在很多其他的语境中。大学可以是私人捐赠的受益机构。你叔叔的遗嘱可能把教堂作为唯一的受益机构，在这种情况下，他死后所有的钱财都将归教堂所有。合同的 third-party beneficiary("第三方受益人")是签署合同(通常是保险单或员工福利计划)的两方希望从中受益的人(通常是儿童)。广义而言，小企业可能是税法改革的受益者；当一家餐馆关张后，它原有的午餐客群就会涌入街对面的另一家餐馆，那家餐馆就成为受益者。

benevolence \bə-ˈnev-ləns\ Kindness, generosity. 善心，仁慈

• In those financially desperate years, the young couple was saved only by the benevolence of her elderly great-uncle. 在经济极端困难的那些年，这对年轻人仅靠她年迈的叔祖父的好心救助才得以度日。

Part of *benevolence* comes from the Latin root meaning "wish." The novels of

UNIT 1

Charles Dickens often include a *benevolent* figure who rescues the main characters at some point—Mr. Brownlow in *Oliver Twist*, Abel Magwitch in *David Copperfield*, Mr. Jarndyce in *Bleak House*, Ebenezer Scrooge in *A Christmas Carol*. To be benevolent, it helps to have money, but it's not necessary; kind assistance of a non financial sort may turn out to be lifesaving benevolence as well.

benevolence 的一部分源自意思是"愿望"的拉丁语词根。查尔斯·狄更斯的小说中经常有这样的 *benevolent* figure（好心人），会在某个时刻搭救小说的主人公——比如，《雾都孤儿》中的布朗洛先生、《大卫·科波菲尔》中的亚伯·马格韦契、《荒凉山庄》中的亚恩代斯先生、《圣诞颂歌》中的埃比尼泽·斯克鲁奇。想成为好心人，有钱财会有所裨益，但钱财也不一定是必需的。钱财之外的帮助有时候也可能成为救命的善举。

AM

AM comes from the Latin *amare*, "to love." The Roman god of love was known by two different names, *Cupid* and *Amor*. *Amiable* means "friendly or good-natured," and *amigo* is Spanish for "friend."

AM 源自拉丁语 *amare*（"爱"）。罗马爱神有两个名字，*Cupid*（丘比特）和 *Amor*（埃莫）。*amiable* 意为"友好的或和善的"。*amigo* 是西班牙语，意思是"朋友"。

amicable \ˈa-mi-kə-bəl\ Friendly, peaceful. 友好的，和平的

• Their relations with their in-laws were generally amicable, despite some bickering during the holidays. 尽管在假期有些口角，但他们与亲家的关系总体上还是很友好的。

Amicable often describes relations between two groups, or especially two nations—for example, the United States and Canada, which are proud of sharing the longest unguarded border in the world. So we often speak of an amicable meeting or an amicable settlement. When *amicable* describes more personal relations, it may indicate a rather formal friendliness. But it's always nice when two friends who've been quarreling manage to have an amicable conversation and to say amicable good-byes at the end.

amicable 通常用来描述两个群体之间，特别是两个国家之间的关系——比如美国和加拿大的关系。两国为拥有世界上最长的、不设防的边境而自豪。所以，我们经常说到一个友好的会议或是一个友好的解决方案。当 *amicable* 用于形容更私人的关系时，它可能表示一种更加形式化的友善。但是，当两个争吵不休的朋友进行一次和平谈话，并在最后友好地了断，这样总归是好的。

enamored \i-ˈna-mərd\ Charmed or fascinated; inflamed with love. 迷恋的，喜爱的

• Rebecca quickly became enamored of the town's rustic surroundings, its slow pace, and its eccentric characters. 瑞贝卡很快就迷恋上了这个小镇的乡村环境，迷上了它慢节奏的生活及其不寻常的个性。

Computer hackers are always *enamored* of their new programs and games. Millions of readers have found themselves enamored with Jane Austen's novels. And Romeo and Juliet were, of course, utterly enamored of each other. But we also often use the word in negative contexts: A friend at work may complain that she's not enamored of the new boss, and when you start talking about how you're not enamored with the neighbors it may be time to move. (Note that both *of* and *with* are commonly used after *enamored*.)

电脑黑客总是迷恋他们的新程序和游戏。数以百万计的读者为简·奥斯汀的小说着迷。当然,罗密欧和朱丽叶完全被对方迷住了。但是,我们也经常把这个词语用在负面的语境中:一个工作上的朋友可能会抱怨她不喜欢新来的老板;当你开始谈论你有多不喜欢邻居时,可能是时候搬家了。(注意:enamored 后面常跟 *of* 和 *with* 。)

amorous\ˈa-mə-rəs\ Having or showing strong feelings of attraction or love. 含情的,示爱的

● It turned out that the amorous Congressman had gotten his girlfriend a good job and was paying for her apartment. 原来,这位多情的国会议员给女友找了份好工作,还为其公寓付钱。

A couple smooching on a park bench could be called amorous, or a young married couple who are always hugging and kissing. But the word is often used a bit sarcastically, as when a tabloid newspaper gets hold of some scandalous photos and calls the participants "the amorous pair." In such cases, we may be encouraged to think the attraction is more physical than emotional.

公园长椅上卿卿我我的情侣也可以被称为 amorous,年轻夫妇经常拥抱亲吻也可以被称为 amorous。但这个词语常带一点儿讽刺的意味,比如某家小报搞到几张丑闻照片,称丑闻主角为"多情的一对"。在这样的情形下,报纸可能想促使我们产生的想法是,他们之间的吸引肉欲多于情感。

paramour\ˈper-ə-ˌmu̇r\ A lover, often secret, not allowed by law or custom. 情人

● He had been coming to the house for two years before her brothers realized that he was actually the paramour of their shy and withdrawn sister. 那个男人常来他们家有两年时间了,她的兄弟们这才意识到,他竟然就是他们害羞而内向的妹妹的情人。

paramour came to English from French (a language based on Latin), though the modern French don't use the word. Since *par amour* meant "through love," it implies a relationship based solely on love, often physical love, rather than on social custom or ceremony. So today it tends to refer to the lover of a married man or woman, but may be used for any lover who isn't obeying the social rules.

paramour 是由法语(一种基于拉丁语的语言)传入英语的,但现代法语不再使用这个词。*par amour* 的意思是"通过爱情",所以该词意味着一种并非基于社会习俗或仪式的关系,而是完全基于爱的关系,这种爱往往是肉体之爱。所以,这个词语今天往往指已婚男女的情人,但也可以用来指不遵守社会规则的情人。

Quizzes

A. Choose the closest synonym:

1. beneficiary   a. benefit   b. prayer   c. recipient   d. contributor
2. amorous   a. friendly   b. sympathetic c. loving   d. kind
3. benediction   a. blessing   b. gift   c. saint   d. favor
4. amicable   a. difficult   b. friendly   c. curious   d. lazy

5. enamored   a. strengthened b. engaged   c. fond   d. free
6. benefactor a. supporter   b. priest   c. donation d. kindness
7. paramour   a. lover   b. husband   c. heaven   d. affection
8. benevolence a. value   b. kindness c. luck   d. approval

B. Complete the analogy:

1. charming : enchanting :: amorous : _____
   a. sublime   b. pleasant   c. likeable   d. passionate
2. greeting : farewell :: benediction : _____
   a. motto   b. speech   c. curse   d. saying
3. lender : borrower :: benefactor : _____
   a. giver   b. beneficiary   c. participant   d. partner
4. gentle : tender :: enamored : _____
   a. lively   b. charmed   c. cozy   d. enraged
5. liking : appreciation :: benevolence : _____
   a. opinion   b. sentimentality c. interest   d. generosity
6. frozen : boiling :: amicable : _____
   a. calm   b. comfortable   c. shy   d. unfriendly
7. patient : doctor :: beneficiary : _____
   a. tycoon   b. investor   c. lover   d. benefactor
8. friend : companion :: paramour : _____
   a. lover   b. theater   c. mother   d. wife

BELL comes from the Latin word meaning "war." *Bellona* was the little-known Roman goddess of war; her husband, Mars, was the god of war.

BELL 源自拉丁语中意思是"战争"的单词。Bellona（贝罗娜）是鲜为人知的罗马战争女神，她的丈夫 Mars（马尔斯）是战争之神。

---

antebellum \ˌan-ti-ˈbe-ləm\ Existing before a war, especially before the American Civil War (1861—1865). 战前的（尤指美国南北战争之前的）

● When World War I was over, the French nobility found it impossible to return to their extravagant antebellum way of life. 第一次世界大战结束后,法国贵族发现他们不可能再回到战前奢靡的生活方式了。

Even countries that win a war often end up worse off than they had been before, and the losers almost always do. So *antebellum* often summons up images of ease, elegance, and entertainment that disappeared in the postwar years. In the American South, the antebellum way of life depended on a social structure, based on slavery, that collapsed after the Civil War; Margaret Mitchell's *Gone with the Wind* shows the nostalgia and bitterness felt by wealthy Southerners after the war more than the relief and anticipation experienced by those released from slavery. In Europe, World War I shattered the grand life of the upper classes, even in victorious France and Britain, and changed society hugely in the space of just four years.

即使是赢得战争的国家,其结果也往往比以前更糟,战败国更是几乎没有例外。因此,*antebellum* 常常让人想起安逸、优雅、欢愉的生活画面,这些在战后岁月中都消失了。在美国南部,战前的生活方式依赖于以奴隶制为基础的社会结构,而这在内战后崩塌了。玛格丽特·米切尔的小说《飘》更多地展现了战后南方富人的怀旧和痛苦,而不是从奴隶制解放出来的人们所感受到的解脱和憧憬。在欧洲,第一次世界大战粉碎了上层阶级的奢华生活,即便是获胜的法国和英国也未能幸免。短短四年,社会巨变。

bellicose \ˈbe-li-ˌkōs\ Warlike, aggressive, quarrelsome. 好战的,好斗的,好争吵的

• The more bellicose party always got elected whenever there was tension along the border and the public believed that military action would lead to security. 每当边境出现紧张局势时,更加好战的政党总能赢得选举,因为公众认为军事行动会带来安定。

Since *bellicose* describes an attitude that hopes for actual war, the word is generally applied to nations and their leaders. In the 20th century, it was commonly used to describe such figures as Germany's Kaiser Wilhelm, Italy's Benito Mussolini, and Japan's General Tojo, leaders who believed their countries had everything to gain by starting wars. The international relations of a nation with a bellicose foreign policy tend to be stormy and difficult, and *bellicosity* usually makes the rest of the world very uneasy.

因为 *bellicose* 指的是一种希望发生真正战争的态度,所以这个词通常适用于某些国家及其领导人。在 20 世纪,这个词常用来形容德皇威廉二世、意大利的贝尼托·墨索里尼和日本的东条英机等人物。这些领导人相信,他们的国家可以通过发动战争获得一切。一个奉行好战外交政策的国家,其国际关系往往是冲突不断、困难重重的。*bellicosity*(好战)通常会使世界上其他国家感到不安。

belligerence \bə-ˈli-jə-rəns\ Aggressiveness, combativeness. 好斗,好战

• The belligerence in Turner's voice told them that the warning was a serious threat. 特纳好战的声音告诉他们,这次警告是一个严重的威胁。

Unlike *bellicose* and *bellicosity*, the word *belligerence* can be used at every level from the personal to the global. The belligerence of Marlon Brando's performances as the violent Stanley Kowalski in *A Streetcar Named Desire* electrified the country in the 1940s and 1950s. At the same time, *belligerent* speeches by leaders of the Soviet Union and the United States throughout the Cold War were keeping the world on edge. *Belligerent* is even a noun; the terrible war in the Congo in recent years, for example, has involved seven nations as belligerents.

与 *bellicose* 和 *bellicosity* 不同,*belligerence* 可以用在从个人到全球的各个层面。马龙·白兰度在《欲望号街车》中饰演狂暴的斯坦利·科瓦尔斯基,他的好斗精神在 20 世纪四五十年代风靡全美国。冷战时期,美苏两国领导人发表的 *belligerent* speeches(战意盎然的演说)让整个世界都紧张不安。*belligerent* 还用作名词。比如,近年来在刚果发生的可怕战争将七个国家卷进来成为交战国。

rebellion \ri-ˈbel-yən\ Open defiance and opposition, sometimes armed,

UNIT 1

to a person or thing in authority. 公开反抗、公开反对

• A student rebellion that afternoon in Room 13 resulted in the new substitute teacher racing out of the building in tears. 那天下午，13号教室里的学生公开反抗，导致新来的代课老师哭着冲出房子。

Plenty of teenagers *rebel* against their parents in all kinds of ways. But a rebellion usually involves a group. *Armed rebellions* are usually put down by a country's armed forces, or at least kept from expanding beyond a small area. The American War of Independence was first viewed by the British as a minor rebellion that would soon run its course, but this particular rebellion led to a full-fledged revolution—that is, the overthrow of a government. Rebellion, armed or otherwise, has often alerted those in power that those they control are very unhappy.

许多青少年以各种各样的方式 *rebel*（反抗）他们的父母。但 *rebellion* 通常涉及一个群体。armed rebellions（武装叛乱）通常会被国家武力量镇压，或至少被阻止扩大到一个小的地区之外。刚开始的时候，美国独立战争被英国人看做一场很快就会结束的小规模叛乱，但这场特殊的叛乱却带来了一场全面的革命——即推翻了一个政府。无论武装与否，反抗常常会提醒当权者，被他们所控制的那些人非常不开心。

PAC

PAC is related to the Latin words for "agree" and "peace." The *Pacific Ocean*—that is, the "Peaceful Ocean"—was named by Ferdinand Magellan because it seemed so calm after he had sailed through the storms near Cape Horn. (Magellan obviously had never witnessed a Pacific typhoon.)

PAC 与拉丁语中表示"同意"和"平静"的单词有关。*Pacific Ocean*（太平洋）——即"平静的海洋"——是费迪南德·麦哲伦命名的，因为在航海穿过好望角附近的暴风雨后，他看到的这个海洋似乎非常平静。（麦哲伦显然从未见过太平洋的台风。）

pacify\ˈpa-sə-ˌfī\ (1) To soothe anger or agitation. 使平静，安抚（2）To subdue by armed action. 平定，平息

• It took the police hours to pacify the angry demonstrators. 警察花了好几个小时才安抚了愤怒的示威者。

Someone stirred up by a strong emotion can usually be pacified by some kind words and the removal of its causes. Unhappy babies are often given a *rubber pacifier for* sucking to make them stop crying. During the Vietnam War, *pacification* of an area meant using armed force to drive out the enemy, which might be followed by bringing the local people over to our side by building schools and providing social services. But an army can often bring "peace" by pure force, without soothing anyone's emotions.

施以温言善语并消除引发情绪的原因，通常可以安抚情绪激动的人。婴儿不开心时，给个 rubber *pacifier*（橡皮奶嘴）来吮吸，他们就不哭了。在越南战争期间，一个地区的 *pacification*（平定）意味着先用武力驱逐敌人，再修建学校和提供社会服务，以此把当地人拉拢过来。但是军队常常纯用武力带来"和平"，而不安抚任何人的情绪。

pacifist\ˈpa-sə-fist\ A person opposed to war or violence, especially

· 7 ·

someone who refuses to bear arms or to fight, on moral or religious grounds. 和平主义者，反战主义者

• Her grandfather had fought in the Marines in World War II, but in his later years he had become almost a pacifist, opposing every war for one reason or another. 第二次世界大战中，她的祖父曾在海军陆战队服役，但他在晚年却几乎成了和平主义者，以种种原因反对每一场战争。

The Quakers and the Jehovah's Witnesses are *pacifist religious groups*, and Henry David Thoreau and Martin Luther King are probably the most famous American *pacifists*. Like these groups and individuals, pacifists haven't always met with sympathy or understanding. Refusing to fight ever, for any reason, calls for strong faith in one's own moral or religious convictions, since *pacifism* during war time has often gotten people persecuted and even thrown in prison. 贵格会和耶和华见证会都是 *pacifist* religious groups（和平主义宗教团体），亨利•戴维•梭罗和和马丁•路德•金都是美国著名的 pacifist（和平主义者）。与这些团体和个人一样，和平主义者并不总能得到同情和理解。由于战争期间的 *pacifism*（和平主义）经常致使人们受到迫害，甚至被关进监狱，因此，无论出于何种理由拒绝战争，都需要有坚定的道德或宗教信仰。

pact\\'pakt\\ An agreement between two or more people or groups; a treaty or formal agreement between nations to deal with a problem or to resolve a dispute. 协议，条约，公约

• The girls made a pact never to reveal what had happened on that terrifying night in the abandoned house. 这些女孩们约定，永远不透露那个可怕的夜晚在那所废弃的房子里所发生的事情。

Pact has "peace" at its root because a pact often ends a period of unfriendly relations. The word is generally used in the field of international relations, where diplomats may speak of an "arms pact," a "trade pact," or a "fishing-rights pact." But it may also be used for any solemn agreement or promise between two people; after all, whenever two parties shake hands on a deal, they're not about to go to war with each other. *pact* 的词根含有"和平"的意思，因为签订一个条约常常会终结一段不友好的关系。这个词语通常用在国际关系领域，外交官们可能会谈到"武器协定""贸易协定"或"捕鱼权协定"等。但它也可以用于两个人之间的庄严的协议或承诺。毕竟，不管什么时候，只要双方握手达成协议，他们都不会准备互相开战了。

pace\\'pā-sē\\ Contrary to the opinion of. 与……的意见相反

• She had only three husbands, pace some Hollywood historians who claim she had as many as six. 与某些研究好莱坞历史的学者的说法相反，她没有六任丈夫，只有三任。

This word looks like another that is much more familiar, but notice how it's pronounced. It is used only by intellectuals, and often printed in italics so that the reader doesn't mistake it for the other word. Writers use it when correcting an opinion that many people believe; for example, "The costs of the program, *pace* some commentators, will not be significant." So what does *pace* have to do with peace? Because it says, "Peace to them (that is, to the people I'm mentioning)—I don't want to start an argument; I just want to correct the facts."

这个词语看起来与另一个非常熟悉的词很像，但请注意其发音。它仅供知识分子使用，且常以斜体印刷，这样读者就不会把它和另一个词混为一谈了。作家们会用它来纠正很多人认同的观点，比如："与一些评论者的观点相反，该项目的成本并不高。"那么，*pace* 与和平有什么关系呢？这是因为它的意思是："给他们和平（此处的'他们'指的是我现在所说的人）——我不想挑起争论，我只想纠正事实。"

Quizzes

A. Match the word on the left to the correct definition on the right:

1. antebellum   a. quarrelsome
2. pace   b. solemn agreement
3. rebellion   c. to make peaceful
4. pacify   d. before the war
5. pacifist   e. aggressiveness
6. belligerence   f. opposition to authority
7. pact   g. contrary to the opinion of
8. bellicose   h. one who opposes war

B. Fill in each blank with the correct letter:

a. antebellum   e. rebellion
b. pacifist   f. bellicose
c. pact   g. pacify
d. pace   h. belligerence

1. The native _____ began at midnight, when a gang of youths massacred the Newton family and set the house afire.

2. The grand _____ mansion has hardly been altered since it was built in 1841.

3. The Senate Republicans, outraged by their treatment, were in a _____ mood.

4. _____ some of the younger scholars, no good evidence has been found that Japan was involved in the incident.

5. The cease-fire _____ that had been reached with such effort was shattered by the news of the slaughter.

6. Their relations during the divorce proceedings had been mostly friendly, so his _____ in the judge's chambers surprised her.

7. The world watched in amazement as the gentle _____ Gandhi won India its independence with almost no bloodshed.

8. Her soft lullabies could always _____ the unhappy infant.

CRIM comes from the Latin words for "fault or crime" or "accusation." It's obvious where the root shows up most commonly in English. A *crime* is an act forbidden by the government, which the government itself will punish you for, and for which you may be branded a *criminal*. A crime is usually more serious than a *tort* (see TORT, p. 526), a "civil wrong" for which the wronged person must himself sue if he wants to get repaid in some way.

CRIM 源自拉丁语中表示"过失、犯罪"或"指控"的单词。这个词根经常出现在哪些英语单词中是显而易见的。crime(犯罪)是政府禁止的行为,政府会为此惩罚你,你可能因此被贴上 criminal(罪犯)的标签。犯罪通常比 tort(侵权行为)更严重(见 TORT,第 526 页),后者是一种"民事过错"。如果受害者想以某种方式得到偿还,他必须自己起诉。

criminology \ˌkri-mə-ˈnä-lə-jē\ The study of crime, criminals, law enforcement, and punishment. 犯罪学

• His growing interest in criminology led him to become a probation officer. 他对犯罪学越来越感兴趣,最后成了缓刑监督官。

Criminology includes the study of all aspects of crime and law enforcement—criminal psychology, the social setting of crime, prohibition and prevention, investigation and detection, capture and punishment. Thus, many of the people involved—legislators, social workers, probation officers, judges, etc.—could possibly be considered *criminologists*, though the word usually refers only to scholars and researchers.

犯罪学研究的是关于犯罪和执法的所有方面——犯罪心理学、犯罪的社会背景、禁止和预防、调查和侦察、逮捕和惩罚等。因此,它所涉及的很多人——诸如立法者、社会工作者、缓刑监督官、法官等——都可以看作是 criminologists(犯罪学家),但这个词通常所指的只是学者和研究人员。

decriminalize \dē-ˈkri-mə-nə-ˌlīz\ To remove or reduce the criminal status of. 使……合法化,使……非刑事化

• An angry debate over decriminalizing doctor-assisted suicide raged all day in the statehouse. 在州议会大厦里,关于是否将医生协助下的自杀行为非刑事化的争论进行了一整天。

Decriminalization of various "victimless crimes"—crimes that don't directly harm others, such as private gambling and drug-taking—has been recommended by conservatives as well as liberals, who often claim that it would ease the burden on the legal system, decrease the amount of money flowing to criminals, and increase persona liberty. Decriminalization is not the same as legalization; decriminalization may still call for a small fine (like a traffic ticket), and may apply only to use or possession of something, leaving the actual sale of goods or services illegal.

"无受害者犯罪"是指那些不直接伤害他人的犯罪,如私人赌博和吸毒等。将各种"无受害者犯罪"decriminalization(非刑事化)的建议是由保守派和自由派所提出来的,他们经常声称此举将减轻法律体系的负担,减少花在罪犯身上的钱,而且会增加个人自由。decriminalization(非刑事化)与 legalization(合法化)不同,前者可能仍然需要交小额罚款(如交通罚单),可能仅适用于使用或拥有某物,而这些东西的实际销售或服务仍是非法的。

UNIT 1

incriminate \ in-ˈkri-mə-ˌnāt \   To show evidence of involvement in a crime or a fault. 证明有罪

• The muddy tracks leading to and from the cookie jar wereenough to incriminate them. 往返于饼干罐的泥泞足迹足以证明他们有罪。

Testimony may incriminate a suspect by placing him at the scene of a crime, and *incriminating* evidence is the kind that strongly links him to it. But the word doesn't always refer to an actual crime. We can say, for instance, that a virus has been incriminated as the cause of a type of cancer, or that video games have been incriminated in the decline in study skills among young people.

证明犯罪嫌疑人在犯罪现场的证词可以将犯罪嫌疑人定罪。*incriminating* evidence(罪证)指的是将犯罪嫌疑人与犯罪强烈地联系在一起的证据。但这个词语并不总是指实际的犯罪。比如,我们可以说,某种病毒已被证明是某种癌症的元凶,或者电子游戏导致年轻人学习技能下降。

recrimination \ rē-ˌkri-mə-ˈnā-shən \   (1) An accusation in answer to an accusation made against oneself. 反诉,反责 (2) The making of such an accusation. 提出反诉

• Their failure to find help led to endless and pointless recriminations over responsibility for the accident. 他们未能找到助力,导致了对该事故责任的无休止、无意义的相互指责。

Defending oneself from a verbal attack by means of a counterattack is as natural as physical self-defense. So a disaster often brings recriminations among those connected with it, and divorces and child-custody battles usually involve recriminations between husband and wife. An actual crime isn't generally involved, but it may be; when two suspects start exchanging angry recriminations after they've been picked up, it often leads to one of them turning against the other in court.

通过反击来保护自己免受言语攻击,与身体上的自卫一样自然。因此,灾难往往会引发相关人士的互相指责,而离婚及子女监护权之争通常也会引发夫妻之间的互相指责。反诉一般不牵涉真实的犯罪,但也有这个可能。当两名被逮捕的嫌疑人开始愤怒地相互指责时,会导致其中一人在法庭上揭露对方。

PROB comes from the Latin words for "prove or proof" and "honesty or integrity." A *probe*, whether it's a little object for testing electrical circuits or a spacecraft headed for Mars, is basically something that's looking for evidence or proof. And *probable* originally described something that wasn't certain but might be "provable."

PROB 源自拉丁语中表示"证明或证据"和"诚实或正直"的单词。无论是用来测试电路的小工具,还是飞往火星的宇宙飞船,probe(探测器)基本上都是用来寻找证据的东西。probable(可能的)最初用来指某些不确定但"可以查明"的事情。

approbation \ ˌa-prə-ˈbā-shən \   A formal or official act of approving; praise, usually given with pleasure or enthusiasm. 批准,核准;赞美,认可

• The senate signaled its approbation of the new plan by voting for it unanimously. 参议院一致投票表示赞同这项新计划。

Approbation is a noun form of *approve*, but approbation is usually stronger than mere *approval*. An official commendation for bravery is an example of approbation; getting reelected to office by a wide margin indicates public approbation; and the social approbation received by a star quarterback in high school usually makes all the pain worthwhile.

approbation 是 *approve* 的一种名词形式,但它通常比 *approval*(赞成、赞许)含义更为强烈。官方对勇敢行为的表彰就是一种认可。以明显优势再次当选表明公众的认可。一位高中的明星四分卫获得社会认可,他为此经历的所有的苦痛就都值了。

probate \ˈprō-ˌbāt\ The process of proving in court that the will of someone who has died is valid, and of administering the estate of a dead person. 遗嘱检验、遗嘱认证

- When her father died, she thought she would be able to avoid probate, but she wasn't that lucky. 她的父亲去世时,她认为可以规避遗嘱认证,但却没有那么幸运。

Ever since people have written wills, those wills have had to be proven genuine by a judge. Without a probate process, greedy acquaintances or relatives could write up a fake will stating that all the person's wealth belonged to them. To establish a will as genuine, it must generally be witnessed and stamped by someone officially licensed to do so (though wills have sometimes been approved even when they were just written on a piece of scrap paper, with no witnesses). Today we use *probate* more broadly to mean everything that's handled in *probate court*, a special court that oversees the handling of estates (the money and property left when someone dies), making sure that everyone eventually receives what is properly theirs.

人们写下遗嘱后,还需要由法官证明其真实性。若没有遗嘱认证的程序,贪婪的熟人或亲戚可能会写一份假遗嘱,声称死去之人的财产都属于他们。要证明遗嘱的真实性,通常必须由官方授权的人见证并盖章。(但是,有时候写在纸片上且没有见证人的遗嘱也会得到认证。)我们现在更多地使用 *probate* 来指 *probate court*(遗嘱认证法庭)处理的所有事情。遗嘱认证法庭负责监督遗产(某人死后留下的钱财)的处理,保证人人都能最终得到应得的部分。

probity \ˈprō-bə-tē\ Absolute honesty and uprightness. 正直、诚实

- Her unquestioned probity helped win her the respect of her fellow judges. 她无可置疑的正直品行赢得了法官同事们的尊重。

Probity is a quality the public generally hopes for in its elected officials but doesn't always get. Bankers, for example, have traditionally been careful to project an air of probity, even though banking scandals and bailouts have made this harder than ever. An aura of probity surrounds such public figures as Warren Buffett and Bill Moyers, men to whom many Americans would entrust their children and their finances.

正直是公众对所选官员必备品质的普遍期望,但并非总是能够得到。以银行家为例,他们传统上都很小心翼翼,摆出一派正直的样子,但银行业丑闻和紧急融资使这样的做派比以往更难。沃伦·巴菲特和比尔·莫耶斯等公众人物身上环绕着正直诚实的光环,许多美国人会把子女和金钱委托给他们。

UNIT 1

reprobate\\ˈre-prə-ˌbāt\\   A person of thoroughly bad character. 恶棍,堕落者

- His wife finally left him, claiming he was a reprobate who would disappear for weeks at a time, gambling and drinking away all his money. 他的妻子最终离开了他,声称他是个恶棍,会一连消失数周,赌博喝酒花光所有的钱。

The related verb of *reprobate* is *reprove*, which originally, as the opposite of approve, meant "to condemn." Thus, a reprobate, as the word was used in Biblical translations, was someone condemned to hell. But for many years *reprobate* has been said in a tone of joshing affection, usually to describe someone of doubtful morals but good humor. Shakespeare's great character Falstaff—a lazy, lying, boastful, sponging drunkard—is the model of a reprobate, but still everyone's favorite Shakespeare character.

与 *reprobate* 相关的动词是 *reprove*,它是 *approve* 的反义词,最初的意思是"谴责"。因此,正如《圣经》译本所使用的那样,堕落者是要遭谴责下地狱的。但是近些年来 *reprobate* 开始带有戏谑、喜爱的意味儿,常用来形容德行存疑但品性幽默之人。莎士比亚笔下的伟大角色福斯塔夫——懒散、撒谎、爱吹牛、好酒贪杯——就是一个无赖的典范,但仍然是人们最喜爱的莎士比亚塑造的角色。

Quizzes

A. Indicate whether the following pairs of words have the same or different meanings:

1. decriminalize / tolerate   same / different
2. probity / fraud   same / different
3. criminology / murder   same / different
4. incriminate / acquit   same / different
5. probate / trial   same / different
6. recrimination / faultfinding   same / different
7. reprobate / scoundrel   same / different
8. approbation / criticism   same / different

B. Match the definition on the left to the correct word on the right:

1. utter honesty   a. approbation
2. approval   b. reprobate
3. rascal   c. recrimination
4. legal process for wills   d. criminology
5. study of illegal behavior   e. probity
6. accuse   f. probate
7. reduce penalty for   g. decriminalize
8. counterattack   h. incriminate

GRAV comes from the Latin word meaning "heavy, weighty, serious." *Gravity* is, of course, what makes things heavy, and without it there wouldn't be any life on earth, since nothing would stay on earth at all. This doesn't stop us from yelling in outrage when the familiar laws of gravity cause something to drop to the floor and break.

GRAV 源自拉丁语中意思是"重的、有重量的、严肃的"的单词。当然,gravity(重力)使物体变重。如果没有重力,地球上就不会有生命,因为没有东西还能在地球上停留。当某物掉落并摔碎时,尽管知道这是我们熟悉的万有引力定律在起作用,但我们还是会禁不住愤怒地大声喊叫。

grave\\'grāv\\   (1) Requiring serious thought or concern. 严重的,严峻的 (2) Serious and formal in appearance or manner. 严肃的,庄重的

• We realized that the situation was grave and that the slightest incident could spark all-out war. 我们意识到形势很严峻,稍有风吹草动就可能引发战争的全面爆发。

Gravity has a familiar physical meaning but also a nonphysical meaning—basically "seriousness." Thus, something *grave* possesses gravity. You can refer to the gravity of a person's manner, though public figures today seem to have a lot less gravity than they used to have. Or you can talk about a grave situation, as in the example sentence. But even though Shakespeare makes a pun on *grave* when a dying character talks about being buried the next day("Ask for me tomorrow and you shall find me a grave man"), the word meaning "hole for burying a body" isn't actually related.

gravity 既有为人熟知的物理意义,但也有非物理意义——基本含义是"严肃性"。因此,something *grave*(严肃的事情)是有分量的。你可以说一个人举止庄重,但现在的公众人物似乎没有以前那么庄重了。你也可以说局势很严峻,正如例句所示。尽管莎士比亚在描绘一个将死之人谈及第二天即将被埋葬的时候用了 grave 的双关语("要是你明天找我,你就会发现我是一个 grave man"),但这个词"坟墓"的含义与词根 GRAV 却没有什么实际上的关系。(译者注:句中 grave 有两义:"坟墓"和"严肃的"。)

gravitas\\'gra-və-ˌtäs\\   Great or very dignified seriousness. 威严,庄重

• The head of the committee never failed to carry herself with the gravitas she felt was appropriate to her office. 这个委员会的主任总是以她认为适合自己职务的庄重态度出现。

This word comes to us straight from Latin. Among the Romans, *gravitas* was thought to be essential to the character and functions of any adult (male) in authority. Even the head of a household or a low-level official would strive for this important quality. We use *gravitas* today to identify the same solemn dignity in men and women, but it seems to come easier in those who are over 60, slow-moving—and a bit overweight.

这个词语直接源自拉丁语。罗马人认为,任何掌权的成年(男)人的性格和角色都必须是庄重的。即使是一家之主或低级官员也会为拥有这一重要品质而努力。如今,我们用 gravitas 形容举止同样庄重的男女,但对于那些 60 岁以上、行动迟缓、还有点胖的人而言,庄重似乎来得要容易一些。

UNIT 1

gravitate \ˈgra-və-ˌtāt\ To move or be drawn toward something, especially by natural tendency or as if by an invisible force. 移向,被吸引到

- On hot evenings, the town's social life gravitated toward the lakefront, where you could stroll the long piers eating ice cream or dance at the old Casino. 炎热的夜晚,小镇的社交生活挪到了湖滨。在那里,你可以边吃冰淇淋边在长长的码头上漫步,也可以在老赌场里跳舞。

To gravitate is to respond, almost unconsciously, to a force that works like *gravity* to draw things steadily to it as if by their own weight. Thus, young people gravitate toward a role model, moths gravitate to a flame, a conversation might gravitate toward politics, and everyone at a party often gravitates to the bar. 被吸引是几乎不自觉地对某种力做出反应,这种力的运作就像是 *gravity*(重力),稳稳地把东西吸引过来,就好像这些东西是被自身重量吸引过来一样。因此,年轻人会靠近行为榜样,飞蛾会扑向火焰,谈话的焦点可能会朝向政治,而聚会上的所有人都聚集于吧台周围。

aggravate \ˈa-grə-ˌvāt\ (1) To make (an injury, problem, etc.) more serious or severe. 使(伤势、问题等)恶化或加重 (2) To annoy or bother. 使恼火或讨厌

- She went back to the soccer team before the knee was completely healed, which naturally aggravated the injury. 她膝伤没有痊愈就回到了足球队,这自然加重了伤势。

Since the *grav-* root means basically "weighty or serious," the original meaning of *aggravate* was "to make more serious." A bad relationship with your parents can be aggravated by marrying someone who nobody likes, for example, or a touchy trade relationship between two countries can be aggravated by their inability to agree on climate-change issues. Depression can be aggravated by insomnia—and insomnia can be aggravated by depression. But when most people use *aggravate* today, they employ its "annoy" sense, as in "What really aggravates my dad is having to listen to that TV all day long." 因为词根 *grav* 的基本意思是"沉重的、严重的",所以 *aggravate* 最初的意思是"使更严重"。比如,和一个大家都不喜欢的人结婚,可能会加剧你和父母之间的不良关系;两国在气候变化问题上无法达成一致,可能会恶化两国间敏感的贸易关系;失眠会加重抑郁,而抑郁又会加重失眠。但是,今天大多数人用 *aggravate* 的时候,用的是其"惹恼"的意思。比如,"让我爸爸真正恼火的是,他必须整天听那电视"。

LEV comes from the Latin adjective *levis*, meaning "light," and the verb *levare*, meaning "to raise or lighten." So a *lever* is a bar used to lift something, by means of *leverage*. And *levitation* is the magician's trick in which a body seems to rise into the air by itself. LEV 源自拉丁语形容词 *levis*,意为"轻的"和动词 *levare*,意为"提升或减轻"。因此,*lever*(杠杆)是一根杆,通过 *leverage*(杠杆作用)举起某物。*levitation*(悬浮)是魔术师的手法,使得身体似乎自己升到了空中。

---

alleviate \ə-ˈlē-vē-ˌāt\ To lighten, lessen, or relieve, especially physical or mental suffering. 减轻,缓解,缓和(尤其是肉体或精神上的痛苦)

- Cold compresses alleviated the pain of the physical injury, but only time could alleviate the effect of the insult. 冷敷能减轻身体损伤带来的疼痛,但只有时间才能减轻侮辱带来的影响。

Physical pain or emotional anguish, or a water shortage or traffic congestion, can all be *alleviated* by providing the appropriate remedy. But some pain or anguish or shortage or congestion will remain: *to alleviate* is not to cure. 身体上的痛苦、精神上的剧痛、水资源匮乏或交通堵塞,所有这些都可以通过适当的补救措施来缓解。但还会残存一些痛苦、剧痛、匮乏或堵塞:缓解并不等于消除。

elevation \ˌe-lə-ˈvā-shən\ (1) The height of a place. 高度.海拔 (2) The act or result of lifting or raising someone or something. 提高.提升

- Her doctor is concerned about the elevation of her blood pressure since her last visit. 自上次她来问诊以来,医生就一直担心她的血压升高问题。

When you're hiking, you may be interested in knowing the highest *elevation* you'll be reaching. Psychologists use the term "mood elevation" to mean improvement in a patient's depression, and some leg ailments require elevation of the limb, usually so that it's higher than the heart for part of each day. *Elevation* can also mean "promotion"; thus, a vice president may be *elevated* to president, or a captain may be elevated to admiral. 远足时,你可能会有兴趣了解你将到达的最高海拔。心理学家使用"情绪提升"这个词来表示患者抑郁症状的改善,而某些腿部疾病需要把腿抬高,通常每天高到心脏以上一段时间。elevation 也有"升职"的意思,比如,副主管可以被 *elevated*(晋升)为主管,海军上校可以晋升为将官。

cantilever \ˈkan-tə-ˌlē-vər\ A long piece of wood, metal, etc., that sticks out from a wall to support something above it. 悬臂

- The house's deck, supported by cantilevers, jutted out dramatically over the rocky slope, and looking over the edge made him dizzy. 这座房子的露台由悬臂支撑,突兀地悬挑在岩石斜坡的上方,从露台边上往下看让他头晕目眩。

Cantilevers hold up a surface or room without themselves being supported at their outer end. Many outdoor balconies are *cantilevered*, and theater balconies may be as well. A cantilevered bridge may have a huge span (as long as 1,800 feet) built out on either side of a single large foundation pier. Architects sometimes use cantilevered construction to produce dramatic effects; Frank Lloyd Wright's "Fallingwater" house, which extends out over a rocky river, is a famous example. But the Grand Canyon's "Skywalk" has become perhaps the best-known piece of cantilevered construction in America. 悬臂用于支撑平台或房间,而悬臂本身的外端却不受支撑。许多露天阳台是 *cantilevered*(悬臂支撑的),剧场的阳台也是这样。悬臂桥跨度可以很大(甚至长达 1800 英尺),从一个大型基础墩起向两侧伸展。建筑师有时会使用悬臂式建筑来营造戏剧效果;弗兰克·劳埃德·赖特的"落水山庄"(又译:流水别墅)就是一个著名的例子。但是,美国最著名的悬臂建筑或许还是科罗拉多大峡谷的"人行天桥"。

levity \ˈle-və-tē\ Lack of appropriate seriousness. 轻率.轻浮

• The Puritan elders tried to ban levity of all sorts from the community's meetings, but found it increasingly difficult to control the younger generation. 年长的清教徒试图禁止各种轻浮的言行出现在社区会议上,但却发现年轻一代越来越难以控制。

Levity originally was thought to be a physical force exactly like gravity but pulling in the opposite direction, like the helium in a balloon. As recently as the 19th century, scientists were still arguing about its existence. Today *levity* refers only to lightness in manner. To stern believers of some religious faiths, levity is often regarded as almost sinful. But the word, like its synonym *frivolity*, now has an old-fashioned ring to it and is usually used only half-seriously.

levity 最初被认为是一种和重力完全一样的物理力,只是方向相反,就像气球中的氦气一样。一直到 19 世纪,科学家们还在争论它是否存在。*levity* 现在只用来形容举止的轻浮。在某些严肃的宗教信徒眼里,轻浮近乎罪恶。但就像它的同义词 *frivolity* 一样,这个词如今有点儿过时的味道了,通常只是被半开玩笑半认真地使用。

Quizzes

A. Fill in each blank with the correct letter:

a. grave   e. alleviate
b. gravitate   f. cantilever
c. gravitas   g. levity
d. aggravate   h. elevation

1. Even the smallest motion would _____ the pain in his shoulder.
2. She hesitated to step onto the balcony, which was supported by a single _____.
3. At their father's funeral they showed the same solemn _____ at which they had often laughed during his lifetime.
4. To relieve the swelling, the doctor recommended _____ of her legs several times a day.
5. Attracted magically by the music, all animals and natural objects would _____ toward the sound of Orpheus's lyre.
6. With the two armies moving toward the border, they knew the situation was _____.
7. The neighboring nations organized an airlift of supplies to _____ the suffering caused by the drought.
8. The board meeting ended in an unusual mood of _____ when a man in a gorilla suit burst in.

B. Match the word on the left to the correct definition on the right:

1. levity   a. solemn dignity
2. gravitas   b. relieve
3. grave   c. raising
4. alleviate   d. support beam

5. elevation
6. aggravate
7. cantilever
8. gravitate

e. move toward as if drawn
f. lack of seriousness
g. serious
h. worsen

Words from Mythology and History 源自神话和历史的词语

cicerone \ˌsi-sə-ˈrō-nē\ A guide, especially one who takes tourists to museums, monuments, or architectural sites and explains what is being seen. 导游，讲解员

• On Crete they sought out a highly recommended cicerone, hoping to receive the best possible introduction to the noteworthy historical sites. 在克里特岛上，他们找了一位别人极力推荐的讲解员，希望能听到著名历史遗迹的最佳介绍。

The Roman statesman and orator Cicero was renowned for his elegant style and great knowledge (and occasional long-windedness). So 18th-century Italians seem to have given the name *cicerone* to the guides who would show well-educated foreigners around the great cultural sites of the ancient Roman empire—guides who sought to be as eloquent and informed as Cicero in explaining the world in which he lived.

罗马政治家、演说家西塞罗以其优雅的风格和渊博的知识而闻名（偶尔也会长篇大论）。因此，18世纪时，意大利人好像已用cicerone来命名那些为受过良好教育的外国人介绍古罗马帝国文化遗迹的导游——他们在解释自己生活的世界时，力求像西塞罗一样口若悬河、学识渊博。

hector \ˈhek-tər\ To bully or harass by bluster or personal pressure. 欺凌，骚扰

• He would swagger around the apartment entrance with his friends and hector the terrified inhabitants going in and out. 他和朋友们会在公寓入口处耀武扬威，骚扰那些惊恐万分的进出公寓的居民。

In Homer's great *Iliad*, Hector was the leader of the Trojan forces, and the very model of nobility and honor. In the Greek war against Troy, he killed several great warriors before being slain by Achilles. His name began to take on its current meaning only after gangs of bullying young rowdies, many of them armed soldiers recently released from service following the end of the English Civil War, began terrorizing the residents of late-17th-century London. The gangs took such names as the Roysters, the Blades, the Bucks, and the Bloods, but the best-known of them was called the Hectors. The names Blades and Hectors may have seemed appropriate because, like Hector and Achilles, they often fought with swords.

在荷马的伟大史诗《伊利亚特》中，赫克托耳是特洛伊军队的领袖，也是高贵与荣誉的典范。在希腊与特洛伊的战争中，他杀死了多位伟大的勇士，最后被阿喀琉斯杀死。17世纪末，英国内战之后，许多恃强凌弱的、粗暴的青年团伙开始恐吓伦敦居民，赫克托耳这个名字就有了现在的含义。这些青年人多半是刚刚退役的武装士兵。他们结成的团伙给自己取名为"罗伊斯特""刀锋""雄鹿""血"等等，其中最有名的就叫"赫克托耳"。"刀锋"和"赫克托耳"这两个名字似乎很合适，因为就像赫克托耳和阿喀琉斯一样，他们也经常用刀剑作战。

UNIT 1

hedonism \ˈhē-də-ˌni-zəm\ An attitude or way of life based on the idea that pleasure or happiness should be the chief goal. 享乐主义.享乐主义的行为

• In her new spirit of hedonism, she went out for a massage, picked up champagne and chocolate truffles, and made a date that evening with an old boyfriend. 她秉持新的享乐主义精神,出去做按摩,买了香槟,吃了巧克力松露,当晚还和前男友约会。

Derived from the Greek word for "pleasure," hedonism over the ages has provided the basis for several philosophies. The ancient Epicureans and the 19th-century Utilitarians both taught and pursued *hedonistic* principles. But although we generally use the word today when talking about immediate pleasures for the senses, philosophers who talk about hedonism are usually talking about quiet pleasures that aren't pursued in a selfish way.

享乐主义源于希腊语中表示"快乐"的单词,它也是几种哲学思想的基础。古代的伊壁鸠鲁主义者和19世纪的功利主义者都教导并且追求*hedonistic*(享乐主义的)原则。但是,尽管我们现在一般用这个词表达感官上的即时快乐,但哲学家们论及快乐主义时,通常指的是不以自私手段所得到的宁静的快乐。

nestor \ˈnes-ˌtȯr\ A senior figure or leader in one's field. 长者.耆宿

• The guest of honor was a nestor among journalists, and after dinner he shared some of his wisdom with the audience. 这位贵宾是资深新闻记者。晚餐过后,他与观众们分享了他的一些智慧。

Nestor was another character from the *Iliad*, the eldest of the Greek leaders in the Trojan War. A great warrior as a young man, he was now noted for his wisdom and his talkativeness, both of which increased as he aged. These days, a nestor is not necessarily long-winded, but merely wise and generous with his advice.

内斯特是《伊利亚特》中的另一个人物,也是特洛伊战争中最年长的一位希腊首领。内斯特在年轻时是个伟大的战士,后来以智慧和健谈而闻名,其智慧和健谈与日俱增。如今,长者并不一定非要长篇大论,只要给出明智而慷慨的建议即可。

spartan \ˈspär-tən\ Marked by simplicity, avoidance of luxury, and often strict self-discipline or self-denial. 简朴的.节约的.自律的.克己的

• When he was single, he had lived a spartan life in a tiny, undecorated apartment with one chair, a table, and a bed. 他单身时过着简朴的生活,住在一个没有装修过的小公寓里,只有一椅、一桌、一床。

In ancient times, the Greek city-state of Sparta had a reputation for the severe and highly disciplined way of life it enforced among its citizens, so as to keep them ready for war at any time. Physical training was required for both men and women. A boy would begin his military training at 7 and would live in army barracks for much of his life, even after he was married. Today, when a cargo ship or a remote beach resort offers "spartan accommodations," some tourists jump at the chance for a refreshing change from the luxuries they've been used to—and no one worries that they'll be forced out of bed at dawn to participate in war games.

古时候,希腊城邦斯巴达以严格而高度自律的生活而闻名,这种生活被强加给它的公民,旨在让他们时刻为战争作

好准备。无论男女,都需要进行体能训练。男孩 7 岁开始军事训练,即使在婚后,大部分时间也住在军营里。如今,当一艘货船或一个偏远的海滩度假胜地提供"斯巴达式食宿"时,有些游客就会抓住机会,让他们业已习惯的奢侈生活来一个令人耳目一新的变化——但不会有人担心会在黎明时分被迫起床,参加战争游戏。

stentorian \sten-ˈtȯr-ē-ən\ Extremely loud, often with especially deep richness of sound. 洪亮的

- Even without a microphone, his stentorian voice was clearly audible in the last rows of the auditorium. 即使没有麦克风,他洪亮的声音在礼堂的后几排也能听得清清楚楚。

Stentor, like Hector, was a warrior in the *Iliad*, but on the Greek side. His unusually powerful voice (Homer calls him "brazenvoiced"—that is, with a voice like a brass instrument) made him the natural choice for delivering announcements and proclamations to the assembled Greek army, in an era when there was no way of artificially increasing the volume of a voice.
斯坦特和赫克托耳一样,也是《伊利亚特》中的战士,但属于希腊一方。他拥有非比寻常的洪亮嗓音(荷马称之为"铜管嗓音"——即跟铜管乐器发出的声音一样),于是他自然就被选为传信者,向集合起来的希腊军队发布公告和宣言。在那个时代可是没有办法人为扩音的。

stoic \ˈstō-ik\ Seemingly indifferent to pleasure or pain. 坚忍的,不以苦乐为意的

- She bore the pain of her broken leg with such stoic patience that most of us had no idea she was suffering. 她以坚忍的毅力承受了断腿之痛,以至于多数人都没有注意到她的煎熬。

The *Stoics* were members of a philosophical movement that first appeared in ancient Greece and lasted well into the Roman era. *Stoicism* taught that humans should seek to free themselves from joy, grief, and passions of all kinds in order to attain wisdom; its teachings thus have much in common with Buddhism. The great Stoics include the statesman Cicero, the playwright Seneca, and the emperor Marcus Aurelius, whose *Meditations* is the most famous book of Stoic philosophy. Today we admire the kind of stoicism that enables some people (who may never have even heard of Marcus Aurelius) to endure both mental and physical pain without complaint.
Stoics(斯多葛学派学者)指的是源于古希腊、延续至罗马时代的一场哲学运动的成员。Stoicism(斯多葛主义)教导人们:为了获得智慧,应该寻求摆脱快乐、悲伤以及各种激情。它的教义也因此与佛教有很多共同之处。斯多葛学派的伟大成员包括政治家西塞罗、剧作家塞内加和皇帝马库斯·奥雷利乌斯,其中马库斯·奥雷利乌斯的《沉思录》是斯多葛哲学最著名的著作。如今,我们钦佩某些人(这些人可能连马库斯·奥雷利乌斯都没有听说过)所拥有的斯多葛派精神,他们忍受着精神和肉体的痛苦,却毫无怨言。

sybaritic \ˌsi-bə-ˈri-tik\ Marked by a luxurious or sensual way of life. 奢靡享乐的,骄奢淫逸的

- When I knew them they were living a sybaritic existence—hopping from resort to resort, each more splendid than the last—but a year later the money ran out. 我认识他们的时候,他们过着奢靡享乐的生活——从一个度假胜地玩到另一个度假胜地,一个比一个豪华。但一年之后,钱花光了。

The ancient city of Sybaris (near modern Terranova di Sibari), founded by the

Greeks on the toe of Italy's "boot," was famous for the wealth and luxury of its citizens in the 6th century B. C. But the *Sybarites'* wealth made them overconfident, and when they went to war with a nearby city, they were defeated by a much smaller army. After the victory, their enemies diverted the course of the river running through Sybaris so that it destroyed the whole city forever.

古城锡巴里斯(靠近现在的泰拉诺瓦达西巴里)由希腊人所建,在"靴"形意大利的足尖位置。在公元前6世纪,它以其公民的富足和奢侈而闻名。但 *Sybarites'* wealth(锡巴里斯居民的富足)使他们过于自信。在与邻城的战争中,他们被规模小很多的敌军打败了。敌人取胜之后,将流经锡巴利斯的河流改道,永远毁掉了整座城市。

Quiz

Choose the closest definition:

1. hedonism
   a. preference for males
   b. habit of gift-giving
   c. tendency to conceal feelings
   d. love of pleasure
2. hector   a. encourage   b. harass   c. deceive
   d. swear
3. cicerone   a. guide   b. cartoon character
   c. orator   d. lawyer
4. spartan   a. cheap   b. Greek   c. severe
   d. luxurious
5. nestor   a. journalist   b. long-winded elder
   c. domestic hen d. judge
6. stoic   a. pleasure-seeking b. bullying   c. repressed
   d. unaffected by pain
7. sybaritic   a. pleasure-seeking b. free of luxury c. sisterly
   d. ice-cold
8. stentorian   a. obnoxious   b. muffled   c. loud
   d. dictated

Review Quizzes

A. Fill in each blank with the correct letter:

a. bellicose   h. benevolence
b. stentorian   i. incriminate
c. pace   j. gravitate
d. sybaritic   k. hector
e. grave   l. enamored
f. alleviate   m. stoic

g. belligerence   n. pacify

1. Her grandfather had a _____ manner, moved slowly, and never laughed.

2. The mood at the resort was _____, and the drinking and dancing continued long into the night.

3. To rattle the other team, they usually _____ them constantly.

4. The judge was known for issuing all his rulings in a _____ voice.

5. He wouldn't even have a place to live if it weren't for the _____ of his wealthy godfather.

6. Thoroughly _____ of the splendid Victorian house, they began to plan their move.

7. She attempted to _____ his anxiety by convincing him he wasn't to blame.

8. Whenever she entered a bar alone, the lonely men would always _____ toward her.

9. Their refusal to cease work on nuclear weapons was seen as a _____ act by the neighboring countries.

10. _____ my many critics, I have never had reason to change my views on the subject.

11. Unable to calm the growing crowd, he finally ordered the police to _____ the area by force.

12. Whenever her boyfriend saw anyone looking at her, his _____ was alarming.

13. He bore all his financial losses with the same _____ calm.

14. Who would have guessed that it would take the killer's own daughter to _____ him.

B. Choose the closest definition:

1. hedonism   a. fear of heights   b. hatred of crowds
   c. liking for children   d. love of pleasure

2. levity   a. lightness   b. policy   c. leverage
   d. literacy

3. aggravate   a. lessen   b. decorate   c. intensify
   d. lighten

4. reprobate   a. researcher   b. commissioner
   c. scoundrel   d. reformer

5. bellicose   a. fun-loving   b. warlike   c. impatient
   d. jolly

6. decriminalize   a. discriminate   b. legalize   c. legislate
   d. decree

7. antebellum   a. preventive   b. unlikely   c. impossible

UNIT 1

    d. prewar

8. benediction   a. slogan   b. prayer   c. greeting
    d. expression
9. pact   a. bundle   b. form   c. agreement
    d. presentation
10. amicable   a. technical   b. sensitive   c. friendly
    d. scenic
11. criminology   a. crime history   b. crime book   c. crime study
    d. crime story
12. approbation   a. approval   b. resolution   c. reputation
    d. substitution

C. Match the definition on the left to the correct word on the right:

1. secret lover   a. elevation
2. estate process   b. gravitas
3. accusation   c. probate
4. integrity   d. probity
5. gift receiver   e. recrimination
6. giver   f. paramour
7. peace lover   g. benefactor
8. promotion   h. beneficiary
9. dignity   i. rebellion
10. revolt   j. pacifist

UNIT 2

MANIA

MANIA in Latin means "madness," and the meaning passed over into English unchanged. Our word *mania* can mean a mental illness, or at least an excessive enthusiasm. We might call someone a *maniac* who was wild, violent, and mentally ill—or maybe just really enthusiastic about something. Too much caffeine might make you a bit *manic*. But the intense mood swings once known as *manic-depressive illness* are now usually called *bipolar disorder* instead.

MANIA 在拉丁语中的意思是"疯狂",这个含义原封不动地传入英语。英语单词 *mania*(躁狂症)可以指一种精神疾病,或者至少是热情过度。我们会称某人为 *maniac*(疯子),这样的人狂野、暴力、有精神疾病,又或许只是对某事很热情。过量的咖啡因可能会让你有点 *manic*(躁狂的)。剧烈的情绪波动在以前被称为 *manic-depressive illness*(躁狂抑郁症),现在常被称为 *bipolar disorder*(双相情感障碍)。

kleptomania \ˌklep-tə-ˈmā-nē-ə\   A mental illness in which a person has a strong desire to steal things. 偷窃狂;盗窃癖

• Kleptomania leads its sufferers to steal items of little value that they don't need anyway. 盗窃癖会迫使患者窃取自己根本不需要的、无价值的东西。

Klepto- comes from the Greek word *kleptein*, "to steal." Even though kleptomania is often the butt of jokes, it's actually a serious mental illness, often associated with mood disorders, anxiety disorders, eating disorders, and substance abuse. Kleptomaniacs tend to be depressed, and many live lives of secret shame because they're afraid to seek treatment.

Klepto- 源自希腊语 *kleptein*(偷窃)。尽管盗窃症常常成为笑柄,但它实际上是一种严重的精神疾病,常与情绪障碍、焦虑症、饮食失调和物品的滥用联系起来。盗窃症患者往往会情绪低落,许多人因为害怕寻求治疗而生活在不为人知的羞耻当中。

dipsomaniac \ˌdip-sə-ˈmā-nē-ˌak\   A person with an extreme and uncontrollable desire for alcohol. 酗酒症患者

• She didn't like the word *alcoholic* being applied to her, and liked *dipsomaniac* even less. 她不喜欢别人用 *alcoholic*(酗酒者)这个词来形容她,更不喜欢别人叫她 *dipsomaniac*(酗酒症患者)。

Dipsomaniac comes from the Greek noun *dipsa*, "thirst," but thirst usually has nothing to do with it. Some experts distinguish between an alcoholic and a dipsomaniac, reserving *dipsomaniac* for someone involved in frequent episodes of binge drinking and blackouts. In any case, there are plenty of less respectful words for a person of similar habits: *sot*, *lush*, *wino*, *souse*, *boozer*, *guzzler*, *tippler*, *tosspot*, *drunkard*, *boozehound*—the list goes on and on and on. *dipsomaniac* 源自希腊语名词 *dipsa*("渴"),但通常与之无关。一些专家将酗酒者和酗酒症患者区分开来,将 *dipsomaniac* 留给经常狂饮乃至喝断片的人。无论如何,有大量不太礼貌的词语来形容有类似习惯的人:*sot*,*lush*,*wino*,*souse*,*boozer*,*guzzler*,*tippler*,*tosspot*,*drunkard*,*boozehound*——不胜枚举啊。

MANIA

megalomaniac \ˌme-gə-lō-ˈmā-nē-ˌak\ A mental disorder marked by feelings of great personal power and importance. 自大狂

• When the governor started calling for arming his National Guard with nuclear weapons, the voters finally realized they had elected a megalomaniac. 州长开始叫嚣用核武器武装其国民警卫队时,选民们终于意识到他们选出来的是一个自大狂。

Since the Greek root *megalo-* means "large," someone who is *megalomaniacal* has a mental disorder marked by feelings of personal grandeur. *Megalomania* has probably afflicted many rulers through out history: The Roman emperor Caligula insisted that he be wor shipped as a living god. J.-B. Bokassa, dictator of a small and extremely poor African nation, proclaimed himself emperor of the country he renamed the Central African Empire. And even democratically elected leaders have often acquired huge egos as a result of public acclaim. But *megalomaniac* is generally thrown around as an insult and rarely refers to real mental illness. 希腊语词根 *megalo-* 的意思是"大的",因此 *megalomaniacal*(狂妄自大的)人患有一种精神障碍,其特征是感觉自己了不起。历史上,*megalomania*(夸大狂)可能折磨了许多统治者:罗马皇帝卡里古拉坚持认为自己是一尊活着的神,应该受到顶礼膜拜;J.-B.博卡萨是一个极其贫穷的非洲小国的独裁者,他将这个国家改名为中非帝国,宣称自己是皇帝;即便是民主选举产生的领导人也常常因民众的夸奖而妄自尊大。但 *megalomaniac* 常用于对别人的辱骂,很少用来指真正的精神疾病。

egomaniac \ˌē-gō-ˈmā-nē-ˌak\ Someone who is extremely self-centered and ignores the problems and concerns of others. 极端自我主义者

• He's a completely unimpressive person, but that doesn't keep him from being an egomaniac. 他是一个很不起眼的人,但这并不妨碍他极度自恋。

Ego is Latin for "I," and in English *ego* usually means "sense of self-worth." Most people's egos stay at a healthy level, but some become exaggerated. *Egomaniacs* may display a grandiose sense of self-importance, with fantasies about their own brilliance or beauty, intense envy of others, a lack of sympathy, and a need to be adored or feared. But, like *megalomaniac*, the word *egomaniac* is thrown around by lots of people who don't mean much more by it than *blowhard* or *know-it-*

all.

　　ego 是拉丁语,表示"我",英语中的 *ego* 通常指的是"自我价值感"。多数人的自我意识保持在健康的水平,但有些人的自我意识有点过头了。极端自我主义者可能会表现出强烈的自负感,幻想自己十分聪明、漂亮、受人强烈地嫉妒,这些人缺乏同情心,需要受人崇拜或让人敬畏。但是,就像 *megalomaniac* 一样,很多人也常用 *egomaniac* 来嘲笑 *blowhard*(自吹自擂者)或 *know-it-all*(自以为无所不知的人)。

PSYCH

PSYCH comes from the Greek word *psyche*, meaning "breath, life, soul." *Psychology* is the science of mind and behavior, and a *psychologist* treats or studies the mental problems of individuals and groups. *Psychiatry* is a branch of medicine that deals with mental and emotional disorders, and a *psychiatrist* (like any other doctor) may prescribe drugs to treat them.

PSYCH 源自希腊语 *psyche*,意为"呼吸、生命、灵魂"。*psychology*(心理学)是研究心理和行为的科学,*psychologist*(心理学家)治疗或研究个人和群体的心理问题。*psychiatry*(精神病学)是治疗精神和情感障碍的医学分支,而 *psychiatrist*(精神病医生,像其他任何医生一样)开药治疗病人。

---

psyche \ˈsī-kē\　Soul, personality, mind. 灵魂,人格,心灵

● Analysts are constantly trying to understand the nation's psyche and why the U.S. often behaves so differently from other countries. 分析家们一直在试图理解民族的心理,以及美国的表现为什么往往与其他国家大相径庭。

　　Sometime back in the 16th century, we borrowed the word *psyche* directly from Greek into English. In Greek mythology, Psyche was a beautiful princess who fell in love with Eros (Cupid), god of love, and went through terrible trials before being allowed to marry him. The story is often understood to be about the soul redeeming itself through love. (To the Greeks, *psyche* also meant "butterfly," which suggests how they imagined the soul.) In English, *psyche* often sounds less spiritual than *soul*, less intellectual than *mind*, and more private than *personality*.

　　早在 16 世纪的某个时候,英语直接向希腊语借用了 *psyche* 一词。在希腊神话中,Psyche(普赛克)是一位美丽的公主,爱上了爱神厄洛斯(丘比特)。她经历了种种残酷的考验,才被允许嫁给爱神。这个故事常被理解为灵魂在爱中得到了救赎。(对希腊人来说,*psyche* 也有"蝴蝶"的意思,这暗示了他们心目中灵魂的样子。)在英语中,*psyche* 听起来往往没有 *soul* 那么有精神,没有 *mind* 那么有知性,但比 *personality* 更私密。

---

psychedelic \ˌsī-kə-ˈde-lik\　(1) Of or relating to a drug (such as LSD) that produces abnormal and often extreme mental effects such as hallucinations. 迷幻药的 (2) Imitating the effects of psychedelic drugs. 引起幻觉的,致幻的

● In her only psychedelic experience, back in 1970, she had watched with horror as the walls began crawling with bizarrely colored creatures. 她唯一的一次迷幻药体验还是在 1970 年,当时她惊恐地看着墙上开始爬满颜色怪异的生物。

　　The most famous—or notorious—of the *psychedelic* drugs is LSD, a compound that can be obtained from various mushrooms and other fungi but is usually created in the lab. The other well-known *psychedelics* are psilocybin (likewise obtained from fungi) and mescaline (obtained from peyote cactus). How psychedelics produce their effects is still fairly mysterious, partly because research ceased for almost 20 years because of their reputation, but scientists are determined to find the answers and much research is now under way. Psychedelics are now used to treat anxiety in patients with cancer, and are being tested in the treatment of such serious conditions as severe depression, alcoholism, and drug addiction.

最有名的——或最臭名昭著的——致幻剂是 LSD,这是一种化合物,可以从各种各样的蘑菇以及其他真菌中获得,但通常在实验室中合成。其他广为人知的 *psychedelics* 还有裸盖菇素(同样从真菌中获得)和麦司卡林(从仙人掌中获得)。迷幻药如何起效仍是未解之谜,部分原因是,相关研究因声誉问题而中断了近 20 年。但是,科学家们决心找到答案,大量的研究正在开展中。迷幻药现在用于治疗癌症患者的焦虑症,也在一些严重疾病的治疗中进行检验,比如重度抑郁、酗酒、药物成瘾等。

psychosomatic \ˌsī-kō-sə-ˈma-tik\ Caused by mental or emotional problems rather than by physical illness. 与心理问题有关的,由精神压力导致的

• Her doctor assumed her stomach problems were psychosomatic but gave her some harmless medication anyway. 医生认为她的胃病是精神压力引起的,但还是给了她一些不会造成伤害的药物。

Since the Greek word *soma* means "body," *psychosomatic* suggests the link between mind and body. Since one's mental state may have an important effect on one's physical state, research on new medicines always involves giving some patients in the experiment a placebo (fake medicine), and some who receive the sugar pills will seem to improve. You may hear someone say of someone else's symptoms, "Oh, it's probably just psychosomatic," implying that the physical pain or illness is imaginary—maybe just an attempt to get sympathy—and that the person could will it away if he or she wanted to. But this can be harsh and unfair, since, whatever the cause is, the pain is usually real.

因为希腊语单词 soma 的意思是"身体",所以 *psychosomatic* 暗示精神和身体之间的联系。人的精神状态可能对身体状况产生重要影响,所以在新药的研究中,通常要给接受实验的病人服用安慰剂(假药),一些病人服用了糖丸后情况似乎有好转。你可能会听到有人说起别人的症状,"哦,这可能只是心理作用",意思是这种生理上的疼痛或疾病是想象出来的——可能是要博得同情——如果他/她想去除病魔,靠意念就可以把它赶走。但这种说法可能很无情且不公平,因为不管是出于什么原因,疼痛通常是真实存在的。

psychotherapist \sī-kō-ˈther-ə-pist\ One who treats mental or emotional disorder or related bodily ills by psychological means. 心理治疗师,精神治疗师

• He's getting medication from a psychiatrist, but it's his sessions with the psychotherapist that he really values. 他从精神科医生那里得到药物,但他认为最有价值的还是他与心理治疗师之间的交流。

Many psychologists offer psychological counseling, and psychological counseling can usually be called *psychotherapy*, so many *psychologists* can be called *psychotherapists*. The most intense form of psychotherapy, called *psychoanalysis*, usually requires several visits a week. A competing type of therapy known as *behavior therapy* focuses on changing a person's behavior (often some individual habit such as stuttering, tics, or phobias) without looking very deeply into his or her mental state.

很多心理学家提供心理咨询,心理咨询通常可以被称为 *psychotherapy*(心理疗法,精神疗法),所以许多心理学家也可以被称为心理治疗师。最强烈的精神治疗方式被称为 *psychoanalysis*(精神分析),通常需要一周数次。有种可以相媲美的疗法被称为 *behavior therapy*(行为治疗),重点在于改变某人的行为(通常是个人习惯,如口吃、抽搐或恐惧症),而不必深入了解他/她的心理状态。

Quizzes

A. Fill in each blank with the correct letter:

a. psychedelic
b. kleptomania
c. psyche
d. egomaniac
e. megalomaniac
f. psychosomatic
g. dipsomaniac
h. psychotherapist

1. Her boss was an _____ who always needed someone around telling him how brilliant he was.

2. Testing _____ drugs on cancer patients was difficult because of their unpredictable mental effects.

3. By now the dictator had begun to strike some observers as a possibly dangerous _____.

4. His fear of AIDS was so intense that he'd been developing _____ symptoms, which his doctor hardly bothered to check out anymore.

5. After finding several of her missing things in the other closet, she began wondering if her roommate was an ordinary thief or actually suffering from _____.

6. They'd only been together two weeks, but already she suspected there was a lot hidden in the depths of her boyfriend's _____.

7. A medical report from 1910 had identified her greatgrandfather as a _____, and ten years later his alcoholism would kill him.

8. He hated the thought of drugs but knew he needed someone to talk to, so his brother recommended a local _____.

B. Match each word on the left to the best definition on the right:

1. psyche   a. alcoholic
2. egomaniac   b. caused by the mind
3. psychotherapist   c. person deluded by thoughts of grandeur
4. psychosomatic   d. producing hallucinations
5. dipsomaniac   e. compulsive thieving
6. megalomaniac   f. mind

7. kleptomania   g. extremely self-centered person
8. psychedelic   h. "talk" doctor

CEPT

CEPT comes from the Latin verb meaning "take, seize." *Capture*, which is what a *captor* has done to a *captive*, has the same meaning. *Captivate* once meant literally "capture," but now means only to capture mentally through charm or appeal. But in some other English words this root produces, such as those below, its meaning is harder to find.

CEPT 源自意思是"拿、抓"的拉丁语动词。capture(俘获)是指 captor(俘获者)对 captive(俘虏)所做的事,这个词语也有同样的含义。captivate 的字面意思曾是"捕获",但现在仅指通过魅力或吸引力在精神上捕获。但在这个词根所构成的其他的一些英语单词中,如下面所列的单词,它的意思就难找到了。

reception \ ri-'sep-shən \ (1) The act of receiving. 反响 (2) A social gathering where guests are formally welcomed. 欢迎会,接待仪式

• Although the reception of her plan by the board of directors was enthusiastic, it was months before anything was done about it. 董事会虽然对她的计划反应热烈,但过了好几个月才有所行动。

Reception is the noun form of *receive*. So at a formal reception, guests are received or welcomed or "taken in." A bad TV reception means the signal isn't being received well. When a new novel receives good reviews, we say it has met with a good critical reception. If it gets a poor reception, on the other hand, that's the same as saying that it wasn't *well-received*.

reception 是 receive 的名词形式。所以,在正式的招待会上,客人受到接待、欢迎或"收留"。电视接收不良意味着信号接收不好。如果一部新小说得到好的书评,那么我们说它受到了好的 critical reception(评价)。另一方面,如果这部小说受到不好的评价,就等于说 it wasn't *well-received*(它没有受到欢迎)。

intercept \ ˌin-tər-'sept \ To stop, seize, or interrupt (something or someone) before arrival. 拦截,截获

• The explosives had been intercepted by police just before being loaded onto the jet. 爆炸物在被装上飞机之前就被警察截获了。

Since the prefix *inter* means "between" (see INTER, p. 703), it's not hard to see how *intercept* was created. Arms shipments coming to a country are sometimes intercepted, but such *interceptions* can sometimes be understood as acts of war. In football, soccer, and basketball, players try to intercept the ball as it's being passed by the other team. In years gone by, letters and documents being carried between officers or officials were sometimes intercepted when the carrier was caught; today, when these communications are generally electronic, an intercepted e-mail isn't actually stopped, but simply read secretly by a third party.

前缀 inter 的意思是"在……之间"(见 INTER,第 703 页),因此不难看出 intercept 是如何产生的。运往某国的武器有时会被拦截,但这种 interceptions(拦截)有时可以被理解为战争行为。在橄榄球、足球和篮球比赛中,一方球员在对方

球员传球时尝试将球拦截。过去,当传递人员被抓获时,官员间往来的信件和文件有时就会被截获;如今的通信通常采用电子方式,被截获的电子邮件实际上并未被拦下,而只是被第三方秘密阅读了。

perceptible \pər-ˈsep-tə-bəl\ Noticeable or able to be felt by the senses.
可察觉的,可感知的

• Her change in attitude toward him was barely perceptible, and he couldn't be sure he wasn't just imagining it. 她对他的态度发生了改变,但几乎觉察不到,因此他不能肯定自己不是在凭空想象。

Perceptible includes the prefix *per-*, meaning "through," so the word refers to whatever can be taken in through the senses. A *perceptive* person picks up minor changes, small clues, or hints and shades of meaning that others can't *perceive*, so one person's *perception*—a tiny sound, a slight change in the weather, a different tone of voice— often won't be perceptible to another.

perceptible 的前缀 *per-* 的意思是"通过",所以这个词指的是可以通过感官感知到的任何东西。一个 *perceptive* person(有洞察力的人)能察觉到别人 *perceive*(察觉)不到的细微变化、小的线索、暗示以及意义上的细微差别,所以一个人的 *perception*(感知)——细微的声音、天气的轻微变化、语调的不同等——常常是另一个人所察觉不到的。

susceptible \sə-ˈsep-tə-bəl\ (1) Open to some influence; responsive. 易受影响的 (2) Able to be submitted to an action or process. 容许的,可能的

• She impressed everyone immediately with her intelligence, so they're now highly susceptible to her influence and usually go along with anything she proposes. 她立刻给大家留下了智慧过人的印象,因此,他们现在很容易受她的影响,通常会赞同她提出的任何建议。

With its prefix *sus-*, "up," *susceptible* refers to something or someone that "takes up" or absorbs like a sponge. A sickly child may be susceptible to colds, and an unlucky adult may be susceptible to back problems. A lonely elderly person may be susceptible to what a con man tells him or her on the phone. And students are usually susceptible to the teaching of an imaginative professor—that is, likely to enjoy and learn from it.

susceptible 的前缀是 *sus-*("向上"),所以这个词用来指能像海绵一样"吸收"某种东西的物或人。体弱多病的孩子可能易患感冒,而运气不好的成年人可能易患背部疾病。孤独的老人可能很容易相信骗子在电话里说的话。学生容易受富有想象力的教授的教学感染——也就是说,他们很可能乐在其中,并从中学到东西。

FIN comes from the Latin word for "end" or "boundary." *Final* describes last things, and a *finale* or a *finish* is an ending. (And at the end of a French film, you may just see the word "Fin.") But its meaning is harder to trace in some of the other English words derived from it.

FIN 源自表示"结束"或"边界"的拉丁语单词。*final* 指的是最后的事情,而 *finale* 或 *finish* 表示的是结尾(在法国电影的结尾,你看到的可能只有"Fin"这个词)。但是,在由这个词根所派生出来的其他的一些英语单词中,该词根的含义很难追溯。

confine \kən-ˈfin\ (1) To keep (someone or something) within limits. 限

制,限定 (2) To hold (someone) in a location. 把(某人)限制在某个地方

• He had heard the bad news from the CEO, but when he spoke to his employees he confined his remarks to a few hints that sales had slipped. 他从首席执行官那里得知了这个坏消息,但在与员工谈话时,他仅仅给出了销量下滑的暗示。

Confine means basically to keep someone or something within borders. Artist Frida Kahlo taught herself to paint when she was confined to bed after a serious bus accident. A person under "house arrest" is confined to his or her house by the government. The discussion at a meeting may be confined to a single topic. A town may keep industrial development confined to one area by means of zoning. And when potholes are being repaired, traffic on a two-way road may be confined to a single lane.

confine 的基本意思是把某人或某物限制在边界之内。艺术家弗里达·卡罗遭遇严重的公共汽车事故后,只得卧床自学绘画。"软禁在家"的人被政府限制在家中。会议上的讨论可能仅限于某个话题。一个小镇可能通过分区的方式把工业发展限制在某一区域。在修复双向道路上的坑洼时,交通可能被限制在一条车道上。

definitive \di-ˈfi-nə-tiv\ (1) Authoritative and final. 权威的,最终的,决定性的 (2) Specifying perfectly or precisely. 最好的,确定的

• The team's brilliant research provided a definitive description of the virus and its strange mutation patterns. 通过出色的研究,这个团队明确地描述了那种病毒及其奇怪的变异模式。

Something *definitive* is complete and final. A definitive example is the perfect example. A definitive answer is usually a strong yes or no. A definitive biography contains everything we'll ever need to know about someone. Ella Fitzgerald's famous 1950s recordings of American songs have even been called definitive—but no one ever wanted them to be the last.

something definitive 指的是完整的、最终的东西。a definitive example 指的是完美的例子。a definitive answer 通常指的是有明确的是或否的答案。a definitive biography 指的是收录了我们所要知道的关于某人的所有信息的传记。20世纪50年代,艾拉·菲茨杰拉德著名的美国歌曲录音被称为 definitive——但没有人希望这些是她最后的歌曲。

finite \ˈfī-ˌnīt\ Having definite limits. 有限的,有尽的

• Her ambitions were infinite, but her wealth was finite. 她的野心无限,但财富有限。

It has come as a shock to many of us to realize that resources such as oil—and the atmosphere's ability to absorb greenhouse gases— are *finite* rather than unlimited. The debate continues as to whether the universe is finite or *infinite* and, if it's finite, how to think about what lies beyond it. Religion has always concerned itself with the question of the finite (that is, human life on earth) versus the infinite (God, eternity, and infinity). But *finite* is mostly used in scientific writing, often with the meaning "definitely measurable."

我们有很多人吃惊地意识到,石油等资源——以及大气层吸收温室气体的能力——是有限的而非无限的。关于宇宙是有限还是 *infinite*(无限)的争论一直持续不断。如果宇宙是有限的,那么宇宙之外到底有什么?宗教一直关注有限(即地球上的人类生命)与无限(上帝、永恒和无穷)之争的问题。但 *finite* 主要用于科技文章中,常带有"确切可以测量"的含义。

infinitesimal \ˌin-ˌfi-nə-ˈte-sə-məl\ Extremely or immeasurably small.
极小的,微量的,无穷小的

• Looking more closely at the research data, he now saw an odd pattern of changes so infinitesimal that they hadn't been noticed before. 他仔细地查看研究数据,发现了一种奇怪的变化模式,这些变化非常之小,之前未被注意到。

Just as *infinite* describes something immeasurable ("without limit"), *infinitesimal* describes something endlessly small. When Antonie van Leeuwenhoek invented the microscope in the 17th century, he was able to see organisms that had been thought too *infinitesimally* small to exist. But today's electron microscope allows us to see infinitesimal aspects of matter that even Leeuwenhoek could not have imagined. 正如 *infinite*(无穷的)描述的是无法测量的东西("没有限制"),*infinitesimal* 描述的是无穷小的东西。17 世纪,安东尼·范·列文虎克发明了显微镜,他能看到许多 *infinitesimally*(无穷地)小到之前被以为不存在的生物体。但是,今天有了电子显微镜,我们能看到连列文虎克都无法想象的物质无穷小的各个方面。

Quizzes

A. Fill in each blank with the correct letter:

a. confine   e. finite
b. susceptible   f. intercept
c. definitive   g. infinitesimal
d. reception   h. perceptible

1. By the fall there had a _____ change in the mood of the students.
2. An _____ speck of dust on the lens can keep a CD player from functioning.
3. They waited weeks to hear about the board's _____ of their proposal.
4. Let's _____ this discussion to just the first part of the proposal.
5. Small children are often _____ to nightmares after hearing ghost stories in the dark.
6. He was at the post office the next morning, hoping to _____ the foolish letter he had sent yesterday.
7. We have a _____ number of choices, in fact maybe only three or four.
8. This may be the best book on the subject so far, but I wouldn't call it _____.

B. Match the word on the left to the correct definition on the right:

1. confine   a. noticeable
2. susceptible   b. ultimate
3. definitive   c. seize
4. reception   d. easily influenced

5. finite   e. tiny
6. intercept   f. limit
7. infinitesimal g. receiving
8. perceptible   h. limited

JECT comes from *jacere*, the Latin verb meaning "throw" or "hurl." To *reject* something is to throw (or push) it back; to *eject* something is to throw (or drive) it out; and to *inject* something is to throw (or squirt) it into something else.
JECT 源自拉丁语动词 *jacere*("投"或"扔")。*reject*(拒绝)某物就是把它扔(或推)回去;*eject*(驱逐)某物就是把它抛(或赶)出去;*inject*(注射)某物就是把它扔进(或喷射到)别的东西中。

interject \ˌin-tər-ˈjekt\   To interrupt a conversation with a comment or remark. 打断,插嘴

• His anger was growing as he listened to the conversation, and every so often he would interject a crude comment. 他越听越气,不时地插进一句粗话。

According to its Latin roots, *interject* ought to mean literally "throw between." For most of the word's history, however, the only things that have been interjected have been comments dropped suddenly into a conversation. *Interjections* are often humorous, and sometimes even insulting, and the best interjections are so quick that the conversation isn't even interrupted.

根据其拉丁语词根,*interject* 的字面意思应该是"抛在中间"。然而,在该词的大部分历史当中,唯一能被"抛在中间"的东西就是突然插入对话中的评论。*interjections*(插入的话语)通常是幽默的,但有时是侮辱性的,最好的插话发生得非常快以至于连谈话都没有被打断。

conjecture \kən-ˈjek-chər\   To guess. 推测,猜测,猜想

• He was last heard of in Bogotá, and they conjectured that he had met his end in the Andes at the hands of the guerrillas. 他们最后一次听到他的消息是在波哥大,因此他们猜测他在安第斯山脉被游击队杀死了。

Formed with the prefix *con-*, "together," *conjecture* means literally "to throw together"—that is, to produce a theory by putting together a number of facts. So, for example, Columbus conjectured from his calculations that he would reach Asia if he sailed westward, and his later *conjecture* that there was a "Northwest Passage" by sea from the Atlantic to the Pacific over the North American continent was proved correct centuries later.

conjecture 的前缀是 *con-*("和……一起"),所以这个词的字面意思是"扔在一起"——也就是说,把一些事实放在一起,从而得出一个理论。比如,哥伦布从计算中推断,一路向西航行就能到达亚洲。后来他有个 *conjecture*:北美大陆有一条连接大西洋和太平洋的海上"西北航道",这个推测几个世纪之后得到证实。

projection \ prə-ˈjek-shən\   An estimate of what might happen in the future based on what is happening now. 预测,估算

• The president has been hearing different deficit projections all week from the members of his economic team. 整个星期,总统已经从他的经济团队中听到了各种不同的赤字预测。

Projection has various meanings, but what they all have in common is that something is sent out or forward. A movie is *projected* onto a screen; a skilled actress projects her voice out into a large theater without seeming to shout; and something sticking out from a wall can be called a projection. But the meaning we focus on here is the one used by businesses and governments. Most projections of this kind are estimates of a company's sales or profits—or of the finances of a town, state, or country—sometime in the future.

projection 有多个含义,但它们的共同之处是把某物发送出去。电影被 projected(投射)到屏幕上;有技巧的女演员不需要喊叫就可以将声音传送到整个大剧院里;从墙上伸出来的东西可称为凸出物。但这里我们所关注的是企业和政府使用该词表达的含义。这种类型的预测大多是对未来某个时间某家公司的销售额或利润的预测,或某个城镇、州或国家财政状况的预测。

trajectory \ trə-ˈjek-tə-rē \ The curved path that an object makes in space, or that a thrown object follows as it rises and falls to earth. 轨道,轨迹

• Considering the likely range, trajectory, and accuracy of a bullet fired from a cheap handgun at 100 yards, the murder seemed incredible. 子弹是用廉价手枪在100码外射出的,考虑到其可能的射程、轨迹、准度,这起谋杀似乎令人难以置信。

Formed with part of the prefix *trans-*, "across," *trajectory* means a "hurling across." By calculating the effect of gravity and other forces, the trajectory of an object launched into space at a known speed can be computed precisely. Missiles stand a chance of hitting their target only if their trajectory has been plotted accurately. The word is used most often in physics and engineering, but not always; we can also say, for example, that the trajectory of a whole life may be set in a person's youth, or that a new book traces the long trajectory of the French empire.

trajectory 由前缀 *trans-*("越过")的一部分构成,它的意思是"抛过……"。通过计算重力和其他力的作用,可以精确计算出以已知速度发射到空间的物体的轨迹。只有准确地绘制出运动轨迹,导弹才有可能击中目标。这个词常用于物理和工程领域,但也不是绝对的。比如,我们也可以说,人一生的轨迹可能在年轻时就确定下来了,某本新书追溯了法兰西帝国的漫长历程。

TRACT comes from *trahere*, the Latin verb meaning "drag or draw." Something *attractive* draws us toward it. Something *distracting* pulls your attention away. And when you *extract* something from behind the sofa, you drag it out.

TRACT 源自拉丁语动词 *trahere*("拖或拉")。something *attractive*(有吸引力的东西)会吸引我们向它靠近。something *distracting*(分散注意力的东西)会把你的注意力拉到一边。当你从沙发后面 *extract* 某物时,你是将它拖出来。

traction \ ˈtrak-shən \ The friction that allows a moving thing to move over a surface without slipping. 附着摩擦力

● The spinning wheels were getting no traction on the ice, and we began to slip backward down the hill. 旋转的车轮无法从冰面上得到附着力,我们开始向后滑下山坡。

A *tractor* is something that pulls something else. We usually use the word for a piece of farm machinery, but it's also the name of the part of a big truck that includes the engine and the cab. Tractors get terrific traction, because of their powerful engines and the deep ridges on their huge wheels. A cross-country skier needs traction to kick herself forward, but doesn't want it to slow her down when she's gliding, so the bottom of the skis may have a "fish-scale" surface that permits both of these at the same time.

tractor(牵引车,拖拉机)被用来拉动别的东西。我们通常用这个词表示一种农用机械,但也可以指大卡车的发动机和驾驶室部分。拖拉机有非常大的附着摩擦力,因为它们有强有力的发动机和有着深脊的巨大车轮。越野滑雪者需要借助附着摩擦力才能前进,但又不希望摩擦力减慢滑行速度,所以滑雪板的底部可以设计成"鱼鳞"状表面,确保二者兼得。

TRACT

retract \ri-ˈtrakt\   (1) To pull back (something) into something larger. 缩回 (2) To take back (something said or written). 收回,撤回(先前的话或文章)

● She was forced to retract her comment about her opponent after it was condemned in the press. 受到媒体谴责后,她被迫撤回针对对手的评论。

The prefix *re-* ("back") gives *retract* the meaning of "draw back." Just as a cat retracts its claws into its paws when they aren't being used, a public figure may issue a *retraction* in order to say that he or she no longer wants to say something that has just been said. But it's sometimes hard to know what a retraction means: Was the original statement an error or an outright lie? Sometimes a politician even has to retract something that everyone actually assumes is the truth. Someone wrongly accused may demand a retraction from his accuser—though today it seems more likely that he'll just go ahead and sue.

前缀 *re-*("后退")赋予 *retract* "收回"之意。正如猫不使用爪子时会将其收进脚掌中一样,某位公众人物可能会发布一个 *retraction*(撤回声明),表明她不想再说曾说过的话。但有时很难明白撤回声明是什么意思:是原话说错了呢,还是原话完全就是一个谎言呢? 有时候,政治家甚至不得不撤回大家实际上已认为是真相的东西。被错误控告的人可能会要求原告撤回指控——但在今天看来,被告更有可能会直接上诉。

protracted \prō-ˈtrak-təd\   Drawn out, continued, or extended. 延长的、持久的

● No one was looking forward to a protracted struggle for custody of the baby. 没有人预料到那个婴儿的监护权之争会旷日持久。

With its prefix *pro-*, "forward," *protracted* usually applies to something drawn out forward in time. A protracted strike may cripple a company; a protracted rainy spell may rot the roots of vegetables; and a protracted lawsuit occasionally outlives the parties involved. Before the invention of the polio vaccines, polio's many victims had no choice but to suffer a protracted illness and its aftereffects.

protracted 的前缀是 *pro-*("向前"),这个词通常指某物持续的时间向前延伸。长期罢工可能拖垮一个公司;连日下雨可能会使蔬菜的根部腐烂;偶尔会有比当事人的生命更长的诉讼案。在脊髓灰质炎疫苗发明之前,许多患者别无选

择，只能忍受长期疾病及其后遗症。

intractable \ˌin-ˈtrak-tə-bəl\ Not easily handled, led, taught, or controlled. 难对付的，难引导的，难教的，难驾驭的，棘手的

• Corruption in the army was the country's intractable problem, and for many years all foreign aid had ended up in the colonels' pockets. 军队腐败是这个国家的棘手问题，多年来所有的外国援助都落入了军官们的口袋。

Intractable simply means "untreatable," and even comes from the same root. The word may describe both people and conditions. A cancer patient may suffer intractable pain that doctors are unable to treat. An intractable alcoholic goes back to the bottle immediately after "drying out." Homelessness, though it hardly existed thirty years ago, is now sometimes regarded as an intractable problem.
intractable 的意思就是"untreatable(不好对付的)"，二者甚至源自同一个词根。这个词同时用来形容人或处境。癌症患者可能要忍受连医生都无能为力的痛苦。无可救药的酒鬼在"戒酒"之后，马上又拿起酒瓶。无家可归现象在30年前几乎不存在，但现在有时候却成了一个棘手的问题。

Quizzes

A. Choose the odd word:

1. conjecture   a. suppose   b. assume   c. guess   d. know
2. protracted   a. lengthened   b. continued   c. circular   d. extended
3. projection   a. survey   b. forecast   c. report   d. history
4. traction   a. grip   b. drive   c. pulling force d. steering
5. trajectory   a. curve   b. path   c. arc   d. target
6. retract   a. unsay   b. withdraw   c. force   d. take back
7. interject   a. insert   b. grab   c. add   d. stick in
8. intractable   a. unbelievable   b. uncontrollable c. stubborn   d. difficult

B. Match each definition on the left to the correct word on the right:

1. pulling force   a. protracted
2. assume   b. interject
3. expectation   c. trajectory
4. difficult   d. traction
5. unsay   e. conjecture
6. drawn out   f. intractable
7. curved path   g. retract
8. interrupt with   h. projection

UNIT 2

DUC/DUCT, from the Latin verb *ducere*, "to lead," shows up regularly in English. *Duke* means basically "leader." The Italian dictator Mussolini was known simply as *Il Duce*, "the leader." But such words as *produce* and *reduce* also contain the root, even though their meanings show it less clearly.

DUC/DUCT 源自拉丁语动词 *ducere*("领路,带领"),在英语中经常出现。Duke(公爵)的基本意思是"领导者"。意大利独裁者墨索里尼的称号就是 *Il Duce*(领袖)。像 *produce* 和 *reduce* 等词语也包含这个词根,但在它们的意思中,该词根的表现并不太清楚。

---

conducive \kən-ˈdü-siv\ Tending to promote, encourage, or assist; helpful. 有利的,有益的,有助的

- She found the atmosphere in the quiet café conducive to study and even to creative thinking. 在这家安静的咖啡馆里,她找到了有利于学习甚至有利于创造性思维的氛围。

Something *conducive* "leads to" a desirable result. A cozy living room may be conducive to relaxed conversation, just as a boardroom may be conducive to more intense discussions. Particular tax policies are often conducive to savings and investment, whereas others are conducive to consumer spending. Notice that *conducive* is almost always followed by *to*.

something conducive(有益的东西)"引出"令人满意的结果。舒适的客厅可能有助于轻松的交谈,就像董事会会议室可能有助于更激烈的讨论一样。某些税收政策往往有助于储蓄和投资,而另一些税收政策则有助于消费支出。注意,conducive 的后面几乎总是跟"to"。

deduction\dē-ˈdək-shēn\ (1) Subtraction. 减去,扣除 (2) The reaching of a conclusion by reasoning. 推论,推断,演绎

- Foretelling the future by deduction based on a political or economic theory has proved to be extremely difficult. 事实证明,通过基于政治或经济理论的推论来预测未来是极其困难的。

To *deduct* is simply to subtract. A tax *deduction* is a subtraction from your taxable income allowed by the government for certain expenses, which will result in your paying lower taxes. Your insurance *deductible* is the amount of a medical bill that the insurance company makes you subtract before it starts to pay—in other words, the amount that will come out of your own pocket. But *deduction* also means "reasoning," and particularly reasoning based on general principles to produce specific findings. Mathematical reasoning is almost always deduction, for instance, since it is based on general rules. But when Dr. Watson exclaims "Brilliant deduction, my dear Holmes!" he simply means "brilliant reasoning," since Sherlock Holmes's solutions are based on specific details he has noticed rather than on general principles.

deduct 就是减除的意思。减税是根据政府规定,从应纳税收入中减少某些特定支出,这将使你的纳税减少。insurance deductible(保险免赔额)指的是,保险公司在开始赔付你的医疗费用之前,先让你减去的一部分金额——换句话说,就是你自己掏腰包的那部分。但 deduction 也有"推论"的意思,尤其是从普遍原则得出特殊结论的推论。比如,数

学推论几乎总是可以叫做 deduction，因为它是基于普遍原则的。但是，当华生医生惊呼，"绝妙的推论啊，我亲爱的福尔摩斯！"他指的仅仅是"绝妙的推理"，因为福尔摩斯的解决方案是基于他所注意到的具体细节之上而非原则之上的。

induce \in-ˈdüs\ （1）Persuade，influence. 劝诱，影响（2）Bring about. 引出，引发

• To induce him to make the call we had to promise we wouldn't do it again. 为了促使他打那个电话，我们不得不承诺再也不会那么做了。

Inducing is usually gentle persuasion; you may, for instance, induce a friend to go to a concert, or induce a child to stop crying. An inducement is something that might lure you to do something, though inducements are occasionally a bit menacing, like the Godfather's offer that you can't refuse. Induce also sometimes means "produce"; thus, doctors must at times induce labor in a pregnant woman. Notice that induct and induction are somewhat different from induce and inducement, though they come from the identical roots.

劝诱通常是温和的劝说。比如，你可以劝朋友去听音乐会，或者劝孩子停止哭泣。inducement（诱因）是可能诱使你做某事的东西，但偶尔诱因会有点威胁性，就像教父所提出来的、你无法拒绝的要求一样。induce 有时也表示"引发"的意思，因此，医生有时候必须为孕妇引产。注意，尽管源自同一个词根，但 induct（给予职位）和 induction（就职）与 induce 和 inducement 有所不同。

seduction \si-ˈdək-shən\ （1）Temptation to sin，especially temptation to sexual intercourse. 引诱（尤指诱奸）（2）Attraction or charm. 吸引力或魅力

• The company began its campaign of seduction of the smaller firm by inviting its top management to a series of weekends at expensive resorts. 该公司邀请那家小公司的最高管理层连续在双休日到豪华度假景点游玩，从而开启了它的引诱活动。

Seduction, with its prefix se-, "aside," means basically "lead aside or astray." In Hawthorne's novel The Scarlet Letter, Hester Prynne is forced to wear a large scarlet A, for "adulteress," after it is revealed that she's been seduced by the Reverend Dimmesdale. Seduction also takes less physical forms. Advertisements constantly try to seduce us (often using sex as a temptation) into buying products we hadn't even known existed.

seduction 的前缀是 se-（"一旁"），这个词的基本意思是"引到一旁或引入歧途"。在霍桑的小说《红字》中，海丝特·白兰被丁梅斯代尔牧师 seduced（诱奸）一事被揭露之后，被迫戴上大大的红色 A 字，意为"奸妇"。引诱也不仅限于肉体上。广告不断地试图引诱我们（经常用性作为诱惑）购买我们甚至不知道存在的产品。

SEQU comes from the Latin verb sequi, meaning "to follow." A sequel follows the original novel, film, or television show.

SEQU 源自拉丁语动词 sequi，意思是"跟随"。sequel 是小说、电影或电视节目的续集。

sequential \si-ˈkwen-shəl\ （1）Arranged in order or in a series. 有序的，按顺序的（2）Following in a series. 依次发生的，相继发生的

• 38 •

- In writing the history of the revolution, his challenge was to put all the events of those fateful days in proper sequential order. 在书写那次革命的历史时,他的挑战是将在这段决定命运的时间里发生的事件按照合适的先后顺序排列。

Things in *sequence*, or regular order, are arranged *sequentially*. Most novels and films move sequentially, but some use techniques such as flashbacks that interrupt the movement forward in time. Sequential courses in college must follow each other in the proper order, just like sequential tasks or steps.

things in *sequence*,即有序的东西,按顺序(*sequentially*)安排。多数小说和电影都是按先后顺序展开的,但也有些会采用倒叙等技巧,从而打断了故事情节的推进。如同连续的任务或步骤一样,大学里的连续课程也必须按照合适的顺序一门接一门进行。

subsequent \səb-si-kwənt\ Following in time, order, or place; later. 随后的,后来的

- Through all her subsequent love affairs, she never stopped thinking about the man who got away. 在所有那些后来的恋情中,她一直念念不忘那个走掉的男人。

The prefix *sub-* normally means "below," and the *sub-* in *subsequent* seems to imply that everything after the first is somehow inferior. As the definition states, *subsequent* can refer to time ("All our subsequent attempts to contact her failed"), order ("The subsequent houses on the list looked even worse"), or place ("The subsequent villages on the river heading east become steadily more primitive"). But *subsequently*, as in "I subsequently learned the real story," simply means "later."

前缀 *sub-* 通常表示"在……之下",所以 *subsequent* 中的 *sub-* 似乎暗示后面的都不如第一个好。正如定义所述,*subsequent* 可以指时间(比如"我们随后联系她的尝试都失败了")、顺序(比如"单子上排在后边的房子看起来更糟")或空间(比如"那条河边向东流去,河边的村庄越往后就越原始")。但 *subsequently* 指的是"后来的",比如"我后来知晓了事情的真相"。

consequential \ˌkän-sə-ˈkwen-shəl\ (1) Resulting. 结果的,随之而来的 (2) Important. 重要的

- None of our discussions thus far has been very consequential; next week's meeting will be the important one. 到目前为止,我们的讨论都无关紧要;下周的会议才重要。

Something consequential follows or comes along with something else. The "resulting" meaning of *consequential* is usually seen in legal writing. For example, "consequential losses" are losses that supposedly resulted from some improper behavior, about which the lawyer's client is suing. But normally *consequential* means "significant" or "important," and it's especially used for events that will produce large *consequences*, or results.

something consequential 紧接着另外一件事发生。*consequential* 表示"后果,结果"的含义时常出现在法律文书中。比如,"后果性损失"指的是某个不当行为造成的损失,这种不当行为是律师的当事人要控告的。通常,*consequential* 的意思是"重大的"或"重要的",常用于描述会产生重大 *consequences*(结果)的事件。

non sequitur \ˈnän-ˈse-kwə-tər\ A statement that does not follow logically from anything previously said. 前后不连贯的陈述,不合逻辑的陈述

• Rattled by the question, his mind went blank, and he blurted out a non sequitur that fetched a few laughs from members of the audience. 他被这个问题吓了一跳,脑子一片空白,脱口而出一句毫不相关的话,引得观众一阵大笑。

Non sequitur is actually a complete sentence in Latin, meaning "It does not follow"—that is, something said or written doesn't logically follow what came before it. It was Aristotle who identified the non sequitur as one of the basic fallacies of logic—that is, one of the ways in which a person's reasoning may go wrong. For Aristotle, the non sequitur is usually a conclusion that doesn't actually result from the reasoning and evidence presented. Sometime when you're listening to politicians answering questions, see how many non sequiturs you can spot.

在拉丁语中,*non sequitur* 实际上是个完整的句子,意思是"与之前所说的并不相关"——也就是说,所说或所写的东西在逻辑上没有承接前面的。亚里士多德将 non sequitur 视为逻辑的基本谬误之一——即推理可能出错的方式之一。对亚里士多德而言,non sequitur 通常指的是无法由前面的推理或证据得出的结论。听听政客们回答问题吧,看你能找出多少 non sequitur。

Quizzes

A. Match the definition on the left to the correct word on the right:

1. out-of-place statement   a. deduction
2. persuade   b. non sequitur
3. temptation   c. induce
4. subtraction   d. subsequent
5. helpful   e. seduction
6. ordered   f. consequential
7. following   g. conducive
8. significant   h. sequential

B. Fill in each blank with the correct letter:

a. conducive   e. consequential
b. deduction   f. subsequent
c. induce   g. non sequitur
d. seduction   h. sequential

1. The detectives insisted on a detailed and _____ account of the evening's events.

2. She fended off all his clumsy attempts at _____.

3. Conditions on the noisy hallway were not at all _____ to sleep.

4. There were a few arguments that first day, but all the _____ meetings went smoothly.

5. He sometimes thought that missing that plane had been the most _____ event of his life.

6. They arrived at the correct conclusion by simple _____.

7. He's hopeless at conversation, since practically everything he says is a _____.

8. He had tried to _____ sleep by all his usual methods, with no success.

Words from Mythology 源自神话的词语

Apollonian \ˌa-pə-ˈlō-nē-ən\ Harmonious, ordered, rational, calm. 和谐的，井然有序的，理智的，冷静的

• After a century of Romantic emotion, some composers adopted a more Apollonian style, producing clearly patterned pieces that avoided extremes of all kinds. 抒发了一个世纪的浪漫情怀之后，一些作曲家采用了更理智的风格，创作出有明显模式的、不走极端的作品。

In Greek mythology, Apollo was the god of the sun, light, prophecy, and music, and the most revered of all the gods. Partly because of the writings of Nietzsche, we now often think of Apollo (in contrast to the god Dionysus) as a model of calm reason, and we may call anything with those qualities *Apollonian*. This isn't the whole story about Apollo, however; he had a terrible temper and could be viciously cruel when he felt like it.

在希腊神话中，Apollo（阿波罗）是太阳、光明、预言和音乐之神，是最受敬仰的神。我们现在常视阿波罗（与狄俄尼索斯神相反）为理性的典范，部分原因在于尼采作品的影响；凡具有此类特质的东西，我们皆可称之为 *Apollonian*。然而，这并非阿波罗的全部；他脾气糟糕，有时还由着性子变得凶残暴虐。

bacchanalian \ˌba-kə-ˈnāl-yən\ Frenzied, orgiastic. 疯狂的，狂欢的

• The bacchanalian partying on graduation night resulted in three wrecked cars, two lawsuits by unamused parents, and more new experiences than most of the participants could remember the next day. 毕业之夜狂欢聚会带来的是三辆汽车被毁、两起由生气的家长提出的控告，以及许多参与者第二天都不会再记得的前所未有的经历。

The Roman god of drama, wine, and ecstasy, Bacchus was the focus of a widespread celebration, the *Bacchanalia*. The festivities were originally secret, and only initiated members could participate. There was wine in abundance, and participants were expected to cut loose from normal restraints and give in to all sorts of wild desires. Eventually the Bacchanalia became more public and uncontrolled, finally getting so out of hand that in 186 B.C. the Roman authorities had it banned. Much the same bacchanalian spirit fills tropical carnivals every year, including New Orleans' Mardi Gras.

Bacchus（巴克斯）是罗马的戏剧、酒和狂欢之神，也是一个被普遍庆祝的节日——*Bacchanalia*（酒神节）上的主角。酒神节的庆祝活动最初是秘密的，只有发起成员才能参与。在庆典上，葡萄酒供应充裕，旨在让参与者摆脱世俗的限制，尽情释放野性的欲望。后来，酒神节终于变得更加公开、不受控制，乃至最终完全失控，以至于公元前186年，酒神节被罗马当局禁止。几乎一样的狂欢精神每年都充斥着各种热带狂欢节，包括新奥尔良的马尔迪·格拉斯狂欢节。

delphic \ˈdel-fik\ Unclear, ambiguous, or confusing. 模棱两可的

• All she could get from the strange old woman were a few delphic comments that left her more confused than ever about the missing documents. 关于那些丢失的文件，她只能从那个奇怪的老妇人那里得到几句模棱两可的话，这些话让她更加困惑了。

Delphi in Greece was the site of a temple to Apollo at which there resided an oracle, a woman through whom Apollo would speak, foretelling the future. The Greeks consulted the oracle frequently on matters both private and public. The prophecies were given in difficult poetry that had to be interpreted by priests, and even the interpretations could be hard to understand. When Croesus, king of Lydia, asked what would happen if he attacked the Persians, the oracle announced that he would destroy a great empire; what she didn't say was that the empire destroyed would be his own. Modernday descendants of the oracle include some political commentators, who utter words of delphic complexity every week. 希腊的 Delphi(特尔斐)是阿波罗神庙所在地，该神庙里住着一位女祭司，阿波罗借她之口预言未来。希腊人经常就私人及公共事务向她请教。女祭司的预言是通过晦涩难懂的诗歌来传达的，这些诗歌须由牧师来解读，但是连神父的解释也让人费解。吕底亚国王克罗伊斯曾问她，如果他进攻波斯人会有什么事情发生。她给出的神谕是，他将毁灭一个伟大的帝国；但她没有明说的是，他毁灭掉的帝国属于他自己。一些政治评论家就像是女祭司的现代传人，他们每周说出来的话都模棱两可、复杂难懂。

Dionysian \ˌdī-ə-ˈni-zhē-ən\   Frenzied, delirious. 发狂的，精神错乱的

● Only in the tropics did such festivals become truly Dionysian, he said, which was why he was booking his flight to Rio. 他说，只有在热带地区，这样的节日才真正疯狂，这也是他订机票去里约热内卢的原因。

Dionysus was the Greek forerunner of Bacchus. He was the inventor of wine, which he gave to the human race. For that gift and for all the wild behavior that it led to, Dionysus became immensely popular, and he appears in a great many myths. He is often shown holding a wine goblet, with his hair full of vine leaves, and attended by a band of goat-footed satyrs and wild female spirits called maenads. In the 19th century, scholars such as Nietzsche claimed that the ancient world could be understood as a continuing conflict between the attitudes represented by Apollo (see *Apollonian* above) and Dionysus—that is, between order and disorder, between moderation and excess, between the controlled and the ecstatic. 希腊酒神 Dionysus(狄俄尼索斯)是罗马酒神 Bacchus(巴克斯)的先驱。他发明了酒并传给人类。由于他的这个礼物以及由此带来的疯狂行为，狄俄尼索斯倍受欢迎，在许多神话中都有他的出现。他的形象经常是这样的：手拿高脚杯，头发上满是葡萄叶，侍奉他左右的是一群有山羊蹄的森林之神萨提尔，还有一群狂野的、被称作 maenad 的小仙女。在19世纪，尼采等学者声称，古代世界可以理解为阿波罗(见上文的 *Apollonian*)和狄俄尼索斯分别代表的两种态度的持续冲突——即秩序与混乱、适度与过度、克制与放纵之间的冲突。

jovial \ˈjō-vē-əl\   Jolly, good-natured. 快乐的，活泼的，和善的

● Their grandfather was as jovial and sociable as their grandmother was quiet and withdrawn. 他们的祖父活泼、合群，但祖母却安静、离群。

Jove, or Jupiter, was the Roman counterpart of the Greek's Zeus, and like Zeus was regarded as chief among the gods. When the Romans were naming the planets, they gave the name Jupiter to the one that, as they may have already known, was the largest of all (though only the second-brightest to the naked eye). When the practice of astrology reached the Roman empire from the East, astrologers declared that those "born under Jupiter" were destined to be merry and generous, and many centuries later this would result in the words *jovial* and *joviality*.

Jove 或 Jupiter(朱庇特)等同于希腊的宙斯,与宙斯一样,也被认为是众神之首。在罗马人命名行星时,他们用朱庇特来命名他们所知道的最大的行星(尽管在肉眼看来亮度只排第二)。当占星术从东方传到罗马帝国时,占星家宣称,"出生在朱庇特星(木星)之下"的人注定是活泼的、慷慨的。许多世纪之后,衍生出了"*jovial*"和"*joviality*"两个词。

mercurial \mər-ˈkyu̇r-ē-əl\ Having rapid and unpredictable changes of mood. 情绪多变的,无常的

• His mother's always mercurial temper became even more unpredictable, to the point where the slightest thing would trigger a violent fit. 他母亲的脾气向来善变,如今更是难以预测,甚至到了一丁点儿小事儿就会强烈爆发的地步。

The god Mercury, with his winged cap and sandals, was the very symbol of speed, and the planet Mercury was named for him by the Romans because it is the fastest-moving of the planets. His name was also given to the liquid silver metal that skitters around on a surface so quickly and unpredictably. And the word *mercurial* seems to have come from the metal, rather than directly from the god (or an astrologer's view of the planet's influence). Mercurial people are usually bright but impulsive and changeable (and sometimes a bit unstable).

Mercury(墨丘利)神头戴有翅膀的帽子,脚穿凉鞋,是速度的象征。罗马人以他的名字命名水星,因为它是运动最快的行星。他的名字也被用来命名一种液态的银色金属,这种金属能在物体表面上快速且不可预测地移动。而 *mercurial* 这个词似乎源自这种金属,而不是直接源自墨丘利神(或者某位占星家对该行星的影响的看法)。情绪多变的人通常欢快、冲动且多变(有时有点情绪不稳定)。

Olympian \ō-ˈlim-pē-ən\ Lofty, superior, and detached. 崇高的,卓越的,超然的

• Now 77, he moved slowly and spoke to the younger lawyers in Olympian tones, but his college friends could remember when he was a brash, crazy risk-taker. 他现年 77 岁,行动缓慢,常以威严的语调与年轻律师对话,但他大学时的朋友们还记得,他以前可是一个冲动、疯狂的冒险家。

The Greek gods lived high atop Mt. Olympus, which allowed them to watch what went on in the human realm below and intervene as they saw fit. They insisted on being properly worshipped by humans, but otherwise tended to treat the affairs of these weak and short-lived creatures almost like a sport. So *Olympian* describes someone who seems "lofty" and "above it all," as if surveying a scene in which other people appear the size of ants. The Olympic Games were first celebrated in the 8th century B.C., at the religious site called Olympia (far from Mt. Olympus), and *Olympian* today actually most often refers to Olympic athletes.

希腊诸神高居奥林匹斯山之巅,这使他们能够看到下面人类世界所发生的事情,并在他们认为合适的时候进行干预。他们坚持要求受到人类虔诚地参拜,但在处理这些弱小而短命的生物的事务时,他们往往将其视作儿戏。*Olympian* 形容一个人看起来"崇高"且"高高在上",好像在扫视下方,下方的其他人微如蝼蚁。公元前 8 世纪,奥林匹克运动会首次举办,地点在一个叫奥林匹亚的宗教圣地(与奥林匹斯山相距甚远),而如今 *Olympian* 实际上常用来指奥林匹克运动员。

venereal \və-ˈnir-ē-əl\ Having to do with sexual intercourse or diseases transmitted by it. 性交的,性病的

• In the 19th century syphilis especially was often fatal, and venereal diseases killed some of the greatest figures of the time. 在 19 世纪,梅毒尤为致命,那个时代最伟大的人物中有些就死于性病。

Venus was the Roman goddess of love, the equivalent of the Greek Aphrodite. Since she governed all aspects of love and desire, a word derived from her name was given to the diseases acquired through sexual contact. Most of these venereal diseases have been around for many centuries, but only in the 20th century did doctors devise tests to identify them or medicines to cure them. Today the official term is *sexually transmitted disease*, or STD; but even this name turns out to be ambiguous, since some of these diseases can be contracted in other ways as well. Venus(维纳斯)是罗马的爱神,相当于希腊的 Aphrodite(阿芙洛狄忒)。她掌管着爱和欲望的各个方面,所以由她的名字衍生出来的 venereal 用来指通过性接触而得的疾病。这些性病大多已经存在了好多个世纪,但直到 20 世纪,医生才设计出诊断方式以及用于治疗的药物。今天,性病的官方术语是 *sexually transmitted disease*(性传播疾病,STD);但就连这个名字也含糊不清,因为有些性病也可以通过其他方式感染。

Quiz

Choose the correct synonym and the correct antonym:

1. Dionysian   a. frenzied   b. angry   c. calm   d. fatal
2. apollonian   a. fruity   b. irrational   c. single   d. harmonious
3. mercurial   a. stable   b. changeable   c. sociable   d. depressed
4. jovial   a. youthful   b. mean-spirited c. merry   d. magical
5. olympian   a. involved   b. lame   c. detached   d. everyday
6. venereal   a. sensual   b. intellectual   c. diseased   d. arthritic
7. bacchanalian   a. restrained   b. dynamic   c. frenzied   d. forthright
8. delphic   a. clear   b. dark   c. stormy   d. ambiguous

UNIT 2

Review Quizzes

A. Choose the closest definition:

1. reprobate   a. prosecution b. scoundrel   c. trial   d. refund
2. intercept   a. throw   b. seize   c. arrest   d. close
3. confine   a. erect   b. restrict   c. ignore   d. lock out
4. deduction   a. addition   b. flirtation   c. total   d. reasoning
5. subsequent   a. unimportant b. early   c. first   d. later
6. sequential   a. important   b. noticeable   c. in order   d. distant
7. non sequitur   a. distrust   b. refusal   c. odd statement   d. denial
8. conjecture   a. ask   b. state   c. guess   d. exclaim
9. perceptible   a. noticeable   b. capable   c. readable   d. thinkable
10. finite   a. vast   b. finished   c. nearby   d. limited

B. Match the definition on the left to the correct word on the right:

1. guess   a. olympian
2. soul   b. perceptible
3. lengthy   c. conjecture
4. godlike   d. definitive
5. ordered   e. protracted
6. clear-cut   f. psyche
7. noticeable   g. susceptible
8. sensitive   h. jovial
9. significant   i. sequential
10. jolly   j. consequential

C. Fill in each blank with the correct letter:

a. mercurial   f. seduction
b. induce   g. bacchanalian
c. intractable   h. traction
d. amicable   i. retract
e. interject   j. trajectory

1. The public isn't aware of the company's _____ of Congress through its huge contributions over many years.

2. The truck was getting almost no _____ on the snowy road.

3. The prison situation is _____, and likely to get worse.

4. He tried to _____ his statement the next day, but the damage had been

done.

5. Surprisingly, her first and second husbands actually have a completely _____ relationship.

6. The argument had gotten fierce, but he somehow managed to _____ a remark about how they were both wrong.

7. The disappointing _____ of his career often puzzled his friends.

8. She again told her family that nothing could _____ her to marry him.

9. By 2:00 a.m. the party was a scene of _____ her frenzy.

10. Her only excuse for her behavior was her well-known _____ temper.

UNIT 3

AMBI means "on both sides" or "around"; *ambi-* comes from Latin. Most of us are either right-handed or left-handed, but *ambidextrous* people can use their right and left hand equally well.
AMBI 的意思是"两边"或"周围"。*ambi-*源自拉丁语。大多数人要么是右撇子，要么是左撇子，但 *ambidextrous* people（左右手都很灵巧的人）可以同样好地使用左手和右手。

ambiguous\am-ˈbi-gyu̇-wəs\ (1) Doubtful or uncertain especially from being obscure or indistinct. 不明确的 (2) Unclear in meaning because of being understandable in more than one way. 含糊其词的，模棱两可的

- Successful politicians are good at giving ambiguous answers to questions on difficult issues. 成功的政治家善于对棘手的问题给出模棱两可的回答。

Ambiguous comes from the Latin verb *ambigere*, "to be undecided." When we say someone's eyes are an ambiguous color, we mean we cannot decide which color they are—blue or green? The *ambiguity* of the Mona Lisa's smile makes us wonder what she's thinking about. An ambiguous order is one that can be taken in at least two ways; on the other hand, the order "Shut up!" may be rude but at least it's *unambiguous*.
ambiguous 源自拉丁语动词 ambigere("不确定的")。用 *ambiguous* 来形容某人眼睛的颜色时，我们的意思是不能确定其眼睛是什么颜色的——蓝色还是绿色？蒙娜丽莎微笑的 ambiguity(含义不明)让我们想知道她在想些什么。不明确的指令至少可以用两种方式解读。而"闭嘴！"这个指令可能很粗鲁，但至少它是 unambiguous(明确的)。

ambient\ˈam-bē-ənt\ Existing or present on all sides. 环绕四周的，周围的

- The ambient lighting in the restaurant was low, and there was a bright candle at each table. 餐厅的背景灯光很暗，每张桌子上都有一根明亮的蜡烛。

Ambient light is the light that fills an area or surrounds something that's being viewed, like a television screen or a painting. Scientists sometimes refer to the ambient temperature, the temperature of the surrounding air. "Ambient music" is the term used today for "atmospheric" background music usually intended for relaxation or meditation. The candlelit restaurant in the example sentence is probably trying for a romantic *ambience*, or "atmosphere."

背景灯光指的是照亮某个区域或围绕被观看的某个东西的灯光，比如电视屏幕或一幅绘画的背景灯光。科学家有时候说到环境温度，即周围空气的温度。如今"氛围音乐"一词指的是营造某种气氛的背景音乐，通常是为了放松或冥想。例句中的烛光餐厅可能是为了营造浪漫的 *ambience*，即"气氛"。

ambivalent \am-ˈbi-və-lənt\ (1) Holding opposite feelings and attitudes at the same time toward someone or something. 有矛盾情绪的 (2) Continually wavering between opposites or alternative courses of action. 摇摆不定的

- He was ambivalent about the trip: he badly wanted to travel but hated to miss the summer activities at home. 他对这次旅行感到摇摆不定：他实在想去旅行，但又不愿意错过家乡的夏日活动。

Ambivalent is a fairly new word, less than a hundred years old, and, not surprisingly, it was first used by psychologists. Since being ambivalent means simply having mixed feelings about some question or issue, some of us spend most of our lives in a state of *ambivalence*. We might feel ambivalence about accepting a high-paying job that requires us to work long hours, about lending money to someone we like but don't know well—or about ordering a Tutti-Frutti Chocolate Banana Sundae El Supremo after we've been starving on a strict diet for weeks.

ambivalent 是一个比较新的单词，只有不到一百年历史。毫不奇怪，它是由心理学家首先使用的。有矛盾情感指的是对某个问题或事件有复杂的情感，所以，有些人一生中的大部分时间都处于 *ambivalence*（情感矛盾）状态。我们可能很纠结是否接受一份高薪但工作时间很长的工作，是否把钱借给喜欢但又不太了解的人，或者要不要在严格节食而饿了几周之后，买一份什锦水果巧克力香蕉圣代。

ambit \ˈam-bət\ The range or limit covered by something (such as a law). 范围，界限，权限

- The treatment of farm animals generally falls outside the ambit of animal-cruelty laws in the U.S. 在美国，如何对待农场的动物一般不在动物虐待法的权限之内。

Ambit is a rather formal term, often used by lawyers, as in, "With this new legislation, tobacco now falls within the ambit of FDA regulation." It almost always refers to something abstract rather than an actual physical range. So, for example, an immigrant might live completely within the ambit of her immigrant community until she started college, where she might find herself in a much broader social ambit. Most of the Latin American colonies were established by Spain, but in the 19th century, as the U.S. became stronger and Spain became weaker, they began to enter the ambit of U.S. power.

ambit 是一个相当正式的术词语，常为律师所用，比如，"根据这个新行法案，烟草现在属于FDA监管的范围"。这个词几乎总是指抽象的、非实际的物质范畴。例如，某个移民可能完全生活在她的移民社区之内，直到她上了大学，才会发现自己的社交范围大多了。多数拉美殖民地是西班牙建立的，但到了19世纪，美国走强，西班牙势弱，这些殖民地开始

进入美国的势力范围。

EPI is a Greek prefix that may mean various things, but usually "on, over" or "attached to." So an earthquake's *epicenter* is the ground right over the center of the quake. And your *epidermis* is the outer layer of your skin, on top of the inner *dermis*.

EPI 是希腊语前缀,可以有很多意思,但通常表示"在……上面,在……上方"或"附着"。所以 earthquake's *epicenter*(震中)指的是地震中心正上方的地面。*epidermis*(表皮)是皮肤的外层,在 *dermis*(真皮层)的上面。

epilogue \ˈe-pə-ˌlȯg\ The final section after the main part of a book or play. 收场白,后记,尾声

• Her editor told her the book really needed an epilogue, to tell where each member of the family is today. 编辑告诉她,这本书确实需要一个后记,告知读者每个家庭成员现在身在何方。

From its Greek roots, *epilogue* means basically "words attached (at the end)." An epilogue often somehow wraps up a story's action, as in the one for a famous Shakespeare play that ends, "For never was a story of more woe / Than this of Juliet and her Romeo." In nonfiction books, we now often use the term *afterword* instead of *epilogue*, just as we now generally use *foreword* instead of *prologue* (see LOG, p. 218). Movies also often have a kind of epilogue—maybe a scene after the exciting climax when the surviving lovers meet in a café to talk about their future. The epilogue of a musical composition, after all the drama is over, is called the *coda* (Italian for "tail").

从希腊语词根来看,*epilogue* 的基本意思是"附加在最后的话"。尾声常以某种方式对故事的发展做出总结,比如莎士比亚的名剧《罗密欧与朱丽叶》的尾声"古今多少事令人悲切/怎比那罗密欧朱丽叶"。在非小说类书籍中,我们现在经常用 *afterword* 来替代 *epilogue*,就像我们用 *foreword* 来替代 *prologue* 一样(见 LOG,第 218 页)。电影常有某种尾声——比如,激动人心的高潮过后的一个场景:劫后余生的恋人在咖啡馆见面,谈论他们的未来。在剧情完结之后,音乐作品的尾声叫做 *coda*(意大利语,表示"尾巴")。

epiphyte \ˈe-pi-ˌfīt\ A plant that obtains its nutrients from the air and the rain and usually grows on another plant for support. 附生植物

• The strangler fig begins life as an epiphyte on a tree branch, drops its tendrils to take root in the ground around the trunk, and slowly covers and strangles the tree to death. 绞杀榕的生命始于树枝上的附生植物。它垂下卷须,在树干周围的地上扎根,然后慢慢包住树木并将它绞杀。

Epiphytic plants are sometimes known as "air plants" because they seemingly survive on thin air. They rely on their host plants merely for physical support, not nourishment. Tropical *epiphytes* include orchids, ferns, and members of the pineapple family. To a newcomer in the tropical rain forest, the first sight of a great tree with large epiphytes hanging from every level can be eerie and astonishing.

Familiar epiphytes of the temperate zone include lichens, mosses, and algae, which may grow on rocks or water without touching the soil.

epiphytic plants（附生植物）有时也叫"气生植物"，因为它们似乎仅靠空气生存。它们对宿主植物的依赖，仅仅为了得到物理支撑，而不是营养。热带附生植物包括兰科植物、蕨类植物和凤梨科植物。对于初到热带雨林的人而言，第一次看到参天大树的每层上都有附生植物垂挂下来，一定会感到神秘又惊奇。温带常见的附生植物包括地衣、苔藓和藻类，它们可以生长在岩石或水上，不需要接触土壤。

epitaph \ˈe-pi-ˌtaf\ An inscription on a grave or tomb in memory of the one buried there. 墓志铭

• The great architect Christopher Wren designed London's majestic St. Paul's Cathedral, the site of his tomb and epitaph: "Si monumentum requiris, circumspice" ("If you seek my monument, look around you"). 伟大的建筑师克里斯托弗·雷恩设计了伦敦壮观的圣保罗大教堂，这里也是他的安葬之地。他的墓志铭是："Si monumentum requiris, circumspice." （"如果你在寻找我的纪念碑，看你的周围。"）

Epitaph includes the root from the Greek word *taphos*, "tomb" or "funeral." Traditionally, *epitaph* refers to a tombstone inscription, but it can also refer to brief memorial statements that resemble such inscriptions. One of the most famous is Henry Lee's epitaph for George Washington: "First in war, first in peace, and first in the hearts of his countrymen."

epitaph 包含有源自希腊语单词 *taphos*（"坟墓"或"葬礼"）的词根。在传统上，*epitaph* 指的是墓碑上的墓志铭，但也可以指类似的简短悼词。最著名的墓志铭之一是亨利·李写给乔治·华盛顿的："战争年代、太平之世、国人心间，皆为冠绝。"

epithet \ˈe-pi-ˌthet\ (1) A descriptive word or phrase occurring with or in place of the name of a person or thing. 绰号，外号 (2) An insulting or demeaning word or phrase. 侮辱、贬低他人的词语

• King Richard I of England earned the epithet "Lionhearted," while his brother, King John, was given the epithet "Lackland." 英国国王理查一世赢得了"狮心王"的绰号，而他弟弟约翰国王则得了个"无地王"的绰号。

From its Greek roots, *epithet* would mean something "put on," or added. Sometimes the added name follows a given name, as in Erik the Red or Billy the Kid. In other cases, the epithet precedes the personal name, as in Mahatma ("Great-souled") Gandhi. In still others, it's used in place of the actual name, as in El Greco ("The Greek") or El Cid ("The Lord"). In its other common meaning, an *epithet* is a mocking or insulting name (like "Lackland" in the example sentence). When enemies are said to be "hurling epithets" at each other, it means they're exchanging angry insults.

从其希腊语词根来看，*epithet* 的意思是被"放在上面"或添加的东西。有时候，绰号跟在名后，比如 Erik the Red（红胡子埃里克）或 Billy the Kid（比利小子）。绰号也可以在名前，比如 Mahatma（"Great-souled"）Gandhi（圣雄甘地）。绰号还可以用来代替真正的名字，如埃尔·格列柯（"希腊人"）或埃尔·熙德（"首领"）。此外，*epithet* 还常用于嘲笑或侮辱某人（比如例句中的"无地王"）。敌对双方相互"叫喊绰号"，就表示在互相怒骂。

（译者注：1. 埃尔·格列柯〔1541—1614〕，西班牙著名画家，原名多米尼柯·狄奥托科普洛，出生于希腊，三十六岁的

时候移居到西班牙。在西班牙,他的名字在日常使用时发音相当拗口,因此,人们称呼他为埃尔·格列柯,"希腊人"之意。2. 埃尔·熙德〔1043—1099〕,西班牙卡斯蒂利亚军事领袖和民族英雄,原名罗德里戈·鲁伊·地亚斯,由于英勇善战,赢得摩尔人的尊敬,被称为埃尔·熙德,阿拉伯语"首领"之意。)

Quizzes

A. Fill in each blank with the correct letter:

a. ambiguous
b. epiphyte
c. ambient
d. epitaph
e. epithet
f. ambivalent
g. epilogue
h. ambit

1. An _____ seems to live on air and water alone.
2. When the _____ light is low, photographers use a flash.
3. She felt _____ about the invitation, and couldn't decide whether to accept or decline.
4. Is any _____ inscribed on Grant's Tomb?
5. Andrew Jackson's _____, describing his lean toughness, was "Old Hickory."
6. Lord Raglan's _____ order confused the commander of the Light Brigade and led to its disastrous charge.
7. Her visit in the spring was a kind of _____ to our relationship, which had really ended two months earlier.
8. The subject really falls within the _____ of economics rather than sociology.

B. Match each word on the left with its correct definition on the right:

1. ambivalent
2. epithet
3. ambit
4. epiphyte
5. ambiguous
6. epitaph
7. ambient
8. epilogue

a. having more than one meaning
b. surrounding
c. wavering
d. grave inscription
e. range
f. descriptive nickname
g. ending
h. non-parasitic plant growing on another

HYP/HYPO is a Greek prefix meaning "below, under." Many *hypo-* words are medical. A *hypodermic* needle injects medication under the skin. *Hypotension*, or low blood pressure, can be just as unhealthy as the better-known *hypertension*, or high blood pressure.

HYP / HYPO 是希腊语前缀，意思是"在……下面，在……下方"。许多带有 hypo 的单词都是医学术语。*hypodermic needle*(皮下注射针)在皮下注射药物。*hypotension*(低血压)和更为人熟知的 *hypertension*(高血压)一样，都有害健康。

hypoglycemia\ˌhī-pō-ˈkän-drē-ˌak\ A person overly concerned with his or her own health who often suffers from delusions of physical disease. 疑病患者

● Hercule Poirot, the detective hero of the Agatha Christie mysteries, is a notorious hypochondriac, always trying to protect himself from drafts. 赫尔克里·波洛是阿加莎·克里斯蒂系列侦探小说中的名侦探。他是个出了名的疑病患者，总是怕自己被抓去服兵役。

One disease a *hypochondriac* really does suffer from is *hypochondria*, the anxiety and depression that come from worrying too much about one's own health. Even though it's easy to joke about hypochondriacs, hypochondria is no joking matter for the sufferer. Somewhat surprisingly, the second part of *hypochondria* derives from *chondros*, the Greek word for "cartilage." The cartilage in question is that of the sternum, or breastbone. From ancient times, doctors believed that certain internal organs or regions were the seat of various diseases, both physical and mental, and the area under the breastbone was thought to be the source of hypochondria.

真正困扰疑病患者的病是 *hypochondria*(疑病症)，即因过度担心自己的健康而产生的焦虑和抑郁。尽管拿疑病患者开玩笑很容易，但疑病症对患者本人而言绝非开玩笑的事情。有点令人惊奇的是，*hypochondria* 一词的第二部分源自希腊语 *chondros*("软骨")。这里讨论的软骨是胸骨下的软骨。从古代开始，医生就认为，特定的内脏器官或部位是生理和心理的各种疾病之所在，而胸骨之下的部位被认为是疑病症之源。

hypoglycemia\ˌhī-pō-glī-ˈsē-mē-ə\ Abnormal decrease of sugar in the blood. 低血糖

● She had been controlling her hypoglycemia through diet and vitamins, but she now realized she needed to add daily exercise as well. 她一直通过饮食和服用维生素来控制低血糖，但她现在意识到，还需要增加日常锻炼。

The root *glyk-* means "sweet" in Greek, so *glyc* shows up in the names of various terms referring to a sugar as a chemical ingredient, such as *glycerine* and *monoglyceride*. People with diabetes have difficulty controlling the sugar in their blood. Too little can be dangerous; its early symptoms may be as minor as nervousness, shaking, and sweating, but it can lead to seizures and unconsciousness. Luckily, it can be taken care of easily by eating or drinking something high in carbohydrates. Its opposite, *hyperglycemia* (see HYPER, p. 493), is the main symptom of diabetes, and usually requires an injection of insulin, which the sufferer usually gives himself. Today many people—though not doctors—use *hypoglycemia* to mean a completely different condition, with some of the same milder symptoms, that doesn't involve low blood sugar.

词根 *glyk-* 在希腊语中的意思是"甜的",所以,许多 *glyc* 所在的词语都有一个含义,即糖是其中的一种化学成分,比如 *glycerine*(甘油)和 *monoglyceride*(单甘油酯)。糖尿病患者很难控制血糖水平。血糖过低会十分危险,其早期症状可能很轻微,如紧张、颤抖、出汗等,但可能导致痉挛惊厥以及意识不清。幸运的是,摄入碳水化合物含量高的食物就能很容易地解决这个问题。相反,*hyperglycemia*(高血糖)(见 HYPER,第 493 页)是糖尿病的主要症状,通常需要注射胰岛素,这通常是患者自己注射的。今天,许多人——但不是医生——用 *hypoglycemia* 表示一种完全不同的疾病,有类似低血糖的轻微症状,但不存在血糖过低的情况。

hypothermia \ˌhī-pō-ˈthər-mē-ə\ Subnormal temperature of the body.
体温过低

• By the time rescuers were able to pull the boy from the pond's icy waters, hypothermia had reached a life-threatening stage. 当救援人员将男孩从池塘冰冷的水中拖出来时,男孩的体温已经低到危及生命的地步。

Hypothermia, which usually results from submersion in icy water or prolonged exposure to cold, may constitute a grave medical emergency. It begins to be a concern when body temperature dips below 95°F, and the pulse, breathing, and blood pressure start to decline. Below 90°, the point at which the normal reaction of shivering ceases, emergency treatment is called for.
体温过低通常是由于浸没在冰冷的水中或长时间暴露在严寒中所导致的,这会造成严重的医疗紧急状况。当体温降到 95 华氏度以下时,就要当心了,这时的脉搏、呼吸和血压开始下降。体温低于 90 华氏度时,正常的颤抖反应停止,此时需要紧急治疗。

hypothetical \ˌhī-pə-ˈthe-tə-kəl\ (1) Involving an assumption made for the sake of argument or for further study or investigation. 假设的 (2) Imagined for purposes of example. 假想的

• The candidate refused to say what she would do if faced with a hypothetical military crisis. 被问及假如遇到军事危机会如何应对时,这位候选人拒绝回答。

The noun *hypothesis* comes straight from the Greek word meaning "foundation" or "base"—that is something "put under" something else. So a hypothesis is something you assume to be true in order that you can use it as the base or basis for a line of reasoning—and any such assumption can be called hypothetical. So, for example, the theory that the dinosaurs became extinct because of a giant meteor that struck the earth near the Yucatán Peninsula involves the hypothesis that such a collision would have had such terrible effects on the earth's climate that the great reptiles would have been doomed. Once a hypothesis has been thoroughly studied and researched without being proved wrong, it generally comes to be called a theory instead.
名词 *hypothesis*(假设)直接源自意思是"基础"的希腊语单词——基础指的是"放在(其他东西)下面"的东西。因此,假设就是你假定为真实的东西,你能用该假设作为推理线索的基础——任何这样的设想都可以称为 hypothetical。比如,有理论认为,恐龙是因为一颗巨大的流星撞击尤卡坦半岛附近区域才灭绝的。这个理论的假设基础是:撞击会对地球的气候产生巨大的影响,足以毁灭恐龙这种大型爬行动物。一旦某个假设被全面研究之后仍未被证实错误,该假设通常可以被称为一个 *theory*(理论)。

THERM/THERMO

THERM/THERMO comes from the Greek word meaning "warm." A *thermometer* measures the amount of warmth in a body, the air, or an oven. A *thermostat* makes sure the temperature stays at the same level. And it's easy to see why the German manufacturers of a vacuum-insulated bottle back in 1904 gave it the name *Thermos*.

THERM / THERMO 源自希腊语,意思是"温暖的"。thermometer(温度计)用来测量身体、空气或烤箱中的温度。thermostat(恒温器)用来确保温度保持在同一水平。1904 年,德国的真空保温瓶制造商把这种保温瓶命名为 Thermos,其原因并不难理解。

thermal \ˈthər-məl\ (1) Of, relating to, or caused by heat. 热的,热量的 (2) Designed to insulate in order to retain body heat. 保暖的,保温的

• A special weave called thermal weave traps insulating air in little pockets to increase the warmth of long underwear and blankets. 一种特殊的热编织法把空气隔绝在小口袋里,从而增加内衣和毯子的保暖性能。

In days gone by, much of the male population of the northern states in the cold months would wear a garment of *thermal* underwear covering the entire body, called a union suit. Union suits kept sodbusters, cowboys, and townsfolk alike not only warm but also itchy and a little on the smelly side (back when bathing once a week was considered the height of cleanliness). Thermal imaging is photography that captures "heat pictures"—rather than ordinary light pictures—of objects. And thermal pollution occurs when industrial water use ends up warming a river in a damaging way. Small-plane pilots use *thermal* as a noun for a warm updraft, often over a plowed field or desert, that lifts their wings, just as it enables hawks to soar upward without moving their wings. 过去,美国北方各州的很多男性会在寒冷的月份穿一种遮盖全身的保暖内衣,称为"连衫裤"。连衫裤能给农夫、牛仔和镇民带来温暖,但也会让他们浑身瘙痒、有汗臭味(在那时候,每周洗澡一次就是干净的最高水准了)。热成像是一种摄影术,能拍到"热量的照片",而不是普通的光成像照片。当工业用水以毁灭性的方式使河流变暖时,热污染就产生了。小型飞机的飞行员把 *thermal* 用作名词,表示上升的热气流,这种气流往往在耕地或沙漠上方,能够托举机翼上升,正如它们能使鹰不扇动翅膀就能在天空翱翔一样。

thermodynamics \ˌthər-mō-dī-ˈna-miks\ Physics that deals with the mechanical actions or relations of heat. 热力学

• With his college major in electrical engineering, he assumed it would be an easy step to a graduate-school concentration in thermodynamics. 因为大学上的是电气工程专业,他认为研究生阶段攻读热力学就很容易了。

Thermodynamics (see DYNAM, p. 422) is based on the fact that all forms of energy, including heat and mechanical energy, are basically the same. Thus, it deals with the ways in which one form of energy is converted into another, when one of the forms is heat. The study of thermodynamics dates from before the invention of the first practical steam engine—an engine that uses steam to produce physical power—in the 18th century. Today most of the world's electrical power is actually produced by steam engines, and the principal use of thermodynamics is in power production.

热力学（见 DYNAM，第 422 页）基于一个事实，即各种形式的能量，包括热能和机械能，本质上都是相同的。因此，热力学研究的是，当其中一个是热能时，一种能量如何转化为另一种能量。热力学研究可以追溯到 18 世纪人类发明第一台实用蒸汽机前——蒸汽机是一种利用蒸汽产生动能的发动机。今天，世界上大部分的电能均是由蒸汽发动机产生的，热力学的主要用处在于电力生产。

thermonuclear \ˌthər-mō-ˈnü-klē-ər\ Of or relating to the changes in the nucleus of atoms with low atomic weight, such as hydrogen, that require a very high temperature to begin. 热核的

● In the 1950s and 1960s, anxious American families built thousands of underground "fallout shelters" to protect themselves from the radiation of a thermonuclear blast. 20 世纪五六十年代，忧心忡忡的美国家庭建造了成千上万的地下"放射性尘降物掩体"，以此保护自己免受热核爆炸的辐射。

Nuclear is the adjective for *nucleus*, the main central part of an atom. The original nuclear explosives, detonated in 1945, were so-called *fission* bombs, since they relied on the fission, or splitting, of the nuclei of uranium atoms. But an even greater source of destructive power lay in nuclear *fusion*, the forcing together of atomic nuclei. The light and heat given off by stars such as the sun come from a sustained fusion—or thermonuclear—reaction deep within it. On earth, such thermonuclear reactions were used to develop the hydrogen bomb, a bomb based on a fusion reaction that merged hydrogen atoms to become helium atoms. The thermonuclear era, which began in 1952, produced bombs hundreds of times more powerful than those exploded at the end of World War II. Why the *thermo-* in *thermonuclear*? Because great heat is required to trigger the fusion process, and the trigger used is actually a fission bomb.

nuclear 是 nucleus（原子核）的形容词，原子核是原子的中心部分。最初的原子弹是 1945 年引爆的原子弹，是所谓的 *fission* bombs（裂变式原子弹），因为它是建立在铀原子核分裂的基础上的。但是更大的破坏力源自 nuclear *fusion*（核聚变），即强迫原子核结合在一起。太阳之类的恒星所发出的光和热来自恒星内部持续的聚变——或热核——反应。在地球上，热核反应被用来制造氢弹，氢弹是基于聚氢为氦的聚变反应。热核时代开始于 1952 年，所造炸弹的威力强于第二次世界大战末期所爆原子弹成百上千倍。为什么 thermonuclear 中有 thermo- 呢？因为触发聚变需要大量的热量，而所用的触发器实际上是一个裂变式原子弹。

British thermal unit The quantity of heat required to raise the temperature of one pound of water one degree Fahrenheit at a specified temperature. 英热单位

● Wood-stove manufacturers compete with each other in their claims of how many British thermal units of heat output their stoves can produce. 柴炉制造商竞相宣称他们的炉子能输出多少的英热单位。

Despite its name, the British thermal unit, or BTU, may be more widely used in North America than in Britain. Air conditioners, furnaces, and stoves are generally

THERM/
THERMO

rated by BTUs. (Though "BTUs" is often short for "BTUs per hour"; in air-conditioner ratings, for instance, "BTUs" really means "BTUs of cooling capacity per hour.") Fuels such as natural gas and propane are also compared using BTUs. The BTU first appeared in 1876 and isn't part of the metric system—the metric unit of energy is the much smaller *joule*—so it isn't much used by scientists, but its practicality keeps it popular for consumer goods and fuels. A better-known heat unit is the *calorie*; a BTU is equal to about 252 calories. (Since the familiar food calorie is actually a *kilocalorie*, a BTU equals only about a quarter of a food calorie.)

虽然名称是英热单位(BTU),但这个词在北美的应用可能比在英国更广泛。空调、熔炉、炉灶通常由 BTUs 来评定。("BTUs"通常是"每小时 BTUs"的简写,但在空调评价中,"BTUs"实际上的意思是"每小时制冷量的BTUs"。)诸如天然气、丙烷之类的燃料也通过 BTU 来比较。BTU 最早出现于 1876 年,它不属于公制计量单位——能量的公制计量单位是要小很多的 *joule*(焦耳)——因此,科学家们很少使用它,但其实用性使它在消费品和燃料领域十分流行。另一个更出名的热量单位是 *calorie*(卡路里),一个 BTU 大约等于 252 卡路里。(因为我们熟知的食物热量实际上是 *kilocalorie* [千卡],所以一个 BTU 仅相当于一千卡的约 1/4。)

Quizzes

THERM/THERMO

A. Choose the closest definition:

1. hypothermia
   a. excitability   b. subnormal temperature
   c. external temperature   d. warmth
2. thermodynamics
   a. science of motion   b. nuclear science
   c. science of explosives   d. science of heat energy
3. hypoglycemia
   a. extreme heat   b. low blood sugar
   c. low energy   d. high blood pressure
4. thermal
   a. boiling   b. heat-related
   c. scorching   d. cooked
5. hypothetical
   a. typical   b. substandard
   c. sympathetic   d. assumed
6. hypochondriac
   a. person with imaginary visions
   b. person with heart congestion
   c. person with imaginary ailments
   d. person with imaginary relatives
7. British thermal unit
   a. unit of electricity   b. heat unit
   c. ocean current unit   d. altitude unit
8. thermonuclear
   a. nuclear reaction requiring high heat
   b. chemical reaction requiring a vacuum
   c. biological reaction producing bright light
   d. nuclear reaction based on distance from the sun

B. Indicate whether the following pairs of words have the same or different meanings:

1. British thermal unit / calorie   same ____ / different ____

2. hypochondriac / wise man   same ____ / different ____
3. thermal / insulating   same ____ / different ____
4. thermonuclear / destructive   same ____ / different ____
5. hypoglycemia / high blood sugar same ____ / different ____
6. hypothetical / supposed   same ____ / different ____
7. thermodynamics / explosives   same ____ / different ____
8. hypothermia / low blood sugar   same ____ / different ____

POLY comes from *polys*, the Greek word for "many." A *polytechnic* institute offers instruction in many technical fields. *Polygamy* is marriage in which one has many spouses, or at least more than the legal limit of one. And *polysyllabic* words are words of many syllables——of which there are quite a few in this book.

POLY 源自希腊语单词 *polys*("很多")。*Polytechnic* institute(理工学院)提供很多种技术领域的教学。*Polygamy*(一夫多妻制)指的是一个人有多个配偶的婚姻，或者至少超过法定的一个配偶。*Polysyllabic* words(多音节单词)指的是由多个音节组成的单词—本书中有很多这样的词。

polyp \ˈpä-ləp\ (1) A sea invertebrate that has a mouth opening at one end surrounded by stinging tentacles. 水螅虫 (2) A growth projecting from a mucous membrane, as on the colon or vocal cords. 息肉

• She had had a polyp removed from her throat, and for two weeks afterward she could only whisper. 她之前切除了咽喉息肉,手术后的两周她只能低声说话。

This term comes from *polypous*, a Greek word for "octopus," which meant literally "many-footed." To the untrained eye, the invertebrate known as the polyp may likewise appear to be many-footed, though it never walks anywhere since its "feet" are tentacles, used for stinging tiny organisms which the polyp then devours. The types of tumor known as polyps got their name because some seem to be attached to the surface by branching "foot"-like roots, even though most do not. Polyps of the nose or vocal cords are usually only inconvenient, causing breathing difficulty or hoarseness, and can be removed easily; however, polyps in the intestines can sometimes turn cancerous.

这个词源自希腊语单词 *polypous*("章鱼"),字面意思是"多足的"。对于非专业人士而言,这种名为水螅虫的无脊椎动物看上去好像有很多脚,但却不能四处走动,因为它的"脚"是触手,用于蜇刺小生物,再吃掉它们。息肉是肿瘤的一种,之所以得名 polyp,是因为有一些息肉似乎是通过分叉的"足"附在组织表面的—就像根——样。但多数息肉非如此。鼻息肉或声带息肉通常仅仅是造成不便,导致呼吸困难或声音嘶哑而已,可轻易去除;但是,肠息肉有时候会变成癌症。

polyglot \ˈpä-lē-ˌglät\ (1) One who can speak or write several languages. 通晓多种语言的人 (2) Having or using several languages. 有多种语言的、使用多种语言的

• As trade between countries increases, there is more need for polyglots who can act as negotiators. 随着国与国之间贸易的增长,人们需要更多的多语言者来担任协商者的角色。

Polyglot contains the root *glot*, meaning "language." It is used both as a noun and as an adjective. Thus, we could say that an international airport is bound to be *polyglot*, with people from all over the world speaking their native languages. One of history's more interesting polyglots was the Holy Roman Emperor Charles V, who claimed that he addressed his horse only in German, conversed with women in Italian and with men in French, but reserved Spanish (his original language) for his talks with God.

Polyglot 包含词根 *glot*("语言")。它既可用作名词也可用作形容词。我们可以说国际机场肯定是 *polyglot*(使用多种语言的),因为来自世界各地的人在机场都说母语。历史上比较有趣的、通晓多种语言的人中,有神圣罗马帝国的皇帝查尔斯五世,他声称他和自己的马说话只用德语,和女人交谈用意大利语,和男人交谈用法语,而和上帝交谈专用西班牙语(他的母语)。

polymer \ˈpä-lə-mər\ A chemical compound formed by a reaction in which two or more molecules combine to form larger molecules with repeating structural units. 聚合体,聚合物

• Nylon, a polymer commercially introduced in 1938, can be spun and woven into fabrics or cast as tough, elastic blocks. 尼龙是一种聚合物,于 1938 年初次商用,可被织成布料,也可以铸成坚硬而有弹性的块状物。

There are many natural *polymers*, including shellac, cellulose, and rubber. But synthetic polymers only came into being around 1870 with Celluloid, known especially for its use in photographic film. After many decades of development, the *polymeric* compounds now include *polypropylene*, used in milk crates, luggage, and hinges; *polyurethane*, used in paints, adhesives, molded items, rubbers, and foams; and *polyvinyl chloride* (PVC), used to make pipes that won't rust. And let's not forget *polyester*, which gave us a lot of uncool clothing in the 1970s but whose strength and resistance to corrosion have ensured that it remains an extremely useful material for all kinds of goods.

自然界有许多天然的聚合物,比如虫胶、纤维素、橡胶等。但人工合成聚合物的出现是 1870 年前后的事了,当时赛璐珞诞生,因在摄影胶片上的应用而出名。经过数十年的发展,现在的 *polymeric* compounds(聚合化合物)包括用于制造牛奶箱、行李箱及铰链的 *polypropylene*(聚丙烯),用于制造颜料、黏合剂、模制品、橡胶及泡沫的 *polyurethane*(聚氨酯),以及用于制造不生锈管道的 *polyvinyl chloride*(聚氯乙烯,PVC)。不要忘了 *polyester*(聚酯纤维),尽管它 20 世纪 70 年代为我们带来许多不太酷的衣服,但其强度和耐腐蚀性确保它仍是一种能制造多种产品的有用材料。

polygraph \ˈpä-lē-ˌgraf\ An instrument for recording changes in several bodily functions (such as blood pressure and rate of breathing) at the same time; lie detector. 多种波动描记器,测谎仪

• My brother-in-law is completely law-abiding, but he's such a nervous type that he's failed two polygraph tests at job interviews. 我的妹夫遵纪守法,但偏偏容易紧张,在求职面试时已经有两次测谎没能通过了。

With its *graph-* root (see GRAPH, p. 298), *polygraph* indicates that it writes out several different results. A polygraph's output consists of a set of squiggly lines on a computer screen, each indicating one function being tested. The functions most commonly measured are blood pressure, breathing rate, pulse, and perspiration, all of which tend to increase when you lie. Polygraphs have been in use since 1924, and have gotten more sensitive over the years, though many experts still believe that they're unreliable and that a prepared liar can fool the machine. They're used not only for law enforcement but perhaps more often by employers—often the police department itself! —who don't want to hire someone who has broken the law in the past but won't admit to it.

polygraph 有词根 graph-(见 GRAPH,第 298 页),它的意思是写出几个不同的结果。测谎仪在电脑屏幕上输出多条波形曲线,每条分别代表一项被测试的生理功能。最常被检测的功能是血压、呼吸、脉搏和排汗,在你说谎的时候,这几项数据往往都会增高。测谎仪自 1924 年开始使用,多年来变得越来越灵敏,但许多专家仍认为测谎仪不可靠,有准备的撒谎者可以骗过机器。测谎仪不只用于执法,也频频被雇主使用——常常是警察部门本身! ——他们不想雇佣那些在过去曾犯过事,但又不肯承认的人。

PRIM

PRIM comes from *primus*, the Latin word for "first." Something *primary* is first in time, rank, or importance. Something *primitive* is in its first stage of development. And something *primeval* had its origin in the first period of world or human history.

PRIM 源自拉丁语单词 primus("第一")。primary 的事物在时间、等级或重要性上是第一位的。primitive 的事物正处于发展的第一阶段。primeval 的事物起源于世界或人类历史的最早时期。

primal \ˈprī-məl\ Basic or primitive. 基础的,原始的

• There was always a primal pleasure in listening to the rain beat on the roof at night and dropping off to sleep in front of the fire. 听夜雨敲打着屋顶,在炉火前酣然入睡,总有一番原始的乐趣。

Primal generally describes something powerful and almost instinctual. So when we speak of the primal innocence of youth or the primal intensity of someone's devotion, we're suggesting that the emotions or conditions being described are basic to our animal nature. Sitting around a campfire may feel like a primal experience, in which we share the emotions of our cave-dwelling ancestors. Intense fear of snakes or spiders may have primal roots, owing to the poison that some species carry. In "primal scream" therapy, popular in the 1970s, patients relive painful childhood experiences and express their frustration and anger through uncontrolled screaming and even violence.

primal 通常用来形容某种强大且近乎本能的东西。因此,当我们说年轻时最原始的纯真或某人发自内心的奉献时,我们想说的是上述这些情感或状况是动物本性的基本特征。坐在篝火周围,感觉就像一种原始的体验,此时我们与穴居的祖先有同样的感受。对蛇或蜘蛛的强烈恐惧可能有原始的根基,或许是因为某些物种携带的毒素。20 世纪 70 年代流行"原始尖叫"疗法,患者通过无拘无束的尖叫甚至暴力行为,释放童年痛苦的经历,表达他们的沮丧和愤怒。

primer \pri-mər\ (1) A small book for teaching children to read. 初级读本 (2) A small introductory book on a subject. 入门读本

• She announced that she'd be passing out a primer on mutual funds at the end of the talk. 她宣布，演讲结束后，她将分发一本关于共同基金的入门读本。

Primers were once a standard part of every child's education. The first primer printed in North America, *The New England Primer* (ca. 1690), was typical; it contained many quotations from the Bible and many moral lessons, and the text was accompanied by numerous woodcut illustrations. We no longer use the word in early education, but it's widely used in everyday speech. Notice how *primer* is pronounced; don't mix it up with the kind of paint that's pronounced with a long *i* sound.

初级读本曾经是儿童教育的一个标配。北美印刷的第一个初级读本是《新英格兰初级读本》（约1690年），很有代表性。书中有许多出自圣经的名言和道德教育，课文还配有许多木刻插图。在早期教育中，我们已不再使用这个词，但它还广泛用于日常语言中。注意 primer 的发音，不要和 paint 之类发长 i 音的词语弄混了。

primate \ˈprī-ˌmāt\ Any member of the group of animals that includes human beings, apes, and monkeys. 灵长目动物

• Dr. Leakey sent three young women to work with individual primates: Jane Goodall with the chimpanzees, Dian Fossey with the gorillas, and Birute Galdakis with the orangutans. 李基博士派三名年轻女性分别研究一种特定的灵长目动物：珍妮·古道尔研究黑猩猩，迪安·福西研究大猩猩，比鲁特·加尔达基斯研究红毛猩猩。

It was the great biologist Carolus Linnaeus who gave the primates their name, to indicate that animals of this order were the most advanced of all. Linnaeus listed human beings with the apes a hundred years before Charles Darwin would publish his famous work on evolution. When people told him that our close relationship to the apes and monkeys was impossible because it disagreed with the Bible, he responded that, from the biological evidence, he simply couldn't come to a different conclusion. Among the mammals, the primates are distinguished by their large brains, weak sense of smell, lack of claws, long pregnancies, and long childhoods, among other things. Along with the apes and monkey, the Primate order includes such interesting animals as the lemurs, tarsiers, galagos, and lorises.

命名灵长目动物的人是大生物学家卡洛勒斯·林奈，灵长目这个名字暗示这一目是最高级的动物。林奈将人类与类人猿并为一类，这比达尔文发表著名的进化论早了一百年。他被告知，人类与猿和猴不可能有这么近的关系，因为这与圣经不符，但他回答道，从生物学证据上来看，不可能有第二种结论。在哺乳动物中，灵长目动物独有的特点是脑袋大、嗅觉弱、没有爪子、孕期长、童年期长等。除了猿和猴子以外，灵长目中还包括许多有趣的动物，比如狐猴、眼镜猴、丛猴、懒猴等等。

primordial \prī-ˈmȯr-dē-əl\ (1) First created or developed. 最初的 (2) Existing in or from the very beginning. 原始的，原生的

• Many astronomers think the universe is continuing to evolve from a primordial cloud of gas. 许多天文学家认为，宇宙从原始气体云演化而来，这一过程仍在继续。

UNIT 3

Primordial can be traced back to the Latin word *primordium*, or "origin," and applies to something that is only the starting point in a course of development or progression. A primordial landscape is one that bears no sign of human use, and a primordial cell is the first formed and least specialized in a line of cells. The substance out of which the earth was formed and from which all life evolved is commonly called "the primordial ooze" or "the primordial soup"—even by scientists.

primordial 可以追溯到拉丁语单词 *primordium*,即"起源",它用于形容在发展或进步历程中作为起点的东西。原始景观是没有人类使用迹象的景观,原始细胞是最先形成且在细胞系中分化最少的细胞。构成地球以及所有生命演化之源的物质被称为"原始浆液"或"原始汤"——甚至连科学家也这样称呼。

Quizzes

A. Fill in each blank with the correct letter:

a. primer   e. polyp
b. polyglot   f. primordial
c. primate   g. polymer
d. polygraph   h. primal

1. The only language instruction the child had ever gotten was from a basic _____, but he was already reading at the fifth-grade level.

2. Rubber is a natural _____ that remains the preferred material for many uses.

3. The asteroids in our solar system may be remnants of a _____ cloud of dust.

4. She had never passed a _____ test, since apparently her heart rate always shot up when she was asked a question.

5. All the _____ species look after their children for much longer than almost any other mammals.

6. Having gone to school in four countries as a child, she was already a fluent _____.

7. They were charmed by the _____ innocence of the little village.

8. The medical tests had revealed a suspicious-looking _____ on his stomach.

B. Indicate whether the following pairs have the same or different meanings:

1. polyp / oyster   same ____ / different ____
2. primate / ape-family member   same ____ / different ____
3. polymer / molecule with repeating units   same ____ / different ____
4. primer / firstborn   same ____ / different ____
5. polyglot / speaking many languages   same ____ / different ____
6. primal / highest   same ____ / different ____
7. polygraph / lie detector   same ____ / different ____

8. primordial / primitive   same ____ / different ____

HOM/HOMO

HOM/HOMO comes from *homos*, the Greek word for "same," which in English words may also mean "similar." A *homograph* is a word spelled like another word but different in meaning or pronunciation, and a *homosexual* is a person who favors others of the same sex. (This root has nothing to do with the Latin *homo*, meaning "person," as in *Homo sapiens*, the French *homme*, and the Spanish *hombre*.)

HOM / HOMO 源自希腊语单词 homos("相同的"),在英语单词中也可以指"相似的"。homograph(同形异义词)是指与另一单词拼写相同、意义或发音不同的单词。homosexual(同性恋)指的是喜欢同性的人。这个词根与拉丁语 homo(人)毫不相关,比如 Homo sapiens(智人),与法语 homme 和西班牙语 hombre 也毫不相关。

homonym \ˈhä-mə-ˌnim\ One of two or more words pronounced and/or spelled alike but different in meaning. 同音及/或同形异义词

• The *pool* of "a pool of water" and the *pool* of "a game of pool" are homonyms.
"A pool of water" 中的 *pool* 和 "a game of pool" 中的 *pool* 是同音同形异义词。

Homonym can be troublesome because it may refer to three distinct classes of words. Homonyms may be words with identical pronunciations but different spellings and meanings, such as *to*, *too*, and *two*. Or they may be words with both identical pronunciations and identical spellings but different meanings, such as *quail* (the bird) and *quail* (to cringe). Finally, they may be words that are spelled alike but are different in pronunciation and meaning, such as the *bow* of a ship and *bow* that shoots arrows. The first and second types are sometimes called *homophones*, and the second and third types are sometimes called *homographs*—which makes naming the second type a bit confusing. Some language scholars prefer to limit *homonym* to the third type.

homonym 有点儿棘手,因为它可以指三种不同类型词语。第一类是发音相同但拼写和意思不同的词语,如 to、too 和 two。第二类是发音及拼写相同但意思不同的词语,比如 quail(鸟)和 quail(畏缩)。最后一类是拼写相同但发音和意思不同的词语,比如船的 bow(船头)和射箭用的 bow(弓)。第一类和第二类有时被称为 homophones(同音异义词),第二类和第三类有时被称为 homographs(同形异义词)——这样一来,第二类的命名就有点令人困惑。一些语言学者倾向于将 homonym 限制在第三类。

homogeneous \ˌhō-mə-ˈjē-nē-əs\ (1) Of the same or a similar kind. 同种的、同类的、相似的 (2) Of uniform structure or composition throughout. 同质的

• Though she was raised in a small town, she found the city more interesting because its population was less homogeneous. 她在小镇长大,但她觉得城市更有意思,因为那里的人口不那么单一。

A slab of rock is *homogeneous* if it consists of the same material throughout, like granite or marble. A neighborhood might be called homogeneous if all the people in it are similar, having pretty much the same background, education, and outlook. Homogeneity is fine in a rock, though some people find it a little boring in a neighborhood (while others find it comforting). Note that many people spell this word homogenous, and pronounce it that way too. 一块岩石如果构成的材料完全相同,就可以称得上是同质的,如花岗岩或大理石。一个街区如果所有的人都相似,有着高度相似的背景、教育和观念,就可以称得上是同质的。岩石的 homogeneity(同质性)固然好,但社区的同质性会使一些人感到有点单调乏味(但也有一些人觉得比较安心)。注意,很多人把这个单词拼写为 homogenous,发音也如此。

homologous \hō-ˈmä-lə-gəs\ Developing from the same or a similar part of a remote ancestor. 同源的

• Arms and wings are homologous structures that reveal the ancient relationship between birds and four-legged animals. 手臂和翅膀是同源性的结构,说明鸟类和四足动物之间的关系年代久远。

In his famous discussion of the panda's thumb, Stephen Jay Gould carefully explains how this thumb is not homologous to the human thumb. Although the two digits are used in much the same way (the panda's thumb is essential for stripping bamboo of its tasty leaves, the staple of the panda's diet), the panda's thumb developed from a bone in its wrist and is an addition to the five "fingers" of its paw. The tiny stirrup and anvil bones of our inner ear, however, do seem to be homologous with the bones that allow a garter snake to swallow a frog whole. 斯蒂芬·杰伊·古尔德在其关于熊猫拇指的著名论述中,仔细地解释了熊猫的拇指与人类的拇指不同源的原因。尽管这两个拇指的作用相似(熊猫的拇指对于剥下鲜美的竹叶而言不可或缺,这些竹叶是熊猫的主食),但熊猫的拇指是一枚腕骨发育而成的,是熊猫爪子的五"指"之外的"指头"。然而,我们内耳中小小的镫骨和砧骨,与能让束带蛇吞下整只青蛙的骨头却是同源的。

homogenize \hō-ˈmä-jə-ˌnīz\ (1) To treat (milk) so that the fat is mixed throughout instead of floating on top. 使(牛奶)均质 (2) To change (something) so that its parts are the same or similar. 使相同,使相似

• By now the suburb had gotten so homogenized that he couldn't tell the families on his street apart. 如今,这个郊区已经变得如此雷同,以至于他都不能区分所住街上的各户人家。

Homogenized milk has been around so long—about a hundred years—that many Americans have never seen milk with the cream on top, and probably think cream separation only happens in expensive yogurt. But homogenize was being used before anyone succeeded in getting milk and cream to mix. People who use the word often dislike the idea that everything is becoming the same, whether it's radio shows that are no longer produced locally or schools that rely too much on standardized testing. 均质牛奶的出现有很长时间了——大约一百年——以至于许多美国人从来没见过表面上有乳脂的牛奶,也许还以为乳脂分离只出现在昂贵的酸奶中。然而,早在有人将乳脂和牛奶成功混合之前,homogenize(均质化处理)就已经被广泛使用了。使用这个词的人通常不喜欢一切趋同的想法,比如不再由当地制作的广播节目以及过分依赖标准化测试的学校。

DIS comes from Latin, where it means "apart." In English, its meanings have increased to include "opposite" or "not" (as in *distaste*, *disagreeable*), "deprive of" (*disinfect*), or "exclude or expel from" (*disbar*). The original meaning can still be seen in a word like *dissipate*, which means "to break up and scatter."

DIS 源自拉丁语,在拉丁语中的意思是"分开"。在英语中,它的含义有所增加,包括"对立"或"不"(如 *distaste*、*disagreeable*)、"剥夺"(如 *disinfect*),或"排除或驱逐"(如 *disbar*)。其最初的含义在一些单词中仍然可以看到,比如 *dissipate*,意思是"散开与消散"。

---

dissuade \di-ˈswād\ To convince (someone) not to do something. 劝阻

• The thought of the danger he might be facing on the journey makes her uneasy, and she's trying to dissuade him from going. 一想到他在旅途中可能面临的危险,她就感到不安,试图劝阻他进行这次旅行。

Dissuade is the opposite of *persuade*, though it's a less common word. The dissuading may be done by a person or by something else: A bad weather forecast may dissuade a fisherman from going out to sea that day, but a warning on a cigarette pack almost never dissuades a real smoker from having his or her next cigarette.

dissuade 是 persuade(说服)的反义词,尽管它是个不那么常用的词。劝阻你的既可能是人,也可能是其他东西;坏天气的预报可能阻止渔民当天出海,但烟盒上的警告几乎从未能阻止真正的烟民再抽一支烟。

disorient \dis-ˈȯr-ē-ˌent\ To cause to be confused or lost. 使迷惑,使迷失方向

• By now the hikers were completely disoriented, and darkness was falling fast. 此刻,徒步旅行者们已经完全迷失了方向,而且夜幕正在迅速降临。

The Orient is the East (just as the Occident is the West). The verb *orient* comes from the traditional practice of building Christian churches so that the altar is at the building's easterly end—in other words, "orienting" the church. One reason for this practice is that the Book of Matthew says, "As the lightning comes from the East … so also will the Son of Man"—that is, just like the sun in the morning, Jesus in his Second Coming will appear in the East. *Orienteering* is participating in a cross-country race in which each person uses a map and compass to navigate the course. *Orient* comes from the word meaning "to rise" (like the sun), and still today it's easy for a hiker to become *disoriented* when an overcast sky hides the sun.

Orient 指的是东方(正如 Occident 指的是西方)。动词 orient(使……向东方)来自建造基督教教堂的传统做法,即圣堂位于教堂最东边的角落——也就是说,"orienting"教堂。这样做有一个原因:《马太福音》说,"如同闪电从东方发出……人子的来临也要这样"——也就是说,就好像早晨的太阳一样,耶稣将从东方再度降临。orienteering(定向比赛)是一种越野比赛,每位选手都会用地图和指南针来导航。orient 源自意思是"升起"(如同太阳)的单词。即便是现在,当阴天遮住太阳时,徒步旅行者仍然十分容易迷失方向。

discredit \dis-ˈkre-dət\ (1) To cause (someone or something) to seem dishonest or untrue. 使(某人或某事物)不可信,受怀疑 (2) To damage the reputation

UNIT 3

of (someone). 败坏(某人)的名声

- His book had been thoroughly discredited by scholars, and his reputation was badly damaged. 他的书遭到了学者们的彻底怀疑,声誉也受到了严重的损害。

Since one meaning of *credit* is "trust," *discredit* means basically "destroy one's trust." A scientific study may be discredited if it turns out it was secretly written up by someone paid by a drug company. An autobiography may be discredited if someone discovers that the best parts came out of a novel. A lawyer may try to discredit testimony in a trial by revealing that the witness just got out of the slammer. Many political campaigns rely on discrediting one's opponents; desperate politicians have learned that, if they can claim that someone attacking them has been completely discredited, it might work even if it isn't true.

credit 有一个"信任"的意思,因此,*discredit* 的基本意思是"摧毁某人的信任"。如果事实表明,某项科学是由收了药厂钱的人秘密撰写的,那么这项研究就可能会受到质疑。如果有人发现某本自传最精彩的部分来自小说,那它可能就不可信了。在审判中,律师可能会揭露目击证人刚从监狱被释放的事实,以此表明他的证词不可信。许多政治竞选靠的就是诋毁对手。孤注一掷的政客们知道,如果他们宣称攻击他们的人完全没有信誉,即便不是事实,这样做也可能会奏效。

dislodge \dis-ˈläj\   To force out of a place, especially a place of rest, hiding, or defense. 强行移开,去除,驱离

- Senators are attempting to dislodge the bill from the committee, where the chairman has failed to act on it for five months. 参议员们正试图废除委员会的这一法案,因为主席已经五个月没有按该法案行事了。

A *lodge* is usually a kind of rooming house or hotel, and the verb *lodge* often means staying or sleeping in such a place. Thus, *dislodge* means removing a person or thing from where it's been staying. So, for instance, you might use a toothpick to dislodge a seed from between your teeth, police might use tear gas to dislodge a sniper from his hiding place, and a slate tile dislodged from a roof could be dangerous to someone hanging out on the street below.

lodge 通常是指一种公寓或旅馆,动词 *lodge* 常指在这样的地方逗留或住宿。因此,*dislodge* 的意思是将某人或某物移出它所在的地方。比如,你可以用牙签剔出牙缝中的一粒种子,警察可能会用催泪瓦斯促使狙击手离开他的藏身之处,屋顶脱落的石板瓦可能会对下面街上闲逛的人造成危险。

Quizzes

A. Choose the closest definition:

1. dislodge   a. drink slowly   b. scatter   c. make pale
   d. remove
2. homonym   a. word meaning the same as another
   b. word spelled and sounded the same as another
   c. one with same name as another
   d. one who loves another of the same sex
3. discredit   a. cancel a bank card   b. show to be untrue

c. dissolve   d. lower one's grade
4. homogeneous   a. self-loving   b. unusually brilliant
   c. having many parts   d. consistent throughout
5. dissuade   a. remove   b. break up   c. advise against
   d. sweep away
6. homologous   a. of different length   b. of similar size
   c. of different stages   d. of similar origin
7. disorient   a. confuse   b. disagree   c. take away
   d. hide
8. homogenize   a. treat as the same   b. explain thoroughly
   c. speak the same language   d. mix thoroughly

B. Match the definition on the left to the correct word on the right:

1. word spelled like another   a. disorient
2. pry loose   b. homogenize
3. having a consistent texture   c. dissuade
4. perplex   d. homonym
5. evolutionarily related   e. discredit
6. damage a reputation   f. homologous
7. make the same throughout   g. dislodge
8. convince otherwise   h. homogeneous

Latin Borrowings

ad hoc \ˈad-ˈhäk\   Formed or used for a particular purpose or for immediate needs. 特别地，专门地

● The faculty formed an ad hoc committee to deal with the question of First Amendment rights on campus. 学院成立了一个专门委员会来处理第一修正案赋予校园的权利问题。

Ad hoc literally means "for this" in Latin, and in English this almost always means "for this specific purpose." Issues that come up in the course of a project often require immediate, ad hoc solutions. An ad hoc investigating committee is authorized to look into a matter of limited scope. An ad hoc ruling by an athletic council is intended to settle a particular case, and is not meant to serve as a model for later rulings. If an organization deals with too many things on an ad hoc basis, it may mean someone hasn't been doing enough planning.

ad hoc 在拉丁语中的字面意思是"为此"，在英语中几乎总是指"为了这个特定的目的"。在一个项目的运作过程中产生的问题，通常需要有迅速的、专门的解决方案。特设调查委员会被授权调查某一限定范围内的事情。运动委员会的特别裁决是为解决一个特案做出的裁决，不作为今后其他裁决的范例。如果某组织有太多的事情要特事特办，这或许意味着某人没有做好充分的规划。

UNIT 3

ad hominem \ˈad-ˈhä-mə-nem\ Marked by an attack on an opponent's character rather than by an answer to the arguments made or the issues raised. 人身攻击的，不理性的

- Presidential campaigns have often relied on ad hominem attacks rather than serious discussion of important issues. 总统竞选往往依靠人身攻击，而不是严肃地讨论重要问题。

Ad hominem in Latin means "to the man"—that is, "against the other person." The term comes from the field of rhetoric (the art of speaking and writing). If you have a weak argument, one easy way to defend yourself has always been to attack your opponent verbally in a personal way. Since such attacks require neither truth nor logic to be effective, their popularity has never waned.

ad hominem 在拉丁语中的意思是"对那个人"——也就是说，"针对别人"。这个词源自修辞学（说话和写作的艺术）领域。如果观点的说服力不强，那就用一种简单的办法为自己辩护，即对你的对手进行口头上的人身攻击。由于此类攻击不讲求事实，也不需要逻辑就能起效，因此其受欢迎程度从未减弱过。

alter ego \ˈȯl-tər-ˈē-gō\ (1) A trusted friend or personal representative. 挚友，知己，个人代表 (2) The opposite side of a personality. 个性的另一面

- The White House chief of staff is a political alter ego, who knows, or should know, who and what the President considers most important. 白宫办公厅主任是总统的政治代言人，他知道或应该知道总统最看重什么人和什么事。

In Latin, *alter ego* literally means "second I." An alter ego can be thought of as a person's clone or second self. A professional alter ego might be a trusted aide who knows exactly what the boss wants done. A personal alter ego might be a close friend who is almost like a twin. *Alter ego* can also refer to the second, hidden side of one's own self. In Robert Louis Stevenson's classic *The Strange Case of Doctor Jekyll and Mr. Hyde*, Dr. Jekyll is a good-hearted, honorable man; but after taking a potion, his alter ego, the loathsome and diabolical Mr. Hyde, takes over his personality.

在拉丁语中，*alter ego* 的字面意思是"第二个我"。alter ego 可以被认为是某人的克隆或第二个自我。职业上的 alter ego 可能是一个值得信赖的助手，他完全明白老板想要做什么。私下里的 alter ego 可能是密友，几乎像双胞胎一样。*alter ego* 也可以指某人秘不示人的第二面。在罗伯特·路易斯·史蒂文森的经典小说《化身博士》中，杰基尔博士是一个善良、可敬的人；但服下一剂魔药后，他的第二个自我，即可恶而又魔鬼般的海德先生，就接管了他的人格。

de facto \dē-ˈfak-tō\ Being such in practice or effect, although not formally recognized; actual. (未被正式认可但)实际上存在的；事实上的

- Although there was never a general declaration of war, the two countries were at war in a de facto sense for almost a decade. 尽管从未有过全面宣战，但两国事实上的战争状态已经持续了近10年。

Literally meaning "from the fact," *de facto* in English can be applied to anything that has the substance of something without its formal name. A de facto government is one that operates with all of the power of a regular government but without official recognition. De facto segregation isn't the result of laws, but can be just as real and deep-rooted as legally enforced segregation. The de facto leader of a group is just the one who all the rest seem to follow. (Compare *de jure*, p. 434.)

de facto 的字面意思是"从事实上看"，在英语中，它被用于形容有实而无名的东西。事实上的政府指的是行使正常政府的全部权力但没有得到官方承认的政府。事实上的种族隔离并非法律的结果，但可以与法律强加的种族隔离一样真实且根深蒂固。一群人事实上的领导者就是其他人都追随的那个人。（比较 *de jure*，第 434 页。）

quid pro quo \ˌkwid-ˌprō-ˈkwō\   Something given or received for something else. 报酬，回报，抵偿物

- He did something very nice for me years ago, so getting him that job was really a quid pro quo. 他几年前为我做了件大好事，所以帮他谋得那份工作实际上是一种回报。

In Latin, *quid pro quo* means literally "something for something." Originally, the phrase was used to mean the substitution of an inferior medicine for a good one. Today it often doesn't suggest anything negative; for most people, it just means "a favor for a favor." But in politics the phrase is often used when, for example, a wealthy corporation gives a lot of money to a candidate and expects to get a big favor in return. In such cases, some of us may prefer to describe the money as a *bribe* and the quid pro quo as a *payoff*.

在拉丁语中，*quid pro quo* 的字面意思是"以物换物"。最初，这个短语指的是用劣质药代替良药，但如今它一般没有任何负面的含义。对多数人来说，它仅仅表示"还个人情"。但在政治上，这个词语经常用在类似下面的例子中：一家有钱的公司给某个候选人一大笔钱，期望他将来回报一个大的好处。在这种情况下，一些人可能更愿意把这笔钱称作 *bribe*（贿赂），而将回报的好处称作 *payoff*（报偿）。

ex post facto \ˌeks-ˌpōst-ˈfak-tō\   Done, made, or formulated after the fact. 事后的

- When Carl tells us his "reasons" for why he behaved badly, they're nothing but ex post facto excuses for impulsive behavior. 卡尔把他行为恶劣的"原因"告诉给了我们，但那不过是为其冲动行为找的事后借口罢了。

Ex post facto is Latin for "from a thing done afterward." Approval for a project that's given ex post facto—after the project already has been begun or completed—may just have been given in order to save face. An ex post facto law is one that declares someone's action to be criminal only after it was committed—a procedure forbidden by our Constitution.

ex post facto 是拉丁语，表示"来自事后做的事"。事后对某项目的批准——在某个项目已经开始或完成后才给予的批准——可能只是为了保住面子。事后法案指的是，在某人已经做了某事之后，才宣布该行为有罪的法令——这种立法程序为我国宪法所禁止。

modus operandi \ˈmō-dəs-ˌä-pə-ˈran-ˌdi\   A usual way of doing something. 惯常做法

- A criminal who commits repeated crimes can often be identified by his modus operandi. 惯犯通常可以通过他惯常的作案手法来辨别。

Modus operandi is Latin for "method of operating." The term is often associated with police work, and it's a favorite of mystery writers. In speech and dialogue, it's often abbreviated to "m. o." (as in "We're beginning to get a handle on the killer's m. o., but we can't go public with it yet"). But it's not only used in criminal contexts. So a frequent gambler who likes to play the horses may have a particular modus operandi for picking winners. And the familiar modus operandi of a cutthroat retailer may be to undersell competitors, drive them out of business, and then raise prices afterwards.

modus operandi 在拉丁语中表示"操作方法"。这个词常与警察的工作联系在一起,也是悬疑作家的最爱。在演讲和对话中,它常被缩写为"m. o."(比如"我们开始了解凶手的 m. o. 了,但还不能将其公之于众")。但它不仅用于犯罪领域。比如,喜欢赌马的老赌徒在挑选胜者时,可能会有某种惯用手法。残酷的零售商的惯用伎俩就是以低于竞争对手的价格出售商品,先把他们挤出市场,然后再提高价格。

modus vivendi \ˈmō-dəs-vi-ˈven-dē\ (1) A practical compromise or arrangement that is acceptable to all concerned. 临时协定,权宜之计 (2) A way of life. 生活方式

● During the budget crisis, the Democratic governor and the Republican legislature established a good working modus vivendi. 在预算危机期间,民主党州长和共和党立法机构确立了一个利于合作的权宜之计。

Modus vivendi literally means "manner of living" in Latin, and it sometimes has that meaning in English as well. Usually, though, a modus vivendi is a working arrangement that disputing parties can live with, at least until a more permanent solution can be found. Typically, a modus vivendi is an arrangement that ignores differences and difficulties. So, for example, two people going through a bitter divorce may be able to arrive at a modus vivendi that allows them to at least maintain an appearance of civility and dignity.

modus vivendi 在拉丁语中的字面意思是"生活方式",有时在英语中也有同样的意思。不过,通常情况下,权宜之计是指争执各方都能接受的合作协定,至少可以持续到更好的方法出台前。一般而言,权宜之计是一种忽视分歧和困难的安排。比如,两个经历着痛苦的离婚过程的人,也许能达成权宜之计,使他们至少能保持表面上的文明和尊严。

Quiz

Choose the closest definition:

1. alter ego
   a. church structure   b. bad conscience
   c. intimate friend   d. self-love
2. modus vivendi
   a. pie with ice cream   b. compromise
   c. stalemate   d. immoral conduct
3. ad hoc
   a. for this purpose   b. permanent
   c. long-range   d. for many reasons
4. ex post facto
   a. in anticipation   b. sooner or later
   c. coming after   d. someday
5. ad hominem
   a. based on personalities   b. based on logic
   c. based on issues   d. based on sexual preference

6. modus operandi   a. procedure   b. way of moving
    c. crime   d. arrest
7. de facto   a. in transit   b. in effect
    c. in debt   d. in theory
8. quid pro quo   a. proven truth   b. philosophical question
    c. mystery   d. something given in return

Review Quizzes

A. Complete the analogy:

1. anxious : calm :: ambivalent : _____
    a. neutral   b. certain   c. funloving   d. jittery
2. prologue : beginning :: epilogue : _____
    a. start   b. end   c. book   d. drama
3. past : previous :: ex post facto : _____
    a. beforehand   b. afterward   c. during   d. actually
4. local : here :: ambient : _____
    a. there   b. somewhere   c. nowhere   d. everywhere
5. rodent : woodchuck :: primate : _____
    a. zoology   b. mammal   c. antelope   d. baboon
6. support : assist :: dissuade : _____
    a. distrust   b. convince   c. soothe   d. discourage
7. personal : impersonal :: ad hominem : _____
    a. to the time   b. to the issue
    c. to the end   d. to the maximum
8. floral : flowers :: thermal : _____
    a. weight   b. pressure   c. terms   d. heat

B. Fill in each blank with the correct letter:

a. ad hoc
b. ambivalent
c. modus operandi
d. epithet
e. thermonuclear
f. quid pro quo
g. polymer
h. homogeneous
i. dissuade
j. modus vivendi
k. primer
l. alter ego
m. polyglot
n. hypochondriac
o. ambit

UNIT 3

1. A real _____, she could speak four languages and read three others.
2. The independent-minded teenager and her overprotective parents struggled to arrive at a _____ that both sides could accept.
3. The usual _____ for the songwriters was for one to write the lyrics first and then for the other to compose the music.
4. She is such a close friend that she seems like my _____.
5. The Congressman's vote was seen as a _____ for the insurance industry's campaign contributions.
6. She's the only person who could possibly _____ him from proceeding with this foolish plan.
7. Much thought has gone into the designing of _____ power plants that run on nuclear fusion.
8. The development of the first synthetic _____ for use as fabric revolutionized the garment industry.
9. "Gray-eyed" is the standard _____ used to describe the goddess Athena.
10. She had written a little _____ on volunteering, which she was now expanding into a full-length book.
11. Jessica was _____ about going to the party: it sounded exciting, but she wouldn't know any of the other guests.
12. In her middle age she became a thorough _____, always convinced she was suffering from some new disease.
13. You should blend all ingredients thoroughly to produce a _____ mixture.
14. An _____ committee was named to come up with ideas for redecorating the waiting room.
15. He reminded the audience that particle physics didn't really fall within the _____ of his expertise.

C. Indicate whether the following pairs have the same or different meanings:

1. de facto / actually   same ____ / different ____
2. hypothermia / heatstroke   same ____ / different ____
3. primordial / existing from the beginning   same ____ / different ____
4. ambient / atmospheric   same ____ / different ____
5. polyphonic / religious   same ____ / different ____
6. primal / first   same ____ / different ____
7. ambiguous / unclear   same ____ / different ____
8. modus operandi / way of life   same ____ / different ____
9. homologous / blended   same ____ / different ____

10. discredit / mislead   same ____ / different ____
11. thermal / soil-related   same ____ / different ____
12. epiphyte / parasite   same ____ / different ____
13. quid pro quo / synonym   same ____ / different ____
14. epitaph / grave inscription   same ____ / different ____
15. dislodge / deflate   same ____ / different ____

UNIT 4

VOR comes from the Latin verb *vorare*, "to eat," and the ending *-ivorous* shows up in words that refer to eaters of certain kinds of food. *Frugivorous* (for "fruit-eating"), *granivorous* (for "grain-eating"), and *graminivorous* (for "grass-eating") aren't too rare, but you won't run across *phytosuccivorous* ("plant-sap-eating") every day.
VOR 源自拉丁语动词 vorare("吃"), 字尾"-ivorous"所在的单词指的是某种食物的食者。frugivorous("食果的")、granivorous("食谷类的")和 graminivorous("食草的")并不罕见, 但你可不会每天都能遇到 phytosuccivorous("吸植物液的")。

carnivorous \kär-ˈni-və-rəs\ Meat-eating or flesh-eating. 食肉的

- He'd gotten tired of his vegetarian guinea pigs and decided he preferred carnivorous pets such as ferrets. 他厌倦了素食的天竺鼠, 准备养雪貂之类的食肉宠物。

The order of mammals that Linnaeus named the *Carnivora* includes such families as the dogs, the bears, the raccoons, the weasels, the hyenas, the cats, and the seals. Most *carnivores* eat only meat in the wild, but some have varied diets; some bears, for instance, normally eat far more vegetation than meat. Carnivores have powerful jaws and complex teeth, and most are highly intelligent. Humans, like their ape cousins, are basically *omnivores* (see p. 372).
林奈命名的食肉目哺乳动物包括犬、熊、浣熊、鼬、鬣狗、猫和海豹等科。大多数 carnivores(食肉动物)只吃野生肉类, 但也有一些食性较杂, 比如, 一些熊类平常吃素多过吃肉。食肉动物拥有强有力的颚和复杂的牙齿, 多数都非常聪明。人类和他们的远房亲戚猿类一样, 基本上是 omnivores(杂食动物)(见第 372 页)。

herbivorous \hər-ˈbi-və-rəs\ Plant-eating. 食草的

- In spite of their frightening appearance, marine iguanas are peaceable herbivorous animals that feed mostly on seaweed. 尽管外表吓人, 但海鬣蜥是一种性情温和的食草动物, 主要吃海藻。

Many *herbivorous* animals, such as rabbits, deer, sheep, and cows, are noted for their gentle and passive ways. But such behavior is not universal among *herbivores*. Rhinoceroses and elephants, for instance, are capable of inflicting serious damage if threatened, and among dinosaurs, the herbivorous Diplodocus had a thick tail that could be used as a lethal weapon against attacking carnivores. Herbivorous humans are usually called *vegetarians*.

许多食草动物，如兔子、鹿、羊和牛，以温顺出名。但这种习性在 *herbivores*（食草动物）中并不普遍。比如犀牛和大象，如果受到威胁，能够造成严重的伤害。恐龙中有一种食草的梁龙，其尾巴粗大，可以用作攻击食肉动物的致命武器。食植物的人类通常被称为 *vegetarians*（素食者）。

insectivorous \ˌin-ˌsek-ˈtiv-rəs\ Feeding on insects. 食虫的

- Their rather odd 12-year-old son kept insectivorous plants in his bedroom and fed them live flies. 他们那 12 岁的儿子很古怪，把食虫植物放在卧室里，喂它们活苍蝇吃。

A wide variety of animals could be called *insectivores*—most of the birds, for example, as well as the spiders. Of the amphibians, frogs and many lizards are largely insectivorous. Even some fish get much of their food from insects. The order of mammals called Insectivora contains the shrews, moles, and hedgehogs, though bats and anteaters are also insectivores. Many insects are themselves insectivores; the dragonfly, for instance, is a swift *insectivorous* terror that lives up to its name. But it's the insectivorous plants that tend to fascinate us; of the over 600 species, the best known are the Venus flytrap (which snaps shut on its prey), the pitcher plants (which drown insects in a tiny pool of water), and the sundews (which capture insects with their sticky surfaces).

很多动物可以被称作 *insectivores*（食虫动物），比如多数的鸟类和蜘蛛。在两栖动物中，青蛙和许多蜥蜴基本属于食虫动物。甚至有些鱼也以昆虫为主要食物。哺乳动物中的食虫目包括鼩鼱、鼹鼠和刺猬，尽管蝙蝠和食蚁兽也是食虫动物。许多昆虫本身就是食虫动物。比如，蜻蜓是一种行动迅速的食虫动物，十分恐怖，配得上它 dragonfly（字面意思是飞龙）之名。但让我们着迷的还是那些食虫植物。600 余种食虫植物中，最著名的是捕蝇草（捕捉猎物时迅速闭合）、猪笼草（将昆虫溺死在一笼液体中）和毛毡苔（利用其黏性表面捕捉昆虫）。

voracious \və-ˈrā-shəs\ Having a huge appetite. 贪吃的，贪婪地

- One of the hardest parts of dieting is watching skinny people with voracious appetites consume large amounts of food without gaining weight. 节食的最痛苦之处就是，看着那些瘦子们大吃特吃，却怎么也长不胖。

Voracious can be applied to people, animals, and even things, and doesn't always refer to consuming food. Thus, teenagers are voracious eaters; you may become a voracious reader on vacation; and Americans have long been voracious consumers. The most voracious bats may eat three-quarters of their weight in insects in a single night. Some countries have a voracious appetite for oil. Voracious corporations keep "swallowing" other companies through mergers.

voracious 可以用来形容人、动物甚至物件，并不总是用来形容吃东西。因此，青少年是 voracious eaters（贪吃的食客），你可能会在假期成为一个 voracious reader（贪婪的读者），美国人长期以来都是 voracious consumers（贪婪的消费

者)。最贪吃的蝙蝠一个晚上就能吃掉相当于自身体重四分之三的昆虫。一些国家对石油胃口很大。贪婪的公司通过兼并不断"吞下"其他公司。

CARN comes from a Latin word meaning "flesh" or "meat." *Carnation* originally meant "the color of flesh," which was once the only color of the flower we call the carnation. In Christian countries, Lent is the period when the faithful traditionally give up something they love, often meat. The days leading up to Lent are known as the *carnival* season, from the Italian *carnelevare*, later shortened to *carnevale*, which meant "removal of meat"—though during carnival, of course, people indulge in just about everything, and the removal of meat only comes later.

CARN 源自拉丁语单词("肉")。carnation(康乃馨)最初的意思是"肉的颜色",肉色曾是康乃馨花的唯一颜色。在基督教国家,按照传统,忠实的信徒会在四旬斋期间放弃他们喜爱的某些东西,通常是肉类。四旬斋前的一段时间被称为 carnival season(狂欢节),这个词源于意大利语 carnelevare,后来简化为 carnevale,意为"去除肉类"——然而,在狂欢节期间,人们当然是纵情享受一切了,去除肉类的事儿还是狂欢节过后再说吧。

carnage \ˈkär-nij\ Great destruction of life (as in a battle); slaughter.
大屠杀

• Countries around the world appealed to all sides of the conflict to stop the carnage of the war in Bosnia. 世界各国呼吁,冲突各方停止波斯尼亚战争的大屠杀。

This word was taken over straight from French (a Latin-based language), and has mostly referred to large-scale killing in wartime. But *carnage* needn't refer only to slaughter on the battlefield. With tens of thousands of people dying each year in automobile accidents, it's appropriate to speak of carnage on the nation's highways. And those concerned about the effects of the violence we see constantly on TV and movie screens may refer to that as carnage as well.

这个词直接从法语(属于拉丁语系)接收过来,主要指战时的大规模屠戮。但是,carnage 并非仅指战场上的屠杀。每年有数万人死于交通事故,所以把交通事故比作美国公路上的大屠杀是恰当的。电视和电影中经常出现暴力场景,对其影响感到担忧的人,也可能将这些场景视为大屠杀。

carnal \ˈkär-nəl\ Having to do with bodily pleasures. 肉欲的

• The news stories about students on Spring Break tend to focus on the carnal pleasures associated with the annual ritual. 学生春假的新闻报道往往会关注这个一年一度的假期中的肉欲之乐。

In Christianity in past centuries, 9 was often used as the opposite of *spiritual*, describing what are sometimes called "the pleasures of the flesh." Thus, gluttony—the consumption of excessive food and drink—was a deadly carnal sin, whereas the holiest monks and hermits might eat hardly anything and never touch wine. Today *carnal* has a somewhat old-fashioned sound; when we use it, we generally mean simply "sexual."

在过去的几个世纪中,基督教经常将 carnal(肉欲的)用作 spiritual(精神的)的反义词,来形容我们有时所说的"肉体的欢愉"。因此，贪食——过量消耗饮食——是一种深重的肉欲之罪。最神圣的僧侣和隐士几乎禁食一切，而且滴酒不沾。今天，carnal 有点儿过时的意味。在我们使用这个单词时，通常指的就是"与性有关的"。

incarnate \in-ˈkär-nət\ Given bodily or actual form; especially, having human body. 具有(人)形的，化身(人)形的

- For the rest of his life, he would regard his childhood nanny as goodness incarnate. 他在余生中把儿时的保姆视为善良的化身。

Incarnate often has a religious ring to it, since for centuries it has been used in the Christian church, which regards Jesus as the *incarnation* of God—that is, as God made human. Surprisingly, neither word appears in Bible translations; instead, the Latin word *incarnatus* appears in the Christian creeds (basic statements of belief) and the Catholic Mass. Regardless, *incarnate* soon began to be used with various nouns: "the devil incarnate," "evil incarnate," etc. Notice that *incarnate* is one of the rare adjectives that usually, but not always, follows its noun. *Incarnate* is also a verb, though with a slightly different pronunciation: "This report simply incarnates the prejudices of its authors," "For her followers, she incarnates the virtue of selflessness," etc.

incarnate 常带有宗教意味，因为它长期以来一直为基督教会所用，基督教会认为耶稣是上帝的化身——也就是说，如同上帝造人。令人惊讶的是，这两个词都没有出现在圣经译本中；相反，拉丁语的 *incarnatus* 出现在基督教教义(基本是信仰条文)和天主教弥撒中。不管怎样，*incarnate* 很快就与许多名词一起使用，比如，"魔鬼的化身""邪恶的化身"等等。注意，罕有形容词用在所修饰的名词之后，*incarnate* 就是其中的一个，但其并不是总要放在后面。*incarnate* 也是一个动词，尽管发音略有不同："这份报告仅仅体现了作者的偏见""对于她的追随者来说，她体现了无私的美德"等等。

reincarnation \ˌrē-ˌin-ˌkär-ˈnā-shən\ (1) Rebirth in new bodies or forms of life. 转世轮回，再生 (2) Someone who has been born again with a new body after death. 转世化身

CARN

- Even as a child he struck everyone as a reincarnation of his grandfather, not in his features but in his manner and personality. 他还是个孩子的时候，人们就吃惊地发现他好像是他爷爷的转世化身，不是说容貌上很像，而主要是举止和个性很像。

It's easy to make fun of people who claim to be the *reincarnation* of Cleopatra or Napoleon, but they don't come from a culture that takes reincarnation seriously. In Hindu belief, a person must pass through a series of reincarnations—some of which may be as insects or fish— before fully realizing that the bodily pleasures are shallow and that only spiritual life is truly valuable; only then do the reincarnations cease. For Hindus, an "old soul" is a person who seems unusually wise from early in life, and whose wisdom must have come from passing through many reincarnations.

那些自称是克利奥帕特拉(埃及艳后)或拿破仑转世的人很容易被人取笑，但他们所处的文化并不把转世当回事。在印度教中，一个人必须经历一系列的转世——其中有几次可能是昆虫或鱼——才能完全意识到身体的快乐是肤浅的，只有精神生活才是真正有价值的。只有到那时，他的轮回才会停止。对印度教徒来说，"古老的灵魂"指的是一个从小看起来就异常聪明的人，他的智慧必定来自很多次的转世。

UNIT 4

Quizzes

A. Indicate whether the following pairs have the same or different meanings:

1. carnage / slaughter   same ____ / different ____
2. insectivorous / buglike   same ____ / different ____
3. reincarnation / rebirth   same ____ / different ____
4. voracious / extremely hungry same ____ / different ____
5. carnal / spiritual   same ____ / different ____
6. herbivorous / vegetarian   same ____ / different ____
7. incarnate / holy   same ____ / different ____
8. carnivorous / meat-eating   same ____ / different ____

B. Fill in each blank with the correct letter:

a. reincarnation   e. voracious
b. insectivorous   f. herbivorous
c. carnage   g. carnal
d. carnivorous   h. incarnate

1. Sheep, cattle, and antelope are _____; unlike dogs and cats, they show no interest in meat.

2. The school tried to shield students from _____ temptations.

3. The smallest mammal is the bumblebee bat, an _____ creature about the size of a dime.

4. Today he speaks of his former stepfather as evil _____, and his mother doesn't argue with him.

5. From the variety of books on his shelves, we could tell he was a _____ reader.

6. Even the ambulance drivers were horrified by the _____ of the accident.

7. As a child she loved to watch them throw meat to the _____ ones, especially the lions and tigers.

CRED

CRED comes from *credere*, the Latin verb meaning "to believe" or "to entrust." We have a good *credit* rating when institutions trust in our ability to repay a loan, and we carry *credentials* so that others will believe that we are who we say we are.

CRED 源自拉丁语动词 *credere*("相信"或"委托")。当一些机构相信我们有能力偿还贷款时,我们就拥有了良好的 *credit* rating(信用评级)。我们带上 *credentials*(证件),别人会相信我们就是自己所说的那个人。

---

credence \ˈkrē-dəns\ Mental acceptance of something as true or real;

· 77 ·

belief. 相信，信任

- He scoffed and said no one still gives any credence to the story of the Loch Ness monster. 他嘲笑说，现在没人还会把尼斯湖怪的故事当真了。

Credence is close in meaning to *belief*, but there are differences. Unlike *belief*, *credence* is seldom used in connection with faith in a religion or philosophy. Instead *credence* is often used in reference to reports, rumors, and opinions. And，unlike *belief*, it tends to be used with the words *give*, *lack*, *lend*, and *gain*. So a new piece of evidence may lend credence to the alibi of a criminal suspect. Claims that a political candidate can become the next President gain credence only after the candidate wins a few primaries. And although stories about Elvis sightings persist，they lack credence for most people.

credence 与 *belief*（信念）意思接近，但也有区别。与 *belief* 不同，*credence* 很少用于宗教或哲学的信仰。相反，*credence* 通常用于指相信报告、传闻和观点。与 *belief* 不同的是，它往往与 *give*、*lack*、*lend* 和 *gain* 连用。因此，新发现的证据可能使犯罪嫌疑人的不在场证明更为可信。只有某政治候选人赢得几场初选后，他成为下届总统的说法才有可信度。尽管不断有传言说见到了猫王，但对大多数人来说，这些说法都缺乏可信度。

credible \ ˈkre-də-bəl \ （1）Able to be believed；reasonable to trust or believe. 可信的，可靠的（2）Good enough to be effective. 足够好的，有明显效果的

- Because of her past criminal record，the defense lawyers knew she wouldn't be a credible witness. 因为她过去有过犯罪记录，辩护律师知道她不是一个可信的目击证人。

Credible evidence is evidence that's likely to be believed. A credible plan is one that might actually work，and a credible excuse is one your parents might actually believe. And just as *credible* means "believable," the noun *credibility* means "believability." (But we no longer use *incredible* to mean the literal opposite of *credible*, just as we no longer use *unbelievable* as the literal opposite of *believable*.) Since *cred* is short for *credibility*, "street cred" is the kind of *credibility* among tough young people that you can only get by proving yourself on the mean streets of the inner city.

可信的证据是能让人信服的证据。可信的计划是可能奏效的计划，可信的借口是父母亲会真正相信的借口。正如 *credible* 的意思是"可信的"，其名词 *credibility* 的意思是"可信度"（但我们不再把 *incredible* 用作 *credible* 完全意义上的反义词，就像我们不再把 *unbelievable* 用作 *believable* 完全意义上的反义词一样）。*Cred* 是 *credibility* 的简写，"street cred（街头信誉）"指的是那种在强壮的年轻人中的信誉，若想得到，只有在市中心区的穷街陋巷中证明自己。

credulity \ kri-ˈdü-lə-tē \ Readiness and willingness to believe on the basis of little evidence. 轻信

- Thrillers and action movies only succeed if they don't strain our credulity too much. 惊悚片和动作片不太过牵强才能取得成功。

A particularly far-fetched story may be said to strain credulity, stretch credulity, put demands on our credulity, or make claims on our credulity. Credulity is a quality of innocent children (of all ages) and isn't always a bad thing; it must have been pure credulity that enabled Chicago White Sox and Philadelphia Phillies fans to wait so long for a World Series victory ("This is the year they're going to take it!"), which probably made life bearable for them. The related adjective is *credulous*. F. Scott Fitzgerald once defined advertising as "making dubious promises to a credulous public."

我们可以说，一个特别牵强附会的故事 strain credulity, stretch credulity, put demands on our credulity 或 make claims on our credulity, 意思是"挑战我们轻信度的底线"。轻信是（所有年龄段）天真的孩子的特点，也并不总是坏事。正是出于纯粹的轻信才让芝加哥白袜队和费城费城人队的球迷为世界职业棒球大赛的胜利等了这么久（"就是今年，他们必定夺冠！"），这可能使他们的生活好受些。它的形容词形式是 credulous。菲茨杰拉德曾将广告定义为"对轻信的公众做出可疑承诺"。

credo \ˈkrē-ˌdō\   (1) A statement of the basic beliefs of a religious faith. 教义 (2) A set of guiding principles or beliefs. 信条

• She claims she made her money on Wall Street just by following the old credo "Buy low, sell high." 她声称，她在华尔街赚钱靠的就是遵循了"低买高卖"的古老信条。

Credo comes straight from the Latin word meaning "I believe," and is the first word of many religious credos, or *creeds*, such as the Apostles' Creed and the Nicene Creed. But the word can be applied to any guiding principle or set of principles. Of course, you may choose a different credo when you're 52 than when you're 19. But here is the credo of the writer H. L. Mencken, written after he had lived quite a few years: "I believe that it is better to tell the truth than to lie. I believe that it is better to be free than to be a slave. And I believe that it is better to know than to be ignorant."

Credo 直接来自拉丁语单词，意思是"我相信"。它是许多宗教教义，即 creeds 的第一个单词，比如《使徒信经》和《尼西亚信经》。但是这个词也可以用于指任何一个或一套指导原则。当然，你可以在 52 岁时选择不同于 19 岁时的信条。下面是作家 H.L.门肯在生活了很多年后写下的信条："我相信说实话好过说谎。我相信自由好过奴役。我还相信了解好过无知。"

FID comes from *fides*, the Latin word for "faith" or "trust." *Fidelity* is another word for "faithfulness." *Confidence* is having faith in someone or something. An *infidel* is someone who lacks a particular kind of religious faith. And the once-popular dog's name *Fido* is Latin for "I trust."

FID 源自拉丁语单词 fides（"信仰"或"信任"）。fidelity 是表示"忠诚"的另一个单词。confidence 指的是对某人或某事有信心。infidel（异教徒）是缺乏某种宗教信仰的人。有个狗名 Fido 一度很流行，这是拉丁语，表示"我信任"。

affidavit \ˌa-fə-ˈdā-vət\   A sworn statement made in writing. 宣誓书

• The whole family had signed affidavits stating that they believed the will to be valid. 全家人都签署了宣誓书,证明他们相信遗嘱是有法律效力的。

In Latin, *affidavit* means "he (she) has sworn an oath," and an affidavit is always a sworn written document. If it contains a lie, the person making it may be prosecuted. Affidavits are often used in court when it isn't possible for someone to appear in person. Police officers must usually file an affidavit with a judge to get a search warrant. Affidavits (unlike similar signed statements called *depositions*) are usually made without an opposing lawyer being present and able to ask questions.

在拉丁语中，*affidavit* 的意思是"他/她已经宣誓"。affidavit 通常是书面的宣誓文件。如果宣誓书中包含谎言，制定者就要遭到诉讼。当某人不能亲自出庭时，法庭上往往就会用到宣誓书。警察通常需要向法官提交宣誓书才能获得搜查令。宣誓书(不同于类似的签署过的声明，称为 *depositions*[证词])的制定往往不需要对方律师在场，对方律师也不能提问。

diffident \ˈdi-fə-dənt\ Lacking confidence; timid, cautious. 缺乏信心的，害羞的，谨慎的

• He always found it a struggle to get his most diffident students to speak in front of the class. 他发现让最害羞的学生在全班人面前发言非常困难。

Diffident means lacking faith in oneself—in other words, the opposite of *confident*. Distrust in your abilities or opinions usually makes you hesitate to speak or act. Patients who feel diffident around their doctors, for example, don't dare ask them many questions. A helpful friend tries to instill confidence in place of *diffidence*.

diffident 指的是对自己缺少信心——换句话说，它是 *confident* 的反义词。若不相信自己的能力或看法，你在说话或行动上通常会犹豫不决。例如，在医生面前缺乏自信的病人不敢问太多问题。乐于助人的朋友会尽力为你注入信心，减少你的 *diffidence*(不自信)。

fiduciary \fi-ˈdü-shē-ˌer-ē\ (1) Having to do with a confidence or trust. 与信任或信任有关的 (2) Held in trust for another. 信托的，信用的

• Pension-fund managers have a fiduciary responsibility to invest the pension's funds for the sole benefit of those who will receive the pensions. 养老基金经理有信托责任，需要完全为了养老金领取者的利益投资他们的老金基金。

A *fiduciary* relationship is one in which one person places faith in another. Stockbrokers and real-estate agents have fiduciary duties to their clients, which means they must act in their clients' best financial interests. Members of a company's board of directors have a *fiduciary* responsibility to protect the financial interests of the company's shareholders. There are legal requirements for those with fiduciary responsibility, and they can be sued for breach of fiduciary duty if they fail.

信托关系指的是某个人寄信任于他人的一种关系。股票经纪人和房地产经纪人对客户负有信托义务，这意味着他们必须从客户的最大经济利益出发行事。公司董事会成员负有信托责任，他们要保护公司股东的财务利益。法律上对信托责任者有一定的要求，如达不到要求，他们就可能因为违背信托责任而遭诉讼。

perfidy \ˈpər-fə-dē\ Faithlessness, disloyalty, or treachery. 背信弃义，不忠或背叛

• While working for the CIA he was lured into becoming a double agent, and it seems he paid a high price for his perfidy. 在为中央情报局工作期间，他受到引诱成为双重间谍。如今看来，他似乎为曾经的不忠付出了高昂的代价。

The *perfidious* Benedict Arnold plotted with the British to surrender West Point to them during the American Revolution—an act that made his name a synonym for *traitor*. In recent years, the perfidy of the double agents Aldrich Ames (of the CIA) and Robert Hanssen (of the FBI) has become notorious.

在美国独立战争期间,*perfidious*(背信弃义的)本尼迪克特·阿诺德与英国人密谋献出西点要塞,这一行为使他的名字成为 *traitor*(背叛者)的同义词。近年来,中央情报局的奥德里奇·艾姆斯和联邦调查局的罗伯特·汉森两位背弃信义的双面间谍已经臭名昭著。

Quizzes

A. Fill in each blank with the correct letter:

a. perfidy   e. credo
b. credible   f. affidavit
c. diffident   g. fiduciary
d. credulity   h. credence

1. She gave little _____ to his story about his deranged girlfriend and the kitchen knife.

2. Their account of the burglary didn't strike investigators as _____, and the insurance company refused to pay.

3. For her own best friend to take up with her former husband was _____ that could never be forgiven.

4. He's so _____ that you'd never believe he gives talks in front of international organizations.

5. The family trust had been so badly mismanaged that it appeared there had been a violation of _____ responsibility.

6. The company's odd but charming _____ was "Don't be evil."

7. The _____ stated that no oral agreement had ever been made.

8. Her _____ is enormous; no story in the supermarket tabloids is too far-fetched for her.

B. Match the definition on the left to the correct word on the right:

1. bad faith   a. perfidy
2. timid   b. credible
3. acceptance   c. diffident
4. trust-based   d. credulity
5. sworn document   e. credo
6. believable   f. affidavit
7. principles   g. fiduciary
8. trustfulness   h. credence

CURR/CURS

CURR/CURS comes from *currere*, the Latin verb meaning "to run." Although words based on this root don't tend to suggest speed, the sense of movement remains. *Current*, for instance, refers to running water in a stream or river, or electrons running through a wire, and an *excursion* is a trip from one place to another.

CURR/CURS 源自拉丁语动词 *currere*(跑)。虽然基于这个词根的单词一般不表示速度,但运动的感觉保了留下来。例如,*current* 指的是小溪或河流中的水流,或电线里的电流,*excursion*(远足、短途旅行)指的是从一地到另一地的旅行。

concurrent \kən-ˈkər-ənt\ Happening or operating at the same time. 同时发生的,并发的

• The killer was sentenced to serve three concurrent life terms in prison. 凶手被判在监狱同时服三项终身监禁。

Things that are *concurrent* usually not only happen at the same time but also are similar to each other. So, for example, multitasking computers are capable of performing concurrent tasks. When we take more than one medication at a time, we run the risks involved with concurrent drug use. And at any multiplex theater several movies are running *concurrently*.

concurrent 的事情通常不仅发生在同一时间,而且彼此相似。例如,多任务计算机能够同时完成多项任务。当我们同时服用一种以上的药物时,就会面临同时用药带来的风险。在任何一家多厅电影院,都有几部电影 *concurrently*(同时地)放映。

cursory \ˈkər-sə-rē\ Hastily and often carelessly done. 仓促的,匆忙的

• Having spent the weekend going to parties, she had only given the chapter a cursory reading before class on Monday. 她周末去参加了聚会,星期一上课前才草草读完这一章。

Unlike the other words in this section, *cursory* always implies speed. But it also stresses a lack of attention to detail. Cursory observations are generally shallow or superficial because of their speed. And when citizens complain about a cursory police investigation of a crime, they're distressed by its lack of thoroughness, not its speed.

与本节的其他单词不同,*cursory* 总是意味着速度。但它也强调对细节的忽视。粗略的观察通常是肤浅的,因为速度很快。当公民们抱怨警方对犯罪行为的调查非常草率时,他们忧虑的是调查不够彻底,而非调查的速度不够快。

discursive \dis-ˈkər-siv\ Passing from one topic to another. 东拉西扯的,不着边际的

• Some days he allowed himself to write long discursive essays in his diary instead of his usual simple reporting of the day's events. 有些天,他任由自己在日记里写些长篇大论的、不着边际的随笔,而不是像往常那样简单地记录当天发生的事情。

The Latin verb *discurrere* meant "to run about," and from this word we get our word *discursive*, which often means rambling about over a wide range of topics. A discursive writing style generally isn't encouraged by writing teachers. But some of the great 19th-century writers, such as Charles Lamb and Thomas de Quincey, show that the discursive essay, especially when gracefully written and somewhat personal in tone, can be a pleasure to read. And the man often called the inventor of the essay, the great Michel de Montaigne, might touch on dozens of different topics in the course of a long discursive essay.

拉丁语动词 discurrere 的意思是"到处跑",由此我们得到 discursive 一词,它的意思是漫谈很多话题。写作老师一般不鼓励漫谈式写作风格。但是,19 世纪的一些大作家,如查尔斯·兰姆和托马斯·德·昆西,向我们展示了漫谈式散文,如果文笔优美且带有个人色彩,读起来也别有一番乐趣。大作家米歇尔·德·蒙田被称为散文的发明者,常常在一篇漫谈式的长篇散文中会涉及几十个不同的话题。

precursor \prē-ˌkər-sər\ One that goes before and indicates the coming of another. 先驱,先兆

• Scientists are trying to identify special geological activity that may be a precursor to an earthquake, which will help them predict the quake's size, time, and location. 科学家们正尝试找出可能是地震前兆的特殊地质活动,这将有助于预测地震的规模、时间和地点。

With its prefix *pre-*, meaning "before," a precursor is literally a "forerunner," and in fact *forerunner* first appeared as the translation of the Latin *praecursor*. But the two words function a little differently today. A forerunner may simply come before another thing, but a precursor generally paves the way for something. So, for example, the Office of Strategic Services in World War II was the immediate precursor of today's Central Intelligence Agency, while the blues music of the 1930s and 1940s was only one of the precursors of the rock and roll of today.

前缀 pre 表示"在……之前",因此,precursor 的字面意思是"先驱者"。事实上,拉丁语单词 praecursor 的最初翻译就是 forerunner。但这两个词如今的作用有所不同。forerunner 指的仅仅是发生在某事之前的事情,而 precursor 一般为某事奠定基础。例如,第二次世界大战时期的战略情报局是今天中央情报局的直接前身,而 20 世纪三四十年代的蓝调音乐只是今天摇滚乐的前身之一。

PED comes from the Latin word for "foot." A *pedal* is pushed by the foot; a *pedicure* is a treatment of the feet, toes, and toenails; and a *pedestal* is what a statue stands on—in a sense, its foot.

PED 源自表示"脚"的拉丁语单词。pedal(踏板)由脚来驱动;pedicure(足疗)是对脚、脚趾和趾甲的治疗;pedestal(基座)用来支撑站立在上面的雕像——从某种意义上说,就是雕像的脚。

quadruped \ˈkwä-drə-ˌped\ An animal having four feet. 四足动物

• She always tells her friends that their farm has five kinds of quadrupeds: sheep, goats, cows, horses, and pigs. 她经常告诉朋友,他们的农场有五种四足动物:绵羊、山羊、奶牛、马和猪。

The *quadrupeds* include almost all the mammals. (Among the exceptions are whales, bats, and humans.) The Greek equivalent of this Latin word is *tetrapod*. However, the two are not identical, since the tetrapod classification includes *bipeds*

• 83 •

such as birds, in which two of the limbs are no longer used for walking. Insects all have six legs, of course, and in the sea there are eight-legged *octopods* (including the octopus). But there are no animals of any kind with an odd number of legs. 四足动物几乎囊括所有的哺乳动物(鲸鱼、蝙蝠和人类例外)。这个拉丁语单词在希腊语中的对等语是 *tetrapod*，但二者并不完全相同，因为 tetrapod 类动物还包括鸟类等 *bipeds*(两足动物)，它们有两肢已不再用于行走了。当然，昆虫都有六条腿，而在海里有八条腿的 *octopods* (包括章鱼)。但是没有一种动物的腿是奇数。

pedigree\pe-də-ˌgrē\ The line of ancestors of a person or animal. 血统，家谱，系谱

● She talks a lot about her pedigree, but never mentions that a couple of her uncles spent time in prison. 她大谈特谈自己的家族背景,但从来不提她的几个叔叔坐过牢的事儿。

What does someone's ancestry have to do with feet? Because someone once thought that a family tree, or genealogical chart, resembled a crane's foot (in French, *pied de grue*), even though cranes' feet only have four talons or claws, no more than any other bird, while a family tree may have hundreds of branches. The word *pedigree* is usually used for purebred animals—cats, racehorses, and dogs, as well as livestock such as cows and sheep. Some people continue to believe that "purity" in human family trees is a good thing as well, though most of us find the idea a little creepy. 世系与脚有什么关系？因为有人认为家谱树或系谱图就像鹤的脚(法语是 *pied de grue*),尽管鹤的脚实际上只有四个脚爪,并不比其他鸟类多,而一个家谱可能有成百上千条支脉。*pedigree* 一词通常用于纯种动物——猫、赛马、狗,以及牛羊等家畜。有人还在相信"纯种"的人类家谱是件好事,但多数人都认为这种想法有点让人毛骨悚然。

impediment\im-ˈpe-də-mənt\ Something that interferes with movement or progress. 妨碍，障碍

● Her poorly developed verbal ability was the most serious impediment to her advancement. 她的语言能力发展得很差,这是她进步的最大障碍。

Impediment comes from a Latin verb that meant "to interfere with" or "to get in the way of progress," as if by tripping up the feet of someone walking. In English, *impediment* still suggests an obstruction or obstacle along a path; for example, a lack of adequate roads and bridges would be called an impediment to economic development. Impediments usually get in the way of something we want. So we may speak of an impediment to communication, marriage, or progress—but something that slows the progress of aging, disease, or decay is rarely called an impediment. *impediment* 源自拉丁语动词,意思是"妨碍"或"阻挡前进",就像把一个正在走路的人绊倒一样。在英语中,*impediment* 指的仍然是路上的障碍物。例如,缺少足够的道路和桥梁可以被称为经济发展的障碍。障碍通常会阻挡我们得到想要的东西。因此,我们可以说沟通的障碍、婚姻的障碍或进步的障碍。但延缓衰老、疾病或衰老进程的东西绝少被称为障碍。

pedestrian\pə-ˈdes-trē-ən\ Commonplace, ordinary, or unimaginative. 平常的，普通的，无想象力的

● While politicians endlessly discussed the great issues facing Russia, the

Russians worried about such pedestrian concerns as finding enough food, shelter, and clothing. 政客们没完没了地讨论俄罗斯面临的重大问题,而俄罗斯人却在担心诸如找到足够的食物、住所和衣服等普通的问题。

Most of us know *pedestrian* as a noun meaning someone who travels on foot. But the adjective sense of *pedestrian* as defined here is actually its original meaning. To be pedestrian was to be drab or dull, as if plodding along on foot rather than speeding on horseback or by coach. *Pedestrian* is often used to describe a colorless or lifeless writing style, but it can also describe politicians, public tastes, personal qualities, or possessions. In comparison with the elaborate stage shows put on by today's rock artists, for instance, most of the stage presentations of 1960s rock stars seem pedestrian.

多数人都知道,*pedestrian* 作为名词指的是徒步旅行的人。但此处所界定的 *pedestrian* 的形容词含义实际上才是它最初的意思。pedestrian 指的乏味无聊,就像迈着沉重的脚走路而不是纵马狂奔或驾车疾驰。pedestrian 通常用来描述某种苍白或没有生气的写作风格,但也可以用来形容政治家、大众审美、个人品质或财产。例如,与当今摇滚艺术家精心制作的舞台表演相比,20 世纪 60 年代摇滚明星的舞台表演大都显得很无聊。

Quizzes

A. Fill in each blank with the correct letter:

a. concurrent
b. pedigree
c. precursor
d. pedestrian
e. cursory
f. impediment
g. discursive
h. quadruped

1. The warm days in March were a _____ to spring floods that were sure to come.
2. His rather snobbish grandmother only seemed to be concerned about his fiancée's _____.
3. After only a _____ look at the new car, he knew he had to have it.
4. The presence of her little sister was a definite to her romantic _____ plans for the evening.
5. She came to enjoy the _____ style of the older, rambling essays.
6. From his fleeting glimpse, all he could tell was that it was a small brown _____ that could move very fast.
7. Convention-goers had to decide which of the _____ meetings to attend.
8. His sister's trips to Borneo made his vacations at the seashore seem _____.

B. Match the definition on the left to the correct word on the right:

1. simultaneous
2. obstacle
3. four-footed animal
4. forerunner

a. impediment
b. precursor
c. quadruped
d. discursive

5. hasty
6. ancestry
7. rambling
8. ordinary

e. pedestrian
f. pedigree
g. cursory
h. concurrent

FLECT

FLECT comes from *flectere*, the Latin verb meaning "to bend." The root sometimes takes the form *flex-*. Things that are *flexible* can be bent, and when you *flex* a muscle, you're usually bending a limb—which, as a trainer at the gym will tell you, requires the use of *flexor* muscles.
FLECT 源自拉丁语动词 *flectere*("使弯曲")。这个词根有时采用 *flex-* 的形式。*flexible*(柔韧的)东西是可以弯曲的,当你 *flex* 肌肉的时候,通常弯曲的是肢体——健身教练会告诉你,这样做需要使用 *flexor* muscles(屈肌)。

deflect \di-ˈflekt\ To turn aside, especially from a straight or fixed course. 转向,偏离

• The stealth technology used on bombers and fighter jets works by deflecting radar energy, making them "invisible." 轰炸机和战斗机使用隐身技术,其工作原理是通过使雷达能量转向来实现"隐形"的目的。

Use of the physical meaning of *deflect* is common. Thus, a soccer goalie's save might involve deflecting the ball rather than catching it, and workers wear eye shields to deflect tiny particles flying out of machines. But the nonphysical meaning may be even more common. A Hollywood actress might deflect criticism about her personal life by giving lavishly to charity, for example, and we've all tried to change the subject to deflect a question we really didn't want to answer.

deflect 的物理意义很常见。比如,足球守门员救球可以通过改变球的方向而不是接球的方式,工人们戴上护目镜来改变机器中飞出的微粒的方向。但这个词的非物理意义可能更常见。比如,好莱坞女演员可能会向慈善机构慷慨捐赠,以此转移人们对她个人生活的批评;我们都尝试过用转移话题的方法来避开实在不想回答的问题。

reflective \ri-ˈflekt\ (1) Capable of reflecting light, images, or sound waves. 反射的(2) Thoughtful. 沉思的

• He likes action movies and going out drinking with friends, but when you get to know him you realize he's basically reflective and serious. 他喜欢看动作片,也喜欢和朋友出去喝酒,但了解他之后,你就知道他本质上是一个喜欢沉思而且很严肃的人。

Reflective people are people who *reflect* on things—that is, look back at things that have been done or said in order to think calmly and quietly about them. Most reflective people would agree with Socrates that (as he told the jury that would soon sentence him to death) "The unexamined life is not worth living." Reflective people tend to be a bit philosophical and intellectual. But almost everyone has reflective moods; gazing into a fireplace or a campfire seems to do it to almost everyone.

喜欢沉思的人会 *reflect*(反思)各种事情——也就是说,回顾做过的事或说过的话,以便冷静地反思。多数沉思者会

同意苏格拉底的话(他告诉即将判他死刑的陪审团),"未经深思熟虑的生活不值得过"。沉思者往往有点儿哲理性,有点儿脑子。但几乎人人都会陷入沉思的状态;凝视着壁炉或篝火时,人人好像都会陷入沉思当中。

genuflect\\'jen-yu̇-ˌflekt\\ To kneel on one knee and then rise as an act of respect. 行屈膝礼

• At religious shrines in China, pilgrims may not only genuflect but actually lie down flat on the ground. 在中国的宗教圣地,朝圣者不仅要行屈膝礼,还要五体投地。

Genuflection, which contains the root *genu–*, "knee," has long been a mark of respect and obedience. King Arthur's Knights of the Round Table genuflected not only when he knighted them but whenever they greeted him formally, and this custom remains in countries today that are still ruled by royalty. In some churches, each worshipper is expected to genuflect whenever entering or leaving a pew on the central aisle. 词根 *genu* 的意思是"膝盖", *genuflection*(屈膝礼)长久以来都是尊敬和服从的标志。亚瑟王的圆桌骑士在封爵时行屈膝礼,在向亚瑟王正式问好时也行屈膝礼。在仍由君主统治的国家,这一习俗至今犹存。在某些教堂里,所有礼拜者在来到或离开中间过道的长椅时,都要行屈膝礼。

inflection\\in-ˈflek-shən\\ (1) A change in the pitch, tone, or loudness of the voice. 抑扬变化 (2) The change in form of a word showing its case, gender, number, person, tense, mood, voice, or comparison. 屈折变化

• She couldn't understand her grandfather's words, but she knew from his inflection that he was asking a question. 她听不懂祖父的话,但从他语调变化中知道他在问一个问题。

Changing the pitch, tone, or loudness of our words are ways we communicate meaning in speech, though not on the printed page. A rising *inflection* at the end of a sentence generally indicates a question, and a falling inflection indicates a statement, for example. Another way of *inflecting* words is by adding endings: *-s* to make a noun plural, *-ed* to put a verb in the past tense, *-er* to form the comparative form of an adjective, and so on. 说话的时候,我们可以改变音高、音调、音量来传达我们的想法,但这种方式不能在印刷品中使用。例如,一句话末尾用升调一般表示疑问,用降调则表示陈述。另一种 *inflecting* words(单词变形)的方法是添加词尾:名词后加-s 表示复数,动词后加-ed 表示过去时,形容词后加-er 表示比较级。

POST comes from a Latin word meaning "after" or "behind." A *postscript* (or PS) is a note that comes after an otherwise completed letter, usually as an afterthought. *Postpartum* refers to the period following childbirth, with any related events and complications. To *postdate* a check is to give it a date after the day it was written. POST 源自拉丁语单词,意为"在……之后"或"在……后面"。*postscript*(或 PS,附笔)指的是在原本已完成的信件后面加上的附言,通常是事后补记。*postpartum*(产后的)指的是分娩后的一段时间以及任何相关事件及并发症。*postdate* a check(把支票日期填迟)是指所填写的日期迟于开票日期。

posterior\pō-'stir-ē-ər\ Situated toward or on the back; rear. 后部的,后面的;后部,后面

• In a human *posterior* and *dorsal* can both refer to the back, but in a fish *posterior* refers to the tail area. 在人身上,posterior 和 dorsal 指的都是背部,但在鱼身上,posterior 指的是尾部。

Posterior comes from the Latin word *posterus*, meaning "coming after." *Posterior* is often used as a technical term in biology and medicine to refer to the back side of things, and is the opposite of *anterior*, which refers to the front side. For example, as more people took up running as a sport, doctors began to see an increase in stress fractures along the posterior as well as the anterior surface of the lower leg bones. In some technical fields, *posterior* may mean "later." When used as a noun, *posterior* simply means "buttocks."
posterior 源自拉丁语单词 posterus,意思是"在……之后"。posterior 常用作生物学或医学领域的术语,指的是背面,与 anterior 相反,后者指的是前面。比如,随着越来越多的人将跑步作为一项运动,医生们开始发现,胫骨前部和后部的应力性骨折增多。在某些技术领域,posterior 可以表示"以后"的意思。用作名词时,posterior 指的就是"臀部"。

posthumous\päs-chə-məs\ (1) Published after the death of the author. 死后出版的 (2) Following or happening after one's death. 死后的

• Though Van Gogh scarcely sold a single painting during his lifetime, he rose to posthumous fame as one of the world's great artists. 尽管梵高生前几乎没有卖出过一幅画,但死后却声名鹊起,成为世界上最伟大的艺术家之一。

Posthumous fame is fame that comes a little late. In fact, its original meaning in English is "born after the death of the father." Bill Clinton was the *posthumous son* of a father who died in an automobile accident. The word is now mostly used of artistic works that appear after the death of the artist, or the changing reputation of a dead artist. Such *posthumous works* as Herman Melville's *Billy Budd*, the diary of Anne Frank, and almost all the poetry of Emily Dickinson have become legendary, and in each case they had a major influence on the writer's reputation.
死后的名声来得有点迟。事实上,这个词在英语中最初的意思是"在父亲死后才出生的"。例如,比尔·克林顿是在他父亲死于车祸后出生的。这个词现在主要用来指艺术家去世后才出现的艺术作品,或者指艺术家死后名声的变化。一些死后出版的作品,诸如赫尔曼·梅尔维尔的《比利·巴德》、安妮·弗兰克的日记以及艾米莉·狄金森的几乎全部诗歌等,都成为了传奇。在上述各例中,这些作品对作家的声誉都产生了重大影响。

postmodern\ˌpōst-'mä-dərn\ Having to do with a movement in architecture, art, or literature that is a reaction against modernism and that reintroduces traditional elements and techniques in odd contexts as well as elements from popular culture. 后现代的

• The postmodern AT&T building in New York, with the "Chippendale" top that reminds viewers of an antique dresser, aroused a storm of criticism. AT&T(美国电话电报公司)后现代风格的大楼位于纽约,有个奇彭德尔式的屋顶,让人想起老式梳妆台。这幢大楼也引发了猛烈的

抨击。

With its prefix *post-*, *postmodern* describes a movement that has reacted against *modernism*. Modernism, dating from around the start of the 20th century, represented a sharp break from 19th-century styles. But in the 1970s architects began to be dissatisfied with the stark simplicity of most modern architecture and began including in their mostly modern designs such traditional elements as columns, arches, and keystones and sometimes startling color contrasts such as might have come from advertising and pop culture. In art and literature, as in architecture, *postmodernism* often seems to be making fun of tradition, especially by denying that there's any real distinction between serious and popular art or writing. Wherever it has shown up, postmodernism has been greeted with a mixture of approval, disapproval, and sometimes amusement.

postmodern 的前缀是 post-，它指的是一场反现代主义的运动。现代主义的出现可以追溯到 20 世纪之初，标志着对 19 世纪风格的重大突破。但是在 20 世纪 70 年代，建筑师们开始对大多数现代主义建筑极简的风格感到不满，于是开始在现代设计中加上诸如石柱、拱门、拱顶石等传统元素，有时还采用惊人的色彩对比，这种对比可能来自广告和流行文化。正如建筑领域一样，在艺术和文学领域，postmodernism（后现代主义）似乎也经常拿传统开涮，尤其是否定在严肃与流行艺术或作品之间存在真正的区别。无论后现代主义出现在何处，迎接它的有赞同，也有反对，还有人觉得好玩。

postmortem \ˌpōst-ˈmȯr-təm\ (1) Occurring after death. 死后的 (2) Following the event. 事后的

• In their postmortem discussion of the election, the reporters tried to explain how the polls and predictions could have been so completely wrong. 在对选举的事后讨论中，记者们尝试解释为什么之前的民调和预测会错得如此离谱。

Post mortem is Latin for "after death." In English, *postmortem* refers to an examination, investigation, or process that takes place after death. A postmortem examination of a body (often simply called a *postmortem*) is often needed to determine the time and cause of death; the stiffening called rigor mortis is one postmortem change that doctors look at to determine when death occurred. Today we've come to use *postmortem* to refer to any examination or discussion that takes place after an event.

post mortem 是拉丁语，表示"死后的"。在英语中，postmortem 指的是死后进行的检查、调查或过程。通常需要对尸体进行尸检（常简称为 postmortem），以确定死亡时间和原因。死后身体变僵，称为尸僵，是医生需要观察的死后变化之一，用来确定死亡发生的时间。今天我们用 postmortem 来指事情发生后所做的任何检查或讨论。

Quizzes

A. Choose the closest definition:

1. posthumous   a. before the event   b. born prematurely
   c. occurring after death   d. early in development
2. reflective   a. merry   b. thoughtful   c. glowing
   d. gloomy

3. posterior   a. on the front   b. on the back   c. underneath   d. on top
4. deflect   a. fold over   b. kneel   c. turn aside   d. protect
5. postmodern   a. ultramodern   b. traditional   c. contemporary   d. mixing styles
6. inflection   a. style in art   b. change in pitch   c. muscle   d. part to the rear
7. genuflect   a. kneel   b. flex a muscle   c. fold back   d. change one's tone of voice
8. postmortem   a. after the event   b. before the event   c. caused by the event   d. causing the event

B. Complete the analogy: _____

1. postscript : letter :: postmortem : _____
   a. examination   b. death   c. body   d. morgue
2. clever : dull :: reflective : _____
   a. lazy   b. educated   c. calm   d. empty-headed
3. prenatal : before birth :: posthumous : _____
   a. after birth   b. before life   c. after death   d. famous
4. reflect : mirror :: deflect : _____
   a. shield   b. laser   c. metal   d. spear
5. accent : syllable :: inflection : _____
   a. note   b. hint   c. turn   d. word
6. wave : friendship :: genuflect : _____
   a. salute   b. knee   c. power   d. obedience
7. exterior : interior :: posterior : _____
   a. frontal   b. behind   c. beside   d. above
8. hip-hop : music :: postmodern : _____
   a. tradition   b. design   c. style   d. architecture

Words from Mythology 源自神话的词语

calypso \kə-ˈlip-sō\   A folk song or style of singing of West Indian origin that has a lively rhythm and words that are often made up by the singer.
卡利普索小调

• If you take a Caribbean vacation in December, you end up listening to a lot of Christmas carols played to a calypso beat. 如果你12月份去加勒比海度假,会听到很多伴着卡利普索节奏的圣诞颂歌。

In Homer's *Odyssey*, the nymph Calypso detains Odysseus for seven years on his way home from the Trojan War, using all her wiles to hold him on her lush island. For many people, the calypso music of the West Indian islands, which was eventually brought to America by singers such as the Andrews Sisters and later Harry Belafonte, has some of the same captivating power as the nymph, though the lyrics that are often improvised to the melodies tend to make fun of local people and happenings. The original name for these songs, however, actually seems to be based on a similar-sounding African word, for which, early in the 20th century, someone began substituting this name from Greek mythology.

荷马史诗《奥德赛》中,在奥德修斯结束特洛伊战争返家途中,海之女神卡利普索用尽诡计把他困在她那奢华的岛上七年。一些歌手,比如安德鲁斯姐妹以及后来的哈里·贝拉等,把西印度群岛的卡利普索小调带到美国。对于许多人来说,卡利普索小调如同海之女神一般,有着令人着迷的力量,虽然歌词是伴着旋律即兴发挥的,其内容还常常取笑当地的人和事。然而,这类歌曲最初的名字实际上好像是基于一个发音相似的非洲单词。20世纪初,有人开始代之以希腊神话中的这个名字。

odyssey \ ˈä-də-sē \ (1) A long, wandering journey full of trials and adventures. 冒险旅行 (2) A spiritual journey or quest. 精神上的长征或探索

● Their six-month camping trip around the country was an odyssey they would always remember. 为期六个月的全国野营之旅是他们终生难忘的冒险旅行。

Odysseus, the hero of Homer's *Odyssey*, spends 20 years traveling home from the Trojan War. He has astonishing adventures and learns a great deal about himself and the world; he even descends to the underworld to talk to the dead. Thus, an odyssey is any long, complicated journey, often a quest for a goal, and may be a spiritual or psychological journey as well as an actual voyage.

奥德修斯是荷马史诗《奥德赛》的主角,他花了20年才从特洛伊战场返回家中。奥德修斯经历了惊心动魄的冒险,从中了解了世界,也了解了自己;他甚至到地下世界与死人说话。因此,奥德赛指的是漫长、复杂的旅程,通常是为了追求某个目标,可能是精神或心理上的旅程,也可能是真实的旅程。

palladium \ pə-ˈlā-dē-əm \ A precious, silver-white metal related to platinum that is used in electrical contacts and as an alloy with gold to form white gold. 钯

● Most wedding rings today are simple bands of gold, platinum, or palladium. 如今,多数婚戒是用金、铂或钯打造的简单的指环。

Pallas Athena was one of the poetical names given to the Greek goddess Athena (although it's no longer clear what Pallas was supposed to mean), and the original palladium was a statue of Athena that was believed to have the power to protect the ancient city of Troy. When an asteroid belt was discovered between Mars and Jupiter, most of the asteroids were named after figures in Greek mythology, and one of the first to be discovered was named Pallas in 1803. In the same year, scientists isolated a new silvery metal element, which they named *palladium* in honor of the recently discovered asteroid.

帕拉斯·雅典娜是希腊女神雅典娜充满诗意的名字之一(但现在帕拉斯是什么意思已经不清楚了)。最初的

palladium 指的是雅典娜的神像,据说有保护特洛伊古城的力量。火星和木星之间的小行星带被发现后,多数小行星以希腊神话中的人物命名,其中最先发现的小行星中有一颗在 1803 年被命名为 Pallas(帕拉斯)。同年,科学家们分离出一种新的银色金属元素,命名为 *palladium*,以纪念这颗当年刚发现的小行星。

Penelope \pə-ˈne-lə-pē\ A modest domestic wife. 贤惠的妻子.端庄的妻子。

● Critics of Hillary Rodham Clinton in the 1990s would perhaps have preferred her to be a Penelope, quietly tending the White House and staying out of politics. 20 世纪 90 年代,希拉里·罗德姆·克林顿的批评者或许更愿意让她做个贤妻良母,安静地照料白宫,远离政治。

In the *Odyssey*, Penelope waits 20 long years for her husband Odysseus to return from Troy. During that time, she must raise their son and fend off the attentions of numerous rough suitors. She preserves herself for a long time by saying she cannot remarry until she has finished weaving a funeral shroud for her aging father-in-law; how- ever, what she weaves each day she secretly unravels each night. A Penelope thus appears to be the perfect, patient, faithful wife (and may be using her clever intelligence to keep herself that way).

在《奥德赛》中,Penelope(佩内洛普)等待丈夫奥德修斯从特洛伊回来等了 20 年。在此期间,她必须抚养他们的儿子,避开众多粗鲁的求婚者。她总是称,要为年迈的公公织好寿衣才能再婚,用这个借口,她得以长时间保全自己;然而,她白天编织的东西,晚上又被她偷偷拆开。佩内洛普于是成为一个完美、耐心、忠诚的妻子(也可能是利用自己的聪明才智才变成这样的)。

procrustean \prō-ˈkrəs-tē-ən\ Ruthlessly disregarding individual differences or special circumstances. 削足适履的.强求一致的

● The school's procrustean approach seemed to assume that all children learned in the same way and at the same rate. 学校采用了强求一致的做法,似乎认定所有的孩子都以同样方法、同样的速度学习。

In the Greek tale of the hero Theseus, Procrustes was a bandit who ambushed travelers and, after robbing them, made them lie on an iron bed. To make sure they "fit" this bed, he would cut off the parts that hung off the ends or stretch the body if it was too short; either way, the unlucky traveler always died. When he made the mistake of confronting Theseus, Procrustes was made to "fit" his own bed. Something procrustean takes no account of individual differences but cruelly and mercilessly makes everything the same.

在关于英雄 Theseus(忒修斯)的希腊故事中,有个强盗叫 Procrustes(普罗克拉斯塔斯),他伏击旅行者,抢劫之后再让他们躺在一张铁床上。为了确保他们"适合"这张床,他会砍掉他们的身体在床之外的部分;如果身体太短,他会用力把他们的身体拉长。不管哪种情况,不幸的旅行者总会死去。当普罗克拉斯塔斯遇到忒修斯的时候,他真是犯了个大错,他被逼去"适合"他自己的床。强求一致的事情指的是不考虑个体差异,残酷无情地强求一致。

protean \ˈprō-tē-ən\ (1) Displaying great versatility or variety. 多才多艺的 (2) Able to take on many different forms or natures. 变化多端的

● A protean athlete, he left college with offers from the professional leagues to play baseball, football, and basketball. 他是个全能的运动员,收到了职业联赛的邀请,从大学退学去打棒球、橄榄球和篮球比赛。

As the story is told in the *Odyssey*, at the end of the Trojan War the sea god Proteus revealed to King Menelaus of Sparta how to get home from Troy with his unfaithful wife, the beautiful Helen of Troy. Before Proteus would give up the information, though, Menelaus had to capture him—no mean feat, since Proteus had the ability to change into any natural shape he chose. The word *protean* came to describe this ability to change into many different shapes or to play many different roles in quick succession.

《奥德赛》的故事中,在特洛伊战争最后,海神 Proteus(普罗透斯)向斯巴达国王 Menelaus(墨涅劳斯)透漏,如何才能把他不忠的妻子,即美丽的特洛伊的海伦,从特洛伊弄回家。但是,要让普罗透斯透漏这些信息,墨涅劳斯必须先要抓住他——绝非易事啊,因为普罗透斯有随心所欲变化成任何自然形状之能。Protean 用来形容这种能变不同样子或快速扮演多种角色的能力。

sibyl \\'si-bəl\\ A female prophet or fortune-teller. 女预言家,女算命师

• The villagers told him about an aged woman who lived alone in a hut on a nearby mountain, a sibyl who knew the future and would prophesy under the right conditions. 村民们告诉他,有个独居在附近山中小屋中的老妇人,她知晓未来,在合适的条件下会给出预言。

Ancient writers refer to the existence of various women in such countries as Babylonia, Greece, Italy, and Egypt, through whom the gods regularly spoke. These sibyls were easy to confuse with the oracles, women who were likewise mouthpieces of the gods, at such sites as Apollo's temple at Delphi. The most famous *sibyl* was the Sibyl of Cumae in Italy, a withered crone who lived in a cave. Her prophecies were collected into twelve books, three of which survived to be consulted by the Romans in times of national emergencies. She is one of the five sibyls memorably depicted by Michelangelo on the ceiling of the Sistine Chapel.

古代的作家们提到过,在巴比伦、希腊、意大利和埃及等国家存在一些能经常代神说话的女人。这些 sibyls(女预言家)和祭司很容易被搞混,后者也同样是神的代言人,她们住在德尔斐的阿波罗神庙这样的地方。最著名的女预言家来自意大利的库马城,她是一个住在山洞里的干瘪老太婆。她的预言被汇编成十二本书,其中三本保存下来,罗马人在遇到全国紧急情况时就会拿来参考。她是被米开朗琪罗画在西斯廷教堂顶上的五个女预言家之一。

siren \\'sī-rən\\ A woman who tempts men with bewitching sweetness. 妖妇,妖冶危险的女人(尤指引诱男子)

• Reporters treated her like a sex symbol, but she lacked the graceful presence and air of mystery of a real siren. 记者们把她当作性感的象征,但她缺乏真正妖妇特有的优雅气质和神秘气息。

The *sirens* were a group of partly human female creatures that lured sailors onto destructive rocks with their singing. Odysseus and his men encountered the sirens on their long journey home from Troy. The only way to sail by them safely was to make oneself deaf to their enchanting song, so Odysseus packed the men's ears with wax, while he himself, ever curious, kept his ears open but had himself tied to the mast to keep from flinging himself into the water or steering his ship toward sure destruction in his desire to see them. A siren today is a sinister but almost irresistible woman. A *siren song*, however, may be any appeal that lures a person to act against his or her better judgment.

塞壬是一群半人形的女性生物,她们用歌声引诱水手们撞上具有毁灭性的礁石。奥德修斯和他的随从们在从特洛

伊返家的漫长旅途中遇到了塞壬。安全从她们身边驶过的唯一办法是,让自己听不到她们诱人的歌声。于是,奥德修斯用蜡封住随从们的耳朵,而他自己更为好奇,没有堵住耳朵,但将自己绑在桅杆上,以防自己因渴望一睹芳容而跳进海里,或是驾船冲向不可避免的灭亡。塞壬一词如今指的是阴险而又令人难以抵抗的女人。然而,*siren song*(塞壬之歌)指的是危险的诱惑,引诱人们逆理性判断行事。

Quiz

Fill in each blank with the correct letter:

a. odyssey　　　　　　　　e. sibyl
b. calypso　　　　　　　　f. procrustean
c. Penelope　　　　　　　　g. siren
d. palladium　　　　　　　　h. protean

1. They danced and sang to the rhythm of the _____ music long into the night.

2. While he was away on maneuvers, his wife stayed loyally at home like a true _____.

3. Critics condemn modern education as _____, forcing all students into narrow and limited modes of thinking.

4. On their four-month _____ they visited most of the major cities of Asia.

5. The wedding rings were white gold, a mixture of gold and _____.

6. She won her reputation as the office _____ after her third successful prediction of who would get married next.

7. Actors like Robin Williams seem _____ in their ability to assume different characters.

8. She was a _____ of the screen in the 1920s, luring men to their doom in movie after movie.

Review Quizzes

A. Choose the closest definition:

1. carnage　　a. meat　　b. slaughter　　c. flesh　　d. battle
2. precursor　　a. shadow　　b. forerunner　　c. follower　　d. oath
3. diffident　　a. angry　　b. different　　c. aggressive　　d. shy
4. pedestrian　　a. useless　　b. footlike　　c. unusual　　d. boring
5. credence　　a. creation　　b. belief　　c. doubt　　d. destruction
6. credible　　a. believable　　b. acceptable　　c. praiseworthy　　d. remarkable
7. pedigree　　a. wealth　　b. education　　c. breeding　　d. purity
8. impediment　　a. help　　b. obstacle　　c. footpath　　d. obligation
9. voracious　　a. vast　　b. hungry　　c. fierce　　d. unsatisfied
10. protean　　a. meaty　　b. powerful　　c. changeable　　d. professional

UNIT 4

B. Indicate whether the following pairs of words have the same or different meanings:

1. procrustean / merciful   same _____ / different ____
2. credulity / distrust   same _____ / different ____
3. concurrent / simultaneous   same _____ / different ____
4. cursory / hurried   same _____ / different ____
5. odyssey / journey   same _____ / different ____
6. deflect / absorb   same _____ / different ____
7. perfidy / disloyalty   same _____ / different ____
8. posterior / front   same _____ / different ____
9. siren / temptress   same _____ / different ____
10. herbivorous / plant-eating   same _____ / different ____

C. Complete the analogy:

1. fiduciary : trust-based :: carnivorous :_____
   a. vegetarian   b. meat-eating   c. greedy   d. hungry
2. cursory : brief :: carnal :_____
   a. musical   b. festive   c. deadly   d. sexual
3. genuflect : kneel :: affidavit :_____
   a. financial affairs   b. courtroom testimony
   c. legal advice   d. sworn statement
4. insectivorous : insects :: herbivorous :_____
   a. plants   b. herbs   c. grains   d. flowers
5. carnage : bloodbath :: Penelope :_____
   a. wife   b. mother   c. daughter   d. siren
6. ambivalent : uncertain :: pedestrian :_____
   a. slow   b. colorful   c. unexciting   d. explosive
7. credence : trust :: discursive :_____
   a. fast   b. slow-moving
   c. wide-ranging   d. all-knowing
8. procrustean : inflexible :: inflection :_____
   a. way of life   b. tone of voice
   c. financial affairs   d. part of speech

UNIT 5

MAL comes from a Latin word meaning "bad." A *malady* is a bad condition—a disease or illness—of the body or mind. *Malpractice* is bad medical practice. *Malodorous* things smell bad. And a *malefactor* is someone guilty of bad deeds.
MAL 源自拉丁语单词,意思是"坏的"。*malady* 指的是身体或精神上的不良状况,即疾病。*malpractice*(玩忽职守)是不好的医疗行为。*malodorous*(恶臭的)东西很难闻。*malefactor*(罪犯)指的是做坏事之人。

malevolent\mə-'le-və-lənt\ Having or showing intense ill will or hatred. 恶意的,恶毒的

• Captain Ahab sees Moby Dick not simply as a whale but as a powerfully malevolent foe. 亚哈船长没有只把莫比·迪克当作一条鲸鱼,而是当成一个恶毒的大敌。

Malevolence runs deep. Malevolent enemies have bitter and lasting feelings of ill will. Malevolent racism and bigotry can erupt in acts of violence against innocent people. Malevolence can also show itself in hurtful words, and can sometimes be seen in something as small as an angry look or gesture.
malevolence(恶意)根深蒂固。恶毒的敌人怀有强烈且持久的恶意。恶毒的种族歧视和偏执可能会在针对无辜人民的暴力行径中爆发出来。恶意也可以表现在伤人的话语中,有时也可以从愤怒的表情或手势之类的小细节中表现出来。

malicious\mə-'li-shəs\ Desiring to cause pain, injury, or distress to another. 有恶意的,恶毒的

• The boys didn't take the apples with any malicious intent; they were just hungry and didn't know any better. 男孩子们拿走苹果并非出于恶意,他们只是饿了,不知还能怎么办。

Malicious and *malevolent* are close in meaning, since both refer to ill will that desires to see someone else suffer. But while *malevolent* suggests deep and lasting dislike, *malicious* usually means petty and spiteful. Malicious gossipers are often simply envious of a neighbor's good fortune. Vandals may take malicious pleasure in destroying and defacing property but usually don't truly hate the owners. *Malice* is an important legal concept, which has to be proved in order to convict someone of certain crimes such as first-degree murder.

malicious 和 *malevolent* 意思接近，都是表示渴望看到别人受苦的恶意。但 *malevolent* 指的是根深且持久的厌恶，而 *malicious* 通常指的是小心眼的、恶意的。恶意搬弄是非的人往往只是嫉妒邻居运气好。破坏他人财产者可能从破坏或污损财产中得到恶意的乐趣，但他们一般并不是真的恨财产的主人。*malice*（预谋）是一个重要的法律概念，若要指控某人犯了某些罪行，比如一级谋杀，就必须证明他有预谋。

malign \mə-ˈlīn\ To make harsh and often false or misleading statements about. 诽谤，污蔑，中伤

• Captain Bligh of the *Bounty* may be one of the most unjustly maligned figures in British naval history. 在英国海军的历史上，赏金号的布莱船长可能是受到最不公正诽谤的人物之一。

Malign is related to verbs like *defame*, *slander*, and *libel*. The person or group being maligned is the victim of false or misleading statements, even if the *maligner* isn't necessarily guilty of deliberate lying. Someone or something that's frequently criticized is often said to be "much maligned," which suggests that the criticism isn't entirely fair or deserved. *Malign* is also an adjective, and writers often refer to a person's malign influence. The very similar *malignant*, which used to be a common synonym of *malign*, today tends to describe dangerous medical conditions, especially cancerous tumors.

malign 与 *defame*、*slander* 和 *libel* 等动词的意思相近。受到诽谤的个人或群体是虚假言论或误导性言论的受害者，尽管 *maligner*（诬蔑者）不一定是在故意说谎。经常受批评的人或事可以说是"过度被黑"，意思是这些批评不完全是公平的或应得的。*Malign* 也用作形容词，作家们常说起某人的有害影响。*malignant* 与它非常相似，也曾是它的常见同义词，但现在一般用来形容危险的医学状况，尤其是恶性肿瘤。

malnourished \ˌmal-ˈnər-isht\ Badly or poorly nourished. 营养不良的

• When they finally found the children in the locked cabin, they were pale and malnourished but unharmed. 他们最后在上了锁的小屋里找到了孩子们，这时的孩子们脸色苍白、营养不良，好在没有受伤。

Malnourished people can be found in all types of societies. Famine and poverty are only two of the common causes of *malnutrition*. In wealthier societies, malnutrition is often the result of poor eating habits. Any diet that fails to provide the nutrients needed for health and growth can lead to malnutrition, and some malnourished people are actually fat.

营养不良的人在各种社会中都有。饥荒和贫穷只是 *malnutrition*（营养不良）的两个常见原因。在比较富裕的社会中，营养不良往往是不健康的饮食习惯所造成的。不能提供健康和生长所需营养的任何饮食都可能导致营养不良，而有些营养不良的人甚至还很胖。

CATA
comes from the Greek *kata*, one of whose meanings was "down." A *catalogue* is a list of items put down on paper, and a *catapult* is a weapon for hurling missiles down on one's enemies.

CATA 源自希腊语 *kata*，它的一个含义是"向下"。*catalogue*（目录）是列在纸上的物品清单，*catapult*（弹弓、石弩、弹射

器)指的是一种武器,用来向敌人发射投掷物。

cataclysm\ˈka-tə-ˌkli-zəm\ (1) A violent and massive change of the earth's surface. 大灾难 (2) A momentous event that results in great upheaval and often destruction. 大动乱,巨变

• World War I was a great cataclysm in modern history, marking the end of the old European social and political order. 在现代历史上,第一次世界大战是一场巨变,标志着旧欧洲社会和政治秩序的终结。

The *-clysm* part of *cataclysm* comes from the Greek word meaning "to wash," so *cataclysm*'s original meaning was "flood, deluge," and especially Noah's Flood itself. A cataclysm causes great and lasting changes. An earthquake or other natural disaster that changes the landscape is one kind of cataclysm, but a violent political revolution may also be a *cataclysmic* event. Many cataclysms could instead be called *catastrophes*.

cataclysm 中的*-clysm* 源自意思是"冲刷"的希腊语单词,所以 *cataclysm* 最初指的是"洪水、洪灾",特别是诸亚大洪水本身。cataclysm 会带来巨大而持久的改变。地震或其他改变地貌的自然灾害是一类 cataclysm,而暴力政治革命也可以被称为 *cataclysmic* event(灾难性的事件)。许多 cataclysms 都可以被称为 *catastrophes*(大灾难)。

catacomb\ˈka-tə-ˌkōm\ An underground cemetery of connecting passageways with recesses for tombs. 地下墓穴

• The early Christian catacombs of Rome provide a striking glimpse into the ancient past for modern-day visitors. 罗马的基督教早期的地下墓穴使得现代参观者们能够一窥遥远的过去。

About forty Christian catacombs have been found near the roads that once led into Rome. After the decline of the Roman empire these cemeteries were forgotten, not to be rediscovered until 1578. *Catacomb* has come to refer to different kinds of underground chambers and passageways. The catacombs of Paris are abandoned stone quarries that were not used for burials until 1787. The catacombs built by a monastery in Palermo, Sicily, for its deceased members later began accepting bodies from outside the monastery; today you may wander through looking at hundreds of mummified corpses propped against the catacomb walls, dressed in tattered clothes that were once fashionable.

曾经通向罗马的大道附近已经发现了约四十个基督教地下墓穴。罗马帝国衰落后,这些墓穴被遗忘,直到1578年才被重新发现。catacomb 指的是各种各样的地下房间和通道。巴黎的地下墓穴曾是废弃的采石场,直到1787年才被用于埋葬死者。西西里首府巴勒莫的地下墓穴是一座修道院为其死去的成员建造的,后来开始接受修道院外的人。今天,你可以漫步其中,看看靠在墓穴墙壁上的成百上千具木乃伊化的尸体,它们身穿着当年流行的衣服,如今已经破破烂烂了。

catalyst\ˈka-tə-list\ (1) A substance that speeds up a chemical reaction or lets it take place under different conditions. 催化剂 (2) Someone or something that brings about or speeds significant change or action. 刺激因

素,导火索

• The assassination of Archduke Ferdinand in Sarajevo in 1914 turned out to be the catalyst for World War I. 1914年费迪南德大公在萨拉热窝遇刺,这件事成为第一次世界大战的导火索。

Chemical catalysts are substances that, in very small amounts, can bring about important chemical changes in large quantities of material. The catalytic converter in your car's exhaust system, for instance, uses tiny amounts of platinum to swiftly convert the engine's dangerous gases to carbon dioxide and water vapor. And it's easy to see how the meaning of catalyst could broaden to include nonchemical situations. We can now say, for example, that the Great Depression served as the catalyst for such important social reforms as Social Security.

化学催化剂这种物质,只需一丁点的量,就可以引发大量材料的重要化学变化。例如,汽车排气系统中的 catalytic converter(催化转化器)使用少量的铂迅速将发动机的有害气体转化为二氧化碳和水蒸气。不难看出,catalyst 一词的含义是如何能够引申到非化学情况的。例如,我们现在可以说,大萧条是诸如社会保障等重要社会改革的催化剂。

catatonic \ˌka-tə-ˈtä-nik\ （1）Relating to or suffering from a form of schizophrenia. 紧张症的,紧张性精神分裂症的（2）Showing an unusual lack of movement, activity, or expression. 不动的

• After an hour, extreme boredom had produced a catatonic stupor in those of the audience who were still awake. 一个小时之后,还没有睡着的观众因极度的无聊而陷入一动不动的恍惚状态。

Catatonia is primarily a form of the terrible mental disease known as schizophrenia, though it may show up in patients with a variety of other mental conditions. A common symptom is extreme muscular rigidity; catatonic patients may be "frozen" for hours or even days in a single position. Its causes remain mysterious. Serious though the condition is, most nondoctors use catatonic humorously to describe people who seem incapable of moving or changing expression.

catatonia(紧张症)是精神分裂症这种可怕的精神疾病的一种主要形式,尽管很多其他种类的精神病患者也有这种症状。紧张症的常见症状之一是肌肉极度僵硬;患者可能会被"冻结"在一个姿势上数小时甚至数日。紧张症的病因至今不明。尽管这种状况很严重,但多数不是医生的人会很幽默地用 catatonic 一词,来形容那些似乎不会动也不会改变表情的人。

CATA

Quizzes

A. Choose the closest definition：

1. malevolent
   a. wishing evil   b. wishing well
   c. blowing violently   d. badly done
2. cataclysm
   a. loud applause   b. feline behavior
   c. disaster   d. inspiration
3. malign
   a. speak well of   b. speak to
   c. speak ill of   d. speak of repeatedly

• 99 •

4. catacomb a. underground road b. underground cemetery
   c. underground spring d. underground treasure
5. malicious a. vague b. explosive
   c. confusing d. mean
6. catatonic a. refreshing b. slow
   c. motionless d. boring
7. malnourished a. fed frequently b. fed poorly
   c. fed excessively d. fed occasionally
8. catalyst a. literary agent b. insurance agent
   c. cleaning agent d. agent of change

B. Indicate whether the following pairs of words have the same or different meanings：

1. catacomb / catastrophe   same ____ / different ____
2. malnourished / overfed   same ____ / different ____
3. cataclysm / disaster   same ____ / different ____
4. malign / slander   same ____ / different ____
5. catatonic / paralyzed   same ____ / different ____
6. catalyst / cemetery   same ____ / different ____
7. malicious / nasty   same ____ / different ____
8. malevolent / pleasant   same ____ / different ____

PROT/PROTO

PROT/PROTO comes from Greek and has the basic meaning "first in time" or "first formed." *Protozoa* are one-celled animals, such as amoebas and paramecia, that are among the most basic members of the biological kingdom. A *proton* is an elementary particle that, along with neutrons, can be found in all atomic nuclei. A *protoplanet* is a whirling mass of gas and dust that astronomers believe may someday become a planet.

PROTO 源自希腊语，基本意思是"最早的"或"最先形成的"。*protozoa*（原生动物）指的是单细胞动物，如变形虫和草履虫，属于生物王国中最基本的成员。*proton*（质子）是一种基本粒子，它与中子一起存在于所有的原子核中。*protoplanet*（原行星）是一团旋转的气体和尘埃，天文学家认为有朝一日原行星会变成行星。

protagonist \prō-ˈta-gə-nist\ The main character in a literary work. （文学作品中的）主人公、主角

• Macbeth is the ruthlessly ambitious protagonist of Shakespeare's play, but it is his wife who pulls the strings. 麦克白是莎士比亚戏剧中的主人公，他冷酷无情、野心勃勃，但幕后操纵者却是他的妻子。

Struggle, or conflict, is central to drama. The *protagonist* or hero of a play, novel, or film is involved in a struggle of some kind, either against someone or something else or even against his or her own emotions. So the hero is the "first struggler," which is the literal meaning of the Greek word *prōtagōnistēs*. A character who opposes the hero is the *antagonist*, from a Greek verb that means literally "to struggle against."

斗争或冲突是戏剧的中心。戏剧、小说或电影中的主角被卷入某种斗争中，要么与人作斗争，要么与物作斗争，甚至与他/她自己的情感作斗争。所以，主角是"第一斗争者"，这是希腊语单词 *prōtagōnistēs* 的字面意思。与主角相对立的人是 *antagonist*（对手），源自一个希腊语动词，其字面意思是"与……斗争"。

protocol \ˈprō-tə-ˌkȯl\ (1) A code of diplomatic or military rules of behavior. 礼仪，礼节 (2) A set of rules for the formatting of data in an electronic communications system. 协议，规则

• The guests at the governor's dinner were introduced and seated according to the strict protocol governing such occasions. 在州长的晚宴上，客人都是按照严格的礼仪被介绍和就座的。

The basic meaning of *proto-* is a little harder to follow in this word. *Protocol* comes from a Greek word for the first sheet of a papyrus roll. In English, *protocol* originally meant "a first draft or record," and later specifically the first draft of a diplomatic document, such as a treaty. The "diplomatic" connection led eventually to its current meaning of "rules of behavior." Someone wearing Bermuda shorts and sandals to a state dinner at the White House would not be acting "according to protocol," and royal protocol forbids touching the queen of England except to shake her hand. But *protocol* is also now used for other sets of rules, such as those for doing a scientific experiment or for handling computer data.

词根 *proto-* 的基本意思在这个单词中有点难寻。*protocol* 源自一个表示纸莎草书卷第一张的希腊语单词。在英语中，*protocol* 最初的意思是"初稿或原始记录"，后来特指外交文件（如条约）的草案。与"外交"的联系最终产生了其现在的含义"行为准则"。如果有人穿着百慕大短裤和凉鞋出席白宫举行的国宴，那他的行为就不"符合礼节"，而按照王室礼节，除了握手外，不得触碰英国女王。然而，*protocol* 现在也用于其他一些规则，比如用于科学实验或处理计算机数据的规则。

protoplasm \ˈprō-tō-ˌpla-zəm\ The substance that makes up the living parts of cells. 原生质

• A mixture of organic and inorganic substances, such as protein and water, protoplasm is regarded as the physical basis of life. 原生质是蛋白质、水等有机物和无机物的混合，被视为生命的物质基础。

After the word *protoplasm* was coined in the mid-19th century for the jellylike material that is the main substance of a cell, it began to be used widely, especially by scientists and others who imagined that the first life-forms must have arisen out of a great seething *protoplasmic* soup. Since protoplasm includes all the cell's living material, inside and outside the nucleus, it is a less useful scientific word today than more precise terms such as *cytoplasm*, which refers only to the living material outside the nucleus. But many remain fascinated by the image of that soup bubbling away as the lightning flashes and the volcanoes erupt.

PROT/ PROTO

19世纪中叶，*protoplasm* 一词被创造出来，表示构成细胞的主要成分的胶状物质。此后，该词开始被科学家及其他人广泛使用，他们认为最早的生命形式一定源自沸腾的 *protoplasmic* soup(原生汤)。因为 protoplasm 包括细胞核内与细胞核外的全部细胞活性成分，所以这个科学词语不如仅表示细胞核外的活性成分的单词 *cytoplasm*（细胞质）有用处。但是，一想到电闪雷鸣、火山喷发、原生质汤咕咕冒泡的画面，很多人就会痴迷不已。

prototype\ˈprō-tō-ˌtīp\ (1) An original model on which some- thing is patterned. 范例，蓝本 (2) A first, full-scale, usually working version of a new type or design. 原型，雏形。

• There was great excitement when, after years of top-secret development, the prototype of the new Stealth bomber first took to the skies. 经过多年的绝密研制，新型隐形轰炸机的原型机首次升空，引起了巨大的轰动。

A *prototype* is someone or something that serves as a model or inspiration. A successful fundraising campaign can serve as a prototype for future campaigns, for example, and the legendary Robin Hood is the *prototypical* honorable outlaw, the inspiration for countless other romantic heroes. But the term is perhaps most widely used in the world of technology; every new "concept car," for example, starts off as a unique prototype.

prototype 指的是被用作范例或激发灵感的人或物。例如，一次成功的筹款活动可以作为将来此类活动的范例；传奇人物罗宾汉就是一个 *prototypical*（典型的）可敬的亡命徒，也是其他无数浪漫英雄的灵感来源。这个词广泛用于科技领域。例如，每一辆新"概念汽车"最初都是以独特的原型车开始的。

ANTE is Latin for "before" or "in front of." *Antediluvian*, which describes something very old or outdated, literally means "before the flood"—that is, Noah's Flood. And *antebellum* literally means "before the war," usually the American Civil War.

ANTE 是拉丁语，表示"在……之前"或"在……前面"。*antediluvian* 用来形容非常古老或过时的东西，其字面意为"大洪水以前的"——即诺亚大洪水之前。*antebellum* 字面意思是"战前的"，通常指的是美国南北战争之前的。

antechamber \an-ti-ˌchām-bər\ An outer room that leads to another and is often used as a waiting room. 前厅，候见室，接待室

• The antechamber to the lawyer's office was both elegant and comfortable, designed to inspire trust and confidence. 通向律师办公室的前厅典雅舒适，这样设计是为了激发信任与信心。

One expects to find an *antechamber* outside the private chambers of a Supreme Court Justice or leading into the great hall of a medieval castle. In the private end of the castle the lord's or lady's bedchamber would have its own antechamber, which served as a dressing room and sitting room, but could also house bodyguards if the castle came under siege. *Anteroom* is a less formal synonym, one that's often applied to the waiting rooms of professional offices today.

在最高法院法官的私室外或者中世纪城堡大厅外，一般会有个 antechamber。在城堡的私人角落的城堡主或夫人的

卧室外,也会有自己的 antechamber,用作更衣室和客厅,在城堡受到围攻时,也可以住保镖。*anteroom* 是它的同义词,但没有那么正式,如今常用来指职业办公室外面的接待室。

antedate \ˈan-ti-ˌdāt\ (1) To date something (such as a check) with a date earlier than that of actual writing. 填写比实际更早的日期 (2) To precede in time. 先于,早于

• Nantucket Island has hundreds of beautifully preserved houses that antedate the Civil War. 南塔开特岛有数百座内战之前就建成的、保存完好的房子。

Dinosaurs antedated the first human beings by almost 65 million years, though this stubborn fact never used to stop cartoonists and screenwriters from having the two species inhabit the same story line. Dictionary editors are constantly noticing how the oral use of a word may antedate its first appearance in print by a number of years. Antedating a check or a contract isn't illegal unless it's done for the purpose of fraud (the same is true of its opposite, *postdating*).
恐龙比人类早出现将近 6500 万年,但这个铁的事实从未阻止漫画家和编剧将这两个物种放在同一个故事情节中。编写词典者常发现,某个词语的口头使用可能比它以书面形式出现要早许多年。把支票或合同的日期填早并非不合法,除非是出于欺诈的目的(其反义词 *postdating*[把日期填迟]亦如此)。

antecedent \ˌan-tə-ˈsē-dənt\ (1) A word or phrase that is referred to by a pronoun that follows it. 先行词 (2) An event or cause coming before something. 前事,前情

• As I remember, she said "My uncle is taking my father, and he's staying overnight," but I'm not sure what the antecedent of "he" was. 我记得,她说的是"我叔叔将带我爸爸出去,他会在外过夜",但我不确定"他"的先行词是什么。

A basic principle of clear writing is to keep your antecedents clear. Pronouns are often used in order not to repeat a noun (so instead of saying "Sheila turns 22 tomorrow, and Sheila is having a party," we replace the second "Sheila" with "she"). But sloppy writers sometimes leave their antecedents unclear (for instance, "Sheila helps Kathleen out, but she doesn't appreciate it," where it isn't clear who "she" is). Watch out for this possible problem when using not just *he* and *she* but also *they*, *them*, *it*, *this*, and *that*. And keep in mind that *antecedent* isn't just a grammar term. You may talk about the antecedents of heart disease (such as bad eating habits), the antecedents of World War II (such as the unwise Treaty of Versailles), and even your own antecedents (your mother, grandfather, etc.).
清晰表达的一个基本原则是要把先行词表达清楚。使用代词通常是为了避免重复使用某个名词(因此,我们不说"希拉明天 22 岁了,希拉要开一个派对",而是将第二个"希拉"替换为"她")。但粗心的作家有时没有交代清楚先行词(比如,在"希拉帮了凯瑟琳,但她并不喜欢这样"中,我们就不清楚"她"指代的是谁)。要注意,不仅是 *he* 和 *she*,在使用 *they*、*them*、*it*、*this* 和 *that* 时,也可能出现这样的问题。要记住,*antecedent* 不只是一个语法术语。也可以谈论心脏病的 antecedent(前因,如不良饮食习惯)、第二次世界大战的 antecedent(前因,如愚蠢的《凡尔赛条约》),甚至你自己的 antecedents(前辈、如母亲、外公等)。

anterior \an-ˈtir-ē-ər\ (1) Located before or toward the front or head. 靠

前的，前部的 (2) **Coming before in time or development.** 先前的，先于的

• When she moved up to join the first-class passengers in the plane's anterior section, she was delighted to recognize the governor in the next seat. 她升到头等舱坐到飞机的前部时，欣喜地认出了邻座的州长。

Anterior generally appears in either medical or scholarly contexts. Anatomy books refer to the anterior lobe of the brain, the anterior cerebral artery, the anterior facial vein, etc. Scholar and lawyers may use *anterior* to mean "earlier in time or order." For example, supporters of states' rights point out that the individual states enjoyed certain rights anterior to their joining the union. And prenuptial agreements are designed to protect the assets that one or both parties acquired anterior to the marriage.

anterior 一般用在医学或学术语境中。解剖学的书会涉及大脑前叶、大脑前动脉、面部前静脉等。学者和律师用 *anterior* 表示"在时间或顺序上更早"。例如，州权利的支持者指出，各州在加入联邦之前就享有某些特定的权利。婚前协议旨在保护一方或双方在婚前获得的财产。

Quizzes

A. Fill in each blank with the correct letter:

a. antedate　　　　　　e. prototype
b. protoplasm　　　　　f. antecedent
c. anterior　　　　　　g. protocol
d. protagonist　　　　　h. antechamber

1. The _____ of *The Wizard of Oz* is a Kansas farm girl named Dorothy.

2. According to official _____, the Ambassador from England ranks higher than the Canadian Consul.

3. A butterfly's antennae are located on the most _____ part of its body.

4. There under the microscope we saw the cell's _____ in all its amazing complexity.

5. She was tempted to _____ the letter to make it seem that she had not forgotten to write it but only to mail it.

6. The engineers have promised to have the _____ of the new sedan finished by March.

7. Please step into the judge's _____; she'll be with you in a few minutes.

8. The British would say "The company are proud of their record," since they treat "the company" as a plural _____.

B. Match the definition on the left to the correct word on the right:

1. to date before　　　　　a. protocol
2. cell contents　　　　　　b. antechamber
3. what comes before　　　c. protagonist
4. rules of behavior　　　　d. antecedent

5. toward the front
6. model
7. waiting room
8. hero or heroine

e. protoplasm
f. antedate
g. prototype
h. anterior

ORTHO comes from *orthos*, the Greek word for "straight," "right," or "true." *Orthotics* is a branch of therapy that straightens out your stance or posture by providing artificial support for weak joints or muscles. And *orthograde* animals, such as human beings, walk with their bodies in a "straight" or vertical position.
ORTHO 源自希腊语单词 orthos("直的""正的"或"真的")。orthotics(矫形术,矫正法)是治疗的一个分科,为虚弱的关节或肌肉提供人工支持,以矫正站姿或坐姿。orthograde animals(直立行走的动物)行走时,身体保持"笔直的"或垂直的姿势,比如人类。

---

orthodontics \ˌȯr-thə-ˈdän-tiks\ A branch of dentistry that deals with the treatment and correction of crooked teeth and other irregularities. 畸齿矫正学

• A specialty in orthodontics would require three more years of study after completing her dentistry degree. 畸齿矫正学专业要求她在修完牙医学学位后再学习三年。

Orthodontics has been practiced since ancient times, but the elaborate techniques familiar to us today were introduced only in recent decades. Braces, retainers, and headgear are used to fix such conditions as crowding of the teeth and overbites. According to a 1939 text, "Speech defects, psychiatric disturbances, personality changes, ... all are correctable through *orthodontic* measures," though many adolescents, having endured the embarrassment of rubber bands breaking and even of entangling their braces while kissing, might disagree.
古代就有畸齿矫正术,但如今为我们所熟知的复杂技术是近几十年才有的。牙箍、牙齿固位体、口外弓被用来纠正牙列拥挤、覆咬合等状况。根据1939年的文本记载,"言语缺陷、精神障碍、性格变化……所有这些都可以通过 orthodontic(牙齿矫正的)措施来改正"。但许多青少年经历过接吻时橡皮筋断裂甚至牙箍互相纠缠的尴尬,他们可能不同意上述观点。

orthodox \ˈȯr-thə-ˌdäks\ (1) Holding established beliefs, especially in religion. 正统的 (2) Conforming to established rules or traditions; conventional. 传统的

• The O'Briens remain orthodox Catholics, faithfully observing the time-honored rituals of their church. 奥布里安人一家是正统天主教徒,虔诚地奉行他们教堂的历史悠久的仪式。

An orthodox religious belief or interpretation is one handed down by a church's founders or leaders. When capitalized, as in *Orthodox Judaism*, *Orthodox* refers to a branch within a larger religious organization that claims to honor the religion's original or traditional beliefs. The steadfast holding of established beliefs that is seen in religious *orthoxy* is apparent also in other kinds of orthodox behavior. Orthodox medical treatment, for example, follows the established practices of mainstream medicine. *Unorthodox* thinking is known in business language as "thinking outside the box."

正统的宗教信仰或解读是由教堂的创始人或领导者传下来的。如果首字母大写,比如在 Orthodox Judaism 中的 Orthodox,指的就是某一庞大宗教组织的一个分支,他们宣称信奉宗教最初的或传统的信仰。religious orthoxy(宗教正统)坚定地遵从既定信念的做法在其他正统行为中也有明显体现。例如,正统医疗方法就是遵循主流医学的既定做法。在商业语言中,unorthodox(非正统的,另类的)思维被说成是"跳脱框架思考",即创造性思维。

orthopedics \ȯr-thə-ˈpē-diks\ The correction or prevention of deformities of the skeleton. 矫形,骨科

• For surgery to correct the child's spinal curvature, they were referred to the hospital's orthopedics section. 人家让他们去医院骨科做手术以矫正孩子的脊柱弯曲。

Just as an orthodontist corrects crookedness in the teeth, an *orthopedist* corrects crookedness in the skeleton. *Orthopedics* is formed in part from the Greek word for "child," and many *orthopedic* patients are in fact children. But adults also often have need of orthopedic therapy, as when suffering from a joint disease like arthritis or when recovering from a broken arm or leg.

正如牙齿矫正师矫正的是畸形的牙齿,orthopedist(矫形外科医师)矫正的是畸形的骨骼。orthopedics 一词有一部分源自希腊语表示"儿童"的单词,许多 orthopedic patients(矫形外科患者)实际上是儿童。但成年人也经常需要接受矫形外科治疗,比如当患有关节炎之类的关节疾病,或者手臂、腿部的骨折康复时。

orthography \ȯr-ˈthä-grə-fē\ The spelling of words, especially spelling according to standard usage. 正字法,拼写法

• Even such eloquent writers as George Washington and Thomas Jefferson were deficient in the skill of orthography. 即使是一些能言善辩的作家,比如乔治·华盛顿和托马斯·杰斐逊,正确拼写的技能也有所欠缺。

Even as recently as the 19th century, the *orthography* of the English language was still unsettled. Not until spelling books like Noah Webster's and textbooks like "McGuffey's Readers" came along did uniform spelling become established in the U. S. Before that, there was much *orthographic* variation, even among the more educated. The many people who still have problems with spelling can take heart from Mark Twain, who once remarked, "I don't give a damn for a man that can spell a word only one way."

即便是到了 19 世纪,英语的正字法仍未确定下来。一直到诺亚·韦伯斯特等的拼写读本和"麦高菲读本"等课本问世,统一的拼写才得以在美国确立。在此之前,即便是在教育程度较高的人群中,也存在很多 orthographic(正确拼写的)变体。那些感到拼写困难的人可以从马克·吐温那里得到鼓舞,他曾说:"能否只用一种方式拼写单词,我才不在乎呢。"

RECT

RECT comes from the Latin word *rectus*, which means "straight" or "right." To *correct* something is to make it right. A *rectangle* is a four-sided figure with straight parallel sides. *Rectus*, short for Latin *rectus musculus*, may refer to any of several straight muscles, such as those of the abdomen.

RECT 源自拉丁语单词 *rectus*，意思是"直的"或"正的"。*correct*（纠正）某物是为了使它正确。*rectangle*（矩形）是有平行直边的四边形。*rectus* 是拉丁语 *rectus musculus* 的简称，指的是几种直肌中的任一种，例如腹部直肌。

rectitude \rek-tə-ˌtüd\ Moral integrity. 正直，诚实

● The school superintendent was stern and not terribly popular, but no one questioned her moral rectitude. 校长很严厉，也不是很受欢迎，但没有人质疑她正直的品性。

We associate straightness with honesty, so if we suspect someone is lying we might ask if they're being "straight" with us, and we might call a lawbreaker *crooked* or label him a *crook*. *Rectitude* may sound a little old-fashioned today, but the virtue it represents never really goes out of style.

我们把率直和诚实联系在一起，所以如果我们怀疑某人在说谎，我们就会问他是否对我们"坦率"，我们也可能会称一个违法分子 *crooked*（不诚实的）或给他贴上 *crook*（骗子）的标签。*Rectitude* 在今天听起来可能有点老套，但它所代表的美德却永远不会过时。

rectify \ˈrek-tə-ˌfī\ To set right; remedy. 纠正，改正，矫正

● The college is moving to rectify this unfortunate situation before anyone else gets hurt. 学院正在采取行动改变这种不幸的状况，以免再有人受伤。

We *rectify* something by straightening it out or making it right. We might rectify an injustice by seeing to it that a wrongly accused person is cleared. An error in a financial record can be rectified by replacing an incorrect number with a correct one. If the error is in our tax return, the Internal Revenue Service will be happy to *rectify* it for us; we might then have to rectify the impression that we were trying to cheat on our taxes.

我们把某个东西弄直或弄对，以此纠正它。我们确保为受冤枉者洗脱罪名，以此纠正不公平。用正确的数字代替错误的，以此来纠正财务记录中的错误。如果纳税申报表上有误，国内收入署会很乐意为我们纠正；而我们以后可能不得不纠正我们企图要偷税漏税的印象。

rectilinear \ˌrek-tə-ˈli-nē-ər\ (1) Moving in or forming a straight line. 直线的（2）Having many straight lines. 有直线的

● After admiring Frank Lloyd Wright's rectilinear buildings for years, the public was astonished by the giant spiral of the Guggenheim Museum. 在赞赏弗兰克·劳埃德·赖特的直线形建筑很多年后，公众被他设计的古根海姆博物馆巨大的螺旋形建筑惊呆了。

Rectilinear patterns or constructions are those in which straight lines are strikingly obvious. In geometry, *rectilinear* usually means "perpendicular"; thus, a *rectilinear polygon* is a many-sided shape whose angles are all right angles (the footprints of most houses, with their extensions and garages, are good examples). But *rectilinear* is particularly used in physics. *Rectilinear motion* is motion in which the speed remains constant and the path is a straight line; and *rectilinear rays*, such as light rays, travel in a straight line.

在直线形模型和建筑中，直线表现得非常明显。在几何学中，rectilinear 通常指"成直角的"；因此，rectilinear polygon（直线多边形）就是全部角都是直角的多边形。（多数房子所占的区域，加上其延伸部分以及车库，都是很好的例子。）rectilinear 在物理学中特别适用。rectilinear motion（直线运动）是速度保持恒定且路线为直线的运动。rectilinear rays（直线射线），比如光线，以直线形式运动。

directive \də-'rek-tiv\ Something that guides or directs; especially, a general instruction from a high-level body or official. 指示，指令

• At the very beginning of the administration, the cabinet secretary had sent out a directive to all border-patrol personnel. 上任伊始，内阁大臣就给所有边境巡逻的人员下达了指令。

As the definition states, a directive *directs*. A directive from a school principal might provide guidance about handling holiday celebrations in class. A directive from the Vatican might specify new wording for the Mass in various languages. Even the European Union issues directives to its member countries, which they often ignore. 正如定义所说，某一指令 directs（给出命令）。学校校长给出指令，指导学生在课堂上开展节日庆祝活动。梵蒂冈给出的指令或许对不同语言弥撒的新措辞有明确的要求。就连欧盟也向其成员国下达指令，但这些指令常常被忽视。

Quizzes

A. Choose the closest definition:

1. orthodox　　　　　a. straight　　　　b. pier　　　　　　c. conventional
   d. waterfowl
2. rectify　　　　　　a. redo　　　　　　b. make right　　　c. modify
   d. make longer
3. orthopedics　　　　a. foot surgery　　　b. children's medicine
   c. medical dictionaries　　　　　　d. treatment of skeletal defects
4. directive　　　　　a. leader　　　　　b. sign　　　　　　c. order
   d. straightener
5. orthography　　　　a. correct color　　　b. correct map
   c. correct direction　d. correct spelling
6. rectitude　　　　　a. roughness　　　　b. integrity　　　　c. certainty
   d. sameness
7. orthodontics　　　　　　　　　　　　a. dentistry for children
   b. dentistry for gums　　　　　　　　c. dentistry for crooked teeth
   d. dentistry for everyone
8. rectilinear　　　　　　　　　　　　　a. employing straight lines
   b. employing curved lines　　　　　　c. employing 45° angles
   d. employing circles

B. Indicate whether the following pairs have the same or different meanings:

1. orthodox / crucial　　　　　　　　　same ____ / different ____
2. rectitude / honesty　　　　　　　　same ____ / different ____

3. orthopedics / broken bones   same ____ / different ____
4. directive / question   same ____ / different ____
5. orthography / architecture   same ____ / different ____
6. rectilinear / straight   same ____ / different ____
7. orthodontics / fixing of crooked teeth   same ____ / different ____
8. rectify / damage   same ____ / different ____

EU comes from the Greek word for "well"; in English words it can also mean "good" or "true." A veterinarian who performs *euthanasia* is providing a very sick or hopelessly injured animal a "good" or easy death.
EU 源自希腊语表示"好"的单词。在英语单词中,它也可以表示"好"或"真"。兽医执行 euthanasia(安乐死)指的是,为病重或伤重无望的动物提供"好的"或容易的死亡。

eugenic \yü-ˈje-nik\ Relating to or fitted for the production of good offspring through controlled breeding. 优生的

• Eugenic techniques have been part of sheep breeding for many years. 多年来,优生技术已经成为绵羊育种的一部分。

The word *eugenic*, like the name *Eugene*, includes the Greek root meaning "born" (see GEN, p. 443). Breeders of farm animals have long used eugenic methods to produce horses that run faster, for example, or pigs that provide more meat. Through *eugenics*, Holstein cows have become one of the world's highest producers of milk. But eugenics also has a dark side. The idea of human eugenics was taken up enthusiastically by the Nazis in the 20th century, with terrible consequences.
如同名字 eugene(尤金)一样,eugenic 一词也含有意思是"出生"的希腊词根 gen-(参见 GEN,第 443 页)。比如,农场动物的育种者长期以来一直通过优生方法来培育跑得更快的马或有更多肉的猪。通过 eugenics(优生学)的方法,荷斯坦奶牛已经成为世界上产奶量最高的奶牛之一。但是优生学也有黑暗的一面。20 世纪,人类优生学的想法被纳粹狂热地吸收,造成了可怕的后果。

euphemism \ˈyü-fə-ˌmi-zəm\ An agreeable or inoffensive word or expression that is substituted for one that may offend or disgust. 委婉语

• The Victorians, uncomfortable with the physical side of human existence, had euphemisms for most bodily functions. 因为对人类存在的生理方面感到不自在,维多利亚时代的人对多数生理功能就已经有了委婉的说法。

The use of *euphemisms* is an ancient part of the English language, and perhaps of all languages, and all of us use them. *Golly* and *gosh* started out as euphemisms for *God*, and *darn* is a familiar euphemism for *damn*. *Shoot*, *shucks*, and *sugar* are all *euphemistic* substitutes for a well-known vulgar word. *Pass away* for *die*, *misspeak* for *lie*, *downsize* for *fire*, *senior citizen* for *old person*—the list goes on and on.

使用委婉语在英语中古已有之，也许所有语言都这样，我们大家也都使用委婉语。*golly* 和 *gosh* 一开始是 *God* 的委婉语，*darn* 是 *damn* 常见的委婉语。*shoot*、*shucks* 和 *sugar* 都是一个众所周知的脏话的 *euphemistic* substitutes（委婉替代语）。*die* 的委婉语是 *pass away*，*lie* 的委婉语是 *misspeak*，*fire* 的委婉语是 *downsize*，*old person* 的委婉语是 *senior citizen*——不胜枚举啊。

euphoria\yu̇-ˈfȯr-ē-ə\ A strong feeling of well-being or happiness. 狂喜，极度愉快，异常兴奋

• Swept up in the euphoria of a Super Bowl victory, the whole city seemed to have poured out into the streets. 沉浸在超级碗比赛胜利的喜悦中,全城人似乎都涌上了街头。

Euphoria is the feeling of an intense (and usually temporary) "high." Doctors use the word for the kind of abnormal or inappropriate high spirits that might be caused by a drug or by mental illness, but euphoria is usually natural and appropriate. When we win enough money in the lottery to buy several small Pacific islands, or even just when the home team wins the championship, we have good reason to feel *euphoric*.

euphoria 指的是一种强烈的（通常是暂时的）"快感"。医生们用这个词来形容可能由药物或精神疾病引起的不正常或不适当的高昂情绪,但 euphoria 通常是自然的而且是恰当的。当我们买彩票赢的钱足够去买几个太平洋岛屿时,或我们的主场球队赢得冠军时,我们有充分的理由感到 *euphoric*（狂喜）。

eulogy\ˈyu̇-lə-jē\ (1) A formal speech or writing especially in honor of a dead person. 悼词，颂词 (2) High praise. 好评

• The book was a fond eulogy to the 1950s, when Americans had joined social organizations of all kinds. 这本书是对 20 世纪 50 年代的深情讴歌,当时的美国人加入了各种各样的社会组织。

With its *-logy* ending (see LOG, p. 218), *eulogy* means literally something like "good speech." We are told to speak only good of the dead, but a *eulogist* actually makes a speech in the dead person's honor—or often instead for someone living, who might actually be there in the audience. The most famous eulogies include Lincoln's Gettysburg Address and Pericles' funeral oration for the Athenian warriors; but these are only two of the many great eulogies, which continue to be delivered not only at funerals and memorial services but at retirement parties, anniversary parties, and birthday parties.

有了词尾 -*logy*（见 LOG，第 218 页），*eulogy* 的字面意思是"美好的言词"。我们被告知只能说死者的好话,但 *eulogist*（致悼词者，致颂词者）实际上是为了表示对死者的敬意而发表演讲——也经常是为了赞颂某个活着的人,这个人可能就在下面的观众中。最著名的颂词有林肯的葛底斯堡演讲和伯里克利为雅典勇士发表的祭文等；但这些只是众多伟大的颂词中的两篇而已,伟大的颂词今后还会出现在葬礼和追悼会上,还会出现在退休派对、周年派对和生日派对上。

DYS

DYS comes from Greek, where it means "bad" or "difficult." So *dysphagia* is difficult swallowing, and *dyspnea* is difficult or labored breathing. *Dysphasia* is an inability to use and understand language because of injury to or disease of the brain. *Dys-* is sometimes close in meaning to *dis-* (see DIS, p. 64), but try not to confuse the two.

DYS 源自希腊语,在希腊语中的意思是"坏的"或"困难的"。因此,*dysphagia* 指的是吞咽困难,*dyspnea* 指的是呼吸困难。*dysphasia*(言语障碍症)指的是由于大脑损伤或疾病而不能使用和理解语言。*dys-* 的意思有时候接近 *dis-*(见 DIS,第 64 页),但尽量不要把两者混为一谈。

dystopia \dis-ˈtō-pē-ə\ An imaginary place where people lead dehumanized and often fearful lives. 反乌托邦,反面乌托邦

• For a 10-year-old British boy, boarding school could be a grim dystopia, with no comforts, harsh punishments, and constant bullying. 对于一个 10 岁的英国男孩来说,寄宿学校可能就是一个可怕的反面乌托邦,没有舒适,只有严厉的惩罚和不断的欺凌。

Dystopia was created from Utopia, the name of an ideal country imagined by Sir Thomas More in 1516. For More, the suffix *-topia* meant "place" (see TOP, p. 366), and *u-* (from the Greek root *ou*) meant "no," but also perhaps "good" (see EU, p. 109). In other words, More's Utopia was too good to be true. It's probably no accident that *dystopia* was first used around 1950, soon after George Orwell published his famous novel *Nineteen Eighty-Four* and 16 years after Aldous Huxley published *Brave New World*. These two are still the most famous of the 20th century's many depressingly *dystopian* novels. And what about all those bleak futuristic films: *Blade Runner*, *Brazil*, *The Matrix*, and the rest? What does it mean when no one will paint a picture of a happy future?

dystopia 由 Utopia(乌托邦)衍生而来,乌托邦是托马斯·莫尔爵士在 1516 年幻想出来的的一个理想中的国家。莫尔认为,后缀 *-topia* 的意思是"地方"(见 TOP,第 366 页),*u-*(源自希腊词根 *ou*)的意思是"无",也可能是"好的"(见 EU,第 109 页)。换句话说,莫尔的乌托邦完好得有些不真实。*dystopia* 在 1950 年前后首次使用,正值乔治·奥威尔出版了他著名的小说《一九八四》之后不久,也就在奥尔德斯·赫胥黎出版《美丽新世界》16 年之后;这恐怕不是巧合。直到现在,这两部小说仍然是 20 世纪众多阴郁的 *dystopian*(反乌托邦)小说中最为著名的。如何看待那些描写无望未来的电影呢?比如:《银翼杀手》《巴西》《黑客帝国》等。没有人描绘未来的幸福画卷意味着什么?

dyslexia \dis-ˈlek-sē-ə\ A disturbance or interference with the ability to read or to use language. 诵读障碍,读写障碍

• She managed to deal with her dyslexia through careful tutoring all throughout elementary school. 通过整个小学期间的认真辅导,她成功地克服了诵读障碍。

Dyslexia is a neurological disorder that usually affects people of average or superior intelligence. *Dyslexic* individuals have an impaired ability to recognize and process words and letters. Dyslexia usually shows itself in the tendency to read and write words and letters in reversed order; sometimes similar reversals occur in the person's speech. Dyslexia has been shown to be treatable through patient instruction in proper reading techniques.

诵读障碍是一种神经疾病,常困扰智力一般或智力超常的人。*dyslexic*(有诵读障碍)的人识别和理解单词和字母的能力有缺陷。诵读障碍患者往往有倒着读写字母和单词的倾向。有时候,他们也会倒着说话。诵读障碍已经被证实可

以通过适当的阅读技巧和耐心的教导治愈。

dyspeptic \dis-ˈpep-tik\ (1) Relating to or suffering from indigestion. 消化不良的 (2) Having an irritable temperament; ill-humored. 脾气暴躁的;坏脾气的

• For decades the dyspeptic columnist served as the newspaper's—and the city's—resident grouch. 几十年来,这位脾气暴躁的专栏作家成为这家报纸的——乃至这座城市的——常住的爱发牢骚的人。

Dyspepsia comes from the Greek word for "bad digestion." Interestingly, the Greek verb *pessein* can mean either "to cook" or "to digest"; bad cooking has been responsible for a lot of dyspepsia. Dyspepsia can be caused by many diseases, but dyspeptic individuals are often the victims of their own habits and appetites. Worry, overeating, inadequate chewing, and excessive smoking and drinking can all bring on dyspepsia. Today we generally use *dyspeptic* to mean "irritable"—that is, in the kind of mood that could be produced by bad digestion.

dyspepsia 源自意思是"消化不良"的希腊语单词。有趣的是,希腊语动词 *pessein* 既可以表示"烹饪",也可以表示"消化"。糟糕的烹饪是消化不良的主要原因。消化不良可能是由许多疾病引起的,但消化不良的人往往是生活习惯和食欲的受害者。烦恼忧愁、暴饮暴食、咀嚼不充分以及过量吸烟饮酒等都会导致消化不良。今天,我们一般用 *dyspeptic* 来表示"易怒的"——也就是说,可能是消化不良所带来的情绪。

dysplasia \dis-ˈplā-zhə\ Abnormal development of cells or organs, or an abnormal structure resulting from such growth. 发育不良,发育异常

• The infant was born with minor hip dysplasia, which was fixed by a routine operation. 那个婴儿出生时髋关节发育不良,已经通过常规手术修复了。

Of the dozens of medical terms that begin with the *dys-* prefix, *dysplasia* (with the suffix *-plasia*, meaning "development") is one of the more common, though not many nondoctors know it. Structural dysplasias are usually something you're born with; they often involve the hip or the kidneys. But cell dysplasia is often associated with cancer. And a *dysplastic* mole—a mole that changes shape in an odd way—is always something to be concerned about.

有几十个医学术语是以前缀 *dys-* 开头的, *dysplasia*(有意思是"发育"的后缀 *-plasia*)是其中比较常见的一个,尽管没有多少外行人知道。结构性发育不良往往是与生俱来的,常涉及臀部或肾脏。但细胞发育异常往往与癌症有关。*dysplastic* mole(发育异常的痣)——形状变化奇怪的痣——通常要引起注意。

Quizzes

A. Fill in each blank with the correct letter:

a. euphemism   e. dyslexia
b. dysplasia   f. euphoria
c. eulogy   g. dystopia
d. dyspeptic   h. eugenic

1. There is many a _____ for the word *die*, and many more for the word

drunk.

2. The novel paints a picture of a _____ in which the effects of climate change have wrecked the social order.

3. Her _____ for her longtime friend was the most moving part of the ceremony.

4. Because his _____ was discovered early, he was able to receive the special reading instruction he needed.

5. The end of the war was marked by widespread _____ and celebration.

6. Ebenezer Scrooge, in *A Christmas Carol*, is a thoroughly _____ character.

7. Though the dog is the product of generations of _____ breeding, she is high-strung and has terrible eyesight.

8. The tests had detected some suspicious cell _____, but her doctors told her not to worry since it was at a very early stage.

B. Match the word on the left to the correct definition on the right:

1. dysplasia   a. nightmarish society
2. euphemism   b. crabby
3. dyslexia   c. abnormal growth
4. eugenic   d. speech of praise
5. dystopia   e. polite term
6. euphoria   f. reading disorder
7. dyspeptic   g. promoting superior offspring
8. eulogy   h. great happiness

Latin Borrowings 拉丁语借词

a fortiori \ˌä-ˌfȯr-tē-ˈȯr-ē\   All the more certainly. 更加肯定,更不必说,更有理由

● If drug users are going to be subject to mandatory sentences, then, a fortiori, drug dealers should be subject to them also. 如果吸毒要被强制性判刑,那贩毒就更应该被判刑了。

A fortiori in Latin literally means "from the stronger (argument)." The term is used when drawing a conclusion that's even more obvious or convincing than the one just drawn. Thus, if teaching English grammar to native speakers is difficult, then, a fortiori, teaching English grammar to nonnative speakers will be even more challenging.

a fortiori 在拉丁语中的字面意思是"来自更充分的(论证)"。它通常用于得出比先前的结论更明显、更令人信服的结论。因此,如果教母语者英语语法都很困难,那毋庸置疑,教非母语者更具挑战性。

a posteriori \ˌä-ˌpōs-tir-ē-ˈȯr-ē\   Relating to or derived by reasoning from known or observed facts. 归纳的,后验的,由果及因的

● Most Presidents will come to the a posteriori conclusion that a booming economy is entirely due to their own economic policies. 许多总统会归纳出一个结论：繁荣的经济完全归功于他们自己的经济政策。

A *posteriori*, Latin for "from the latter," is a term from logic, which usually refers to reasoning that works backward from an effect to its causes. This kind of reasoning can sometimes lead to false conclusions. The fact that sunrise follows the crowing of a rooster, for example, doesn't necessarily mean that the rooster's crowing caused the sun to rise.

a posteriori 在拉丁语中表示"从后者"，这是一个逻辑学术语，通常指的是由果及因的逆向推理。这种推理有时会导致错误的结论。例如，太阳总是会在公鸡打鸣后升起，但这并不意味着是公鸡打鸣导致太阳升起。

a priori \ˌä-prē-ˈȯr-ē\ Relating to or derived by reasoning from self-evident propositions. 演绎的，由因及果的，先验的

- Her colleagues rejected the a priori argument because it rested on assumptions they felt weren't necessarily true. 她的同事们拒绝了这个先验的论证，因为他们认为该论证所基于的假设不一定正确。

A *priori*, Latin for "from the former," is traditionally contrasted with *a posteriori* (see above). The term usually describes lines of reasoning or arguments that proceed from the general to the particular, or from causes to effects. Whereas a posteriori knowledge is knowledge based solely on experience or personal observation, a priori knowledge is knowledge that comes from the power of reasoning based on self-evident truths. So, for example, "Every mother has had a child" is an a priori statement, since it shows simple logical reasoning and isn't a statement of fact about a specific case (such as "This woman is the mother of five children") that the speaker knew about from experience.

a priori 在拉丁语中表示"从前者"，传统上与 *a posteriori*（见上文）形成对照。这个术语通常指从一般到特殊，或原因到结果的推理或论证。归纳的知识完全是基于经验和个人观察而来的，而先验的知识则是基于"公理"推断而来的。例如，"每个母亲都有孩子"是一个先验的陈述，因为它仅仅是一个简单的逻辑推理，而不是说话人凭经验知道的关于特定情况（例如，"这个女人是五个孩子的母亲"）的事实陈述。

bona fide \ˈbō-nə-ˌfīd\ (1) Made in good faith, without deceit. 真诚的，不欺骗 (2) Authentic or genuine. 真实的，真正地

- According to the broker, they've made a bona fide offer to buy the property. 根据经纪人的说法，他们是真心想买下这处房产。

Bona fide means "in good faith" in Latin. When applied to business deals and the like, it stresses the absence of fraud or deception. A bona fide sale of securities is an entirely aboveboard transaction. Outside of business and law, *bona fide* implies mere sincerity and earnestness. A bona fide promise is one that the person has every intention of keeping. A bona fide proposal of marriage is one made by a suitor who isn't kidding around. *Bona fide* also has the noun form *bona fides*; when someone asks about someone else's *bona fides*, it usually means evidence of their qualifications or achievements.

bona fide 在拉丁语中的意思是"有诚意"。当这个词被用于商品交易及类似情况时,它强调的是没有欺骗。真诚的证券销售指的是完全光明正大的交易。在商业和法律领域之外,bona fide 指的是完全的真挚与诚恳。真正的承诺是真心想遵守的诺言。真正的求婚是由一个认真的追求者提出的。bona fide 也有名词形式 bona fides。当有人问起别人的 bona fides 时,通常指的是他们资历或成果的证明。

carpe diem \ˈkär-pā-ˈdē-ˌem\   Enjoy the pleasures or opportunities of the moment without concern about the future. 及时行乐

● When he learned the phrase "Carpe diem" in high-school Latin class, he knew he'd found the motto he would live by for the rest of his life. 当他在高中拉丁语课上学到"及时行乐"这个短语时,他知道自己找到了余生所要奉行的座右铭。

Carpe diem, a phrase that comes from the Roman poet Horace, means literally "Pluck the day," though it's usually translated as "Seize the day." A free translation might be "Enjoy yourself while you have the chance." For some people, Carpe diem serves as the closest thing to a philosophy of life as they'll ever have.

carpe diem 这个短语源自罗马诗人贺拉斯,字面意思是"拉住这一天",但通常被翻译成"抓住当下"。这个短语也可以意译为"趁你还有机会,尽情享受当下吧"。对某些人来说,carpe diem 是最接近他们人生哲学的东西。

caveat emptor \ˈka-vē-ˌät-ˈemp-tər\   Let the buyer beware. 顾客留心,买者自负

● The best rule to keep in mind when buying anything from a pushcart is: "Caveat emptor." 从手推车上买东西时要牢记在心中的最好准则就是:"顾客留心。"

"Without a warranty, the buyer must take the risk" is the basic meaning of the phrase caveat emptor. In the days when buying and selling was carried on in the local marketplace, the rule was a practical one. Buyer and seller knew each other and were on equal footing. The nature of modern commerce and technology placed the buyer at a disadvantage, however, so a stack of regulations have been written by federal, state, and local agencies to protect the consumer against dangerous or defective products, fraudulent practices, and the like. But the principle that a buyer needs a warranty if he is to avoid risk remains an important legal concept. Note that a caveat is a small warning or explanation intended to avoid misinterpretation.

"如果没有保证单,买者必须承担风险"是 caveat emptor 的基本意思。买卖在本地市场进行的年代里,这条规则是很实用的。那时候,买卖双方相互了解、平起平坐。然而,现代商业和技术的本质把消费者放到了一个不利的位置上,因此联邦、州和地方机构都制定了一系列规章制度,以保护消费者免受危险、有缺陷的产品、欺诈行为等的侵害。但是,如果买方想避免风险,就需要一张保证单,这一原则仍然是一个重要的法律概念。注意,caveat 指的是一个小小的警告或解释,意在避免误解。

corpus delicti \ˈkȯr-pəs-di-ˈlik-ˌtī\   (1) The substantial and basic fact or facts necessary to prove that a crime has been committed. 犯罪构成 (2) The material substance, such as the murdered body, on which a crime has been committed. 犯罪事实

● The police believed they had solved the crime, but couldn't prove their case without the corpus delicti. 警方认为他们已经侦破了那个犯罪案件,但因缺少犯罪事实,案件就无法证实。

Corpus delicti literally means "body of the crime" in Latin. In its original sense, the body in question refers not to a corpse but to the body of essential facts that, taken together, prove that a crime has been committed. In popular usage, *corpus delicti* also refers to the actual physical object upon which a crime has been committed. In a case of arson, it would be a ruined building; in a murder case, the victim's corpse.

corpus delicti 在拉丁语中的字面意思是"犯罪的 body"。从它最初的意思来看,所说的 body 不是指尸体,而是重要事实的实体,这些事实聚在一起,就能证明犯罪已经发生。在流行的用法中,*corpus delicti* 也指被实施犯罪的实际的物质对象。在纵火案中,它指的是被毁的建筑;在谋杀案中,它指的是受害者的尸体。

curriculum vitae \ kə-ˈri-kyü-ləm-ˈvē-ˌtī \ A short summary of one's career and qualifications, typically prepared by an applicant for a position; résumé. 简历,履历

- The job advertisement asked for an up-to-date curriculum vitae and three recommendations. 这个招聘广告要求应聘者提供一份最新的简历和三封推荐信。

The Latin phrase *curriculum vitae*, often abbreviated CV, literally means "the course of one's life." The term is usually used for applications for jobs in the sciences and medicine and for teaching positions in colleges and universities. A shorter term is simply *vita*, meaning "life." In other fields, *résumé* is more commonly used in the U.S.; in England, however, *curriculum vitae* is the usual term for any job application.

拉丁短语 *curriculum vitae*,常缩写为 CV,字面意思是"某人生活的经历"。这个词通常在应聘科学和医学领域的工作,以及应聘大学教师职位时使用。它的简写是 *vita*,意思是"生活"。在其他领域应聘时,*résumé* 在美国更常用;然而,在英国,任何领域应聘都用 curriculum vitae。

Quiz

Fill in each blank with the correct letter:

a. a priori   e. carpe diem
b. curriculum vitae   f. a fortiori
c. caveat emptor   g. corpus delicti
d. a posteriori   h. bona fide

1. To ensure that all reservations are _____, the cruise line requires a nonrefundable deposit.

2. If Britain can't afford a space program, then _____ neither can a much poorer country like India.

3. The philosopher published his own _____ proof of the existence of God.

4. Their motto is "_____," and the two of them have more fun than anyone else I know.

5. She sent out a _____ full of impressive educational and professional credentials.

6. All of the elements were available to establish the _____ of the defendant's crime.

7. This art critic takes the _____ position that if Pablo Picasso painted it, it's a masterpiece of modern art.

8. When you go out to buy a used car, the best advice, warranty or no warranty, is still "_____."

Review Quizzes

A. Complete the analogy:

1. antagonist : villain :: protagonist : _____
   a. maiden   b. wizard   c. knight   d. hero
2. radical : rebellious :: orthodox : _____
   a. routine   b. conventional   c. sane   d. typical
3. fake : fraudulent :: bona fide : _____
   a. copied   b. certain   c. authentic   d. desirable
4. slang : vulgar :: euphemism : _____
   a. habitual   b. polite   c. dirty   d. dumb
5. identify : name :: rectify : _____
   a. make over   b. make new   c. make right   d. make up
6. better : inferior :: anterior : _____
   a. before   b. beside   c. above   d. behind
7. warranty : guarantee :: caveat emptor : _____
   a. explanation   b. warning   c. endorsement   d. contract
8. jovial : merry :: dyspeptic : _____
   a. grumpy   b. sleepy   c. dopey   d. happy
9. lively : sluggish :: catatonic : _____
   a. active   b. petrified   c. feline   d. tired
10. benevolent : wicked :: malevolent : _____
    a. evil   b. silly   c. noisy   d. kindly

B. Fill in each blank with the correct letter:

a. antechamber
b. a posteriori
c. euphoria
d. malign
e. a fortiori
f. orthography
g. prototype
h. directive
i. curriculum vitae
j. catacomb
k. dysplasia
l. eugenic
m. malnourished
n. protoplasm
o. orthodontics

1. Before car makers produce a new model, they always build and test a _____.

2. Her short stories are her main qualification for the job, but the college needs her _____ as well.

3. They were shown into an elegant _____ where they awaited their audience with the king.

4. After graduation from dental school, Kyle took a postgraduate course in _____.

5. That yappy little dog makes the _____ assumption that he's what keeps me from breaking into the house.

6. The jellylike substance in cells is called _____.

7. These abused and _____ children can't be expected to pay attention in class.

8. In poor countries, hip _____ is rarely fixed in the early years.

9. They felt such _____ that they almost wept with joy.

10. Since they earned high honors for achieving a 3.7 average, _____ we should do so for getting a 3.8.

11. He argues that _____ is more important than ever, since the success of your Web searches depends on your spelling.

12. It is common for boxers to _____ each other in crude terms before a big match.

13. Their department had received a _____ that morning regarding flexibility in the work schedule.

14. When they went to Rome, they made sure to visit at least one underground _____.

15. _____ experimentation has produced a new breed of sheep with thick, fast-growing wool.

C. Indicate whether the following pairs have the same or different meanings:

1. corpus delicti / basic evidence   same ____ / different ____
2. rectify / straighten   same ____ / different ____
3. malicious / mean   same ____ / different ____
4. protocol / rules of behavior   same ____ / different ____
5. a priori / determined later   same ____ / different ____
6. dyslexia / speech patterns   same ____ / different ____
7. cataclysm / religious teachings   same ____ / different ____
8. antedate / occur before   same ____ / different ____
9. orthopedics / shoe repair   same ____ / different ____

10. rectilinear / curvy   same ____ / different ____
11. orthodox / Christian   same ____ / different ____
12. carpe diem / look ahead   same ____ / different ____
13. prototype / model   same ____ / different ____
14. catalyst / distributor   same ____ / different ____
15. rectitude / stubbornness   same ____ / different ____

UNIT 6

EQU comes from the Latin word *aequus*, meaning "equal." To *equalize* means to make things equal. Things that are *equivalent* have the same value, use, or meaning. All three sides of an *equilateral* triangle are of the same length. And an *equation* (for instance, 21 + 47 = 68) is a statement that two mathematical expressions are equal.

EQU 源自拉丁语单词 *aequus*，意思是"相等的"。*equalize* 的意思是使事物相等。如果说一些事物是 *equivalent*（相等的），则表示他们在价值、用途或者意义上是相同的。*equilateral* triangle(等边三角形)的三条边长度相同。*equation*（等式，比如 21+47＝68)是两个数学表达式相等的陈述。

equable \\'e-kwə-bəl\\ (1) Tending to remain calm. (1)宁静的，平和的 (2) Free from harsh changes or extreme variation. (2)稳定的，变化小的

• Her friends thought it odd that such an equable woman had married a man so moody and unpredictable. 她的朋友们都觉得奇怪，这么一个性情温和的女人竟然嫁给了一个喜怒无常、捉摸不定的男人。

Equable usually describes either climate or personality. The word seems to be used less today than in decades past, maybe because the personality type is less admired than it used to be. A steady, calm, equable personality may not produce much excitement but usually makes for a good worker and a good parent, and maybe even a longer life. In the words of the poet Robert Service: "Avoid extremes: be moderate / In saving and in spending. / An equable and easy gait / Will win an easy ending."

equable 通常形容气候或个性。这个词好像比几十年前用得要少，也许是因为这种性格类型不再那么受人推崇了。稳定、冷静、平和的性格可能不会带来太多的刺激，但通常能造就好职工、好家长，甚至可能让你活得更长。罗伯特·瑟维斯在诗中写道："不走极端：适中就好/储蓄还是消费/平静而轻松的步态/赢得舒适的结尾。"

adequacy \\'a-di-kwə-sē\\ Being equal to some need or requirement. 足够。

充分
- Environmentalists doubt the adequacy of these regulations to protect the wilderness areas. 环保人士怀疑这些法规是否足以保护荒野地区。

When we question the adequacy of health-care coverage, or parking facilities, or school funding, we're asking if they are *equal* to our need. The adjective *adequate* means "enough" or "acceptable"— though in sentences like "His performance was adequate," it really means "no better than acceptable."

当我们质疑医疗保险、停车场设施或学校资金是否充足时,我们是在问 if they are *equal* to our need(能不能满足我们的需要)。形容词 *adequate* 的意思是"足够的"或"可接受的"——但在像"His performance was adequate"这样的句子中,它真正的意思是"差强人意的"。

equilibrium \ˌē-kwə-ˈli-brē-əm\ (1) A state in which opposing forces are balanced so that one is not stronger or greater than the other. 均势,均衡,平衡 (2) A state of emotional balance or calmness. (心情或情绪的)平静

- The news had come as a shock, and it took him several minutes to recover his equilibrium. 这消息使他非常震惊,过了几分钟才恢复平静。

Equilibrium contains a root from the Latin *libra*, meaning "weight" or "balance." As a constellation, zodiac symbol, and astrological sign, Libra is usually pictured as a set of balance scales, often held by the blindfolded goddess of justice, which symbolizes fairness, equality, and justice. *Equilibrium* has special meanings in biology, chemistry, physics, and economics, but in all of them it refers to the balance of competing influences.

equilibrium 中包含拉丁语词根 *libra*,意思是"重量"或"平衡"。Libra 是星座,是黄道十二宫之一,也是占星学符号之一,常常被画成天平的样子,被蒙着眼睛的女神拿在手中,象征公正、公平和正义。*equilibrium*(均衡)在生物学、化学、物理学和经济学中都有特殊意义,但在上述全部领域中,它指的都是对抗力量之间的平衡。

equinox \ˈē-kwə-ˌnäks\ A day when day and night are the same length.
春分,秋分,昼夜平分日

- She and her friends got together for an equinox party twice a year to celebrate the arrival of the fall and the spring. 她和朋友们举办春分、秋分派对,每年聚会两次,以庆祝春天和秋天的到来。

If you know that *nox* means "night" in Latin, it's not hard to remember the meaning of *equinox*. There are two equinoxes in the year: the spring equinox, around March 21, and the fall equinox, around September 23. The equinoxes are contrasted with the *solstices*, when the sun is farthest north and south of the equator. The summer solstice occurs around June 22 (the longest day of the year), the winter solstice around December 22 (the shortest day).

如果你知道 *nox* 在拉丁语中是"夜晚"的意思,就不难记住 *equinox* 的含义了。一年中有两个昼夜平分日:春分(3月21日左右)和秋分(9月23日左右)。与昼夜平分日相对的是 *solstices*(至日),此时太阳在赤道外的最北边和最南边。夏至发生在6月22日左右(一年中白天最长),冬至在12月22日左右(白天最短)。

QUIS

QUIS is derived from the Latin verb meaning "to seek or obtain." The roots *quer*, *quir*, and *ques* are derived from the same Latin verb and give us words such as *inquiry* and *question*.

QUIS 源自意思是"寻求或获得"的拉丁语动词。词根 *quer*、*quir* 和 *ques* 的都源自这个拉丁语动词，衍生出 *inquiry*、*question* 等单词。

inquisition \ˌin-kwə-ˈzi-shən\ A questioning or examining that is often harsh or severe. 审讯，盘问

• The President's first choice for the job turned him down, fearing the Senate hearings would turn into an inquisition into her past. 总统把她作为该职位的第一人选，但被她拒绝了，因为她担心参议院的听证会会变成一场对她过往经历的质询。

While an *inquiry* can be almost any search for truth, the related word *inquisition* suggests a long, thorough investigation that involves extensive and harsh questioning. Though the two words originally had about the same meaning, today *inquisition* tends to remind us of the Spanish Inquisition, an ongoing trial conducted by church-appointed *inquisitors* that began in the Middle Ages and sought out nonbelievers, Jews, and Muslims, thousands of whom were sentenced to torture and to burning at the stake.

inquiry（调查）可以是对几乎任何真相的追寻，而其近义词 *inquisition*（审讯）则是冗长而彻底的调查，需要进行广泛而严厉的盘问。这两个词最初的含义几乎相同，但现在 *inquisition* 一词往往让我们想到西班牙宗教审讯，那是一场始于中世纪的持续的审判，由教堂任命的 *inquisitors*（审讯者）来完成。他们搜捕无信仰者、犹太教徒、穆斯林，成千上万的人被课以酷刑，被判烧死于火刑柱上。

perquisite \ˈpər-kwə-zət\ (1) A privilege or profit that is provided in addition to one's base salary. 额外补贴，福利 (2) Something claimed as an exclusive possession or right. 优待，特权

• A new car, a big house, and yearly trips to Europe were among the perquisites that made the presidency of Wyndam College such an attractive position. 新车、大房、每年去欧洲旅行等等，这些福利使温德姆学院校长职位变得如此诱人。

Though the Latin source of *perquisite* originally meant "something insistently asked for," the "ask" meaning has mostly vanished from the English word. A perquisite, often called simply a *perk*, is instead something of value that the holder of a particular job or position is entitled to, usually without even asking. The President of the United States, for instance, enjoys as perquisites the use of Camp David and Air Force One. Perhaps because perquisites are usually available to only a small number of people, the word sometimes refers to non-job-related privileges that are claimed as exclusive rights.

尽管 *perquisite* 的拉丁语词源最初的意思是"坚持要求得到的东西"，但"要求"之意在这个英语单词中已基本消失。perquisite 常简写为 *perk*，用来指拥有某工作或职位的人有资格得到的某种有价值的福利，通常无须再开口要。例如，美国总统享有使用戴维营和空军一号的权利。也许因为通常只有少数人能得到 perquisites，所以该词有时也指与工作不相

122

关的特权,被称为专有权。

acquisitive \ə-ˈkwi-zə-tiv\ Eager to acquire; greedy. 渴望得到的,贪得无厌的

- With each year the couple became more madly acquisitive, buying jewelry, a huge yacht, and two country estates. 年复一年,这对夫妇变得越来越贪婪,他们购买珠宝、大游艇,还有两处乡村庄园。

Unlike most tribal peoples and the populations of some older countries, we Americans live in an acquisitive society, a society devoted to getting and spending. And America often makes successfully acquisitive people into heroes; even Ebenezer Scrooge, that model of miserly greed and *acquisitiveness*, was once defended by a White House chief of staff. An acquisitive nation may seek to acquire other territories by force. But mental acquisition of specialized knowledge or skills—or new vocabulary!—doesn't deprive others of the same information.

与多数部落和某些古老国度的人不同,我们美国人生活在一个贪婪的社会,即一个醉心于索取和消费的社会。美国常常把成功的贪婪者变成英雄,就连埃比尼泽·斯克鲁奇这么一个贪得无厌、*acquisitiveness*(利欲熏心)的守财奴典型,也曾得到某位白宫幕僚长的辩护。贪得无厌的国家也许会寻求以武力 acquire(获得)别国领土。但是,mental acquisition(脑力上获取)专业知识、技能——或新的词汇!——却不会剥夺其他人获取同样信息的权利。

requisition \ˌre-kwə-ˈzi-shən\ A demand or request (such as for supplies) made with proper authority. 征用,申请书

- The teachers had grown impatient with having to submit a requisition for even routine classroom supplies. 连常规课堂用品都要提交申请书,教师们对此已经不耐烦了。

Requisition was originally a noun but is now probably more common as a verb. So we either can speak of sending our office's purchasing department a requisition for computers, or of *requisitioning* more computers from the department. The word has an official sound to it. However, one of Hollywood's bittersweet love stories begins when Omar Sharif, playing a World War II freedom fighter, says to Ingrid Bergman, who is the owner of a stately old yellow Rolls Royce, "I've come to requisition your car."

requisition 起初是名词,但现在可能更常用作动词。因此,我们可以说向办公室采购部门提交购买电脑的申请书,也可以说向该部门 *requisitioning* 更多的电脑。这个词听上去有一点官方的意味。然而,好莱坞电影中有个苦乐参半的爱情故事,开头是这样的:奥马尔·沙里夫扮演的第二次世界大战自由战士,对英格丽·褒曼扮演的气派的黄色旧劳斯莱斯汽车的主人说:"我来征用你的车。"

Quizzes

A. Indicate whether the following pairs of terms have the same or different meanings:

1. equilibrium / weight   same ____ / different ____
2. inquisition / curiosity   same ____ / different ____
3. equable / steady   same ____ / different ____
4. perquisite / salary   same ____ / different ____

5. equinox / May Day same ____ / different ____
6. acquisitive / greedy same ____ / different ____
7. requisition / requirement same ____ / different ____
8. adequacy / surplus same ____ / different ____

B. Fill in each blank with the correct letter:

a. equinox   e. adequacy
b. requisition   f. acquisitive
c. equilibrium   g. equable
d. perquisite   h. inquisition

1. They're a quiet, pleasant couple, with very _____ temperaments.
2. You couldn't even get a pencil unless you filled out a _____.
3. In a healthy economy, supply and demand are in a state of approximate _____.
4. Daylight saving time begins in March, shortly before the _____ and the arrival of spring.
5. There was more than enough water, but he worried about the _____ of their food supplies.
6. The whole family was _____ by nature, and there were bitter legal battles over the will.
7. His status as newcomer did carry the special _____ of being able to ask a lot of questions.
8. Louisa feared an _____ into her background and previous involvements.

PLE/PLEN

PLE/PLEN comes from a Latin word meaning "to fill." It can be seen in the words *plenty*, meaning basically "filled," and *complete*, meaning "thoroughly filled."

PLE/PLEN 源自意思是"充满"的拉丁语单词。这个词根可以从 *plenty*（基本意思是"充满的"）和 *complete*（"完全充满的"）等单词看出来。

plenary \ˈplē-nə-rē\ (1) Including all who have a right to attend. 全体出席的 (2) Complete in all ways. 完全的

• For the convention's plenary session, five thousand members gathered to hear a star speaker. 在该大会的全体会议上，五千成员济济一堂，听一位著名演讲者讲话。

Plenary often shows up in writing referring to the "plenary power" held by a government, and is particularly used for powers mentioned in a constitution. For example, under the U.S. Constitution, the Congress has plenary power to wage war, which means that no one else—not the courts, not the states, not the president—has any power whatsoever to second-guess Congress about warmaking. But in recent years, that hasn't stopped some presidents from starting conflicts that looked a lot like wars to most people. At a conference, the plenary sessions (unlike the various smaller "presentations," "workshops," "forums," and "seminars" that otherwise fill the day) try to bring everyone together in the same room.

plenary 在书面语中常常指政府所拥有的"绝对权力",尤其是用于宪法规定的权力。例如,根据美国宪法,国会拥有发动战争的绝对权力,意思就是没有任何别的部门——包括法院、各州和总统在内——有权对国会所做的战争决策事后批评。但是,近年来,这一宪法条款并未阻止某些总统挑起在多数人看来类似于战争的冲突。大会的全体会议(不像各种规模较小的"讲座""工作坊""论坛"和"研讨会",如果不举行全体会议,它们就会占满一天时间)要求全部人员共同出席。

complement \ˈkäm-plə-mənt\ (1) Something that fills up or makes perfect; the amount needed to make something complete. 补充物,补足物,足额,定额 (2) A counterpart. 配对物

• On the committee, the two young people provided an energetic complement to the older members. 在委员会中,这两位年轻人很好地弥补了年长委员们活力的不足。

A *complement* fills out or balances something. We think of salt as the complement of pepper (maybe mostly because of their colors), and the right necktie is a perfect complement to a good suit. *Complement* can also mean "the full quantity, number, or amount"; thus, a ship's complement of officers and crew is the whole force necessary for full operation. *Complement* is actually most common as a verb; we may say, for example, that a bright blue scarf *complements* a cream-colored outfit beautifully. Don't confuse *complement* with *compliment*, which means an expression of respect or affection.

complement 补充或平衡某个东西。我们认为盐与胡椒相配(可能主要因为两者的颜色,黑白搭配),合适的领带配高档套装,堪称完美。*complement* 也可以指"数量的全部"。比如,一艘船上的全体官员和船员就是该船完全运行所需的全部力量。实际上,*complement* 最常用作动词。例如,我们可以说,明蓝色的围巾是奶油色外套的完美搭配。别把 *complement* 和 *compliment* 混淆了,后者用来表达尊敬或喜爱。

deplete \di-ˈplēt\ To reduce in amount by using up. 耗尽,用尽

• Years of farming on the same small plot of land had left the soil depleted of minerals. 多年来在同一小块土地上耕作使得土壤中的矿物质已经枯竭。

The *de-* prefix often means "do the opposite of," so *deplete* means the opposite of "fill." Thus, for example, a kitchen's food supplies can be rapidly depleted by hungry teenagers. But *deplete* often suggests something more serious. Desertions can deplete an army; layoffs can deplete an office staff; and too much time in bed can rapidly deplete your muscular strength.

前缀 *de* 通常表示"做与……相反的事",所以 *deplete* 的意思与"充满"相反。例如,厨房的食物可能很快被饥饿的青少年耗尽。但是 *deplete* 通常表示更严重的情况。逃兵会严重削弱军队的力量,裁员会使办公室职员人数大大减少,卧床时间太多会大量消耗你肌肉的力量。

replete \ri-ˈplēt\ Fully or abundantly filled or supplied. 充满的,充足的

• The professor's autobiography was replete with scandalous anecdotes about campus life in the 1950s. 那个教授的自传中充满了20世纪50年代校园生活中的丑闻轶事。

Replete implies that something is filled almost to capacity. Autumn landscapes in New England are replete with colorful foliage. Supermarket tabloids are always replete with details of stars' lives, whether real or imaginary. And a professor may complain that most of the papers she received were replete with errors in grammar and punctuation.

replete 指的是某物几乎被完全装满。新英格兰的秋天满眼都是五彩缤纷的树叶。超市小报上总是充满明星生活的细节，有真有假。教授可能会抱怨，她收到的大多数论文中满是语法和标点错误。

METR/METER

comes to us from Greek by way of Latin; in both languages it refers to "measure." A *thermometer* measures heat; a *perimeter* is the measure around something; and things that are *isometric* are equal in measure.

METR / METER 经由拉丁语从希腊语传入英语。在希腊语和拉丁语中，它指的都是"测量"。*thermometer*（温度计）测量的是温度；*perimeter*（周长）是测量某物的周边得到的结果；*isometric*（等量的）指的是测量的结果相等。

metric \ˈme-trik\ (1) Relating to or based on the metric system. 公制的 (2) Relating to or arranged in meter. 格律的，韵律的

• Americans have resisted using the metric system for years, but are now slowly getting accustomed to a few of the metric units. 美国人多年来一直抵制使用公制，但现在正慢慢地习惯一些公制单位。

The *metric* system was invented in France in the years following the French Revolution, and a version of it is now used in most of the world to measure distance, weight, and volume. Basic metric units include the *kilogram* (the basic unit of weight), the *liter* (the basic unit of volume), and of course the *meter* (the basic unit of length—see below). *Metric*—or more often *metrical*—can also refer to the basic underlying rhythm of songs and poetry. So while the scientists' measurements are usually metric, the poets' are usually metrical.

公制诞生于法国，在法国大革命之后的数年，它的某一版本现在为世界上多数国家所用，以测量长度、重量和体积。基本的公制单位包括 kilogram（千克，重量的基本单位）、liter（升，体积的基本单位），当然还有 meter（米，长度的基本单位——见下文）。metric——或更常用的 metrical——也可以指歌曲和诗歌基本的节奏韵律。科学家的度量通常用 metric，而诗人通常用 metrical。

meter \ˈmē-tər\ (1) The basic metric unit of length, equal to about 39.37 inches. 米 (2) A systematic rhythm in poetry or music. （诗歌或音乐的）韵律、格律、节奏、节拍

• The basic meter of the piece was 3/4, but its rhythms were so complicated that the 3/4 was sometimes hard to hear. 这首曲子的基本节奏是3/4拍，但其节奏太过于复杂，有时候很难听出3/4拍来。

Meter is a metric measurement slightly longer than a yard; thus, a 100-meter dash might take you a second longer than a 100-yard dash. But the word has a different sense in music, where people aren't separated by whether they use the metric system. For a musician, the *meter* is the regular background rhythm, expressed by the "time signature" written at the beginning of a piece or section: 2/2, 2/4, 3/8, 4/4, 6/8, etc. Within a meter, you can create rhythms that range from the simple to the complex. So, for example, "America the Beautiful" is in 4/4 meter (or "4/4 time"), but so are most of the rhythmically complex songs written by Paul Simon, Burt Bacharach, or Stevie Wonder. In ordinary conversation, though, most people use "rhythm" to include meter and everything that's built on top of it. In poetry, meter has much the same meaning; however, poetic meters aren't named with numbers but instead with traditional Greek and Latin terms such as *iambic* and *dactylic*.

<small>*meter* 是公制度量单位，比英制单位码略长；因此，百米冲刺可能比百码冲刺要多花一秒钟的时间。但是这个词在音乐中的含义有所不同，在音乐领域，不会因为是否使用 metric system 而把人分成两类。对于音乐家来说，节拍是有规律的背景节奏，用"拍号"表达，写在曲子或章节的开头：2/2、2/4、3/8、4/4、6/8 等等。同样的节拍中，你可以创造出从简到繁的各种节奏。比如《美丽的亚美利加》是 4/4 拍，由保罗·西蒙、伯特·巴沙拉克和史提夫·旺德创作的大多数节奏复杂曲子也是。然而，在日常对话中，多数人所说的"rhythm"包括了 meter 以及与之相关的东西。在诗歌中，meter 的意思与音乐中大致相同；然而，诗歌的 meter 并不是用数字来命名的，而是用传统的希腊语和拉丁语来命名的，比如 *iambic* （抑扬格）和 *dactylic* （扬抑抑格）。</small>

odometer \ō-ˈdä-mə-tər\ An instrument used to measure distance traveled. 里程表，里程计

• Jennifer watched the odometer to see how far she would have to drive to her new job. 詹妮弗看了看里程计，她想知道到新的工作地点有多远。

odometer includes the root from the Greek word *hodos*, meaning "road" or "trip." An odometer shares space on your dashboard with a speedometer, a tachometer, and maybe a "tripmeter." The odometer is what crooked car salesmen tamper with when they want to reduce the mileage a car registers as having traveled. One of life's little pleasures is watching the odometer as all the numbers change at the same time.

<small>Odometer 包含源自希腊语的词根 *hodos*（"路"或"旅行"）。里程计与速度计、转速计，也许还有"短距离里程计"共享你仪表盘上的空间。狡猾的汽车销售人员会篡改里程计，让汽车所行的里程看起来少一些。看着里程表上各个数字在同一时间变化也不失为生活中的一个乐趣啊。</small>

tachometer \ta-ˈkä-mə-tər\ A device used to measure speed of rotation. 转速计，转速表

• Even though one purpose of a tachometer is to help drivers keep their engine speeds down, some of us occasionally try to see how high we can make the needle go. 尽管转速计的唯一目的是让司机减慢引擎的速度，但有些人偶尔也想看看指针能指到多大的速度。

A *tachometer* is literally a "speed-measurer," since the Greek root *tach-* means "speed." This is clear in the names of the *tachyon*, a particle of matter that travels faster than the speed of light (if it actually exists, it's so fast that it's impossible to

METR/ METER

see with any instrument), and *tachycardia*, a medical condition in which the heart races uncontrollably. Since the speed that an auto tachometer measures is speed of rotation of the crankshaft, the numbers it reports are revolutions per minute, or rpm's.

希腊语词根 *tach-* 的意思是"速度",所以 tachometer 的字面意思就是"速度测量器"。这一含义在 *tachyon*(超光速粒子)一词中显而易见,超光速粒子是比光运动更快的粒子(如果它确实存在,也没办法通过仪器看到,因为速度太快了);这一含义在 *tachycardia*(心动过速)一词中也显而易见,心动过速是一种心脏不受控制地跳动的医学状况。因为汽车转速计测量的是曲轴的转速,所以它显示的是 revolutions per minute(每分钟转数),缩写为 rpm。

Quizzes

A. Match the word on the left to the correct definition on the right:

1. meter   a. drain
2. tachometer   b. brimming
3. metric   c. counterpart
4. replete   d. beat pattern
5. odometer   e. distance measurer
6. deplete   f. rotation meter
7. plenary   g. general
8. complement   h. relating to a measuring system

B. Choose the closest definition:

1. deplete   a. straighten out   b. draw down   c. fold
   d. abandon
2. replete   a. refold   b. repeat
   c. abundantly provided   d. fully clothed
3. odometer   a. intelligence measurer
   b. heart-rate measurer   c. height measurer
   d. mile measurer
4. tachometer   a. rpm measurer   b. sharpness measurer
   c. fatigue measurer   d. size measurer
5. complement   a. praise   b. number required
   c. abundance   d. usual dress
6. metric   a. relating to poetic rhythm
   b. relating to ocean depth   c. relating to books
   d. relating to particles of matter
7. plenary   a. for hours   b. for life   c. for officials
   d. for everyone
8. meter   a. weight   b. rhythm   c. speed
   d. force

UNIT 6

AUD, from the Latin verb *audire*, is the root that has to do with hearing. What is *audible* can be heard. An *audience* is a group of listeners, sometimes seated in an *auditorium*. And *audio* today can mean almost anything that has to do with sound.

AUD 源自拉丁语动词 *audire*，是个与听力有关的词根。*audible* 的意思是能听见的。*audience* 指的是一群听众，有时坐在 *auditorium*（礼堂）里。*audio* 现在可以表示几乎所有与声音有关的东西。

auditor \ˈȯ-də-tər\ A person who formally examines and verifies financial accounts. 审计员，查账人员

• It seems impossible that so many banks could have gotten into so much trouble if their auditors had been doing their jobs. 如果审计人员能做好本职工作，恐怕就没有那么多银行陷入这么多的麻烦中了。

The *auditing* of a company's financial records by independent examiners on a regular basis is necessary to prevent "cooking the books," and thus to keep the company honest. We don't normally think of *auditors* as listening, since looking at and adding up numbers is their basic line of work, but auditors do have to listen to people's explanations, and perhaps that's the historical link. Hearing is more obviously part of another meaning of *audit*, the kind that college students do when they sit in on a class without taking exams or receiving an official grade.

由独立的审计人员定期 *auditing*（审核）公司的财务报表是必要的，可以防止"做假账"，从而使公司能诚实运作。我们通常认为审计人员不是在听，因为审查和计算数字才是他们的基本工作，然而，审计员的确要听取人们的解释，也许这就是历史渊源。在 *audit* 的另一个意思中，"听"的含义更为明显。旁听是指大学生在教室中听课，但无须参加考试，也无须取得正式的分数。

auditory \ˈȯ-də-ˌtȯr-ē\ (1) Perceived or experienced through hearing. 听觉的 (2) Of or relating to the sense or organs of hearing. 听的

• With the "surround-sound" systems in most theaters, going to a movie is now an auditory experience as much as a visual one. 多数影院都配有"环绕立体声"系统，看电影如今既是视觉的体验也是听觉体验。

Auditory is close in meaning to *acoustic* and *acoustical*, but *auditory* usually refers more to hearing than to sound. For instance, many dogs have great auditory (not acoustic) powers, and the *auditory nerve* lets us hear by connecting the inner ear to the brain. *Acoustic* and *acoustical* instead refer especially to instruments and the conditions under which sound can be heard; so architects concern themselves with the acoustic properties of an auditorium, and instrument makers with those of a clarinet or piano.

auditory 与 *acoustic* 和 *acoustical* 意思相近，但 *auditory* 通常与听觉相关，而不是与声音相关。例如，许多狗有很强的 auditory（而非是 acoustic）能力，*auditory nerve*（听觉神经）将内耳与大脑相连，使我们能够听到声音。而 *acoustic* 和 *acoustical* 则主要指乐器和传音条件；因此，建筑师关注的是礼堂的声学特性，乐器制造商关注的是单簧管或钢琴的声学特性。

audition \ȯ-ˈdi-shən\　A trial performance to evaluate a performer's skills. 试镜，试演

• Auditions for Broadway shows attract so many hopeful unknown performers that everyone in the business calls them "cattle calls." 百老汇演出的试演吸引了非常多有希望的无名演员，业内称他们为"cattle calls"，即临时演员应募者。

Most stars are discovered at auditions, where a number of candidates read the same part and the director chooses. Lana Turner famously skipped the audition process and was instead discovered by an agent sipping a soda in a Sunset Boulevard café at age 16. Audition can also be a verb; so, for example, after Miss Turner gained her stardom, actors had to audition to be her leading man. But when musicians audition for a job in an orchestra, it's usually behind a screen so that the judges won't even know their sex and therefore can't do anything but listen. 多数明星都是在试镜时被发掘的。许多候选演员试镜时会读同一段台词，由导演挑选。众所周知，拉娜·特纳没有参加试镜，16岁那年，她在日落大道的一家咖啡馆里，被一个喝苏打汽水的经纪人发现。audition 同时也是动词，例如，特纳小姐成名后，演员想成为她的男一号必须试镜才行。然而，当音乐家们参加管弦乐队面试时，他们通常是在幕后，评委们甚至连他们的性别都不知道，只能听。

inaudible \i-ˈnȯ-də-bəl\　Not heard or capable of being heard. 听不见的

• The coach spoke to her in a low voice that was inaudible to the rest of the gymnastics team. 教练同她说话的声音很低，其他的体操队员听不见。

With its negative prefix in-, inaudible means the opposite of audible. What's clearly audible to you may be inaudible to your elderly grandfather. Modern spy technology can turn inaudible conversations into audible ones with the use of high-powered directional microphones, so if you think you're being spied on, make sure there's a lot of other noise around you. And if you don't want everyone around you to know you're bored, keep your sighs inaudible. 前缀 in- 表示否定，因此 inaudible 的意思与 audible（听得见的）相反。你能清楚听见的声音也许你年迈的祖父听不见。借助高功率定向麦克风，现代间谍技术可以变听不见的对话为听得见的对话，所以如果你觉得自己被监视了，一定要待在周围吵闹的地方。如果你不想让周围的人知道你很无聊，那就不要让别人听到你长吁短叹。

SON is the Latin root meaning "sound." *Sonata*, meaning a piece for one or two instruments, was originally an Italian verb meaning "sounded" (when singers were involved, the Italians used a different verb). And *sonorous* means full, loud, or rich in sound.

SON 是意为"声音"的拉丁语词根。Sonata（奏鸣曲）指的是供一种或两种乐器演奏的乐曲，它最初是一个意大利语动词，意思是"听起来"（当涉及歌手时，意大利人使用了另一个动词）。Sonorous（洪亮的）的意思是声音饱满、响亮或圆润。

---

sonic \ˈsä-nik\　(1) Having to do with sound. 声音的 (2) Having to do with the speed of sound in air (about 750 miles per hour). 音速的

• A sonic depth finder can easily determine the depth of a lake by bouncing a

· 130 ·

sound signal off the bottom. 回声测深仪通过水底反弹声音信号很容易就能测得湖水的深度。

A sonic boom is an explosive sound created by a shock wave formed at the nose of an aircraft. In 1947 a plane piloted by Chuck Yeager burst the "sound barrier" and created the first sonic boom. In the decades afterward sonic booms became a familiar sound to Americans. (Because of steps that were eventually taken, sonic booms are rarely heard anymore.) Today sonic is often used by ambitious rock musicians to describe their experimental sounds.

音爆是飞机头部形成的冲击波所产生的爆炸声。1947年,查克·耶格尔驾驶的一架飞机突破了音障,创造出了第一个音爆。此后的几十年里,美国人听惯了音爆声。(由于最终采取了措施,现在音爆声已经很少听到了。)如今,sonic 一词常被雄心勃勃的摇滚乐手用来形容他们的实验音乐。

dissonant \ˈdi-sə-nənt\ (1) Clashing or discordant, especially in music. 不和谐的,不悦耳的 (2) Incompatible or disagreeing. 不一致的,不协调的

• Critics of the health-care plan pointed to its two seemingly dissonant goals: cost containment, which would try to control spending, and universal coverage, which could increase spending. 这项医疗保健计划的批评者们指出了该计划两个似乎自相矛盾的目标:降低成本与全民覆盖。前者旨在控制开支,而后者却要增加开支。

Since *dissonant* includes the negative prefix *dis-*, what is dissonant sounds or feels unresolved, unharmonic, and clashing. Early in the 20th century, composers such as Arnold Schoenberg and his students developed the use of *dissonance* in music as a style in itself. But to many listeners, the sounds in such music are still unbearable, and most continue to prefer music based on traditional tonality. *Dissonant* is now often used without referring to sound at all. *Cognitive dissonance*, for example, is what happens when you believe two different things that can't actually both be true.

前缀 dis- 表示否定,所以 dissonant 的声音听起来或感觉上是不协调的、不和谐的、刺耳的。在20世纪初,像阿诺德·勋伯格和他的学生这样的作曲家把 dissonance(不和谐)的音用在音乐中,自成风格。但对许多听众来说,这类音乐中的音依然让人难以忍受,他们还是更喜欢基于传统调性的音乐。dissonant 现在不仅仅用于音乐上,例如,cognitive dissonance(认知失调)指的就是你相信两件不同的事情都是真的,但实际上两者不可能同时为真。

resonance \ˈre-zə-nəns\ (1) A continuing or echoing of sound. 共振,共鸣 (2) A richness and variety in the depth and quality of sound. 洪亮,响亮

• The resonance of James Earl Jones's vocal tones in such roles as Darth Vader made his voice one of the most recognizable of its time. 詹姆斯·厄尔·琼斯扮演的达斯·维德等角色声音洪亮,他的声音也因此成为在那个时代最具辨识度的声音之一。

Many of the finest musical instruments possess a high degree of resonance which, by producing additional vibrations and echoes of the original sound, enriches and amplifies it. Violins made by the Italian masters Stradivari and Guarneri possess a quality of resonance that later violinmakers have never precisely duplicated. And you may have noticed how a particular note will start something in a room buzzing, as one of the touching surfaces begins to resonate with the note. Because of that, *resonance* and *resonate*—along with the adjective *resonant*—aren't always used to describe sound. For example, you may say that a novel resonates strongly with you because the author seems to be describing your own experiences and feelings.

许多上乘的乐器具有高度的共振性，即通过增加振动和回声，使原始的声音更加饱满、响亮。意大利大师斯特拉迪瓦里和瓜纳里制作的小提琴拥有的共鸣品质，后来者难以精确复制。你或许已经注意到，某个特定的音符可以让房间中的某样东西嗡嗡作响，这是因为该物体的接触面与音符 *resonate*（产生共振）。因此，*resonance* 和 *resonate*——与形容词 *resonant* 一起——不仅用来形容声音。例如，你可能会说某部小说与你产生了强烈的共鸣，因为作者好像写的就是你的个人经历和情感一样。

ultrasonic \ˌəl-trə-ˈsä-nik\ Having a frequency higher than what can be heard by the human ear. 超声的

• My grandfather's dog is always pricking up its ears at some ultrasonic signal, while he himself is so deaf he can't even hear a bird singing. 我爷爷的狗在听到某个超声信号时总是竖起耳朵，而爷爷自己却耳背得很，鸟叫声都听不见。

Ultrasound, or *ultrasonography*, works on the principle that sound is reflected at different speeds by tissues or substances of different densities. Ultrasound technology has been used medically since the 1940s. *Sonograms*, the pictures produced by ultrasound, can reveal heart defects, tumors, and gallstones; since low-power ultrasonic waves don't present any risks to a body, they're most often used to display fetuses during pregnancy in order to make sure they're healthy. *Ultrasonics* has many other uses, including underwater *sonar* sensing. High-power ultrasonics are so intense that they're actually used for drilling and welding.

ultrasound（超声波）或 *ultrasonography*（超声波扫描）的工作原理是，不同密度的组织或物体所反射声波的速度不同。自 20 世纪 40 年代以来，超声波技术就被用于医疗。*sonograms*（超声波图）是由超声波绘制的图像，可以用来检测心脏疾病、肿瘤和胆结石；低功率超声波不会对人体造成任何损害，所以常用于孕期胎儿检查，以确保胎儿健康成长。*ultrasonics*（超声学）还有许多其他用途，包括水下 *sonar*（声呐）传感。高功率超声波强大到竟然可以用来钻孔和焊接。

Quizzes

A. Indicate whether the following pairs of words have the same or different meanings:

1. dissonant / jarring   same ____ / different ____
2. inaudible / invisible   same ____ / different ____
3. resonance / richness   same ____ / different ____
4. audition / tryout   same ____ / different ____
5. ultrasonic / radical   same ____ / different ____
6. auditor / performer   same ____ / different ____
7. sonic / loud   same ____ / different ____
8. auditory / hearing-related same ____ / different ____

B. Match the word on the left to the correct definition on the right:

1. inaudible   a. involving sound
2. auditory   b. impossible to hear

3. ultrasonic
4. resonance
5. auditor
6. sonic
7. dissonant
8. audition

c. beyond the hearing range
d. a critical hearing
e. relating to hearing
f. unharmonious
g. financial examiner
h. continuing or echoing sound

ERR, from the Latin verb *errare*, means "to wander" or "to stray." The root is seen in the word *error*, meaning a wandering or straying from what is correct or true. *Erratum* (plural, *errata*) is Latin for "mistake"; so an errata page is a book page that lists mistakes found too late to correct before the book's publication.
ERR 源自拉丁语动词 errare,意为"迷路"或"偏离"。该词根见于 error(错误)一词中,意为偏离正道。erratum(复数形式是 errata)是拉丁语,表示"错误";因此,书的勘误页列出书中所发现的错误,因太晚而无法在出版前纠正。

---

errant \ˈer-ənt\ (1) Wandering or moving about aimlessly. 漫游的,游走的,游历的 (2) Straying outside proper bounds, or away from an accepted pattern or standard. 迷失的,偏离正道的

• Modern-day cowboys have been known to use helicopters to spot errant calves. 据说,现代牛仔利用直升机来寻走失的小牛。

Errant means both "wandering" and "mistaken." A *knight-errant* was a wandering knight who went about slaying dragons or rescuing damsels in distress (at least when he was on good behavior). *Arrant* is a old-fashioned spelling of *errant*; an *arrant knave* (the phrase comes from Shakespeare) is an extremely untrustworthy individual. An errant sock might be one that's gotten lost; an errant politician might be one who's been caught cheating; and an errant cloud might be one that floats by all alone in a deep-blue sky on a summer day.
errant 同时有"漫游的"和"错误的"之意。knight-errant(游侠骑士)指的是周游各地的骑士,他们屠杀巨龙、拯救少女于困境之中(至少他们行为端正时是这么做的)。arrant 是 errant 的旧式拼写,arrant knave(这个短语源自莎士比亚)指的是完全不值得信赖的人。errant sock 可能就是那只丢失的袜子;errant politician 可能是被发现在说谎的政治家;errant cloud 指的可能是夏日里独自飘浮在深蓝色天空中的云。

aberrant \ə-ˈber-ənt\ Straying or differing from the right, normal, or natural type. 异常的,反常的,不循常轨的

• Sullivan's increasingly aberrant behavior was leading his friends to question his mental stability. 沙利文越来越反常的行为让朋友们怀疑他的心理稳定性。

Something aberrant has wandered away from the usual path or form. The word is generally used in a negative way; aberrant behavior, for example, may be a symptom of other problems. But the discovery of an aberrant variety of a species can be exciting news to a biologist, and identifying an aberrant gene has led the way to new treatments for diseases.

something aberrant（异常的东西）已经偏离了平常的道路或形态。这个词一般用于消极语境，例如，aberrant behavior（反常的举止）指的可能是其他问题的某个症状。但是，对生物学家来说，发现一种不寻常的物种是令人激动的消息，而识别异常的基因已经带来新的疾病治疗方法。

erratic\i-ˈra-tik\ (1) Having no fixed course. 无规律的，不规则的 (2) Lacking in consistency. 不稳定的

• In the 1993 World Series, the Phillies weren't helped by the erratic performance of their ace relief pitcher, "Wild Thing." 在1993年的世界职业棒球大赛上，费城人队的王牌替补投手"野东西"发挥不稳，未能帮到球队。

Erratic can refer to literal "wandering." A missile that loses its guidance system may follow an erratic path, and a river with lots of twists and bends is said to have an erratic course. *Erratic* can also mean "inconsistent" or "irregular." So a stock market that often changes direction is said to be acting *erratically*; an erratic heartbeat can be cause for concern; and if your car idles erratically it may mean that something's wrong with the spark-plug wiring.

erratic 的字面意思是"漫游的"。失去制导系统的导弹可能会沿着飘忽不定的路线飞行，弯弯曲曲的河流被认为河道不稳定。Erratic 也可以指"不一致的"或"不规则的"。因此，经常变换风向的股市被称为 be acting erratically（表现不稳定）；心律不齐需要引起警惕；如果你的车不正常地空转，可能是火花塞线有毛病。

erroneous\i-ˈrō-nē-əs\ Mistaken, incorrect. 错误的

• For years her parents had had an erroneous idea of her intelligence, because she didn't begin to talk until the age of six. 由于她直到六岁才开始说话，父母多年来对她的智力一直有错误的认识。

Erroneous basically means "containing errors," and, since most of us are constantly suffering from mistaken notions, the word is often used in front of words such as "assumption" and "idea." It's also used to describe the kind of mistaken information that can lead to erroneous theories, erroneous conclusions, and erroneous decisions.

erroneous 的基本意思是"包含错误的"。由于多数人的观念经常有错，所以这个词常用于"假设""想法"等词语之前。它也用来指可以导致错误理论、错误结论以及错误决定的那类错误信息。

CED comes from the Latin verb *cedere*, meaning "to proceed" or "to yield." *Proceed* itself employs the root, as does *recede*, and their related nouns *procession* and *recession* employ another form of the Latin verb.

CED 源自拉丁语动词 cedere，意思是"行进"或"退让"。与 recede 一样，proceed 本身也使用这个词根，但它们的名词 progress 和 recession 用是却是这个拉丁动词的另一种形式。

---

cede\ˈsēd\ To give up, especially by treaty; yield. 放弃，割让，屈服

• Their 88-year-old father reluctantly ceded control over his finances to two of the children this year. 今年,他们 88 岁的父亲十分勉强地把财务控制权让给了两个孩子。

Cede is often a formal term used in discussing territory and rights, but is also used less formally. So, for example, Spain ceded Puerto Rico to the U. S. in 1898, following the Spanish-American War, and the U. S. ceded control of the Panama Canal to Panama in 1999. Critics warn that we are ceding leadership in alternative-energy technology to China. Citizens of one European country or another are always worrying that their own country is ceding too much power to the European Union. A tennis player doesn't have any choice when she cedes her no. 1 ranking to a rival.

cede 常作为讨论领土和权利的正式词语使用,但也可以用于不那么正式的场合。例如,1898 年美西战争之后,西班牙将波多黎各割让给美国;1999 年,美国将巴拿马运河的控制权转让给巴拿马。批评者警告说,我们(美国)正在把在替代能源技术方面的领先地位让给中国。某个欧洲国家的公民总是担心,他们的国家将太多的权力拱手让给欧盟。网球运动员将第一的排名让与对手,但也别无选择。

concede \kən-'sēd\ To admit grudgingly; yield. 不情愿地承认,屈服

• To his friends, Senator Beasley concedes that his reelection campaign was badly run and that he made several damaging errors. 比斯利参议员不情愿地向他的朋友们承认,他的连任竞选没搞好,他犯了几个毁灭性的错误。

After the votes have been counted, one candidate traditionally concedes the election to his or her opponent by giving a *concession* speech. If you're lucky, your boss will concede that she was wrong the last time she criticized you. But in the middle of an argument, we're not all so good at conceding that the other guy might have a good point.

计票结束后,失败的候选人传统上会发表 *concession* speech(败选演说),向对手承认选举结果。幸运的话,你的老板会承认上次错怪你了。但是在争论的过程中,我们并非都很善于承认对方的理由可能会更为充分。

accede \ak'-sēd\ (1) To give in to a request or demand. 让步 (2) To give approval or consent. 同意

• This time Congress refused to accede to the demands of the president, and began cutting the funding for the war. 这一次,国会拒绝同意总统的要求,开始削减战争经费。

To accede usually means to yield, often under pressure and with some reluctance, to the needs or requests of others. Voters usually accede to a tax increase only when they're convinced it's the only real solution to a shortfall in government funding. A patient may accede to surgery only after the doctor assures him it's better than the alternatives. If you accede to your spouse's plea to watch the new reality show at 9:00, you may get to choose something better at 10:00.

accede 通常的意思是对他人的需要或要求做出让步,往往是屈服于压力且很不情愿。通常情况下,选民们只有在相信增税是解决政府资金短缺唯一可行的方法时,才会勉强同意增税。只有在医生保证做手术比不做手术好的时候,病人才可能接受手术。如果你同意配偶看 9 点真人秀的请求,到 10 点的时候也许才轮到你选择更好的节目。

precedent \'pre-sə-dənt\ Something done or said that may be an example or rule to guide later acts of a similar kind. 先例,前例

● When Judy bought Christmas presents for all her relatives one year, she claimed that it set no precedent, but it did. 有一年,朱迪给她所有的亲戚都买了圣诞礼物,她说不要把这次送礼成为先例,但最终还是成了先例。

A *precedent* is something that *precedes*, or comes before. The Supreme Court relies on precedents—that is, earlier laws or decisions that provide some example or rule to guide them in the case they're actually deciding. When hostages are being held for ransom, a government may worry about setting a bad precedent if it gives in. And a company might "break with precedent" by naming a foreigner as its president for the first time.

先例指的是 *precedes*(之前发生)的事情。最高法院依靠先例——也就是说,先前的法律或决定,为他们判决现在的案件提供了例子或规则。当被要挟付赎金解救人质时,政府会担心,做出让步会开创一个不好的先例。某公司任命外国人担任总裁,或许就是在"打破先例"。

Quizzes

A. Complete the analogy:

1. descending : ascending :: errant : _____
   a. moving   b. wandering   c. fixed   d. straying
2. grab : seize :: cede : _____
   a. hang on   b. hand over   c. hang up   d. head out
3. fruitful : barren :: erroneous : _____
   a. productive   b. pleasant   c. targeted   d. correct
4. disagree : argue :: concede : _____
   a. drive   b. hover   c. yield   d. refuse
5. stable : constant :: erratic : _____
   a. fast   b. invisible   c. mistaken   d. unpredictable
6. swerve : veer :: accede : _____
   a. agree   b. descent   c. reject   d. demand
7. typical : normal :: aberrant : _____
   a. burdened   b. roving   c. odd   d. missing
8. etiquette : manners :: precedent : _____
   a. courtesy   b. tradition   c. rudeness   d. behavior

B. Fill in each blank with the correct letter:

a. aberrant   e. erratic
b. errant   f. erroneous
c. precedent   g. cede
d. concede   h. accede

1. Her low opinion of him turned out to be based on several _____ assumptions.
2. The judges could find no _____ to guide them in deciding how to deal with

the case.

3. Like many malaria sufferers, she experienced _____ changes in her temperature.

4. Occasionally an _____ cow would be found on the back lawn, happily grazing on the fresh clover.

5. She's very stubborn, and in an argument she'll never _____ a single point.

6. After several incidents of disturbingly _____ behavior, his parents began taking him to a psychiatrist.

7. After lengthy negotiations, the union will probably _____ to several of the company's terms.

8. The treaty requires that both sides _____ several small tracts of land.

Words from Mythology and History 源自神话和历史的词语

Augean stable \ȯ-ˈjē-ən-ˈstā-bəl\ A condition or place marked by great accumulation of filth or corruption. 奥吉斯的牛舍，污秽腐败之所

• Leaders of many of the newly formed nations of Eastern Europe found that the old governments of their countries had become Augean stables that they must now clean out. 东欧许多新成立的国家的领导人发现，他们国家的旧政府已成为他们现在必须清理的"污秽腐败之所"。

Augeus, the mythical king of Elis, kept great *stables* that held 3,000 oxen and had not been cleaned for thirty years when Hercules was assigned the job as one of his famous "twelve labors." This task was enormous even for someone so mighty, so Hercules shifted the course of two rivers to make them pour through the stables. *Augean* by itself has come to mean "extremely difficult or distasteful," and to "clean the Augean stable" usually means either to clear away corruption or to perform a large and unpleasant task that has long called for attention. So today we refer to "*Augean tasks*," "*Augean labor*," or even "*Augean clutter*." And the British firm *Augean PLC* is—what else?—a waste-management company.

Augeus（奥吉斯）是神话中埃利斯的国王，他有一个巨大的牛舍，养着3000头牛。赫拉克勒斯被指派清理之时，已有30年未曾清理，这也是赫拉克勒斯有名的"十二项考验"之一。这项任务对即便像他那样孔武有力的人来说也十分艰巨。于是，赫拉克勒斯将两条河流改道，用河水冲洗牛舍。Augean 本身就有"十分艰巨或令人不快"的意思。"清理奥吉斯的牛舍"通常意味着整治腐败，或者执行一项早就引起关注的、艰巨而令人不快的任务。所以今天我们说"Augean tasks"（艰巨的任务）、"Augean labor"（困难的工作），甚至"Augean clutter"（凌乱不堪）。英国公司 Augean PLC 是——还能是别的什么？——垃圾处理公司而已。

Croesus \ˈkrē-səs\ A very rich person. 克里萨斯王，富豪

• Warren Buffett's extraordinary record of acquiring and investing made him an American Croesus. 沃伦•巴菲特收购和投资的非凡记录使他成为美国大富豪。

Croesus, which tends to appear in the phrase "*rich as Croesus*," was the name of a king of Lydia, an ancient kingdom in what is now western Turkey, who died

• 137 •

around 546 B.C. Lydia was probably the first country in history to use coins, and under the wealthy and powerful Croesus the first coins of pure silver and gold were produced, which may have added to the legends surrounding his wealth. But it was Croesus who the Greek lawgiver Solon was thinking about when he said "Count no man happy until his death"—and indeed Croesus was finally overthrown and may even have been burned alive.

Croesus(克里萨斯)常出现在短语"rich as Croesus"(像克里萨斯一样富裕)中,他是吕底亚王国的一位国王,在大约公元前546年去世。吕底亚是一个古老的王国,位于现在的土耳其西部。这可能是历史上第一个使用硬币的国家,在富有而强大的克里萨斯王的统治下,铸造了最早的纯金币和纯银币,也为他的财富传奇又添上一笔。然而,古希腊的立法者梭伦曾说:"到死方知是否幸福。"他说这话的时候想到的正是克里萨斯——事实上,克里萨斯最终被推翻,甚至还可能是被活活烧死的。

dragon's teeth \ˈdra-gənz-ˈtēth\ Seeds of conflict. 冲突的种子,争斗的根源

• Many experts believed that, in invading a Middle Eastern country that hadn't attacked us, we were sowing dragon's teeth. 许多专家认为,入侵一个根本没有侵犯过我们的中东国家,是在播下冲突的种子。

The Phoenician prince Cadmus once killed a dragon, and was instructed by the goddess Athena to plant its teeth in the ground. From the many teeth, there immediately sprang up an army of fierce armed men. The goddess then directed him to throw a precious stone into their midst, and they proceeded to slaughter each other until only the five greatest warriors were left; these became Cadmus's generals, with whom he constructed the great city-state of Thebes. When we "sow dragon's teeth," we're creating the conditions for future trouble.

腓尼基王子卡德摩斯曾杀死了一条龙,雅典娜女神指示他把龙牙埋在地里。这些龙牙立刻冒出一支全副武装的凶猛的军队。雅典娜女神接着吩咐他把一块宝石扔到士兵中间,他们开始互相厮杀,直到只剩下五个最强大的战士才住手。这五个人后来成为卡德摩斯的将军,与卡德摩斯一起建立了伟大的底比斯城邦。当我们"种下龙牙"的时候,我们正在为未来的麻烦创造条件。

Hades \ˈhā-dēz\ The underground home of the dead in Greek mythology. 冥界,阴间

• In a dramatic scene, he crawls up out of the ground coated in black petroleum as though emerging from Hades. 在一个戏剧性的场景中,他从地下钻出来,裹着一层黑色的石油,就像从冥界钻出来一样。

In Greek mythology, Hades is both the land of the dead and the god who rules there. Hades the god (who the Greeks also called Pluto) is the brother of Zeus and Poseidon, who rule the skies and the seas. The realm called Hades, where he rules with his wife Persephone, is the region under the earth, full of mineral wealth and fertility and home to dead souls. Hades today is sometimes used as a polite term for Hell ("It's hotter than Hades in here!").

在古希腊神话中,Hades(哈得斯)既是死者的国度,又是统治该地之神。哈得斯神(希腊人也叫普路托)是天神宙斯和海神波塞冬的兄弟。他与妻子珀尔塞福涅统治着一个叫做哈得斯的王国,这个地下之域矿产资源丰富、土地肥沃,是亡灵的家园。如今,Hades(冥界)有时用作Hell(地狱)的文雅的说法("这里可比Hades热啊!")。

lethargic \ lə-'thär-jik \　　（1）Lazily sluggish. 懒洋洋地,无精打采的（2）Indifferent or apathetic. 漠不关心的,缺乏兴趣的

● Once again the long Sunday dinner had left most of the family feeling stuffed and lethargic. 漫长的周日晚餐又一次让多数家人感觉肚中饱胀、昏昏欲睡。

The philosopher Plato wrote that before a dead person could leave the underworld to begin a new life, he or she had to drink from the river Lethe, whose name means "forgetfulness" in Greek, and forget all aspects of one's former life and the time spent in Hades (usually pretty awful, according to Plato). But *lethargic* and its noun *lethargy* never actually refer to forgetting; instead, they describe the weak, ghostly state of the dead spirits—so weak that they may require a drink of blood before they can even speak. 哲学家柏拉图写道,死去的人在离开地下重新开始新生活之前,必须喝下 river Lethe（忘川河）的水,这条河的名字在希腊语中是"健忘"的意思。他于是就会忘记从前的全部生活以及在冥界度过的时光（柏拉图认为,冥界的生活通常是很可怕的）。然而, lethargic 及其名词 lethargy 所指的实际上从来都不是忘却；相反,它们指的是死亡灵魂的虚弱、幽灵般的状态——虚弱到必须喝点血才能力气说话。

Midas touch \ 'mī-dəs-'təch \　　The talent for making money in every venture. 点石成金

● Investors are always looking for an investment adviser with the Midas touch, but after a couple of good years each adviser's brilliance usually seems to vanish. 投资者总是在寻找能点石成金的投资顾问,但业绩好了几年之后,顾问们的才华似乎都消失了。

Midas was a legendary king of Phrygia (in modern-day Turkey). In return for a good deed, he was granted one wish by the god Dionysus, and asked for the power to turn everything he touched into gold. When he discovered to his horror that his touch had turned his food and drink—and even his daughter—to gold, he begged Dionysus to take back the gift, and Dionysus agreed to do so. When "Midas touch" is used today, the moral of this tale of greed is usually ignored. Midas（迈达斯）是弗里吉亚（在今土耳其）的一个富有传奇色彩的国王。酒神狄俄尼索斯为了报恩,答应满足他的一个愿望,迈达斯希望拥有能将所有触碰过的东西都变成金子的能力。他惊恐地发现,凡是他触碰过的东西,食物、饮料——甚至女儿——都变成了金子,于是他恳求狄俄尼索斯收回他的能力,狄俄尼索斯答应了。我们今天还在用"Midas touch"（点石成金）这个词语,但这个故事贪婪的寓意通常被忽略了。

Pyrrhic victory \ 'pir-ik-'vik-tə-rē \　　A victory won at excessive cost. 皮拉斯式的胜利,惨胜,付出极大代价的胜利

● That win turned out to be a Pyrrhic victory, since our best players sustained injuries that would sideline them for weeks. 我们为那场胜利付出了极大的代价,因为我们的主力队员们受伤了,不得不缺阵数周。

In 279 B.C. Pyrrhus, the king of Epirus, a country in northwest Greece, defeated the Romans at the Battle of Ausculum, but lost all of his best officers and many men. He is said to have exclaimed after the battle, "One more such victory and we are lost." Pyrrhic victories are more common than we tend to think. Whenever we win an argument but in so doing manage to offend the friend we were arguing with, or whenever a country invades another country but rouses widespread opposition in surrounding countries in the process, it's probably a Pyrrhic victory that has been achieved.

公元前 279 年,古希腊西北部伊庇鲁斯的国王 Pyrrhus(皮拉斯)在奥斯库伦战役中打败了罗马人,但他却失去了所有最好的军官以及很多士兵。据说,他在战斗结束后喊道:"再有一次这样的胜利,我们就完了。"皮拉斯式的胜利比我们想象的还要常见。我们跟朋友争辩赢了,但却冒犯了他们,或者某个国家入侵他国,却引发了周边国家的普遍反对,这样的胜利恐怕就是 Pyrrhic victory 了。

stygian \\ˈsti-jē-ən\\ Extremely dark, dank, gloomy, and forbidding. 黑魆魆的,阴森的

- When the power went out in the building, the halls and stairwells were plunged in stygian darkness. 大楼停电了,大厅和楼梯井都陷入了阴森的黑暗之中。

The Greek underworld of Hades was cold and dark, rather than blazing like the Christian image of Hell. The river Styx, whose name meant "hateful" in Greek, was the chief river of the underground, and the souls of the dead were ferried across its poisonous waters into Hades by the boatman Charon. The Styx was so terrible that even the gods swore by its name in their most solemn oaths. The name Stygia, borrowed from *stygian*, is used for a country in fantasy games today; but a stygian atmosphere, a stygian tunnel, stygian darkness, and so on, still describe the dreary cheerlessness of the Greek underworld.

希腊冥界的地下世界寒冷而黑暗,而基督教中的地狱形象却是极为灼热。River Styx(斯堤克斯河)的名字在希腊语中的意思是"可憎的",它是冥界的主要河流,死者的灵魂需要由船夫卡隆摆渡过这条有毒的河,才得以进入冥界。斯堤克斯实在可怕,连众神发下最郑重的誓言时,都会用上它的名义。Stygia 这个名字是从 *stygian* 借来的,今天用作魔幻游戏中某个国家的名称;但是,a stygian atmosphere、a stygian tunnel、stygian darkness 等等,用来形容的依然是如同古希腊地下世界般的沉闷和阴暗。

Quiz

Choose the word that does not belong:

1. lethargic   a. lazy   b. sluggish   c. energetic   d. indifferent
2. Croesus   a. rich   b. powerful   c. impoverished   d. successful
3. Midas touch   a. talented   b. unsuccessful   c. rich   d. prosperous
4. Pyrrhic victory   a. unqualified   b. costly   c. dangerous   d. destructive
5. Augean stable   a. purity   b. corruption   c. filth   d. Herculean
6. Hades   a. underworld   b. heaven   c. dead

d. eternity
7. dragon's teeth a. dangerous b. troublesome c. sensible
   d. conflict
8. stygian a. glamorous b. gloomy c. grim
   d. dank

Review Quizzes

A. Match each word on the left to its antonym on the right:

1. cede
2. erroneous
3. dissonant
4. lethargic
5. replete
6. acquisitive
7. deplete
8. equilibrium
9. inaudible
10. aberrant

a. true
b. generous
c. energetic
d. fill
e. imbalance
f. typical
g. acquire
h. hearable
i. empty
j. harmonious

B. Complete the analogies:

1. allow : forbid :: cede : _____
   a. take   b. agree   c. soothe   d. permit
2. lively : energetic :: erratic : _____
   a. calm   b. changeable   c. steady   d. weary
3. complain : whine :: accede : _____
   a. go over   b. give in   c. give out   d. go along
4. noisy : raucous :: dissonant : _____
   a. musical   b. symphonic   c. harsh   d. loud
5. amount : quantity :: complement _____
   a. remainder   b. extra   c. extension   d. minority
6. spendthrift : thrifty :: acquisitive : _____
   a. wealthy   b. uncertain   c. curious   d. unselfish

C. Fill in each blank with the correct letter:

a. auditor
b. tachometer
c. dragon's teeth
d. complement
e. Croesus

f. erratic
g. Midas touch
h. accede
i. Pyrrhic victory
j. metric

1. My grandfather has never had any money, but his brother is rich as _____.

2. Every scientist in the world uses a version of the _____ system, but the American public has always resisted it.

3. An _____ had been going over the company's financial records all week.

4. The triumphant corporate takeover proved to be a _____, since the resulting debt crippled the corporation for years.

5. The children made only _____ progress because they kept stopping to pick flowers.

6. Some of the faculty have decided to quietly _____ to the students' request for less homework.

7. She's been sowing _____ with her mean gossip, and by now no one in the department is speaking to anyone else.

8. When the traffic gets too noisy, I have to glance at the _____ to see if the engine is racing.

9. Fresh, hot bread is the perfect _____ to any dinner.

10. Her wealthy father had always had the _____, and his money-making genius was still a mystery to her.

UNIT 7

VIS comes from a Latin verb meaning "see." *Vision* is what enables us to see, *visual* images are *visible* to our eyes, and a *visitor* is someone who comes to see something. The same verb actually gives us another root, *vid-*, as in Julius Caesar's famous statement about his military exploits, "Veni, vidi, vici" ("I came, I saw, I conquered"), and such common English words as *video*.

VIS 源自意思是"看见"的拉丁语动词。有了 vision（视力），我们就能看见东西，visual images（视觉图像）对眼睛来说是 visible（可见的），而 visitor（访客）是来看东西的人。同一个拉丁语动词实际上还提供了另一词根 vid-，比如，该词根出现在尤利乌斯·恺撒炫耀自己军事功绩的著名宣言"Veni, vidi, vici（我来了，我看到了，我征服了）"中，还出现在 video（视频）等常见的英语单词中。

vista \ˈvi-stə\ (1) A distant view. 远景 (2) An extensive mental view, as over a stretch of time. 展望

• The economic vista for the next two years looks excellent, according to a poll of business economists. 据商业经济学家的一项调查，未来两年的经济前景看好。

Vista is generally used today for broad sweeping views of the kind you might see from a mountaintop. But the word originally meant an avenue-like view, narrowed by a line of trees on either side. And *vista* has also long been used (like *view* and *outlook*) to mean a mental scan of the future—as if you were riding down a long grand avenue and what you could see a mile or so ahead of you was where you'd be in the very near future.

vista 现在一般用来指从山顶上可以看到的那种一望无际的景色。但这个词最初指的是因两边各有一排树木而变得狭窄的林荫道般的景色。vista（像 view 和 outlook 一样）也一直用来形容对未来的展望——就好像你行进在一条壮观的大道上，远处约一英里以外所看到的就是你不久的将来要到的地方。

vis-à-vis \ˌvē-zä-ˈvē\ In relation to or compared with. 关于，与……相比。

• Many financial reporters worry about the loss of U.S. economic strength vis-à-vis our principal trading partners. 许多财经记者都担心，与主要贸易伙伴相比，美国的经济实力会减弱。

Vis-à-vis comes from Latin by way of French, where it means literally "face-to-face." In English it was first used to mean a little horse-drawn carriage in which two people sat opposite each other. From there it acquired various other meanings, such as "dancing partner." Today it no longer refers to actual physical faces and bodies, but its modern meaning comes from the fact that things that are face-to-face can easily be compared or contrasted. So, for example, a greyhound is very tall vis-à-vis a Scottie, and the Red Sox have often fared badly vis-à-vis the Yankees. vis-à-vis 源自拉丁语，是从法语传到英语中的，在法语中的字面意思是"面对面"。在英语中，它最初指两个人面对面就座的小马车。由此引申出其他含义，比如"舞伴"。它如今不再表示实际意义上的脸和身体，但其现代意义来自这样的事实：面对面的东西很容易进行比较或对比。比如，灵提比苏格兰猎犬要高大，红袜队打得不如扬基队。

visionary \ˈvi-zhə-ˌner-ē\ (1) A person with foresight and imagination. 有远见和有想象力的人 (2) A dreamer whose ideas are often impractical. 梦想家，空想家

• His followers regarded him as an inspired visionary; his opponents saw him as either a con man or a lunatic. 追随者们将他视为受神灵启示的有远见者，而反对者则视他为骗子或疯子。

A visionary is someone with a strong *vision* of the future. Since such visions aren't always accurate, a visionary's ideas may either work brilliantly or fail miserably. Even so, *visionary* is usually a positive word. Martin Luther King, Jr., for instance, was a visionary in his hopes and ideas for a just society. The word is also an adjective; thus, for example, we may speak of a *visionary* project, a visionary leader, a visionary painter, or a visionary company. 有远见的人指的是对未来有明确的 *vision*（想象，幻想）之人。这些想象并不总是准确无误，因此有远见之人的想法可能十分奏效也可能失败得很惨。即便如此，*visionary* 通常是个积极的单词。例如，小马丁·路德·金是一个追求构建公平社会的梦想家。这个单词也是形容词；例如，我们可以说 *visionary* project（有远见的方案）、有远见卓识的领导者、充满想象力的画家、有远见的公司。

envisage \in-ˈvi-zij\ To have a mental picture of; visualize. 想象，设想

• A mere three weeks after they had started dating, the two were already arguing, and none of us could envisage the relationship lasting for long. 他们约会才三周就开始吵架，我们难以想象这段关系能长久。

One of the imagination's most valuable uses is its ability to see something in the "mind's eye"—that is, to *visualize*, *envision*, or *envisage* something. Envisaging a possibility may be one of the chief abilities that separate human beings from the other animals. What we envisage may be physical (such as a completed piece of furniture) or nonphysical (such as finishing college). Envisaging life with a puppy might lead us down to the pound to buy one, and envisaging the sinking of an island nation may focus our minds on climate change. 想象力最有价值的作用之一就是，它能使我们看到"想象中的"东西——也就是说，可以 *visualize*、*envision* 或 envisage（设想）某样东西。设想某种可能是将人类与其他动物区分开来的主要能力之一。我们想象出来的东西可以是

实物(如一件成型的家具),也可以是非实物(如读完大学)。想象有小狗的生活可能会促使我们到动物收容所买上一只;想象一个岛国的沉没可能促使我们关注气候的变化。

SPECT

SPECT comes from the Latin verb *specere*, meaning "to look at," and produces several familiar English words. *Spectacles* can be glasses that you look through; but a spectacle can also be a remarkable sight—in Roman times, perhaps a *spectacular* chariot race or a *spectacularly* bloody battle between gladiators and wild beasts, mounted for the pleasure of its *spectators*.

SPECT 源自拉丁语动词 *specere*,意思是"看",产生了几个熟悉的英语单词。*spectacles* 可以指用来看东西的眼镜;但 spectacle 也可以是一种非凡的景象——在罗马时代,也许 *spectacular* chariot race(壮观的战车比赛)或角斗士和野兽之间的 *spectacularly*(壮观地)血腥战斗,能为 *spectators*(观众)增添不少乐趣。

aspect \ˈa-ˌspekt\ (1) A part of something. 方面 (2) A certain way in which something appears or may be regarded. 角度,视点

• Many experts believe the mental aspect of distance racing is more important than the physical aspect. 许多专家相信,长跑的心理方面比身体方面更重要。

Since *aspectus* in Latin means "looked at," an aspect of something is basically the direction from which it's looked at. So we may say that travel is your favorite aspect of your job, or that eating well is one aspect of a healthy life. If you look at a stage set from the front, it looks completely different than from behind, where all the mechanisms are visible, and both aspects are important. The word can be very useful when you're analyzing something, and it's used a great deal in the writings of scholars.

aspectus 在拉丁语中的意思是"看",因此 aspect of something 的基本意思是看某个东西的方向角度。因此我们可以说,旅行是你对这个工作最喜欢的方面,或者说健康饮食是健康生活的一个方面。从前面看舞台与从后面看完全不同,因为在后面,所有的构造都一目了然,但两个视角都重要。分析某样东西的时候,这个词会非常有用,它在学者的文章中用得也很多。

prospect \ˈprä-ˌspekt\ (1) The possibility that something will happen in the future. 可能性,前景 (2) An opportunity for something to happen. 机会

• There was little prospect of a breakthrough in the negotiations before the elections. 在选举前,谈判取得突破的可能性微乎其微。

Since the Latin prefix *pro-* often means "forward" (see PRO, p. 677), *prospect* refers to looking forward. The prospect of a recession may lead investors to pull their money out of the stock market. Graduates of a good law school usually have excellent prospects for finding employment. *Prospective* students roam campuses with their parents in the year before they plan to enter college.

拉丁语前缀 *pro-* 常表示"向前"(参见 PRO,第 677 页)的意思,因此 *prospect* 指的就是向前看。经济衰退的前景可能会促使投资者将资金从股市中转出来。法律名校的毕业生的就业前景良好。*prospective* students(可能上大学的学生)打算上大学前一年会与父母到大学校园参观一下。

SPECT

• 145 •

perspective\pər-ˈspek-tiv\ (1) Point of view; the angle, direction, or standpoint from which a person looks at something. 观点，视角 (2) The art or technique of painting or drawing a scene so that objects in it seem to have depth and distance. 透视法

• From the perspective of the lowly soldier, the war looked very different. 从地位低下的士兵的角度来看，这场战争就大为不同了。

To the modern mind, it's hard to believe that perspective had to be "discovered," but before the 1400s paintings simply lacked accurate perspective. Instead, important people and objects were simply shown larger than less important ones; and although distant objects were sometimes shown smaller than near ones, this wasn't done in a regular and accurate way. Just as odd, many paintings didn't represent the other meaning of *perspective* either—that is, a scene might not be shown as if it were being seen from one single place. Today, *perspective* is used much like *standpoint*. Just as *standpoint* once used to mean simply the physical place where you stand but today also means the way you "see" things as a result of who you are and what you do, the same could be said about *perspective*.

现代人很难相信，透视法在过去还需要"被发现"，但在 15 世纪以前，绘画就是缺乏准确的透视。重要的人或物只是画得大一些，尽管远处的物体有时画得比近处的小一些，但这种画法不常用，也不准确。同样奇怪的是，过去的很多画作也没有体现出 perspective 一词的另一个含义"视角"——也就是说，所展示的场景也不像是从一个角度所观察到的。今天，perspective 与 standpoint 的用法很像。standpoint 过去用来表示你站立的实际位置，而现在也表示基于你的身份和职业所"看"东西的角度，perspective 也是如此。

prospectus\prə-ˈspek-təs\ A printed statement that describes something (such as a new business or a stock offering) and is sent out to people who may be interested in buying or investing. 章程，简章，广告宣传资料

• The prospectus for the mutual fund says nothing about how its profit forecasts were calculated. 那个共同基金的简章没有说明其预期利润是如何计算出来的。

Like *prospect*, *prospectus* looks forward. Thus, a prospectus originally outlined something that didn't yet exist, describing what it would become. This might even be a book; the great dictionary of Noah Webster, like that of Samuel Johnson, was first announced in the form of a prospectus, so that well-to-do people might actually subscribe to it—that is, pay for it in advance so that Webster would have money to live on while writing it. Soon, *prospectus* was being used to mean a description of a private school or college, intended to attract new students. Today the word very often means a description of a stock offering or mutual fund, whether new or not.

像 prospect 一样，prospectus 的意思也是"向前看"。因此，prospectus 最初勾勒的是尚未被生产出来的东西，描述这将会是个什么样的东西。它甚至有可能是一本书；诺亚·韦伯斯特的伟大的词典，正如塞缪尔·约翰逊的词典一样，一开始也是以 prospectus 的形式对外宣布的，这样的话，有钱人就可以订阅——也就是所，提前掏钱支付，韦伯斯特就可以在撰写词典时能有钱活下去。很快，prospectus 用来指私立学校或大学制作的招生简章，目的是吸引新学生。今天，这个词常表示指对股票发行或共同基金的介绍，无论新旧。

UNIT 7

Quizzes

A. Fill in each blank with the correct letter:

a. perspective
b. vis-à-vis
c. prospectus
d. prospect
e. envisage
f. aspect
g. visionary
h. vista

1. When she considered Cleveland _____ other cities where she might have to live, she always chose Cleveland.
2. The _____ of spending an evening with such an unhappy couple was just depressing.
3. His ambitious plans for the city marked him as a true _____.
4. The most troubling _____ of the whole incident was the public reaction.
5. The _____ for the new development was full of glowing descriptions that made both of us suspicious.
6. Turning a corner, they found themselves gazing out on the broad _____ of the river valley.
7. Some judges only look at crimes like these from the _____ of the police.
8. Her therapist keeps asking her if she could _____ getting back together with her husband.

B. Match the definition on the left to the correct word on the right:

1. compared to
2. advance description
3. prophet
4. imagine
5. standpoint
6. outlook
7. element
8. view

a. perspective
b. envisage
c. vis-à-vis
d. aspect
e. prospectus
f. visionary
g. prospect
h. vista

VOC comes from the Latin words meaning "voice" and "speak." So a *vocal* ensemble is a singing group. A *vocation* was originally a "calling" from God to do religious work as a priest, monk, or nun, though today most people use the word just to mean a career. And a *vocabulary* is a set of words for speaking.

VOC 源自意是"声音"和"说话"的拉丁语单词。所以，*vocal* ensemble 指的是合唱团。*vocation*（神召，天命，职业）最初指的是来接受自上帝的"召唤"，担负起牧师、修士或修女等宗教工作，但今天多数人用它仅表示职业。*vocabulary*（词汇表）是指说话用的一组词语。

equivocate \i-ˈkwi-və-ˌkāt\ (1) To use ambiguous language, especially in order to deceive. 含糊其词 (2) To avoid giving a direct answer. 躲闪

• As the company directors continued to equivocate, the union prepared to return to the picket lines. 由于公司领导们不断含糊其辞,工会成员们准备退回到纠察线之后。

With its root *equi-*, meaning "equal," *equivocate* suggests speaking on both sides of an issue at the same time. An *equivocal* answer is one that manages not to take a stand; an *unequivocal* answer, by contrast, is strong and clear. Politicians are famous for equivocating, but *equivocation* is also typical of used-car salesmen, nervous witnesses in a courtroom, and guys whose girlfriends ask them how committed they are to a relationship. 词根 *equi-* 表示"平等的",因此 *equivocate* 指的是在同一时间为一件事情的两面说话。*equivocal* answer(模棱两可的回答)就是设法不选立场的回答;相反,*unequivocal* answer(明确的回答)则坚定而清晰。政治家以说话含糊其辞而出名,但是 *equivocation*(含糊其辞)也常用于二手车推销员、法庭上紧张的证人以及被女朋友问及对感情有多忠诚的男人。

irrevocable \i-ˈre-və-kə-bəl\ Impossible to call back or retract. 不可收回的、不可撤销的。

• She had told him she wasn't going to see him again, but he couldn't believe her decision was irrevocable. 她告诉他再不来见他了,但他无法相信这一决定是不能改变的。

Irrevocable has a formal sound to it and is often used in legal contexts. Irrevocable trusts are trust funds that cannot be dissolved by the people who created them (the other kind is a *revocable* trust). An irrevocable credit is an absolute obligation from a bank to provide credit to a customer. Irrevocable gifts, under U.S. tax law, are gifts that are given by one living person to another and can't be reclaimed by the giver. But the word isn't always legal; we've all had to make irrevocable decisions, decisions that commit us absolutely to something. *irrevocable* 一词听起来比较正式,常用于法律语境中。irrevocable trusts(不可撤销信托)是不能被设立信托者解除的信托(另一种是 revocable trust[可撤销信托])。irrevocable credit(不可撤销信用证)指的是银行为客户提供信贷的绝对义务。根据美国的税法,irrevocable gifts(不可撤销的礼物)指的是活着的某个人送给另一个人的礼物,送礼的一方不得要回。但这个词不仅用于法律领域。我们每个人都不得不做出 irrevocable decisions(不可撤销的决定),即绝对不能更改的做某事的决定。

advocate \ˈad-və-ˌkāt\ To speak in favor of. 拥护,主张

• Our lawyer is advocating a suit against the state, but most of us would rather try some other approaches first. 我们的律师主张要起诉这个州,但多数人宁愿先尝试别的方法。

The verb *advocate* may be followed by *for* ("advocated for better roads," "advocated for merging the two school districts") or by a noun or gerund ("advocating an increase in the military budget," "advocated closing the budget gap"). But *advocate* isn't only a verb; An *advocate* is someone who advocates for you, or argues on your side. Originally, this was often a lawyer in court, and in Britain *advocate* is still a term for "lawyer."

动词 *advocate* 可以跟 for 连用(比如,"主张建更好的道路""主张合并两个学区"),也可以跟名词或动名词连用(比如,"主张增加军事预算""主张削减预算赤字")。但 *advocate* 不只是动词;*advocate* 指的是支持你,或为你说话的人。这个词最初常指法庭上的律师,在英国,*advocate* 仍是用来表示"律师"的一个术语。

vociferous \vō-ˈsi-fə-rəs\ Making noisy or emphatic outcries. 叫喊的,吵闹的

• Whenever the referee at these soccer games makes a questionable call, you hear vociferous protests from half the parents. 每当足球裁判做出有争议判罚时,就能听到一半的家长们大声抗议。

A vociferous group shouts loudly and insistently, and they're usually not too happy about something. So, for example, we often hear about vociferous critics, vociferous demands, vociferous opponents, or a vociferous minority. When a small group makes itself vociferous enough, everyone else may even start thinking it's actually a majority.
一群吵闹的人会不停地大喊大叫,他们通常对某件事情不高兴。因此,我们经常听说吵闹的批评者、大声的要求、喧闹的反对者,或吵嚷的少数群体。当一个小群体喊叫的声音足够响亮时,其他人就会开始认为他们实际上代表了多数人。

PHON
is a Greek root meaning "sound," "voice," or "speech." It's probably most familiar in the form of the English suffix *-phone*, in words that begin with a Greek or Latin root as well. Thus, the *tele-* in *telephone* means "far," the *micro-* in *microphone* means "small," the *xylo-* in *xylophone* means "wood," and so on.
PHON 是希腊语词根,意为"声音""嗓音"或"言语"。它最为人熟知的形式可能是英语后缀 *-phone*,用在一些以希腊语或拉丁语词根开头的单词中。*telephone*(电话)中的 *tele-* 意思是"远的",*microphone*(麦克风)中的 *micro-* 意思是"小的",*xylophone*(木琴)中的 *xylo-* 意思是"木制的"等等。

---

phonics \ˈfä-niks\ A method of teaching beginners to read and pronounce words by learning the characteristic sounds of letters, letter groups, and especially syllables. 读音法

• My son's school switched to phonics instruction several years ago, and reading achievement in the early grades has been improving. 我儿子的学校几年前转为使用读音法教学,此后低年级的阅读水平一直在提高。

In the field of beginning reading, there are two basic schools of thought in the U. S. today. One emphasizes "whole language" teaching, which relies on teaching a lot of reading; the other emphasizes phonics, teaching how letters and syllables correspond to sounds. Phonics instruction may be especially difficult in English, since English has the most difficult spelling of any Western language. Consider the various ways we create the *f* sound in *cough*, *photo*, and *giraffe*, or the *sh* sound in *special*, *issue*, *vicious*, and *portion*, or the *k* sound in *tack*, *quite*, and *shellac*, and how we pronounce the *o* in *do*, *core*, *lock*, and *bone*, or the *ea* in *lead*, *ocean*, *idea*, and *early*. Teaching phonics obviously isn't an easy job, but it's probably an important one.

在启蒙阅读领域,美国现在基本上有两个思想流派。一个强调"整体语言"教学,依赖大量的阅读;另一个强调读音法教学,教字母及音节与声音之间的对应关系。读音法教学在英语学习中尤为困难,因为在西方各语言中,英语的拼写最难。想想看吧,同一个音我们有多少种表达方式,比如在 cough、photo、giraffe 中都有 f 音,在 special、issue、vicious、portion 中都有 sh 音,在 tack、quite、shellac 中都有 k 音;(再想想同一个字母又有多少发音吧)比如 o 在 do、core、lock、bone 中发音不同,ea 在 lead、ocean、idea、early 中发音也不同。语音法教学殊为不易,但或许很重要。

phonetic \ fə-'ne-tik \ Relating to or representing the sounds of the spoken language. 语音的

• In almost every Spanish word the pronunciation is clear from the spelling, so the phonetic part of learning Spanish isn't usually a big challenge. 几乎每个西班牙语单词的读音都可以从拼写中清楚地看出来,因此,学习西班牙语时,语音部分通常并不是很困难。

The English alphabet is phonetic—that is, the letters represent sounds. The Chinese alphabet, however, isn't phonetic, since its symbols represent ideas rather than sounds. But even in English, a letter doesn't always represent the same sound; the "a" in *cat*, *father*, and *mate*, for example, represents three different sounds. Because of this, books about words often use specially created phonetic alphabets in which each symbol stands for a single sound in order to represent pronunciations. So in this book, *cat*, *father*, and *mate* would be *phonetically* represented as 'kat, ' fä-thə, and 'māt.

英语的字母是表音的——也就是说,字母代表发音。然而,汉字不是表音的,因为每个符号代表的是意思而不是声音。但即便在英文中,一个字母也并不总代表同一个音;例如,cat、father、mate 中的"a"就代表了三个不同的音。由于这个原因,词汇书常使用专门创造的音标字母表,其中的每个符号代表一种读音,由此来表达发音。因此,在本书中,cat、father、mate 等单词会 phonetically 用 'kat、'fä-thər 和 'māt 表示。

polyphonic \ˌpä-lē-'fä-nik\ Referring to a style of music in which two or more melodies are sung or played against each other in harmony. 复调的

• Whenever he needed something calming, he would put on some quiet polyphonic music from the Renaissance and just let the voices waft over him. 每当需要有东西让自己平静下来时,他都会播放文艺复兴时代安静的复调音乐,让音乐声在自己上方飘荡。

Since *poly-* means "many" (see POLY, p. 57), polyphonic music has "many voices." In *polyphony*, each part has its own melody, and they weave together in a web that may become very dense; a famous piece by Thomas Tallis, composed around 1570, has 40 separate voice parts. Polyphony reached its height during the 16th century with Italian madrigals and the sacred music of such composers as Tallis, Palestrina, and Byrd. Usually when we speak of polyphony we're talking about music of Bach's time and earlier; but the principles remain the same today, and songwriters such as the Beatles have sometimes used polyphony as well.

Poly- 的意思是"多"(参见 POLY,第 57 页),因此复调音乐有"多个声音"。在 polyphony(复调)中,每个部分都有自己的旋律,全部旋律交织成一张紧密的网。托马斯·塔利斯在 1570 年前后创作的一首曲子有 40 个不同的声部。随着意大利牧歌和诸如塔利斯、帕莱斯特里那、伯德等作曲家创作的圣歌的出现,复调音乐在 16 世纪达到了巅峰。提起复调音乐时,我们通常指的是巴赫及其之前时代的音乐;然而,音乐的法则至今未变,诸如披头士乐队之类的歌曲作家有时也会使用复调。

cacophony \kə-ˈkä-fə-nē\ Harsh or unpleasant sound. 刺耳的声音

● In New York she was often dragged off by her boyfriend to downtown jazz concerts, where she struggled to make sense of what sounded like nothing but cacophony. 在纽约,她常被男朋友拉着去市中心看爵士音乐会,在那儿,她竭力想弄懂那些听上去不过是噪音的东西。

Cacophony employs the Greek prefix *caco-*, meaning "bad," but not everything we call *cacophonous* is necessarily bad. Grunge, thrash, hardcore, and goth music are unlistenable to some people and very popular to others. Open-air food markets may be marked by a cacophony of voices but also by wonderful sights and sounds. On the other hand, few people can really enjoy, for more than a few minutes, the cacophony of jackhammers, car horns, and truck engines that assaults the city pedestrian on a hot day in August.

cacophony 包含希腊语前缀 *caco-*("坏"),但并非所有被我们称作 *cacophonous* 的东西都是坏的。有人觉得垃圾音乐、打击乐、硬核音乐和哥特音乐不堪入耳,而别人却非常爱听。露天食品市场可能一片嘈杂,但也不乏美妙景象和动听的声音。另一方面,在炎热的八月,手提钻的声音、汽车喇叭声,还有卡车发动机声音充斥着行人的耳膜,也很少有人真的爱听这样的嘈杂之声,哪怕只听上几分钟。

Quizzes

A. Complete the analogy:

1. initial : beginning :: irrevocable : _____
   a. usual   b. noisy   c. final   d. reversible
2. arithmetic : numbers :: phonics : _____
   a. letters   b. notes   c. meanings   d. music
3. prefer : dislike :: advocate : _____
   a. oppose   b. support   c. assist   d. boost
4. multistoried : floor :: polyphonic : _____
   a. poetry   b. melody   c. story   d. harmony
5. reject : accept :: equivocate : _____
   a. decide   b. specify   c. detect   d. delay
6. melodic : notes :: phonetic : _____
   a. sounds   b. signs   c. ideas   d. pages
7. monotonous : boring :: vociferous : _____
   a. vegetarian   b. angry   c. favorable   d. noisy
8. stillness : quiet :: cacophony : _____
   a. melodious   b. dissonant   c. creative   d. birdlike

B. Indicate whether the following pairs have the same or different meanings:

1. advocate / describe   same ____ / different ____

2. phonetic / phonelike   same ____ / different ____
3. equivocate / refuse   same ____ / different ____
4. polyphonic / many-voiced   same ____ / different ____
5. irrevocable / unfortunate   same ____ / different ____
6. cacophony / din   same ____ / different ____
7. vociferous / calm   same ____ / different ____
8. phonics / audio   same ____ / different ____

CUR, from the Latin verb *curare*, means basically "care for." Our verb *cure* comes from this root, as do *manicure* ("care of the hands") and *pedicure* ("care of the feet").

CUR 源自拉丁语动词 *curare*，基本意思是"关心，照料"。动词 *cure*（治疗）源自这个词根，*manicure*（字面意思是"手部护理"）和 *pedicure*（"足部护理"）亦如此。

curative \ˈkyùr-ə-tiv\ Having to do with curing diseases. 治疗的

• As soon as the antibiotic entered his system, he imagined he could begin to feel its curative effects. 抗生素刚一进入他身体，他就想象自己能感受到其治疗效果了。

Medical researchers are finding curative substances in places that surprise them. Folklore has led to some "new" *cures* of old diseases, and natural substances never before tried have often proved effective. Quinine, which comes from a tree in the Andes, was the original drug for malaria; aspirin's main ingredient came from willow bark; and Taxol, a drug used in treating several cancers, was originally extracted from the bark of a yew tree. The curative properties of these natural drugs are today duplicated in the laboratory.

医学研究人员正在一些想不到的地方发现有疗效的物质。民间传说为许多老的疾病提供了"新的" *cures*（疗法，药物），以前从未试过的天然物质也常被证明是有疗效的。奎宁来源于安第斯山脉的一棵树，是抗疟疾的原药；阿司匹林的主要成分源自柳树皮；紫杉醇用于治疗数种癌症，它最初是从一棵紫杉树的树皮中提取出来的。如今，这些天然药物的疗效在实验室中得到了复制。

curator \ˈkyùr-ˌā-tər\ Someone in charge of something where things are on exhibit, such as a collection, a museum, or a zoo. 馆长，负责人，管理人

• In recent decades, zoo curators have tried to make the animals' surroundings more and more like their natural homes. 近几十年来，动物园园长们尝试着将动物们的生活环境变得越来越像它们的自然家园。

In a good-sized art museum, each curator is generally responsible for a single department or collection: European painting, Asian sculpture, Native American art, and so on. *Curatorial* duties include acquiring new artworks, caring for and repairing objects already owned, discovering frauds and counterfeits, lending artworks to other museums, and mounting exhibitions of everything from Greek sculpture to 20th-century clothing. 在大型的艺术博物馆中，每位管理人一般都负责一个部门或展区：欧洲绘画、亚洲雕塑、美洲原住民艺术等。*curatorial* duties(管理者的职责)包括获取新作品，保养和维修已经拥有的艺术品，发现欺诈和赝品，向其他博物馆出借展品以及举办从希腊雕塑到 20 世纪服饰等的各种展览。

procure \prō-ˈkyu̇r\ To get possession of; obtain. 取得，获得

• Investigators were looking into the question of how the governor had procured such a huge loan at such a favorable rate. 调查人员正在调查州长是如何以这么优惠的价格得到这笔巨额贷款的。

While *procure* has the general meaning of "obtain," it usually implies that some effort is required. It may also suggest getting something through a formal set of procedures. In many business offices, a particular person is responsible for procuring supplies, and government agencies have formal *procurement* policies. When teenagers use an older friend to procure the wrong kind of supplies for their parties, they often risk getting into trouble. *procure* 的一般含义是"获得"，但它通常暗示要付出努力。这个词也可能意味着要通过一套正式的程序来获取某个东西。在许多商业办公室，某个特定的人负责采购所需物品；政府机构有正式的 *procurement* policies(采购政策)。当青少年利用年长一些的朋友为他们的派对弄到不合适的物品时，他们往往冒着陷入麻烦的风险。

sinecure \ˈsi-nə-ˌkyu̇r\ A job or position requiring little work but usually providing some income. 闲职，挂名职位

• The job of Dean of Students at any college is no sinecure; the hours can be long and the work draining. 任何大学的教导主任的职位都绝非闲职，这个职位工作时间长且劳神费力。

Sinecure contains the Latin word *sine*, "without," and thus means "without care." In some countries, the government in power may be free to award sinecure positions to their valued supporters; in other countries, this would be regarded as corruption. The positions occupied by British royalty are called sinecures by some people, who claim they enjoy their enormous wealth in return for nothing at all. But their many supporters point to the amount of public-service, charitable, and ceremonial work they perform, not to mention the effort they put into promoting Britain to the world. *sinecure* 中包含拉丁语单词 *sine*("没有")，因此这个词语的意思是"无须操心的"。在某些国家，执政政府可以随意将一些挂名职位授予他们的重要支持者；而这样做在另一些国家会被视为腐败。英国皇室所居的职位被一些人称为挂名职位，他们认为皇室不需要付出就可以得到巨大的财富。而很多支持者却指出，皇室成员在公共服务、慈善和仪式等方面做了许多工作，更不用说他们在向全世界宣传英国方面所付出的努力了。

PERI, in both Latin and Greek, means "around." A *period* is often a span of time that keeps coming around regularly, day after day or year after year. With a *periscope*, you can see around corners. *Peristalsis* is the process that moves food around the intestines; without it, digestion would grind to a halt.

PERI 在拉丁语和希腊语中都是"周围"的意思。*period*（一段时间）通常指的是有规律来到的一段时间，日复一日，年复一年。用 *periscope*（潜望镜），你可以看清拐角处。*peristalsis*（蠕动）是使食物在肠道内移动的过程；没有蠕动，消化就会停止。

perimeter \ pə-ˈri-mə-tər \ The boundary or distance around a body or figure. 周边，周长

● In a medieval siege, an army would surround the perimeter of a city's high walls, denying the population any food from outside as it assaulted the walls with catapults and battering rams. 在中世纪的围攻中，军队会围在城市高墙的四周，用投石器和攻城锤攻击城墙，同时切断城市居民来自城外的食物补给。

The perimeter of a prison is ringed with high walls and watchtowers, and the entire perimeter of Australia is bounded by water. In geometry, you may be asked to calculate the perimeter of various geometrical shapes. In basketball, the perimeter is the area beyond the free-throw circle; a "perimeter player" tends to stay outside that circle. Try not to confuse this word with *parameter*, which usually means a rule or limit that controls what something is or how it can be done.
监狱的四周环绕着高墙和瞭望塔，澳大利亚的整个周边都被水包围。在几何中，你可能会被要求计算各种几何图形的周长。在篮球方面，perimeter 指的是罚球圈之外的区域；"外线球员"往往会留在罚球圈外。不要将这个词与 *parameter*（参数）混淆，后者通常指用来决定某物是什么和应该怎么做的规则或限制。

periodontal \ ˌper-ē-ō-ˈdän-təl \ Concerning or affecting the tissues around the teeth. 牙周的

● Years of bad living had filled his teeth with cavities, but it was periodontal disease that finished them off. 多年的糟糕生活使他的牙齿满是蛀洞，但最终毁了所有牙齿的是牙周疾病。

In dentistry, cavities are important but they aren't the whole story; what happens to your gums is every bit as vital to your dental health. When you don't floss regularly to keep plaque from forming on your teeth and gums, the gums will slowly deteriorate. Dentists called *periodontists* specialize in the treatment of periodontal problems, and when the gums have broken down to the point where they can't hold the teeth in place a periodontist may need to provide dental implants, a costly and unpleasant process. But even a periodontist can't keep your gums healthy; that job is up to you.
在牙科领域，龋齿问题很重要，但并非全部；牙龈问题对于牙齿健康也同等重要。如果不经常用牙线剔除牙齿和牙龈上的牙菌斑，牙龈就会慢慢恶化。牙医中的 *periodontists*（牙周病医师）专治牙周问题。当牙龈已经坏到无法再固定牙齿的时候，牙周病医生可能需要采取植牙的措施，植牙花费高昂且不舒适。然而，即便是牙周病医师也不能保证你的牙龈健康；牙龈的健康要靠你自己。

peripatetic \ ˌper-ə-pə-ˈte-tik \ (1) Having to do with walking. 漫步的 (2) Moving or traveling from place to place. 巡游的

● She spent her early adult years as a peripatetic musician, traveling from one engagement to another. 她刚成年那会儿是个巡游音乐家，到处巡回演出。

UNIT 7

The philosopher Aristotle had his school at the Lyceum gymnasium in Athens. The Lyceum may have resembled the Parthenon in being surrounded by a row of columns, or colonnade, which the Greeks would have called a *peripatoi*. Aristotle was also said to have paced slowly while teaching, and the Greek word for "pacing" was *peripatos*. And finally, *peripatos* meant simply "discussion." Whatever the source of the word, Aristotle and his followers became known as the *Peripatetics*, and the "pacing" sense led to *peripatetic*'s English meaning of traveling or moving about. Johnny Appleseed is a good example of a peripatetic soul, and peripatetic executives and salespeople today stare into their laptop computers while endlessly flying from city to city.

哲学家亚里士多德将学校办在雅典的吕克昂体育馆。吕克昂与帕台农神殿可能很像,周围都有一圈石柱或柱廊,古希腊人称之为 peripatoi。据说,亚里士多德教学时会慢慢踱步,希腊语中表示"踱步"的单词是 peripatos。peripatos 最后仅表示"讨论"的意思。无论这个词的起源是什么,亚里士多德及其追随者都被称为 Peripatetics(逍遥派),"踱步"的含义也使 peripatetic 在英语中有旅行或四处走动的意思。约翰尼·阿普塞德就是一个流浪灵魂的范例;奔波的主管和销售人员一边无休止地在城市之间飞来飞去,一边还要紧盯着笔记本电脑。

peripheral \ pə-ˈri-fə-rəl \ (1) Having to do with the outer edges, especially of the field of vision. 外围的 (2) Secondary or supplemental. 次要的,辅助的

- Like most good fourth-grade teachers, he had excellent peripheral vision, and the kids were convinced that he had eyes in the back of his head. 像大多数优秀的四年级教师一样,他有出色的周边视觉,孩子们都相信他的后脑勺长了眼睛。

Your peripheral vision is the outer area of your field of vision, where you can still detect movement and shapes. It can be very valuable when, for instance, you're driving into Chicago at rush hour, especially when switching lanes. When people call an issue in a discussion peripheral, they mean that it's not of primary importance, and they're probably suggesting that everyone get back to the main topic. *Peripheral* is now also a noun: computer peripherals are the added components—printers, webcams, microphones, etc.—that increase a computer's capacities.

周边视觉指的是视野的外部区域,你在该区域仍可以看到物体的运动和形状。如果在高峰时段驶入芝加哥,尤其是在你换道时,周边视觉可能会非常有用。在讨论问题时,如果有人称某事儿是 peripheral,意思就是这事儿不重要,言下之意是让大家回归正题。peripheral(辅助设备)也是个名词:电脑辅助设备是那些附加在电脑之外的、可以增加性能的东西——打印机、网络摄像头、麦克风等等。

Quizzes

A. Fill in each blank with the correct letter:

a. curative   e. peripheral
b. sinecure   f. perimeter
c. procure   g. peripatetic
d. curator   h. periodontal

1. The _____ benefits of antibiotics have saved many lives.

2. _____ vision is part of what most eye doctors test in their patients.

3. What he had hoped to be an undemanding _____ turned out to be the hardest but most rewarding job of his career.

4. Because of deer, she needed to put up a fence along the _____ of the garden.

5. We asked our purchasing manager to _____ new chairs for the office.

6. In his youth he had been amazingly _____, hitchhiking thousands of miles on three continents.

7. The museum's _____ of African art narrates a guided tour of the exhibit.

8. Regular flossing can prevent most _____ disease.

B. Choose the closest definition:

1. sinecure   a. hopeful sign   b. unsuccessful search
   c. careless act   d. easy job

2. curator   a. doctor   b. lawyer   c. caretaker
   d. spectator

3. periodontal   a. visual   b. inside a tooth
   c. around a tooth   d. wandering

4. peripatetic   a. wandering   b. unemployed
   c. surrounding   d. old-fashioned

5. procure   a. say   b. obtain   c. look after
   d. heal

6. curative   a. purifying   b. healing   c. saving
   d. repairing

7. perimeter   a. factor   b. characteristic   c. supplement
   d. boundary

8. peripheral   a. supplementary   b. around a tooth
   c. wandering   d. dangerous

SENS comes from the Latin noun *sensus*, meaning "feeling" or "sense." *Sense* itself obviously comes straight from the Latin. A *sensation* is something you sense. And if you're *sensitive*, you feel or sense things sharply, maybe even too sharply. SENS 源自拉丁语名词 *sensus*，意思是"感觉"。sense 本身明显是直接源自拉丁语的。sensation 是所感知到的东西。如果你很 sensitive，你能敏锐地感觉到事物，甚至可能会过于敏锐。

---

sensor\ˈsen-ˌsȯr\   A device that detects a physical quantity (such as a movement or a beam of light) and responds by transmitting a signal. 传感器

• The outdoor lights are triggered by a motion sensor that detects changes in infrared energy given off by moving human bodies. 户外灯由运动传感器触发,该传感器可以探测到移动的人体所释放的红外能量的变化。

Sensors are used today almost everywhere. Radar guns bounce microwaves off moving cars. A burglar alarm may use a photosensor to detect when a beam of light has been broken, or may use ultrasonic sound waves that bounce off moving objects. Still other sensors may detect pressure (barometers) or chemicals (Breathalyzers and smoke detectors). Stud finders, used by carpenters to locate wooden studs under a wall, may employ magnets or radar. Wired gloves, which relay information about the position of the fingers, are used in virtual-reality environments. A cheap car alarm may be nothing but a shock sensor, in which a strong vibration will cause two metal surfaces to come together.

传感器现在几乎是无处不在。雷达枪可以接收行驶的汽车反射回来的微波。防盗警报器可以利用光传感器探测被打断的光线,也可以利用移动的物体反射回来的超声波。还有其他的传感器,用来探测压力(气压计)或化学物质(酒精测试仪、烟雾报警器)。木匠用来找到墙下面木头壁骨位置的探测器,可能利用磁铁或者雷达。在虚拟现实环境中使用的数据手套,可以传递关于手指位置的信息。廉价的汽车报警器可能只不过是一个震动传感器,原理在于,强烈的震动可以让两个金属表面相接触。

desensitize \dē-'sen-sə-ˌtīz\ To cause (someone or something) to react less to or be less affected by something. 使不敏感,使脱敏,使麻木

• Even squeamish nursing students report becoming desensitized to the sight of blood after a few months of training. 即便是晕血的护理专业学生,在几个月的训练后,看到血也不敏感了。

Physical desensitizing is something that biologists have long been aware of. Basic training in the armed forces tries to desensitize new recruits to pain. We can desensitize ourselves to the summer heat by turning off the air conditioning, or become desensitized to the cold by walking barefoot in the snow. But desensitize is more often used when talking about negative emotions. Parents worry that their children will be desensitized to violence by playing video games. Soldiers may become desensitized to death on the battlefield. Desensitizing may be natural and desirable under some circumstances, but maybe not so good in others.

生物学家很早就意识到生理脱敏现象的存在。武装部队的基本训练是为了让新兵对痛苦感到麻木;通过关闭空调的办法,我们可以减轻对酷暑的敏感性;我们也可以通过赤脚在雪地里行走的办法,减少对寒冷的敏感性。然而,desensitize 更经常用于谈论消极情绪。比如,家长们担心,玩电子游戏会让孩子们对暴力感到麻木。战场上的士兵可能会对死亡变得麻木。desensitizing 在某些情况下可能是自然的、有利的,在另一些情况下就不那么好了。

extrasensory \ˌek-strə-'sens-rē\ Not acting or occurring through any of the known senses. 超感觉的

• A kind of extrasensory capacity seems to tell some soldiers when danger is near. 某种超感能力似乎能让一些士兵意识到危险正在靠近。

Since extra means "outside, beyond" (see EXTRA, p. 175), extrasensory means basically "beyond the senses." Extrasensory perception, or ESP, usually includes communication between minds involving no obvious contact (*telepathy*), gaining information about something without using the normal senses (*clairvoyance*), or predicting the future (*precognition*). According to polls, about 40% of Americans believe in ESP, and many of them have had personal experiences that seem to prove its existence. When someone jumps into your mind months or years after you had last thought of him or her, and the next day you learn that the person has just died, it can be hard to convince yourself it was just coincidence. Still, scientific attempts to prove the existence of ESP have never been terribly successful.

  extra 的意思是"在……以外，超越"(参见 EXTRA，第 175 页)，因此 *extrasensory* 的基本含义是"超越感官的"。超感知觉简称 ESP，通常包括不需要明显接触就能进行心灵交流(*telepathy*[心灵感应])，不用常规感官就能获取事物的信息(*clairvoyance*[超视，神视])，或能够预测未来(*precognition*[预知力])。据调查，约 40% 的美国人相信 ESP，其中还有很多人有亲身经历以证明 ESP 的存在。好几个月或好几年都没想起过的某个人突然跃入你的脑海，而第二天，你就得知这个人刚刚去世，这样的事情很难让我们相信只是巧合。尽管如此，科学家想要证实 ESP 存在的尝试却从未取得多么大的成功。

sensuous \ˈsen-shü-wəs\   (1) Highly pleasing to the senses. 美好感觉的，愉悦感官的 (2) Relating to the senses. 感觉的

  • Part of what audiences loved about her was the delight she took in the sensuous pleasures of well-prepared food. 观众们喜欢她，一定程度上是因为她很享受精致食物带来的美好感觉。

  Sensuous and *sensual* are close in meaning but not identical, and *sensuous* was actually coined by the poet John Milton so that he wouldn't have to use *sensual*. *Sensuous* usually implies pleasing of the senses by art or similar means; great music, for example, can be a source of sensuous delight. *Sensual*, on the other hand, usually describes gratification of the senses or physical appetites as an end in itself; thus we often think (perhaps unfairly) of wealthy Romans leading lives devoted to sensual pleasure. You can see why the Puritan Milton might have wanted another word.

  sensuous 和 *sensual* 的意思接近但不完全相同，*sensuous* 一词是由诗人约翰·弥尔顿创造的，这样他就不必再使用 *sensual* 一词了。*sensuous* 通常指的是艺术之类的方法所带来的感官的愉悦；例如，优美的音乐可能成为感官愉悦的源泉。而 *sensual* 通常指的是把以感官的满足或肉体欲望的满足作为终极目标，因此，我们常常认为(也许不公平)富裕的罗马人过着追求感官享受的生活。你能明白清教徒弥尔顿为什么想要另造一个词了吧。

SOPH

SOPH come from the Greek words meaning "wise" and "wisdom." In English the root sometimes appears in words where the wisdom is of the "wise guy" variety, but in words such as *philosophy* we see it used more respectfully.

  SOPH 源自意思是"聪明"和"智慧"的希腊词单词。在英语中，这个词根有时候出现在一些带点儿"自作聪明者"的聪明之意的单词中，但在 *philosophy* 这样的词语中，这个词根用得就很恭敬了。

sophistry \ˈsä-fə-strē\   Cleverly deceptive reasoning or argument. 诡辩

- For lawyers and politicians, the practice of sophistry from time to time is almost unavoidable. 对于律师和政治家来说,时不时地使用诡辩几乎是难以避免的。

The Sophists were a group of Greek teachers of rhetoric and philosophy, famous during the 5th Century B.C., who moved from town to town offering their teaching for a fee. The Sophists originally represented a respectable school of philosophy, but some critics claimed that they tried to persuade by means of clever but misleading arguments. The philosopher Plato wrote negatively about them, and the comic dramatist Aristophanes made fun of them, showing them making ridiculously fine distinctions about word meanings. We get our modern meanings of *sophist*, *sophistry*, and the adjective *sophistical* mostly from the opinions of these two men. 智者派是古希腊的一群教授辞学和哲学的教师,在公元前5世纪很有名气。他们从一个城市到另外一个城市,以教学来换取酬金。智者派最初代表的是一个受人尊敬的哲学学派,但某些批评者认为,他们说服他人靠的是巧妙但有误导性的言论。哲学家柏拉图对他们有负面看法,喜剧作家阿里斯托芬则取笑他们,认为他们过细地区分词义的差别。*sophist*(诡辩家)、*sophistry*(诡辩)以及形容词*sophistical*(诡辩的)的(消极的)现代含义主要源自上述这两人的看法。

sophisticated \sə-ˈfis-tə-ˌkā-təd\ (1) Having a thorough knowledge of the ways of society. 老于世故的 (2) Highly complex or developed. 非常复杂的,高级的

- In *Woman of the Year*, Katharine Hepburn plays a sophisticated journalist who can handle everything except Spencer Tracy. 在电影《风云女性》(又译《小姑居处》)中,凯瑟琳·赫本扮演一位老于世故的记者,除斯宾塞·特雷西外,她可以搞定一切。

A *sophisticated argument* is thorough and well-worked-out. A satellite is a *sophisticated* piece of technology, complex and designed to accomplish difficult tasks. A *sophisticated* person, such as Humphrey Bogart in *Casablanca*, knows how to get around in the world. But *sophistication* isn't always admired. As you might guess, the word is closely related to *sophistry* (see above), and its original meanings weren't very positive, and still today many of us aren't sure we really like *sophisticates*. sophisticated argument(严密的论证)是完整的、精心构思的。卫星是尖端的科技,非常复杂,用来完成困难的任务。老练的人,比如《卡萨布兰卡》中的亨弗莱·鲍嘉,明白整个社会的生存之道。但sophistication(老于世故)不总是令人艳羡。你可能已经猜到了,这个词与*sophistry*关系紧密(见上文),其最初的含义并不是很积极,直到今天很多人仍不确定是否真的喜欢 *sophisticates*(老于世故的人)。

sophomoric \ˌsä-fə-ˈmȯr-ik\ Overly impressed with one's own knowledge, but in fact undereducated and immature. 一知半解的,幼稚的

- We can't even listen to those sophomoric songs of his, with their attempts at profound wisdom that just demonstrate how little he knows about life. 我们听不了他的那些幼稚的歌,那些歌想显摆自己大智大慧,却只暴露出他对生活的知之甚少。

Sophomoric seems to include the roots *soph-*, "wise," and *moros*, "fool" (seen in words such as *moron*), so the contrast between wisdom and ignorance is built right into the word. Cambridge University introduced the term *sophomore* for its second-year students in the 17th century (though it's no longer used in Britain), maybe to suggest that a sophomore has delusions of wisdom since he's no longer an ignorant freshman. In America today, *sophomore* is ambiguous since it can refer to either high school or college. But *sophomoric* should properly describe something—wit, behavior, arguments, etc.—that is at least trying to be *sophisticated*.

sophomoric 有词根 soph-("聪明的")和 *moros*("愚蠢的"),因此,智慧和无知两个对照鲜明的含义并存于这个单词中。剑桥大学在 17 世纪首次用 *sophomore* 表示该校二年级的学生(但英国现在已经不再使用这个单词),也许是为了暗示大二学生自以为有了智慧,不再是一个无知的新生。在当今美国,*sophomore* 不止一种含义,可以指高中也可以指大学(的二年级学生)。但是,*sophomoric* 应该恰如其分地描述某个东西——智慧、行为、观点等——这个东西至少在努力变得 *sophisticated*。

theosophy \ thē-ˈä-sə-fē \   A set of teachings about God and the world based on mystical insight, especially teachings founded on a blend of Buddhist and Hindu beliefs. 通神学,神智学

• He had experimented with a number of faiths, starting with Buddhism and ending with a mixture of Eastern and Western thought that could best be called theosophy. 他尝试过多种信仰,始于佛教,终于一种东西方信仰的混合物,后者最恰当的称呼是通神学。

The word *theosophy*, combining roots meaning "God" and "wisdom," appeared back in the 17th century, but the well-known religious movement by that name, under the leadership of the Russian Helena Blavatsky, appeared only around 1875. Blavatsky's theosophy combined elements of Plato's philosophy with Christian, Buddhist, and Hindu thought (including reincarnation), in a way that she claimed had been divinely revealed to her. The *Theosophical* Society, founded in 1875 to promote her beliefs, still exists, as does the *Anthroposophical* Society, founded by her follower Rudolf Steiner.

theosophy 一词结合了意思是"上帝"和"智慧"的两个词根,出现在 17 世纪。然而,俄罗斯的海伦娜·布拉瓦茨基领导的以该词命名的著名宗教运动,直到 1875 年前后才出现。布拉瓦茨基的通神学以她声称的神谕的方式,把柏拉图哲学因素与基督教、佛教和印度教思想(包括转世)结合起来。Theosophical Society(通神学会)成立于 1875 年,旨在宣传她的教义,至今尚存;而由她的追随者鲁道夫·施泰纳所创立的 Anthroposophical Society(人智学学会),也同样至今尚存。

Quizzes

A. Indicate whether the following pairs of words have the same or different meanings:

1. sophisticated / worldly-wise   same ____ / different ____
2. sensuous / sensitive   same ____ / different ____
3. theosophy / mythology   same ____ / different ____
4. extrasensory / extreme   same ____ / different ____
5. sophistry / wisdom   same ____ / different ____
6. desensitize / deaden   same ____ / different ____
7. sophomoric / wise   same ____ / different ____
8. sensor / scale   same ____ / different ____

B. Match the word on the left to the correct definition on the right:

1. theosophy   a. immaturely overconfident
2. extrasensory   b. detector
3. sensuous   c. doctrine of God and the world
4. sophomoric   d. pleasing to the senses
5. sophistry   e. false reasoning
6. desensitize   f. not using the senses
7. sophisticated   g. make numb
8. sensor   h. highly complex

Words from Mythology and History 源自神话和历史的词语

Achilles' heel \ə-ˈki-lēz-ˈhēl\   A vulnerable point. 阿喀琉斯之踵（又译阿基里斯之踵）

• By now his rival for the Senate seat had discovered his Achilles' heel, the court records of the terrible divorce he had gone through ten years earlier. 现在，他的参议院席位的竞争对手已经发现了他的弱点，就是10年前他经历的糟糕的离婚在法庭留下的记录。

When the hero Achilles was an infant, his sea-nymph mother dipped him into the river Styx to make him immortal. But since she held him by one heel, this spot did not touch the water and so remained mortal and vulnerable, and it was here that Achilles was eventually mortally wounded. Today, the tendon that stretches up the calf from the heel is called the Achilles tendon. But the term Achilles' heel isn't used in medicine; instead, it's only used with the general meaning "weak point"—for instance, to refer to a section of a country's borders that aren't militarily protected, or to a Jeopardy contestant's ignorance in the Sports category.
当英雄 Achilles（阿喀琉斯）还是个婴儿时，他那位海洋仙女母亲为了让他永生，把他浸泡在冥河中。但有一只脚踵被母亲握在手里，没有浸到冥河水，因此这只脚踵不能永生，成为弱点，阿喀琉斯最终也是在这个位置受到了致命伤的。从脚后跟延伸到小腿的肌腱现在被称为 Achilles tendon（阿喀琉斯肌腱）。然而，Achilles' heel 一词却并不用在医学领域，只用于一般意义上的"弱点"——例如，某国没有受到军事保护的一段边界，或者《危险边缘》（智力问答节目）的选手对运动领域一无所知，都可以叫做"阿喀琉斯之踵"。

arcadia \är-ˈkā-dē-ə\   A region or setting of rural pleasure and peacefulness.
世外桃源

• The Pocono Mountains of Pennsylvania are a vacationer's arcadia. 宾夕法尼亚州的科波诺山是度假者的世外桃源。

Arcadia, a beautiful rural area in Greece, became the favorite setting for poems about ideal innocence unaffected by the passions of the larger world, beginning with the works of the Roman poet Virgil. There, shepherds play their pipes and sigh with longing for flirtatious nymphs; shepherdesses sing to their flocks; and goat-footed nature gods play in the fields and woods. Today, city dwellers who hope to retire to a country house often indulge in arcadian fantasies about what rural life will be like.

Arcadia(阿卡狄亚)是古希腊景色优美的乡村地区。从罗马诗人维吉尔开始,这里就是诗人最喜爱的诗歌背景,象征着不受大世界激情影响的理想的纯真。在那里,牧羊人吹着笛子,对善于调情的小仙女发出渴望的叹息;牧羊女对着羊群歌唱,而有着山羊足的自然之神在田野和丛林间嬉戏。如今,想要退隐乡间的城市居民常常对乡村生活抱有 *arcadian*(世外桃源般的)幻想。

Cassandra\kə-ˈsan-drə\ A person who predicts misfortune or disaster.
凶事预言家

• They used to call him a Cassandra because he often expected the worst, but his predictions tended to come true. 因为他经常预测最糟糕的事情,所以他们常称他为凶事预言家,但他的预测往往会成真。

Cassandra, the daughter of King Priam of Troy, was one of those beautiful young maidens with whom Apollo fell in love. He gave her the gift of prophecy in return for the promise of her sexual favors, but at the last minute she refused him. Though he could not take back his gift, he angrily pronounced that no one would ever believe her predictions; so when she prophesied the fall of her city to the Greeks and the death of its heroes, she was laughed at by the Trojans. A modern-day Cassandra goes around predicting gloom and doom—and may turn out to be right some of the time. Cassandra(卡桑德拉)是特洛伊王普里阿摩斯之女,也是阿波罗爱上的那些美女中的一位。阿波罗送给她预言能力作为礼物,以交换与她发生关系的承诺。然而,卡桑德拉在最后时刻拒绝了阿波罗。尽管阿波罗无法收回礼物,但他愤怒地宣告,永远不会有人相信她的预言;所以,当她预言她所在的特洛伊城将陷落在希腊人手中,该城的英雄都将死去时,遭到了特洛伊人的嘲笑。现代的卡桑德拉常会预言厄运——预言有时候也会成真。

cyclopean\ˌsī-klə-ˈpē-ən\ Huge or massive. 巨大的,庞大的

• They're imagining a new medical center on a cyclopean scale—a vast ten-block campus with thirty high-rise buildings. 他们想象的是一个规模巨大的医疗中心——占地十个街区,有三十座高楼。

The Cyclopes of Greek mythology were huge, crude giants, each with a single eye in the middle of his forehead. Odysseus and his men had a terrible encounter with a Cyclops, and escaped utter disaster only by stabbing a burning stick into the monster's eye. The great stone walls at such ancient sites as Troy and Mycenae are called cyclopean because the stones are so massive and the construction (which uses no cement) is so expert that it was assumed that only a superhuman race such as the Cyclopes could have achieved such a feat. Cyclopes(库克罗普斯)是古希腊神话中的巨人,他们高大而粗鲁,每个巨人的额头正中都长有一只独眼。奥德修斯和他的随从曾与一个独眼巨人发生了可怕的遭遇,他们将一根燃烧的木棒刺入巨人的眼中才逃过一劫。特洛伊和迈锡尼等古代遗址上壮观的石墙堪称 cyclopean,原因在于筑墙的石头是如此之大,墙又砌得如此之精(没有用水泥),以至于似乎只有像库克罗普斯这样的超人才能够完成这一壮举。

draconian\drə-ˈkō-nē-ən\ Extremely severe or cruel. 极度严苛的

• The severe punishments carried out in Saudi Arabia, including flogging for drunkenness, hand amputation for robbery, and beheading for drug trafficking, strike most of the world as draconian. 沙特阿拉伯实施严刑峻法，被全世界多数地方视为过分严苛，包括对醉酒者施以鞭刑，抢劫者砍下手掌，毒品走私者砍头等等。

Draconian comes from the name of Draco, a leader of Athens in the 7th century B. C. who in 621 B. C. produced its first legal code. The punishments he prescribed were extraordinarily harsh; almost anyone who couldn't pay his debts became a slave, and even minor crimes were punishable by death. So severe were these penalties that it was said that the code was written in blood. In the next century, the wise leader Solon would revise all of Draco's code, retaining the death penalty only for the crime of murder.

Draconian 源自德拉古的名字，他是公元前 7 世纪时雅典的一位领袖，在公元前 621 年制定了雅典的第一部法典。他所制定的惩罚极度严苛；无力偿还债务的人几乎都成了奴隶，即使是轻微的罪过也判处死刑。这些惩罚如此严厉，以至于人们说这部法典就是用鲜血写就的。在之后的一个世纪，聪明的领导人索伦修改了德拉古的整个法典，死刑只适用于谋杀罪。

myrmidon \ˈmər-mə-ˌdän\   A loyal follower, especially one who executes orders unquestioningly. 忠诚的追随者

- To an American, these soldiers were like myrmidons, all too eager to do the Beloved Leader's bidding. 在美国人看来，这些士兵就像忠仆一样，急切地想要执行敬爱领袖的指令。

In the Trojan War, the troops of the great hero Achilles were called Myrmidons. As bloodthirsty as wolves, they were the fiercest fighters in all Greece. They were said to have come from the island of Aegina, where, after the island's entire population had been killed by a plague, it was said to have been repopulated by Zeus, by turning all the ants in a great anthill into men. Because of their insect origin, the Myrmidons were blindly loyal to Achilles, so loyal that they would die without resisting if ordered to. The Trojans would not be the last fighting force to believe that a terrifying opposing army was made up of men who were not quite human.

在特洛伊战争中，伟大的英雄阿喀琉斯的军队被称为 Myrmidons（迈密登）。他们像狼一样嗜血，是全希腊最凶悍的战士。据说，这些人来自埃伊纳岛，该岛的居民全部死于一场瘟疫，宙斯将一座蚁冢的蚂蚁全变成人，使岛上重新有人居住。由于其昆虫起源，这些 Myrmidons 盲目效忠于阿喀琉斯，就是让他们去死也不会反抗。令人恐惧的敌军竟然由非人类组成，特洛伊军绝不会是最后一支有此想法的作战力量。

nemesis \ˈne-mə-səs\   A powerful, frightening opponent or rival who is usually victorious. 强劲对手

- During the 1970s and 1980s, Japanese carmakers became the nemesis of the U. S. auto industry. 在 20 世纪 70 年代和 80 年代，日本汽车制造商成为美国汽车制造业的强劲对手。

The Greek goddess Nemesis doled out rewards for noble acts and vengeance for evil ones, but it's only her vengeance that anyone remembers. According to the Greeks, Nemesis did not always punish an offender right away, but might wait as much as five generations to avenge a crime. Regardless, her cause was always just and her eventual victory was sure. But today a nemesis doesn't always dispense justice; a powerful drug lord may be the nemesis of a Mexican police chief, for instance, just as Ernst Stavro Blofeld was James Bond's nemesis in three of Ian Fleming's novels.

希腊女神 Nemesis(涅墨西斯)对高尚的行为给予奖励,对邪恶的行为予以报复,但人们只记得她的报复。根据古希腊人的说法,复仇女神并不总是立刻惩罚罪犯,而是要等到五代才报复。无论如何,她的理由总是正义的,她最终的复仇胜利也是毫无疑问的。然而,当今的 nemesis(强劲对手)并不总是伸张正义。例如,某个强大的毒枭可能是墨西哥警察局长的强劲对手,正如在伊恩·弗莱明三部小说中,恩斯特·斯塔夫罗·布洛菲尔德就是詹姆斯·邦德的强劲对手一样。

Trojan horse \ˈtrō-jən-ˈhȯrs\ Someone or something that works from within to weaken or defeat. 特洛伊木马

• Researchers are working on a kind of Trojan horse that will be welcomed into the diseased cells and then destroy them from within. 研究者们正在研制一种类似于特洛伊木马的东西,能顺利进入病变细胞,然后从内部摧毁它们。

After besieging the walls of Troy for ten years, the Greeks built a huge, hollow wooden horse, secretly filled it with armed warriors, and presented it to the Trojans as a gift for the goddess Athena, and the Trojans took the horse inside the city's walls. That night, the armed Greeks swarmed out and captured and burned the city. A Trojan horse is thus anything that looks innocent but, once accepted, has power to harm or destroy—for example, a computer program that seems helpful but ends up corrupting or demolishing the computer's software.

在包围了特洛伊城十年之后,希腊人造了一个巨大的空心木马,在里面秘密地装满武装战士,再将它送给特洛伊人作为给雅典娜女神的礼物,特洛伊人把木马运入了城中。当天晚上,希腊人蜂拥而出,攻陷并烧毁了这座城市。特洛伊木马由此成为看起来无害,可一旦接受,就有伤害或毁灭力量的东西——比如某个看起来有用,结果却会使电脑软件受损、瘫痪的电脑程序。

Quiz

Fill in each blank with the correct letter:

a. myrmidon   e. Achilles' heel
b. draconian   f. nemesis
c. cyclopean   g. Cassandra
d. Trojan horse   h. arcadia

1. He's nothing but a _____ of the CEO, one of those creepy aides who's always following him down the hall wearing aviator sunglasses.

2. A "balloon mortgage," in which the low rates for the first couple of years suddenly explode into something completely unaffordable, should be feared as a _____.

3. They marveled at the massive ancient _____ walls, which truly seemed to have been built by giants.

4. On weekends they would flee to their little _____ in rural New Hampshire,

UNIT 7

leaving behind the trials of the working week.

5. In eighth grade his _____ was a disagreeable girl named Rita who liked playing horrible little tricks.

6. His gloomy economic forecasts earned him a reputation as a _____.

7. Historians point to the _____ treaty terms of World War I as a major cause of World War II.

8. Believing the flattery of others and enjoying the trappings of power have often been the _____ of successful politicians.

Review Quizzes

A. Choose the correct synonym and the correct antonym:

1. peripheral   a. central   b. logical   c. sincere
   d. secondary
2. curative   a. humane   b. unhealthful   c. sensible
   d. healing
3. irrevocable   a. final   b. undoable   c. unbelievable
   d. vocal
4. perimeter   a. essence   b. edge   c. center
   d. spurt
5. nemesis   a. ally   b. no one   c. enemy
   d. bacteria
6. sophomoric   a. silly   b. wise   c. cacophonous
   d. collegiate
7. Achilles' heel   a. paradise   b. heroism   c. strong point
   d. vulnerability
8. peripatetic   a. stay-at-home   b. exact   c. wandering
   d. imprecise
9. vociferous   a. speechless   b. steely
   c. sweet-sounding d. loud
10. visionary   a. idealist   b. cinematographer
    c. conservative d. writer
11. sophisticated   a. rejected   b. advanced   c. worldly-wise
    d. innocent
12. equivocate   a. equalize   b. dither   c. decide
    d. enjoy

B. Choose the closest definition:

1. phonetic   a. called   b. twitched   c. sounded

• 165 •

d. remembered
2. sophistry   a. deception   b. musical composition
   c. sound reasoning d. pleasure
3. procure   a. appoint   b. obtain   c. decide
   d. lose
4. vista   a. summit   b. outlook   c. mountain
   d. avenue
5. cacophony   a. fraud   b. argument   c. racket
   d. panic
6. vis-à-vis   a. compared to   b. allowed to   c. rented to
   d. talked to
7. perspective   a. judgment   b. self-examination
   c. standpoint   d. landscape
8. peripheral   a. auxiliary   b. central
   c. relating to the sun   d. philosophical
9. draconian   a. clever   b. massive   c. disastrous
   d. severe
10. polyphonic   a. multi-melodic   b. uniformly harmonic
    c. relatively boring d. musically varied
11. cyclopean   a. whirling   b. gigantic   c. rapid
    d. circular
12. envisage   a. surround   b. imagine   c. investigate
    d. envy
13. periodontal   a. relating to feet b. around the sun
    c. around the teeth d. around a corner
14. curator   a. caretaker   b. watcher   c. doctor
    d. purchaser
15. Cassandra   a. optimist   b. economist   c. pessimist
    d. oculist

C. Fill in each blank with the correct letter：

a. equivocate   f. Trojan horse
b. sensuous   g. arcadia
c. cacophony   h. theosophy
d. extrasensory   i. sinecure
e. nemesis   j. desensitize

1. The job turned out to be a _____, and no one cared if he played golf twice a week.

2. The huge Senate bill was a _____, filled with items that almost none of the

senators were aware of.

3. We opened the door onto a haze of cigarette smoke and a _____ of music and laughter.

4. In an old book on _____ she found a philosophy very similar to the one she and her boyfriend were exploring.

5. She was sure her old _____ was plotting to get her fired.

6. After a month of barefoot running, he had managed to thoroughly _____ the soles of his feet.

7. The letter described their new Virginia farm as a kind of _____ of unspoiled nature.

8. Whenever they asked for a definite date, he would _____ and try to change the subject.

9. She lay in the bath with her eyes closed in a kind of _____ daydream.

10. Husband and wife seemed to communicate by _____ means, each always guessing what the other needed before anything was said.

UNIT 8

PORT comes from the Latin verb *portare*, meaning "to carry." Thus, something *portable* can be carried around. A *porter* carries your luggage, whether through a train station or high into the Himalayas. When we *transport* something, we have it carried from one place to another. And goods for *export* are carried away to another country.

PORT 源自拉丁语动词 *portare*，意思是"搬运，携带"。因此，something *portable* 是可以携带的东西。无论是通过火车站还是在喜马拉雅山的高处，*porter*（搬运工）搬运行李。当我们 *transport*（运送）某物时，我们把它从一个地方运到另一个地方。goods for *export*（出口的货物）被运往另一个国家。

portage\\'pȯr-tij\\ The carrying of boats or goods overland from one body of water to another; also, a regular route for such carrying. （两水路间的）陆运

- The only portage on the whole canoe route would be the one around the great waterfall on our second day. 整个独木舟航线上仅有一次陆运，就是我们第二天绕过大瀑布的那一次。

Portage was borrowed from French back in the 15th century to mean "carrying, transporting" or "freight," and it has kept its simple "carrying" sense to the present day. But its first known use in its "carrying of boats" sense came in 1698, and the obstacle that the canoes couldn't be steered over was none other than Niagara Falls. Though canoes are much lighter today than they used to be, a long portage that includes a lot of camping gear can still test a camper's strength.

portage 借自法语，最早可以追溯到 15 世纪，意为"搬运、运输"或"运货"，其"搬运"这个简单的含义沿用至今。但已知最早使用"船只搬运"的含义出现在 1698 年，当时，独木舟无法逾越的障碍正是尼亚加拉大瀑布。尽管如今的独木舟比以前轻很多，但长途搬运很多野营装备仍能考验野营者的体力。

portfolio\\ pȯrt-ˈfō-lē-ō \\ (1) A flat case for carrying documents or artworks. 公文包 (2) The investments owned by a person or organization. 投资组合

- In those days, a graphic artist who had recently moved to New York would just schlep his portfolio around to every magazine office in the city. 那时候,刚搬到纽约的平面艺术家会费力地提着公文包穿梭于纽约一家家杂志社的办公室。

Portfolio is partly based on the Latin *folium*, meaning "leaf, sheet." A portfolio usually represents a portable showcase of your talents. Today actual portfolios are used less than they used to be by artists, since most commercial artists have a Web site dedicated to showing off their art. But *portfolio* in its other common meaning is extremely common. Not so long ago, a broker would keep each of his or her clients' investments in a separate notebook or portfolio. Today the investment portfolio, like an artist's portfolio, usually takes the form of a Web page, even though everyone still uses the same old word.

portfolio 的一部分基于拉丁语 *folium*("叶,片")。公文包就像一个便携式陈列柜,里面装的是能显示你才能的东西。如今,实物公文包不如过去那样常用了,因为多数商业艺术家都有一个专门展示其艺术作品的网址。然而,*portfolio* 的另外一个常见的意思却极为常用。曾几何时,经纪人还会将客户的每一个投资项目都分开记录在笔记本中或放在公文包里。而现在,如同展示艺术家作品的方式一样,记录投资组合的方式往往以网站的形式呈现,但大家都还在使用这个旧词。

comport \kəm-ˈpȯrt\ (1) To be in agreement with. 与……相符,与……一致(2) To behave. 表现,举止。

- This new evidence comports with everything we know about what happened that night. 新证据与我们了解到的那天晚上所发生的一切都吻合。

With its prefix *com*-, "with," the Latin word *comportare* meant "to bring together." So it's easy to see how in English we could say that a college's policy comports with state law, or that a visit to your parents doesn't comport with your other weekend plans, or that your aunt and uncle won't listen to anything on TV that doesn't comport with their prejudices. The "behave" sense of the word comes through French, and its essential meaning is how a person "carries" him- or herself. So you may say, for instance, that your 17-year-old comported himself well (for once!) at the wedding reception, or that an ambassador always comports herself with dignity—that is, her *comportment* is always dignified—or that your class comported itself in a way that was a credit to the school.

前缀 *com* 的意思是"和……一起",因此拉丁语单词 *comportare* 的意思是"使在一起"。所以,英语中的下列说法很容易理解:大学的政策符合州的法律;看望父母与自己其他的周末计划不相符;你叔叔阿姨不想看与他们的成见不符的电视。该词的"表现、举止"含义源自法语,其核心意思是一个人如何"展现"他/她自己。比如可以说:你17岁的孩子在婚宴上表现得很好(就这一次!);这个大使总是举止优雅——也就是说,她的 *comportment*(举止)总是很高贵;你班的学生表现很好,给学校争光了。

deportment \di-ˈpȯrt-mənt\ Manner of conducting oneself socially. 举止,风度,仪态

- At social events she would constantly sneak glances at Alexandra, in quiet admiration of her elegant and graceful deportment. 在社交活动中,她会不时地偷偷看亚历桑德拉一眼,暗自羡慕她优雅的举止。

We've all seen pictures of girls walking around balancing books on their heads in an effort to achieve the poise of a princess or a film star. Classes in *deportment* were once a standard part of a young lady's upbringing, offered in all the girls' colleges; and you can still take private *deportment* classes, where you'll learn about posture and body language, how to move, sit, stand, shake hands, dress, drink and eat, and much more. But deportment isn't all about refined female grace. In fact, *deport* is often used as a synonym for *comport*, but usually in a positive way; thus, people are often said to deport themselves well, confidently, with dignity, like gentlemen or ladies, and so on.

我们都看到过女孩头顶书本走路的场景,她们这样做是为了达到像公主或电影明星般的身姿优雅。女子学院都曾开过仪态课,这在以前是女孩教育的标准环节。如今,你仍然可以上私人仪态课,学习仪态和肢体语言,如何动、坐、站、握手、穿衣、饮食等等。然而,deportment 并不只表示女性的优雅风度。事实上,*deport* 常用作 *comport* 的同义词,但更为积极;因此,我们经常说人们举止得体、自信、庄重、像绅士或淑女等等。

PEND comes from the Latin verb *pendere*, meaning "to hang" or "to weigh." (In the Roman era, weighing something large often required hanging it from a hook on one side of the balance scales.) We find the root in English words like *appendix*, referring to that useless and sometimes troublesome tube that hangs from the intestine, or that section at the back of some books that might contain some useful additional information.

PEND 源自拉丁语动词 *pendere*,意思是"悬挂"或"衡量"。(在罗马时期,给一个大东西称重时,通常需要将其挂在天平秤一侧的钩子上。)我们在英语单词中可以找到这个词根,比如 *appendix* 一词,指的是挂在肠子上的、无用且有时麻烦的管状器官,或是某些书后面包含的一些有用的附加信息。

---

pendant \ˈpen-dənt\ Something that hangs down, especially as an ornament.
垂饰,挂件

• Around her neck she was wearing the antique French pendant he had given her, with its three rubies set in silver filigree. 她脖子上戴着他送的古色古香的法国挂件,是一个镶嵌着三颗红宝石的银丝饰品。

Most pendants are purely decorative. But a pendant may also hold a picture or a lock of hair of a lover or a child. And, perhaps because they hang protectively in front of the body and near the heart, pendants have often had symbolic and magical purposes. Thus, a pendant may be a charm or amulet, or its gems or metals may be felt to have health-giving properties. In architecture, a pendant is an ornament that hangs down from a structure, but unlike a necklace pendant it's usually solid and inflexible.

多数垂饰都是纯装饰性的,但有的挂件中也可以放照片,或放情人、孩子的一绺头发。另外,也许是出于保护的目的,挂件常常悬挂在身前靠近心脏的位置,因此,它们常常带有象征性和神秘的作用。挂件有可能是个护身符,上面的宝石或金属常给人以有益健康的感觉。在建筑学中,垂饰是从建筑物垂下的装饰品,但与项链的吊坠不同,它通常是实心的且不能弯曲。

append \ə-'pend\ To add as something extra. 附加，添加

- She appended to the memo a list of the specific items that the school was most in need of. 在备忘录中，她附上了学校最需要的详细物品清单。

Append is a somewhat formal word. Lawyers, for example, often speak of appending items to other documents, and lawmakers frequently append small bills to big ones, hoping that everyone will be paying attention only to the main part of the big bill and won't notice. When we append a small separate section to the end of a report or a book, we call it an *appendix*. But in the early years of e-mail, the words we decided on were *attach* and *attachment*, probably because appendixes are thought of as unimportant, whereas the attachment is often the whole reason for sending an e-mail.

append 是比较正式的词语。例如，律师经常会说，要将一些条款附加到之前的文件中，而立法者常常会将小的法案附加到大的中，希望大家只关注大法案的主要部分而不会注意到添加的小法案。当我们将一个小的、独立的部分添加到报告或书的末尾时，我们称之为 *appendix*（附录，附件）。但在电子邮件早期，我们决定使用的却是 *attach* 或 *attachment*，可能是因为 appendixes 听起来不重要，而 attachment 经常是发邮件的唯一目的。

appendage \ə-'pen-dij\ (1) Something joined on to a larger or more important body or thing. 附加物，附属物 (2) A secondary body part, such as an arm or a leg. 附器，附肢

- She often complained that she felt like a mere appendage of her husband when they socialized with his business partners. 她经常抱怨说，在她和丈夫与他的商业伙伴交往时，感觉自己就像是他的附属品。

Appendix isn't the only noun that comes from *append*. Unlike *appendix*, *appendage* doesn't suggest the end of something, but simply something attached. The word is often used in biology to refer to parts of an animal's body: an insect's antennae, mouthparts, or wings, for example. The appendages of some animals will grow back after they've been removed; a salamander, for example, can regrow a finger, and the tiny sea squirt can regrow all its appendages—and even its brain.

appendix 并非 *append* 的唯一名词形式。与 *appendix* 不同的是，*appendage* 并不表示某个东西的尾部，而只是附加上去的东西。在生物学中，这个词常指动物身体的某些部分，例如昆虫的触角、口器或翅膀。某些动物的附器被移除后会重新长出来，例如，蝾螈可以重新长出指头，而小小的海鞘可以重新长出所有的附器——甚至大脑。

suspend \sə-'spend\ (1) To stop something, or to force someone to give up some right or position, for a limited time. 暂停 (2) To hang something so that it is free on all sides. 悬挂，悬浮

- The country has been suspended from the major trade organizations, and the effects on its economy are beginning to be felt. 该国已被暂时排除在主要贸易组织之外，这对其经济的影响开始显现。

When something is *suspended*, it is "left hanging"; it is neither in full operation nor permanently ended. *Suspense* is a state of uncertainty and maybe anxiety. When we watch a play or movie, we enjoy experiencing a "suspension of disbelief"; that is, we allow ourselves to believe we're watching reality, even though we aren't truly fooled. *Suspension* can also mean physical hanging; thus, in a suspension bridge, the roadway actually hangs from huge cables. When some substance is "in suspension," its particles are "hanging" in another substance, mixed into it but not actually dissolved, like fine sand in water, or sea spray in the air at the seashore.

某物被 suspended，意为它被"悬置"，既没有完全运转也没有永久结束。suspense（悬念）是一种不确定和焦虑的情感状态。当我们看戏剧或电影时，我们享受"暂停怀疑"的体验；也就是说，我们让自己暂时相信所看到的都是真实的，尽管我们并不是真地受骗。*suspension* 也可以表示物理意义上的悬挂，因此，吊桥的桥面实际上是悬挂在巨大的缆索上的。当某种物质处在"悬浮状态"时，其颗粒"悬置"于另一物质之中，与之混合但实际上没有溶解，比如水中的细沙，或海边空气中的浪花。

Quizzes

A. Choose the closest definition:

1. pendant   a. porch   b. salary   c. flag
   d. ornament
2. portfolio   a. mushroom   b. folder   c. painting
   d. carriage
3. suspend   a. study carefully   b. watch closely   c. slip gradually
   d. stop temporarily
4. deportment   a. manner   b. section   c. departure
   d. promotion
5. append   a. close up   b. predict   c. attach
   d. reconsider
6. portage   a. small dock   b. river obstacle   c. light boat
   d. short carry
7. comport   a. bend   b. behave   c. join
   d. transport
8. appendage   a. hanger   b. body organ   c. limb
   d. companion

B. Fill in each blank with the correct letter:

a. portage   e. appendage
b. portfolio   f. pendant
c. deportment   g. append
d. comport   h. suspend

1. He found himself peering at her silver _____, trying to make out the odd symbols that formed the design.

2. Their _____ consisted mostly of high-tech stocks.

3. On the organizational chart, the group appears way down in the lower left corner, looking like a minor _____ of the company.

4. The biggest challenge would be the half-mile _____ around the river's worst rapids.

5. This is the entire report, to which we'll _____ the complete financial data when we submit it.

6. She never fails to impress people with her elegant _____ in the most difficult social situations.

7. Whenever his mother got wind of more bad behavior, she would _____ his allowance for a month.

8. These figures don't _____ with the ones you showed us yesterday.

PAN comes from a Greek word meaning "all"; as an English prefix, it can also mean "completely," "whole," or "general." A *panoramic* view is a complete view in every direction. A *pantheon* is a temple dedicated to all the gods of a religion. A *pandemic* outbreak of a disease may not affect the entire human population, but enough to produce a catastrophe.

PAN 源自意思是"全部"的希腊语单词;作为英语前缀,它也可以表示"完全的""总的"或"全面的"之意。*panoramic* view(全景)是全方位的完整视图。*pantheon*(万神殿)是供奉某宗教所有神灵的殿堂。某种疾病的 *pandemic* outbreak(大爆发)也许不会影响整个人类,但足以造成一场灾难。

---

panacea \ˌpa-nə-ˈsē-ə\ A remedy for all ills or difficulties; cure-all. 万能之计,灵丹妙药

• Educational reform is sometimes viewed as the panacea for all of society's problems. 教育改革有时被视为解决所有社会问题的灵丹妙药。

Panacea comes from a Greek word meaning "all-healing," and Panacea was the goddess of healing. In the Middle Ages and the Renaissance, alchemists who sought to concoct the "elixir of life" (which would give eternal life) and the "philosopher's stone" (which would turn ordinary metals into gold) also labored to find the panacea. But no such medicine was ever found, just as no solution to all of a society's difficulties has ever been found. Thus, *panacea* is almost always used to criticize the very idea of a total solution ("There's no panacea for the current problems plaguing Wall Street").

panacea 源自意思是"治愈全部"的希腊语单词,Panacea(帕那刻亚)也是治愈女神(又译:医药女神)的名字。在中世纪和文艺复兴时期,炼金术士试图配置出"长生不老药"(带来永生)和"点金石"(将普通金属变成黄金),他们也竭力寻找万能药。然而,人们从来并没有找到过这样的万灵药,正如人们从来都找不到解决所有社会问题的万能方法一样。因此,*panacea* 常用于批评某种万全之策的想法("不存在能解决目前困扰华尔街的所有问题的万能药")。

---

pandemonium \ˌpan-də-ˈmō-nē-əm\ A wild uproar or commotion. 骚动,群情沸腾

• Pandemonium erupted in the stadium as the ball shot past the goalie into the net. 当球越过守门员射入球网时,体育场顿时一阵喧闹。

In John Milton's *Paradise Lost*, the fallen Satan has his heralds proclaim "A solemn Councel forthwith to be held/At Pandaemonium, the high Capital/Of Satan and his Peers." Milton got the name for his capital of hell, where Satan gathered together all his demons, by linking *pan* with the Latin word *daemonium*, "evil spirit." For later writers, *pandemonium* became a synonym for hell itself, since hell was then often seen as a place of constant noise and confusion, but also for any wicked and lawless place. Nowadays it's used to refer to the uproar itself rather than the place where it occurs. 在约翰·弥尔顿的《失乐园》中,堕落的撒旦让他的传令官传达消息:"即刻召开庄严的会议/在万魔殿/撒旦和伙伴们的最高首府。"弥尔顿把 *pan* 与拉丁语单词 *daemonium*(恶灵)结合,用以命名地狱的首府,也就是撒旦召集手下恶魔们的地方。对后来的作家而言,*pandemonium* 是地狱的代名词,因为地狱常被视为一个吵吵闹闹、混乱不堪的地方,这个词语也用来指代任何邪恶的、无法无天的地方。今天,它用于指代混乱本身,而非混乱之所。

pantheism \ˈpan-thē-ˌi-zəm\ A system of belief that regards God as identical with the forces and laws of the universe. 泛神论

• Most of her students seemed to accept a vague kind of pantheism, without any real belief that God had ever appeared in human form. 她的多数学生似乎都接受了一种模糊的泛神论,并不真正相信上帝曾以人形出现过。

Pantheistic ideas—and most importantly the belief that God is equal to the universe, its physical matter, and the forces that govern it—are found in the ancient books of Hinduism, in the works of many Greek philosophers, and in later works of philosophy and religion over the centuries. Much modern New Age spirituality is pantheistic. But most Christian thinkers reject *pantheism* because it makes God too impersonal, doesn't allow for any difference between the creation and the creator, and doesn't seem to allow for humans to make meaningful moral choices. *pantheistic*(泛神论的)思想——核心内容是认为上帝等同于宇宙,等同于宇宙万物,等同于支配宇宙的力量——存在于印度教的古书中、希腊很多哲学家的著作中、后世的哲学和宗教著作中。现代的新时代精神在很大程度上就是泛神论思想。但多数基督教思想家都拒绝泛神论,因为泛神论使上帝不具有人格,将造物主和造物混为一谈,似乎也让人类不可能做出有意义的道德选择。

panoply \ˈpa-nə-plē\ (1) A magnificent or impressive array. 雄伟的阵式,盛况 (2) A display of all appropriate accessory items. 全套

• The full panoply of a royal coronation was a thrilling sight for the throngs of sidewalk onlookers and the millions of television viewers. 对人行道上成群的旁观者和数百万电视观众而言,观看国王加冕典礼的盛况可真是激动人心啊。

The fully armed Greek soldier was an impressive sight, even if Greek armor never became as heavy as that of medieval knights on horseback (who couldn't possibly have marched in such outfits). *Panoplia* was the Greek word for the full suit of armor, and the English *panoply* originally likewise referred to the full suit of armor worn by a soldier or knight. Today *panoply* may refer to full ceremonial dress or lavish ceremonial decoration of any kind. And it can also refer to striking spectacle of almost any kind: the breathtaking panoply of autumn foliage, or the stirring panoply of a military parade, for example.

全副武装的希腊士兵令人难忘,尽管他们的盔甲没有中世纪骑兵的沉重(穿着这么重的盔甲要想行军也难)。*panoplia* 是希腊语,指的是全副盔甲。英语的 *panoply* 最初指的也是士兵或骑兵的全副盔甲。现在,panoply 可以表示全套礼服或各种奢华的庆典装饰。它也可以指几乎所有引人注目的场景;例如,秋天树叶的壮观全景,或者阅兵式激动人心的场景。

EXTRA is Latin for "outside" or "beyond." So anything *extraterrestrial* or *extragalactic* takes place beyond the earth or the galaxy. Something *extravagant*, such as an *extravaganza*, goes way beyond the normal. And *extra* is naturally a word itself, a shortening of *extraordinary*, "beyond the ordinary."

EXTRA 是拉丁语,表示"以外"或"超越"。所以,anything *extraterrestrial* or *extragalactic*(地球外的或银河外的任何事情)都发生在地球或银河系之外。something *extravagant*(奢侈的东西),比如一场 *extravaganza*(盛大的娱乐表演),远远超出正常标准。*extra* 本身自然就是一个单词,是 *extraordinary*("非凡的")一词的简写。

extradite \ˈek-strə-ˌdīt\ To deliver an accused criminal from one place to another where the trial will be held. 引渡

• Picked up by the Colorado police for burglary, he's being extradited to Mississippi to face trial for murder. 因入室盗窃被科罗拉多警方逮捕后,他被引渡到密西西比州,面临谋杀罪审判。

Extradition from one state to another is generally a straightforward process. But extradition may become more complicated when two countries are involved, even though most countries have signed treaties stating that they will send criminals to the country where they are wanted. Many countries often won't send their own citizens to another country for trial; countries that don't permit the death penalty may not agree to send a suspect back to face such a penalty; and most countries won't extradite someone accused of political crimes. When extradition seems unlikely, a country may actually kidnap someone from another country, but this is illegal and rare.

一般来说,将犯人从一州引渡到另一州不难。但是,当涉及两个国家时,引渡可能就会很复杂了,尽管多数国家都签署了条约,表示会送犯人到通缉他们的国家。许多国家往往不会把自己的公民送到另一国家接受审讯;没有死刑的国家可能不同意把嫌疑人送回去,面临这样的刑罚;多数国家都不会引渡政治犯。当引渡无望时,某个国家可能会采取绑架的措施把人带回来,但这样做是非法的,也很罕见。

extrapolate \ik-ˈstra-pə-ˌlāt\ To extend or project facts or data into an area not known in order to make assumptions or to predict facts or trends. 推断,外推

• Economists predict future buying trends partly by extrapolating from current economic data. 经济学家对未来购买趋势的预测有一部分是通过对当前经济数据外推得来的。

Scientists worry about the greenhouse effect because they have *extrapolated* the rate of carbon-dioxide buildup and predicted that its effect on the atmosphere will become increasingly severe. On the basis of their *extrapolations*, they have urged governments and businesses to limit factory and automobile emissions. Notice that it's acceptable to speak of extrapolating existing data (to produce new data), extrapolating *from* existing data (to produce new data), or extrapolating new data (from existing data)—in other words, it isn't easy to use this word wrong.
科学家们很担心温室效应，因为他们推断出了二氧化碳积累的速度，并且预言，它对大气的影响将会越来越严重。基于 *extrapolations*(推断)，他们已经敦促政府和企业限制工厂和汽车的排放。注意:"从已知数据推断出新数据"既可以说 extrapolating existing data (to produce new data)，也可以说 extrapolating *from* existing data (to produce new data)，还可以说 extrapolating new data (from existing data)——换句话说，这个单词不容易用错。

extrovert \ˈek-strə-ˌvərt\ A person mainly concerned with things outside him- or herself; a sociable and outgoing person. 性格外向的人

• These parties are always full of loud extroverts, and I always find myself hiding in a corner with my drink. 这些派对上总有许多吵闹的、性格外向的人，而我自己则总是躲在角落里喝酒。

Extrovert (sometimes spelled *extravert*) means basically "turned outward"—that is, toward things outside oneself. The word was coined by the eminent psychologist C. G. Jung in the early 20th century. The opposite personality type, in Jung's view, was the *introvert*. Extroverts seem to be favored by societies such as ours, even though introverts seem to be on average more mentally gifted. Psychologists have said that the only personality traits that can be identified in newborn infants are shyness and lack of shyness, which are fairly close to—but not really the same as—*introversion* and *extroversion*.
extrovert(有时拼写为 *extravert*)的基本意思是"向外面"——也就是说，关注自身以外的东西。这个词是著名心理学家 C. G. 荣格在 20 世纪初创造的。荣格认为，与此相反的性格类型是 *introvert*(内向的)。外向者好像更受我们这样的社会青睐，但一般来说，内向的人似乎更有智力天赋。心理学家认为，新生儿唯一可以识别的性格特征就是害羞或者不害羞，这很接近于——但不完全等同于——*introversion*(内向)和 *extroversion*(外向)。

extraneous\ek-ˈstrā-nē-əs\ (1) Existing or coming from the outside. 外来的 (2) Not forming an essential part; irrelevant. 枝节的,无关联的

• Be sure your essays are well focused, with any discussion of extraneous topics kept to a minimum. 要确保你的文章中心明确,尽量少写无关的内容。

Extraneous and *strange* both come from the same Latin word, *extraneus*, which basically meant "external" or "coming from outside." But unlike *strange*, *extraneous* is a slightly formal word, often used by scientists and social scientists. Researchers always try to eliminate extraneous factors (or "extraneous variables") from their studies. A researcher conducting a psychological test, for example, would try to make sure that the people were tested under the same conditions, and were properly divided according to gender, age, health, and so on.

extraneous 和 *strange* 源自同一个拉丁语单词 *extraneus*,该词的基本含义是"外部的"或"源自外部的"。与 *strange* 的不同之处在于,*extraneous* 稍微正式一些,常为科学家和社会学家所用。研究人员做研究时,总要尽量消除不相关因素(或"无关变量")。例如,进行心理测试的研究人员要尽量确保受试条件相同,并根据性别、年龄、健康等对受试者合理分组。

Quizzes

A. Fill in each blank with the correct letter:

a. extrapolate   e. extradite
b. panoply   f. pantheism
c. extraneous   g. extrovert
d. panacea   h. pandemonium

1. From these figures, economists can _____ data that shows a steady increase in employment.

2. Being a natural _____, he took to his new career as a salesman easily.

3. The new voice-mail system comes with the usual full _____ of options.

4. _____ broke out at the news of the victory.

5. The treaty with Brazil doesn't require us to _____ a criminal who's a native-born American.

6. He's locked himself in his studio to ensure that there won't be any _____ distractions.

7. She had always believed in vitamins as a _____, but they weren't always able to fight off infections.

8. He attended the Presbyterian church, even though for many years his real beliefs had been a mixture of Buddhism and _____.

B. Indicate whether the following pairs of terms have the same or different meanings:

1. panacea / antibiotic   same ____ / different ____
2. pandemonium / chaos   same ____ / different ____
3. pantheism / priesthood   same ____ / different ____
4. panoply / display   same ____ / different ____
5. extrapolate / project   same ____ / different ____
6. extraneous / necessary   same ____ / different ____
7. extradite / hand over   same ____ / different ____
8. extrovert / schizophrenic   same ____ / different ____

PHOT comes from the Greek word for "light." *Photography* uses light to create an image on film or paper, and a *photocopy* is an image made by using light and tiny electrically charged ink particles.

PHOT 源自希腊语表示"光"的单词。*photography*（摄影）是利用光在胶片或纸上形成图像，*photocopy*（复印件）指的是利用光和微小的带电墨水颗粒制成的图像。

photoelectric \ˌfō-tō-i-ˈlek-trik\　Involving an electrical effect produced by the action of light or other radiation. 光电的

• They wanted to avoid the kind of smoke detector that uses radioactive materials, so they've installed the photoelectric kind instead. 他们不想使用带有放射性物质的那类烟雾报警器，所以他们安装了光电型的烟雾报警器。

The *photoelectric effect* occurs when light (or similar radiation such as X-rays) falls on a material such as a metal plate and causes it to emit electrons. The discovery of the photoelectric effect led to important new theories about matter (and to a Nobel Prize for Albert Einstein). *Photoelectric cells*, or *photocells*, are used in burglar-alarm light detectors and garage-door openers (both employ a beam of light that is broken when something moves across it), and also to play soundtracks on movie film (where a light beam shines through the soundtrack encoded on the film and is "read" by the photocells). 光（或 X 射线之类的放射线）照射到金属板等材料上，促使其释放出电子，就产生了 *photoelectric effect*（光电效应）。光电效应的发现带来了关于物质的重要新理论的出现（也为阿尔伯特·爱因斯坦带来了诺贝尔奖）。*photoelectric cells* 或 *photocells*（光电池）用于防盗报警的光传感器和车库门开启感应器上（两者所利用的都是一束光线，当有东西经过时，光线会被阻断），光电池也用于播放电影胶片上的声音（光线照射到胶片上，光电池"读取"胶片上面编码的音轨）。

photovoltaic \ˌfō-tō-väl-ˈtā-ik\　Involving the direct generation of electricity when sunlight or other radiant energy falls on the boundary between dissimilar substances (such as two different semiconductors). 光伏的

• Photovoltaic technology is being applied to thin film that can produce as much energy as solar cells while using far less semiconducting material. 光伏技术被运用在薄膜上，可以产生与太阳能电池一样多的能量，但使用的半导体材料要少得多。

The *-voltaic* part of *photovoltaic* comes from the name of Alessandro Volta, inventor of the electric battery. Thus, unlike photoelectric cells, which use electricity for certain small tasks, photovoltaic (or PV) cells actually produce electricity. Solar cells, the standard type of photovoltaic cells (often called simply *photocells*), operate without chemicals and with no moving parts to create energy directly from sunlight. Much research is now being done on creating an alternative technology—solar film, which could be stuck onto almost any surface, or possibly even sprayed on. *photovoltaic* 中的 *-voltaic* 源自电池的发明者亚历山德罗·沃尔塔的名字。光电池需要用电才能完成某些小任务，而光伏（或 PV）电池就不同了，竟然能用来发电。太阳能电池是标准类型的光伏电池（通常简称 *photocells*），无须化学物质，也无须活动部件，直接利用太阳光来产生能量。目前，人们开展了大量的研究，要创造一种替代技术——太阳能发电膜。它可以固定在几乎任何表面上，甚至可以喷涂上去。

photon \ˈfō-ˌtän\　A tiny particle or bundle of radiant energy. 光子

- The idea that light consists of photons is difficult until you begin to think of a ray of light as being caused by a stream of tiny particles. 光由光子组成的想法很难理解，除非你开始将一道光想象成是由微小粒子流所造成的。

It was Albert Einstein who first theorized that the energy in a light beam exists in small bits or particles, and scientists today know that light sometimes behaves like a wave (somewhat like sound or water) and sometimes like a stream of particles. The energies of *photons* range from high-energy gamma rays and X-rays down to low-energy infrared and radio waves, though all travel at the same speed. The amazing power of lasers is the result of a concentration of photons that have been made to travel together in order to hit their target at the same time. 阿尔伯特·爱因斯坦首先提出，光中的能量存在于细小的粒子中，而当今的科学家们知道光有时像波浪（有点像声音或水），有时像粒子流。光子的能量范围从高能量的伽马射线和X射线到低能量的红外和无线电波之间不等，但它们的运动速度相同。激光的惊人力量就是光子集中的结果，即让这些光子向同一方向运动，同时击中一个目标。

photosynthesis \ˌfō-tō-ˈsin-thə-sis\ The process by which green plants use light to produce organic matter from carbon dioxide and water. 光合作用

- Sagebrush survives in harsh climates because it's capable of carrying on photosynthesis at very low temperatures. 灌木蒿可以在恶劣的气候条件下生存，是因为它能够在非常低的温度下进行光合作用。

The Greek roots of *photosynthesis* combine to produce the basic meaning "to put together with the help of light." Photosynthesis is what first produced oxygen in the atmosphere billions of years ago, and it's still what keeps it there. Sunlight splits the water molecules (made of hydrogen and oxygen) held in a plant's leaves and releases the oxygen in them into the air. The leftover hydrogen combines with carbon dioxide to produce carbohydrates, which the plant uses as food—as do any animals or humans who might eat the plant. *photosynthesis*（光合作用）的希腊词根合起来，产生了该词的基本意思"在光的帮助下结合"。数十亿年前，大气中最早的氧气就是光合作用的结果，光合作用使大气中一直有氧气存在。阳光分解植物叶片中的水分子（由氢气和氧气构成），再将其中的氧气释放到空气中。剩下的氢与二氧化碳结合产生碳水化合物，被植物用作养分——就像植物被动物或人类用作食物一样。

LUC

LUC comes from the Latin noun *lux*, "light," and the verb *lucere*, "to shine or glitter." In ancient Rome, *Lucifer*, meaning "Light-bearer," was the name given to the morning star, but the name was eventually transferred by Christians to Satan. This tradition, which dates back to the period before Christ, said that Lucifer had once been among the angels but had wanted to be the great light in the sky, and for his pride had been cast out of heaven and thus became the opponent of everything good. LUC源自拉丁语名词 *lux*（"光"）和动词 *lucere*（"照亮或闪光"）。在古罗马，*Lucifer*（路西法）的意思是"光的使者"，是启明星的名字，但这个名字最终却被基督徒转变成撒旦。这个传说可以追溯到耶稣基督之前，路西法曾是一位天使，但想

成为天上最亮的光,他因骄傲而被逐出天堂,成为一切美好事物的敌人。

lucid\ˈlü-səd\　(1) Very clear and easy to understand. 浅显易懂的 (2) Able to think clearly. 头脑清醒的

• On his last visit he had noticed that his elderly mother hadn't seemed completely lucid. 他上次看望母亲时,注意到年迈的母亲好像头脑并不完全清醒。

Mental *lucidity* is easy to take for granted when we're young, though alcohol, drugs, and psychological instability can confuse the mind at any age. We all hope to live to 100 with our mental abilities intact, which is entirely possible; avoiding the condition called dementia (which includes the well-known Alzheimer's disease) often involves a combination of decent genes, physical and mental activity, and a good diet. Writing *lucidly*, on the other hand, can take a lot of work at any age; you've probably had the experience of trying to read a set of instructions and wondering if the writer even grew up speaking English.

mental *lucidity*(思维清晰)在年轻的时候很容易被认为是理所当然的,尽管酒精、药物和心理问题会使任何年龄的人都思维混乱。我们都希望,活到100岁时心智能力仍然健全,这是完全可能的;避免痴呆症(包括众所周知的阿尔茨海默病)需要的是良好的基因、身心活动以及健康的饮食。另一方面,在任何年龄段,*lucidly*(清晰地)写作都需要非常努力才行;你可能有过这样的经验:在读一套说明书时,你会怀疑它的作者到底是不是说英语长大的。

elucidate\i-ˈlü-sə-ˌdāt\　To clarify by explaining; explain. 阐明

• A good doctor should always be willing to elucidate any medical jargon he or she uses. 好医生应该总是乐意解释他/她所用的任何医学术语。

The basic meaning of *elucidate* is "to shed light on." So when you elucidate, you make transparent or clear something that had been murky or confusing. *Elucidation* of a complex new health-care policy may be a challenge. Elucidation of the terms of use for a credit card may be the last thing its provider wants to do. The physicist Carl Sagan had a gift for elucidating astronomical science to a large audience, his *lucid* explanations making clear how stars are born and die and how the universe may have begun.

elucidate 的基本意思是"使清楚"。所以,当你进行阐释时,你会将之前不清楚、不明白的东西变得透明或清晰。对一个复杂的新医保政策进行 *elucidation*(阐释)可能是一项挑战。阐释信用卡的使用条款可能是提供信用卡的人最不想做的事情。物理学家卡尔·萨根拥有可以向大众阐释天文科学知识的天赋,他那 *lucid* explanations(浅显易懂的解释),使人们清楚地知道了星球是怎样产生的、又是怎样消亡的以及宇宙可能是怎样诞生的。

lucubration\ˌlü-kyu̇-ˈbrā-shən\　(1) Hard and difficult study. 刻苦研究 (2) The product of such study. 苦心的著作,心血之作

• Our professor admitted that he wasn't looking forward to reading through any more of our lucubrations on novels that no one enjoyed. 教授承认,他不希望再读我们苦心研究那些无人欣赏的小说得来的成果。

Lucubration came to mean "hard study" because it originally meant study done by lamplight, and in a world without electric lights, such study was likely to be the

UNIT 8

kind of hard work that would only a dedicated student like Abe Lincoln would make a habit of. The word has a literary feel to it, and it's often used with a touch of sarcasm.

lucubration 的意思是"刻苦的学习",因为它最初的意思是在灯光下学习,在没有电灯的年代,这样的学习可能会很辛苦,恐怕只有像亚伯拉罕·林肯这样勤奋的学生才能养成这种习惯。这个词有点书卷气,也常带点儿讽刺意味儿。

translucent \tranz-ˈlü-sənt\ Partly transparent; allowing light to pass through without permitting objects beyond to be seen clearly. 半透明的

● Architects today often use industrial glass bricks in their home designs, because translucent walls admit daylight while guarding privacy. 现在的建筑师在家居设计中经常使用工业玻璃砖,因为半透明的墙可以透过光线,同时又可以保护隐私。

With its prefix *trans-*, meaning "through," *translucent* describes material that light shines through without making anything on the other side clearly visible, unlike a *transparent* material. Frosted glass, often used in bathroom windows, is translucent, as is stained glass. Red wine in a crystal goblet, when held before a candle in a dark corner of a quiet restaurant, usually proves to be translucent as well.

前缀 *trans-* 的意思是"通过", *translucent* 描述某种材料,光线可以透过,但不会使另一面的东西清晰可见,这与 *transparent* material(透明的材料)不同。磨砂玻璃和彩色玻璃一样,都是半透明的,常用在浴室的窗户上。当你端起透明的高脚杯,在安安静静的餐厅里,对着黑暗角落里的烛火看时,就会发现里面的红酒也是半透明的。

Quizzes

A. Fill in each blank with the correct letter:

a. photovoltaic   e. photoelectric
b. lucid   f. lucubration
c. photon   g. photosynthesis
d. translucent   h. elucidate

1. A soft light filtered through the _____ white curtains separating the two rooms.

2. _____ cells on the roof capture the sun's energy, and with the small windmill nearby they produce more energy than the house needs.

3. Few of us can truly imagine that light can be reduced to a tiny packet of energy called a _____.

4. In graduate school, his lively social life was replaced with three years of intense _____.

5. A large tree with a 40-inch trunk may produce two-thirds of a pound of oxygen every day through _____.

6. His 88-year-old aunt is in a nursing home, and he never knows which days she'll be _____.

7. The alarm system depends on _____ technology that detects when someone breaks a beam of light in a doorway.

8. Whenever anyone asks the professor to _____, he just makes everything more complicated instead of less.

B. Match the definition on the left to the correct word on the right:

1. involving the interaction of light with matter   a. lucubration
2. production of carbohydrates   b. photoelectric
3. clarify   c. translucent
4. passing light but only blurred images   d. elucidate
5. elemental particle   e. photovoltaic
6. brightly clear   f. photosynthesis
7. hard study   g. photon
8. using light to generate electricity   h. lucid

MOR/MORT

MOR/MORT comes from Latin words meaning "to die" and "death." A *mortuary* is a place where dead bodies are kept until burial, and a *postmortem* examination is one conducted on a recently dead body. The Latin phrase "Memento mori" means "Remember that you must die"; so a *memento mori* is the name we give to a reminder of death; the skulls you can find carved on gravestones in old cemeteries are examples.

MOR / MORT 源自意思是"死去"和"死亡"的拉丁语单词。mortuary(太平间)指的是将尸体一直存放到下葬的地方，postmortem(尸检)是指对新近死亡的尸体进行的检查。拉丁语短语"Memento mori"的意思是"记住,你必须死";因此，memento mori(死亡象征)是我们给那些让我们想起死亡的东西起的名字;刻在古老墓地墓碑上的骷髅头就是例子。

mortality \mȯr-ˈta-lə-tē\ (1) The quality or state of being alive and therefore certain to die. 必死性 (2) The number of deaths that occur in a particular time or place. 死亡率

• Mortality rates were highest among those who lived closest to the plant. 住得离那家工厂最近的人群死亡率最高。

Young people tend to assume they will never die; but a person's sense of his or her *mortality* generally increases year by year, and often increases greatly after a serious accident or illness. Still, many people refuse to change behaviors that would improve their chances of living into old age. *Mortality rates* are calculated by government agencies, insurance companies, and medical researchers. *Infant mortality rates* provide a good indicator of a country's overall health; in recent years, the rates in countries like Iceland, Singapore, and Japan have been much better than in the U. S.

年轻人往往以为他们永远不会死;但人们对自己的必死之感一般会逐年增加,遭遇了严重事故或得过一场大病之后，这种感觉会大大增加。尽管如此，很多人还是不愿意养成能提升长寿概率的生活习惯。死亡率是由政府机构、保险公司和医学研究人员来计算的。婴儿死亡率是衡量一个国家整体健康水平的很好的指标；近年来，冰岛、新加坡和日本等国家的死亡率远远低于美国。

moribund \ˈmȯr-ə-bənd\ （1）In the process of dying or approaching death. 临近死亡的（2）Inactive or becoming outmoded. 停滞的，过时的

- Church attendance in Britain has fallen in recent years, but no one would say the Anglican church is moribund. 近年来，英国的教堂出席率有所下降，但没人会说英国国教已行将消亡。

Moribund is still sometimes used in its original literal sense of "approaching death," but it's much more often used to describe things. When the economy goes bad, we hear about moribund mills and factories and towns; the economy itself may even be called moribund. Critics may speak of the moribund state of poetry, or lament the moribund record or newspaper industry.

moribund 有时仍然表示它最初的字面意思"接近死亡的"，但它更多地用来形容某样东西。当经济不景气时，我们会听人说起，濒临倒闭的工厂以及凋敝的城镇；经济本身也可以说成是停滞不前的。批评者可能会说，诗歌停滞不前，也可能哀叹唱片业或新闻业停滞不前。

amortize \ˈa-mər-ˌtīz\ To pay off (something such as a mortgage) by making small payments over a period of time. 分期偿还

- For tax purposes, they chose to amortize most of the business's start-up costs over a three-year period. 考虑到税金问题，他们选择在三年内分期偿还这项生意的大部分启动资金。

Amortize is most common as a legal term, and many of us first come across it when we take out a mortgage or start a business. Financial officers and tax lawyers can choose how to legally amortize various types of business expenses, some of which may seem much better than others. In mortgage *amortization*, much of what you pay month by month is actually interest on the mortgage debt, especially at the beginning. So what does amortizing have to do with death? Basically, to amortize a debt means to "kill" it slowly over time.

amortize 最常用作法律术语，很多人第一次接触这个词是在办理抵押贷款或创业的时候。财务人员和税务律师可以选择如何合法地分期偿还各种类型的业务费用，其中一些似乎比其他的要好得多。在偿还抵押贷款时，你每月支付的很多钱实际上是贷款的利息，特别是在刚开始的时候。那么，分期偿还这个词与死亡有什么关系呢？从根本上讲，偿还抵押贷款就好像是在一天天慢慢地"杀死"这项债务。

mortify \ˈmȯr-tə-ˌfī\ （1）To subdue or deaden (the body) especially by self-discipline or self-inflicted pain. 约束，克制（2）To embarrass greatly. 使（某人）很尴尬

- Our 14-year-old is mortified whenever he sees us dancing, especially if any of his school friends are around. 我们家14岁的孩子一看到我们跳舞就会颇为尴尬，特别是他学校的朋友也在旁边时。

Mortify once actually meant "put to death," but no longer. Its "deaden" sense is most familiar to us in the phrase "mortifying the flesh," which refers to a custom once followed by devout Christians, who would starve themselves, deprive

MOR/
MORT

themselves of every comfort, and even whip themselves in order to subdue their bodily desires and punish themselves for their sins. But the most common use of *mortify* today is the "humiliate" sense; its connection with death is still apparent when we speak of "dying of embarrassment."

实际上，*mortify* 曾表示"杀死"的意思，但现在没有了。它的"使……死亡"之意最为我们熟知的还是出现在短语 "mortifying the flesh"(禁欲)中，这个短语所指的是虔诚的基督徒曾遵循的一个习俗，他们会忍饥挨饿，剥夺自己的一切享受，甚至鞭打自己，来抑制身体的欲望以及惩罚自己的罪恶。但 *mortify* 现在最常用来表示"使……尴尬"；当我们说 "尴尬死了"的时候，它与死亡的联系依旧很明显。

TROPH

TROPH comes from the Greek *trophe*, meaning "nourishment." This particular *troph-* root doesn't show up in many everyday English words (the *troph-* in words like *trophy*, *apostrophe*, and *catastrophe* has a different meaning), but instead tends to appear in scientific terms.

TROPH 源自希腊语 *trophe*，意思是"营养"。Troph- 这个词根并未出现在许多日常英语词语中(*troph-* 在 *trophy*、*apostrophe*、*catastrophe* 等单词中有不同的意思)，反而经常出现在科学术语中。

atrophy \ˈa-trə-fē\ (1) Gradual loss of muscle or flesh, usually because of disease or lack of use. 萎缩 (2) A decline or degeneration. 衰退或退化。

• After a month in a hospital bed, my father required a round of physical therapy to deal with his muscular atrophy. 在医院的病床上躺了一个月后，我父亲需要进行一轮理疗来治疗肌肉萎缩。

From its literal Greek roots, *atrophy* would mean basically "lack of nourishment." Although the English word doesn't usually imply any lack of food, it always refers to a wasting away. Those who have been bedridden for a period of time will notice that their muscles have *atrophied*. And muscular atrophy is a frequent result of such diseases as cancer and AIDS. We also use *atrophy* in a much more general sense. After being out of work a few years, you may find your work skills have atrophied; someone who's been living an isolated life may discover the same thing about his or her social skills; and a democracy can atrophy when its citizens cease to pay attention to how they're being governed.

从其希腊语词根来看，*atrophy* 的基本意思是"缺乏营养"。然而，这个英语单词所指的并不是缺乏食物，而是变得消瘦。卧床一段时间之后的人会注意到，their muscles have *atrophied*(他们的肌肉已经萎缩)。肌肉萎缩是癌症和艾滋病等的常见后果。我们也在更一般的意义上使用 *atrophy*。比如，失业几年后，你可能会发现你的工作技能退步了；孤独生活的人可能会发现他/她的社交技能也退步了；当民众不再关注自己如何被治理时，民主就会衰退。

hypertrophy \hī-ˈpər-trə-fē\ (1) Excessive development of an organ or part. 肥大 (2) Exaggerated growth or complexity. 过度生长

• Opponents claimed that the Defense Department, after years of being given too much money by the Congress, was now suffering from hypertrophy. 反对者声称，国防部多年来得到国会太多的拨款，现在患上了"肥大症"。

When the prefix *hyper*, "above, beyond" (see HYPER, p. 493), is joined to *-trophy*, we get the opposite of *atrophy*. An organ or part becomes *hypertrophic* when it grows so extremely that its function is affected. Muscle hypertrophy is common in men who do strength training, and is often harmless; but extreme muscle hypertrophy generally involves taking steroids, which can do great damage to the body. Hypertrophy of the heart sounds as if it might be healthy, but instead it's usually a bad sign. As the example sentence shows, *hypertrophy*, like *atrophy*, can be used in nonmedical ways as well.

前缀 *hyper* 的意思是"在……之上,超越"(参见 HYPER,第493页),与 *-trophy* 结合,构成 *atrophy* 的反义词。当某器官或身体某部位过度生长导致功能受到影响时,它就是 *hypertrophic*(肥大的)。肌肉肥大在进行力量训练的男性身上很常见,通常是无害的;但肌肉过度肥大通常是服用类固醇所致,这对身体危害很大。心脏肥大听起来好像是健康的,但通常却不是什么好征兆。如例句所示,*hypertrophy* 和 *atrophy* 一样,也可以用于非医学领域。

dystrophy \ˈdi-strə-fē\ Any of several disorders involving the nerves and muscles, especially muscular dystrophy. 营养障碍;营养不良

• The most common of the muscular dystrophies affects only males, who rarely live to the age of 40. 最常见的肌肉营养不良只见于男性,这些人很少活到40岁。

Since the prefix *dys-* means "bad" or "difficult" (see DYS, p. 110), *dystrophy* is always a negative term. Originally it meant "a condition caused by improper nutrition," but today the term is instead used for a variety of other conditions, particularly conditions that noticeably affect the muscles. Of the many types of muscular dystrophy, the best known is Duchenne's, a terrible disease that strikes about one in 3,300 males and produces severe wasting of the muscles. However, the muscular dystrophies generally affect many other organs and systems as well. And the other dystrophies, which tend to involve the eyes or hands, don't much resemble the muscular dystrophies.

前缀 *dys* 的意思是"坏的"或"困难的"(参见 DYS,第110页),因此 *dystrophy* 是一个消极的词语。它最初的含义是"由营养不良引起的疾病",但这个词语现在用于其他很多疾病,特别是明显影响到肌肉的疾病。在许多种肌肉营养不良中,最常见的是杜氏肌营养不良症,这是一种可怕的疾病,约1/3300的男性患上这种可怕的疾病,会有严重的肌肉萎缩。然而,肌肉营养不良一般也影响其他许多器官和系统。此外,还有其他的营养不良,往往涉及眼睛或手,与肌肉营养不良不太一样。

eutrophication \yü-ˌtrō-fə-ˈkā-shən\ The process by which a body of water becomes enriched in dissolved nutrients. 水体富营养化

• Local naturalists are getting worried about the increasing eutrophication they've been noticing in the lake. 当地的自然主义者注意到,那个湖泊的富营养化程度越来越高,他们对此忧心忡忡。

Eutrophication, which comes from the Greek *eutrophos*, "well-nourished" (see EU, p. 109), has become a major environmental problem. Nitrates and phosphates, especially from lawn fertilizers, run off the land into rivers and lakes, promoting the growth of algae and other plant life, which take oxygen from the water, causing the death of fish and mollusks. Cow manure, agricultural fertilizer, detergents, and human waste are often to blame as well. In the 1960s and 1970s, the eutrophication of Lake Erie advanced so extremely that it became known as the "dead lake." And many areas of the oceans worldwide—some more than 20,000 square miles in extent—have become "dead zones," where almost no life of any kind exists.

eutrophication 源自希腊语 *eutrophos*（"营养良好的"）（见 EU, 第 109 页），水体富营养化已成为一个主要的环境问题。硝酸盐和磷酸盐，尤其是来自草地肥料中的硝酸盐和磷酸盐，从陆地流入河流、湖泊，促进藻类和其他植物的生长，而这些植物从水中吸收氧气，导致鱼类和软体动物死亡。牛粪、农业肥料、洗涤剂和人类粪便也常造成水体富营养化。在 20 世纪 60 年代和 70 年代，伊利湖的富营养化发展迅速，以至于成了"死湖"。全球海洋的许多区域——约 20,000 平方英里以上——已成为"死海"，几乎没有任何生命存在。

Quizzes

A. Choose the closest definition:

1. mortality   a. deadliness   b. danger   c. disease   d. death rate
2. hypertrophy   a. excessive growth   b. low birth rate   c. increased speed   d. inadequate nutrition
3. amortize   a. bring back   b. pay down   c. make love   d. die off
4. atrophy   a. expansion   b. swelling   c. exercise   d. wasting
5. mortify   a. weaken   b. bury   c. embarrass   d. kill
6. dystrophy   a. bone development   b. muscular wasting   c. nerve growth   d. muscle therapy
7. moribund   a. deathlike   b. unhealthy   c. lethal   d. dying
8. eutrophication   a. inadequate moisture   b. excessive growth   c. loss of sunlight   d. healthy nourishment

B. Fill in each blank with the correct letter:

a. eutrophication
b. atrophy
c. hypertrophy
d. dystrophy
e. moribund
f. mortify
g. mortality
h. amortize

1. By the 1960s, most of the textile industry had moved south, and the mill town seemed _____.
2. In muscular _____, the wasting begins in the legs and advances to the arms.
3. Most people don't spend much time thinking about their _____ until they're

in their thirties or forties.

4. They should be able to _____ their mortgage completely by the time they retire.

5. Muscular _____ as extreme as that is only possible with steroids.

6. Some religious sects still engage in acts designed to _____ the flesh.

7. By then the pond had almost entirely filled in with plant life, a result of the _____ caused by the factory's discharges.

8. In the four weeks before he has the cast taken off, his muscles will _____ quite a lot.

Words from Mythology and History 源自神话和历史的词语

aeolian harp \ē-'ō-lē-ən-'härp\ A box-shaped instrument with strings that produce musical sounds when the wind blows on them. 风弦琴

• Poets have long been fascinated by the aeolian harp, the only instrument that produces music without a human performer. 诗人们长期以来都痴迷于风弦琴,这是唯一不用人类就能奏出音乐的乐器。

According to the ancient Greeks, Aeolus was the king or guardian of the winds. He lived in a cave with his many, many sons and daughters, and sent forth whatever wind Zeus asked for. When Odysseus stopped there on his way home from Troy, he received a bag of winds to fill his sails. But while he was asleep, his men, thinking it contained treasure, opened the bag and released the raging winds, which blew their ships all the way back to their starting point. An aeolian harp produces enchanting harmonies when the wind passes over it. According to Homer, it was the god Hermes who invented the harp, by having the wind blow over the dried sinews attached to the shell of a dead tortoise.

根据古希腊人的说法,Aeolus(埃奥罗斯)是风之王或风的守护神。他和自己的许多儿女住在一个山洞里,按照宙斯的要求刮风。奥德修斯从特洛伊城回家,途中停在山洞那里,他收到一袋帮他扬帆的风。但是当他睡着的时候,他的手下以为袋子里装的是财宝,就打开了袋子,狂风被释放了出来,将船一直吹回起到了旅途的起点。当风吹过时,风鸣琴就会奏出迷人的和声。根据荷马的说法,赫尔墨斯神让风吹过绑在死龟壳上干燥的肌腱,风弦琴就此诞生。

cynosure \'sī-nə-ˌshu̇r\ (1) A guide. 导游 (2) A center of attention. (关注的)焦点。

• Near the club's dance floor, a young rock star was hanging out, the cynosure of a small crowd of admirers. 俱乐部的舞池旁,有个年轻的摇滚明星待在那里,他成了一小群崇拜者关注的焦点。

In Greek *kynosoura* means "dog's tail," and in Latin *Cynosura* came to mean the constellation Ursa Minor (Little Bear)—what we usually call the Little Dipper. The first star on the dog's or bear's "tail," or the dipper's "handle," is Polaris, the North Star, long used as a guide for seamen or travelers lost on a clear night, since, unlike the other stars, it always remains in the same position in the northern sky, while the other constellations (and even the rest of its own constellation) slowly revolve around it. Since *Cynosura* also came to mean the star itself, the English *cynosure* now may mean both "guide" and "center of attention."

希腊语 *kynosoura* 的意思是"狗尾巴",而在拉丁语中,*Cynosura* 指的是小熊星座——我们通常称之为小北斗星。狗或熊的"尾巴"或北斗的"勺柄"上的第一颗星是北极星。在晴朗的夜晚,北极星很早就被迷路的海员或旅行者用来指引方向了,这是因为它和别的星星不同,总是在北方天空的同一个位置,而其他星座(甚至本星座的其他星星)则围绕它慢慢旋转。因为 *Cynosura* 也指代这颗星本身,所以英语中的 *cynosure* 现在表示"导游",或者"关注的焦点"。

laconic \lə-ˈkä-nik\   Using extremely few words. 话极少的,言简意赅的

● Action-film scripts usually seem to call for laconic leading men who avoid conversation but get the job done. 动作电影剧本需要的好像通常是话少的男主角,他们不用对话也照样能完成工作。

Ancient Sparta was located in the region of Greece known as *Laconia*, and the Greek word *lakonikos* could mean both "*Laconian*" and "Spartan." The disciplined and militaristic Spartans, the finest warriors of their time, were known for putting up with extreme conditions without complaint. So English writers who knew their ancient history came to use *laconic* to describe the habit of saying few words. Today we can refer not only to a laconic person but also to laconic wit, a laconic answer, or a laconic phrase—such as "Men of few words require few laws," uttered by a Spartan king.

古斯巴达位于古希腊一个叫拉哥尼亚的地区,希腊语 *lakonikos* 可以同时表示"拉哥尼亚人"和"斯巴达人"。纪律严明、尚武好战的斯巴达人,是当时最优秀的勇士,以忍受极端条件却毫无怨言而闻名。因此,了解其古代历史的英国作家开始用 *laconic* 来形容沉默寡言的习惯。今天,我们不仅可以说 *laconic* 的人,还可以说 *laconic* 的机智,*laconic* 的答案,或 *laconic* 的短语——比如斯巴达国王所说的"话少的人不需要法律"。

mnemonic \ni-ˈmä-nik\   Having to do with the memory; assisting the memory. 记忆的,帮助记忆的

● Sales-training courses recommend various mnemonic devices as a way of remembering peoples' names. 销售培训课程推荐大家使用各种助记方法来记忆人名。

The Greek word for memory is *mnemosyne*, and *Mnemosyne* was the goddess of memory and the mother of the Muses. So something that helps the memory is a mnemonic aid, or simply a *mnemonic*. Such traditional mnemonic devices as "Every Good Boy Does Fine" (for the notes on the lines of a musical staff with a treble clef) or the "Thirty days hath September" rhyme help to recall simple rules or complicated series that might otherwise slip away. (For extra credit, guess what "King Henry Died Drinking Chocolate Milk" or "King Philip Could Only Find Green Socks" stands for.) Notice that the first *m* isn't pronounced, unlike in other *-mne-* words such as *amnesia* and *amnesty*.

希腊语中表示记忆的单词是 *mnemosyne*,Mnemosyne(摩涅莫辛涅)是记忆女神,也是缪斯们的母亲。有助于记忆的东西被称作 mnemonic aid(助记方法),简称 *mnemonic*。有一些传统的助记方法,比如,"Every Good Boy Does Fine"(指

代五线谱高音谱号的线上音符）或童谣"Thirty days hath September",有助于回忆起简单的规则或复杂的系列,不这样记就会忘掉。（额外奖赏你一下,猜猜"King Henry Died Drinking Chocolate Milk"或者"King Philip Could Only Find Green Socks"表示什么意思吧。）请注意,第一个 m 不发音,这与含有-mne-的其他单词不同,比如 *amnesia*（健忘症）和 *amnesty*（大赦）。

platonic\ plə-ˈtä-nik \　（1）Relating to the philosopher Plato or his teachings. 柏拉图的（2）Involving a close relationship from which romance and sex are absent. 纯友谊的

● The male and female leads in sitcoms often keep their relationship platonic for the first few seasons, but romance almost always wins out in the end. 在情景喜剧的前几季中,男女主角常常保持着柏拉图式的关系,但最后,两人的爱情差不多都能修成正果。

The philosopher Plato presented his theories in a series of dramatic conversations between Socrates and other people, now called the "Platonic dialogues." Among many other important concepts, he taught that everything here on earth is a pale imitation—like a shadow—of its ideal form, and this ideal form is now often called the "platonic form." But *platonic* is probably usually seen in the phrase "platonic love." Because Socrates (through Plato) teaches that the philosophical person should turn his passion for a lover into appreciation of beauty and love of a higher power and of the universe, close but nonsexual friendship between two people who might be thought to be romantically attracted is today known as platonic love or friendship.

哲学家柏拉图通过苏格拉底和他人的一系列戏剧性对话提出了自己的理论,后世称之为"柏拉图式对话"。他教给人们许多重要的概念,其中有一点是,世间万物皆是对其理想形式的苍白模仿——就像影子一样,这种理想的形式现在常被称为"柏拉图形式"。但 *platonic* 一词可能最常见于短语"柏拉图式恋爱"中。苏格拉底（通过柏拉图）教诲道,贤明者应化情欲为对美的欣赏和对更高力量及宇宙的热爱,因此,相互爱慕之人的那种亲密但无性的友谊如今被视为柏拉图式的爱恋或友谊。

sapphic\ ˈsa-fik \　（1）Lesbian. 女同性恋的（2）Relating to a poetic verse pattern associated with Sappho. 萨福体的

● The Roman poets Catullus and Horace composed wonderful love poems in sapphic verse. 罗马诗人卡图卢斯和霍勒斯写了萨福体风格的美妙爱情诗篇。

The poet Sappho wrote poems of self-reflection but also of passion, some of it directed to the women attending the school she conducted on the Greek island of Lesbos around 600 B.C. Even though most of the poems survive only as fragments, they have been greatly admired for many centuries. They were written in an original rhythmical pattern, which has become known as sapphic verse. Later admirers, such as the Roman poets Catullus and Horace, honored her by adopting the sapphic meter for their own poetry. Because of Sappho, the island of Lesbos also gave its name to lesbianism, which writers often used to call sapphic love.

诗人萨福写了许多自我反省又充满激情的诗,其中一些写于公元前 600 年前后,写给那些在希腊莱斯博斯岛上她开设的学校上学的女性。尽管多数诗歌只存片段,但已经享誉诸多世纪。这些诗是以一种原始的韵律模式写成的,被称为萨福诗体。后世的崇拜者,如罗马诗人卡图卢斯和贺拉斯,为表敬意,将萨福诗体的韵律用于自己的诗歌中。因为萨福的原因,the island of Lesbos（莱斯博斯岛）的名字也用来命名 lesbianism（女同性恋关系）,作家们常称之为 sapphic love

（萨福式恋爱）。

Socratic \ sō-ˈkra-tik \
Having to do with the philosopher Socrates or with his teaching method, in which he systematically questioned the student in conversation in order to draw forth truths. 苏格拉底的,问答法的

- She challenges her students by using the Socratic method, requiring them to think and respond constantly in every class. 她用苏格拉底问答法激励学生,要求他们每堂课都不断思考和回应。

Socrates lived and taught in Athens in the 5th Century B. C., but left no writings behind, so all we know of him comes through the works of his disciple Plato, almost all of which claim to be accounts of Socrates' conversations with others. Today Socrates is best remembered for his method of teaching by asking increasingly difficult questions, the so-called *Socratic method*. This generally involves the use of *Socratic induction*, a way of gradually arriving at generalizations through a process of questions and answers, and *Socratic irony*, in which the teacher pretends ignorance while questioning his students skillfully to make them aware of their errors in understanding.

苏格拉底于公元前5世纪在雅典生活和教学,但没有留下任何著作,所以我们对他的了解都源自他的弟子柏拉图的著作。据说,柏拉图记录的几乎都是苏格拉底与他人的对话。今天,人们记得苏格拉底是因为他的教学方法,他会向学生提出越来越难的问题,这就是所谓的 *Socratic method*（苏格拉底教学法）。该方法常使用 *Socratic induction*（苏格拉底式诱导）,即在问答过程逐渐得出结论,还使用 *Socratic irony*（苏格拉底式反讽）,即教师假装一无所知,通过巧妙的提问,使学生意识到自己的理解错误。

solecism \ ˈsō-lə-ˌsi-zəm \
(1) A grammatical mistake in speaking or writing. 语法错误 (2) A blunder in etiquette or proper behavior. 失礼

- The poor boy committed his first solecism immediately on entering by tracking mud over the Persian rug in the dining room. 可怜的男孩一进餐厅就在波斯地毯上留下了泥印,第一次失礼了。

In ancient Asia Minor (now Turkey), there was a city called Soloi where the inhabitants spoke Greek that was full of grammatical errors. So errors in grammar, and later also small errors in formal social behavior, came to be known (at least by intellectuals) as solecisms. The British magazine *The Economist* publishes a list of solecisms to be avoided in its prose, including the use of "try and" when you mean "try to," "hone in on" when you mean "home in on," and so forth. Social solecisms, such as mentioning how inferior the wine is to someone who turns out to be the hostess's sister, are more commonly called by a French name, *faux pas*.

在古代小亚细亚（现在的土耳其）,有一个城市叫作 Soloi（索罗伊）,那里的居民说希腊语,但满是语法错误。因此,语法错误以及后来在正式社交场合的小失误,都被（至少是被知识分子）称为 solecisms。英国杂志《经济学人》刊登了一张语法错误表,上面所列的都是要避免使用的错误,比如,不要把"try to"写成"try and",不要把"home in on"写成"hone in on"等等。social solecisms（社交失礼）,比如你居然向女主人的妹妹抱怨酒有多么不好,常用法语词 *faux pas* 来代替。

UNIT 8

Quiz

Fill in each blank with the correct letter:

a. solecism
b. sapphic
c. platonic
d. Socratic
e. cynosure
f. aeolian harp
g. mnemonic
h. laconic

1. She always learns her students' names quickly by using her own _____ devices.

2. Every so often, a breeze would spring up and the _____ in the window would emit its beautiful harmonies.

3. New Yorkers tend to think of their city as the _____ of the nation.

4. The _____ method is inappropriate for normal courtroom interrogation.

5. After encountering the fifth _____ in the report, we began to lose faith in the writer.

6. Her father-in-law was _____ in her presence but extremely talkative around his son.

7. As an experiment, he had written a poem in _____ verse, but he suspected that the rhythm was more suited to Greek.

8. The dinner was good, but saying that it approached the _____ ideal of a meal was probably too much.

Review Quizzes

A. Fill in each blank with the correct letter.

a. elucidate
b. appendage
c. solecism
d. pantheism
e. comport
f. laconic
g. moribund
h. deportment
i. mortality
j. atrophy

1. After spending four years at home, she's afraid her professional skills have begun to _____.

2. Her impressive résumé doesn't _____ well with her ignorance of some basic facts about the business.

3. He can't go to a cocktail party without committing at least one _____ and offending a couple of people.

4. Like most farmers, he's fairly _____, but when he says something it's usually worth listening to.

5. For kids their age they have excellent manners, and everyone admires their _____ around adults.

6. It was a large beetle with an odd _____ coming off the top of its head.

7. The book's introduction helps _____ how the reader can make the best use of it.

8. _____ has been a common element in religious belief in the West over many centuries.

9. The newspaper has suffered declines in both advertisements and readership over the last few years and is clearly _____.

10. The _____ rates from these kinds of cancer have been going down as new treatments have been adopted.

B. Indicate whether the following pairs of words have the same or different meanings:

1. mnemonic / ideal   same ____ / different ____
2. hypertrophy / overgrowth   same ____ / different ____
3. extrapolate / project   same ____ / different ____
4. mortify / stiffen   same ____ / different ____
5. appendage / attachment   same ____ / different ____
6. cynosure / guide   same ____ / different ____
7. extrovert / champion   same ____ / different ____
8. append / attach   same ____ / different ____
9. amortize / pay down   same ____ / different ____
10. lucid / glittering   same ____ / different ____
11. atrophy / enlarge   same ____ / different ____
12. translucent / cross-lighted same ____ / different ____
13. solecism / goof   same ____ / different ____
14. pandemonium / uproar   same ____ / different ____
15. extraneous / superb   same ____ / different ____
16. lucubration / nightmare   same ____ / different ____
17. photosynthesis / reproduction same ____ / different ____
18. panacea / remedy   same ____ / different ____
19. elucidate / charm   same ____ / different ____
20. deportment / behavior   same ____ / different ____

C. Match the definition on the left to the correct word on the right:

1. question-and-answer   a. panoply
2. elementary particle of light   b. pendant
3. stop temporarily   c. sapphic
4. hanging ornament   d. comport
5. impressive display   e. translucent

6. nonsexual   f. platonic
7. behave   g. photon
8. dying   h. Socratic
9. lesbian   i. suspend
10. light-diffusing   j. moribund

UNIT 9

HER comes from the Latin verb *haerere*, meaning "to stick." Another form of the verb produces the root *hes-*, seen in such words as *adhesive*, which means basically "sticky" or "sticking," and *hesitate*, which means more or less "stuck in one place."
HER 源自拉丁语动词 *haerere*，意思是"粘着，黏附"。这个动词的另一种形式产生了词根 *hes-*，见于 *adhesive* 和 *hesitate* 这样的单词中，*adhesive* 的基本意思是"粘的"或"粘住的"，*hesitate* 或多或少有"粘在一个地方"的意思。

adherent\ad-ˈhir-ənt\ (1) Someone who follows a leader, a party, or a profession. 追随者，支持者 (2) One who believes in a particular philosophy or religion. 信徒

• The general's adherents heavily outnumbered his opponents and managed to shout them down repeatedly. 那位将军的支持者人数远远超过反对者，他们的喊声一次又一次压倒对方。

Just as tape *adheres* to paper, a person may adhere to a cause, a faith, or a belief. Thus, you may be an *adherent* of Hinduism, an adherent of environmentalism, or an adherent of the Republican Party. A plan for cutting taxes always attracts adherents easily, regardless of what the cuts may result in.
就像胶带 *adheres* to（粘到）纸上一样，某个人可能会坚持一项事业、一种信仰或一个信念。因此，你可能是印度教的信徒、环境保护主义的支持者，或者是共和党的追随者。不管减税会带来什么样的结果，减税计划总是很容易吸引支持者。

cohere\kō-ˈhir\ To hold together firmly as parts of the same mass. 黏合，连贯

• His novels never really cohere; the chapters always seem like separate short stories. 他的小说从没真正做到情节连贯，各个章节总是看起来像独立的短篇故事。

When you finish writing a paper, you may feel that it *coheres* well, since it's sharply focused and all the ideas seem to support each other. When all the soldiers in an army platoon feel like buddies, the platoon has become a *cohesive* unit. In science

• 194 •

class you may learn the difference between *cohesion* (the tendency of a chemical's molecules to stick together) and *adhesion* (the tendency of the molecules of two different substances to stick together). Water molecules tend to cohere, so water falls from the sky in drops, not as separate molecules. But water molecules also *adhere* to molecules of other substances, so raindrops will often cling to the underside of a clothesline for a while before gravity pulls them down.

写完一篇文章后,你可能会觉得它的连贯性很强,这是因为文章的中心明确,所有的想法看起来都相互支撑。军队里一个排的所有士兵都感觉像兄弟,这个排就成为 cohesive unit(有凝聚力的单位)。在科学课上,你会了解到 cohesion(内聚力,即同一化学物质的分子粘在一起的趋势)和 adhesion(附着力,即两种不同物质的分子粘在一起的趋势)的区别。水分子会凝聚起来,所以水以雨滴的形式从天而落,而不是以单个分子的形式落下。但是水分子也会 adhere(附着)在其他物质的分子上,所以雨滴会先附着在晾衣绳下面,然后才因重力而落下。

incoherent \in-kō-ˈhir-ənt\ (1) Unclear or difficult to understand. 不清楚的,不易理解的 (2) Loosely organized or inconsistent. 无条理的,不一致的。

• The police had found him in an abandoned warehouse, and they reported that he was dirty, hungry, and incoherent. 警方在一个废弃的仓库里找到了他,他们说他又脏又饿、语无伦次。

Incoherent is the opposite of *coherent*, and both commonly refer to words and thoughts. Just as *coherent* means well ordered and clear, *incoherent* means disordered and hard to follow. *Incoherence* in speech may result from emotional stress, especially anxiety or anger. Incoherence in writing may simply result from poor planning; a twelve-page term paper that isn't written until the night before it's due will generally suffer from incoherence.

incoherent 是 coherent 的反义词,通常指的都是词语和思想。正如 coherent 指的是有序的、清楚的,incoherent 指的则是无序的、不易理解的。incoherence in speech(说话条理不清)可能是情绪压力所致,尤其是焦虑或愤怒。作品条理不清可能只是计划不周所致;一篇12页的学期论文,如果直到截止日期的前一晚才撰写,通常会出现条理不清的情况。

inherent \in-ˈhir-ənt\ Part of something by nature or habit. 固有的,与生俱来的

• A guiding belief behind our Constitution is that individuals have certain inherent rights that can't be taken away. 我们宪法背后的指导思想是,人人都有某些不可剥夺的与生俱来的权利。

Inherent literally refers to something that is "stuck in" something else so firmly that they can't be separated. A plan may have an inherent flaw that will cause it to fail; a person may have inherent virtues that everyone admires. Since the flaw and the virtues can't be removed, the plan may simply have to be thrown out and the person will remain virtuous forever.

inherent 的字面意是某个东西被紧紧地"卡在"另一东西中,无法分开。比如,某项计划可能因为有内在的缺陷而失败;某个人可能有天生的美德,人人都很羡慕。因为这样的缺陷和美德是无法消除的,所以该计划可能不得不被抛弃,而这个人的美德将永远保持下去。

FUG comes from the Latin verb *fugere*, meaning "to flee or escape." Thus, a *refugee* flees from some threat or danger, while a *fugitive* is usually fleeing from the law.

FUG 源自拉丁语动词 *fugere*，意思是"逃跑或逃走"。因此，*refugee*（难民）要逃避某种威胁或危险，而 *fugitive*（逃亡者）通常逃避法律。

centrifugal\sen-ˈtri-fyu̇-gəl\ Moving outward from a center or central focus. 离心的

• Their favorite carnival ride was the Round-up, in which centrifugal force flattened them against the outer wall of a rapidly spinning cage. 他们在游乐场最喜欢乘坐"聚拢转圈"，在离心力的作用下，身体平贴在快速旋转的笼子的外壁上。

Centrifugal force is what keeps a string with a ball on the end taut when you whirl it around. A *centrifuge* is a machine that uses centrifugal force. At the end of a washing machine's cycle, it becomes a weak and simple centrifuge as it whirls the water out of your clothes. Centrifuges hundreds of thousands of times as powerful are essential to nuclear technology and drug manufacturing. Part of an astronaut's training occurs in a centrifuge that generates force equal to several times the force of gravity (about like a washing machine) to get them used to the forces they'll encounter in a real space mission.

旋转一根头上连着小球的绳子，在离心力的作用下，绳子会一直绷紧。*centrifuge*（离心机）利用的就是离心力。在洗衣机整个工作的最后一步，水从衣服里甩出来，这时的洗衣机就成了一个简单的小功率离心机。而数十万倍速的离心机对核技术和药品生产来说至关重要。宇航员有一部分训练是在离心机中进行的，该机产生的力量是地球引力的数倍（大致相当于洗衣机），这样做是为了让宇航员能习惯在真实航天任务会遇到的那种力量。

refuge\ˈre-ˌfyüj\ Shelter or protection from danger or distress, or a place that provides shelter or protection. 保护，庇护，庇护所

• Caught in a storm by surprise, they took refuge in an abandoned barn. 他们突遭暴风雨，躲避在一个废弃的谷仓里。

The *re-* in *refuge* means basically "back" or "backward" rather than "again" (see RE, p. 683); thus, a *refugee* is someone who is "fleeing backward." *Refuge* tends to appear with certain other words: you generally "seek refuge," "take refuge," or "find refuge." Religion may be a refuge from the woes of your life; a beautiful park may be a refuge from the noise of the city; and your bedroom may be a refuge from the madness of your family.

refuge 的 *re-* 基本意思是"后退"或"向后"，而不是"再次"（参见 RE，第 683 页）；因此，*refugee*（难民）就是"向后逃跑"的人。*refuge* 往往与一些特定的词连用，比如你一般会"seek refuge""take refuge"或"find refuge"。宗教可以是你逃避生活不幸的避难所；美丽的公园可以是躲避城市喧嚣的避难所；卧室可以是避开家人疯狂行为的避难所。

fugue\ˈfyüg\ A musical form in which a theme is echoed and imitated by voices or instruments that enter one after another and interweave as the piece proceeds. 赋格曲

• For his debut on the church's new organ, the organist chose a fugue by J. S.

UNIT 9

Bach. 那个风琴师选择了 J. S. 巴赫的一首赋格曲,在教堂的新风琴上进行首次公开演奏。

Bach and Handel composed many fugues for harpsichord and organ in which the various parts (or voices) seem to flee from and chase each other in an intricate dance. Each part, after it has stated the theme or melody, apparently flees from the next part, which takes up the same theme and sets off in pursuit. Simple rounds such as "Three Blind Mice" or "Row, Row, Row Your Boat" could be called fugues for children, but a true fugue can be long and extremely complex.
巴赫和亨德尔为大键琴和风琴创作了许多赋格曲,曲子的各个部分(或声部)仿佛在复杂的舞蹈中相互逃避和追逐。每个部分陈述完主旋律后,都明显逃离下一部分,而下一部分又采用同一主旋律开始追逐。"三只盲鼠"或者"划船歌"之类的简单轮唱曲可以称儿童赋格曲,但真正的赋格曲一般很长,且极为复杂。

subterfuge\\'səb-tər-ˌfyüj\\ (1) A trick designed to help conceal, escape, or evade. 诡计,花招 (2) A deceptive trick. 骗人的把戏

- The conservatives' subterfuge of funding a liberal third-party candidate in order to take votes away from the main liberal candidate almost worked that year. 那年,为了抢走那个自由派主要候选人的选票,保守党资助了一个自由派第三方候选人,这招儿几乎奏效了。

With its "flee" root, the Latin verb *subterfugere* meant "to escape or avoid." Thus, a subterfuge is a way of escaping blame, embarrassment, inconvenience—or even prison—by tricky means. The life of spies consists of an endless series of subterfuges. In the more everyday world, putting words like "heart-healthy" on junk-food packaging is a subterfuge to trick unwary shoppers. And getting a friend to call about an "emergency" in order to get out of an evening engagement is about the oldest subterfuge in the book.
因为含有意为"逃跑"的词根,拉丁语动词 *subterfugere* 的意思是"逃跑或逃避"。因此,subterfuge 是一种以狡猾的手段来逃避谴责、尴尬、不便,甚至牢狱的办法。间谍的生活里有无穷无尽的、一环套一环的诡计。而在平常的生活中,垃圾食品的包装上写上"有益心脏健康"之类的话就是欺骗粗心购物者的伎俩。为了从晚上的约会中脱身,就让朋友打电话说有"紧急情况",这是书上最老的花招了。

Quizzes

A. Fill in each blank with the correct letter:

a. cohere   e. centrifugal
b. refuge   f. adherent
c. incoherent   g. subterfuge
d. fugue   h. inherent

1. The author tries to take on so many different subjects that the book really doesn't _____ very well.

2. All the plans for the surprise party were in place except the _____ for keeping her out of the house until 6:30.

3. She had left Scientology and was now an _____ of the Unification Church.

4. Fleeing the Nazis, he had found _____ in the barn of a wealthy family in

northern Italy.

5. By the time his fever reached 105°, the boy was mumbling _____ sentences.

6. A rock tied to a string and whirled about exerts _____ force on the string.

7. Mahatma Gandhi believed goodness was _____ in humans.

8. As the last piece in the recital, she had chosen a particularly difficult _____ by Bach.

B. Choose the closest definition:

1. inherent   a. built-in   b. inherited   c. confused   d. loyal
2. fugue   a. mathematical formula   b. musical form   c. marginal figure   d. masonry foundation
3. adherent   a. sticker   b. stinker   c. follower   d. flower
4. centrifugal   a. moving upward   b. moving backward   c. moving downward   d. moving outward
5. cohere   a. control   b. react   c. pause   d. unite
6. subterfuge   a. overhead serve   b. underhanded plot   c. powerful force   d. secret supporter
7. incoherent   a. attached   b. constant   c. controlled   d. confused
8. refuge   a. starting point   b. hideout   c. goal   d. return

---

COSM

COSM comes from the Greek word for "order." Since the Greeks believed the universe was an orderly place, words in this group usually relate to the universe. So *cosmonaut* was the word for a space traveler from the former Soviet Union. (The roots of our own word, *astronaut*, suggest "star traveler" instead.) Oddly enough, *cosmetics* comes from the same root, since putting things in order is similar to decorating something—such as your face.

COSM 源自希腊语中意思是"秩序"的单词。古希腊人相信宇宙是一个有序的地方,所以下文的几个词通常和宇宙有关。比如,*cosmonaut* 指的是苏联的太空旅行者(我们用的单词是 *astronaut*,其词根让人想到的是"星际旅行者")。奇怪的是,*cosmetics*(化妆品)也源自同一个词根,这是因为,把东西有序地摆放好如同是在装饰某个东西——比如你的脸。

---

cosmos \ˈkäz-ˌmōs\ (1) The universe, especially when it is viewed as orderly and systematic. （视作有序体系的）宇宙（2）Any orderly system that is complete in itself. 任何本身完备的有序体系

• The astronomer, the biologist, and the philosopher all try in their own ways to make sense of the cosmos. 天文学家、生物学家和哲学家都尝试以自己的方式理解宇宙。

Cosmos often simply means "universe." But the word is generally used to suggest an orderly or harmonious universe, as it was originally used by Pythagoras in the 6th century B.C. Thus, a religious mystic may help put us in touch with the cosmos, and so may a physicist. The same is often true of the adjective *cosmic*: Cosmic rays (really particles rather than rays) bombard us from outer space, but cosmic questions come from human attempts to find order in the universe.

cosmos 通常指的就是"宇宙"。但这个词一般用来表示一个有序或和谐的宇宙，这也是毕达哥拉斯在公元前6世纪最早使用该词的原义。因此，宗教神秘主义者可能会帮助我们与宇宙建立联系，物理学家可能也这样。形容词 *cosmic*（宇宙的）的情况往往也是如此，比如宇宙射线（实际上是粒子而不是射线）从外太空轰击我们，但宇宙问题源自人类试图在宇宙中寻找秩序。

cosmology \käz-ˈmä-lə-jē\ （1）A theory that describes the nature of the universe. 宇宙论（2）A branch of astronomy that deals with the origin and structure of the universe. 宇宙学

• New Age teachers propose a cosmology quite unlike the traditional Jewish, Christian, or Islamic ways of viewing the universe. 新时代的教师提出了一种与传统的犹太教、基督教或伊斯兰教截然不同的宇宙论。

Most religions and cultures include some kind of cosmology to explain the nature of the universe. In modern astronomy, the leading cosmology is still the Big Bang theory, which claims that the universe began with a huge explosion that sent matter and energy spreading out in all directions. One reason why fans watch *Star Trek* is for the various cosmologies depicted in the show, including different conceptions of space, time, and the meaning of life.

多数宗教和文化都有某种宇宙论来解释宇宙的本质。在现代天文学中，首要的宇宙论仍然是大爆炸理论，该理论认为，宇宙开始于一次巨大的爆炸，将物质和能量向四面八方扩散。《星际迷航》的粉丝之所以观看这部电影，有一个原因是它所描绘的各种宇宙论，包括关于空间、时间和生命意义的不同概念。

microcosm \ˈmī-krə-ˌkä-zəm\ Something (such as a place or an event) that is seen as a small version of something much larger. 缩影

• The large hippie communes of the 1960s and 1970s were microcosms of socialist systems, with most of socialism's advantages and disadvantages. 20世纪六七十年代的大型嬉皮士公社是社会主义制度的缩影，拥有社会主义的大部分优点和缺点。

A troubled urban school can look like a microcosm of America's educational system. A company's problems may be so typical that they can represent an entire small country's economic woes "in microcosm." *Microcosm*, and especially its synonym *microcosmos*, are also sometimes used when talking about the microscopic world. The documentary film *Microcosmos* is devoted to the remarkable insect life in an ordinary meadow on a single summer's day. 陷入困境的城市学校看起来就是美国教育体系的缩影。某家公司的问题可能非常典型,是整个小国家经济困境的缩影。*microcosm*,尤其是它的同义词 *microcosmos*,有时也被用来谈论微观世界。纪录片《微观世界》展示了在一个夏日的一块普通草地上的奇妙昆虫世界。

cosmopolitan \ˌkäz-mə-ˈpä-lə-tən\   (1) Having international sophistication and experience. 四海为家的,游历世界的(2) Made up of persons, elements, or influences from many different parts of the world. 世界性的,国际化的

• New York, like most cosmopolitan cities, offers a wonderful array of restaurants featuring foods from around the world. 纽约像多数国际大都市一样,有各种各样很棒的餐厅,各国美食琳琅满目。

Since *cosmopolitan* includes the root *polit-*, from the Greek word for "citizen," someone who is cosmopolitan is a "citizen of the world." She may be able to read the morning paper in Rio de Janeiro, attend a lecture in Madrid, and assist at a refugee camp in Uganda with equal ease—and maybe all in the same week. And a city or a country that is cosmopolitan has aspects and elements that come from various countries.

cosmopolitan 含有希腊语词根 *polit-*("公民"),所以 someone who is cosmopolitan 指的是"世界公民"。她可以在巴西里约热内卢读晨报,在西班牙马德里听讲座,在乌干达难民营提供帮助,同样得心应手——这一切可能就发生在同一周之内。一个国际化的城市或国家有源自不同国家的特征和元素。

SCI

SCI comes from the Latin verb *scire*, "to know" or "to understand." The root appears in such common words as *science*, which originally meant simply "knowledge," and *conscience*, meaning "moral knowledge." And to be *conscious* is to be in a state where you are able to know or understand.

SCI 源自拉丁语动词 *scire*("知道"或"理解")。这个词根出现在像 science(科学)和 conscience(良知)这样的常用单词中,前者最初的意思就是"知识",后者的意思是"道德知识"。conscious(有意识的)指的是处于一种你能够知道或理解的状态。

conscientious\ˌkän-shē-ˈen-shəs\   (1) Governed by morality; scrupulous. 本着良心的,一丝不苟的(2) Resulting from painstaking or exact attention. 认真的,尽责的

• New employees should be especially conscientious about turning in all their assignments on time. 新员工应该格外认真负责,按时完成分配的任务。

Conscience and its adjective *conscientious* both come from a Latin verb meaning "to be aware of guilt." *Conscientious* indicates extreme care, either in observing moral laws or in performing assigned duties. A conscientious person is someone with a strong moral sense, who has feelings of guilt when he or she violates it. A conscientious worker has a sense of duty that forces him or her to do a careful job. A conscientious report shows painstaking work on the part of the writer. And a *conscientious objector* is someone who, for reasons of conscience, refuses to fight in an army.

conscience(良心)及其形容词 conscientious 都源自拉丁语中意思是"意识到有罪"的动词。conscientious 表示极其认真,无论是在遵守道德法则方面,还是在完成所分配的任务方面。conscientious person 指的是有强烈道德意识的人,在违反道德法则时,他/她有罪恶感。conscientious worker 有种迫使他/她认真工作的责任感。conscientious report 体现出作者的辛勤工作。conscientious objector 是出于良知而拒绝当兵打仗的人。

nescience\ˈne-shəns\ Lack of knowledge or awareness: ignorance. 知识或认识缺乏,无知

• About once every class period, my political-science professor would angrily denounce the nescience of the American public. 我的政治学教授大约每节课都会愤怒地谴责一次美国公众的无知。

This word, which means literally "non-knowledge," is only used by intellectuals, and the same is true of its adjective, *nescient*. We all have heard the remarkable facts: 40% of us believe that humans and dinosaurs lived on earth at the same time; 49% believe that the President can ignore the Constitution; 60% can't name the three branches of government; 75% can't find Israel on a map; and so on. Is it any wonder we Americans are sometimes called nescient?

这个词的字面意思是"无知识",只有知识分子使用,其形容词 nescient 也是如此。我们都听说过一些惊人的事实:我们有 40% 的人认为人类和恐龙在同一时间生活在地球上;49% 的人认为总统可以无视宪法;60% 的人叫不上来政府三个分支的名字;75% 的人在地图上找不到以色列,等等。我们美国人有时被称为 nescient,有什么奇怪的吗?

prescient\ˈpre-shənt\ Having or showing advance knowledge of what is going to happen. 有先见之明的,能预知未来的

• For years she had read the *Wall Street Journal* every morning, looking for prescient warnings about crashes, crises, and catastrophes on the horizon. 她多年来每天早上都读《华尔街日报》,从中找寻有关崩溃、危机和灾难即将来临的预警。

Being truly prescient would require supernatural powers. But wellinformed people may have such good judgment as to appear prescient, and *prescient* is often used to mean "having good foresight." Some newspaper columnists may seem prescient in their predictions, but we can't help suspecting that any apparent *prescience* is usually the result of leaks from people with inside knowledge.

要想真能预知未来就需要有超自然的力量。但是,消息灵通的人可能因为判断能力强,所以给人以有先见之明的样子,prescient 通常用来表示"很有远见"。有些报纸专栏作家的预测好像很有先见之明,但我们不由得要怀疑,任何明显的 prescience(预见)通常都是由知道内幕消息的人泄露所致。

unconscionable\ən-ˈkän-shə-nə-bəl\ (1) Not guided by any moral sense; unscrupulous. 昧良心的,肆无忌惮的 (2) Shockingly excessive, unreasonable, or unfair. 过度的,不合理的或不公平的

• When the facts about how the cigarette industry had lied about its practices for decades finally came out, most Americans found the behavior unconscionable. 当有关烟草行业几十年来撒谎的事实最终浮出水面时,多数美国人都认为这样做是肆无忌惮。

Something that can't be done in good *conscience* is *unconscionable*, and such acts can range from betraying a confidence to mass murder. For a five-syllable word, *unconscionable* is actually quite common. This is partly because it isn't always used very seriously; so, for example, a critic is free to call a fat new book "an unconscionable waste of trees." In law, an unconscionable contract is one that, even though it was signed by both parties, is so ridiculous that a judge will just throw it out.

不能 in good conscience（凭良心）做事情就是昧良心的，这类事情很多，从泄露秘密到大屠杀，不一而足。*unconscionable* 一词有五个音节，居然还很常用。部分原因在于，这个词的使用并不都很严肃，比如，评论家可以随意称一本厚厚的新书是"对树木的过度浪费"。在法律上，unconscionable contract 是指，这个合同尽管由双方签署，但却荒谬到连法官都想一把扔掉的地步。

Quizzes

A. Complete the analogy:

1. clever : brainy :: prescient : _____
   a. evil　　　　　b. wise　　　　　c. existing　　　　　d. painstaking
2. village : city :: microcosm : _____
   a. flea circus　　b. universe　　　c. scale model　　　d. bacteria
3. bold : shy :: cosmopolitan : _____
   a. planetary　　b. naive V　　　c. unique　　　　d. nearby
4. informed : ignorant :: conscientious : _____
   a. careful　　　b. all-seeing　　c. well-informed　　d. scientific
5. geology : earth :: cosmology : _____
   a. sophistication　b. universe　　c. explanation　　d. appearance
6. data : information :: nescience : _____
   a. wisdom　　　b. ignorance　　c. judgment　　　d. learning
7. forest : trees :: cosmos : _____
   a. stars　　　　b. earth　　　　c. orbits　　　　d. universe
8. corrupt : honest :: unconscionable : _____
   a. orderly　　　b. attractive　　c. universal　　　d. moral

B. Match the definition on the right to the correct word on the left:

1. cosmopolitan   a. having foresight
2. nescience   b. universe
3. microcosm   c. lack of knowledge
4. conscientious   d. well-traveled
5. unconscionable   e. small world
6. cosmology   f. scrupulous
7. prescient   g. inexcusable
8. cosmos   h. description of the universe

UNIT 9

JUNCT comes from the Latin verb *jungere*, meaning "to join." A *junction* is a place where roads or railways come together. A *conjunction* is a word that joins two other words or groups of words: "this *and* that," "to be *or* not to be."
JUNCT 源自拉丁语动词 *jungere*，意思是"连接"。junction（交叉点）指的是公路或铁路交会的地方。conjunction（连词）是指将两个或两组词连接起来的词语，比如"this *and* that"中的"and"，"to be *or* not to be"中的"or"。

juncture \\ˈjəŋk-chər\\ (1) An important point in a process or activity. 关键时刻，紧要关头 (2) A place where things join; junction. 接合点，交接处

• The architect claims his design for the new Islamic Museum represents a juncture of Muslim and Western culture. 那个建筑师声称，他设计的新伊斯兰博物馆代表了穆斯林文化和西方文化的结合。

The meaning of *juncture* can be entirely physical; thus, you can speak of the juncture of the turnpike and Route 116, or the juncture of the Shenandoah and Potomac Rivers. But it more often means something nonphysical. This may be a moment in time, especially a moment when important events are "crossing" ("At this critical juncture, the President called together his top security advisers"). But *juncture* also often refers to the coming together of two or more ideas, systems, styles, or fields ("These churches seem to operate at the juncture of religion and patriotism," "Her job is at the juncture of product design and marketing," etc.).
juncture 的意思可以完全是物质的；比如，这条收费高速公路和 116 号公路的交汇点、谢南多厄河和波多马克河的交汇处。但它所指的更多还是非物质的东西。可能是某一时刻，特别是重大事件发生的时刻（"在这个关键时刻，总统把他的高级安全顾问召集起来"）。但是 *juncture* 通常也指两种及以上的思想、制度、风格或领域的结合（"这些教堂的运作似乎结合了宗教和爱国主义""她的工作结合了产品设计和营销"，等等）。

adjunct \\ˈa-ˌjəŋkt\\ Something joined or added to another thing of which it is not a part. 附属物，辅助物

• All technical-school students learn that classroom instruction can be a valuable adjunct to hands-on training. 所有的技术学校学生都知道，课堂教学是实操培训的宝贵辅助手段。

With its prefix, *ad-*, meaning "to or toward," *adjunct* implies that one thing is "joined to" another. A car wash may be operated as an adjunct to a gas station. An *adjunct* professor is one who's attached to the college without being a full member of the salaried faculty. And anyone trying to expand his or her vocabulary will find that daily reading of a newspaper is a worthwhile adjunct to actual vocabulary study.
前缀 *ad-* 的意思是"朝向……"，*adjunct* 指的是某个东西"接合到"另一个东西上。洗车间可以作为加油站的附属设施运作。*adjunct* professor（兼职教授）依附于学院但不是该学院带薪教师的正式成员。尝试扩大词汇量的人会发现，每天读报对于实际的词汇学习是有价值的辅助手段。

disjunction \\dis-ˈjəŋk-shən\\ A break, separation, or sharp difference between two things. 分离，分裂，不一致

• By now she realized there was a serious disjunction between the accounts of his personal life that his two best friends were giving her. 她现在意识到,他的两个最好的朋友关于他个人生活的讲述明显不同。

A *disjunction* may be a mere lack of connection between two things, or a large gulf. There's often a huge disjunction between what people expect from computers and what they know about them, and the disjunction between a star's public image and her actual character may be just as big. We may speak of the disjunction between science and morality, between doing and telling, or between knowing and explaining. In recent years, *disjunction* seem to have been losing out to a newer synonym, the noun *disconnect*.

disjunction 指的可能只是两个事物之间缺少联系,或有巨大的鸿沟。人们对电脑的期待和对电脑的了解之间往往差距很大,某明星的公众形象和她的真实品行之间的差距或许也很大。科学与道德、行动与言语、所知与所释之间也有不一致的地方。近年来,disjunction 似乎要被一个新一些的同义词取代了,即名词 disconnect。

conjunct\kən-ˈjəŋkt\ Bound together; joined, united. 结合的、连接的

• Politics and religion were conjunct in 18th-century England, and the American colonists were intent on separating the two. 在18世纪的英国,政治和宗教是结合在一起的,而在美洲的殖民者却一心想要把两者分开。

With its prefix *con-*, meaning "with, together," *conjunct* means basically "joined together." A rather intellectual word, it has special meanings in music (referring to a smooth melodic line that doesn't skip up or down) and astronomy (referring to two stars or planets that appear next to each other), but its more general "bound together" meaning is rarer. A *conjunction* is a word (particularly *and*, *or*, or *but*) that joins together words or groups of words, and an adverb that joins two clauses or sentences (such as *so*, *however*, *meanwhile*, *therefore*, or *also*) is called a *conjunctive adverb*—or simply a *conjunct*.

前缀 con 的意思是"和……一起",所以 conjunct 的基本意思就是"结合在一起"。这是一个很知性的词语,它在音乐(指的是平稳的、没有上下跃动的旋律线)和天文学(指的是紧挨着出现的两颗恒星或行星)领域都有特殊的含义,但它更一般的含义——"绑在一起"——反而不那么常用。conjunction(连接词)是用来连接单词或词组的词(特别是 and、or 或 but)。而用来连接两个从句或句子的副词(例如 so、however、meanwhile、therefore 或 also)被称为 conjunctive adverb(连接副词)——简称为 conjunct。

PART, from the Latin word *pars*, meaning "part," comes into English most obviously in our word *part*. An *apartment* or *compartment* is part of a larger whole. The same is usually true of a *particle*.

PART 源自拉丁语单词 pars,意思是"部分",进入英语中最明显地体现于单词 part。apartment(公寓套房)或 compartment(隔间)是更大整体的部分。particle(粒子)通常也是如此。

---

bipartite\bī-ˈpär-ˌtīt\ (1) Being in two parts. 两部分的 (2) Shared by two. 双方共有的

- The report is a bipartite document, and all the important findings are in the second section. 这个报告是由两个部分组成的文件,重要的调查结果全在第二部分。

Usually a technical word, *bipartite* is common in medicine and biology. A bipartite patella, for example, is a split kneecap; many people are born with them. Many creatures have a bipartite life cycle, living life in two very distinct forms. As one example, the velella begins life as a creature that travels with thousands of others in the form of a kind of sailboat, blown across the ocean's surface with the wind; only later does each velella turn into a tiny jellyfish. *bipartite* 是技术用语,在医学和生物学领域很常见。比如,二分髌骨指的是裂开的膝盖骨,很多人天生就有。许多生物的生命周期是由两部分构成的,先后以两种截然不同的形式生活。例如,帆水母这种生物,一开始呈帆船的形式,数以万计地集体游动,随风飘过海面;后来,这种船形的生命变成了小小的水母。

impartial \im-'pär-shəl\ Fair and not biased; treating or affecting all equally. 公正的,不偏不倚的

- Representatives of labor and management agreed to have the matter decided by an impartial third party. 劳资双方的代表同意由公正的第三方来决定此事。

To be "*partial to*" or "*partial toward*" someone or something is to be somewhat biased or prejudiced, which means that a person who is partial really only sees part of the whole picture. To be *impartial* is the opposite. The United Nations sends impartial observers to monitor elections in troubled countries. We hope judges and juries will be impartial when they hand down verdicts. But grandparents aren't expected to be impartial when describing their new grandchild. to be "Partial to" or "partial toward" someone or something 指的是存有一些偏见,意思是有偏见的人所真正看到的只是总体情况的一部分。to be impartial 的意思正好相反。联合国派公正的观察员监督在陷入困境的国家举行的选举。我们希望法官和陪审团在作裁决时要保持公正。但是,人们不会期待祖父母在描述刚出生的孙子时,能够没有任何偏爱。

participle \'pär-tə-ˌsi-pəl\ A word that is formed from a verb but used like an adjective. 分词

- In the phrase "the crying child," "crying" is a present participle; in "satisfaction guaranteed," "guaranteed" is a past participle. 在短语"the crying child"中,"crying"是现在分词;在"satisfaction guaranteed"中,"guaranteed"是过去分词。

English verbs can take several basic forms, which we call their *principal parts*: the infinitive ("to move," "to speak," etc.), the past tense ("moved," "spoke"), the past participle ("moved," "spoken"), and the present participle ("moving," "speaking"). The *participles* are words that "take part" in two different word classes; that is, verb forms that can also act like adjectives ("the spoken word," "a moving experience"). A grammatical error called a *dangling participle* occurs when a sentence begins with a participle that doesn't modify the subject; in the sentence "Climbing the mountain, the cabin came in view," for example, "climbing" is a dangling participle since it doesn't modify "cabin."

英语的动词可以有几种基本形式,我们称之为 principal parts(主要变化形式);不定式(比如,"to move""to speak"等),过去时("moved""spoke"),过去分词("moved""spoken"),现在分词("moving""speaking")。分词是指那些"扮演"两个不同词类的词;即动词形式也具有形容词的功能("the spoken word" "a moving experience")。当句子开头的分词不修饰主语时,就出现一种名为 dangling participle(垂悬分词)的语法错误。比如,在"Climbing the mountain, the cabin came in view"中,"climbing"是垂悬分词,因为它没有修饰"cabin"。

partisan\ˈpär-tə-zən\ (1) A person who is strongly devoted to a particular cause or group. 坚定支持者(2) A guerrilla fighter. 游击队员

● Throughout his career on the Supreme Court, he had been a forthright partisan of the cause of free speech. 他在最高法院的整个职业生涯中,一直是自由言论事业的直言不讳的坚定支持者。

A partisan is someone who supports one *part* or *party*. Sometimes the support takes the form of military action, as when guerrilla fighters take on government forces. But *partisan* is actually most often used as an adjective, usually referring to support of a political party. so if you're accused of being too partisan, or of practicing partisan politics, it means you're mainly interested in boosting your own party and attacking the other one.

partisan 指的是支持 one *part*(一方)或 *party*(党派)的人。他们有时候是以军事行动的形式提供支持,比如游击队战士与政府军的较量。但 *partisan* 实际上常用作形容词,通常指某个政党的支持。所以,如果你被指责党派色彩太浓,或者实行党派政治,意思就是你的主要兴趣在于壮大自己的党派,抨击对方的党派。

Quizzes

A. Choose the closest definition:

1. juncture a. opening b. crossroads c. end
   d. combination
2. impartial a. fair b. biased c. accurate
   d. opinionated
3. adjunct a. warning b. addition c. disclosure
   d. difference
4. participle a. verb part b. warning c. supplement
   d. guerrilla fighter
5. conjunct a. joined b. difficult c. spread out
   d. simplified
6. bipartite a. double-edged b. twice-married
   c. two-part d. having two parties
7. disjunction a. prohibition b. break c. requirement
   d. intersection
8. partisan a. judge b. teacher c. supporter
   d. leader

B. Indicate whether the following pairs of words have the same or different meanings:

1. impart / give   same ____ / different ____
2. conjunct / split   same ____ / different ____
3. participle / verb part   same ____ / different ____
4. impartial / supportive   same ____ / different ____
5. adjunct / supplement   same ____ / different ____
6. juncture / train station   same ____ / different ____
7. partisan / fighter   same ____ / different ____
8. disjunction / connection   same ____ / different ____

MIS comes from the Latin verb *mittere*, "to send." A *missile* is something sent speeding through the air or water. And when your class is *dismissed* at the end of the day, you're sent home.

MIS 源自拉丁语动词 *mittere*，意思是"送"。*Missile*（投掷物）是发射的东西，在空中或水中快速飞行。在一天结束的时候，你的班级被 *dismissed* 的时候，你就被打发回家了。

---

mission\\'mi-shən\ (1) A task that someone is given to do, especially a military task. 任务，尤其是军事任务 (2) A task that someone considers an important duty. 使命

• She considers it her mission to prevent unwanted puppies and kittens from being born. 她认为，防止不想要的小狗小猫出生是她的任务。

Your own *mission* in life can be anything you pursue with almost religious enthusiasm. People with a mission—whether it's stopping drunk driving, keeping the town's public areas clean, increasing local recycling, or building a community center—very often succeed in really changing things.

你自己的人生 *mission*（使命）可以是以近乎宗教般的狂热追求的任何事情。肩负使命的人——无论是制止醉驾、保持城镇公共区域的清洁、增加当地的回收利用，还是建立社区中心——往往能够真正改变一些东西。

missionary\\'mi-shə-ˌner-ē\ A person undertaking a mission, and especially a religious missionary. 传教士

• North American missionaries have been working in Central America for decades, and you can find their churches in even the most remote jungle regions. 北美传教士在中美洲一直工作了几十年，甚至可以在最偏远的丛林地区找到他们的教堂。

Beginning around 1540, an order of Catholic priests known as the Jesuits began to send its members to many parts of the world to convert peoples who believed in other gods to Christianity. Wherever they went, the Catholic *missionaries* built central buildings for their religious work, and the buildings themselves became known as *missions*; many 17th-century missions in the American West and Southwest are now preserved as museums. Their foes, the Protestants, soon began sending out their own missionaries, and today Protestant missionaries are probably far more numerous. 从约 1540 年起,一个名为耶稣会的天主教牧师会开始派遣成员到世界各地,使信仰其他神的人皈依基督教。无论这些天主教传教士走到哪里,他们都会建立传教中心,传教中心的建筑本身被称为 *missions*(传教所);在美国西部和西南部,许多 17 世纪的传教所现在作为博物馆被保存下来。与耶稣会敌对的新教徒很快开始派遣自己的传教士,到了今天,新教传教士在人数上可能要多得多。

emissary \\ˈe-mə-ˌser-ē\\ Someone sent out to represent another; an agent. 使者,代理

• Now in his 70s, he had served over many years as a presidential emissary to many troubled regions of the world. 他如今 70 多岁了,曾一直担任总统特使很多年时间,去过世界上许多动乱地区。

Like *missionaries*, *emissaries* are sent on missions. However, emissaries are more likely to be representing governments, political leaders, and nonreligious institutions, and an emissary's mission is usually to negotiate or to gather information. So a president may send a trusted emissary to a war-torn region to discuss peace terms. A company's CEO may send an emissary to check out another company that they may be thinking of buying. And a politician may send out an emissary to persuade a wealthy individual to become a supporter. 就像 *missionaries*(传教士)一样,*emissaries* 也被派去执行任务。然而,使者所代表的更有可能是政府、政治领导人和非宗教机构,他们的任务通常是谈判或收集信息。因此,总统可能会派可靠的特使到饱受战争蹂躏的地区,商谈和平条款。公司的首席执行官可能会派使者去考察另一家他们想收购的公司。政治家可能会派使者去说服某个富人成为他的支持者。

transmission \\trans-ˈmi-shən\\ (1) The act or process of sending something from one point to another, especially sending electrical signals to a radio, television, computer, etc. 传送,传输 (2) The gears by which the power is passed from the engine to the axle in a motor vehicle. 传动装置

• Even in the Middle Ages, transmission of news of a ruler's death across the Asian continent could be accomplished by sun reflectors within 24 hours. 即使在中世纪,统治者的死讯也可以在 24 小时内通过太阳光反射装置传遍整个亚洲大陆。

Since *trans-* means "across" (see TRANS, p. 674), it's not hard to see the meaning of *transmission*. Disease transmission occurs when an infection passes from one living thing to another. TV signal transmission can be interrupted by tree leaves, including moving leaves and branches during a storm. Your car's transmission *transmits* the engine's power to the axle, changing the gears to keep the engine working with maximum efficiency at various speeds. 因为 *trans-* 的意思是"横过,越过"(参见 TRANS,第 674 页),所以 *transmission* 的意思不难搞懂。疾病传播指的是某种传染病从一种生物传给另一种生物。电视信号传输可能会被树叶打断,包括在暴风雨中飞舞的树枝树叶。汽车的变速器把引擎的动力 *transmits*(传递)到车轴上,改变齿轮使发动机在各种速度下都保持最大效能。

UNIT 9

PEL comes from the Latin verb *pellere*, meaning "to move or drive." So a *propeller* moves a small airplane forward. And if you *dispel* someone's fears, you "drive them away."

PEL 源自拉丁语动词 *pellere*,意思是"移动或驱动"。Propeller(螺旋桨)可以推动小飞机前进。如果你 *dispel*(消除)某人的恐惧,你就"赶走了恐惧"。

compel \kəm-ˈpel\ (1) To force (someone) to do something. 强迫,迫使 (2) To make (something) happen. 使(某事)发生

- After returning from the lecture, they felt compelled to contribute to one of the refugee relief agencies. 听完讲座回来后,他们觉得有必要向一家难民救济机构捐款。

The prefix *com-* acts as a strengthener in this word; thus, to *compel* is to drive powerfully, or force. So you may feel *compelled* to speak to a friend about his drinking, or compelled to reveal a secret in order to prevent something from happening. A *compulsion* is usually a powerful inner urge; a *compulsive* shopper or a compulsive gambler usually can't hold onto money for long. You might not want to do something unless there's a *compelling* reason; however, a compelling film is simply one that seems serious and important.

前缀 com- 在这个词中起增强作用,因此 compel 就是有力地驱赶或迫使。比如,你可能会觉得有必要和朋友谈谈他喝酒的事,或者为了防止某事发生而不得不透露一个秘密。compulsion 通常指一种有力的内心冲动;compulsive shopper(上瘾的购物者)或上瘾的赌徒手里通常放不住钱。除非有 compelling reason(令人信服的理由),否则你可能不想做某事;然而,一部 compelling 电影只是看似严肃且重要的电影。

expel \ik-ˈspel\ (1) To drive or force out. 驱赶,赶走 (2) To force to leave, usually by official action. 开除,除名

- For repeatedly ignoring important agreements over several years, the two countries were eventually expelled from the trade organization. 由于几年来一再无视重要的协议,这两个国家最终被该贸易组织除名。

To *expel* is to drive out, and its usual noun is *expulsion*. *Expel* is similar to *eject*, but *expel* suggests pushing out while *eject* suggests throwing out. Also, ejecting may only be temporary: the player ejected from a game may be back tomorrow, but the student expelled from school is probably out forever.

expel 表示驱逐出去,其常用的名词是 *expulsion*。expel 与 eject 相似,但是 expel 表示推出,而 eject 表示逐出。此外,ejecting 可能只是暂时的,比如,被逐出比赛的球员明天可能就会回来,但被学校开除的学生可能永远回不来了。

impel \im-ˈpel\ To urge or drive forward by strong moral force. 推动,促使,驱使

- As the meeting wore on without any real progress being made, she felt impelled to stand and speak. 会议沉闷地进行着,没有任何实质性的进展,她觉得有必要站起来发言。

Impel is very similar in meaning to *compel*, and often a perfect synonym, though it tends to suggest even more strongly an inner drive to do something and a greater urgency to act, especially for moral reasons. But when *impel* takes its noun and adjective forms, it changes slightly. So an *impulse*—such as "impulse buying," when you suddenly see something cool and know you've got to have it—often isn't based on anything very serious. And *impulsive* behavior in general, such as blurting out something stupid on the spur of the moment, is the kind of thing you're supposed to get over when you grow up.

  impel 与 *compel* 的意思非常相似,通常是其完美的同义词,但它往往暗示做某事的更强烈的内在动力——以及要采取行动的更大紧迫性,尤其是出于道德原因。*impel* 的名词形式和形容词形式的含义略有不同。因此,*impulse*(冲动)——比如,你突然看到一个很酷的东西,觉得必须得到它时,会"冲动购物"——常常不是因为什么严肃的事情。而一般来说,*impulsive* behavior(冲动的行为)往往是你长大后应该克服的东西,比如因一时冲动脱口而出一些蠢话。

repel \ri-ˈpel\ (1) To keep (something) out or away. 赶走,排斥 (2) To drive back. 驱除,击退

• Her son, knowing how she was repelled by rats and snakes, had started keeping them in his bedroom. 她儿子知道她非常讨厌老鼠和蛇,开始把它们放在自己的卧室里。

  Since *re-* can mean not just "again" but also "back" (see RE-, p. 684), *repel* means "drive back." *Repel* has two common adjective forms; thus, a *repellent* or *repulsive* odor may drive us into the other room. Its main noun form is *repulsion*. Magnets exhibit both attraction and repulsion, and the goal of an armed defense is the repulsion of an enemy; but we generally use *repulsion* to mean "strong dislike." In recent years, *repulse* has been increasingly used as a synonym for *repel* ("That guy repulses me").

  re- 不只表示"再次",还表示"向后"(参见 RE-,第 684 页),因此 *repel* 的意思是"驱除"。*repel* 有两种常见的形容词形式;因此,*repellent* 或 *repulsive*(令人反感的)气味可以把我们赶到另一个房间。它的主要名词形式是 *repulsion*。比如,磁铁既有吸引力又有排斥力,而武装防御的目的就是击退敌人。但是我们一般用 *repulsion* 来表示"强烈的厌恶"。近年来,*repulse*(使讨厌)越来越多地被用作 *repel* 的同义词("那个家伙让我讨厌")。

Quizzes

A. Fill in each blank with the correct letter:

a. mission   e. expel
b. missionary   f. impel
c. emissary   g. repel
d. transmission   h. compel

1. They knew that hunger would eventually _____ the grizzly to wake up.

2. An _____ was sent to the Duke with a new offer.

3. Men like him normally _____ her, so I'm surprised that she seems interested.

4. _____ of the bacteria usually occurs through close personal contact.

5. Though the Senate can _____ a member for certain crimes, it's almost never been done.

6. The only people in the village who could speak English were a Peace Corps volunteer and a _____ at the little church.

7. Don't count on conscience to _____ most people to make the right choice under such difficult circumstances.

8. Their _____ on this occasion was to convince their elderly father to surrender his driver's license.

B. Match the definition on the left to the correct word on the right：

1. force by moral pressure   a. transmission
2. evangelist   b. compel
3. drive irresistibly   c. repel
4. disgust   d. mission
5. agent   e. expel
6. sending   f. missionary
7. drive out   g. impel
8. errand   h. emissary

Words from Mythology 源自神话的词语

arachnid \ə-ˈrak-ˌnid\

A member of the class Arachnida, which principally includes animals with four pairs of legs and no antennae, such as spiders, scorpions, mites, and ticks. 蛛形纲动物

• His interest in arachnids began when, as a child, he would watch spiders build their gorgeous webs in the corners of the porch. 他还是个孩子的时候就会观看蜘蛛在门廊的角落里结起漂亮的蛛网，他对蛛形纲的动物的兴趣从那时就开始了。

The Greek word for "spider" is *arachne*, and, according to Greek mythology, the original arachnid was a girl named Arachne. A marvelous weaver, she made the mistake of claiming she was better at her craft than the goddess Athena. In a contest between the two, she angered the goddess by weaving a remarkable tapestry showing the gods behaving badly. As punishment, Athena changed Arachne into a spider, fated to spend her life weaving. With their eight legs, arachnids are easily distinguished from the six-legged insects, on which they feed by injecting digesting juices and then sucking up the liquefied remains.

希腊语中的"蜘蛛"是 arachne，根据希腊神话，最早的 arachnid 是一个叫 Arachne(阿拉克涅)的女孩。她编织技艺精湛，但她宣称自己比雅典娜女神的技艺更高明，由此铸成大错。在两人的比赛中，她织了一幅表现众神行为不端的毯子，惹怒了雅典娜。作为惩罚，雅典娜把她变成了一只蜘蛛，注定要用一生编织。蛛形纲的动物有八条腿，很容易与六条腿的昆虫区别开来。它们以昆虫为食，先对猎物注入消化液，再吸吮液化的尸体。

calliope \kə-ˈlī-ə-pē\

A musical instrument similar to an organ in which whistles are sounded by steam or compressed air. 汽笛风琴

- The town's old calliope, with its unmistakable sound, summoned them to the fair every summer. 这个小镇的老汽笛风琴的声音永远不会出错,每个夏天都把他们召唤到集市上。

To the ancient Greeks, the Muses were nine goddesses, each of whom was the spirit of one or more of the arts and sciences. Calliope was the Muse of heroic or epic poetry, who inspired poets to write such epics as the *Iliad* and the *Odyssey*. Since the lengthy epics were generally sung from beginning to end, she was responsible for a great deal of musical reciting. But she wouldn't necessarily have approved of having her name used for the hooting organlike instrument that was invented in America around 1855. Calliopes gave a festive air to the great showboats that floated up and down the Mississippi and Ohio Rivers giving theatrical performances; the loudest could supposedly be heard eight miles away, attracting customers from all around. Today they are mostly heard on merry-go-rounds and at circuses. 古希腊人认为,缪斯女神有九位,每一位女神都代表了一种或多种艺术和科学。Calliope(卡利俄珀)是英雄诗或史诗的缪斯女神,她给诗人们以灵感,从而创作出诸如《伊利亚特》《奥德赛》之类的史诗。由于长篇史诗一般从头唱到尾,她承担大量的演唱工作。但她并不一定会赞成用自己名字命名那种发出汽笛声的、像风琴的乐器,那种乐器是1855年左右在美国发明。汽笛风琴为来往于密西西比河和俄亥俄河上提供戏剧表演的大型演艺船增添了节日的气氛。据说,汽笛风琴的声音可以传出八英里以外,吸引四面八方的来客。今天,人们通常能在旋转木马和马戏场上听到这种乐器。

dryad \ˈdrī-əd\   A wood nymph. 树神,林中仙女

- The ancient Greeks' love of trees can be seen in their belief that every tree contained a dryad, which died when the tree was cut. 古希腊人对树木的喜爱可以从他们的信仰中看出来,他们相信每棵树上都有一个仙女,树被砍掉,仙女就死了。

The term *dryad* comes from the Greek word for "oak tree." As the Greeks saw it, every tree (not only oaks) had a spirit. The best known of the dryads was Daphne. The beautiful daughter of a river god, she was desired by the god Apollo; as he was about to capture her, she prayed to her father to save her, and he transformed her into a laurel tree. In her honor, Apollo commanded that the poet who won the highest prize every year be crowned with a laurel wreath. The Greeks' respect for trees unfortunately failed to keep Greece's forests from shrinking greatly over the centuries, and those that remain produce little wood of good quality. *Dryad* 一词源自意思是"橡树"的希腊语单词。希腊人认为,每棵树(不仅是橡树)都有一个精灵。最出名的树精是达芙妮(Daphne)。她是一个河神的漂亮女儿,受到阿波罗神的追求;在快要被阿波罗抓住的时候,她祈祷父亲施救,被父亲变成了一棵月桂树。阿波罗下令,每年获得最高奖的诗人戴上月桂花环,以此来纪念她。不幸的是,希腊人对树木的尊重也没能阻止希腊森林在过去几个世纪以来大幅减少,而保留下来的那些森林几乎没有生产出优质木材。

fauna \ˈfȯ-nə\   Animal life, especially the animals that live naturally in a given area or environment. 动物群

- The larger fauna of the county include coyotes, black bear, deer, moose, wild turkey, hawks, and vultures. 那个县的大动物群有郊狼、黑熊、鹿、驼鹿、野火鸡、鹰和秃鹫等。

Faunus and Fauna were the Roman woodland god and goddess for whom animals were a particular concern. Faunus was the Roman equivalent of the Greek god Pan, and like Pan, he had goats' legs. Their goat-legged helpers, called *fauns*, were known for their love of pleasure and mischief. The fauna of a continent are often very similar across a broad east-west band; from north to south, however, they may vary greatly.

Faunus(福纳斯)和Fauna(福纳)是罗马的森林男神和女神,他们特别关心动物。福纳斯在罗马神话里相当于古希腊的潘神,他和潘神一样也有山羊腿。他们的帮手 *fauns*(农牧神)也长着山羊腿,以贪图享乐、爱玩恶作剧而出名。一个大陆上的动物群在宽阔的东西地带十分相似,但南北地带则差异巨大。

flora\ˈflȯr-ə\ Plant life, especially the flowering plants that live naturally in a specific area or environment. 植物群

● Scientists are busily identifying the flora of the Amazon rain forest before the rapid expansion of commercial interests consumes it. 趁着亚马孙雨林还没有因商业利益的迅速扩张而被吞噬,科学家们正忙着鉴别其植物群。

Flora means "flower" in Latin, and Flora was the Roman goddess of spring and flowering plants, especially wildflowers and plants not raised for food. She was shown as a beautiful young woman in a long, flowing dress with flowers in her hair, strewing flowers over the earth. English preserves her name in such words as *floral*, *floret*, and *flourish*. A region's flora may range from tiny violets to towering trees. The common phrase "flora and fauna" covers just about every visible living thing.

Flora 在拉丁语中的意思是"花", Flora(芙罗拉)是罗马神话里的女神,代表春天和开花的植物,尤其是野花和非食用的植物。芙罗拉以年轻貌美的女子形象示人,身穿飘逸的长裙,头发上插着鲜花,她把鲜花撒满大地。在英语中,芙罗拉的名字保留在"flower""floret"和"flourish"等单词中。某一地区的植物群种类可能很多,从小小的紫罗兰到参天大树。"flora and fauna"(动植物群)这个常用短语几乎涵盖了所有看得见的生物。

herculean\ˌhər-kyu̇-ˈlē-ən\ (1) Extremely strong. 非常强大的 (2) Extremely extensive, intense, or difficult. 极其广泛的、激烈的或艰巨的。

● Accomplishing all the things he promised during the presidential campaign will be a herculean task. 要兑现他在总统竞选期间的全部承诺将是十分艰巨的任务。

The hero Hercules, son of the god Zeus by a human mother, was famous for his superhuman strength. To pacify the wrath of the god Apollo, he was forced to perform twelve enormously difficult tasks, or "labors." These ranged from descending into the underworld to bring back the terrifying dog that guarded its entrance to destroying the many-headed monster called the Hydra. Any job or task that's extremely difficult or calls for enormous strength is therefore called *herculean*.

英雄 Hercules(赫拉克勒斯)是宙斯的儿子,母亲是人类,他以超人的力量而出名。为了平息阿波罗神的愤怒,他被迫执行了十二项极其艰巨的任务。从潜入地下世界,把守卫入口的可怕的狗带回来,再到消灭名为九头蛇的多头怪兽,不一而足。因此,任何极其困难或需要巨大力量的工作或任务都被称为 herculean。

Pandora's box\pan-ˈdȯr-əz-ˈbäks\ A source of many troubles. 潘多拉之盒,灾难之源

● In a thundering speech, he predicted that, if the bill was passed, the new policy would open a Pandora's box of economic problems. 他在一个令人震惊的演讲中预测道，如果该法案获得通过，这项新政策将打开经济问题的潘多拉之盒。

The god Prometheus stole fire from heaven to give to the human race, which originally consisted only of men. To punish humanity, the other gods created the first woman, the beautiful Pandora. As a gift, Zeus gave her a box, which she was told never to open. However, as soon as he was out of sight she took off the lid, and out swarmed all the troubles of the world, never to be recaptured. Only Hope was left in the box, stuck under the lid. Anything that looks ordinary but may produce unpredictable harmful results can thus be called a Pandora's box. Prometheus(普罗米修斯)神窃走了天火并带给了最初只有男人的人类。为了惩罚人类，其他的神创造了第一个女人，漂亮的Pandora(潘多拉)。宙斯送给她一个盒子作为礼物，告诉她永远不要打开。然而，宙斯刚离开，她就打开了盒盖，世上所有的烦恼都蜂拥而出，再也没有回来，只剩下希望被盖在盒子里。有些东西看起来很普通却可能产生难以预测的有害结果，任何这样的东西都可以被称为潘多拉之盒。

Scylla and Charybdis \ˈsi-lə-and-kə-ˈrib-dəs\ Two equally dangerous alternatives. 左右为难，进退两难

• Doctors and patients who need to calculate the ideal dosage of the medication, knowing how it can trigger a different dangerous condition, often feel caught between Scylla and Charybdis. 医生和病人需要计算药物的理想剂量，他们知道，一不小心就会引发不同的危险状况，因此常常感到左右为难。

The Strait of Messina is the narrow passage between the island of Sicily and the "toe" of Italy's "boot." In Greek mythology, two monsters hovered on either side of the strait. Scylla, a female monster with six snake-like heads, each with pointed teeth, barked like a dog from the rocks on the Italian side. Charybdis, on the Sicilian side, caused a whirlpool by swallowing the waters of the sea three times a day. When Odysseus attempted to sail between them, he encountered disaster on both sides. Being caught between Scylla and Charybdis is a lot like being between a rock and a hard place. 墨西拿海峡是西西里岛和意大利"靴尖"之间的狭窄通道。在古希腊神话中，有两个怪物各据海峡一侧。Scylla(锡拉)是一只雌怪，有六个蛇头，每个蛇头都有尖利的牙齿。它盘踞在意大利一侧的岩石上，像狗一样狂吠。Charybdis(喀里布底斯)居西西里岛一侧，一天三次吞下海水，形成漩涡。当奥德修斯尝试在他们之间航行时，遭遇到了来自墨西拿海峡两侧的灾难。夹在锡拉和喀里布底斯之间，就像夹在岩石和坚硬的地方之间一样让人左右为难。

Quiz

Complete the analogy:

1. hobgoblin : imp :: dryad : _____
   a. moth　　　　　b. oak tree　　　　c. nymph　　　　d. dragonfly
2. difficult : simple :: herculean : _____
   a. intense　　　　b. easy　　　　　　c. mammoth　　　d. strong
3. wrath : anger :: Scylla and Charybdis : _____

a. rage   b. double peril   c. ferocity   d. whirlpools
4. piano : nightclub :: calliope : _____
   a. organ   b. circus   c. church   d. steam
5. canine : dog :: flora : _____
   a. oak trees   b. wood nymphs   c. plants   d. animals
6. reptile : snake :: arachnid : _____
   a. toad   b. salamander   c. bird   d. scorpion
7. cabinet : china :: Pandora's box : _____
   a. pleasures   b. troubles   c. taxes   d. music
8. cattle : livestock :: fauna : _____
   a. meadows   b. flowers   c. wildlife   d. trees

Review Quizzes

A. Choose the correct synonym:

1. impartial   a. fair   b. biased   c. cautious
   d. undecided
2. cosmopolitan   a. bored   b. intelligent
   c. inexperienced d. well-traveled
3. incoherent   a. clear   b. uncertain   c. confused
   d. unknown
4. mission   a. greeting   b. assignment   c. support
   d. departure
5. compel   a. drive   b. prevent   c. eject
   d. compare
6. inherent   a. local   b. inherited   c. acquired
   d. built-in
7. cosmos   a. chaos   b. order   c. universe
   d. beauty
8. impart   a. grant   b. stick   c. combine
   d. withhold
9. adjunct   a. addition   b. neighbor   c. connection
   d. acquaintance
10. repel   a. attract   b. greet   c. offend
    d. send

B. Match the definition on the right to the correct word on the left:

1. emissary   a. verb part
2. conscientious   b. cause to act

3. participle c. equal perils
4. impel d. agent
5. dryad e. foresighted
6. prescient f. attachment
7. Scylla and Charybdis g. careful
8. subterfuge h. very difficult
9. herculean i. trick
10. adjunct j. tree spirit

C. Fill in each blank with the correct letter:

a. adherent f. flora
b. centrifugal g. expel
c. conscientious h. prescient
d. arachnid i. disjunction
e. transmission j. subterfuge

1. He's no longer really an _____ of that economic philosophy.

2. The most successful stockbrokers have the reputation of being almost eerily _____ .

3. Most philosophers see no _____ between science and morality.

4. _____ force keeps roller-coaster cars from crashing to the ground.

5. _____ of electric power over long distances always involves considerable losses.

6. Unlike the spiders, the _____ we call the daddy longlegs has no waist.

7. The archerfish can _____ sudden jets of water at insects, knocking them into the lake or river.

8. She won praise for her _____ handling of details.

9. He always used to be able to get hold of Grateful Dead tickets by some kind of _____ .

10. The _____ of the West Creek Valley includes at least a dozen rare species.

UNIT 10

PUT comes from the Latin verb *putare*, meaning "to think, consider, or believe." So, for example, a *reputation* is what others think of you. But when the root shows up in such words as *compute*, *dispute*, and *deputy*, its meaning is harder to trace.
PUT 源自拉丁语动词 *putare*，意思是"认为、考虑或相信"。例如，*reputation*（名声）指的是别人对你的看法。但当这个词根出现在 *compute*（计算）、*dispute*（争论）、*deputy*（代理）等词语中时，其含义就比较难追溯了。

reputed \ri-ˈpyü-təd\ Believed to be a certain way by popular opinion. 据说的，号称的，普遍认为的

• The 15th-century prince Vlad the Impaler is reputed to have inspired the character Dracula, though in fact, evil though Vlad was, Dracula's creator only borrowed his nickname. 人们普遍认为，15世纪的王子穿刺王伏勒德是德古拉这个角色的灵感来源，尽管伏勒德也很邪恶，但德古拉的创造者只是借用了他的绰号。

Reputed is used constantly today by reporters, and almost always to describe suspected criminals—"the reputed mobster," "the reputed drug kingpin," "the reputed gang leader," etc. But the word shouldn't be left to journalists; your elderly aunt may, for instance, be reputed to have made a large fortune in oil, or to have had four husbands who all died mysteriously. *Reputed* is easy to confuse with *reputable*, and they used to mean the same thing—that is, "having a good reputation"—but it's become rare to hear *reputed* used with that meaning today.
如今，*reputed* 一词经常为记者所使用，几乎总是用来描述犯罪嫌疑人——"公认的匪徒""公认的毒枭""公认的黑帮头目"等等。但这个词不应该只为记者所用。比如，据说你那上了年纪的姑母在石油上大赚了一笔，或者说她有四个丈夫都死得很神秘。*reputed* 和 *reputable* 很容易混淆，它们以前表示相同的东西——即"有好名声"——但现在很少听到 *reputed* 再用于这个含义了。

disrepute \ˌdis-ri-ˈpyüt\ Loss or lack of good reputation; disgrace. 名誉丧失，耻辱

• The family had fallen into disrepute after the conviction and imprisonment of his father and uncle. 在他的父亲和叔叔被定罪下狱之后，这家人已经声誉丧失了。

A *reputation* can be easy to lose, and someone who is no longer respectable may eventually find he's become genuinely *disreputable*—the kind of person that almost no one wants to be seen with. Disrepute isn't only for individuals: A company may fall into disrepute as a result of news stories about its products' defects; drug scandals have brought entire sports into disrepute; and a scientific theory may fall into disrepute as a result of new discoveries.

reputation（声誉）很容易丧失，某个人不再受尊敬，他可能最终会发现自己真正是 *disreputable*（声名狼藉的）——这类人让别人觉得羞与为伍。声誉受损不仅仅是个人的问题：某家公司可能会因其产品缺陷的新闻报道而丧失声誉；毒品丑闻使整个体育运动丧失声誉了；某个科学理论可能因新的发现而名声扫地。

impute \im-'pyüt\ To attribute. 归咎于，归因于

- The British imputed motives of piracy to American ships trying to prevent them from interfering with American trade during the War of 1812. 1812年战争期间，一些美国船只试图阻止英国妨碍对美贸易，英国人就指责他们有海上劫掠动机。

Imputing something to someone (or something) usually means observing something invisible in that person (or thing). We may impute meaning to a play or novel, or to a casual remark by a friend, that was never intended. Many of us like to impute bad motives to others, while always regarding our own motives as pure. In tax law, imputed income is something that isn't actual money but might as well be—for example, the free use of a car lent to you by your employer.

将某物归因于某人（或物）通常指的是，注意到那个人（或物）身上看不见的东西。我们可以把某个用意加之于某个戏剧或小说，或加之于某个朋友无意中说的话。许多人喜欢把不好的动机加之于他人，而总是认为自己的动机很纯洁。在税法中，imputed income（推算收入）指的不是实际的钱，但很可能是——比如雇主免费借给你使用的汽车。

putative \'pyü-tə-tiv\ Generally supposed; assumed to exist. 公认的，假定的，推定的

- To strengthen the case for the defense, a putative expert took the stand. 为了加强辩方的力量，一位公认的专家出庭作证。

Putative is almost always used to express doubt or skepticism about a common belief. Thus, Tintagel Castle in Cornwall, a picturesque ruin, is the putative fortress of the medieval King Arthur. The residents of New York City are *putatively* chic, neurotic, rude, and dangerous. And cable TV is full of putative experts, who often turn out not to have much knowledge of the subjects they're talking about.

putative 几乎总是用来表达对某一普遍看法的怀疑。比如，康沃尔有个风景如画的廷塔格尔城堡废墟，被说成是中世纪亚瑟王的堡垒。纽约市的居民 are *putatively* chic（被推定为时尚）、神经质、粗鲁、危险。有线电视上有很多被认为是专家的人，事实表明，他们往往对所谈话题知之甚少。

LOG, from the Greek word *logos*, meaning "word," "speech," or "reason," is found particularly in English words that end in *-logy* and *-logue*. The ending *-logy* often means "the study of"; so, for instance, *biology* is the study of life, and *anthropology* is the study of humans. And *-logue* usually indicates a type of discussion; thus, *dialogue* is conversation between two people or groups, and an *epilogue* is an author's last words on a subject. But exceptions aren't hard to find.

LOG 源自希腊语单词 logos，意为"词""说话"或"推理"，尤其出现在以-logy 和-logue 结尾的英语单词中。词尾-logy 常指"对……的研究"，例如，biology(生物学)是对生命的研究，anthropology(人类学)是对人类的研究。词尾-logue 通常表示某类讨论；因此，dialogue(对话)是两个或两组人之间的对话，epilogue(结语)是作者就某个话题最后所说的话。但例外的情况不难找到。

physiology \ˌfi-zē-ˈä-lə-jē\ (1) A branch of biology dealing with the processes and activities by which living things, tissues, and cells function. 生理学 (2) The life processes and activities of a living thing or any of its parts. 生理，生理机能

• For students planning to go to medical school, the university's most popular major is Human Physiology. 对于打算上医学院的学生来说，这所大学最受欢迎的专业是人体生理学。

The Latin root *physio-* generally means "physical," so human physiology deals with just about everything that keeps us alive and working, and other physiology specialties do the same for other animals and for plants. To do anything serious in the field of health, you've obviously got to know how the body's organs and cells function normally. Physiology used to be considered separately from anatomy, which focuses on the body's structures; however, it's now known that structure and function can't easily be separated in a scientific way, so "anatomy and physiology" are often spoken of in the same breath.

拉丁词根 physio 一般表示"生理的"，因此，人体生理学研究的是一切维持我们生存和工作的东西，其他的生理学专业亦如此，只是研究对象换成了其他动物和植物。要在保健领域做些严肃的事情，你显然必须知道身体的器官和细胞是如何正常工作的。生理学以前被看做与解剖学是分开的，后者关注的是身体的结构。但现在我们知道，结构和功能不能用科学的方法轻易分开，所以，"解剖学和生理学"经常相提并论。

methodology \ˌme-thə-ˈdä-lə-jē\ A set of methods or rules followed in a science or field. 方法，规则

• Some researchers claimed that Dr. Keller's methodology was sloppy and had led to unreliable conclusions. 有些研究人员声称，凯勒博士的方法很随意，导致了不可靠的结论。

The methodology employed in an experiment is essential to its success, and bad methodology has spoiled thousands of research projects. So whenever a piece of research is published in a scientific or medical journal, the researchers always carefully describe their methodology; otherwise, other scientists couldn't possibly judge the quality of what they've done.

实验方法对实验的成功至关重要，糟糕的方法已经毁掉了成千上万的研究项目。因此，在科学或医学杂志上发表研究成果时，研究人员总是仔细地描述他们的研究方法；否则，其他科学家就无法判断成果的质量。

ideology \ˌī-dē-ˈä-lə-jē\ The set of ideas and beliefs of a group or political

party. 思想(体系)，意识形态

- By the time she turned 19, she realized she no longer believed in her family's political ideology. 到了19岁时，她意识到自己不再相信家人的政治意识形态。

The root *ideo-*, as you might guess, means "idea." Ideas and theories about human behavior can always be carried too far, since such behavior is very hard to pin down. So *ideological* thinkers—people who come up with large theories about how the world works and try to explain everything (and maybe even predict the future) according to those theories—are almost always disappointed, sooner or later, to find that it doesn't really work out. A person intensely devoted to a set of political ideas or theories can be called an *ideologue*—a translation of the French *idéologue*, a word actually coined by Napoleon as a label for those political thinkers full of ideas he had no use for.

你可能猜到了，词根 *ideo* 的意思是"想法"。关于人类行为的想法和理论总是有点儿过头，因为这些行为很难说清楚。因此，*ideological*（意识形态的）思想家们——提出关于世界运作的大理论，并试图以此解释一切（甚至预测未来）的那些人——几乎早晚都会失望地发现，这些理论不能真正奏效。对一套政治思想或理论非常投入的人可以称为 *ideologue*（空想家）——这是从法语 *idéologue* 翻译过来的词，而这个法语词竟然是拿破仑所造的，用来称呼那些有满脑子思想但对他都无用的政治思想家。

LOG

cardiology \ˌkär-dē-ˈä-lə-jē\ The study of the heart and its action and diseases. 心脏病学

- After his heart attack, he actually bought himself a cardiology textbook and set about learning everything he could about his unreliable organ. 在心脏病发作后，他竟买了本心脏病学课本，开始学习一切能学到的、关于自己那颗不可靠心脏的知识。

The root *card-* (closely related to *cord*—see CORD, p. 290) shows up in many heart-related words. *Cardiologists* frequently find themselves studying *cardiograms*, the charts of heart activity, made by machines called *cardiographs*. Heart attacks, and deaths caused by them, have both declined as a result of better medical emergency procedures, cholesterol-lowering drugs, and a decline in smoking. But the factors likely to actually improve heart health, such as better diets and more *cardiovascular* exercise (exercise, such as running, that improves the heart and blood vessels), haven't made any progress at all. So we should all be prepared to perform *cardiopulmonary resuscitation* (an emergency procedure done on someone whose heart has stopped, to get the heart and lungs working again).

词根 *card-*（与 *cord* 密切相关—见 CORD，第 290 页）出现在许多与心脏相关的单词中。*Cardiologists*（心脏病学家）经常研究 *cardiograms*（心电图），心电图是由 *cardiographs*（心电图仪）所记录的心脏活动图表。由于有了更好的医疗急救程序、使用降胆固醇药物以及减少吸烟，心脏病发作和心脏病致死率也有所减少。但关于能实际提升心脏健康的可能性因素的研究，比如更合理的饮食以及多做 *cardiovascular*（心血管的）运动（如跑步等能改善心脏和血管的运动），却没有任何进展。因此，我们都应该准备好实施 *cardiopulmonary resuscitation*（心肺复苏术，一种对心脏停止跳动的人进行的紧急手术，以使心肺重新工作）。

UNIT 10

Quizzes

A. Indicate whether the following pairs of words have the same or different meanings:

1. putative / supposed   same ____ / different ____
2. ideology / beliefs   same ____ / different ____
3. reputed / questioned   same ____ / different ____
4. cardiology / game theory   same ____ / different ____
5. disrepute / shame   same ____ / different ____
6. methodology / carefulness   same ____ / different ____
7. impute / compute   same ____ / different ____
8. physiology / bodybuilding   same ____ / different ____

B. Choose the closest definition:

1. methodology   a. endurance   b. patience   c. authority
   d. system
2. impute   a. imply   b. revise   c. attribute
   d. defy
3. reputed   a. famous   b. accused   c. determined
   d. supposed
4. ideology   a. notion   b. philosophy   c. standard
   d. concept
5. putative   a. assumed   b. appointed   c. solved
   d. ignored
6. cardiology   a. ear specialty   b. heart specialty
   c. brain specialty d. nerve specialty
7. disrepute   a. argument   b. violence   c. untruth
   d. disgrace
8. physiology   a. sports medicine b. body language
   c. study of medicine d. study of organisms

TERR comes from the Latin *terra*, "earth." A *territory* is a large expanse of land. *Terra firma* is Latin for "firm ground" as opposed to the swaying seas. A *terrace* is a leveled area, often one created for farming on a sloping hill. And the French word for potato, *pomme de terre*, means literally "apple of the earth."

TERR 源自拉丁语 *terra*,意思是"地"。*territory*(领土)是一大片土地。*terra firma* 是拉丁语,表示"坚实的土地",与摇摆的海洋形成对照。*terrace*(梯田)是一块平整好的地方,通常在山坡上,用于耕种。而表示土豆的法语单词是 *pomme de terre*,它的字面意思是"地下的苹果"。

parterre\pär-'ter\ (1) A decorative garden with paths between the beds of plants. 花坛，花圃 (2) The back area of the ground floor of a theater, often under the balcony. （尤指剧院楼厅底下的）正厅后座

• The city's park boasts a beautiful parterre with many varieties of roses. 这个城市公园有一个美丽的花坛，里面有很多种类的玫瑰。

Parterre comes to English by way of French, where it means "on the ground." And in the early years of the theater, the parterre was truly on the ground. In Shakespeare's day, an English theater's parterre was the cheap standing-room area right in front of the stage, normally filled with rowdy spectators. The original idea of the French parterre garden, with its carefully designed plots and walkways, was to present an artistic pattern when seen from above—from a balcony, a raised terrace, or the top of an outdoor staircase. English gardeners responded with garden designs that tried to make their viewers half-forget that they were seeing something created by humans rather than untamed nature itself.

parterre 由法语传入英语，法语中的意思是"在地上"。早期剧院的 parterre 确实是在地面上。在莎士比亚时代，英国剧院的 parterre 指的是舞台正前方的廉价站立区域，往往挤满了吵吵嚷嚷的观众。法国花坛花园有精心设计的小块花园和人行道，这种设计的最初想法是，从上方——比如从阳台、露台或室外楼梯的顶部——俯瞰整个花园要呈现出某种艺术图案。作为回应，英国园丁设计的花园，尽量让观赏者在一定程度上忘记自己看到的是人类创造的东西，而不是未驯服的大自然本身。

subterranean\ˌsəb-tə-'rā-nē-ən\ Underground. 地下的

• In Carlsbad Caverns National Park there is an astonishing subterranean chamber over half a mile long. 在卡尔斯巴德洞穴国家公园里，有一个让人十分吃惊的地下洞穴，长度超过半英里。

A tunnel is a subterranean road or pathway, and a subway is a subterranean railway. The subterranean vaults at Fort Knox hold billions of dollars of gold reserves. Subterranean reservoirs called *aquifers* are tapped for water; in places where the pressure on the subterranean water is great enough, a hole drilled in the ground will bring it bubbling to the surface.

隧道是地下道路，地铁是地下铁路。诺克斯堡的地下金库拥有价值数十亿美元的黄金储备。地下蓄水层被称为 *aquifers*，可用来取水。在地下水压力足够大的地方，钻一个洞，水就会汩汩冒出地面。

terrarium\tə-'rer-ē-əm\ An enclosure, usually transparent, with a layer of dirt in the bottom in which plants and sometimes small animals are kept indoors. 动植物培养箱

• When no one was watching, they dropped their snake in the fifth-grade terrarium, and then waited in the hall to hear the screams. 他们趁没人注意把蛇扔进五年级的动植物培养箱，然后就在大厅里等尖叫声。

The turtle exhibit at a zoo is often in the form of a terrarium, as are some of the exhibits at a plant conservatory. In an ant terrarium, elementary-school students watch the ants dig their network of tunnels as if no one were watching. Terrariums try to create conditions as close as possible to a natural habitat. A covered terrarium can often sustain itself for months on the moisture trapped inside. But creating a good terrarium requires careful control not only of humidity but also of temperature, as well as good ventilation; the lighting should include the full spectrum of sunlight as well as a day-night regulator.

动物园里的龟展常采用培养箱的形式,如同植物温室里的一些展览一样。小学生们看着蚂蚁在培养箱里旁若无人地挖洞。培养箱试图营造出尽可能接近自然栖息地的环境。一个封闭的培养箱通常可以依靠自身的水分维持数月。但是要创造一个良好培养箱需要小心控制湿度、温度,还要通风良好,照明应该包括全光谱以及昼夜调节器。

terrestrial\tə-ˈres-trē-əl\ (1) Having to do with Earth or its inhab- itants. 地球的 (2) Living or growing on land instead of in water or air. 陆生的,陆栖的

• The roadrunner, although a largely terrestrial bird, can take flight for short periods when necessary. 走鹃虽然基本上属于陆栖鸟类,但在必要的时候能短时间飞行。

Everything on or having to do with Earth can be called terrestrial. Mercury, Venus, and Mars are often called the terrestrial planets, since they are rocky balls somewhat like Earth rather than great globes of gas like Jupiter, Saturn, Uranus, and Neptune. Something *extraterrestrial* comes from beyond the earth and its atmosphere; the word can be used to describe anything "out of this world," from moon rocks to meteors. Turning to the second sense of *terrestrial*, animals are often divided into the *terrestrial* (land-living) and the *aquatic* (water-living). And sometimes terrestrial animals are contrasted with *arboreal* animals, those that live in trees.

地球上的或与地球有关的一切都可以称为 terrestrial。水星、金星和火星通常被称为类地行星,因为它们是岩石球体,有点像地球,而不是像木星、土星、天王星和海王星那样的由气体组成的大球体。something extraterrestrial(外星的东西)是源自地球和大气层之外的东西,这个词可以用来描述"这个世界之外的"任何东西,如月球岩石、流星等。再来谈谈 terrestrial 的第二个含义:动物通常分为陆栖的(生活在陆地上)和水栖的(生活在水中)。有时陆栖动物与 arboreal (树栖)动物又有不同,后者是指生活在树上的动物。

MAR

MAR, from the Latin word *mare*, meaning "sea," brings its salty tang to several English words. A *submarine* is an undersea ship. *Marine* means basically "relating to the sea," so when the Continental Marines were established back in 1775, their job was to provide on-board security on naval ships; but they immediately began to be used on land as well, and the marines have continued to operate on both land and sea ever since.

MAR 源自拉丁语 mare,意思是"海",给几个英语单词带来了海洋的气息。submarine(潜水艇)是海面下航行的船。Marine 的基本意思是"与海洋有关的",所以当大陆海军陆战队早在 1775 年成立时,他们的工作是为海军舰艇提供船上安全保障;但他们随即被用于陆地,从那以后,海军陆战队就一直在海上和陆地都开展行动。

marina\mə-ˈrē-nə\ A dock or harbor where pleasure boats can be moored securely, often with facilities offering supplies or repairs. 游艇停泊区,码头

- The coast of Florida has marinas all along it for the use of anything from flimsy sailboats to enormous yachts. 佛罗里达州沿海岸有很多码头，可以停泊从单薄的帆船到巨大的游艇等各种船只。

Marina comes straight from Latin, where it means simply "of the sea." At a modern marina, sailors can acquire whatever they need for their next excursion, or they can tie up their boats until the next weekend comes along. Some even imitate John D. MacDonald's famous detective hero Travis McGee, who lives on his boat in Miami and rarely leaves the marina. marina 直接源自拉丁语，在拉丁语中的意思就是"海洋的"。在现代化码头，水手们可以获得下一段航行需要的所有东西，他们也可以把船停泊好，直到下个周末到来。有些人甚至模仿约翰·D.麦克唐纳的著名侦探英雄特拉维斯·麦基，住在迈阿密的船上，很少离开码头。

aquamarine \\ˌä-kwə-mə-ˈrēn\\ (1) A transparent blue or bluegreen gem. 海蓝宝石 (2) A pale blue or greenish blue that is the color of clear seawater in sunlight. 海蓝色

- Many of the houses on the Italian Riviera are painted aquamarine to match the Mediterranean. 意大利里维埃拉的许多房屋被漆成海蓝色，与地中海相得益彰。

Aqua marina is Latin for "seawater," so when a lovely blue-green form of the semiprecious gem known as beryl was given an English name several centuries ago, *aquamarine* seemed appropriate. Aquamarine is the ideal color that most of us carry around in our heads when we imagine the waters that lap the shores of the Greek and Caribbean islands on a sunny day. But even the Mediterranean and the Caribbean can take on lots of other colors depending on weather conditions. aqua marina 是拉丁语，表示"海水"，因此在几个世纪前，人们在给一种被称为绿柱石的可爱的、蓝绿色准宝石起英文名时，aquamarine 看起来很合适。当我们想象在明媚的阳光下拍打着希腊和加勒比群岛海岸的海水时，海蓝色是多数人脑海中最理想的颜色。但即使是在地中海和加勒比地区，海水的颜色也会因天气状况的不同而千变万化。

mariner \\ˈmer-ə-nər\\ A seaman or sailor. 海员，水手

- When he signed on as a mariner, the young Ishmael never suspected that the ship would be pursuing a great white whale. 当年轻的以实玛利受雇成为一名水手时，他从没有想到这艘船会追逐一条大白鲸。

In Coleridge's *Rime of the Ancient Mariner*, an old seaman tells of how, by shooting a friendly albatross, he had brought storms and disaster to his ship, and how as punishment his shipmates hung the great seabird around the mariner's neck and made him wear it until it rotted. The word *mariner* has occasionally been used to mean simply "explorer," as in the famous Mariner spaceflights in the 1960s and 1970s, the first to fly close to Mars, Venus, and Mercury. 在柯勒律治的《老水手之歌》中，一个老水手讲述道，他射死了一只友好的信天翁，给船招来风暴和灾难，同船的水手把死鸟挂在他脖子上作为惩罚，直至鸟腐烂。mariner 这个词偶尔被用来指"探险家"，20世纪60年代和70年代著名的水手号探测器航天之旅用的就是此意。水手号首次接近火星、金星和水星。

UNIT 10

maritime \ˈmer-ə-ˌtim\ (1) Bordering on or having to do with the sea. 沿海的，近海的，海的 (2) Having to do with navigation or commerce on the sea. 海运的，海上贸易的

- As a result of the ocean, Canada's Maritime Provinces—New Brunswick, Nova Scotia, and Prince Edward Island—have a late spring but a mild winter. 由于海洋的原因，加拿大的沿海省份——新不伦瑞克、新斯科舍省和爱德华王子岛——春天来得迟，但冬天气候温和。

The maritime countries of Portugal and England produced many seafaring explorers during the 16th and 17th centuries, many of whom sailed under the flags of other countries. Sailing for the Spanish, Ferdinand Magellan captained the ship that was the first to circle the world, charting many new maritime routes as it went. Henry Hudson, funded by the Dutch, sailed up what we call today the Hudson River, claiming the maritime area that now includes New York City for the Netherlands.

16世纪和17世纪，海洋国家葡萄牙和英国诞生了许多航海探险家，其中有许多人在其他国家的旗帜下航行。葡萄牙人费迪南德·麦哲伦为西班牙航行，他作为船长，进行了首次环球航行，绘制了许多新的海上航线。英国人亨利·哈德逊，由荷兰人资助，沿我们现在所称的哈德逊河逆流而上，宣称荷兰对包括现在纽约市在内的海域拥有主权。

Quizzes

A. Complete the analogy:

1. crepe : pancake :: parterre : _____
   a. balcony   b. planet   c. garden   d. parachute
2. motel : motorist :: marina : _____
   a. dock   b. pier   c. sailor   d. boat
3. aquarium : water :: terrarium : _____
   a. plants   b. turtles   c. rocks   d. earth
4. urban : city :: maritime : _____
   a. beach   b. dock   c. sea   d. harbor
5. aquatic : water :: terrestrial : _____
   a. sea   b. land   c. forest   d. mountain
6. pink : red :: aquamarine : _____
   a. blue   b. watery   c. turquoise   d. yellow
7. submarine : underwater :: subterranean : _____
   a. blue   b. belowground   c. hollow   d. rumbling
8. logger : lumberjack :: mariner : _____
   a. doctor   b. lawyer   c. chief   d. sailor

B. Match the definition on the left to the correct word on the right:

1. theater area   a. mariner
2. blue-green gem   b. terrestrial
3. under the ground   c. marina

4. near the sea
5. contained habitat
6. seaman
7. small harbor
8. earthly

d. terrarium
e. maritime
f. parterre
g. subterranean
h. aquamarine

PATH

PATH comes from the Greek word *pathos*, which means "feeling" or "suffering." So a *pathetic* sight moves us to pity, and a *sympathetic* friend "feels with" you when you yourself are suffering.

PATH 源自希腊语单词 *pathos*，意思是"感受"或"受苦"。因此，*pathetic* sight（悲惨的景象）让我们深感同情。当你自己在受苦时，*sympathetic* friend（有同情心的朋友）也"感同身受"。

pathos \ˈpā-ˌthäs\ (1) An element in life or drama that produces sympathetic pity. 引起怜悯的因素 (2) An emotion of sympathetic pity. 悲悯

- The pathos of the blind child beggars she had seen in India could still keep her awake at night. 她在印度目睹了盲童乞丐的悲惨遭遇，至今依然夜不能寐。

Pathos comes directly from Greek. According to Aristotle, the persuasive power of public speaking relies on three elements: the speaker's authority, the logic of the speech, and the speech's pathos. Aristotle claims that pathos is the appeal to the audience's sense of right and wrong, and that it is this (unlike authority and logic) that moves the audience's emotions. Today we usually speak of pathos as an element in fiction, film, drama, music, or even painting, or the real-life pathos of a situation or personality. Since *pathos* is closely related to *pathetic*, it's not surprising that, like *pathetic*, *pathos* may occasionally be used a bit sarcastically.

pathos 直接源自希腊语。亚里士多德认为，公众演讲的说服力取决于三个因素：演讲者的权威性、演讲的逻辑性和演讲的悲悯性。亚里士多德称，悲悯是对观众是非感的感召，而正是这种感召（不像权威和逻辑）触动了观众的情感。今天，我们通常把悲悯作为小说、电影、戏剧、音乐，甚至绘画的一个因素来谈论，或者谈及现实生活中某一情景或性格让人哀怜。既然 *pathos* 和 *pathetic* 是密切相关的，所以就像 *pathetic* 一样，*pathos* 有时带点讽刺意味也就不足为奇了。

apathetic \ˌa-pə-ˈthe-tik\ (1) Showing or feeling little or no emotion. 冷淡的，漠然的 (2) Having no interest. 不感兴趣的，无动于衷的

- His apathetic response to the victory bewildered his friends. 他对这场胜利无动于衷，这让朋友们很不理解。

Apathy, or lack of emotion, is central to Albert Camus's famous novel *The Stranger*, in which the main character's indifference toward almost everything, including his mother's death, results in his imprisonment. We feel little *sympathy* for him, and may even feel *antipathy*, or dislike. The American voter is often called apathetic; of all the industrial democracies, only in America does half the adult population fail to vote in major elections. As you can see, *apathetic* isn't the opposite of *pathetic*, even though the *a-* that it begins with means "not" or "without."

 apathy,即冷漠,是阿尔贝·加缪著名小说《陌生人》的核心。在这部小说中,主人公对包括母亲死亡在内的几乎一切都漠不关心,这导致他被捕入狱。我们对他没有多少 *sympathy*(同情),甚至可能感到 *antipathy*,即反感。美国选民通常被称为冷漠的,在所有工业民主国家中,只有美国有一半的成年人在重大选举中不投票。*apathetic* 并不是 *pathetic*(可怜的)的反义词,尽管开头的 *a-* 意思是"不"或"没有"。

empathy \\'em-pə-thē\\   The feeling of, or the ability to feel, the emotions and sensations of another. 同情,同感,共鸣,同理心

 ● Her maternal empathy was so strong that she often seemed to be living her son's life emotionally. 她作为母亲的同理心非常强,从情绪方面讲,她似乎常常过着儿子的生活。

 In the 19th century, Charles Dickens counted on producing an *empathetic* response in his readers strong enough to make them buy the next newspaper installment of each novel. Today, when reading a novel such as *A Tale of Two Cities*, only the most hard-hearted reader could fail to feel empathy for Sidney Carton as he approaches the guillotine. One who *empathizes* suffers along with the one who feels the sensations directly. *Empathy* is similar to *sympathy*, but empathy usually suggests stronger, more instinctive feeling. So a person who feels sympathy, or pity, for victims of a war in Asia may feel empathy for a close friend going through the much smaller disaster of a divorce.

 19世纪,查尔斯·狄更斯指望读者能产生强烈的 *empathetic* response(共鸣反应),强烈到足以让他们购买刊载自己小说的下一期报纸。如今,当读到像《双城记》这样的小说时,只有最铁石心肠的读者才不会对西德尼·卡登在走向断头台时候的心情产生共鸣。one who *empathizes*(有同理心的人)会对他人的悲喜感同身受。*empathy* 与 *sympathy* 相似,但前者常表示更强、更本能的感觉。因此,对亚洲战争的受害者感到同情或怜悯的人,对其好友所经历的离婚这样的小灾小难也能感同身受。

telepathic \\ˌte-lə-ˈpa-thik\\   Involving apparent communication from one mind to another without speech or signs. 心灵感应的

 ● After ten years of marriage, their communication is virtually telepathic, and each always seems to know what the other is thinking. 经过了十年婚姻,他们之间的交流几乎是心灵感应的,似乎总能知道对方的心思。

 Since *tele-* means "distant" (see TELE, p. 452), you can see how *telepathy* means basically "feeling communicated from a distance." The word was coined around 1880, when odd psychic phenomena were being widely discussed by people hoping that researchers might find a scientific basis for what they believed they themselves were experiencing. Today, when people talk about extrasensory perception, or ESP, telepathy is usually what they're talking about. In recent years, the notion of *memes*—ideas that might somehow physically fly from brain to brain so that people all over the world might have the same idea at about the same time without any obvious communication—has been widely discussed. Even though scientists haven't been able to establish the existence of telepathy, about 30% of

Americans continue to believe in it.

*tele*的意思是"远的"（见 TELE，第 452 页），所以 *telepathy* 的基本意思是"远距离的感情交流"。这个词是在 1880 年左右创造的，当时人们普遍讨论一些奇怪的心理现象，他们希望，研究人员能够为他们相信自己正在经历的事情找到科学依据。今天，当人们谈论超感知觉（ESP）时，通常指的是心灵感应。近年来，人们广泛讨论 *memes*（模因）这一概念——即思想不知何故犹如实质地从一个人的大脑传到另一个人的大脑，于是，世界各地的人不需要有任何明显的交流，就能在几乎同一时间有了相同的想法。尽管科学家们还不能证实心灵感应的存在，但大约 30％的美国人一直相信它。

PEN/PUN

PEN/PUN comes from the Latin words *poena*, "penalty," and *punire*, "to punish." A *penalty* is, of course, a *punishment*.

PEN / PUN 源自拉丁语单词 *poena*（处罚）和 *punire*（施加处罚）。当然了，*penalty* 指的是 *punishment*。

penal \ˈpē-nəl\ Having to do with punishment or penalties, or institutions where punishment is given. 刑事的，刑罚的

• The classic novels *Les Misérables* and *The Count of Monte Cristo* portray the terrible conditions in French penal institutions in the 19th century. 经典小说《悲惨世界》和《基督山伯爵》描述了 19 世纪法国监狱的恶劣状况。

A state or country's *penal code* defines its crimes and describes its punishments. During the 18th and 19th centuries, many countries established penal colonies, where criminals were sent as punishment. Often these were unbearably severe; but it was to such colonies that some of Australia's and the United States' early white inhabitants came, and the convicts provided labor for the European settlement of these lands.

一个州或国家的 *penal code*（刑法）规定了罪行及惩罚。在 18 和 19 世纪，许多国家建立了流放地，罪犯被送到那里作为惩罚。这些流放地的环境极其恶劣；但是，澳大利亚和美国早期的白人居民去的正是这样的地方，流放的罪犯们为这些土地上的欧洲殖民地提供了劳动力。

impunity \im-ˈpyü-nə-tē\ Freedom from punishment, harm, or loss. 免受惩罚、伤害或损失

• Under the flag of truce, the soldiers crossed the field with impunity. 那些士兵们打着休战的旗子穿过战场，没有受到惩罚。

Impunity is protection from punishment, just as immunity is protection from disease. Tom Sawyer, in Mark Twain's novel, broke his Aunt Polly's rules with near impunity because he could usually sweet-talk her into forgiving him; if that failed, he had enjoyed himself so much he didn't care what *punishment* she gave him.

impunity 是免于惩罚，正如免疫是免受疾病一样。在马克·吐温的小说《汤姆·索亚》中，汤姆·索亚违反了他的波莉姨妈的规矩，却几乎不受惩罚，因为他通常可以用甜言蜜语讨得谅解；如果甜言蜜语也没用，他之前已经玩痛快了，也就不在乎她会给他什么样的 *punishment*（惩罚）。

penance\\'pe-nəns\\ An act of self-punishment or religious devotion to show sorrow or regret for sin or wrongdoing. 忏悔

- In the Middle Ages bands of pilgrims would trudge to distant holy sites as penance for their sins. 在中世纪，朝圣者为了赎罪会成群结队地跋涉到遥远的圣地。

Penance as a form of apology for a mistake can be either voluntary or ordered by someone else. Many religions include penance among the ways in which believers can show *repentance* or regret for a misdeed. The Christian season of Lent，40 days long，is traditionally a time for doing penance.

忏悔是为犯错而道歉的一种形式，可以是自愿的，也可以是别人命令的。许多宗教都将忏悔作为信徒对错误行为表达 *repentance*（悔悟）或后悔的一种方式。基督教四旬斋长达 40 天，传统上是忏悔的时间。

punitive\\'pyü-nə-tiv\\ Giving，involving，or aiming at punishment. 惩罚性的

- The least popular teachers are usually the ones with punitive attitudes，those who seem to enjoy punishing more than teaching. 最不受欢迎的老师通常是那些具有惩罚性态度的人，他们似乎喜欢惩罚学生胜过教学。

Punitive is an important word in the law. When you sue a person or company for having wronged you in some way，you normally ask for something of value equal to what you were deprived of by the other party. But when the defendant has done something particularly bad，you may also ask for *punitive damages*，money over and above the actual cost of the harm done，intended to teach the defendant a lesson. Punitive damages are fairly rare，but when they're actually granted they may be as much as four times the size of the basic damages.

punitive 是一个重要法律词汇。当你起诉某人或某公司以某种方式伤害了你时，你通常会要求得到一些与你被对方拿走的东西同等价值的东西。但当被告做了特别糟糕的事情时，你也可以要求 *punitive damages*（惩罚性赔偿），金额超过实际伤害的费用，意在给被告一个教训。惩罚性赔偿是相当罕见的，但真正给予受害者的话，其金额可能高达基本损害的四倍。

Quizzes

A. Fill in each blank with the correct letter：

a. impunity
b. apathetic
c. punitive
d. telepathic
e. empathy
f. penal
g. pathos
h. penance

1. You can't go on breaking the speed limit with _____ forever.
2. He had covered disasters before，but the _____ of the situation in Haiti was beyond description.
3. In some households，grounding is a severe form of _____ action.
4. The mildest of the federal _____ institutions are the so-called "country club" prisons.

5. The public's response to studies predicting dangerous climate change was _____ for many years.

6. As _____ during the period of Lent, Christians may give up a favorite food.

7. Almost everyone feels some _____ for a child's misery.

8. Identical twins have claimed to experience _____ communication about important events.

B. Complete the analogy:

1. passionate : emotional :: apathetic : _____
   a. caring   b. unjust   c. indifferent   d. dominant
2. fine : speeding :: penance : _____
   a. misdeed   b. credit card c. fee   d. behavior
3. humor : laughter :: pathos : _____
   a. comedy   b. ridicule   c. death   d. pity
4. immunity : sickness :: impunity : _____
   a. death   b. flood   c. punishment   d. sleep
5. kindness : cruelty :: empathy : _____
   a. pity   b. heartlessness c. emotion   d. tears
6. educational : school :: penal : _____
   a. judge   b. police   c. prison   d. sentence
7. telephonic : electric :: telepathic : _____
   a. extrasensory b. superhuman c. airborne   d. sci-fi
8. encouraging : reward :: punitive : _____
   a. damage   b. penalty   c. praise   d. jury

MATR/MATER

MATR/MATER comes from the Greek and Latin words for "mother." A *matron* is a mature woman with children. And *matrimony* is marriage itself, the traditional first step toward motherhood.

MATR / MATER 源自希腊语和拉丁语单词,表示"母"。matron 指有孩子的成熟女人。matrimony 本身是婚姻的意思,在传统上是成为母亲的第一步。

maternity \mə-ˈtər-nə-tē\ The state of being a mother; motherhood. 母亲身份

• It's quite possible that the *Mona Lisa* is a portrait of maternity, and that the painting marks the recent birth of her child Andrea. 《蒙娜丽莎》很可能是一幅为人之母者的肖像画,这幅画用来庆祝刚出生的孩子安德里亚。

Maternity is used as both a noun and an adjective. *Maternity benefits* are benefits specially provided by employers for women having babies, and usually include *maternity leave*, time off work. With maternity come *maternal* feelings, which are shown by all species of warm-blooded animals as well as a few reptiles such as crocodiles and alligators.

<small>maternity 兼做名词和形容词。maternity benefits（产妇福利/生育津贴）是雇主为孕产妇特别提供的福利，通常包括 maternity leave（产假），即不用上班。伴随 maternity 而来的是 maternal feelings（母性），所有温血动物以及鳄鱼和短吻鳄等几种爬行动物都表现出这样的感情。</small>

matriarch \ˈmā-trē-ˌärk\ A woman who controls a family, group, or government. 女家长，女族长，女政府首脑

MATR/
MATER

• Every August all the grown children and their families are summoned to the estate by the matriarch. 每年八月，所有成年的孩子和他们的家人都会被女族长召集到庄园里。

A *matriarchy* is a social unit governed by a woman or group of women. It isn't certain that a true *matriarchal* society has ever existed, so matriarchy is usually treated as an imaginative concept. But there are societies in which relatedness through women rather than men is stressed, and elements of matriarchy may be stronger in certain societies than they are in most of the Western world. And most of us can point to families in which a woman has become the dominant figure, or grande dame, or matriarch.

<small>matriarchy（母权社会）是由一个或一群女人统治的社会单位。真正的 matriarchal society（母系氏族社会）是否存在还不确定，因此母权社会通常被认为是一个想象出来的概念。但也有一些社会强调通过女性而非男性建立联系，母权制因素在某些社会中可能比在多数西方世界中更强。多数人都能指出女性为主导的家庭，这样的女性又被称为 grande dame（贵妇人），或 matriarch（女家长）。</small>

matrilineal \ˌma-trə-ˈli-nē-əl\ Based on or tracing the family through the mother. 母系的

• Many of the peoples of Ghana in Africa trace their family through matrilineal connections. 非洲加纳的许多民族都通过母系的关系来追溯他们的家庭。

A person's *lineage* is his or her *line* of ancestors. So *matrilineal* means basically "through the mother's line," just as *patrilineal* means "through the father's line." *Matrilineality* is an important concept in anthropology; among other things, it usually determines who will inherit property on a person's death. Though families that follow the European model take the father's name and are therefore patrilineal, matrilineal societies have existed around the world, including among various American Indian tribes.

<small>一个人的 lineage 是他/她的世系，所以 matrilineal 的意思基本上是"通过母系"，正如 patrilineal 是"通过父系"一样。matrilineality（母系社会）是人类学的一个重要概念，它通常决定谁将在某人死后继承财产。遵循欧洲模式的家庭以父亲的名字命名，也因此是父系的，但母系社会存在于世界各地，在各种美洲印第安部落中也有存在。</small>

matrix \ˈmā-triks\ (1) Something (such as a situation or a set of conditions) in which something else develops or forms. 母体，环境 (2) Something shaped like a pattern of lines and spaces. 线路网，矩阵

- The country's political matrix is so complex that no one who hasn't lived there could possibly understand it. 这个国家的政治环境非常复杂，没在那里生活过的人不可能理解它。

In ancient Rome, a *matrix* was a female animal kept for breeding, or a plant (sometimes called a "parent plant" or "mother plant") whose seeds were used for producing other plants. In English the word has taken on many related meanings. Mathematicians use it for a rectangular organization of numbers or symbols that can be used to make various calculations; geologists use it for the soil or rock in which a fossil is discovered, like a baby in the womb. And *matrix* was a good choice as the name of the reality in which all humans find themselves living in a famous series of science-fiction films.

在古罗马，*matrix* 指的是用于繁殖的雌性动物，或以种子繁殖的植物（有时称为"亲本植物"或"母本植物"）。这个词在英语中有许多相关的意思。数学家用它来表示数字或符号的矩阵，可以用来进行各种计算；地质学家用它来表示能在里面发现化石的土壤或岩石，这就像子宫里的胎儿一样。在著名的《黑客帝国》科幻电影系列中，用 *matrix*（母体）来命名人类发现自己生活的那个真实世界是个不错的选择。

AQU

AQU comes from *aqua*, the Latin word for "water." We keep pet fish in an *aquarium* at home or visit larger sea animals in a building with that name. Water sports such as swimming, canoeing, and sailing are sometimes called *aquatics*. In Scandinavia there's a popular drink called *aquavit*, the name coming from the Latin *aqua vitae*, "water of life"—though instead of water it mostly consists of alcohol.

AQU 源自拉丁词中表示"水"的单词 aqua。我们把宠物鱼养在家里的 *aquarium*（鱼缸，水族箱）里，或者去 *aquarium*（水族馆）参观更大的海洋动物。游泳、皮划艇和帆船等水上运动有时被称为 *aquatics*（水上运动）。在斯堪的纳维亚，有一种很受欢迎的饮料称为 *aquavit*，这个名字源自拉丁语 *aqua vitae*（生命之水）——但它并不是水，通常含有酒精。

aquaculture \ˈä-kwə-ˌkəl-chər\ The farming of plants and animals (such as kelp, fish, and shellfish) that live in the water. 水产养殖

- The farming of oysters by the Romans was an early form of aquaculture that has continued to the present day. 古罗马人的牡蛎养殖是水产养殖的早期形式，一直延续至今。

For most of the modern history of *aquaculture*, only costly fish and shellfish like salmon and shrimp were harvested. But new technologies are allowing cheaper and more efficient cultivation of fish for food, and such common fish as cod are now being farmed. Seaweeds and other algae are also being grown—for food (mostly in Asia), cattle feed, fertilizer, and experimentally as a source of energy. Aquaculture is now the world's fastest-growing form of food production.

在现代水产养殖史上的大部分时间里，人们只收获价值高的鱼类和甲壳类水产品，如鲑鱼、虾等。但是，新技术的应用使养殖食用鱼类变得更便宜、更有效，像鳕鱼这样的普通鱼类也开始被养殖。人们还养殖海藻及其他藻类——用作食物（主要在亚洲）、牛饲料、肥料，并尝试作为能源。水产养殖现在是世界上增长最快的食品生产形式。

aquanaut \ˈä-kwə-ˌnȯt\ A scuba diver who lives and works both inside and outside an underwater shelter for an extended time. 海底观察员，海底实验室工

作人员，深海操作人员
- Each scientist at the laboratory spent two weeks a year as an aquanaut living in the deep-sea station. 实验室里的每一位科学家每年都要在深海工作站作为海底观察员生活两周时间。

Aquanaut combines *aqua* with the Greek *nautes*, meaning "sailor." Like *astronaut* and *aeronaut*, the word may remind you of those mythical Greek heroes known as the Argonauts, who sailed with Jason on his ship, the *Argo*, in quest of the Golden Fleece. Various underwater habitats for aquanauts, such as Conshelf, SEALAB, and MarineLab, have captured the public imagination since the 1960s. aquanaut 将 aqua 和希腊语 nautes（"水手"）结合。像 astronaut（宇航员）和 aeronaut（飞艇驾驶员）一样，这个词也会让你想起那些被称为阿尔戈号船员的希腊神话英雄，他们和詹森一起乘坐 Argo（阿尔戈号）船去寻找金羊毛。自 20 世纪 60 年代以来，海底观察员的各种水下栖息地，如大陆架站、海底实验室和海洋实验室，使公众着迷。

aqueduct\ˈa-kwə-ˌdəkt\　(1) A pipe or channel for water. 导水管，沟渠 (2) A bridgelike structure for carrying water over a valley. 高架渠，渡槽

- Roman aqueducts were built throughout the empire, and their spectacular arches can still be seen in Greece, France, Spain, and North Africa. 罗马高架渠曾遍布整个帝国，其壮观的拱券至今在希腊、法国、西班牙和北非仍可看到。

Based party on the Latin *ducere*, meaning "lead" or "conduct" (see DUC, p. 37), the word *aqueduct* named an ancient civil-engineering marvel. You may have seen photos of the great arches of ancient aqueducts spanning valleys in countries throughout the old Roman Empire, practical pipelines that are also regarded as works of timeless beauty. From the 20th century, the 242-mile Colorado River Aqueduct, the 336-mile Central Arizona Project, and the 444-mile California Aqueduct are considered wonders of American engineering, but they are not renowned for their beauty. Most aqueducts today either are riverlike channels or run underground, perhaps appearing simply as a long mound. aqueduct 的一部分源自拉丁语 ducere（"带领"或"引导"）（参见 DUC，第 37 页），这个词用以命名古代的一项土木工程的奇迹。你可能见过古代高架渠的巨大拱券的照片，这些拱券跨越整个古罗马帝国的各地的山谷，这种实用的输水管道也被视为具有永恒之美的艺术品。从 20 世纪开始，全长 242 英里的科罗拉多河渡槽、全长 336 英里的中央亚利桑那工程和全长 444 英里的加利福尼亚渡槽被认为是美国工程的奇迹，但它们并不以美观而闻名。今天的多数渡槽要么是像河流一样的渠道，要么是在地下运行，外表看起来或许就像一个长长的土丘而已。

aquifer\ˈa-kwə-fər\　A layer of rock, sand, or gravel that can absorb and hold water. 地下蓄水层

- Cities without access to a nearby lake or river must rely on underground aquifers to meet their water needs. 有些城市的附近没有湖泊或河流可用，它们必须依靠地下蓄水层来满足居民的用水需求。

The vast but relatively shallow Ogallala *Aquifer* lies beneath the Great Plains, under portions of eight states. Its thickness ranges from a few feet to more than a thousand feet. The Ogallala yields about 30 percent of the nation's groundwater used for irrigation in agriculture, and provides drinking water for most of the people within the area. But for many years more water has been extracted from the Ogallala than has been returned, and the situation today is of great concern.

广阔而相对较浅的奥加拉蓄水层位于北美大平原之下，即美国八个州的部分地区的下面。该蓄水层的厚度从几英尺到一千多英尺不等。奥加拉提供全美30%的农业灌溉地下用水，也为该地区的多数居民提供饮用水。但多年来，从奥加拉抽取的水比返回的水多，如今的情况备受关注。

Quizzes

A. Choose the closest definition:

1. matriarch   a. goddess   b. mermaid   c. bride
   d. grande dame
2. aquaculture   a. aquarium design   b. reef diving
   c. pearl fishing   d. water farming
3. matrilineal   a. through the mother's family
   b. graduating   c. adopted   d. female
4. aqueduct   a. channel   b. dam   c. dike
   d. reservoir
5. matrix   a. formula   b. alternate reality   c. scheme
   d. source
6. aquanaut   a. swimmer   b. diver   c. surfer
   d. pilot
7. maternity   a. motherhood   b. nightgown
   c. women's club   d. marriage
8. aquifer   a. waterway   b. fishpond   c. spring
   d. underground reservoir

B. Fill in each blank with the correct letter:

a. aquifer   e. matrilineal
b. aquaculture   f. matriarch
c. maternity   g. aqueduct
d. matrix   h. aquanaut

1. Marriage didn't seem to affect her much, but _____ has changed her completely.

2. After five years living in the suburb, they felt they had become part of a complex social _____.

3. As an _____ she often lives underwater for several days at a time.

4. The _____ they depend on for irrigation is slowly being depleted, and _____ the farmers are being forced to cut back on water use.

5. Wild salmon has become an expensive rarity, and _____ is the source of

most of the salmon we now eat.

6. The tribe seemed to be _____, with all inheritances passing through the females rather than the males.

7. The _____ that runs through the city is an open concrete-lined river.

8. He'd been married to Cynthia for three years, but she hadn't yet dared to introduce him to her great-aunt, the family _____.

Words from Mythology 源自神话的词语

cereal\ˈsir-ē-əl\ (1) A plant that produces grain that can be eaten as food, or the grain it produces. 谷类植物 (2) The food made from grain. 谷类食物

• Rice is the main food cereal of Asia, whereas wheat and corn are the main food cereals of the West. 大米是亚洲的主要粮食作物，而小麦和玉米是西方的主要粮食作物。

The Roman goddess Ceres, the equivalent of the Greek Demeter, was a calm goddess who didn't take part in the quarrels of the other gods. Her particular responsibility was the food-giving plants, and for that reason the food grains came to carry her name. Cereals of the ancient Romans included wheat, barley, spelt, oats, and millet—but not corn (maize), which was a cereal of the Americas.
罗马女神克瑞斯，相当于希腊神话中的德墨忒耳，她生性恬静，不参与其他神之间的争吵。她专门负责粮食作物，正因为如此，食粮才以她的名字命名。古罗马人的粮食作物包括小麦、大麦、斯佩尔特小麦、燕麦和小米——但不包括玉米，玉米是美洲的一种粮食作物。

Junoesque\ˌjü-nō-ˈesk\ Having mature, poised, and dignified beauty.
有优雅高贵之美的(似罗马女神朱诺的)

• In 1876, as a centennial gift, the French sent to America a massive statue of a robed Junoesque figure representing Liberty, to be erected in New York Harbor. 1876年，法国人送给美国一尊巨大的雕像作为百年纪念礼物，这是一尊身着长袍、象征自由的优雅高贵的人像，被竖立在纽约港。

Juno was the wife of Jupiter, the chief of the Roman gods. As the first among goddesses, her power gave her particular dignity; and as goddess of women and marriage, she was a mature matron. But such younger goddesses as Diana, goddess of the hunt, perhaps came closer to today's ideals of slim and athletic female beauty.
朱诺是罗马众神之首朱庇特的妻子。作为第一女神，她的力量赋予她特殊的尊严；作为女性和婚姻女神，她是一位成熟的中年女子。但是，狩猎女神黛安娜这样的年轻女神，也许更接近今天理想的苗条健美的女性美。

martial\ˈmär-shəl\ Having to do with war and military life. 战争的；军事的

• The stirring, martial strains of "The British Grenadiers" echoed down the snowy street just as dawn was breaking. 拂晓时分，《英国掷弹兵进行曲》那激动人心的军乐旋律回荡在白雪皑皑的街道上。

Mars was the Roman god of war and one of the patron gods of Rome itself. He was responsible for everything military, from warriors to weapons to marching music. Thus, *martial arts* are skills of combat and self-defense also practiced as sport. When *martial law* is declared, a country's armed forces take over the functions of the police. And a *court-martial* is a military court or trial.

马尔斯是罗马的战神,也是罗马本身的守护神之一。他负责一切军务,包括士兵、武器、行军音乐等等。*martial arts*（武术）指的是战斗和自卫的技能,也作为一项运动来习练。*martial law*（戒严令）宣布之后,国家的武装部队将接管警察的职能。*court-martial* 是指军事法庭或军事审判。

Promethean \prə-ˈmē-thē-ən\ New or creative in a daring way. 勇于创造的

• The Promethean energy of Beethoven's symphonies was a revelation to European audiences in the early years of the 19th century. 贝多芬交响乐大胆创新的能量对19世纪早期的欧洲听众而言是一种启示。

Prometheus was a Titan, a generation older than Zeus. When Zeus overthrew his own father Cronus and seized power, Prometheus fought on the side of the gods and against his fellow Titans. But when Zeus later wanted to destroy the race of humans, Prometheus saved them by stealing fire for them from the gods. He also taught them how to write, farm, build houses, read the stars and weather, cure themselves when sick, and tame animals—in short, all the arts and skills that make humans unique. So inventive was he that anything of great creativity and originality can still be called Promethean. But Prometheus had taken a terrible risk; enraged by his disobedience, Zeus had him chained to a rocky cliff, where for many long centuries an eagle daily tore at his liver.

Prometheus(普罗米修斯)是一个泰坦巨人,比宙斯年长一代。当宙斯推翻自己的父亲克罗诺斯夺得权力时,普罗米修斯站在众神的一边,与他的泰坦巨人同胞作战。但当宙斯后来想毁灭人类时,普罗米修斯从众神那里偷来天火拯救他们。他还教给人类如何写作、种田、盖房子、看星星和天气、生病时自己治病、驯养动物——总之就是所有那些使人类变得独一无二的艺术和技能。他创造力极强,因此具有伟大的创造性和创新性的一切东西仍然可以称为 Promethean。但是普罗米修斯冒了很大的风险;宙斯对他的违逆行为感到愤怒,把他锁在一个岩石峭壁上,每天有一只老鹰撕咬他的肝脏,持续了漫长的岁月。

Sisyphean \ˌsi-sə-ˈfē-ən\ Endless and difficult, involving many disappointments. 永无休止的,徒劳的

• After twenty years, many researchers had begun to think that defeating the virus was a Sisyphean task that would never succeed. 二十年后,许多研究人员开始认为,战胜病毒是一项无休止的、永难取胜的任务。

Reputedly the cleverest man on earth, King Sisyphus of Corinth tricked the gods into bringing him back to life after he had died. For this they punished him by sending him back to the underworld, where he must eternally roll a huge rock up a long, steep hill, only to watch it roll back to where he started. Something Sisyphean demands the same kind of unending, thankless, and ultimately unsuccessful efforts.

科林斯国王 Sisyphus(西西弗斯)据说是地球上最聪明的人,他欺骗众神让他死后复生。诸神为此而惩罚他,把他送回了地狱。在那里,他必须永无休止地把一块巨石推上一个又长又陡的山坡,再眼睁睁看着石头滚回开始的地方。something Sisyphean 指的是需要像西西弗斯那样无休止的、费力不讨好的、最终却不成功的努力的事。

titanic\tī-'ta-nik\ Having great size, strength, or power; colossal. 巨大的
- The titanic floods of 1993 destroyed whole towns on the Mississippi River. 1993年的特大洪水摧毁了密西西比河上的所有城镇。

In Greek mythology, the Titans were the generation of giant creators that produced the younger, stronger, cleverer gods, who soon overpowered and replaced them (see *Promethean* above). In 1911 the largest ship that had ever been built was christened the *Titanic* for its unmatched size and strength. But the name may have proved unlucky; on its maiden voyage in 1912 a massive iceberg ripped a fatal hole in the great ship, and it sank in the icy waters off Newfoundland.

在希腊神话中，Titans（泰坦）这一代巨神创造出了一代更年轻、更强壮、更聪明的神，新一代神很快胜出并取而代之（见上文的 *Promethean*）。1911年，当时史上最大的船因其无与伦比的规模和动力而被命名为 *Titanic*（泰坦尼克号）。但事实证明，这个名字可能并不吉利。在1912年的首航中，这艘巨轮被一座巨大的冰山撕开一个致命的洞，沉没在纽芬兰附近冰冷的海水中。

Triton\'trī-tən\ (1) A being with a human upper body and the lower body of a fish; a merman. 特里同，男性人鱼 (2) Any of various large mollusks with a heavy, conical shell. 梭尾螺
- In one corner of the painting, a robust Triton emerges from the sea with his conch to announce the coming of the radiant queen. 在这幅画的一角，一个强壮的人鱼带着他的海螺从大海中浮现，宣告光芒四射的女王的到来。

Triton was originally the son of the sea god Poseidon (or Neptune). A guardian of the fish and other creatures of the sea, he is usually shown as hearty, muscular, and cheerful. Like his father, he often carries a trident (three-pronged fork) and may ride in a chariot drawn by seahorses. Blowing on his conch shell, he creates the roar of the ocean. As a decorative image, Tritons are simply the male version of mermaids. The handsome seashells that bear their name are the very conchs on which they blow. Triton has also given his name to the planet Neptune's largest moon.

Triton（特里同，又译特赖登）本是海神波塞冬（或尼普顿）的儿子。他是鱼类及其他海洋生物的守护者，其形象通常表现为精力充沛、肌肉发达、性格开朗。就像父亲一样，他也经常带着三叉戟（三根齿的叉子），乘坐由海马牵引的战车。他吹响海螺壳，由此创造出海洋的轰鸣声。作为装饰性形象，特里同就是男性版本的美人鱼。那些以 triton 命名的好看的海贝壳正是它们用来吹的海螺。Triton 还被用来命名海王星最大的卫星（海卫一）。

vulcanize\'vəl-kə-ˌnīz\ To treat crude or synthetic rubber or plastic so that it becomes elastic and strong and resists decay. 硫化，硬化
- The native islanders had even discovered how to vulcanize the rubber from the local trees in a primitive way. 岛上的土著居民甚至发现了一种硫化当地树木所产橡胶的原始方法。

The Roman god Vulcan (the Greek Hephaestus) was in charge of fire and the skills that use fire, especially blacksmithing. When Charles Goodyear almost accidentally discovered how to vulcanize rubber in 1839, he revolutionized the rubber industry. He called his process *vulcanization* because it used fire to heat a mix of rubber and sulfur. Vulcanized rubber was soon being used for shoes and other products, and in the Civil War balloons made of this new, stronger rubber carried Union spies over the Confederate armies. The material's importance increased greatly over the years, and today vulcanized rubber remains in use for automobile tires and numerous other products.

罗马的火神伍尔坎(希腊的赫菲斯托斯)掌管火和使用火的技能,尤其是锻冶技能。1839 年,查尔斯·古德伊尔差不多是偶然之中发现了硫化橡胶的方法,彻底改变了橡胶行业。他把这个过程称为 *vulcanization*(硫化),因为该过程用火加热橡胶和硫磺的混合物。硫化橡胶很快就被用于鞋子和其他产品,在美国南北战争时期,由这种更结实的新橡胶制成的气球载着联邦间谍越过南部邦联军队。这种材料的重要性随时间的推移而大大提高,硫化橡胶如今仍然用于汽车轮胎和许多其他产品。

Quiz

Fill in each blank with the correct letter:

a. Promethean
b. titanic
c. Triton
d. Junoesque
e. Sisyphean
f. vulcanize
g. cereal
h. martial

1. For a mother of nine, laundry and ironing can seem _____ in their endlessness and drudgery.

2. One clear and beautiful morning, a series of _____ waves swept the entire village into the sea.

3. The aging jazz singer acquired a certain _____ quality in her mature years.

4. On each arm of the great candelabra was carved a _____ blowing on his conch.

5. Corn, unknown in ancient Europe, has become a staple _____ of the modern world.

6. When Goodyear discovered how to _____ rubber, he made Henry Ford's Model T possible.

7. In some ways, Edison's mind may have been the most _____ since Leonardo da Vinci's.

8. The _____ arts of the Far East have become popular in the West as means of self-defense.

Review Quizzes

A. Indicate whether the following pairs of words have the same or different meanings:

1. aquamarine / navy blue   same ____ / different ____
2. subterranean / underground same ____ / different ____
3. physiology / sports medicine same ____ / different ____

4. disrepute / disgrace			same ____ / different ____
5. empathy / sentimentality		same ____ / different ____
6. Junoesque / slender			same ____ / different ____
7. Promethean / creative		same ____ / different ____
8. penance / regret			same ____ / different ____
9. mariner / sailor			same ____ / different ____
10. pathos / anger			same ____ / different ____
11. titanic / powerful			same ____ / different ____
12. vulcanize / organize		same ____ / different ____
13. terrestrial / earthly		same ____ / different ____
14. impunity / freedom from harm	same ____ / different ____
15. penal / legal			same ____ / different ____
16. matrix / puzzle			same ____ / different ____
17. marina / dock			same ____ / different ____
18. putative / natural			same ____ / different ____
19. terrarium / garden			same ____ / different ____
20. apathetic / indifferent		same ____ / different ____

B. Choose the word that does not belong:

1. Sisyphean   a. difficult   b. unending   c. demanding
   d. rolling
2. maternity   a. femininity   b. parenthood
   c. motherliness d. motherhood
3. mariner   a. sailor   b. seaman   c. crew member
   d. archer
4. cereal   a. corn   b. eggplant   c. rice
   d. barley
5. reputed   a. known   b. reported   c. believed
   d. thought
6. ideology   a. essay   b. philosophy   c. principles
   d. beliefs
7. punitive   a. disciplinary   b. punishing
   c. correctional d. encouraging
8. empathy   a. fascination   b. pity   c. concern
   d. compassion
9. maritime   a. coastal   b. nautical   c. oceangoing
   d. lakeside
10. apathetic   a. unfortunate   b. unconcerned
    c. uncaring   d. uninterested

C. Match the definition on the right to the correct word on the left:

1. impute
2. martial
3. parterre
4. maritime
5. penal
6. matrilineal
7. terrestrial
8. methodology

a. fancy garden
b. through the mother's line
c. assign
d. nautical
e. related to war
f. disciplinary
g. procedure
h. earthly

UNIT 11

CANT

CANT, from the Latin verb *cantare*, meaning "sing," produces several words that come directly from Latin. But some others came to English by way of French, which added an *h* to the root, giving us such words as *chant* and *chantey*.
CANT 源自拉丁语动词 *cantare*，意思是"歌唱"，衍生出几个直接源于拉丁语的单词。还有一些单词经法语进入英语，给这个词根上加了个字母 *h*，衍生出 *chant* 和 *chantey* 等单词。

---

cantata \ kən-ˈtä-tə \   A musical composition, particularly a religious work from the 17th or 18th century, for one or more voices accompanied by instruments. 康塔塔（通常为宗教题材的音乐作品，一个或多个声部，由乐器伴奏）

• Composers of the 18th century composed sacred cantatas by the dozen, and Bach's friend G. P. Telemann actually wrote over a thousand. 18 世纪的作曲家创作了许多神圣康塔塔，巴赫的朋友 G. P. 特勒曼竟然创作了一千多首。

A *cantata* is sung, unlike a *sonata*, which is played on instruments only. The most famous cantatas are by Johann Sebastian Bach, who wrote the music for about 200 religious cantatas, using hymns and new religious poems as his texts. His cantatas consisted of several different sections for different voices—solos, duets, and choruses. Some of his nonreligious cantatas have been performed like mini-operas. 康塔塔与奏鸣曲不同，是被唱出来的，而后者只在乐器上演奏。最著名的康塔塔是由约翰·塞巴斯蒂安·巴赫创作的，他创作了大约 200 首宗教康塔塔谱曲，以赞美诗和新的宗教诗歌为文本。他的康塔塔由几个不同段落组成，对应不同的声部——独唱、二重唱、合唱。他的一些非宗教的康塔塔表演起来就像是小型歌剧一样。

incantation \ ˌin-ˌkan-ˈtā-shən \   (1) A use of spells or verbal charms spoken or sung as part of a ritual of magic. 念咒 (2) A formula of words used in, or as if in, such a ritual. 咒语

• He repeated the words slowly over and over like an incantation. 他像念咒语一样一遍遍慢悠悠地重复着这些词。

Incantation comes directly from the Latin word *incantare*, "enchant." *Incantare* itself has *cantare* as a root, which reminds us that magic and ritual have always been associated with chanting and music. Incantations have often been in strange languages; "Abracadabra" is a not-so-serious version of an incantation.

incantation 直接源自拉丁语 incantare（对……施魔法）。incantare 本身有一个词根 cantare，它提醒我们，魔法和仪式总是与吟诵和音乐联系在一起。咒语经常用奇怪的语言；"Abracadabra"是一个不那么严肃的咒语版本。

cantor \\'kan-tər\\ An official of a Jewish synagogue who sings or chants the music of the services and leads the congregation in prayer. 领诵人，领唱人

- The congregation waited for the cantor to begin the prayers before joining in. 这些会众们等领诵人开始祈祷后才加入进来。

The cantor is, after the rabbi, the most important figure in a Jewish worship service. A cantor not only must possess an excellent singing voice but also must know by heart long passages of Hebrew. Cantors such as Jan Peerce and Richard Tucker became international opera stars. The comedian and singer Edward Israel Iskowitz renamed himself Eddie Cantor for his original profession and became enormously popular on stage, screen, radio, and television for over 40 years.

在犹太人的礼拜仪式中，领诵人是仅次于拉比的重要人物。领诵人不仅要有一副好嗓子，而且要能熟记希伯来语的长段。简•皮尔斯和理查德•塔克这样的领唱人成了国际歌剧明星。喜剧演员兼歌手爱德华•以色列•伊斯科维茨以其最初的职业将自己的名字改为埃迪•康托尔(Cantor)，在舞台、银幕、广播和电视上备受欢迎，时间长达40多年。

descant \\'des-ˌkant\\ An additional melody sung above the principal melody. （高声部）伴唱，伴奏

- The soprano added a soaring descant to the final chorus that held the listeners spellbound. 女高音在最后的合唱中加入了高亢的高音伴唱，使听众入迷。

The prefix *des-*, meaning "two" or "apart," indicates that the descant is a "second song" apart from the main melody. In popular songs a descant will often be sung at the very end to produce a thrilling climax.

前缀 des- 的意思是"两个"或"分开"，这表明 descant 是除主旋律外的"第二首歌"。在流行歌曲中，高声部往往会在结尾唱出一个惊心动魄的高潮。

LINGU comes from the Latin word that means both "tongue" and "language," and in English today *tongue* can still mean "language" (as in "her native tongue"). Our expression "slip of the tongue" is just a translation of the Latin phrase *lapsus linguae*. The root even shows up in a slangy-sounding word like *lingo*. And since *lingu-* changed to *langu-* in French, our word *language* is related as well.

LINGU 源自兼有"舌头"和"语言"之意的拉丁语单词，在当今的英语中，tongue（舌头）仍然可以表示"语言"（比如"她的母语"）。短语"slip of the tongue"（口误）正是从拉丁语短语 lapsus linguae 翻译而来的。这个词根甚至出现在像 lingo（行话）这样的有点儿俚语味道的单词中。由于在法语里 lingu 变成了 langu，英语单词 language 也跟着改变。

UNIT 11

linguistics \liŋ-ˈgwi-ˌstiks\ The study of human speech. 语言学

• The new speechwriter, who had majored in linguistics, was soon putting his knowledge of the deceptive tricks of language to good use. 这位新来的演讲撰稿人主修语言学，他很快就好好利用了一下语言欺骗技巧的知识。

Any analysis of language, including 8th-grade grammar, can be called linguistics. As recently as 200 years ago, ordinary grammar was about the only kind of linguistics there was. Today a *linguist* may be a person who learns foreign languages, but the term usually refers to people who devote themselves to analyzing the structure of language. Many linguists concentrate on the history of a language; others study the way children learn to speak; others analyze the sounds of a language—and still others just study English grammar, a subject so big that you could easily spend your entire life on it.

LINGU

任何对语言的分析，包括八年级语法在内，都可以称为语言学。就在200年前，普通语法还是唯一的语言学。如今，*linguist* 可以指外语学习者，但通常指那些致力于分析语言结构的人。许多语言学家专注于研究某种语言的历史，有些语言学家研究儿童学习说话的方式，也有些语言学家分析某种语言的声音——此外，还有一些语言学家只是研究英语语法。语法这个领域太大了，他们很容易就会穷其一生钻研语法。

multilingual \məl-tē-ˈliŋ-gwəl\ Using or able to use several languages.
使用多种语言的，会多种语言的

• She soon discovered that he was truly multilingual, fluent in not only the German and Polish he had grown up speaking but in English and Arabic as well. 她很快发现他真的会说多种语言，从小就说的德语和波兰语很流利，英语和阿拉伯语也很流利。

The roots of *multilingual* come from Latin (see MULTI, p. 627). If you happen to prefer Greek, use the synonym *polyglot*, in which *poly-* has the same meaning as *multi-*, and *-glot* means the same thing as *-lingual*. The best way to become multilingual is probably to be born in a *bilingual* (two-language) household; learning those first two seems to give the mind the kind of exercise that makes later language-learning easy.

multilingual 的词根源自拉丁语（参见 MULTI，第627页）。如果你碰巧更加喜欢希腊语，可以使用它的同义词 *polyglot*，其中的 *poly-* 与 *multi-* 意思相同，*-glot* 与 *lingual* 意思相同。学会多种语言的最好方法可能是生在一个 *bilingual*（双语）家庭。学习前两种语言似乎给大脑提供了一种锻炼，以后的语言学习就会容易了。

lingua franca \ˈliŋ-gwə-ˈfraŋ-kə\ A language used as a common or commercial language among peoples who speak different languages. 通用语

• That first evening in Tokyo, she heard English being spoken at the next table, and realized it was serving as a lingua franca for a party of Korean and Japanese businessmen. 在东京的第一个晚上，她听到邻桌的人在说英语，意识到这是韩国和日本商人聚会的通用语言。

In the Middle Ages, the Arabs of the eastern Mediterranean referred to all Europeans as Franks (the name of the tribe that once occupied the land we call France). Since there was plenty of Arab-European trade, the traders in the Mediterranean ports eventually developed a trading language combining Italian,

• 243 •

Arabic, and other languages, which almost everyone could more or less understand, and it became known as the "Frankish language," or *lingua franca*. Some languages actually succeed in becoming lingua francas without changing much. So, when the Roman empire became vast and mighty, Latin became the important lingua franca; and at a meeting between Japanese and Vietnamese businesspeople today, English may well be the only language spoken.

在中世纪,地中海东部的阿拉伯人将所有欧洲人都称为法兰克人(以这个名字命名的那个部落曾经占据了我们称之为法国的土地)。由于有大量的阿拉伯——欧洲贸易往来,地中海港口的商人们最终形成了一种结合意大利语、阿拉伯语和其他语言的贸易语言,称为"法兰克语"或 lingua franca(通用语),几乎每个人都能或多或少地理解这种语言。事实上,有些语言在没有太多变化的情况下成功地变为通用语。因此,当罗马帝国变得庞大而强大时,拉丁语成了重要的通用语;而在如今的日本和越南商人的会议上,英语很可能是唯一的交流语言。

linguine\liŋ-ˈgwē-ˈnē\　A narrow, flat pasta. 意大利扁面条

• As a test of her clients' table manners, she would serve them challenging dishes and watch to see how gracefully they could handle chopsticks or deal with long, slithery linguine. 为了测试客户的餐桌礼仪,她会给他们上一些有挑战性的菜肴,观察他们如何优雅地使用筷子或怎样对付又长又滑的扁面条。

The modern language closest to Latin is Italian, and the Italian word *linguine* means literally "little tongues." Linguine is only one of the types of pasta whose names describes their shapes. Others include *spaghetti* ("little strings"), *fettuccine* ("little ribbons"), *penne* ("little quills"), *orzo* ("barley"), *farfalle* ("butterflies"), *vermicelli* ("little worms"), *capellini* ("little hairs"), *fusilli* ("little spindles"), and *radiatori* ("little radiators"). If you're thinking about learning Italian, you could make a good start by just visiting an Italian restaurant.

最接近拉丁语的现代语言是意大利语,意大利语单词 *linguine* 的字面意思是"小舌头"。扁面条只是意大利面的一种,这些面以其形状命名。其他还包括 *spaghetti*(形似"细绳"的面食)、*fettuccine*(形似"细丝带")、*penne*(形似"小翎管")、*orzo*(形似"大麦粒")、*farfalle*(形似"蝴蝶")、*vermicelli*(形似"小蠕虫")、*capellini*(形似"细毛")、*fusilli*(形似"小纺锤")和 *radiatori*(形似"小天线")。如果想学意大利语,可以先去意大利餐厅开个好头。

Quizzes

A. Choose the closest definition:

1. descant
   a. climb downward　b. added melody
   c. supposed inability　d. writing table
2. linguistics
   a. language study　b. reading
   c. mouth surgery　d. tongue exercise
3. incantation
   a. ritual chant　b. ceremony
   c. solemn march　d. recorded song
4. linguine
   a. slang　b. pasta
   c. Italian dessert　d. common language
5. cantata
   a. snack bar　b. pasta dish

UNIT 11

    c. sung composition d. farewell gesture
6. lingua franca   a. Old French   b. common language
    c. Italian casserole d. French coin
7. cantor   a. singer   b. refusal   c. traitor
    d. gallop
8. multilingual   a. highly varied   b. in separate parts
    c. born with multiple tongues   d. fluent in several languages

B. Indicate whether the following pairs of words have the same or different meanings:

1. lingua franca / pasta dish   same ____ / different ____
2. incantation / sacred dance   same ____ / different ____
3. linguine / Italian language   same ____ / different ____
4. descant / enchant   same ____ / different ____
5. linguistics / science of singing   same ____ / different ____
6. cantata / sonata   same ____ / different ____
7. cantor / conductor   same ____ / different ____
8. multilingual / using several fingers same ____ / different ____

SPIR

SPIR comes from the Latin words meaning "breath" and "breathe." When we *inspire* others—that is, give them *inspiration*—it's as though we're breathing new energy and imagination into them. When you *expire*, or die, you "breathe out" your soul in your last breath. A license, membership, credit card, or free offer may also expire, at a time indicated by its *expiration* date.

SPIR 源自意思是"呼吸"的拉丁语单词。当我们 *inspire*(激励)他人时——也就是说,给他们以 *inspiration*(灵感)时——就像为他们注入新的能量和想象力一样。当你 *expire*,即死亡时,最后一口气"呼出"了你的灵魂。在 *expiration* date(有效期限)所标明的时间点,许可证、会员资格、信用卡、免费优惠等可能也会到期。

---

spirited \ˈspir-ə-təd\ Full of energy or courage; very lively or determined. 精神饱满的,充满活力的,坚定的

- The team put up a spirited defense, but they were doomed from the start. 这个球队进行了顽强的防守,但他们从一开始就注定要失败。

You may see *spirited* used to describe a conversation, a debate, a horse, or a campaign. And it often shows up in such words as *high-spirited* ("bold and energetic"), *mean-spirited* ("spiteful"), and *public-spirited* ("generous to a community"), all of which reflect the original meaning of *spirit*, a notion much like "soul" or "personality."

spirited 用来形容对话、辩论、赛马或运动。它经常出现在 *high-spirited*("大胆而充满活力的"), *mean-spirited*("怀有恶意的")和 *public-spirited*("对社区慷慨的")等词语中,这些词都反映了 *spirit*(精神)的本义,即一种与"灵魂"或"人格"非常相似的概念。

· 245 ·

dispiriting \di-'spir-ə-tiŋ\ Causing a loss of hope or enthusiasm. 令人沮丧的，令人气馁的

- It was terribly dispiriting for them to lose yet another game, and he had to reassure his daughter that she'd actually done a great job as goalie. 又输掉一场比赛让他们十分沮丧，而他还得安慰女儿说，作为守门员她实际上干得很不错了。

Lots of things can be dispiriting: a bad job interview, an awful film, a relationship going sour. Maybe for that reason, *dispiriting* has lots of synonyms: *discouraging*, *disheartening*, *demoralizing*, *depressing*, etc.

许多事情都会是 *dispiriting*（令人沮丧的）：糟糕的面试、糟糕的电影、恶化的关系等。也许正是因为这个原因，*dispiriting* 有很多同义词：*discouraging*、*disheartening*、*demoralizing*、*depressing* 等等。

respirator \'re-spə-ˌrā-tər\ (1) A device worn over the nose and mouth to filter out dangerous substances from the air. 防毒面具，口罩 (2) A device for maintaining artificial respiration. 呼吸器，呼吸机

- His lungs had been terribly damaged by decades of heavy smoking, and he'd been living on a respirator for the last year. 由于几十年大量吸烟，他的肺受损严重，去年他一直靠呼吸机维持生命。

Respiration means simply "breathing." We usually come across the word in *artificial respiration*, the lifesaving technique in which you force air into the lungs of someone who's stopped breathing. Respirators can take several different forms. Scuba-diving equipment always includes a respirator, though it doesn't actually do the breathing for the diver. Medical respirators, which are used especially for babies and for emergency care and actually take over the job of getting oxygen into the lungs, are today usually called ventilators, so as to distinguish them from simple oxygen systems (which merely provide a steady flow of oxygen into the nostrils) and face masks.

respiration 的意思就是"呼吸"。我们通常会在 *artificial respiration*（人工呼吸）中见到这个词，人工呼吸是一种挽救生命的技术，即迫使空气进入呼吸停止之人的肺部。呼吸器有几种不同的形式。潜水设备总是包括一个呼吸器，但它实际上并没有为潜水员提供呼吸功能。医用呼吸器尤其用于婴儿以及紧急护理，实际上承担着把氧气送入肺部的工作，现在通常被称为 ventilator，以区别于简单的氧气系统（只提供稳定的氧气流进入鼻孔）和面罩。

transpire \tran-'spīr\ (1) To happen. 发生 (2) To become known. 为人所知，透漏

- We kept up our questioning, and it soon transpired that the boys had known about the murder all along. 我们不停地追问，很快就得知那些男孩一直都知道这起谋杀案。

Since the prefix *trans-* means "through" (see TRANS, p. 674), *transpire*'s most literal meaning is something like "breathe through." Thus, the original meaning of the English word—still used today—is to give off a watery vapor through a surface such as a leaf. From there, it came to mean also the gradual appearance of previously secret information, as if leaking out of the pores of a leaf (as in "It transpired that she was not only his employee but also his girlfriend"). And soon it was being used to mean simply "happen" (as in "I wondered what had transpired in the cafeteria at lunchtime").

由于前缀 trans-意为"通过"（参见 TRANS，第 674 页），因此 transpire 最字面的意思类似于"通过……呼吸"。因此，这个英语单词的最初含义——至今仍在使用——是通过叶子等的表面散发水蒸气。由此，它也用来表示以前的秘密信息逐渐公开，就像从叶子的毛孔里逸出一样（比如"我们得知，她不仅是他的雇员，还是他的女朋友"）。很快，这个词用来表示"发生"（比如"我想知道午餐时间在自助餐厅发生了什么事情"）。

VER comes from the Latin word for "truth." A *verdict* in a trial is "the truth spoken" (see DICT, p. 294). But a just verdict may depend on the *veracity*, or "truthfulness," of the witnesses.

VER 源自表示"真实"的拉丁语单词。在审判中的 *verdict*（裁定）指的是"说出来的真相"（见 DICT，第 294 页）。但公正的裁定可能取决于目击证人的 *veracity*，即"诚实"。

---

verify \ˈver-ə-ˌfī\ (1) To prove to be true or correct. 证明，核实 (2) To check or test the accuracy of. 查证

• It is the bank teller's job to verify the signature on a check. 核对支票上的签名是银行出纳的工作。

During talks between the United States and the former Soviet Union on nuclear weapons reduction, one big problem was how to *verify* that weapons had been eliminated. Since neither side wanted the other to know its secrets, *verification* of the facts became a difficult issue. Because of the distrust on both sides, many doubted that the real numbers would ever be *verifiable*.

在美国和苏联关于削减核武器的会谈中，有一个大问题是如何核实核武器是否已被销毁。彼此都不想让对方知道自己的秘密，因此对事实的 verification（核实）成了难题。由于互不信任，很多人怀疑真实的数字是否是 verifiable（能核实的）。

---

aver \ə-ˈvər\ To state positively as true; declare. 断言，坚称

• The defendant averred that she was nowhere near the scene of the crime on the night in question. 被告坚称，案发当晚她根本不在犯罪现场附近。

Since *aver* contains the "truth" root, it basically means "confirm as true." You may aver anything that you're sure of. In legal situations, *aver* means to state positively as a fact; thus, Perry Mason's clients aver that they are innocent, while the district attorney avers the opposite. If you make such a statement while under oath, and it turns out that you lied, you may have committed the crime of perjury.

由于 *aver* 包含意思是"真相"的词根，所以它的基本意思是"确认为真"。你可能会咬定你确信的事情。在法律情境中，*aver* 指断言某事属实；因此，佩里·梅森的当事人坚称无罪，而地区检察官所坚称的恰恰相反。如果你宣誓做出这样的陈述，而事实证明你撒谎，你可能已经犯了伪证罪。

---

verisimilitude \ˌver-ə-sə-ˈmi-lə-ˌtüd\ (1) The appearance of being true or probable. 貌似真实 (2) The depiction of realism in art or literature. 逼真，真实性

• By the beginning of the 20th century, the leading European painters were losing interest in verisimilitude and beginning to experiment with abstraction. 到了20世纪初,欧洲的主要画家对逼真性失去了兴趣,开始尝试抽象风格。

From its roots, *verisimilitude* means basically "similarity to the truth." Most fiction writers and filmmakers aim at some kind of verisimilitude to give their stories an air of reality. They need not show something actually true, or even very common, but simply something believable. A mass of good details in a play, novel, painting, or film may add verisimilitude. A spy novel without some verisimilitude won't interest many readers, but a fantastical novel may not even attempt to seem true to life.

就词根而言,*verisimilitude* 的基本意思是"与真相相似"。大多数小说家和电影制作人追求的目标是某种逼真性,以使故事有真实感。他们不需要展示实际上真实的东西,甚至不需要展示非常普遍的东西,要展示的只是可信的东西。戏剧、小说、绘画或电影中的大量细节会增加真实性。没有真实感的间谍小说不会引起很多读者的兴趣,但奇幻小说甚至不会尝试让自己看起来更真实。

veracity \ və-ˈra-sə-tē \ (1) Truth or accuracy. 真实(性),准确(性) (2) The quality of being truthful or honest. 诚实,老实

• We haven't been able to check the veracity of most of his story, but we know he wasn't at the motel that night. 我们还没能核实他的故事的大部分情节是否准确,但我们知道那天晚上他不在汽车旅馆。

People often claim that a frog placed in cold water that then is gradually heated will let itself be boiled to death, but the story actually lacks *veracity*. We often hear that the Eskimo (Inuit) peoples have dozens of words for "snow," but the veracity of the statement is doubtful, since Eskimo languages seem to have no more snow words than English (with *flake*, *blizzard*, *powder*, *drift*, *freezing rain*, etc.). In 2009 millions accepted the veracity of the claim that, against all the evidence, the elected president wasn't a native-born American. Not all the "facts" we accept without thinking are harmless.

人们常说,把青蛙放在冷水中,逐渐加热,它就会被煮死,但这个故事实际上缺乏真实性。我们经常听说爱斯基摩人(因纽特人)拥有几十个形容雪的单词,但是这种说法的真实性令人生疑,因为爱斯基摩语中表示雪的单词似乎并不比英语多(比如 *flake*、*blizzard*、*powder*、*drift*、*freezing rain* 等)。2009年,数百万人罔顾所有证据,接受了下面说法的真实性,即当选的总统并非土生土长的美国人。并非所有我们不假思索就接受的"事实"都是无害的。

Quizzes

A. Fill in each blank with the correct letter:

a. transpire
b. aver
c. respirator
d. verify
e. spirited
f. veracity
g. dispiriting
h. verisimilitude

1. Maybe some new information will _____ when they question the family

tomorrow.

2. The company was doing badly, and she'd been having problems with her boss, so all in all it had been a _____ week at work.

3. The prosecutor expected the witness to _____ that the suspect was guilty.

4. Critics complained about the lack of _____ in his crime writing, saying it sounded as if he'd never even been inside a police station.

5. There's always a _____ exchange of opinions around the Thanksgiving table, but nobody ever takes offense.

6. His father has been living on a _____ for the last two weeks, but now his lungs seem to be improving.

7. She was never able to _____ anything he had told her about his past.

8. The boys claim they never went near the river that afternoon, but we suspect their _____.

B. Complete the analogy:

1. believe : doubt :: aver : _____
   a. state   b. mean   c. deny   d. subtract
2. transfer : hand over :: transpire : _____
   a. breathe out   b. cross   c. encourage   d. come to light
3. illusion : fantasy :: verisimilitude : _____
   a. appearance   b. realism   c. style   d. proof
4. gloomy : glum :: spirited : _____
   a. spiraling   b. alcoholic   c. lively   d. complex
5. loyalty : treason :: veracity : _____
   a. dishonesty   b. truthfulness   c. ideals   d. safekeeping
6. exciting : thrilling :: dispiriting : _____
   a. dreary   b. calming   c. relaxing   d. soothing
7. praise : ridicule :: verify : _____
   a. testify   b. contradict   c. establish   d. foretell
8. pacemaker : heart :: respirator : _____
   a. kidneys   b. brain   c. liver   d. lungs

TURB comes from the Latin verb *turbare*, "to throw into confusion or upset," and the noun *turba*, "crowd" or "confusion." So a *disturbance*, for example, confuses and upsets normal order or routine.

TURB 源自拉丁语动词 *turbare*(引起混乱)和名词 *turba*(人群或混乱)。比如，*disturbance*(社会动乱，骚乱)会搅乱正常秩序或常规。

turbid\\ˈtər-bid\\ (1) Thick or murky, especially with churned-up sediment. 浑浊的,污浊的 (2) Unclear, confused, muddled. 不清的,混乱的。

- The mood of the crowd was restless and turbid, and any spark could have turned them into a mob. 人群情绪不安迷乱,任何煽风点火都可能让他们变成暴徒。

The Colorado River in spring, swollen by melting snow from the high mountains, races through the Grand Canyon, *turbid* and churning. A chemical solution may be described as turbid rather than clear. And your emotions may be turbid as well, especially where love is involved: What did he mean by that glance? Why did she say it like that?
春天,科罗拉多河由于高山融雪而涨水,奔腾穿过大峡谷,河水浑浊,波涛汹涌。某种化学溶液可以被描述为混浊而非清澈的。你也可能会胡思乱想,尤其是涉及爱情的时候:他那一瞥是什么意思? 她为什么那样说?

perturb\\pər-ˈtərb\\ To upset, confuse, or disarrange. 使不安,使担心,使紊乱

- News of the new peace accord was enough to perturb some radical opponents of any settlements. 新和平协议的消息足以使一些反对任何和解的激进分子感到不安。

With its *per-* prefix, *perturb* meant originally "thoroughly upset," though today the word has lost most of its intense edge. *Perturb* and *perturbation* are often used by scientists, usually when speaking of a change in their data indicating that something has affected some normal process. When someone is referred to as *imperturbable*, it means he or she manages to remain calm through the most trying experiences.
perturb 的前缀是 *per-*,它最初的意思是"彻底心烦意乱",但如今这个单词表示的强烈不安感已失大半。科学家经常使用 *perturb* 和 *perturbation*,通常指数据发生的变化,该变化说明有个东西影响了某一正常的过程。当某人被称为 *imperturbable*(沉着的,冷静的)时,意思是他/她能在最艰难的时候保持冷静。

turbine\\ˈtər-ˌbin\\ A rotary engine with blades made to turn and generate power by a current of water, steam, or air under pressure. 涡轮机,汽轮机

- The power plant used huge turbines powered by water going over the dam to generate electricity. 这座发电厂使用巨大的涡轮机,由流过大坝的水驱动发电。

The oldest and simplest form of *turbine* is the waterwheel, which is made to rotate by water falling across its blades and into buckets suspended from them. Hero of Alexandria invented the first steam-driven turbine in the 1st century A.D., but a commercially practical steam turbine wasn't developed until 1884; steam turbines are now the main elements of electric power stations. Jet engines are gas turbines. A *turbojet* engine uses a turbine to compress the incom-ing air that feeds the engine before being ejected to push the plane forward; a *turboprop* engine uses its exhaust to drive a turbine that spins a propeller. A wind turbine generates electricity by being turned by the wind; the largest now have vanes with a turning diameter of over 400 feet.
最古老、最简单的涡轮机是水车,河水流过水车的叶片,落入叶片上悬挂的桶中,推动水车旋转。公元1世纪,亚历

UNIT 11

山大港的希罗发明了第一台蒸汽驱动的涡轮机,但直到1884年,实用商业汽轮机才被开发出来;汽轮机现在是发电站的主要设备。喷气发动机是燃气轮机。*turbojet* engine(涡轮喷气发动机)使用涡轮压缩进入发动机的空气,然后喷射出去推动飞机前进;*turboprop* engine(涡轮螺旋桨发动机)用其排出的气体驱动涡轮旋转螺旋桨。风力涡轮机通过风力驱动来发电;现在最大的风力涡轮机的叶片回旋直径超过400英尺。

turbulent \ˈtər-byü-lənt\ (1) Stirred up, agitated. 汹涌的,湍急的,猛烈的 (2) Stirring up unrest, violence, or disturbance. 骚乱的,动荡的,混乱的

• The huge ocean liner *Queen Elizabeth II* was never much troubled by turbulent seas that might have sunk smaller boats. 巨大的远洋班轮伊丽莎白女王二世号从来没有被波涛汹涌的大海所困扰,而如此汹涌的大海可能会导致较小的船只沉没。

Some people lead turbulent lives, and some are constantly in the grip of turbulent emotions. The late 1960s are remembered as turbulent years of social revolution in America and Europe. Often the captain of an airplane will warn passengers to fasten their seatbelts because of upper-air *turbulence*, which can make for a bumpy ride. El Niño, a seasonal current of warm water in the Pacific Ocean, may create turbulence in the winds across the United States, affecting patterns of rainfall and temperature as well.

有些人过着动荡不安的生活,有些人不断被动荡不安的情绪所控制。20世纪60年后期被认为是美国和欧洲动荡的社会革命年代。机长通常会警告乘客,由于高空 *turbulence*(湍流)导致颠簸,要系好安全带。厄尔尼诺是太平洋的一种季节性暖流,可能会在吹过美国的风中产生气流,影响降雨和气温的模式。

VOLU/VOLV comes from the Latin verb *volvere*, meaning "to roll, wind, turn around, or twist around." Thus, *revolve* simply means "turn in circles." And a *volume* was originally a scroll or roll of papyrus.
VOLU / VOLV 源自拉丁语动词 *volvere*,意思是"滚动、缠绕、转身或转动"。因此,*resolve* 的意思就是"转圈"。而 *volume* 最初指的是羊皮纸卷或莎草纸卷轴。

---

voluble \ˈväl-yə-bəl\ Speaking readily and rapidly; talkative. 滔滔不绝的,口若悬河的,健谈的

• He proved to be a voluble informer who would tell stories of bookies, smugglers, and hit men to the detectives for hours. 事实证明,他是一个健谈的告密者,会连续几个小时向侦探们讲述关于赌徒、走私犯以及杀手的故事。

A voluble person has words "rolling" off his or her tongue. In O. Henry's famous story "The Ransom of Red Chief," the kidnappers nab a boy who turns out to be so unbearably voluble that they can hardly wait to turn him loose again.
健谈者说话滔滔不绝。在欧·亨利的著名故事《红酋长的赎金》中,绑架者捉住了一个男孩,结果这个男孩口若悬河,令人无法忍受,他们迫不及待地要释放了他。

devolve \di-ˈvälv\ (1) To pass (responsibility, power, etc.) from one person or group to another person or group at a lower level of authority. 移交,下放(责任、权力等) (2) To gradually go from an advanced state to a less

· 251 ·

advanced state. 退化

• Since 1998, considerable power has been devolving from the British government in London to the new Scottish Parliament in Edinburgh. 自1998年以来,相当多的权力已经从伦敦的英国政府移交给爱丁堡的新苏格兰议会。

With its *de-* prefix (see DE-, p. 646), *devolution* implies moving backward. Once powers have been centralized in a unified government, giving any powers back—that is, devolving the power—to a smaller governmental unit can seem to be reversing a natural development. In a somewhat similar way, a job that your boss doesn't want to do may devolve upon you. But *devolve* and *devolution* are also treated nowadays as the opposites of *evolve* and *evolution*. So we may also speak of moral devolution, such as occurred in Germany in the 1930s, when a country with an extraordinary culture became a brutal dictatorship. And parents may watch their slacker teenager and wonder if devolution is occurring right in front of their eyes.

devolution 的前缀是 *de-*(参见 DE-,第646页),它的意思是向后移动。一旦权力集中在一个统一的政府手中,交回权力——也就是说,移交权力——给小一些的政府单位的做法似乎是在逆转自然的发展。与此类似,老板可能会把不想做的工作移交给你。但是,*devolve* 和 *devolution*(退化)如今也被当成 *evolve* 和 *evolution*(进化)的对立面。因此,我们也可以说道德退化,比如20世纪30年代的德国,一个拥有非凡文化的国家变成了残酷的独裁国家。家长们可能会看着他们懒散的孩子,想知道退化现象是不是就在眼前发生。

evolution \ˌe-və-ˈlü-shən\ A process of change from a lower, simpler, or worse state to one that is higher, more complex, or better. 进化,演变

• Thomas Jefferson and the other Founding Fathers believed that political evolution reached its highest form in democracy. 托马斯·杰斐逊和其他开国元勋认为,民主是政治发展的最高形式。

Part of the humor of the old *Flintstones* cartoon show is that it contradicts what is known about biological evolution, since humans actually *evolved* long after dinosaurs were extinct. *Evolution* can also be used more broadly to refer to technology, society, and other human creations. For example, an idea may evolve, even in your own mind, as the months or years pass. And though many people don't believe that human beings truly become better with the passing centuries, many will argue that our societies tend to evolve, producing more goods and providing more protection for more people.

《摩登原始人》这部老卡通片的幽默之处在于,它与已知的生物进化论相悖,因为人类实际上是在恐龙灭绝很久以后才 *evolved*(进化)而来的。*evolution* 也可以更广泛地用于指技术、社会以及人类创造的其他东西。甚至于在你头脑中,有个想法会随着时间的推移而逐渐形成。虽然许多人不相信人类真的会随着时间的流逝变得更好,但许多人会认为我们的社会在不断发展,生产更多的商品,为更多人提供更多的保护。

convoluted \ˈkän-və-ˌlü-təd\ (1) Having a pattern of curved windings. 盘绕的,曲折的 (2) Involved, intricate. 错综复杂的,难理解的

• After 10 minutes, Mr. Collins's strange story had become so convoluted that none of us could follow it. 十分钟后,柯林斯先生的奇怪故事变得离奇曲折,没人能够听懂。

UNIT 11

Convolution originally meant a complex winding pattern such as those visible on the surface of the brain. So a convoluted argument or a convoluted explanation is one that winds this way and that. An official document may have to wind its way through a convoluted process and be stamped by eight people before being approved. Convoluted language makes many people suspicious; as a great philosopher once said, "Anything that can be said can be said clearly."

VOLU/
VOLV

convolution 最初指的是一种复杂的缠绕模式,比如在大脑皮层上可见的脑回。复杂的推论或复杂的解释会绕来绕去。某份官方文件可能要经过复杂的程序,要有八个人盖章才能获得批准。繁复的语言会让很多人生疑;一位伟大的哲学家曾经说过:"凡是能够言说的,都能说得清楚。"

Quizzes

A. Choose the closest definition:

1. convoluted   a. spinning   b. babbling   c. grinding   d. winding
2. turbine   a. whirlpool   b. engine   c. headdress   d. carousel
3. evolution   a. process of development   b. process of democracy   c. process of election   d. process of elimination
4. perturb   a. reset   b. inset   c. preset   d. upset
5. voluble   a. whirling   b. unpleasant   c. talkative   d. garbled
6. turbulent   a. churning   b. turning   c. yearning   d. burning
7. turbid   a. flat   b. calm   c. confused   d. slow
8. devolve   a. hand down   b. hand in   c. turn up   d. turn around

B. Match the word on the left to the correct definition on the right:

1. voluble   a. murky
2. turbine   b. chatty
3. evolution   c. seething
4. turbid   d. complicated
5. devolve   e. turning engine
6. perturb   f. degenerate
7. convoluted   g. disturb
8. turbulent   h. progress

FAC

FAC comes from the Latin verb *facere*, meaning "to make or do." Thus, a *fact* was originally simply "something done." A *benefactor* is someone who does good. And to *manufacture* is to make, usually in a *factory*.

FAC 源自拉丁语动词 *facere*，意思是"做"。因此，*fact* 最初指的就是"所做的事情"。*benefactor* 指的是做善事的人。*manufacture* 通常指的是在工厂里制作。

---

factor \ˈfak-tər\ Something that contributes to producing a result; ingredient. 因素，成分。

• The most important factor in the success of the treaty talks was the physical presence of the two presidents. 条约谈判成功的最重要因素是两位总统的出席。

In Latin *factor* means simply "doer." So in English a factor is an "actor" or element or ingredient in some situation or quantity. Charm can be a factor in someone's success, and lack of exercise can be a factor in producing a poor physique. In math we use *factor* to mean a number that can be multiplied or divided to produce a given number (for example, 5 and 8 are factors of 40). And in biology a gene may be called a factor, since genes are ingredients in the total organism.

拉丁语 *factor* 的意思就是"做某事的人"。所以在英语中，factor 指的是在某个情景或某个量中的一个"参与者"、因素或成分。魅力可能是某人成功的一个因素，缺乏锻炼可能是导致体质较差的一个因素。在数学中，我们用 *factor*（因数）来表示一个数字，可以乘或除得出一个给定的数（比如，5 和 8 是 40 的因数）。在生物学中，基因可称为 factor，因为基因是整个生物体的组成部分。

---

factotum \fak-ˈtō-təm\ A person whose job involves doing many different kinds of work. 事务总管，勤杂人员

• Over the years she had become the office factotum, who might be doing legal research one day and organizing the company picnic the next. 多年来，她已成为办公室的事务总管，今天可能在做法律研究，明天可能在组织公司野餐。

This odd word doesn't come from ancient Latin, but it was coined to look as if it did. The term *Johannes factotum*, meaning "Jack-of-all-trades," first shows up in writing in 1592 to describe none other than Shakespeare himself. The word *gofer* is similar to *factotum* but a bit less dignified. In other words, a factotum is an assistant, but one who may have taken over some fairly important functions.

这个奇怪的词并非源自古拉丁语，但它被造出来之后，看起来又像是源自古拉丁语。*Johannes factotum* 的意思是"万事通"，最早出现在 1592 年的作品中，用来形容的就是莎士比亚本人。*Gofer* 这个词和 *factotum* 很像，但是没有那么高贵。换句话说，factotum 是个助手，但可能已经接管了一些相当重要的功能。

---

facile \ˈfa-səl\ (1) Easily accomplished. 容易得到的，轻易做到的 (2) Shallow, superficial. 肤浅的，表面的

• The principal made a facile argument for the school's policy, but no one was convinced. 校长为学校的政策给了一个浅显的理由，但没有人信服。

A facile suggestion doesn't deal with the issue in any depth, and a facile solution

may be only temporarily effective. A facile writer is one who seems to write too quickly and easily, and a careful reader may discover that the writer hasn't really said very much.
肤浅的建议并不能解决有深度的问题,肤浅的解决方案可能只是暂时有效。浅薄的作家似乎写得太快、太容易,而细心的读者可能会发现这个作家废话连篇。

facilitate\fə-ˈsi-lə-ˌtāt\ To make (something) easier; to make (something) run more smoothly. 使更容易,促进,推动

• Her uncle hadn't exactly gotten her the job, but he had certainly facilitated the process. 确切地说,她叔叔并没有让她得到那份工作,但他确实促进了这个过程。

Facilitating is about getting things done. Clever employees are quietly facilitating all kinds of useful activity within their organizations all the time. People who lead therapy groups or workshops are often called *facilitators*, since their job isn't to teach or to order but rather to make the meetings as productive as possible. Even businesses now use facilitators in meetings where they don't want any person's particular desires to outweigh anyone else's. The *facilitation* of a rewarding discussion should be a facilitator's only goal. Today, in recognition of the many different situations that may call for a facilitator, there is even an International Association of Facilitators.
facilitating 就是把事情做好。聪明的员工一直在悄悄地为他们组织内各种有用的活动提供便利。领导治疗小组或研讨会的人通常被称为 *facilitators*(推动者),因为他们的工作不是教导或下令,而是尽可能使会议富有成效。如今,连企业都会在会议上使用 facilitators,他们不希望在会上有任何人自己的欲望盖过其他人的。*facilitation*(推动)有益的讨论应该是 facilitators 的唯一目标。今天,由于认识到许多情况都需要 facilitators,人们甚至还成立了一个国际建导师协会。

LUM

LUM comes from the Latin noun *lumen*, meaning "light." Thus, our word *illuminate* means "to supply with light" or "make clear," and *illumination* is light that shines on something.
LUM 源自拉丁文名词 *lumen*,意思是"光"。因此,英语单词 *illuminate* 指的是"照亮"或"使……清楚",*illumination* 指的是照亮某物的光。

lumen\ˈlü-mən\ In physics, the standard unit for measuring the rate of the flow of light. 流明(光通量单位)

• The lumen is a measure of the perceived power of light. 流明是所感知到的光能的计量单位。

There are two common units for measuring light, the candela and the lumen. Both are recognized as standard international units, which also include the second (for time), the kilogram (for weight), and the meter (for length). The *candela* is a measure of intensity; an ordinary candle gives off light with the intensity of about one candela. The lumen is a measure of "luminous flux"; a standard 100-watt lightbulb gives off 1500-1700 lumens. Luminous flux indicates how much light is actually perceived by the human eye. Technologies vary in how efficiently they turn electricity into light; halogen lights produce about 12 lumens per watt, ordinary incandescent lightbulbs produce about 15 lumens per watt, and compact fluorescent bulbs produce about 50 lumens per watt.

测量光有两种常用的单位——坎德拉和流明。两者都是公认的标准国际单位,标准国际单位还包括秒(表示时间)、千克(表示重量)、米(表示长度)等。*Candela*(坎德拉)是发光强度的计量单位,一只普通蜡烛的发光强度约为一坎德拉。流明是"光通量"的计量单位,标准的 100 瓦灯泡的光通量是 1500—1700 流明。光通量表示人眼实际感知到的光量。电能转化为光的技术有很多,但效率各不相同。卤素灯每瓦产生约 12 流明,普通的白炽灯泡每瓦产生约 15 流明,紧凑型荧光灯每瓦产生约 50 流明。

luminous \ˈlü-mə-nəs\ (1) Producing or seeming to produce light. 发光的。(2) Filled with light. 照亮的。照明的。

• She ended her recital with a luminous performance of Ravel's song cycle, and the crowd called her back for repeated encores. 她精彩地演唱了拉威尔的组歌,以此结束独唱会,但观众们却要她一次次返场加唱。

Luminous, like its synonyms *radiant*, *shining*, *glowing*, and *lustrous*, is generally a positive adjective, especially when it describes something that doesn't literally glow, such as a face, a performance, or a poem. Luminous signs depend on a gas such as neon, krypton, argon, xenon, or radon—and you can use luminous (DayGlo) paint to make your own signs. New technologies have now given us luminous fabrics, which are being used to produce striking or creepy effects in clothing, upholstery, and interior surfaces.

luminous 与同义词 *radiant*、*shining*、*glowing*、*lustrous* 一样,通常是积极的形容词,特别是当它用来描述某个实际并不发光的东西时,比如脸、表演、诗等。发光标志靠的是某种气体,比如氖、氪、氩、氙、氡——你也可以使用发光涂料(DayGlo)制作自己的发光标志。现在,新技术为我们提供了发光面料,这些面料用于服装、室内装潢、内饰表面等,可以产生惊艳的或惊恐的效果。

bioluminescent \ˌbī-ō-ˌlü-mə-ˈne-sᵊnt\ Relating to light given off by living organisms. 生物发光的

• Most of the light emitted by bioluminescent marine organisms is blue or blue-green. 海洋生物发光发出的光大多是蓝色或蓝绿色。

Bio- comes from the Greek word for "life" (see BIO, p. 407). On land, fireflies, glowworms, and the fox-fire fungus are all known for their *bioluminescence*. In the sea, bioluminescent life-forms include plankton, squid, and comb jellies, as well as some unusual fish. Most deep-sea animals are bioluminescent, but single-celled algae living at or near the surface can also create a remarkable show, as they often do in Bioluminescent Bay on the Puerto Rican island of Vieques. But bioluminescence is unknown in true plants, and mammals, birds, reptiles, and amphibians never got the knack of it either.

bio- 源自希腊语中表示"生命"的单词(参见 BIO,第 407 页)。在陆地上,萤火虫、狐火真菌等都以其 *bioluminescence*

(生物发光)而闻名。在海洋中，发光生物包括浮游生物、鱿鱼、栉水母以及一些不寻常的鱼类。大多数深海动物都具有生物发光功能，但生活在海面或海面附近的单细胞藻类也可以有令人瞩目的表现，就像它们在波多黎各的别克斯岛的生物发光湾所做的那样。但在真正的植物中，生物发光尚未被发现，哺乳动物、鸟类、爬行动物和两栖动物也从未掌握过这种技术。

luminary \ lü-mə-ˌner-ē \ A very famous or distinguished person. 名人，杰出人物

• Entering the glittering reception room, she immediately spotted several luminaries of the art world. 走进熠熠生辉的接待室，她立即发现了几位艺术界的名流。

The Latin word *luminaria* could mean either "lamps" or "heavenly bodies." For medieval astrologers, the luminaries were the sun and the moon, the brightest objects in the heavens. Today a luminary is usually a person of "brilliant" achievement: a celebrity, a "leading light," or a "star."

拉丁语 *luminaria* 既可以指"灯"，也可以指"天体"。对于中世纪的占星师来说，发光体是太阳和月亮，是天空中最明亮的物体。如今，杰出人物通常是有"辉煌"成就的人：名人、"要人""明星"。

Quizzes

A. Fill in each blank with the correct letter:

a. lumen
b. bioluminescent
c. luminary
d. luminous

e. facile
f. factor
g. factotum
h. facilitate

1. The light output of an ordinary candle provided the basis for the light unit called the _____.
2. Her _____ voice was all the critics could talk about in their reviews of the musical's opening night.
3. She was quick-witted, but her reasoning was often _____ and not deeply thoughtful.
4. The _____ insects that he studies use their light for mating.
5. The support of the financial industry would greatly _____ the passage of the bill.
6. He had just been introduced to another _____ of the literary world and was feeling rather dazzled.
7. The main _____ in their decision to build was their desire for a completely "green" home.
8. As the company's _____, she often felt overworked and underappreciated.

B. Indicate whether the following pairs of words have the same or different meanings:

1. facilitate / ease   same ____ / different ____
2. lumen / lighting   same ____ / different ____

3. factor / element   same _____ / different _____
4. luminary / star   same _____ / different _____
5. factotum / expert   same _____ / different _____
6. luminous / glowing   same _____ / different _____
7. facile / practical   same _____ / different _____
8. bioluminescent / brilliant   same _____ / different _____

Words from Mythology and History 源自神话和历史的词语

muse \\'myüz\   A source of inspiration; a guiding spirit. 缪斯,灵感源泉;指导精神

• At 8:00 each morning he sat down at his desk and summoned his muse, and she almost always responded. 每天早上8点,他坐在办公桌前,召唤自己的缪斯,而她几乎都会有所回应。

The Muses were the nine Greek goddesses who presided over the arts (including *music*) and literature. A shrine to the Muses was called in Latin a *museum*. An artist or poet about to begin work would call on his particular Muse to inspire him, and a poem itself might begin with such a call; thus, Homer's *Odyssey* begins, "Sing to me of the man, Muse" (that is, of Odysseus). Today a muse may be one's special creative spirit, but some artists and writers have also chosen living human beings to serve as their muses.

缪斯是九位希腊女神,掌管艺术(包括 *music*)和文学。缪斯们的神庙在拉丁语中被称作 *museum*。艺术家或者诗人在开始工作前,会召唤某位缪斯给予灵感,而诗歌本身也可能以这种方式开头。因此,荷马《奥德赛》的首句是:"给我歌颂那个男人吧,缪斯女神"(那个男人指的是奥德修斯)。今天,缪斯可以指某人的特殊创造精神,但一些艺术家和作家也会选择活着的人类来当作他们的缪斯。

iridescent \ˌir-ə-ˈde-sənt\   Having a glowing, rainbowlike play of color that seems to change as the light shifts. 彩虹色的,色彩斑斓的

• The children shrieked with glee as the iridescent soap bubbles floated away in the gentle breeze. 看到彩虹色的肥皂泡在微风中飞走,孩子们高兴地尖叫起来。

Iris, the Greek goddess of the rainbow, took messages from Mount Olympus to earth, and from gods to mortals or other gods, using the rainbow as her stairway. *Iridescence* is thus the glowing, shifting, colorful quality of a rainbow, also seen in an opal, a light oil slick, a butterfly wing, or the mother-of-pearl that lines an oyster shell.

Iris(艾丽丝)是希腊的彩虹女神,她用彩虹作阶梯,把消息从奥林匹斯山传向人间,从天神传向凡人或其他天神。因此,*iridescence*(彩虹色)指的是彩虹的闪亮、变幻和色彩缤纷的属性,也可见于蛋白石、浮油、蝴蝶翅膀或牡蛎壳中的珍珠母。

mausoleum \ˌmo-zə-ˈlē-əm\   (1) A large tomb, especially one built aboveground with shelves for the dead. 陵墓 (2) A large, gloomy building or room. 大而阴森的建筑物或房间

- The family's grand mausoleum occupied a prominent spot in the cemetery, for all the good it did the silent dead within. 这个家族宏大的陵墓位于墓地中显耀的位置,那是因为该家族对安息在墓地中的人做出过巨大贡献。

Mausolus was ruler of a kingdom in Asia Minor in the 4th century B. C. He beautified the capital, Halicarnassus, with all sorts of fine public buildings, but he is best known for the magnificent monument, the Mausoleum, that was built by his wife Artemisia after his death. With its great height (perhaps 140 feet) and many beautiful sculptures, the Mausoleum was declared one of the Seven Wonders of the Ancient World. Though Halicarnassus was repeatedly attacked, the Mausoleum would survive for well over 1,000 years. Mausolus(摩索拉斯)是公元前4世纪小亚细亚一个王国的统治者。他用各式各样的公共建筑来美化首都哈利卡那索斯,但最为人们熟知的还是在他去世之后,妻子阿忒米西娅为纪念他而建造的宏伟的摩索拉斯王陵墓。陵墓高约140英尺,有许多精美的雕塑,被誉为古代世界的七大奇观之一。尽管哈利卡纳索斯后来不断受到攻击,但摩索拉斯王陵墓却存在长达千年之久。

mentor\ˈmen-ˌtȯr\ A trusted counselor, guide, tutor, or coach. 导师,指导者

- This pleasant old gentleman had served as friend and mentor to a series of young lawyers in the firm. 这位和蔼可亲的老绅士曾是公司中一批又一批年轻律师的导师和朋友。

Odysseus was away from home fighting and journeying for 20 years, according to Homer. During that time, the son he left as a babe in arms grew up under the supervision of Mentor, an old and trusted friend. When the goddess Athena decided it was time to complete young Telemachus's education by sending him off to learn about his father, she visited him disguised as Mentor and they set out together. Today, anyone such as a coach or tutor who gives another (usually younger) person help and advice on how to achieve success in the larger world is called a mentor. And in recent years we've even been using the word as a verb, and now in business we often speak of an experienced employee *mentoring* someone who has just arrived. 根据荷马的讲述,奥德修斯离家战斗,旅行时间长达20年之久。在此期间,他离开时还在襁褓中的儿子在Mentor(孟托)的监护下长大了,孟托是他信任的一个老朋友。当女神雅典娜觉得是时候送忒勒马科斯去见父亲,完成教育的时候,她就扮成孟托一起出发了。如今,任何能给别人(通常年轻一些的人)帮助和建议,让他们在大世界中取得成功的教练或导师都可以称作mentor。近年来,我们还一直把它用作动词,比如在商业中,我们常说,一个有经验的雇员正在 *mentoring*(指导)某个新员工。

narcissism\ˈnär-sə-ˌsi-zəm\ (1) Extreme self-centeredness or fascination with oneself. 极度自我,自恋 (2) Love or desire for one's own body. (对身体)自恋,自我陶醉

- His girlfriend would complain about his narcissism, saying he spent more time looking at himself in the mirror than at her. 他的女朋友抱怨他太自恋了,说他照镜子的时间比看她的时间还长。

Narcissus was a handsome youth in Greek mythology who inspired love in many who saw him. One was the nymph Echo, who could only repeat the last thing that anyone said. When Narcissus cruelly rejected her, she wasted away to nothing but her voice. Though he played with the affections of others, Narcissus became a victim of his own attractiveness. When he caught sight of his own reflection in a pool, he sat gazing at it in fascination, wasting away without food or drink, unable to touch or kiss the image he saw. When he finally died, the gods turned him into the flower we call the *narcissus*, which stands with its head bent as though gazing at its reflection. People with "*narcissistic* personality disorder" have a somewhat serious mental condition, according to psychologists, but the rest of us are free to call anyone who seems vain and self-centered a *narcissist*.

Narcissus(纳西索斯)是希腊神话中的美少年,很多人对他一见倾心。其中有一个是仙女 Echo(伊可),她只能重复别人说的最后一句话。当遭到那喀索斯残忍拒绝后,她便日渐消瘦,直到身体完全消失,仅留下声音。尽管那喀索斯玩弄别人的感情,但他也成了自己魅力的受害者。在池水中看到自己的倒影后,他便沉迷其中,不吃不喝日渐消瘦,却又无法触碰或吻到所看见的影子。他最终死去,众神将他变成了水仙花,花的头部弯曲,仿佛在凝视着自己的倒影。心理学家认为,"自恋型人格障碍"患者有严重的精神问题,而我们可以称那些自负而又以自我为中心的人为自恋者。

tantalize\ˈtan-tə-ˌlīz\   To tease or torment by offering something desirable but keeping it out of reach. 逗引,撩拨,惹弄

• The sight of a warm fire through the window tantalized the little match girl almost unbearably. 透过窗户看到暖烘烘的炉火,卖火柴的小女孩心动不已。

King Tantalus, according to Greek mythology, killed his son Pelops and served him to the gods in a stew for dinner. Almost all the gods realized what was happening and refused the meal, though only after Demeter had taken a nibble out of Pelops's shoulder. After they had reconstructed him, replacing the missing shoulder with a piece of ivory, they turned to punishing Tantalus. In Hades he stands in water up to his neck under a tree laden with fruit. Each time he stoops to drink, the water moves out of reach; each time he reaches up to pick something, the branches move beyond his grasp. He is thus eternally tantalized by the water and fruit. Today anything or anyone that tempts but is unobtainable is tantalizing.

根据希腊神话,国王 Tantalus(坦塔罗斯)杀死了自己的儿子佩洛普斯,并将他的肉炖成汤来招待众神。在农业之神德墨忒耳吃了一小口佩洛普斯的肩部的肉后,几乎所有天神都意识到了发生的事情,他们拒绝了这顿饭。天神们将佩洛普斯的身体重新拼凑起来,用一块儿象牙替代缺失的一小块肩膀,转而惩罚坦塔罗斯。在冥府,坦塔罗斯站在齐颈深的水中的一棵结满果实的树下。每当他俯身喝水时,河水就会退去;每当他伸手摘果子时,树枝就会移开。因此,他永远被水和水果逗引。如今,任何有诱惑力但又无法得到的人或物都可以被称作是"逗弄人的"。

thespian\ˈthes-pē-ən\   An actor. 演员。

• In summer the towns of New England welcome troupes of thespians dedicated to presenting plays of all kinds. 夏季,新英格兰的城镇会迎来很多戏班子,表演各种各样的戏剧。

Greek drama was originally entirely performed by choruses. According to tradition, the Greek dramatist Thespis, of the 6th century B. C., was the inventor of tragedy and the first to write roles for the individual actor as distinct from the chorus, and the actor's exchanges with the chorus were the first dramatic dialogue. Since Thespis himself performed the individual parts in his own plays, he was also the first true actor. Ever since choruses disappeared from drama, thespians have filled all the roles in plays. *Thespian* is also an adjective; thus, we can speak of "thespian ambitions" and "thespian traditions," for example.

希腊戏剧最初完全是由合唱团表演的。根据传统说法,公元前 6 世纪的希腊剧作家 Thespis(泰斯庇斯)是悲剧的创造者,也是第一个为演员个人写角色的人,这与合唱截然不同,演员与合唱者的对唱就是最早的戏剧台词。因为泰斯庇斯本人参演了自己的剧作,他也成为第一位真正的演员。合唱从戏剧中消失之后,演员们承担了戏剧的全部角色。*Thespian* 也是形容词,比如我们可以说"戏剧的目标""戏剧的传统"等。

zephyr \\'ze-fər\\ (1) A breeze from the west. 西风 (2) A gentle breeze. 和风,微风

● Columbus left Genoa sailing against the zephyrs that continually blow across the Mediterranean. 哥伦布离开了热内亚,逆着吹过地中海的西风向前航行。

The ancient Greeks called the west wind Zephyrus and regarded him and his fellows—Boreas (god of the north wind), Eurus (god of the east wind), and Notus (god of the south wind)—as gods. A zephyr is a kind wind, bringer of clear skies and beautiful weather.

古希腊人称西风为 Zephyrus(泽费罗斯),并将他和他的兄弟们称为风神——波瑞阿斯(北风之神)、欧里斯(东风之神)、诺鲁斯(南风之神)。西风是一种温和的风,会带来晴朗的天空和美好的天气。

Quiz

Fill in each blank with the correct letter:

a. mausoleum
b. thespian
c. iridescent
d. tantalize
e. muse
f. mentor
g. zephyr
h. narcissism

1. At the middle of the cemetery stood the grand _____ of the city's wealthiest family.

2. On fair days a gentle _____ would blow from morning until night.

3. The company president took the new recruit under her wing and acted as her _____ for the next several years.

4. He would often _____ her with talk of traveling to Brazil or India, but nothing ever came of it.

5. The oil slick on the puddle's surface became beautifully _____ in the slanting light.

6. After his last book of poetry was published, his _____ seemed to have abandoned him.

7. In everyone there is a bit of the _____ yearning for a stage.

8. By working as a model, she could satisfy her _____ while getting paid for it.

Review Quizzes

A. Choose the correct definition:

1. voluble   a. argumentative   b. mumbly   c. speechless   d. talkative
2. facilitate   a. guide   b. build   c. order   d. obstruct
3. verify   a. reverse   b. mislead   c. prove   d. test
4. zephyr   a. stormy blast   b. icy rain   c. light shower   d. gentle breeze
5. aver   a. reject   b. detract   c. deny   d. assert
6. turbulent   a. unending   b. swirling   c. muddy   d. angry
7. facile   a. tough   b. quiet   c. familiar   d. easy
8. perturb   a. soothe   b. restore   c. park   d. upset
9. devolve   a. decay   b. turn into   c. suggest   d. improve
10. convoluted   a. disorderly   b. complex   c. discouraged   d. superior
11. muse   a. singer   b. poetry   c. inspiration   d. philosopher
12. tantalize   a. visit   b. satisfy   c. tease   d. watch
13. iridescent   a. shimmering   b. drab   c. striped   d. watery
14. mentor   a. translator   b. interpreter   c. guide   d. student
15. factotum   a. manufacturer   b. untruth   c. dilemma   d. assistant

B. Indicate whether the following pairs of terms have the same or different meanings:

1. thespian / teacher   same ____ / different ____
2. facile / handy   same ____ / different ____
3. evolution / extinction   same ____ / different ____

4. verify / prove   same ____ / different ____
5. turbine / plow   same ____ / different ____
6. spirited / energetic   same ____ / different ____
7. incantation / chant   same ____ / different ____
8. turbid / muddy   same ____ / different ____
9. transpire / ooze   same ____ / different ____
10. aver / claim   same ____ / different ____

C. Fill in each blank with the correct letter:

a. lingua franca   g. facilitate
b. narcissism   h. linguistics
c. descant   i. cantor
d. verisimilitude   j. devolve
e. cantata   k. turbine
f. veracity   l. mausoleum

1. The defense lawyers knew the jury might be doubtful about the next witness's _____.

2. They were a very attractive couple, but their _____ often annoyed other people.

3. The university chorus was going to perform a Bach _____ along with the Mozart Requiem.

4. They finally realized they would need a real-estate agent to _____ the sale of the property.

5. He began his singing career as a _____ in Brooklyn and ended it as an international opera star.

6. She had hired a highly experienced deputy, hoping to _____ many of her responsibilities onto him.

7. One day in the cemetery the _____ door was open, and he peered in with horrified fascination.

8. Never having studied _____, he didn't feel able to discuss word histories in much depth.

9. The Spaniards and Germans at the next table were using English as a _____.

10. Her films showed her own reality, and she had no interest in _____.

11. The roar of the _____ was so loud they couldn't hear each other.

12. As part of their musical training, she always encouraged them to sing their own _____ over the main melody.

UNIT 12

UMBR comes from the Latin *umbra*, meaning "shadow." Thus, the familiar *umbrella*, with its ending meaning "little," casts a "little shadow" to keep off the sun or the rain.
UMBR 源自拉丁语 umbra，意思是"阴影"。我们所熟悉的 umbrella(伞)的词尾的意思是"小的"，因此这个词指的是投下一个"小的阴影"，以遮挡太阳或雨水。

umber\ˈəm-bər\ (1) A darkish brown mineral containing manganese and iron oxides used for coloring paint. 棕土，赭土 (2) A color that is greenish brown to dark reddish brown. 棕土色

• Van Dyke prized umber as a pigment and used it constantly in his oil paintings.
范·戴克很看重赭土，把它作为颜料经常用在绘画中。

The mineral deposits of Italy provided sources of a number of natural pigments, among them umber. Since the late Renaissance, umber has been in great demand as a coloring agent. When crushed and mixed with paint, it produces an olive color known as *raw umber*; when crushed and burnt, it produces a darker tone known as *burnt umber*.
意大利的矿藏有许多可作为天然颜料的来源，其中就有赭土。自文艺复兴晚期以来，赭土作为着色剂需求一直大。赭土粉碎后与颜料混合产生一种黄褐色，称为 raw umber (生赭色)；粉碎并烧焦后产生一种稍暗的色调，称为 burnt umber (焦赭色)。

adumbrate\ˈa-dəm-brāt\ (1) To give a sketchy outline or disclose in part. 勾画轮廓 (2) To hint at or foretell. 暗示，预示

• The Secretary of State would only adumbrate his ideas for bringing peace to Bosnia. 国务卿只是扼要地讲了他要为波斯尼亚带来和平的一些想法。

A synonym for *adumbrate* is *foreshadow*, which means to present a shadowy version of something before it becomes reality or is provided in full. Tough questioning by a Supreme Court justice may adumbrate the way he or she is planning to rule on a case. A bad review by a critic may adumbrate the failure of a new film. And rats scurrying off a ship were believed to adumbrate a coming disaster at sea.

adumbrate 的一个同义词是 *foreshadow*，其含义是在某事物成为现实或被完全展示出来之前，给出其模糊的版本。最高法院法官的严厉质询可能预示着他/她正在计划如何对案件做出裁决。影评人给出不好的评价可能预示着一部新电影的失败。据说，老鼠从船上匆匆跑掉预示着一场海上灾难即将来临。

penumbra \ pə-ˈnəm-brə \   (1) The partial shadow surrounding a complete shadow, as in an eclipse. （日、月食等的）半影 (2) The fringe or surrounding area where something exists less fully. 外部、边缘区域

- This area of the investigation was the penumbra where both the FBI and the CIA wanted to pursue their leads. 这项调查是在联邦调查局和中央情报局都想要追踪的线索的外部区域开展的。

Every solar eclipse casts an *umbra*, the darker central area in which almost no light reaches the earth, and a penumbra, the area of partial shadow where part of the sun is still visible. *Penumbra* can thus be used to describe any "gray area" where things aren't all black and white. For example, the right to privacy falls under the penumbra of the U.S. Constitution; though it isn't specifically guaranteed there, the Supreme Court has held that it is implied, and thus that the government may not intrude into certain areas of a citizen's private life. Because its existence is still shadowy, however, the Court is still determining how much of an individual's life is protected by the right to privacy.

每次日食都会产生 *umbra*（本影）和 *penumbra*（半影）。本影是几乎没有光线照射到地球的黑暗的中心区域，半影是仍可见部分太阳的半阴影区域。因此，*penumbra* 可以用来描述任何"灰色区域"，在这个区域中事物并非都是黑和白。比如，隐私权属于美国宪法的边缘区域；尽管这个权利没有得到特别的保护，但最高法院认为这种保护是隐含的，因此政府不得侵入公民私生活的某些领域。然而，由于它的存在仍然是模糊的，法院仍在决定个人生活中有多少可受隐私权的保护。

umbrage \ ˈəm-brij \   A feeling of resentment at some slight or insult, often one that is imagined rather than real. 不悦、怨恨

- She often took umbrage at his treatment of her, without being able to pinpoint what was offensive about it. 她经常因他对自己的态度而不悦，但却无法明确指出其中的冒犯之处。

An *umbrage* was originally a shadow, and soon the word also began to mean "a shadowy suspicion." Then it came to mean "displeasure" as well—that is, a kind of shadow blocking the sunlight. *Umbrage* is now generally used in the phrase "take umbrage at." An overly sensitive person may take umbrage at something as small as having his or her name pronounced wrong.

umbrage 最初指的是阴影，很快这个词开始表示"阴暗的怀疑"的意思。随后它也有了"不悦"的含义——也就是说，某种阴影遮住阳光。*umbrage* 现在通常被用在短语 "take umbrage at（）感到受到了冒犯或怠慢"中。过度敏感的人可能会对他/她的名字被念错这样小的事情而生气。

VEST comes from the Latin verb *vestire*, "to clothe" or "to dress," and the noun *vestis*, "clothing" or "garment." *Vest* is the shortest English word we have from this root, and is the name of a rather small piece of clothing. VEST 源自拉丁语动词 *vestire*("穿衣")以及名词 *vestis*("衣服")。Vest 是这个词根所衍生的最短的英语单词,用作一种小件衣服的名字。

divest \dī-ˈvest\ (1) To get rid of or free oneself of property, authority, or title. 剥夺(财产、权力、头衔等) (2) To strip of clothing, ornaments, or equipment. 脱去

• In protest against apartheid, many universities in the 1980s divested themselves of all stock in South African companies. 为了抗议种族隔离,许多大学在 20 世纪 80 年代从南非公司全部撤资。

If you decide to enter a monastery, you may *divest* yourself of most of your possessions. When a church is officially abandoned, it's usually divested of its ornaments and furnishings. A company that's going through hard times may divest itself of several stores, and investors are constantly divesting themselves of stocks that aren't performing well enough. And when it turns out that athletes have been using steroids, they're usually divested of any awards they may have won. 如果决定进入修道院,你可能会放弃自己的大部分财物。当教堂被正式废弃时,通常会失去饰品和家具。处于艰难时期的公司可能会关闭几家门店,投资者会不断卖掉表现不佳的股票。如果有结果表明运动员一直在服用兴奋剂,他们通常会被剥夺所获的全部奖项。

investiture \in-ˈves-tə-ˌchür\ The formal placing of someone in office. 授职仪式,授权仪式

• At an English monarch's investiture, he or she is presented with the crown, scepter, and sword, the symbols of power. 在英国君主的授职仪式上,他/她会被授予象征权力的王冠、权杖和国剑。

In its original meaning, an *investiture* was the clothing of a new officeholder in garments that symbolized power. The Middle Ages saw much debate over the investiture of bishops by kings and emperors. These rulers felt that high religious offices were theirs to give as rewards for someone's loyal service or as bribes for someone's future support; the popes, on the other hand, regarded these investitures as the improper buying and selling of church offices. The investiture struggle caused tension between popes and monarchs and even led to wars. *investiture* 最初指的是新上任的官员所穿的象征权力的官服。中世纪出现了很多关于由国王和皇帝授权主教的争论。这些统治者认为,高级宗教职位是他们的,是作为对某人忠诚服务的奖赏,也可以作为贿赂品以换取某个人未来的支持;而教皇则认为这种授权是对教会职务的不正当买卖。授权之争导致了教皇和君主之间的紧张关系,甚至引发了战争。

transvestite \tranz-ˈves-ˌtīt\ A person, especially a male, who wears clothes designed for the opposite sex. 异装癖者

• In Handel's operas, the heroic male leading roles are today often sung by female transvestites, since he originally wrote them for the soprano range. 在韩德尔的歌剧中，男主角如今常常由女扮男装者演唱，因为这些歌剧最初是为女高音演员创作的。

Transvestite includes the prefix *trans-*, "across," and thus means literally "cross-dresser" (and the word *cross-dresser* is in fact now commonly used in place of *transvestite*). In the theater, from ancient Greece to Elizabethan England, *transvestism* was common because all parts—even Juliet—were played by men. Traditional Japanese Kabuki and Noh drama still employ transvestism of this sort. In everyday life, women's clothing includes fashions so similar to men's fashions that both *transvestite* and *cross-dresser* are generally applied only to men. The much newer word *transgender* describes people whose gender identity differs from the sex they had or were identified as having at birth.

VEST

transvestite 的前缀是 trans-("跨越")，因此它的字面意思是"跨性别穿衣的人"(事实上，cross-dresser 现在通常用来替代 transvestite)。在从古希腊到伊丽莎白时代的英格兰剧院中，transvestism(异性装扮现象)很常见，因为所有的角色——甚至是朱丽叶——都由男性扮演。传统的日本歌舞伎和能剧仍雇佣异装演员。在日常生活中，女性服装中有些时装与男性时装极为相似，因此 transvestite 和 cross-dresser 一般只适用于男性。transgender(跨性别者，变性人)这个很新的词描述的是那些性别认同与他们出生时的性别不同的人。

travesty \ˈtra-vəs-tē\ (1) An inferior or distorted imitation. 拙劣的模仿，扭曲 (2) A broadly comic imitation in drama, literature, or art that is usually grotesque and ridiculous. 滑稽的模仿

• The senator was shouting that the new tax bill represented a travesty of tax reform. 这位参议员大声疾呼，他声称新税法是对税改的歪曲。

The word *travesty* comes from the same prefix and root as *transvestite*. Since cross-dressing often isn't very convincing, the word has usually referred to something absurd. So a verdict that angers people may be denounced as a "travesty of justice." *Saturday Night Live* specializes in dramatic travesties mocking everything from political figures and issues to popular culture—"disguised" versions intended for entertainment. *Travesty* may also be a verb; thus, Mel Brooks has travestied movie genres of all kinds—westerns, thrillers, and silent films, among others.

travesty 源自与 transtriteite 相同的前缀及词根。由于异装现象往往不是很让人信服，所以这个词通常指的是荒谬的东西。因此，某项引发民众不满的裁决可能会被谴责为"对正义的歪曲"。《周六夜现场》擅长戏剧性的滑稽模仿，讽刺从政治人物、政治问题到流行文化等一切事情——是一档"伪装"版的娱乐节目。travesty 也用作动词，因此，梅尔·布鲁克斯模仿了各种电影类别——西部片、惊悚片、默片等等。

Quizzes

A. Fill in the blank with the correct letter:

a. penumbra   e. divest

b. transvestite
c. investiture
d. travesty
f. umber
g. umbrage
h. adumbrate

1. All the pigments—crimson, russet, _____, cobalt blue, and the rest—were mixed by his assistants.

2. The _____ of the prime minister was an occasion of pomp and ceremony.

3. Some people are quick to take _____ the moment they think someone might have been disrespectful.

4. Since all the judges were cronies of the dictator, the court proceedings were a _____ of justice.

5. The new director planned to _____ the museum of two of its Picassos.

6. The farther away a source of light is from the object casting a shadow, the wider will be that shadow's _____.

7. The young model became a notorious success when she was discovered to be a _____.

8. The increasing cloudiness and the damp wind seemed to _____ a stormy night.

B. Match the definition on the left to the correct word on the right:

1. resentment
2. brownish color
3. installing in office
4. cross-dresser
5. bad imitation
6. get rid of
7. near shadow
8. partially disclose

a. penumbra
b. travesty
c. transvestite
d. adumbrate
e. divest
f. umbrage
g. investiture
h. umber

THE/THEO

THE/THEO comes from the Greek word meaning "god." *Theology*, the study of religion, is practiced by *theologians*. *Monotheism* is the worship of a single god; Christianity, Islam, and Judaism are *monotheistic* religions, and all three worship the same god. *Polytheistic* religions such as those of ancient Greece and Rome, on the other hand, worship many gods.

THE / THEO 源自意思是"神"的希腊语单词。Theology(神学)是 theologians(神学家)所从事的宗教研究。Monotheism(一神论)是对唯一神的崇拜；基督教、伊斯兰教和犹太教都是 monotheistic religions(一神论的宗教)，三者都信仰同一个神。另一方面，古希腊和古罗马等的 polytheistic religions(多神论的宗教)则崇拜很多神。

apotheosis \ə-ˌpä-thē-ˈō-səs\ (1) Transformation into a god. 神化 (2) The perfect example. 完美的榜样,典范

- Abraham Lincoln's apotheosis after his assassination transformed the controversial politician into the saintly savior of his country. 亚伯拉罕·林肯遭暗杀后被神化,这位备受争议的政治家变成了国家的神圣的救世主。

In ancient Greece, historical figures were sometimes worshipped as gods. In Rome, *apotheosis* was rare until the emperor Augustus declared the dead Julius Caesar to be a god, and soon other dead emperors were being *apotheosized* as well. In older paintings you may see a heroic figure—Napoleon, George Washington, or Shakespeare, for example—being raised into the clouds, symbolizing his or her apotheosis. But today any great classic example of something can be called its apotheosis. You might hear it said, for example, that Baroque music reached its apotheosis in the works of J. S. Bach, or that the Duesenberg Phaeton was the apotheosis of the touring car.

THE/THEO

在古希腊,历史人物有时被当作神来崇拜。在罗马,奥古斯都皇帝宣布死去的尤利乌斯·恺撒为神之前,神化现象是罕见的,很快其他死去的皇帝也被 *apotheosized*(神化)。你可能会在比较老的画作中,看到英雄人物——比如拿破仑、乔治·华盛顿或莎士比亚等——被升到云端,象征着他/她的神化。但是,如今任何关于某事物的了不起的经典例子都可称 apotheosis。比如,你可能会听人说,巴洛克音乐在巴赫的作品作中堪称封神之作,或者杜森伯格辉腾是旅行车的完美典范。

atheistic\ˌā-thē-ˈis-tik\ Denying the existence of God or divine power. 无神论的

- The atheistic Madalyn Murray O'Hair successfully sought the removal of prayer from American public schools in the 1960s. 20世纪60年代,在无神论者马德琳·默里·奥海尔的努力下,美国公立学校取消了祈祷活动。

In the Roman Empire, early Christians were called atheistic because they denied the existence of the Roman gods. And once the Christian church was firmly established, it condemned the Romans as *atheists* because they didn't believe in the Christian God. In later centuries, English-speaking Christians would often use the words *pagan* and *heathen* to describe such non-Christians, while *atheist* would be reserved for those who actually denied the existence of any god. *Atheism* is different from *agnosticism*, which claims that the existence of any higher power is unknowable; and lots of people who simply don't think much about religion often call themselves *agnostics* as well.

在罗马帝国,早期的基督徒被看作无神论者,因为他们否认罗马诸神的存在。基督教会根基稳固之后,开始谴责罗马人是 *atheists*(无神论者),因为罗马人不相信基督教的上帝。在后来的几个世纪中,说英语的基督徒经常用 *pagan*(异教徒)和 *heathen*(异教徒)来描述这些非基督徒,而 *atheist* 留给那些实际上否认上帝存在的人。Atheism(无神论)不同于 *agnosticism*(不可知论),后者认为任何更高力量的存在都是不可知的。许多根本不怎么思考宗教的人也常自称为 *agnostics*(不可知论者)。

pantheon\ˈpan-thē-än\ (1) A building serving as the burial place of or containing memorials to the famous dead of a nation. 万神殿,先贤祠 (2) A group of notable persons or things. 名流,要人

- A Hall of Fame serves as a kind of pantheon for its field, and those admitted in the early years are often the greatest of all. 名人堂在各自的领域里就是一种万神殿,而那些早期的入选者往往是最伟大的。

Each of the important Roman gods and goddesses had many temples erected in their name. But in 27 B. C. a temple to all the gods together was completed in Rome; twice destroyed, it was ultimately replaced by a third temple around A. D. 126. This extraordinary domed structure is still one of the important sights of Rome, and the burial place for the painters Raphael and Carracci and two kings. In Paris, a great church was completed in 1789—1990; named the Panthéon, it was announced as the future resting place of France's great figures, and the bodies of Victor Hugo, Louis Pasteur, Marie Curie, and many others now rest within its walls.

每一位重要的罗马男神和女神都有很多为他们建立的神庙。但在公元前 27 年,罗马建成了一座供奉所有神灵的神庙;它两次被毁,最终在公元 126 年左右被第三座神庙取代。这座非凡的穹顶建筑如今仍是罗马的重要景观之一,也是著名画家拉斐尔、卡拉契和两位国王的墓地。在巴黎,一座大教堂在 1789—1990 年间建成,命名为万神殿,被宣布为未来法国伟大人物的安息之所,维克多・雨果、路易・巴斯德、玛丽・居里和其他许多人的遗体如今都长眠于此。

theocracy\thē-ˈä-krə-sē\ (1) Government by officials who are regarded as divinely inspired. 神权政治,神权政体 (2) A state governed by a theocracy. 神权制国家

- The ancient Aztecs lived in a theocracy in which guidance came directly from the gods through the priests. 古老的阿兹特克人生活在神权政治中,他们通过祭司直接从众神那里获得指引。

In the Middle Ages, the Muslim empires stretching around much of the Mediterranean were theocracies, and the pope ruled most of modern-day Italy. But theocracies are rare today. When a government tries to follow all the teachings of a single religion, things usually don't work out terribly well, so U. S. Constitution and Bill of Rights forbid using religion as the principal basis for democracy.

在中世纪,穆斯林帝国延伸到地中海大部分地区,实行神权政治,而教皇则统治现代意大利的大部分地区。然而,神权政治如今已经很少见了。当一个政府试图遵循单一宗教的所有教义时,事情通常不太顺利,因此美国宪法和权利法案禁止将宗教作为民主的主要基础。

ICON

ICON comes from the Greek *eikon*, which led to the Latin *icon*, both meaning "image." Though the *icon-* root hasn't produced many English words, the words that is does appear in tend to be interesting.

ICON 源自希腊语 *eikon*,而 *eikon* 又衍生出拉丁语 *icon*,两者的意思都是"形象"。虽然词根 *icon-* 没有产生很多英语单词,但有这个词根出现的单词往往很有趣。

icon\ˈī-ˌkän\ (1) A religious image usually painted on a small wooden panel; idol. 圣像,神像 (2) Emblem, symbol. 标志,象征

- Henry Ford's assembly line captured the imagination of the world, and he and his company became icons of industrial capitalism. 福特的流水生产线激发了全世界的想象力,他和他的公司成为工业资本主义的象征。

In the Eastern Orthodox church, much importance is given to *icons*, usually small portraits on wood—sometimes with gold-leaf paint—of Jesus, Mary, or a saint, which hang in churches and in the houses of the faithful. The Orthodox church favors icons partly because they communicate directly and forcefully even to uneducated people. They are regarded as sacred; some believers actually pray to them, and many believe that icons have carried out miracles. The common modern uses of *icon* grew out of this original sense. The fact that Orthodox icons have a symbolic role led to *icon* being used to mean simply "symbol." Because of the icon's sacredness, the term also came to mean "idol." And once we began to use *idol* to refer to pop-culture stars, it wasn't long before we began using *icon* the same way. But for the little computer-desktop images that you click on, the older meaning of "symbol" is the one we're thinking of.

东正教会非常重视神像,通常是些画在木头上的耶稣、玛丽或圣徒的小肖像——有时用金叶漆画。东正教会偏爱神像的部分原因是,即使是对没有受过教育的人,神像也能直接有力地传达信息。神像被认为是神圣的;一些信徒向神像祈祷,许多人相信神像创造了奇迹。icon 的现代常见用法正是源于这种原始意义。东正教神像具有象征性的作用,这一事实赋予 icon "象征"之意。由于神像的神圣性,这个词也指"偶像"。我们开始使用 idol 来表示流行文化明星不久后,也开始用 icon 表示同样的含义。但是对于你点击的电脑桌面小图标,我们想到的还是其"象征"这个旧的含义。

iconic \ī-ˈkä-nik\ (1) Symbolic. 象征的 (2) Relating to a greatly admired and successful person or thing. 偶像的

- The 1963 March on Washington was the iconic event in the history of the civil-rights movement, now familiar to all American schoolchildren. 1963年的华盛顿大游行是民权运动历史上的标志性事件,如今已为美国所有学童熟知。

The original meaning of *iconic* was essentially "resembling an icon," but today it more often seems to mean "so admired that it could be the subject of an icon." And with that meaning, *iconic* has become part of the language of advertising and publicity; today companies and magazines and TV hosts are constantly encouraging us to think of some consumer item or pop star or show as first-rate or immortal or flawless—absolutely "iconic"—when he or she or it is actually nothing of the kind. iconic 最初的意思在本质上是"像神像一样",但如今,它更多的时候意味着"备受崇拜以至于可以成为偶像的主题"。有了这个意义,iconic 就成了广告和宣传语言的一部分。如今,公司、杂志和电视主持人不断鼓动人们相信某些消费产品、流行歌星、节目等是一流的,是流芳百世的,或是完美无缺的——绝对"偶像性"的——而实际上根本不是这样。

iconoclast \ī-ˈkä-nə-ˌklast\ (1) A person who destroys religious images or opposes their use. 破坏宗教神像者 (2) A person who attacks settled beliefs or institutions. 打破传统信仰者

- She's always rattling her friends by saying outrageous things, and she enjoys her reputation as an iconoclast. 她总说些令人震惊的话让朋友们害怕,也很享受她的叛逆者的名声。

ICON

When the early books of the Bible were being written, most of the other Middle Eastern religions had more than one god; these religions generally encouraged the worship of idols of the various gods, which were often regarded as magical objects. But in the Ten Commandments given to Moses in the Old Testament, God prohibits the making of "graven images" or "idols" for worship, proclaiming that the Jews are to worship only one God, who is too great to be represented in an idol. However, by the 6th century A.D., Christians had begun to create religious images in order to focus the prayers of the faithful. Opposition to icons led to the *Iconoclastic* Controversy in A.D. 726, when, supported by the pope, iconoclasts began smashing and burning the images in churches and monasteries (*clast-* comes from the Greek word meaning "to break"). In time, peace was restored, and almost all Christians have since accepted depictions of Jesus, Mary, and the saints. Today an iconoclast is someone who constantly argues with conventional thinking, refusing to "worship" the objects of everyone else's "faith."

在《圣经》早期几卷成书的过程中,中东多数其他宗教的神不止一个。这些宗教一般鼓励膜拜众神的神像,这些神像常被视为神奇之物。然而,在《旧约》的摩西十诫中,上帝禁止制作"雕像"或"神像"来供奉,宣称犹太人只崇拜唯一的上帝,上帝太伟大,无法用神像来表达。然而,到了公元 6 世纪,基督徒开始创造宗教形象,让忠实的信徒集体祈祷。公元 726 年,在教皇的支持下,*iconoclasts* 开始砸毁并焚烧教堂和寺院中的图像(*clast-* 来源于希腊语,意思是"破坏"),反对圣像导致了 *Iconoclastic* Controversy(圣像崇拜之争)。最后,和平得以恢复,几乎所有基督徒自此以后都接受了耶稣、玛利亚和圣徒的神像。如今,iconoclast 指的是与传统思想不断斗争的人,他们拒绝"崇拜"人人都"信仰"的对象。

iconography \ ˌī-kə-ˈnä-grə-fē \ (1) The imagery and symbolism of a work of art or an artist. 图示(法)。象征(手法) (2) The study of artistic symbolism. 图像学。

• Today scholars pore over the advertisements in glossy magazines, studying the iconography for clues to the ads' hidden meanings. 学者们如今仔细查看印刷精美的杂志上的广告,研究其象征手法以寻找线索破解广告背后的意义。

If you saw a 17th-century painting of a man writing at a desk with a lion at his feet, would you know you were looking at St. Jerome, translator of the Bible, who, according to legend, once pulled a thorn from the paw of a lion, which thereafter became his devoted friend? And if a painting showed a young woman reclining on a bed with a shower of gold descending on her, would you recognize her as Danaë, locked up in a tower to keep her away from the lustful Zeus, who then managed to gain access to her by transforming himself into golden light (or golden coins)? An *iconographic* approach to art can make museum-going a lot of fun—and amateur *iconographers* know there are also plenty of symbols lurking in the images that advertisers bombard us with daily.

有一幅 17 世纪的画作,画的是一个男人伏案写作,脚边卧着一头狮子。看到这幅画,你是否知道这个人是翻译《圣经》的圣杰罗姆?据传说,他曾经帮狮子拔去爪子上的一根刺,狮子此后成了他忠实的朋友。还有一幅画,画的是一个年轻的女人躺在床上,金雨水落在身上,你能认出她是达娜厄吗?她被锁在塔里以避开好色的宙斯,而宙斯则化身为金光(或金币)一亲芳泽。艺术的 *iconographic* approach(图解方法)可以使博物馆之行变得很有趣。连非专业的

iconographers(图像研究者)都知道,广告商每天都在用潜藏着大量象征意象的图像对我们进行狂轰滥炸。

Quizzes

A. Fill in each blank with the correct letter:

a. pantheon   e. icon
b. iconic   f. apotheosis
c. atheistic   g. iconoclast
d. iconography   h. theocracy

1. Her personal _____ of actresses included Vanessa Redgrave, Helen Mirren, Emma Thompson, and Maggie Smith.

2. He enjoyed being an _____, since he had a lot of odd ideas and arguing suited his personality well.

3. His well-known _____ beliefs meant that he couldn't hope for great success in politics.

4. Thirty years later, his great speech was viewed as an _____ moment in modern American history.

5. Being inducted into the Hall of Fame is as close as a modern ballplayer can come to _____.

6. The strange _____ of the painting had caught her attention years ago, and she continued to puzzle over the obviously symbolic appearance of various odd objects.

7. They had come back from Russia with a beautiful _____ of Mary and another of St. Basil.

8. The high priest in this medieval _____ was equivalent to a dictator.

B. Match the word on the left to its definition on the right:

1. icon   a. state ruled by religion
2. pantheon   b. symbolic
3. apotheosis   c. symbol
4. iconography   d. nonbelieving
5. atheistic   e. artistic symbolism
6. iconoclast   f. hall of fame
7. theocracy   g. dissenter
8. iconic   h. perfect example

URB comes from the Latin noun for "city." Our word *urban* describes cities and the people who live in them. With its *sub-* prefix (see SUB, p. 491), a *suburb* is a

town "near" or "under" a larger city, and *suburban* houses are home to *suburbanites*.
URB 源自表示"城市"的拉丁语名词。英语单词 urban 描述的是城市及其居民。Suburb(郊区)的前缀是 sub-(参见 SUB, 第 491 页),这个词指的是"临近"或"附属于"较大城市的城镇,*suburban* houses(郊区的房屋)是 *suburbanites*(郊区居民)的住所。

urbane \ˌər-ˈbān\ Sophisticated and with polished manners. 温文尔雅的,彬彬有礼的

● He was remembered as a gentlemanly and urbane host of elegant dinner parties. 人们的印象中,在他主办的优雅的晚宴上,他温文尔雅,颇有绅士风度。

Urbane's synonyms include *suave*, *debonair*, and especially *cosmopolitan*. *Urbanity* was a trait of such classic movie stars as Fred Astaire, Cary Grant, William Powell, Leslie Howard, Charles Boyer, and George Sanders. (Notice that, for some reason, *urbane* is almost always used to describe men rather than women.) Teenagers in the 1960s read James Bond novels and watched his character onscreen to get tips about acquiring an urbane identity. But it's hard to acquire urbanity without actually having had wide social experience in sophisticated cities. And, since times have changed, the whole notion doesn't seem to attract young people quite the way it used to.

Urbane 的同义词包括 suave、debonair,特别是 cosmopolitan。urbanity(彬彬有礼)是弗雷德·阿斯泰尔、加里·格兰特、威廉·鲍威尔、莱斯利·霍华德、查尔斯·博耶尔和乔治·桑德斯等经典电影明星的特征(注意,出于某种原因,urbane 几乎总是用来形容男性,而不是女性)。20 世纪 60 年代的青少年阅读詹姆斯·邦德小说,在银幕上观看他扮演的角色,以获得成为温文尔雅之人的技巧。但如果没有在关系复杂的城市获得到丰富的社会体验,就很难做到温文尔雅。而且,随着时代的变迁,这种观念似乎不再像过去那样吸引年轻人了。

exurban \ek-ˈsər-bən\ Relating to a region or settlement that lies outside a city and usually beyond its suburbs and often is inhabited chiefly by well-to-do families. 城市远郊的

● Exurban areas typically show much higher education and income levels than closer-in suburbs or nearby rural counties. 远郊地区的教育和收入水平通常高于近郊地区或附近的农村地区。

With its prefix *ex-*, ("outside of,") the noun *exurb* was coined around 1955 to describe the ring of well-off communities beyond the suburbs that were becoming commuter towns for an urban area. Most exurbs were probably quiet little towns before being discovered by young city dwellers with good incomes looking for a pleasant place to raise their children. Planners, advertisers, and political strategists today often talk about such topics as *exurban* development, exurban trends, exurban migration, and exurban voters.

exurb 的前缀是 *ex-*(在……外面),这个名词是在 1955 年前后新造的,用来描述郊区以外的富裕社区圈,这些社区正在成为城区的通勤城镇。大多数远郊地区以前可能都是安静的小镇,后来被收入丰厚的年轻城市居民发现,他们希望找到一个能让孩子快乐成长的地方。如今的城市规划者、广告商和政治战略家经常谈论远郊的发展、远郊的趋势、远郊的移民、远郊的选民等话题。

interurban \ˌin-tər-ˈər-bən\ Going between or connecting cities or towns. 城际的，市际的

• Businesspeople in the two cities have been waiting for decades for a true high-speed interurban railway on the Japanese model. 为开通日本模式的真正的高速城际铁路，这两个城市的商人已经等了几十年。

Interurban is generally used to describe transportation. As a noun (as in "In those days you could take the interurban from Seattle to Tacoma"), *interurban* has meant a fairly heavy but fast electric train, something between an urban trolley and a full-fledged long-distance train, that offers more frequent service than an ordinary railway. Interurban transit today may include bus, ferry, and limousine—and, in a few lucky areas, a regional railway. With oil supplies dwindling, there's hope that interurban railways will be coming back into wider use.
interurban 通常用来描述交通。作为一个名词（比如"在那个年代，你可以乘坐城际列车从西雅图到塔科"），*interurban* 指的是相当重但速度很快的电气列车，介于城市电车和成熟的长途列车之间，提供比普通铁路更频繁的服务。当今的城际交通可能包括公共汽车、渡轮、大型豪华轿车——在少数幸运地区，还可能有区域性铁路。随着石油供应的减少，城际铁路有望重新得到更广泛的使用。

urbanization \ˌər-bə-nə-ˈzā-shən\ The process by which towns and cities are formed and become larger as more and more people begin living and working in central areas. 城市化

• The area has been undergoing rapid urbanization, and six or seven of the old small towns are now genuine suburbs. 这个地区正在经历快速的城市化，有六七个古老的小镇现在成了真正的郊区。

The word *urbanization* started appearing in print way back in the 1880s, which says something about the growth of American cities. The expansion of Los Angeles was an early example of uncontrolled urbanization. Urbanization is often seen as a negative trend, with bad effects on quality of life and the environment. But apartments require much less heat than houses, and commuting by mass transit rather than cars can reduce pollution and energy use, and cities offer improved opportunities for jobs (and often for education and housing as well), so city growth doesn't make everyone unhappy.
urbanization 早在 19 世纪 80 年代就开始出现在出版物中，它反映了美国城市的发展。洛杉矶的扩张是城市化失控的一个早期的例子。城市化往往被视为一种消极的趋势，会对生活质量和环境产生不良影响。但是公寓需要的供热量远远低于独立住宅，使用公共交通而非汽车通勤可以减少污染、减少能源的使用，城市还能提供更好的就业机会（通常也有更好的教育和房地产机会），因此城市的发展并没有让每个人都不开心。

CULT comes from the Latin *cultus*, meaning "care." So *cultivation* is care of something, such as a garden, in a way that encourages its growth. And *culture* is what is produced by cultivating human knowledge, skills, beliefs, manners, science, and art over many years.

CULT 源自拉丁语 *cultus*，意思是"照料"。因此，*cultivation*（培养）指的是照料某个东西，比如花园，以促进其生长。*culture*（文化）是通过多年培养人类知识、技能、信仰、礼仪、科学和艺术所形成的产物。

acculturation \ə-ˌkəl-chə-ˈrā-shən\
(1) Modification of the culture of an individual, group, or people by adapting to or borrowing traits from another culture. 文化适应 (2) The process by which a human being acquires the culture of a particular society from infancy. 文化移入

• The old Eastern European bagel has gone through an acculturation in America, where it has acquired a soft texture, a white interior, and fillers like eggs and peanut butter. 古老的东欧百吉饼在美国已经历了文化适应，在美国，百吉饼质地柔软、内里雪白，以鸡蛋和花生酱等为填料。

Whenever people come in close contact with a population that's more powerful, they're generally forced to *acculturate* in order to survive. Learning a new language is usually part of the *acculturation* process, which may also include adopting new clothing, a new diet, new occupations, and even a new religion. An older generation often fails to acculturate thoroughly, but their children often pick up the new ways quickly.

每当人们与更强大的人群密切接触时，他们一般会为了生存而被迫 *acculturate*（适应文化）。学习一门新语言通常是文化适应过程的一部分，文化适应可能还包括接受新的服装、新的饮食、新的职业，甚至新的宗教。老一代人一般做不到彻底的文化适应，但他们的孩子往往很快就能适应新环境。

cross-cultural \ˈkrȯs-ˈkəlch-rəl\
Dealing with or offering comparison between two or more different cultures or cultural areas. 跨文化的

• A cross-cultural study of 49 tribes revealed a tight relationship between the closeness of mother-infant bonding in a given tribe and that tribe's peacefulness toward its neighbors. 一项针对 49 个部落的跨文化研究表明，部落中母子亲情的亲密程度与该部落和相邻部落的和睦程度之间存在密切关系。

If you've ever traveled in a foreign country, you've found yourself making some *cross-cultural* comparisons: Why are huge family dinners so much more common in Italy than back home? Why do Mexican teenagers seem to play with their little relatives so much more than teenagers in the U.S.? Cross-cultural analysis has produced extremely interesting data about such things as the effects of various nations' diets on their populations' health. Though *cross-cultural* was originally used by anthropologists to refer to research comparing aspects of different cultures, it's also often used to describe the reality that lots of us face daily while simply walking the streets of a big American city.

如果曾到国外旅行过，你会发现自己会做一些跨文化的比较：为什么在意大利家庭聚餐比在国内更常见？为什么墨西哥的青少年似乎比美国的青少年更喜欢和他们的小亲戚玩耍？跨文化分析产生了非常有趣的数据，比如各国饮食习惯对其人口健康的影响。最初，人类学家用 *cross-cultural* 表示对不同文化的各个方面所进行的比较研究，但现在，人们也常常用这个词表示许多人每天只要在美国大城市的街上走一走，就能看到的现实情况。

horticulture \ˈhȯr-tə-ˌkəl-chər\   The science and art of growing fruits, vegetables, flowers, or ornamental plants. 园艺学。

• He considered majoring in botany, but has decided instead on horticulture, hoping he can spend more time in a greenhouse than in the library or the lab. 他曾考虑主修植物学,但最终选择了园艺,希望自己能在温室中而不是在图书馆或实验室里花费更多时间。

Hortus is Latin for "garden," and the first gardens were planted about 10,000 years ago in what is often called the Fertile Crescent—the crescent-shaped area stretching from Israel north through Syria and down Iraq's two great rivers to the Persian Gulf. Probably more fertile in previous centuries than it is today, it was the original home of such food plants as wheat, barley, peas, and lentils or their ancient ancestors (not to mention the ancestors of cows, pigs, sheep, and goats as well). Many *horticulturists* today work as researchers or plant breeders or tend orchards and greenhouses—but most American households contain at least one amateur horticulturist. *Hortus* 在拉丁语中表示"种植园",在大约一万年前,最早的种植园出现在被称为新月沃土的地方——这片新月形的地区从以色列向北,穿过叙利亚,南下到伊拉克两河流域,再到波斯湾。在以前的诸多世纪,这片土地可能比现在更肥沃,它是一些粮食作物最早的家园,比如小麦、大麦、豌豆、扁豆,甚至包括这些作物的先祖(更不用说牛、猪、绵羊和山羊的先祖了)。如今,许多 *horticulturists*(园艺家)从事研究或植物育种工作,或照料果园和温室等。然而,多数美国家庭中至少都有一人堪称业余园艺家。

subculture \ˈsəb-ˌkəl-chər\   A group whose beliefs and behaviors are different from the main groups within a culture or society. 亚文化群。

• Members of the emo subculture at her high school recognized each other by their skinny jeans, dyed hair, and canvas sneakers. 她所在高中的情绪硬核亚文化群成员通过紧身牛仔裤、染发和帆布运动鞋相互认可。

This common meaning of *subculture* (it has an older biological meaning) only appeared in the 1930s, and for about 20 years it was used mostly by sociologists, psychologists, and anthropologists. But in the 1950s, as America's wealth led to more and more teenagers getting their own cars and thus their independence, not to mention the arrival of rock 'n' roll, people noticed something unusual happening among young people, and began to speak of the "youth subculture." As the country's wealth and freedom of movement continued to increase, we realized that the U.S. had become home to a large number of subcultures. Today the Web makes possible more than anyone could have dreamed of back in the 1950s. When we happen to stumble on a subculture—bodybuilders, Trekkies, hackers, Airstreamers, anime lovers, motocross enthusiasts—we may realize with astonishment that we had never even imagined that it might exist. *subculture* 的这个常见含义(它还有一个更早的生物学意义)在 20 世纪 30 年代才出现,在随后的约 20 年中主要为社会学家、心理学家和人类学家所使用。但到了 20 世纪 50 年代,随着美国的富裕,越来越多的青少年拥有自己的汽车,从而获得了独立。而随着摇滚乐的到来,人们注意到年轻人身上发生了一些不寻常的事情,开始谈论"青年亚文化"。随着美国越来越富有,人口流动越来越自由,我们意识到美国已经成为众多亚文化的家园。今天,网络使诸多事情成为可

能,这在20世纪50年代是任何人都无法想象的。当我们偶然遇到某个亚文化群体时——比如健美者、《星际》迷、黑客、清风族、日本动漫迷、摩托车越野赛爱好者——我们可能会惊讶地发现,以前甚至从未想过居然会有这种亚文化。

Quizzes

A. Choose the closest definition:

1. cross-cultural　a. combining art and music　b. between two or more cultures
   c. combining fruits and vegetables　d. intensively cultivated
2. interurban　　a. densely populated
   b. between cities　c. from the inner city
   d. within the city
3. urbanization　　a. moving to cities　b. street construction
   c. becoming citylike　d. mass transit
4. horticulture　　a. intellectual knowledge
   b. science of growing plants　c. animal science
   d. horse breeding
5. acculturation　　a. developing cultural institutions
   b. turning woods into farmland
   c. acquiring aspects of another culture
   d. appreciation of music and dance
6. urbane　　a. foolish　b. old-fashioned　c. dependable
   d. sophisticated
7. subculture　　a. group within a culture
   b. cultivation below ground　c. goth kids　d. small garden
8. exurban　　a. high-rise　b. crowded
   c. above the city　d. beyond the suburbs

B. Fill in each blank with the correct letter:

a. exurban　　　　　　　　e. interurban
b. urbane　　　　　　　　f. urbanization
c. acculturation　　　　　g. horticulture
d. cross-cultural　　　　　h. subculture

1. In their _____ home, 25 miles from the city, they looked out on a small field and woods.

2. _____ had proceeded swiftly over the previous ten years, and shopping malls had replaced the cozy streets of the old suburb.

3. A _____ study had revealed far greater levels of anxiety in middle-class Americans than in middle-class Scandinavians.

4. Their next-door neighbors were an _____ couple who threw lively parties where you could meet writers, artists, designers, and media people.

5. His wife's background in _____ led them to plant a large fruit orchard and build a huge greenhouse for flower cultivation.

6. After the island was acquired by Japan around 1910, the population began undergoing rapid _____, eventually giving up its native language.

7. In his teens he became part of a Web-based _____ whose members were devoted to raising poisonous reptiles.

8. _____ railways have begun making a comeback as city dwellers have become increasingly concerned about climate change.

DEM/DEMO

DEM/DEMO comes from the Greek word meaning "people." "Government by the people" was invented by the ancient Greeks, so it's appropriate that they were the first to come up with a word for it: *demokratia*, or *democracy*.

DEM / DEMO 源自意思是"人民"的希腊语单词。"民治政府"的理念是古希腊人的发明，因此毫不夸张地说，他们最先想出表示这个理念的单词：*demokratia*，即 *democracy*（民主）。

---

demographic \ˌde-mə-ˈgra-fik\ Having to do with the study of human populations, especially their size, growth, density, and patterns of living. 人口学的，人口统计的。

• Each year the state government uses the most current demographic figures to determine how to distribute its funding for education. 该州政府每年都会使用最新的人口统计数据来确定如何分配教育经费。

Demographic analysis, the statistical description of human populations, is a tool used by government agencies, political parties, and manufacturers of consumer goods. Polls conducted on every topic imaginable, from age to toothpaste preference, give the government and corporations an idea of who the public is and what it needs and wants. The government's census, which is conducted every ten years, is the largest demographic survey of all. Today *demographic* is also being used as a noun; so, for example, TV advertisers are constantly worrying about how to appeal to "the 18-to-24-year-old demographic."

人口统计分析是对人口所做的统计性描述，是政府机构、政党和消费品制造商使用的一种工具。对所有可以想象到的话题进行的民意调查，从年龄到牙膏偏好等，可以让政府和企业了解公众是谁、他们需要什么、想要什么。政府的人口普查每十年进行一次，是最大规模的人口调查。现在，*demographic* 也用作名词；比如，电视广告客户一直在为如何吸引"18 至 24 岁年龄阶段的人口"而发愁。

---

endemic \en-ˈde-mik\ (1) Found only in a given place or region. 某地特有的，地方性的 (2) Often found in a given occupation, area, or environment. 某职业、地区或环境特有的

• Malaria remains endemic in tropical regions around the world. 疟疾仍是世界上热带地区的地方病。

With its *en-* prefix, *endemic* means literally "in the population." Since the Tasmanian devil is found in the wild exclusively in Tasmania, scientists say it is "endemic to" that island. But the word can also mean simply "common" or "typical"; so we can say that corruption is endemic in the government of a country, that colds are "endemic in" nursery school, or that love of Barbie dolls is "endemic among" young American girls. Don't confuse *endemic* with *epidemic*; something can be endemic in a region for centuries without ever "exploding."

endemic 的前缀是 en-，它的字面意思是"在人群中"。由于塔斯马尼亚恶魔(袋獾)只在塔斯马尼亚的野外被发现，所以科学家们说它是该岛"特有的"。但这个词也可以简单地表示"常见的"或"典型的"；所以我们可以说腐败现象是一个国家政府的"常见病"，感冒是幼儿园的"通病"，或者对芭比娃娃的喜爱是美国年轻女孩的"通病"。不要把 endemic(地方病)与 epidemic(流行病)混为一谈；某些东西可以在一个地区流行若干世纪，但从未"爆发"。

demagogue \ˈde-mə-ˌgäg\ A political leader who appeals to the emotions and prejudices of people in order to arouse discontent and to advance his or her own political purposes. 蛊惑民心的政客

• His supporters called him a "man of the people"; his enemies called him a lying demagogue. 支持者称他为"人民公仆"，敌人则称他为"谎话连篇、蛊惑民心的政客"。

Demagogue was once defined by the writer H. L. Mencken as "one who will preach doctrines he knows to be untrue to men he knows to be idiots," and Mencken's definition still works quite well. The "doctrines" (ideas) preached by demagogues will naturally always be the kind that appeal directly to the ordinary voter, the "common man" or "little guy." Appealing to the common people is not itself a bad thing, but it has often been used by those who calculate that *demagoguery* (or *demagogy*) is the easiest way to power. In most countries, fear of *demagogic* leaders is so strong that voters aren't even permitted to vote directly for the nation's leader, but instead vote only for a local representative.

作家亨利·路易斯·门肯曾将 demagogue 定义为"给白痴传布伪经的人"。门肯的定义今天仍然有效。煽动者所传布的"教义"(思想)自然总是那种能直接吸引普通选民("普通人"或"小人物")的东西。吸引普通民众本身并不是一件坏事，但它经常为一些人所利用，那些人认为 demagoguery (蛊惑民心，或 demagogy) 是最容易获得权力的方式。在多数国家，人们十分害怕 demagogic leaders(蛊惑民心的领导人)，因此不允许选民直接投票选举国家领导人，而只能投票选地方代表。

demotic \di-ˈmä-tik\ Popular or common. 大众化的，通俗的

• Partly because of television, the demotic language and accents of America's various regions have become more and more similar. 一定程度上是因为有了电视，美国各个地区民众的语言和口音才变得越来越雷同。

For many years *demotic* was used only to describe the writing of ancient Egypt, as the name of the script used by ordinary Egyptians rather than by their priests. *Demotic* is still an intellectual word, but it can now be used to describe any popular style in contrast to a style associated with a higher class, especially a style of speech or writing. So, for example, demotic Californian is different from demotic Texan.

The most demotic dress today is probably blue jeans and sneakers, and those who wear them have demotic taste in fashion. The problem is, in American society it can sometimes be hard to find a style that *can't* be described as demotic.

在很多年里，demotic 只用来描述古埃及的文字，是普通埃及人而非祭司所使用的文字的名称。demotic 现在仍是知识分子用的词，但可以用来描述任何通俗的风格，尤其是口语和文字的风格，这和那种与更高阶层社会相联系的风格正好相反。比如，加利福尼亚人的风格不同于得克萨斯人。如今，最大众化的服装可能是牛仔裤和运动鞋，而那些如此打扮的人对时尚也有大众化的品位。问题是，在美国社会中，有时很难找到一种不能用 demotic 来形容的风格。

POPUL
comes from the Latin word meaning "people," and in fact forms the basis of the word *people* itself. So the *population* is the people of an area, and *popular* means not only "liked by many people" but also (as in *popular culture*) "relating to the general public."

POPUL 源自意思是"人民"的拉丁语单词，这个词根实际上构成了 people 一词本身的基础。因此，population 指的是一个地区的人民，popular 不仅仅有"为众人所喜爱"的意思，而且有"与大众有关"的意思（比如 popular culture）。

---

populist \ˈpä-pyə-list\ A believer in the rights, wisdom, or virtues of the common people. 平民主义者，民粹主义者

● He knew he would have to campaign as a populist in order to appeal to the working-class voters. 他知道，必须以平民主义者的身份参加竞选活动，才能受到工薪阶层选民青睐。

The word *populist* first appeared in the 1890s with the founding of the Populist Party, which stood for the interests of the farmers against the big-money interests. In later years *populism* came to be associated with the blue-collar class in the cities as well. Populism can be hard to predict. It sometimes has a religious tendency; it usually isn't very interested in international affairs; it has sometimes been unfriendly to immigrants and blacks; and it's often anti-intellectual. So populism often switches between liberal and conservative. But the *populist* style always shows its concern with Americans with average incomes as opposed to the rich and powerful.

populist 一词最早出现在 19 世纪 90 年代，当时平民党成立，代表的是农民的利益，与富人的利益相对立。此后，populism（平民主义，民粹主义）也开始与城市的蓝领阶层联系起来。平民主义很难预测。它有时有宗教倾向，通常对国际事务不太感兴趣；有时对移民和黑人不友好，而且常常是反对知识分子的。因此，民粹主义经常游移于自由派和保守派之间。但 populist 的风格始终表现出对平均收入的美国人而非富人和当权者的关注。

populace \ˈpä-pyü-ləs\ (1) The common people or masses. 民众，平民百姓 (2) Population. 人口

● Perhaps Henry Ford's major achievement was to manufacture a car that practically the entire populace could afford—the Model T. 福特的主要成就是制造一辆几乎可以让所有民众买得起的汽车——福特 T 型车。

Populace is usually used to refer to all the people of a country. Thus, we're often told that an educated and informed populace is essential for a healthy American democracy. Franklin D. Roosevelt's famous radio "Fireside Chats" informed and reassured the American populace in the 1930s as we struggled through the Great Depression. We often hear about what "the general populace" is thinking or doing, but generalizing about something so huge can be tricky.

populace 通常用来指一个国家的所有人。因此,我们经常听到这样的说法,受过良好教育和消息灵通的民众对美国民主的健康至关重要。20 世纪 30 年代,当我们在大萧条中挣扎时,富兰克林·罗斯福通过收音机发表了著名的"炉边谈话",让美国民众了解情况,重拾信心。我们经常听到"普通民众"在想什么或在做什么,但对如此巨大的群体进行概述可能会非常棘手。

populous \ˈpä-pyu̇-ləs\ Numerous, densely settled, or having a large population. 人口稠密的,人口众多的

POPUL

- Most Americans can't locate Indonesia, the fourth most populous country in the world, on a map. 多数美国人在地图上找不出世界上人口第四多的国家——印度尼西亚。

With a metropolitan area of more than 20 million people, Mexico City could be called the world's second or third most populous city. And the nearby Aztec city of Tenochtitlán was one of the largest cities in the world even when Hernán Cortés arrived there in 1519. But by the time Cortés conquered the city in 1521 it wasn't nearly so populous, since European diseases had greatly reduced the population. Avoid confusing *populous* and *populace*, which are pronounced exactly the same.

墨西哥城的大都市区拥有 2000 多万人口,堪称世界人口第二或第三多的城市。附近阿兹特克的特诺奇蒂特兰城,甚至当赫尔南多·科尔特斯于 1519 年到达那里时,它还是世界上最大的城市之一。但是,当科尔特斯于 1521 年征服这座城市时,就根本算不上人口众多了,因为来自欧洲的疾病导致人口锐减。*populous* 和 *populace* 发音完全相同,但不要将两者混为一谈。

vox populi \ˈväks-ˈpä-pyü-ˌlī\ Popular sentiment or opinion. 公众舆论

- Successful politicians are always listening to the vox populi and adjusting their opinions or language accordingly. 成功的政治家总是倾听公众舆论,并对自己的观点和措辞做出相应的调整。

Dating from at least the time of Charlemagne, the Latin saying "Vox populi, vox Dei" means literally "The voice of the people is the voice of God"—in other words, the people's voice is sacred, or the people are always right. Today, by means of modern opinion polls, we seem to hear the vox populi (or *vox pop* for short) year-round on every possible issue. But maybe we should occasionally keep in mind that full Charlemagne-era quotation: "Those people should not be listened to who keep saying the voice of the people is the voice of God, since the riotousness of the crowd is always very close to madness."

至少从查理曼大帝时代开始,拉丁语"Vox populi, vox Dei"的字面意思就是"人民的声音就是上帝的声音"——换句话说,人民的声音是神圣的,或者人民总是正确的。今天,通过现代民意调查的手段,我们似乎一年到头都能听到关于每一个可能的问题的 vox populi(简称为 *vox pop*)。但有时候我们也要记住查理曼时代的那句完整语录:"不应该听信那些一直将人民的声音就是上帝的声音挂在嘴边的人,因为群众的放纵总是非常接近疯狂的。"

UNIT 12

Quizzes

A. Choose the closest definition:

1. demagogue   a. medium-sized city   b. fiery politician
   c. democratic socialist   d. new democracy
2. populace   a. politics   b. numerous   c. masses
   d. popularity
3. endemic   a. common   b. absent   c. infectious
   d. occasional
4. demotic   a. devilish   b. common   c. cultural
   d. useful
5. populous   a. well-liked   b. foreign   c. numerous
   d. obscure
6. demographic   a. describing politics   b. describing populations
   c. describing policies   d. describing epidemics
7. populist   a. communist   b. campaigner   c. socialist
   d. believer in the people
8. vox populi   a. public policy   b. public survey
   c. public opinion   d. public outrage

B. Indicate whether the following pairs of words have the same or different meanings:

1. demotic / common   same ____ / different ____
2. populist / politician   same ____ / different ____
3. endemic / locally common   same ____ / different ____
4. populace / popularity   same ____ / different ____
5. demographic / phonetic   same ____ / different ____
6. vox populi / mass sentiment   same ____ / different ____
7. demagogue / prophet   same ____ / different ____
8. populous / well-loved   same ____ / different ____

Animal Words 动物词语

aquiline \ˈa-kwə-ˌlīn\ （1）Relating to eagles. 与老鹰有关的（2）Curving like an eagle's beak. 像鹰嘴一样弯曲的

• The surviving busts of noble Romans show that many of the men had strong aquiline noses. 幸存的罗马贵族半身像表明，许多罗马男人都有明显的鹰钩鼻。

Aquiline, from the Latin word meaning "eagle," is most often used to describe a nose that has a broad curve and is slightly hooked, like a beak. The aquiline figure on the U. S. seal brandishes the arrows of war and the olive branch of peace. The word for eagle itself, *Aquila*, has been given to a constellation in the northern hemisphere.

<small>aquiline 源自拉丁语中意思是"鹰"的单词,最常用来表示有宽阔曲线、轻微钩状的鼻子,像鹰喙一样。美国国徽上的鹰挥舞着象征战争的箭头和象征和平的橄榄枝。aquila 这个词本身表示鹰,已被用来命名北半球的一个星座(天鹰座)。</small>

asinine \ˈa-sə-ˌnīn\ Foolish, brainless. 愚蠢的,无头脑的

- He's not so great when he's sober, but when he's drunk he gets truly asinine. <small>他清醒的时候虽不那么出色,但喝醉的时候却是愚蠢至极。</small>

The donkey, or *ass*, has often been accused of stubborn, willful, and stupid behavior lacking in logic and common sense. *Asinine* behavior exhibits similar qualities. Idiotic or rude remarks, aggressive stupidity, and general immaturity can all earn someone (usually a man) this description. If you call him this to his face, however, he might behave even worse.

<small>驴(即 ass)经常被人指责为顽固、任性,会做出缺乏逻辑和常识的愚蠢举动。asinine behavior(愚蠢的行为)表现出相似的特点。愚蠢或粗鲁的言论、咄咄逼人的蠢行以及总体上的不成熟都会给某个人(通常是男人)招来这样的评价。然而,如果你当面这么说他,他的表现会更糟。</small>

bovine \ˈbō-ˌvīn\ (1) Relating to cows and oxen. 牛的,与牛有关的 (2) Placid, dull, unemotional. 恬静的、迟钝的、没有感情的

- In that part of Texas, many of the veterinarians specialize in bovine conditions and won't even deal with dogs or cats. <small>在得克萨斯州的那个地区,许多兽医专治牛病,连狗和猫都不理会。</small>

Bovine comes from the Latin word for "cow," though the biological family called the *Bovidae* actually includes not only cows and oxen but also goats, sheep, bison, and buffalo. So *bovine* is often used technically, when discussing "bovine diseases," "bovine anatomy," and so on. It can also describe a human personality, though it can be a rather unkind way to describe someone. When Hera, the wife of Zeus, is called "cow-eyed," though, it's definitely a compliment, and Zeus fairly melts when she turns those big bovine eyes on him.

<small>bovine 源自拉丁语中表示"牛"的词,但牛科动物实际上不仅包括母牛和公牛,还包括山羊、绵羊、野牛和水牛。因此,在讨论"牛病""牛解剖学"等时,bovine 经常被用作科技术语。它也可以用来描述人的性格,但用它来形容一个人可能是相当不友善的方式。当宙斯的妻子赫拉被称为"牛眼睛的"时,这绝对是一种赞美,当她把大牛眼转向宙斯时,宙斯的心全都融化了。</small>

canine \ˈkā-ˌnīn\ Relating to dogs or the dog family; doglike. 犬的,似犬的

- Pleasure in getting their tummies rubbed must be a basic canine trait, since all our dogs have loved it. <small>喜欢被人抚摸肚子肯定是犬的一个基本特征,因为我们的所有狗都已经喜欢上了。</small>

Dogs are prized for their talents and intelligence but aren't always given credit for their independence. Instead, tales of canine devotion and attachment are legendary; the old *Lassie* and *Rin-Tin-Tin* television series featured at least one heroic act of devotion per show. So we often hear people described as having "doglike devotion" or "doglike loyalty." But *canine* itself, unlike *doglike*, usually refers to four-legged creatures. *Canine* is not only an adjective but also a noun. Dogs and their relatives in the Canidae family—the wolves, jackals, foxes, and coyotes—are often called canines. And so are those two slightly pointed teeth a bit to the right and left of your front teeth.

<small>狗因其天赋和智慧而受到人类的褒奖,但并不总是因其独立性而受到褒奖。相反,关于狗的忠诚和依恋的故事是传奇性的,老版电影《灵犬莱西》和《任丁丁》电视系列的每集都至少有一次奉献的英雄壮举。因此,我们经常听到有人被形容"奉献如狗"或"忠诚如狗"。但是 canine 这个词本身,与 doglike 不同,通常指四条腿的动物。canine 不仅是形容词,而且是名词。狗与它的犬科亲缘动物——狼、豺、狐狸和郊狼——通常被称为 canines(犬科动物)。而你门牙左右的两颗稍微有点尖的牙通常也被称为 canines(犬齿)。</small>

feline\\'fē-ˌlīn\ (1) Relating to cats or the cat family. 猫的 (2) Like a cat in being sleek, graceful, sly, treacherous, or stealthy. 像猫的

● The performers moved across the high wire with feline grace and agility. <small>表演者像猫一样优雅而敏捷地走过高空钢丝。</small>

Cats have always provoked a strong reaction from humans. The Egyptians worshipped them, leaving thousands of *feline* mummies and idols as evidence. In the Middle Ages, *felines* were feared as agents of the devil, and were thought to creep around silently at night doing evil. (Notice that *feline* is also a noun.) The fascinating family called the *Felidae* includes about 40 species of superb hunters, including the lions, tigers, jaguars, cheetahs, cougars, bobcats, and lynxes, and almost all of them are smooth, silent, and independent.

<small>猫总是引起人类的强烈反应。埃及人崇拜它们,留下的成千上万猫木乃伊和雕像便是证据。在中世纪,人们害怕 felines(猫科动物),认为它们是魔鬼的代理人,在夜间悄悄地到处作恶(注意,feline 也可用作名词)。令人惊叹着迷的猫科动物包括大约 40 种优秀猎手,像狮子、老虎、美洲虎、猎豹、美洲狮、北美山猫、猞猁等,几乎所有猫科动物都沉着、安静、独立。</small>

leonine\\'lē-ə-ˌnīn\ Relating to lions; lionlike. 狮子的,像狮子的

● As he conducted, Leonard Bernstein would fling his leonine mane wildly about. <small>伯恩斯坦指挥时会疯狂地甩着他狮子鬃毛般的长发。</small>

The Latin word for "lion" is *leon*, so the names *Leon*, *Leo*, and *Leona* all mean "lion" as well. A *leonine* head usually has magnificent hair, like a male lion's mane. The leonine strength of Heracles (Hercules) is symbolized by the lion's pelt that he wears, the pelt of the fabled Nemean Lion which he had slain as one of his Twelve Labors. But leonine courage is what is so notably lacking in *The Wizard of Oz*'s Cowardly Lion.

<small>拉丁语单词 leon 表示"狮子",因此 Leon、Leo 和 Leona 都是"狮子"的意思。狮子头上通常有华丽的毛发,就像雄狮的鬃毛。赫拉克勒斯身穿狮皮,象征他拥有狮子般的巨大力量,这狮子皮取自传说中的涅墨亚狮子,是赫拉克勒斯在完成十二项任务之一时杀死的。但《绿野仙踪》中胆小的狮子却明显缺乏勇气。</small>

porcine\\'pȯr-ˌsīn\ Relating to pigs or swine; piglike. 猪的;像猪的

• She describes her landlord's shape as porcine, and claims he has manners to match. 她说房东长得像猪，连举止都匹配。

Pigs are rarely given credit for their high intelligence or their friendliness as pets, but instead are mocked for their habit of cooling themselves in mud puddles and the aggressive way they often go after food. While *porcine* isn't as negative a term as *swinish*, it may describe things that are fat, greedy, pushy, or generally piggish—but primarily fat. Porky Pig and Miss Piggy aren't particularly porcine in their behavior, only in their appearance—that is, pink and pudgy.

猪很少因为它们智商高或作为宠物很友善而受到赞扬，反而因它们习惯在泥坑里降温以及它们抢食时表现出的咄咄逼人而受到嘲笑。虽然 porcine 不像 swinish 那样负面，但它描述的东西可能会肥胖、贪婪、爱占便宜，总的来讲就是像猪一样——但主要还是肥胖。动画里的猪小弟和猪小姐的行为并不像猪，像猪的地方只在它们外表——粉红色、矮胖。

vulpine\ˈvəl-ˌpin\ （1）Relating to foxes; foxlike. 狐狸的，像狐狸的（2）Sneaky, clever, or crafty; foxy. 偷偷摸摸的，聪明的，诡计多端的，狡猾的。

• She'd already decided she didn't like anything about him, especially the twitchiness, that vulpine face, and those darting eyes. 她已经决定不再喜欢他了，尤其是他情绪焦躁、面相狡诈、目光游移。

Foxes may be sleek and graceful runners with beautiful coats and tails, but they're almost impossible to keep out of the henhouse. Over the centuries they have "outfoxed" countless farmers. Because of the quick intelligence in their faces and their cunning nighttime raids, *vulpine* today almost always describes a face or manner that suggests a person capable of the same kind of sly scheming.

狐狸有漂亮的皮毛和尾巴，跑起来流畅而优雅，但它们几乎不可能被关在鸡舍之外。很多世纪以来，它们"智胜"无数农民。由于狐狸脸上展现出来的机敏，加上它们善于狡猾地夜间突袭，vulpine 现在几乎总是用来形容某个像狐狸般诡计多端之人的面孔或举止。

Quizzes

Fill in each blank with the correct letter:

a. leonine   e. canine
b. aquiline   f. feline
c. porcine   g. vulpine
d. asinine   h. bovine

1. Collies and chow chows often have splendid _____ neck ruffs.
2. The dancers, in their black leotards, performed the piece with slinky, _____ grace.
3. Proud of the _____ curve of his nose, the star presents his profile to the camera in old silent films at every opportunity.
4. The slick fellow offering his services as guide had a disturbingly _____ air about him.

5. Some of the most beloved _____ traits, such as loyalty and playfulness, are often lacking in humans.

6. The last applicant she had interviewed struck her as passive and _____ and completely lacking in ambition.

7. Jeff and his crowd were in the balcony, catcalling, throwing down cans, and being generally _____.

8. She peeked out to see her _____ landlord climbing the stairs slowly, gasping for breath, with the eviction notice in his hand.

Review Quizzes

A. Choose the closest definition:

1. vulpine   a. reddish   b. sly   c. trustworthy   d. furry
2. atheistic   a. boring   b. godless   c. roundabout   d. contagious
3. adumbrate   a. revise   b. punish   c. advertise   d. outline
4. populous   a. numerous   b. populated   c. popular   d. common
5. iconoclast   a. icon painter   b. dictator   c. dissident   d. tycoon
6. endemic   a. local   b. neighborly   c. sensational   d. foreign
7. iconic   a. wealthy   b. famous   c. indirect   d. symbolic
8. feline   a. sleek   b. clumsy   c. crazy   d. fancy
9. pantheon   a. mall   b. road race   c. trouser store   d. hall of fame
10. icon   a. psychic   b. leader   c. symbol   d. prophet
11. urbane   a. calm   b. elegant   c. excited   d. secure
12. horticulture   a. interior decoration   b. food science   c. horse breeding   d. plant growing

13. demotic   a. reduced   b. common   c. upper-class   d. demented

14. luminary   a. ruler   b. lantern   c. lighting designer   d. celebrity

15. travesty   a. farce   b. outfit   c. transportation   d. success

16. divest   a. add on   b. take off   c. take in   d. add up

B. Fill in each blank with the correct letter:

a. populist
b. demographic
c. theocracy
d. investiture
e. aquiline
f. apotheosis
g. bovine
h. populace
i. vulpine
j. cross-cultural

1. The _____ of the great Albert Einstein seemed to occur while he was still living.

2. _____ surveys often divide the U. S. population by income and education.

3. Nothing ever seemed to disturb her pleasant but _____ manner.

4. He was interested in _____ studies that showed that these kinds of cancers don't appear in African tribal populations.

5. The _____ of the society's new leader was a secret and solemn event.

6. With his _____ nose, he looked like a member of the ancient Roman senate.

7. He had a nervous, _____ manner, with a tense alertness and shifty eyes.

8. She ran her campaigns as a _____, a champion of the common man, though she herself had a great deal of money.

9. The general _____ has never cared much about foreign policy except when the country goes to war.

10. In a true _____, the legal punishments are often those called for in the holy books.

C. Match the word on the left to the correct definition on the right:

1. porcine   a. half-shadow
2. divest   b. doglike
3. asinine   c. brown
4. penumbra   d. public opinion

5. leonine
6. umber
7. vox populi
8. iconic
9. transvestite
10. canine

e. cross-dresser
f. symbolic
g. foolish
h. plump
i. lionlike
j. get rid of

UNIT 13

CORD

CORD, from the Latin word for "heart," turns up in several common English words. So does its Greek relative *card-*, which is familiar to us in words such as *cardiac*, "relating to the heart."

CORD 源自拉丁语中表示"心脏"的单词,出现在几个常用的英语单词中。希腊语中与其相关的 *card-* 也是这样,出现在 *cardiac*("与心脏有关的")这样的单词中,我们对此很熟悉。

accord \ə-ˈkȯrd\ (1) To grant. 给予,授予 (2) To be in harmony; agree. 与……一致,符合

- What she told police under questioning didn't accord with the accounts of the other witnesses. 她在警察盘问时的说法与其他证人不一致。

A new federal law may accord with—or be in *accordance* with— the guidelines that a company has already established. The rowdy behavior of the hero Beowulf accords with Norse ideals of the early Middle Ages; but such behavior wouldn't have been in accordance with the ideals of a later young lord from the same general region, Shakespeare's Prince Hamlet. *Accord* is also a noun, meaning "agreement." Thus, we often hear of two countries signing a peace accord; and we also frequently hear of two things or people being "in accord with" each other.

新的联邦法律能 accord with——或者 be in *accordance* with(与……一致)——某公司已确立的方针。英雄贝奥武夫的粗暴行为符合中世纪早期挪威人的完美标准;但这样的行为并不符合莎士比亚笔下哈姆雷特王子的标准,尽管后来的这位年轻贵族也来自同一个大区。*accord* 也是名词,意为"协议"。因此,我们经常听到两国签署和平协议,也经常听到两个事物或人"相一致"。

concord \ˈkän-ˌkȯrd\ (1) A state of agreement; harmony. 一致,和谐 (2) A formal agreement. 正式协议。

- In 1801 Napoleon signed a concord with the pope reestablishing the Catholic Church in France. 1801 年,拿破仑与教皇就法国重建天主教会一事签订了协议。

The roots of *concord* suggest the meaning "hearts together." At the very outset of the American Revolution, the town of Concord, Massachusetts, was the site of a famous battle—obviously not exactly in keeping with its name. It shares that name with the capital of New Hampshire and a few other towns and cities, and *Concordia*, the original Latin word for "concord," is the name of several Lutheran universities. Today *concord* is a rather formal term, probably most often used to mean a specific agreement; thus, two countries may sign a concord on matters that have led to trouble in the past.

concord 的词根暗示它的意思是"心连心"。在美国革命的最初阶段,马萨诸塞州的康科德镇(Concord)就是一场著名战役的发生地——这显然名不副实。它与新罕什尔州的首府及其他几个市、镇同名。concordia 是"cordcord"的拉丁语源词,也是几所路德教大学的名称。现在的 concord 是一个很正式的术语,可能最常用来表示特定的协议;因此,两个国家或许会就过去导致纠纷的问题签署一项协议。

CORD

cordial \ˈkȯr-jəl\ Warm, friendly, gracious. 热情的,友好的,亲切的

• After the meeting, the president extended a cordial invitation to everyone for coffee at her own house. 会议结束后,总裁热情地邀请大家去她家喝咖啡。

Anything that is *cordial* comes from the heart. Cordial greetings to friends on the street, or cordial relations between two countries, are warm without being passionate. *Cordial* is also a noun, which originally meant any stimulating medicine or drink that was thought to be good for the heart. Today a cordial is a liqueur, a sweetened alcoholic drink with interesting flavoring. Cordials such as crème de menthe, Drambuie, or Benedictine are alcoholic enough to warm the spirits and the heart.

任何 cordial 的东西皆源自内心。在街上向朋友们热情地打招呼,或两国之间的友好关系,均热情但不激情。cordial 也是名词,最初指的是被认为有益于心脏的刺激性药物或饮料。现在的 cordial 指的是某种添加了有趣的调味品的甜酒饮料。诸如 crème de menthe、Drambuie、Benedictine 之类的饮料都含有酒精,足以温暖精神和心灵。

discordant \dis-ˈkȯr-dənt\ Being at odds, conflicting, not in harmony.
不一致的,不和谐的

• The first discordant note at dinner was struck by my cousin, when he claimed the president was only interested in taking away our guns. 表兄声称总统只对拿走我们的枪支感兴趣,这话奏响了晚餐的第一个不和谐音符。

Discord, a word more common in earlier centuries than today, means basically "conflict," so *discordant* often means "conflicting." The opinions of Supreme Court justices are frequently discordant; justices who disagree with the Court's decision usually write a dissenting opinion. *Discordant* is often used with a somewhat musical meaning, suggesting that a single wrong note or harmony has been heard in the middle of a performance—even though musical words such as *chord* actually come from a different Latin word, meaning "cord" or "string" (a reference to the strings of ancient instruments such as the lyre).

discord 这个词在早先几个世纪更常见,其基本意思是"冲突",因此 discordant 通常表示"冲突的"。最高法院大法

官们的意见经常不一致。法官如果不同意法院的裁决,通常会写反对意见书。*discordant* 的使用通常带有某种音乐的意义,暗示听到了演奏过程中的一个错误音符或和声。但 *chord*(和弦)等表示音乐的词实际上源自另一个拉丁语单词,该词的意思是"细绳"或"琴弦"(参见七弦琴等古代弦乐器)。

CULP comes from the Latin word for "guilt." Its best-known appearance in English is probably in *culprit*, meaning someone who is guilty of a crime.
CULP 源自拉丁语中表示"罪"的单词。它在英语中最出名的存在或许是 *culprit*,意思是犯罪者。

culpable \ˈkəl-pə-bəl\ Deserving to be condemned or blamed. 应受谴责的

• The company was found guilty of culpable negligence in allowing the chemical waste to leak into the groundwater. 该公司被判过失罪,因其导致化学废料泄漏到地下水中。

Culpable normally means simply "guilty." To a lawyer, "culpable negligence" is carelessness so serious that it becomes a crime—for instance, building a swimming pool in your suburban yard with no fence around it, so that a neighbor's child could fall in and drown. But degrees of *culpability* are important in the law; someone who intended to do harm always faces a more serious challenge in court than someone who was merely careless.

culpable 通常的意思是"有罪的"。对律师来说,"culpable negligence"是太过于粗心大意,到了犯罪的程度——比如,在郊区院子里建造一个游泳池,周围没有围栏,邻居的孩子就可能会掉进去淹死。但是,*culpability* 的轻重程度在法律上很重要。法庭上蓄意伤害往往比无意伤害面临的判罚更重。

exculpate \ˈek-skəl-ˌpāt\ To clear from accusations of fault or guilt. 使……无罪,证明……无罪

• The girls aren't proud of what they did that night, but they've been exculpated by witnesses and won't be facing criminal charges. 那些女孩对那晚所做的事儿并非感到问心无愧,但因为有目击者的无罪证明,她们不会面临刑事指控。

Exculpate gets its meaning from the prefix *ex-*, which here means "out of" or "away from." A suspected murderer may be exculpated by the confession of another person. And *exculpatory* evidence is the kind that defense lawyers are always looking for.

exculpate 的含义来自前缀 *ex-*(此处意为"在……外"或"远离……")。一个涉嫌杀人的犯罪嫌疑人可能由于另一个人的供认而免罪。*exculpatory* evidence(无罪证据)是辩护律师总在寻找的东西。

inculpate \in-ˈkəl-ˌpāt\ To accuse or incriminate; to show evidence of someone's involvement in a fault or crime. 控告,指控,证明有罪。

• It was his own father who finally inculpated him, though without intending to. 最终指控他的正是他父亲,但并非蓄意而为。

Inculpate is the opposite of *exculpate*, just as *inculpatory* evidence is the opposite of *exculpatory* evidence. By inculpating someone else, an accused person may manage to exculpate himself. Through plea bargaining, the prosecution can often encourage a defendant to inculpate his friends in return for a lighter sentence.

inculpate 是 *exculpate* 的反义词，正如 *inculpatory* evidence（定罪证据）是 *exculpatory* evidence（无罪证据）的反义词一样。通过指控他人，被告可能会设法自我开脱。通过辩诉交易，检方经常能够鼓励被告指控他的朋友以换取轻判。

mea culpa \ˌmā-ə-ˈku̇l-pə\   An admission of personal fault or error. 认错，道歉

- The principal said his mea culpa at the school board meeting, but not all the parents were satisfied. 那个校长在学校董事会上承认了错误，但是并非所有父母都满意。

Mea culpa, Latin for "through my fault," comes from the prayer in the Catholic mass in which, back when Latin was still the language of the mass, one would confess to having sinned "mea culpa, mea culpa, mea maxima culpa" ("through my fault, through my fault, through my most grievous fault"). When we say "Mea culpa" today, it means "I apologize" or "It was my fault." But *mea culpa* is also common as a noun. So, for instance, a book may be a long mea culpa for the author's past treatment of women, or an oil company may issue a mea culpa after a tanker runs aground.

CULP

mea culpa 是拉丁语，表示"因我的错"，源自天主教弥撒中的祈祷文。回到拉丁语仍然是弥撒用语的时代，某个人会承认犯了罪"mea culpa, mea culpa, mea maxima culpa"（"因我的错，因我的错，因我最严重的错"）。现在我们说"Mea culpa"时，意思是"我道歉"或"这是我的错"。但 *mea culpa* 也常用作名词。例如，某本书可能是作者为过去对女性的态度所做的长篇检讨，或者某个石油公司可能会在油轮搁浅后承认错误。

Quizzes

A. Choose the closest definition:

1. exculpate   a. convict   b. prove innocent   c. suspect   d. prove absent
2. discordant   a. insulting   b. relieved   c. unlimited   d. conflicting
3. culpable   a. disposable   b. refundable   c. guilty   d. harmless
4. cordial   a. hateful   b. friendly   c. fiendish   d. cool
5. inculpate   a. incorporate   b. resist   c. accuse   d. offend
6. concord   a. generosity   b. straightness   c. agreement   d. pleasure
7. mea culpa   a. rejection   b. apology   c. excuse   d. forgiveness
8. accord   a. harmonize   b. accept   c. distress   d. convince

B. Match the definition on the left to the correct word on the right:

1. accuse   a. accord

2. excuse
3. goodwill
4. heartfelt
5. grant
6. blamable
7. disagreeing
8. confession

b. concord
c. mea culpa
d. discordant
e. culpable
f. cordial
g. inculpate
h. exculpate

DICT

DICT comes from *dicere*, the Latin word meaning "to speak." So a *dictionary* is a treasury of words for speaking. And a *contradiction* (with its prefix *contra-*, "against") speaks against or denies something.

DICT 源自拉丁语单词 dicere(说话)。所以 dictionary(词典)是说话用词的宝库。contradiction(其前缀 contra- 的意思是"反对")指的是反驳或否认某事。

diction \ˈdik-shən\ (1) Choice of words, especially with regard to correctness, clearness, or effectiveness. 措辞 (2) Clarity of speech. 清晰的发音

• Our CEO is determined to appear in some TV ads, but he first needs to work on his diction with a vocal coach. 我们的首席执行官决心在一些电视广告中出镜,但他首先需要与声乐教练合作练习发音。

When your English teacher complains about some of the words you chose to use in an essay, she's talking about your *diction*. She may also use the term when commenting on the word choices made by a poet, and why a particular word was the best one possible in a particular line. (Compare *syntax*, p. 710.) But the second meaning of *diction* is just as common, and your English teacher might use that one on you as well, especially when she's asked you to read something aloud and you mumble your way through it.

当英语老师批评你的文章选用的某些单词时,她谈论的是你的 diction(措辞)。她也用这个术语来评论某个诗人的用词,为什么某行诗中的某个词可能是最好的那一个(比较 syntax,第 710 页)。但是 diction 的第二个含义同样常用,尤其是当她要求你大声朗读某个材料,而你又读得磕磕绊绊时,她可能把这个含义用到你身上。

edict \ˈē-ˌdikt\ (1) An official announcement that has the force of a law. 法令 (2) An order or command. 命令。

• In 1989 an edict by the leader of Iran pronouncing a death sentence on a British novelist stunned the world. 1989 年,伊朗领导人宣布判处一名英国小说家死刑,震惊了世界。

Edicts are few and far between in a democracy, since very few important laws can be made by a president or prime minister acting alone. But when a crisis arose in the Roman Republic, the senate would appoint a *dictator*, who would have the power to rule by edict. The idea was that the dictator could make decisions quickly, issuing his edicts faster than the senate could act. When the crisis was over, the edicts were canceled and the dictator usually retired from public life. Things are different today: dictators almost always install themselves in power, and they never give it up.

法令在民主国家少之又少,因为罕有重要的法律是由总统或首相单独制定的。但当罗马共和国出现危机时,元老院会任命一个 *dictator*(行政长官),他有权通过法令进行统治。当时的想法是,行政长官可以迅速做出裁决,发布命令的速度快于元老院。危机结束后,法令被撤销,行政长官通常会退出公众生活。但现在的情况不同了:dictators(独裁者们)几乎一直掌权,从不放弃。

jurisdiction \ˌjur-is-ˈdik-shən\ (1) The power or right to control or exercise authority. 管辖权 (2) The territory where power may be exercised. 管辖区域。

• Unluckily for the defendants, the case fell within the jurisdiction of the federal court rather than the more tolerant state court. 对被告而言不幸的是,这个案件属于联邦法院的管辖范围,而不是更宽容的州法院。

Questions of *jurisdiction* are generally technical legal matters. The most important ones include which court will hear a given case and which law-enforcement agency can get involved. But although they may seem like mere technicalities, *jurisdictional* matters sometimes turn out to be all-important in the final outcome. Jurisdiction may depend on where you are (for example, in which state), on who you are (if you're a juvenile, for example, you may only be tried in juvenile court), and on what the subject is (for example, cases involving the estate left by someone who has died are dealt with in probate court).

管辖权问题一般是技术性的法律事项。最重要的问题包括:某一特定案例由哪个法院审理,哪个执法机构可以参与其中等。但是,尽管看起来只是技术性细节,*jurisdictional* matters(管辖权事项)有时对最终的结果起至关重要的作用。管辖权可能取决于你所在的地方(比如,在哪个州),你是谁(比如,如果未成年可能只在少年法庭受审),以及主题是什么(比如,涉及死者遗产的案件在遗嘱检验法庭处理)。

dictum \ˈdik-təm\ A formal and authoritative statement. 声明

• It has long been a dictum of American foreign policy that the government doesn't negotiate with kidnappers and terrorists. 政府不与绑匪和恐怖分子谈判,这早已成为美国外交政策的铁律。

The word *dictum* is frequently used in philosophy, but also in economics, political science, and other fields. Almost any condensed piece of wisdom—"The perfect is the enemy of the good," "Buy low, sell high," "All politics is local," etc.—can be called a dictum. In the law, judges may often add to a written opinion an *obiter dictum*, or "statement made in passing"—a strong statement that isn't directly relevant to the case being decided. If they're well thought out and eloquent, *obiter dicta* (notice the plural form) may be referred to by later judges and lawyers for years afterward.

dictum 一词常用于哲学,但也用于经济学、政治学及其他领域。几乎任何浓缩的智慧——"完美是优秀的敌人""低买高卖""所有政治都是地方政治"等——都可以称之为格言。在法律上,法官可能经常在书面意见上添加 *obiter dictum*,意思是"附带意见"——即与正在审理的案子不直接相关的有力的看法。如果是深思熟虑的结果且有很强的说服力,*obiter dicta*(注意,这是复数形式)可能会被后来的法官和律师用作参考。

GNI/GNO comes from a Greek and Latin verb meaning "to know," and can be found at the root of *know* itself. Among other words built from this root, you may *recognize* ("know again") some and be *ignorant* of ("not know") others. But only an *ignoramus* would know absolutely none of them.

GNI / GNO 源自意思是"知道"的希腊语和拉丁语动词，可以在 know 本身的词根中找到它。关于这个词根衍生出的其他单词，你可能会 recognize（"再次知道[认出]"）一些，而 be ignorant of（"不知道"）其他的。但只有 ignoramus（无知的人）才会一个都不认识。

cognitive\ˈkäg-nə-tiv\ (1) Having to do with the process of knowing, including awareness, judgment, and understanding. 认知的 (2) Based on factual knowledge that has been or can be gained by experience. 认知力的

• A child isn't a computer; a third-grader's cognitive abilities are highly dependent on his or her upbringing and happiness. 孩子不是电脑，三年级学生的认知能力高度依赖于他/她的教养和快乐。

Cognitive skills and knowledge involve the ability to acquire factual information, often the kind of knowledge that can easily be tested. So *cognition* should be distinguished from social, emotional, and creative development and ability. *Cognitive science* is a growing field of study that deals with human perception, thinking, and learning.

认知技能和知识涉及获取事实信息的能力，通常这类知识易于测试。因此，应该将 cognition（认知力）与社会、情感、创造性发展和能力区分开来。cognitive science（认知科学）是一个不断发展的研究领域，涉及人类的感知、思考和学习。

agnostic\ag-ˈnä-stik\ A person who believes that whether God exists is not known and probably cannot be known. 不可知论者

• Both of them were always agnostics, but after they had children they started attending church again. 他们两人一直都是不可知论者，但有了孩子以后，他们又开始去教堂了。

The words *agnostic* and *agnosticism* were coined around 1870 by the great English biologist T. H. Huxley, who had just spent a decade defending the works of Charles Darwin against the attacks of the church. Scientists often put a high value on evidence when arguing about religion, and many *agnostic* thinkers believe that human minds simply aren't equipped to grasp the nature of God. But agnostics differ from *atheists*, who actually claim that no God exists and may even think they can prove it. You may have seen the similar word *gnostic*, the name for followers of certain religious sects from around the time of Christ that sought spiritual knowledge and rejected the material world. An increasing interest in *gnosticism* today can be seen in the popular novels of Philip Pullman, Dan Brown, and Neil Gaiman.

agnostic（不可知论者）和 agnosticism（不可知论）两个词是在 1870 年左右由英国伟大的生物学家托马斯·亨利·赫胥黎创造的，他用了十年时间反对教会的抨击，捍卫查尔斯·达尔文的进化论。在关于宗教的争论中，科学家常高度重

视证据，许多 agnostic thinkers（不可知论思想家）认为，人类的大脑没有能力掌握上帝的本质。但 agnostics 不同于 atheists（无神论者），后者声称上帝不存在，甚至认为可以证明这一点。你可能见过类似的词 gnostic（诺斯替主义信徒），这是基督时代某些宗教派别追随者的名字，这些教派寻求灵性知识而拒绝物质世界。人们如今对 gnosticism（诺斯替主义）的兴趣日益浓厚，可以在菲利普·普尔曼、丹·布朗和尼尔·盖曼的流行小说中窥见一斑。

incognito \ˌin-ˌkäg-ˈnē-tō\   In disguise, or with one's identity concealed. 伪装，隐藏个人身份

• Years after her reign as a top Hollywood star, she was discovered working incognito as a bartender in Manhattan while living in cheap hotels. 人们发现，她在成为顶级的好莱坞明星多年之后，居然隐藏身份在曼哈顿一家酒吧当招待，还住廉价的酒店。

In a famous myth, Zeus and Hermes visit a village incognito to test the villagers. The seemingly poor travelers are turned away from every household except that of Baucis and Philemon. This elderly couple, though very poor themselves, provide the disguised gods with a feast. When the gods finally reveal themselves, they reward the couple generously for their hospitality, but destroy the rest of the village. 在一个著名的神话中，宙斯和赫尔墨斯乔装打扮到一个村庄来考验村民。这两个看起来很穷的旅行者被全村人拒之门外，只有博西斯和腓力门一家例外。这对上了年纪的夫妇虽然自己很穷，却让乔装打扮的两位神灵饱餐一顿。最终，两位神灵表明了身份，慷慨地回馈了热情好客的这对夫妇，却杀掉了其他村民。

GNI/
GNO

prognosis \präg-ˈnō-səs\   (1) The chance of recovery from a given disease or condition. 预后 (2) A forecast or prophecy. 预测，预言

• The prognosis for a patient with chicken pox is usually excellent; the prognosis for someone with liver cancer is terrible. 水痘患者的预后通常不错，而肝癌患者的预后则很糟糕。

With its prefix *pro-*, meaning "before," *prognosis* means basically "knowledge beforehand" of how a situation is likely to turn out. *Prognosis* was originally a strictly medical term, but it soon broadened to include predictions made by experts of all kinds. Thus, for example, economists are constantly offering prognoses (notice the irregular plural form) about where the economy is going, and climate scientists regularly *prognosticate* about how quickly the earth's atmosphere is warming. prognosis 的前缀 pro- 意思是"在……之前"，这个词的基本意思是"事先知道"情况可能会如何发展。prognosis 最初是一个严格的医学用语，但很快拓展到包括各行各业的专家所做的预测。例如，经济学家不断提供有关经济发展方向的预测（注意其不规则的复数形式），气候科学家经常 prognosticate（预测）地球大气变暖的速度有多快。

Quizzes

A. Fill in each blank with the correct letter：

a. agnostic   e. diction
b. dictum   f. incognito
c. cognitive   g. edict
d. jurisdiction   h. prognosis

1. Psychology is not entirely a _____ science, since it deals with behavior as

well as the mind.

2. He often repeated Balzac's famous _____: "Behind every great fortune is a great crime."

3. Movie stars often go out in public _____, in faded sweatshirts, worn-out pants, and sunglasses.

4. When their dictatorial grandfather issued an _____, everyone obeyed it.

5. She has strong opinions about lots of public issues, but she's an _____ about foreign policy.

6. The _____ for the world's climate in the next century is uncertain.

7. He complains about his students' _____, saying they mumble so much that he often can't understand them.

8. The judge refused to consider two elements in the case, saying that they lay outside his _____.

B. Indicate whether the following pairs of words have the same or different meanings:

1. agnostic / complex   same ____ / different ____
2. cognitive / digestive   same ____ / different ____
3. diction / wordiness   same ____ / different ____
4. dictum / declaration   same ____ / different ____
5. incognito / hospitable   same ____ / different ____
6. jurisdiction / authority   same ____ / different ____
7. prognosis / outlook   same ____ / different ____
8. edict / order   same ____ / different ____

GRAPH comes from the Greek verb *graphein*, "to write." Thus, a *biography* is a written account of someone's life (see BIO, p. 441), a *discography* is a written list of recordings on disc (records or CDs), and a *filmography* is a list of motion pictures. But lots of uses of *-graph* and *-graphy* don't mean literally "writing" (as in *autograph* or *paragraph*), but instead something more like "recording," as in *photography*, *seismograph*, or *graph* itself.

GRAPH 源自希腊语动词 *graphein*（"书写"）。因此，*biography*（传记）是对某个人生活的书面记录（见 BIO，第 441 页），*discography*（唱片分类目录）指的是写在光盘（唱片或 CD）上面的录音目录，*filmography* 指的是影片目录。但很多词语所用的 -graph 和 -graphy 表示的并不是字面意思"书写"（如 *autograph*、*paragraph*），而更像是"记录"的某个东西，如 *photography*、*seismograph*，或 *graph* 本身。

---

calligraphy \kə-ˈli-grə-fē\   The art of producing beautiful hand- writing. 书法艺术

● Calligraphy can be seen today in event invitations, logo designs, and stone inscriptions.   如今，我们可以在活动请柬、标志设计和石刻上见到书法艺术。

Kalli- is a Greek root meaning "beautiful," and "beautiful" in the case of *calligraphy* means artistic, stylized, and elegant. Calligraphy has existed in many cultures, including Indian, Persian, and Islamic cultures; Arabic puts a particularly high value on beautiful script, and in East Asia calligraphy has long been considered a major art. Calligraphers in the West use pens with wide nibs, with which they produce strokes of widely differing width within a single letter.

kalli-是希腊语词根,意思是"美丽的"。就 calligraphy 而言,"美丽的"所指的是艺术的、风格化的、优雅的。书法存在于许多文化中,包括印度文化、波斯文化和伊斯兰文化等,阿拉伯文化尤为重视文字之美。在东亚,书法一直被认为是一种重要的艺术。西方的书法家使用有宽笔尖的笔,以便在一个字母内产生宽度差异很大的笔画。

hagiography\ˌha-gē-ˈä-grə-fē\ (1) Biography of saints. 圣徒传记 (2) Biography that idealizes or idolizes. 理想化或偶像化的传记

• According to the new biography, which should really be called a hagiography, the former prime minister doesn't seem to have done anything small-minded or improper in his entire life. 根据那本真该被称作圣徒传记的新传记,这位前首相似乎一生都没做过任何狭隘的或不恰当的事情。

For those able to read, reading stories of the lives of the saints was a popular pastime for centuries, and books collecting short saints' biographies were best sellers. These often included terrifically colorful stories (about slaying dragons, magically traveling through space, etc.) that were perhaps a bit too good to be strictly true, and after finding God not one of them ever did a single thing that wasn't saintly—and some of them may not have actually existed. Still today, *hagiographic* accounts of the lives of politicians and pop-culture stars are being written, though there now seems to be a bigger audience for biographies that seek out the not-so-wholesome secrets of the person's life, sometimes even making up a few of them.

对于那些有阅读能力的人而言,读圣徒的生活故事很多世纪以来都是一种受欢迎的消遣方式,而收录了短篇圣徒传记的书籍曾经都是畅销书。这些书里通常有丰富多彩的故事(关于屠龙、神奇的空间穿越等),这些故事可能过于好了点儿,很难让人全信。在找到上帝之后,没有一个圣徒做过一件不神圣的事情——其中有些圣徒实际上可能并不存在。时至今日,仍有人在撰写关于政治家和流行文化明星生活的 hagiographic(理想化的)报道,尽管现在似乎有更多读者喜欢那些揭露某个人不太健康的生活秘密的传记,而有些秘密甚至是凭空捏造的。

choreography\ˌkȯr-ē-ˈä-grə-fē\ (1) The art of composing and arranging dances and of representing them in symbolic notation. 舞蹈设计 (2) The movements by dancers in a performance. 舞蹈动作

• The reviews praised the show for its eye-catching choreography, calling it the best element of the whole musical. 剧评赞扬了这场表演引人注目的舞蹈设计,称其为整部音乐剧的最佳元素。

In ancient Greece, a *choreia* was a circular dance accompanied by a singing *chorus*. But the actual notating of dances by means of symbols didn't begin until the 17th or 18th century, when ballet developed into a complex art form in France. The *choreographer* of a major ballet, which might run to an hour or more, will always record his or her work in notation, though *choreographing* a five-minute segment for a TV talent show usually doesn't require any record at all.

在古希腊，*choreia*（诗乐舞）是一种由 *chorus* 伴唱的圆圈舞。但是，真正用符号记录舞蹈的做法直到 17 或 18 世纪才出现，当时芭蕾舞在法国发展成为一种复杂的艺术形式。一场大型的芭蕾舞表演可能会持续一个小时或更长时间，*choreographer*（编舞者）总会用符号记录他/她的作品，但为电视才艺秀 *choreographing*（编舞）五分钟长的片段通常不需要什么记录。

lithograph \ˈli-thə-ˌgraf\ A picture made by printing from a flat surface (such as a smooth stone) prepared so that the ink will only stick to the design that will be printed. 平版画，石版画

- To make a lithograph, the artist first draws an image, in reverse, on a fine-grained limestone or aluminum plate. 为了制作石版画，那个艺术家首先在细粒石灰岩或铝板上绘制相反的图像。

Lithos is Greek for "stone," and a stone surface has traditionally been involved in lithography, though a metal plate may take its place today. The *lithographic process* was invented around 1796 and soon became the main method of printing books and newspapers. Artists use *lithography* to produce prints (works intended to be sold in many copies), and art lithographs sometimes resemble older types of prints, including etchings, engravings, and woodcuts. Pablo Picasso, Marc Chagall, Joan Miró, and M. C. Escher are among the many artists who have used lithography to produce important original works. Today lithographic printing accounts for over 40% of all printing, packaging, and publishing.

lithos 是希腊语，意思是"石头"，石板在传统上一直被用于平版印刷术，尽管如今可以被金属板取代。*lithographic process*（平版印刷工艺）发明于 1796 年左右，很快成为印刷书籍和报纸的主要方法。艺术家使用 *lithography*（平版印刷术）印制作品（打算有很多份用来出售），艺术版画有时类似于更早的印制品类型，包括蚀刻、雕刻和木刻。很多艺术家用平板印刷术制作重要的原创作品，其中包括巴勃罗·毕加索、马克·夏加尔、胡安·米罗和 M. C. 埃舍尔等。如今，平版印刷占印刷、包装和出版总量的 40% 以上。

ART
comes from the Latin word for "skill." This reminds us that, until a few centuries ago, almost no one made a strong distinction between skilled craftsmanship and what we would now call "art." And the word *art* itself could also mean simply "cleverness." The result is that this root appears in some words where we might not expect it.

ART 源自拉丁语中表示"技巧"的词。这提醒我们，直到几个世纪前，还几乎没有人明确区分需要技能的手艺和我们如今称之为"艺术"的东西。*art* 一词本身也可能仅仅表示"聪明"。其结果是，这个词根出现在我们可能没有想到的一些单词中。

artful \ˈärt-fəl\ (1) Skillful. 精湛的，巧妙的 (2) Wily, crafty, sly. 狡猾的，狡诈的

- It was an artful solution: each side was pleased with the agreement, but it was the lawyer himself who stood to make the most money off of it. 这是一个巧妙的解决方案:各方都对协议感到满意,但律师本人很可能才是从中获利最多的一方。

A writer may produce an artful piece of prose, one that's clearly and elegantly written. The same writer might also make an artful argument, one that cleverly leaves out certain details and plays up others so as to make a stronger case. In the first instance, the prose is well crafted; in the second, the argument might instead be called crafty. But even though both uses are correct, most of us still use *artful* somewhat differently from *artistic*.

一位作家可能会写出精湛的散文,即清晰、优雅的散文。这位作家也可能会进行巧妙的论证,即聪明地省略某些细节而突出其他细节,以便使理由更充分。在第一个例子中,那篇散文是 well crafted(精心设计的);而在第二个例子中,那个论证也可以被称为 crafty(狡猾的)。但即便两种用法都对,多数人在 artful 和 artistic(艺术的)的使用上还是有所不同。

artifact \ˈär-ti-ˌfakt\ A usually simple object made by human workmanship, such as a tool or ornament, that represents a culture or a stage in a culture's development. 人工制品,手工制品

● Through the artifacts found by archaeologists, we now know a considerable amount about how the early Anasazi people of the Southwest lived. 通过考古学家发掘的这些人工制品,我们现在对早期西南部的阿纳萨齐人的生活方式已有相当多的了解。

One of the things that make humans unique is their ability to make and use tools, and ever since the first rough stone axes began to appear about 700,000 years ago, human cultures have left behind *artifacts* from which we've tried to draw a picture of their everyday life. The roots of artifact mean basically "something made with skill"; thus, a mere stone that was used for pounding isn't an artifact, since it wasn't shaped by humans for its purpose—unlike a ram's horn that was polished and given a brass mouthpiece and was blown as part of a religious ritual.

人类之所以独一无二,有一个原因是能够制造工具和使用工具。自从约 70 万年前出现第一个粗糙的石斧以来,人类文化就已经留下了人工制品,从中我们已经尝试绘出他们日常生活的画面。从 artifact 的词根可以知道,这个词的基本意思是"用技巧制作的东西";因此,仅仅用于敲击的石头不能被称为人工制品,因为它不是人类为此目的而制作的——这不同于公羊的角,人类将羊角磨光,装上铜嘴吹奏,成为宗教仪式的一个部分。

artifice \ˈär-tə-fəs\ (1) Clever skill. 技巧,策略 (2) A clever trick. 诡计

● By his cunning and artifice, Iago convinces Othello that Desdemona has been unfaithful. 凭借他的狡诈和诡计,伊阿古使奥赛罗相信苔丝狄蒙娜一直不忠。

Artifice can be a tricky word to use. It combines the same roots as *artifact*, so it's sometimes seen in descriptions of craftsmanship ("The artifice that went into this jewelry can still astound us," "The chef had used all his artifice to disguise the nature of the meat"). But it can also be used for many situations that don't involve physical materials ("They had gotten around the rules by a clever artifice," "The artifice of the plot is ingenious"). Like its adjective, *artificial*, *artifice* isn't necessarily either positive nor negative. But both words can make us slightly uncomfortable if we like to think of simplicity and naturalness as important values.

artifice 是个使用起来很棘手的词。构成该词的词根与 *artifact* 的词根相同，所以有时可以在对技艺的描述中见到它("制作珠宝的技巧仍然让我们震惊""厨师倾尽所有的技艺来掩盖肉的本质")。但这个词也可以用于许多不涉及物质材料的情况("他们通过聪明的技巧绕过了规则""这个情节的技巧新颖独特")。就像它的形容词 *artificial* 一样，*artifice* 也不一定是褒义词或贬义词。但如果我们认为简单和自然是重要的价值观念，这两个词可能会让我们有点不舒服。

artisan \ˈär-tə-zən\   A skilled worker or craftsperson. 技工，工匠

● At the fair, they saw examples of the best carving, pottery, and jewelry by local artisans. 在那个展会上，他们看到了能代表当地工匠最高水平的雕刻、陶器和珠宝。

Artisans aren't the same as *artists*, but it can sometimes be hard to tell the difference. In the Middle Ages, artisans organized themselves into guilds. In every city each group of artisans—weavers, carpenters, shoemakers, and so on—had its own guild, which set wages and prices, kept standards high, and protected its members from outside competitors. In America, however, most artisans have always been fiercely independent. Today, when factories produce almost all of our goods, artisans usually make only fine objects for those who can afford them. And we now even include food among the artisan's crafts, so you can buy *artisanal* cheeses, breads, and chocolates—but probably not if you're watching your budget.

工匠与 *artists*（艺术家）不同，但有时候很难区分。在中世纪，工匠们自己会组织成行会。在每个城市，各种工匠群体——织工、木匠、鞋匠等——都有自己的行会，行会规定工资和价格，保持高标准，保护其会员免受外部竞争者的侵害。然而，美国的多数工匠一直高度独立。如今，工厂几乎能生产我们需要的所有商品，而工匠通常只制作精美的物品，卖给那些买得起的人。我们现在甚至将食物纳入工匠的手艺范畴，所以你可以买手工奶酪、手工面包、手工巧克力——但如果预算有限，也许就不买。

Quizzes

A. Fill in each blank with the correct letter:

a. choreography   e. calligraphy
b. lithograph   f. hagiography
c. artful   g. artifact
d. artisan   h. artifice

1. The strangest _____ they had dug up was a bowl on which an extremely odd animal was painted.

2. A signed _____ by Picasso wouldn't be valued nearly as highly as one of his paintings.

3. She admired the _____, but the dancers didn't seem to have practiced enough.

4. He'd done an _____ job of writing the proposal so as to appeal to each board member who would have to approve it.

5. In his spare time he practiced _____, using special pens to write short

quotations suitable for framing.

6. Each room in the palace was a masterpiece of _____, from its wall paintings to its chandeliers to its delicate furniture.

7. Each worker at the tiny textile workshop thought of himself or herself as an _____.

8. The book was pure _____, painting its statesman hero as not only brilliant but saintly.

B. Match the definition on the left to the correct word on the right:

1. craftsperson   a. artful
2. saint's biography   b. artifice
3. ingenious   c. lithograph
4. print   d. choreography
5. clever skill   e. artisan
6. beautiful handwriting f. hagiography
7. man-made object   g. calligraphy
8. dance design   h. artifact

FORT

FORT comes from *fortis*, Latin for "strong." The familiar noun *fort*, meaning a building strengthened against possible attacks, comes directly from it. And our verb *comfort* actually means "to give strength and hope to."

FORT 源自拉丁语 *fortis*（"强大"）。我们熟知的名词 *fort*（堡垒）直接来自这个词根，意思是经过加固的建筑物，用以阻挡可能发生的进攻。英语动词 *comfort* 实际指的是"给……力量和希望"。

---

fortify \ˈfȯr-tə-ˌfī\   To strengthen. 加强，增强，防御

• Fortified by a good night's sleep and a big breakfast, they set off for the final 20 miles of their journey. 经过一夜好睡眠和丰盛早餐的补充,他们开始了最后20英里的旅程。

Medieval cities were fortified against attack by high walls, and volunteers may fortify a levee against an overflowing river by means of sandbags. Foods can be fortified by adding vitamins, but "fortified wines," such as sherry and port, have brandy (a "stronger" drink) rather than vitamins added to them. By adopting good exercise habits, you can fortify your body against illness. And fortifying needn't always be physical. An author's reputation may be fortified by the success of his new book, or a prosecutor can fortify a case against a suspect by finding more evidence.

中世纪的城市用高墙作防抵御袭击，而志愿者用沙袋来加固防洪堤，防止河水泛滥。食物可以通过添加维生素来强化，但是"强化葡萄酒"，如雪利酒和波特酒，添加的是白兰地（一种"更烈的"酒）而不是维生素。养成良好的运动习惯，你可以增强体质以抵御疾病。而强化并不总是物质的。作家的声誉可能会因其新书的成功而得到提升，检察官可以找更多证据来加强对犯罪嫌疑人的指控。

fortification\ˌfȯr-tə-fə-ˈkā-shən\ (1) The building of military defenses to protect a place against attack. 建造堡垒,设防 (2) A structure built to protect a place. 防御工事

• The city's fortifications had withstood powerful assaults by catapults, battering rams, and tall siege towers that rolled up to release soldiers onto the top of the walls. 这个城市的防御工事经受了石弩、攻城锤以及高大的攻城塔的强大攻击,攻城塔能被推到城墙边并将士兵投放到城墙顶上。

In the Middle Ages, many European cities were entirely enclosed by sturdy walls, with walkways along the top and towers at intervals, designed to make an invasion impossible. A water-filled ditch, or moat, might run alongside the wall for added defense. Such defenses turned the entire city into a *fort*, or *fortress*. Over the centuries, *fortifications* changed steadily with the development of new weaponry. In World War II, the German fortification of the French coast included antitank barriers, bunkers, minefields, and underwater obstacles, but it wasn't enough to turn back the immense force of the Allied invasion on D-day. 中世纪的很多欧洲城市完全被坚固的城墙围住,墙顶有走道,每隔一段距离有塔楼,这样的设计是为了杜绝入侵。墙外是护城河,以增加防御能力。这种防御将整个城市变成一个 *fort* 或 *fortress*(堡垒)。很多世纪以来,防御工事随新武器的发展而不断改变。在第二次世界大战中,德国在法国海岸的防御体系包括反坦克屏障、掩体、雷区和水下障碍物,但这不足以抵御在诺曼底登陆日盟军入侵的强大力量。

forte\ˈfȯrt, ˈfȯr-ˌtā, fȯr-ˈtā\ Something that a person does particularly well; one's strong point. 特长,专长,强项

• Her forte was statistics, and she was always at a disadvantage when the discussion turned to public policy. 她的强项是统计数据,但当讨论到公共政策时,她就处于劣势了。

In the Middle Ages, swords were often known to break in battle, so the strongest part of a sword's blade—the part between the handle (or hilt) and the middle of the blade—was given a name, the *forte*. Today a forte is usually a special strength. But no one can agree on how to pronounce it: all three pronunciations shown above are heard frequently. Part of the problem is confusion with the Italian musical term *forte* (always pronounced /ˈfȯr-ˌtā/), meaning "loud." 中世纪时,人们知道剑在战斗中常会折断,因此剑最结实的部分——即介于柄(或剑柄)与剑刃中段之间的部分——被赋予了一个名称 *forte*(剑身最强的部分)。今天,强项通常指一种特殊的力量。但没有人能就这个词的发音达成一致:上面显示的三个发音经常都能听到。部分问题在于,这个词常与意大利语中意思是"响亮"的音乐术语 *forte*(总是读作/ˈfȯr-ˌtā/)相混淆。

fortitude\ˈfȯr-tə-ˌtüd\ Mental strength that allows one to face danger, pain, or hardship with courage. 坚忍,刚毅,勇气

• He's just too nice, and we worry that he won't have the fortitude to deal with the monsters in that office. 他实在是太善良了,我们担心他没有勇气应对办公室里那些恶人。

How many people know that the famous marble lions that guard the steps of the New York Public Library in Manhattan are named Patience and *Fortitude*? In Latin, the quality of *fortitudo* combines physical strength, vigor, courage, and boldness, but the English *fortitude* usually means simply firmness and steadiness of will, or "backbone." The philosopher Plato long ago listed four essential human virtues—prudence (i. e., good judgment), justice (i. e., ability to be fair in balancing between one's own interests and others'), temperance (i. e., moderation or restraint), and fortitude, and in Christian tradition these became known as the four "cardinal virtues."

有多少人知道，守卫在曼哈顿纽约公共图书馆台阶旁的著名石狮被命名为"耐心"和"毅力"? 在拉丁语中，*fortitudo* 这种品质融合了体力、活力、勇气和胆量，但英语中的 *fortitude* 通常只表示意志坚定不动摇，或表示"骨气"。古代哲学家柏拉图早就列出了人类的四个基本的美德——谨慎(即良好的判断力)，正义(即公正地平衡自己和他人的利益的能力)，克制(即适度或克制)和刚毅。在基督教传统中，这些被称为四个"cardinal virtues"(基本美德)。

CIS comes from the Latin verb meaning "to cut, cut down, or slay." An *incisor* is one of the big front biting teeth; beavers and woodchucks have especially large ones. A *decision* "cuts off" previous discussion and uncertainty.

CIS 源自意思是"切、砍倒或杀"的拉丁语动词。*incisor*(门牙)是位于前部用于撕咬的大牙之一，海狸和土拨鼠的门牙特别大。一项 *decision*(决定)"结束"了之前的讨论和不确定状态。

concise\kən-ˈsīs\ Brief and condensed, especially in expression or statement. 简明的，简洁的

 • Professor Childs's exam asked for a concise, one-page summary of the causes of the American Revolution. 蔡尔兹教授的考试要求简要概述美国革命的原因，长度不超过一页纸。

 Many students think that adding unnecessary sentences with long words will make their writing more impressive. But in fact almost every reader values *concision*, since concise writing is usually easier to read, better thought out, and better organized—that is, simply better writing. Words such as *short* don't have the full meaning of *concise*, which usually means not just "brief" but "packed with information."

许多学生认为添加带有长单词的、不必要的句子会让他们的作文更令人印象深刻。但实际上，几乎每个读者都看重 *concision*(简洁)，因为简洁的作品通常更易于阅读、考虑更周详、结构更合理——简而言之，就是更好。像 *short* 这样的词不具有 *concise* 的全部意义，后者的含义通常包括"简短的"，还包括"富含信息的"。

excise\ˈek-ˌsīz\ To cut out, especially surgically. (尤指手术上)切除

 • The ancient Minoans from the island of Crete apparently excised the hearts of their human sacrifices. 很显然，克里特岛的古代米诺斯人切除了献祭人的心脏。

 Excise takes part of its meaning from the prefix *ex-*, "out." A writer may excise long passages of a novel to reduce it to a reasonable length, or a film director may excise a scene that might give offense. A surgeon may excise a large cancerous tumor, or make a tiny *excision* to examine an organ's tissue. *Excise* is also a noun, meaning a tax paid on something manufactured and sold in the U. S. Much of what consumers pay for tobacco or alcohol products go to cover the excise taxes that the state and federal government charge the manufacturers. But it's only accidental that this noun is spelled like the verb, since it comes from a completely different source.

excise 从前缀 ex-("向外")中得到了部分含义。作者可以大段删除小说的内容,将其压缩到合理的长度;电影导演可以删除某个可能冒犯观众的场景;外科医生可以切除大的癌性肿瘤,或做一个小小的 excision(切片)来检查某器官的组织。excise 也作名词,意思是为在美国生产和销售的产品所支付的税。消费者为烟草或酒精产品支付的钱,很多都用来支付州和联邦政府向制造商征收的货物税。这个名词的拼写像动词完全出于偶然,因为它的来源全然不同。

incisive \in-ˈsī-siv\ Impressively direct and decisive. 直截了当的

• A few incisive questions were all that was needed to expose the weakness in the prosecutor's case. 要暴露出控方案件的弱点,几个直截了当的问题足矣。

From its roots, *incise* means basically "to cut into." So just as a doctor uses a scalpel to make an *incision* in the skin, an *incisive* remark cuts into the matter at hand. A good analyst makes incisive comments about a news story, cutting through the unimportant details, and a good critic *incisively* identifies a book's strengths and weaknesses.

从词根来看,*incise* 的基本含义是"切入"。因此,正如医生使用手术刀在皮肤上做个 *incision*(切口)一样,一句精辟的评论切入当前的问题。好的分析家能透过不重要的细节,做出切中要害的新闻报道;好的评论家能 *incisively*(敏锐地)指出一本书的优缺点。

precision \pri-ˈsi-zhən\ Exactness and accuracy. 准确,精确

• By junior year she was speaking with greater precision, searching for exact words in place of the crude, awkward language of her friends. 到了大三,她说话更精准,会找一些妥帖的词语代替朋友粗俗、笨拙的语言。

Many of us often use *precision* and *accuracy* as synonyms, but not scientists and engineers. For them, accuracy describes a particular measurement—that is, how close it is to the truth. But precision describes a measurement system—that is, how good it is at giving the same result every time it measures the same thing. This may be why even nonscientists now often speak of "precision instruments" for measuring, "precision landings" made by airplanes, "precision drilling" for natural gas, and so on.

许多人经常把 *precision* 和 *accuracy* 用作同义词,但科学家和工程师不会。对于他们来说,*accuracy* 描述一种特定的度量——也就是说,它离有多么接近真相。但 *precision* 描述一个度量系统——也就是说,它有多么善于在测量相同东西时每每都能得出相同的结果来。这或许能解释,为什么即便不是科学家的人如今也常谈到用于测量的"精密仪器"、飞机"精确着陆"、天然气"精密钻井"等等。

Quizzes

A. Fill in each blank with the correct letter:

a. forte
b. fortify
c. fortification

e. concise
f. excise
g. incisive

d. precision   h. fortitude

1. Ms. Raymond's report was _____ but managed to discuss all the issues.

2. Carpentry isn't his _____, but he could probably build something simple like a bed.

3. They could _____ their theory by positive results from some more experiments.

4. The judge was deeply knowledgeable about the case, and his questions to both lawyers were _____.

5. The last Spanish _____ along the river proved to be the most difficult one for the French forces to take.

6. Whenever she was on the verge of despair, she remembered her grandfather's words about _____ being the character trait most important for success.

7. Before eating an apple, some people carefully _____ the brown spots.

8. What the tipsy darts players lacked in _____ they made up for in enthusiasm.

B. Choose the closest definition:

1. precision   a. accuracy   b. beauty   c. brilliance
   d. dependence
2. fortitude   a. armor   b. endurance   c. skill
   d. weapon
3. excise   a. add   b. examine   c. refuse
   d. cut out
4. forte   a. discipline   b. force   c. castle
   d. special strength
5. incisive   a. damaging   b. sharp   c. lengthy
   d. definite
6. fortification   a. diet   b. exercise   c. stronghold
   d. belief
7. concise   a. concentrated   b. sure   c. shifting
   d. blunt
8. fortify   a. attack   b. strengthen   c. struggle
   d. excite

Animal Words 动物词语

apiary \ˈā-pē-ˌer-ē\   A place where bees are kept for their honey. 养蜂场

• Apple orchards are excellent sites for apiaries, since the bees keep the apple trees productive by pollinating them. 苹果园是养蜂场的绝佳场所,因为蜜蜂通过授粉能让苹果树丰产。

Beekeeping, or *apiculture*, is the care of honeybees that ensures that they produce more honey than they can use. An apiary usually consists of many separate beehives. The social life of a hive is strange and marvelous. The queen bee, who will become the mother of an entire colony, is actually created by being fed "royal jelly" while she is still only a larva. The tens of thousands of worker bees are underdeveloped females; only a handful of the bees are male, and they do no work at all. The workers defend the hive by kamikaze means, stinging any intruder and dying as they do so. There's more drama in a quiet-looking apiary than the casual observer might notice.

养蜂，即 *apiculture*，指的是照料蜜蜂，确保它们生产的蜂蜜比它们食用的多。养蜂场通常由许多单独的蜂箱组成。蜂群的社会生活很奇妙。蜂王是整个蜂群的母亲，在还是幼虫时，就被喂食"蜂王浆"。数以万计的工蜂是发育不完全的雌蜂；只有为数极少的蜜蜂是雄性的，它们根本不工作。工蜂们用自杀性的方式来保卫蜂箱，它们用蜂针蜇入侵者，代价是死亡。看似安静的养蜂场里好戏连台，不细心观察可是注意不到的啊。

caper\\ˈkā-pər\\ (1) A playful leap. 雀跃，蹦跳 (2) A prank or mischievous adventure. 恶作剧

• For their caper in the girls' bathroom, all three seniors were suspended for a week. 因为在女生浴室搞恶作剧，三个大四学生全部被勒令停学一周。

Caper in Latin means "a male goat." Anyone who has watched a young goat frolic in a field or clamber onto the roof of a car knows the kind of crazy fun the English word *caper*—which is also a verb—is referring to. A *capriole* is a backward kick done in midair by a trained horse. *Capricorn*, meaning "horned goat," is a constellation and one of the signs of the zodiac. And a *capricious* act is one that's done with as little thought as a frisky goat might give it.

caper 在拉丁语中的意思是"公山羊"。只要看到过小山羊在田野中嬉戏或费力地爬到汽车顶上，任何人都会知道英语单词 *caper*——也用作动词——所指的那种无比的快乐。*capriole*（原地腾跃）指的是训练有素的马跳跃起来向后踢的动作。*capricorn* 的意思是"长角的山羊"，它是星座名，也是黄道十二宫之一。*capricious* act（任性的行为）指的是做事情不假思考，就像活泼好动的山羊那样。

equestrian\\i-ˈkwes-trē-ən\\ Of or relating to horseback riding. 骑马的

• The circus's equestrian acts, in which bareback riders performed daring acrobatic feats atop prancing horses, were her favorites. 她最爱看马戏团的马术表演，其中有无鞍马骑手在欢蹦乱跳的马上表演大胆的特技。

Equestrian comes from *equus*, Latin for "horse." Old statues of military heroes, like the famous one of General Sherman on New York's Fifth Avenue, are frequently equestrian. In these sculptures the man always sits nobly upright on a horse, but the horse's stance varies; depending on whether the rider was killed in battle or survived, was victorious or defeated, the horse traditionally stands with four, three, or two hooves on the ground. Equestrian statues have been popular through the centuries, because until the 20th century almost every officer in Europe and America was trained in equestrian skills and combat.

equestrian 源自拉丁语 *equus*（"马"）。过去的战争英雄雕像，如纽约第五大道上著名的谢尔曼将军，通常都是骑马的。在这些雕塑中，男人总是高贵笔直地端坐在马上，但马的站姿却有所不同；根据骑者在战斗中丧生或幸存、胜利或失败，雕像中的马传统上会有四只、三只或两只蹄着地。很多世纪以来，骑马的雕像一直颇受欢迎，因为直到 20 世纪，几乎每个欧美军官还都要接受马术技巧及格斗训练。

lupine\\'lü-ˌpīn\   Like a wolf; wolfish. 似狼的

● Doctors reported that the boy showed lupine behavior such as snarling and biting, and walked with his knees bent in a kind of crouch. 医生报告说，那个男孩表现出像狼一样的行为，如咆哮、咬人，行走时膝盖弯曲呈蹲伏状。

Lupine comes from *lupus*, Latin for "wolf," and its related adjective *lupinus*, "wolfish." Lupine groups have a highly organized social structure, with leaders and followers clearly distinguished; dogs, since they're descended from wolves, often show these lupine patterns when living in groups. Stories of children raised by wolves (the most famous being Romulus, the legendary founder of Rome) have generally been hard to prove, partly because "wild" children lack human language abilities and can't describe their experiences. *Lupine* is also a noun, the name of a well-known garden flower, which was once thought to drain, or "wolf," the soil of its nutrients.

lupine 源自拉丁语 *lupus*（"狼"）及其相关的形容词 *lupinus*（"似狼的"）。狼群具有高度组织化的社会结构，领导者和追随者区别明显。狗是狼的后裔，群体生活时也常表现出这些狼的特点。关于狼抚养孩子的故事（最著名的是罗马的传奇创始人罗穆卢斯）一般很难证明，一定程度上是因为"野"孩子缺乏人类的语言能力，无法描述他们的经历。*lupine* 也是名词，指的是一种有名的园艺花卉（羽扇豆），曾经被认为会耗尽或"狼吞虎咽"土壤的营养物质。

ovine\\'ō-ˌvīn\   Of, relating to, or resembling sheep. 绵羊的，像绵羊的

● In her veterinary practice she specialized in ovine medicine, but often treated cows and pigs as well. 在兽医工作中，她专门从事绵羊医学，但也经常医治牛和猪。

Sheep belong to the same family of mammals as goats, antelope, bison, buffalo, and cows. The genus *Ovis* includes at least five species, including the domestic sheep. Some 12,000 years ago, in the area now known as Iraq, sheep became one of the first animals to be domesticated; only the dog is known to have been tamed earlier. At first, they were valued for their milk, skin, and meat (mutton and lamb); not until about 1500 B.C. did the weaving of wool begin. Today a billion sheep are being farmed worldwide. The term *ovine* (which is a noun as well as an adjective) is mostly used in scientific and medical writing—which means you could impress your friends by dropping it into a casual conversation.

绵羊与山羊、羚羊、野牛、水牛和奶牛同属哺乳动物的一个科。genus *Ovis*（羊属）拥有包括家羊在内的至少五个物种。大约 12000 年前，在伊拉克的地区，绵羊成为最早被驯化的动物之一，据说只有狗的驯化更早一些。人类一开始看重的是它们的奶、皮和肉（mutton 和 lamb）。直到公元前 1500 年左右，人们才开始编织羊毛。全世界现在饲养十亿只绵羊。*Ovine* 这个术语（既是名词又是形容词）主要用于科学和医学写作——这意味着，如果把这个词用在闲聊中，朋友会对你钦佩不已。

ornithologist\\ˌȯr-nə-'thä-lə-jist\   A person who studies birds. 鸟类学者，鸟类

学家

- John James Audubon, the great painter of the birds of early America, was also a writing ornithologist of great importance. 约翰·詹姆斯·奥杜邦是美国早期鸟类的伟大画家,也是一位重要的鸟类学作家。

The Greek root *ornith-* means "bird," so *ornithology* is the study of birds. Amateur ornithology, usually called *birding* or *birdwatching*, is an extraordinarily popular pastime in America, where over 40 million people pursue it. Roger Tory Peterson's many field guides have long been some of the amateur ornithologist's most useful tools. Amateurs often make essential contributions to serious ornithology, as in the annual Christmas Bird Count, when tens of thousands of birders fan out across North and South America to produce a kind of census of all the species in the New World. 希腊语词根 *ornith-* 意为"鸟",因此 *ornithology*(鸟类学)是对鸟的研究。业余鸟类研究通常被称为 *birding* 或 *birdwatching*(观鸟),是美国非常受欢迎的一种消遣方式。在美国,观鸟者的人数超过 4000 万。罗杰·托瑞·彼得森的许多野外观鸟指南一直是业余鸟类学家最有用的工具。业余爱好者经常为严肃的鸟类学做出重要贡献,比如一年一度的圣诞节鸟口调查中,数以万计的观鸟者散布在南北美洲,对"新大陆"的所有鸟类进行一次普查。

serpentine\ˈsər-pən-ˌtīn\ Like a snake or serpent in shape or movement; winding. 蛇形的、蛇形移动的、蜿蜒的

- The Great Wall of China, the greatest construction of all time, wends its serpentine way for some 4,000 miles across the Chinese landscape. 中国的长城是有史以来最伟大的建筑,它在中国大地上蜿蜒前行,绵延 4000 多英里。

A snake moves by curving and winding along the ground. Roads through the Pyrenees, the mountains that separate Spain from France, tend to be *serpentine*, curving back and forth on themselves up and down the steep slopes. *Serpentine* has other meanings as well. As a noun, it's the name for a soft green mineral, and also for the party streamers you might throw at midnight on New Year's Eve. The *serpentine belt* under the hood in your car is the long, looping belt that most of the car's accessories—the AC, the power steering, the alternator, and so on—depend on to get their power. 蛇在地面上蜿蜒移动。将西班牙与法国分开的比利牛斯山脉的山路往往是蛇形的,在陡峭的山坡上曲曲折折、起起伏伏。*serpentine* 也有其他含义。作为名词,它指的是一种绿色的软矿物,亦指在新年前夕的午夜时分抛出的派对飘带。汽车引擎盖下的 *serpentine belt*(蛇形皮带)是环形长皮带,汽车的大部分附件——AC、动力转向、交流发电机等——都靠它来获取动力。

simian\ˈsi-mē-ən\ Having to do with monkeys or apes; monkeylike. 猴或猿的、像猿的、像猴的

- Every afternoon the pale youth could be found watching the simian antics in the Monkey House with strange intensity. 每天下午都可以看到那个脸色苍白的青年,他神情怪异地使劲盯着猴舍的猴子,看它们的滑稽动作。

The Latin word for "ape" is *simia*, which itself comes from *simus*, "snub-nosed." *Simian* is usually a scientific word; thus, for instance, biologists study simian viruses in the search for cures to AIDS and other diseases. But *simian* can be used by the rest of us to describe human behavior. Human babies often cling to their mothers in a simian way, and kids playing on a jungle gym may look like *simians*. But if you notice that a friend has a simian style of walking or eating bananas, it might be best not to tell him.

拉丁语中表示"猿"的词语是 *simia*,它又源自 *simus*("塌鼻梁的")。*simian* 通常是一个科学用词,比如,生物学家研究猿猴病毒,以寻找治疗艾滋病和其他疾病的方法。但其他人可以使用 *simian* 描述人类行为。人类的婴儿经常以类似猿猴的方式依附母亲,而在攀登架上玩耍的孩子看起来可能像 *simians*。但如果你注意到,某个朋友走路或吃香蕉的方式与猿猴相像,最好不要告诉他。

Quiz

Indicate whether the following pairs have the same or different meanings:

1. equestrian / horselike   same ____ / different ____
2. ornithologist / studier of birds same ____ / different ____
3. lupine / apelike   same ____ / different ____
4. apiary / monkey colony   same ____ / different ____
5. ovine / goatlike   same ____ / different ____
6. caper / leap   same ____ / different ____
7. simian / catlike   same ____ / different ____
8. serpentine / winding   same ____ / different ____

Review Quizzes

A. Fill in each blank with the correct letter:

a. artisan
b. edict
c. equestrian
d. artifact
e. discordant
f. cognitive
g. apiary
h. exculpate
i. inculpate
j. serpentine
k. precision
l. artifice
m. prognosis
n. simian
o. jurisdiction

1. The farmer tended his _____ lovingly and gathered delicious wildflower honey every year.

2. In trying to _____ herself, she only made herself look guiltier.

3. They arrived in time to see the top riders compete in the championship _____ event.

4. The doctor's _____ is guarded, but she is cautiously optimistic that recovery will be complete.

5. It was a tall vase, with elaborate _____ shapes winding around it from top to bottom.

6. Each side's anger at the other has set a sadly _____ tone for the negotiations.

7. We set the clock with great _____ on the first day of every new year.

8. He's trying hard to _____ as many of his friends in the crime as he can.

9. These beautiful handblown goblets were obviously made by a talented _____.

10. The final _____ from the presidential palace commanded every citizen to wear a baseball cap at all times.

11. The child scrambled over the wall with _____ agility.

12. They're worried about their son's mental health, though the doctors say his _____ skills are fine.

13. She found a small clay _____ in the shape of a bear at the site of the ancient temple.

14. He used every _____ imaginable to hide his real age from the television cameras.

15. Firing local teachers falls outside the superintendant's actual _____.

B. Choose the correct antonym:

1. accord   a. harmonize   b. strengthen   c. differ
   d. agree
2. incisive   a. dull   b. noble   c. faulty
   d. exceptional
3. artful   a. lovely   b. sly   c. talented
   d. awkward
4. forte   a. weak point   b. sword   c. quarrel
   d. pinnacle
5. cordial   a. lazy   b. cool   c. terrific
   d. heartfelt
6. incognito   a. indoors   b. in disguise
   c. as oneself   d. as you were
7. fortify   a. construct   b. reinforce   c. supply
   d. weaken
8. concise   a. lengthy   b. wide   c. dated
   d. brief
9. culpable   a. prisonlike   b. misleading   c. guilty
   d. innocent
10. concord   a. belief   b. conflict   c. deception
    d. peace

C. Choose the closest definition:

1. ornithologist   a. student of fish   b. student of words
   c. student of birds   d. student of wolves
2. mea culpa   a. through my eyes   b. through my fault
   c. through my door   d. through my work
3. lupine   a. foxy   b. horselike
   c. sheepish   d. wolfish
4. discordant   a. energetic   b. temporary
   c. phony   d. clashing
5. jurisdiction   a. area of power   b. area of coverage
   c. area of damage   d. area of target
6. excise   a. call out   b. hold out   c. cut out
   d. fold out
7. choreography   a. book design   b. dance script
   c. choir practice   d. bird study
8. ovine   a. oval   b. egglike   c. sheep-related
   d. birdlike
9. dictum   a. word   b. statement   c. update
   d. answer
10. caper   a. wolf   b. goat   c. character
    d. prank

UNIT 14

CRYPT

CRYPT comes from the Greek word for "hidden." To *encrypt* a message is to encode it—that is, to hide its meaning in code language. When a scientific term begins with *crypto-*, it always means that there's something hidden about it.
CRYPT源自表示"隐藏"的希腊语单词。encrypt（加密）信息就是为其编码——也就是将它的含义隐藏在代码语言中。如果一个科学术语以 crypto- 开头，它通常表示里面隐藏了某些东西。

crypt \ˈkript\ (1) A room completely or partly underground, especially under the main floor of a church. 教堂地下室 (2) A room or area in a large aboveground tomb. 地上墓室

• His old nightmare was of being locked in a crypt with corpses as his only companions. 他以前的噩梦是被锁在地窖里，只有尸体为伴。

Hidden under the main floor of a great church is often a large room, often with a tomb as its centerpiece. Many major European churches were built over the remains of a saint—the Vatican's great St. Peter's Basilica is an example—and instead of having the coffin buried, it was often given its spacious room below ground level. In a large aboveground tomb, or *mausoleum*, there may be several small chambers for individual coffins, also called crypts; when the comic book *Tales from the Crypt* made its first appearance in 1950, it was this meaning that the authors were referring to.
大教堂的主楼下面通常隐藏着一个大房间，其中央通常是一个坟墓。欧洲许多大教堂都是建在一位圣徒的遗体上的——梵蒂冈的圣彼得大教堂就是一个例子——圣徒的棺材没有埋起来，而是安放在地下一个宽敞的房间中。在大型地上坟墓或 *mausoleum*（陵墓）中，可能会有几个单独存放棺材的小墓穴，也称为 crypts。当漫画书《墓穴故事》（又译《魔界奇谈》）在1950年首次出版时，作者所用的 crypt 就是指的这个意思。

encrypt \in-ˈkript\ (1) To convert into cipher. 密码,加密 (2) To convert a message into code. 将……译成代码。

- Messages on the group's Web site are encrypted in code words to keep law-enforcement agents from understanding them. 该组织网站上的信息是用密码字加密的,以防止执法人员看懂这些信息。

Codes aren't always in another language; people have always been able to communicate in ways that conceal their real meaning. In countries ruled by dictators, novelists and playwrights have sometimes managed to encrypt their messages, conveying political ideas to their audiences so that the authorities never notice. But encryption today usually refers to a complex procedure performed on electronic text to make sure the wrong people—whether a nation's enemies or a business competitor (most businesses use encryption today)—can't read it. And sensitive data that merely resides on a company's own computers is often encrypted as well.
代码并不总是用另一种语言编写的,人们总是能够以隐藏其真实含义的方式进行交流。在独裁者统治的国家,小说家和剧作家有时会设法加密他们的信息,向读者传达政治思想,这样统治当局就不会注意到。但是,现在的 encryption (加密)通常是指对电子文本进行复杂的处理,以确保没有资格的人——无论是国家的敌人还是商业竞争者(大多数企业如今使用加密)——无法读取。另外,仅仅存放于公司自己电脑上的敏感数据也经常被加密。

cryptic \ˈkrip-tik\ (1) Mysterious; puzzlingly short. 神秘的,费解的 (2) Acting to hide or conceal. 隐藏的,秘密的

- From across the room, Louisa threw Philip a cryptic look, and he puzzled over what she was trying to tell him. 路易莎从房间那头神秘地瞥了菲利普一眼,但菲利普不明白她到底想告诉他什么。

Until the writing on the famous Rosetta Stone was finally translated in the early 19th century, Egyptian hieroglyphic writing was entirely cryptic, its meaning hidden from the modern world. In the same way, a cryptic comment is one whose meaning is unclear, and a cryptic note may leave you wondering. Cryptic coloring among plants and animals acts like camouflage; so, for example, some moths that are tasty to blue jays are cryptically colored to look like bugs that jays won't touch.
直到19世纪初著名的罗塞塔石碑上的文字被破译出来之前,埃及的象形文字还是非常神秘的,现代世界难解其意。同样,含糊其辞的评论所表达的意思不清楚,而含糊不清的注释会让人不知所云。植物和动物的 cryptic coloring(保护色)起到伪装的作用,比如冠蓝鸦喜欢吃的某些飞蛾会 cryptically(隐秘地)变色,这样看起来就像是冠蓝鸦不会碰的虫子。

cryptography \krip-ˈtä-grə-fē\ (1) Secret writing. 密文 (2) The encoding and decoding of messages. 密码术

- As a graduate student in mathematics, she never dreamed she would end up working in cryptography for the Defense Department. 作为一名数学研究生,她从未想过自己最终会在国防部从事密码工作。

During World War II, cryptography became an extremely complex science for both the Allied and Axis powers. The Allies managed to secretly crack the code produced by the Nazis' Enigma machine, and thereby may have shortened the war by two years. The Axis *cryptographers*, on the other hand, never managed to crack the Americans' ultimate code—the spoken languages of the Navajo and other American Indians. In the age of computers, cryptography has become almost unbelievably complex; it's widely used in peacetime in such areas as banking telecommunications.

在第二次世界大战期间,密码学对同盟国和轴心国而言都是极其复杂的科学。同盟国成功地破解了纳粹的恩尼格玛密码机的代码,从而将战争缩短了可能有两年。而另一边,轴心国的 *cryptographers*(密码员)从未成功破解过美国人的终极代码——纳瓦霍人和其他印第安人的口语。在计算机时代,密码学的复杂程度令人难以置信。密码学在和平时期被广泛用于银行、电信等领域。

AB/ABS
comes to us from Latin, and means "from," "away," or "off." *Abuse* is the use of something in the wrong way. To *abduct* is to "lead away from" or kidnap. *Aberrant* behavior is behavior that "wanders away from" what is acceptable. But there are so many words that include these roots that it would be *absurd* to try to list them all here.

AB / ABS 源自拉丁语,意思是"离开""分离"或"分开"。*abuse*(滥用)是指以错误的方式使用某物。*abduct*(诱拐)是"带离"或绑架。*aberrant* behavior(异常的行为)是"偏离"可接受范围的行为。有太多的词含有该词根,想在此处全部列出会显得很荒唐。

abscond \ab-ˈskänd\ To depart in secret and hide. 潜逃,逃遁,逃走

● They discovered the next morning that their guest had absconded with most of the silverware during the night. 第二天早上,他们发现客人携带大部分银器连夜潜逃了。

Wagner's massive four-part opera *The Ring of the Nibelung* begins with a dwarf absconding with gold which he turns into a magic ring. And in J. R. R. Tolkien's *The Hobbit*, Bilbo Baggins *absconds* from Gollum's caves with the ring he has found, the ring Gollum calls "my precious"; what follows is detailed in the three-volume *Lord of the Rings*. (Tolkien knew Wagner's opera well.) A young couple might abscond from their parents to get married, but sooner or later they must face those parents again.

瓦格纳的大型歌剧《尼贝隆之戒》由四部分组成,开场是一个侏儒带着被他变成魔法戒指的黄金潜逃。在 J. R. R. 托尔金的《霍比特人》中,比尔博·巴金斯带着他找到的戒指从咕噜的洞穴里逃走了,咕噜称戒指为"我的宝贝",接下来就是三卷本《指环王》的详细内容。(托尔金太了解瓦格纳的歌剧了。)一对年轻的情侣可能会逃离他们的父母去结婚,但他们早晚还必须要再次面对父母。

abstemious \ab-ˈstē-mē-əs\ Restrained, especially in the consumption of food or alcohol. (饮食或饮酒)有节制的,有度的

● Her parents had left her two million dollars when they died, having been so abstemious for years that their neighbors all assumed they were poor. 父母去世时给她留下了 200 万美元,他们多年来一直非常节俭,邻居们都以为他们很穷。

Many 14th-century monks lived by the Rule of St. Benedict, which demands an

abstemious life of obedience and poverty. But not all monks could maintain such abstemious habits. Chaucer's *Canterbury Tales* contains a portrait of a fat monk who is supposed to follow a vegetarian diet but instead is an enthusiastic hunter who loves a juicy swan best. He justifies breaking the Rule by saying that it's old-fashioned and that he's just keeping up with modern times. *Abstemious* itself has a slightly old-fashioned sound today, especially in a country where everyone is constantly encouraged to consume.

14世纪的许多修道士在圣本笃会规的约束下生活,会规要求他们过服从和贫穷的有节制的生活。但并非所有修道士都能保持这种有节制的习惯。乔叟的《坎特伯雷故事集》中描写了一个胖修道士,他本应吃素,但却是一位狂热的猎人,最喜欢吃多汁的天鹅肉。他为自己打破会规辩解说,规定早过时了,他只是跟上了现代的步伐而已。如今,*abstemious* 一词本身听起来有点过时了,在一个鼓励人人不断消费的国家更是如此。

abstraction \ab-'strak-shən\ The consideration of a thing or idea without associating it with a particular example. 抽象

- All the ideas she came up with in class were abstractions, since she had no experience of actual nursing at all. 她在课堂上提出的所有想法都是抽象的,因为她根本没有实际护理的经验。

From its roots, *abstraction* should mean basically "something pulled or drawn away." So *abstract* art is art that has moved away from painting objects of the ordinary physical world in order to show something beyond it. Theories are often abstractions; so a theory about economics, for instance, may "pull back" to take a broad view that somehow explains all of economics (but maybe doesn't end up explaining any of it very successfully). An *abstract* of a medical or scientific article is a one-paragraph summary of its contents—that is, the basic findings "pulled out" of the article.

从词根来看,*abstraction* 的基本意思应该是"被抽离的东西"。因此,*abstract* art(抽象的艺术)是一种艺术,但已经脱离普通物质世界的描绘对象,目的是要展示超越物质世界的东西。理论通常是抽象的,比如,一个关于经济学的理论可能会"退一步",以一种宽泛的视角来解释经济学的全部内容(但最终可能无法很成功地解释其任何一点)。医学或科学文章的 *abstract*(摘要)是概括文章内容的一段话——也就是说,从文中提取出来的基本结论。

abstruse \ab-'strüs\ Hard to understand; deep or complex. 难以理解的,深奥的

- In every class he fills the blackboard with abstruse calculations, and we usually leave more confused than ever. 他每堂课都在黑板上写满了深奥的计算,而我们通常在离开时比之前更糊涂。

The original meaning of *abstruse*, coming almost straight from the Latin, was "concealed, hidden." It's easy to see how the word soon came to describe the kind of language used by those who possess certain kinds of expert knowledge (and don't necessarily want to share it with other people). Scientific writing is often filled with the kind of abstruse special vocabulary that's necessary for exact and precise descriptions. Unfortunately, the language of a science like quantum physics can make an already difficult subject even more abstruse to the average person.

abstruse 最初的意思是"隐藏的",几乎直接来自拉丁语。很容易看出,这个词如何很快用来描述拥有某种专业知识的人所使用的那类语言(他们不一定想与他人分享这些知识)。科学文章往往充满了深奥的专门词汇,这些词汇是进行精确描述所必需的。不幸的是,像量子物理学这样的科学所使用的语言,会使一个本来就已经很难的学科对普通人来说更是难上加难。

Quizzes

A. Match the definition on the left to the correct word on the right:

1. mysterious
2. code writing
3. translate to code
4. difficult
5. tomb
6. generalization
7. self-controlled
8. flee

a. encrypt
b. abstraction
c. abscond
d. cryptic
e. abstruse
f. crypt
g. cryptography
h. abstemious

B. Fill in each blank with the correct letter:

a. cryptic
b. abscond
c. abstraction
d. crypt

e. cryptography
f. abstemious
g. encrypt
h. abstruse

1. She had failed to _____ the file when she put it on her hard drive, and her secretary had secretly copied it.

2. His answer was so short and _____ that I have no idea what he meant.

3. The great, echoing _____ of St. Stephen's Cathedral could have held hundreds of people.

4. That's a clever _____, but in the real world things work very differently.

5. The _____ vocabulary of the literature professor led many students to drop her class.

6. He's given up drinking and leads an _____ life these days, rarely thinking about his former high living.

7. Their _____ hasn't been revised in two years, and we've been worried about the security of the data.

8. The bride is so shy that her mother fears she'll _____ from the reception.

PED comes from the Greek word for "child." The same root also has the meaning "foot" (see p. 83), but in English words it usually isn't hard to tell the two apart.
PED 源自表示"孩子"的希腊语单词。同一词根也具有"脚"的含义(参见第 83 页),但在英语单词中,两者通常不难区分。

pedagogy \ˈpe-də-ˌgō-jē\　The art, science, or profession of teaching. 教育学，教学法

• His own pedagogy is extremely original; it sometimes alarms school officials but his students love it. 他自己的教学方法极具独创性，有时会引起校方官员的警惕，但学生们很喜欢。

Since in Greek *agogos* means "leader," a *paidagogos* was a slave who led boys to school and back, but also taught them manners and tutored them after school. In time, *pedagogue* came to mean simply "teacher"; today the word has an old-fashioned ring to it, so it often means a stuffy, boring teacher. The word *pedagogy*, though, is still widely used, and often means simply "teaching." And *pedagogic* training is what everyone majoring in education receives.

因为在希腊语中 *agogos* 的意思是"领导者"，所以 *paidagogos* 指的是一个奴隶，带着男孩子们上下学，放学后还教他们礼貌，并且辅导他们。随着时间的推移，*pedagogue* 的意思逐渐变成"教师"。今天这个词听起来有点过时，所以它通常用来形容一个古板、无聊的老师。然而，*pedagogy* 这个词现在仍广泛使用，通常的意思就是"教学"。*pedagogic* 培训是每个教育专业的人所接受的培训。

pedant \pe-dənt\　(1) A formal, unimaginative teacher. 学究 (2) A person who shows off his or her learning. 卖弄学问的人

• At one time or another, every student encounters a pedant who can make even the most interesting subject tedious. 每个学生都免不了会遇到一个学究，他甚至能使最有趣的科目变得枯燥乏味。

It isn't always easy to tell a *pedantic* teacher from one who is simply thorough. Some professors get an undeserved reputation for *pedantry* from students who just don't like the subject much. Regardless of that, a pedant need not be a teacher; anyone who goes around displaying his or her knowledge in a boring way can qualify.

区分 *pedantic* teacher(学究式的老师)和一丝不苟的老师并不总是那么容易。有些教授得了不实的 *pedantry*(迂腐)之名，而实际上那些学生只是不太喜欢这门课而已。不管怎样，pedant 不一定就是老师，任何无聊地到处炫耀自己知识的人都有资格成为 pedant(卖弄学问的人)。

pediatrician \ˌpē-dē-ə-ˈtri-shən\　A doctor who specializes in the diseases, development, and care of children. 儿科医生

• Children in the U.S. usually see a pediatrician until they turn at least 15 or 16. 在美国，孩子们看儿科医生通常要持续到至少 15 或 16 岁。

Since *iatros* means "physician" in Greek (see IATR, p. 662), words such as *pediatric* naturally refer to "children's medicine." *Pediatrics* is a fairly new medical specialty; until about 1900, children were considered small adults and given the same medical treatment, only milder. Benjamin Spock was the most famous pediatrician of the 20th century, and his book *Baby and Child Care* changed the way millions of Americans raised their children.

由于 *iatros* 在希腊语中的意思是"医生"(参见 IATR，第 662 页)，所以 *pediatric* 这样的词自然指的就是"儿科医学"。*Pediatrics*(儿科学)是一种比较新的医学专业；直到约 1900 年，儿童还被认为是小大人，接受同样的治疗，只是比

较温和一些。本杰明•斯波克是 20 世纪最著名的儿科医生,他的著作《婴幼儿护理》改变了数百万美国人抚养孩子的方式。

encyclopedic\in-ˌsī-klə-ˈpē-dik\　(1) Of or relating to an encyclopedia. 百科全书的 (2) Covering a wide range of subjects. 包括各种学科的,渊博的

• Someone with the kind of encyclopedic knowledge she has should be competing on *Jeopardy*. 有她那样渊博知识的人应该参加《危险边缘》的比赛。

In Greek, *paidaea* meant not simply "childrearing" but also "educa- tion," and *kyklios* meant "general"; thus, an encyclopedia is a work broad enough to provide a kind of general education. The world's most eminent general encyclopedia, the *Encyclopaedia Britannica*, is a huge work that covers every field of human knowledge. But *encyclopedic* doesn't have to refer to books; it's often used to describe the wide-ranging knowledge that certain types of minds just can't stop acquiring.

在希腊语中,*paidaea* 不仅有"抚养孩子",还有"教育"的意思,*kyklios* 的意思是"全面的";因此,百科全书是内容宽泛、足以提供通识教育的一类著作。世界上最著名的百科全书是《大英百科全书》,这是一部涵盖人类知识的各个领域的巨著。但是 encyclopedic 并不一定指书,它也经常被用来描述某些类型的大脑无法停止获取的广博知识。

TROP comes from the Greek *tropos*, meaning "turn" or "change." The *troposphere* is the level of the atmosphere where most weather changes—or "turns in the weather"—occur. And the *Tropics of Cancer and Capricorn* are the lines of latitude where the sun is directly overhead when it reaches its northernmost and southernmost points, on about June 22 and December 22 every year—that is, the point where it seems to turn and go back the other way.

TROP 源自希腊语 *tropos*,意思是"转"或"变"。*troposphere*(对流层)是大气的一层,大部分天气变化或"天气转变"都在这一层发生。*Tropics* of Cancer and Capricorn(北回归线和南回归线)指的是每年 6 月 22 日和 12 月 22 日太阳直射到的最北端和最南端的纬线——即太阳由此后要转到反方向。

---

tropism\ˈtrō-ˌpi-zəm\　Automatic movement by an organism unable to move about from place to place, especially a plant, that involves turning or growing toward or away from a stimulus. (尤其是植物的)向性

• The new president was soon showing a tropism for bold action, a tendency that seemed more the result of instinct than of careful thought. 新总统很快就表现出了行动大胆的倾向性,这种倾向与其说是深思熟虑的结果,不如说是本能的结果。

In *hydrotropism*, a plant's roots grow in the direction of increasing moisture, hoping to obtain water. In *phototropism*, a plant (or fungus) moves toward light, usually the sun—perhaps because, in the colder climates where such plants are usually found, concentrating the sun's warmth within the sun-seeking flower can create a warm and inviting environment for the insects that fertilize it. In *thigmotropism*, the organism moves in response to being touched; most climbing plants, for example, put out tiny tendrils that feel around for something solid and then attach themselves or curl around it. When microbiologists talk about *tropism*, however, they're often referring instead to the way a virus will seek out a particular type of cell to infect. And when intellectuals use the word, they usually mean a tendency shown by a person or group which they themselves might not even be aware of.

<small>*hydrotropism*（向水性）指的是植物向水分增多的方向生长，因为它想汲取水分。*phototropism*（向光性）指的是植物（或真菌）向光生长，通常是阳光——这也许是因为，在这类植物通常生存的比较寒冷环境中，把太阳的热量集中在向日的花朵中，可以为使其受精的昆虫创造一个温暖而诱人的环境。*thigmotropism*（向触性）指的是有机体对触碰做出反应有，比如，大多数攀缘植物会伸出微小的卷须，感知周围坚硬的东西，然后附着在上面或卷曲在其周围。然而，当微生物学家谈论向性时，他们通常指的是病毒寻找特定类型的细胞来感染的方式。可能当知识分子使用这个词时，通常指的是某个人或团体所表现出的一种倾向，这种倾向连他们自己都没有意识到。</small>

entropy\\'en-trə-pē\ (1) The decomposition of the matter and energy in the universe to an ultimate state of inactive uniformity. 熵 (2) Chaos, randomness. 混乱，无序

• The apartment had been reduced to an advanced state of entropy, as if a tiny tornado had torn through it, shattering its contents and mixing the pieces together in a crazy soup. <small>这个公寓已陷入高度混乱的状态，仿佛有一股小小的龙卷风将其撕裂，把里面的东西吹得粉碎，再把碎片搅到乱七八糟的汤里。</small>

With its Greek prefix *en-*, meaning "within," and the *trop-* root here meaning "change," *entropy* basically means "change within (a closed system)." The closed system we usually think of when speaking of entropy (especially if we're not physicists) is the entire universe. But entropy applies to closed systems of any size. Entropy is seen when the ice in a glass of water in a warm room melts—that is, as the temperature of everything in the room evens out. In a slightly different type of entropy, a drop of food coloring in that glass of water soon spreads out evenly. However, when a nonphysicist uses the word, he or she is usually trying to describe a large-scale collapse.

<small>*entropy* 的希腊语前缀 *en-* 表示"内部"，词根 *trop-* 表示"变化"，这个词的基本含义是"在（一个封闭系统）内部的变化"。谈到熵时，我们通常想到的封闭系统（特别是当我们不是物理学家时）是整个宇宙。但熵适用于任何规模的封闭系统。当温暖的房间里的一杯水中的冰融化时——也就是说，当房间里所有东西的温度均等时——我们可以看到熵。在另一种类型稍有不同的熵中，一杯水中的一滴食用色素很快均匀地扩散开来。然而，当一个非物理学家使用这个词时，他/她通常是在试图描述一次大规模的崩溃。</small>

heliotrope\ˈhē-lē-ə-ˌtrōp\ Any of a genus of herbs or shrubs having small white or purple flowers. 天芥菜属植物

• A long bank of purple heliotrope lined the walkway, and her guests were always remarking on the flowers' glorious fragrance. <small>人行道边有一长排紫色的天芥菜属植物，她的客人们总在谈论这种花的芬芳。</small>

Helios was the god of the sun in Greek mythology, and *helio-* came to appear in a number of sun-related English words. The genus known as the heliotropes consists of about 250 species; many are thought of as weeds, but the best-known species, garden heliotrope, is a popular and fragrant perennial that resembles the forget-me-not. The heliotrope tends to follow the sun—that is, turn its blossoms toward the sun as it travels from East to West every day. But the fact is, *heliotropism*—turning toward the sun—is common among flowers (and even leaves), and some, like the sunflower, are more dramatically *heliotropic* than the heliotrope. Those in the far North actually use their petals to reflect the sun's heat onto the flower's central ovary during the short growing season.

<small>Helios(赫利俄斯)是希腊神话中的太阳神，helio 出现在许多与太阳有关的英语单词中。天芥菜属植物约有 250 种，许多被认为是杂草，但其中最有名的缬草，是一种为人喜爱的多年生芳香植物，与勿忘我相似。天芥菜喜欢跟随太阳——也就是说，太阳每天从东向西移动时，天芥菜转动花朵一直朝向太阳。但事实是，heliotropism（向日性）——即转向太阳——在花（甚至叶子）中很常见。有些植物，比如向日葵，明显比天芥菜更 heliotropic（向日性的）。在遥远的北方，植物在短促的生长季节里用花瓣将太阳的热量反射到花的中央子房。</small>

psychotropic \sī-kə-ˈtrō-pik\ Acting on the mind. 作用于精神的

● My mother is taking two drugs that may produce psychotropic side effects, and I'm worried that they might be interacting. 我母亲正在服用两种可能产生精神副作用的药物，我担心它们会可能相互影响。

Psychotropic is used almost always to describe substances that we consume. Such substances are more numerous than you might think, and some have been known for thousands of years. Native American religions, for example, have used psychotropic substances derived from certain cactuses and mushrooms for centuries. Caffeine and nicotine can be called psychotropic. Psychotropic prescription drugs include antidepressants (such as Prozac) and tranquilizers (such as Valium). Any medication that blocks pain, from aspirin to the anesthetics used during surgery, can be considered a psychotropic drug. Even children are now prescribed psychotropic drugs, often to treat attention deficit disorder. And all recreational drugs are psychotropic. *Psychoactive* is a common synonym of *psychotropic*.

<small>psychotropic 几乎总是用来描述我们所消耗的物质。这些物质的数量比你想象的要多，有些已经存在了数千年。比如，几个世纪以来，美洲原住民宗教一直使用从某些仙人掌和蘑菇中提取的精神药物。咖啡因和尼古丁可称为精神药物。精神类处方药包括抗抑郁药（如百忧解）和镇静剂（如安定）。任何能阻止疼痛的药物，从阿司匹林到手术用的麻醉药，都可以被认为是精神药物。如今甚至给儿童也开精神药物，常用来治疗注意力缺陷障碍。所有的娱乐性药物都是作用于精神的。psychoactive 是 psychotropic 的常用同义词。</small>

Quizzes

A. Indicate whether the following pairs of words have the same or different meanings:

1. psychotropic / mind-altering   same ____ / different ____
2. encyclopedic / important   same ____ / different ____
3. entropy / disorder   same ____ / different ____
4. heliotrope / sunflower   same ____ / different ____

5. pediatrician / foot doctor   same ____ / different ____
6. tropism / growth   same ____ / different ____
7. pedagogy / teaching   same ____ / different ____
8. pedant / know-it-all   same ____ / different ____

B. Match the definition on the left to the correct word on the right:

1. thorough   a. entropy
2. decay   b. pediatrician
3. boring teacher   c. heliotrope
4. fragrant flower   d. encyclopedic
5. automatic motion   e. tropism
6. education   f. pedant
7. affecting the mind   g. psychotropic
8. children's doctor   h. pedagogy

NEO comes from the Greek *neos*, meaning "new." *Neo-* has become a part of many English words. Some are easy to understand; for example, *neo-Nazi*. Some are less so; you might not immediately guess that *neotropical* means "from the tropics of the New World," or that a *neophyte* is a "newcomer." When William Ramsay discovered four new gases, he named them all using Greek roots that at first glance might sound slightly mysterious: *argon* ("idle"), *krypton* ("hidden"), *xenon* ("strange")—and *neon* ("new").

NEO 源自希腊语 neos，意思是"新的"。Neo-已经成为许多英语单词的组成部分。有些很容易理解，比如 neo-Nazi（新纳粹）。有些就不那么容易理解了。你也许不能一下子就猜到，neotropical（新热带区的）的意思是"来自新大陆的热带地区"，或者 neophyte 的意思是"新来者"。当威廉·拉姆齐发现了四种新气体时，他全部用希腊语词根命名，这些词根第一眼看上去可能有点神秘：argon（氩，意为"懒惰的"）、krypton（氪，意为"隐藏的"）、xenon（氙，意为"奇怪的"）——还有，neon（氖，意为"新的"）。

---

neoclassic \ˌnē-ō-ˈkla-sik\ Relating to a revival or adaptation of the styles of ancient Greece and Roman, especially in music, art, or architecture. 新古典主义的

• He had always admired the paintings of the French neoclassical masters, especially Poussin and Ingres. 他一直很欣赏法国新古典主义大师的绘画作品，尤其是普桑和安格尔的作品。

In the arts and architecture, a style that has existed for a long time usually produces a reaction against it. So after the showy style of Europe's so-called baroque era (from about 1600s to the early 1700s), the reaction came in the form of the neoclassical movement, bringing order, restraint, and simpler and more conservative structures, whether in plays, sonatas, sculptures, or public buildings. Its inspiration was the art of ancient Greece and Rome—that is, of *classical* antiquity. Why *classical*? In Latin *classicus* meant "of the highest *class*," so in English *classic* and *classical* originally described the best ancient Greek and Latin literature, but soon came to mean simply "of ancient Greek and Rome," since these were already seen as the highest and best cultures. *Neoclassic* generally describes artworks from the 1700s or early 1800s (by the painter David, the composer Mozart, the sculptor Canova, etc.), but also works from the 20th century that seem to have been inspired by the ideals of Greece and Rome.

在艺术和建筑中,某一风格若长期存在,通常会引起反感。在欧洲所谓的巴洛克时代(从17世纪至18世纪初)的浮华风格之后,人们的反感以新古典主义运动的形式出现,带来秩序、克制以及更简单、更保守的结构,体现在戏剧、奏鸣曲、雕塑、公共建筑等方面。其灵感源自古希腊和罗马的艺术——即 classical antiquity(古典时代)的艺术。为何是 classical(古典的)? 在拉丁语中,classicus 的意思是"of the highest class"(最高阶层的),因此在英语中,classic 和 classical 最初用来描述最好的古希腊和拉丁文学,但很快就只表示"古希腊和罗马的",因为它们已经被视为最高和最好的文化。Neoclassic(新古典主义)一般描述18世纪或19世纪初期的作品(画家大卫、作曲家莫扎特、雕塑家卡诺瓦等),也包括20世纪的作品,这些作品似乎受到了希腊和罗马典范的启发。

Neolithic \ˌnē-ə-ˈlith-ik\ Of or relating to the latest period of the Stone Age, when polished stone tools were used. 新石器时代的

• Around the Mediterranean, the Neolithic period was a time of trade, of stock breeding, and of the first use of pottery. 在地中海沿岸,新石器时期指的是一个贸易、畜牧和最早使用陶器的时期。

Since *lithos* in Greek means "stone," the Neolithic period is the "new" or "late" period of the Stone Age, in contrast to the Paleolithic period ("old" or "early" period—see PALEO, p. 695) and the Mesolithic period ("middle" period) of the Stone Age. The use of polished stone tools came to different parts of the world at different times, but the Neolithic Age is usually said to begin around 9000 B.C. and to end around 3000 B.C., when the Bronze Age begins. The Neolithic is the era when the farming of plants and animals begins, and when, as a result, humans first begin to create permanent settlements.

由于 lithos 在希腊语中的意思是"石头",所以新石器时代是指石器时代的"新的"或"晚的"时期,与旧石器时代("旧的"或"早的"时期——见 PALEO,第695页)以及中石器时代("中间的"时期)相反。磨制石器的使用在世界上不同的地方出现的时代有所不同,但通常认为,新石器时代始于公元前9000年左右,止于青铜时代开始的公元前3000年左右。在新石器时代,人类开始种植植物、养殖动物,也因此首次开始建立永久定居点。

neoconservative \ˌnē-ō-kən-ˈsər-və-tiv\ A conservative who favors strongly encouraging democracy and the U.S. national interest in world affairs, including through military means. 新保守主义者

• Many believed that foreign policy in those years had fallen into the hands of the neoconservatives, and that the war in Iraq was one result. 很多人认为,那些年的外交政策落入了新保守派手中,伊拉克战争就是其中一个结果。

In the 1960s several well-known socialist intellectuals, including Norman Podhoretz and Irving Kristol, alarmed by growing political extremism on the left, began to move in the other direction. Soon the term *neoconservative* (or *neocon* for short) was being attached to them. Rather than simply drifting toward the political center, Podhoretz and Kristol actually moved far to the right, especially on the issue of maintaining a strong military stance toward the rest of the world. The main magazine of *neoconservatism* became Podhoretz's *Commentary*; it was later joined by the *Weekly Standard*, edited by Kristol's son William. Not everyone agrees on how to define these terms; still, it's clear that today you don't have to be a former liberal in order to be a neoconservative.

在20世纪60年代,几位著名的社会主义知识分子,包括诺曼·波德霍雷茨和欧文·克里斯托尔在内,对左翼日益增长的政治极端主义感到震惊,开始转向反方向。很快,*neoconservative*(新保守主义,或简称 *neocon*)一词就与他们联系在了一起。实际上,波德霍雷茨和克里斯托尔并没有简单地向政治中心靠拢,而是向右翼靠拢了很多,在对世界其他地区保持强硬军事立场的问题上更是如此。*neoconservatism*(新保守主义)的主要杂志为波德霍雷茨的《评论》,后来,克里斯托尔的儿子威廉姆编辑的《旗帜周刊》也加入了这一行列。不是每个人都同意这些术语的定义;尽管如此,如今要成为新保守主义者,你不必是前自由派人士,这是显而易见的。

neonatal \ˌnē-ō-ˈnā-t^əl\ Of or relating to babies in the first month after their birth. 新生儿的

- The hospital's newest addition is a neonatal intensive-care unit, and newborns in critical condition are already being sent there from considerable distances. 该医院最新增加了新生儿重症监护室,情况危急的新生儿已经从很远的地方被送到那里。

Partly based on the Latin *natus*, "born," *neonatal* means "newly born." Neonatal babies themselves are called *neonates*. Most hospitals now offer neonatal screening, which is used to detect diseases that are treatable only if identified during the first days of life, and specialized neonatal nursing as well. But despite spending much money on neonatal care, the U.S. still ranks lower than some much less wealthy countries (such as the Czech Republic, Portugal, and Cuba) in *infant mortality* (infant deaths).

neonatal 部分基于拉丁语 *natus*("出生"),它的意思是"新生的"。新生儿本身被称为 *neonates*。现在,大多数医院都提供新生儿筛查,以查明某些只有在婴儿出生后的前几天查出来才可以医治的疾病;此外,还提供专门的新生儿护理。但是,尽管美国在新生儿护理方面投入了大量资金,在 infant mortality(婴儿死亡率)方面,美国的排名仍然低于某些不那么富裕的国家(如捷克共和国、葡萄牙和古巴)。

NOV

NOV comes from the Latin word *novus*, meaning "new." To *renovate* an old house is to "make it new again"—that is, put it back in tip-top shape. The long-running PBS show *Nova* keeps its large audience up to date on what's new in the world of science. And when the British king sent Scottish settlers to a large island off Canada's Atlantic coast in the 17th century, he named it *Nova Scotia*, or "New Scotland."

NOV 源自拉丁语单词 *novus*,意思是"新的"。*Renovate*(修复)一栋老房子就是"让它焕然一新"——也就是说,把它恢复到很好的状态。美国公共广播公司(PBS)长期播出的节目《新星》让广大观众了解科学界的最新动态。17世纪,当英国国王把苏格兰移民送到加拿大的大西洋海岸附近的一个大岛上时,他把这个岛命名为 Nova Scotia(新斯科舍),意思是

"新苏格兰"。

novice\ˈnä-vəs\ (1) One who has no previous training or experience in a specific field or activity; beginner. 新手,初学者 (2) A new member of a religious order who is preparing to become a nun or monk. 初学修女,初学修士

● It's hard to believe that a year ago she was a complete novice as a gardener, who couldn't identify a cornstalk. 很难相信她一年前还是一个菜鸟园丁,连玉米秆都认不出来。

Among the ancient Romans, a novice (*novicius*) was usually a newly imported slave, who had to be trained in his or her duties. Among Catholics and Buddhists, if you desire to become a priest, monk, or nun, you must serve as a novice for a period of time, often a year (called your *novitiate*), before being ordained or fully professing your vows. No matter what kind of novice you are—at computers, at writing, at politics, etc. —you've got a lot to learn. 在古罗马人中,新手(*novicius*)通常指的是刚从他国购进的奴隶,他们必须在工作中接受培训。在天主教徒和佛教徒中,如果你想成为牧师、修士/僧侣或修女/尼姑,必须先见习一段时间,通常为一年(称为 *novitiate*),然后才能被授予圣职或完全宣誓入教。无论你是哪个领域的新手——电脑、写作、政治等——你都有很多东西要学。

novel\nä-vəl\ (1) New and not resembling something formerly known or used. 新的,新颖的。(2) Original and striking, especially in conception or style. 创新的

● His techniques for dealing with these disturbed young people were novel, and they caught the attention of the institute's director. 他对付这些心理不正常的年轻人的方法很新颖,引起了研究所所长的注意。

If someone tells you that you've come up with a novel idea or a novel interpretation of something, it's probably a compliment: not everyone is capable of original thinking. But not everything new is terribly worthwhile; a *novelty*, for example, is often a cute (or maybe just silly) little object that you might put on a display shelf in your house. It may seem surprising that the familiar noun novel is related as well. In the 14th century, Italian writers began writing collections of short tales, each of which they called a *novella* because it represented a new literary form; from this word, three centuries later, the English coined the noun novel. 如果有人告诉你,你给出的想法很新颖或对某事的解释很新颖,这可能是在赞美你;不是每个人都有原创思维的能力。但并不是所有新的事物都非常值得,比如,*novelty*(小玩具、小饰品)通常指的是可爱的(或者只是傻傻的)小物件,可以放在你家的陈列架上。令人惊讶的是,我们所熟悉的名词 novel(小说)也有关联。在 14 世纪,意大利作家开始创作短篇故事集,他们称之为 *novella*,因为它代表了一种新的文学形式。三个世纪之后,英国人根据该词创造了名词 *novel*。

innovation\i-nə-ˈvā-shən\ (1) A new idea, device, or method. 新观念,新手段,新方法 (2) The introduction of new ideas, devices, or methods. 革新,创新,改革

● "Smooshing" bits of candy into ice cream while the customer watched was just one of his innovations that later got copied by chains of ice-cream outlets. 当着顾客的面把糖果"磨碎"放进冰淇淋里只是他的创新之一,后来被连锁冰淇淋店效仿。

UNIT 14

Innovation is a word that's almost always connected with business. In business today, it's almost a rule that a company that doesn't *innovate* is destined for failure. The most important and successful businesses were usually started by *innovators*. And company managers should always at least listen to the *innovative* ideas of their employees.

innovation 这个词几乎总与商业联系在一起。在今天的商业中,不进行 innovate(创新,革新)的公司注定要失败。最重要、最成功的企业通常是由 innovators(创新者)创办的。公司的管理者至少应该倾听员工的 innovative ideas(创新的想法)。

supernova\ˌsü-pər-ˈnō-və\ (1) The explosion of a star that causes it to become extremely bright. 超新星(爆发) (2) Something that explodes into prominence or popularity. 突然崭露头角或流行起来的东西

- After exploding, a nova leaves a "white dwarf" which may explode again in the future, but a supernova destroys the entire star. 新星爆炸后会留下"白矮星",白矮星未来可能会再次爆炸,但超新星爆发会摧毁整个恒星。

A *nova*, despite its name, isn't actually a "new" star, but rather one that wasn't noticed until it exploded, when it may increase in brightness by a million times before returning to its previous state a few days later. A supernova is far larger; a star in its supernova state may emit a billion times as much light as previously. After a few weeks it begins to dim, until it eventually ceases to exist; it's often replaced by a black hole. (Though remains that were shot out into space may survive; those of a great supernova seen in A.D. 1054 are now known as the Crab Nebula.) All this may serve as a warning to those human stars whose fame explodes too rapidly; supernovas of this kind have sometimes vanished by the following year.

尽管 nova 名为新星,但实际上并不是"新的"星,而是一颗直到爆炸时才被人注意到的恒星,此时,它的亮度可能会增加百万倍,几天后才恢复到原来的状态。supernova 则要大得多,一颗处于超新星状态的恒星所发出的光可能是以前的十亿倍。几周后,它开始变暗,直到最终消失。超新星常被黑洞取代(但抛入太空的残骸可能仍以幸存。公元 1054 年发现了一颗超新星,其残骸现在被称为蟹状星云)。上述一切也给那些名气来得太快的人类明星提个醒,这种人类超级新星可能在第二年就会从公众的视线中消失。

Quizzes

A. Fill in each blank with the correct letter:

a. Neolithic   e. supernova
b. novice   f. neoconservative
c. novel   g. neoclassic
d. neonatal   h. innovation

1. My father subscribes to the _____ magazines and still thinks we had no choice but to invade Iraq.

2. The building's style is _____, with Roman columns and with white statues on either side of the entrance.

3. In his youth he had intended to join the priesthood, and he even served as a _____ for six months before giving it up.

4. They're now working at a _____ site in Syria, where they've found evidence of goat, pig, and sheep farming.

5. The baby might not have survived if the hospital hadn't had an excellent _____ ward.

6. The _____ seen by Asian astronomers in 1054 was four times as bright as the brightest planet.

7. The company had a history of _____ that had earned it immense respect and attracted many of the brightest young engineers.

8. She often comes up with _____ interpretations of the evidence in cases like this, and she's sometimes proven correct.

B. Match the word on the left to the correct definition on the right:

1. novice   a. star explosion
2. innovation   b. new invention or method
3. neoclassic   c. beginner
4. neoconservative   d. newborn
5. neonatal   e. ancient
6. novel   f. cleverly new
7. supernova   g. favoring aggressive
8. Neolithic foreign policy   h. resembling Greek and
                                 Roman style

POS

POS comes from the Latin verb *ponere*, meaning "to put" or "to place." You *expose* film by "placing it out" in the light. You *compose* a song by "putting together" a series of notes. And you *oppose* locating a new prison in your town by "putting yourself against" it.

POS 源自拉丁语动词 *ponere*,意思是"放"或"置"。你"把胶卷放在外边"的光下,就会 *expose* film(使胶卷曝光)。你把一系列音符"放在一起",就可以 *compose*(创作)歌曲。你"把自己放在新监狱的对立面",就是 *oppose*(反对)将新监狱建在你住的小镇。

impose\im-ˈpōz\ (1) To establish or apply as a charge or penalty or in a forceful or harmful way. 把……强加于 (2) To take unfair advantage. 占便宜,利用

• After seeing her latest grades, her parents imposed new rules about how much time she had to spend on homework every night. 看到她的最新成绩后,父母定了新规则,规定她每晚必须花多少时间做家庭作业。

The Latin *imposui* meant "put upon," and that meaning carried over into English in *impose*. A CEO may impose a new manager on one of the company's plants. A

• 328 •

state may impose new taxes on luxury items or cigarettes, and the federal government sometimes imposes trade restrictions on another country to punish it. A polite apology might begin with "I hope I'm not imposing on you" (that is, "forcing my presence on you"). And a *self-imposed* deadline is one that you decide to hold yourself to.

拉丁语 *imposui* 的意思是"强加于",这一含义延续到英语中,体现在 *impose* 上。首席执行官可能会在公司的某家工厂安插一名新经理。某个州可能对奢侈品或香烟征收新税,而联邦政府有时会对另一个国家实施贸易限制以做惩罚。礼貌的道歉可以这样开始:"我希望没打扰到你(也就是说,"把我的存在强加于你")。"而 *self-imposed* deadline(自我强加的最后期限)是你决定让自己遵守的最后期限。

juxtapose \ˈjək-stə-ˌpōz\ To place side by side. 把……并置,把……并列

● You won't notice the difference between the original and the copy unless you juxtapose them. 除非你把原件和复印件放在一起,否则注意不到两者的区别。

Since *juxta* means "near" in Latin, it's easy to see how *juxtapose* was formed. Juxtaposing is generally done for examination or effect. Interior designers constantly make decisions about juxtaposing objects and colors for the best effect. Juxtaposing two video clips showing the different things that a politician said about the same subject at two different times can be an effective means of criticizing. The *juxtaposition* of two similar X-rays can help medical students distinguish between two conditions that may be hard to tell apart. And advertisements frequently juxtapose "before" and "after" images to show a thrilling transformation.

由于 *juxta* 在拉丁语中的意思是"接近的",因此很容易看出 *juxtapose* 是如何构成的。并列放置一般是为了检查或为了达到某种效果。室内设计师时常决定该如何搭配物品和颜色才能达到最佳效果。将两段视频剪辑放在一起,显示出某政客在不同的两个时间点就同一话题发表的不同看法,这样做可能是一种有效的批评手段。两张相似 X 光片的 *juxtaposition*(对比),可以帮助医科学生区分两种很难区分的状况。广告经常把"之前"和"之后"的图像放在一起,以显示出激动人心的变化。

POS

transpose \trans-ˈpōz\ (1) To change the position or order of (two things). 使变换位置,使变换顺序 (2) To move from one place or period to another. 转移

● She rechecked the phone number and discovered that two digits had been transposed. 她重新核对了电话号码,发现有两个数字被调换了。

Though transposing two digits can be disastrous, transposing two letters in a word often doesn't matter too much. (You can prboalby raed tihs setnence witohut too mcuh toruble.) Transposing two words or sounds—as in "Can I sew you to another sheet?"—has been a good source of humor over the years. Doctors sometimes discover that something in the body—a nerve, an organ, etc.—has been transposed, or moved away from its proper place. For musicians, transposing means changing the key of a piece; if you can do this at a moment's notice, you've been well trained.

尽管调换两个数字可能会带来灾难性的后果,但调换某个单词的两个字母通常无关紧要(比如,在"You can

• 329 •

prboalby raed tihs setnence witohut too mcuh toruble"这句话中，有几个单词的字母被调换了顺序，但不妨碍理解）。将两个单词或两个音节换一下——比如"Can I sew you to another sheet?"（即"Can I show you to another seat？"）——多年来一直是幽默之源。医生有时会发现，病人身体里的某个东西——神经、器官等等——调换了位置，或者离开了原位。对于音乐家来说，transposing 的意思是改变乐曲的调子。如果你能在片刻之间做到这一点，那说明你受过良好的训练。

superimpose\ˌsü-pər-im-ˈpōz\ To put or place one thing over something else. 添加，叠加，使重叠

• Using transparent sheets, she superimposes territory boundaries on an outline of Africa, showing us how these changed in the late 19th and early 20th century. 她用透明片在非洲的轮廓上叠加了领土边界，向我们展示了这些边界在 19 世纪末和 20 世纪初是如何变化的。

Superimposition was one of the magical effects employed by early filmmakers. Using "mirror shots," with semitransparent mirrors set at 45° angles to the scene, they would superimpose shadowy images of ghosts or scenes from a character's past onto scenes from the present. Superimposing your own ideas on something, such as a historical event, has to be done carefully, since your ideas may change whenever you learn something new about the event.

superimposition（叠加）是早期电影人运用的魔法效果之一。使用"镜像拍摄"，将半透明的镜子设置成与场景呈 45 度角，可以将模糊的鬼魂的图像或角色过去的场景叠加到现在的场景上。把你自己的想法叠加到某件事上，比如某个历史事件上，你必须要小心行事，因为每当你对这件事有了新的认识，你的想法就会有所改变。

TEN

TEN, from the Latin verb *tenere*, basically means "hold" or "hold on to." A *tenant* is the "holder" of an apartment, house, or land, but not necessarily the owner. A *lieutenant governor* may "hold the position" ("serve in lieu") of the governor when necessary.

TEN 源自拉丁语动词 *tenere*，基本的意思是"握"或"抓住"。*Tenant* 指的是公寓、房屋或土地的"占用者"，但不一定是所有者。在必要时，*lieutenant* governor（副总督）可以"担任"（"代替任职"）总督的职务。

tenure\ˈten-yər\ (1) The amount of time that a person holds a job, office, or title. 任期 (2) The right to keep a job, especially the job of teacher or professor. 终身职位

• I know two assistant professors who are so worried about being denied tenure this year that they can't sleep. 我认识两位助理教授，他们因过于担心今年会被剥夺终身教职而无法入眠。

Tenure is about holding on to something, almost always a job or position. So you can speak of someone's 30-year tenure as chairman, or someone's brief tenure in the sales manager's office. But *tenure* means something slightly different in the academic world. In American colleges and universities, the best (or luckiest) teachers have traditionally been granted a lifetime appointment known as tenure after about six years of teaching. Almost nobody has as secure a job as a *tenured* professor, but getting tenure can be difficult, and most of them have earned it.

tenure 指的是拥有某个东西,一般是工作或职位。因此,你可以说某人有 30 年的主席任期,或者某人在销售经理办公室短期任职。但是,tenure 在学术界的意思略有不同。在美国的大学和学院中,按照惯例,最优秀的(或最幸运的)教师六年教学工作后会被终身任用,称为终身教职。几乎没有人能像 tenured professor(终身教授)那样拥有稳定的工作,但获得终身职位可能会很困难,他们中的多数人都是靠努力获得的。

tenacious \tə-'nā-shəs\ Stubborn or determined in clinging to something. 坚持的,顽强的,坚定的

• He was known as a tenacious reporter who would stay with a story for months, risking his health and sometimes even his life. 他被认为是一个坚持不懈的记者,会冒着健康甚至生命的危险一连几个月坚持报道某件事。

Success in most fields requires a *tenacious* spirit and a drive to achieve. Nowhere is this more apparent than in the entertainment business. Thousands of actors and actresses work *tenaciously* to build a TV or film career. But without talent or beauty, *tenacity* is rarely rewarded, and only a few become stars. 在多数领域,要想取得成功就需要有顽强的精神和达成目标的动力。这一点在娱乐业表现得最为明显。成千上万的演员 tenaciously(坚持不懈地)工作,开创电视或电影事业。但没有天赋和美貌,tenacity(坚持)罕有回报,成为明星者只有少数几个人。

tenable \'te-nə-bəl\ Capable of being held or defended; reasonable. 站得住脚的,合理的

• She was depressed for weeks after her professor said that her theory wasn't tenable. 教授说她的理论站不住脚之后,她沮丧了好几个星期。

Tenable means "holdable." In the past it was often used in a physical sense—for example, to refer to a city that an army was trying to "hold" militarily against an enemy force. But nowadays it's almost always used when speaking of "held" ideas and theories. If you hold an opinion but evidence appears that completely contradicts it, your opinion is no longer tenable. So, for example, the old ideas that cancer is infectious or that being bled by leeches can cure your whooping cough now seem *untenable*. tenable 指的是"可持有的"。在过去,它通常用于物理意义上——例如,可以用来指一个城市,某军队抵御敌军的进攻,努力在军事上"持有"该城市。但这个词现在通常用来谈论"持有的"观点和理论。如果你持有某一观点,但证据却与之完全相反,你的观点就站不住脚了。举例来说,过去认为癌症有传染性,用水蛭吸血可以治愈百日咳,这些旧的观点现在看来是 untenable(站不住脚的)。

tenet \'te-nət\ A widely held principle or belief, especially one held in common by members of a group or profession. 原则,信条,宗旨

• It was soon obvious that the new owners didn't share the tenets that the company's founders had held to all those years. 没多久就看得出,新老板并不认同公司创始人多年来坚持的信条。

A *tenet* is something we hold, but not with our hands. Tenets are often ideals, but also often statements of faith. Thus, we may speak of the tenets of Islam or Hinduism, the tenets of Western democracy, or the tenets of the scientific method, and in each case these tenets may combine elements of both faith and ideals.

tenet 是我们所持有的东西，但不是用手。信条往往是理想，但也也往往是信仰的宣言。因此，我们可以谈论伊斯兰教或印度教的 tenets、西方民主的 tenets、科学方法的 tenets 等，无论是哪一种情况，这些 tenets 都可能结合了信仰和理想的元素。

Quizzes

A. Choose the closest definition:

1. impose   a. force   b. request   c. seek   d. hint
2. tenacious   a. stubborn   b. intelligent   c. loving   d. helping
3. superimpose   a. surpass   b. put into   c. place over   d. amaze
4. juxtapose   a. place on top of   b. put away   c. place side by side   d. put into storage
5. transpose   a. emerge   b. change into   c. cross   d. switch
6. tenable   a. decent   b. tough   c. reasonable   d. controllable
7. tenet   a. claw   b. belief   c. renter   d. shelter
8. tenure   a. strong hold   b. permanent appointment   c. lengthy period   d. male voice

B. Indicate whether the following pairs have the same or different meanings:

1. impose / remove   same ____ / different ____
2. tenet / principle   same ____ / different ____
3. transpose / exchange   same ____ / different ____
4. tenure / absence   same ____ / different ____
5. superimpose / offend deeply   same ____ / different ____
6. tenacious / sensible   same ____ / different ____
7. juxtapose / switch   same ____ / different ____
8. tenable / reasonable   same ____ / different ____

UNIT 14

Number Words 数字词语

MONO comes from the Greek *monos*, meaning "alone" or "single." So a *monorail* is a railroad that has only one rail; a *monocle* is an old-fashioned eyeglass that a gentleman used to squeeze into his eye socket; a *monotonous* voice seems to have only one tone; and a *monopoly* puts all ownership of a type of product or service in the hands of a single company.

MONO 源自希腊语 monos，意思是"单独"或"单一"。monorail（单轨铁路）是只有单一轨道的铁路；monocle（单片眼镜）是一种老式的眼镜，绅士常把它夹进眼窝里；monotonous voice（单调的声音）似乎只有一个音调；monopoly（垄断）指的是将一类产品或服务的所有权集中在一家公司手中。

monogamous \mə-ˈnä-gə-məs\ Being married to one person or having one mate at a time. 单配偶的，单配性的

• Geese, swans, and most other birds are monogamous and mate for life. 鹅、天鹅和多数其他鸟类都是单配性的，一生只有一个伴侣。

American marriage is by law monogamous; people are permitted to have only one spouse at a time. There are cultures with laws that permit marriage to more than one person at a time, or *polygamy*. Although the term *polygamy* may refer to *polyandry* (marriage to more than one man), it is more often used as a synonym for *polygyny* (marriage to more than one woman), which appears to have once been common in most of the world and is still found widely in some cultures.

根据法律，美国的婚姻是单配偶性的，人们一次只能有一个配偶。而在有些文化中，法律允许一次与一个以上的人结婚，即 polygamy（多配偶制，一夫多妻制）。尽管 polygamy 一词可以指 polyandry（嫁给一个以上的男人），但它更常用作 polygyny（娶一个以上的女人）的同义词。一夫多妻曾在世界上多数地方很常见，在某些文化中现在仍然广泛存在。

monoculture \ˈmä-nə-ˌkəl-chər\ (1) The cultivation of a single crop to the exclusion of other uses of land. 单作 (2) A culture dominated by a single element. 单文化

• Monoculture is practiced on a vast scale in the American Midwest, where nothing but corn can be seen in the fields for hundreds of square miles. 美国中西部地区实行大规模的单一栽培模式，数百平方英里的田地上除了玉米什么也看不见。

The Irish Potato Famine of 1845—1849, which led to the deaths of over a million people, resulted from the monoculture of potatoes, which were destroyed by a terrible blight, leaving farmers nothing else to eat. Almost every traditional farming society has practiced crop rotation, the planting of different crops on a given piece of land from year to year, so as to keep the soil from losing its quality. But in the modern world, monoculture has become the rule on the largest commercial farms, where the same crop can be planted year after year by means of the intensive use of fertilizers. Modern monoculture has produced huge crops; on a large scale, it permits great efficiency in planting, pest control, and harvesting. But many experts believe this all comes at a huge cost to the environment.

1845年至1849年的爱尔兰马铃薯大饥荒导致了一百多万人死亡,大饥荒是马铃薯单一栽培所造成的,马铃薯毁于可怕的枯萎病,农民没有其他东西可吃。几乎每个传统的农业社会都会实行轮作,即在某块田地上在年度间种植不同作物,以防止土壤质量下降。但在现代世界,单一栽培已成为最大规模的商业农场的惯例,同一种作物可以通过集约使用化肥年复一年地种植。现代单一栽培产量巨大,大规模单一栽培在种植、虫害防治和收获方面效率很高。但许多专家认为,这一切都付出了巨大的环境代价。

monolithic \ˌmä-nə-ˈli-thik\ (1) Appearing to be a huge, featureless, often rigid whole. 庞大的,大一统的 (2) Made up of material with no joints or seams. 独块儿的,单体的,构成整料的

- The sheer monolithic rock face of Yosemite's El Capitan looks impossible to climb, but its cracks and seams are enough for experienced rock climbers. 约塞米蒂国家公园有块酋长巨石,它的单体岩壁看起来是不可能攀登的,但其裂缝和接缝足以让经验丰富的攀岩者攀登。

The *-lith* in *monolith* comes from the Greek *lithos*, "stone," so *monolith* in its original sense means a huge stone like those at Stonehenge. What's so impressive about monoliths is that they have no separate parts or pieces. To the lone individual, any huge institution or government bureaucracy can seem monolithic. But the truth may be different: The former U. S. S. R. once seemed monolithic and indestructible to the West, but in the 1990s it crumbled into a number of independent republics.

monolith 中的 *-lith* 源自希腊语 *lithos*(石头),所以 *monolith* 最初的意思是巨石,就像巨石阵中的石头一样。巨石令人印象深刻之处在于它没有分离出的部分或碎片。对一个孤立的人来说,任何大型机构或政府官僚机构都可能显得铁板一块。但事实可能有所不同:苏联曾在西方看来是铁板一块、坚不可摧的,但在20世纪90年代,它分裂了许多独立的共和国。

MONO

monotheism \ˈmä-nō-thē-ˌi-zəm\ The doctrine or belief that there is a single god. 一神论

- The earliest known instance of monotheism dates to the reign of Akhenaton of Egypt in the 14th century B. C. 已知最早的一神论可以追溯到公元前14世纪埃及阿赫那顿统治时期。

Monotheism, which is characteristic of Judaism, Islam, and Christianity, is distinguished from *polytheism*, belief in or worship of more than one god. The monotheism that characterizes Judaism began in ancient Israel with the adoption of Yahweh as the single object of worship and the rejection of the gods of other tribes and nations without, initially, denying their existence. Islam is clear in acknowledging one, eternal, unbegotten, unequaled God, while Christianity holds that a single God is reflected in the three persons of the Holy Trinity.

monotheism 是犹太教、伊斯兰教和基督教的特征,它有别于 *polytheism*(多神论),即信仰或崇拜不止一位神。犹太教的一神论始于古以色列,以耶和华为唯一崇拜对象,拒绝其他部落和国家的神,但最初并不否认他们的存在。伊斯兰教明确承认只有一个永恒的、自生的、无与伦比的神,而基督教则认为,唯一的上帝体现在为三位一体。

UNIT 14

UNI comes from the Latin word for "one." A *uniform* is a single design worn by everyone. A *united* group has one single opinion, or forms a single *unit*. A *unitard* is a one-piece combination leotard and tights, very good for skating, skiing, dancing—or riding a one-wheeled *unicycle*.
UNI 源自表示"一个"的拉丁语单词。uniform(制服)是每个人都穿的同一种款式。united group(团结的群体)持有同一个观点,或形成一个独立的 unit(单位)。unitard(全身紧身衣)是紧身衣和紧身衣裤结合的一件衣服,非常适合滑冰、滑雪、跳舞——或骑一个轮子的 unicycle(独轮车)。

unicameral \ˌyü-ni-ˈka-mə-rəl\ Having only one lawmaking chamber. 一院制的,单一的

● In this country, with its unicameral system of government, a single group of legislators meets to make the laws. 这个国家实行一院制政府,由单一立法者群体开会制定法律。

Unicameral means "one-chambered," and the term almost always describes a governing body. Our federal legislature, like those of most democracies, is *bicameral*, with two legislative (lawmaking) bodies—the Senate and the House of Representatives. And except for Nebraska, all the state legislatures are also bicameral. So why did the nation decide on a bicameral system? Partly in order to keep some power out of the hands of ordinary voters, who the Founding Fathers didn't completely trust. For that reason, the original Constitution states that senators are to be elected by the state legislatures; not until 1914, after passage of a Constitutional amendment, did we first cast direct votes for our senators.
unicameral 的意思是"一院的",这个词几乎总是描述一个管理机构。与大多数民主国家一样,美国的联邦立法机构是 bicameral 两院制的,有两个立法(制定法律的)机关——参议院和众议院。除内布拉斯加州外,其他所有州的立法机构也都是两院制的。为什么国家决定采用两院制呢? 部分原因是为了不让某些权力落入普通选民之手,因为开国元勋们并不完全信任这些选民。因此,最初的宪法规定,参议员由州议会选举产生。直到 1914 年,宪法修正案通过后,我们才第一次直接投票选举参议员。

unilateral \ˌyü-ni-ˈla-tə-rəl\ (1) Done by one person or party; one-sided. 单方面做出的,单边的 (2) Affecting one side of the body. 仅影响身体一侧的

● The Japanese Constitution of 1947 includes a unilateral rejection of warfare as an option for their country. 1947 年的日本宪法把单方面拒绝战争作为日本的选择。

The world is a smaller place than it used to be, and we get uncomfortable when a single nation adopts a policy of *unilateralism*—that is, acting independently with little regard for what the rest of the world thinks. A *unilateral* invasion of another country, for instance, usually looks like a grab for power and resources. But occasionally the world welcomes a unilateral action, as when the U.S. announced unilateral nuclear-arms reductions in the early 1990s. Previously, such reductions had only happened as part of *bilateral* ("two-sided") agreements with the old Soviet Union. *Multilateral* agreements, on issues such as climate change, often involve most of the world's nations.

世界变小了,当某个国家采取 *unilateralism*(单边主义)政策——即不顾世界其他国家的想法,独立行动时,我们就会感到不安。比如,单方面入侵另一个国家,通常看起来像是要攫取权力和资源。但单边行动在世界上偶尔也受欢迎,比如美国在20世纪90年代初宣布单方面削减核武器。此前,这种削减只是作为与苏联 *bilateral*("双边的")协议的一部分。在气候变化等问题上达成的 *multilateral* agreements(多边协议),往往涉及世界上大多数国家。

unison \ˈyü-nə-sən\ (1) Perfect agreement. 一致,协调 (2) Sameness of musical pitch. 同度,同音

• Unable to read music well enough to harmonize, the village choir sang only in unison. 由于不能很好地理解音乐以配和声,村里的唱诗班只能齐唱。

This word usually appears in the phrase "in unison," which means "together, at the same time" or "at the same musical pitch." So an excited crowd responding to a speaker may shout in unison, and a group of demonstrators may chant in unison. The old church music called Gregorian chant was written to be sung in unison, with no harmonizing voices, and kindergarten kids always sing in unison (at least when they can all find the same pitch). In a similar way, an aerobics class moves in unison following the instructor, and a group or even a whole town may work in unison when everyone agrees on a common goal.

这个词通常出现在短语"in unison"中,意思是"和……一起,在同一时刻"或"在同一音高"。因此,兴奋的人群会齐声叫喊来回应演讲者,示威人群会有节奏地反复喊叫。"格里高利圣咏"是为了合唱而创作的,这种古老的教堂音乐没有和声;幼儿园的孩子总是合唱(至少是当他们都能找到相同音高时)。同样,健美操班会跟着老师一起做动作;如果大家达成共同目标,一群人乃至整个小镇都会一起行动起来。

unitarian \ˌyü-nə-ˈter-ē-ən\ Relating or belonging to a religious group that believes that God exists only in one person and stresses individual freedom of belief. (基督教中不信仰三位一体的)一位论派信徒

• With his unitarian tendencies, he wasn't likely to get into fights over religious beliefs. 由于有一位论倾向,他不太可能卷入宗教信仰的斗争。

Unitarianism, originally a sect of Christianity believing in a single or *unitary God*, grew up in 18th-century England and developed in America in the early 19th century. Though they believe in Christ's teaching, they reject the idea of the three-part Trinity—God as father, son, and holy spirit—and thus deny that Christ was divine, so some people don't consider them truly Christian. In this century the Unitarians joined with the *Universalist Church*, a movement founded on a belief in *universal salvation*—that is, the saving of every soul from damnation after death. Both have always been liberal and fairly small; today they count about half a million members. Without a capital letter, *unitarian* refers simply to belief in a *unitary* God, or in *unity* within some nonreligious system.

Unitarianism(上帝一位论)最初是基督教的一个派别,信仰单一的上帝,即 *unitary* God。这一派别成长于18世纪的英国,19世纪初期在美国得到发展。虽然他们相信基督的教导,但他们拒绝三位一体——圣父、圣子、圣灵——的观念,从而否认基督是神圣的,所以有些人并不认为他们是真正的基督徒。在20世纪,一位论派信徒加入了 *Universalist*

Church(普救派教会),普救派教会建立在 *universal* salvation(普遍救赎)信仰的基础上——即把每一个灵魂从死后的诅咒中拯救出来。两派一直都信奉自由主义且规模较小,如今他们有大约 50 万会员。如果首字母不大写,*unitarian* 所指的只是相信单一的上帝,或者相信某个非宗教体系内部的 *unity*(统一)。

Quiz

Fill in each blank with the correct letter:

a. monotheism
b. unilateral
c. monolithic
d. unison
e. unitarian
f. monoculture
g. unicameral
h. monogamous

1. The president is allowed to make some _____ decisions without asking Congress's permission.

2. The relationship was unbalanced: she was perfectly _____, while he had two other women in his life.

3. In rejecting a _____ legislature, America seemed to follow Britain's lead.

4. The sheer mountain face, _____ and forbidding, loomed over the town.

5. As a strict Catholic, she found _____ beliefs unacceptable.

6. Most religious groups in this country practice one or another form of _____.

7. Corn was a _____ in the village, and the farmers would simply move to a new field each year to keep the soil from wearing out.

8. At Halloween and Thanksgiving assemblies, the children would recite holiday poems in _____.

Review Quizzes

A. Choose the correct synonym:

1. unilateral   a. one-sided   b. sideways   c. complete
   d. multiple

2. cryptography   a. gravestone writing   b. physics writing
   c. code writing   d. mathematical writing

3. monotheism   a. nature worship   b. worship of one god
   c. worship of pleasure   d. sun worship

4. abscond   a. steal   b. discover   c. retire
   d. flee

5. transpose   a. send out   b. take place   c. overcome
   d. switch

6. tenet   a. shelter   b. principle   c. choice
   d. landlord

7. pedagogy   a. study   b. teaching   c. research   d. child abuse
8. unison   a. solitude   b. melody   c. collection   d. agreement
9. crypt   a. code   b. granite   c. tomb   d. church
10. superimpose   a. increase   b. lay over   c. improve   d. excel
11. monogamous   a. with one spouse   b. without a spouse   c. with several spouses   d. with someone else's spouse
12. tenable   a. available   b. unbearable   c. agreeable   d. reasonable

B. Fill in each blank with the correct letter:

a. tenure
b. pediatrician
c. pedant
d. unitarian
e. impose
f. abstraction
g. tenacious
h. cryptic
i. encyclopedic
j. abstruse

1. Their son had just called to tell them that the university had decided to grant him _____.

2. Tuesday the baby sees the _____ for her immunizations and checkups.

3. The only clues for the treasure hunt were in a _____ poem that his father had written.

4. By the time she was 25 she had an _____ knowledge of her state's history.

5. The notion of a savior was foreign to his _____ beliefs.

6. The legislature is threatening to _____ strict limits on this kind of borrowing.

7. The speech contained one _____ after another, but never a specific example.

8. At the age of 72 he was regarded by most of the students as a boring _____.

9. The sick child's _____ grip on life was their only hope now.

10. The researcher's writing was _____ but it was worth the effort to read it.

C. Indicate whether the following pairs of words have the same or different meanings:

1. monotheism / growing of one crop   same ____ / different ____
2. unison / unitedness   same ____ / different ____
3. cryptic / gravelike   same ____ / different ____
4. monolithic / boring   same ____ / different ____

5. abstemious / self-controlled   same ____ / different ____
6. tenet / ideal   same ____ / different ____
7. crypt / tomb   same ____ / different ____
8. tenable / reasonable   same ____ / different ____
9. unicameral / one-chambered   same ____ / different ____
10. abstruse / difficult   same ____ / different ____

UNIT 15

TERM/TERMIN comes from the Latin verb *terminare*, "to limit, bound, or set limits to," and the noun *terminus*, "limit or boundary." In English, those boundaries or limits tend to be final. A *term* goes on for a given amount of time and then ends, and to *terminate* a sentence or a meeting or a ballgame means to end it. TERM/TERMIN 源自拉丁语动词 *terminare*("限制,约束或设限")和名词 *terminus*("限制或边界")。在英语中,这些边界或限制往往表示结束。一个 *term*(任期或学期)会持续一段时间然后结束,*terminate*(使结束)一个刑期、会议或球赛指的是结束这些活动。

terminal\ˈtər-mə-nəl\ (1) Forming or relating to an end or limit. 末端的,最后的,终点的 (2) Fatal. 致命的

• She knows she's in the late stages of a terminal illness, and has already drawn up a will. 她知道自己到了绝症晚期,已经立好了遗嘱。

A terminal disease ends in death. If you're *terminally* bored, you're "bored to death." For many students, a high-school diploma is their terminal degree (others finish college before *terminating* their education). A bus or train *terminal* is the endpoint of the line. A computer terminal was originally the endpoint of a line connecting to a central computer. A terminal ornament may mark the end of a building, and terminal punctuation ends this sentence. 绝症最终会导致死亡。如果你 *terminally* 无聊,你就是"无聊得要死"。对多数学生来说,高中文凭是他们的终极文凭(还有些则上完大学才 *terminate* 他们的教育)。公交车或火车的 *terminal*(终点站)是该线路的终点;计算机终端最初是连接到中央计算机线路的端点;尖顶饰标志一个建筑物的末端;句末标点符号可以结束这个句子。

indeterminate\ˌin-di-ˈtər-mə-nət\ Not precisely determined; vague. 不确定的,模糊的

• The police are looking for a tall white bearded man of indeterminate age who should be considered armed and dangerous. 警方正在寻找一个年龄不明、留着白胡子的高个男子,他

被认为是持有武器的危险分子。

When you *determine* something, you decide on what it is, which means you put limits or boundaries on its identity. So something indeterminate lacks identifying limits. A mutt is usually the product of indeterminate breeding, since at least the father's identity is generally a mystery. A painting of indeterminate origins is normally less valued than one with the painter's name on it. And if negotiations are left in an indeterminate state, nothing has been decided.

当你 *determine* 某个东西时，你决定它是什么，这意味着你为它的身份设置限制或边界。所以不确定的东西缺乏身份识别的限制。杂种狗通常是不确定血统的产物，因为至少父亲的身份是个谜。来历不明的画通常比上面有画家名字的画价值要低。如果谈判处于不确定的状态，则什么都还没有决定。

interminable \ in-ˈtər-mə-nə-bəl \ Having or seeming to have no end; tiresomely drawn out. 无休止的，冗长乏味的

• The preacher was making another of his interminable pleas for money, so she snapped off the TV. 牧师又一次没完没了地呼吁捐钱，她于是啪的一声关掉了电视。

Nothing is literally endless, except maybe the universe and time itself, so *interminable* as we use it is always an exaggeration. On an unlucky day you might sit through an interminable meeting, have an interminable drive home in heavy traffic, and watch an interminable film—all in less than 24 hours.

没有什么东西是无穷尽的，或许宇宙和时间本身除外，因此我们使用 *interminable* 一词通常是一种夸张。在某个不幸的一天里，你可能开了一个冗长乏味的会，然后在拥挤的道路上无休无止地开车回家，后来又看了一部冗长无聊的电影——这一切都在不到 24 小时内完成。

terminus \ˈtər-mə-nəs\ （1）The end of a travel route (such as a rail or bus line), or the station at the end of a route. 终点，终点站（2）An extreme point; tip. 终端，尖端

• They've been tracking the terminus of the glacier for 20 years, in which time it has retreated 500 yards. 他们二十年来一直在追踪那个冰川的终点，而在此期间，冰川已经后退了 500 码。

This word comes straight from Latin. In the Roman empire, a terminus was a boundary stone, and all boundary stones had a minor god associated with them, whose name was Terminus. Terminus was a kind of keeper of the peace, since wherever there was a terminus there could be no arguments about where your property ended and your neighbor's property began. So Terminus even had his own festival, the Terminalia, when images of the god were draped with flower garlands. Today the word shows up in all kinds of places, including in the name of numerous hotels worldwide built near a city's railway terminus.

这个单词直接源自拉丁语。在罗马帝国，terminus 指的是界石，所有的界石都与一个小神相关，名叫特米纳斯。界神特米纳斯在某种程度上是和平的守护者，因为只要有界石地方，你房地产的终点和邻居房地产的起点就不会有任何争议。因此，特米纳斯甚至有自己的节日，名为 Terminalia。这时，特米纳斯的雕像会被披上花环。如今，这个词出现在各种各样的地方，全世界很多建在城市的铁路终点站附近的酒店名字里都有它。

TERM/
TERMIN

GEO comes from the Greek word for "Earth." *Geography* is the science that deals with features of the Earth's surface. *Geologists* study rocks and soil to learn about the Earth's history and resources. *Geometry* was originally about measuring portions of the Earth's surface, probably originally in order to determine where the boundaries of Egyptians' farms lay after the annual flooding by the Nile River.

GEO 源自希腊语中表示"地球"的单词。*geography*(地理学)是研究地球表面特征的科学。*geologists*(地质学家)通过研究岩石和土壤来了解地球的历史和资源。*geometry*(几何学)最初是关于测量地球表面的各部分的学科,可能最初是为了确定在每年尼罗河泛滥之后,埃及人农场的边界位置。

geocentric \ ˌjē-ō-ˈsen-trik \ Having or relating to the Earth as the center. 以地球为中心的,地心的

• He claims that, if you aren't a scientist, your consciousness is mostly geocentric for your entire life. 他声称,如果你不是科学家,那么你的意识在一生中基本上都是以地球为中心的。

The idea that the Earth is the center of the universe and that the sun revolves around it is an ancient one, probably dating back to the earliest humans. Not until 1543 did the Polish astronomer Copernicus publish his calculations proving that the Earth actually revolves around the sun, thus replacing the geocentric model with a *heliocentric* model (from *Helios*, the Greek god of the sun). But *geocentrism* remains central to various religious sects around the world, and still today one in five adult Americans believes the sun revolves around the Earth.

地球是宇宙的中心,太阳围绕着地球转,这是一个古老的观点,也许可以追溯到最早的人类。直到 1543 年,波兰天文学家哥白尼才发表了他的计算结果,证明地球实际上是围绕太阳旋转的,从而用 *heliocentric* model 日心说模型(源自希腊太阳神 *Helios*)取代了地心说模型。但是,*geocentrism*(地心说)仍然是世界各地不同宗教派别的核心内容。时至今日,仍有五分之一的成年美国人相信,太阳绕着地球转。

geophysics \ ˌjē-ə-ˈfi-ziks \ The science that deals with the physical processes and phenomena occurring especially in the Earth and in its vicinity. 地球物理学

• Located in the heart of oil and gas country, the university offers a degree in geophysics and many of its graduates go straight to work for the oil and gas industry. 该大学位于那个石油和天然气国家的中心,提供地球物理学学位,许多毕业生直接进入油气行业工作。

Geophysics applies the principles of physics to the study of the Earth. It deals with such things as the movement of the Earth's crust and the temperatures of its interior. Another subject is the behavior of the still-mysterious *geomagnetic* field. Some *geophysicists* seek out deposits of ores or petroleum; others specialize in earthquakes; still others study the water beneath the Earth's surface, where it collects and how it flows.

地球物理学将物理学原理应用于地球研究。地球物理学研究诸如地壳运动及其内部温度等问题。另一个研究领域是依然神秘的 *geomagnetic* field(地磁场)活动。有些 *geophysicists*(地球物理学家)寻找矿石或石油的矿床;有些专门研

究地震；还有些研究地表以下的水，地下水在哪里聚集、如何流动等。

geostationary \ˌjē-ō-ˈstā-shə-ˌner-ē\ Being or having an orbit such that a satellite remains in a fixed position above the Earth, especially having such an orbit above the equator. （人造卫星）相对地球是静止的

- It was the science-fiction writer Arthur C. Clarke who first conceived of a set of geostationary satellites as a means of worldwide communication. 正是科幻小说家阿瑟·克拉克首次设想，将一组对地静止卫星作为全球通信的一种手段。

We don't give much thought to geostationary satellites, but many of us rely on them daily. Anyone who watches satellite TV or listens to satellite radio is dependent on them; the weather photos you see on TV are taken from geostationary satellites; and military information gathering via satellite goes on quietly day after day. (Though the satellites that provide GPS service for your car or cell phone actually aren't geostationary, since they orbit the Earth twice a day.) By 2009 there were about 300 geostationary satellites in operation, all of them moving at an altitude of about 22,000 miles. Since they hover above the same spot on Earth, your receiving dish or antenna doesn't have to turn in order to track them.

我们不会仔细考虑对地静止卫星，但许多人每天都依赖它们。看卫星电视、听卫星广播的人，都要依靠这些卫星。你在电视上看到的天气照片是对地静止卫星拍摄的；通过卫星收集军事信息的工作日复一日地悄然进行着。（但为你的汽车或手机提供 GPS 服务的卫星实际上不是对地静止卫星，因为它们每天绕地球转两次。）到 2009 年，大约有 300 颗对地静止卫星在运行，它们都在大约 22,000 英里的高空移动。由于它们停留在地球上的同一地点，所以卫星信号接收盘或天线不需要通过转动来跟踪它们。

geothermal \ˌjē-ō-ˈthər-məl\ Of, relating to, or using the natural heat produced inside the Earth. 地热的

- Geothermal power plants convert underground water or steam to electricity. 地热发电厂将地下水或蒸汽转化为电能。

Geothermal comes partly from the Greek *thermos*, "hot" (see THERM/THERMO, p. 54). Most geothermal electricity is provided by power plants situated in areas where there is significant activity of the Earth's great tectonic plates—often the same areas where volcanoes are found. But hot water from deep underground may be used by cities far from volcanoes to heat buildings or sidewalks. And a newer source of geothermal energy relies on a less dramatic kind of heat: Individual homeowners can now install heat pumps that take advantage of the 50°-60° temperature of the soil near the surface to provide heating in cold weather (and air-conditioning in the warm months). These very small-scale geothermal systems may eventually supply more useful energy than the large power plants.

geothermal 部分源自希腊语 *thermos*（"热"）（见 Therm/Thermo，第 54 页）。多数地热发电都是由发电厂提供的，这些发电厂位于地球大板块活动显著的地区——通常也是火山所在的区域。但地下深处的热水也可以为远离火山的城市用来为建筑物或人行道供热。还有一种新的地热能源，依赖的是一种不太引人注目的热量：个人业主现在可以安装热泵，利用地表附近 50°—60° 的土壤温度，在冷天供暖（在暖和的月份制冷）。这些极小规模的地热系统最终可能提供比大发电厂更有用的能源。

Quizzes

A. Choose the closest definition:

1. terminus   a. heat source   b. endpoint   c. final exam   d. period
2. interminable   a. remarkable   b. unthinkable   c. reliable   d. eternal
3. geocentric   a. moonlike   b. near earth's core   c. mathematical   d. earth-centered
4. geophysics   a. physical geometry   b. earth science   c. material science   d. science of shapes
5. geostationary   a. polar   b. hovering over one location   c. space-station-related   d. equatorial
6. terminal   a. fatal   b. technical   c. verbal   d. similar
7. indeterminate   a. lengthy   b. uncertain   c. unending   d. likely
8. geothermal   a. globally warmed   b. using earth's heat   c. solar-powered   d. tropical

B. Fill in each blank with the correct letter:

a. geophysics   e. indeterminate
b. terminus   f. geocentric
c. geothermal   g. terminal
d. interminable   h. geostationary

1. Tens of millions of people couldn't watch TV if it weren't for a fleet of _____ satellites.
2. Their house is mostly heated by a _____ heat pump, so they pay almost nothing for fuel.
3. Most of us are _____ in our thinking until a grade-school teacher tells us about how the earth revolves around the sun.
4. Their land extends all the way out to the _____ of the little peninsula.
5. He was a man of _____ age, and mysterious in other ways as well.
6. It was the mystery of the earth's magnetic field that eventually led him into the field of _____.
7. He gave _____ lectures, and I usually dozed off in the middle.
8. Last week we assumed his condition was _____; today no one is making predictions.

UNIT 15

SPHER comes from the Greek word for "ball." A ball is itself a *sphere*, as is the ball that we call Earth. So is the *atmosphere*, and so are several other invisible "spheres" that encircle the Earth. SPHER 源自希腊语中表示"球"的单词。球本身就是一个 *sphere*，就像我们称之为地球的那个球体一样。*atmosphere*（大气层）也是如此，围绕地球的其他几个看不见的"spheres"亦如此。

---

spherical \ˈsfir-ə-kəl\ Relating to a sphere; shaped like a sphere or one of its segments. 关于球体的，球形的

- The girls agreed that the spacecraft had been deep blue and perfectly spherical, and that its alien passengers had resembled large praying mantises. 那些女孩们一致认为，飞船是深蓝色的，是完美的球形，飞船上的外星乘客就像巨大的螳螂。

Something spherical is like a *sphere* in being round, or more or less round, in three dimensions. Apples and oranges are both spherical, for example, even though they're never perfectly round. A *spheroid* has a roughly spherical shape; so an asteroid, for instance, is often *spheroidal*—fairly round, but lumpy. something spherical（球形的东西）像一个 *sphere*，是三维的球形或近似于球形。比如，苹果和橙子都是球形的，但它们从来都不是完美的球形。椭球体大致呈球形，比如，小行星通常是 *spheroidal*（类似球体的）——大致是球形的，但表面有块状物。

stratosphere \ˈstra-tə-ˌsfir\ (1) The part of the earth's atmosphere that extends from about seven to about 30 miles above the surface. 平流层，同温层 (2) A very high or the highest region. 高层，最高水平

- In the celebrity stratosphere she now occupied, a fee of 12 million dollars per film was a reasonable rate. 在她现在所处的顶级名人圈里，拍一部电影要价 1200 万美元很合理。

The stratosphere (*strato-* simply means "layer" or "level") lies above the earth's weather and mostly changes very little. It contains the ozone layer, which shields us from the sun's ultraviolet radiation except where it's been harmed by manmade chemicals. The levels of the *atmosphere* are marked particularly by their temperatures; stratospheric temperatures rise only to around 32°—very moderate considering that temperatures in the *troposphere* below may descend to about – 70° and those in the *ionosphere* above may rise to 1000°. 同温层（*strato-* 的意思就是"层"）不受地球气象的影响，且通常变化极小。它包含臭氧层，臭氧层保护我们免受太阳紫外线辐射的伤害，但臭氧层受到人造化学物质破坏的地方除外。*atmosphere*（大气）的各层尤以温度为标志，stratospheric temperatures（平流层的温度）上升到仅 32°左右——相比平流层下面的 *troposphere*（对流层）的温度可能下降到约 – 70°，而上面的 *troposphere*（电离层）的温度可能上升到 1000°，这是非常温和的了。

biosphere \ˈbī-ə-ˌsfir\ (1) The part of the world in which life can exist. 生物圈 (2) Living things and their environment. 生物及其环境

- The moon has no biosphere, so an artificial one would have to be constructed

SPHER

for any long-term stay. 月球没有生物圈，所以想要长期驻留，必须建一个人造生物圈。

The *lithosphere* is the solid surface of the earth (*lith-* meaning "rock"); the *hydrosphere* is the earth's water (*hydro-* means "water"), including the clouds and water vapor in the air; and the *atmosphere* is the earth's air (*atmos-* meaning "vapor"). The term *biosphere* can include all of these, along with the 10 million species of living things they contain. The biosphere recycles its air, water, organisms, and minerals constantly to maintain an amazingly balanced state; human beings should probably do their best to imitate it. Though the word has a new sound to it, it was first used over a hundred years ago.

lithosphere（岩石圈）指的是地球的固体表面（lith- 的意思是"岩石"）；hydrosphere（水圈）指的是地球的水（hydro- 意为"水"），包括空中的云和水蒸气；atmosphere（大气层）指的是地球的空气（atmos- 的意思是"蒸汽"）。Biosphere（生物圈）可以包括所有这些，还包括里面的 1000 万种生物。生物圈不断地循环其空气、水、生物和矿物质，以保持惊人的平衡状态，人类应该尽可能地效仿它。尽管这个词听上去很新，但距第一次使用也有一百多年了。

hemisphere \\'he-mə-ˌsfir\\ Half a sphere, especially half the global sphere as divided by the equator or a meridian. 半球

• A sailor who crosses the equator from the northern to the southern hemisphere for the first time is traditionally given a special initiation. 对于首次跨越赤道从北半球来到南半球的水手，传统上要专门举行一个"新体验仪式"。

Hemisphere includes the prefix *hemi-*, meaning "half." The northern and southern hemispheres are divided by the equator, the circle halfway between Earth's two poles. The eastern and western hemispheres aren't divided so exactly, since there are no poles in the Earth's east-west dimension. Often the dividing line is said to be the "prime meridian"—the imaginary north-south line that runs through Greenwich, England, from which all longitude is calculated (itself being the 0° meridian). But for simplicity's sake, the eastern hemisphere is often said to include all of Europe, Africa, Australia, and Asia, while the western hemisphere contains North and South America and a great deal of ocean.

Hemisphere（半球）的前缀是 hemi-（"半"）。赤道是地球两极正中间的一个圆圈，将北半球和南半球分开。由于地球的东西维度上没有两极，所以东西半球并没有这么精确的划分。东西半球的分界线通常被称为"本初子午线"——即贯穿英格兰格林尼治的假想的南北线，所有经度都是从这条线计算出来的（它本身是 0°子午线）。但为了简单起见，人们一般认为东半球包括整个欧洲、非洲、大洋洲和亚洲，西半球包括南北美洲以及许多海洋。

VERT

VERT comes from the Latin verb *vertere*, meaning "to turn" or "to turn around." *Vertigo* is the dizziness that makes it seem as if everything is turning around you. And an *advertisement* turns your attention to a product or service.

VERT 源自拉丁语动词 vertere，意思是"转"或"转向"。Vertigo 是眩晕，让人觉得好像一切都在绕着你旋转。advertisement（广告）把你的注意力转移到某个产品或服务上。

divert \\dī-ˈvərt\\ (1) To turn from one purpose or course to another. 转变

（目的或路线）(2) To give pleasure to by distracting from burdens or distress. 娱乐,消遣

• The farmers had successfully diverted some of the river's water to irrigate their crops during the drought. 旱灾期间,农民们成功地将部分河水分流来灌溉农作物。

The Roman circus was used to provide *diversion* for its citizens—and sometimes to divert their attention from the government's failings as well. The diversion was often in the form of a fight—men pitted against lions, bears, or each other—and the audience was sure to see blood and death. A *diverting* evening these days might instead include watching the same kind of mayhem on a movie screen. 罗马马戏团用来为市民提供 diversion(娱乐)——有时也用来 divert(转移)市民对政府缺陷的注意力。这种娱乐的形式通常是打斗——人与狮子、熊或其他动物较量——观众肯定会目睹流血与死亡。如今,一个 diverting evening(愉快的夜晚)可能会包括在电影屏幕上观看同类的暴力场面。

converter \kən-ˈvər-tər\ A device that changes something (such as radio signals, radio frequencies, or data) from one form to another. 变频器,变流器,转换器

• She was so indifferent to television that she hadn't even bought a converter, and her old TV sat there useless until she finally lugged it down to the recycling center. 她对电视漠不关心,甚至连电视转换器都没有买,旧电视一直闲置在那里,直到最终被拖到回收中心。

Converters come in many forms. Travelers to foreign countries who bring along their electric razors or hair dryers always pack a small electric converter, which can change direct current to alternating current or vice versa. In 2009 millions of Americans bought digital analog converters, small box-shaped devices that change the new broadcast digital signal to the analog signal that older TV sets were made to receive. A *catalytic converter* is the pollution-control device attached to your car's exhaust system that converts pollutants such as carbon monoxide into harmless form. 转换器有多种形式。到国外旅行的人,如果带着电动剃须刀或吹风机,总会带上一个小型电源转换器。它可以把直流电变成交流电,也可以把交流电变成直流电。2009年,数以百万计的美国人购买了数模转换器。这是一种盒状的小装置,可以将新的广播数字信号转换成供老式电视机接收的模拟信号。catalytic converter(催化转化器)是一种污染控制装置,安装在汽车排气系统上,可以将一氧化碳等污染物转化为无害物。

avert \ə-ˈvərt\ (1) To turn (your eyes or gaze) away or aside. 转移(目光或视线) (2) To avoid or prevent. 避免,防止

• General Camacho's announcement of lower food prices averted an immediate worker's revolt. 卡马乔将军宣布降低食品价格,避免了工人马上就要开始的反抗。

Sensitive people *avert* their eyes from gory accidents and scenes of disaster. But the accident or disaster might itself have been averted if someone had been alert enough. Negotiators may avert a strike by all-night talks. In the Cuban missile crisis of 1962, it seemed that nuclear catastrophe was barely averted. *Aversion* means "dislike or disgust"—that is, your feeling about something you can't stand to look at.

敏感的人把目光从血淋淋的事故和灾难现场移开。但如果某人足够警觉的话,事故或灾难本身可能已经被避免了。谈判人员可以通宵谈判来避免罢工。在 1962 年的古巴导弹危机中,核灾难堪堪躲过。*aversion* 的意思是"讨厌或厌恶"——也就是说,你对不忍直视的某个东西的感觉。

revert \ri-ˈvərt\ (1) To go back or return (to an earlier state, condition, situation, etc.). 恢复,回返 (2) To be given back to (a former owner). 归还

• Control of the Panama Canal Zone, first acquired by the U. S. in 1903, reverted to the local government in 1999. 美国先是在 1903 年获取了巴拿马运河区的控制权,后于 1999 年归还当地政府。

Since the prefix *re-* often means "back" (see RE-, p. 684), the basic meaning of *revert* is "turn back." *Revert* and *reversion* often show up in legal documents, since property is often given to another person on the condition that it will revert to the original owner at some future date or when something happens (usually the death of the second person). In nonlegal uses, the word tends to show up in negative contexts. Many reformed drinkers, for example, eventually revert to their old ways, and most people revert to smoking at least once or twice before succeeding in quitting for good.

由于前缀 *re-* 通常表示"回"(参见 RE-,第 684 页),所以 *revert* 的基本含义是"返回"。法律文件中经常出现 *revert*(复归)和 *reversion*(复归权),因为把财产给予另一个人的条件通常是,在未来的某一天或发生某事时(通常指第二个人去世),财产要归还给原主人。在非法律用途中,这个词往往出现在负面语境中。比如,许多改过自新的饮酒者最终又旧态复萌;多数人至少还会复吸一两次,才能成功地永久戒烟。

Quizzes

A. Fill in each blank with the correct letter:

a. revert   e. divert
b. avert   f. converter
c. hemisphere   g. spherical
d. biosphere   h. stratosphere

1. Every living thing that we know of inhabits the earth's _____.

2. The generals had discussed what would be involved if they tried to _____ 10,000 troops from Afghanistan to Iraq.

3. The _____ contains the ozone layer, which guards the earth against excessive ultraviolet radiation.

4. She's praying that her daughter doesn't _____ to her old habit of partying several nights a week.

5. As soon as his normal baseball season is over, my nephew joins a team in the southern _____, where spring training is just starting.

6. Only by seizing a cord dangling beside the window did he manage to _____ disaster.

7. By federal law, every gasoline-powered vehicle must have a catalytic _____ to reduce pollution.

8. Football and rugby balls are ovoid, unlike the _____ balls used in other sports.

B. Match the word on the left to the correct definition on the right:

1. avert   a. go back
2. spherical   b. upper atmosphere
3. divert   c. device for adapting
4. hemisphere   d. avoid
5. revert   e. half-sphere
6. biosphere   f. entertain
7. stratosphere   g. globelike
8. converter   h. life zone

MORPH comes from the Greek word for "shape." *Morph* is itself an English word with a brand-new meaning, which was needed when we began to digitally alter photographic images or shapes to make them move or transform themselves in often astonishing ways.
MORPH 源自希腊语中表示"形状"的单词。*morph*（变形,图像变形）本身就是一个有着全新含义的英语单词,当我们开始用数字技术改变照片的图像或形状,使其以令人吃惊的方式移动或变形时,就需要它。

---

amorphous \ə-ˈmȯr-fəs\   Without a definite shape or form; shapeless. 无定形的,无形状的

• Picking up an amorphous lump of clay, she molded it swiftly into a rough human shape. 她拿起一块无定形的黏土,迅速捏成一个大致的人形。

According to the Greek myths of the creation, the world began in an amorphous state; and the Bible states that, at the beginning, "the earth was without form, and void." Most of us have had nightmares that consist mostly of just a looming amorphous but terrifying thing. A plan may have so little detail that critics call it amorphous. And a new word may appear to name a previously amorphous group of people, such as *yuppie* in 1983 and *Generation X* six years later.
根据希腊神话的创世传说,世界开始于无定形状态;圣经有云,起初"地是空虚混沌"。多数人都做过噩梦,梦里大都是一种无形的、可怕的、森森然逼近的东西。一项计划可能细节太少,以至于批评者称其没有定型。一个新词可能会出现,用来给以前不固定的一群人命名,比如 1983 年的 *yuppie*（雅皮士）以及六年后的 *Generation X*（X 一代）。

anthropomorphic \ˌan-thrə-pə-ˈmȯr-fik\   (1) Having or described as having human form or traits. 人形的,有人类特征的 (2) Seeing human traits in nonhuman things. 拟人化的,认为（非人类）有人性的,赋予人性的

● The old, diseased tree had always been like a companion to her, though she didn't really approve of such anthropomorphic feelings. 这棵有病的老树一直像她的伙伴,虽然她并不赞成将物视为人。

Anthropomorphic means a couple of different things. In its first sense, an anthropomorphic cup is a cup in the shape of a human, and anthropomorphic gods are human in appearance—like the Greek and Roman gods, for example, even though Socrates and others believed that their fellow Greeks had created the gods in their own image rather than the other way around. In its second sense, the animal characters in Aesop's fables are anthropomorphic since they all have human feelings and thoughts even though they don't look like humans. Thus, when the fox calls the grapes sour simply because they're out of reach, it's a very human response. Thousands of years after Aesop, *anthropomorphism* is still alive and well, in the animal stories of Beatrix Potter, George Orwell's *Animal Farm*, and hundreds of cartoons and comic strips.

anthropomorphic 有两个不同的含义。其一,anthropomorphic cup 是人形的杯子,anthropomorphic gods 是具有人的外表的神——比如,希腊和罗马的神,但苏格拉底等人认为,希腊人按照自己的形象创造了众神,而不是倒过来。其二,伊索寓言中的动物角色是拟人化的,因为他们都有人类的情感和思想,尽管看起来不像人类。因此,狐狸仅仅因为够不到葡萄就说葡萄酸,这是一种非常人性化的反应。在伊索寓言问世之后的几千年里,在比阿特丽克斯·波特的动物故事、乔治·奥威尔的《动物庄园》以及成百上千的漫画和连环漫画中,*anthropomorphism*(拟人创作手法,拟人化)依然存在。

metamorphosis\ˌme-tə-ˈmȯr-fə-səs\ (1) A physical change, especially one supernaturally caused. 形变(尤指超自然引起的)(2) A developmental change in an animal that occurs after birth or hatching. 蜕变

● Day by day the class watched the gradual metamorphosis of the tadpoles into frogs. 全班学生一天天观察从蝌蚪到青蛙的缓慢蜕变过程。

Many ancient myths end in a metamorphosis. As Apollo is chasing the nymph Daphne, she calls on her river-god father for help and he turns her into a laurel tree to save her. Out of anger and jealousy, the goddess Athena turns the marvelous weaver Arachne into a spider that will spin only beautiful webs. But natural substances may also *metamorphose*, or undergo metamorphosis. Heat and pressure over thousands of years may eventually turn tiny organisms into petroleum, and coal into diamonds. And the most beloved of natural metamorphoses (notice how this plural is formed) is probably the transformation of caterpillars into butterflies.

许多古老的神话都以形变而告终。当阿波罗追逐女神达芙妮时,她请求河神父亲的帮助,父亲把她变成一棵月桂树。出于愤怒和嫉妒,女神雅典娜把神奇的织布女子阿拉克涅变成了会织漂亮蛛网的蜘蛛。但天然物质也可能 *metamorphose*(发生质变),或经历 metamorphosis。几千年的高温和高压可能最终会把微生物变成石油,把煤变成钻石。最可爱的自然 metamorphoses(注意这个复数是如何形成的)可能是毛虫变成蝴蝶。

morphology\mȯr-ˈfä-lə-jē\ (1) The study of the structure and form of plants and animals. (生物)形态学 (2) The study of word formation. (语言)形态学,词

法研究

- The morphology of the mouthparts of the different mayfly species turns out to be closely related to what they feed on and their methods of eating. 不同种类蜉蝣口器的形态与它们的食物和进食方式密切相关。

Within the field of biology, *morphology* is the study of the shapes and arrangement of parts of organisms, in order to determine their function, their development, and how they may have been shaped by evolution. Morphology is particularly important in classifying species, since it can often reveal how closely one species is related to another. Morphology is studied within other sciences as well, including astronomy and geology. And in language, morphology considers where words come from and why they look the way they do.

在生物学领域中,形态学研究生物体各部分的形状和排列顺序,以确定它们的功能、发育以及它们是如何进化成形的。形态学在物种分类中尤为重要,因为它常可以揭示物种之间关系的密切程度。形态学在其他科学中也有研究,包括天文学、地质学等。而在语言学中,形态学研究的是单词从何而来以及为什么它们看起来是那样的。

FORM is the Latin root meaning "shape" or "form." When you *march in formation*, you're moving in ordered patterns. And a *formula* is a standard form for expressing information, such as a rule written in mathematical symbols, or the "Sincerely yours" that often ends a letter.

FORM 是拉丁语词根,意思是"形状"。当你 march in formation(编队前进)时,你就在按照有序的队形前进。formula 是表达信息的标准化形式,比如用数学符号写的公式,或者结束信件时常用的"谨致问候"之类的套话。

format\ˈfȯr-ˌmat\ (1) The shape, size, and general makeup of something. 版式,格式 (2) A general plan, arrangement, or choice of material. 总体规划、安排或材料选择。

- The new thesaurus would be published in three formats: as a hardcover book, a large paperback, and a CD-ROM. 这本新同义词词典将以三种格式出版:精装书、大型平装书和CD-ROM。

Format is a word that seems to gain more uses with every decade. Traditionally, people used the word simply to refer to the design of a book or newspaper page, but today that's only one of its many meanings. TV news shows seem to change their format, or general form, as often as their anchorpeople, and show types such as situation comedy and crime drama are often called formats. When a radio station gives up playing pop music to became a talk station, it's said to be switching formats. In the electronic age, *format* has also become widely used as a verb; thus, organizing electronic data for storage or other special uses is called formatting (or *reformatting*).

format 一词似乎每十年会新增更多含义。传统上,人们使用这个词只是用来指代书籍或报纸页面的设计,但如今这只是它众多含义中的一个。电视新闻节目好像经常改变编排方式,就像它们的主持人一样。情景喜剧和犯罪剧等节目类型通常被称为 formats(节目形式)。当一个广播电台停止播放流行音乐而变成一个聊天电台时,就被称为改版。在电子时代，*format* 也被广泛用作动词；因此，安排用于储存或其他特殊目的的电子数据称为格式化（或 *reformatting*［重新格式化］）。

conform\kən-ˈfȯrm\ (1) To be similar or identical; to be in agreement or harmony. 相似，一致，符合 (2) To follow ordinary standards or customs. 遵循（普通的标准或习俗）

• My family was too odd to really conform to the little town's ideas about proper behavior, but it didn't seem to bother our neighbors too much. 我的家人太古怪，不遵循这个小镇人心目中的正常行为标准，但好像也没有太影响邻居。

Conform, with its prefix *con-*, "with" or "together," means basically "to adopt the form of those around you." Thus, employee behavior must usually conform with basic company policies. A certain philosophy may be said to conform with American values (even if we sometimes have a hard time agreeing on exactly what those are). And a Maine Coon cat or a Dandie Dinmont terrier must conform to its breed requirements in order to be registered for breeding purposes. Being a *conformist* is usually a safe bet; being a *nonconformist*, who ignores society's standards and the whole idea of *conformity*, can be a bit dangerous but also sometimes more fun.

conform 的前缀是 *con-*（"和……一起"），这个词的基本意思是"采用周围人的样子"。因此，员工的行为通常必须符合公司的基本政策。某种哲学据说符合美国的价值观（即使我们有时很难就这些价值观究竟是什么达成一致）。缅因库恩猫或丹迪丁蒙特犬必须符合其品种要求才能登记用于育种目的。做一个 *conformist*（墨守成规的人）通常能万无一失；而 *nonconformist*（不墨守成规的人）会无视社会的标准以及 *conformity*（从众）的总体思想，这可能有点危险，但有时也更有趣。

formality\fȯr-ˈma-lə-tē\ (1) An established custom or way of behaving that is required or standard. 礼节，俗套 (2) The following of conventional rules. 遵循成规

• The bride and groom wanted a small, intimate wedding without all the usual formalities. 新娘和新郎想要一个非正式的小型婚礼，不要所有那些繁文缛节。

Formal behavior follows the proper *forms* or customs, and *informal* behavior feels free to ignore them. The formality of a dinner party is indicated by such formalities as invitations, required dress, and full table settings. Legal *formalities*, or technicalities, may turn out to be all-important even if they often seem minor. America requires fewer formalities than many other countries (in Germany, for example, you may know someone for years before using his or her first name), but even in relaxed situations Americans may be observing invisible formalities.

formal behavior（正式的行为）遵循适当的 *forms*（行为方式）或习惯，而 *informal* behavior（非正式的行为）可以随意忽略它们。晚宴的正式性表现为请柬、着装要求和全套餐具等规矩。法律程序或技术细节可能是最重要的，即使它们通常看起来微不足道。美国比其他许多国家要求的礼节更少（比如，在德国，你可能认识一个人很多年后才会直呼其名），但即使在放松的情况下，美国人也可能在遵守一些无形的礼节。

formative\ˈfȯr-mə-tiv\ (1) Giving or able to give form or shape; constructive. 赋予形式或形状的，有助于成长的 (2) Having to do with important

UNIT 15

growth or development. 与重要的成长或发展有关的
• She lived in Venezuela during her formative years and grew up speaking both Spanish and English. 她的在委内瑞拉度过了性格形成期,从小说西班牙语和英语。

Whatever gives shape to something else may be called formative; for example, the Grand Canyon is a product of the formative power of water, and the automobile was a huge formative influence on the design of America's cities. But it usually applies to some kind of shaping that isn't physical. An ambitious plan, for example, goes through a formative stage of development. The formative years of the U. S. included experimentation with various forms of government. And the most important formative experiences in our own lives tend to take place in the first 20 years or so.

任何能赋予其他事物形状的东西都可以被称为 formative;比如,大峡谷是水的塑形之力的产物,而汽车对美国城市的设计产生了巨大的形成性影响。但这个词通常适用于一些非物质的塑形。比如,雄心勃勃的计划要经过发展形成阶段。在美国的形成期,进行了各种形式的政府的尝试。我们生活中最重要的形成经历往往发生在前 20 年左右。

Quizzes

A. Indicate whether the following pairs of words have the same or different meanings:

1. formative / form-giving   same ____ / different ____
2. morphology / shapeliness   same ____ / different ____
3. conform / agree   same ____ / different ____
4. anthropomorphic / man-shaped   same ____ / different ____
5. format / arrangement   same ____ / different ____
6. amorphous / shapeless   same ____ / different ____
7. formality / convention   same ____ / different ____
8. metamorphosis / hibernation   same ____ / different ____

B. Fill in each blank with the correct letter:

a. morphology   e. conform
b. formative   f. amorphous
c. metamorphosis   g. formality
d. format   h. anthropomorphic

1. No one was surprised when WTFX's new _____ turned out to be exactly the same as that of the company's 70 other stations.

2. The job description seemed a bit _____, and she wondered what she would really be doing.

3. While on the base, visitors are expected to _____ with all official rules and regulations.

4. Her poodle really does have some _____ traits, but I'm not sure he really appreciates Beethoven.

5. He seemed to undergo a complete _____ from child to young adult in just a few months.

6. The new couple found the _____ of the elegant dinner a little overwhelming.

7. He had written his senior thesis on the _____ of a species of dragonfly.

8. Among her _____ influences she included her favorite uncle, her ballet classes, and the Nancy Drew series.

DOC/DOCT comes from the Latin *docere*, which means "to teach." So, for instance, a *doctor* was originally a highly educated person capable of instructing others in a field—which usually wasn't medicine.

DOC/DOCT 源自拉丁语 docere("教")。比如,doctor 最初指的是受过良好教育的人,能够教某领域的其他人——通常不是医学领域。

doctrine \ˈdäk-trən\ (1) Something that is taught. 所教的东西,教义,信条 (2) An official principle, opinion, or belief. 正式声明,官方的原则、意见或信仰

• According to the 19th-century doctrine of "papal infallibility," a pope's official statements on matters of faith and morals must be regarded as the absolute truth. 根据 19 世纪"教皇无谬论"的教义,教皇对信仰和道德问题的官方声明必须被视为绝对真理。

The original doctrines were those of the Catholic Church, especially as taught by the so-called *doctors* (religious scholars) of the Church. But today a doctrine can come from many other sources. Old and established legal principles are called legal doctrine. Traditional psychiatrists still follow the doctrines of Sigmund Freud. U. S. presidents have given their names to doctrines as well: In 1823 the Monroe Doctrine stated that the United States would oppose European influence in the Americas, and in 1947 the Truman Doctrine held that America would support free countries against enemies outside and inside.

最初的 doctrines 指的是天主教的教义,特别是教会的那些被称作 doctors(神学家,即宗教学者)的人所教的教义。但今天的 doctrine 可以有很多别的来源。旧的、既定的法律原则被称为 legal doctrine。传统的精神病医生仍然遵循西格蒙德·弗洛伊德的学说。美国总统也曾以自己的名字命名某些主义;1823 年,门罗主义声称美国将反对欧洲对美洲施加影响;1947 年,杜鲁门主义认为美国应当支持那些自由国家对抗国内外的敌人。

docent \ˈdō-sᵊnt\ (1) Teacher, lecturer. 教师,讲师 (2) A person who leads guided tours, especially through a museum. 讲解员,向导

• Visitors to Istanbul's great Topkapi Museum often decide they need to hire an English-speaking docent. 伟大的托普卡帕宫博物馆位于伊斯坦布尔,来参观的游客经常决定要聘请一位会说英语的讲解员。

The title of docent is used in many countries for what Americans would call an associate professor—that is, a college or university teacher who has been given tenure (see *tenure*, p. 330) but hasn't yet achieved the rank of full professor. But in the U.S. a docent is a guide who works at a museum, a historical site, or even a zoo or a park. Docents are usually volunteers, and their services are often free of charge.

在许多国家,docent 这个头衔用来指美国人所说的 associate professor(副教授)——也就是已经获得终身职位(见 tenure,330 页)但还没有达到教授级别的大学教师。但是在美国,docent 指的是在博物馆、历史遗迹、甚至动物园或公园工作的讲解员。讲解员通常是志愿者,其服务通常是免费的。

doctrinaire \ˌdäk-trə-'ner\ Tending to apply principles or theories without regard for practical difficulties or individual circumstance. 教条的

• She had never taken a doctrinaire approach to teaching, since education theories didn't always match the reality of instructing 25 lively students. 她从来没有采取过教条主义的教学方法,因为教育理论并不总是与教导 25 名活泼的学生的实际情况相匹配。

Someone *doctrinaire* sticks closely to official doctrines or principles. A doctrinaire judge will give identical sentences to everyone found guilty of a particular crime. A doctrinaire feminist may treat all men as if they were identical. A doctrinaire economist might call for a single solution for the economic problems in all countries, regardless of their social and cultural history. As you might guess, the word isn't often used in positive contexts.

教条主义者严格遵守官方的教条或原则。教条主义的法官会对所有犯了某一罪行的人做出完全一样的判决。教条主义的女权主义者可能会把所有的男人都看成是一样的。教条主义的经济学家可能会呼吁对所有国家的经济问题采取同一种解决办法,而不考虑它们的社会和文化历史。正如你可能猜测的那样,这个词不常用在积极的语境中。

indoctrinate \in-'däk-trə-ˌnāt\ (1) To teach, especially basics or fundamentals. 教导,传授 (2) To fill someone with a particular opinion or point of view. 向……灌输(观点)

• In the Army's basic training, sergeants have 11 weeks to indoctrinate their new recruits with army attitudes and discipline. 在陆军的基础训练中,中士有 11 周的时间向新兵灌输军队的态度和纪律。

Indoctrinate simply means "brainwash" to many people today. We frequently hear, for example, of religious cults that indoctrinate their members to give up their freedom and individuality and to work hard only for a leader's goals. But its meaning wasn't originally negative at all. And the fact is that every society indoctrinates its young people with the values of its culture; in the U.S. we tend to be indoctrinated to love freedom, to be individuals, and to work hard for success, among many other things. But we now rarely use *indoctrinate* (or its noun, *indoctrination*) in a positive way; instead we usually stick to the simpler and safer *teach* or *instruct*.

对今天的许多人来说,indoctrinate 指的就是"洗脑"。比如,我们经常听到一些宗教教派教导他们的成员放弃自由和个性,只为领导者的目标而奋斗。但其含义在最初一点也不消极。事实上,每个社会都向年轻人灌输其文化价值观。在美国,我们往往被灌输热爱自由、成为独立个体、为成功而努力等观念。但是我们现在很少积极地使用 indoctrinate (或者它的名词 indoctrination);相反,我们通常用更简单、更安全的词:teach 或 instruct。

TUT/TUI comes from a Latin verb meaning "to look after," and in English the root generally shows up in words that include the meaning "guide," "guard," or "teach"—such as *tutor*, the name for a private teacher who guides a student (or *tutee*) through a subject.
TUT/TUI 源自拉丁中意思是"照管"的动词，在英语中，这个词根通常出现在含有"指导""保护"或"教"等意思的单词中——比如，*tutor* 用来命名指导学生（或 *tutee*[受辅导者]）完成某个科目的私人教师。

tutorial \tü-ˈtȯr-ē-əl\ (1) A class for one student or a small group of students. 个别辅导课 (2) An instructional program that gives information about a specific subject. （某一特定学科的）学习指南，教程

- He'd been taking tutorials with the same graduate student for two years, and learning far more than he'd ever learned in his large classes. 他跟同一个研究生一起上了两年的辅导课，学到的东西比他在大班学到的要多得多。

Tutorials with live tutors are useful for both advanced students and struggling ones. Many computer programs include electronic tutorials to help the new user get used to the program, leading him or her through all its functions, often by means of pictures and short videos. But a really difficult program may still require a real-life tutor to be fully understood.
导师现场个别辅导对高年级的学生和学习有困难的学生都很有用。许多计算机程序包含了电子教程，通过图片和短视频帮助新用户习惯这个程序，引导他/她了解程序的所有功能。但真正困难的程序可能仍然需要现实生活中的导师指导才能完全理解。

tuition \tü-ˈwi-shən\ (1) The act of teaching; instruction. 授课；讲授 (2) The cost of or payment for instruction. 学费

- As she happily flipped through her college catalogs, her parents sat quietly but uneasily calculating the total tuition costs. 她愉快地翻阅大学概况手册，而她的父母则静静地坐着，不安地计算着学费总额。

The sense of *tuition* meaning "teaching" or "instruction" is mostly used in Britain today. In the U.S., *tuition* almost always means the costs charged by a school, college, or university for that teaching. Those costs have tended to rise at an alarming rate in recent years. Around 2010 a student could receive a four-year college education (tuition, room, and board) at an inexpensive public university for less than $50,000, but might have to pay more than $200,000 at an expensive private college or university.
tuition 的"教学"或"指示"含义在当今英国用得最多。而在美国，*tuition* 几乎总是指学校、学院或大学收取的教学费用。近年来，教育费用呈惊人的上涨趋势。2010 年左右，一个学生在便宜的公立大学接受四年教育（包括学费、住宿费和伙食费）的花销不到 50,000 美元，但在昂贵的私立大学，可能需要支付超过 200,000 美元。

intuition \ˌin-tü-ˈwi-shən\ (1) The power of knowing something immediately without mental effort; quick insight. 直觉（力），敏锐的洞察力 (2) Something known in this way. 凭直觉感知的事

• She scoffed at the notion of "women's intuition," special powers of insight and understanding in personal relations that women are supposed to have. 她嘲笑"女性直觉"这一概念，即女性在人际关系中被认为拥有的洞察力和理解力。

Intuition is very close in meaning to *instinct*. The moment a man enters a room you may feel you know *intuitively* or instinctively everything about him—that is, you may *intuit* his basic personality. Highly rational people may try to ignore their intuition and insist on being able to explain everything they think, but artists and creative thinkers often tend to rely on their *intuitive* sense of things. Intuition can be closely related to their imagination, which seems to come from somewhere just as mysterious. Some psychologists claim that the left brain is mainly involved in logical thinking and the right brain in intuitive thinking; but the brain is terribly complex, and even if there's some truth to this idea, it's not terribly obvious how to make use of it.

intuition 与 instinct 意思非常接近。一个男人刚走进房间，你可能会感到凭直觉或 *instinctively* 就知道关于他的一切——也就是说，你可以 *intuit*（凭直觉知晓）他的基本个性。高度理性的人可能会尽量忽视直觉，而坚持认为能解释自己所思考的一切，但艺术家和富有创意的思想家往往依赖对事物的 *intuitive* sense（直觉）。直觉可能与想象力密切相关，而想象力似乎也来自同样神秘的地方。一些心理学家认为，左脑主要进行逻辑思维，而右脑主要进行直觉思维；但是大脑极为复杂，即使这个想法有些道理，我们也不太清楚该如何利用它。

tutelage \'tü-tə-lij\ Instruction or guidance of an individual; guardianship. 个人辅导；监护。

• Under the old man's expert tutelage, they had learned to carve and paint beautiful and realistic duck decoys. 在那位老人的专业指导下，他们学会了雕刻和绘制美丽而逼真的诱饵鸭。

Tutelage usually means specialized and individual guidance. Alexander the Great was under the tutelage of the philosopher Aristotle between the ages of 13 and 16, and his *tutor* inspired him with a love of philosophy, medicine, and science. At 16 he commanded his first army, and by his death 16 years later he had founded the greatest empire ever seen. But it's not so easy to trace the effects of the brilliant tutelage he had received in his youth.

tutelage 通常指的是专门的个人辅导。亚历山大大帝在 13 至 16 岁时接受了哲学家亚里士多德的指导，这位 *tutor*（导师）激发了他对哲学、医学和科学的热爱。16 岁时，亚历山大大大帝指挥了自己的第一支军队，在 16 年之后他死前，已建立了有史以来最伟大的帝国。但要追溯年轻时受到的非凡的教导对他产生的影响却实属不易。

Quizzes

A. Choose the closest definition:

1. docent   a. leader   b. scholar   c. guide   d. minister
2. tuition   a. requirement   b. instruction   c. resolution

TUT/
TUI

    d. housing
3. indoctrinate   a. medicate thoroughly
    b. research thoroughly   c. instruct thoroughly
    d. consider thoroughly
4. tutelage   a. responsibility   b. protection
    c. instruction   d. safeguard
5. doctrine   a. solution   b. principle   c. religion
    d. report
6. tutorial   a. small class   b. large class   c. night class
    d. canceled class
7. doctrinaire   a. by the way   b. by the by   c. by the rule
    d. by the glass
8. intuition   a. ignorance   b. quick understanding
    c. payment   d. consideration

B. Match the word on the left to the correct definition on the right：

1. indoctrinate   a. instruction costs
2. tutelage   b. guide
3. doctrine   c. fill with a point of view
4. tutorial   d. insight
5. doctrinaire   e. guardianship
6. intuition   f. official teaching
7. docent   g. individual instruction
8. tuition   h. rigidly principled

Number Words 数字词语

DI/DUP，Greek and Latin prefixes meaning "two," show up in both technical and nontechnical terms，with *dup-* sometimes shortened to *du-*. So a *duel* is a battle between two people. A *duet* is music for a *duo*, or pair of musicians. A *duplicate* is an exact copy，or twin. And if you have *dual* citizenship，you belong to two countries at once.

DI/DUP 是希腊语和拉丁语前缀，意思是"二"，在技术用语和非技术用语中均出现，*dup-* 有时简写为 *du-*。所以 *duel*（决斗）是两个人之间的战斗。*duet*（二重奏或二重唱）是为 *duo*，即两位音乐家，所写的音乐作品。*duplicate* 指的是精确的复制品或成对的东西。如果你有 *dual* citizenship（双重国籍），你就同时属于两个国家。

dichotomy \ dī-ˈkä-tə-mē \ （1）A division into two often contradictory groups. 一分为二，二分法 （2）Something with qualities that seem to contradict each other. 对立的事物

• Already in her first job, she noticed a dichotomy between the theories she'd been taught in college and the realities of professional life. 她在从事第一份工作时就已经注意到，大学里所学的理论与职业生活的现实是对立的。

In the modern world there's a dichotomy between fast and intense big-city life and the slower and more relaxed life in the country. But the dichotomy is nothing new: the Roman poet Horace was complaining about it in the 1st century B.C. Among other eternal dichotomies, there's the dichotomy between wealth and poverty, between the policies of the leading political parties, between a government's words and its actions—and between what would be most fun to do right this minute and what would be the mature and sensible alternative.

在现代世界里，大城市的生活节奏快而紧张，而乡村的生活节奏慢而轻松，两种生活截然不同。但是这种对立并不新鲜：早在公元前1世纪，罗马诗人贺拉斯就对此有所抱怨。此外，还有一些永恒的对立存在，比如，富裕与贫困、两大政党的政策、政府的言与行——还有，此时此刻是做些非常好玩的事情还是做些别的成熟明智的事情。

dimorphic\dī-'mòr-fik\ Occurring in two distinguishable forms (as of color or size). 二态的

• One of a birder's challenges is identifying birds of the less colorful sex in dimorphic species. 观鸟者的困难之一，是识别二态鸟类中颜色不那么鲜艳的性别的鸟。

Dimorphism varies greatly in the animal kingdom. Among mammals, the male is generally larger than the female, but other differences in appearance tend to be modest. But birds are usually noticeably dimorphic, with the male being the more colorful sex; when we imagine a pheasant, a mallard, a cardinal, or a peacock, we're almost always picturing the male rather than the female. Among spiders the situation is often reversed. The golden orb-weaver spider, for example, is spectacularly dimorphic: the female may be 20 times the size of the male, and she usually ends up eating him, sometimes even while he's mating with her. Many sea creatures, including many fish, take care of gender problems by simply chang- ing from one sex into the other.

动物王国的二态性差异很大。在哺乳动物中，雄性的体型通常比雌性大，但其他外观上的差异往往不大。但是鸟类通常有明显的二态性，雄鸟身体的颜色更艳丽。当我们想象野鸡、野鸭、主红雀、孔雀时，脑海里的画面几乎总是雄鸟而非雌鸟。蜘蛛的情况常常是相反的。比如，黄金圆蛛有着惊人的二态性：雌性蜘蛛的体型可能是雄性的20倍，且通常会最终吃掉雄蜘蛛，有时甚至在交配时吃掉它。许多海洋生物，包括许多鱼类，只需从一个性别转成另一性别就能处理好性别问题。

duplex\'dü-ˌpleks\ (1) Having two principal elements; double. 有两部分的，复式的，双倍的 (2) Allowing electronic communication in two directions at the same time. 双工的

• The upper floor of their splendid duplex apartment had a panoramic view of Paradise Park. 在他们富丽堂皇的复式公寓的上层，可以看到天堂公园的全景。

Duplex can describe a confusing variety of things, depending on the technical field. Most of us use it as a noun: a *duplex* can be either a two-family house or a two-story apartment. In computer science and telecommunications, duplex (or *full-duplex*) communication can go in both directions at once, while *half-duplex* communication can go only one way at a time. In other areas, just translate *duplex* as "double" and see if the sentence makes sense.

根据技术领域的不同，*duplex* 可以描述各种各样令人困惑的事情。多数人都把它用作名词：*duplex*（复式公寓）可以是两户的联式房屋，也可以是两层楼的公寓。在计算机科学和通信技术中，双工（或 *full-duplex*[全双工]）通信可以同时双向进行，而 *half-duplex*（半双工）通信每次只能单向进行。在其他领域，只需将 *duplex* 变成 "double"，再看这个句子是否讲得通。

duplicity \dủ-ˈpli-sə-tē\ Deception by pretending to feel and act one way while acting in another. 表里不一，口是心非，两面派

• By the time Jackie's duplicity in the whole matter had come to light, she had left town, leaving no forwarding address. 在整件事上耍两面派的行为暴露时，杰基已经离开了小镇，没有留下任何转寄地址。

The Greek god Zeus often resorted to *duplicity* to get what he wanted, and most of the time what he wanted was some woman. His duplicity usually involved a disguise: he appeared to Leda as a swan, and to Europa as a bull. Sometimes he had to be *duplicitous* to get around his wife, Hera. After he had had his way with Io and was about to get caught, he turned her into a cow to avoid Hera's anger. 希腊神宙斯为了得到他想要的东西，常常采取欺骗的手段，而多数时候他想要的是某个女子。宙斯的口是心非通常会用到伪装：在勒达看来他是一只天鹅，在欧罗巴看来他是一头公牛。有时他不得不 be *duplicitous* to（耍两面派）才能绕过妻子赫拉。当他和爱娥走到一起，正要被抓住时，他把爱娥变成了一头母牛，以躲避赫拉的愤怒。

BI/BIN also means "two" or "double." A *bicycle* has two wheels, and *binoculars* consist of two little telescopes. *Bigamy* is marriage to two people at once. And a road built through the middle of a neighborhood *bisects* it into two pieces.

BI/BIN 指的也是"二"或"双"。*bicycle*（自行车）有两个轮子，*binoculars*（双筒望远镜）由两个小望远镜组成。*bigamy*（重婚）是同时和两个人结婚。一条从街区正中间穿过的路把这个街区 *bisect*（均分）为两个部分。

bipartisan \ˌbī-ˈpär-tə-zən\ Involving members of two political parties.
两党的，涉及两党的

• The president named a bipartisan commission of three Republicans and three Democrats to look into the issue. 总统任命一个由三名共和党人和三个民主党人组成的两党委员会来调查这个问题。

Partisan means basically "belonging to a party," so something *bipartisan* combines two parties. Since the United States today operates with a two-party system of government (even though the Constitution says nothing about parties at all), legislation often must have some bipartisan support in order to pass into law.

UNIT 15

Bipartisan committees review legislation, compromising on some points and removing or adding others in order to make the bill more agreeable to both parties and make bipartisan support from the entire legislature or Congress more likely.

partisan 的基本意思是"属于一个政党",所以涉及两党的东西把两个党联系起来。由于美国现在实行的是两党制政府(尽管宪法对政党没有任何规定),立法通常得到两党的支持才能成为法律。两党委员会审查立法,在某些内容上做出妥协、删除或增加其他内容,以便使该法案更符合两党的利益,使两党更有可能得到整个立法机构或国会的支持。

binary \ˈbī-nə-rē\ (1) Consisting of two things or parts; double. 由两部分组成的;双重的 (2) Involving a choice between two alternatives. 涉及两个选项的

• The Milky Way contains numerous binary stars, each consisting of two stars orbiting each other. 银河系中有许多双星,均由两颗互相环绕的星组成。

Binary has many uses, most of them in technical terms. Almost all computer software, for example, is written in *binary code*, which uses only two digits, 0 and 1, 0 standing for a low-voltage impulse ("off") and 1 standing for a high-voltage impulse ("on"). All information is kept in this form. The word "HELLO," for example, looks like this: 1001000 1000101 1001100 1001100 1001111.

binary 有很多用法,但多数用在技术术语中。比如,几乎所有计算机软件都用 *binary code*(二进制代码)编写,二进制代码使用 0 和 1 两个数字,0 代表低压脉冲("关"),1 代表高压脉冲("开")。所有信息都以这种形式保存。比如,"HELLO"一词看起来是这样的:1001000 1000101 1001100 1001100 1001111。

biennial \ˌbī-ˈe-nē-əl\ (1) Occurring every two years. 两年一次的,每两年的 (2) Continuing or lasting over two years. 持续两年以上的

• The great biennial show of new art in Venice usually either puzzles or angers the critics. 威尼斯两年一次的新艺术大展通常会让批评家要么困惑,要么愤怒。

Biennial conventions, celebrations, competitions, and sports events come every two years. *Biennials* are plants that live two years, bearing flowers and fruit only in the second year. (Carrots and sugar beets are two examples; since we're only interested in their roots, we don't wait another year to see their flower and fruit.) In contrast, *semiannual* means "twice a year." But no one can agree whether *biweekly* means "twice a week" or "every two weeks," and whether *bimonthly* means "twice a month" or "every two months." Maybe we should stop using both of them until we can decide.

biennial 的大会、庆典、比赛和体育赛事每两年举行一次。*biennials*(二年生植物)指的是生活两年的植物,这些植物第二年开花结果(比如胡萝卜和甜菜。因为我们只对它们的根感兴趣,所以不会再等一年去看花和果实)。相反,*semiannual* 的意思是"一年两次"。但是没有人能确定 *biweekly* 指的是"一周两次"还是"两周一次",*bimonthly* 指的是"一月两次"还是"两月一次"。也许我们应该停用这两个词,直到我们能明确其含义。

bipolar \ˌbī-ˈpō-lər\ Having two opposed forces or views; having two poles or opposed points of attraction. 两强对立的,两极的

• Our bipolar Earth spins on an axis that extends between the North and South Poles. 我们的两极地球绕着南北两极之间的轴线旋转。

Magnets are always *bipolar*: one pole attracts and the other repels or drives away. And the Cold War arms race was bipolar, since it mainly involved the opposing powers of the U. S. and the Soviet Union. But the word is encountered most often today in *bipolar disorder*, the newer name of what used to be called *manic-depressive illness*, in which the person tends to swing between the two extremes, or poles, of high intensity and deep depression, with depression being the main condition. Though an extremely serious illness, bipolar disorder can often be controlled by the drug lithium.

磁铁总是两极的:一个磁极吸引,另一磁极排斥。冷战时期的军备竞赛是两极的,因为冷战主要涉及美国和苏联两大对头。但如今这个词最常出现在 *bipolar disorder*(双相情感障碍)中,这种疾病过去常被称为 *manic-depressive illness*(躁郁症),患者往往在极度焦虑和重度抑郁两个极端或两极之间反复,其主要症状是抑郁。虽然双相情感障碍是一种非常严重的疾病,但往往可以用锂类药物控制。

Quiz

Fill in each blank with the correct letter:

a. bipolar
b. duplex
c. biennial
d. duplicity
e. dimorphic
f. binary
g. dichotomy
h. bipartisan

1. The new bill, with its thoroughly _____ backing, passed through Congress easily.

2. Parrots are strikingly _____, unlike canaries, in which you can't tell the sexes apart until the male starts singing.

3. Powerful drugs like lithium are often prescribed for _____ depression.

4. A liar's _____ usually catches up with him sooner or later.

5. At the very heart of the computer revolution was the _____ number system.

6. Democracies must always deal with the difficult _____ between individual liberties and social order.

7. They shared the modest _____ with another family of four, who they often met when going in and out.

8. Every two years we get to hear Mildred McDermot sing "Moonlight in Vermont" at the _____ town picnic.

Review Quizzes

A. Fill in each blank with the correct letter:

a. anthropomorphic
b. doctrine
k. avert
l. revert

c. tuition
d. interminable
e. duplex
f. binary
g. formative
h. biennial
i. doctrinaire
j. spherical
m. conform
n. intuition
o. indeterminate
p. bipartisan
q. metamorphosis
r. dichotomy
s. tutelage
t. hemisphere

1. This marble was limestone before it underwent _____.
2. The computer works by making choices between _____ opposites.
3. The main piano competition is _____, but there are smaller ones on the off-years.
4. The lab results were _____, and he was told to wait a week before having another blood test.
5. We failed to get the contract because our equipment didn't _____ to the company's specifications.
6. She managed to _____ a very awkward meeting by slipping out a side door just as he was coming in.
7. I had an _____ wait in the doctor's office and didn't get home until 6:00.
8. What he later learned about her past had confirmed his original _____ that she was not to be trusted.
9. The _____ between good and evil has been dealt with by different religions in many different ways.
10. Let's not _____ to the kind of name-calling we had to put up with at the last meeting.
11. To keep the issue as nonpolitical as possible, the governor named a _____ committee to study it.
12. At boarding schools, _____ isn't separated from fees for room and board.
13. The _____ was roomy, but a great deal of noise came through the wall separating them from the other family.
14. Under the great man's _____, he slowly learned how to develop his musical ideas into full-fledged sonatas.
15. As a practicing Catholic, she thought frequently about the church _____ that life begins at conception.
16. Michelangelo's great painting shows an _____ God touching Adam's finger.
17. A _____ interpretation of these rules will leave no room for fun at all.
18. My trip to Australia was the first time I had left this _____.
19. The assignment was to write an essay about the most _____ experience of

her later teenage years.

20. The stone was roughly _____, but it didn't roll easily.

B. Choose the correct synonym and the correct antonym：

1. intuition   a. instruction   b. payment   c. logic
   d. sixth sense
2. divert   a. please   b. entertain   c. bore
   d. send
3. amorphous   a. beginning   b. shapeless   c. shaping
   d. formed
4. terminal   a. first   b. final   c. highest
   d. deathlike
5. duplicity   a. desire   b. two-facedness   c. honesty
   d. complexity
6. formality   a. convention   b. black tie   c. rationality
   d. casualness
7. conform   a. rebel   b. shape   c. greet
   d. fit in
8. dichotomy   a. operation   b. negotiation   c. contradiction
   d. agreement
9. avert   a. face   b. wonder   c. avoid
   d. claim
10. doctrinaire   a. relaxed   b. strict   c. written
    d. religious

C. Choose the closest definition：

1. format   a. design   b. formality   c. formation
   d. concept
2. biosphere   a. life cycle   b. environment
   c. natural bubble   d. evolution
3. morphology
   a. study of structure
   b. study of woods
   c. study of butterflies
   d. study of geometry
4. avert   a. embrace   b. prevent   c. claim
   d. escape
5. bipolar   a. double-jointed   b. snowy   c. opposing
   d. two-handed
6. indoctrinate   a. teach   b. demonstrate   c. infiltrate
   d. consider
7. metamorphosis   a. condition   b. independence

c. technique   d. transformation
8. duplicity   a. doubleness   b. dishonesty   c. photocopy
   d. second opinion
9. tutorial   a. penalty   b. teacher   c. classroom
   d. small class
10. stratosphere   a. cloud level   b. sea level
    c. atmospheric layer   d. outer space

UNIT 16

TOP comes from *topos*, the Greek word for "place." A *topic* is a subject rather than a place; to the Greeks, the original word meant more or less "about one place or subject (rather than another)"—which just goes to show that it's not always easy to trace a word's meaning from its roots.

TOP 源自希腊语中表示"地方"的 *topos* 一词。topic 是一个话题而不是地方。对古希腊人来说,最初那个词语的意思大概是"关于一个地方或者话题(而不是另一个)"——这正好可以表明,将一个词语的意思追溯至根源,并不总是那么容易。

topical\tä-pə-kəl\ (1) Designed for local application to or treatment of a bodily part. (身体用药或治疗的)局部的 (2) Referring to the topics of the day. 有关时事的;热门话题的

• If the topical ointment doesn't work on the rash, the doctor will prescribe an antibiotic pill. 如果这种局部药膏治不了麻疹,医生就会开一个抗生素片。

Like a *topical* medicine, a topical reference or story applies to something specific, focusing on a *topic* that's currently in the news. TV comedians often use topical humor, making jokes about a currently popular movie or the latest political scandal—if possible, one that just broke that same day. Topical humor has a short lifespan, though, because the news keeps changing and the new hot topics just keep coming. The medical meaning of *topical* stays closer to the meaning of the root, since it describes something that's put right on the place that seems to need it.

像 topical 药物一样,topical 参考或故事适用于特定的东西,关注新闻报道中出现的 topic(话题)。电视喜剧通常使用 topical 幽默,就当前某一深受欢迎的电影或者最新的政治丑闻开玩笑——如果可能的话,就当天爆出的丑闻开玩笑。不过,topical 幽默生命期不长,因为新闻不断变化,新的热门话题不断涌现。topical 在医学方面的意思与词根的意思比较贴近,因为它描述的东西用在似乎需要它的那个部位。

ectopic\ek-ˈtä-pik\ Occurring or originating in an abnormal place. 异位的

• A pacemaker was installed to correct her ectopic heartbeat. 安装了一个起搏器,用来纠

正她的异位心跳。

Ectopic is a medical word that means basically "out of place." An ectopic kidney is located in an abnormal position. In patients with an ectopic heartbeat, the electrical signals that trigger the heart muscles originate in an abnormal area of the heart. But *ectopic* most commonly describes a pregnancy in which the fertilized egg begins to develop in an area outside the uterus, such as in a fallopian tube; such pregnancies may lead to serious problems if not treated.

ectopic 是一个医学词语，基本意思是"不在正确位置"。ectopic 肾脏处于不正常的位置。在异位心跳的病人体内，触发心脏肌肉的电信号源自心脏中不正常的部位。但是 ectopic 最主要用来描述的，是受精卵在子宫外(比如输卵管)开始发育的妊娠。这样的妊娠，如果不予以治疗，可能导致严重问题。

utopian \yü-'tō-pē-ən\ Relating to an imaginary place in which the government, laws, and social conditions are perfect. 乌托邦的；完美社会的

• Some of the new mayor's supporters had gotten increasingly unrealistic, and seemed to expect that she could turn the city into a utopian community. 新市长的一些支持者越来越不现实，似乎希望她能把这座城市变成一个完美社会。

In 1516 Thomas More published *Utopia*, a description of a fictional island in the Atlantic with an ideal society, in order to draw a sharp contrast with the disorderly political situation of his own time. He created the name from *topos* ("place") and *ou*, Greek for "no," since he was well aware that nowhere so perfect was likely to exist on earth. People have long dreamed of creating utopian communities; some of them have joined communes, societies where other idealists like themselves have chosen to live in a cooperative way according to certain principles. Not just communes but plans of all kinds have been labeled utopian by critics. But we can dream, can't we?

1516 年，托马斯·莫尔出版了 *Utopia*(《乌托邦》)一书，描述的是一个虚构的大西洋岛屿，那里有一个理想社会。他这样做，是为了与自己那个时代混乱的政治状况进行对比。他用 topos("地方")和 ou(希腊语"不")创造了这个名字，因为他很清楚，那么完美的社会地球上根本不存在。人们很久以来就梦想着创造完美的社会，他们有些人加入了公社，也就是其他跟自己一样的理想主义者组成的社会，决定按照某些原则以合作方式生活在一起。不仅是公社，各种计划也都被评论家说成是 *utopian*(乌托邦的)。但我们可以有梦想，是不是？

topography \tə-'pä-grə-fē\ (1) The art of showing the natural and man-made features of a region on a map or chart. 地形描绘 (2) The features of a surface, including both natural and man-made features. 地形；地势

• Planning the expedition involved careful study of the region's topography. 计划进行这次考察，需要仔细研究该地区的地形。

Topography combines *top-* with *graph-*, a root meaning "write" or "describe." The topography of the Sahara Desert features shifting sand dunes and dry, rocky mountains. A *topographic* (or *topo*) map not only shows the surface features of a region but also indicates the contours and approximate altitude of every location, by means of numerous curving lines, each indicating a single elevation. In other words, it shows a "three-dimensional" picture on a two-dimensional surface. Topo maps are commonly used by hikers, surveyors, government workers, and engineers, among other people.

topography 把 *top*- 和 *graph*- 这个表示"写"或者"描述"的词根结合起来了。撒哈拉沙漠的地形特征是流动的沙丘和干燥、多岩的山。*topographic*(或者 *topo*)地图不但展示了某个地区的地表特征,也显示了每个地点的等高线和大致纬度,方法是利用很多曲线,每一条表明一个高度。换句话说,它在二维表面展示了一个"三维"图画。使用地形图的,一般是远足者、勘测员、政府工作人员和工程师等等。

CENTR/CENTER

CENTR/CENTER comes from the Greek *kentron* and the Latin *centrum*, meaning "sharp point" or "center point of a circle." A *centrifuge* is a spinning machine that throws things outward from the *center*; the apparent force that pushes them outward is called centrifugal force.

CENTR/CENTER 源自希腊语 *kentron* 和拉丁语 *centrum*("锐利的尖端"或者"圆圈的中心点")。*centrifuge*(离心机;离心分离机)是一个旋转的机器,把东西从中心向外抛去。将它们向外推去的惯性力称为 *centrifugal force*(离心力)。

eccentric \ ik-ˈsen-trik \ (1) Not following an established or usual style or conduct. 古怪的;反常的 (2) Straying from a circular path; off-center. 离心的;偏离圆形轨道的

• She keeps a dozen stray cats in her house and is rather eccentric, but her neighbors say she's very pleasant and completely harmless. 她在房子养了十多只流浪猫,很是古怪。不过,邻居都说她彬彬有礼,完全不会伤害谁。

An eccentric wheel spins unevenly, and an eccentric person is similarly a little off-center. Most eccentricities are inoffensive to others, and some may even do some good. For instance, riding a bicycle to work might be considered eccentric by some people, but it's good exercise and it cuts down on pollution. Some eccentrics are just ahead of their time.

eccentric(偏心的)轮子转动不平稳,*eccentric*(古怪的)人同样有些异常。大多数 eccentricities(怪癖;古怪行为)并不让他人厌恶,有些甚至还有些好处。比如,骑车子上班可能让些人觉得古怪,但是它能锻炼身体,也减少了污染。有些 eccentrics(古怪的人)只是超越了时代。

epicenter \ ˈe-pi-ˌsen-tər \ (1) The location on the earth's surface directly above the focus of an earthquake. 震中 (2) The center or focus of activity. (活动)的中心;焦点

• The destruction caused by Mexico City's earthquake was extensive because the city was at the quake's epicenter. 墨西哥城的地震引起的破坏很严重,因为该城市位于震中。

The meaning of *epi*- in *epicenter* is "over," so the epicenter of an earthquake lies over the center or "focus" of the quake. *Epicenter* can also refer to the centers of things that may seem in their own way as powerful—though not as destructive—as earthquakes. Wall Street, for example, might be said to lie at the epicenter of the financial world.

epicenter 中的 *epi* 意思是"在……上方",所以地震的 *epicenter* 位于地震"中心"的上面。*epicenter* 也可以指事物的

UNIT 16

中心，这些事物的强大有其自己的方式，虽然不像地震那样具有破坏力。比如华尔街可以说是位于金融世界的中心。

egocentric \ˌē-gō-ˈsen-trik\ Overly concerned with oneself; self-centered. 以自我为中心的；自私的

• He's brilliant but completely egocentric, and the only things he'll talk about are his own life and work. 他很出色，但是极其自私，唯一谈论的就是自己的生活和工作。

Ego means "I" in Latin. To an *egocentric* person, *I* is the most important word in the language. Great artists and writers are often *egocentrics*; such people can be hard to live with, though their *egocentricity*, an unfortunate side effect of their talent, is often forgiven. But ordinary egocentricity, which shows up as selfishness, lack of sympathy, and lack of interest in other people, usually has little to do with any personal talent or success.

ego 在拉丁语中意思是"我"。对于 *egocentric*(以自我为中心的)人来说，"我"是语言中最重要的词语。伟大的艺术家和作家常常是 egocentrics(以自我为中心的人)。这样的人，要跟他一起生活是很难的，不过，他们的 *egocentgricity*(以自我为中心)是其天才的不幸的副产品，常常可以原谅。一般的 *egocentricity* 的表现是自私、缺乏同情心、对他人缺乏兴趣，通常与个人天才或成功没有多大关系。

ethnocentric \ˌeth-nō-ˈsen-trik\ Marked by or based on the attitude that one's own group is superior to others. 种族(民族)中心主义的；有种族(民族)优越感的

• Some reviewers criticized the ethnocentric bias that came through in the way the film portrayed immigrants. 有些评论家批评了这部电影描绘移民的方式所传达的民族优越感。

The Greek word *ethnos* means "nation" or "people." So *ethnocentricity* shows itself in a lack of respect for other ways of life, and an ethnocentric person feels that his or her own nation or group is the cultural center of the world. *Ethnocentric* describes the kind of person who behaves badly when traveling in foreign countries, often called an "Ugly American" (from a book and movie of the same name). Whenever you hear someone making fun of the way a foreigner speaks English, just remember that it's the foreigner, not the person laughing at him, who actually can speak a foreign language.

希腊语词语 *ethnos* 意思是"民族"或"人民"。所以，*ethnocentricity* 表现出来就是缺乏对其他生活方式的尊重，*ethnocentric*(有民族优越感的)人觉得自己的民族或群体是世界的文化中心。*ethnocentric* 描述的是一个在国外旅游时表现恶劣的人，通常称为"丑陋的美国人"(来自同名书籍和电影)。每当你听到有人拿外国人说英语的方式开玩笑，你就记住，是那个外国人能说外语，而不是那个嘲笑他的人。

Quizzes

A. Fill in each blank with the correct letter:

a. epicenter   e. topography
b. ectopic   f. egocentric
c. ethnocentric   g. topical
d. utopian   h. eccentric

1. She claims that his remarks show an _____ bias against foreign cultures.
2. The _____ of a river valley often includes a wide, fertile floodplain.
3. The earth's orbit around the sun is _____ rather than perfectly circular.
4. An _____ pregnancy is an unusual event that poses serious medical problems.
5. Since he hates needles, he asks his dentist to use only a _____ anesthetic inside his mouth.
6. There's nothing wrong with liking yourself so long as you don't become _____.
7. In 1970 they founded a _____ community on a 400-acre farm, where all property was to be owned in common.
8. Luckily, the quake's _____ was far away from any human settlement.

B. Match the word on the left to the correct definition on the right:

1. topical   a. central point
2. egocentric   b. centered on one's own group
3. utopian   c. away from its usual place
4. ethnocentric   d. self-centered
5. topography   e. of current interest
6. eccentric   f. ideal
7. ectopic   g. placed off-center
8. epicenter   h. landscape features

DOM comes from the Latin *domus*, "house," and *dominus*, "master," and the two are indeed related. In the Bible, King Ahasuerus, angered by his queen's disobedience, proclaims that "every man is to be master of his own house," and in the Roman empire no one doubted that this was how it was meant to be. A *domain* is the area where a person has authority or is *dominant*—but we no longer think of a house as the domain of a single dominant member of a family.

DOM 源自拉丁语 domus("房子")和 dominus("主人"),而且这两者是有关系的。在《圣经》中,亚哈随鲁国王因为王后不听话,就宣布"每个男人都是自己房子的主人",在罗马帝国,没有人质疑这就是它应有的意思。domain(领地;势力范围)是某个人在那里当权的或者是 dominant(处于支配地位的)地方——不过,我们已经不再把房子视为家庭中一个处于支配地位的成员的 domain 了。

---

dominion\də-ˈmin-yən\ (1) An area over which one rules; domain. 领土; 领地 (2) Supreme authority. 最高权力;统治权

● The Roman empire had dominion over the entire Mediterranean, which the Romans called *mare nostrum*, "our sea." 罗马帝国统治整个地中海,他们把它称为 mare nostrum,"我们的海"。

The ruler of a region has dominion over it, and the area itself may be called the ruler's dominion. In the days of the British Empire, England had dominion over many countries throughout the world. Though Canada has been quite independent of Great Britain since the 19th century, it was generally referred to as the Dominion of Canada in official documents until at least the 1950s. The word has an old-fashioned sound today, and probably shows up in history books, historical novels, and fantasy video games more often than in discussions of modern nations.

某一地区的统治者对其有 dominion(统治权),这一地区本身可以叫做这位统治者的 dominion(领土)。在大英帝国时期,英格兰对全世界很多国家都有 dominion(统治权)。虽然加拿大从 19 世纪就在很大程度上独立于英国了,但直到 20 世纪 50 年代,在官方文件中它通常仍被称为 the Dominion of Canada(加拿大领地)。这个词语今天听起来过时了,它出现的频率,在历史书、历史小说和幻想电子游戏中可能超过对当代国家的讨论。

predominant \prē-ˈdä-mə-nənt\ Greater in importance, strength, influence, or authority. 占优势的;最重要的;主导的

• The predominant color of the desert landscape was a rusty brown. 沙漠景色中最主要的颜色是锈棕色。

Something predominant stands out above all the rest. The predominant theme in an essay is the one that predominates—the main idea that the writer wants to express. (Notice the difference between the adjective and the verb; be sure not to spell the adjective with an -ate ending.) The word is widely used in many fields. For example, the predominant language of Switzerland is German; the predominant cause of obesity in children is a bad diet; and your predominant reason for wanting a larger vocabulary may be to simply be a better-educated person—though the positive effects of a large vocabulary on one's romantic life are well known.

predominant 东西比其他所有的都突出。一篇散文的 predominant(最重要的)主题就是 predominates(占优势)的那个——作者想要表达的主要观点。(注意形容词和动词;拼写形容词时,结尾不是 -ate。)这一词语广泛使用于多个领域。比如,瑞士的 predominant 语言是德语;儿童肥胖的 predominant 原因是糟糕的饮食;你想要词汇量更大的 predominant 理由,可能只是做一个受过更好教育的人,不过很多人都知道,词汇量更大,在爱情生活中也很有好处。

domineering \ˌdä-mə-ˈnir-iŋ\ Tending to control the behavior of others in a bossy manner. 专横的;专断的

• His mother was a domineering type, and not even his stepfather dared do anything without her permission. 他妈妈是那种很专横的人,连他继父未经允许都不敢做什么。

To be domineering is to behave like a lord. (The word lordly doesn't express quite the same thing.) Someone who tells you what you can wear or what friends you can spend time with could be called domineering; so could someone who always decides what you're going to do with your free time. Those of us who grow up with a domineering parent usually flee as soon as we're old enough.

domineering 就是表现得像个君王一样。(Lordly 这个词语意思很不一样。)告诉你能穿什么,或者可以跟什么样的朋友交往,这样的人可以说是 domineering;老是决定你在空闲时间干什么的人也是这样。我们当中有些人,成长过程中有个 domineering 爸爸或者妈妈,通常是年龄一到就尽快逃走。

domination\ˌdä-mə-ˈnā-shən\ (1) Supremacy or power over another. 主宰；控制；支配 (2) The exercise of governing or controlling influence. 实施统治；实施控制

- The region was under the domination of a single nation, even though it hadn't yet invaded its neighbors. 这一地区在一个国家的控制之下，虽然它还没有侵略过邻国。

Domination may sound like something that's achieved by military force. The total domination of Europe, for example, has never been achieved: The Roman empire could never fully *dominate* the northern Germanic tribes; Napoleon couldn't conquer Spain; and although Adolf Hitler was briefly *dominant* over most of the continent, he never managed to overpower England. But the word's earliest appear- ances don't necessarily involve physical force; Chaucer, for instance, speaks of a mind's domination by strong drink. So we may observe that a great tennis player has continued his domination of the world's courts this season, or that the domination of popular music by rock and roll was obvious by the end of the 1950s.

domination 听起来好像是通过军事力量取得的。比如对整个欧洲的 *domination* 从未实现过：罗马帝国一直没有完全 *dominate*（统治）北方的日耳曼部落；拿破仑未能征服西班牙；虽然阿道夫·希特勒短暂 *dominant*（统治）了欧洲大陆大部分地区，但他从未能够征服英国。但是，这一词语最早出现未必都涉及武力，比如，乔叟谈到了烈酒对精神的 *domination*（控制）。所以，我们可以说，这个赛季，有个伟大的网球手一直主宰世界网球场，或者摇滚乐到20世纪50年代已经明显统治了流行乐坛。

OMNI comes from the Latin word *omnis*, meaning "all." So in English words, *omni-* can mean "in all ways," "in all places," or "without limits." An *omnidirectional* antenna, for example, is one that receives or sends radio waves equally well in all directions. And *Omni* by itself has been used repeatedly as a brand name for things as different as a hotel chain and a science magazine.

OMNI 源自拉丁语 *omnis*（"所有"）。因此，在英语单词中，*omni-* 可以表示"在所有方面""在所有地方"或者"无限"。比如，*omnidiretional*（全方向的）天线在所有方向接收或发送电波都一样好。Omni 本身一直频繁被用作商标名称，用于连锁酒店和科学杂志这样不同的东西。

omnivore\ˈäm-ni-ˌvȯr\ An animal that eats both plants and other animals. 杂食动物

- If we're all natural omnivores, she kept asking herself, then why wouldn't her toddler eat anything but cashews and peanut butter until the age of four? 她老是问自己，如果我们天生都是杂食动物，为什么她蹒跚学步的孩子四岁前只吃腰果和花生酱呢？

Human beings seem to be classic *omnivores*. Originally living as "hunter-gatherers," we hunted and fished when possible but also gathered nuts, berries, fruits, seeds, and roots for much of our diet. We're physically well suited for both tasks; our hands are perfect for picking things, and our build is ideal for running down even the fastest game animals because of our great stamina. Some 10,000 years ago humans began practicing agriculture involving both animals and plants. The other *omnivorous* mammals include chimpanzees, pigs, opossums, porcupines, bears, raccoons, skunks, chipmunks, mice and rats, and skunks. But even many mammals classed as *carnivorous* (see VOR, p. 73) turn out to be capable of shifting to plant foods when necessary.

人类似乎是典型的杂食动物。最初，我们过着狩猎和采集的生活，可能的话就打猎、捕鱼，但也采集坚果、浆果、水果、种子和根，作为日常饮食的很大一部分。从身体上来说，我们适合这两个任务；我们的手对采摘来说是完美的，我们的身材对追获最快的猎物来说是理想的，因为我们有巨大的耐力。大约一万年前，人类开始从事包括动物和植物的农业。其他 omnivorous 哺乳动物包括长臂猿、猪、负鼠、豪猪、熊、浣熊、臭鼬、花栗鼠、大小不同的老鼠。但是，即使是很多被归类为 carnivorous（肉食的）（见 VOR，第 73 页）动物，必要时也能转吃植物性食物。

omnipotent \äm-ˈni-pə-tənt\ Having complete or unlimited power; all-powerful. 万能的；无所不能的

• What really scares these men is the nightmare of an omnipotent state, and they think that with their guns they'll be able to keep the government's forces at bay when the time comes. 真正让这些男人害怕的是一个噩梦般的万能社会，他们认为到时候凭着自己的枪支，政府军就难以接近。

If you know that *potens* means "power" in Latin (see POT, p. 557), it's not hard to guess the meaning of *omnipotent*. In Christian services and prayers, the Latin *omnipotens* is translated as "almighty" and always applied to God. But *omnipotence* in a government or ruler is naturally a bit scary; as a British lord observed a century ago, "Power tends to corrupt, and absolute power corrupts absolutely." So democracies do their best to make omnipotence impossible.

如果你知道 potens 在拉丁语中意思是"力量"（见 POT，第 557 页），猜出 omnipotent 的意思并不难。在基督教的宗教仪式和祈祷中，拉丁语的 omnipotens 被翻译成"万能的"，而且几乎总是用在上帝身上。但是政府或者统治者的 omnipotence 自然有些让人害怕，就像一个英国贵族一个世纪前说的，"权力往往使人堕落，绝对的权力绝对使人堕落"。所以，民主国家尽量使 omnipotence 不要存在。

omnibus \ˈäm-ni-bəs\ Of or including many things. 众多事物的；包括众多事物的

• Eager to go home for vacation, Senate leaders assembled an omnibus bill to tie up the loose ends on dozens of unrelated projects. 参议院领导急着回家度假，凑了一个综合议案，以了结很多毫不相干的项目的扫尾工作。

In Latin, *omnibus* means "for all." So an omnibus bill in Congress packages several measures together, an omnibus survey may poll the public on a wide range of issues, and an omnibus edition of a writer's stories may bring together just about all of them. As a noun, *omnibus* used to mean a large vehicle for public transportation—that is, "for all" who could pay the fare—but around 1900 the word began to be shortened to simply *bus*.

在拉丁语中，omnibus 意思是"为所有"。所以，国会的 omnibus（综合）议案将几个提案组合在一起，omnibus（多项）调查就一系列问题对公众进行民意调查，作家的 omnibus（汇编）版会将其所有短篇小说搜集在一起。作为名词，omnibus（公共汽车）曾经的意思是用于公共交通的大型车辆——也就是"为了所有"付得起车费的人——但是大概在 1900 年，这一词语缩略为简单的 bus 了。

OMNI

omniscient \äm-ˈni-shənt\ Knowing everything; having unlimited understanding or knowledge. 无所不知的

● Brought up in a strict Christian family, he knew that an omniscient God was watching him every second of his life. 他在严格的基督教家庭长大，知道无所不知的上帝每一秒都在看着他。

Omniscience is something that a totalitarian state may try to achieve by means of informers, cameras, and monitoring of electronic communication. If your English teacher tells you that a novel has an "omniscient narrator," she means that the voice telling the story isn't one of the characters but instead knows what each of them is doing and thinking, with the point of view constantly shifting from one to another.

Omniscience 是集权国家想通过告密者、照相机和电子交流监控达到的目的。如果英语老师告诉你某一部小说有一个"omniscient narrator"（全知叙述者），她意思是，讲述故事的人不是小说人物，但知道每个人物的所做所想，其观察点从一个人物到另一个人物不断转换。

Quizzes

A. Choose the closest definition:

1. domination a. name b. control c. attraction d. movement
2. omnipotent a. almighty b. all-knowing c. all-seeing d. all-round
3. domineering a. owning b. homelike c. royal d. bossy
4. omniscient a. immense b. all-knowing c. universal d. unlimited
5. dominion a. weakness b. kingdom c. game d. habit
6. omnibus a. immense b. transporting c. all-inclusive d. worldwide
7. predominant a. longest b. lightest c. strongest d. earliest
8. omnivore a. world traveler b. meat- and plant-eater c. universe d. bottom-feeder

B. Complete the analogy:

1. educated : unschooled :: omniscient : _____
   a. commanding b. lazy c. ignorant d. know-it-all
2. selective : limited :: omnibus : _____
   a. everyday b. all-time c. oversized d. comprehensive

3. persuasion : influence :: domination : _____
   a. household   b. country   c. command   d. outlaw
4. weak : feeble :: omnipotent : _____
   a. timid   b. all-powerful   c. global   d. huge
5. obedient : tame :: domineering : _____
   a. sweet   b. easygoing   c. obnoxious   d. controlling
6. human : deer :: omnivore : _____
   a. plant-eater   b. elk   c. ape   d. dieter
7. property : estate :: dominion : _____
   a. attitude   b. difference   c. realm   d. country
8. larger : smaller :: predominant : _____
   a. secondary   b. necessary   c. primary   d. demanding

HOL/HOLO, meaning "whole," comes from the Greek word *holos*, with the same meaning. The root can be found in *catholic*. When capitalized, *Catholic* refers to the worldwide Christian church based in Rome, which was once the "whole"—that is, the only—Christian church. Without the capital letter, *catholic* means simply "universal" or, when describing a person, "broad in one's interests or tastes."

HOL/HOLO 意思是"整个",源自希腊语单词 *holos*,意思相同。这一词根可以在 *catholic*(包罗万象的;广泛的)中看到。第一个字母大写时,Catholic(天主教)指的是总部位于罗马的世界范围的那个基督教会,它曾经是"整个"——也就是唯一的——基督教会。没有这个大写字母, *catholic* 意思很简单,就是"普遍的;广泛的"或者,在描述一个人时,"兴趣活爱好广泛的"。

---

holistic \ hō-'lis-tik \ Relating to or concerned with wholes or with complete systems rather than with the analysis of, treatment of, or dissection into parts. 全体的;整体的

• Environmental scientists tend to be holistic in their views, even when they're only studying a tiny patch of ground. 环境科学家的观点往往是整体性的,即使只是研究一小块地面时也是这样。

"The whole is greater than the sum of its parts" expresses the essence of *holism*, a term coined by the great South African general and statesman Jan Smuts in 1926. Holism generally opposes the Western tendency toward analysis, the breaking down of wholes into parts sometimes to the point that "you can't see the forest for the trees." Holism is an important concept in the sciences and social sciences, and especially in medicine. Holistic medicine tries to treat the "whole person" rather than focusing too narrowly on single symptoms. It emphasizes the connections between the mind and the body, avoids the overuse of drugs, and has borrowed such practices from Eastern traditions as acupuncture and yoga.

"整体大于部分之和"表达了 holism(整体论)的实质内容，holism 一词是 1926 年南非伟大的将军和政治家简·斯默茨创造的。holism 通常反对西方的分析倾向，因为分析将整体分裂为部分，有时候到了"见树不见林"的程度。Holism 在自然科学和社会科学中是一个很重要的概念，在医学中尤其如此。holistic medicine(整体医学)努力治疗"整个人"，而不是狭隘地关注一个个症状。它强调心灵和肉体之间的联系，避免过多使用药物，还从东方传统中借用了针灸和瑜伽这样的做法。

hologram \ˈhō-lə-ˌgram\ A three-dimensional image reproduced from a pattern of interference produced by a beam of radiation such as a laser. 全息图

• When holograms are used for data storage, the entire bulk of the storage material can be used rather than just its surface. 全息图用于数据储存时，全部储存的材料就都可以利用了，而不仅仅是其表面。

A *hologram* is a picture of a "whole" object, showing it in three dimensions. We've all seen cheap *holographic* images on credit cards and ID cards (where they help prevent copying). Far more impressive are large holograms that take the form of a ghostly 3-D moving figure that you can walk around to see from all angles. Holograms were invented in 1947 but only perfected after the invention of the laser in 1960. Today they're used in such technologies as compactdisc players and checkout scanners, and holograms can be created of the inside of live internal organs to permit doctors to examine the organs in great detail. And soon televisions with hologram technology may enable us to watch in "3-D."

hologram 是"整个"事物的图画，以三维来对其进行展示。我们都见过信用卡和身份证(可以有助于防止伪造)上廉价的 *holographic images*(全息图像)。更让人惊叹的是巨大的全息图，是一个幽灵般的三维移动人物，你可以在周围走着从各个角度观看。全息图发明于 1947 年，不过到 1960 年激光发明后才得到改进。今天，全息图用于激光唱机和条码阅读器之类的设备，有生命的内部器官内部的全息图可以让医生仔细检查这些器官。不久，使用全息技术的电视机或许就可以让我们用三维观看了。

Holocene \ˈhō-lə-ˌsēn\ Of, relating to, or being the present geologic epoch. 全新世的

• As the Holocene epoch began, the glaciers were swiftly retreating, forests were taking over the bare land, and human beings were moving northward again in large numbers. 随着全新世的开始，冰川正急剧后退，森林正占领光秃秃的土地，人类又大批正向北迁移了。

To geologists, we live today in the *Holocene epoch*, the period that began about 10,000 years ago, at the end of the last ice age, when humans first began practicing agriculture. But what does *Holocene* have to do with "whole"? Well, in geological language, the Holocene epoch follows the *Paleocene* ("remotely recent"), the *Eocene* ("early recent"), the *Oligocene* ("scarcely recent"), the *Miocene* ("less recent"), the *Pliocene* ("more recent"), and the *Pleistocene* ("most recent") epochs—so the Holocene is the "wholly recent" period of geological time.

对地质学家来说，我们今天生活在 *Holocene epoch*(全新世)。这一时期开始于大约 10,000 年前冰川时代结束时。当时，人类刚刚开始从事农业生产。但是 *Holocene* 为什么跟"全部"有关呢？用地质学语言来说，*Holocene epoch* 在

UNIT 16

Paleocene（古新世）、*Eocene*（始新世）、*Oligocene*（渐新世）和 *Pleistocene*（更新世）之后——所以，*Holocene* 是地质时代上的"全新"时期。

holocaust \hō-lə-ˌkȯst\ (1) (usually capitalized) The mass slaughter of European civilians and especially Jews by the Nazis during World War II. （通常大写）（第二次世界大战期间纳粹对欧洲人尤其是犹太人的）大屠杀 (2) A thorough destruction involving extensive loss of life, especially through fire. （尤其是大火引起的）彻底破坏

• Her parents had escaped the Holocaust in Poland by fleeing into the forest and surviving there with hundreds of others for two years. 她父母逃到了森林里，跟其他数百个人一起活了下来，逃脱了波兰的大屠杀。

The Greek word *holokaustos* means "burnt whole." For the early Jews who followed the laws given in the first books of the Bible, a *holocaust* was a sacrifice to God, the burning on an altar of a lamb, goat, or young bull. The word is used about 200 times in the traditional Greek version of the Old Testament, though it rarely appears in English translations. In the 1700s *holocaust* began to be used to refer to the mass destruction of life. But no mass murder in Western history ever approached the scale achieved by the Nazis. As many as 6 million Jews may have died at their hands; when the slaughter of non-Jews is included, the number of murdered victims may have amounted to over 15 million.

希腊语词语 *holokaustos* 意思是"整个焚烧"。早期犹太人遵守《圣经》前几卷中的法律，对他们来说，holocaust 是向上帝献祭，在祭坛上焚烧羔羊、山羊或者小牛。这一词语在《旧约》的传统的希腊语版本中用了大约二百次，不过在英语版本中很少出现。18 世纪，*holocaust* 开始用来指大批毁灭生命。但是，西方历史上没有哪一次屠杀赶得上纳粹的杀人规模。多达六百万犹太人可能死于他们手下；如果非犹太人包括进去的话，被屠杀者的数目可能高达一千五百万。

RETRO means "back," "backward," or "behind" in Latin. *Retro* in English is generally a prefix, but has also become a word in its own right, usually used to describe old styles or fashions.

RETRO 意思是"回""向后"或者"在……之后"。Retro 在英语中一般情况下是前缀，但本身也成了词语，通常用来描述过时的款式。

retroactive \ˌre-trō-ˈak-tiv\ Intended to apply or take effect at a date in the past. 有追溯效力的；溯及既往的

• The fact that the tax hike was retroactive annoyed the public the most. 增税有追溯效力，这是让公众最生气的。

We normally think of time as constantly moving forward. Since *retroactive* seems to defy time's forward movement, retroactive taxes, laws, and regulations are often seen as particularly obnoxious and unfair. (See also *ex post facto*, p. 68.) But nobody ever objects to receiving a retroactive raise at work. When we judge historical people and events in terms of present-day morality and attitudes, our retroactive judgments may indicate that we're too impressed with ourselves and ignorant of history.

我们通常认为时间是不断前进的。由于 retroactive 似乎藐视时间的前进，具有追溯效力的税、法律和规章制度常常特别令人厌恶、很不公正(亦见 ex post facto，第 68 页)。但是，没有人反对收到追溯的加薪。根据今天的道德和态度去判断历史人物和事件时，我们的追溯判断可能会表明，我们太自以为了不起了，而且对历史一无所知。

retrofit\re-trō-ˌfit\ To furnish something with new or modified parts or equipment that was optional or unavailable at the time of manufacture. 装配新部件(或设备)

• The office building has been retrofitted with air-conditioning，but the result has been a mixed success. 办公楼翻新时装上了空调，但是结果又好又不好。

The concept of *retrofitting* became an urgent necessity during World War II，when weapons technology was advancing at an intense pace and planes and ships were becoming outdated even before their construction was complete，and the only solution was to *retrofit* the completed craft with the brand-new technology. Retrofitting was revived on a massive scale during the energy crisis of the 1970s，when new features were added to millions of old houses to make them more energy-efficient. Retrofitting is thus different from merely *renovating*，which may not involve any new technology at all.

retrofitting 在第二次世界大战期间极其必要。当时，武器技术发展迅猛，飞机和轮船尚未制造完成就已经过时了，唯一的办法，就是为造好的产品配置崭新的部件。在 20 世纪 70 年代的能源危机时期，retrofitting 大规模复苏了。当时，众多旧房屋增加了新特色，使其更加节省能源。于是，retrofitting 跟单纯的 renovating(翻新)是不一样的，因为后者可能根本不涉及新技术。

retrogress\ˌre-trō-ˈgres\ To return to an earlier and usually worse or more primitive state. 退步；倒退

• According to the tests，the sophomores had actually retrogressed in the course of spring term. 根据测试，二年级学生实际上在春季学期成绩有所退步。

As you might guess，*retrogress* is the opposite of *progress*. *Retrogression* is usually an undesirable decline from a higher or advanced level. So，for instance，in difficult social situations an adolescent can retrogress to a childish level of maturity. And under the extreme conditions of total war，a whole society may retrogress to a primitive state. The increasing number of poor or homeless people has been seen as evidence of modern social retrogression，and the rise of loud，name-calling TV and radio personalities strikes many people as a sign of political retrogression.

你可以猜到，retrogress 是 progress 的反义词。retrogression 通常是人们不想看到的高水平的下降。所以，比如在不同的社交场合，一位青少年可能还不如小时候成熟。在全面战争这一极端情况下，整个社会可能会倒退到很落后的状态。穷人和无家可归者越来越多，一直被视为现代社会倒退的证明。电视和电台名人咋咋呼呼、满嘴脏话，让很多人感到这是政治倒退的迹象。

retrospective\ˌre-trə-ˈspek-tiv\ A generally comprehensive exhibition or performance usually covering an artist's output to date. (艺术家作品的)回顾展

- A retrospective covering the photographer's entire career is forcing critics to revise their earlier estimates of her status as an artist. 一个涵盖她整个摄影生涯的回顾展，使评论家不得不改变原来对她作为艺术家地位的估计。

Retrospective is partly rooted in the Latin verb *specere*, "to look," so a retrospective is a look back at an artist's career. The subject of a retrospective is usually an older living artist, or one who has recently died. Galleries and museums honor painters and sculptors, film festivals honor directors and actors, and concert organizations honor composers. Retrospectives can be difficult and expensive to assemble, so they're rarely put together except for deserving artists; the result is that they frequently win many new fans for the person's achievement.

retrospective 的一部分词根是拉丁语动词 *specere*（"看"），所以，retrospective 就是对艺术家生涯的回顾。回顾展的对象往往是一位在世的老年艺术家，或者最近去世的艺术家。画廊和博物馆向画家和雕刻家致敬，电影节向导演和演员致敬，音乐会机构向作曲家致敬。组织一场回顾展很困难，也很花钱，所以，除了为了劳苦功高的艺术家，人们很少这样做。回顾展的结果，往往是为该人的成就赢得了很多新的粉丝。

Quizzes

A. Fill in each blank with the correct letter:

a. retrospective   e. hologram
b. holistic   f. retrogress
c. retrofit   g. Holocene
d. holocaust   h. retroactive

1. She turns 70 this year, and the museum is honoring her with a huge _____.

2. He likes wearing a T-shirt with a large _____ on the chest and watching people's reactions to the way it changes as they walk by.

3. The navy plans to _____ a fleet of 25-year-old ships to increase their speed and monitoring capacity.

4. His doctor favors a _____ approach to achieving wellness, but she'll prescribe standard drugs for serious illnesses.

5. In *Lord of the Flies*, a group of English schoolboys manages to _____ to a barely civilized state within a few months.

6. There are still a few hunting-and-gathering tribes on earth who live the way all of humankind lived at the beginning of the _____.

7. Although the tax increase wasn't passed until June, its effect was _____ to the first of the year.

8. The creation of the United Nations was intended to, among other things, prevent another _____ from ever occurring.

B. Match the word on the left to the correct definition on the right:

1. retrogress   a. 3-D image
2. holocaust   b. effective as of earlier

3. retrospective
4. retrofit
5. holistic
6. Holocene
7. retroactive
8. hologram

c. mass destruction
d. concerned with the whole
e. review of a body of work
f. revert to an earlier state
g. current human era
h. modernize

TEMPOR comes from the Latin *tempus*, meaning "time." A *temporary* repair is meant to last only a short time. The *tempo*, or speed, of a country-and-western ballad is usually different from that of a hip-hop number. The Latin phrase *Tempus fugit* means "Time flies," an observation that seems more true during summer vacation than in the dead of winter.

TEMPOR 源自拉丁语 *tempus*("时间")。*temporary* 修理只持续很短的时间。乡村和西部民谣的 *tempo*，或者速度，通常与嘻哈歌曲的不一样。拉丁语短语 *Tempus fugit* 意思是"时间飞逝"。这一说法在暑假期间似乎比在寒冬期间更为正确。

---

temporal \ ˈtem-pə-rəl \ (1) Having to do with time as opposed to eternity; having to do with earthly life as opposed to heavenly existence. 时间有限的；凡间生活的；尘世的 (2) Having to do with time as distinguished from space. 时间的（而非空间的）

• The quick passing of the seasons as we grow older makes us feel the fleeting nature of temporal existence. 随着我们的成长，季节飞逝，让我们感到凡间生存的短暂。

Temporal existence is often contrasted with spiritual existence, which many religions teach is eternal. The American system of government features a separation of church and state—that is, a separation of spiritual and temporal authority. But such separation is relatively recent. In past centuries, the Roman Catholic Church exerted temporal authority—that is, political power—throughout much of Europe, and the Church of England has always been officially headed by the temporal ruler of Great Britain. Temporal isn't always used in religious contexts; for example, child psychologists often measure "temporal processing"—that is, speed of thinking—in children with mental difficulties. Note that temporal may also mean "near the temples (of the head)"; thus, your brain's temporal lobes are situated at your temples. But this temporal is based on a different Latin root.

尘世间的生存往往与精神的存在形成对比，因为很多宗教教导我们，后者是永恒的。美国政府体制的特点是政教分离，也就是说，精神和尘世的权力是分开的。但是，这样的分离相对来说是最近的事情。在过去多个世纪，罗马天主教会在整个欧洲实施的是尘世的权力，也就是政治权力，而英国国教的正式首领一直是大不列颠王国的尘世领袖。*temporal* 并不总是用于宗教语境，比如儿童心理学家经常测量有智力问题的儿童的 "temporal processing"，也就是思考速度。注意，*temporal* 的意思也可以是 "在太阳穴附近"，所以，你大脑的 *temporal lobes*（颞叶）在太阳穴那里。但是，这个 *temporal* 以另一个拉丁语词根为基础。

contemporary \kən-'tem-pə-ˌrer-ē\ (1) Occurring or existing during the same period of time. 同一时期的 (2) Having to do with the present period; modern or current. 当代的;当前的

• The two scientists were contemporary with each other, but neither seemed to have heard of the other's existence. 两位科学家生活在同一时期,但是谁也没有听说过对方的存在。

Contemporary can be confusing because of its slightly different meanings. In everyday use, it generally means simply "modern" or "new." But before the 20th century it instead referred only to things from the same era as certain other things; so, for instance, Jesus was contemporary with the Roman emperors Augustus and Tiberius, and Muhammad was contemporary with Pope Gregory the Great. And *contemporary* is also a noun; thus, Jane Austen's *contemporaries* included Coleridge and Wordsworth, and your own contemporaries were born around the same year that you were.

contemporary 让人迷惑,因为它与其他意思稍有不同。在日常使用中,它通常的意思很简单,就是"当代的"或者"新的"。但在 20 世纪之前,它仅仅指的是与其他事物同一时代的事物;所以,比如耶稣与罗马皇帝奥古斯都和提比略生活在同一时期,穆罕默德与教皇格列高利一世生活在同一时期。contemporary 也用作名词,这样,简·奥斯汀的 *contemporaries* 包括柯勒律治和华兹华斯,你的 *contemporaries* 和你出生年份基本一样。

extemporaneous \ek-ˌstem-pə-'rā-nē-əs\ (1) Composed, performed, spoken, or done on the spur of the moment; impromptu or improvised. 即兴的;即席的;临场的;没有准备的 (2) Carefully prepared but delivered without notes. (精心准备但)脱稿的;不用讲稿的

• It was once common in middle-class homes to make extemporaneous speeches, recite poetry, and give little solo song recitals after a dinner with guests. 在中产阶级家庭中,做即兴演讲、背诵诗歌,以及在与客人共进晚餐后进行小型独唱,曾经是很常见的。

• The ability to speak well *extemporaneously* is an important talent for politicians, especially when participating in debates. (Though it's also a good idea to have a "spin doctor" who can go out afterward and tell everyone what the candidate *really* meant to say.) Some people claim there's a difference between *extemporaneous* and *impromptu*, saying that an extemporaneous speech is planned beforehand but not written down, while an impromptu speech is genuinely unprepared or off-the-cuff, but today the two words are mostly used as synonyms.

extemporaneously 讲话的本领是政治家的重要能力,尤其是参加辩论时。(不过,能有一个舆论导向专家,后来出去告诉大家候选人 *really*[真的]想说什么,也是个不错的主意。)有些人声称,*extemporaneous* 和 *impromptu* 是有区别的,一个 *extemporaneous* 演讲是事先准备好但没有写下来,而一个 *impromptu* 演讲是真的没有事先准备或者未经思考,但是今天,这两个词语多数时候是当作同义词使用的。

TEMPOR

temporize \'tem-pə-ˌrīz\ (1) To act in a way that fits the time or occasion; to give way to current opinion. 随潮流;见风使舵 (2) To draw out discussions to gain time. 拖延

• The legislature was accused of temporizing while the budget deficit continued to worsen. 人们指责立法机构在预算赤字持续恶化时拖延时间。

The Latin word that *temporize* comes from meant simply "to pass the time"; the meaning of the English word is different but obviously related. People aren't usually admired for temporizing. A political leader faced with a difficult issue may temporize by talking vaguely about possible solutions without actually doing anything. The point is to avoid taking an action that lots of people aren't going to like, in hopes that the problem will somehow go away, but the effect is often just to make matters worse.

衍生出 *temporize* 一词的拉丁语词语意思很简单,就是"打发时间";这个英语单词的意思则不同,但是显然有联系。人们常常并不会因为拖延时间受人敬佩。面临困难问题的政治家,可能会含糊其辞地谈论可能的解决办法,但不会真正采取什么措施,以此拖延时间。这么做的关键是避免采取很多人不会喜欢的行动,希望这一问题会不知怎么就消失了,但是结果往往会使情况更糟糕。

CHRON comes from the Greek word for "time." A *chronicle* records the events of a particular time, which is why so many newspapers have the name *Chronicle*. A *chronometer* is a device for measuring time, usually one that's more accurate (and more expensive) than an ordinary watch or clock.

CHRON源自希腊语中表示"时间"的那个词语。*chronicle*(编年史)记录某个特定时间发生的那些事件,因此很多报纸都取名为 *Chronicle*。*chronometer*(精密计时表)是一个测量时间的仪器,通常比普通的手表或钟表更准确。

---

chronic \\ˈkrä-nik\\ (1) Lasting a long time or recurring frequently. 慢性的;复发的 (2) Always present; constantly annoying or troubling; habitual. 一直有的;一直令人厌烦的;习惯性的

- He had stopped to pick up ice-cream cones for the kids, hoping it would give him a temporary rest from their chronic bickering. 他停下来给孩子买了蛋卷冰淇淋,希望他们停止吵闹,让他有片刻安宁。

Chronic coughing goes on and on; chronic lateness occurs day after day; chronic lameness never seems to get any better. Unfortunately, situations that we call chronic almost always seem to be unpleasant. We never hear about chronic peace, but we do hear about chronic warfare. And we never speak of chronic health, only of chronic illness.

chronic(慢性)咳嗽绵延不断;chronic(习惯性的)迟到每天发生;chronic(长期的)跛足似乎永远没有什么好转。不幸的是,我们称为 chronic 的情况似乎总是令人讨厌的。我们从未听到过有谁说 chronic 和平,但是的确听到过有人说 chronic 战争。我们从不说 chronic 健康,只会说 chronic 病。

chronology \\krə-ˈnä-lə-jē\\ (1) A sequence of events in the order they occurred. 年表;按发生时间顺序的一系列事件 (2) A table, list, or account that presents events in order. 事件顺序表

- The scandal had gotten so complex that the newspaper had to print a chronology showing the order of the numerous events involved. 丑闻变得太复杂了,以至于这

家报纸不得不印出一个时间顺序表,展示涉及的众多事件的顺序。

History is much more than a simple *chronology* of events, but keeping events in *chronological* order is the first essential step in thinking about it. When, for example, historians try to show how World War I prepared the way for World War II, tracking the chronology of the events in the years between the two wars can help in explaining a complicated historical era.

历史远远不止是一个简单时间顺序表,但是在思考历史的时候,按 *chronological*(按时间顺序的)顺序编排事件是第一个重要步骤。比如,当历史学家想要展示第一次世界大战如何为第二次世界大战铺平道路时,追踪两次战争期间的事件发生的顺序,有助于解释这个复杂的历史时代。

anachronism \ə-ˈna-krə-ˌni-zəm\ (1) The error of placing a person or thing in the wrong time period. 时代错误 (2) A person or thing that is out of its own time. 不在自己时代的人或物

• A Model T Ford putt-putting down the highway at 25 miles per hour was an anachronism by 1940. 一辆 1940 年的福特 T 型车,以每小时 25 英里的速度,嘟嘟嘟嘟沿着公路行驶,与今天这个时代很不相称。

In Shakespeare's time, playwrights didn't worry much about *anachronisms*. When Shakespeare saw his plays performed, all the characters, even Romans and Greeks, would have been dressed in the clothes of his own period. *Macbeth*, which is set in the 11th century, contains *anachronistic* references to clocks and cannons, which the real Macbeth would have known nothing about. Today, a writer may spend months doing research in order to avoid anachronisms in the historical novel she's working on. Using the second meaning of the word, we could say that manual typewriters and slide rules are anachronisms in these days of computers and calculators, and a person who likes doing things the old-fashioned way might himself be described as an anachronism.

在莎士比亚时代,戏剧家不担心时代错误。莎士比亚看到自己的剧本演出时,所有的人物,甚至是古罗马人和古希腊人,都能穿着他那个时代的服装。《麦克白》的时代背景是 11 世纪,里面包含了 *anachronistic*(时代错误的)钟表和大炮,而这些东西,真正的麦克白根本不知道。今天,一位作家如果正在写一部历史小说,可能花上几个月时间从事研究工作,以免发生时代错误。使用该词第二个意思,我们可以说手动打字机和滑尺在今天这个电脑时代都是 anachronisms(不符合时代的事物)。一个喜欢用老办法做事的人本身也可以说是个 anachronism(不合潮流的人)。

synchronous \ˈsiŋ-krə-nəs\ (1) Happening or existing at exactly the same time; simultaneous. 同时发生的;同时存在的;同时的 (2) Recurring or acting at exactly the same intervals. 同周期的

• The theory depends on whether the chemical appeared in synchronous deposits worldwide seven million years ago. 这一理论成败与否,要看七百万年前这一化学物质是否出现在世界各地的同步沉积层中。

Communications satellites are usually put into a *synchronous* (or *geosynchronous*) orbit, circling the earth once every 24 hours and so appearing to hover over a single spot on the surface. This type of *synchronized* movement is important, since you have to know where to aim your satellite dish. In the computer field, *synchronous* usually refers to the use of a simple timing signal that permits very rapid exchange of data between computers. The kind of mysterious coincidence sometimes called *synchronicity*—such as the appearance of two different comic-book characters named Dennis the Menace in the U. S. and Britain within three days of each other in 1951—has fascinated people for centuries.

通信卫星通常被放入 synchronous（同步的）（或者 geosynchronous，对地同步的）轨道，二十四小时环绕地球，所以看起来似乎停留在地球表面同一地点的上空。这种类型的 synchronized（同步的）运动很重要，因为你必须知道朝哪里对准你的圆盘式卫星电视天线。在计算机领域，synchronous 通常指使用一个简单的定时信号，它能让电脑之间进行快速信息交流。有时被称为 synchronicity（同时性；同时发生）的那种神秘巧合，几个世纪以来一直让人很感兴趣。比如在 1951 年，有两个都叫淘气阿丹的漫画书人物，三天之内出现在美国和英国。

Quizzes

A. Complete the analogy：

1. antique : ancient :: contemporary : _____
   a. simultaneous   b. modern   c. fragile   d. warped
2. foreigner : country :: anachronism : _____
   a. antique   b. novelty   c. watch   d. time period
3. argue : agree :: temporize : _____
   a. discuss   b. negotiate   c. conclude   d. grow cold
4. drama : scenes :: chronology : _____
   a. events   b. clock   c. length   d. sequence
5. sudden : expected :: extemporaneous : _____
   a. sudden   b. rehearsed   c. off-the-cuff   d. off-the-wall
6. infrequent : occasional :: chronic : _____
   a. short   b. surprising   c. continuous   d. noisy
7. temporary : enduring :: temporal : _____
   a. modern   b. existing   c. arising   d. eternal
8. amorphous : shapeless :: synchronous : _____
   a. simultaneous   b. in sequence   c. out of order   d. always late

B. Match the word on the left to the correct definition on the right：

1. chronic   a. current
2. temporal   b. order of events
3. anachronism   c. ongoing
4. extemporaneous   d. happening at the same time
5. synchronous   e. talk to fill time
6. temporize   f. improvised
7. chronology   g. measurable by time

8. contemporary   h. misplacement in time

Number Words 数字词语

TRI means "three," whether derived from Greek or Latin. A *tricycle* has three wheels. A *triangle* has three sides and three angles. And a *triumvirate* is a board or government of three people.
TRI 不论源自希腊语还是拉丁语，意思都是"三"。tricycle(三轮车)有三个轮子。triangle(三角形)有三条边和三个角。triumvirate(三人领导小组)是三个人组成的理事会或者政府。

---

triad\ˈtrī-ˌad\   (1) A group of three usually related people or things. 三人组合，三人小组；三件一套(或组)；三位一体 (2) A secret Chinese criminal organization. 三合会(中国第一个秘密犯罪组织)

• The kids in the garage band next door seemed to know six or seven triads and a couple of seventh chords. 隔壁车库乐队的孩子们似乎知道六七个三和弦和两三个七和弦。

The best-known type of *triad* is a type of musical chord consisting of three notes. A D-major triad is made up of the notes D, F-sharp, and A; an F-minor triad is made up of F, A-flat, and C; and so on. Major and minor triads form the basis of tonal music, and songs and other pieces usually end with a *triadic* harmony. In medicine, a triad is a set of three symptoms that appear together.
最有名的 triad 类型就是一种由三个音符构成的和弦。D 大三和弦由 D, F 升 A 三个音符构成，F 大三和弦由 F、降 A 和 C 构成，等等。大三和弦和小三和弦构成了调性音乐的基础，歌曲和其他乐曲通常以一个 *triadic harmony*(三和弦)结束。在医学上，triad(三征)就是同时出现的三个的症状。

trilogy\ˈtri-lə-jē\   A series of three creative works that are closely related and develop a single theme. 三部曲；三联剧

• William Faulkner's famous "Snopes trilogy" consists of the novels *The Hamlet*, *The Town*, and *The Mansion*. 威廉·福克纳著名的《斯诺普斯三部曲》由《村子》《小镇》《大宅》三部小说组成。

Dozens of tragic *trilogies* were written for the Greek stage, though only one, Aeschylus's great *Oresteia* (consisting of *Agamemnon*, *The Libation Bearers*, and *The Eumenides*), has survived complete. Authors in later years have occasionally chosen to create trilogies to allow themselves to develop a highly complex story or cover a long span of time. Tolkien's *Lord of the Rings* wasn't actually intended as a trilogy, but since it was published in three volumes it's usually called one. George Lucas's three original *Star Wars* movies are an example of a film trilogy (which he followed many years later by another).

希腊戏剧有很多悲剧三联剧，不过只有一个完整保留下来了，那就是埃斯库罗斯的《奥瑞斯提亚》(由《阿伽门农》《奠酒人》和《报仇神》组成)。后来的作者偶尔决定创造三部曲，让自己叙述一个非常复杂的故事，或者时间跨度很长的故事。托尔金的《指环王》本来并不是要成为三部曲的，但是，由于它出版时有三册，也就被称为三部曲了。乔治·卢卡斯的三部新颖的《星球大战》电影是电影三部曲的一个例子(多年后他又指导了一个)。

triceratops \ ˌtrī-ˈser-ə-ˌtäps \ One of a group of large dinosaurs that lived during the Cretaceous period and had three horns, a bony crest or hood, and hoofed toes. 三角恐龙(生活在白垩纪的巨大恐龙)

• The triceratops probably used its three horns for defense against the attacks of meat-eating dinosaurs. 三角恐龙可能用自己的三个角抵抗食肉恐龙的袭击。

The name *triceratops*, meaning literally "three-horned face," refers to the two horns above its eyes and the smaller third horn on its snout. Just as striking was the frilled hood or ruff that rose behind its head, though no one is quite sure what it was for. The triceratops was one of the last dinosaurs to evolve and also one of the last to become extinct. It could reach lengths of 30 feet and could stand nearly eight feet high. Despite its ferocious looks and three-foot-long horns, the triceratops was actually a vegetarian.

triceratops 这个名字的字面意思是"三个角的脸"，指的是三角恐龙眼睛上方的两个角和鼻子上的一个角。同样引人注意的是其头部后边立起的颈部褶边，不过谁也无法确定其用途。三角恐龙是最后演化出来的恐龙之一，也是最后灭绝的恐龙之一。它身长可达三十英尺，身高将近八英尺。虽然它样子凶猛，而且有三英尺长的角，但三角恐龙实际上食草动物。

trident \ ˈtri-dənt \ A three-pronged spear, especially one carried by various sea gods in classical mythology. 三叉戟

• The bronze statue at the middle of the great fountain depicted a sea god emerging from the water, wreathed in seaweed and carrying a large trident. 这个大喷泉中央的青铜雕像，描绘的是一个从水中出现的海神，身上挂着海草，手握一把巨大的三叉戟。

A *trident* has three prongs or teeth, as the root *dent*, "tooth," tells us. The trident has long been used to spear fish in different parts of the world, so there's no mystery about why the Greek sea god Poseidon and his Roman counterpart Neptune both carry a trident as their symbol. In some gladiator exhibitions in ancient Rome, one gladiator, called a *retiarius* ("net man"), would be equipped as though he were a fisherman, with a weighted net and a trident; with his net he would snare his sword-wielding opponent, and with his trident he would spear his helpless foe.

trident 有三个叉齿，就像 *dent*("牙齿")这一词根告诉我们的那样。三叉戟长久以来就在世界各地用来插鱼，所以，希腊神话中的海神波塞冬以及他在罗马神话中对应的尼普顿，都拿着三叉戟作为其象征符号，也就不难理解了。在古罗马某些角斗士表演中有一个被称为 *retiarius*("网人")的角斗士，其装备就是要让他看起来似乎是个渔民，拿着一个带铅块的渔网和一把三叉戟。他用渔网捉住舞剑的对手，用三叉戟猛插那个无助的敌人。

trimester \ trī-ˈmes-tər \ (1) A period of about three months, especially one of three such periods in a human pregnancy. 三个月(尤指妊娠期三个阶段中的一个) (2) One of three terms into which an academic year is sometimes divided. (三学期制的)一学期

• Most women experience morning sickness in the first trimester of pregnancy.

大多数妇女在怀孕的前三个月会有恶心现象。

Semester, which comes from the Latin words for "six" and "month," has come to mean half an academic year when the year is divided into two segments. When an academic year is divided into three segments, each is called a trimester (which is usually a bit more accurate, since each segment often is close to three months in length). Some colleges operate on the "quarter" system, with the summer being the fourth quarter, but this just means that each quarter is basically a trimester. In a human pregnancy, a trimester is three months long, representing one-third of the nine months that a typical pregnancy lasts.

semester 源自拉丁语中表示"六"和"月"的两个词语。这个单词逐渐表示一年分成两个学期时的半个学年。当一个学年分成三部分时,每一个叫做 trimester(这通常更准确一些,因为每个部分常常更接近三个月)。有些大学实施"学季"制度,夏天是第四个学季,但是这仅仅意味着每个学季基本上是一个 trimester。在人类妊娠过程中,trimester 是三个月,代表正常孕期九个月的三分之一。

trinity \ˈtri-nə-tē\ (1) (capitalized) The unity of Father, Son, and Holy Spirit as three persons in one God in Christian belief. (基督教的)三位一体 (2) A group of three people. 三人组

• In Christian art depicting the Trinity, the Holy Spirit is almost always shown as a radiant dove. 在描绘三位一体的基督教艺术中,圣灵几乎总是显示为光芒四射的鸽子。

The nature of the Trinity (or Holy Trinity) has caused centuries of argument and division within the Christian faith. The word doesn't actually appear in the Bible itself, but the New Testament does speak of the Father, Son, and Holy Spirit together; the Father is understood as the protector of the Jews, the Son as the savior of mankind, and the Holy Spirit as the preserver of the church. Almost all the major Christian sects may be called *trinitarian*. The island of Trinidad is one of many places named with the Spanish translation of *Trinity*.

Trinity 的性质已经在基督教这一信仰内引发了几个世纪的争吵和分裂。这一词语实际上并未出现在《圣经》中,但是《新约》的确说到了圣父、圣子和圣灵一体。圣父被理解为犹太人的保护者,圣子被理解为人类的拯救者,圣灵被理解为这一宗教的保护者。几乎所有主要的基督教教派都可以说是 trinitarian(信奉三位一体论的)。Trinidad(特立尼达)这一岛屿是用 Trinity 的西班牙语对应词命名的诸多地方之一。

triptych \ˈtrip-tik\ (1) A picture or carving made in the form of three panels side by side. 三联画 (2) Something composed or presented in three sections. 三部相联的艺术作品

• The Renaissance produced many beautiful triptychs portraying religious scenes that are still used as altarpieces. 文艺复兴产生了诸多描绘宗教场景的三联画,至今仍用作圣坛画。

Triptych contains the root -*ptyche*, the Greek word for "fold." So a traditional painted or carved triptych has three hinged panels, and the two outer panels fold in toward the central one. Most triptychs were intended to be mounted over a church altar. Many great triptychs were produced in the Renaissance, perhaps the most famous being Hieronymus Bosch's *Garden of Earthly Delights*. But major triptychs continued to be produced throughout the 20th century by such painters as Francis Bacon.

triptych 一词包含词根-*pthche*(希腊语,"折叠")。所以,传统的绘画或者雕刻的三联画有合叶连起来的三个方形板子,外侧的两个朝中间的那个折叠。大多数三联画都是为了被用来固定在教堂圣坛的上方。很多伟大的三联画都是文艺复兴时期产生的,可能最著名的是耶罗尼米斯·博斯的《人间乐园》。但是,在整个 20 世纪,弗朗西斯·培根这样的画家继续创作了重要的三联画。

trivial \ˈtri-vē-əl\ Of little value or importance. 没什么价值的;不重要的;不值一提的;琐碎的

• She was so caught up in the trivial details of the trip that she hardly noticed the beautiful scenery. 她只顾忙于这次旅行的琐碎小事,几乎没有注意到美景。

Trivial comes from a Latin word meaning "crossroads"—that is, where three roads come together. Since a crossroads is a very public place where all kinds of people might show up, *trivialis* came to mean "commonplace" or "vulgar." Today the English word has changed slightly in meaning and instead usually describes something barely worth mentioning. Mathematicians use the word to refer to some part of a proof or definition that's extremely simple and needn't be explained, but the rest of us tend to use it just to mean "unimportant." "Small talk" at a party, for example, is usually trivial conversation, though a trivial excuse for not going on a date ("I have to wash my hair") might hide an emotion that isn't so trivial ("I can't stand the sight of you"). To *trivialize* something is to treat it as if it didn't matter, as if it were just another *triviality*.

trivial 源自拉丁语中表示"十字路口"的一个词语。交叉路口就是三条路相遇汇聚的地方。交叉路口是繁忙的公共场所,各种人都会出现,所以,*trivialis* 后来的意思是"普通"或者"粗俗"。今天,这个英语单词的意思稍微有些变化,通常描述几乎不值一提的事物。数学家用这一词语来指算或定义的某个非常简单、无须解释的部分。不过,其他人往往用它只是表示"不重要的"。比如聚会上的"闲聊"通常都是不重要谈话,但是拒绝参加约会的不重要的借口("我得洗头"),则可能隐藏着不那么无足轻重的情绪("我看到你就受不了")。*trivialize* 某物就是不把它当回事,好像它就是另外一件 *triviality*(琐事)。

Quizzes

Choose the closest definition:

1. trimester a. a three-masted sailing ship
   b. a period of about three months c. a three-cornered hat
   d. a three-minute egg
2. trivial a. crossed b. indented
   c. unimportant d. found
3. triad a. three-striped flag
   b. three-headed monster c. three-note chord
   d. three-month delay
4. trinity a. romantic triangle

b. three-part recipe
c. group of three
d. triplets
5. trident
a. three-toothed hag
b. three-pronged spear
c. triple portion
d. threesome
6. trilogy
a. three-person conversation
b. three-hour nap
c. three-volume story
d. three-ton truck
7. triceratops
a. three-foot alligator
b. three-set tennis match
c. three-topped tree
d. three-horned dinosaur
8. triptych
a. three-week travel voucher
b. three-part painting
c. three-phase rocket
d. three-handed clock

Review Quizzes

A. Fill in each blank with the correct letter:

a. topical
b. contemporary
c. temporize
d. synchronous
e. topiary
f. epicenter
g. dominion
h. chronic
i. retrofit
j. trivial
k. eccentric
l. retroactive
m. extemporaneous
n. predominant
o. trilogy

1. She constantly assured her employees that their opinions were never _____ or unimportant.

2. England, though a small nation, once had _____ over a great empire.

3. It cost millions to _____ each fighter jet with new navigational instruments.

4. For high-school dancers, their movements were remarkably _____.

5. When the last volume of her _____ was published, her fans snapped it up eagerly.

6. Before beginning to drill, the dentist applies a _____ anesthetic.

7. The doctor told him his condition was _____ and untreatable but not life-threatening.

8. Having left his notes at home, he had to give an entirely _____ lecture.

9. The book was criticized for having too many subjects and no _____ theme.

10. The city maintains a small _____ garden full of trees and bushes in all sorts of shapes.

11. No matter how long you _____ and stall for time, the problem won't go away.

12. Since his salary review was delayed by a few weeks, his boss made the raise _____ to the beginning of the month.

13. His habit of wearing purple socks and white sneakers to the office was considered harmlessly _____.

14. Several other great Dutch artists were _____ with Rembrandt.

15. She works hard at being outrageous, and it's not the first time she's been at the _____ of a controversy.

B. Choose the closest definition:

1. egocentric   a. group-centered   b. centered on the mind
    c. self-centered   d. mentally ill.
2. retrofit   a. insert   b. dress up
    c. update   d. move back
3. retrospective   a. backward glance   b. exhibit of an artist's work
    c. illusion of depth   d. difference of opinion
4. anachronism   a. electronic clock   b. literary theory
    c. misplacement in time   d. current topic
5. triceratops   a. winged dragon   b. dinosaur
    c. three-part work   d. climbing gear
6. triad   a. triplet   b. chord   c. third rail
    d. three-pointed star
7. temporal   a. religious   b. ideal   c. time-related
    d. durable
8. holistic   a. wholesome   b. herbal   c. complete
    d. whole-oriented
9. ectopic   a. amazing   b. current   c. reserved
    d. out of place
10. triptych   a. three-part painting   b. triple window
    c. computer switch   d. multivolume work

C. Match each word on the left to the correct definition on the right:

1. Holocene   a. land's features
2. predominant   b. group-centered
3. retrogress   c. three-pronged spear
4. domination   d. principal

5. chronology
6. ethnocentric
7. trimester
8. topography
9. trinity
10. trident

e. group of three
f. go backward
g. order of events
h. school-year term
i. recent era
j. control

UNIT 17

ANIM comes from the Latin *anima*, meaning "breath" or "soul." So, for example, an *animal* is a living, breathing thing—though human animals have often argued about whether other species actually have souls.
ANIM 源自拉丁语 anima（呼吸或灵魂）。所以，比如 animal（动物）指的是一个活着的、会呼吸的事物，不过人类这种动物曾常常就其他物种是否有灵魂进行辩论。

animated \ˈa-nə-ˌmā-təd\ (1) Full of life; lively, vigorous, active. 充满生命力的，活泼的，活跃的 (2) Seeming or appearing to be alive. 似乎是活着的

• Her gestures as she talked were so animated that even people across the room were watching her. 她说话时的手势非常活泼，甚至连房间另一头的人都在看着她。

Animated cartoon characters have been "given life" by film techniques, though the *animation* of drawings actually goes back to handheld toys in the 1830s. A child watching the cartoon may also be animated—squealing, laughing, and jumping around—as can a crowd of hockey fans or a rock-concert audience. And the best discussions and arguments are often highly animated.
动画片中的人物被电影技术"赋予生命"了，不过图画 animaition（被赋予生命）可以追溯到 19 世纪 30 年代的手握玩偶。看动画片的孩子也可以是 animated（活跃的）——尖叫、大笑、跳来跳去——就像一群曲棍球粉丝或者摇滚音乐会观众那样。最好的讨论和争论通常都是极其 animated（热烈的）。

magnanimous \mag-ˈna-nə-məs\ (1) Showing a lofty and courageous spirit. 高尚的；有勇气的 (2) Generous and forgiving. 宽宏大度的

• She was magnanimous in victory, saying she'd been lucky to win and praising her opponent's effort. 她取胜时表现得很高尚，说赢了是运气好，还赞扬了对手所付出的努力。

The basic meaning of *magnanimity* is "greatness of spirit." Thus, magnanimity is the opposite of pettiness or "smallness." A truly magnanimous person can lose without complaining and win without gloating. Angry disputes can sometimes be resolved when one side makes a magnanimous gesture toward the other. And it's the mark of magnanimity to give credit to everyone who worked on a project even if you'd rather it all went to you.

magnanimity 的基本意思是"精神的伟大",因此 magnanimity 就是小气或者"渺小"的反义词。一个真正崇高的人输了不怨天尤人,赢了不洋洋自得。愤怒的争论,如果一方对另一方做出高尚的姿态,有时就可以得到解决。即使你宁愿某个项目的重担几乎全部落在你肩上,也要对付出努力的每一个人表示赞扬,这是高尚的标志。

animosity \ˌa-nə-ˈmä-sə-tē\ Ill will or resentment. 恶意;愤恨;仇

- Legend has it that the animosity between the Greeks and the Trojans began with the stealing of the beautiful Helen from her husband, Menelaus. 根据传说,希腊人和特罗伊人之间的愤恨之情的原因是美丽的海伦被人从她丈夫那里偷走了。

The important Latin word *animus* (very closely related to *anima*) could mean a great many things having to do with the soul and the emotions, one of them being "anger." As an English word, *animus* has generally meant "ill will," so it isn't mysterious that *animosity* means basically the same thing. Animosity can exist between two people, two groups or organizations, or two countries, and can sometimes lie hidden for years before reappearing. The deep animosities that exist between certain ethnic and religious groups sometimes seem as if they will last forever.

animus(跟 anima 有紧密联系)是一个重要的拉丁语单词。它可以表示许许多多东西,都与灵魂和情绪有关,其中之一是"愤怒"。作为英语单词,animus 通常的意思是"恶意,仇恨",所以,animosity 基本上表示同样的意思,并不难以理解。animosity 可以存在于两个人、两个群体、两个组织或者两个国家之间,有时也可以隐藏多年才会再次出现。某些种族和宗教群体之间深深的 animosities(仇恨)似乎永远不会消除。

inanimate \i-ˈna-nə-mət\ (1) Not alive; lifeless. 没有生命的;死的 (2) Not lively; dull. 不活泼的;沉闷的

- The sculptures of Rodin are so expressive that, although inanimate, they seem full of life and emotion. The couch you sit on while you watch TV is an inanimate object, as is your footrest, your bag of snacks, and your remote control. Spend too much time on that couch and you risk becoming a couch potato. (A potato is an inanimate object.)

罗丹的雕塑虽是没有生命的,但都极富表现力,充满生机,饱含情绪。你看电视坐的沙发是没有生命的,脚凳、你那一袋零食、遥控器都是如此。在沙发上花时间太多,就有可能变成沙发土豆(土豆是没有生命的东西)。

FIG comes from a Latin verb meaning "to shape or mold" and a noun meaning "a form or shape." So a *figure* is usually a shape. A *transfiguration* transforms the shape or appearance of something. And a *disfiguring* injury changes the appearance of part of the body for the worse.

FIG 源自拉丁语中一个表示"塑造"的动词和一个表示"形式或形状"的名词。所以,一个 figure 通常是一个形状。一次 transfiguration(变形)会改变某一事物的形状或者外表。一次 disfiguring(损毁外表)伤会使身体一部分的外表变得难看。

figurative\ˈfi-gyù-rə-tiv\ (1) Representing form or figure in art. 形式的；形状的 (2) Saying one thing in terms normally meaning or describing another thing. 比喻的

• When the poet says he's been living in the desert, it's a figurative reference to his emotional life. 当诗人说他一直生活在沙漠中时,这是对他情感生活的比喻。

Words and phrases can have both literal and *figurative* meanings, and we all use words with both kinds of meanings every day of our lives. We can literally close the door to a room, or we can *figuratively* close the door to further negotiations—that is, refuse to take part in them. Figurative language includes *figures of speech*, such as similes ("she's been like a sister to me") and metaphors ("a storm of protest"). And sometimes it's hard to tell whether a phrase is literal or figurative: If I say I "*picked up*" a little Spanish in Mexico, is that literal or figurative? You've probably noticed that lots of the definitions in this book show both a literal meaning (often something physical) and a figurative meaning (often nonphysical).

单词和短语会有字面意义和比喻意义。日常生活中我们都使用词语的两种意义。我们可以真的关上房间的门,或者 *figuratively*(用比喻的手法)关上进一步谈判的门——也就是说,拒绝参与谈判。比喻性的语言包括 *figures of speech*(修辞格),比如明喻("她对我像姐姐一样")和暗喻("抗议的暴风雨")。有时,很难说清楚一个短语是用的字面意义还是比喻意义。如果我说我在墨西哥"*picked up*"(学会了)一点西班牙语,这是字面意义还是比喻意义? 你可能曾经注意到,这本书中很多定义既显示了字面意义(通常是具体事物),也显示了比喻意义(通常是抽象事物)。

configuration\kən-ˌfi-gyù-ˈrā-shən\ An arrangement of parts or elements; shape, design. 布局；结构；形状；设计

• We've changed the configuration of the office so that employees will have more privacy at their desks. 我们已经改变了办公室的布局,这样,职员们在桌子那里就能有更多隐私。

The term is very common in computer science and mathematics, and in scientific and technological fields in general. Thus, for example, two scientists won a 1962 Nobel Prize for their description of the *configuration* of the DNA molecule. Since then, researchers have studied what different configurations within the DNA strands mean and what they control, and genetic engineers have tried to *configure* or *reconfigure* DNA in new ways to prevent or treat diseases.

这个词语在计算机科学和数学上很常见,在整个科学和技术领域都是这样。所以,比如两个科学家因为描述了DNA 分子的 *configaration*(结构),于 1962 年获得了诺贝尔奖。从此以后,研究人员一直研究 DNA 链中的不同结构意味着什么以及它们控制什么。遗传工程学家已经在努力以新的方式 *configure*(安排)或者 *reconfigure*(重新安排)DNA,从而防止或者治疗疾病。

effigy\ˈe-fə-jē\ An image of a person, especially a crude representation of a hated person. (尤指可恨的人简单粗糙的)形象；雕像；塑像

• The night before the big game, an effigy of the rival coach was burned on a huge bonfire. 这次重大比赛的前夜,对方球队教练的塑像在一大堆篝火上被烧掉了。

It was the practice of the ancient Egyptians to bury an *effigy* of a dead person along with that person's body. The idea was that if anything happened to the body in the afterlife, the effigy could be used as a spare. *Effigy* now usually refers to crude stuffed figures of the kind that get abused by angry protestors and unruly college students. But the small dolls that witches have used to bring pain and death on their victims can be called effigies as well. Actually, those witches and college kids seem to use their effigies for pretty much the same thing.

古埃及人有一个做法,是将死者的 effigy 与其身体一起埋葬。这样做的目的是,如果尸体在后世发生什么意外了,effigy 可以用作备用品。*effigy* 现在通常指那种粗糙简单的填充形象,让愤怒的抗议者和无法无天的大学生用来侮辱、践踏。但是,巫婆用来给人带来痛苦和死亡的小玩偶也可以叫做 effigies。实际上,那些巫婆和大学生用这些 effigies 目的差不多。

figment \ˈfig-mənt\ Something made up or imagined. 想象的事物;编造的事物

● His preference for Cindy is a figment of your imagination; believe me, he barely knows she exists. 他偏爱辛迪是你想象出来的。相信我,他几乎不知道有她这么一个人。

A figment is something formed from imaginary elements. Daydreams are figments; nightmares are figments that can seem very real. Most figments are everyday fears and hopes about small things that turn out to be imaginary. But when the radio play "The War of the Worlds" aired in 1938, it caused a panic among thousands of people who didn't realize the Martian invasion was just a figment of the author's imagination.

figment 是利用想象元素构成的东西。白日梦是 figments,噩梦是看来很真实的 figments。大多数 figments 都是日常生活中对小事儿的恐惧和希望,实际上是想象出来的。但是,当广播剧"世界大战"在 1938 年播出时,在很多人中间引起了恐慌,他们没有意识到火星人的进攻只是作者想象力的 figment。

Quizzes

A. Fill in each blank with the correct letter:

a. inanimate   e. figment
b. figurative   f. magnanimous
c. animated   g. configuration
d. effigy   h. animosity

1. The _____ form of the dog lay stretched in front of the fire for hours.

2. The _____ of the new aircraft's wings was one of the Defense Department's most closely held secrets.

3. Inviting her former rival to take part in the conference was a _____ gesture.

4. Don't tell him, but his popularity is just a _____ of his imagination.

5. He only meant the remark in a _____ sense, but lots of people thought he meant it literally.

6. Another _____ discussion about politics was going on when they arrived at the bar that evening.

7. The best negotiators always make a serious study of the basic causes of the _____ between feuding partners.

8. Every Halloween they would set a crude _____ of a farmer on their porch, though they never really knew why.

B. **Indicate whether the following pairs of terms have the same or different meanings:**

1. figment / fruitcake same ____ / different ____
2. animosity / hatred same ____ / different ____
3. figurative / mathematical same ____ / different ____
4. magnanimous / petty same ____ / different ____
5. effigy / bonfire same ____ / different ____
6. animated / lively same ____ / different ____
7. configuration / list of parts same ____ / different ____
8. inanimate / not alive same ____ / different ____

ANN/ENN

ANN/ENN comes from Latin *annus*, meaning "year." An *annual* event occurs yearly. An *anniversary* is an example of an annual event, although the older you get the more frequent they seem to be.

ANN/ENN 源自拉丁语 annus("年")。Annual 事件每年发生。anniversary(周年纪念)就是每年发生的事件的一个例子。不过,你年龄越大,周年纪念似乎越频繁。

annuity \ə-ˈnü-ə-tē\ Money that is payable yearly or on some regular basis, or a contract providing for such payment. 年金;年金合同

• Throughout her working career she invested regularly in annuities that would support her after retirement. 在整个工作生涯中,她根据年金合同定期交钱,退休后就可以领钱了。

Annuities are handy things to have when you retire, since they provide an income on an *annual* basis or more frequently. Annuities are normally contracts with life-insurance companies that specify that payments begin at retirement. Company pensions are traditionally doled out in the form of annuities, and sweepstakes jackpots may also come as annuities. An annuity can be a wise idea if you think you're going to live a long time; however, annuities can be tricky and should only be purchased after carefully comparing the products offered by various companies.

退休后,annuities(年金合同)是很有用的,因为它可以提供一笔收入,按 annual(每年)一次或多次的方式支付给你。annuities 通常是跟保险公司签订的合同,其中明确规定,退休时开始支付。公司的养老金传统上以年金的方式进行发放,赌金全赢制比赛的累加奖金也可能是以年金的形式发放的。如果你觉得自己会很长寿,年金合同是个聪明的主意;不过,它也可能有很多问题,应该仔细比较五花八门的公司提供的产品之后才能购买。

superannuated \ˌsü-pər-ˈan-yü-ˌwā-təd\ (1) Outworn, old-fashioned, or out-of-date. 用旧的;老式的;过时的 (2) Forced to retire because of old age or

UNIT 17

infirmity.（因为年老或虚弱）被迫退休的

• He called himself a car collector, but his backyard looked like a cemetery for superannuated clunkers. 他自称搜集汽车,但是他后院看着像个老车公墓。

A *superannuated* style is out-of-date—its time has come and gone. And a person who has passed an age limit and been forced to retire may technically be called superannuated. But more often *superannuated* describes people who seem somehow to belong to the past. So a 55-year-old surfer might be regarded as superannuated by the young crowd riding the waves in Santa Cruz, and a superannuated hippie might still be dressing the way he did in 1972.

superannuated 样式是过时的——其流行时期来了又走了。过了某一年龄期限、被迫退休的人,严格地说可以称为 superannuated。但是,superannuated 更多地用于描述不知为什么似乎属于过去的人。所以,一个 55 岁的冲浪者,可以被那些在圣克鲁斯冲浪者年轻人视为 superannuated 了。一个 superannuated 嬉皮士,穿着打扮可能还跟他 1972 年一样。

millennium \mə-'le-nē-əm\ (1) A period of time lasting 1,000 years, or the celebration of a 1,000-year anniversary. 一千年,一千周年纪念 (2) A period of great happiness and perfection on earth. 地球上的幸福时期

• The first millennium B.C. saw the rise of important civilizations in Greece, Rome, India, Central America, and China. 在公元前一千年期间,希腊、罗马、印度美洲中部和中国文明崛起了。

Since in Latin *mille* means "thousand" (see MILL, p. 484), a *millennium* lasts 1,000 years. Thus, we're living today at the beginning of the third millennium since the birth of Christ. But some religious sects, relying on a prophecy in the biblical Book of Revelation, speak of a coming millennium when Jesus will return to reign on earth for 1,000 years, evil will be banished, and all will live in peace and happiness. Members of these sects who keep themselves in a constant state of preparedness are called *millenarians* or *millennialists*.

在拉丁语中,mille 的意思是"千"(见 MILL,第 484 页),所以一个 millennium 持续一千年。这样,我们就正生活在基督出生后第三个 millennium 初期。但是,有些宗教派别根据《圣经·启示录》中的一个预言,说将有一个 millennium,那时耶稣将回到地球,统治一千年,邪恶的人将被赶走,所有人的生活将会安宁、幸福。这些宗教派别的成员使自己一直处于准备状态,他们被称为 millenarians 或者 millennialists (千禧年主义者)。

ANN / ENN

perennial \pə-'re-nē-əl\ (1) Continuing to grow for several years. 多年生的 (2) Enduring or continuing without interruption. 持续不断的

• "See You in September" is a perennial summertime hit among lovesick teenagers. 《九月份见》在单相思的青少年中间一直都是夏天最受欢迎的电影。

A *perennial* garden is full of *perennials* like delphiniums and asters, flowers that continue to bloom year after year. (*Annuals*, by contrast, grow for only a single season and must be replanted *annually*, and *biennials* die after two years.) Evergreens are *perennially* green; for that reason, they're perennial favorites for Christmas wreaths and decorations. In a similar way, taxes are a perennial political issue; and a perennial political candidate may come back over and over claiming he's

· 397 ·

the only one who can save us from them.

一个 perennial garden(多年生植物花园)里面都是 perennials(多年生植物)，比如飞燕草和紫苑，都是每年开花的植物。(然而,annuals[一年生植物]只生长一个季节，必须 annually[每年]种植；biennials[两年生植物]两年后死掉。)常绿植物是 perennially green,因此，它们是圣诞节花环和点缀物最喜欢用的。同样，税收是个 perennial 政治问题；一个 perennial 政治候选人每年都回来说，只有他可以使我们免于交税。

EV comes from the Latin *aevum*, "age" or "lifetime." Though the root occurs in only a few English words, it's related to the Greek *aion*, "age," from which we get the word *eon*, meaning "a very long period of time."

EV 源自拉丁语 *aevum*("年龄"或者"一生")。尽管这一词根只出现在几个英语单词中，但它跟希腊语的 *aion*("年龄")有关，从这个词语我们有了 *eon* 这个单词，意思是"漫长的一段时间"。

coeval \kō-ˈē-vəl\   Having the same age or lasting the same amount of time; contemporary. 年龄一样的；时间一样长的；当代的

• Homer's *Iliad* and *Odyssey*, probably written around 700 B.C., are coeval with portions of the Hebrew Bible, or Old Testament. 荷马的《伊利亚特》和《奥德赛》可能写于公元前 700 年，跟《希伯来圣经》(也就是《旧约》)的某些部分一样古老。

Coeval usually describes things that existed together for a very long time or that originated at the same time in the distant past. Thus, astronomers might speak of one galaxy as being coeval with another, and a period in the history of one civilization might be coeval with a similar period in another. As a noun, however, *coeval* may describe people as well; so, for example, two artists who lived and worked at the same time might be described as *coevals*.

coeval 通常描述存在时间很久或者同时起源于遥远的过去的事物。这样，天文学家可能说一个星系与另一个星系同样古老，一个文明的某一历史阶段可能与另一个文明的相似阶段持续时间相同。然而，作为名词时，coeval 也可用来描述人；所以，比如两个同时生活、工作的艺术家可以说是 *coevals*。

longevity \län-ˈje-və-tē\   (1) A long duration of life. 长寿 (2) Length of life; long continuance. 寿命；持续时长；长久的持续

• Picasso had a career of remarkable longevity, and was producing plentifully until his death at 91. 毕加索有着很长的艺术生涯，直到 91 岁去世前都在创作大量作品。

As living conditions improve and the science of medicine advances, the longevity of the average American has increased greatly, from about 45 years in 1900 to over 75 years today. But the most impressive human longevity is nothing compared to the 400-year lifespan of an ocean clam found near Iceland, or the 5,000-year lifespan of the bristlecone pine, a tree found in the western U.S. We may use *longevity* to talk not only about actual lives but also of the useful "life" of things: the life of your car's tires or the shingles on your roof, for example.

随着生活条件的改善和医学的进步，普通美国人的寿命已经大大延长，从 1900 年的 45 岁延长到了现在的 75 岁。但是，与冰岛附近发现的一个四百年的海蛤相比，或者与美国西部的一棵 5000 年的刺果松相比，最令人赞叹的人类寿命也不算什么。我们不但可以使用 *longevity* 谈论实际寿命,也可以谈论事物的有用"生命期",比如你的车胎或者房顶木瓦的寿命。

medieval\ˌmē-dē-ˈē-vəl\ (1) Relating to the Middle Ages of European history, from about A.D. 500 to 1500. 中世纪的 (2) Extremely out-of-date. 极其过时的;老掉牙的

• The great cathedral at Chartres in France, finished in 1220, is a masterpiece of medieval architecture. 法国沙特尔那座大教堂建成于1220年,是中世纪建筑的杰作。

With its roots *medi-*, meaning "middle," and *ev-*, meaning "age," *medieval* literally means "of the Middle Ages." In this case, *middle* means "between the Roman empire and the Renaissance"—that is, after the fall of the great Roman state and before the "rebirth" of culture that we call the Renaissance. This same period used to be called the "Dark Ages," since it was believed that in these years civilization all but vanished. And indeed, for most Europeans in these centuries, it was a time of poverty, famine, plague, and superstition, rather than the age of magic, dazzling swordplay, towering castles, and knights in splendid armor displayed in today's graphic novels and video games. 有了 *medi-*("中")和 *ev-*("时代")这两个词根,*medieval* 字面意思就是"of the Middle Ages"("中世纪的")。自这一情况中,*middle* 意思是"在罗马帝国和文艺复兴之间"——也就是在罗马这个伟大的国家崩溃后和被称为"文艺复兴"的文化的"再生"之前。这一时期过去常常被称为"黑暗时代",因为人们相信,在那些岁月中,文明几乎消失了。实际上,对那几个世纪的多数欧洲人来说,那个时代充满了贫穷、饥荒、瘟疫和迷信,而不是今天情节生动的小说和电子游戏中展示的神奇而耀眼的击剑、高高耸立的城堡以及盔甲闪亮的骑士。

primeval\prī-ˈmē-vəl\ (1) Having to do with the earliest ages; primitive or ancient. 原始的;古老的 (2) Existing from the beginning. 从开始就存在的

• When European settlers first arrived in North America, they found vast tracts of primeval forest, seemingly untouched by human influence. 当欧洲移民首次到达北美洲时,他们发现那里有大片的原始森林,似乎从未受到过人类的影响。

With its *prim-* prefix, meaning "first," *primeval* obviously refers to an original age. So the word often suggests the earliest periods in the earth's history. Myths are often stories of the creation of the world and of its primeval beings. The trees in a primeval forest (few of which remain today in most countries) may be 400 years old—not as old as the world, but maybe as old as they ever live to. According to scientists, life on earth began in the protein-rich waters of the primeval seas and swamps, and the decay of their tiny organisms and plant matter over millions of years produced our petroleum and coal. 有了 *prim-*("第一,最早")这一前缀,*primeval* 显然指一个最早的时代。所以这个词语常常暗示着地球历史的最早时期。神话常常是世界诞生及其古老的生物的故事。原始森林的树木(在大多数国家,它们很少存在了)可能有四百年了——没有这个世界古老,但确实是它们能够活着的时间。根据科学家所说,地球上的生命产生于原始海洋和沼泽富含蛋白质的水中,微生物在数百年的腐烂过程中产生了我们的石油和煤。

Quizzes

A. Choose the closest definition:

1. perennial   a. flowerlike   b. excellent   c. everlasting   d. thorough
2. longevity   a. extent   b. life length   c. longitude   d. longing
3. superannuated   a. amazing   b. huge   c. aged   d. perennial
4. coeval   a. ancient   b. simultaneous   c. same-sized   d. continuing
5. millennium   a. thousand   b. century   c. era   d. a thousand years
6. annuity   a. annual event   b. annual payment   c. annual income   d. annual garden
7. medieval   a. antiquated   b. middle-aged   c. romantic   d. knightly
8. primeval   a. wicked   b. elderly   c. primitive   d. muddy

B. Match the definition on the left to the correct word on the right:

1. ancient   a. perennial
2. of the same age   b. longevity
3. yearly payment   c. primeval
4. era of earthly paradise   d. coeval
5. of the Middle Ages   e. millennium
6. worn out   f. annuity
7. length of life   g. medieval
8. continuing   h. superannuated

CORP

CORP comes from *corpus*, the Latin word for "body." A *corpse* is a dead body. A *corporation* is also a kind of body, since it may act almost like an individual. And a *corps* is a "body" of soldiers.

CORP 源自拉丁语中表示"身体"的词语 *corpus*。*corpse* 就是尸体，*corporation*（公司）也是一种身体，因为其行为几乎会像人一样。*corps*（兵团）是士兵的群体。

---

corporeal \kȯr-ˈpȯr-ē-əl\   Having or relating to a physical body; substantial.

身体的，肉体的，物质的

• In paintings, angels usually look very much like corporeal beings, often with actual feathered wings. 在绘画作品中，天使通常看起来很像肉体构成的生物，往往长着翅膀。

In various religions, including Christianity, *corporeal* existence is often called the opposite of *spiritual* existence, and corporeal existence, unlike spiritual existence, is often said to be contaminated with evil. The word is also often used by philosophers, especially when considering the nature of reality. For lawyers, *corporeal* describes physical property such as houses or cars, as opposed to something valuable but nonphysical like a good reputation.

在各种宗教里，包括基督教，*corporeal*（肉体的）存在常常被称为 *spiritual*（精神的）存在的对立物。而肉体的存在，与精神的存在不同的是，据说常常被邪恶污染了。这个词语也常常被哲学家使用，尤其是考虑现实的本质时。对律师来说，*corporeal* 描述实体财产，比如房屋、汽车，与其相对的是珍贵但并非实体的东西，比如良好的声誉。

corpulent \ˈkȯr-pyu̇-lənt\　Having a large, bulky body; obese. 身材巨大的；肥胖的

• Squire Jenkins had often been described as "stout" or "portly," but more recently the word his acquaintances were using was usually "corpulent," or even "fat." 詹金斯先生常常被人描述为"粗壮"或者"富态"，但是最近，他认识的人使用的词语通常是"胖"，甚至是"肥"。

The Duchess of Windsor may have said that you can never be too rich or too thin, but that's a rather modern point of view. In earlier times in Europe, being overweight was considered a sign of wealth and well-being, as demonstrated by the *corpulence* of many European kings. Still today, corpulence is thought to be superior to thinness in some of the world's cultures. But *corpulent* and *corpulence* are less often used than they once were, and we're now probably more likely to say "obese" and "obesity."

温莎公爵夫人也许说过，你再有钱或者再瘦都不过分，不过这是很现代的看法。在欧洲的早期，超重被认为是富有、幸福的标志，正如欧洲列国国王的 *corpulence*（肥胖）所证明的那样。今天，在世界多数文化中，肥胖仍被认为胜过瘦弱。但是，*corpulent* 和 *corpulence* 现在用得没有以前多了，而且我们现在可能更有可能说"obese"和"obesity"。

corporal \ˈkȯr-pə-rəl\　Relating to or affecting the body. 身体的，影响身体的

• She was reminded that, in the public-school system, shaking a child was now regarded as unacceptable corporal punishment. 有人提醒她，现在在公立学校体制内，抓着孩子摇晃被认为是无法接受的体罚。

The adjective *corporal* today usually appears in the phrase *corporal punishment*, which means "bodily punishment." This used to include such acts as mutilation, branding, imprisonment, and even death. But today execution comes under the separate heading of "*capital punishment*," which originally involved losing your head (*capit-* meaning "head"). Milder forms of corporal punishment are used by American parents, and were once common in schools as well. *Corporal* is occasionally used in other ways; in the traditional church, the "corporal works of mercy" include seven helpful acts such as sheltering the homeless and burying the dead. *Corporal* as a military rank actually comes from *caporal*—which has the same root as *capital*.

corporal 这个形容词通常出现在 corporal punishment 这一短语中，意思是"体罚"。以前，体罚包括伤害身体、打烙印、监禁，甚至致死。但是今天，处决被另外归在了 capital punishment（"极刑"）下面。极刑最初包括丢掉脑袋（capit-意思是"头"）。今天，美国父母使用较轻形式的体罚，而以前它在学校也是很普遍的。corporal 偶尔有其他使用方式。在传统的教会中，"corporal works of mercy"（肉体慈善）包括七种助人行为，比如为无家可归者提供房屋和埋葬死人。corporal 作为一个军衔实际上源自 caporal—它跟 capital 词根相同。

incorporate\in-ˈkȯr-pə-ˌrāt\ (1) To blend or combine into something already existing to form one whole. 并入；纳入 (2) To form or form into a corporation. 组成公司

• The new edition incorporates many suggestions and corrections received by the author from his readers. 新版包含了作者从读者那里得到的许多建议和更正。

From its roots, *incorporate* means basically "add into a body" or "form into a body." So, for example, a chef might decide to incorporate a couple of new ingredients into an old recipe, and then might incorporate that new item into the restaurant's dinner menu. The restaurant itself was probably *incorporated* at the beginning, and so is now a *corporation*—that is, a "body" that's legally allowed to act like a single person in certain ways, even if it may have many individual employees. As you can see, the two meanings turn out to be fairly different.

因为其两个词根，incorporate 意思基本上就是"加在一起成为一体"或者"组成一个团体"。所以，比如一位厨师可能决定要把几种新的调料加入一个旧的食物做法，之后可能把那个新菜加到餐厅的菜单上。这个餐厅本身最初可能也是 incorporated（组成公司的），所以现在是一个 corporation，也就是说，在某些方面像一个人那样被允许合法行动的"体"，虽然它可能有很多雇员。你可以看到，这两个意思竟然很不相同。

TANG/TACT

TANG/TACT comes from the Latin words *tangere*, "to touch," and *tactus*, "sense of touch." So, for instance, to make *contact* is to touch or "get in touch with."

TANG/TACT 源自拉丁语词语 tangere（"接触"）和 tactus（"触觉"）。所以，比如 make contact 就是接触或者"与……有联系"。

tact\ˈtakt\ The ability to deal with others without offending them. 善于打交道；善于交往

• Already at 16 his daughter showed remarkable tact in dealing with adults, which she certainly hadn't gotten from him. 他女儿16岁就在与人交往方面表现出色，这显然并非从他身上继承的。

This word came to English directly from French (a Latin-based language), where it can also mean simply "sense of touch." Dealing with difficult situations involving other people can require the kind of extreme sensitivity that our fingertips possess. As Lincoln once said, "*Tact* is the ability to describe others as they see themselves," which doesn't usually come naturally. Someone *tactful* can soothe the feelings of the most difficult people; a *tactless* person will gener- ally make a bad situation worse.

这一词语直接从法语(以拉丁语为基础的一种语言)进入英语。在法语中，它的意思很简单，就是"触觉"。处理人际交往方面的棘手情况，需要我们的手指尖拥有的极度敏感。就像林肯曾经说的，"善于交往就是能像别人看自己那样描述他们"，但这种本领通常不是天生的。tactful(言行得体的)人能安慰最难以应付的人的情感；tactless(言行不当的)人通常让糟糕的情况更糟糕。

tactile \ˈtak-təl\ (1) Able to be perceived by touching. 可触知的;能摸到的 (2) Relating to the sense of touch. 触觉的

• He always enjoyed the tactile sensation of running his hand over the lush turf. 他总是喜欢把手抚过茂密的草皮那种触摸的感觉。

If you set your cell phone to vibrate rather than ring, you're taking the tactile option. Educators believe that some students are naturally "tactile learners," much better at "hands-on" learning than at tasks that involve patient listening and reading. Many longtime readers resist using e-books, saying they miss the tactile sensations of leafing through an actual book. And the blind, using the raised dots of the braille alphabet, rely entirely on their tactile sense to read; some can actually read as fast as the average person can read out loud.

如果你把手机设为震动模式而不是响铃模式，你就是在做出 tactile(触觉)选择。教育工作者认为有些学生是天生的"触觉学习者"，更善于"动手操作的"学习，而不那么善于完成需要耐心听和读的任务。很多读书多年的人不愿使用电子书，说他们怀念翻阅真实书籍的触摸感觉。盲人要利用布莱叶文凸起的小圆点，就得完全依赖触觉进行阅读。有的盲人读起书来，速度不亚于普通人朗读的速度。

tangential \tan-ˈjen-shəl\ Touching lightly; incidental. 轻轻触摸的;偶然的

• The government is trying to determine if the extremists were deeply involved or if their relationship to the suspect was merely tangential. 政府正努力确定这些极端主义者是深陷其中了，还是他们与嫌疑人的关系只是偶然的。

In geometry, a *tangent* is a straight line that touches a curve at a single point. So we say that someone who starts talking about one thing and gets sidetracked has gone off on a tangent. The new subject is tangential to the first subject—it touches it and moves off in a different direction.

在几何学中，tangent(切线)是在一个点上接触弧线的直线。所以我们说，开始谈论一件事但转变话题的人 has gone off on a tangent(跑题了)。这一新话题 is tangential to(接触后离开了)第一个话题——它接触了第一个话题，又转到另一个方向了。

tangible \ˈtan-jə-bəl\ Able to be perceived, especially by touch; physical, substantial. 可触摸到的;实体的;物质的

• The snow was tangible evidence that winter had really come. 这场雪是冬天已经到来的具体证据。

Something that's literally tangible can be touched. A rock is tangible, and so is a broken window; if the rock is lying next to the window, it could be tangible evidence of vandalism. When we say that the tension in a room is tangible, we mean we feel it so strongly that it seems almost physical. But if we're being literal, tension, like

TANG/
TACT

hope, happiness, and hunger, is literally *intangible*—it may be real, but it can't be touched. When lawyers talk about an *intangible* asset, they might mean something like a company's good reputation—very valuable, but not quite touchable.

<small>tangible 东西就是可以触摸到的。岩石是 tangible,砸烂的窗户也是。如果岩石就躺在窗户旁边,它就是故意破坏公物的 tangible 证据。当我们说房间的紧张气氛是 tangible,我们的意思是我们对它的感觉太强烈了,它好像几乎是具体的。但是,如果我们不夸张的话,紧张就像希望、幸福和饥饿,是 intangible——它是真实的,但却无法触摸到。当律师谈到某一 intangible asset(无形资产)时,他可能是指像公司的盛名这样的东西——很珍贵,但却无法触摸。</small>

Quizzes

A. Fill in each blank with the correct letter:

a. incorporate   e. corporeal
b. tangible   f. tangential
c. corporal   g. tact
d. tactile   h. corpulent

1. The question was only _____ to the main subject, but he answered it anyway.

2. The flogging of sailors was once a common form of _____ punishment in the British navy.

3. The district attorney realizes that they don't have much _____ evidence, and he's desperate to dig up more.

4. At 300 pounds, President Taft was often referred to as _____, especially by his enemies.

5. Brain surgeons have highly developed _____ sensitivities.

6. We hope to _____ suggestions from everyone on the board into our final proposal.

7. The footprints on the rug suggested that their mysterious nighttime visitor had been something more _____ than a ghost.

8. She's never had much _____, and her big mouth is always getting her into trouble.

B. Indicate whether the following pairs of terms have the same or different meanings:

1. corpulent / boring   same ____ / different ____
2. tangential / touching lightly   same ____ / different ____
3. incorporate / leave out   same ____ / different ____
4. tact / cleverness   same ____ / different ____
5. corporeal / substantial   same ____ / different ____
6. corporal / military   same ____ / different ____
7. tactile / sticky   same ____ / different ____
8. tangible / touchable   same ____ / different ____

UNIT 17

CODI/CODE comes from the Latin *codex*, meaning "trunk of a tree" or "document written on wooden tablets." A *code* can be either a set of laws or a system of symbols used to write messages. To *encode* a message is to write it in code. A genetic code, transmitted by genes, is a set of instructions for everything from blood type to eye color.

CODI/CODE 源自拉丁语 *codex*("树干"或者"木牍上写的文件")。*Code* 可以是一套法律或者用来书写信息的符号系统。*Encode* 一条信息就是用 code(密码)书写这条信息。遗传密码是通过基因传递的,是一套决定从血型到瞳孔颜色等各种东西的指令。

codex \ˈkō-ˌdeks\ A book in handwritten form, especially a book of Scripture, classics, or ancient texts. (尤指《圣经》、经典著作或者古代文本的)古书手抄本

• There on the shelves of the monastery library they saw codex after codex, all carefully copied and illustrated by hand. 在修道院的书架上,他们看到了一卷又一卷的古书手抄本,抄写、配图都很仔细。

In the 3rd and 4th centuries A.D., the codex began to replace the older scroll as the preferred form for longer writings. Unlike the scroll, this wonderful invention permitted writing on both sides of a sheet, made it easy to locate a particular passage, and could contain a very long piece of writing. Codices (note this unusual plural form) were usually written on parchment, the specially prepared skin of a sheep or goat, or papyrus, the ancestor of paper. Because codices were handwritten, there were few copies of any single codex, and sometimes only a single copy. Today we no longer write our books in longhand, but the modern book has kept basically the same form as the original codices.

在公元三、四世纪,手抄本开始代替更古老的卷轴,成为较长文本更为主要的形式。与卷轴不同的是,这一了不起的发明让人可以在一张纸的两面进行书写,这样就可以很容易找到某一特定段落,也能容纳一篇更长的文字。codices(注意这一奇怪的复数形式)通常写在羊皮纸或者羊纸莎草纸上。羊皮纸是一种以特殊方法加工的绵羊或山羊皮,而纸莎草纸是纸的最早形式。由于古书手抄本是手写的,任何一本古书的数量都很少,有时只有一本。今天我们不再用手写书了,但是当代书籍保留了和最初的手抄本基本一样的内容。

codicil \kä-də-səl\ (1) An amendment or addition made to a will. 遗嘱的修改(或补充) (2) An appendix or supplement. 附录;补充

• With the birth of each new grandchild, the old man added a new codicil to his will. 随着每一个孙子、孙女的出生,这位老人都在遗嘱上增加一点内容。

A codicil is literally a "little *codex*," a little bit of writing on a small piece of writing material, used to add to or change something about a larger piece of writing. A codicil to a will can change the terms of the original will completely, so it generally requires witnesses just like the will itself, though in some states a handwritten codicil may not. In mystery novels, such changes have been known to cause murders; in real life, codicils aren't usually quite that exciting.

codicil 从字面来说就是一个"*little* codex(小手抄本)",也就是一小片书写材料上写的一点文字,通常是要在更长的一篇文字上增添些什么,或者修改些什么。遗嘱的 codicil 可以彻底改变原先遗嘱的条款,所以它一般需要证人在场,就像立遗嘱那样,不过在有些州,手写的 codicil 可以不需要这样。在推理小说中,这样的修改会引发谋杀;在现实生活中,codicils 通常没那么惊心动魄。

codify \ˈkä-də-ˌfī\ To arrange according to a system; classify. 编排;归类

● In the 6th century B.C., the great statesman Solon newly codified the laws of Athens, replacing the harsh legal code of Draco. 公元前 6 世纪,最伟大的政治家索伦以新的方式编排了雅典的法律,取代了德拉古的严厉法典。

A *code* is a collection of laws arranged in an orderly way; famous examples include the Code of Hammurabi, from about 1760 B.C. in ancient Babylon, and the Napoleonic Code, produced at Napoleon's orders in 1804. Laws that have been included in a code have been codified. The rules of baseball differed greatly from one place to another until they were codified by Alexander Cartwright in 1845; they haven't changed much since, though we don't know what Cartwright would say about the designated hitter.

code 就是井然有序地安排在一起的一套法律,著名的例子包括公元前 1760 年古巴比伦的《汉谟拉比法典》、1804 年按照拿破仑的命令编排的《拿破仑法典》。包括在法典中的法律已经被 codified(编排)。以前,不同地方的棒球规则差异很大,直到亚历山大·卡特莱特在 1845 年将其编排后,这种局面才结束。它们此后没有多大变化,不过我们不知道卡特莱特会就那个指定击球员说些什么。

decode \di-ˈkōd\ (1) To put a coded message into an understandable form. 解码;破译(密码)(2) To find the underlying meaning of; decipher. 理解深层含义

● The Allies were able to decode many important secret messages sent by the Germans and Japanese in World War II. 第二次世界大战期间,盟军破解了德国人发送给日本人的很多重要秘密信息。

To *decode* is to take out of *code* and put into understandable language. (Its opposite is *encode*, "to put into coded form.") But dreams may sometimes also be decoded; psychologists often try to decode the images of their patients' dreams so as to understand the emotions behind them. And readers must often decode what a novel or story or poem is telling them, which may require two or three readings. *Decipher* is often a synonym, though we now use it when talking about reading difficult handwriting.

decode 就是从 *code*(密码)中取出,翻译成可以理解的语言。(其反义词是 *encode*,"译成密码"。)但是,梦有时也可以被 decoded(解析)。心理学家经常努力 decode(解析)病人梦中的形象,以了解其背后的情绪。读者必须经常 decode(理解)一部长篇小说、一篇短篇小说或者一首诗歌要告诉他们什么话,这需要读上两三遍。*decipher* 常常与 *decode* 同义,不过现在谈论识别难以明白的字迹时用它。

UNIT 17

SIGN comes from the Latin noun *signum*, "mark or sign." A *signal* is a kind of sign. Your *signature* is your own personal sign. And an architect's *design* marks out the pattern for a building.
SIGN源自拉丁语名词 *signum*("做标记或签名")。*Signal* 是一种符号。你的 *signature*(签名)是你的个人符号。建筑师的 *design*(设计)画出一栋建筑的图案。

---

signify \ˈsig-nə-ˌfī\ (1) To be a sign of something; to mean something. 表示;说明;意味着 (2) To show or make known, especially by a sign. (尤指用符号)表明

- The improved performance of the students signifies that the new approach may be working. 学生们表现进步了,说明这种新方法是有效的。

Signify basically means "to make a sign or signal." One of its synonyms is *indicate*; the *index finger* is the finger you point with, so to indicate is essentially to point to something. *Significant* means "important" and *significance* means "importance"; similarly, *insignificant* means "unimportant" and *insignificance* means "lack of importance."
signify 基本意思是"做手势或发出信号"。其同义词之一是 *indicate*(表明)。*index finger*(食指)就是指东西的那个指头,所以 *indicate* 基本上就是指什么东西。*Significant* 意思是"重要的",*significance* 意思是"重要性";同样,*insignificant* 意思是"不重要的",*insignificance* 意思是"缺乏重要性"。

insignia \in-ˈsig-nē-ə\ A badge of authority or honor; a distinguishing sign or mark. 徽章;标记;标志

- Peering closely at the photograph, he could now see clearly the insignia of the Nazi SS on his grandfather's chest. 仔细看照片,他现在才看到祖父胸前的纳粹黑衫队的徽章。

Insignia are the official signs of rank, titles, or awards. Medals are an example, as are the crowns of monarchs. The Catholic church employs such insignia as the red robes of cardinals. U.S. presidents have the presidential seal, which appears on the stand when they're giving a speech. But most of us think first of the bars, stripes, badges, and patches of military rank.
徽章是职位、头衔或者奖项的官方标志。奖牌是一个例子,君主的王冠也是。天主教会使用诸如红衣主教的红袍子这样的 *insignia*。美国总统有总统印章,在他们演讲时会出现在台子上。但是,我们大多数人首先想到的是军衔的色带、条纹、勋章和标记。

signatory \ˈsig-nə-ˌtȯr-ē\ A person or government that signs an agreement with others; especially a government that agrees with others to abide by a signed agreement. (协议的)签署者;签署方;签署国

- More than a dozen countries were signatories to the agreement setting limits on fishing in international waters. 在限制国际水域捕鱼的协议上,十多个国家签字了。

A *signatory* puts his or her *signature* on a document that is also *signed* by others. In 1215 the English barons revolted against King John and forced him to join them as a signatory to the Magna Carta. This agreement stated the barons' own duties to the King but also *assigned* the barons clear rights and limited the King's power over them. Though the Magna Carta did nothing for the common people, it's often been called the first step toward democracy in the English-speaking countries.

signatory 在其他人也 *sign*（签署）的文件上写上他或她的 *signature*（签名）。1215 年，英国贵族反抗英国国王，迫使他作为 signatory 跟他们一起签署《大宪章》。这个协议陈述了贵族们对国王应尽的义务，但也 *assigned*（分配）给他们权利了，而且限制了国王对他们的控制权。虽然《大宪章》没有为普通人民带来利益，但它也经常被誉为英语国家朝着民主迈出的第一步。

signet\\'sig-nət\\ （1）A seal used instead of a signature to give personal or official authority to a document. 印章；图章（2）A small engraved seal, often in the form of a ring. 图章戒指

• The charters of lands and rights of the early American colonies were confirmed with the king's signet. 早期北美殖民地的土地和权利宪章盖上国王的印章得到批准。

Signets have been used for thousands of years. The design of a signet is personalized for its owner, and no two are alike. The ancients used signets to mark their possessions and to sign contracts. In later years signets were used to stamp a blob of hot wax sealing a folded secret document so that it couldn't be opened and read without the design being broken. The Pope still wears a signet, called the Fisherman's Ring, which is carved with a figure of St. Peter encircled with the Pope's name; after a Pope's death, the ring is destroyed and a new one is made.

印章已经使用了数千年了。印章的图案是专为其主人设计的，没有哪两个是一样的。古人用印章在其财产上做标记、签合同。后来，印章被用来盖在密封折叠起来的秘密文件上的一滴热蜡上，这样，只要打开阅读文件，就必然弄坏图案。教皇仍然戴着被称为渔人戒指的图章戒指，上面刻有圣彼得的身形，外加教皇的名字。教皇去世后，这枚戒指被销毁，一枚新的被制作出来。

Quizzes

A. Choose the closest definition:

1. codify
   a. conceal   b. list   c. disobey
   d. interpret
2. signet
   a. stamp   b. gold ring   c. Pope's sign
   d. baby swan
3. codicil
   a. small fish   b. one-tenth
   c. amendment to a will   d. legal objection
4. signify
   a. sense   b. remind   c. sign
   d. mean
5. insignia
   a. indication   b. signal   c. badge
   d. rank
6. codex
   a. private seal   b. handwritten book
   c. secret letter   d. coded message

7. signatory   a. document   b. agreement   c. banner
    d. cosigner
8. decode   a. explain   b. conceal   c. symbolize
    d. disguise

B. Match the word on the left to the correct definition on the right:

1. insignia   a. interpret
2. codex   b. addition
3. signatory   c. emblem of honor
4. decode   d. engraved seal
5. signet   e. old type of book
6. codify   f. signer
7. signify   g. organize laws
8. codicil   h. indicate

Number Words 数字词语

QUADR/QUART

comes from Latin words meaning "four" or "fourth." In English, a *quart* is one-fourth of a gallon, just as a *quarter* is one-fourth of a dollar. A *quadrangle* has four sides and angles but isn't necessarily square. And *quadruplets* are four babies born at the same time.

QUADR/QUART 源自拉丁语中表示"四"或者"第四"的词语。在英语中，quart 是四分之一加仑，就像 quarter 是四分之一美元那样。quadrangle（四边形）有四条边、四个角，但不一定是正方形的。quadruplets（四胞胎）是同时出生的四个婴儿。

quadrant \'kwä-drənt\

(1) A quarter of a circle. 四分之一圆 (2) Any of the four quarters into which something is divided by two lines intersecting at right angles. （被两条交叉的垂直线分开的任何东西的）四分之一部分

• Washington, D. C. , like a number of other cities, is divided into quadrants called Northwest, Northeast, Southwest, and Southeast. 华盛顿特区跟一些其他城市一样，被两条垂直线分为四个部分，分别称为西北、东北、西南和东南。

This word is used for a traditional instrument, used to make calculations of altitude and traditionally employed by sailors to navigate, which has a piece shaped like a quarter of a circle. A *quadrant shower* is a shower that fits snugly into a bathroom corner and displays a curved front, making a quadrant shape on the floor. But perhaps *quadrant* is used most often today to name a particular quarter of a city. 这一词语用来指一种传统仪器。这用仪器用来计算纬度，传统上是水手用于航行的，上面有一块像是圆的四分之一。quadrant shower（扇形喷头）是安安稳稳装在卫生间一个角落的喷头，前面是弧形，水喷在地上，会出现一个四分之一圆的形状。但是今天，quadrant 或许更多地用于命名城市的某一特定四分之一的部分。

quadrille\ kwä-'dril \   A square dance popular in the 18th and 19th century, made up of five or six patterns for four couples. 方形舞；卡德利尔舞

• Quadrilles were very popular at balls in the American South before the Civil War. 美国南北战争以前，方形舞在南方的舞厅非常流行。

The *quadrille*, named for its four couples that form the sides of a square, seems to have begun as a French country dance. In the 18th century it became fashionable among the French nobility; as performed by elegantly dressed aristocrats, it became slow and formal. It crossed over to England and from there to New England, where it turned back into a dance for the common people. It soon evolved into the American square dance, a lively type of dance that employs a "caller" to make sure everyone remembers the steps.

方形舞的命名，来源于构成正方形四条边的四对舞者。它最早是法国乡村的一种舞蹈。18世纪，这种舞蹈在法国贵族中很时尚。因为表演者是衣着优雅的贵族，它变得缓慢而正式。方形舞传到了英格兰，又从那里传到了新英格兰，又变成了普通人的舞蹈。很快，它演变成了美国方形舞。这是一种活泼的舞蹈，有一位喊出舞步的指挥，来确保每个人都记着自己的步子。

quadriplegic\ˌkwä-drə-'plē-jik\   Paralyzed in both arms and both legs. 四肢瘫痪的

• A motorcycle accident in her teens had killed her boyfriend and left her a quadriplegic. 她十几岁时遭遇摩托车事故，男友死了，自己四肢瘫痪。

Quadriplegia is the result of injury or illness, almost always affecting the spine. Though a *paraplegic* has lost the use only of his or her legs, *quadriplegics* are paralyzed in all four limbs. Today voice-activated wheelchairs help the quadriplegic get around, and houses can be equipped with similar systems to operate lights and appliances; monkeys have even been trained to assist quadriplegics with everyday tasks. The work of the quadriplegic actor Christopher Reeve has led to remarkable advances in developing new nerve connections, enabling some determined paraplegics and quadriplegics to walk again.

quadriplegia（四肢瘫痪）源于受伤或者疾病，几乎总是影响到脊椎。paraplegic（截瘫病人）只是不能使用双腿，但quadriplegic（四肢瘫痪病人）四肢都不能用了。今天，声控轮椅帮助四肢瘫痪患者四处活动，房子可以配备类似的系统来操纵灯和家电，甚至有猴子得到训练后在日常生活中帮助四肢瘫痪患者。四肢瘫痪的演员克里斯托弗·里夫的努力促进了神经连接开发方面的进步，使有些意志坚强的截瘫病人和四肢瘫痪病人重新行走了。

quartile\'kwȯr-ˌtīl\   One of four equal groups each containing a quarter of a statistical population. 四分位值

• The schools in our town always average in the lowest quartile in both reading and math achievement. 我们镇上的学校在阅读和数学平均成绩方面总是属于第四分位值。

A *quartile* is a *quarter* of a specific group that has been tested or evaluated in specific ways. The first quartile is the one that scores highest and the fourth quartile scores lowest. For achievement and proficiency tests, the first quartile is the place to be; for blood pressure or cholesterol, the third quartile is healthier.

UNIT 17

quartile 是已接受测试或以特定方式接受评价的一组人的 *quarter*(四分之一)。第一四分位值是得分最高的,第四分位值是得分最低的。对于成绩测试和水平测试来说,第一四分位值是人们向往的;对于血压或者胆固醇来说,第三四分位值更健康。

TETR comes from the Greek word for "four." In the immensely popular video game *Tetris*, for example, each of the pieces the game is played with has four segments. But the root usually shows up in long chemical names.
TETR 源自希腊语中表示"四"的那个词语。比如,在大受欢迎的电子游戏"Tetris"(俄罗斯方块)中,游戏使用的每个棋子都有四部分。但是,这个词根通常出现在长长的化学名词中。

---

tetracycline \ˌte-trə-ˈsī-ˌklēn\   A yellow broad-spectrum antibiotic. 四环素

● He was sent home with a prescription for tetracycline and some advice about how to avoid Lyme disease in the future. 医生让他回家之前,开了四环素,提供了以后如何避免莱姆病的建议。

Most chemical names are made up of two or more Greek and Latin roots strung together. Thus, *tetracycline*, with its *cycl-* root from the Greek word for "circle," means "four-ringed"—that is, "consisting of four fused hydrocarbon rings." Antibiotics work against bacteria and other tiny organisms (but not viruses); tetracycline, which comes from a kind of soil bacteria, is one of the most used of the antibiotics. "Broad-spectrum" antibiotics work well on numerous organisms; thus, tetracycline has proved effective against acne, chlamydia, cholera, rickets, and various lung and eye infections, among many other conditions.
大多数化学名称都由两个或更多希腊语和拉丁语词根连在一起。这样,*tetrecline* 因为其词根 *cycl-*源自希腊语中表示"圆圈"的那个词语,意思就是"四个圆圈",也就是"由四个熔融烃环组成"。抗生素抵抗细菌及其他微生物(但不包括病毒)。四环素源自一种土壤细菌,是使用最多的抗生素之一。"广谱"抗生素对很多微生物都有用,这样,四环素就已证明可以有效治疗痤疮、衣原体、霍乱、佝偻病和各种肺部和眼部感染,等等。

tetrahedron \ˌte-trə-ˈhē-drən\   A solid shape formed by four flat faces.
四面体

● Her son's box kite was a tetrahedron, and its pyramid shape was easy to pick out among the traditional designs flown by the other children. 她儿子的箱型风筝是个四面体,在其他孩子的很多传统风格的风筝中,其棱锥形状很容易被辨认出来。

The simplest tetrahedron is made of four equal-sided triangles: one is used as the base, and the other three are fitted to it and each other to make a pyramid. But the great pyramids of Egypt aren't tetrahedrons: they instead have a square base and four triangular faces, and thus are five-sided rather than four-sided.
最简单的四面体由四个等边三角形组成:一个用作基底,其他三个与基底固定在一起,而且相互之间也固定起来,构成一个棱锥体。但是,埃及的大金字塔不是四面体,而是有一个正方形基底和四个三角形的面,这样它就有五个面,而不是四个面。

tetralogy \te-ˈtra-lə-jē\   A set of four connected literary, artistic, or

TETR

· 411 ·

musical works. (文学、美术或者音乐的)四部曲；四联剧

• *The Raj Quartet*, Paul Scott's long and complex tetralogy of India, was made into a highly praised television series. 《泰姬四部曲》是保罗•斯科特的长而复杂的印度四部曲,已经改编成电视剧,受到了高度赞扬。

Vivaldi's *Four Seasons* could be called a tetralogy, since it's a set of four violin concertos, one for each season of the year. Eight of Shakespeare's history plays are often grouped into two tetralogies. Wagner's great *Ring of the Nibelung*, an opera tetralogy based on Norse mythology, contains about 18 hours of music. The original tetralogies, however, were sets of four plays by the same author performed together in ancient Greece; the first three were always tragedies, and the last was a wild comedy. Tetralogies were written by such great dramatists as Aeschylus, Sophocles, and Euripedes; unfortunately, none of them have survived in their entirety. 维瓦尔第的《四季》可以称为一个 tetralogy,因为它是一组四首小提琴协奏曲,一个季节一首曲子。莎士比亚八部历史剧通常分为两个 tetralogies。瓦格纳伟大的《尼伯龙根的指环》是一个歌剧 tetralogy,以北欧神话为基础,包含长达十八个小时的音乐。不过,最早的 tetralogies(四联剧)是古希腊同一个作者创作的四个一组的戏剧;前三个总是悲剧,最后一个是热闹的喜剧。tetralogies 是由埃斯库罗斯、索福克勒斯和欧里庇得斯这样的伟大戏剧家创作的,不幸的是,它们没有一个完整地保留下来。

tetrapod \ˈte-trə-ˌpäd\ A vertebrate with two pairs of limbs. 四足动物

TETR

• His special study was the great seismosaurus, probably the largest tetrapod—and the largest land animal—that ever lived. 他专门研究巨大的地震龙。这可能是存在过的最大的四足动物,也是最大的陆地动物。

The earliest tetrapods, or "four-footed" animals, were mammal-like reptiles that evolved before the rise of the dinosaurs and ranged from mouse-sized to cow-sized. Today the tetrapods include the reptiles, the amphibians, the birds, and the mammals—including humans. Though the fish aren't classified as tetrapods, it's quite possible that our own limbs began as paired fins hundreds of millions of years ago. 最早的 tetrapods,或者"四足动物",是类似哺乳动物的爬行动物,在恐龙兴盛前演化出来,从老鼠那么小到牛那么大的都有。今天的四足动物包括爬行动物、两栖动物、鸟类和哺乳动物(包括人)。虽然鱼类没有被归为四足动物,但很可能的是,数百万年前,我们的四肢最初是成对的鳍。

Quiz

Match the definition on the left to the correct word on the right:

1. four-sided solid   a. quadriplegic
2. square dance   b. tetralogy
3. one-fourth of a group   c. quadrant
4. four connected works   d. tetrapod
5. paralyzed in four limbs   e. quartile

6. quarter
7. antibiotic
8. four-limbed animal

f. tetrahedron
g. quadrille
h. tetracycline

Review Quizzes

A. Choose the correct synonym and the correct antonym:

1. decode   a. translate   b. recover   c. encode
   d. transmit
2. animated   a. colorful   b. lifeless   c. smiling
   d. vigorous
3. tangible   a. readable   b. touchable   c. eternal
   d. nonphysical
4. animosity   a. affection   b. mammal   c. dedication
   d. hatred
5. corpulent   a. slim   b. spiritual   c. overweight
   d. bodily
6. figurative   a. modeled   b. literal   c. painted
   d. symbolic
7. corporal   a. military   b. bodily   c. nonphysical
   d. reasonable
8. perennial   a. two-year   b. lasting   c. temporary
   d. flowering
9. longevity   a. anniversary   b. shortness
   c. uncertainty   d. permanence
10. primeval   a. recent   b. antique   c. ancient
    d. swamplike

B. Fill in each blank with the correct letter:

a. magnanimous
b. codicil
c. corporeal
d. intact
e. quadriplegic
f. effigy
g. inanimate
h. tactile
i. millennium
j. tetrahedron

k. medieval
l. codex
m. figment
n. quartile
o. tetrapod
p. coeval
q. tetracycline
r. superannuated
s. incorporate
t. signify

1. When she woke from her coma, she reported the experience of floating in the air and looking down on her _____ body.

2. The year 2000 marked the start of the third _____ A.D.

3. In _____ Europe, great walls were erected around entire cities for the protection of the people.

4. Every large land animal is a _____, as is every bird.

5. In his victory speech he was _____ to his opponents, promising them an important role in his government.

6. In these auctions, bidders _____ that they're raising their bids by holding up a paddle with a number on it.

7. In this report she hoped to _____ all the research she'd been doing for the last year.

8. In the rare-book room of the library, he found another _____ containing three long poems in Old English.

9. A grade-point average that falls in the top _____ earns a student special privileges.

10. A _____ can be a strong and stable structure, since it's made of four triangles.

11. For the homecoming celebration, we made an _____ of our opponents' mascot and draped it in black.

12. We all know it's ridiculous to curse at _____ objects when it's just our own clumsiness that's at fault.

13. A _____ to the environmental treaty provided for a special exception for three African countries.

14. Because of technological advances and access laws, the life of a _____ is far less restricted than it once was.

15. Being blind, his _____ sense was extremely well developed.

16. It was a terrible experience, but they came through it with their sense of humor _____.

17. The idea that my parents don't like you is a _____ of your imagination.

18. She knows that creaky old chair is _____, but she loves it and wouldn't give it up for anything.

19. That tree was planted when I was born, so it and I are _____.

20. Penicillin and _____ are among the most useful of the antibiotics.

C. Match the definition on the left to the correct word on the right:

1. incidental   a. configuration
2. will addition   b. tetralogy
3. politeness   c. annuity

4. arrangement
5. regular payment
6. formal dance
7. four-part work
8. seal
9. signer
10. classify

d. tact
e. codify
f. quadrille
g. tangential
h. signet
i. codicil
j. signatory

UNIT 18

CAPIT, from the Latin word for "head," *caput*, turns up in some important places. The head of a ship is its *captain*, and the *capital* of a state or country is where the "head of state" works. A *capital* letter stands head and shoulders above a lowercase letter, as well as at the head (beginning) of a sentence.
CAPIT 源自拉丁语表示"头"的单词 *caput*，出现在一些重要地方。一艘船的首领就是其 *captain*（船长），*capital*（首都）是一个国家的元首工作的地方。*capital* letter（大写字母）除了位于句首，也是比小写字母高的字母。

CAPIT

capitalism \ˈka-pə-tə-ˌli-zəm\   An economic system based on private ownership, private decisions, and open competition in a free market. 资本主义

• In the 1980s, the leaders of the free world had faith that capitalism and a free-market economy would solve all our problems. 20世纪80年代，自由世界的领导们相信，资本主义和自由市场经济会解决所有问题。

Capital is wealth—that is, money and goods—that's used to produce more wealth. Capitalism is practiced enthusiastically by *capitalists*, people who use capital to increase production and make more goods and money. Capitalism works by encouraging competition in a fair and open market. Where a *capitalist* economy encourages private actions and ownership, socialism prefers public or government ownership and control of parts of the economy. In a pure capitalist system, there would be no public schools or public parks, no government programs such as Social Security and Medicare, and maybe not even any public highways or police. In a pure socialist system, there wouldn't be any private corporations. In other words, there's just about no such thing as pure capitalism or pure socialism in the modern world.
capital（资本）是产生更多财富的财富——也就是金钱和物质。*capitalists*（资本家）是增加生产、制造更多物质和金钱的人，热衷于搞资本主义。资本主义运转的途径据称是鼓励在公平、公开的市场上进行竞争。*capitalist* economy（资本主义经济）鼓励私人行为和私有，社会主义更加鼓励公有或者政府所有，控制经济的一部分。在纯粹的资本主义制度中，没有公立学校或者公园，没有社保和医保之类的政府项目，甚至没有任何公路或者警察。在纯粹的社会主义制度中，

不会有任何私有企业。换句话说,在当代世界,几乎没有纯粹的资本主义或者纯粹的社会主义这样的东西。

capitulate\kə-'pi-chə-ˌlāt\ To surrender or stop resisting; give up. 投降;停止抵抗;放弃;

• At 2:00 a.m. the last three senators finally capitulated, allowing the bill to move forward. 凌晨两点钟,最后三位参议员放弃了,允许这个法案进展下去。

Capitulation often refers to surrender on the battlefield. Originally it only referred to surrender according to an agreement, though that part of the meaning is often absent. Today a teacher can capitulate to her students' cries of protest against a homework assignment, or a father can capitulate to his kids' pleas to stop for ice cream, when the only terms of the agreement are that they'll stop complaining. *capitulation*(投降)通常指的是在战场上停止抵抗。最初,它仅仅指根据协议放弃抵抗,不过目前,这一部分意思常常并不出现。今天,教师面对学生对家庭作业的抗议会投降,或者父亲面对孩子们停下来买冰淇淋的请求会投降,这时,协议的唯一条件就是他们同意不再抱怨。

decapitate\di-'ka-pə-ˌtāt\ (1) To cut off the head; behead. 砍头;杀头 (2) To destroy or make useless. 毁掉;使无用

• The leaders of the uprising were decapitated, and their heads were mounted on long poles on London Bridge as a warning to the people. 起义领袖都被砍头了,脑袋挂在了伦敦桥上高高的杆子上,以示警告。

Decapitation is a quick and fairly painless way to go, so it was once considered suitable only for nobles like Sir Walter Raleigh, Mary Queen of Scots, and two of Henry VIII's unfortunate wives. The invention of the guillotine in the 18th century was meant to make execution swifter and more painless than hanging or a badly aimed blow by the executioner's sword. *decapitation*(斩首)是快速而相当没有痛苦的死法,所以它曾经被认为只适合于贵族,比如沃尔特·罗利爵士、苏格兰玛丽女王和亨利八世两个不幸的妻子。18世纪发明了断头台,目的是要让处决比绞刑或者刽子手瞄得很不准确的一剑更为快捷、痛苦更少。

recapitulate\ˌrē-kə-'pi-chə-ˌlāt\ To repeat or summarize the most important points or stages. 重复;总结

• At the end of his talk, the president carefully recapitulated the main points in order. 在讲话结束时,总裁仔细有条理地总结了要点。

Capitulation originally meant the organizing of material under headings. So *recapitulation* usually involves the gathering of the main ideas in a brief summary. But a recapitulation may be a complete restatement as well. In many pieces of classical music, the recapitulation, or *recap*, is the long final section of a movement, where the earlier music is restated in the main key. *capitulation*(摘要,概要)最早的意思是在标题下组织材料,所以 *recapitulation*(摘要重述)通常包括简要总结要点。但是一个 recapitulation 也可能是一个完整的重述。在很多古典乐曲中,recapitulation(再现部)或者 *recap*,是一个乐章长长的最后一部分,在这一部分,早先的音乐以主音的形式重奏一次。

ANTHROP comes from the Greek word for "human being." So an *anthropomorphic* god, such as Zeus or Athena, basically looks and acts like a human. And in Aesop's fables and many animated cartoons, animals are usually *anthropomorphized* and behave exactly like furry, four-legged human beings.
ANTHROP 源自希腊语中表示"人"的那个词语。所以,*anthropomorphic*(拟人的)神祇,比如宙斯或者雅典娜,基本上看起来像人,行为也像人。在伊索寓言和很多动画片中,动物通常是 *anthropomorphized*(被人格化的),行为恰恰就像长着毛、四条腿的人。

anthropoid \ˈan-thrə-ˌpȯid\ Any of several large, tailless apes. 类人猿

● The chimpanzees, gorillas, orangutans, gibbons, and bonobos are all classified as anthropoids. 黑猩猩、大猩猩、红毛猩猩、长臂猿和矮黑猩猩都被归为类人猿。

With its suffix *-oid*, meaning "resembling," the word *anthropoid* means literally "resembling a human being." Anthropoid apes are so called because they resemble humans more closely than do other primates such as monkeys and lemurs. Some even spend a good deal of time walking on their hind legs. Anthropoids are, of course, highly intelligent (though maybe no more so than many monkeys), and some of them use sticks and stones as tools. (But if you call someone an anthropoid, you're probably not complimenting his intelligence.)

因为有了意思是"类似"的后缀 *-oid*,*anthropoid* 一词字面意思是"类似人"。类人猿之所以这样命名,是因为他们比猴子和狐猴这样的灵长类动物更接近人类。有些类人猿甚至有很多时间都用后腿行走。当然了,类人猿是非常聪明的(虽然可能并不比很多猴子更聪明),有一些用棍子和石头作为工具。(不过,如果你把某人称为类人猿,你可不是在称赞他聪明。)

anthropology \ an-thrə-ˈpä-lə-jē\ The science and study of human beings.
人类学

● By studying the cultures of primitive peoples, anthropology may give us a better understanding of our own culture. 通过研究原始人的文化,人类学可以让我们更好地理解我们自己的文化。

Anthropologists, those who study the whys and wherefores of human existence, today look not only at the tribes of the Amazon but also at the neighborhoods of Brooklyn or Santa Monica. Every group and every culture now seems to be possible material for *anthropology*. Some anthropologists specialize in the study of human evolution, some study human language, some study archaeology, and some study human culture through the ages. Unlike historians, they tend to focus less on what has been recorded in writings than on what can be discovered in other ways.

anthropologists 指的是那些研究人类生存的原因和理由的人,他们今天不但研究亚马孙河的部落,也研究布鲁克林或者圣莫妮卡的城区。每个群体以及每个文化现在似乎都可能成为人类学的研究材料。有些人类学家专门研究人类的进化,有些研究人类语言,有些研究考古学,有些则对人类文化进行历时研究。跟历史学家不同的是,他们往往不那么关注已有文字记载的东西,而更多地关注以其他方式可以发现什么。

misanthropic \ ˌmi-sən-ˈthrä-pik \   Hating or distrusting humans. 憎恨人类的;怀疑人类的

• Few characters in literature are more misanthropic than Ebenezer Scrooge, who cares for nothing but money. 在文学作品人物中,埃比尼泽·斯克鲁奇只在乎钱,很少有谁比他更憎恶人类了。

Jonathan Swift was famous for the *misanthropy* of works such as *Gulliver's Travels* which make fun of all kinds of human foolishness. But in spite of his apparent misanthropic attitude, he spent a third of his income on founding a hospital and another third on other charities—certainly not the acts of a true *misanthrope*. Today we often use synonyms such as *cynic* and *grinch* for misanthropic types—while hoping we don't meet too many of them.
乔纳森·斯威夫特以其作品中对人类的憎恶著称。比如在《格列佛游记》中,他嘲弄各种人的愚蠢。但是,尽管他有着明显的憎恨人类的态度,他花去三分之一的收入创建了一家医院,又把另外三分之一的收入花在了慈善事业上。这毫无疑问不是一个真正的 *misanthrope*(憎恶人类者)的行为。今天,我们经常使用 *cynic* 和 *grinch* 这样的同义词,指几种憎恶人类的人,同时并不希望遇到太多这样的人。

lycanthropy \ lī-ˈkan-thrə-pē \   (1) A delusion that one has become a wolf. (自己)变狼妄想 (2) Transformation into a wolf through witchcraft or magic. (通过巫术或魔术)变成狼

• The local farmers avoided the residents of the village in the next valley, who had long been suspected of grave robbing and lycanthropy. 当地农民避开了邻近山谷的村民,因为这些村民长期以来一直被怀疑从事盗墓活动,而且会变成狼。

The Greek word for "wolf," *lykos*, combines with the *anthro-* root to produce the meaning "wolfman." In European folklore, dating back to the ancient Greeks and Romans, there are men who change into wolves at night and devour animals, people, or graveyard corpses before returning to human form at dawn. Werewolves, or *lycanthropes*, may be evil and possessed by the devil, or may instead be the victims of a werewolf bite and thereby cursed to change into wolf form at the full moon. The werewolf's evil intention is shown by its eating only part of the animal or corpse, rather than all of it like a truly hungry wolf.
希腊语中表示"狼"的词语 *lykos* 与 *anthropo-* 这一词根结合,就有了"狼人"这个意思。在欧洲民俗文化中,如果追溯到古希腊人和古罗马人时期,有些人夜晚变成狼,吞食动物、人或者墓园尸体,黎明前变回人形。狼人,或者 *lycanthopes*,可能是邪恶的,而且被魔鬼附身,或者自己被狼人咬了之后,在满月时变成狼的形状,于是成了受害者。狼人的邪恶意图,表现于它只吃掉动物或尸体的一部分,而不是像真正饥饿的狼那样将其全部吃掉。

ANTHROP

Quizzes

A. Fill in each blank with the correct letter:

a. misanthropic

b. capitalism

c. lycanthropy

e. recapitulate

f. anthropology

g. decapitate

d. capitulate   h. anthropoid

1. She's too proud to _____ to her rivals on this point without getting something major in return.

2. In the years when new primitive cultures were being discovered regularly, _____ must have been a very exciting field.

3. _____ is the economic system in most of the world's countries today, but in many of these the government also plays a large role.

4. The gorilla is classified as an _____ because of its relatively close resemblance to humans.

5. The guillotine was used in France to _____ criminals before capital punishment was outlawed there.

6. By the time he turned 80 he was genuinely bitter and _____ and disliked by all his neighbors.

7. All the sports channels constantly _____ the highlights of recent games.

8. In these mountains, where wolves can be heard baying at the moon every night, many of the villagers believe in _____.

B. Match the word on the left to the correct definition on the right:

1. recapitulate   a. free-market system
2. misanthropic   b. human-wolf transformation
3. capitalism   c. surrender
4. anthropoid   d. summarize
5. decapitate   e. antisocial
6. anthropology   f. study of cultures
7. capitulate   g. ape
8. lycanthropy   h. behead

KINE

KINE comes from the Greek word *kinesis*, meaning "movement." Kinetic energy is the energy of motion (as opposed to potential energy, the kind of energy held by a stretched elastic band). Kinetic art is art that has moving parts, such as Alexander Calder's famous mobiles. And *cinema*, the art of moving pictures, actually comes from the same *kine-* root as well.

KINE 源自希腊语 *kenesis*("运动")。Kinetic energy(动能)是运动中的能量(与潜能相反,因为潜能是伸展的皮筋具有的能量)。kinetic art(动态艺术)有移动的部分,比如亚历山大·考尔德著名的悬挂饰物,cinema 是电影艺术,这个词语实际上也源自词根 *kine-*。

---

kinesiology\kə-ˌnē-sē-ˈä-lə-jē\ The scientific study of human movement. 人体运动学

● With a kinesiology degree in hand, she landed a job as a rehab therapist for patients following heart surgery. 因为拥有人体运动学学位,她得到了一份康复治疗师的工作,为心脏手术后的病人服务。

Kinesiologists study the acquisition of motor skills, the mechanical aspects of movement, and the body's responses to physical activity. A kinesiologist may work in a public-school fitness program, design exercise programs for people with and without disabilities, or work with patients recovering from disease, accidents, and surgery. As a field of research, *kinesiology* focuses particularly on the mechanics of muscular activity.

kinesiologists(人体运动学家)研究运动技巧的获得、运动的机械学的方方面面以及身体对体力活动的反应。kinesiologist 可能教授公立学校的健身课,为残疾或非残疾人设计运动计划,或者帮助生病、遭受事故或者手术后的病人。作为一个研究领域,人体运动学特别注重肌肉活动的技术性细节。

hyperkinetic \ˌhi-pər-kə-ˈne-tik\ (1) Relating to or affected with hyperactivity. 过分活跃的 (2) Characterized by fast-paced or frantic activity. 快节奏的;紧张忙乱的

• *Noises Off* is a hyperkinetic stage farce that moves at a breathless pace for a full hour and a half. 《幕后音》是一个快节奏的舞台闹剧,持续一个半小时,节奏快得让人喘不过气。

Since the prefix *hyper-* means "above, beyond" (see HYPER, p. 493), *hyperkinetic* describes motion beyond the usual. The word is usually applied to children, and often describes the condition of almost uncontrollable activity or muscular movements called *attention-deficit/hyperactivity disorder* (ADHD). Kids with ADHD are usually not just hyperkinetic but also inattentive, forgetful, and flighty. Though they're often treated with drugs, many experts believe there are better ways of dealing with the problem. Lots of people now shorten both *hyperactive* and *hyperkinetic* to simply *hyper* ("He's been hyper all morning"), but usually don't mean it too seriously.

由于前缀 *hyper* 意思是"在……上面,超过"(见 HYPER,第 493 页),*hyperkinetic* 描述超常的运动。这个词语通常用于描述儿童,也常常描述 *attention-deficit/hyperactivity disorder*(ADHD,多动症)这种活动或者肌肉运动几乎无法控制的状况。有多动症的孩子通常不仅仅 hyperkinetic(过分活跃),而且注意力不集中、健忘而且容易激动。尽管他们常常接受药物治疗,很多专家认为,处理这一问题还有更好的办法。很多人现在把 *hyperactive* 和 *hyperkinetic* 都缩略为 *hyper*("He's been hyper all morning"他一个上午都很活跃),但是,通常并不是太严肃。

kinescope \ˈki-nə-ˌskōp\ A motion picture made from an image on a picture tube. 电视屏幕纪录片

• In the archives she turned up several kinescopes of Ernie Kovacs's 1950s show, which she thought had been dumped into New York Harbor decades ago. 在档案馆里,她找到了几张厄尼·科瓦奇 20 世纪 50 年代时装秀的录像。

Kinescope, originally a trademark for the cathode-ray tube in a TV, later became the name for a film of a TV screen showing a live broadcast. In order for a program to be seen beyond New York in the early days of TV, a kinescope had to be shipped from station to station. Though grainy and fuzzy, these were for a time the only way of capturing live shows. But in 1951 Desi Arnaz and Lucille Ball decided to film their comedy show rather than to broadcast it live, and in a few years live broadcast comedy and drama had vanished from the airwaves.

　　Kinescope 最初是一个电视机阴极射线管的商标,后来成了电视屏幕纪录片的名称。在电视的早期阶段,为了让某个节目在纽约以外也能看到,电视屏幕纪录片不得不从一个电视台送到另一个电视台。虽然多粒而模糊,这些纪录片曾一度是唯一能拍现场表演的方法。但是在 1951 年,戴西•阿那斯和露茜丽•鲍尔决定摄制自己的喜剧节目,而不是直播。几年后,直播的广播喜剧和戏剧从无线电波中消失了。

telekinesis\ˌte-li-kə-ˈnē-səs\　The movement of objects without contact or other physical means, as by the exercise of an occult power. 心灵致动

　　● Fascinated by telekinesis as a boy, he'd spent hours in his room trying to push a pencil off the table using only his mind. 他小时候对无接触运动很着迷,会在房间花上几个小时,想仅仅利用心灵作用把铅笔从桌子上推下去。

　　Tele- in Greek means "far off" (see TELE, p. 452). The eternally appealing idea of moving an object remotely, using only psychic powers, has had a long life in films, TV shows, stories and novels, video games, and comics. But although some researchers believe in the existence of *telekinesis* (also known as *psychokinesis*), most scientists believe that any reported experiences have been the result of fraud, wishful thinking, or naturally explainable events.

　　tele- 在希腊语中意思是"遥远"(见 TELE,第 452 页)。利用心灵的力量,从远方移动物体,这一迷人的想法,长期存在于电影、电视节目、故事和小说、电子游戏和连环画中。但是,虽然一些研究人员认为存在着无接触运动(也称为 *psychokinesis*),大多数科学家认为,任何已经报道的这种事情,都源自欺骗、痴心妄想或者可以合理解释的事件。

DYNAM

DYNAM comes from the Greek *dynamis*, meaning "power." A *dyne* is a unit used in measuring force; an instrument that measures force is called a *dynamometer*. And when Alfred Nobel invented a powerful explosive in 1867, he named it *dynamite*.

　　DYNAM 源自表示"力量"的希腊语词语 *dynamis*。Dyne 是一个用于测量力量的单位;测量力量的仪器称为 *dynamometer*(测力计)。阿尔弗雷德•诺贝尔在 1867 年发明强力炸药后,将其命名为 *dynamite*。

dynamic\dī-ˈna-mik\　(1) Relating to physical force or energy. 动力的 (2) Continuously and productively active and changing; energetic or forceful. 活跃多变的;充满活力的;有力的

　　● The situation has entered a dynamic phase, and what we knew about it last week has changed considerably by now. 这种情况已经进入活跃多变阶段。我们上周了解的一切,现在已经有很大变化了。

　　Dynamic is the opposite of *static*, which means "not moving or active." So all living languages, for example, are dynamic rather than static, changing from year to year even when they don't appear to be. A bustling commercial city like Hong Kong is intensely dynamic, constantly changing and adapting. A dynamic relationship—for example, the relationship between housing values and interest rates charged by banks—is one that changes all the time. Unfortunately, the word has been used so much by advertisers that we tend to forget its basic meaning.

dynamic 的反义词是 *static*，这个词意思是"静止的；不动的"。因此，比如所有的活语言都是 dynamic，而不是 static。即使看起来并没有变化时，它们也在逐年变化。像香港这样的繁忙商业城市极有活力，不断变化。活跃多变的关系，比如房价和银行所收取利率之间的关系，是一直变化的。不幸的是，这个词语已经被广告商用得太多，结果我们常常忘记它的基本意思了。

dynamo \ˈdī-nə-ˌmō\ (1) A power generator, especially one that produces direct electric current. (直流)发电机 (2) A forceful, energetic person. 精力充沛的人

• Even as they entered the power plant, the roar of the water covered the sound of the immense dynamos. 即使在他们进入发电厂的时候，水的呼啸声就已淹没了巨大发电机的声音。

The dynamo was introduced in 1832 to produce electricity for commercial use. Like all later generators, the original dynamos changed mechanical energy (produced by steam, which was itself produced by burning coal) into electricity. The word is less used today than it once was, since it's often applied only to generators that produced direct electric current (DC) rather than alternating current (AC), which is now the standard. A human dynamo is a person who seems to have unlimited energy, such as New York's legendary mayor Fiorello La Guardia, whose forcefulness and vigor matched that of his intensely *dynamic* city.

发电机是 1832 年开始使用的，用来为商业目的服务。就像所有后来的 generators(发电机)一样，最初的 dynamos 将机械能(由水蒸气产生，而水蒸气由烧煤产生)转变成电。这个词语今天不如以前使用那么频繁了，因为它经常仅用于指产生直流电(DC)而不是交流电(AC)的 generators(发电机)，而目前使用交流电才是标准做法。一个 human dynamo 指一个似乎精力无穷的人，比如鼎鼎有名的纽约市长菲奥雷拉·瓜迪亚。他言辞有力、精力充沛，跟他那座极有活力的城市很是般配。

aerodynamics \ˌer-ō-dī-ˈna-miks\ (1) A science that studies the movement of gases such as air and the way that objects move through such gases. 空气动力学 (2) The qualities of an object that affect how easily it is able to move through the air. 空气动力特性

• Early automobile designs were based on the boxlike carriages drawn by horses, back when no one was even thinking about aerodynamics. 早期的汽车设计以马匹牵引的箱子一样的马车为基础，当时甚至没人考虑空气动力特性。

Aerodynamics began as a science around the time of the Wright brothers' first manned flights. Since then, it's become important to the building not only of aircraft and automobiles but also of rockets and missiles, trains, ships, and even such structures as bridges and tall buildings, which often have to withstand strong winds. An *aerodynamic* vehicle is one whose design helps it achieve the greatest speed and most efficient use of fuel. But although we might casually call any sleek car design aerodynamic, true aerodynamics is practiced not by artistic product designers but instead by highly trained scientists, and many people's lives depend on their work.

空气动力学开始成为一门科学大约是在莱特兄弟最早的载人飞行时期。从此以后，它对飞机和汽车制造很重要，对火

箭和导弹、火车、轮船制造也很重要，甚至对桥梁和高楼建筑来说也很重要，因为它们不得不抵抗强风。一个 aerodynamic（符合空气动力特性的）交通工具，其设计有助于获得最高速度和燃料的最高使用率。但是，虽然我们可以不够严谨地把任何流线型汽车设计都说成是 aerodynamic，真正的空气动力学工作不是艺术产品设计者而是接受过严格训练的科学家从事的，而且很多人的生活都要依靠这些科学家的工作。

hydrodynamic \ ˌhī-drō-dī-ˈna-mik \ Having to do with the science that studies fluids in motion and the forces that act on bodies surrounded by fluids.
流体动力学的

● Building levees to contain a flood presents complicated hydrodynamic problems. 修建防洪大堤是一个复杂的水动力问题。

Bernoulli's principle, which is basic to the science of *hydrodynamics*, says that the faster a fluid substance flows, the less outward pressure it exerts. It shows the close relationship between *hydrodynamics* and *aerodynamics* (which deals with the movement of air and other gases), since it can partly explain how air will "lift" an airplane by the way it flows over the wings, and how a spoiler helps keep a race car's wheels pressed to the ground as it accelerates. Hydrodynamics is sometimes applied today in studying the surface of the planets and even the stars. As used informally by boaters, *hydrodynamic* often means "hydrodynamically efficient."

伯努利的原则以 *hydrodynamics*（流体动力学）为基础。这一原则认为，流体速度越快，对外界施加的压力越小。它表明 *hydrodynamics* 与 *aerodynamics* 有着紧密关系，因为后者可以部分解释空气如何流过机翼上方、"抬起"飞机，也可以部分解释气流偏导器如何在赛车加速时有助于其轮子压在地面上。今天，流体动力学有时应用于对行星甚至星星表面的研究。在船工不正式的用法中，*hydrodynamic* 常常表示"从空气动力学角度来看很有效"。

Quizzes

A. Choose the closest definition:

1. dynamo   a. powerhouse   b. force unit   c. time interval
      d. power outage
2. kinesiology   a. science of planetary motion
      b. atomic motion   c. study of human movement
      d. history of film
3. aerodynamic   a. glamorously smooth
      b. relating to movement through air   c. using oxygen for power
      d. atmospherically charged
4. telekinesis   a. moving of objects by mental power
      b. broadcasting of films   c. distant motion
      d. electronic control from afar
5. hyperkinetic   a. overgrown   b. large-bodied
      c. intensely active   d. projected on a large screen
6. hydrodynamic   a. relating to moving fluids
      b. water-resistant   c. relating to boats   d. relating to water

7. kinescope   a. light meter   b. peep show   c. early movie camera   d. camera for live TV

8. dynamic   a. explosive   b. energetic   c. excited   d. dangerous

B. Indicate whether the following pairs have the same or different meanings:

1. hydrodynamic / tidal   same ____ / different ____
2. hyperkinetic / overactive   same ____ / different ____
3. kinescope / motion-triggered camera   same ____ / different ____
4. aerodynamic / air-powered   same ____ / different ____
5. kinesiology / sports history   same ____ / different ____
6. dynamo / generator   same ____ / different ____
7. telekinesis / electronic broadcasting   same ____ / different ____
8. dynamic / electric   same ____ / different ____

GRAD comes from the Latin noun *gradus*, "step" or "degree," and the verb *gradi*, "to step, walk." A *grade* is a step up or down on a scale of some kind, and a *gradual* change takes place in small steps.

GRAD 源自拉丁语名词 gradus("脚步"或"程度")和动词 gradi("跨步,走")。grade 是某种刻度尺上向上或向下的一格,gradual 变化是一点点发生的。

---

gradation \grā-ˈdā-shən\ (1) A series made up of successive stages. 逐渐变化 (2) A step in an ordered scale. 阶段;步骤

• In the fall, the leaves show gradations of color from deepest red to brightest yellow. 秋天,叶子显示出从最深的红色到最艳丽的黄色之间颜色变化。

In the Boy Scouts, gradations of rank move upward from Tenderfoot to Eagle Scout. A violin or a voice can produce gradations of musical pitch too small to appear in written music. In the 18th century Jonathan Swift could even write of "the several kinds and gradations of laughter, which ladies must daily practice by the looking-glass."

在童子军中,职务的变化从新加入的童子军向上直到鹰级童子军。一把小提琴或者一个声音可以产生小得在乐谱中难以显示的音调的逐步变化。在 18 世纪,乔纳森·斯威夫特甚至写到了"贵族妇女必须对着镜子天天训练的几种逐步变化的笑声"。

degrade \di-ˈgrād\ (1) To treat someone or something poorly and without respect. 恶劣对待;不尊重 (2) To make the quality of something worse. 降低质量

• They had feared for years that television was degrading the mental capacities of their children. 他们有几年时间都害怕电视正在毁掉儿童的智力。

In Shakespeare's *King Lear*, the old king is degraded by the daughters he has given his kingdom to. He finds it *degrading*, for instance, when the number of his guards is reduced from 100 to 25. His *degradation* seems complete when, after going mad, he's reduced to living in the wilderness. As you can see, *degrade* is often a synonym for *humiliate*.

在莎士比亚的戏剧《李尔王》中，老国王把自己的王国送给几个女儿，却得不到她们的敬重。比如，他发现自己的卫兵从一百个减到二十五个是很 *degrading*（丢脸的）事情。在发疯后，他竟沦落到在野外流浪的境地，遭受的恶劣待遇到了顶点。你可以发现，*degrade* 常常是 *humiliate* 的同义词。

gradient \\ˈgrā-dē-ənt\\ (1) Slope, grade. 坡；斜坡；坡度 (2) A continuous change in measure, activity, or substance. 持续变化

- Steep temperature gradients in the atmosphere are usually associated with unstable conditions. 大气温度的急剧变化通常与不稳定的大气状况有关。

Any slope can be called a *gradient*. In the interstate highway system, the maximum gradient is 6 percent; in other words, the highway may never ascend more than 6 vertical feet over a distance of 100 feet. Any rate of change that's shown on a graph may have a sloped gradient. Suppose the graph's horizontal axis shows the passage of time and its vertical axis shows some activity; if the activity is happening very fast, then the gradient of the line on the graph will be steep, but if it's slow the gradient will be gentle, or *gradual*.

任何一个斜坡都可以被称为 gradient。在州际公路系统中，最大的坡度是六度；换句话说，公路在一百英尺距离内上升的高度不得超过六英尺。图标上显示的任何变化率都可能会有一个坡度。假如这个图标的水平轴显示时间变化，垂直轴显示某种活动，如果活动进展很快，那么图标上那条线的坡度就会很陡，但是如果活动发生缓慢，坡度就会平缓，或者说 gradual（逐渐的；逐步的）。

retrograde \\ˈre-trō-ˌgrād\\ (1) Moving or performed in a direction that is backward or opposite to the usual direction. 朝后的；往不正常方向的 (2) Moving toward a worse or earlier state. 恶化的；倒退的

- For the government to cover up the findings of its scientific research institutes was clearly a retrograde step. 政府掩盖其科研机构的发现结果，显然是一次堕落行为。

Retrograde describes backwardness of one kind or another. If a country decided to go back to amputating the limbs of criminals, we might call that policy retrograde. A retrograde view of women might be one that sees them basically as housekeepers. Mars and Jupiter show retrograde (backward) motion at some stages of their orbits, though this is only because of the way we see them from the earth, not because of any real backward movement.

retrograde 描述某种倒退。如果一个国家决定回到过去，砍掉罪犯的肢体，我们可以说这是政策的倒退。对女性的倒退看法，可能就是认为女性基本上是家庭主妇。在其运行轨道某些阶段，火星和水星显示出后退的（向后的）运动，不过，原因只是我们是从地球看两颗行星的，不是因为其有任何倒退运动。

UNIT 18

REG, from the Latin *regula*, meaning "rule," has given us many English words. Something *regular* follows a rule of some kind, even if it's just a law of nature. A *regime* can be a form of rule or government. To *regulate* an industry means to make and enforce rules, or *regulations*, for it; removing such rules is called *deregulation*.

REG 源自拉丁语 *regula*("规则"),给我们提供了很多英语词语。*regular*(规则的)东西遵循某种规则,即使只是某一自然规律。一个 *regime*(政体)是一种统治形式。*regulate*(管理,控制)某一行业就是为其制定并实施一些规章制度,或称 *regulations*;撤销这些规章制度这一做法被称为 *deregulation*(撤销管制)。

regimen\ˈre-jə-mən\ A regular course of treatment, usually involving food, exercise, or medicine. 治疗法;养生法

- As part of his training regimen, he was now swimming two miles, running seven miles, and bicycling 15 miles every day. 作为这一训练养生法的一部分,他现在每天游泳两英里,跑步七英里,骑车十五英里。

Americans love self-improvement, so they're constantly adopting *regimens*: skin-care regimens, low-cholesterol regimens, weight-loss regimens, and the like. A course of medication may be complicated enough to deserve the name *regimen*, and a rehab regimen may require having your activities monitored at a treatment center. Mental regimens can also be valuable; researchers are finding that minds that get the most exercise seem to last the longest.

美国人喜欢自我改善,所以他们不断采用养生法:皮肤养生法、低胆固醇养生法、减肥养生法,等等。某个服药过程可能较为复杂,值得被称为 *regimen*,某个康复治疗法可能需要在诊疗中心对你的活动进行监控。精神治疗法也可以是很重要的;研究人员发现,使用最多的头脑似乎持续时间最长。

interregnum\ˌin-tə-ˈreg-nəm\ (1) The time during which a throne is vacant between two successive reigns or regimes. 职位空置期;政体空置期 (2) A period during which the normal functions of government or control are suspended. 政权空白期

- During the weeklong interregnum between the CEO's death and the appointment of a new CEO, she felt that she was really running the whole show. 在首席执行官去世和任命新首席执行官之间长达一周的过渡期,她觉得自己真的在掌控一切。

Every time a pope dies, there's an *interregnum* period before a new one is elected by the cardinals. In most democratic systems, however, the law specifies who should take office when a president or prime minister dies unexpectedly, and since the power usually passes automatically, there's no true interregnum. The question of succession—that is, of who should take over when a country's leader dies—has often presented huge problems for countries that lacked a constitution, and in monarchies it hasn't always been clear who should become king or queen when a monarch dies. The interregnum following the death of Edward VI in 1553, for instance, was briefly suspended when Lady Jane Grey was installed as Queen; nine days later she was replaced by Mary Tudor, who sent her straight to the Tower of London.

每次有教皇去世了,红衣主教选出新教皇之前,都有一个职位空置期。不过,在大多数民主体制中,总统或首相突然去世时,由法律指定谁应该就职。因为权力通常自动传下去,所以总统或首相没有真正的职位空置期。继位这一问题——也就是一个国家的领导去世了,谁应该接任——在没有宪法的国家往往是一个重大问题。在君主立宪制国家,君主去世了,谁应该成为国王或女王也常常并不清楚。比如,1553 年爱德华六世去世后出现了职位空置期,在简·格雷夫人被任命为女王后,职位空置期短暂中止了。九天后,她被玛丽·都铎取代,玛丽直接将其送进了伦敦塔。

regalia\ri-ˈgāl-yə\ (1) The emblems and symbols of royalty. 王权标志 (2) Special or official dress. 特别服装;职位服装

• The governor seems to enjoy life in the governor's mansion and all the regalia of office more than actually doing his job. 州长似乎在享受州长官邸的生活和该职位的标志,而不是踏踏实实做自己的工作。

Just as *regal* describes a king or queen—that is, a ruler—*regalia* originally meant the things, and especially the dress and decoration, that belong exclusively to a monarch. The British monarchy's regalia include the crown jewels (crown, scepter, orb, sword, etc.) that lend luster to royal coronations. Academic regalia—the caps, gowns, and hoods worn by students receiving their degrees—link institutions to their past by preserving the dress worn at universities since their beginnings in the Middle Ages, when long hooded robes were needed for warmth.

就像 *regal* 描述国王或女王——也就是一个统治者——*regalia*(王权标志)最早指君主专有的东西,尤其是服装和装饰物。英国君主制的 regalia,包括使加冕典礼熠熠生辉的王权珠宝,比如王冠、权杖、宝球、宝剑等等。学术 regalia(特别服装),也就是学位帽、学位服以及接受学位证书时戴的兜帽。这些东西将学府与其过去联系起来,方法是保留中世纪时大学开办时人们穿的衣服。当时需要带兜帽的袍子来保暖。

regency\ˈrē-jən-sē\ A government or period of time in which a regent rules in place of a king or queen. 摄政;摄政期

• Since the future king was only four when Louis XIV died, France spent eight years under a regency before he took the throne at 13 as Louis XV. 路易十四去世时,未来的国王只有四岁。在他以路易十五的身份登基前,在法国有过八年的摄政期。

In Britain, the years from the time when George III was declared insane until his death (1811-1820) are known as the Regency period, since in these years his son, the future George IV, served as Prince Regent, or acting monarch. (Sometimes the term covers the period up to the end of George IV's own reign in 1830.) The Regency is remembered for its elegant architecture and fashions, its literature (especially the works of Jane Austen) and its politics. Today hotels, furniture, and businesses on both sides of the Atlantic carry the name "Regency" to identify with the period's style, and hundreds of modern romance novels—called simply "Regencies"—have been set in the period. Though there have been dozens of

European regencies over the centuries, for Americans today there seems to be only one Regency.

在英国，从乔治三世被宣布精神失常到他去世(1811—1820)，这几年称为摄政期。因为在这几年中，他的儿子，也就是未来的乔治四世，身份是 Prince Regent(摄政王)，或者代理君主(有时候，这一词语涵盖的时间一直到乔治四世在1830年统治结束时)。这一摄政时期以其优雅的建筑和时尚、文学(尤其是简·奥斯丁的作品)、政治为人所铭记。今天，大西洋两岸的宾馆、家具和公司名称中带有 *Regency*(摄政时期)，目的是为了对那个时代的风格表示认同。成百上千的现代爱情小说——简单地称为"Regencies"(摄政时期风格的小说)——背景都是这一时期。虽然数个世纪以来有许许多多欧洲的摄政时期，但对今天的美国人来说，似乎只有一个。

Quizzes

A. Choose the closest definition:

1. regency   a. monarch   b. acting government   c. crowning   d. royal style
2. degrade   a. reduce in size   b. raise in esteem   c. lower in rank   d. increase in importance
3. regimen   a. army unit   b. dynasty   c. rule book   d. routine
4. gradient   a. graph   b. slope   c. road   d. steps
5. interregnum   a. vacation   b. recess   c. period without a leader   d. period of peace
6. gradation   a. program in a series   b. stage in a series   c. eventual decline   d. definite improvement
7. regalia   a. royalty   b. set of rules   c. training schedule   d. trappings of office
8. retrograde   a. moving in reverse   b. grading again   c. primitive   d. switching grades

B. Fill in each blank with the correct letter:

a. regimen
b. gradation
c. regency
d. degrade
e. retrograde
f. interregnum
g. gradient
h. regalia

1. At a ceremonial occasion such as this, every officer would be present, in full _____.
2. Each subtle _____ of color seemed more beautiful as the sun slowly set.
3. Every pope's death is followed by a short _____ while the cardinals prepare to choose a new pope.

4. The trail's _____ for the first part of the race was gentle, but after three miles it became quite steep.

5. His 20-year-old daughter took over the company when he died, but her first couple of years were really a _____ under the senior vice president.

6. Once a thriving democracy, the country lapsed into dictatorship in the 1970s, a _____ step that it's still recovering from.

7. Her new _____ included a yoga session and a one-hour bike ride every day.

8. By all means apologize for your mistake, but don't _____ yourself.

CRIT

CRIT comes from a Greek verb that means "to judge" or "to decide." So a film *critic* judges a movie and tells us what's good or bad about it. Her *critical* opinion may convince us not to go, or we may overlook any negative *criticism* and see it anyway.

CRIT 源自希腊语中表示"判断"或"决定"的一个动词。所以,电影 critic(评论家)对一部电影进行评判,之后告诉我们它的优点和缺点。她的 critical(评论的)看法可能会说服我们不要去看,或者我们可能会无视任何负面的 criticism(评论),只管去看。

criterion \krī-ˈtir-ē-ən\ A standard by which a judgment or decision is made. 标准

• He's one of those readers whose main criterion for liking a book is whether it confirms his prejudices. 有些人是否喜欢一部书,主要标准就是它是否能够证实自己的偏见。他就是这样一个读者。

One person's principal criterion for a new car may be its gas mileage, while someone else's may be whether it has room for four children. When filling a job opening, employers usually look for several criteria (notice the plural form) in the applicants; and when college admissions officers are reading student applications, they likewise always keep a few basic criteria in mind. And when interviewing an applicant, one criterion for both the employer and the admissions officer might include the size of the applicant's vocabulary! 一个人判断一辆新车的主要标准就是其是否省油,而另一个人的标准可能是这辆车是否能够坐四个孩子。要填补空缺时,雇主通常在求职者身上寻找几个 criteria(标准;注意复数形式)。当大学招生人员阅读学生的申请书时,他们同样总是在头脑中有几个基本标准。在面试申请人时,雇主和招生人员共有的一个标准可能就包括申请人的词汇量!

critique \kri-ˈtēk\ A judgment or evaluation, especially a rating or discussion of merits and faults. 判断;评价

• Whenever he reads his latest story in the fiction-writing seminar, one of the other students always delivers a nasty critique. 无论什么时候他在小说写作研讨课上朗读自己最近写的短篇小说时,其他学生总有一个会进行很苛刻的评价。

Even though *criticize* means to judge something negatively, a critique can be completely positive—or completely negative. Usually it's somewhere in between. When a paper of yours receives a critique from a teacher, you should read it carefully, and then reread it; getting mad or offended is the worst way to react. *Critique* is often a verb as well. Thus, writers and artists often form groups solely to critique each other's work, and scientific articles frequently get critiqued in letters to the editor in the following issue of the journal.

尽管 criticize 意思是进行否定性判断，critique 却可能完全是肯定性的——或者完全否定性的。通常，它在两者之间。当你的论文得到老师的评价时，你应该仔细阅读，之后再次阅读；生气是最差的反应方式。critique 也经常用作动词。这样，作家和艺术家经常组成团体，唯一的目的就是相互评价作品。科学文章常常在期刊下一期写给编辑的信中受到评价。

hypercritical\ˌhī-pər-ˈkri-tə-kəl\   Overly critical. 过分挑剔

● Most teachers do their best to correct their students' mistakes without seeming hypercritical. 大多数教师都尽量帮助学生改正错误，而不会显得过于挑剔。

The important prefix *hyper-* means "excessive" or "beyond" (see HYPER, p. 494), so *hypercritical* means basically "too fussy." In TV and film comedies, the mother-in-law is just about always hypercritical, since the person her child married is never good enough for her. But other parents, spouses, and even children can be just as bad, so we should all be careful. If your father asks what you think of his new experimental meatloaf and you say it needs a pinch of oregano, you're being constructive; if you say he should cut down on the sawdust next time, you're probably being hypercritical.

hyper 这一重要前缀意思是"过度"或者"超过"（见 HYPER, 494 页），所以 *hypercritical* 这个词的基本意思就是"过于挑剔"。在电视和电影喜剧中，岳母或者婆婆几乎总是过于挑剔，因为跟她孩子结婚的人对她来说总是不够令人满意。但是其他的父母、配偶甚至孩子也可能同样糟糕，所以我们都应该小心翼翼。如果你爸爸问你他尝试着做的肉丸子怎么样，你说还需要一点点牛至，你的话是具有建设性的；如果你说下一次应该少用些锯末儿，你可能就是过分苛刻了。

hematocrit\hi-ˈma-tə-ˌkrit\   The ratio of the volume of red blood cells to whole blood. 血细胞比容；分血器

● The latest blood test had revealed that her hematocrit had risen considerably and was almost back to normal. 最新的血液测试显示，她的红细胞压积已大幅上升，几乎恢复正常。

Our blood is mostly made up of four components: plasma, red blood cells, white blood cells, and colorless blood cells called platelets. An instrument called a hematocrit (because it "judges" the blood) is used to separate a sample of blood into its components. The normal hematocrit for men is about 48%, for women about 38%. An abnormal proportion of red blood cells, either too many or too few, is a good early indicator of many diseases. So when you give blood as part of a physical exam, your hematocrit is one of the findings your doctor will often check.

我们的血液有四种成分：血浆、红细胞、白细胞和叫做血小板的无色的血细胞。有一种仪器称为 hematocrit（分血器）（因为它"评判"血液），用来将一个血液样本分成其各个成分。男性的正常血细胞比容大约是 48%，女性的大约是 38%。不正常的血细胞比例要么太高，要么太低，可以很好地提前显示很多疾病。所以，当你为体检提供血液时，你的血细胞比容是医生通常要查看的结果之一。

JUR comes from the Latin verb *jurare*, "to swear, take an oath," and the noun *jus*, "right or law." A *jury*, made up of *jurors*, makes judgments based on the law. And a personal *injury* was originally something done to you that a court would find unjust.

JUR 源自拉丁语动词 *jurare*("发誓")以及名词 *jus*("权利"或"法律")。*jury*(陪审团)由 *jurors*(陪审员)组成,以法律为基础进行裁决。人身 *injury*(伤害)最初指法庭认定的他人对你做的不公平的事情。

jurisprudence\ˌju̇r-is-ˈprü-dəns\ (1) A system of law. 法律体系 (2) The study and philosophy of law. 法学

• As a young lawyer his heroes were the crusaders of 20th-century jurisprudence, especially Louis Brandeis and Thurgood Marshall. 作为一名青年律师,他的偶像是那些20世纪法律体系的斗士,尤其是路易·布兰德和瑟古德·马歇尔。

Jurisprudence as a study may have begun in the Roman empire, where schools of law were first established. And Roman jurisprudence, like so many other things the Romans created, served as the model in later centuries throughout the Western world. And like many other legal words, *jurisprudence* is used only in formal writing.

法学作为一门学位可能起始于罗马帝国,因为那里首先建立了法律学校。罗马的法律体系,就像罗马人创造的其他很多东西一样,成了后来整个西方世界的榜样。就像很多其他法律词语一样,*jurisprudence* 只用于正式文体。

abjure\ab-ˈju̇r\ To reject formally. 公开放弃;正式放弃

• The Spanish Inquisition forced many Jews to abjure their religion and adopt Christianity or be burned at the stake. 西班牙宗教裁判所迫使众多犹太人公开放弃自己的宗教,要么信仰基督教,要么被烧死在火刑柱上。

From its Latin roots, *abjure* would mean literally "to swear away." Thus, after the holidays many people abjure all sweets and fattening foods, often making their vow in front of friends or relatives. *Abjure* is often confused with *adjure*, which means "to command solemnly, as if under oath." Thus, a judge might adjure a criminal to change his ways; but it's up to the criminal to abjure a life of crime.

由于其两个拉丁语词根,*abjure* 字面意思会是"发誓放弃"。这样,假期后,很多人发誓放弃所有糖果以及让人发胖的食物。他们通常在朋友或者亲属面前发誓。人们常常把 *abjure* 跟 *adjure* 搞混,而后者的意思是"严肃地命令"。这样,法官可能命令罪犯改邪归正;但是,要由罪犯决定是否放弃罪恶的生活。

perjury\ˈpər-jə-rē\ The crime of telling a lie under oath. 作伪证;发假誓

• Found guilty of perjury for lying under oath in front of a Congressional committee, he was sentenced to two years in prison. 因为在一国会委员会面前发誓后又撒谎,他被裁决发假誓罪,被判处两年徒刑。

The prefix *per-* in Latin often meant "harmfully." So witnesses who *perjure* themselves do harm to the truth by knowingly telling a lie. Not all lying is perjury, only lying under oath; so perjury generally takes place either in court or before a legislative body such as Congress. To avoid committing perjury, a witness or defendant may "take the Fifth"; that is, refuse to answer a question because the answer might be an admission of guilt, and the Fifth Amendment to the Constitution forbids forcing a citizen to admit to being guilty of a crime.

拉丁语中的 per 这一前缀通常的意思是"有害地",所以,作伪证的证人因为故意撒谎而损害事实真相。不是所有的撒谎都是发假誓,只有发誓了又撒谎才是;所以发假誓通常发生在法庭上或者一个立法团体(比如国会)面前。要避免这一罪行,证人或者被告可以"以美国宪法第五条修正案为庇护";也就是拒绝回答问题,因为回答了可能等于承认有罪。宪法第五条修正案禁止强迫公民承认有罪。

de jure \dē-ˈju̇r-ē\ Based on or according to the law. 以法律为基础;根据法律

• The country is a de jure democracy, but since one party controls all the media outlets it really isn't one. 这是一个以法律为基础的民主国家,但由于一个政党控制了所有媒体,它名不副实。

Coming straight from Latin, *de jure* is a term used mostly, but not always, in legal writing. Sometimes it's not enough to have something written into law; if a law isn't enforced, it might as well not exist. And if ordinary citizens are too scared of what would happen to them if they exercised their rights, then they don't really have those rights at all. Unfortunately, many countries have constitutions and laws that sound good but turn out not to have much effect. So *de jure* is almost always used in contrast to something else; its opposite is *de facto* (see p. 67).

de jure 这一术语直接源自拉丁语,多数情况下用在法律写作中。有时,仅仅将条文写进法律还不够;法律如果不能得到执行,还不如不存在。如果普通公民行使了自己的权利,又很害怕会出什么事,那他们并不是真正享有这些权利。不幸的是,很多国家都有着听起来很好,实际上没有什么效力的宪法和法律。所以,*de jure* 的使用几乎总是与另外某种东西形成对比,其反义词是 *de facto*(见第 67 页)。

Quizzes

A. Indicate whether the following pairs have the same or different meanings:

1. de jure / based on law   same ____ / different ____
2. hematocrit / test tube   same ____ / different ____
3. jurisprudence / legal beliefs   same ____ / different ____
4. hypercritical / untruthful   same ____ / different ____
5. perjury / testimony   same ____ / different ____
6. criterion / standard   same ____ / different ____
7. abjure / reject   same ____ / different ____
8. critique / evaluation   same ____ / different ____

B. Fill in each blank with the correct letter:

a. hematocrit   e. abjure
b. jurisprudence   f. hypercritical
c. criterion   g. perjury

d. de jure   h. critique

1. He had never learned how to make his criticism seem constructive rather than _____.

2. As soon as the party agrees to _____ violence, we're ready to allow them to participate in elections.

3. The judges gave a thorough and helpful _____ of each contestant's work.

4. Although her own philosophy of _____ is liberal, most observers think her interpretations of the law as a judge have been balanced.

5. What shall we use as the basic _____ for this award?

6. The _____ power of the prime minister was considerable, but all real power was held by the army.

7. The _____ showed an abnormal ratio of red blood cells.

8. She was probably committing _____ when she swore that she had spent the night alone at home.

Number Words 数字词语

PENT comes from the Greek word for "five." The *Pentagon* in Washington, D. C., the world's largest office building, has five sides just like any other pentagon. And a *pentatonic* scale in music has only five notes, rather than the seven notes of the major or minor scale.

PENT 源自希腊语中表示"五"的那个单词。华盛顿特区的 *Pentagon*（五角大楼）是世界最大的办公楼，有五个边，就像任何五边形一样。音乐中的 *pentatonic scale*（五声音阶）只有五个音符，而没有大音阶或小音阶的七个音符。

pentathlon \pen-ˈtath-lən\ An athletic contest in which each athlete competes in five different events. 五项全能比赛

● The modern Olympic pentathlon includes swimming, cross-country running, horseback riding, fencing, and target shooting. 现代奥运五项全能比赛包括游泳、越野跑、马术、击剑和射击。

The Greek word *athlos* means "contest or trial," so to be an *athlete* you had to compete in physical contests. The ancient Greek pentathlon tested warriors' skills in sprinting, long jumping, javelin throwing, discus throwing, and wrestling, none of which are part of today's Olympic pentathlon. But a *pentathlete* must still have muscles and reflexes suited to almost any kind of physical feat. See also *decathlon*, p. 460.

希腊语单词 *athlos* 意思是"竞赛或选拔赛"。所以，要做 *athlete*（运动员），你得在体育竞赛中竞争。古希腊人的五项全能比赛考验的是战士在短跑、跳远、掷标枪、掷铅球和摔跤方面的技能。但是，这五个方面都不是今天的奥运会的一部分。然而，*pentathlete*（五项全能运动员）仍然必须拥有适合于每种身体技能的肌肉和反应能力。（见 *decathlon*，第 460

页）

Pentateuch \ˈpen-tə-ˌtük\ The first five books of the Old Testament, traditionally said to have been written by Moses. 《五经》(《旧约》的前五卷,传统上认为是摩西所写)

• The Pentateuch takes us from the creation of the world up to the Israelites' arrival in the Promised Land. 《五经》将我们从创造世界之初带到了以色列人到达应许之地之时。

Pentateuch means simply "five books." In Greek, the Pentateuch (which Jews call the Torah) includes the books of Genesis, Exodus, Leviticus, Numbers, and Deuteronomy. These contain some of the oldest and most famous stories in the Bible, including those of Adam and Eve, Jacob and his brothers, and Moses, as well as some of the oldest codes of law known, including the Ten Commandments. Pentateuch 意思很简单,就是"五部书"。在希腊语中,《五经》(犹太人称为《律法书》)包括《创世记》《出埃及记》《利未记》《民数记》和《申命记》。这几卷书有《圣经》中最古老、最有名的一些故事,包括亚当和夏娃的故事、雅各与其兄弟们的故事、摩西的故事,还有已知的最古老的一些法律,包括《十诫》。

pentameter \pen-ˈta-mə-tər\ A line of poetry consisting of five metrical feet. 五音步诗行；五音步

• Shakespeare's tragedies are written mainly in blank verse, which is unrhymed iambic pentameter. 莎士比亚创作其悲剧主要用的是无韵诗,也就是不押韵的抑扬格五音步诗行。

In a line of poetry written in perfect *iambic pentameter*, there are five unstressed syllables, each of which is followed by a stressed syllable. Each pair of syllables is a metrical foot called an *iamb*. Much of the greatest poetry in English has been written in iambic pentameter; Chaucer, Shakespeare, and Milton used it more than any other meter. Robert Frost's line "I'm going out to clean the pasture spring" is an example of it; his "And miles to go before I sleep" is instead an example of iambic *tetrameter*, with only four accented syllables. 在一行用完美的 *iambic pentameter*(抑扬格五音步诗行)写的诗歌中,有五个非重读音节,每一个后面紧接着是一个重读音节。每一对音节是一个被称为 *iamb*(抑扬格)的韵步。用英语创作的伟大诗歌,很多都使用抑扬格五音步诗行。乔叟、莎士比亚和弥尔顿使用抑扬格五音步诗多于其他格律。罗伯特·弗洛斯特的诗行"And miles to go before I sleep"(睡前还有很多路要走)则是抑扬格 *tetremeter*(四音步诗),只有四个重读音节。

Pentecostal \ˌpen-ti-ˈkäs-tᵊl\ Of or relating to any of various fundamentalist sects that stress personal experience of God and vocal expression in worship. 五旬节派教会的

• Their neighbors belonged to a Pentecostal sect and homeschooled their daughters, who never wore clothes more revealing than floor-length skirts and long pants. 他们的邻居们属于一个五旬节教派,在家教育女儿。这些女孩子从未穿过比长到脚的裙子和长裤更暴露的衣服。

In ancient Greek, *pentekoste* meant "fiftieth day"—that is, the fiftieth day after Easter (counting Easter itself). On that day, Christians celebrate an event described in the Bible that took place fifty days after Christ's resurrection, when the apostles heard the rush of a mighty wind, saw tongues of fire descending on them, and heard the Holy Spirit speaking from their own mouths but in other tongues (languages). "Speaking in tongues," when everyone in a congregation may begin talking in languages that no one can understand, is the best-known practice of *Pentecostals*. Pentecostals belong to many different denominations; with growing numbers especially in Latin America and Africa, there may be over 500 million Pentecostals worldwide.

在希腊语中,*pentekoste* 意思是"第五十天",也就是复活节后第五十天(包括复活节当天)。那一天,基督徒庆祝《圣经》中讲述的一个事件。这个事件发生在基督复活后第五十天,当时他的门徒听到了大风的呼啸声,看到火舌从天而降,扑向他们,听到了圣灵从他们自己口中说话,但用的是其他"舌头"(即语言)。"用舌头说话",就是会众里每一个人开始用没人懂得的语言说话,是五旬节派教会成员最有名的做法。五旬节派教会成员属于很多不同的教派。随着成员数量的增加,尤其是在拉丁美洲和非洲,全世界可能会有超过五亿人的五旬节派教会成员。

QUINT

QUINT comes from the Latin word meaning "five." *Quintuplets* are babies that come in sets of five; about 60 U.S. families increase in size by that number every year.

QUINT 源自拉丁语中表示"五"的那个词语。*quintuplets* 就是五胞胎婴儿;每年大约有六十个美国家庭增加五个成员。

quincentennial \ˌkwin-sen-ˈte-nē-əl\ A 500th anniversary, or the celebration of such an event. 五百周年纪念;五百周年纪念活动

• In 1992 Americans celebrated the quincentennial of Christopher Columbus's first voyage to the New World. 1992 年,美国人庆祝了克里斯托弗·哥伦布首次航行到达新世界的五百周年纪念。

The United States is such a young country that it will be quite some time before we reach our quincentennial as a nation: 2276 A.D., to be exact. Some American cities will celebrate their quincentennials long before that, but even St. Augustine, Florida, the nation's oldest city, will have to wait until 2065. Meanwhile, many young people can look forward happily to our national *tricentennial* in 2076; and their grandchildren may be around for our *quadricentennial* in 2176.

美国是一个很年轻的国家。我们作为一个国家,要过很久才能庆祝五百周年纪念,确切地说是在公元 2276 年。有些美国城市在这很久之前就将庆祝他们的五百周年纪念。不过,即使是这个国家最古老的城市佛罗里达的圣奥古斯丁,也不得不等到 2065 年。同时,很多年轻人可以高兴地期待我们国家将于 2076 年庆祝 *tricentennial*(三百周年纪念)。他们的曾孙们或许可以在 2176 年庆祝我们的 *quadricentennial*(四百周年纪念)。

quintessential \ˌkwin-tə-ˈsen-chəl\ Representing the purest or most perfect example of something. 典范的

• As a boy, he had thought of steak, eggs, and home fries as the quintessential Saturday breakfast. 童年时代,他就想在最好的周日早餐吃牛排、鸡蛋和家常炸土豆片。

The philosophers and scientists of the ancient world and the Middle Ages believed that the world we inhabit was entirely made up of four elements: earth, air, fire, and water. Aristotle added a fifth element, the *aether* or *ether*, by which he meant the material that fills the rest of space, mostly invisibly but sometimes taking the form of stars and planets. Many writers described the element as a kind of invisible light or fire. In the Middle Ages, it was referred to as the *quinta essentia* ("fifth element"). It isn't surprising that the *quinta essentia* came to stand for anything so perfect that it seemed to surpass the limitations of earth. Today we generally use *quintessential* rather freely to describe just about anything that represents the best of its kind.

古代世界和中世纪的哲学家和科学家认为，我们居住的这个世界完全由四种元素构成：土、空气、火和水。亚里士多德增加了第五个元素：aether 或者 ether，他用这个词语表示充满宇宙其他空间的材料，很大程度上是看不见的，但有时候以星星和行星的形式出现。很多作家将这一元素描述为一种看不见的光或者火。在中世纪，人们把它说成是 quinta essenia（"第五种元素"）。quinta essentia 后来代表非常完美，似乎超越地球局限的任何事物，这并不奇怪。今天，我们通常很自由地使用 quintessential 来描述能代表各项种类事物的最佳者。

QUINT

quintet\kwin-'tet\ (1) A musical piece for five instruments or voices. 五重奏乐曲；五重唱歌曲 (2) A group of five, such as the performers of a quintet or a basketball team. 五人组（比如五重奏或五重唱表演者或者篮球队）

● The team's five starters are considered one of the most talented quintets in professional basketball. 这个球队的五个参赛者被认为是职业篮球最有天赋的五人组。

A classical *quintet* is usually written for strings (usually two violins, two violas, and a cello) or woodwinds (flute, oboe, clarinet, bassoon, and horn), but brass quintets (two trumpets, horn, trombone, and tuba) have also become popular in North America recently. In jazz, Miles Davis led two famous quintets. In pop music, the Miracles, the Temptations, and the Jackson 5 were immensely popular vocal quintets. In rock, one of the most common instrumental lineups has been a quintet consisting of two guitars, a bass, a keyboard, and drums; famous rock quintets have included the Grateful Dead and the Beach Boys.

古典五重奏曲通常是为弦乐器组写的（通常有两个小提琴、两个中提琴和一个大提琴），或者为木管乐器组写的（笛子、双簧管、单簧管、低音管和大号），但是铜管五重奏（两个喇叭、号、长号和大号）最近在北美也很流行。在爵士乐界，迈尔斯·戴维斯领导两个著名五重奏乐队。在流行乐界，奇迹乐队、诱惑乐队和杰克逊五人乐队曾经是极其流行的声乐五重唱乐队。在摇滚乐界，最普通的乐器阵容包括两把吉他、一个低音号、一个键盘和几个鼓。著名的摇滚五人组包括"感恩而死"和"海滩男孩"。

quintile\'kwin-ˌtīl\ One or another of the values that divide a tested population into five evenly distributed classes, or one of these classes. 五分位值

● According to the tests, their one-year-old boy ranks high in the second quintile for motor skills. 根据这些测试，他们一岁的儿子在运动技能的第二个五分位值中名列前茅。

Americans love statistics about themselves, whether they inform us about our income, ice-cream consumption, or trash production. And any such rating can be

• 437 •

divided into fifths, or quintiles. The fifth or lowest quintile would include the 20 percent of the population who make the least money or eat the least ice cream or generate the least trash, and the first quintile would include the 20 percent who make, eat, or generate the most.

美国人喜欢关于自己的统计数字,不管这些数字告诉我们的是我们的收入,冰淇淋消费量还是垃圾产生量。任何这种等级都可以分成五个五分之一,或者五分位值。第五个,也就是最低的五分位值,包括人口中挣钱最少,或者吃的冰淇淋最少,或者产生垃圾最少的人。第一个五分位值则包括百分之二十挣钱最多、吃冰淇淋最多、产生垃圾最多的人。

Quiz

Match the definition on the left to the correct word on the right:

1. evangelically Christian　　　　a. quintet
2. most typical　　　　　　　　　b. quintile
3. event with five contests　　　　c. Pentateuch
4. 500th birthday　　　　　　　　d. pentathlon
5. composition for five　　　　　e. quincentennial
6. poetic rhythm　　　　　　　　f. Pentecostal
7. first books of the Bible　　　　g. quintessential
8. one fifth of a group　　　　　h. pentameter

Review Quizzes

A. Choose the correct synonym:

1. degrade　　　　a. praise　　　　b. outclass　　　　c. lose
   d. lower
2. capitulate　　　a. nod　　　　　b. yield　　　　　c. resist
   d. fall in
3. hypercritical　　a. pretended　　b. complimentary
   c. underdeveloped　d. overly harsh
4. criterion　　　　a. argument　　b. scolding　　　　c. standard
   d. critical review
5. retrograde　　　a. failing　　　b. forward　　　　c. sideways
   d. backward
6. abjure　　　　　a. take up　　　b. damn　　　　　c. reject
   d. include
7. perjury　　　　a. cleansing　　b. lying under oath　c. theft
   d. court decision
8. misanthropic　　a. humanitarian　b. wretched
   c. antisocial　　　d. monumental

UNIT 18

9. de jure   a. by a judge   b. by a lawyer   c. by law
   d. by a jury
10. pentathlon   a. five competitions
    b. five-note scale   c. five-month period
    d. five-sided figure

B. Fill in each blank with the correct letter:

a. decapitate   i. recapitulate
b. anthropology   j. hyperkinetic
c. dynamic   k. criterion
d. gradient   l. quintessential
e. regency   m. hematocrit
f. critique   n. pentathlon
g. Pentecostal   o. quintet
h. quintile

1. Her main _____ for a boyfriend was a great sense of humor.

2. In Japan, the track for a mountain cable car climbs at a _____ of an astonishing 31 degrees.

3. Our professor is always careful to _____ her main points at the end of each class.

4. He would write a lengthy _____ on every term paper, though he suspected few of the students ever read them.

5. For her, *The Night of the Living Dead* remained the _____ horror film, against which she judged all the others.

6. The _____ lasted several years, as the boy king passed through an awkward preadolescent stage to emerge as a serious and dignified 20-year-old.

7. The concert ended with a string _____ by Beethoven.

8. For his graduate work in _____, he's been doing research on societies in India's tribal areas.

9. She's having her bloodwork done and is waiting anxiously to hear her _____.

10. In their harsh justice system, the standard practice was to lop off the hands of minor offenders and _____ serious criminals.

11. The test results placed her in the highest _____ of the population.

12. By all accounts, he was a _____ and forceful individual.

13. At 25 he was still as _____ as a 14-year-old, constantly fidgeting at his desk, with his leg bouncing up and down.

14. They grew up attending a _____ church, watching their father speak in tongues on most Sundays.

15. Track stars with superb all-round training usually try out for the _____ competition.

C. Choose the closest definition:

1. anthropoid
   a. tapirs and antelopes
   b. cats and dogs
   c. chimpanzees and gorillas
   d. salamanders and chameleons
2. gradation
   a. step in a series
   b. show in a series
   c. novel in series
   d. speech in a series
3. quintile
   a. fifteenth
   b. five-spot
   c. group of five
   d. one fifth
4. quintessential
   a. fifth
   b. being
   c. ideal
   d. important
5. Pentateuch
   a. New Testament books
   b. five-sided figure
   c. Old Testament books
   d. five-pointed star
6. capitalism
   a. free-enterprise system
   b. common-property state
   c. socialist democracy
   d. controlled economy
7. dynamo
   a. explosive
   b. missile
   c. generator
   d. electric weapon
8. quincentennial
   a. 5th anniversary
   b. 15th anniversary
   c. 50th anniversary
   d. 500th anniversary
9. pentameter
   a. five-line stanza
   b. five-word sentence
   c. five-beat poetic line
   d. five-sided shape
10. regalia
    a. monarchy
    b. official costume
    c. regularity
    d. solemn dignity
11. criterion
    a. dinosaur
    b. mourning
    c. criticism
    d. gauge
12. jurisprudence
    a. legal philosophy
    b. legal agreement
    c. senior judge
    d. cautious ruling
13. regimen
    a. daily plan
    b. strict order
    c. ruling family
    d. officers' club
14. perjury
    a. suing
    b. cursing
    c. misleading
    d. lying
15. critique
    a. mystique
    b. commentary
    c. argument
    d. defense

UNIT 19

BIO comes from the Greek word for "life," and forms the base for many English words. *Biology*, for instance, is the study of living forms and life processes; the *biosphere* is the entire area of and above the earth where life can exist; and *biotechnology* is the use of living organisms to create useful products.

BIO 源自希腊语中表示"生命"的那个词语，构成了很多英语单词的基础。比如 biology（生物学）这个单词，意思是对生活形式和生命过程进行研究的学问；biosphere（生物圈）是位于地球上面生物存在的整个区域；biotechnology（生物技术）就是利用生物生产有用产品。

bionic \bī-'ä-nik\ Made stronger or more capable by electronic or mechanical devices. （因电子或机械装置而变得）更加强大的；能力更强的

• Bionic feet and hands for amputees have ceased to be mere sci-fi fantasies and are becoming realities. 为截肢者提供能力更强的手和脚不再仅仅是科学幻想了，而正在成为现实。

The science of *bionics* uses knowledge about how biological systems work to help solve engineering problems. The material Velcro, for example, was inspired by the way burrs behave when they stick to your clothes, and some computer chips are now wired in ways that imitate the "wiring" of the brain and nervous system. But in popular use, the adjective *bionic* almost always describes artificial limbs or other bodily parts that work as much like real ones as possible. A perfect bionic arm would move and function as easily as a real arm—a goal we're rapidly getting closer to.

bionics（仿生学）利用对生物系统如何运转的知识帮助解决工程问题。比如维可牢这种材料，其灵感来源于带芒刺的小果实粘在衣服上的原理，有些计算机芯片现在的安装方式模仿大脑和神经系统的"线路"。但是在流行的用法中，形容词 bionicd 几乎总是描述尽可能像真实器官那样工作的假肢或者其他器官。完美的仿生胳膊会跟真的胳膊一样移动和发挥其功能——这是我们正在快速接近的目标。

biopsy \'bī-ˌäp-sē\ The removal and examination of tissue, cells, or fluids from a living body. 活组织检查

• Everyone felt relieved when the results of the biopsy showed the tumor wasn't cancerous. 当活组织检查结果表明肿瘤没有发生癌变时,大家放心了。

Matter examined in a *biopsy* is always taken from a living organism. Most biopsies are done by using a needle to extract tissue or fluid, but some may instead require cutting, and others may amount to nothing more than swabbing the inside of the patient's cheek. Biopsies are best known as a means of detecting cancer, but a doctor may also take a biopsy of heart muscle to investigate suspected heart disease, for example, or perform a biopsy on a pregnant woman to test for disorders in the fetus.

活组织检查中的物质总是采自活着的生物。进行大多数活组织检查,都用一根针来提取组织或体液,但是有些需要进行切割,其他的可能仅仅是用试纸擦拭病人脸颊内面。活组织检查最为人所知的,就是它是一种发现癌症的方式,但是,医生也可能对心脏肌肉进行活组织检查,以了解他怀疑存在的心脏病,或者对孕妇进行活组织检查,来检查胎儿是否存在疾病。

biodegradable \ˌbī-ō-di-ˈgrā-də-bəl\ Able to be broken down into harmless substances by microorganisms or other living things. 可生物降解的

• Though the advertisements promised that the entire package was biodegradable, environmentalists expressed their doubts. 虽然这些广告承诺整个包装盒都是可生物降解的,但是环境保护主义者表示怀疑。

In *biodegradable*, with its root *grad*, "to step or move," and its prefix *de-* "downward," we get an adjective describing things that can be broken down into basic substances through normal environmental processes. Animal and plant products are normally biodegradable, but mineral substances such as metals, glass, and plastics usually are not. Newly developed biodegradable plastics are now appearing in numerous products. However, "biodegradable" products can vary greatly in how long they take to break down. A loaf of bread may require only a couple of weeks, and a piece of paper may vanish in a couple of months, but some "biodegradable" plastic milk cartons may take four or five years.

biodegradable 这一单词,因为含有词根 *grad* ("迈步;移动")以及前缀 *de-* ("向下"),让我们有了一个形容词,来描绘通过正常环境过程可分解成基本物质的事物。动植物产品通常是可生物降解的,但是矿物质,比如金属、玻璃和塑料,常常并不是这样的。新开发的可生物降解的塑料正出现在很多产品中。然而,"可生物降解的"产品多久可以分解,差异就很大了。一个面包可能只需要几个星期,一张纸可能在几个月之内就消失了,可是有些"可生物降解的"塑料牛奶盒可能需要四五年的时间。

symbiosis \ˌsim-bē-ˈō-səs\ (1) The close living together of two different forms of life in a way that benefits both. 共生 (2) A cooperative relationship between two people or groups. 合作关系

• The lichen that grows on rocks is produced by the symbiosis of a fungus and an alga, two very different organisms. 生长在岩石上的地衣是一种真菌和一种藻共生的结果,而这两者是差异很大的生物。

With its prefix *sym-*, "with," *symbiosis* expresses the notion of cooperation between living things. *Symbiotic* associations are found throughout the plant and animal world. You may have read, for instance, of the little blackbird plover, which picks the teeth of the fierce African crocodile. Or the bird called the African honeyguide, which leads a little mammal called the ratel to a bees' nest, which the ratel, protected from the bees by its thick fur, then breaks open, and both it and the honeyguide feast on the honey. Or even our own bodies, which are home to millions of bacteria—especially the bacterium *E. coli* in our intestines—and neither we nor *E. coli* could live without the other. You can probably think of plenty of human relationships that could be called *symbiotic* as well.

因为有了前缀 *sym-*（跟……在一起），*symbiosis* 就表达了生物之间的合作这一概念。比如，你可能通过阅读了解到，千鸟为凶猛的非洲犀牛剔牙。或者非洲向蜜鸟将蜜獾这种小型哺乳动物引向蜂巢（蜜獾皮毛厚实不怕被蜜蜂叮，能打开蜂巢向蜜鸟可趁机获取蜂蜜），或者甚至是我们自己的身体生存着数百万细菌（尤其是我们肠内的大肠杆菌），我们自己和细菌离开对方都不能生存。你可能会想到很多也可称为 *symbiotic* 的人类关系。

GEN

GEN, which comes from the Greek *genos*, meaning "birth," has *generated* dozens of English words. A set of *genes*, for instance, gives birth to a living being. And a *genealogy* is a historical map of your family, showing how each *generation* gave birth to the next.

GEN 源自希腊语 *genos*（"生"），*generated*（产生）了很多英语单词。比如一组基因会产生一个生物。*genealogy*（系谱）就是家庭的历史地图，表明每一 *generation*（代）是如何产生下一代的。

genesis \ˈje-nə-səs\ Origin, beginning. 起源，开端

- The genesis of the project dates back to 1976, when the two young men were roommates at Cornell University. 这一项目的起源可追溯至 1976 年，当时这两个年轻人在康奈尔大学是舍友。

The traditional Greek name for the first and best-known book of the Bible is *Genesis*, meaning "origin." Genesis tells the stories of the creation, Adam and Eve, Cain and Abel, Noah's ark, the Tower of Babel, Abraham and his sons, and more—the stories that explain how the world and humanity were created, as well as much about how humanity, and especially the descendants of Abraham, relate to the rest of the world. Today we use *genesis* to refer to the creative beginnings of much smaller things, but never unimportant ones.

《圣经》第一卷也是最著名的一卷，其传统的希腊语名称是 *Genesis*（《创世记》），意思是"起源"。《创世记》讲述了上帝创造世界、亚当和夏娃、该隐与亚伯、诺亚方舟、巴别塔、亚伯拉罕和儿子们等等许多故事。这些故事解释了世界和人类是如何产生的，还对人类，尤其是亚伯拉罕的后裔与世上其他人之间的联系解释了不少。今天，我们用 *genesis* 来指那些小得多但一直很重要的事物的起源。

generator \ˈje-nə-ˌrā-tər\ A machine by which mechanical energy is changed into electrical energy. 发电机

- The jungle settlement depended on a large generator, which provided electricity for a couple of hours each morning and evening. 这个丛林定居点依靠一台巨大的发电机,每天早晚提供几小时的电。

Generators work by rotating a coil of wire in a magnetic field, causing a current to flow in the wire. A generator may be a huge spinning turbine powered by water, wind, steam, gas, or nuclear reactions, which sends electricity out through power lines to thousands of customers. But normally when we use the word, we're thinking of a small machine powered by gasoline or diesel, such as you might keep in your basement for those times when a storm knocks out your power, to create electricity right in front of your eyes. A special kind of generator called an alternator powers a car's electrical system (including its lights, power steering, etc.) while the car is running. 发电机转动处于磁场中的一卷电线,使电能在电线中流动。发电机可能是一台巨大的旋转涡轮机,由水、风、蒸汽、天然气或者核反应来提供动力。它通过输电线把电能送给千万个客户。不过,我们通常使用这个词语时,想到的是一台小机器,由汽油或柴油提供动力。这种机器就像你放在地下室的那种,预备着在暴风雨中断电力时就在你眼前发电。汽车行驶的时候,为其电力系统提供能量的是一种特殊的叫做交流发电机的机器。

genre\ˈzhän-rə\ Kind, sort; especially a distinctive type or category of literature, art, or music. 种类;(文学、美术、音乐的)体裁;类型

• Opera was a new genre for her, since all her compositions up until then had been songs and chamber music. 歌剧对她来说是一种新的类型,因为直到当时,陪伴她的都是歌曲和室内乐。

Genre, as you might guess from the way it sounds, comes straight from French, a language based on Latin. It's closely related to genus, a word you may have encountered in biology class. Both words contain the gen- root because they indicate that everything in a particular category (a genre or a genus) belongs to the same "family" and thus has the same origins. So the main genres of classical music would include symphonies, sonatas, and opera, and the major genres of literature would include novels, short stories, poetry, and drama. But within the category of novels, we could also say that detective novels, sci-fi novels, romance novels, and young-adult novels are separate genres. 你从其发音方式就可以猜到,genre 直接来自法语这种以拉丁语为基础的语言。跟它有密切关系的 genus(属)这一词语,你可能在生物学课堂遇到过。两个词语都含有 gen- 这一词根,因为它们表明某一种类(genre 或者 genus)中的一切都属于同一"family"("科"),所以有着同样的来源。因此,古典音乐的主要体裁会包括交响乐、奏鸣曲和歌剧,而文学的体裁则包括长篇小说、短篇小说、诗歌和戏剧。但是,在长篇小说这一种类中,我们也可以说侦探小说、科幻小说、爱情小说以及青少年小说是不同的体裁。

carcinogenic\ˌkär-sə-nō-ˈje-nik\ Producing or causing cancer. 致癌的

• Although she knows all too well that the tobacco in cigarettes is carcinogenic, she's too addicted to quit. 虽然她很清楚香烟中的烟草能够致癌,但是太上瘾了,没法戒烟。

It sometimes seems as if the list of carcinogenic substances gets longer every day. A substance such as a food additive that's been in common use for years may unexpectedly show signs of being carcinogenic in laboratory experiments. When that happens, the suspected *carcinogen* will often have to be withdrawn from the market. When a building material like asbestos turns out to be a carcinogen, it may also have to be physically removed from buildings. English has hundreds of other scientific words ending in *-genic* (such as *allergenic*), and in almost all of them the ending means "causing."

<small>有时候,致癌物质的单子好像越来越长。在实验室的实验中,被普遍使用多年的物质,比如某种食物添加剂,竟然显示出致癌的迹象。发生这种情况时,这种令人怀疑的 carcinogen(致癌物)往往要从市场收回了,它甚至可能被人从建筑物中除去。英语中有数百个其他科学术语的词尾也是 -genic(比如 allergenic,过敏的)。在几乎所有这些词语中,这一词尾的意思都是"引起"。</small>

Quizzes

A. Fill in each blank with the correct letter:

a. genre   e. biopsy
b. symbiosis   f. genesis
c. carcinogenic   g. bionic
d. biodegradable   h. generator

1. The _____ of the idea for his first novel lay in a casual remark by a stranger one afternoon in the park.

2. Scientists are working on new _____ devices to enable amputees to do detailed manual work.

3. Any insecticides that are known to be _____ have supposedly been banned by the federal government.

4. Just about everything in our bodies is _____ except the fillings in our teeth.

5. She had a physical last week, and the doctor ordered a _____ of a suspicious-looking patch of skin.

6. After 50 years of marriage, the _____ between them is just about total.

7. About once a year, an ice storm knocks out the electricity, and we haul out the _____ to get everything going again.

8. She loved various kinds of classical music, but the string quartet was one _____ that she could never warm up to.

B. Indicate whether the following pairs have the same or different meanings:

1. genesis / birth   same ____ / different ____
2. biopsy / life story   same ____ / different ____
3. generator / electricity-producing machine   same ____ / different ____
4. biodegradable / readily broken down   same ____ / different ____
5. carcinogenic / cancer-causing   same ____ / different ____
6. symbiosis / shared existence   same ____ / different ____
7. genre / animal group   same ____ / different ____
8. bionic / fantastic   same ____ / different ____

FUNCT comes from the Latin verb *fungi*, "to perform, carry out." If your car is *functional*, it's able to perform its *function* of providing transportation. But a *functional illiterate* is a person who, for all practical or functional purposes, might as well not be able to read or write at all.
FUNCT源自拉丁语动词*fungi*(进行,做)。如果你的车是*functional*(能起作用的,工作的,运转的),它就能够发挥其运输*function*(功能)。但是,*functional illiterate*(半文盲)是一个实际上几乎不会读、写的人。

functionary \ˈfəŋk-shə-ˌner-ē\ (1) Someone who performs a certain function. 履行某一职责的人 (2) Someone who holds a position in a political party or government. 官员;公职人员

• He was one of a group of party functionaries assigned to do the dirty work of the campaign. 他是被指派在这次运动中执行肮脏任务的党内官员之一。

For most of us, being described as a *functionary* wouldn't be a compliment. The word refers especially to a person of lower rank, with little or no authority, who must carry out someone else's orders. *Bureaucrat* is often a synonym. However, *functionary* can also refer to the world beyond government and offices; a character in a play, for example, could be called a functionary if it was obvious that her sole function was to keep the plot moving.
对我们大多数人来说,被称作一个*functionary*不是什么赞扬的话。这个词语特别指一个职务较低、根本没有或者没有多少权力、必须执行某人命令的人。*bureaucrat*(官僚)常常是它的一个同义词。不过,*functionary*也可以指政府和办公室之外的世界。比如戏剧中的一个人物,如果她唯一的作用就是让阴谋继续下去,就可以被称为*functionary*。

malfunction\ˌmal-ˈfəŋk-shən\ To fail to operate in the normal or usual manner. 失灵;出现故障;运转失常

• An examination of the wreck revealed that the brakes may have malfunctioned as the truck started down the hill. 对残骸进行仔细检查后可以发现,卡车顺山坡向下行驶的时候,车闸失灵了。

A *malfunctioning* switch might keep us from turning on a light. A malfunctioning heart valve might require replacement with an artificial valve, and if your immune system *malfunctions* it may start to attack healthy cells. And a *malfunction* in a voting machine could result in hundreds of votes being miscounted.
malfunctioning(出现故障的)开关会让我们无法开灯。malfunctioning(不正常的)心脏瓣膜可能需要用人工瓣膜进行更换。如果人体免疫系统malfunctions(出现问题),可能会开始袭击健康细胞。自动选票机出现*malfunction*(故障)就会使大量选票被数错。

defunct\di-ˈfəŋkt\ No longer, living, existing, or functioning. 已灭绝的;已消失的;不再运转的

• The company, which had once had annual sales of $150 million, was now defunct. 这家公司曾经有一亿五千万美元的年销售额，现在却已消失了。

  If you know that *de-* often means "the opposite of" (see DE-, p. 646), it's easy to guess the meaning of *defunct*. Shakespeare seems to have been the first writer to use this adjective, in *Henry V*. Defunct American political parties include the Greenback Party, the Readjuster Party, and the Nullifier Party. Defunct Academy Awards categories include Best Dance Direction and Best Assistant Director. Defunct U. S. auto models include the Dudly Bug, the LuLu, the Hupmobile, the Gas-au-lec, and the Nu-Klea Starlite. But to speak of a person as defunct would sound disrespectful—which is how it sounds in E. Cummings's famous poem "Buffalo Bill's defunct."

  如果你知道 *de-* 通常的意思是"……的对立"(见 DE-，第 646 页)，就很容易猜到 *defunct* 的意思。莎士比亚似乎在《亨利五世》中首次使用了这个词语。已经消失的美国政党包括绿背党、重新调整者党以及废弃党。已消失的学院奖种类包括最佳舞蹈指导奖和最佳副导演奖。已消失的美国车型包括达德利小虫、鲁鲁、哈普车、嘎斯奥莱克以及努克利星光。但是，说一个人 defunct 听起来会很不尊重人——在卡明斯那首著名的诗歌"*Buffalo Bill's defunct*"("野牛比尔死了")中听起来就这样。

> MUT

dysfunctional \dis-ˈfəŋ(k)-shnəl\
(1) Showing abnormal or unhealthy behaviors and attitudes within a group of people. 难以处理正常社会关系的 (2) Being unable to function in a normal way. 运转不正常的

  • A psychologist would call their family dysfunctional, but even though there's a lot of yelling and slamming of doors, they seem pretty happy to me. 一位心理学家会说他们的家庭不正常，但即使他们常常又是喊叫又是摔门，在我看来还是蛮幸福的。

  Dysfunctional and *dysfunction* have been used for almost a hundred years, often in medical writing ("brain dysfunction," "a dysfunctional liver") but also by social scientists ("a dysfunctional city council," "diplomatic dysfunction"). But they only really entered the general vocabulary in the 1980s, when therapists and talk-show hosts began talking about dysfunctional families. The signs of family dysfunction turned out to be numerous, and it soon began to seem as if pretty much all our families could be called dysfunctional.

  dysfunctional 和 *dysfunction* 被使用快一百年了，经常出现在医学文字中("brain dysfunction""a dysfunctional liver")，但社会科学家也用("a dysfunctional city council""diplomatic dysfunction")。不过，它们在 20 世纪 80 年代才进入一般词汇。当时，治疗师和脱口秀主持人开始谈到了 dysfunctional 家庭。家庭 disfunction 有很多迹象，不久，在很大程度上我们所有家庭似乎都可以是 dysfunctional 了。

MUT comes from the Latin *mutare*, "to change."
Plenty of sciencefiction movies—*Godzilla*, *The Fly*, *The Incredible Shrinking Man*—used to be made on the subject of weird *mutations*, changes in normal people or animals that usually end up causing death and destruction. What causes the unfortunate victim to *mutate* may be a mysterious or alien force, or perhaps invisible radiation. Though the science in these films isn't always right on target, the scare factor of an army of *mutants* can be

• 447 •

hard to beat.

MUT 源自拉丁语的 *mutare*（"变化"）。很多科幻电影——《哥斯拉》《变蝇人》《奇怪的收缩人》——依据的都是奇怪的 *mutations*（变异），也就是正常人或动物发生的变化,通常的结局是引起死亡和毁灭。使不幸的受害者发生变化的,可能是一种神秘的或者外来的力量,或者可能是看不见的辐射。虽然这些电影中的科学并非总是正确,但一群异形这一恐惧因素是很难超越的。

commute \kə-ˈmyüt\ (1) To exchange or substitute; especially to change a penalty to another one that is less severe. 替换;替代;(尤其是)减刑 (2) To travel back and forth regularly. 通勤

- There was a public outcry at the harshness of the prison sentence, and two days later the governor commuted it to five years. 公众对这一严厉的判刑表示抗议。两天后,州长将其减为五年。

When you *commute* between a suburb and a city, you're "exchanging" one location for another. When a chief executive substitutes a life sentence for the death sentence handed down by a court, he or she is commuting the original sentence. Most such *commutations* are the result of the prisoner's good behavior. A *commutator* is a device in many electric motors that regularly changes alternating current to direct current. 当你在郊区和城市之间来回坐车时,你就是在用一个地点"替代"另一个地点。当一位州长（或市长）用无期徒刑代替法庭公布的死刑时,他或她就是在减轻最初的判决。大多数这样的 *commutations*（减刑）的原因都是因犯表现良好。*commutator*（电流转向器）是很多电动机里的一个装置,将交流电有规律地变成直流电。

immutable \i-ˈmyü-tə-bəl\ Not able or liable to change. 不能变化的;不大可能变化的

- Early philosophers believed there was an immutable substance at the root of all existence. 早期的哲学家认为,所有存在的起因是一种不变的物质。

Mutable means simply "changeable," so when the negative prefix *im-* is added we get its opposite. In computer programming, an *immutable* object is one that can't be changed after it's been created. In a constantly changing world, people who hunger for things as immutable as the laws of nature may try to observe an immutable moral code and set of values. Unfortunately, *immutability* isn't a basic quality of many things in this world. *mutable* 意思很简单,就是"能变化的",所以加上 *im-* 这一否定前缀后,我们就得到了其反义词。在计算机编程中,一个 immutable 目标就是设计后不能改变的目标。在这个不断变化的世界上,渴望一切都像自然规律那样不变的人,可能想要遵守不变的道德准则和价值观。不幸的是,*immutability*（不变性）不是这个世界上很多事物的基本特点。

permutation \ˌpər-myü-ˈtā-shən\ A change in the order of a set of objects; rearrangement, variation. 顺序的变化;重新排列;变化

- They had rearranged the rooms in the house plans four or five times already, but the architect had come up with yet another permutation. 他们把房屋平面图上的房间重新安排四五次了,但建筑师又有了新的安排方式。

There are six *permutations* of the letters A, B, and C, selected two at a time;

AB, AC, BC, BA, CA, and CB. As you see, order is important in permutations. (By contrast, there are only three *combinations*: AB, AC, and BC.) Permutation is an important concept in mathematics, especially in the field of probability. But we can use the word more generally to mean any change produced by rearranging existing parts without introducing new ones. Some soap operas, for example, love permutations; the cast of regulars is constantly being rearranged into new pairs, and even triangles.

字母 A、B、C 有六种排列方式,每次选择两个:AB、AC、BC、BA、CA 和 CB。可以看到,顺序在排列中很重要。(与此截然不同的是,它们只有三种 *combinations*[组合]:AB、AC 和 BC)。排列在数学上似乎是一个重要概念,尤其是在概率领域。但是,我们可以更广泛地使用这一词语,表示没有引入新部分而重新安排现存部分引起的任何变化。比如说某些肥皂剧喜欢重新组合,一直出现的演员被不断重新安排成新的两人组合,甚至三人组合。

MUT

transmute \ trans-'myüt \ (1) To change in shape, appearance, or nature, especially for the better; to transform. (形状、外貌或性质的)变化;改善 (2) To experience such a change. 经历变化(或改善)

• Working alone in his cluttered laboratory in 15th-century Milan, he spent twenty years searching for a method of transmuting lead into gold. 在 15 世纪的米兰,他在自己那个堆满东西的实验室里工作,花了二十年时间寻找一种将铅变成金子的方法。

Transmutation changes something over into something else. Thus, a writer may transmute his life into stories or novels, and an arranger might transmute a lively march tune into a quiet lullaby. In the "Myth of Er" at the end of Plato's *Republic*, for example, human souls are transmuted into the body and existence of their choice. Having learned from their last life what they do *not* want to be, many choose transmutation into something that seems better. A meek man chooses to be transmuted into a tyrant, a farmer into a dashing (but short-lived) warrior, and so on. But very few seem to have learned anything from their former life that would make their choice a real improvement.

transmutation 将一种事物变成另一种事物。这样,作家会将自己的生活经历变成故事或者小说,编曲者会将活泼的进行曲变成轻柔的摇篮曲。比如,在柏拉图的《共和国》结尾处的"厄尔神话"中,人类的灵魂被变成了自己想要的身体和生活。从上一次生活中知道了自己不想成为什么之后,很多人决定变成看上去更好的东西。一个温顺的男人决定变成暴君,一个农民决定变成自信潇洒(但活不长)的士兵,等等。但是,好像很少有人从前世学到什么东西能让自己的选择变得确实更好了。

Quizzes

A. Choose the closest definition:

1. defunct   a. dead   b. depressed   c. defective
   d. deserted
2. permutation   a. evolution   b. rearrangement
   c. approval   d. inflation
3. functionary   a. bureaucrat   b. hard worker

c. activist   d. executive
4. transmute   a. reconsider   b. send away   c. silence
   d. convert
5. dysfunctional   a. untrained   b. divorced
   c. performing poorly   d. unfamiliar
6. immutable   a. unchangeable   b. immature   c. noisy
   d. defiant
7. malfunction   a. work slowly   b. work improperly
   c. work efficiently   d. work mechanically
8. commute   a. deposit   b. invest   c. discuss
   d. change

B. Complete the analogies:

1. hostile : friendly :: immutable : _____
   a. changeable   b. decaying   c. breathable   d. out of date
2. wounded : healed :: dysfunctional : _____
   a. lame   b. healthy   c. crippled   d. unsteady
3. permit : allow :: commute : _____
   a. review   b. claim   c. substitute   d. send
4. healthy : vigorous :: defunct : _____
   a. brainless   b. failed   c. strong   d. unhappy
5. order : sequence :: permutation : _____
   a. addition   b. notion   c. rearrangement   d. removal
6. soldier : army :: functionary : _____
   a. anthill   b. stadium   c. vacation   d. organization
7. transmit : send :: transmute : _____
   a. transit   b. transform   c. transfer   d. transport
8. misbehave : scold :: malfunction : _____
   a. function   b. fix   c. exchange   d. rearrange

FRACT

FRACT comes from the Latin verb *frangere*, "to break or shatter." A *fraction* is one of the pieces into which a whole can be broken, and a *fracture* is a break in a wall, a rock, or a bone.

FRACT 源自拉丁语动词 *frangere*("断裂或破碎")。*fraction* 指整个事物破裂成的碎块之一,*fracture* 指墙壁、岩石或者骨头发生的断裂。

---

fractious\ˈfrak-shəs\   (1) Apt to cause trouble or be unruly. 捣乱的;惹是生非的;难以管教的 (2) Stirring up quarrels; irritable. 引发吵闹的;暴躁的;易怒的

- Shopping with a fractious child is next to impossible. 带一个喜欢捣蛋的孩子购物几乎让人无法忍受。

One of the earliest meanings of *fraction* was "a break in good feeling"—that is, an argument or conflict. So a person who starts fights could be called fractious. A fractious horse is one that hasn't been properly broken or trained. A fractious political party is one whose members keep fighting among themselves. And a fractious baby is one that's always breaking the home's peace and quiet with angry squalling. *fraction* 最早的意思之一是"感情出现裂缝",也就是争吵了或者发生冲突了。所以,引发打斗的人可以说是 fractious。*fractious* 马是没有正确驯服或训练的马。fractious 政党是成员总是内斗的政党。fractious 婴儿是总是生气地哭叫、打破家庭安静的婴儿。

FRACT

fractal \ˈfrak-tᵊl\ An irregular shape that looks much the same at any scale on which it is examined. 分形

- He was showing her the fractals in the local ferns, in which each leaf reproduced the shape of the entire fern. 他正给她看当地蕨类植物上的分形,每个叶子再现了整棵蕨类植物的形状。

This term was coined in 1975 to describe shapes that seem to exist at both the small-scale and large-scale levels in the same natural object. Fractals can be seen in snowflakes, in which the microscopic crystals that make up a flake look much like the flake itself. They can also be seen in tree bark and in broccoli buds. Coastlines often represent fractals as well, being highly uneven at both a large scale and a very small scale. Fractal geometry has been important in many fields, including astronomy, physical chemistry, and fluid mechanics. And even some artists are benefiting, creating beautiful and interesting abstract designs by means of fractals. 这一术语创造于 1975 年,用来形容在同一个自然物体中,似乎既存在于小规模又存在于大规模水平的形状。不规则碎片形可以在雪花中看到,构成雪花的每个微小晶体看上去跟雪花很相似。这种形状也可在树皮和西蓝花花苞中见到。海岸线也常常再现不规则碎片形。分形几何在很多领域都很重要,包括天文学、物理化学和流体力学。甚至一些艺术家也从中受益了,用分形创造了美丽、有趣的抽象图案。

infraction \ in-ˈfrak-shən \ The breaking of a law or a violation of another's rights. 违法;犯法;违反他人权利

- The assistant principal dealt with any students who had committed minor infractions of the rules. 副校长处理轻微违反校规的学生。

An infraction is usually the breaking of a law, rule, or agreement. So a nation charged with an infraction of an international treaty will usually have to pay a penalty. In Federal law, an infraction is even smaller than a misdemeanor, and the only penalty is a fine. Most of us occasionally commit infractions of parking laws and get ticketed; speeding tickets are usually for infractions as well, though they go on a permanent record and can end up costing you money for years to come. The closely related word *infringement* generally refers to a violation of a right or privilege; use of another's writings without permission, for example, may be an infringement of the copyright.

infraction 通常是违法、违反规则或者协定。所以被指控违反国际条约的国家通常不得不接受处罚。在《联邦法》中，*infraction* 甚至比 *misdemeanor*(轻罪)还小，唯一的处罚就是罚款。我们大多数人都曾违章停车，为此收到罚款单；超速罚款单通常也是违规的结果，不过会记录在案，可能让你在后面几年一直花钱。与 *infraction* 密切相关的词语 *infringement* 一般指侵犯权利或者特权，比如未经允许使用他人文字可能是侵犯版权。

refraction \ri-ˈfrak-shən\ The change of direction of a ray of light or wave of energy as it passes at an angle from one substance into another in which its speed is different. 折射

TELE

- From where I was standing, the refraction made it look as if her legs underwater were half their actual length. 从我站的地方来看，折射现象好像让她双腿的水下部分只有实际长度的一半。

The root of *refraction* is seen in the notion that the path of a ray of light or wave of energy is "broken" when it is deflected or turned. The effects of refraction can be seen in a rainbow, which is formed when light rays passing into (and reflecting out of) water droplets are bent at different angles depending on their color, so that the light separates into bands of color. The amount of refraction depends on the angle and the type of matter; refraction can occur even when passing through different kinds of air. A mirage, such as you might see in the desert or over a patch of asphalt in the summer, occurs when light passing through warm air meets the very hot air near the surface; reflecting the sky, it often resembles a lake.

refraction 的词根可以在这一概念中看到：光线或者能量波在被转向或返回时"折断了"。折射的效果可以在彩虹中看到，而彩虹的形成是这样的：光线由于颜色不同，照进(并反射出)小水滴时向各个角度弯曲，结果光分成了光带。折射量要看角度和物质的类型，即使通过不同种类的空气也会发生折射。海市蜃楼——就像你夏天可能会在沙漠或者一片沥青地面上空看到的那样——当穿过温暖空气的光线遇到靠近地面的热空气时就会发生。反射到天空时，它看起来就像湖泊。

TELE has as its basic meanings "distant" or "at a distance." A *telescope* is for looking at far-off objects; a camera's *telephoto* lens magnifies a distant scene for a photograph; and a *television* lets us watch things taking place far away.

TELE 基本意思是"遥远的"或者"在远处的"。*telescope*(望远镜)用来观看遥远的事物；照相机的远摄镜头能放大远处的景色以供拍照；*television*(电视)让我们观看遥远的地方发生的事情。

---

telegenic \ˌte-lə-ˈje-nik\ Well-suited to appear on television, especially by having an appearance and manner attractive to viewers. (尤指因为吸引人而)适合出现在电视上的

- The local anchorpeople all have telegenic faces and great hair, though they don't always seem to know a lot about the economy or political science. 当地主持人都有迷人的脸庞和漂亮的头发，不过他们好像并不总是很了解经济或者政治。

The word *telegenic*, a blend of "*tele*vision" and "photo*genic*," first appeared back in the 1930s, before hardly anyone owned a TV. With the supreme importance of TV cameras in politics, people running for political office today worry about being telegenic enough to have a successful career. Even events have been described as telegenic; unfortunately, such events are often human tragedies, such as fires, earthquakes, or floods, which happen to broadcast well and capture the interest of the viewers.

telegenic 一词由"*tele*vision"和"photo*genic*"混合而成,20世纪30年代首次出现,当时大家几乎都没有电视机。由于电视摄像机在政治方面非常重要,竞选政治职位的人今天都很担心不够 *telegenic* 事业就不会成功。甚至连事件都被描述成 *telegenic* 了,不幸的是,这样的事件常常是人类的悲剧,比如火灾、地震或者洪水。这些事情收视率很高,让观众很感兴趣。

teleological \ ˌtē-lē-ə-ˈlä-ji-kəl \ Showing or relating to design or purpose, especially in nature. 目的论的

• Many naturalists object to the teleological view that sees everything in nature as part of a grand design or plan. 很多博物学家都反对将自然界的一切视为某一宏伟目标或计划一部分的目的论看法。

Teleology has the basic meaning "the study of ends or purposes." So Aristotle's famous "teleological argument" claims that anything complex must have a creator, and thus that God exists. And a teleological explanation of evolutionary changes claims that all such changes occur for a definite purpose. But the type of morality called "teleological ethics" doesn't involve God at all: instead, it claims that we should judge whether an act is good or bad by seeing if it produces a good or bad result, even if the act involves harming or killing another person.

teleology 的基本意思是"对目的的研究"。所以,亚里士多德著名的"目的论论点"声称,一切复杂的东西都有创造者,所以上帝是存在的。对进化中的变化的目的论解释声称,所有这些变化的发生都有一个确定的目的。但是,所谓的"目的论道德"这种道德根本不涉及上帝;相反,它声称,我们应该看某一行为产生的结果是好是坏来判断其好坏,即使这一行为伤害或者害死了另一个人也无所谓。

telemetry \ tə-ˈle-mə-trē \ The science or process of measuring such things as pressure, speed, or temperature, sending the result usually by radio to a distant station, and recording the measurements there. 遥测

• The telemetry of the satellite had gone dead in 1999, and its fate remains a mystery. 这一卫星的遥测在1999年无声无息了,卫星的命运成了一个谜。

Telemetry is used to obtain data on the internal functioning of missiles, rockets, unmanned planes, satellites, and probes, providing data on such factors as position, altitude, and speed as well as conditions like temperature, air pressure, wind speed, and radiation. Weather forecasters rely on telemetry to map weather patterns. Astronauts on the space shuttle are monitored with telemetry that measures and transmits readings on their blood pressure, respiration, and heart rates. Similar kinds of telemetry are used by biologists to study animals in the wild and keep track of their populations and movements. Telemetry is also widely used in modern agriculture, often to regulate irrigation.

遥测用于获得导弹、火箭、无人飞机、卫星和空间探测器内部的运转数据,提供有关其位置、维度和速度方面的数据以及维度、气压、风速和辐射状况。天气预报依靠遥测来提供天气变化模式信息。密切关注宇宙飞船上的宇航员的就是遥测,它能够测量其血压、呼吸、心率,并发送这些信息。生物学家也利用相似种类的遥测来研究野生动物,了解其数量和动态。遥测也广泛用于现代农业,通常是为了调节灌溉。

telecommute \ˈte-li-kə-ˌmyüt\ To work at home using an electronic link with a central office. 远距离工作;家庭办公

● A dozen of our employees are now telecommuting, and we calculate that altogether they're saving 25 gallons of gasoline and its pollution every day. 我们有十来个雇员目前在远距离办公。我们计算了一下,他们每天总共节约二十五加仑的汽油并减少其污染。

This word has been around since the early 1970s, when computer terminals in the home first began to be connected to so-called mainframe computers by telephone lines. Since the creation of the World Wide Web in 1991, and with the widening access to broadband connections, *telecommuting* has grown to the point that the U. S. is now home to many millions of occasional *telecommuters*. Telecommuting can make work much easier for people with young children and people with disabilities, and because of its obvious environmental benefits and the lessening of traffic congestion, telecommuting is now officially encouraged by federal legislation. Still, only a fraction of those who could be telecommuting are actually doing so.

这个词语从 20 世纪 70 年代早期开始使用,那时,家庭电脑终端刚开始利用电话线跟所谓的主机连在一起。随着 1991 年万维网的产生,也随着宽带连接日益广泛的使用,远距离办公发展迅猛,美国现在有数以百万计的 occasional *telecommuters*(偶尔进行远距离办公者)。家里有小孩和残疾人的话,远距离办公可以使工作更容易些,而且由于其在环境方面有明显好处,并且减少交通堵塞,联邦立法对其公开鼓励。不过,只有小部分有条件的人才这样做。

Quizzes

A. Fill in each blank with the correct letter:

a. telecommute   e. infraction
b. fractious   f. teleological
c. telegenic   g. refraction
d. fractal   h. telemetry

1. Under the microscope, the bark revealed its _____ nature, reproducing its visible surface at the microscopic level.

2. The philosopher's argument was _____ in that it looked for a design or purpose in natural phenomena.

3. It's _____ a team, and there often seems to be no cooperation between them at all.

4. Her boss has given her permission to _____ two days a week, using a computer hookup from home.

5. _____ of sunlight through water droplets is what produces rainbows.

6. Wildlife zoologists use _____ to track the migration habits of the caribou.
7. That last _____ of the rules cost their team 15 yards.
8. Some newscasters seem to have been hired for nothing more than their _____ smiles.

B. Match each word on the left to the correct definition on the right:

1. telecommute   a. self-reproducing shape
2. refraction   b. quarrelsome
3. telemetry   c. work electronically from home
4. fractal   d. bending of light rays
5. telegenic   e. violation
6. fractious   f. well-suited to television
7. teleological   g. long-distance measurement
8. infraction   h. relating to design or purpose

PHIL comes from the Greek word meaning "love." In *philosophy*, it's joined with *sophia*, "wisdom," so philosophy means literally "love of wisdom." When joined with *biblio-*, "book," the result is *bibliophile*, or "lover of books." And *Philadelphia*, containing the Greek word *adelphos*, "brother," was named by its Quaker founder, William Penn, as the city of "brotherly love."

PHIL 源自希腊语中表示"爱"的那个词语。在 philosophy 一词中，它跟 sophia（"智慧"）连在一起，所以 philosophy 字面意思就是"爱智慧"。跟 biblio-（"书"）连在一起，结果就是 bibliophile（"爱书者"）。Philadelphia 含有希腊词语 adelphios（"兄弟"），由贵格会创建者威廉·佩恩命名为"兄弟之爱"之城。

---

oenophile \ˈē-nə-ˌfīl\   A person with an appreciation and usually knowledge of fine wine. 酒行家；品酒家

• As an amateur oenophile, he was constantly talking to his friends in the vocabulary of wine tasting. 作为一个业余酒行家，他总是用品酒术语跟朋友谈话。

The root *oeno-* comes from the Greek word meaning "wine." The oenophile should be distinguished from the *oenologist*, or "student of wine," who has a technical knowledge of the cultivation of wine grapes and of the whole winemaking process. Oenophiles may not know how to make a great wine, but they know one when they taste it. Not only that, but they can describe it using nouns like *nose*, *finish*, and *bouquet*, as well as adjectives such as *woody*, *full-bodied*, *robust*, and *noble*.

词根 oeno- 源自希腊语中意思是"酒"的那个词语。oenophile 应该跟 oenologist（葡萄酒专家）分开，因为后者对酿酒葡萄的种植及整个酿酒过程都有专业知识。品酒家不一定知道如何酿造好酒，但是尝到了就知道是好酒。不仅如此，他们还能用 nose（气味）、finish（最后一道工序）和 bouquet（香味）等名词以及 woody（有木桶味的）、full-bodied（浓烈的）、noble（上等的）等形容词描述好酒。

philatelist\fə-'la-tə-list\　A person who collects or studies stamps. 集邮家

• The U. S. Postal Service issues first-day covers of each new stamp design especially for philatelists. 美国邮政总局特别为集邮家发行每种新邮票设计的首日封。

The first postage stamps were made available on May 1, 1840, in England, and it didn't take long for the hobby of stamp collecting to arise. Within a year, a young London lady was letting it be known in a newspaper advertisement that she was "desirous of covering her dressing room with cancelled postage stamps." *Philately* has been alive and well ever since, though modern philatelists—including rock stars, English kings, and American presidents—are more likely to put the stamps they collect in special albums. 第一批邮票于1840年5月出现在英国,没有多久,就产生了集邮这一爱好。一年之内,一位年轻的伦敦女性就在报纸广告中告知人们,她"很想拿用过的邮票盖满整个梳妆室"。*philately*一词从此具有了生命力,不过当代philatelists(集邮爱好者)——包括摇滚歌星、英国国王和美国总统——更可能将邮票放进专门的集邮册里。

Anglophile\'aŋ-glə-ˌfīl\　A person who greatly admires or favors England and English things. 英国迷;崇英者

• His grandparents were Anglophiles, and whenever they had guests in the afternoon the beautiful silver tea service would come out. 他祖父母都是英国迷,只要下午来客人了,漂亮的银茶具就摆出来了。

Even after fighting two wars against Britain, Americans continued to regard England with more fondness than perhaps any other country. For much of our history, Americans have sought to imitate the British in any number of ways—American movie stars even used to adopt British accents—and the two countries have long been close allies. But Britain isn't the only country Americans fall in love with; *Francophiles* (France-lovers), *Germanophiles* (Germany-lovers), and *Italophiles* (Italy-lovers) are also common. In the 19th century, Russian *Slavophiles* called for rejecting European culture in favor of homegrown Russian culture (Slavs being those who speak a Slavic language such as Russian or Polish). Occasionally *phil-* words are turned around; thus, someone who is *philosemitic* is a lover of Jewish culture. 虽然跟英国打过两次仗,美国人还是最喜欢英国。在我们历史上大多数时间,美国人都在无数方面努力模仿英国——美国影星以前甚至使用英国口音——而且两个国家一直是关系密切的联盟。但是英国不是美国人唯一爱上的国家;*Francophiles*(法国迷)、*Germanophiles*(德国迷)和*Italophiles*(意大利迷)也很常见。在19世纪,俄国的*Slavophiles*(斯拉夫迷)要求拒绝接受欧洲文化而支持土生土长的俄罗斯文化(斯拉夫人指那些讲俄语、波兰语等斯拉夫语的人)。有时,带*phil-*的词语倒过来了,这样,*philosemitic*就是热爱犹太文化的人。

philanthropy\fə-'lan(t)-thrə-pē\　(1) A charitable act or gift. 捐赠;善举 (2) An organization that distributes or is supported by charitable contributions. 慈善机构;慈善团体

• Her last philanthropy was dedicated to protecting a vast area in central Africa where many of the great apes lived. 她的最后一次捐赠专门用于保护非洲中部一大片地区,那里生活着很多大猩猩。

With its *anthro-* root (see ANTHROP, p. 418), *philanthropy* means literally "love of mankind." Thus, philanthropy is giving money for a purpose or cause benefiting people who you don't personally know. (Animals are usually included as well.) Individuals have often set up their own permanent *philanthropic* organizations in the form of foundations. The greatest American *philanthropists* have included Warren Buffett, Bill Gates, Andrew Carnegie, and John D. Rockefeller, but tens of millions of us could be considered philanthropists on a much smaller scale.

有了 *anthro-* 这一词根(见 ANTHROP,第418页), *philanthropy* 表示"对人类的爱"。因此, philanthropy 就是为某一目的或事业捐款,从而有利于你不认识的那些人(动物通常也包括在内)。常常有些个人建立自己永久性的 *philanthropic* (慈善的)机构,其形式是基金会。伟大的美国 *philanthropists* (慈善家)包括沃伦·巴菲特、比尔·盖茨、安德鲁·卡耐基以及约翰·D.洛克菲勒,但是我们中很多人在较小的程度上也可被视为慈善家。

NEG

NEG and its variants *nec-* and *ne-* are prefixes of denial or refusal in Latin, and the Latin verb *negare* means "to say no." To *negate* something is to make it ineffective, and something *negative* denies, contradicts, refuses, or reverses.

NEG 及其变体 *nec-* 和 *ne-* 都是拉丁语中表示否定或者拒绝的前缀。拉丁语动词 *ngeare* 意思是"说不"。*negate* 什么东西就是使其无效,*negative* 东西能够否定、抵牾、决绝或者反转。

negligent \ˈne-gli-jənt\ (1) Failing to take proper or normal care. 疏忽的; 失职的 (2) Marked by or likely to show neglect. 受到忽视的;可能显示出受到忽视的

• The Army Corps of Engineers was found negligent for having failed to keep the New Orleans levees in good repair. 人们发现陆军工程兵团失职了,因为它未能维护好奥尔良码头。

To be *negligent* is to be *neglectful*. *Negligence* is an important legal concept; it's usually defined as the failure to use the care that a normally careful person would in a given situation. *Negligence* is a common claim in lawsuits regarding medical malpractice, auto accidents, and workplace injuries. But you can also be negligent about answering your e-mail, or negligent in the way you dress. (The original garment called a *negligee* was worn by women who had neglected to get fully dressed.) The legal meanings of *negligent* and *negligence*, however, tend to be the ones we most often encounter nowadays.

某人 negligent 就是 *neglectful* (疏忽的;失职的)。*negligence* (疏忽;失职)是一个重要法律概念,它通常被定义为在某一特定情形中,未能像正常情况下那样细心。*negligence* 也是跟医疗过失、交通事故和工伤有关的诉讼中常见的索赔理由。但是你也可能在回复电子邮件方面 negligent,或者着装方面 negligent(原先称为 *negligee* [长晨衣]的衣服就是未能穿戴整齐的妇女穿的)。然而,*negligent* 和 *negligence* 的法律方面的意思往往是我们目前常常碰到的。

abnegation \ˌab-ni-ˈgā-shən\ Self-denial. 拒绝享乐;过清苦生活

• She's been denying herself pleasures since she was a child, so she's actually attracted by the life of abnegation that a nun leads. 从童年时代起,她就不让自己享受快乐,所以实际上,尼姑过的清苦生活很吸引她。

Abnegation plays an important part in the teachings of all the major religions. The founder of Buddhism was a prince who gave up all his worldly goods when he discovered the world of poverty that lay outside the palace gates, and abnegation has been a Buddhism practice ever since. Hinduism has an even older tradition of abnegation. Special periods of abnegation and fasting may even be included in a religion's yearly calendar; serious Christians give up some pleasure for the 40-day period of Lent, for instance, and Muslims are forbidden to eat during daylight hours during the month of Ramadan. 拒绝享乐在所有主要宗教的教义中都很重要。佛教的创始人是一位王子,他发现宫门外的贫穷世界后,就放弃了所有世间财物,从此,过清苦生活就成了佛教的一种做法。印度教有着更加古老的拒绝享乐的传统。宗教每年的日历上甚至都有特定清苦和斋戒时期。比如,严肃的基督徒在四旬斋期间放弃四十天的快乐,穆斯林在斋月期间的白天不得进食。

negligible \ˈne-gli-jə-bəl\ So small as to be neglected or disregarded. 无足轻重的;无不足道的

• Local weather forecasters had made it sound like the blizzard of the century, but the amount of snow turned out to be negligible. 当地天气预报员的话,让人感觉这是本世纪最严重的暴风雪,可是结果呢,降雪量少得可以忽略。

Negligible comes from the same Latin verb as neglect, so something negligible is literally "neglectable." If an accident results in negligible damage to your car, you should be thankful. If two years of intense focus on testing in the classroom results in a negligible improvement in student test scores, it's probably time to try something new. *negligible* 跟 *neglect* 源自同一拉丁语动词,所以 negligible 东西简直是"neglectable"(可以忽视的)。如果一次事故对你汽车的损伤是 negligible,你应该心怀感激。如果课堂上有两年时间对考试非常重视,结果学生的成绩进步却几乎可以忽略,则可能该试试别的方法了。

renege \ri-ˈneg\ To go back on a promise or commitment. 食言;违背承诺

• If his partners renege at this point, the whole project will probably fall through. 如果他的合作伙伴在此刻不履行承诺,整个项目可能就要成为泡影了。

To renege on a bet is to refuse to pay up when you lose. To renege on a promise of marriage, or on a deal of any kind, is to pull out. History is full of promises and commitments and treaties that were reneged on, such as the many treaties with Native Americans that American settlers and the U.S. government went back on over a period of almost 300 years. A synonym is welsh ("He always welshes on his deals"); however, since that word may have come from Welsh, meaning a native of Wales in Britain, some people think it might be offensive. 打赌食言就是拒绝不给对方你输掉的东西。违背婚约,或者违背任何种类的协议,就是退出。历史上有很多承诺和条约没有被履行,比如在将近三百年的时间内,北美移民和美国政府违背了很多跟北美原住民签订的条约。有个同义词是 welsh("He always welshed on his deals");然而,由于这个词语可能源自 Welsh(威尔士语),表示在大不列颠的威尔士本土人,有些人觉得它会冒犯他人。

UNIT 19

Quizzes

A. Choose the closest definition:

1. Anglophile   a. amateur fisherman   b. geometry fan   c. England-lover   d. non-Hispanic
2. negligible   a. small   b. correctable   c. noteworthy   d. considerate
3. oenophile   a. pig lover   b. book lover   c. word lover   d. wine lover
4. negligent   a. penniless   b. careless   c. criminal   d. decent
5. philatelist   a. stamp collector   b. gem collector   c. wine collector   d. coin collector
6. abnegation   a. abundance   b. abruptness   c. self-denial   d. self-satisfaction
7. philanthropy   a. stamp collecting   b. pleasure   c. dignity   d. generosity
8. renege   a. repeat   b. go back on   c. renegotiate   d. overturn

B. Indicate whether the following pairs have the same or different meanings:

1. negligent / neglectful   same ____ / different ____
2. philatelist / postman   same ____ / different ____
3. philanthropy / wealth   same ____ / different ____
4. renege / return   same ____ / different ____
5. oenophile / wine expert   same ____ / different ____
6. abnegation / absence   same ____ / different ____
7. Anglophile / fish-lover   same ____ / different ____
8. negligible / unimportant   same ____ / different ____

Number Words 数字词语

DEC comes from both Greek and Latin and means "ten." So a *decade* lasts for ten years; the *decimal* system is based on ten; and a *decahedron* is a geometrical shape with ten sides.

DEC 源自希腊语和拉丁语,意思是"十"。所以,一个 *decade* 长达十年;*decimal* system(十进制)以十为基础;一个 *decathedron* 就是一个有十条边的几何图形。

decalogue\\ˈde-kə-ˌlȯg\\ (1) (capitalized) The Ten Commandments. (大写时表示)《十诫》(2) Any basic set of rules that must be obeyed. 一套准则

• At 15 she posted a decalogue of life rules on her bedroom door, starting with "1. Be respectful to teachers." 十五岁时，她在卧室门上贴了一张生活准则，打头的是"第一条：尊敬老师"。

In *decalogue* the root *deca-* is combined with *logos*, Greek for "word." In the Biblical book of Exodus, the original Decalogue, or Ten Commandments, was handed to Moses by God atop Mount Sinai. In Jewish and Christian tradition, the Ten Commandments are regarded as laws handed down from the highest authority and as the foundation of morality. They include commands to honor God, the Sabbath day, and one's parents, and bans on worshiping images, swearing, murder, adultery, theft, lying about others, and envying what others have. Individuals have often had their own personal decalogues; Thomas Jefferson's "ten commandments" started off with "Never put off till tomorrow what you can do today."

在 *decalogue* 一词中，与词根 *deca-* 结合的是希腊语 *logos*，意思是"词"。在《圣经》的《出埃及记》这一卷，最早的 Decalogue，或者说"十诫"，由上帝在西奈山顶交给了摩西。在犹太教和基督教传统中，十诫被认为是从最高权威传下来的法律，并被看作道德的基础。它们包括尊敬上帝、安息日和父母这样的命令，以及对崇拜形象、辱骂、谋杀、通奸、偷盗、说别人谎话、嫉妒他人所有的禁止。个人也常常有自己的准则，托马斯·杰斐逊的"十诫"第一条是"今日事，今日毕"。

decathlon\\di-ˈkath-ˌlän\\ An athletic contest made up of ten parts. 十项全能比赛

• Though the U.S. has dominated the Olympic decathlon for its whole modern history, the 1948 victory by the 17-year-old Bob Mathias still astonished the world. 在奥运会现代史上，虽然美国一直在十项全能中占据优势，但17岁的鲍勃·马赛厄斯在1948年取得的胜利还是震惊了世界。

Decathlon from *deca-* and *athlon*, "contest," means "ten contests." The ancient Greek Olympics held five-contest competitions, or *pentathlons*, that were based on the skills needed in battle. The modern Olympic decathlon, which was born in 1912, consists of the 100-meter run, 400-meter run, 1500-meter run, 110-meter high hurdles, javelin throw, discus throw, shot put, pole vault, high jump, and long jump. The original winner was the legendary Jim Thorpe, who would later be judged the greatest American athlete of the 20th century. And ever since, the Olympic decathlon winner has been called the finest all-around athlete in the world.

decathlon 由 *deca-* 和 *athlon*（"竞赛"）构成，意思是"十项竞赛"。古希腊奥运会举行五项比赛的竞赛，或者说是 *pentathlons*，以战场上需要的技能为基础。现代奥运会的十项全能比赛诞生于1912年，由100米赛跑、400米赛跑、1500米赛跑、110米跨栏、掷标枪、掷铁饼、推铅球、撑竿跳、跳高和跳远组成。最早的获胜者是传奇人物吉姆·索普，他后来被认为是20世纪最伟大的美国运动员。从此以后，奥运会十项全能比赛获胜者一直被称为世界最好的全能运动员。

decibel\\ˈde-sə-bəl\\ A unit based on a scale ranging from 0 to about 130 used to measure the loudness of sound, with 0 indicating the least sound that can be heard and 130 the average level that causes pain. 分贝

• She worries about the damage that high decibel levels can cause, and always wears ear protection when mowing the lawn. 她担心高分贝声音会引起伤害,所以在草坪割草时总是带着护耳。

The *bel* in *decibel* honors the inventor of the telephone, Alexander Graham Bell. Decibels work on a *logarithmic scale* (you may need to look up *logarithm*), so 20 decibels is 10 times as strong as 10 decibels, and 50 decibels is 1,000 times as strong as 20 decibels. The decibel readings of some everyday sounds make for interesting comparisons. Whispers and rustling leaves usually register under 20 decibels, the average level of conversation is about 50 decibels, and noisy factories or office machinery may have decibel levels of 90 to 100. In the category of sounds between 100 and 120 decibels, which can eventually cause deafness, we find elevated trains, artillery—and rock concerts.

decibel 中的 *bel* 表达了对电话发明者亚历山大·贝尔(Bell)的敬意。分贝是用 logarithmic scale(对数标尺)(你可能需要查一下 logarithm 这个词语)测量的,所以 20 分贝就是 10 分贝 10 倍的强度,50 分贝是 20 分贝 1,000 倍的强度。比较一下有些日常声音的分贝的读数是很有意思的。窃窃私语和树叶的沙沙声通常低于 20 分贝,一般谈话的声音大约是 50 分贝,吵闹的工厂或者办公室机器的声音可能达到 90 到 100 分贝。在 100 到 120 分贝这一类的声音中,我们发现有高架列车、大炮和摇滚音乐会的声音。这类声音最终可以引起失聪。

decimate \\ˈde-sə-ˌmāt\\ To reduce drastically or destroy most of. 大量减少;毁灭大部分

• Before the developments of modern medicine, diphtheria and typhoid could decimate the populations of entire towns and cities. 在现代医学发展起来之前,白喉和伤寒可以让整个城镇失去大量人口。

Commanders in the Roman army took discipline seriously. Mutiny in the ranks was dealt with by selecting, through drawing lots, one soldier in every ten and making the other nine club or stone the unfortunate winner of this gruesome lottery to death. The *dec-* in *decimate* thus reflects this Roman practice, which was ordered by such well-known leaders as Crassus, Mark Antony, and Augustus. But over time, the word's meaning has shifted, and today it almost always describes great destruction or loss of life. So, for example, we can say that a wave of layoffs has decimated a company's workforce, the populations of some of Africa's greatest wild animals have been decimated by poaching, or aerial bombardment has decimated whole sections of a city.

罗马军队的指挥官很看重纪律,处理士兵反叛用的是抓阄挑选法。在这一可怕的碰运气的事情中,十个士兵有一个不幸的获胜者,被其他九个士兵用棍棒或者石头打死。decimate 中的 dec- 就这样反映了罗马人的做法,这一做法是著名的领导克拉苏、马克·安东尼和高古斯都命令的。随着时间的推移,这一词语的意义转变了,今天几乎总是描述毁灭或失去众多生命。所以,比如我们可以说大批人失业,使该公司失去大批劳动力;偷猎使非洲某些最大的野生动物数量大减;或者空袭炸毁了一座城市的大片城区。

CENT

CENT, from the Latin *centum*, means "one hundred." A dollar is made up of a hundred *cents*, though other monetary systems use *centavos* or *centimes* as the smallest coin. A *centipede* has what appears to be a hundred feet, though the actual number varies greatly. But there really are a hundred years in a *century*.

CENT 源自拉丁语 *centum*("一百")。一美元由一百 *cents*(分)构成,不过其他币制使用 *centavos* 或者 *centimes* 作为最小的硬币。*centipede*(百足虫)的脚看起来似乎有一百,不过实际数字相差大。可是,一个 *century*(世纪)确实有一百年。

CENT

centenary \sen-'te-nə-rē\ A 100th anniversary or the celebration of it; a centennial. 一百周年纪念

● The company is celebrating the centenary of its founding with a lavish banquet. 该公司正以豪华盛宴庆祝创建一百周年。

A *centenary*, like its cousin *centennial*, is an anniversary. Thus, the year 2013 may mark the centenary of a town's founding, and the yearlong calendar of public events that the town sponsors for the occasion—that is, the celebration of the anniversary—can also be called a centenary. Individuals have their own centenaries, which usually celebrate their births; thus, Gerald Ford's centenary will occur in 2013, and John Kennedy's in 2017. And if you live long enough to be a *centenarian*, you'll be around to join the celebrations.

一个 *centenary*,就像与该词有亲缘关系的 *centennial* 一样,是一个周年纪念。因此 2013 年可能标志着某个城镇建立一百周年,而全城人为此赞助的持续一年的公共活动,也就是一百周年纪念庆典,也可被称为一个 centenary。个人也有自己的 centenaries,通常是庆祝自己的生日。这样,杰拉德·福特的一百岁纪念发生在 2013 年,约翰·肯尼迪的一百岁纪年发生在 2017 年。如果你活得足够长到,可以被称为 centenarian(百岁老人),将来就会加入这样的纪念活动。

centigrade \'sen-tə-ˌgrād\ Relating to a temperature scale in which 0° is the freezing point of water and 100° is its boiling point. 摄氏的

● The normal temperature of a human body is 37° centigrade. 人体正常温度是 37 摄氏度。

The *centigrade* scale is essentially identical to the *Celsius* scale, the standard scale by which temperature is measured in most of the world. Anders Celsius of Sweden first devised the centigrade scale in the early 18th *century*. But in his version, 100° marked the freezing point of water, and 0° its boiling point. Later users found it less confusing to reverse these two. To convert Fahrenheit degrees to centigrade, subtract 32 and multiply by 5/9. To convert centigrade to Fahrenheit, multiply by 9/5 and add 32.

centigrade 温标基本上等于 Celsius 温标,后者是世界大多数地方测量温度的标准温标。瑞典的安德斯·摄尔修斯在 18 世纪早期提出了摄氏温标。但是在他那个方法中,100°标志着水冰点,0°是沸点。后来的使用者发现将两者倒过来就不那么让人迷惑了。要将华氏温度转为摄氏温度,减 32 再乘 5/9 即可。要将摄氏温度转为华氏温度,就乘 9/5 再加 32。

centimeter \'sen-tə-ˌmē-tər\ A length measuring 1/100th of a meter, or about 0.39 inch. 厘米

● There are 2.54 centimeters in an inch, 30.48 centimeters in a foot. 1 英寸相当于 2.54 厘米,1 英尺相当于 30.48 厘米。

In the metric system, which is used in most countries of the world, each basic unit of measure of length, area, or volume can be divided into centimeters. A meter consists of 100 centimeters, a square meter consists of 10,000 square centimeters, and a cubic meter consists of 1,000,000 cubic centimeters.

世界上大多数国家使用米制。在米制中,长度、面积或者体积的每个基本测量单位都可以分成厘米。1米等于100厘米,1平方米等于10,000平方厘米,1立方米等于1,000,000立方厘米。

centurion \ˈsen-ˈchür-ē-ən\   The officer in command of a Roman century, originally a troop of 100 soldiers. 百夫长(罗马军队中管理一个百人对的军官)

• Centurions and their centuries were the backbone of the great Roman armies.
百夫长及其百人队是强大的罗马军队的骨干。

In ancient Rome, a *century* was approximately equal to a company in the U. S. Army, and a centurion was roughly equivalent to a captain. Centurions play a role in the New Testament; Jesus performs a miracle for a centurion in Capernaum, centurions are present at the crucifixion, and in later years St. Paul is arrested by centurions. According to a writer of the time, centurions were chosen for their size and strength, their abilities at swordplay and at throwing missiles, and the quality of their discipline, which was partly shown by how well their soldiers kept their own armor polished.

在古罗马,一个*century*(百人队)大约相当于美国军队一个连队,百夫长大约相当于一个上尉。百夫长有在《新约》中出现;基督在迦百农为一个百夫长制造了神迹;基督被钉在十字架上时,几位百夫长就在现场;后来的岁月中,圣保罗被百夫长逮捕了。根据当时一位作家所说,选择百夫长要看个头和力气、击剑和扔掷物的本领,还有纪律如何。纪律如何一定程度上要看其士兵的盔甲的光亮度保持得怎样。

Quiz

Fill in each blank with the correct letter:

a. centurion
b. decimate
c. centigrade
d. decibel
e. decathlon
f. centimeter
g. Decalogue
h. centenary

1. The ear can usually hear the difference between noises that differ in intensity by a single _____.
2. No one bothers to compete in the _____ who isn't an extraordinary natural athlete.
3. The company celebrated its _____ this month, and one of the founder's elderly children was able to come.
4. The _____ in the Old Testament is matched by the Beatitudes in the New Testament.
5. Rain is likely to become snow at about 0° _____ .
6. An earthquake can easily _____ the buildings of an entire city.
7. The legion commanders decided that each _____ should divide up the food

within his own century.

8. Last week's rainfall in Paris measured less than a _____.

Review Quizzes

A. Choose the correct synonym:

1. immutable   a. unalterable   b. transformable
   c. inaudible   d. audible
2. dysfunctional   a. working badly   b. unresponsive
   c. healthy   d. uncaring
3. permutation   a. continuation   b. splendor   c. disorder
   d. rearrangement
4. defunct   a. working   b. rotten   c. useless
   d. dreary
5. fractious   a. smiling   b. peaceable   c. angry
   d. troublesome
6. infraction   a. lawful act   b. arrest   c. piece
   d. violation
7. abnegation   a. position   b. self-indulgence   c. self-denial
   d. refusal
8. symbiosis   a. musical instrument   b. independence
   c. community   d. interdependence
9. decimate   a. destroy   b. pair up   c. multiply
   d. remove
10. renege   a. afford   b. honor   c. flee
    d. deny

B. Fill in each blank with the correct letter:

a. commute
b. functionary
c. telegenic
d. carcinogenic
e. Anglophile
f. biodegradable
g. decibel
h. centenary

i. refraction
j. telepathic
k. malfunction
l. oenophile
m. biopsy
n. decathlon
o. centurion

1. Their bags are made of _____ plastic that they claim will break down within two months.

2. Somethng that was downloaded is causing parts of the operating system

to _____.

3. Since tobacco is well known to be a _____ substance, it's surprising that smoking is still legal.

4. He's so serious about wines that it's hard to be his friend if you're not an _____.

5. That music might sound better if the sound were turned down a _____ or two.

6. Which of the ten events in the _____ is your favorite?

7. The _____ of light in a glass of water appears to bend a pencil or spoon where it enters the water.

8. Doctors recommended a _____ in case the X-ray had missed something.

9. A low-level _____ in the company handles such complaints.

10. The experiment showed that her claim to have _____ powers was false.

11. My grandfather celebrates his _____ in May.

12. He was successful in radio but not _____ enough to succeed on television.

13. The _____ and his soldiers had proved themselves skilled fighters in the battles on the eastern frontier.

14. Filled with books about Queen Victoria, Churchill, and Henry VIII, the house was clearly home to an _____.

15. After having reviewed the new evidence that had come to light, the governor decided to _____ the sentence.

C. Indicate whether the following pairs of terms have the same or different meanings:

1. transmute / endanger   same ____ / different ____
2. bionic / artificial   same ____ / different ____
3. telemetry / space travel   same ____ / different ____
4. centimeter / 1/1000 of a meter same ____ / different ____
5. philatelist / dancer   same ____ / different ____
6. teleological / systematic   same ____ / different ____
7. decalogue / set of rules   same ____ / different ____
8. negligible / ignorable   same ____ / different ____
9. infraction / split   same ____ / different ____
10. functionary / bureaucrat   same ____ / different ____

NOM

UNIT 20

NOM comes from the Latin word for "name." A *nominee* is a person "named"—or *nominated*—to run for or serve in office. A *binomial* ("two names") is the scientific name for a species: *Felis catus* for the house cat, for example. A *polynomial*, with "many names," is an algebra expression involving several terms: $2x+9y-z^3$, for instance. NOM 源自拉丁语中表示"名字"的那个词语。nominee 就是被"提名"——或者 nominated——去竞选或者担任职位的人。binominal("两个名字")是某一物种的学名：比如 *felis catus* 指家猫。polynominal(多项式)，就是有"很多名字"，是一个涉及几项的代数式，比如 $2x+9y-z^3$。

nominal \ˈnä-mə-nəl\ (1) Existing in name or form only and not in reality. 名义上的；有名无实的 (2) So small as to be unimportant; insignificant. 渺小的；无足轻重的

- The actor himself was the nominal author, but 90 percent of the prose was the work of his ghostwriter. 这位演员本人是名义上的作者，但该文章的百分之九十都是捉刀人写的。

Something nominal exists only in name. So the nominal ruler in a constitutional monarchy is the king or queen, but the real power is in the hands of the elected prime minister. In the United Kingdom, the British monarch is also the nominal head of the Church of England; and those baptized in the Church who aren't really churchgoers might be called nominal Christians. A fee can be called nominal when it's small in comparison to the value of what it buys. So, for example, you might sell a friend a good piece of furniture for a nominal amount. And the charge for a doctor's visit might be a nominal $20, since most of the cost is covered by an insurance plan. nominal 东西只是名义上存在。所以，君主立宪制国家的 nominal 统治者是国王或者女王，但实际权力在选举任职的首相手中。在大不列颠王国，英国君主也是英国国教的名义首领。那些在教堂洗礼过但并不去做礼拜的人可称为 nominal 基督徒。一笔费用的价值，如果比用它购买的东西的价值要小，就可以说是 nominal。所以，比如你可能只收

nominal 钱就把家具很便宜地卖给朋友。由于大部分费用由保险计划承担，医生上门服务所收费用只是 nominal 20 元。

nomenclature\ˈnō-mən-ˌklā-ˌchür\　(1) A name or designation, or the act of naming. 名称；称号；命名 (2) A system of terms or symbols used in biology, where New Latin names are given to kinds and groups of animals and plants. 生物学术语(或符号)集

• Naming newly discovered plants or animals requires close study of the system of nomenclature. 给新发现的植物或动物命名需要对生物学术语集进行仔细研究。

Various specialized fields have their own particular nomenclatures, or sets of terms. In particle physics, for instance, the elementary particles known as quarks, which are believed to come in pairs, have acquired such names as "up" and "down," "strange" and "charm," and "truth" and "beauty"—which is all most of us know about quarks and all we need to know. But *nomenclature* is used most often for the system of biological classification created by Linnaeus. In Linnaeus's system, each species has its own two-word name, the first word being the name of its genus. Thus, the genus *Equus* includes the horse (*Equus caballus*) and the mountain zebra (*Equus zebra*). But since broccoli, cauliflower, and cabbage actually all belong to the same species (*Brassica oleracea*), they each need a third name to distinguish themselves.

各个专门领域都有自己特殊的 nomenclatures，或者术语集。比如在粒子物理学中，人们相信被称为夸克的基本粒子是一对一对的。这样，它们就有了"上"和"下"、"奇特"和"魅力"以及"真理"和"美"之类的名字。这是我们大多数人对夸克的了解，也是我们需要知道的全部。但是，nomenclature 主要用于卡罗鲁斯·林奈乌斯所创造的生物学分类系统。在林奈乌斯的系统中，每个物种都有其自己的两个词构成的名字，第一个词是它那个属的名称。这样 *Equus*（马属）这个属就包括马（*Equuscaballu*）以及山斑马（*Equus zebra*）。但是，由于西蓝花、花菜和卷心菜实际上都属于同一个物种（*Brassica oleracea*），它们每一个都需要第三个名字加以区别。

ignominious\ˌig-nə-ˈmi-nē-əs\　(1) Marked with shame or disgrace; dishonorable. 可耻的；丢脸的 (2) Humiliating or degrading. 耻辱的；有辱人格的

• If Attila the Hun was truly murdered by his bride on their wedding night, it was a most ignominious death for a warrior. 如果匈奴人阿提拉真的被自己的新娘在婚礼上杀死了，这对一位勇士来说就死得太丢人了。

The Latin *nomen* could mean both "name" and "good reputation," and even today we can say that someone who has been disgraced has "lost his good name." With its negative prefix *ig-*, *ignominious* indicates the "namelessness" that goes with shame or dishonor. A person who suffers an ignominious fate may die nameless and forgotten.

拉丁语的 *nomen* 可以表示"名字"和"好名声"。即使在今天，我们也可以说某个被羞辱的人"失去了好名声"。因为 *ig-* 这个表示否定的前缀，*ignominious* 表示伴随的耻辱的"无名"。一个遭受可耻命运的人可能死了之后被人忘记了名字。

misnomer\ˌmis-ˈnō-mər\　A wrong name, or the use of a wrong name. 错误的名称；使用错误名称

- Calling the native peoples of the western hemisphere "Indians" was one of the great misnomers in recorded history. 把西半球的本地人叫做"Indians"是有文字记录的历史上使用名称方面最大的错误之一。

Historians have long noted that the Holy Roman Empire in its later years was neither holy, Roman, nor an empire. The Battle of Bunker Hill was actually fought on nearby Breed's Hill. And the famous Woodstock Festival was actually held in the town of Bethel. But misnomers aren't limited to history. The Pennsylvania Dutch are actually of German ancestry. Koala bears aren't bears—they're marsupials. And in the world of food, the Rocky Mountain oyster, as diners have sometimes discovered too late, aren't really oysters. 历史学家很长时间以来都注意到,神圣罗马帝国在后期既不神圣,也跟罗马无关,也不是帝国。邦克山战役实际上发生在布里德山附近。著名的伍德斯托克音乐节实际上在贝塞尔城举行。但是错误的名称不仅仅局限于历史方面。宾夕法尼亚荷兰裔人实际上祖先是德国人。考拉熊不是熊,而是有袋类动物。在美食领域,落基山牡蛎实际上并不是牡蛎,然而美食家们发现得太晚了。

PATER/PATR

PATER/PATR comes from both the Greek and the Latin word for "father." So a *patron*, for example, is someone who assumes a fatherly role toward an institution or project or individual, giving moral and financial support. PATER/PATR 源自希腊语和拉丁语中表示"父亲"的那个词。所以,比如 *patron*,对某个机构或者工程或者个人来说,承担着父亲一样的角色,给予精神和经济上支持。

patrician \pə-ˈtri-shən\ A person of high birth or of good breeding and cultivation; an aristocrat. 出身高贵的人;教养良好的人;贵族

- They passed themselves off as patricians, and no one looked too closely at where their money came from. 他们假装贵族,没有人仔细调查他们的钱都是从哪儿来的。

A patrician was originally a descendant of one of the original citizen families of ancient Rome. Until about 350 B.C., only patricians could hold the office of senator, consul, or pontifex (priest). Later, the word was applied to members of the nobility created by the Roman emperor Constantine. As time went by, other nobles, such as those in medieval Italian republics and in German city-states, also came to be known as patricians. Today someone's appearance, manners, or tastes can be described as *patrician*, whether the person is actually of high birth or not. The actress Grace Kelly, an immigrant's daughter, was admired for her *patrician* beauty even before she became Princess Grace of Monaco, with classic features worthy of ancient Rome's finest sculptors. patrician 最初是古罗马最早的市民家庭的后裔。在公元前 350 年之前,只有贵族才能当上元老院议员、执政官或者大祭司。后来,这一词语用于罗马皇帝康斯坦丁创立的贵族阶层的成员。随着时间的流逝,其他贵族,比如中世纪意大利那些共和国和德国那些城邦国家的贵族,也被称为 patricians 了。今天某人的外貌、举止或者品位可以被描述为 *patrician*(高贵的;有教养的),不管他是否出身高贵。女演员格蕾丝·凯丽是个移民的女儿,她那具有古典美的五官值得古罗马最好的雕刻家去雕刻。她在成为摩纳哥格蕾丝王妃之前,就以其 *patrician*(高贵的)美受人崇拜了。

PATER/PATR

patriarchy \\'pā-trē-,är-kē\\ (1) A family, group, or government controlled by a man or a group of men. 男性统治的家庭、群体或者政府 (2) A social system in which family members are related to each other through their fathers. 父系社会体制

• She spent the 1980s raging against the patriarchy, which she claimed had destroyed the lives of millions of women. 她在整个20世纪80年代一直抨击父系社会体制,说它毁了众多妇女的生活。

With its root *-arch*, meaning "ruler, leader," a *patriarch* is a man who dominates something, even if it's just a family. In Christianity, the term is used for a few leading figures who appear early in the Old Testament, including Methuselah, Abraham, Isaac, and Jacob; in the Eastern Orthodox church, a patriarch is usually the equivalent of a bishop. Outside of the field of anthropology, *patriarchy* didn't start to be used much until the 1970s, when the women's movement gained a huge following. Many feminists have claimed that all Western societies are *patriarchal*—that is, that they systematically enable men to dominate women. But there's plenty of disagreement about how this is done, and the word isn't discussed as often as it used to be.

词根-arch 的意思是"统治者,领导"。有了这个词根,patriarch 就指一个主宰某物(即使只是一个家庭)的男性。在基督教世界,这一词语用于《旧约》中出现最早的几个领袖人物,包括马土撒拉、亚伯拉罕、以撒和雅各;在东正教中,patriarch 通常相当于主教。在人类学领域之外,patriarchy 这个词语直到20世纪70年代才开始使用,当时妇女运动有了很多追随者。很多女性主义者声称,所有西方社会都是 patriarchal(男人统治的;男性主导的),也就是说它们有计划地使男性主宰女性。但是,关于这到底是怎么做到的,有很多不一致的看法,这一词语也不像原来那么经常被人讨论了。

expatriate \\ek-'spā-trē-ət\\ A person who has moved to a foreign land. 移居国外的人;侨民

• As he got to know his fellow expatriates in Morocco, he found himself wondering what had led each of them to leave America. 随着对那些移居摩洛哥的同胞的了解,他发现自己很想知道他们每个人离开美国的原因。

Expatriate combines the prefix *ex-*, "out of" or "away from," with the Latin *patria*, "fatherland." A famous colony of expatriates was the group of writers and artists who gathered in Paris between the two world wars, including Ernest Hemingway, F. Scott Fitzgerald, and Gertrude Stein. Unlike an exile or an emigrant, an expatriate's residence abroad is usually voluntary and extended but not permanent, and expatriates—often called *expats*—generally keep their original national identity and eventually end their self-imposed exiles by *repatriating* themselves.

expatriate 由前缀 ex-(在……外;远离……)和拉丁语的 patria(祖国)构成。有一群侨民很有名,就是两次世界大战期间聚居在巴黎的那些作家和艺术家。这些人包括欧内斯特·海明威、F. 斯科特·菲茨杰拉德和葛楚德·斯坦。跟流放的人或者移民不同的是,侨民在国外居住通常是自愿的、长期的,但不是永远。侨民——经常叫做 expats——普遍保留自己原来的国民身份,最终通过 repatriating(遣返)自己结束自我流放。

PATER/ PATR

paternalistic \ pə-ˌtər-nə-ˈlis-tik \ Tending to supply the needs of or regulate the activities of those under one's control. 家长式统治的；家长式的

• Some still accuse the university of being too paternalistic in regulating student living arrangements. 有些人仍然责怪这所大学在管理学生的生活安排方面家长作风太严重。

A good father shows *paternal* concern about his children, just as a good mother often acts out of *maternal* feeling. But *paternalistic* has a negative sound nowadays, since paternalistic people or institutions seek—often with decent intentions—to control many aspects of the lives of those under their control. In the 19th century, mill owners actually often provided cheap housing for the mill's employees. Today companies frequently have strict rules regarding personal appearance, or against marriages within the company. Colleges and universities used to practice a kind of *paternalism*, especially in trying to keep men and women out of each other's dorms, but a changing society has mostly put an end to that.

好爸爸对孩子表现出 *paternal*（父亲的）关心，正如好妈妈的行为经常是出于 *maternal*（母亲的）的恩爱感。但是，*paternalistic* 这个词语目前听来有贬义，因为 paternalistic 人或者机构想方设法（通常是带着体面的愿望）去控制下面那些人的生活的很多方面。在 19 世纪，磨坊主实际上经常给雇工提供廉价劣质的住房。今天，公司经常在个人外表方面制定严格的规章制度，或者禁止公司人员之间结婚。大学过去有一种 *paternalism*（家长作风），尤其是设法让男女学生不要进入对方宿舍，但是，变化的社会使这种做法在大多数情况下已经结束了。

Quizzes

A. Fill in each blank with the correct letter：

a. patriarchy   e. ignominious
b. misnomer   f. paternalistic
c. expatriate   g. nomenclature
d. nominal   h. patrician

1. It's a community pool, and the fee we pay each time we use it is only _____.

2. At Christian colleges, policies tend to be rather strict and _____.

3. "Friend" is a _____ for Charlotte; "rival" is more like it.

4. The country could still be called a _____, with men being completely dominant both at home and in the government.

5. The first public attempts to test the antiballistic missiles ended in _____ failure.

6. He soon discovered that he wasn't the only American _____ living in the Guatemalan village.

7. The person who discovers a previously unknown plant usually gets to name it, but the _____ must follow a strict set of rules.

8. His family and upbringing were _____, but he still considered himself a man of the people.

B. Match the word on the left to the correct definition on the right:

1. paternalistic
2. nomenclature
3. patriarchy
4. misnomer
5. expatriate
6. nominal
7. ignominious
8. patrician

a. wrong name
b. aristocrat
c. exercising fatherly authority
d. rule by men
e. naming system
f. humiliating
g. in name only
h. person living abroad

LEGA

LEGA comes from the Latin *legare*, meaning "to appoint" or "to send as a deputy." The same root actually shows up in such words as *legal*—but how the law connects with sending deputies can get awfully complicated and probably isn't worth going into.

LEGA 源自拉丁语 *legare*("任命"或者"将……作为代表派遣")。这同一个词根实际上出现在 *legal*(合法的;法律的)这样的词语中。不过,法律怎么会跟派遣代表有关,真是太复杂了,可能不值得深究。

---

legate \ˈle-gət\ An official representative, such as an ambassador. 官方代表;大使

• All the important European powers sent legates of some kind to the peace conference. 所有重要的欧洲强国都派遣了这样那样的代表参加这次和谈。

Legate is a somewhat old-fashioned word, less used today than it was a century ago. More common is the synonym *envoy*. In the days before electronic communications, a legate often had particularly large responsibilities, since he couldn't check with his government to be sure he was doing the right thing. The Vatican still sends papal legates to represent the pope's point of view in negotiations.

legate 是个有些过时的词语,没有一个世纪前那么常用了。更常见的词语是 *envoy*。在电子通信时代之前,legate 常常肩负特别重大的责任,因为他没办法跟政府进行商讨以确保自己做的是正确的。梵蒂冈仍然派遣教皇使节,在谈判中代表教皇的观点。

legacy \ˈle-gə-sē\ (1) Something left to a person in a will. (遗嘱中留给某人的)遗产 (2) Something handed down by an ancestor or predecessor or received from the past. (祖先、前任的)遗留物;历史遗产

• The Stradivarius family of violin makers left a priceless legacy of remarkable instruments. 制作小提琴的斯特拉迪瓦里斯家族留下了价值无法估计的精美乐器。

In its basic meaning, a legacy is a gift of money or other personal property that's granted by the terms of a will—often a substantial gift that needs to be properly managed. But the word is used much more broadly as well. So, for instance, much of Western civilization—law, philosophy, aesthetics—could be called the undying legacy of ancient Greece. And the rights and opportunities that women enjoy today are partly the legacy of the early suffragists and feminists.

legacy 的基本意思是按照遗嘱中的条款给予的钱或其他个人财产，常常是需要好好管理的丰厚赠品。但是这个词语也有更广泛的意思。比如，西方文明中很多东西——法律、哲学、美学——可以被称为古希腊的永恒遗产。今天的女性享受的权利和机会一定程度上是早期的争取选举权者和女性主义者的遗产。

delegation \ˌde-li-ˈgā-shən\ A group of people chosen to represent the interests or opinions of others. 代表团

● Each American colony sent a delegation to the Second Continental Congress, and in its second year all 56 delegates approved Jefferson's Declaration of Independence. 每一个美国殖民地都派代表团参加了第二次大陆会议。第二年，所有 56 位代表通过了杰弗逊起草的《独立宣言》。

The task of a *delegation*—each member of which can be called a *delegate*—is to represent a larger group, often at a conference. Thus, a delegation of nondoctors to a medical convention may want to make sure the rights and needs of patients aren't ignored, just as a delegation of laypeople may attend a religious conference to express the concerns of other laypeople.

delegation(代表团)的每一位成员可以称为 *delegate*(代表)。代表团的任务常常是在会议上代表一个更大的群体。因此，非医生组成的代表团参加医学会议，可能是要确保病人的权利和需要不会受到忽视，就像平信徒代表团参加宗教会议是为了表达其他平信徒所关心的问题一样。

relegate \ˈre-lə-ˌgāt\ (1) To remove or assign to a less important place. 使……降职/降级；使……处于较低地位 (2) To refer or hand over for decision or for carrying out. 提交；托付

● First-year students were relegated to the back of the line so that all the upper classes could eat first. 一年级学生被赶到了队伍后面，好让高年级学生先吃。

Originally *relegate* meant "to send into exile, banish." So when you relegate an old sofa to the basement, you're sending it to home-decorating Siberia. When confronted with a matter that no one really wants to face, a chief executive may relegate it to a committee "for further study," which may manage to ignore it for years. It may be annoying to read a newspaper article about a pet project and find that your own contributions have been relegated to a short sentence near the end.

relegate 最早的意思是"流放、赶走"。所以，你把一个破沙发 relegate(发配)到地下室的时候，就是在把它送到房屋装修的西伯利亚。遇到了无人想要面对的问题，行政总裁可能会将其 relegate(提交)给一个委员会做"进一步研究"，而委员会可能会将其搁置几年。读报纸知道有一个宠物计划，发现你贡献的宠物被 relegated 到了差不多最后的短短一句话，你会挺生气。

GREG comes from the Latin *grex*, "herd" or "flock." Bees, starlings, cows—any creatures that like to live together in flocks or herds—are called *gregarious*, and

the same word is used for people who enjoy companionship and are happiest when they're in the middle of a rowdy herd.

GREG 源自拉丁语 grex(群)。蜜蜂、椋鸟、牛——任何喜欢群居的动物——都被描述为 gregrious(群居的)。这个词语也用于人,用于那些喜欢他人陪伴、在吵闹的人群中情绪最好的人。

aggregate\\ˈa-grə-gət\\   A collection or sum of units or parts. 总数;集合

● His lawyers realize that the aggregate of incriminating details is now pointing toward a conviction. 他的律师意识到,所有显示有罪的细节加起来可能会使他被判有罪。

An *aggregate* is often an example of something being greater than the sum of its parts. For instance, even if no individual element in a person's background would assure a criminal career, the aggregate of factors could make a life of crime seem unavoidable. *Aggregate* is often used in the phrase "in the aggregate," as in "Her achievements were, in the aggregate, impressive enough to earn her a scholarship." *Aggregate* is also an adjective, meaning "total"; so, for instance, economists often discuss aggregate demand for goods and services in the country's economy, just as you yourself might speak about your father's aggregate income from his three jobs.

aggregate 常常是整体大于部分之和的例子。比如,即使一个人的背景中没有一个元素可以使其从事犯罪职业,因素之和也会使犯罪生涯不可避免。*aggregate* 常常用于"in the aggregate"(加在一起;总共)这一短语中,比如"Her achievements were, in the aggregate, impressive enough to earn her a scholarship"(她所有成就加起来令人赞叹,足以让她获得奖学金)。*aggregate* 也用作形容词,意思是"总的"。所以,比如经济学家常常探讨一个国家的经济中商品和服务的总需求,这就像你可能会说到你爸爸三份工作的总收入。

congregation\\ˌkän-gri-ˈgā-shən\\   (1) A gathering of people, espe- cially for worship or religious instruction. (教堂做礼拜或接受宗教学习的)会众 (2) The membership of a church or temple. (教堂或寺庙的)会众数量

● That Sunday the congregation was especially large, and the minister delivered one of his best sermons. 那个星期天,会众人数特别多,牧师进行了最好的布道之一。

The verb *congregate* may be used for spontaneous gatherings. A crowd quickly congregates at the scene of an accident, for example, just as cows, sheep, or horses tend to congregate during a storm. And under military rule, citizens are often forbidden to congregate on street corners or anywhere else. But a congregation is generally a group that has gathered for a formal purpose, usually in church. The Congregational Church was originally the church of the Puritan settlers, in which each congregation governed its own church independent of any higher authority.

动词 *congregate* 可用于自发的聚会。比如一群人很快就聚集在事故现场,就像牛、羊或者马可能在暴风雨期间聚集起来那样。根据军事规则,公民不得聚集在街角或其他任何地方。但是 congregation 常常是为了正式目的聚在一起的,通常是在教堂。The Congregational Church(公理会)最初是清教徒移民的教会。在这个教会,每一群会众管理自己的教堂,不受更高权力的约束。

egregious\\i-ˈgrē-jəs\\   Standing out, especially in a bad way; flagrant. 极坏的;非常糟糕的

- Many of the term papers contained egregious grammatical errors. 很多学期论文中都有很糟糕的语法错误。

Since *egregious* begins with a short version of *ex-*, meaning "out of," the word should mean literally "out of the herd." So something egregious possesses some quality that sets it apart from others. Originally, that distinguishing quality was something good, but by the 16th century the word's meaning had taken a U-turn and the word was being applied to things that were outrageously bad. This has remained the most common sense. Thus, an egregious fool is one who manages to outdo run-of-the-mill fools, and egregious rudeness sets a new standard for unpleasant salesclerks.

由于 *egregious* 以 *ex-* 的节略写法开始,而 *ex-* 意思是"在……之外",这个单词字面意思应该是"在群体之外"。所以,egregious 东西有着某种良好的品质,但是到了 16 世纪,这个单词的意思彻底发生了转变,开始用于极坏的事物。从此这一直是其最常用的意思。这样,egregious 傻瓜就是要超过一半傻瓜的傻瓜,egregious 粗鲁为令人讨厌的售货员设立了新标准。

segregate \ˈse-grə-ˌgāt\　(1) To separate from others or from the general mass; isolate. 隔离 (2) To separate along racial lines. 按种族对……进行隔离

- Some schools are experimenting with gender segregation, claiming that both sexes learn better in classrooms from which the other sex is absent. 有些学校尝试着进行性别隔离,说没有异性在场,两种性别的学生在课堂上都学得更好。

The prefix *se-* means "apart," so when you *segregate* something you set it apart from the herd. The word typically means separating something undesirable from the healthy majority. During the apple harvest, damaged fruit is segregated from the main crop and used for cider. In prisons, hardened criminals are segregated from youthful offenders. Lepers used to be segregated from the general population because they were thought to be highly infectious. The opposite of *segregate* is often *integrate*, and the two words were in the news almost daily for decades as African-Americans struggled to be admitted into all-white schools and neighborhoods.

前缀 *se-* 意思是"分开",所以,当你 segregate 某物时,你将其与他者分开。这个词语通常意思是将不想要的东西与健康的大多数分开。在苹果收获期间,损坏的苹果跟大多数苹果分开,用来酿造苹果酒。在监狱中,坐牢时间长的囚犯跟年轻囚犯分开。麻风病人过去是跟大众隔离开的,因为人们认为这些人传染性很强。*segregate* 的反义词是 *integrate*,美国黑人争取进入全白人学校和全白人城区的几十年期间,这两个词语几乎天天出现在新闻中。

Quizzes

A. Complete the analogy:

1. habit : custom :: legacy : _____
   a. descendant　　b. tradition　　c. transit　　d. deputy
2. obedient : tame :: egregious : _____
   a. crowded　　b. uncrowded　　c. blatant　　d. fair
3. governor : executive :: legate : _____

a. letter b. priest c. deputy d. bandit

4. series : sequence :: aggregate : _____
   a. individual b. collection c. attack d. annoyance
5. flock : group of sheep :: delegation : _____
   a. group of candidates b. group of worshippers
   c. group of runners d. group of representatives
6. tear : mend :: segregate : _____
   a. mix b. sort c. send away d. refine
7. revise : amend :: relegate : _____
   a. vanish b. banish c. tarnish d. varnish
8. location : place :: congregation : _____
   a. birds b. whales c. group d. temple

B. Fill in each blank with the correct letter:

a. congregation e. legacy
b. relegate f. aggregate
c. segregate g. legate
d. delegation h. egregious

1. The child had tried to hide his mistake with an _____ lie.
2. The king's _____ arrived two weeks early in order to negotiate the agreement that the king would later sign in person.
3. Battlefield medics were forced to _____ the hopeless cases from the other casualties.
4. The government is struggling to overcome a _____ of corruption that goes back a hundred years or more.
5. Taken in the _____, these statistics are very disturbing.
6. At the conference a carefully chosen _____ presented its views to the president.
7. The _____ grew silent as the first strains of the wedding march sounded.
8. There in the corner, where the shopkeeper had decided to _____ him, sat a stuffed bear with a mournful face.

FLU comes from the Latin verb *fluere*, "to flow." So a *flume* is a narrow gorge with a stream flowing through it. A *fluent* speaker is one from whom words *flow* easily. *Influence* originally referred to an invisible *fluid* that was believed to flow from the stars and to affect the actions of humans. A mysterious outbreak of disease in 15th-century Italy led Italians to blame it on the stars' *influenza*—and the name stuck.

FLU 源自拉丁语动词 *fluere*("流")。所以，*flume* 是小溪流过的窄窄的峡谷。说话 *fluent*(流利)的人，词语从他口中很容易 *flow*(流畅说出)。*influence* 最早指看不见的 *fluid*(流体)，据说从星星流出来，影响人类的行动。15 世纪意大利神秘爆发的疾病让意大利人将其怪罪在星星的 *influenza*(影响)上，*influenza*(流感)这个词语就沿用至今。

affluence \ˈa-ˌflü-əns\ An abundance of wealth. 财富；富裕

● The affluence of the city's northern suburbs is indicated by the huge houses there. 这座城市北部郊区的富有从那些大房子就可以看出来。

Affluence comes from the Latin verb *affluere*, "to flow abundantly." Thus, someone or something blessed with affluence has received an incoming *flood* of riches. Since the *affluent* residents of suburbs often work in the central city but pay taxes back home, the wealth of some metropolitan areas tends to *flow* in one direction—out.

affluence 源自拉丁语动词 *affluere*(大量地流)。这样，幸运地拥有财富的人或物已经接受了涌入的 *flood*(大量)财富。由于 *affluent*(富裕的)郊区居民常常在市中心工作，但在家庭所在地交税，一些都市区的财富往往 *flow*(流)向一个方向——向外。

effluent \ˈe-ˌflü-ənt\ Polluting waste material discharged into the environment. 污染环境的废物；污水

● The effluent from the mill had long ago turned this once-beautiful stream into a foul-smelling open-air sewer. 这座工厂排出的废物很早以前就将这个曾经美丽的小河变成了难闻的露天下水道。

Effluent comes from the Latin verb *effluere*, "to flow out." In an older meaning, an effluent was a stream flowing out of a river or lake. But nowadays *effluent* almost always means wastes that pour into our water and air. Liquid factory waste, smoke, and raw sewage can all be called effluents. An effluent filter keeps treated waste flowing out of a septic tank from clogging up its drainage pipes.

effluent 源自拉丁语动词 *effluere*("流出")。它有一个更古老的意思，是从河流或者湖泊流出的小河。但是今天，*effluent* 几乎总是指排到水里和空中的废物。effluent(污水)过滤器使化粪池流出的处理过的水不会堵塞排水管。

confluence \ˈkän-ˌflü-əns\ (1) A coming or flowing together at one point. 汇合；汇集 (2) A place of meeting, especially of two streams. (尤指两条河流的)汇合处

● The confluence of several large economic forces led to the "perfect storm" that shook the world economy in 2008. 几股强大的经济力量汇集在一起，导致了 2008 年动摇世界经济的"极致风暴"。

The joining of rivers—as at Harpers Ferry, West Virginia, where the Shenandoah and Potomac Rivers flow together spectacularly—was the original meaning of *confluence*, and in its later meanings we still hear a strong echo of the physical merging of waters. So today we can speak of a confluence of events, a confluence of interests, a confluence of cultures, and so on, from which something important often emerges.

河流的汇合——比如在西弗吉尼亚的哈珀斯河那里，谢南多亚河跟波托马克河汇合了，非常壮观——是 *confluence*

的原始意思，而在其后来的意思中，我们还可以听到水流汇合的强烈暗示。所以，今天我们可以说事件的 confluence、兴趣的 confluence、文化的 confluence 等等，重要的东西常常从中出现。

mellifluous \me-ˈli-flü-wəs\ Flowing like honey; sweetened as if with honey.
像蜂蜜一样流淌的；(仿佛加入蜂蜜而)变甜了的

• His rich, mellifluous voice is familiar to us from countless voice-overs for commercials, station breaks, and documentaries. 从广告、电台播出中断和纪录片的无数解说中，我们已经熟悉了他那浑厚、流畅的声音。

With its root *mel-*, meaning "honey," *mellifluous* means literally "flowing like honey." The word usually applies to sound; it has often been used to describe voices such as Renee Fleming's or Barbra Streisand's, or pieces by composers such as Ravel and Debussy. The DJ on a radio station that plays soft music may have a voice so mellifluous that it almost puts the listener to sleep.
因为有了表示"蜂蜜"的词根 *mel-*，*mellifluous* 字面意思就是"像蜂蜜一样流动"。这个词语通常用于声音，它常常用来形容人的声音，比如雷妮·弗莱明或者芭芭拉·史翠珊的声音，或者作曲家拉威尔和德彪西的曲子。在电台播放轻柔音乐的节目主持人会有非常甜美流畅的声音，几乎可以让听众睡着。

PREHEND/PREHENS

PREHEND/PREHENS comes from the Latin verb *prehendere*, "to seize." Most of the English words where it appears are closely related to the ones discussed below.
PREHEND/PREHENS 源自拉丁语动词 *prehendere*("抓")。有这一词根出现的大多数英语单词都跟下面讨论到的这些有紧密关系。

---

prehensile \prē-ˈhen-səl\ Adapted for grasping, especially by wrapping around. 抓握的

• The squid has eight short "arms" but also two long prehensile tentacles that it uses for catching its prey. 鱿鱼有八条短短的"胳膊"，但也有两条长长的适合抓握的触须，用来抓捕猎物。

Howler monkeys are among the American monkeys with prehensile tails. Famous for their booming howls, howlers can wrap their tails around a nearby branch while using their prehensile feet and hands for picking lice from their fur or lobbing a coconut at an unwelcome tourist. Our own hands are prehensile, of course. Our feet are not; on the other hand, they're much better for running than the prehensile feet of a monkey or ape.
吼猴是美国有 prehensile tail(卷尾)的猴子之一。这些以深沉叫声闻名的猴子，在使用 prehensile 手和脚捉毛里的虱子，或者从高处向不受欢迎的游客扔椰子时，能将尾巴缠在附近的树枝上。当然，我们的手也是 prehensile。我们的脚不能这样，不过它们比猿猴的 prehensile 脚更适合奔跑。

apprehend \ˌa-pri-ˈhend\ (1) Arrest, seize. 逮捕 (2) Understand. 理解

• It was a few minutes before she managed to apprehend the meaning of what she had just seen. 几分钟后，她才好不容易明白自己所看到的一切意味着什么。

PREHEND
PREHENS

To *apprehend* is to seize, either physically or mentally. So to apprehend a thief is to nab him. But to apprehend a confusing news story, or to apprehend a difficult concept in physics, is to understand it—that is, to "grasp" it mentally. If you're *apprehensive* about something that's about to happen, it means you've grasped all the unpleasant possibilities and are waiting with anxiety or dread.

apprehend 就是抓住，要么是身体的，要么是精神的。所以，apprehend 一个小偷就是逮住他。但是 apprehend 一个让人难以明白的新闻故事，或者 apprehend 一个难懂的物理概念，就是理解它——也就是在精神方面"抓住"它。如果你 *apprehensive* 就要发生的事情，意思就是你已经明白所有不好的可能性，正担心或者恐惧地等待着。

comprehend\ˌkäm-pri-ˈhend\ (1) To grasp the meaning of; understand. 理解；明白 (2) To take in or include. 包括

● In the days following the dropping of the atomic bomb on Hiroshima, the public slowly began to comprehend the fact that the nuclear age had arrived. 在原子弹投放广岛之后的日子里，公众慢慢开始明白核能时代已经到来这一事实。

To *comprehend* is to mentally grasp something's complete nature or meaning. *Comprehend* is thus often a bit stronger than *understand*: for example, you may understand the instructions in a handbook without completely comprehending their purpose. *Comprehend*'s second meaning is much less common. Using that sense of the word, we could say that good manners comprehends (that is, includes) more than simple table etiquette, for example, or that true courage comprehends more than just physical showing off. And something *comprehensive* includes a great deal: so a comprehensive exam, for instance, includes all the material that was studied in the course.

comprehend 就是在精神上抓住某物的全部性质或者意思。所以，comprehend 常常比 understand 意思更强一些；比如，你可能会 understand 手册里的使用说明，却并不完全 comprehend 其目的。comprehend 第二个意思更为常用。使用这个意思，我们可以说良好的举止 comprehend（包括）的不只是，比如说吧，简单的餐桌礼仪，或者真正的勇气包括的不只是身体上的显摆。comprehensive（无所不包的）东西包括很多；比如 comprehensive 考试包括学习过程中的所有内容。

reprehensible\ˌre-pri-ˈhen-sə-bəl\ Deserving stern criticism or blame. 应该严厉批评的；应该严厉责备的

● Whether or not he ever broke the law, his treatment of his first wife was thoroughly reprehensible. 不管他是否曾经违法，他这样对待第一任妻子都应该严厉批评。

From its prefix *re-*, meaning "back," *reprehend* would mean literally "to hold back, restrain"; but even the Latin version of the verb had come to mean "to scold, blame"—in other words, to restrain bad behavior by expressing disapproval. *Reprehensible* is applied to both things and people—that is, both the sin and the sinner. So a senator might be scolded for reprehensible conduct, but might also be called a thoroughly reprehensible person. And most of us would call dogfighting morally reprehensible, and would use the same word to describe those who put the dogs up to it.

从其前缀 re-（"回"）来看，reprehend 字面意思会是"阻挡；控制"；但是，即使是这个动词的拉丁写法也已开始表示

• 478 •

"责备,指责"了——换句话说,就是通过表示反对来阻止不良行为。reprehensible 用于事物也用于人,也就是说,恶行和作恶者。所以,一位参议院可能因为 reprehensible 行为受到责备,但也可能被骂成一个彻底 reprehensible 人。我们大多数人会说斗狗是道德上 reprehensible,会用这同一个词语形容那些怂恿斗狗的人。

Quizzes

TEMPER

A. **Choose the closest definition:**

1. apprehend   a. seize   b. insist   c. understand   d. deny
2. confluence   a. support   b. joining   c. certainty   d. outflow
3. reprehensible   a. understandable   b. worthy of blame   c. worthy of return   d. inclusive
4. comprehend   a. take   b. understand   c. compress   d. remove
5. mellifluous   a. flowing slowly   b. flowing outward   c. flowing smoothly   d. flowing downward
6. effluent   a. wastewater   b. wealth   c. trash   d. sewer
7. prehensile   a. able to peel   b. able to swing   c. able to howl   d. able to grasp
8. affluence   a. suburb   b. excess   c. wealth   d. mall

B. **Indicate whether the following pairs of words have the same or different meanings:**

1. prehensile / dropping   same ____ / different ____
2. mellifluous / smooth   same ____ / different ____
3. reprehensible / unusual   same ____ / different ____
4. effluent / pollutant   same ____ / different ____
5. comprehend / include   same ____ / different ____
6. confluence / understanding   same ____ / different ____
7. apprehend / arrest   same ____ / different ____
8. affluence / wealth   same ____ / different ____

TEMPER comes from the Latin verb *temperare*, "to moderate or keep within limits" or "to mix." Most of the world's people live in the *temperate* zone—that is, the zone where the *temperature* is moderate, between the hot tropics and the icy Arctic and Antarctic Circles. It's less easy to see how we get *temperature* from this root; the word actually used to refer to the mixing of different basic elements in the body, and only slowly came to mean how hot or cold that body was.

TEMPER 源自拉丁语动词 *temperare*("使适中;使不过分;混合")。世界上大多数人生活在 *temperate*(温带)的地区,也就是 *temperature*(温度)适中的地区,在热带和寒冷的北极圈和南极圈之间。要想明白我们是怎么从这一词根得到 *temperature* 这一词语的,就不那么容易了。这个词语实际上曾用来指身体里不同的基本元素的混合,后来才逐渐表示身体多么热或者多么冷。

TEMPER

temper \ˈtem-pər\   To dilute, qualify, or soften by adding something more agreeable; to moderate. 使变淡;使缓和;使温和

● A wise parent tempers discipline with love. 明智的父母将惩罚与关爱并用。

The *temper* root keeps its basic meaning—"to mix" or "to keep within limits"—in the English word *temper*. When you temper something, you mix it with some balancing quality or substance so as to avoid anything extreme. Thus, it's often said that a judge must temper justice with mercy. Young people only gradually learn to temper their natural enthusiasms with caution. And in dealing with others, we all try to temper our honesty with sensitivity.

temper 这一词根在英语单词 *temper* 中保持着其基本意思——"混合"或者"使不过分"。当你 temper 什么东西时,你混入一些起平衡作用的品质或物质,以避免走向极端。因此,据说法官要公平与怜悯并用。年轻人只能逐渐明白,做自己天生热衷的事情也要谨慎。在处理与他人的关系时,我们都努力做到既要诚实,又要体谅他人情感。

temperance \ˈtem-prəns\   (1) Moderation in satisfying appetites or passions. 节制;适度 (2) The drinking of little or no alcohol. (几乎)滴酒不沾

● Buddhism teaches humankind to follow "the middle way"—that is, temperance in all things. 佛教教导人类要走"中道"——也就是说,一切都要适度。

Since *temperance* means basically "moderation," you might assume that, with respect to alcohol, *temperance* would mean moderate consumption, or "social drinking." Instead, the word has usually meant the prohibition of all alcohol. To temperance leaders such as Carry Nation, the safest form of drinking was no alcohol at all. Believing she was upholding the law, Nation began her hatchet-swinging attacks on saloons, known as "hatchetations," in the 1890s. National prohibition did eventually come—and go—but largely through the efforts of more *temperate* (that is, moderate) reformers.

由于 *temperance* 的基本意思是"适度",你或许会认为,就酒而言,*temperance* 会意味着适度饮酒,或者"社交饮酒"。可是,这个词语通常意思是禁止所有的酒。对于凯瑞·内森这样的禁酒领袖来说,最安全的饮酒方式是根本没酒。内森认为自己在支持法律,开始了对酒吧的猛烈攻击,这就是 20 世纪 90 年代人们所知道的"hatchetations"(挥斧攻击),国家禁令最终还是来了……又走了……但是主要是通过更加 *temperate*(温和)的改革家的努力。

intemperate \in-ˈtem-pə-rət\   Not moderate or mild; excessive, extreme. 过度的;过分的;极端的

● Lovers of fine wines and scotches are almost never intemperate drinkers. 喜欢上等葡萄酒和苏格兰威士忌的人从来不过度饮酒。

Since the prefix *in-* generally means "not," *intemperate* is the opposite of *temperate*. Someone intemperate rejects moderation in favor of excess. A religious fanatic is likely to preach with intemperate zeal, and a mean theater critic may become intemperate in her criticism of a new play, filling her review with intemperate language. And both *temperate* and *intemperate* also often refer to weather; a region with an intemperate climate isn't where all of us would choose to build a house.

由于 *in-* 这一前缀通常表示"不", *intemperate* 就是 *temperate* 的反义词。intemperate 的人愿意过度,不愿意适度。宗教狂热分子可能极端热情地进行宣传活动,刻薄的戏剧评论家对一部新戏进行评论时很是过分,评论文章中满是极端的语言。*temperate* 和 *intemperate* 也经常指天气,有 intemperate 气候的地区不是我们都愿意去盖房子的地方。

distemper\dis-ˈtem-pər\ (1) A highly contagious viral disease, especially of dogs. 犬瘟热 (2) A highly contagious and usually fatal viral disease, especially of cats, marked by the destruction of white blood cells. 猫瘟热

• An epidemic of feline distemper had swept the country, and its cat population had plummeted. 一场猫瘟热传染病横扫该国,猫的数量急剧下降。

Back when doctors believed that our moods were affected by an imbalance of mysterious fluids in the body, or "humors," distemper often meant moodiness, as when Shakespeare's Hamlet is asked "What is the source of your distemper?" Today the word is used only for true physical conditions. The *distemper* that affects dogs, often called *canine distemper*, also affects foxes, wolves, mink, raccoons, and ferrets. It can be treated with medication, but is generally fatal if not treated. Distemper in cats, known as feline distemper or *panleukopenia*, actually isn't related to canine distemper. If caught quickly, it too can be treated. And both types can be prevented by vaccination, so all responsible pet owners get their animals vaccinated.

医生们一度相信,体内神秘流体(或者"体液")不平衡会影响我们的情绪。当时,distemper 常常意味着情绪多变,就像莎士比亚笔下的哈姆雷特被问及"你为何情绪失调?"时那样。今天,这一词语只用来指真实的身体状况。侵袭狗的 distemper(犬瘟热),常常称为"canine distemper"也侵袭狐狸、狼、水貂、浣熊和雪貂。这种病可用药物进行治疗,但如果不治疗常常是致命的。猫瘟热,feline distemper 或者 panleukopenia,实际上跟犬瘟热无关。如果及早发现,该病也是可以治愈的。两种疾病都可以通过注射疫苗进行预防,因此,所有负责任的宠物主人都给自己的宠物注射疫苗。

PURG comes from the Latin verb *purgare*, "to clean or cleanse." Almost all the English words where it shows up are closely related to those discussed below.

PURE 源自拉丁语动词 *purgare*("打扫;清洁")。几乎全部有它出现的英语单词都与下面讨论的词语联系紧密。

---

purge\ˈpərj\ (1) To clear of guilt or sin. 免除罪责 (2) To free of something unwanted or considered impure. 清除

• His first act as leader was to purge the party of estremists. 他当上领导的一件事就是清除党内的极端分子。

In some cultures, a ritual bath or prayer is performed to purge guilt or evil spirits. The Minoans of ancient Crete may have used human sacrifice as a way of purging the entire community, which is fine for the community but rough on the victims. In many cultures, people periodically purge themselves physically—that is, clean out their digestive tracts—by taking strong laxatives; this used to be a popular springtime ritual, and herbal *purgatives* were readily available.

在有些文化中,人们举行仪式性的洗浴或祈祷来免罪或驱除恶鬼。古代克里特岛的米诺人用人进行祭祀,作为清洁整个社会的一种方式。这对社会来说很好,但对受害者来说则很残酷。在很多文化中,人们服用强效通便剂,定期清洁自己的身体,也就是说,彻底清理自己的消化道。这在过去常常是很流行的春季习俗,药草 *purgatives*(泻药)很容易找到。

expurgate\ˈek-spər-ˌgāt\ To cleanse of something morally harmful or offensive; to remove objectionable parts from. 净化(道德上有害或冒犯的东西);去除(不受欢迎的部分)。

• In those years, high-school English classes only used expurgated editions of Chaucer's *Canterbury Tales*. 在那些年里,高中英语课只使用删节版的乔叟的《坎特伯雷故事集》。

Expurgation has a long and questionable history. Perhaps history's most famous *expurgator*, or censor, was the English editor Thomas Bowdler, who in 1818 published the *Family Shakespeare*, an expurgated edition of Shakespeare's plays that omitted or changed any passages that, in Bowdler's opinion, couldn't decently be read aloud in a family. As a result, the term bowdlerize is now a synonym of *expurgate*.

expurgation 有着悠久而可疑的历史。英国编辑托马斯·鲍德勒也许是历史上最著名的 *expurgator*(净化者),或者说审查者。他在 1818 年出版了《家庭莎士比亚戏剧》,这是莎士比亚戏剧的删节版,删去或修改了鲍德勒认为在一个家庭里不能体面朗读的任何段落。因此,术语 bowdlerize 现在是 *expurgate* 的同义词。

purgative\ˈpər-gə-tiv\ (1) Cleansing or purifying, especially from sin. 洗罪的;除罪的 (2) Causing a significant looseness of the bowels. 引起腹泻的

• I'm afraid my ten-year-old discovered the purgative effect of too many apples after a lazy afternoon in the orchard. 恐怕我那个十岁的孩子在果园懒洋洋地待了一个下午之后,发现了吃太多苹果的通便效果。

Purgative can be used as a noun as well as an adjective. For centuries, doctors prescribed purgatives—that is, laxatives—for all kinds of ailments, not knowing anything better to do. Physical cleansing has always reminded people of emotional and spiritual cleansing, as expressed in the saying "Cleanliness is next to godliness." So we may say, for example, that confession has a purgative effect on the soul. Some psychologists used to claim that expressing your anger is purgative; but in fact it may generally be no better for your emotional life than taking a laxative, and can sometimes really foul things up.

purgative 除了用作形容词,也可用作名词。有数个世纪,医生们都为各种小病开 purgatives——也就是 laxatives(通便药)——而不知道还有什么更好的办法。清洁身体一直都让人们想到清洁情绪和精神,就像谚语"清洁仅次于圣洁"说的那样。所以,比如我们可以说,告罪有着清洁灵魂的作用。有些心理学家过去曾说,表达愤怒之情有清洁作用;但实际上,它对你精神生活的效果,通常并不会比服用泻药更好,有时候真的会把事情搞砸。

purgatory\ˈpər-gə-ˌtȯr-ē\ (1) According to Roman Catholic doctrine, the place where the souls of those who have died in God's grace must pay

for their sins through suffering before ascending to heaven. 炼狱（2）A place or state of temporary suffering or misery. 经受暂时折磨或痛苦的地方或状态

• For both of them, filled with anxiety, the long, sleepless night felt like purgatory. 对他们两个来说,因为心里充满焦虑,这漫长、无眠的夜晚感觉像是炼狱。

Purgatory is the place where the soul is cleansed of all impurities, as Dante described in his great poem *The Divine Comedy*. Today *purgatory* can refer to any place or situation in which suffering and misery are felt to be sharp but temporary. Waiting to hear the results of a test, or whether you got a good job, can be a purgatory. And an endless after-dinner speech can make an entire roomful of people feel as if they're in purgatory.

purgatory 是灵魂的不洁得到清洗的地方,就像但丁在他伟大的诗歌《神曲》中所描述的那样。今天,*purgatory* 可用来指任何折磨或痛苦感到更加强烈但短暂的地方或处境。等着听到考试结果,或者听到你是否得到了一份好工作,都可能是短暂而痛苦的。晚宴后没完没了的演说,会使整个房间的人感觉好像在炼狱中。

Quizzes

A. Fill in each blank with the correct letter:

a. intemperate
b. expurgate
c. temperance
d. purge
e. purgatory
f. temper
g. purgative
h. distemper

1. For a sick person, waiting for medical test results can feel like _____.

2. Don thinks we had better _____ our enthusiasm for this scheme with a large dose of skepticism.

3. When taken in moderate quantities, the _____ effects of bran can be healthful.

4. The widow leaped to her feet and launched into a shockingly _____ tirade at the jury.

5. Filmmakers must sometimes _____ entire scenes from their films to receive an acceptable rating.

6. Her eternal watchword was _____, and no one ever saw her upset, worn out, angry, or tipsy.

7. Concerned that the workers might be forming a union, the president considered trying to _____ the entire department.

8. That year, the local raccoon population had been severely reduced by an epidemic of _____.

B. Match the definition on the left to the correct word on the right:

1. place of misery   a. distemper
2. unrestrained   b. purge

3. remove offensive material
4. mix or moderate
5. purifying
6. moderation
7. remove impure elements
8. animal disease

c. temperance
d. purgative
e. temper
f. expurgate
g. intemperate
h. purgatory

Number Words 数字词语

MILL means either "a thousand" or "a thousandth." A *millennium* is a thousand years, and a *million* is a thousand thousands. But a *milligram* is a thousandth of a gram, a *milliliter* a thousandth of a liter, and a *millimeter* a thousandth of a meter. MILL 要么表示"一千",要么表示"第一千"。*millennium* 是一千年,*million* 是一千个一千。但是 *milligram* 是千分之一克,*milliliter* 是千分之一升,*millimeter* 是千分之一米。

millefleur \mēl-ˈflər\ Having a pattern of small flowers and plants all over. 满是小花草图案的

● She was painstakingly embroidering a millefleur pattern on a pillow casing. 她正细心地往枕套上绣着小花草图案。

Millefleur came into French from the Latin *mille flores* ("a thousand flowers"), and from French directly into English. You may have seen the famed Unicorn Tapestries, in which the unicorn is seen frolicking, relaxing, being hunted, and being caught, all against a beautiful millefleur background. Italian has given us the similar word *millefiori*; though *fiori*, like *fleurs*, means "flowers," *millefiori* actually refers to a type of multicolored ornamental glass. And the borrowed French word *millefeuille* (*feuille* meaning "leaf") is the name of a dish made with puff pastry, the kind of pastry whose flakes resemble thin dry leaves.

millefleur 从拉丁语的 *mille flores*("一千朵花")进入法语,又从法语直接进入英语。你可能见过著名的麒麟挂毯,上面是麒麟在嬉戏、在放松、被追猎、被捕捉,背景是美丽的小花草图案。意大利语给我们了相似的 *millefiori* 这个词。虽然 *fiori* 跟 *fleurs* 一样,意思是"花,"但 *millefiori* 实际上指一种杂色的装饰性玻璃。借来的法语单词 *mille-feuille*(*feuille* 意思是"叶子")是一道菜的名字。这道菜的材料是泡芙面团,它的薄片像薄而干的叶子。

millenarianism \ˌmi-lə-ˈner-ē-ə-ˌni-zəm\ (1) Belief in the 1,000 year era of holiness foretold in the Book of Revelation. 《圣经·启示录》中预言的圣洁千年这一信念 (2) Belief in an ideal society to come, especially one brought about by revolution. 未来理想社会这一信念

● Millenarianism is one of the future-oriented beliefs common in the New Age movement. 未来理想社会这一信念是新时代运动中面向未来的常见信仰之一。

Originally the *millennium* was not simply any thousand-year period, but instead the thousand years prophesied in the biblical Book of Revelation, when holiness will prevail on earth and Jesus Christ will preside over all. Later, *millennium* was extended to mean any period—always in the future—marked by universal happiness and human perfection. On several occasions over the centuries, members of Christian sects have become convinced that the biblical millennium was arriving and gathered together to await it. But nonreligious millenarians have also believed in a future society marked by human perfection. Even if they regard this future as certain, they've generally been willing to help it along by working for a political, social, or economic revolution. The millennium always seems to be approaching; to date, it hasn't arrived.

millennium(千年)最初并非随便哪一千年,而是《圣经·启示录》中预言的那一千年。在这一千年中,地球上到处一片圣洁,耶稣会掌管一切。后来,*millennium* 意义扩大了,包括任何其特征是举世幸福、人类完美的阶段,这种阶段总是在未来。在过去的世世代代,基督教教派的成员有几次都坚信,《圣经》中预言的千年就要到来,还聚在一起等待着。但是,不信仰宗教的 millenarians(未来理想社会信仰者)也认为有一个未来的、特征是人类完美的社会。即使他们认为肯定有这样一个未来社会,他们也一直普遍乐意通过为一个政治的、社会的或者经济的革命而奋斗来帮助它到来。

millipede\ˈmi-lə-ˌpēd\ Any of a class of many-footed arthropods that have a cylindrical, segmented body with two pairs of legs on each segment, and, unlike centipedes, no poison fangs. 千足虫

• As they turned over rocks and bricks in their search for the lost bracelet, millipedes of various sizes went scurrying off. 在他们翻遍岩石和砖头寻找丢失的手镯时,大小不一的千足虫到处逃窜。

The earth is home to about 10,000 species of millipedes. Though they have no poison fangs, many of them can, when threatened, emit a liquid or gas poisonous to their enemies. If their structure were true to their name, millipedes would have a thousand legs, but in fact they have far fewer. Even so, a millipede in motion is a sight to ponder: How can it possibly coordinate all those legs so that it doesn't trip over itself? Like some tiny conga line or bunny hop, it scuttles away to a rhythm only it can hear.

地球上大约有一万种千足虫。虽然它们没有毒牙,但在生命安全受到威胁时,很多千足虫会释放对敌人有毒的液体或气体。如果其结构与名字相符的话,千足虫就会有一千条腿,但实际上,它们的腿要少得多。即使这样,行动中的千足虫也是值得考虑的景象:它怎么可能协调所有的腿,而不会被自己绊倒? 就像一个小型的康茄舞或者兔子跳一样,它随着只有自己听得到的节奏匆忙逃走。

millisecond\ˈmi-lə-ˌse-kənd\ One thousandth of a second. 千分之一秒;毫秒

• A lightning bolt lasts only about 20 milliseconds, though the image may stay in one's eye for much longer. 闪电仅仅持续二十毫秒,不过其形象在人眼中留下的时间会长得多。

A millisecond isn't long enough for the blink of an eye, but a few milliseconds may determine the winner of a swim race or a hundred-yard dash. With the ever-increasing speed of modern technology, even a millisecond has started to seem a little sluggish; computer operations are now measured in nanoseconds—that is, billionths of a second.

一毫秒还不够眨一次眼睛,但是几毫秒或许可以确定游泳比赛或一百码短跑中的获胜者。随着现代技术日益加速的发展,即使一毫秒也开始看起来有点缓慢了。电脑操作现在是按微秒(也就是一秒的十亿分之一)测量的。

HEMI/SEMI

HEMI/SEMI means "half." *Hemi-* comes from Greek, *semi-* from Latin. A *hemisphere* is half a sphere, and a *semicircle* is half a circle. (The French prefix *demi-*, which probably developed from Latin as well, also means "half"—as in *demitasse*, a little after-dinner coffee cup half the size of a regular cup.)

HEMI/SEMI 意思是"半"。hemi-源自希腊语,semi-源自拉丁语。hemisphere 就是半个球体,semicircle 就是半圈。(法语前缀 demi-可能是从拉丁语发展而来的。它的意思也是"半",比如在 demitasse 这个单词中。这个单词指一种小小的饭后咖啡杯子,只有正常杯子一半大小。)

semitone \ˈse-mē-ˌtōn\ The tone at a half step. 半音

● The ancient piano in the great music room had been allowed to fall terribly out of tune, with every note at least a semitone flat. 这间巨大的音乐室中的古老钢琴走调很厉害,每个音符至少降了半音。

A *semitone* (sometimes called a *half tone* or a *half step*) is the distance from a white key to a neighboring black key on the piano keyboard—for example, from G to G-sharp or from E to E-flat. In an octave (from G to the next G above, for instance), there are twelve semitones. Semitones are the smallest intervals that are used intentionally in almost any of the music you'll normally hear. Two semitones equal a *whole tone*—the distance from G up to A or from E down to D, for example.

semitone(有时候叫做 half tone 或者 half step)是钢琴键盘上从白色键到邻近的黑色键之间的距离,比如从 G 调到升 G 调,或者从 E 调到降 E 调。在一个八度(比如从 G 调到下一个 G 调)里有十二个半音。半音是有意用在几乎你能听到的任何音乐中的最小的音程中的,两个半音等于一个 whole tone(全音)——比如从 G 调升到 A 调或者从 E 降调降到 D 调的距离。

semicolon \ˈse-mē-ˌkō-lən\ The punctuation mark, used chiefly to separate major sentence elements such as independent clauses. 分号

● Some young vandal had done a search-and-replace on Mr. Marsh's computer file, and in place of every semicolon was the mysterious message "Hendrix RULES!" 一些故意破坏公物的年轻人在马什先生的计算机文件上做了一个搜寻与替代,替代每个分号的是"Hendrix RULES!"这条神秘信息。

The *semicolon* was introduced into modern type by an Italian printer around 1566. But since it's actually the same symbol as the ancient Greek question mark, it's older than the colon (:), which first appears around 1450. Don't mix the two up. A colon introduces something: usually a list, sometimes a statement. A semicolon separates two independent but related clauses; it may also replace the comma to separate items in a complicated list.

大约在 1566 年,一位意大利印刷商在现代印刷字符中首次使用分号。但是,由于它实际上跟古代希腊的问号是一

个符号,它比 1450 年左右出现的冒号(:)还要古老。不要把这两个标点符号弄混了。冒号引出某种内容:通常是一个名单,有时候是一句话。分号将两个独立但相关的从句分开,它也可能代替逗号将复杂列表中的每一项分开。

hemiplegia \ˌhe-mi-ˈplē-jə\ Total or partial paralysis of one side of the body that results from disease of or injury to the motor centers of the brain. 偏瘫

- She's starting to regain the use of her right hand, and some of the therapists think her hemiplegia might eventually be reversed. 她开始能用右手了,一些治疗师认为她的偏瘫最终可能好转。

Hemi-, unlike *semi*, almost always appears in scientific or technical words, including medical terms such as this one. A *hemiplegic*, like a paraplegic (who has lost the use of both legs), has usually suffered brain damage, often from a wound or blood clot. Other conditions that affect one side of the body are *hemihypertrophy* (excessive growth on one side), *hemiatrophy* (wasting on one side), and *hemiparesis* (weakness or partial paralysis).

hemi- 跟 semi- 不一样,几乎总是出现在科学或专门术语中,包括像这个词语一样的医学术语。hemiplegic(偏瘫病人)就像 paraplegic(截瘫病人;不能使用双腿的人),通常遭受过脑伤害,多是由受伤或者血块导致的。影响身体一侧的其他疾病包括 hemihypertrophy(偏侧肥大)、hemiatrophy(偏侧萎缩)以及 hemiparesis(轻偏瘫)。

HEMI/SEMI

semiconductor \ˌse-ˌmē-kən-ˈdək-tər\ A solid that conducts electricity like a metal at high temperatures and insulates like a nonmetal at low temperatures. 半导体

- Silicon, which makes up 25% of the earth's crust, is the most widely used semiconductor, and as such has formed the basis for a revolution in human culture. 硅占地球外壳的 25%,是应用最广泛的半导体,并因此构成了人类文化中一次革命的基础。

A semiconductor is a crystal material whose ability to conduct electricity rises as its temperature goes up. That is, it sometimes acts as a conductor and sometimes as an insulator. Its conducting ability can be much increased by chemical treatment. A manufactured chip of silicon, less than half an inch square, may contain millions of microscopic transistors, which can serve control and memory functions when installed in a computer, automobile, cell phone, DVD player, or microwave oven.

半导体是一种晶体材料,随着其温度上升,导电能力也会提高。也就是说,它的作用有时候相当于导体,有时候相当于绝缘体。其导电能力经过化学处理可以大大增强。生产的硅片,虽然不到半平方英寸,却可能包含数百万个微小的导体。这些导体安装在计算机、汽车、手机、DVD 播放机或者微波炉中,能够发挥控制和记忆功能。

Quiz

Fill in each blank with the correct letter:

a. millefleur   e. semicolon
b. semiconductor   f. millenarianism
c. millisecond   g. hemiplegia
d. semitone   h. millipede

1. _____ increased dramatically as the year 2000 approached.

2. In most integrated circuits, silicon is used as the _____.

3. The poison from the largest tropical centipedes can be lethal to small children, but a _____ could never kill a human.

4. Seeing that the highest note was out of her comfortable range, she asked her pianist to play the whole song a _____ lower.

5. For the baby's room they chose wallpaper with a dainty _____ design.

6. A childhood disease had resulted in the crippling _____ that had confined him to a wheelchair for ten years.

7. Some Olympic races have been extremely close, but no one has ever won by a single _____.

8. The meaning of a clause rarely depends on whether it ends with a colon or a _____.

Review Quizzes

A. Complete the analogy:

1. repulsive : attractive :: ignominious : _____
   a. favorite   b. honorable   c. horrible   d. disgraceful
2. obnoxious : pleasant :: egregious : _____
   a. boring   b. bothersome   c. unpleasant   d. unnoticeable
3. milliliter : volume :: millisecond : _____
   a. distance   b. weight   c. time   d. mass
4. enthusiastic : eager :: intemperate : _____
   a. calm   b. amused   c. restrained   d. uncontrolled
5. paraplegia : legs :: hemiplegia : _____
   a. paralysis   b. stroke   c. lungs   d. left or right side
6. erase : delete :: expurgate : _____
   a. confess   b. read   c. censor   d. scrub
7. allow : permit :: apprehend : _____
   a. accept   b. ignore   c. figure out   d. examine
8. split : separation :: confluence : _____
   a. breakup   b. division   c. flow   d. merging
9. repair : fix :: purge : _____
   a. purify   b. smooth   c. weaken   d. support
10. present : gift :: legacy : _____
    a. ownership   b. legal settlement c. will   d. inheritance

UNIT 20

B. Choose the closest definition:

1. patrician   a. patriot   b. aristocrat   c. father
   d. grandfather
2. congregation   a. anthill   b. gathering   c. hearing
   d. church
3. temperance   a. wrath   b. modesty   c. moderation
   d. character
4. nominal   a. trifling   b. important   c. by name
   d. serious
5. legate   a. heritage   b. gift   c. ambassador
   d. letter
6. comprehend   a. misjudge   b. confirm   c. grasp
   d. gather
7. effluent   a. discharge   b. effort   c. excess
   d. wealth
8. purgative   a. secret agent   b. bleaching agent
   c. road agent   d. cleansing agent
9. semicolon   a. small intestine   b. punctuation mark
   c. low hill   d. small bush
10. reprehensible   a. understandable   b. reptilian
    c. disgraceful   d. approachable
11. distemper   a. anger   b. hysteria   c. disease
    d. weakness
12. millipede   a. thousand-year blight
    b. many-legged arthropod   c. hundred million
    d. obstacle
13. purgatory   a. near heaven   b. place of punishment
    c. evacuation   d. place of earthly delights
14. semitone   a. soft sound   b. half note   c. shade of color
    d. half step
15. aggregate   a. nuisance   b. assembly   c. pile   d. sum total

C. Fill in each blank with the correct letter:

a. mellifluous
b. expatriate
c. millefleur
d. paternalistic
e. affluence
f. purge

i. temper
j. misnomer
k. semiconductor
l. legacy
m. prehensile
n. millenarianism

g. nomenclature
o. delegation
h. segregate

1. Thousands of microscopic transistors partly made of the same _____ are embedded in each chip.

2. Each generation hopes to leave the next a _____ of peace and prosperity.

3. Each time a new insect is discovered, strict rules of _____ help determine what its name will be.

4. We sent a two-person _____ off to the restaurant to choose supper for everyone.

5. The hands of even a newborn infant are _____ and surprisingly strong.

6. Let's _____ the bad fruit from the rest to prevent the rot from spreading.

7. The company's _____ attitudes toward its employees were at times helpful and at times just irritating.

8. The _____ tones of a Mozart flute concerto poured from the window.

9. "Panama hat" is a _____, since the hats have actually always been made in Ecuador.

10. Imperial Rome was a city of great _____ as well as terrible poverty.

11. Many of us take milk or cream with our coffee to _____ its acidity.

12. The outburst seemed to _____ the crowd of its anger.

13. Since everyone interprets the Bible's prophecies differently, _____ has broken out at many different times through the centuries.

14. She soon realized that she wasn't the only American _____ in her Kenyan village.

15. A design with a detailed _____ background is a challenge for even a needlepoint expert.

UNIT 21

SUB

SUB means "under." So a *subway* runs under the streets, and a *submarine* moves under the ocean's surface. A *subject* is a person under the authority of another. A movie's *subplot* is lower in importance than the main plot. *Subscribe* once meant "to write one's name underneath," so *subscription* was the act of signing a document or agreement.

SUB 意思是"在……下面",因此,*subway*(地铁)在街道下延伸,*submarine*(潜水艇)在海面下行驶。*subject*(臣民)是处于另一个人的权威之下的人。电影的 *subplot*(次要情节)的重要性在主要情节之下。*subscribe* 曾经的意思是"在……下面写下自己的名字",所以,*subscription* 指代在文件或协定上签字这一行为。

---

subconscious\ˌsəb-ˈkän-shəs\ Existing in the mind just below the level of awareness. 下意识的;潜意识的

• After dropping three dishes in a week, she began thinking there might be some kind of subconscious agitation behind her case of butterfingers. 一星期让三个盘子掉在地上之后,她开始想,也许她笨手笨脚的背后有某种潜意识的焦虑。

We're rarely aware, or at least fully aware, of our subconscious mental activity. But subconscious thought does affect our feelings and behavior, and it's often revealed in dreams, artistic expression, and slips of the tongue. The subconscious mind can be a hiding place for anxiety, a source of creativity, and often the reason behind our own mysterious behavior. 我们很少意识到自己的潜意识精神活动,或者至少是很少充分意识到。但是,潜意识的思想并不影响我们的情感和行为,而是常常在睡梦、艺术表达和口误中表现出来。潜意识可以成为忧虑这一创造力源泉的隐蔽所,也常常是我们神秘行为背后的原因。

subjugate\ˈsəb-jə-ˌgāt\ To bring under control and rule as a subject; conquer, subdue. 征服;控制

• The country's government claimed it was just trying to protect national security, but some saw its actions as an attempt to subjugate the news media. 该国政府声称自己正努力保护国家安全,但是有人看到其采取行动,试图控制新闻媒体。

Since *jugus* means "yoke" in Latin, *subjugate* means literally "bring under the yoke." Farmers control oxen by means of a heavy wooden yoke over their shoulders. In ancient Rome, conquered soldiers, stripped of their uniforms, might actually be forced to pass under an ox yoke as a sign of submission to the Roman victors. Even without an actual yoke, what happens to a population that has come under the control of another can be every bit as humiliating. In dozens of countries throughout the world, ethnic minorities are denied basic rights and view themselves as subjugated by their country's government, army, and police.

由于 *jugus* 在拉丁语中意思是"牛轭", *subjugate* 字面意思就是"使处于牛轭之下"。农民把沉重的木头牛轭套在牛的肩膀上来控制它们。在古罗马,被征服的士兵被扒光衣服,可能真的被迫从牛轭下通过,表示服从罗马胜利者。即使没有真的牛轭,被征服的人民也会因为另一方的所作所为遭受同样的羞辱。在世界上数十个国家,少数民族得不到基本权利,认为自己被国家政府、军队和警察所控制。

subliminal \ sə-ˈbli-mə-nəl \ Not quite strong enough to be sensed or perceived consciously. 下意识的;潜意识的

• A few worried parents claimed that some heavy-metal songs contain subliminal messages—in the form of words recorded backwards—that urge young fans to take up devil worship. 有几位忧心忡忡的父母说,有些重金属歌曲含有潜意识的信息,以倒着录制的词语的形式出现,鼓动年轻的粉丝崇拜魔鬼。

Since the Latin word *limen* means "threshold," something subliminal exists just below the threshold of conscious awareness. The classic example of a subliminal message is "Eat popcorn" flashed on a movie screen so quickly that the audience doesn't even notice it consciously. Actually, no such advertising has ever been shown to work. But ordinary ads, both in print and on TV, do contain all kinds of images that shape our response to the product being advertised even when we don't realize it. Try looking carefully at some ads that you like, in order to discover how many ways they may be *subliminally* affecting you.

由于拉丁语的 *limen* 意思是"门槛",潜意识的东西就存在于意识的门槛之下。潜意识信息的经典例子是电影银幕上闪现的"吃爆米花"几个字。它们迅速闪过,观众甚至不能有意识地注意到。实际上,没有什么表明这样的广告会产生效果。但是普通的广告,印刷的以及电视上的,确实包含各种形象,在我们没有意识到的时候,就影响了我们对广告中产品的反应。为了发现有多少方式可以对你 *subliminally*(潜意识地)产生影响,试着仔细看看你喜欢的一些广告吧。

subversion \ səb-ˈvər-zhən \ (1) An attempt to overthrow a government by working secretly from within. 颠覆 (2) The corrupting of someone or something by weakening their morals, loyalty, or faith. 削弱

• It's sometimes easier for a government to combat attack from outside than subversion from within. 有时,对一个政府来说,对抗外界攻击比对抗内部颠覆更容易些。

Subversion is literally the "turning over" of something. In the 1950s and 1960s, many people worried about communist subversion of the U.S. government, though they often saw *subversive* activities where none existed. Nondemocratic governments often claim that anyone who disagrees with them or joins a demonstration is a *subversive*. But subversion isn't always quite so serious a matter; when words like *weekend*, *sandwich*, *job*, and *camping* started being used by the French, for example, some of them began claiming that America was *subverting* their language.

subversion 字面意思是将某物"翻过来"。在 20 世纪 50 年代和 60 年代,很多人担心美国政府受到共产主义的颠覆,虽然他们常常看到的只是无人存在的 *subversive*(颠覆性的)活动。非民主政府常常声称,任何人只要不同意政府的观点,或者参加了游行示威活动,就是 *subversive*(破坏分子)。但是,颠覆活动并非总是很严重的事情。比如,当法国人开始使用 weekend、sandwich、job 和 camping 这些词语时,有些人声称美国正在破坏他们的语言。

HYPER

HYPER is a Greek prefix that means "above or beyond," so *hyper-* often means about the same thing as *super-*. *Hyperinflation* is inflation that's growing at a very high rate. To be *hypercritical* or *hypersensitive* is to be critical or sensitive beyond the normal. And if you *hyperextend* a knee or elbow, it means you're actually bending it backward.

HYPER 是一个希腊语前缀,意思是"在……上面或者在……较远的一边",所以 *hyper-* 通常与 *super-* 同义。*hyperinflaion* 是速度很快的通货膨胀。*hypercritical* 或者 *hypersensitive* 意思是过分吹毛求疵或者过分敏感。如果你 *hyperextend* 一个膝盖或者胳膊肘,意思是说你竟然在让它反向弯曲。

hyperactive \ˌhī-pər-ˈak-tiv\ Excessively active. 极度活跃的

● Stephen King's hyperactive imagination has produced dozens of fantastical stories, not to mention countless nightmares in his readers. 斯蒂芬·金那极度活跃的想象力产生了众多奇幻故事,更不用说读者做的无数噩梦了。

For doctors and psychologists, *hyperactive* describes a condition with unpleasant consequences. Hyperactive children usually have a very short attention span and can't sit still, and *hyperactivity* can lead to difficulty in learning or just get them in trouble for disturbing their classes. But not every high-spirited child is hyperactive. Having a high energy level is pretty normal for children, and some parents think that prescribing drugs for hyperactivity is mostly just good for the drug companies.

对医生和心理学家来说,*hyperactive* 描述一种具有不良后果的疾病。hyperactive 孩子通常注意力持续时间很短,难以安静地坐着。*hyperactivity*(极度活跃)会导致学习困难,或者让孩子因为破坏班级秩序而陷入麻烦。不过,不是每个活跃的孩子都是 hyperactive。对于孩子来说,精力高度充沛是很正常的。有些父母认为,为 hyperactivity 开药主要有利于制药公司。

hyperbole \hī-ˈpər-bə-lē\ Extreme exaggeration. 夸张

● The food at Chez Pierre was good, but it couldn't live up to the hyperbole of the restaurant critics. 切兹·皮埃尔餐厅的食物很不错,但没有餐厅评论家讲的那么夸张。

Advertisers and sports commentators make their living by their skillful use of *hyperbole*. Presenting each year's Superbowl as "the greatest contest in the history of sports" certainly qualifies as hyperbole, especially since the final scores are usually so lopsided. Equally *hyperbolic* are advertisers' claims that this year's new car model is "the revolutionary vehicle you've been waiting for" when it's barely different from last year's—which of course was once described in the same glowing terms. Politicians love hyperbole too; some of them seem convinced that calling a new bill "the worst bill ever passed by Congress" or comparing the president to Hitler is a great way to win votes.

广告商和体育评论员靠着自己的夸张技能过日子。他们把每年的超级碗说成是"体育史上最伟大的比赛",肯定说得上是夸张,尤其是因为最后的分数通常都很不平衡。同样 *hyperbolic*(夸张的)是广告商的吹嘘,说今年的这款车是"您一直期盼的革命性新车",尽管它跟去年的几乎没什么区别,而去年的当然也曾被他们用同样热烈赞扬的话语吹嘘过。政治家也喜欢夸张。其中一些人似乎确信,说一个新法案是"国会通过的最糟糕的法案",或者将总统跟希特勒加以比较,是赢得选票的良方。

hypertension\ˌhī-pər-ˈten-shən\ High blood pressure. 高血压

● Pregnancy is often accompanied by mild hypertension that doesn't threaten the mother's life. 怀孕常常伴有轻微的高血压,但并不威胁母亲的生命。

You might have thought that hypertension was what a movie audience feels near the climax of a thriller, but you would have been wrong. High blood pressure—that is high pressure against the walls of your veins and arteries caused by blood flow—often occurs when the arteries or veins become blocked or narrowed, making the heart work harder to pump blood. But many cases seem to be the result of smoking or taking in too much salt, and many are genetically caused. Hypertension is serious, since it can lead to heart attacks and strokes. Though it often produces no warning symptoms, your blood pressure can be checked quickly and easily by a nurse. If it's high, it can usually be controlled by stopping smoking, losing weight, lowering your salt intake, and exercising—and if all else fails, by medication.

你可能曾经认为高血压是惊悚片达到高潮时电影观众的感觉,但其实你错了。高血压,也就是血流导致的静脉和动脉血管壁的高压,常常发生在动脉或静脉堵塞或变窄的时候,从而使心脏泵血时更为费力。但是,很多高血压的原因似乎是抽烟或者食用盐摄入过量,还有很多是遗传导致的。高血压是严重疾病,因为它能导致心脏病发作和中风。尽管它常常并没有产生报警症状,护士也可以很容易地迅速检查你的血压。如果血压高,通常可以通过戒烟、减肥、减少盐的摄入量、运动加以控制;如果其他方法都没有效果,那就利用药物。

hyperventilate\ˌhī-pər-ˈven-tə-ˌlāt\ To breathe rapidly and deeply. 强力呼吸

● They laughed so hard they began to hyperventilate and feel giddy. 他们笑得太厉害了,结果开始强力呼吸并感到眩晕。

Hyperventilating can be a response to fear and anxiety. A test pilot who panics and hyperventilates faces a dangerous situation. When the level of carbon dioxide in your blood goes down and the oxygen level goes up, blood vessels constrict because of the chemical changes and the body can't get enough oxygen (even though it's there in the blood), and the pilot can become lightheaded and may even faint. To guard against this, pilots are taught to control their breathing. On the ground, the usual remedy for *hyperventilation* is breathing into a paper bag, which raises the level of carbon dioxide and restores normal breathing.

  hyperventilating 可能是对恐惧和忧虑做出的反应。恐惧并强力呼吸的试飞员可能会面临危险。当血液中的二氧化碳水平下降、氧气水平上升时,由于体内的化学变化,血管就会收缩,身体就不能得到足够的氧气(尽管氧气就在血液中),飞行员就会头晕,甚至可能昏迷。要防止这种情况,就要教飞行员控制自己的呼吸。在地面上,*hyperventilation*(清理呼吸)通常的疗法是对着纸袋子呼吸,因袋子可以提供二氧化碳水平,使呼吸恢复正常。

Quizzes

A. Fill in each blank with the correct letter:

a. hyperactive   e. subjugate
b. subliminal   f. hyperventilate
c. hypertension   g. subconscious
d. subversion   h. hyperbole

  1. Stealing elections through fraud represents a _____ of democracy.

  2. She's warned me that there's plenty of _____ in her brother's big talk and that I shouldn't take it too seriously.

  3. Accident-prone people may have a _____ desire to do themselves harm.

  4. In yoga class we're often warned not to _____ during our breathing exercises.

  5. Napoleon hoped to _____ all of Europe and make it his empire.

  6. Both my parents are on medication for _____, and the doctor monitors their blood pressure regularly.

  7. He claims the ice cubes in whiskey ads contain images that send _____ messages to readers.

  8. A _____ imagination can transform every creak and rustle in a dark house into a threat.

B. Match the word on the left to the correct definition on the right:

1. hyperactive   a. breathe deeply and rapidly
2. subjugate   b. secret effort to overthrow
3. hyperventilate   c. extreme overstatement
4. subconscious   d. not strong enough to be sensed
5. hypertension   e. beneath the level of consciousness
6. subversion   f. overly active
7. hyperbole   g. conquer
8. subliminal   h. high blood pressure

PRE, one of the most common of all English *prefixes*, comes from *prae*, the Latin word meaning "before" or "in front of." So a *prediction* forecasts what will happen before it occurs. The 5:00 TV news *precedes* the 6:00 news. And someone with a *prejudice* against a class of people has judged them before having even met them.

PRE 是最常见的英语前缀之一,源自意思是"在……之前"或者"在…前面"的拉丁语词语 prae。因此,prediction(预言)可以告诉人们会发生什么事情。五点的电视新闻 precedes(先于)六点的新闻。对某一社会阶层有 prejudice(先入之见、偏见)的人,甚至没有接触他们之前就对其做出了判断。

preclude\pri-ˈklüd\ To make impossible beforehand; prevent. 使……不可能;阻止

• If we accept this cash offer from the company, that will preclude our joining in the big suit against it with the other investors. 如果我们接受该公司的现金,就无法与其他投资者一起进行这次重要起诉了。

Preclude is often used in legal writing, where it usually refers to making something legally impossible. A new law may be passed by Congress to preclude any suits of a certain kind against a federal agency, for example. Some judges have found that the warnings on cigarette packs preclude any suits against the tobacco companies by lung-cancer sufferers. But there are plenty of nonlegal uses as well. Bad weather often precludes trips to the beach, and a lack of cash might preclude any beach vacation at all.

preclude 常常用于法律文本,通常指使某事在法律上不可能发生或存在。比如,国会可能通过一项新的法律,以阻止对某一联邦机构任何种类的起诉。有的法官发现,烟盒上的警告语使肺癌患者无法起诉烟草公司。但是,这一词语也有很多与法律无关的用法。恶劣天气常常让人们无法到达海岸,缺乏现金可能使人们根本无法到海滩度假。

precocious\prē-ˈkō-shəs\ Showing the qualities or abilities of an adult at an unusually early age. (人)早熟的

• Everyone agrees that their seven-year-old daughter is smart and precocious, but she's also getting rather full of herself. 人们都一致认为,他们那个七岁的女儿聪明、早熟,但她也越来越自高自大了。

Growing from a child to an adult is like the slow ripening of fruit, and that's the image that gave us *precocious*. The word is based on the Latin verb *coquere*, meaning "to ripen" or "to cook," but it comes most directly from the adjective *praecox*, which means "ripening early or before its time." *Precocity* can occasionally be annoying; but precocious children don't come precooked, only "preripened."

孩童长大成人就像水果慢慢成熟,这就是让我们有了 *precocious* 这一词语的形象。这一词语的基础是意为"成熟"或者"烹调"的拉丁语动词 coquere,但它主要直接源自意为"早熟的"形容词 praecox。precocity 偶尔会让人不高兴;但是 precocious 孩子并不是预先烹制的,而是"提前成熟的"。

predispose\ˌprē-di-ˈspōz\ (1) To influence in advance in order to create a particular attitude. 提前影响以产生某一特定印象 (2) To make one more likely to develop a particular disease or physical condition. 使……更可能染上某种疾病或身体状况

• Growing up in a house full of sisters had predisposed her to find her friendships with other women. 在一个有很多姐妹的家庭成长,使她更容易与其他女性成为朋友。

Predispose usually means putting someone in a frame of mind to be willing to do something. So a longtime belief in the essential goodness of people, for example, will predispose us to trust a stranger. Teachers know that coming from a stable family generally predisposes children to learn. And viewing television violence for years may leave young people with a *predisposition* to accept real violence as normal. The medical sense of the word is similar. Thus, a person's genes may predispose her to diabetes or arthritis, and malnutrition over a long period can predispose you to all kinds of infections.

predispose 通常的意思是让某人处于某种心情,从而愿意做某事。因此,比如由于长久以来我们都相信人们本质上是善良的,这使我们更有可能信任陌生人。教师都知道,来自稳固家庭的孩子更有可能努力学习。多年观看电视上的暴力行为,可能让年轻人有一种 *predisposition*(倾向),认为暴力是正常行为。这一词语的医学意思与此相似。这样,一个人的基因可能使她更有可能患上糖尿病或者关节炎,长时间营养不良可能使你患上各种感染。

prerequisite \prē-ˈre-kwə-zət\ Something that is required in advance to achieve a goal or to carry out a function. 前提;前提条件

• In most states, minimal insurance coverage is a prerequisite for registering an automobile. 在大多数州,最小保险责任范围是登记车辆的前提。

Prerequisite is partly based on *requirere*, the Latin verb meaning "to need or require." So a prerequisite can be anything that must be accomplished or acquired before something else can be done. Possessing a valid credit card is a prerequisite for renting a car. A physical exam may be a prerequisite for receiving a life-insurance policy. And successful completion of an introductory course is often a prerequisite for enrolling in a higher-level course.

Prerequisite 一定程度上以 *requirere*("需要或者要求")这一拉丁语动词为基础。所以,prerequisite 可以是实现目标或者得到某物前必须做的任何事情。拥有一张有效的信用卡是租车的前提条件。体格检查可能是取得人寿保险的前提条件。完成入门课程常常是报名学习更高级课程的前提条件。

PARA is a Greek prefix usually meaning "beside" or "closely related to." So *parallel* lines run beside each other. And a Greek *paragraphos* was originally a line written beside the main text of a play to show where a new person begins speaking; today we just start a new *paragraph* on a new line.

PARA 是一个希腊语前缀,通常的意思是"在……旁边"或者"与……有密切关系"。因此,*parallel*(平行的)线相互平行。希腊的 *paragraphos* 最初指写在剧本主要文本旁边的一行字,用以表明一个新的角色要说话了;今天,我们只是在新的一行开始一个新 *paragraph*(段落)。

---

paraphrase \ˈper-ə-ˌfrāz\ To restate the meaning (of something written or spoken) in different words. 复述

• She started off the class by asking one of the students to paraphrase the Tennyson poem, to make sure everyone understood its basic meaning. 她开始那堂课的办

法,是让一位学生复述坦尼森那首诗歌,要保证每个人都能听懂其基本意思。

When we *paraphrase*, we provide a version that can exist beside the original (rather than replace it). We paraphrase all the time. When you tell a friend what someone else has said, you're almost always paraphrasing, since you're not repeating the exact words. If you go to hear a talk, you might paraphrase the speaker's main points afterward for your friends. And when writing a paper on a short story, you might start off your essay with a *paraphrase* of the plot. Paraphrasing is especially useful when dealing with poetry, since poetic language is often difficult and poems may have meanings that are hard to pin down.

当我们 paraphrase(复述)时,我们在提供一个可与原始版本同时存在的版本(而不是代替它)。我们总是在复述。当你告诉一位朋友另一个人说了什么,你几乎总是在复述,因为你不是在一字不差地重复。如果听了一个讲座,你可能会在后来向朋友们重述讲座人的要点。写一篇有关某一短篇小说的论文时,你可能会在一开始提供情节的 paraphrase(重述)。paraphrasing 在处理诗歌时尤其有用,因为诗歌的语言常常比较难懂,诗歌可能有难以确定的意思。

paralegal\ˌpa-rə-ˈlē-gəl\ Of, relating to, or being a trained assistant to a lawyer. 律师助理的

• Part of the firm's business involved researching real-estate properties, which the senior lawyers regarded as paralegal work. 该公司一部分业务涉及房地产研究,高级律师认为这是律师助理的工作。

Much of the work in a law office can be done by *paralegal* assistants, also called legal aides or simply *paralegals*, who work alongside licensed lawyers. Often a paralegal is trained in a narrow field and then entrusted with it. In this respect, paralegals are similar to *paraprofessionals* in other fields, such as engineering. Paraprofessionals used to be trained in the office itself, but today it's common to study for a paraprofessional certificate or degree at a community college or university.

律师事务所很多工作可由 paralegal assistants(律师助理)完成,这些人也称为 legal aides 或者简单地称为 *paralegals*,他们与执业律师一起工作。通常,paralegal 在某一狭隘的领域受过训练,之后承担这一领域的工作。在这一点上,paralegals 类似于其他领域(比如工程)的 *paraprofessionals*(专职人员的助手)。paraprofessionals 过去常常由机构自己进行培训,但是今天,常见的做法是他们在社区学院或大学学习,之后获得 paraprofessional certificate(专业人员助手证书)或者学位。

paramedic\ˌpa-rə-ˈme-dik\ A specially trained medical technician licensed to provide a wide range of emergency services before or during transportation to a hospital. 医务辅助人员;护理人员

• Five ambulances had already arrived, and a dozen paramedics were crouched over the victims with bandages and IVs. 五辆救护车到了,十多个护理人员拿着绷带和静脉注射器蹲在受害人旁边。

In ground warfare, wounded troops must usually be transported from the front lines back to field hospitals, and trained *paramedical* personnel—that is, nondoctors, usually known as *medics* or *corpsmen*—were first widely used in such situations. It took many decades for the wartime model to be applied effectively to ordinary peacetime medicine. With advances in medical technology (such as defibrillators, for restarting a heart after a heart attack), *paramedics* became an essential part of emergency medicine, and today hundreds of thousands of people owe their lives to paramedics. *Paraprofessionals* who work only in hospitals and clinics usually go by other titles.

在地面战争中,伤兵通常必须从前线转移到野战医院,接受过训练的 *paramedical* personnel(护理人员)——即非医生,通常称为 *medics* 或者 *corpsmen*——首次在这种情况下得到广泛使用。好几十年过去了,这种战争模式才有效应用于和平时期的一般医疗。随着医疗技术(比如用于心脏病发作后让心脏重新跳动的除颤器)的进步,paramedics 成了急救医学重要的一部分,而且今天,很多人多亏了护理人员才保住了性命。只在医院和诊所工作的 *paraprofessionals* 通常有其他称呼。

paramilitary \ˌpa-rə-ˈmi-lə-ˌter-ē\ Relating to a force formed on a military pattern, especially as a possible backup military force. 辅助军事的;准军事的

• In the country's most remote regions, the real power was held by large landowners, who actually kept paramilitary forces, their own private armies, on their estates. 在该国那些最偏远地区,真正的权力由大地主执掌。这些人竟然在自己的土地上拥有准军事力量,也就是他们的私人部队。

This term *paramilitary* can take in a wide range of organizations, but is usually applied to forces formed by a government. Groups opposing a government, even when organized along military lines, are more often referred to as guerrillas or insurgents. In countries with weak central governments (such as, in recent times, Afghanistan, Somalia, Iraq, or Congo), warlords may form their own paramilitary forces and take over all local police and military functions. *Paramilitary* often has a sinister sound today, since it's also applied to groups of off-duty military or police personnel who carry out illegal violence, often at night, with the quiet support of a government.

paramilitary 这一术语可以包括多种机构,但通常用于某一政府建立的部队。反对政府的那些群体,即使是按照军事方式组织起来的,也常常被称为游击队或者叛乱者。在中央政府(比如,在近代的阿富汗、索马里、伊拉克或者刚果政府)势单力薄的国家,军阀可能组成自己的准军事部队,接手所有当地的警察和军事职能。*paramilitary* 在今天通常听起来有些险恶,因为它也可用于实施非法暴力的非执勤的军事或警察群体,这样的非法暴力常常是在夜间,在政府默不作声的支持下进行的。

Quizzes

A. Choose the closest definition:

1. prerequisite   a. pattern   b. requirement   c. preference
   d. direction
2. paramedic   a. medical technician   b. hypodermic
   c. surgeon   d. nurse's aide
3. predispose   a. recycle   b. eliminate   c. demonstrate
   d. influence

4. paraphrase   a. spell out   b. shorten   c. lengthen   d. reword

5. preclude   a. come before   b. come after   c. prevent   d. predict

6. paralegal   a. lawful   b. lawyer-assisting   c. above the law   d. barely legal

7. precocious   a. nearly cooked   b. maturing early   c. self-contradictory   d. necessary

8. paramilitary   a. basic-training   b. skydiving   c. semimilitary   d. police

META

B. Fill in each blank with the correct letter:

a. paraphrase   e. predispose
b. preclude   f. paramedic
c. precocious   g. prerequisite
d. paralegal   h. paramilitary

1. No one in her class of high-school seniors was able to _____ the proverb "Blood is thicker than water."

2. At 13 she was _____ enough to mingle with the guests at her parents' cocktail parties.

3. Everything I had heard about the guy from my friends didn't exactly _____ me to like him.

4. After a year as a _____ she knew she had the stomach for anything a doctor might have to face.

5. Any felony conviction in your past would _____ your getting a job with the state government.

6. At his law firm they treated almost everything involving real estate as _____ work.

7. The only _____ for taking the Galaxies course is a strong background in high-school math and physics.

8. Many of the crimes are apparently being carried out by members of secret _____ organizations made up of off-duty police and former soldiers.

META is a prefix in English that generally means "behind" or "beyond." In medicine, for example, the *metacarpal* bones are the hand bones that come right after, or beyond, the *carpal* or wrist bones. And *metalanguage* is language used to talk about language, which requires going beyond normal language.

META 是一个英语前缀，通常的意思是"在……之后"或者"在……较远处，超越"。比如在医学上，*metacarpal* bones（掌骨）是位于 *carpal* bones（腕骨）之后或较远处的手骨。*metalanguage* 是用于谈论语言的语言，要求超越正常语言。

metadata \ˌme-tə-ˈdā-tə\ Data that provides information about other data.
元数据

• Before putting videos up on the Web site, she always tags them with a decent set of metadata. 在把视频放在网站上之前，她总是要用一组很体面的元数据作为标签。

Metadata is electronic data that somehow describes an electronic file or its contents, and is usually included in the file itself. An important use for metadata is for searching. A piece of metadata might identify the file, its size, the date it was compiled, its nature, and so on. Metadata is particularly important for making pictures searchable; since a picture of a landscape in the Southwest, for example, can't be "read" by a search engine, data tags such as "Southwest," "mesa," and "arroyo" might be included in the digitized image file. The same can be done for audio files; the tags for a speech might read "Gore," "climate," and "Copenhagen." Metadata tags for a Web page, including tags identifying its most important content, ensure that the page won't be overlooked by a search engine.

元数据是以某种方式描述电子文件或其内容的电子数据，通常包括在文件本身之内。元数据的一个重要用途是搜索。元数据可以识别文件、文件的大小、编写文件的数据、文件的性质等等。元数据特别重要的用途是让图画变得可以检索。比如，由于西南部风景图画无法让搜索引擎"阅读"，像"西南""方山""旱谷"这样的数据标签可以被包括在数字化的图像文件中。语音文件也可以这样处理，演讲的标签可以是"戈尔""气候""哥本哈根"。网页的元数据标签，包括识别其最重要内容的标签，可以确保这一网页不会被搜索引擎忽视。

metaphorical \ˌme-tə-ˈfȯr-i-kəl\ Relating to a figure of speech in which a word or phrase meaning one kind of object or idea is used in place of another to suggest a similarity between them. 暗喻的

• He always points out to his classes that metaphors can be found in poetry of all kinds, from "The eyes are the windows of the soul" to "You ain't nothin' but a hound dog." 他总是对几个班的学生说，暗喻存在于各种诗歌中，从"The eyes are the windows of the soul"（"眼睛是心灵的窗口"）到"You ain't nothing but a hound dog"（"你只是一条猎犬"）。

Metaphor comes from a Greek word meaning "transfer" (or, to stay close to its roots, "carry beyond"). Thus, a metaphor transfers the meaning of one word or phrase to another. Metaphors often include a form of the verb *be* (as in the examples above), and they're often contrasted with similes, which are usually introduced by *like* or *as* ("O, my luve's like a red, red rose"). But, they don't have to include *be*; when you say that the teacher gave us a mountain of homework or that we're drowning in paperwork, these too are *metaphorical* statements.

metaphor 源自一个意思是"转移"（或者为了不要脱离其词根，"运到远处"）的希腊语单词，这样，暗喻就转移了某个单词或短语的意思。暗喻通常包含动词 *be*（是）的某种形式（就像在上面的例子中那样），而且常常与明喻形成对比，而明喻常常由 *like* 或者 *as* 引导（"O, my luve's like a red, red rose"）（"我的爱人像红红的玫瑰"）。但是，暗喻也不是必须包含动词 *be*。当你说老师给我们布置的作业跟山一样多，或者我们正淹死在日常文书工作中时，这些也是 *metaphorical*（暗喻的）说法。

metaphysics \ˌme-tə-ˈfi-ziks\ The part of philosophy having to do with the ultimate causes and basic nature of things. 形而上学；玄学

• Most of the congregation prefers to hear their minister preach about virtue, and they get restless when his sermons head in the direction of metaphysics. 大多数教堂会众更想听牧师宣讲美德，而当他布道的内容朝玄学方向转移时，大家就坐立不安了。

Just as *physics* deals with the laws that govern the physical world (such as those of gravity or the properties of waves), *metaphysics* describes what is beyond physics—the nature and origin of reality itself, the immortal soul, and the existence of a supreme being. Opinions about these *metaphysical* topics vary widely, since what's being discussed can't be observed or measured or even truly known to exist. So most metaphysical questions are still as far from a final answer as they were when Plato and Aristotle were asking them. 就像 *physics* 涉及的是控制物理世界的定律（比如万有引力定律或者波动性定律）那样，玄学描述物理世界以外的东西——现实本身的性质和来源、不朽的灵魂、上帝的存在。关于这些 *metaphysical*（玄学的）话题的看法有很大差异，因为正在讨论的内容无法观察、无法测量，甚至无法知道是否真的存在。所以，大多数玄学问题都远远没有最终答案，就像柏拉图和亚里士多德问这些问题时那样。

metonymy \mə-ˈtä-nə-mē\ A figure of speech in which the name of one thing is used for the name of something else that is associated with it or related to it. 转喻

• When Wall Street has the jitters, the White House issues a statement, and the people wait for answers from City Hall, metonymy is having a busy day. 当华尔街神经紧张时，白宫发布了一项声明，人们等待着市政厅的回答。这时，转喻正度过忙碌的一天。

At first glance, *metaphor* and *metonymy* seem close in meaning, but there are differences. In a metaphor we substitute one thing for something else that's usually quite different; for example, *Web* for a worldwide network of linked computers and their technology. In metonymy, we replace one word or phrase (such as "stock market" or "local government officials" in the examples above) with another word or phrase associated with it. Most familiar *metonyms* are place-names, such as *Hollywood* for "the film industry," or *K Street* for "Washington lobbyists." But saying "the press" to refer to the news media, or "sweat" to refer to hard work, could also be called metonymy. 乍一看，*metaphor* 和 *metonymy* 似乎意思相近，但还是有区别的。在暗喻中，我们用一个事物代替另一个事物，而且这一事物通常很不相同，比如 *Web* 代表一个世界范围内将电脑及其技术联系在一起的网络。在转喻中，我们用一个与某一单词或短语（比如"股市"或者"当地政府官员"）相关的另一单词或短语代替它。大多数人们熟悉的 *metonyms*（转喻词）都是地名，比如 *Hollywood*（好莱坞）代表"电影业"，或者"K Street"代表"华盛顿说客"。但是，用"报刊"来指新闻媒体，或者"汗水"来指辛勤劳动，也可以称为转喻。

UNIT 21

PER is a Latin preposition that generally means "through," "throughout," or "thoroughly." Thus, *perforate* means "to bore through," *perennial* means "throughout the years," and *permanent* means "remaining throughout." And the "thoroughly" sense shows up in *persuade*, for "thoroughly advise," and *perverted*, "thoroughly turned around."

PER 是一个拉丁语介词，通常的意思是"通过""贯穿"或者"彻底地"。这样 *perforate* 意思就是"打孔；穿孔"，*perennial* 就是"贯穿多年的"，*permanent* 就是"永久的"。"彻底"这一意思存在于 *persuade* 当中，表示"彻底建议"，也存在于 *perverted*，表示"彻底转过来的"。

percolate \ˈpər-kə-ˌlāt\ (1) To trickle or filter through something porous. 渗透；滤过 (2) To become spread through. 遍及

• She tells herself that the money she spends on luxuries eventually percolates down to the needy. 她告诉自己，她花在奢侈品上的钱最终会到穷人手里。

Percolate comes from a Latin verb meaning "to put through a sieve." Something that percolates filters through something else, just as small particles pass through a sieve. Water is drawn downward through the soil, and this *percolation* usually cleans the water. A slow rain is ideal for percolating into the soil, since in a violent rainstorm most of it quickly runs off. For this reason, drip irrigation is the most effective and water-conserving form of irrigation. Percolation isn't always a physical process; awareness of an issue may percolate slowly into the minds of the public, just as Spanish words may gradually percolate into English, often starting in the Southwest.

percolate 源自一个意思是"筛"的拉丁语动词。能够 percolates 的事物滤过另一事物，就像小颗粒穿过筛子那样。水通过土壤被向下吸引，这一 percolation（过滤）通常可以使水得以净化。缓慢降落的雨水最有利于渗入土壤，因为在下暴雨时，大部分水都迅速流走了。因此，滴灌是最有效、最省水的灌溉形式。percolation 并不总是一个物理过程；对某一问题的认识会慢慢渗入公众的头脑，就像西班牙语单词会逐渐渗入英语一样，常常在西南部开始。

pervade \pər-ˈvād\ To spread through all parts of something. 渗透；弥漫；遍及

• We all knew that more job cuts were coming, and the entire office was pervaded with anxiety. 我们都知道就要裁员了，整个办公室都是忧虑的气氛。

Pervade can be used to describe something physical: a chemical odor may pervade a building, for example, and most scientists believe that outer space is pervaded by mysterious "dark matter." But the word usually doesn't refer to anything that could be detected by scientific instruments. Thus, humor may pervade a novel, gloom may pervade a gathering, and corruption may pervade a government. And something *pervasive* exists in every part of something: fatherlessness may be a pervasive problem in poor neighborhoods, for instance, and pervasive optimism sometimes

• 503 •

causes the stock market to soar.

pervade 可以用来描述客观存在的事物：比如，化学物质的气味会 pervade 整个建筑物，大多数科学家都认为外太空 pervaded(弥漫着)神秘的"暗物质"。但是，这一词语通常并不指任何科学仪器可以探测到的事物。这样，幽默可能 pervade 整部小说，忧郁可能 pervade 某个聚会，腐败可能 pervade 整个政府。pervasive(无处不在的；普遍的)事物存在于某事物的各个部分：比如，没有父亲是贫穷城区的 pervasive 问题，pervasive 乐观情绪有时让股市飙升。

permeate\\'pər-mē-ˌāt\\ (1) To spread throughout. 遍及 (2) To pass through the pores or small openings of. 渗透；滤过

- On Saturday mornings back in those days, the aroma of fresh pies and breads would permeate almost every house on the block. 那时，在星期六的上午，新鲜馅饼和面包的香味会弥漫于这个街区的几乎每一栋房子。

Permeate is often a synonym for *pervade*. We could say, for example, that at exam time the campus is either "permeated" or "pervaded" by a sense of dread. But the two words aren't identical. For one thing, *permeate* can mean simply "pass through," and is often used when talking about liquids; thus, a boot can be permeated by water, though certain oils make leather less *permeable*, and you might just want to buy boots made of *impermeable* material. And things may "pass through" in a nonphysical way as well; so you might say that anxiety about climate change has started to permeate into the public's consciousness—but once anxiety has become *pervasive* it's pretty much taken over.

permeate 与 *pervade* 通常是同义词。比如，我们可以说，在考试时间，整个校园 "permeated"或者"pervaded"了恐惧感。但是这两个词语并不完全一样。一方面，*permeate* 可以仅仅表示"滤过"，常常用于谈论液体的时候；这样，一只靴子可以被水 permeated(渗透)，虽然某些种类的油可以使皮革不太 *permeable*(可渗透的)，而你可能只是想要购买由 *impermeable*(不可渗透的)材料制成的靴子。事物也可能以非物理的方式"穿过"；所以，你可以说对气候变化的忧虑开始渗入公众的意识——但是一旦忧虑变得 *pervasive*(无处不在的)，它就在很大程度上 taken over(被占领)了。

persevere\\ˌpər-sə-'vir\\ To keep at something in spite of difficulties, opposition, or discouragement. 坚持不懈；不屈不挠

- For ten years she persevered in her effort to find out what the government knew about her husband's disappearance. 有十年时间，她坚持不懈，要发现政府对丈夫失踪所了解的信息。

The early settlers of the New World persevered in the face of constant hardship and danger. The Pilgrims of Plymouth Plantation lost half their number in the first winter to disease and hunger, but their *perseverance* paid off, and within five years their community was healthy and self-sufficient. Perhaps more remarkable are all the solitary inventors who have persevered in pursuing their visions for years, lacking any financial support and laughed at by the public.

面对艰难困苦和危险，新世界的早期定居者不屈不挠。因为疾病和饥饿，第一个冬天，普利茅斯种植园的清教徒有一半人失去了生命，但他们的 *perseverance*(毅力)有了好结果。在最初五年内，他们身体健康，自给自足。也许更了不起的，是所有孤军奋战的发明家。他们缺乏财政支持，遭人嘲笑，仍然不屈不挠，多年来追求自己的理想。

UNIT 21

Quizzes

A. Fill in each blank with the correct letter:

a. metaphorical
b. persevere
c. metaphysics
d. percolate
e. permeate
f. metonymy
g. pervade
h. metadata

1. None of his audio or photo files have any _____ associated with them, so it's impossible to find them via an ordinary Web search.
2. She's extremely stubborn, so I'm sure she's going to _____ until the whole thing is completed.
3. When the Gypsy Carmen sings "Love is a wild bird," she's being _____.
4. We know that drugs now _____ the blue-collar workplace in many small Midwestern towns.
5. "Green Berets," the nickname for the U.S. Army Special Forces, is a good example of _____.
6. Before the Internet, it took many years before these ideas began to _____ the barriers that the government had set up.
7. In philosophy he loved _____ most, because it dealt with the deepest mysteries.
8. The liquid began to _____ through the blend of herbs and spices, giving off a delicious scent.

B. Match the word on the left to the correct definition on the right:

1. persevere   a. seep
2. metonymy   b. equating one thing with another
3. permeate   c. spread into
4. metaphysics   d. keep going
5. pervade   e. use of an associated term
6. percolate   f. study of the nature of things
7. metaphorical   g. information about other information
8. metadata   h. fill with something

ANT/ANTI

ANT/ANTI is a Latin prefix meaning "against." An *anticlimax* is the opposite of a climax. An *antiseptic* or *antibiotic* fights germs. An *antacid* attacks acid in the stomach. And an *antidote* works against the effects of a poison.

ANT/ANTI 是一个拉丁语前缀,意思是"反对"。*anticlimax*(扫兴的结局)是 *climax*(高潮)的反义词。*antiseptic*(防腐剂;抗菌剂)或者 *antibiotic*(抗生素)与细菌作斗争。*antacid*(抗酸剂;解酸药)在胃中攻击酸。*antidote*(解毒剂)对抗毒药,使其难以奏效。

antagonist\ an-ˈta-gə-nist\　A person who opposes or is unfriendly toward another; an opponent. 对手；敌手

• With supplies ordered from the Acme Company, Road Runner's constant antagonist, Wile E. Coyote, attempts one dastardly deed after another. 有了从顶峰公司订购的补给品，跑路者一直以来的对手大笨狼怀尔采取了一次又一次卑鄙行动。

On the stage or screen, in a story or a novel, the *protagonist* is the main character and the antagonist is the opposing one. *Pro-* and *ant-* usually mark the good and bad characters, but not always; there may occasionally be an evil protagonist and a good antagonist. In the drama of the real world, it's especially hard to sort out which is which, so we usually speak of both parties to a conflict as antagonists. During a strike, for example, representatives of labor and management become antagonists; they often manage to *antagonize* each other, and the *antagonism* often remains after the strike is over.

在舞台或屏幕上，在故事或小说中，*protagonist* 是主角，而 antagonist 是其对立者。*pro* 和 *ant-* 通常标明好的和坏的人物，但并非总是如此，偶尔也有邪恶的 protagonist 和善良的 *antagonist*。在现实世界这部戏剧中，尤其难以分出哪个是哪个，所以我们通常把一场冲突的双方都叫做 antagonists。比如在一场罢工期间，劳资双方的代表就成了 antagonists，他们经常设法 *antagonize*（激起……的敌意）对方，*antagonism*（敌对情绪）即使在罢工之后依然存在。

antigen\ ˈan-ti-jen\　A chemical substance (such as a protein) that, when introduced into the body, causes the body to form antibodies against it. 抗原

• When the immune system is weak, it may not be able to produce enough antibodies to combat the invading antigens. 当免疫系统脆弱时，可能会产生足够的抗体以对抗入侵的抗原。

An *antibody* is a protein produced by your immune system to fight outside invaders. Since the enemy substance actually triggers the production of antibodies, such substances are called antigens—*anti-* being short for *antibody*, and *-gen* meaning "producer." (In a similar way, an *allergen* produces an allergy, and a *pathogen* produces a pathology or disease.) Antigens are often rodlike structures that stick out from the surface of an invading organism—usually a bacterium or a virus—and allow it to attach itself to cells in the invaded body. But unfortunately for them, in doing so they let the immune system know they're present, and the body is flooded with an army of Pac-Man-like antibodies.

antibody（抗体）是免疫系统产生的与外来入侵者对抗的蛋白质。由于敌对物质激发了抗体的产生，这些物质被称为 antigens（抗原）。*anti-* 是 *antibody*（抗体）的缩略，而 *-gen* 意思是"产生者"。（同样，*allergen*［过敏原］产生过敏，*pathogen*［病原体］产生疾病。）抗原通常是棒状结构，从入侵微生物（通常是细菌或病毒）的表面伸出来，使其能够附着在被入侵的机体的细胞上。但对它们来说不幸的是，这样做也让免疫系统知道了它们的存在，这个机体就会充满像吃豆人那样的抗体。

antipathy\ an-ˈti-pə-thē\　A strong dislike. 反感；憎恶；厌恶

• It seemed odd that he could feel such intense antipathy for someone he'd only met once, and we suspected there was more to the story. 他对刚刚认识的人就如此反感，似乎很

奇怪,我们都怀疑这背后还有更多的原因。

When the nation of Yugoslavia was created in 1945, it combined a number of ethnic groups with a history of violent antipathy toward each other. In 1991-1992 four regions of the country announced that they would become independent nations; a bloody six-year war followed, fueled by these ancient and powerful antipathies. The American Civil War similarly resulted from antipathy between the North and the South. But in the U. S.'s relations with its next-door neighbors, it's been a long time since emotions have gotten much stronger than annoyance. 当南斯拉夫这个国家在 1945 年出现时,它将几个相互之间有着强烈 antipathy 的少数民族结合在了一起。在 1991—1992 年之间,该国四个地区宣布他们要成为独立国家,接着是一场长达六年的血战,因为强烈的 antipathy 而加剧了。美国南北战争同样源于南北之间的 antipathy。但是在美国与隔壁邻国之间的关系中,厌烦的情绪已经存在很久了。

antithesis \an-'ti-thə-səs\ (1) The contrast or opposition of ideas. (观点之间的)对照;对立 (2) The exact opposite. 对立面

CONTRA

• Life on the small college campus, with its personal freedom and responsibility, was the antithesis of what many students had known in high school. 小小的大学校园里的生活,及其个人的自由和责任,是许多学生在高中所知道的对立面。

Writers and speechmakers use the traditional pattern known as antithesis for its resounding effect; John Kennedy's famous "ask not what your country can do for you—ask what you can do for your country" is an example. But antithesis normally means simply "opposite." Thus, war is the antithesis of peace, wealth is the antithesis of poverty, and love is the antithesis of hate. Holding two antithetical ideas in one's head at the same time—for example, that you're the sole master of your fate but also the helpless victim of your terrible upbringing—is so common as to be almost normal. 作家和演讲者利用称为 antithesis 的传统模式来达到强烈的效果,约翰·肯尼迪那句著名的话就是例子:"不要问祖国可以为你做什么,问一问你能为祖国做什么。"但是 antithesis 通常的意思是"对立面"。这样,战争就是和平的 antithesis,富裕就是贫穷的 antithesis,爱就是恨的 antithesis。同时在头脑中怀有 antithetical(对立的)两个观点——比如你是自己命运唯一的主宰,但是又是不良家庭教养的受害者——太普遍了,几乎可以说是正常的。

CONTRA is the Latin equivalent of anti-, and it too means essentially "against" or "contrary to." A contrast "stands against" something else that it's compared to. And contrapuntal music, as in the music of Bach, sets one melody against another played at the same time and produces harmony (which no one is opposed to).

CONTRA 是相当于 anti- 的拉丁语词语,也基本上有着"反对"或者"与……相对"的意思。contrast(迥然不同的事物)跟一个与其进行比较的事物"对立"。contrapuntal(对位的)音乐,就像巴赫的音乐中的那些,使一个旋律与另一个同时演奏的旋律形成对立,并产生和声(没有人反对这一点)。

contraband \ˈkän-trə-ˌband\ Goods that are forbidden by law to be owned or brought into or out of a country; smuggled goods. 走私；走私货

• Late at night he would go driving through the desert on the interstate, peddling his contraband to wary gas-station attendants. 深夜，他开车穿过沙漠，在州际公路上向警惕的加油站服务员兜售违禁品。

In Latin a *bannus* was an order or decree, so a *contrabannum* was something that went against a decree. This led to the Italian word *contrabbando*, from which we get *contraband*. Contraband items aren't always illegal; they may simply be things (such as cigarettes) that are meant to be taxed. So a dealer in untaxed contraband can charge a little less and still make enormous profits. Of course, if the item is actually forbidden, like illegal drugs, then the profits could be much greater.

在拉丁语中，*bannus* 是一个命令或者法令，所以，*contrabannum* 就是与法令对立的事物。这就产生了意大利语单词 *contrabbando*，从这一单词我们有了 *contraband*（禁运品；走私货）这一单词。禁运品并非总是非法的，它们可能仅仅是需要征税的东西（比如香烟）。所以，经销未征税禁运品的商人，即使要价低一些，仍然可以获得很大的利润。当然，如果这一商品实际上是禁止的，比如非法药品，那么利润就可以大得多。

contraindication\ˌkän-trə-ˌin-də-ˈkā-shən\ Something (such as a symptom or condition) that makes a particular treatment, medication, or procedure likely to be unsafe. 禁忌症

• A history of stomach ulcers is a contraindication to regular use of aspirin. 胃溃疡病史是定期服用阿司匹林的禁忌症。

For doctors, an *indication* is a symptom or circumstance that makes a particular medical treatment desirable. Serious anxiety, for example, is often an indication for prescribing a tranquilizer. A *contraindication*, then, is a symptom or condition that makes a treatment risky, such as taking certain other medications at the same time. Drugs and conditions that are *contraindicated* for a medication are listed on its label, and reeled off at high speed in TV ads. Patients can guard against the dangers of drug interaction by reading labels carefully and making sure their doctors know what else they're currently taking.

对医生来说，*indication*（适应症）是让某一特定治疗可行的症状或者情况。比如，严重忧虑常常是开镇静剂的 indication。那么，contraindication 就是让治疗有风险的症状或者情况，比如同时服用某些其他药物。对某一药物来说 *contraindicated*（被禁忌的）的禁忌症的药物和状况都列在标签上了，在电视广告中快速地一口气说出来。病人可以通过仔细阅读标签，以及确保医生了解自己目前在服用何种药物，来预防药物相互作用的危险。

contravene\ˌkän-trə-ˈvēn\ (1) To go against or act contrary to; to violate. 违背；违反 (2) To oppose in an argument, to contradict. 反驳

• The power company was found to be contravening state and federal environmental standards for wastewater discharged into bodies of water. 这一发电公司被发现违反了州和联邦废水排入水体方面的环境标准。

Contravene is most often used in reference to laws. So a government may take a company to court claiming that its policies are *in contravention* of national labor

UNIT 21

laws. The contravention of copyright laws is a big topic today especially where electronic information is involved. And a country might be punished if a trade organization finds that it's contravening international trade agreements.

<small>contravene 用于法律方面的时候最多。所以某一政府可能将某一公司告上法庭，声称其策略 in contravention of（违反了）国家劳动法。版权法的 contravention（违反）在今天是个重要话题，尤其是涉及电子信息的时候。如果一个贸易组织发现某一国家 contravening（正违反）国家贸易协定，这个国家可能会受到制裁。</small>

contrarian \ kən-ˈtrer-ē-ən \ A person who takes a contrary position or attitude, especially an investor who buys shares of stock when most others are selling or sells when others are buying. 采取对立立场或态度者；（股票买卖中）多数人抛售时反而吃进（或多数人吃进时反而抛售）的投资者

• My father was basically a contrarian, who never accepted the com- mon wisdom and loved nothing so much as a good argument. 我爸爸基本上总是采取对立态度，从不接受大众的看法，最喜欢争论个过瘾。

Anyone who thinks that most of what the public believes is wrong would be called a contrarian. And *contrarian* is a basic term in the vocabulary of investing. In fact, most successful investors often behave like contrarians by "buying low and selling high"—that is, buying stocks that are cheap because most investors put a low value on them but that have the possibility of rising, and selling stocks that most investors are valuing highly but that seem likely to decline. The word may be most common as an adjective; so you may express a *contrarian* opinion, hold a contrarian view, or pursue a contrarian investment strategy.

<small>任何觉得公众相信的东西是错误的人都可以叫做 contrarian。contrarian 是投资词汇中一个基本术语。实际上，大多数成功的投资者都像 contrarians，"低价购入高价售出"，也就是说，因为众人对股票股价很低但它却有涨价的可能而购买低价股票，并抛售多数投资者估价很高但却有降价可能的股票。这一词语作为形容词时最为常用，所以，你可能表达 contrarian 观点，有 contrarian 看法，或者采取 contrarian 投资策略。</small>

CONTRA

Quizzes

A. Complete the analogy:

1. champion : hero :: antagonist : _____
    a. comrade   b. supporter   c. opponent   d. thug
2. harm : benefit :: contraindication : _____
    a. denial   b. refusal   c. injection   d. indication
3. truth : fact :: antithesis : _____
    a. same   b. opposite   c. enemy   d. friend
4. opposite : equal :: contrarian : _____
    a. contrast   b. conformist   c. contradiction   d. conflict
5. misery : joy :: antipathy : _____
    a. disgust   b. confusion   c. opposition   d. liking
6. accept : oppose :: contravene : _____

a. go around　　　b. violate　　　c. obey　　　d. distrust
7. cause : effect :: antigen : _____
　　　a. germs　　　b. blood　　　c. antibody　　　d. genes
8. idol : adored :: contraband : _____
　　　a. useful　　　b. opposed　　　c. smuggled　　　d. expensive

B. Indicate whether the following pairs of words have the same or different meanings:

1. antithesis / opposite　　　　　same ____ / different ____
2. contrarian / opponent　　　　　same ____ / different ____
3. antipathy / affection　　　　　same ____ / different ____
4. contraindication / benefit　　　same ____ / different ____
5. contravene / violate　　　　　same ____ / different ____
6. antigen / antibody　　　　　　same ____ / different ____
7. antagonist / enemy　　　　　　same ____ / different ____
8. contraband / antidote　　　　　same ____ / different ____

Greek and Latin Borrowings 希腊语和拉丁语借词

in memoriam \ˌin-mə-ˈmȯr-ē-əm\　　In memory of. 纪念

● The message on the pedestal begins "In memoriam" and then lists the names of the local young men who died in World War I. 基座上的信息以"纪念"开始，之后列出了第一次世界大战中牺牲的年轻人的姓名。

　　Since the days of the Roman empire, the words *In memoriam*, followed by a name, have been found on monuments and gravestones. They may also appear in the dedication of a book or poem; Alfred Tennyson's greatest poem is his immense *In Memoriam*, written over a period of 17 years to mourn the death of his dear friend Arthur Hallam. 从罗马帝国时代以来，*In memoriam* 这两个字，紧随其后是一个名就出现在纪念碑和墓碑上。它们也可能出现在书籍或者诗歌的赠言中。阿尔弗雷德·坦尼森最伟大的诗歌是其非常出色的 *In Memoriam*，这是他在十七年的时间内为悼念挚友阿瑟·哈勒姆而写的。

magnum opus \ˈmag-nəm-ˈō-pəs\　　A great work, especially the greatest achievement of an artist, composer, or writer. 杰作；代表作

● No one was exactly sure what the massive novel was about, but everyone was certain that it was his magnum opus. 没人可以确定这部伟大的小说讲的是什么，但是大家都可以肯定这是他的杰作。

　　The greatest work of a great artist may be hard to agree on. Many would pick Rembrandt's *The Night Watch*, Mozart's *Don Giovanni*, Ovid's *Metamorphoses*, Dante's *Divine Comedy*, Wren's St. Paul's Cathedral, and Michelangelo's Sistine Chapel murals. But for Shakespeare, would it be *Hamlet* or *King Lear*? For

Mahler, *The Song of the Earth* or *The Ninth Symphony*? For the Marx Brothers, *A Day at the Races* or *A Night at the Opera*?

一位伟大的艺术家最伟大的作品是什么,大家可能有不同的看法。很多人选择伦勃朗的《夜巡》、莫扎特的《唐璜》、奥维德的《变形记》、但丁的《神曲》、雷恩的圣保罗大教堂、米开朗琪罗的西斯廷教堂的壁画。但是对莎士比亚来说,是《哈姆雷特》还是《李尔王》? 对马勒来说,是《大地之歌》还是《第九交响曲》? 对马克斯兄弟来说,是《赌场风波》还是《歌声俪影》?

memento mori \mə-ˈmen-tō-ˈmȯr-ē\   A reminder of mortality, especially a human skull symbolizing death. 死亡象征;骷髅头

- The first twinges of arthritis often serve as a vivid memento mori for middle-aged jocks trying to ignore their advancing years. 对于那些想要忽视自己日渐衰老这一事实的职业赛马骑师来说,关节炎最初的一阵阵疼痛就是生动的死亡象征。

Memento mori literally means "Remember you must die." The early Puritan settlers were particularly aware of death and fearful of what it might mean, so a Puritan tombstone will often display a memento mori intended for the living. These death's-heads or skulls may strike us as ghoulish, but they helped keep the living on the straight and narrow for fear of eternal punishment. In earlier centuries, an educated European might place an actual skull on his desk to keep the idea of death always present in his mind.

memento mori 字面意思是"记着你一定会死"。早期的清教徒移民特别能意识到死亡,害怕它意味的内容,所以清教徒的墓碑上常常向活着的人们展示一个死亡象征。这些骷髅头可能让我们感觉毛骨悚然,但是,它们有助于让活着的人因为害怕永久惩罚而为人正直。在早先几个世纪,受过良好教育的欧洲人可能把真的骷髅头放在桌子上,让自己一直铭记死亡。

habeas corpus \ˈhā-bē-əs-ˈkȯr-pəs\   An order to bring a jailed person before a judge or court to find out if that person should really be in jail. 人身保护令

- The country has a primitive legal system with no right of habeas corpus, and suspects often are shot before they ever see a judge. 这个国家有一个很原始的法律体系,根本不包含享受人身保护令的权利,犯罪嫌疑人常常没有见到法官就被枪毙了。

The literal meaning of *habeas corpus* is "You shall have the body"—that is, the judge must have the person charged with a crime brought into the courtroom to hear what he's been charged with. Through much of human history, and in many countries still today, a person may be imprisoned on the orders of someone in the government and kept behind bars for years without ever getting a chance to defend himself, or even knowing what he's done wrong. In England, the right to be brought before a judge to hear the charges and answer them was written into law over 300 years ago, and the U.S. adopted the British practice in its Constitution.

habeas corpus 的字面意思是"你将拥有身体",也就是说,法官必须让人把被指控有某种罪行的人带到法庭上,听一听他被指控犯了什么罪。在人类历史长时期内,一个人可能因为政府某个人的命令而被关进监狱,在狱中多年却没有机会为自己辩护,甚至没有机会知道自己做了什么,在很多国家今天仍然如此。在英国,三百年前,被带到法官面前听听他人的指控并做出回答的权利就被写进了法律。美国在宪法中采用了英国的做法。

rigor mortis\ˈri-gər-ˈmȯr-təs\ The temporary rigidity of muscles that sets in after death. 尸体僵硬

• The coroner could tell from the progress of rigor mortis that death had occurred no more than six hours earlier. 验尸官从尸体僵硬的进展可以判断,死亡发生的时间在六个小时之前。

Rigor mortis, which translates from Latin as "stiffness of death," sets in quickly and usually ends three or four days after death. The condition results from a lack of certain chemicals in the muscles; it may be affected by muscular activity before death as well as the external temperature. Mystery writers frequently make use of rigor mortis as a means by which the detective or the examiner can determine the time of the victim's death, which often turns out to be all-important in solving the case. rigor mortis,从拉丁语翻译为"死亡的僵硬",开始得很快,通常在死后三天或四天结束。这种状况的原因是肌肉缺乏某些化学物质,它可以受到死亡前肌肉活动以及外界温度的影响。推理小说作家常常将尸体僵硬作为侦探或者验尸官确定受害者死亡时间的方式,这一方式最终被证明对破案来说十分重要。

sine qua non\si-ni-ˌkwä-ˈnōn\ An essential thing. 必要条件;必不可少的事物

• Good planning is the sine qua non of a successful dinner party. 计划周密是晚宴成功的必要条件。

Sine qua non can be translated literally as "Without which, not." Though this may sound like gibberish, it means more or less "Without (something), (something else) won't be possible." Sine qua non sounds slightly literary, and it shouldn't be used just anywhere. But it actually shows up in many contexts, including business ("A solid customer base is the sine qua non to success"), show business ("A good agent is a sine qua non for an actor's career"), and politics ("His support was really the sine qua non for her candidacy"). sine qua non 可以从字面翻译为"没有这个就不行"。尽管这或许听起来像是令人费解的话,但其意思大概是"没有(某物),(另一物)就不可能"。sine qua non 听起来有些文学气息,而且不应该随便使用。但是,它竟然出现在很多环境中,包括商业("A solid customer base is the sine qua non to success"["稳固的顾客基础是成功的必要条件"])、娱乐业("A good agent is a sine qua non for an actor's career"["好的经纪人对演员的职业生涯来说必不可少"])、政治("His support was really the sine qua non for her candidacy"["他的支持真的是她获得候选人资格的必要条件"])。

tabula rasa\ˈta-byu̇-lə-ˈrä-sə\ (1) The mind in its blank or unmarked state before receiving any impressions from outside. 白板状的心灵 (2) Something existing in its original pure state. 纯洁的事物

• As for knowing what life outside of his little village was like, he was practically a tabula rasa. 至于他的小村庄外的生活是什么样子的,他一无所知,简直就是一张白纸。

In ancient Rome, a student in class would write on a wax-covered wooden tablet, or tabula, using a sticklike implement. At the end of the day, the marks could be scraped off, leaving a fresh, unmarked tablet—a tabula rasa—for the next day's lessons. But even before the Romans, the Greek philosopher Aristotle had called the mind at birth an "unmarked tablet." We still use the term today, but usually not very seriously; with what we know about biology and genetics, most of us don't really think there's nothing in a mind at birth.

在古罗马，上课的学生会用小棍子一样的东西在涂有一层蜡的木头板子（或者 *tabula*）上写字。一天结束后，写字的痕迹可以刮掉，为第二天留下一个没有痕迹的板子，也就是 *tabula rasa*。不过，即使在罗马人之前，希腊哲学家亚里士多德就已经把人出生时的心灵叫做"没有痕迹的板子"了。今天，我们仍然使用这一说法，不过通常不是很严肃。有了对生物学和遗传学的了解，我们大多数人并不真的认为人出生时心灵空空如也。

terra incognita \ˈter-ə-ˌin-ˌkäg-ˈnē-tə\ An unexplored country or field of knowledge. 未知的土地；未知的领域

• We've been to Phoenix once, but otherwise Arizona is terra incognita. 我们去过菲尼克斯一次，除此以外，亚利桑那就那我们来讲就一片未知的土地。

When Roman mapmakers drew a land area that no one had yet explored, they often labeled it "Terra Incognita"—that is, "Unknown Territory"—and the term continued to be used for centuries afterward. When Columbus and his successors first crossed the Atlantic, they entered upon terra incognita, a land that came to be called the "New World." But the term is just as useful for mental exploration. For most of us, subjects such as particle physics, French 17th-century drama, and soil mechanics are terra incognita, and we can only hope to live long enough to be able to explore some of them someday.

如果一片土地尚不为人所知，罗马的地图制作者画地图时，就将其标为"Terra Incognita"——也就是"未知的土地"——这一名称此后继续使用了多个世纪。当哥伦布及其继承者首次穿越大西洋时，他们踏上了 terra incognito，一片后来被称为"新世界"的土地。但是这一名称对于精神上的探索来说也同样有用。对于大多数人来说，像粒子物理学、法国17世纪喜剧以及土壤力学这样的学科，都是 terra incognito，我们只能希望活得很久，将来有一天能探索其中一部分。

Quiz

Fill in each blank with the correct letter:

a. rigor mortis
b. magnum opus
c. sine qua non
d. habeas corpus
e. in memoriam
f. terra incognita
g. memento mori
h. tabula rasa

1. The entire field of quantum physics is _____ to me.
2. She claimed there was no such thing as the _____ of a successful novel, since great novels are so different.
3. *The Rite of Spring* is often regarded as Igor Stravinsky's _____.
4. To judge from the degree of _____, she appeared to have died no later than 4:00 a.m.
5. The monument listed the brave men and women who had died in the war, under the words "_____."
6. As for knowledge about home repair, his mind is a _____.
7. In legal systems without _____, individuals are often locked up for years

without ever knowing the charges against them.

8. Just accept those first gray hairs as a little _____.

Review Quizzes

A. Complete the analogy:

1. brief : extended :: hyperactive : _____
   a. exaggerated   b. young   c. required   d. calm
2. unconscious : aware :: subliminal : _____
   a. underneath   b. noticeable   c. deep   d. regular
3. prefer : favor :: preclude : _____
   a. assume   b. expect   c. prevent   d. avoid
4. awareness : ignorance :: hyperbole : _____
   a. exaggeration   b. understatement   c. calm   d. excitement
5. permit : allow :: permeate : _____
   a. ignore   b. move   c. penetrate   d. recover
6. night : dark :: sine qua non : _____
   a. necessary   b. nonessential   c. thorough   d. objective
7. fondness : affection :: antipathy : _____
   a. love   b. rejection   c. solution   d. distaste
8. edit : revise :: paraphrase : _____
   a. dedicate   b. praise   c. restate   d. compose
9. tolerate : accept :: contravene : _____
   a. argue   b. violate   c. oppose   d. throw out
10. dispute : argument :: antithesis : _____
    a. dislike   b. agreement   c. danger   d. opposite

B. Fill in each blank with the correct letter:

a. pervade
b. memento mori
c. metaphysics
d. antagonist
e. metadata
f. in memoriam
g. precocious
h. hyperventilate

i. rigor mortis
j. contraindication
k. antigen
l. subconscious
m. metaphorical
n. contrarian
o. subjugate

1. She was a smart and _____ child who could read by the age of three.
2. He senses that a negative tone has begun to _____ the school in the last couple of years.

UNIT 21

3. The preserved body sits on a chair behind glass in public view like a strange _____.

4. In Iraq, many years of government brutality failed to fully _____ the people called the Kurds.

5. There's so much difficult _____ language in the poem that critics have had a hard time interpreting it.

6. The death was so recent that _____ hadn't yet set in.

7. Late-night discussions in the dorm often became arguments about deep topics such as _____.

8. Pregnancy is a _____ to taking the measles vaccine.

9. The initial tests look for the _____ associated with tumors of this kind.

10. The _____ for the photos on his blog site includes identification of every single person in them.

11. At the end of each year, the magazine includes a section called "_____," which lists all the important figures who died that year.

12. The chief _____ of the Republican Party is the Democratic Party, and vice versa.

13. He keeps dinner parties lively with his _____ arguments, which nobody ever agrees with.

14. When my 12-year-old gets anxious, he often starts to _____, and it's caused him to pass out a couple of times.

15. Was it some _____ fear that made her forget the interview?

C. Choose the closest definition:

1. metaphorical   a. symbolic   b. literary   c. descriptive
  d. extensive
2. subversion   a. sabotage   b. undertow   c. turnover
  d. overture
3. predispose   a. recycle   b. subdue   c. spread
  d. influence
4. sine qua non   a. requirement   b. exception
  c. allowance   d. objection
5. antithesis   a. opponent   b. opposite   c. disadvantage
  d. argument
6. precocious   a. previous   b. ripe   c. early-maturing
  d. clever
7. tabula rasa   a. partial truth   b. complete ignorance
  c. slight contamination   d. pure trash
8. percolate   a. boil   b. spread   c. restore

d. seep
9. contravene   a. go against   b. retrieve   c. dance
   d. object
10. terra incognita   a. new information
    b. unknown cause   c. unexplored territory
    d. old suspicion
11. contraband   a. smuggled goods
    b. trade surplus   c. customs
    d. imports
12. prerequisite   a. requirement   b. reservation
    c. influence   d. decision
13. metonymy   a. rate of growth
    b. exaggeration   c. model of perfection
    d. use of a related word
14. persevere   a. carry off   b. resume   c. inquire
    d. carry on
15. hypertension   a. anxiety   b. tightness
    c. high blood pressure   d. duodenal ulcer

UNIT 22

ACER/ACR comes from the Latin adjective *acer*, meaning "sharp" or "sour." Grapefruit and limes have an *acid* taste; *acid* can also describe a person's sense of humor (other words for it might be *sharp* or *biting*). The *acidity* of the soil often indicates whether it's good for growing certain crops; blueberries, for instance, love acid soil, so they're more likely to be found east of the Mississippi River, where acid soil is the rule.

ACER/ACR 源自拉丁语形容词 acer("浓烈的"或者"酸的")。柚子和酸橙有 acid(酸的)味道；acid 也可以用来描述人的幽默感(其他用来描述幽默感的词语可能是 sharp 或者 biting)。土壤的 acidity(酸性)常常表明它是否适合种植某些农作物，比如蓝莓喜欢酸性土壤，所以更可能在密西西比河以东地区看到它们，因为那里酸性土壤很常见。

acerbic \ə-ˈsər-bik\ Sharp or biting in temper, mood, or tone. 尖刻的；辛辣的

• She had enjoyed his acerbic humor for years, but then a friend told her about the nasty jokes he was making about her behind her back. 她喜欢他那辛辣的幽默多年了，但是之后，有位朋友告诉她，他背后拿她开了很多恶意玩笑。

Acerbic often describes wit. An acerbic critic won't make many friends among the writers or artists whose work is being criticized, but often keeps his or her readers amused and entertained. *Acerbity* may be slightly less sharp than *sarcasm*, but not much; both words have roots meaning basically "cut."

acerbic 常常用来描述智慧。acerbic 评论家如果批评了作家或艺术家的作品，在他们当中就不会有很多朋友，但却会让自己的读者很高兴。acerbity 可能会比 sarcasm(讽刺)稍稍温和些，但也不会好多少，两个词都有着意为"砍、切、割"的词根。

acrid \ˈa-krəd\ Unpleasantly sharp and harsh; bitter. 尖刻的；辛辣的

• The acrid odor of gunpowder hung in the air long after the shots' echoes had died away. 枪声消逝很久之后，枪药那辛辣的气味仍然飘在空气中。

Acrid exactly fits the smoke from a fire—a burning building or forest, for example. Dense smog may cast an acrid pall over a city, making throats burn and eyes sting. But, like *acid* and *acerbic*, *acrid* sometimes also describes nonphysical things, such as the remarks of a bitter person.

acrid 很适合烧火冒的烟——比如燃烧的建筑物或者森林。浓浓的烟雾覆盖着城市上空,让喉咙火辣辣的,让眼睛刺痛。但是,就像 acid 和 acerbic 那样,acrid 有时也用来描述并不以实体存在的事物,比如刻薄的人说的话。

acrimony\ˈa-krə-ˌmō-nē\ Harsh or bitter sharpness in words, manner, or temper. 尖刻;辛辣

• Town meetings here were usually civilized, and no one could recall an issue that had ever aroused such intense acrimony as the new pulp mill. 这里的镇民大会通常是很文明的,没有谁能想起有哪个问题像这个新造纸厂那样让人们如此尖酸刻薄。

Acrimony is angry harshness that usually springs from intense personal dislike. An *acrimonious* exchange is full of cutting, unpleasant remarks designed to hurt. Civil wars are often more acrimonious and bloody than foreign wars. In the same way, a bad divorce may be more acrimonious than any other kind of legal battle.

acrimony 是源自强烈个人厌恶感的愤怒、尖酸的言辞、态度。acrimonious(尖酸刻薄的)对话充满伤人的令人不快的尖刻言辞。内战常常比对外战争更加 acrimonious(激烈的)、血腥。同样,糟糕的离婚比其他任何种类的官司更加 acrimonious(令人充满怨恨)。

exacerbate\ig-ˈza-sər-ˌbāt\ To make worse, more violent, or more severe. 使恶化;使加重

• The increase in coal-burning power plants has greatly exacerbated the buildup of greenhouse gases. 电厂烧煤量增加,使温室气体的积累更加严重。

To *exacerbate* is not to cause, but only to make something bad even worse. So the loss of a major industry in a city may exacerbate its already serious unemployment problem. A vicious remark can exacerbate a quarrel. Building a new mall may exacerbate an area's existing traffic problems. A new drug can exacerbate the side effects of the drug a patient is already taking. It used to be thought that too much blood in the body exacerbated a fever, so the patient's blood would be drained, often by means of leeches—and not all patients survived.

exacerbate 不是引发问题,而是让糟糕的情况更加严重。所以一个城市失去了一个主要行业,可能会 exacerbate (使……更加严重)已经严重的失业问题。一句恶毒的话可以 exacerbate(使……更加激烈)争吵。一种新药能够 exacerbate(使……更加严重)病人所服药物的副作用。人们以前认为体内血液过多会 exacerbate(使……更加严重)发烧,所以病人的血液要释放一下,通常是利用水蛭,但并非所有病人都能活下来。

STRICT

STRICT comes from the Latin verb meaning "to draw tight, bind, or tie." So the English word *strict* means "tightly controlled." And when someone begins a sentence "Strictly speaking, ..." you know he or she is going to be talking about a word or idea in its most limited sense, "drawing tight" the meaning till it's as narrow as possible.

STRICT 源自意思是"拉紧,绑起来,捆好"的那个拉丁语动词。所以,英语词语 *strict* 意思是"紧紧控制"。当某人说话时一开口就是"*strictly speaking*"(严格说来),你就会知道他或她要从狭义上谈论某个词语或观点了,即"收紧"其意思,直到它尽可能狭窄。

stricture \ˈstrik-chər\ (1) A law or rule that limits or controls something; restriction. 限制;约束;控制 (2) A strong criticism. 批评;指责

• There are severe legal strictures on the selling of marijuana in almost every state. 有几项法律对几乎各州的大麻销售活动都进行了严格限制。

Stricture has meant many things through the centuries, and its "restriction" meaning—probably the most common one today—is actually the most recent. High-school teachers often put strictures on texting during class. Cities concerned about their murder rate have slapped strictures on the possession of handguns. And the United Nations may vote to put strictures on arms sales to a country that keeps violating international treaties. With the meaning "strong criticism," *stricture* is slightly old-fashioned today, but it's still used by intellectuals. So, for example, an article may amount to a harsh stricture on the whole medical profession, or an art review may just express the critic's strictures on sentimental paintings of cute little houses with glowing windows.

stricture 多个世纪以来有很多意思,但表示"限制"的意思在今天是最常见的,实际上也是最新产生的。高中教师经常 put strictures on(限制)上课发短信这一行为。担心其谋杀率的城市已 slapped strictures on(对……进行严格限制)拥有手枪。联合国可能会投票 put strictures on(限制)向屡屡违反国际条约的国家销售武器。表示"强烈批评"这一意思时,*stricture* 在今天有些过时了。因此,比如一篇文章可能是对整个医疗行业的尖锐批评,或者一篇艺术评论可能要表达的,只是评论家对窗户泛着红光的小屋的伤感画作的批评。

restrictive \ri-ˈstrik-tiv\ (1) Serving or likely to keep within bounds. 限制的;约束的 (2) Serving or tending to place under limits as to use. 限制使用的

• The deed to the property had a restrictive covenant forbidding any development of the land for 50 years. 这一地产的契约有一条限制性协约,禁止五十年内开发这片土地。

Restrictive covenants (that is, agreements) in real-estate deeds were once used to forbid the buyer from ever selling the property to anyone of another race. These are now illegal, though other kinds of restrictive covenants are very common; in some neighborhoods, they may even tell you what colors you can't paint your house. In grammar, a restrictive clause is one that limits the meaning of something that comes before it. In the sentence "That's the professor who I'm trying to avoid," "who I'm trying to avoid" is a restrictive clause, since it's what identifies the professor. But in the sentence "That's my History professor, who I'm trying to avoid," the same clause is *nonrestrictive*, since the professor has already been identified as "my History professor." There should always be a comma before a nonrestrictive clause, but not before a restrictive clause.

房地产契约中的 restrictive covenants(限制性协约)(covenants 也就是 agreements)曾用于禁止购买者将房地产卖给另一种族的任何人。这些协约现在是非法的,虽然其他种类的限制性协约很常见。在城市有些区域,这些协约可能会告诉你房子不能刷成什么颜色。在语法中,限定性从句限制前面出现的成分的意思。在"That's the professor who I'm trying to avoid"这个句子中,"who I'm trying to avoid"是限定性从句,因为它说明了 *the professor* 是哪一个。但是,在"That's my History professor, who I'm trying to avoid"中,这同一个从句却是非限定性从句,因为已经说明了 the professor 是"my History professor"。非限定性从句前面总是要有一个逗号,但限定性从句前面没有。

constrict \kən-ˈstrikt\　(1) To draw together or make narrow. 收紧;使变窄 (2) To limit. 限制

• She felt that small towns, where everyone seems to know every move you make and is just waiting to gossip about it, can constrict your life terribly. 她觉得,在小城镇每个人似乎都对你的一举一动了如指掌,就等着说闲话了,这会严重限制人的生活。

Arteries constricted by cholesterol slow the flow of blood, just as traffic arteries or highways constricted by accidents slow the flow of traffic. But constriction isn't always physical. Economic growth may be constricted by trade barriers. A narrow, constricted life may be the result of poverty or lack of opportunity. And an actress may feel constricted by a role she played as a child or by her TV character from years ago, which the public refuses to forget. 血管因为胆固醇而 constricted(变窄)会使血液流通缓慢,就像交通干线或者公路因为交通事故而 constricted(受限)会使车流缓慢。但是 constriction 并非总是涉及实物。经济发展会受到贸易壁垒的 constricted(限制)。狭隘、constricted(受限的)生活可能是贫穷或者缺少机会的结果。女演员可能感觉 restricted(受到限制),是因为小时候扮演的一个角色或者多年前她的电视角色难以被公众忘记。

STRICT

vasoconstrictor \ˌvā-zō-kən-ˈstrik-tər\　Something such as a nerve fiber or a drug that narrows a blood vessel. 血管收缩神经;血管收缩药

• For operations like this, my dentist likes to use a vasoconstrictor to keep bleeding to a minimum. 对那些与此类似的手术来说,我的牙医喜欢使用血管收缩药,使流血保持最小量。

Our blood vessels are constantly narrowing and widening in response to our activity or our environment, constricting in order to retain body heat and widening to get rid of excess heat. So when we're hot our skin flushes, and when we're very cold we become pale. Since the width of the blood vessels affects blood pressure, vasoconstrictors are prescribed to treat low blood pressure. Vasoconstrictors include antihistamines and amphetamines, as well as nicotine and caffeine; we commonly buy them for our runny noses and bloodshot eyes as well. The opposite of vasoconstrictors are *vasodilators*, which are commonly used to treat high blood pressure. 我们的血管不断收缩、扩张,以对我们的活动或者环境做出反应。收缩是为了保持血液热量,扩张是为了除去多余热量。所以,我们热的时候,皮肤泛红;我们冷的时候,皮肤苍白。由于血管的宽度影响血压,医生就开 vasoconstrictors(血管收缩药)来治疗低血压。Vasoconstrictors(血管收缩药)除了尼古丁和咖啡因,还包括抗组胺药和苯丙胺,我们常常购买这些药治疗流鼻涕以及眼睛布满血丝。与 vasoconstrictors 相对的是 *vasodilators*(血管扩张药),它们通常被用来治疗高血压。

UNIT 22

Quizzes

A. Indicate whether the following pairs of words have the same or different meanings:

1. exacerbate / worsen   same ____ / different ____
2. acrid / dry   same ____ / different ____
3. acrimony / divorce payment   same ____ / different ____
4. acerbic / harsh   same ____ / different ____
5. constrict / assemble   same ____ / different ____
6. restrictive / limiting   same ____ / different ____
7. vasoconstrictor / Amazon snake   same ____ / different ____
8. stricture / tightening   same ____ / different ____

B. Fill in each blank with the correct letter:

a. stricture   e. acerbic
b. vasoconstrictor   f. acrimony
c. constrict   g. acrid
d. stringent   h. exacerbate

1. The list of new demands only served to _____ the crisis.
2. The _____ that Olympic athletes be amateurs would sometimes get an athlete banned because of a few dollars he or she had earned as a professional.
3. The _____ fumes in the plant irritated his eyes and nose for several days.
4. With four or five _____ comments she managed to annoy or insult almost everyone in the room.
5. Soon after the banking scandal hit the newspapers, a new set of _____ regulations was announced.
6. She was given a _____ for the tooth extraction, but there was some bleeding anyway.
7. These deposits are beginning to _____ the coronary arteries to a dangerous degree.
8. Even for a child-custody case, the _____ between the parties was unusual.

STRU/STRUCT

STRU/STRUCT comes from the Latin verb *struere*, meaning "to put together, build, arrange." A *structure* is something that's been *constructed*,—that is, built or put together. *Instructions* tell how the pieces should be arranged. Something that *obstructs* is a barrier that's been "built" to stand in your way. And something *destructive* "unbuilds."

STRU/STRUCT 源自拉丁语动词 *struere*("放在一起,建筑,安排")。structure(建筑物)就是 constructed(被建造的)东西,也就是建造或者组合在一起的东西。instructions(指令)告诉人们各个部分如何安排在一起。obstructs(阻碍)的东西就是"建起来"的障碍,阻挡你的路。*destructive*(破坏性的)东西能"拆毁"东西。

deconstruction\ˌdē-kən-ˈstrək-shən\ Analysis of texts, works of art, and cultural patterns that is intended to expose the assumptions on which they are based, especially by exposing the limitations of language.
解构

• Deconstruction has been performed on *Huckleberry Finn* by English professors so many times that it's a wonder there's anything left of it. 解构已经被英语教授们用在《哈克贝利·费恩历险记》上很多次了,再有什么东西剩下就是奇迹了。

Deconstruction doesn't actually mean "demolition"; instead it means "breaking down" or analyzing something (especially the words in a work of fiction or nonfiction) to discover its true significance, which is supposedly almost never exactly what the author intended. A feminist may *deconstruct* an old novel to show how even an innocent-seeming story somehow depends on the oppression of women. A new western may deconstruct the myths of the old West and show lawmen as vicious and criminals as flawed but decent. Table manners, *The Sound of Music*, and cosmetics ads have all been the subjects of *deconstructionist* analysis. Of course, not everyone agrees with deconstructionist interpretations, and some people reject the whole idea of deconstruction, but most of us have run into it by now even if we didn't realize it.

deconstruction 实际上并不意味着"拆毁",而表示"分解"或者分析某物(尤其是小说或者非小说作品中的词语)来发现其真实意义,但它几乎常常并非作者的原意。女性主义者可能会 *deconstruct*(拆析)一部旧小说,以表明即使一部看似天真的小说,也是以某种方式根据对妇女的压迫而创作的。一部新的西部电影可能 deconstruct(解构)古老西部的神话,说明女治安官是邪恶的,而罪犯是有缺陷但正派的。餐桌礼仪、《音乐之声》和化妆品广告都已成为 deconstructionist(解构主义的)分析对象。当然,不是每个人都同意 deconstructionist(解构主义者)解释,有些人拒绝接受整个 deconstruction(解构主义),但是大多数人即使没有意识到,到现在也已经遇到过 deconstruction(解构主义)。

infrastructure\ˈin-frə-ˌstrək-chər\ (1) The underlying foundation or basic framework. 基础;基本框架 (2) A system of public works. 基础设施

• The public loved her speeches about crime but dozed off when she brought up highway repair and infrastructure deterioration. 公众喜欢她关于犯罪的演讲,但是,当她讲到公路修补和基础设施恶化问题时,大家打起盹来。

Infra- means "below"; so the infrastructure is the "underlying structure" of a country and its economy, the fixed installations that it needs in order to function. These include roads, bridges, dams, the water and sewer systems, railways and subways, airports, and harbors. These are generally government-built and publicly owned. Some people also speak about such things as the intellectual *infrastructure* or the infrastructure of science research, but the meaning of such notions can be extremely vague.

infra-意思是"在……下面",所以 infrastructure(基础设施)是一个国家及其经济的 underlying structure("基底结构"),是它运作所需要的固定设施。这些设施包括道路、桥梁、水坝、供水及排水系统、铁路和地铁、机场和海港。这些通

常是政府建造、公众拥有的东西。有些人也谈到 intellectual infrastructure（智力基础设施）或者 the infrastructure of science research（科研基础设施）之类的东西，但是这些概念的意思是极其模糊的。

construe \ kən-'strü \ (1) To explain the arrangement and meaning of words in a sentence. 解释（句中词语的安排和意义）(2) To understand or explain; interpret. 理解；解释；阐释

• She asked how I had construed his last e-mail, and I told her that something about it had left me very worried. 她问我是怎样理解他最后一封电子邮件的，我告诉她有关这封邮件的某些东西让我很是担心。

Construe can usually be translated as "interpret." It's often used in law; thus, an Attorney General might construe the term "serious injury" in a child-abuse law to include bruises, or a judge might construe language about gifts to "heirs" to include spouses. The IRS's *construal* of some of your activities might be different from your own—and much more expensive at tax time. Construing is also close to translating; so when the British say "public school," for instance, it should be construed or translated as "prep school" in American terms.

construe 通常可以解释为"interpret"（解释；理解）。它常常用于法律领域；这样，司法部长可能将儿童虐待法中"严重伤害"这一短语 construe（理解为）包括瘀伤，或者一位法官可能将关于留给"继承人"的礼物 construe（理解为）包括配偶。美国国家税务局对你的一些活动的 construal（解释；理解）可能与你自己的理解不一样——在征税时要昂贵得多。construing 也接近于翻译，所以，比如当英国人说"public school"（公学）时，应该用美国的说法将其理解或翻译为"prep school"（预科学校）。

instrumental \ ˌin-strə-'men-təl \ (1) Acting as a means, agent, or tool. 发挥重要作用的 (2) Relating to an instrument, especially a musical instrument. 乐器的

• His mother had been instrumental in starting the new arts program at the school, for which she was honored at the spring ceremony. 他妈妈对这所学校开办新的艺术课程发挥了重要作用，为此在春季开学典礼上受到了表扬。

An *instrument* is a tool, something used to *construct*. It's often a tool for making music. A musical saw happens to be a carpenter's tool that can be played with a violin bow (though you probably wouldn't want to play a wrench or a pair of pliers). The musical meanings of *instrumental*, as in "It starts with an instrumental piece" or "a jazz *instrumental*," are common. But the meanings "helpful," "useful," and "essential," as in "He was instrumental in getting my book published," are just as common.

instrument 就是工具，也就是用来 construct（建造）的东西。它通常是产生音乐的工具。乐锯碰巧就是可以用小提琴琴弓演奏的木匠的工具（虽然你可能不想演奏一把扳手或者一把钳子）。instrumental 音乐方面的意思，比如在"It starts with an instrumental piece"（"它以一首器乐曲开始"）或者"a jazz *instrumental*"（"器乐爵士"）中，是很常见的。但是"有帮助的""有用的"以及"必不可少的"这些意思，就像在"He was instrumental in getting my book published"中，也同样常见。

PROP/PROPRI comes from the Latin word *proprius*, meaning "own." A

• 523 •

proprietor is an owner, and *property* is what he or she owns. And the original meaning of *proper* was "belonging to oneself'," so a writer around the year 1400 could say "With his own proper sword he was slain," even if we might not say it quite the same way today.

PROP/PROPRI 源自拉丁语单词 *proprius*("自己的")。*proprietor* 就是物主, *property* 就是他或她拥有的东西。*proper* 最初的意思是"属于自己",所以大约生活在 1400 年的作家会说"With his own proper sword he was slain"("他死在自己的剑下"),即使我们不会以同样的方式这样表达。

proprietary \ prə-ˈprī-ə-ˌter-ē \ (1) Relating to an owner or proprietor; made or sold by one who has the sole right to do so. 所有人的 (2) Privately owned and run as a profit-making organization. (作为营利机构而)由私人经营的

• The local hospital was a not-for-profit institution, whereas the nearby nursing homes were proprietary. 当地医院是一家非营利机构,而附近那些私立养老院则是私人经营的营利机构。

A *proprietary* process is a manufacturing process that others are forbidden to use, and a proprietary trademark is a name that only the owner can use. Legal rights of this kind are ensured by copyrights and patents. After a certain period of time, inventions and processes lose their legal protection, cease to be proprietary, and enter the "public domain," meaning that everyone can use them freely. Baseball fans often take a proprietary attitude toward their favorite team—that is, they behave more or less as if they own it, even though the only thing they may own is the right to yell from a bleacher seat till the end of a game.

proprietary(所有人的)生产过程是禁止其他人使用的生产过程,proprietary(所有人的)商标是只有主人才能使用的名称。这种法律权利由版权和专利确保。过了特定的一段时间,发明和过程失去法律保护,不再是 proprietary(所有人专有的)了,就进入了"公共领域",意思是每个人都能自由使用。棒球迷经常对自己最爱的球队采取一种 proprietary attitude(所有人态度),就是说,好像他们拥有这个球队一样,尽管他们的权利只是在露天看台的座位上喊叫,直到比赛结束。

propriety \ prə-ˈprī-ə-tē \ (1) The state of being proper; appropriateness. 适当 (2) Acting according to what is socially acceptable, especially in conduct between the sexes. 举止得当;得体

• Propriety used to forbid a young unmarried man and woman to go almost anywhere without an adult. 举止得当过去常常意味着禁止年轻的单身男女在没有成年人的情况下去任何地方。

In an earlier era, when social manners were far more elaborate than they are today, *propriety* and *impropriety* were words in constant use. Today we're more likely to use them in other contexts. We may talk about the propriety of government officials' dealings with private citizens, the propriety of the relationship between a lawyer and a judge, or the impropriety of speaking out of turn in a meeting that follows Robert's rules of order. Relations between men and women still present questions of propriety, but today it's often in the workplace rather than in social settings. Wherever rules, principles, and standard procedures have been clearly stated, propriety can become an issue. Something *improper* usually isn't actually illegal, but it makes people uncomfortable by giving the impression that something isn't quite right.

在早些时期,当社会礼仪比今天复杂很多的时候,*propriety* 和 *impropriety* 是不断使用的两个词语。今天,我们更可能将其用于其他环境。我们可能谈论政府官员对公民私人的 propriety(得体性)、律师和法官之间关系的 propriety(得体性),或者在遵循罗伯特议事规则的会议上不按顺序发言的 impropriety(不得体)。男女之间的关系仍然向我们提出 propriety(得体性)问题,但是今天它经常存在于工作场所,而不是社交环境。在规则、原则以及标准程序已明确陈述的任何地方,propriety(得体性)都会成为问题。*improper*(不得体)的东西未必不合法,但是它给人的印象是不太恰当的,从而让人不舒服。

appropriate \ə-ˈprō-prē-ˌāt\ (1) To take exclusive possession of, often without right. 独占;盗用 (2) To set apart for a particular purpose or use. 专用.

• It was one of those insulting words that sometimes get appropriated by a group that it's meant to insult, which then starts using it proudly and defiantly. 这是那些要用来污辱某个群体但有时却被其占有、之后自豪而放肆地使用的词语之一。

From its roots, the verb *appropriate* would mean basically "make one's own"—that is, "take," or sometimes "grab." Each year the President and Congress create a budget and appropriate funds for each item in it, funds which mostly come in the form of taxes from the public. In the House of Representatives, the powerful *Appropriations* Committee often gets the last word on how much money goes to each program. "*Misappropriation* of funds," on the other hand, is a nice way of saying "theft." If someone appropriated pieces of your novel, you might take him or her to court; and if you appropriated trade secrets from your former employers, you might be the one sued.

从其词根来看,动词 *appropriate* 的基本意思会是"使成为自己的"——也就是"占有",或者有时候是"攫取"。每年,总统和国会都会做好一个预算,为其中每一项拨款。在下议院,权力巨大的 *Appropriations Committee*(拨款委员会)在每项计划分配多少钱方面常常拥有最终决定权。另一方面,"*misappropriation of funds*"("盗用资金")是"偷窃"的委婉说法。如果某人 appropriated(剽窃)你小说中的片段,你可能将其告上法庭;如果你从以前的雇主那里 appropriated(盗取)商业信息,你可能受到起诉。

expropriate \ek-ˈsprō-prē-ˌāt\ (1) To take away the right of possession or ownership. 剥夺(拥有权);没收;征用 (2) To transfer to oneself. 据为己有;侵占

• It was only when the country's new government threatened to expropriate the American oil refineries that Congress became alarmed. 只当该国新政府说要占有美国炼油厂时,国会才害怕起来。

In ancient Rome, an emperor could condemn a wealthy senator, have him killed, and expropriate his property. In 1536 Henry VIII declared himself head of the new Church of England and expropriated the lands and wealth of the Roman Catholic monasteries. And nearly all of North America was expropriated from the American Indians, usually without any payment at all. Today, democratic governments only carry out legal *expropriations*, in which the owners are *properly* paid for their land—for example, when a highway or other public project needs to be built.

在古罗马,皇帝可以给富有的元老院议员判刑、将其处死、没收其财产。1536 年,亨利八世宣布自己为新的英格兰教会首领,*expropriated*(没收了)罗马天主教修道院的土地和财富。几乎整个北美洲都从印第安人那里 *expropriated*(被抢走了),通常没有任何报偿。今天,民主国家政府仅仅实行合法的 *expropriations*(征用),土地的主人会得到适当赔付,比如需要建造公路或者其他公共工程的时候。

Quizzes

A. Complete the analogy:

1. grant : award :: expropriate : _____
   a. find b. want c. move d. claim
2. consumer goods : cars :: infrastructure : _____
   a. foundation b. surface c. bridges d. boats
3. accept : receive :: appropriate : _____
   a. send b. lose c. take d. offer
4. solve : figure out :: construe : _____
   a. build b. misspell c. tighten d. interpret
5. habit : practice :: propriety : _____
   a. appropriateness b. property c. behavior d. proportion
6. description : portrayal :: deconstruction : _____
   a. demolition b. interpretation c. transference d. translation
7. monetary : money :: proprietary : _____
   a. prosperity b. property c. profit d. protection
8. practical : effective :: instrumental : _____
   a. hardworking b. tool-shaped c. instructional d. useful

B. Indicate whether the following pairs of terms have the same or different meanings:

1. proprietary / public   same ____ / different ____
2. construe / explain   same ____ / different ____
3. appropriate / take   same ____ / different ____
4. infrastructure / dome   same ____ / different ____
5. propriety / ownership   same ____ / different ____
6. instrumental / melodic   same ____ / different ____
7. expropriate / seize   same ____ / different ____
8. deconstruction / demolition same ____ / different ____

TORT

TORT comes from a form of the Latin verb *torquere*, meaning "to twist, wind, or wrench." In *torture*, parts of the body may be wrenched or twisted or stretched; so those "Indian sunburns" that schoolkids give by twisting in different directions on some unlucky guy's wrist stay pretty close to *torture*'s original meaning.

UNIT 22

TORT 源自拉丁语动词 *torquere*("扭曲,缠绕或者猛拉")的一种形式。在 *torture*(酷刑)中,身体的某些部分可能被猛拉或者扭曲或者伸展;所以,男学生抓住某个不幸的男孩的手腕,往各个不同方向扭,这种称为 *Indian sunburns*(印度晒伤)的折磨与 *torture* 的最初意思很相近。

tort \ˈtȯrt\ A wrongful act that does not involve breach of contract and for which the injured party can receive damages in a civil action. (不构成刑事犯罪但可引起民事诉讼的)侵权行为

• The manufacturer was almost bankrupted by the massive tort actions brought by employees harmed by asbestos. 因为受到石棉伤害的员工引起了大规模的侵权诉讼,这家工厂几乎破产。

Tort came into English straight from French many centuries ago, and it still looks a little odd. Its root meaning of "twisted" (as opposed to "straight") obviously came to mean "wrong" (as opposed to "right"). Every first-year law student takes a course in the important subject of torts. Torts include all the so-called "product-liability" cases, against manufacturers of cars, household products, children's toys, and so on. They also cover dog bites, slander and libel, and a huge variety of other very personal cases of injury, both mental and physical—Torts class is never dull. If you're sued for a tort and lose, you usually have to pay "damages"—that is, a sum of money—to the person who you wronged.

tort 在数个世纪前直接从法语进入英语,现在看起来还是有些怪异。其"扭曲的"这一词根意义(与"直的"相对)后来显然用来表示"错误的"(与"正确"相对)。每一位一年级法律专业学生都学习一门侵权方面的重要课程。侵权包括全部所谓的"产品责任"案件,指控的是汽车、家用制品、儿童玩具等商品的生产厂家。侵权也包括犬咬伤、文字或口头诽谤,以及多种多样的其他个人伤害案件,包括精神的和身体的——侵权课从来不会无聊。如果你因为侵权受到指控并且输掉了官司,你通常不得不向你伤害的人支付"赔偿金"——也就是一笔钱。

extort \ik-ˈstȯrt\ To obtain from a person by force, threats, or illegal power. 抢夺;勒索;敲诈

• She had tried to extort money from a film star, claiming that he was the father of her baby. 她曾想从一位电影明星那里敲诈一笔钱,说他是她婴儿的父亲。

To extort is literally to wrench something out of someone. *Extortion* is a mainstay of organized crime. Just as the school bully extorts lunch money from the smaller kids in exchange for not beating them up, thugs extort "protection" money from business owners with threats of violence. But that's only one kind of extortion; a mobster might extort favors from a politician with threats of revealing some dark secret, just as you might extort a favor from a brother or sister by promising not to tell on them.

extort 从字面来看就是将某物从某人手中夺走。*extortion* 是有组织犯罪主要依靠的一个手段。就像校园恶霸从小一些的学生那里 extort(勒索)午餐费而不再欺负他们一样,恶棍通过扬言要使用暴力向商人 extort(勒索)"保护"费。但是,这只是一种 extortion(勒索行为)。匪徒会威胁说要揭露某一不可告人的秘密,从政客那里 extort(索取)利益,就像你通过承诺不打小报告,从哥哥/弟弟或姐姐/妹妹那里 extort(索取)好处一样。

contort \kən-ˈtȯrt\ To twist in a violent manner. 用力扭

● The governor's explanation of his affair was so contorted that it only made matters worse for him. 州长对自己风流韵事的解释太走样了,结果情况对他更为不利。

Circus *contortionists* are known for twisting their bodies into pretzels; such *contortions* tend to be easier for females than for males, and much easier for the young than for the old. When trying to say something uncomfortable or dishonest, people often go through verbal contortions. But when someone else "twists" something you said or did, we usually say instead that they've *distorted* it. 马戏团的 *contortionists*（柔术演员）以将身体扭曲成椒盐卷饼状而著称。这样的 *contortions*（扭曲）对女性来说比男性往往更容易些,对年轻人来说比对老年容易得多。人们想说让人不舒服或者不诚实的话时,往往会 go through verbal contortions（扭曲语言）。但是当另一个人"扭曲"了你所说的话或者所做的事,我们通常则说他们已经"*distorted*"（"歪曲了"）事实。

tortuous \ˈtȯr-chə-wəs\ (1) Having many twists, bends, or turns; winding. 弯弯曲曲的;蜿蜒曲折的 (2) Crooked or tricky; involved, complex. 不正直的;骗人的;复杂的

● The road over the mountains was long and dangerously tortuous, and as you rounded the sharp corners you could never see whether a huge truck might be barreling down toward you. 山上的路长的曲折,在急转弯时,你可能从来都看不到是否有巨大的卡车向你奔驰而来。

A labyrinth is a *tortuous* maze. The first labyrinth was built as a prison for the monstrous Minotaur, half bull and half man; only by holding one end of a thread was the heroic Theseus able to enter and slay the Minotaur and then exit. A tortuous problem, a tortuous history, and the tortuous path of a bill through Congress all have many unexpected twists and turns; a tortuous explanation or argument may be too crooked for its own good. Don't confuse *tortuous* with *torturous*, which means "tortured" or "painfully unpleasant"; *tortuous* has nothing to do with torture. 迷宫里面是 tortuous（曲曲折折的）路。第一座迷宫是为囚禁半牛半人怪物米诺托而建造的。抓着一根线的一头,英雄特修斯才能走进去杀死了米诺托,之后走了出来。tortuous（复杂的）问题、tortuous（复杂的）历史、一个法案经过国会的 tortuous（曲折的）程序,都有很多意想不到的迂回曲折;tortuous（复杂的）解释或者论据可能太过复杂而对自己不利。不要将 tortuous 与 torturous 搞混了。torturous 意思是"遭受折磨的"或者"极其令人不愉快的";tortuous 与折磨无关。

VIV comes from *vivere*, the Latin verb meaning "to live or be alive." A *survivor* has lived through something terrible. A *revival* brings something back to life, whether it's an old film, interest in a long-dead novelist, or religious enthusiasm in a group, maybe in a huge tent in the countryside. VIV 源自意为"活着或者活的"拉丁动词 vivere。survivor（幸存者）经历了可怕的事件而大难不死。revival（复活）让死去的某物恢复活力,不管是老电影人们对一位早已去世的小说家的作品的兴趣,还是聚集在乡间一个大帐篷里的一个群体的宗教热情。

---

vivacious \vī-ˈvā-shəs\ Lively in an attractive way. 活泼可爱的

● For the cheerleading squad, only the most outgoing, energetic, and vivacious

UNIT 22

of the students get chosen. 对这个拉拉队来说，只有最外向的、精力充沛的、活泼可爱的学生才有可能被选上。

Vivacious can be used to describe a piece of music or writing, but it's generally used today to describe people, and particularly women. The main female characters in Shakespeare's plays—Beatrice in *Much Ado About Nothing*, Rosalind in *As You Like It*, and Portia in *The Merchant of Venice*, for example—are often full of humor, spirit, and *vivacity*.

vivacious 可以用来形容一曲音乐或者一篇文字，但是今天通常用于形容人，尤其是女性。莎士比亚戏剧中的主要女性角色，比如《无事生非》中的核经典译本、《皆大欢喜》中的罗瑟琳以及《威尼斯商人》中的鲍西亚，都非常幽默风趣、精力充沛、vivacity（活泼可爱）。

bon vivant \ˌbän-vē-ˈvänt\ A sociable person with a love of excellent food and drink. 喜欢精美饮食和社交的人

• My uncle and aunt were bons vivants, and could usually be found in the evening at a swank midtown bar surrounded by a crowd of tipsy merrymakers. 我姑父和姑妈都是爱吃爱玩的人，晚上常常出现在市区中心的时尚酒吧，周围是一群略有醉意的寻欢作乐的人。

Bon vivant comes straight from French, where it means literally "good liver," and is still pronounced in the French way, though we've actually been using it in English since the 17th century. A proper bon vivant has some money and lots of friends and plenty of style and knows a good wine and can tell a great story and loves to laugh. Because of all these requirements, true bons vivants are rather rare—but that doesn't mean there aren't plenty of people who hope to be one someday.

bon vivant 直接来自法语，在法语中字面意思是"过得很好的人"。现在，这一词语仍然按照法语的方式发音，虽然我们从 17 世纪就开始在英语中使用了。一个正儿八经的 bon vivant 有些钱财，朋友众多，相当时尚，很懂好酒，能讲故事，喜欢大笑。由于所有这些要求，真正的 bons vivants 是相当少见的，但有很多人希望将来成为这种人。

revivify \rē-ˈvi-və-ˌfī\ To give new life to; bring back to life. 使再生，使复活

• All their efforts to revivify the boys' club seemed to be getting them nowhere, till one of the board members had a great idea. 他们为振兴男孩俱乐部所作的一切努力似乎都毫无结果，直到有一个董事会成员想出了一个好主意。

Worn-out soil may be by careful organic tending. A terrific new recruit can revivify a discouraged football team, and an imaginative and energetic new principal can revivify a failing high school. After World War II, one European country after another was slowly revivified, their economies and cultural life gradually coming back to life. Notice that *revivify* looks like some other words with very similar meanings, such as *revive*, *revitalize*, and *reinvigorate*.

经过精心的有机照料，磨损的土壤可以恢复原状。一个出色的新成员可以重振一支士气低落的足球队，一个富有想象力和活力的新校长可以重振一所失败的高中。第二次世界大战后，一个又一个欧洲国家慢慢复兴起来，他们的经济和文化生活逐渐恢复了生机。注意 revivify 看起来和其他一些含义非常相似的词很像，比如 revive（复苏）、revitalize（振兴）和 reinvigorate（振兴）。

vivisection \ˈvi-və-ˌsek-shən\ Operation on living animals, often for experimental purposes. (动物)解剖

• The lab attempts to avoid vivisection in its research, concentrating instead on alternative methods that have been developed. 实验室人员想在研究工作中避免动物解剖，而把精力集中在已经开发出的其他方法上。

Vivisection includes the Latin root *sect*, meaning "cut." The Greek physician Galen, who lived during the 2nd century A.D., practiced vivisection on live monkeys and dogs to learn such things as the role of the spinal cord in muscle activity and whether veins and arteries carry air or blood; his findings formed the basis of medical practice for more than a thousand years. Vivisection continues to be used in drug and medical research today, but often in secret, since it makes most people very uncomfortable and some groups are violently opposed to it.

vivisection 中有意为"切、割"的拉丁词根 *sect*。生活在公元2世纪的希腊医生盖伦，曾 practiced vivisections on(解剖)猴子和狗，以了解脊髓在肌肉活动中的作用，以及静脉和动脉是运输空气还是血液。他的发现结果有一千多年都是医疗工作的基础。vivisection(动物解剖)今天仍然应用于药物和医学研究工作，但常常是秘密进行的，因为这使大多数人很不舒服，而且有些团体激烈反对这一做法。

Quizzes

A. Fill in each blank with the correct letter:

a. revivify
b. tort
c. vivacious
d. tortuous
e. extort
f. vivisection
g. contort
h. bon vivant

1. He was horrified by _____, and even protested the dissecting of frogs in biology class.

2. She was able to _____ her body so as to fit entirely into a box 20 inches square.

3. As the daughter of a _____, she was used to having her parents leave her with a babysitter most evenings while they enjoyed themselves in the downtown bars and restaurants.

4. A group of new young teachers had managed to _____ the school.

5. In a _____ case, unlike a criminal case, the government doesn't get involved.

6. We carefully made our way down the steep and _____ trail.

7. Marie is the _____ one and Jan is the serious one.

8. He tried to _____ a B from his math teacher by saying that, if he couldn't play because of bad grades, they'd lose and everyone would blame her.

B. Choose the closest definition:

1. vivacious   a. sweet-tempered   b. loud   c. lively

    d. gluttonous
2. extort   a. obtain by force   b. pay up
   c. engage in crime   d. exterminate
3. vivisection   a. living area   b. animal experimentation
   c. experimental treatment   d. removal of organs
4. contort   a. perform   b. twist   c. squeeze
   d. expand
5. bon vivant   a. dieter   b. partyer
   c. chocolate candy   d. nightclub act
6. tortuous   a. painful   b. winding   c. harmful
   d. monstrous
7. revivify   a. revive   b. reclaim   c. retain
   d. restrain
8. tort   a. deformity   b. law   c. product
   d. wrongful act

SERV means "to be subject to." A *servant* is the person who *serves* you with meals and provides other necessary *services*. A tennis or volleyball *serve* puts the ball in play, much as a servant puts food on the table.

SERV 意思是"从属于"。*servant* 是用饭菜 *serves*(服侍)你并提供其他必要 *services*(服务)的人。网球或排球的 *serve*(发球)将球发出去,很像 *servant*(仆人)将食物端到桌子上一样。

SERV

serviceable \ˈsər-və-sə-bəl\ (1) Helpful or useful. 有帮助的;有用的 (2) Usable. 可用的

- In the attic they found some chairs and a table, which, with a new coat of paint, became quite serviceable for informal get-togethers. 在阁楼里,他们发现了一些椅子和一张桌子,刷漆之后,举行非正式聚会时还是很有用的。

Someone who speaks serviceable Spanish isn't fluent in it but gets by pretty well. A serviceable jacket is practical and maybe even rugged. But *serviceable* sometimes damns with faint praise. A serviceable performance is all right but not inspired. Serviceable curtains aren't the ideal color or pattern, but they *serve* their purpose. A serviceable pair of shoes is sturdy but won't win you any fashion points. 说 serviceable 西班牙语的人说得不流利,但可以很好地应付过去。serviceable 夹克衫很实用,可能甚至结实耐用。但是 *serviceable* 有时候表明褒实贬。serviceable 表演还不错,但并不优秀。serviceable 窗帘没有最理想的颜色或图案,但能 serve their purpose(满足需要)。一双 serviceable 鞋子很结实,但不会让人觉得你很时尚。

servile \ˈsər-ˌvīl\ (1) Suitable to a servant. 适合于仆人的 (2) Humbly submissive. 奴性的;恭顺的

- The dog's manner was servile, and it lacked a healthy independence. 狗的态度是奴

性的,缺乏健康的独立性。

During the Middle Ages, most of the farming was done by a *servile* class known as *serfs*, who enjoyed hardly any personal freedom. This began to change in the 14th century; but the Russian serfs weren't freed until the 1860s, when the servile class in the U. S. was also freed. But *servile* today usually refers to a personal manner; a person who shows *servility* usually isn't a *servant*, but simply seems too eager to please and seems to lack self-respect.

在中世纪,大部分农活是由被称为 *serfs*(农奴)的一个 servile 阶层完成的,他们几乎没有任何个人自由。在 14 世纪,这种状况开始改变了,但是俄国农奴直到 19 世纪 60 年代才得到自由。不过,今天 *servile*(逢迎的;恭顺的)通常指个人举止。一个表现出 *servility*(奴性)的人通常不是 *servant*(仆人),只是看上去太急于讨好他人,好像缺少自尊。

servitude \ˈsər-və-ˌtüd\ A state or condition of slavery or bondage to another. 奴役

• She spent an entire summer working at a resort under conditions that felt like utter servitude. 她整个夏天都在一个度假胜地工作,工作条件让她觉得是彻头彻尾的奴役。

Servitude is slavery or anything resembling it. The entire black population of colonial America lived in permanent servitude. And millions of the whites who populated this country arrived in "indentured servitude," obliged to pay off the cost of their journey with several years of labor. Servitude comes in many forms, of course: in the bad old days of the British navy, it was said that the difference between going to sea and going to jail was that you were less likely to drown in jail.

servitude 就是奴役或者任何与其相似的情况。在殖民时代的美国,全部黑人生活在 servitude 中。生活在这片土地上的数百万白人在"indentured servitude"(契约奴役)中到达这里,被迫劳动几年付清路费。当然,servitude 有多种形式:在英国海军的恶劣时代,据说出航和坐牢的差异是,你坐牢淹死的可能性小一些。

subservient\səb-ˈsər-vē-ənt\ (1) Serving or useful in an inferior situation or capacity. 充当下手的 (2) Slavishly obedient. 恭顺的;卑躬屈膝的

• Many have wondered why Congress always seems subservient to the financial industry, supporting it even when the voters are angrily calling for reforms. 很多人都想知道,为什么国会总是看上去对金融行业卑躬屈膝,甚至在投票人大声疾呼要求改革时,仍然对其进行支持。

Since *sub-* means "below," it emphasizes the lower position of the person in the subservient one. Soldiers of a given rank are always subservient to those of a higher rank; this *subservience* is symbolized by the requirement that they salute their superior at every opportunity. Women have often been forced into subservient relationships with men. A small nation may feel subservient to its more powerful neighbor, obliged to obey even when it doesn't want to. So subservience usually brings with it a good dose of resentment.

由于 *sub-* 意思是"在……下面",它强调处于下级地位者的较低地位。某一军阶的士兵总是对更高军阶的士兵毕恭毕敬,这种 *subservience*(恭顺;卑躬屈膝)的象征,就是有机会就向更高一级者敬礼这一要求。女性经常被迫处于向男性 subservient relations(卑躬屈膝的关系)中。小国可能 feel subservient to(感觉屈居于……之下)强大的邻国,被迫在即使不情愿时也要俯首听命。所以,subservience 通常会带来很多怨恨。

UNIT 22

CLUS comes from the Latin *claudere*, "to close." Words based on the Latin verb often have forms in which the *d* becomes an *s*. So, for example, *include*, which once meant "to shut up or enclose" and now means "to contain," has the related word *inclusive*, which means "including everything."
CLUB 源自意为"关闭"的拉丁语词语 *claudere*。以这一动词为基础的词语，通常具有其中的 *d* 变为 *s* 的情况。所以，比如 *include* 曾经的意思是"关闭或包围"，现在的意思是"包含"。它有相关词语 *inclusive*，意思是"无所不包的"。

occlusion \ə-ˈklü-zhən\ An obstruction or blockage; the act of obstructing or closing off. 障碍；堵塞；阻挡；封死

• The doctors worry that a loosened piece of plaque from the artery wall could lead to an occlusion of a brain artery, resulting in a stroke. 医生担心的是，动脉壁上脱落的一个斑块，会导致脑动脉堵塞，进而出现中风。

Occlusion, formed with the prefix *ob-*, here meaning "in the way," occurs when something has been closed up or blocked off. Almost all heart attacks are the result of the occlusion of a coronary (heart) artery by a blood clot, and many strokes are caused by an occlusion in an artery serving the brain. When a person's upper and lower teeth form a *malocclusion*, they close incorrectly or badly. An occlusion, or *occluded* front, happens when a fast-moving cold front overtakes a slow-moving warm front and slides underneath it, lifting the warm air and blocking its movement.
occlusion 用前缀 ob-（这里的意思是"妨碍"）构成，出现于某物被堵住或封闭时。几乎所有的心脏病发作都由冠状动脉被血块堵塞所致，很多中风都由于为大脑供血的某根动脉出现堵塞引起。当人的上下牙齿形成 *malocclusion*（咬合不正）时，它们没有正确闭合或闭合不佳。occlusion（锢囚锋），或者 *occluded* front 发生的原因是，快速移动的冷锋追上慢速移动的暖锋，并滑到其下方，将其抬起，阻碍其运动。

exclusive \iks-ˈklü-siv\ (1) Not shared; available to only one person or group, especially those from a high social class. 独有的；专用的；排外的 (2) Full and complete. 完整的

• That technology is exclusive to one cell-phone manufacturer, but some of the others are dying to use it. 那一技术是某一手机生产商独有的，但是其他生产商都很想使用。

In words such as *expel*, *export*, and *exclusive*, the prefix *ex-* means "out of, outside." Thus, to *exclude* means basically to close the door in order to keep someone or something out. When the word appears in an advertisement, it's often making an appeal to snobs. An "exclusive" offer is supposedly made to only a few people; not so many years ago, "exclusive" housing developments excluded those of a certain race or color. If a product is being sold *exclusively* by one store, you won't be able to find it anywhere else. When a newspaper or news show has an *exclusive*, it's a story that no one else has yet reported. *Exclusive*'s antonym is *inclusive*; an inclusive policy, an inclusive church, or an inclusive approach is one that aims to include as many people as possible.

· 533 ·

在 *expel*,*export* 和 *exclusive* 这样的词语中,前缀 *ex* 的意思是"离开,在……外面"。这样,*exclude* 的基本上意思是关上门,让某人待在外面。这一词语在广告中出现时,就是在吸引自命不凡的人。"exclusive"("专用的")东西只给少数人,就在几年前,"exclusive"("专有")房产开发将某一种族或肤色的人排除在外。如果一种产品由某一商店 *exclusively*(独家)销售,你在别的地方是看不到的。当某一报纸或新闻节目有一个 *exclusive*(独家新闻),那就是一个别人尚未报道的故事。*exclusive* 的反义词是 *inclusive*。一个 inclusive 方针、一个 inclusive 教堂、一个 inclusive 处理方法,旨在包括尽可能多的人。

recluse \ˈre-ˌklüs\   A person who lives withdrawn from society. 隐士

* The lonely farmhouse was home to a middle-aged recluse, a stooped, bearded man who would never answer the door when someone knocked. 这个孤零零的农舍住着一个中年隐士,一个弯腰驼背、留着小胡子的男人,谁敲门也不开门。

Greta Garbo and Howard Hughes were two of the most famously *reclusive* celebrities of modern times. She had been a great international star, called the most beautiful woman in the world; he had been an aircraft manufacturer and film producer, with one of the greatest fortunes in the world. It seems that Garbo's *reclusiveness* resulted from her desire to leave her public with only the youthful image of her face. Hughes was terrified of germs, though that was the least of his problems.

葛丽泰·嘉宝和霍华德·修斯是当代最著名的 *reclusive* celebrities(隐士名人)。她曾是伟大的国际明星,被称为世界最美丽的女性;他曾是一位飞机制造商和电影制片人,是世界上最富裕的人之一。嘉宝的 *reclusiveness*(离群索居)源自她要留给公众一个年轻的容颜的愿望。修斯对细菌感到惊恐,虽然这是他最小的问题。

seclusion \si-ˈklü-zhən\   (1) A screening or hiding from view. 隐藏 (2) A place that is isolated or hidden. 孤立之地;隐藏之地

* The police immediately placed him in seclusion in a hospital room, with armed guards at the door. 警察马上就发现他隐藏在一个医院病房,门口是荷枪实弹的卫兵。

With its prefix *se-*, "apart," *seclusion* has the basic meaning of a place or condition that's "closed away." A lone island may be *secluded*, and its seclusion might be what its owner prizes most about it. Presidents and their staffs may go into seclusion before making critical decisions. Monastery life is purposely secluded, and monks may have taken vows to live lives of seclusion. The deadly brown *recluse* spider prefers seclusion but is sometimes disturbed by very unlucky people.

有了前缀 *se*-("分离的"),*seclusion* 的基本意思是一个"分隔在外"的地方或状况。一个孤零零的岛屿会是 *secluded*(与世隔绝的),其 seclusion(与世隔绝)可能是其主人最自豪的。总统及其工作人员在做出重要决定之前会 go into seclusion(隐藏起来)。修道院的生活是专门要 secluded(与世隔绝的),修道士可能曾发誓要过 lives of seclusion(隐居生活)。致命的 brown recluse spider(隐士蜘蛛)更喜欢 seclusion(隐居),但有时候会被很不幸的人打扰。

Quizzes

A. Complete the analogy:

1. freedom : liberty :: servitude : _____
   a. determination   b. arrangement   c. slavery   d. work

2. inclusive : many :: exclusive : _____
   a. everyone   b. numerous   c. few   d. snobbish
3. considerate : thoughtless :: subservient : _____
   a. boastful   b. bossy   c. decisive   d. unique
4. monk : pray :: recluse : _____
   a. deny   b. receive   c. reclaim   d. hide
5. fashionable : stylish :: serviceable : _____
   a. useless   b. devoted   c. fundamental   d. adequate
6. progress : advance :: occlusion : _____
   a. dismissal   b. obstruction   c. prevention   d. denial
7. dominant : aggressive :: servile : _____
   a. saving   b. sensitive   c. obedient   d. forgetful
8. conclusion : ending :: seclusion : _____
   a. refusal   b. relaxation   c. isolation   d. denial

B. Indicate whether the following pairs of words have the same or different meanings:

1. occlusion / stroke   same ____ / different ____
2. subservient / military   same ____ / different ____
3. recluse / hermit   same ____ / different ____
4. serviceable / usable   same ____ / different ____
5. exclusive / sole   same ____ / different ____
6. servitude / enslavement   same ____ / different ____
7. seclusion / solitude   same ____ / different ____
8. servile / humble   same ____ / different ____

Greek and Latin Borrowings 希腊语和拉丁语借词

acme \ˈak-mē\   Highest point; summit, peak. 顶峰；巅峰；高峰

• Last Saturday's upset victory over Michigan may prove to have been the acme of the entire season. 上周六芝加哥公牛队被意外战胜可能会是整个赛季的巅峰。

In Greek, *acme* meant a mountain peak, but in English we hardly ever use it in the physical sense. Instead we speak of someone's new job as the acme of her career, or of a certain leap as the acme of classical dance technique. In old Road Runner cartoons, the Acme Company is the provider of every ingenious device imaginable. But the word can't always be taken quite literally as a brand or company name; it's possible, for instance, that something called the Acme Bar & Grill may not be the absolutely highest and best example of a bar and grill. And don't confuse *acme* with *acne*, the skin disorder—even though both actually come from the same word.

在希腊语中，*acme* 意思是山峰，但在英语中，我们几乎不会使用其与具体事物相关的意思。相反，我们说某人的新工作是其生涯的顶峰，或者某一跳跃动作是古典舞技术的顶峰。在以前的跑路者卡通片中，顶峰公司提供你能想到的

每一种巧妙装置。但是,这一词语并不总是可以从字面意思理解为一个商标或公司名称。比如,有可能叫做 Acme Bar & Grill (顶峰烧烤) 的餐厅不一定是最高明、最好的烧烤餐厅。不要把 acme 和表示皮肤疾病的 acne (痤疮;粉刺) 搞混了,虽然两者实际上源自同一个词语。

catharsis\kə-'thär-səs\ A cleansing or purification of the body, emotions, or spirit. 净化;精神宣泄

● Having broken down sobbing at the funeral, he said afterwards that it had felt like a catharsis. 难以自控地葬礼上抽泣之后,他后来说那感觉像一次精神宣泄。

One of the earliest uses of *catharsis* is in Aristotle's *Poetics*, where the philosopher claims that watching a tragedy provides the spectators with a desirable catharsis because of the buildup and release of the emotions of pity and fear. Sigmund Freud borrowed the term as a name for the process of bringing a set of unconscious desires and ideas back into consciousness in order to eliminate their bad effects. Today some people claim it's cathartic to merely express your anger or grief, since it "gets it out of your system." Laxatives are also called cathartic, since they provide a physical catharsis that some people believe to be healthful. But there's no general agreement about any of this, and the notion of catharsis remains a very personal one.

catharsis 最早的使用之一是在亚里士多德的《诗学》中。这位哲学家在作品中声称,观看一出悲剧会给观众提供一次他们渴望的 catharsis (精神宣泄),原因是同情和恐惧情绪积累之后得到了释放。西格蒙德•弗洛伊德把该词借来,用来命名那个为了除去其不良效果而将一系列无意识的欲望和想法带回到意识当中的过程。今天,有些人声称,仅仅表达愤怒或者悲伤就是 cathartic (起宣泄作用的),因为它"让它离开了你的身体"。缓泻药也被称为是 cathartic (导泻的),因为这些药能提供一个有些人认为有利于健康的身体的 catharsis (净化)。但是,有关这几点,哪个也没有一个一致看法,catharsis 这一观念仍然是很个人化的。

colossus\kə-'lä-səs\ (1) A gigantic statue. 巨大雕像 (2) A person or thing that resembles such a statue in size or activity or influence. 巨人;庞然大物;伟人;影响巨大的事物

● Even if *Citizen Kane* had been his only movie, Orson Welles would be regarded as a colossus in the history of film. 即使《公民凯恩》是他唯一的一部电影,奥森•威尔斯也会成为电影史上的伟人。

The original *colossi* (notice the plural form) were the larger-than-life statues made by the Greeks and Romans. The most famous of these was the *Colossus* of Rhodes, a statue of the sun god Helios built on the Greek island of Rhodes around 280 B.C. that was over 100 feet tall and took more than 12 years to build. The Statue of Liberty is a modern colossus, enormous and stately, at the entrance to New York Harbor. And someone who has played a *colossal* role in history, such as Winston Churchill, may be called a colossus as well.

最早的 colossi (巨大雕像) (注意复数形式) 是古希腊人和古罗马人制作的巨大雕像。其中最著名的是罗德岛巨像,这是太阳神赫利俄斯的雕像,于公元前 280 年被建在希腊的罗德岛上。雕像高度超过 100 英尺,花了超过 12 年的时间才建成。自由女神像是一个当代巨像,高大而端庄,位于纽约港的入口处。在历史上发挥 colossal (巨大的) 作用的人,比如温斯顿•丘吉尔,也可以称为 colossus (伟人)。

detritus \ di-ˈtrī-təs \   Loose material that results from disintegration; debris. 岩屑；碎片
• The base of the cliff was littered with the detritus of centuries of erosion. 悬崖底部散落着几个世纪以来侵蚀留下的碎石。

After the first hard freeze of fall, gardens are sadly littered with the detritus of the summer's plants and produce: stalks, leaves, vines, rotted vegetables, and maybe even a hand trowel left behind. As the flooding Mississippi River retreats back to its ordinary course, it leaves detritus behind in its wake, debris gathered from everywhere by the raging waters. The detritus of civilization may include junkyards and abandoned buildings; mental detritus may includes all kinds of useless trivia. Notice how this word is pronounced; for some reason, people often try to accent the first syllable rather than the second. 秋天第一次坚冻之后，园子里凄惨地散落着夏天植物和农产品的残留物：茎秆、叶子、藤蔓、腐烂的蔬菜，可能甚至还有丢下的泥铲。随着泛滥的密西西比河水退回到原来的河道，后面留下的是 detritus，也就是汹涌的河水从各处聚集来的杂物。文明的 detritus 可能包括废物堆积场和遗弃的建筑物，金属 detritus 可能包括各种没用的琐碎物品。注意这一词语的发音；由于某种原因，人们常常想要重读第一个音而不是第二个音。

hoi polloi \ ˌhȯi-pə-ˈlȯi \   The general population; the masses. 民众；大众
• He's a terrible snob, the kind of person who thinks it's funny to say things like "the riffraff" and "the hoi polloi" and "the great unwashed." 他很势利，是那种觉得说了"the riffraff"（乌合之众）和"the hoi polloi"以及"the great unwashed"（下层民众）就很滑稽的人。

In Greek, *hoi polloi* means simply "the many." (Even though *hoi* itself means "the," in English we almost always say "the hoi polloi.") It comes originally from the famous Funeral Oration by Pericles, where it was actually used in a positive way. Today it's generally used by people who think of themselves as superior—though it's also sometimes used in Pericles' democratic spirit. By the way, it has no relation to *hoity-toity*, meaning "stuck-up," which starts with the same sound but has nothing to do with Greek. 在希腊语中，*hoi polloi* 意思很简单，就是"众多人"。(尽管 *hoi* 本身意思是"the"，我们在英语中几乎总是说"the hoi polloi"。) 它最初源自伯里克利著名的《祭文》，实际上意思是肯定的。今天，它通常被那些自认为高人一等的人使用——虽然它有时也按照伯里克利的民主精神使用。顺便说一下，它与 *hoity-toity*（自大的）没有关系，后者第一个音与它是一样的，但是跟希腊语毫无关系。

kudos \ ˈkü-ˌdōz \   (1) Fame and renown that result from an achievement; prestige. (成就带来的)声誉；声望 (2) Praise. 赞扬
• His first film earned him kudos at the independent film festivals, and the big studios were soon calling him up. 他的第一部电影在独立电影节上为他赢得了声誉，大型电影制片厂很快就给他打电话了。

Kudos is an odd word in English. In Greek, *kydos* meant "glory" or "prestige"; in other words, it wasn't something you could count. But in English *kudos* looks like a plural and is therefore often treated as one. So people now sometimes use the form *kudo*, with *kudos* as its plural.

kudos 在英语中是个奇怪的词语。在希腊语中，*kydos* 意思是"荣耀"或者"声望"，换句话说，它不是可以数的东西。但是，在英语中，*kudos* 看起来像是复数形式，因此常常被当做复数形式。所以，人们有时候使用 *kudo* 这一形式，把 *kudos* 当做复数形式。

onus \ˈō-nəs\   A disagreeable necessity or obligation; responsibility. 负担；责任

● Now that Congress has passed the bill, the onus is on the President to live up to his promise and sign it into law. 既然国会已经通过了这样法案，总统的责任就是履行承诺，签名使其成为法律。

In Latin *onus* means literally a "burden," like a particularly heavy backpack. But in English an onus is more often a burden of responsibility or blame. In legal language, the *onus probandi* is the "burden of proof," meaning the big job of assembling enough evidence to prove a person's guilt, since the accused is innocent until proved guilty.

在拉丁语中，*onus* 字面意思是"负担"，就像一个特别沉重的背包。但是，在英语中，*onus* 更多的时候表示成为负担的责任或者职责。在法律语言中，*onus probandi* 是"举证责任"，意思是搜集足够证据来证明某人有罪这项重大工作，因为被指控者在证明有罪之前是无辜的。

stigma \ˈstig-mə\   A mark of shame; stain. 耻辱；污点

● In these small villages, the stigma of pregnancy is a terrible thing for an unmarried girl. 在这些小村庄，未婚先孕这一耻辱对未婚女孩来说是一件可怕的事情。

In Greek and Latin, a *stigma* was a mark or brand, especially one that marked a slave, so a stigma marked a person as inferior. When the plural form *stigmata* is used, it usually refers to the nail wounds on Christ's hands and feet, wounds which have sometimes reappeared on the hands or feet of later worshippers such as St. Francis. When *stigma* began to be used in English, it usually meant the kind of mark or stain you can't actually see. So today we hear about the stigma of homelessness, the stigma of overweight, and the stigma of mental illness. People may be so afraid of being *stigmatized* for losing a job that they'll put on their office clothes and drive out their driveways every weekday morning so that the neighbors won't know.

在希腊语和拉丁语中，*stigma* 是记号或者烙印，尤其是标明奴隶身份的那种。所以，*stigma* 标明某人地位低下。其复数形式 *stigmata* 通常指基督手上和脚上的钉伤。这种伤有时重现在后来的崇拜者比如圣弗朗西斯的手脚上。*stigma* 在英语中开始使用时，通常指我们实际上看不到的标记或污点。所以，今天我们会听到人们说无家可归的耻辱、身体肥胖的耻辱、精神病的耻辱。人们也可能害怕因为失去工作而 *stigmatized*（被人羞辱），于是，工作日的每天早上，他们穿上办公室工作服，把车开出私家车道，这样邻居就被蒙在鼓里了。

Quizzes

Fill in each blank with the correct letter:

a. kudos
b. colossus
c. acme
d. catharsis
e. hoi polloi
f. detritus
g. stigma
h. onus

1. Now that they have apologized, the _____ is on you to do the same.
2. The storm waves had left the beach littered with _____.
3. For many years Microsoft has remained the _____ of the software industry, feared by all its competitors.
4. In the 1950s the _____ of divorce was strong enough that a divorced man almost couldn't run for high office.
5. She says she and her fellow stars would never go near a restaurant where the _____ might be eating.
6. At the _____ of his racing career, Bold Ruler won the Kentucky Derby.
7. His painting is obviously a kind of _____ for him, and his works are filled with violent images.
8. A young Korean pianist has been winning _____ from critics worldwide.

Review Quizzes

A. Complete the analogy:

1. rule : regulation :: stricture : _____
   a. criticism   b. injury   c. dislike   d. bravery
2. demanding : effortless :: tortuous : _____
   a. twisting   b. winding   c. straight   d. descending
3. expensive : costly :: exclusive : _____
   a. indirect   b. fantastic   c. experienced   d. fashionable
4. criticism : error :: kudos : _____
   a. praise   b. prestige   c. blame   d. achievement
5. experiment : subject :: vivisection : _____
   a. botany   b. biology   c. bacteria   d. animals
6. inspect : examine :: construe : _____
   a. condemn   b. continue   c. contend   d. interpret
7. appropriate : take :: expropriate : _____
   a. proclaim   b. seize   c. expel   d. complete
8. funny : comical :: acerbic : _____

a. distrustful   b. sarcastic   c. witty   d. cheerful
9. praise : compliment :: onus : _____
   a. load   b. habit   c. obligation   d. reputation
10. capable : helpless :: serviceable : _____
    a. useless   b. useful   c. practical   d. formal

B. Fill in each blank with the correct letter:

a. extort
b. exacerbate
c. appropriate
d. constrict
e. detritus
f. convivial
g. servitude
h. infrastructure
i. tortuous
j. seclusion
k. vivacious
l. colossus
m. restrictive
n. propriety
o. occlusion

1. The collapsing bridge was only the latest evidence of the city's deteriorating _____.

2. She began a long and _____ explanation of why she had stayed out so late, but her parents weren't buying it.

3. The _____ of the mountain hut was just what she needed to begin serious work on her book.

4. The children at the orphanage lived in a condition of genuine _____, often working from dawn to dusk.

5. They often joined their neighbors for a _____ evening of scrabble or charades.

6. The steep bank had become a dumping ground, and _____ of all kinds lay at the bottom.

7. His diet had been terrible for years, so he wasn't surprised when the doctor reported a near _____ of one coronary artery.

8. The company's new standards of _____ prohibited taking any large gifts from salespeople.

9. There were several _____ clauses in the house contract, including one that required weekly mowing of the lawn.

10. The statue for the plaza would be a 30-foot-high _____ representing Atlas holding the globe.

11. She had been a _____ teenager, but had become rather quiet and serious by her thirties.

12. She was forced to practically _____ the money from her husband with threats.

13. Dr. Moss warned him that any drinking would only _____ his condition.
14. The legislature had decided to _____ funds for new harbor facilities.
15. She feared that marriage and a family would _____ her life unbearably.

C. Choose the closest definition:

1. acerbic   a. spicy   b. tangy   c. mild
   d. stinging
2. deconstruction   a. analysis   b. destruction
   c. breaking   d. theory
3. acme   a. monument   b. peak   c. honor
   d. award
4. subservient   a. arrogant   b. submissive
   c. demanding   d. underneath
5. contort   a. torture   b. twist   c. turn
   d. twirl
6. instrumental   a. instructive   b. intelligent
   c. helpful   d. fortunate
7. catharsis   a. explosion   b. cleansing   c. pollution
   d. cough
8. acrid   a. pleasant   b. crazed   c. irritating
   d. soothing
9. stigma   a. sting   b. statue   c. stain
   d. stalk
10. recluse   a. spider   b. hermit   c. request
    d. hiding place
11. acrimony   a. breakup   b. dispute   c. bitterness
    d. custody
12. propriety   a. misbehavior   b. suitability   c. harassment
    d. drama
13. servile   a. efficient   b. pleasant   c. humble
    d. unnerving
14. tort   a. cake   b. twist   c. wrong
    d. law
15. revivify   a. retreat   b. rewrite   c. reappear
    d. refresh

UNIT 23

TEXT comes from a Latin verb that means "to weave." So a *textile* is a woven or knitted cloth. The material it's made from determines its *texture*, the smoothness or roughness of its surface. And individual words are "woven" into sentences and paragraphs to form a *text*.

TEXT 源自拉丁语中表示"织"的一个动词。所以一块 *textile* 就是一块纺织或者编织的布料。布料的材料决定其 *texture*（质地），也就是其表面光滑还是粗糙。单个的词语"织"成句子和段落，从而构成 *text*（文本）。

textual\ˈteks-chə-wəl\ Having to do with or based on a text. 文本的；以文本为基础的

- A textual analysis of 1,700 lipstick names, including Hot Mama and Raisin Hell, suggested to the author that the women buying them lack a healthy sense of self-worth. 对一千七百个唇膏（包括 Hot Mama 和 Raisin Hell）名称进行的文本分析让作者知道，购买这些唇膏的女性缺乏健康的自我价值感。

Before the invention of the printing press, books were produced by hand. When the *text* of a book is copied this way, *textual* errors can creep in, and a text that's been copied again and again can contain many such errors. By comparing different copies of a work, textual critics try to figure out where the copyists went wrong and restore the text to its original form so that modern readers can again enjoy the correct versions of ancient texts. When a class performs textual analysis of a poem, however, they are looking closely at its individual words and phrases in an effort to determine the poem's meanings.

印刷机发明之前，书籍是手工制作的。书的 *text*（文本）被手工抄写时，文本错误就会悄然出现，一再抄写的文本就会包含很多这样的错误。通过对同一作品的不同副本进行比较，文本评论家努力发现抄写人出错的地方，并将文本恢复到最初的形式，从而使当代读者享受古老文本的正确版本。然而，当全班学生对一首诗歌进行文本分析时，他们仔细查看的是单个的词语和短语，以此来努力分析诗歌的意思。

context\ˈkän-ˌtekst\ （1）The surrounding spoken or written material in which a word or remark occurs. (一个词语或一句话的)语境 (2) The conditions or circumstances in which an event occurs; environment or setting. (事件发生的)环境；背景

• The governor claimed that his remarks were taken out of context and that anyone looking at the whole speech would get a different impression. 州长说,他的话被人从语境中孤立出来了,所以任何人看了整个演讲就会获得不同的印象。

Context reveals meaning. The context of an unfamiliar word can give us *contextual* clues to help us determine what the word means. Taking a remark out of context can change its meaning entirely. Likewise, people's actions sometimes have to be understood as having occurred in a particular context. The behavior of historical figures should be seen in the context of their time, when standards may have been very different from our own.

context(语境)揭示意义。生词的语境可以给予我们 contextual(语境的)线索,帮助我们确定词语的意思。使一句话脱离语境可能会彻底改变其意思。同样,人们的行动有时候必须理解为发生在一定的 context(环境)中。历史人物的行为应该放在他们的时代环境中来看待,因为当时的标准跟我们今天的差异很大。

hypertext \ˈhī-pər-ˌtekst\ A database format in which information related to that on a display screen can be accessed directly from the screen (as by a mouse click). 超文本

• Three days ago my mother was asking me why some of the words are underlined in blue, but by yesterday she was already an expert in hypertext. 三天前,我妈妈还在问我为什么有些词语下面画蓝线,可是到了昨天,她已经是超文本方面的专家了。

Since *hyper-* generally means "above, beyond" (see HYPER, p. 493), hypertext is something that's gone beyond the limitations of ordinary text. Thus, unlike the text in a book, hypertext permits you, by clicking with a mouse, to immediately access text in one of millions of different electronic sources. Hypertext is now so familiar that most computer users may not even know the word, which was coined by Ted Nelson back in the early 1960s. It took a few more years for hypertext to actually be created, by Douglas Engelbart, and then quite a few more years before the introduction of the World Wide Web in 1991.

由于 *hyper* 的意思一般来说是"在……上方,超越"(见 HYPER,第 493 页),超文本就是超越一般文本限制的文本。因此,与书籍文本不同的是,超文本可以让你通过用鼠标点击就可以马上在数百万不同的电子文本来源中找到所需文本。现在人们对超文本太熟悉了,大多数电脑用户甚至不知道 20 世纪 60 年代泰德·纳尔逊发明的这个词语。又过了几年,超文本才被道格拉斯·恩格尔巴特真正创建出来。之后,又过了好几年,万维网才于 1991 年开始使用。

subtext \ˈsəb-ˌtekst\ The underlying meaning of a spoken or written passage. (话语或文字)暗含的意思

• The tough and cynical tone of the story is contradicted by its romantic subtext. 这一故事粗犷、悲观的情调与其浪漫的暗含意义相矛盾。

A literary text often has more than one meaning: the literal meaning of the words on the page, and their hidden meaning, what exists "between the lines"—the subtext. Arthur Miller's play *The Crucible*, for example, is about the Salem witchcraft trials of the 17th century, but its subtext is the comparison of those trials with the "witch hunts" of the 1950s, when many people were unfairly accused of being communists. Even a social conversation between a man and a woman may have a subtext, but you may have to listen very closely to figure out what it is. Don't confuse *subtext* with *subplot*, a less important plot that moves along in parallel with the main plot.

文学文本常常有不止一种意义:页面上词语的字面意义,还有隐含的意思,也就是存在于"字里行间"的意思。比如,阿瑟·米勒的戏剧《熔炉》讲的是 17 世纪塞勒姆的女巫审判,但是,其背后动机是将这些审判与 20 世纪 50 年代的"猎巫行动"进行比较。当时,很多人被不公正地指责为共产主义者。即使男女之间社交性的谈话也可能有隐含意义,但是你必须仔细倾听才能明白是什么。不要将 subtext 与 subplot 弄混了,后者的意思是与主要情节平行发展的次要情节。

PLAC comes from the Latin *placere*, "to please or be agreeable to," or *placare*, "to soothe or calm." *Pleasant*, *pleasurable*, and *pleasing* all derive from this root, even though their spelling makes it hard to see.

PLAC 源自拉丁语 *placere*,意思是"讨好或者讨某人欢心",或者 *placare*,意思是"安慰或者使某人平静"。*pleasant*, *pleasurable* 以及 *pleasing* 都源自这一词根,尽管他们的拼写很难让人看出这一点。

---

placate \ˈplā-ˌkāt\ To calm the anger or bitterness of someone. 安慰;抚慰

• The Romans had a number of ways of placating the gods, which occasionally included burying slaves alive. 罗马人有几种方式来抚慰诸神,偶尔包括活埋奴隶。

Politicians are constantly having to placate angry voters. Diplomats frequently need to placate a country's allies or possible enemies. Parents are always placating kids who think they've been unfairly denied something. And lovers and spouses are some of the champion placaters. It's no secret that people with the best social skills are often the best at placating other people—and that they themselves may be the ones who benefit the most by it.

政客总是不得不安慰愤怒的选民。外交官时不时地需要安慰一个国家的盟国或者可能成为敌人的国家。父母总是安慰索要某个东西遭到拒绝而感觉委屈的孩子。恋人和夫妻也最善于安慰彼此。社交技能最好的人常常最会安慰他人,自己最能从中受益,这已经不是什么秘密了。

---

placebo \plə-ˈsē-bō\ A harmless substance given to a patient in place of genuine medication, either for experimental purposes or to soothe the patient. (为达到实验目的或者安慰病人而使用的无害的)安慰剂

• The placebo worked miraculously: his skin rash cleared up, his sleep improved, and he even ceased to hear voices. 这种安慰剂效果神奇;他的皮疹消失了,睡眠改善了,他甚至不再听到人声了。

Doctors doing research on new treatments for disease often give one group a placebo while a second group takes the new medication. Since those in the placebo group usually believe they're getting the real thing, their own hopeful attitude may bring about improvement in their condition. Thus, for the real drug to be considered effective, it must produce even better results than the placebo. Placebos have another use as well. A doctor who suspects that a patient's physical symptoms are psychologically produced may prescribe a placebo in the hope that mentally produced symptoms can also be mentally cured.

研究疾病新疗法的医生常常给一组人使用安慰剂,给第二组人使用新药。由于使用安慰剂的那组人通常相信自己使用的是真药,他们满怀信心的态度可能使其病情改善。这样,要使真药让人觉得有效,它就得产生比安慰剂更好的疗效。安慰剂还有另外一种用途。医生如果怀疑病人的身体症状是心理引起的,可能会开一些安慰剂,希望精神产生的症状也可以精神治疗。

placidity \ pla-ˈsi-də-tē \ Serene freedom from interruption or disturbance; calmness. 平静

• Her placidity seemed eerie in view of the destruction she had witnessed and the huge loss she had suffered. 她目睹了这次大破坏以及自己遭受的巨大损失。考虑到这一点,她能够如此平静,似乎很奇怪。

A *placid* lake has a smooth surface untouched by wind. A placid scene is one in which everything seems calm; it may even include a meadow with a few placid cows grazing on it. Someone with a *placid* personality has an inner peacefulness that isn't easily disturbed. As a personality trait, *placidity* is surely a lot better than some of the alternatives; however, the word sometimes describes people who are also a bit passive, like those contented cows.

一个 placid 湖泊水面平滑,没有风的干扰。一个 placid 场面,其中一切都是平静的,甚至包括草坪,上面有几头 placid 牛在吃草。性格 placid 的人,其内心的宁静不易被打破。作为一种性格特点,placidity 毫无疑问要比某些其他特点好很多;不过,这一词语有时候用来描述有点被动的人,就像那些心满意足的牛一样。

implacable \ im-ˈpla-kə-bəl \ Not capable of being pleased, satisfied, or changed. 无法讨好的;无法满足的;无法改变的

• Attempts to negotiate a peace settlement between such implacable enemies seem doomed to failure. 要在这样不共戴天的敌对双方之间努力达成和平协议,注定是要失败的。

Implacable, with its negative prefix *im-*, describes something or someone that can't be calmed or soothed or altered. A person who carries a grudge feels an implacable resentment—a resentment that can't be soothed. An implacable foe is one you can't negotiate with, perhaps one who's fueled by implacable hatred. And *implacable* sometimes describes things that only seem to be alive: an implacable storm is one that seems as if it will never let up, and an implacable fate is one that you can't outrun or hide from.

implacable 因为有 im- 这一表示否定的前缀,所以用来描述无法安慰、抚慰或者改变的人或物。怀恨在心的人感到的是 implacable 愤恨——无法平息的愤恨。implacable 敌人是你无法与其谈判的人,可能是一个为 implacable 怨恨所刺激的人。implacable 有时用来描述只是似乎有生命力的事物:一场 implacable 暴风雨就是看似永远不会减弱的暴风雨,一个 implacable 命运是你无法逃避的命运。

PLAC

Quizzes

A. Fill in each blank with the correct letter:

a. placebo   e. subtext
b. textual   f. implacable
c. placate   g. hypertext
d. context   h. placidity

1. When the sentence was taken out of _____, it sounded quite different.

2. An _____ mob had been demonstrating outside the presidential palace for two weeks now, with their numbers growing from day to day.

3. Many young people wonder how anyone ever did research without the benefit of _____ links.

4. It took a week of bringing flowers home every day to _____ his wife.

5. The deeper meaning of many literary works lies in their _____.

6. The group of patients who were given a _____ did as well as those who were given the real drug.

7. The study of poetry normally requires careful _____ analysis.

8. The _____ of the quiet countryside was soothing after a week in the city.

B. Match the word on the left to the correct definition on the right:

1. placate   a. relating to written matter
2. context   b. unyielding
3. placebo   c. underlying meaning
4. textual   d. soothe
5. placidity   e. setting of spoken or written words
6. subtext   f. harmless substitute
7. implacable   g. computer links
8. hypertext   h. peacefulness

AUT/AUTO

AUT/AUTO comes from the Greek word for "same" or "self." Something *automatic* operates by itself, and an *automobile* moves by itself, without the help of a horse. An *autograph* is in the handwriting of the person him- or herself, and an *autopsy* is an inspection of a corpse by an examiner's own eyes.

AUT/AUTO 源自希腊语表示"同样"或"自己"的词语。automatic(自动的)事物不需外力操作,automobile(汽车)自己即可移动,无需马匹牵引。autograph(亲笔签名)是某人亲笔写的,autopsy(尸检)是检查者用自己的眼睛对尸体进行的检查。

UNIT 23

automaton \ȯ-ˈtä-mə-tən\ (1) An automatic machine, especially a robot. 自动操作装置;机器人 (2) An individual who acts mechanically. 机械行事的人

• The work he used to do as a welder in the assembly plant has been taken over by a sophisticated automaton designed overseas. 他过去在装配厂当焊工时做的工作已被国外设计的一种精密的自动化机器所取代。

The idea of the automaton has fascinated people for many centuries. A traveler to the emperor's court in Byzantium in A.D. 949 reported that mechanical birds sat in a golden tree singing the songs of their species; that mechanical lions flanked the throne, roaring and switching their great tails; and that, as he stood watching, the emperor's throne suddenly shot upward toward the high ceiling, and when it slowly descended the emperor was wearing new robes. Early automata (notice the common plural form) often relied on water, steam, or falling weights to power them. Today automata, often called robots, are used in manufacturing plants to build not only vehicles but also much smaller electronic equipment. 自动操作装置这一想法让人们着迷数个世纪了。公元949年,到过拜占庭皇帝朝廷的一位旅行家报告说:自动鸟站在一棵黄金树上唱着它们自己的歌曲;自动狮子站在宝座两旁,吼叫着而且摆动着巨大的尾巴;他站在那里观看时,皇帝的宝座突然朝天花板射了出去,慢慢降落时,皇帝却穿上了新袍子。早期的 *automata*(注意这一常见复数形式)常常依赖水、汽或者落下的重物来提供动力。今天,automata 通常称为机器人,用在工厂,不但制造交通工具,也制造小得多的电子设备。

autoimmune\ˌȯ-tō-im-ˈyün\ Of, relating to, or caused by antibodies that attack molecules, cells, or tissues of the organism producing them. 自体免疫的;自身免疫的

• His doctors suspected that the strange combination of symptoms might be those of an autoimmune disease. 医生怀疑,他这奇怪的混合症状可能是一种自体免疫疾病的症状。

Any healthy body produces a variety of antibodies, proteins in the blood whose job is to protect the body from unwanted bacteria, viruses, and cancer cells. The cells and organs that deal with such infections make up the immune system. In some people and animals, for various reasons, the antibodies become overactive and turn on the body's healthy tissues as well; the result is an autoimmune disease—an immune response directed against one's own self. More than eighty autoimmune diseases have been identified, the best-known being type 1 diabetes, multiple sclerosis, lupus, and rheumatoid arthritis. 任何健康的身体都产生各种各样的抗体,也就是血液中的蛋白质,其职责是保护身体免受不必要的细菌、病毒和癌细胞的侵袭。由于各种原因,在某些人和动物体内,抗体过于活跃,也会攻击体内健康的组织,结果就产生了一种 autoimmune(自体免疫的)疾病——针对自身的免疫反应。目前已经识别出了八十多种自身免疫疾病,最有名的是1型糖尿病、多发性硬化、狼疮和类风湿性关节炎。

autonomy\ȯ-ˈtä-nə-mē\ (1) The power or right of self-government. 自治权 (2) Self-directing freedom, especially moral independence. 自主;自主权

• Though normally respectful of their son's autonomy, the Slocums drew the line at his request to take a cross-country motorcycle trip. 虽然通常情况下尊重儿子的自主权,

斯洛克姆夫妇还是不允许他进行越野摩托车旅行。

Since *nomos* is Greek for "law," something *autonomous* makes its own laws. The amount of *autonomy* enjoyed by French-speaking Quebec, or of Palestinians in certain towns in Israel, have become major issues. The autonomy of individual states in the United States has posed serious constitutional questions for two centuries. The autonomy of children is almost always limited by their parents. But when those parents are elderly and begin driving poorly and getting confused about their finances, their children may see the need to limit their autonomy in much the same way.

由于 *nomos* 在希腊语中意思是"法律",*autonomous*(自治的,自主的)事物制定自己的法律。说法语的魁北克省、以色列某些城镇的巴勒斯坦人所享受的自主程度,已经成为重要话题。美国各州的自主权在过去两个世纪已经构成了宪法问题。孩子的自主权几乎总是受到父母的限制。但是,当父母年迈、开车技术下降、经济问题搞不清楚时,孩子可能会发现有必要以相似的方式限制其自主权。

autism \ˈȯ-ˌti-zəm\

A condition that begins in childhood and causes problems in forming social relationships and in communicating with others and includes behavior in which certain activities are constantly repeated. 自闭症;孤独症

• She was beginning to think that her four-year-old's strange behavior and complete lack of interest in his playmates might be due to autism. 她开始想,自己四岁的孩子行为古怪,对小伙伴完全没有兴趣,原因可能是自闭症。

Autism, in its strict sense, becomes evident before the age of 3. The *autistic* child generally refuses to talk, becomes obsessive about toys, resists any change vehemently, and sometimes flies into unexplained rages. Autism is believed to be biological in origin, and seems to be related to several milder conditions such as Asperger's syndrome. As many as 1 in 100 children, mostly boys, may have autism, Asperger's, or a related condition. About one in ten autistic children turns out to have a remarkable mental gift, such as the ability to play a difficult piece on the piano after a single hearing or repair a complex machine without any training. Many *autistic* children seem to grow out of it as they become adults, and some autistic adults manage to live independently. *Autistic* is sometimes used loosely to describe a much more common kind of psychological withdrawal in adults.

autism(自闭症),从严格意义上说,三岁前就变得明显了。autistic(患有自闭症的)孩子通常拒绝交谈,对玩具变得着迷,强烈反对任何变化,有时会无端地发火。人们相信,自闭症来自遗传,似乎与几种轻微的疾病有关,比如亚斯伯格综合征。一百个孩子当中(其中大多数是男孩),就可能有一个患有自闭症、亚斯伯格综合征,或者相关疾病。患有自闭症的孩子当中,可能十分之一有着不一般的天赋,比如一段音乐听一遍就能够用钢琴演奏出来,或者未经培训就能修理复杂的机器。很多 *autistic*(患有自闭症的)孩子成年后似乎自闭症就消失了,而且有些患有自闭症的成年人能够独立生活。*autistic* 有时用来不太精确地描述一种更常见的成年人的性格孤僻。

GRAT

GRAT comes from the Latin words *gratus*, meaning "pleasing, welcome, or agreeable," and *gratia*, meaning "grace, agreeableness, or pleasantness." A meal that's served *graciously* will be received with *gratitude* by *grateful* guests; those who show no appreciation could be called *ingrates*.

GRAT 源自拉丁语单词 *gratus*,意思是"令人高兴的、受欢迎的、或者令人愉悦的",以及 *gratia*,意思是"优雅、令人愉悦、令人欢喜"。*graciously*(和蔼优雅地)端上的饭菜会得到 *grateful*(心怀感激的)客人的 *gratitude*(感谢),那些不知感恩的人可以称为 *ingrates*(忘恩负义之人)。

gratify \ˈɡra-tə-ˌfī\ (1) To be a source of pleasure or satisfaction; give pleasure or satisfaction to. 令人愉悦或满足 (2) To give in to; indulge or satisfy. 屈服于;沉溺;满足

• It gratified him immensely to see his daughter bloom so beautifully in high school. 看到女儿上高中时出落得楚楚动人,他很高兴。

A *gratifying* experience is quietly pleasing or satisfying. But gratifying an impulse means giving in to it, which isn't always such a good idea, and "instant *gratification*" of every desire will result in a life based on junk food and worse. Truly gratifying experiences and accomplishments usually are the result of time and effort.

一次 *gratifying* 经历让人心中愉快或者满足。但是 gratifying 自己的冲动就是屈服于它,这并非总是明智之举。"instant *gratification*"(立刻满足)每个欲望的结果就是依赖垃圾食品过日子,或者更糟糕。真正 gratifying(令人满足的)经历和成就通常源于时间和努力。

gratuity \ɡrə-ˈtü-ə-tē\ Something, especially a tip, given freely. 赠予物(尤指小费)

• After sitting for three hours over a six-course meal at Le Passage, we always leave the waiter a very generous gratuity. 在通道酒店坐了三个小时吃了六道菜大餐之后,我们通常会给服务员一笔不菲的小费。

Gratuity is a fancier and more formal word than *tip*. It occurs most often in written notices along the lines of "Gratuities accepted." Its formality makes it best suited for describing tips of the dignified, expensive variety. For the taxi driver who takes you to the superb Belgian restaurant, it's a tip; for the restaurant's maitre d', it's a gratuity.

gratuity 是比 *tip* 更花哨、更正式的说法。它通常出现在手写通知中的"Gratuity accepted"(小费收到)这一行。其正式性使其最适用于描述庄重、慷慨的那种小费。对于开车送你到比利时一家高级餐厅的出租车司机来说,那是 tip;对于餐厅侍者总管来说,那是 gratuity。

gratuitous \ɡrə-ˈtü-ə-təs\ Not called for by the circumstances. 无谓的

• Members of the committee were objecting to what they considered gratuitous violence on television. 委员会成员正在电视上谴责他们觉得是无谓的暴力。

In its original sense, *gratuitous* can refer to anything given freely, like a tip. But the word now almost always applies to something that's seen as not only unnecessary (like a tip, which you don't really have to give) but also unwelcome. To insult or criticize someone *gratuitously* is to make a hurtful remark that's uncalled for and undeserved. But scenes in a film that you yourself might call gratuitous were, unfortunately, probably put there to attract an audience that wants to see them.

按照其原始意义,*gratuitous* 可用来指任何赠予的东西,比如小费。但是现在,这个词语几乎总是用于不但被认为不必要(比如小费,你其实没必要给)而且不受欢迎的事物。*gratuitously*(无谓地)侮辱或者批评某人,就是说了不必要的、也不该说的伤人的话。但不幸的是,电影中你认为无谓的场景,可能只是为了吸引想看到这些场景的观众。

ingratiate \ in-'grā-shē-ˌāt \ To gain favor or acceptance by making a deliberate effort. 讨好;巴结;迎合

• None of her attempts to ingratiate herself with the professor seemed to improve her grades. 她多次努力讨好教授,似乎是为了得高分。

To *ingratiate* yourself is to put yourself in someone's good *graces*—that is, to gain someone's approval. People often try to ingratiate themselves by engaging in an activity known by such names as *bootlicking*, *apple-polishing*, and *brownnosing*. But some people are able to win favor just by relying on their *ingratiating* smiles.

ingratiate yourself(巴结别人)就是让你 in someone's good *graces*,也就是说,得到那个人的欢心。人们经常想方设法,通过做被称为 *bootlicking*(拍马屁)、*apple-polishing*(讨好)和 *brownnosing*(巴结)这样的事情讨人欢心。但有些人仅仅凭着 *ingratiating*(谄媚的)微笑就赢得欢心了。

Quizzes

A. Complete the analogy:

1. favor : prefer :: gratify : _____
   a. use b. please c. thank d. repay
2. liberty : freedom :: autonomy : _____
   a. government b. car science c. independence d. robot
3. entertain : joke :: ingratiate : _____
   a. flatter b. devour c. vibrate d. criticize
4. worker : laborer :: automaton : _____
   a. robot b. computer c. gadget d. employee
5. necessary : needed :: gratuitous : _____
   a. thankless b. unthinking c. welcome d. uncalled-for
6. immune : infections :: autoimmune : _____
   a. bacteria b. viruses c. epidemic d. body tissues
7. bonus : salary :: gratuity : _____
   a. obligation b. thankfulness c. refusal d. bill
8. paranoia : suspicion :: autism : _____
   a. sleep b. withdrawal c. anger d. fear of cars

B. Indicate whether the following pairs of words have the same or different meanings:

1. automaton / robot   same ____ / different ____
2. gratuity / tip   same ____ / different ____
3. autoimmune / invulnerable same ____ / different ____
4. gratuitous / deserved   same ____ / different ____

5. autonomy / freedom　　　　　　　same ____ / different ____
6. gratify / gladden　　　　　　　　same ____ / different ____
7. autism / dictatorship　　　　　　same ____ / different ____
8. ingratiate / contribute　　　　　same ____ / different ____

CLAM/CLAIM comes from the Latin verb *clamare*, meaning "to shout or cry out." To *claim* often means "to call for." And an *exclamation* is a cry of shock, joy, or surprise.

CLAM/CLAIM 源自拉丁语动词 *clamare*，意思是"喊叫"。*claim* 通常的意思是"要求"。*exclamation* 指因震惊、快乐或感到意外而发出的声音。

clamor \ˈkla-mər\ (1) Noisy shouting; loud, continuous noise. 喊叫；音量大而持续的噪声 (2) Strong and active protest or demand. 抗议；要求

• The clamor in the hallways between classes was particularly loud that morning as news of the state championship swept through the student body. 那天上午,当州锦标赛的消息在学生中间传开时,班级之间的走廊里噪声特别大。

The clamor on Broadway at midday can be astonishing to a tourist from a midwestern town; if they happen to be digging up the street with jackhammers, the clamor can be even worse. The clamor on the floor of a stock exchange goes on without stopping for seven hours every day. A clamor of protest may sometimes be quieter, but is often just as hard to ignore. A politican who receives a thousand e-mails a day *clamoring* for his resignation might as well be listening to an angry crowd.

对于来自中西部城镇的游客来说,百老汇大街中午时分的 clamor(噪声)是令人吃惊的,如果碰巧有人用风钻挖开路面,噪声就更让人受不了了。股票交易所的交易厅内,噪声一天可以连续不断持续七个小时。抗议的声音有时候可能低一些,但常常也是无法忽视的。政治家一天收到一千封电子邮件,clamoring(吵着)让他辞职,这跟听着愤怒的人群的声音是一样的。

acclamation \ˌa-klə-ˈmā-shən\ (1) A loud, eager indication of approval, praise, or agreement. 喝彩；欢呼；赞同 (2) An overwhelming yes vote by cheers, shouts, or applause. 拥护；赞成

• To the principal's suggestion that Friday be a holiday to honor the victors in the national math olympics, the students yelled their approval in a long and loud acclamation. 校长建议把周五设为节日,向全国数学奥赛获奖者致敬。对此,学生们长久高呼着表示赞同。

Approval can come from a single person, but *acclamation* requires a larger audience. An *acclaimed* movie is widely praised, and critical *acclaim* can lead to box-office success. When a popular proposal comes up in a legislature, the speaker may ask that it be passed "by acclamation," which means that everyone just gets to yell and cheer in approval and no one bothers counting the votes at all.

表示赞成的可以是一个人,但是高呼表示赞同则需要大批观众。一部 *acclaimed* 电影是普遍受到赞扬的电影,critical acclaim(评论家的赞扬)可以让票房率很高。当一项受欢迎的提案在立法机构进行讨论时,议长会要求"by acclamation"通过,意思是大家都欢呼表示赞同,根本没人去数选票。

declaim \di-ˈklām\   To speak in the formal manner of someone delivering a speech. 慷慨激昂地说;大声而有力地说

• Almost any opinion can sound convincing if it's declaimed loudly and with conviction. 几乎任何看法,只要大声而坚定地说出来,听起来就会令人信服。

Declaiming suggests an unnatural style of speech best suited to a stage or podium. Listening to an actor declaim a passage in a Shakespeare play can be enjoyable. Listening to Aunt Ida at Sunday dinner declaiming on the virtues of roughage might not be. Most people don't appreciate being treated as an audience, and good advice is usually more welcome when it's not given in a *declamatory* style. declaiming(大声而有力地说)暗示一种不自然的说话方式,最适合用于舞台或者讲台。听着演员慷慨激昂地背诵莎士比亚戏剧中的段落,是很令人愉快的。星期天吃饭时听着爱达姨妈庄重地说着食物中粗纤维的好处,却不是这样。大多数人并不喜欢被人当作听众,不用 declamatory(慷慨陈词的)方式提供好的建议会更受欢迎。

proclaim \prō-ˈklām\   To declare or announce publicly, officially, or definitely. 宣布;宣告;声明

• He burst into the dorm room, jumped onto his bed, and proclaimed that he had just aced the sociology exam. 他冲进宿舍,跳到床上,宣布说他社会学考试取得了好成绩。

The *pro-* in *proclaim* means "forward, out," so a *proclamation* is an "outward" statement intended for the public. We often think of proclamations as something issued by monarchs or dictators, but Lincoln was able to issue his Emancipation Proclamation because as president he had the power to free the slaves in certain areas. At a slightly lower level, a governor may proclaim a day in honor of the state's firemen, a movie critic may proclaim a director to be the best of all, or you may proclaim your New Year's resolutions to a crowd of friends. proclaim 中的 pro-意思是"向前,出来",所以 proclamation 是一种面向公众的"向外的"话。我们经常认为 proclamations 是君主或者独裁者颁布的东西,但是林肯也颁布《解放黑人奴隶宣言》,因为作为总统,他有权使奴隶在某些地区获得自由。在较低的水平上,一位州长会宣布某一天是向该州消防员致敬的日子,一位电影评论家可以声明某位导演是最好的导演,或者你可以向一群朋友宣布自己的新年决心。

CRAC/CRAT comes from the Greek word meaning "power." Attached to another root, it indicates which group holds the power. With *demos*, the Greek word for "people," it forms *democracy*, a form of government in which the people rule. A *theocracy*, from the Greek *theos*, "god," is government based on divine guidance. In a *meritocracy*, people earn power by their own merit.

CRAC/CRAT 源自希腊语表示"权力"的那个词语。跟另一词根连用,它表明哪一个群体掌握权力。它与 *demos* 这一表示"人民"的词语构成 democracy(民主政体),意思是一种由人民来统治的政体。theocracy(神权政体)源自希腊语中表示"神"的 theos,意思是一种以神的指引为基础的政体。在 meritocracy(精英领导体制)这种政体中,人民用自己的美德赢

得权力。

aristocrat \ə-ˈris-tə-ˌkrat\ The highest social class in a country, usually because of birth and wealth. 贵族

• A wealthy aristocrat from a famous European family, she surprised everyone by becoming a supporter of little-known jazz musicians. 作为欧洲一个著名家族的有钱贵族,她却资助一个鲜为人知的爵士乐队,令人吃惊。

Since *aristos* means "best" in Greek, ancient Greeks such as Plato and Aristotle used the word *aristocracy* to mean a system of rule by the best people—that is, those who deserved to rule because of their intelligence and moral excellence. But this kind of "best" soon became something you could inherit from your parents. The United States has no formal aristocracy—no noble titles such as *baron* or *marquis* that stay in the family—but certain American families have achieved an almost *aristocratic* status because of the wealth they've held onto for generations.

由于 *aristos* 在希腊语中意思是"最好的",像柏拉图和亚里士多德这样的古希腊人,使用 *aristocracy* 来指一种贤人统治的制度,也就是那些因为智力超群、道德高尚而值得拥有统治权的人。但是这种"最好"很快就变成了可以从父母那里遗传而来的东西。美国没有正式的贵族,没有 *baron*(男爵)或者 *marquis*(侯爵)这样的贵族头衔,但是某些美国家庭,由于其数代拥有的财富,几乎获得了 *aristocratic*(贵族的)地位。

autocratic \ˌȯ-tə-ˈkra-tik\ (1) Having to do with a form of government in which one person rules. 独裁的;专制的 (2) Resembling the ruler of such a government. 独断专行的

• It's hard to believe that a guy who seems so nice to his friends is an autocratic boss who sometimes fires people just because he's in a bad mood. 很难相信,一个对朋友似乎很好的人,作为老板却很独断专行,有时不高兴了就把人解雇了。

Autos in Greek means "same" or "self," so in an *autocratic* government all the power is held by the leader him- or herself. Autocratic governments are often called dictatorships, or sometimes *autocracies*. In everyday life, a teacher, a parent, or a football coach can all behave like *autocrats* as well.

autos 在希腊语中意思是"同一"或者"自己",所以在专制政府中,所有权力都由领导自己掌握。独裁政府常常称为 dictatorships,有时候也称为 *autocracies*。在日常生活中,教师、父母或者足球教练也可能很专制。

bureaucrat \ˈbyu̇r-ə-ˌkrat\ (1) An appointed government official. 政府官员 (2) An official of a government or system that is marked by fixed and complex rules that often result in long delays. 官僚

• To settle his insurance claim he had to make his way through four or five bureaucrats, every one of them with a new form to fill out. 为了解决保险索赔问题,他不得不过几个官僚的关,每一次都有新表格要填写。

In French, a *bureau* is a desk, so *bureaucracy* means basically "government by people at desks." Despite the bad-mouthing they often get, partly because they usually have to stick so close to the rules, bureaucrats do almost all the day-to-day work that keeps a government running. The idea of a bureaucracy is to split up the complicated task of governing a large country into smaller jobs that can be handled by specialists. *Bureaucratic* government is nothing new; the Roman empire had an enormous and complex bureaucracy, with the bureaucrats at lower levels reporting to bureaucrats above them, and so on up to the emperor himself.

在法语中,*bureau* 是桌子,所以 *bureaucracy* 的基本意思是"坐在桌子旁边的人的统治"。虽然经常被人说坏话,官僚们却做着让政府运转的日常工作。官僚体制这一想法目的是将治理一个大国家的复杂任务分成专家可以处理的小任务。*bureaucratic*(官僚的)体制不是什么新事物;罗马帝国有着庞大而复杂的官僚体制,下级官僚向上级官僚汇报工作,以此类推一直到皇帝本人。

plutocracy \plü-ˈtä-krə-sē\ (1) Government by the wealthy. 富豪统治;财阀当政 (2) A controlling class of wealthy people. 富豪阶级

• Theodore Roosevelt sought to limit the power held by the plutocracy of wealthy industrialists. 西奥多·罗斯福努力限制工业家构成的富豪阶级掌握的权力。

Ploutos was Greek for "wealth," and *Plouton*, or *Pluto*, was one of the names used for the Greek god of the underworld, where all the earth's mineral wealth was stored. So a *plutocracy* governs or wields power through its money. The economic growth in the U.S. in the late 19th century produced a group of enormously wealthy *plutocrats*. Huge companies like John D. Rockefeller's Standard Oil gained serious political power, and Rockefeller was able to influence lawmakers in states where his businesses operated. For this reason, it was said in 1905 that Ohio and New Jersey were plutocracies, not democracies.

Ploutos 在希腊语中意思是"财富",而 *Plouton*,或者 *Pluto*,是希腊神话中冥王的名字之一,因为地球所有矿物都在地下。所以,富豪阶级利用金钱统治或者运用权力。美国 19 世纪晚期的经济发展产生了一群极其富有的 *plutocrats*(财阀)。像戴·洛克菲勒的标准石油公司这样的大公司获得了不可轻视的政治权力,洛克菲勒本人可以影响其公司所在的各州的立法人员。因此,据说 1905 年俄亥俄州和新泽西州都是财富统治的州,而不是民主统治的州。

Quizzes

A. Fill in each blank with the correct letter:

a. plutocracy   e. proclaim
b. declaim   f. bureaucrat
c. aristocrat   g. acclamation
d. clamor   h. autocratic

1. She hates being thought of as a _____, but in these huge government offices with long rows of desks it's hard for her to think of herself as anything else.

2. The assembly approved the proposal by enthusiastic _____.

3. Her father had been harsh and _____, and her mother and brothers had barely opened their mouths when he was around.

4. I got tired of hearing him _____ about how much better things were when he was young.

• 554 •

5. His parents had been London shopkeepers, but many who met him assumed from his fine manners and accent and dress that he was an _____.

6. The networks could _____ the winner of the election as early as 7:00 p.m.

7. The country is supposedly a democracy, but it's really run as a _____ by about twenty extremely wealthy families.

8. The proposed new tax was met with a _____ of protest.

B. Match the word on the left to the correct definition on the right:

1. autocratic   a. declare
2. declaim   b. noble
3. plutocracy   c. noisy din
4. acclamation   d. government official
5. proclaim   e. speak formally
6. bureaucrat   f. ruled by one person
7. clamor   g. rule by the rich
8. aristocrat   h. acceptance with cheers

PUNC comes from the Latin noun *punctum*, meaning "point." A period is a form of *punctuation* that's literally a point, and a *punctured* tire has been pricked by a sharp point.

PUNC 源自拉丁语名词 punctum，意思是"点"。句号就是一种 punctuation（标点）形式，的确是一个点，而 punctured（被刺破的）轮胎被尖头刺破了。

punctilious \ˌpəŋk-ˈti-lē-əs\ Very careful about the details of codes or conventions. 一丝不苟的

● A proofreader has to be punctilious about spelling and punctuation. 校对员在拼写和标点方面必须一丝不苟。

A *punctilio* is a small point—a minor rule, or a little detail of conduct in a ceremony. A person who pays close attention to such minor details is punctilious. *Punctiliousness* can be valuable, especially for certain kinds of tasks, as long as you don't become so concerned about small points that you fail to pay attention to the large ones.

一个 punctilio 就是一个小点，一条次要的规则，或者典礼中一个行为细节。对这些小事儿非常注意的人就是 punctilious。只要你不至于过分担心小事儿而忽视了大事儿，punctiliousness（一丝不苟）就是很重要的，尤其是对某些任务来说。

punctual \ˈpəŋk-chə-wəl\ Being on time; prompt. 准时的

● The company had become much more punctual under the new president, and every meeting started precisely on time. 在新任总裁的领导下，公司全体人员比以前准时多了，每次会

议都准时开始。

The original meaning of *punctual* described a *puncture* made by a surgeon. The word has meant lots of other things through the centuries, usually involving being precise about small points. And today *punctuality* is all about time; a punctual train or a punctual payment or a punctual person shows up "on the dot."
punctual 最早的意思用来描述外科医生刺的小孔。这个词语数个世纪以来有多种意思,通常涉及在细节上很准确。今天,punctuality 都跟时间有关:punctual 火车,或者 punctual 付款,或者 punctual 人"on the dot"("准点")到来。

compunction \kəm-ˈpəŋk-shən\ (1) Anxiety caused by guilt. 内疚;愧疚 (2) A slight misgiving. 疑虑;顾虑

• Speeding is something many people seem to do without compunction, their only concern being whether they'll get caught. 很多人超速了似乎毫不愧疚,只是担心是否会被抓住。

Compunction is most often used in describing people who don't feel it—that is, who aren't "stung" or "pricked" by conscience. Ruthless businessmen steal clients and contracts from other businessmen without compunction, and hardened criminals have no compunctions about armed robbery and worse. Notice how compunction can be used in a noncountable way, like *guilt* ("He killed without compunction"), or in the plural, like *qualm* ("She had no compunctions about lying"). But words like *guilt*, *qualm*, *regret*, *remorse*, *doubt*, and *unease*, unlike *compunction*, are often used when talking about people who actually suffer from them.
compunction 主要用来描述没有这种感觉的人,也就是那些不会被良心"叮咬"或者"刺痛"的人。无情的商人毫不愧疚地从其他公司偷走顾客及合同,死不悔改的罪犯进行武装抢劫甚至干更坏的事情也不会内疚。注意 compunction 做不可数名词时的用法,类似于 guilt("He killed without compunction""他杀人了也毫不愧疚"),或者复数形式的用法,类似于 qualm("She had no compunctions about lying""她撒起谎来毫不愧疚")。但是,像 guilt,qualm,regret,doubt 和 unease 这样的词语,与 compunction 不同,经常用于谈论深受其苦的人们的时候。

acupuncture \ˈa-kyə-ˌpəŋ(k)-chər\ A method of relieving pain or curing illness by inserting fine needles through the skin at specific points. 针灸

• As a last resort he agreed to try acupuncture treatment with Dr. Lu, and his pain vanished like magic. 无计可施了,他就同意试一下陆大夫的针灸治疗法,结果疼痛神奇地消失了。

In Latin, *acus* means "needle," and the English word *acupuncture* was coined way back in the 17th century to describe a technique the Chinese had already been using for 2,000 years. An *acupuncturist* may insert many extremely fine needles at a time; the treatment is usually uncomfortable but not truly painful. In China today, even major surgery is often carried out using only acupuncture to kill the pain; it's also used for many other conditions, including insomnia, depression, smoking, and overweight. Acupuncture is based on ancient theories of bodily energy that few Western doctors have ever accepted; but even though attempts to explain its effects by Western science have been unsuccessful, it's now widely recognized by doctors as effective for pain reduction.

在拉丁语中,*acus* 意思是"针"。英语单词 *acupuncture*(针灸)是 17 世纪发明的词语,用来描述中国人使用了两千多年的一种技术。*acupuncturist*(针灸医生)一次会插入很多根纤细的针。这一治疗方法通常很不舒服,但并不是很疼痛。在今天的中国,即使重要的外科手术也常常只用针灸来止痛。针灸也用于其他很多疾病,包括失眠、抑郁、抽烟和超重。针灸是以古老的身体能量理论为基础的,这些理论很少被西方医生接受过;但是,即使西方科学未能解释其效果,现在医生们也普遍认为它能有效止痛。

POT comes from the Latin adjective *potens*, meaning "able." Our English word *potent* means "powerful" or "effective," whether for good or bad. A potent new antibiotic might be able to deal with infections that have developed resistance to older drugs; an industrial gas might be identified as a potent contributor to climate change; and a potent drink might leave you staggering.

POT 源自拉丁语形容词 *potens*,意思是"有能力的"。我们的英语单词 *potent* 意思是"强大的"或者"有效的",不管是好是坏。*potent* 新抗生素或许可以对付已经对药物有抵抗能力的感染;工业废气或许可以被认定为气候变化 *potent* 贡献因素;*potent* 饮料可能让你走路摇摇晃晃。

potential\pə-ˈten-shəl\ (1) The possibility that something will happen in the future. 可能性 (2) A cause for hope. 希望的诱因

● If the plan works we'll be millionaires, but the potential for disaster is high. 如果这个计划有用的话,我们就会成为百万富翁,不过失败的可能性也很大。

Potential can be either good or bad. Studying hard increases the potential for success, but wet roads increase the potential for accidents. But when a person or thing "has potential," we always expect something good from it in the future. As an adjective (as in "potential losses," "potential benefits," etc.), *potential* usually means simply "possible." In science, however, the adjective has a special meaning: *Potential energy* is the kind of stored energy that a boulder sitting at the top of a cliff has (the opposite of *kinetic energy*, which is what it has as it rolls down that cliff).

potential 可以好,也可以不好。努力学习会提高成功的可能性,但是道路湿滑会提高事故的可能性。但是,当人或事物"has potential",我们总是希望未来会有好结果。作为形容词(比如在"potential losses""potential benefits"等短语中),*potential* 通常的意思只是"可能的"。在科学领域,这一形容词具有特殊的意思:*potential energy*(势能)指悬崖顶部的大岩石中储存的那种能量(与其相对的是 *kinetic energy* 也就是动能,指的是它滚下悬崖时具有的能量)。

impotent\ˈim-pə-tənt\ Lacking power or strength. 没有力量的;无力的

● The government now knows it's utterly impotent to stop the violence raging in the countryside, and has basically retreated to the capital city. 政府现在知道,他们无力阻止乡村地区嚣张的暴力活动,于是基本上撤回到了州府。

A police department may be impotent to stop the flow of drugs into a neighborhood. A group of countries may be impotent to force another country to change its human-rights policies. The *impotence* of a prime minister may be shown by her inability to get an important piece of legislation passed. *Impotent* and *impotence* may also have a special meaning, when they refer to a man's inability to have sexual intercourse.

警察局的某个部门可能 impotent(无力的)阻止毒品流入附近地区。一些国家可能无力迫使另一国家改变其人权政策。一位总理无力使一项重要的立法得到通过，就会显示出其 *impotence*。*impotent* 和 *impotence* 也有一个特殊的意思，也就是指男性无法性交。

plenipotentiary \ˌple-nə-pə-ˈten-shə-rē\ A person, such as a diplomat, who has complete power to do business for a government. 全权代表；全权大使

• In the Great Hall, in the presence of the Empress, the plenipotentiaries of four European nations put their signatures on the treaty. 在大厅中，当着女皇的面，四个欧洲国家的全权代表在条约上签字了。

Back in the 12th century, when the Roman Catholic Church in some ways resembled the powerful Roman empire that had come before it, the Church revived the Roman concept of an official with *plena potens*—"full powers"—to negotiate agreements (see PLE/ PLEN, p. 124). Whereas an ambassador could only make offers that a faraway ruler had specified, often weeks or months earlier, a *plenipotentiary* could negotiate an entire agreement without checking back constantly with his ruler. Today, with instant electronic communications, this distinction has generally lost its importance, but there are still ambassadors who wouldn't be allowed at a negotiating table.

早在12世纪，罗马天主教会在某些方面类似于之前出现的很有权力的罗马皇帝。当时，教会恢复了罗马有着 *plena potens* "全权"——的官员这一概念，让他们去商讨各种协议（见 PLE/PLEN，第124页）。虽然大使只能表达几周或几个月前远方统治者明确的旨意，全权大使则不必总是与统治者商议即可达成整个协议。今天，由于电子通信非常迅速，这一区别基本失去了意义，但是仍然有不被允许坐在谈判桌旁的大使。

potentate \ˈpō-tᵊn-ˌtāt\ A powerful ruler. 统治者

• After 18 years as president of the college, he wielded power like a medieval potentate, and no one on the faculty or staff dared to challenge him. 在该学院任校长十八年后，他行使起权力来就跟中世纪的统治者一样，全体教师或管理人员谁也不敢质疑他。

Like such titles as *grand vizier*, *caliph*, and *khan*, *potentate* summons up thoughts of absolute rulers of an earlier age in such lands as Turkey, Persia, and India. It often suggests a person who uses power or authority in a cruel and unjust way—that is, a tyrant. Today, though it's still used as a title by the organization called the Shriners, it's more often used humorously ("Supreme Intergalactic Potentate," "Potentate of Pasta," etc.).

就像 *grand vizier*, *caliph* 和 *khan* 这样的头衔一样，*potentate* 让人想到诸如土耳其、波斯和印度这些国家早期的独裁统治者。它常常暗示一个残忍而且不公正地行使权力的人，也就是一个暴君。今天，尽管称为圣地兄弟会的组织仍然用它作为一个头衔，但它更常以幽默的方式被使用（"Supreme Intergalactic Potentate""Potentate of Pasta"等等）。

UNIT 23

Quizzes

A. Choose the closest definition:

1. impotent   a. antique   b. weak   c. broken   d. skimpy
2. punctual   a. deflated   b. cranky   c. prompt   d. careful
3. potentate   a. ruler   b. bully   c. warrior   d. prime minister
4. acupuncture   a. massage technique   b. arrow hole   c. pinprick   d. needle therapy
5. punctilious   a. pointed   b. careful   c. prompt   d. unusual
6. plenipotentiary   a. monarch   b. ambassador   c. fullness   d. likely possibility
7. compunction   a. desire   b. bravery   c. qualm   d. conviction
8. potential   a. privilege   b. prestige   c. power   d. possibility

B. Indicate whether the following pairs of words have the same or different meanings:

1. acupuncture / precision   same _____ / different _____
2. plenipotentiary / emperor   same _____ / different _____
3. punctual / on time   same _____ / different _____
4. potentate / monarch   same _____ / different _____
5. compunction / threat   same _____ / different _____
6. impotent / powerless   same _____ / different _____
7. punctilious / speedy   same _____ / different _____
8. potential / influence   same _____ / different _____

Greek and Latin Borrowings 希腊语和拉丁语借词

ambrosia \am-ˈbrō-zhə\ (1) The food of the Greek and Roman gods. (希腊和罗马神祇的)神食;仙馐 (2) Something extremely pleasant to taste or smell. 美食;美味佳肴

• After two days lost in the woods, the simple stew tasted like ambrosia to them. 在树林中迷失两天后,简单的炖菜对他们来说如同美味一般。

Ambrosia literally means "immortality" in Greek, and in Greek and Roman mythology only the immortals—the gods and goddesses— could eat ambrosia or drink *nectar*. Both may have been divine forms of honey. The gods also used nectar and ambrosia like oils for ceremonial anointing, and a mixture of water, oil, and fruits called ambrosia came to be used in human ceremonies as well. Since we can't know what the mythical ambrosia tasted or smelled like, we mere mortals are free to give the name to our favorite *ambrosial* dessert—perhaps one involving oranges, coconut, and heavy cream.

ambrosia 在希腊语中字面意思是"永生",在希腊和罗马神话中只有永生者,也就是男神和女神,才能食用 ambrosia,或者饮用 *nectar*。两者可能都是仙界的蜂蜜。诸神也像使用油那样在涂油仪式上使用 nectar 和 ambrosia,称为 ambrosia 的一种水、油和水果的混合物也用于人类的仪式上。由于我们不知道神话中的 ambrosia 的味道或气味如何,我们可以自由命名最喜欢的 ambrosial(极其美味的)饭后甜点——也许里面有橘子、椰蓉和油腻的奶油。

dogma\ˈdȯg-mə\ (1) Something treated as established and accepted opinion. 真理 (2) A principle or set of principles taught by a religious organization. 教义;教条

• New findings about how animals communicate are challenging the current dogma in the field. 动物如何交流这一方面的新发现正挑战这一领域的真理。

Religious *dogma* and scientific dogma are sometimes at odds, as in arguments between those who believe in the biblical story of creation and those who believe in evolution. Since all dogma resists change, arguments of any kind are harder to resolve when both sides are *dogmatic* in their beliefs. *Dogma* and *dogmatic* are generally used disapprovingly; it's always other people who believe unquestioningly in dogma and who take a dogmatic approach to important issues.

宗教教义和科学定理有时相悖,比如在相信《圣经》创世故事的人和相信进化理论的人之间的争论中。由于所有教条抗拒变化,当双方在自己的看法方面 *dogmatic*(武断)时,任何种类的争论都更难以得到解决。*dogma* 和 *dogmatic* 通常有不以为然的味道:毫无保留地相信 dogma、对重要问题采取 dogmatic 处理方式的总是别人。

gratis\ˈgra-təs\ Without charge;free. 免费的

• The service is gratis, since it comes as part of a package deal. 这服务是免费的,因为它是一项一揽子交易的一部分。

Gratis comes from the Latin word for "favor"; so in English a *party favor* is a small item given gratis to everyone attending a party. *Gratis* is used as both an adjective ("The drinks were gratis") and an adverb ("Drinks were served gratis"). But however it's used, it means "free."

gratis 源自拉丁语中表示"恩惠"的词语,所以,在英语中,party favor 是送给参加聚会的每个人的小礼物。*gratis* 既用作形容词("The drinks were gratis"),也用作副词("Drinks were served gratis")。但是,不管怎么使用,它的意思都是"免费"。

eureka\yu̇-ˈrē-kə\ An exclamation used to express triumph and delight on a discovery. 我发现啦;我找到啦(用于做出发现时表达愉悦的感叹词)

• The mountain town of Eureka, California, was named for the cries of delight by prospectors when they discovered gold in them thar hills. 加利福尼亚州的山城尤里卡市,是用探矿者在山里发现黄金时高兴的叫声命名的。

Eureka means "I have found" in Greek. The story goes that the Greek inventor Archimedes, given the task of determining the purity of gold in a crown, shouted "Eureka!" one day after stepping into a bath and making water slop over the side, when he suddenly realized that the weight of water displaced indicated the bulk of his body, but that a larger body made of lighter matter might weigh the same but would displace more water. Thus, a crown in which lighter metal had secretly been mixed with the gold would reveal itself in the same way. The story may not be true, but we still shout "Eureka!" when we make a sudden, welcome discovery.

Eureka 在希腊语中意思是"我发现了"。有个故事说,希腊发明家阿基米德接到一个任务,要确定一个王冠的黄金纯度。有一天,他踏进浴池时,水漫了出来。他突然意识到,被替代的水的重量表明了他身体的体积,但是用更轻的物质制造的更大的物体可能重量一样,但会替代更多的水。于是他大叫:"Eureka!"这样,在皇冠的黄金中偷偷掺入的较轻金属,也会以同样的方式暴露自己。这个故事未必真实,但是我们有了突然而令人高兴的发现,仍然会大叫"Eureka!"

per se \pər-ˈsā\ By, of, or in itself; as such. 本身

• He claims that the reason for the invasion wasn't oil per se, but rather the country's dangerous military power, which had been made possible by its oil. 他声称入侵的原因不是为了石油本身,而是该国因为石油而很危险的军事力量。

We generally use *per se* to distinguish between something in its narrow sense and some larger thing that it represents. Thus, you may have no objection to educational testing per se, but rather to the way testing is done. An opposition party may attack a president's policy not because they dislike the policy per se but because they want to weaken the president. And when New York's police chief decided to crack down on small crimes, it wasn't the small crimes per se that were his target, but instead the larger crimes which he believed would be reduced because of this new approach.

我们通常用 *per se* 来区分狭隘意义上的某事物和其代表的更大的事物。因此,你对教育考试本身可能没有异议,但是会对考试的方式有异议。反对党攻击总统的政策,可能不是因为他们不喜欢这一政策本身,而是想要削弱总统的力量。当纽约警察局长决定打击轻罪时,轻罪本身不是其目标,而是因为他认为这么做可以减少重罪的发生。

opus \ˈō-pəs\ A creative work, especially a musical composition or set of compositions numbered in order of publication. 创作的作品;编号乐曲

• Beethoven's Ninth Symphony is also known as Opus (Op.) 125. 贝多芬第九交响曲也被称为第 125 号作品。

A literary *opus* is often a single novel, though the word may sometimes refer to all of a writer's works. But *opus* normally is used for musical works. Mendelssohn's Opus 90 is his *Italian Symphony*, for example, and Brahms's Op. 77 is his Violin Concerto. Since many composers' works were never given opus numbers in an orderly way, they now often have catalog numbers assigned by later scholars. So Haydn's Symphony No. 104 is Hob. 104 (Hob. is short for Anthony van Hoboken, the cataloger), and Mozart's *Marriage of Figaro* is K. 492 (K. stands for Ludwig Köchel).

文学 opus 常常是一部单独的小说,虽然这个词语可能有时用来指一位作家的全部作品。但是 opus 通常用于音乐作品。比如门德尔松的第 90 号作品就是其《意大利交响曲》,勃拉姆斯的第 77 号作品就是其《小提琴协奏曲》。由于很多

作曲家的作品从未以有序的方式加上作品序号,现在常常有后来学者加上的目录编号。所以海顿的第一百零四交响乐就是 Hob. 104(Hob. 是编目人 Anthony van Hoboken 姓氏的缩写),而莫扎特的《费加罗的婚礼》是 K. 492(K. 代表 Ludwig Köchel)。

impetus \\ˈim-pə-təs\\ (1) A driving force or impulse; something that makes a person try or work hard; incentive. 动力;刺激 (2) Momentum. 动量

• The promise of a nice bonus gave us all an added impetus for finishing the project on time. 给一笔丰厚的奖金这一承诺,让我们大家更有动力准时完成项目了。

An *impetus* can be something positive and pleasant, or something negative and unpleasant, but in either case it stimulates action. The need to earn a living provides many people with the impetus to drag themselves out of bed five mornings a week. On the other two days, the impetus might be the smell of bacon cooking, or the idea of an early-morning round of golf. *Impetus* can be used either with *an* or *the* in front of it ("The accident provided an impetus for changing the safety regulations") or without them ("His discoveries have given impetus to further research").

impetus 可以是正面的、令人愉悦的东西,也可以是负面的、令人不悦的东西,但两种情况都可以激发人们采取行动。谋生的需要让很多人有了每周五天早上从床上爬起来的动力。在其他两天早上,这一动力可能是做熏肉的香味,或者一大早打一场高尔夫球这一想法。*impetus* 前面可以用 *an* 或者 *the*("The accident provided an impetus for changing the safety regulations""这次事故为改变安全法规提供了动力"),也可以不用("His discoveries have given impetus to further research""他的发现促进了进一步的研究工作")。

thesis \\ˈthē-səs\\ (1) An opinion or proposition that a person presents and tries to prove by argument. 论点 (2) An extended paper that contains the results of original research, especially one written by a candidate for an academic degree. 论文

• She's done all the coursework needed for her master's degree but hasn't yet completed her thesis. 她完成了所有硕士学位课程,但是还没有完成论文。

In high school, college, or graduate school, students often have to write a *thesis* on a topic in their major field of study. In many fields, a final thesis is the biggest challenge involved in getting a master's degree, and the same is true for students studying for a Ph. D. (a Ph. D. thesis is often called a *dissertation*). But a thesis may also be an idea; so in the course of the paper the student may put forth several theses (notice the plural form) and attempt to prove them.

在中学、大学或者研究生院,学生经常不得不撰写其主要研究领域某一论题方面的 thesis(论文)。在很多领域,要获得硕士学位,学位论文是最大的挑战。这一点对博士研究生来说也一样(博士论文通常称为 *dissertation*)。但是,一个 thesis 也可能是一个观点;所以在一篇论文中,学生可能要提出几个 theses(注意复数形式),并努力加以证明。

Quiz

Fill in each blank with the correct letter:

a. gratis   e. thesis
b. ambrosia   f. opus

c. per se
d. impetus
g. eureka
h. dogma

1. His latest _____ is a set of songs on poetry by Pablo Neruda.
2. This sauce tastes like _____!
3. Treating epilepsy and depression by stimulating the muscles with electrical current was medical _____ for years, but today no one is doing it anymore.
4. The article isn't really about surgery _____, but it talks about several issues that are closely related to it.
5. She wrote her _____ on the portrayal of women in the works of Nathaniel Hawthorne.
6. _____! I knew I'd find that file sooner or later!
7. The souvenirs were distributed _____ to anyone who stopped to see the display.
8. The _____ for this latest big research effort is a prize that's being offered by a foundation.

Review Quizzes

A. Complete the analogy:

1. shout : whisper :: clamor : _____
   a. noise   b. din   c. murmur   d. confusion
2. barrier : stop :: impetus : _____
   a. force   b. drive   c. trip   d. work
3. approval : permission :: autonomy : _____
   a. satisfaction   b. independence c. slavery   d. poverty
4. helpful : servant :: autocratic : _____
   a. friend   b. enemy   c. teacher   d. tyrant
5. turmoil : conflict :: placidity : _____
   a. peace   b. dullness   c. trouble   d. smoothness
6. alas : disappointment :: eureka : _____
   a. distress   b. woe   c. distance   d. discovery
7. gladden : delight :: gratify : _____
   a. please   b. depress   c. amaze   d. surprise
8. strong : vigorous :: impotent : _____
   a. healthy   b. fragile   c. powerful   d. weak

B. Fill in each blank with the correct letter:

a. acclamation
b. ingratiate
c. potentate

i. plutocracy
j. thesis
k. autonomy

d. context
e. declaim
f. ambrosia
g. automaton
h. dogma
l. placate
m. punctilious
n. subtext
o. autocratic

1. She can work like an _____ for eight hours a day, in constant motion, never pausing to speak to a fellow worker.

2. Her boss had flown into a rage that morning, and it had taken her two hours to _____ him.

3. By taking his remarks out of _____, the papers made him look like a crook.

4. The _____ that controls the government also controls all the country's news media.

5. Her attempts to _____ herself with the new management were resented by the other workers.

6. She was so _____ about the smallest office policies that everyone went to her when they had forgotten one of them.

7. He had to revise his _____ twice before being granted his master's degree.

8. He holds court in his vast 15th-floor office like an oriental _____, signing documents and issuing commands.

9. Huge cheering crowds in the streets greeted him on his return from exile, and he was swept into office almost by _____.

10. The dinner was nothing special, but the dessert was pure _____.

11. Replacing an _____ government with a democracy is never easy if the country is unfamiliar with democratic procedures.

12. She stood before the crowd and began to _____ in the tones of a practiced politician.

13. Several remote tribes have been granted limited _____, including self-policing rights and freedom from taxation.

14. Her theory was hotly debated, since it disagreed with the established _____.

15. She claims that the novel has a _____ that no one has ever noticed, and pointed out the clues that the author had provided.

C. Choose the closest definition:

1. aristocrat   a. noble   b. power   c. ruler
     d. office worker
2. gratuitous   a. pleasant   b. unnecessary   c. happy
     d. satisfying
3. gratuity   a. fee   b. service   c. obligation
     d. tip

UNIT 23

4. opus   a. achievement   b. composition   c. burden
   d. talent
5. per se   a. if not   b. of course   c. free of charge
   d. as such
6. compunction   a. confidence   b. misgiving
   c. condition   d. surprise
7. autism   a. self-absorption   b. self-governance
   c. authenticity   d. authority
8. gratis   a. irritating   b. grateful   c. inexpensive
   d. free
9. gratify   a. unify   b. donate   c. satisfy
   d. modify
10. factotum   a. computer printout   b. carved pole
    c. plumber   d. assistant
11. implacable   a. impossible to place   b. impossible to change
    c. impossible to say   d. impossible to like
12. textual   a. of an idea   b. of a manuscript
    c. on an assumption   d. on a hunch
13. placebo   a. one-celled animal   b. medical instrument
    c. harmless substance   d. peaceful mood
14. potential   a. regulation   b. influence   c. impact
    d. possibility
15. bureaucrat   a. furniture maker   b. politician   c. official
    d. servant

UNIT 24

MAND comes from *mandare*, Latin for "entrust" or "order." A *command* is an order; a *commandment* is also an order, but usually one that comes from God. And a *commando* unit carries out orders for special military actions.
MAND 源自拉丁语 *mandare*，意思是"委托"或者"命令"。一个 *command* 就是一个命令，一个 *commandment* 也是一个命令，但往往指上帝的命令。一个 *commando* unit（突击队）执行特殊军事行动命令。

mandate\ˈman-ˌdāt\ (1) A formal command. 正式命令 (2) Permission to act, given by the people to their representatives.（人们给予代表的）授权

- The new president claimed his landslide victory was a mandate from the voters to end the war. 新任总统声称，他凭借压倒性优势取得的选举胜利是选举人结束战争的授权。

A *mandate* from a leader is a command you can't refuse. But that kind of personal command is rarely the meaning of *mandate* today; much more common are connected with institutions. Thus, the Clean Air Act was a mandate from Congress to clean up air pollution—and since *mandate* is also a verb, we could say instead that the Clear Air Act *mandated* new restrictions on air pollution. Elections are often interpreted as mandates from the public for certain kinds of action. But since a politician is not just a symbol of certain policies but also an individual who might happen to have an awfully nice smile, it can be risky to interpret most elections as mandating anything at all.
来自领导的 mandate 是你不能拒绝服从的命令。但是那种个人命令在今天很少是 mandate 的意思，更多的是与机构有关系。这样，《清洁空气法案》是国会清除空气污染的 mandate。由于 mandate 也用作动词，我们可以说《清洁空气法案》mandated（规定）对空气污染实施新的限制措施。选举通常可以理解为公众要求采取某些行动的授权。但是，由于政治家不仅是某些政策的象征符号，而且是可能碰巧有着迷人微笑的个人，将大多数选举理解为规定什么，是有风险的。

mandatory\ˈman-də-ˌtȯr-ē\ Required. 要求的；强制的

- If attendance at the meeting hadn't been mandatory, she would have just gone home. 如果不要求出席会议，她可能早就回家了。

Something *mandatory* is the result of a *mandate* or order, which usually comes in the form of a law, rule, or regulation. Today there seem to be a lot of these mandates, so mandatory seat belts, mandatory inspections for industries, and mandatory prison sentences for violent crimes are regularly in the news. But mandatory retirement at age 65, which used to be common, is now illegal in most cases.

要求的东西就是 *mandate* 或者命令的结果,通常是以法律、规则或者法规的形式出现(在美国)。今天似乎有很多这种命令,所以强制的安全带、强制的行业检查和强制的暴力犯罪判刑频繁出现在新闻中。但是强制的六十五岁退休,过去很常见,如今在很多情况下却是不合法的。

commandeer \ˌkä-mən-ˈdir\ To take possession of something by force, especially for military purposes. 强征;征用

• No sooner had they started their meeting than the boss showed up and commandeered the conference room. 他们的会议刚刚开始,老板就出现了,强行使用会议室。

Military forces have always had the power to commandeer houses. The Declaration of Independence complains about the way the British soldiers have done it, and the third Amendment to the Constitution states that the commandeering of people's houses shall be done only in a way prescribed by law. Almost anything—food, supplies, livestock, etc.—can be militarily commandeered when the need arises. But you don't have to be in the military for someone to "pull rank" on you: Your father may commandeer the car just when you were about to take it out for the evening, your teacher may commandeer your cell phone as you're texting in the middle of class, or your older sister may commandeer the TV remote to watch some lousy dancing competition.

军队一直都有权力 commandeer(征用)房子。《独立宣言》抗议了英国士兵强征房子的行为,《美国宪法》第三条修正案声明,commandeering(征用)房屋只能按照法律规定的方式进行。几乎任何东西,食物、补给品、牲畜等等,必要时都可以被军队 commandeered(征用)。但是,你不一定要在军队才会有人"仗势欺侮"你:你今晚正要开车出去,你爸爸可能会 commandeer(强行使用)那辆车;你上课时发短信,老师也可以 commandeer(没收)手机;你姐姐可能 commandeer(抢走)电视遥控器,看某个糟糕的舞蹈比赛。

remand \ri-ˈmand\ (1) To order a case sent back to another court or agency for further action. 将(案件)发回原审法院重审 (2) To send a prisoner back into custody to await further trial or sentencing. 将(嫌疑人)还押候审

• The state supreme court had remanded the case to the superior court, instructing it to consider the new evidence. 州最高法院已将案件发回高等法院,命令他们考虑新证据。

Remand means "order back" or "send back." After losing a case in a lower court, lawyers will frequently appeal it to a higher court. If the higher court looks at the case and sees that the lower court made certain kinds of errors, it will simply remand it, while telling the lower court how it fell short the first time: by not instructing the jury thoroughly, for example, or by not taking into account a recent related court decision.

remand 意思是"命令送回"或"送回"。在下级法院打输官司后,律师会频繁向高级法院上诉。如果高级法院检查了案子,认为下级法院犯了某些错误,就会将其送回重审,并告知他们第一次如何没有达到预期标准:比如没有详细指示陪审团,或者没有考虑最近的相关的法院审判结果。

UND comes into English from the Latin words *unda*, "wave," and *undare*, "to rise in waves," "to surge or flood." *Undulations* are waves or wavelike things or motions, and to *undulate* is to rise and fall in a wavelike way.

UND 源自拉丁语 *unda*,意思是"波浪",和 *undare*,意思是"往上涌"或者"涌动或淹没"。*undulations* 指波浪或类似波浪的事物或动作,*undulate* 意思是像波浪一样起伏。

undulant\\ˈən-jə-lənt\\ （1）Rising and falling in waves. 波浪般起伏的（2）Wavy in form, outline, or surface. (形式、轮廓或表面)波浪形的

• The man's undulant, sinister movements reminded her of a poisonous snake about to strike. 这个男人的起伏不定的凶险动作让她想到了准备攻击的毒蛇。

The surface of a freshly plowed field is undulant. A range of rolling hills could be called undulant, as could the shifting sands of the Sahara. A waterbed mattress is often literally undulant. And a field of wheat will *undulate* or sway in the wind, like the waves of the sea.

刚刚犁过的田野表面 undulant(像波浪一样起伏)。一系列起伏的山丘可以描述为 undulant,撒哈拉移动的沙丘也可以这样描述。水床的垫子往往是 undulant(波浪般起伏的)。风中的麦田就像海浪一样 *undulate* 或摆动。

inundate\\ˈi-nən-ˌdāt\\ （1）To cover with a flood or overflow. 淹没（2）To overwhelm. 使……难以承受;使……应接不暇

• As news of the singer's death spread, retailers were inundated with orders for all his old recordings. 随着这位歌手去世消息的传播,订购其旧唱片的订单让零售商应接不暇。

In the summer of 1993, record rains in the Midwest caused the Mississippi River to overflow its banks, break through levees, and *inundate* the entire countryside; such an *inundation* hadn't been seen for at least a hundred years. By contrast, the Nile River inundated its entire valley every year, bringing the rich black silt that made the valley one of the most fertile places on earth. (The inundations ceased with the completion of the Aswan High Dam in 1970.) Whenever a critical issue is being debated, the White House and Congressional offices are inundated with phone calls and e-mails, just as a town may be inundated with complaints when it starts charging a fee for garbage pickup.

1993 年夏天,美国中西部史无前例的降雨使密西西比河的河水溢出河岸,冲破防洪堤,inundate(淹没)整个乡野,这样的 *inundation*(洪水泛滥;水灾)至少一百年没有见过。与此形成对比的是,尼罗河曾经每年 inundated(淹没)整个河谷,带来了肥沃的泥沙,使河谷成为世界上最丰产的地方之一。(阿斯旺大坝于 1970 年建成后,inundations[河水泛滥]不再出现了。)只要就某一重要问题进行辩论,白宫和国会办公室的电话和电子邮件就会 inundated(泛滥成灾),就像一座城镇,开始为垃圾收集收费时,人们的抱怨就会 inundated(泛滥成灾)。

redound \ri-ˈdaůnd\ (1) To have an effect for good or bad. 起作用；产生影响 (2) To rebound or reflect. 反弹；反射

• Each new military victory redounded to the glory of the king, whose brilliance as a leader was now praised and feared throughout Europe. 每一次军事胜利都会提高国王的声誉，其作为领导的出色才能受到赞扬，让整个欧洲惧怕。

Redound has had a confusing history. Its original meaning was simply "overflow." But since the prefix *re-* often means "back," the later meaning "result" may have arisen because flowing back—on a beach, for example—is a result of the original flowing. *Redound* has long been confused with other words such as *resound* and *rebound*, so today "rebound" is another of its standard meanings. As examples of its usual meaning, we could say that the prohibition of alcohol in 1919 redounded unintentionally to the benefit of gangsters such as Al Capone—and that Capone's jailing on tax-evasion charges redounded to the credit of the famous "Untouchables."

redound 的历史令人迷惑不解。其原始意义只是"溢出"。但是，由于 *re-* 这一前缀意思是"回"，后来的"结果"这一意思可能就出现了，因为，比如说，海ект上海水流回去是最初流到海滩上的结果。人们一直都将 *redound* 跟其他词语搞混，比如 *resound* 和 *rebound*，所以，今天"rebound"成了其标准意义之一。作为其通常意思的例子，我们可以说 1919 年的禁酒无意之中反而对艾尔·卡彭之类的歹徒很有利，而且卡彭因为受到逃税指控而坐牢，反而让那些有名的"碰不得的人"获得了赞同。

redundancy \ri-ˈdən-dən-sē\ (1) The state of being extra or unnecessary. 多余；冗余 (2) Needless repetition. 不必要的重复

• A certain amount of redundancy can help make a speaker's points clear, but too much can be annoying. 适当的重复有助于阐明发言者的观点，但是太多了会令人不快。

Redundancy, closely related to *redound*, has stayed close to the original meaning of "overflow" or "more than necessary." Avoiding redundancy is one of the prime rules of good writing. "In the modern world of today" contains a redundancy; so does "He died of fatal wounds" and "For the mutual benefit of both parties." But redundancy doesn't just occur in language. "Data redundancy" means keeping the same computer data in more than one place as a safety measure, and a backup system in an airplane may provide redundancy, again for the sake of safety.

redundancy 与 *redound* 有密切联系，而且一直没有远离"溢出"或者"多余"这个原始意义。避免重复是正确写作的主要原则之一。"In the modern world of today"就含有一处重复，"He died of fatal wounds"和"For the mutual benefit of both parties"也一样。但是，重复不仅仅出现在语言中。"Data redundancy"（"信息重复"）的意思是，作为安全措施，将同样的电脑信息储存在不止一处。飞机上的备用系统也是为了安全起见。

Quizzes

A. Fill in each blank with the correct letter:

a. redound   e. remand
b. commandeer   f. inundate
c. undulant   g. mandate

d. mandatory h. redundancy

1. "Each and every" is an example of a _____ that almost everyone uses.
2. A group of four gunmen tried to _____ the jet soon after takeoff.
3. In the second movement, the composer depicts the waves of the ocean by means of lines that rise and fall in _____ patterns.
4. The court's decision represents a _____ to continue working toward absolute equality in the workplace.
5. Sportsmanship and generosity always _____ to the credit of both the team and the school.
6. The judge will probably _____ this case to the lower court for further study.
7. Piles of job applications _____ the office every day.
8. The session on business ethics is _____ for all employees.

B. Match the definition on the left to the correct word on the right:

1. needless repetition   a. mandate
2. required   b. undulant
3. flood   c. commandeer
4. take over   d. redundancy
5. reflect   e. inundate
6. command   f. remand
7. wavy   g. mandatory
8. send back   h. redound

SANCT, meaning "holy," comes from the Latin word *sanctus*. Thus, *sanctity* means "holiness." In ancient Greece, a spot could be *sanctified*, or "made holy," by a group of priests who carried out a solemn ritual; these might be spots where fumes arose from a crack in the earth or where a spring of clear water flowed out of the ground, and a temple might be built there for worship of a god.

SANCT 意思是"神圣的",源自拉丁语 sanctus。所以, sanctity 意思是"神圣"。在古希腊,一群祭司举行一个宗教仪式,就可使某一地点 sanctified (神圣化),或者"被变得神圣";这些地方可能是地缝里冒出烟气的地点,或者清清泉水流出来的地点,而且可能会建造寺庙崇拜某个神祇。

SANCT

sanction\ˈsaŋk-shən\ To give approval to. 批准;准许;许可

● The bill's opponents claimed that removing criminal penalties for drug possession would amount to sanctioning drug use. 反对这一法案的人声称,取消对私藏毒品的刑罚等于允许吸毒。

Sanction originally meant "make holy" or "give official church approval to." The word still has a solemn sound to it, so *sanctioning* is something generally done by an institution or government, though not necessarily by a church. So a college may sanction—or "give its blessing to"—the use of office space by a gay organization, or a hotrod association may sanction two new tracks for official races. But *sanction* is also a noun, which may have two near-opposite meanings, "approval" and "penalty." Thus, a company may be accused of giving its *sanction* to illegal activities. But when two or more countries impose sanctions on another country, it often involves cutting off trade. No wonder *sanction* is such a tricky word for so many of us.

sanction 最初的意思是"使……神圣"或者"给予……正式的教会批准"。这个词语听起来仍然有庄重之感,所以 sanctioning 通常是某一机构或政府的行为,虽然不一定是教会的行为。因此,一所大学可以 sanction——或者说"许可"——某一同性恋组织使用其办公空间,或者某一改装汽车协会 sanction 两个新车道用来进行正式赛车。但是, sanction 也可用作名词,有两个几乎相反的意思:"批准"和"惩罚"。这样,某一公司可被指控对非法活动给予 sanction。但是,当两个或者更多国家对另一国家实施惩罚时,通常意味着切断贸易。难怪 sanction 对我们很多人来说是这么一个难以应付的词语。

sanctimonious \ˌsaŋk-tə-ˈmō-nē-əs\ Pretending to be more religiously observant or morally better than other people. 假装圣洁的;伪善的;道貌岸然的

• The candidates' speeches were sanctimonious from beginning to end, filled with stories about how their deep faith was the basis for everything they did. 这些候选人的演讲从头到尾都是虚伪的,他们讲了很多故事,说自己的深沉信仰是一切行为的基础。

Making a show of your religious morality has always struck some people the wrong way, including Jesus. In his Sermon on the Mount, Jesus preaches that, when we give away money for charity, we shouldn't let our left hand know what our right hand is doing—that is, the giving should be done for its own sake and other people shouldn't be told about it. Those who make a display of how good and pious they are are called hypocrites. But *sanctimony*, or *sanctimoniousness*, has often been a good strategy for American politicians, many of whom have found it a great way to win votes.

炫耀自己的宗教道德总是让一些人有相反的感觉,包括耶稣。在登山宝训中,他宣讲说,当我们为慈善事业捐钱时,不应该让左手知道右手在干什么,也就是说,施舍应该仅仅为了施舍这一目的,不应该告诉他人。那些炫耀自己多么善良、多么虔诚的人称为伪善者。但是 *sanctimony*,或者 *sanctimoniousness*,常常是美国政治家的有效策略,其中很多人发现这是赢得选票的良方。

sacrosanct \ˈsa-krō-ˌsaŋkt\ (1) Most sacred or holy. 极其神圣的 (2) Treated as if holy and therefore immune from criticism or disturbance of any kind. 仿佛神圣不容置疑或干扰的

• Lots of experts have criticized the governor's education program, but it's regarded as sacrosanct by members of her own party. 很多专家批评了州长的教育计划,但她所在政党的一些成员认为该计划神圣不可更改。

Sacrosanct means literally "made holy by a sacred rite," and in its original use the word was reserved for things of the utmost holiness. But *sacrosanct* is now used to describe a questionable sacredness which nevertheless makes something immune from

SANCT

attack or violation; that is, the person using the word usually doesn't regard the thing as sacred at all. So to call a government program sacrosanct is to imply that others regard it as untouchable. And a piece of writing is more likely to be thought of as sacrosanct by its author than by the editor who has to fix it up.

sacrosanct 字面意思是"因神圣的仪式而神圣",最初该词仅用于最神圣的事物。但是 *sacrosanct* 现在用于描述值得质疑的神圣,不过还是能使其免遭攻击或者违反。也就是说,使用这一词语的人通常并不认为该事物很神圣。因此,说政府某一计划 sacrosanct 就是在暗示其他人它是不可更改的。一篇文字,其作者更可能认为它是 sacrosanct,不得不加以修改准备发表的编辑则不那么肯定。

sanctuary \ ˈsaŋk-chə-ˌwer-ē \ (1) A holy place, such as a church or temple, or the most holy part of one. 圣所;圣殿 (2) A place of safety, refuge, and protection. 庇护所;避难所;保护区

• The midtown park is a tranquil sanctuary amidst the city's heat, noise, and bustle. 市中心区那个公园是个宁静的地方,可以躲避炎热、噪声和嘈杂。

Historically, churches have been places where fugitives could seek at least temporary protection from the law. In Anglo-Saxon England, churches and churchyards generally provided 40 days of immunity, and neither the sheriffs nor the army would enter to seize the outlaw. But gradually the right of *sanctuary* was eroded. In 1486 sanctuary for the crime of treason was disallowed, and sanctuary for most other crimes was severely restricted by Henry VIII and later abolished. In the 1980s many U.S. churches provided sanctuary to political refugees from Central America, and the U.S. government mostly chose not to interfere. Today, wildlife sanctuaries provide protection for the species within its boundaries, and farm-animal sanctuaries now rescue livestock from abuse and starvation.

古往今来,教堂一直是逃亡者至少可以暂时躲避法律惩罚的地方。在盎格鲁—撒克逊时代的英国,教堂和教堂大院通常提供四十天的保护,无论是郡督还是军队,谁也不会进去抓捕逃犯。但是慢慢地,提供 *sanctuary*(庇护)的权利被削弱了。1486年,庇护叛国罪的权力被官方拒绝接受,庇护多数其他罪行的权力也被亨利八世严重限制了,后来彻底废除了。20 世纪 80 年代,很多美国教堂为中美洲的政治逃犯提供庇护,美国政府多数情况下不予干涉。今天,野生动物保护区为其中的物种提供保护,家畜 sanctuaries(保护区)现在拯救家畜,使其免于虐待和饥饿。

LOQU comes from the Latin verb *loqui*, "to talk." An *eloquent* preacher speaks fluently, forcefully, and expressively. And a dummy's words come out of a *ventriloquist's* mouth—or perhaps out of his belly (in Latin, *venter*).

LOQU 源自拉丁语动词 *loqui*,意思是"谈话"。*eloquent* 的牧师讲话流畅、有力、富有表达力。人体模型的话语从 *ventriloquist*(口技表演者)的嘴里——或者可能是从他的肚子里——讲了出来。

colloquium \ kə-ˈlō-kwē-əm \ A conference in which various speakers take turns lecturing on a subject and then answering questions about it. 学术研讨会;学术会议

• There's a colloquium at Yale on Noah Webster in September, where she's scheduled to deliver a paper. 九月份，耶鲁大学将举行一次关于诺亚·韦伯斯特的研讨会，已经安排她宣读论文了。

A *colloquy* is a conversation, and especially an important, high-level discussion. *Colloquy* and *colloquium* once meant the same thing, though today *colloquium* always refers to a conference. Because of its old "conversation" meaning, however, a colloquium is a type of conference with important question-and-answer periods.
colloquy 就是一次谈话，尤其是重要的、高水准的讨论。colloquy 和 colloquium 曾经有着同样的意思，虽然今天 colloquium 总是指学术研讨会。当时，由于它具有"谈话"这一古老的意思，colloquium 这种学术会议有提问和回答这种阶段，而且很重要。

soliloquy \sə-ˈli-lə-kwē\ A dramatic speech that represents a series of unspoken thoughts. 独白

- Film characters never have onscreen soliloquies, though they may tell us their thoughts in a voiceover. 电影中的人物从来没有显示在屏幕上的独白，尽管他们可能会通过解说者说出自己的想法。

Since *solus* means "alone" in Latin, soliloquies take place when a character is alone onstage, or maybe spotlighted off to one side of a dark stage. Novels have no trouble in expressing to the reader a character's personal thoughts, but such expression is less natural to stage drama. The soliloquies of Shakespeare—in *Hamlet* ("To be or not to be"), *Macbeth* ("Tomorrow and tomorrow and tomorrow"), *Romeo and Juliet* ("But soft! what light from yonder window breaks"), etc.—are the most famous, but modern playwrights such as Tennessee Williams, Arthur Miller, and Sam Shepard have also employed them.
由于 solus 在拉丁语中意思是"单独"，所以独白发生在某一人物单独站在舞台上的时候，或者在黑暗的舞台一侧被聚光灯照亮的时候。长篇小说很容易向读者表达人物的个人想法，但是这样的表达在舞台戏剧中是不正常的。莎士比亚戏剧中的 soliloquies（独白）——《哈姆雷特》中的"To be or not to be"（"生存还是毁灭"）、《麦克白》中的"Tomorrow and tomorrow and tomorrow"（"明天，又一个明天，又一个明天"）、《罗密欧与朱丽叶》中的"But soft! what light from yonder window breaks"（"嘘！那边窗户里亮起的是什么光"），等等——是最有名的，但是当代戏剧家，比如田纳西·威廉姆斯、阿瑟·米勒和萨姆·谢泼德，也使用了独白。

colloquial \kə-ˈlō-kwē-əl\ Conversational in style. 谈话风格的；像谈话一样的

- The author, though obviously a professional writer, uses a colloquial style in this new book. 虽然作者显然是一位职业作家，却在新书中使用了白话风格的语言。

Since *colloquy* means basically "conversation," colloquial language is the language almost all of us speak. It uses contractions ("can't," "it's," "they've"), possibly some slang, lots of short words and not many long ones. But our language usually changes when we write, becoming more formal and sometimes even "literary." Except in e-mails and text messages, many people never write a contraction or use the word "I", and avoid informal words completely. But colloquial language isn't necessarily bad in writing, and it's sometimes more appropriate than the alternative.

由于 *colloquy* 的基本意思是"谈话",谈话风格的语言是我们几乎所有人说的。这种语言使用缩约词("can't"、"it's"、"they've"),可能还有一些俚语、很多短词和很少长词。但是,我们写作时,我们的语言通常会发生变化,变得更加正式,有时候甚至是"文学风格的"。除了电子邮件和手机短信,很多人从来不会写一段谈话或者使用"我"这个词,并完全避免使用非正式词语。但是,谈话风格的语言在写作中不一定就不好,有时候反而合适。

loquacious \lō-ˈkwā-shəs\   Apt to talk too much; talkative. 善于言谈的;说话过多的

• She had hoped to read quietly on the plane, but the loquacious salesman in the next seat made it nearly impossible. 她本来希望在飞机上安静地看书,但是旁边座位上那个销售员话太多了,她几乎没法看书。

A *loquacious* speaker can leave a big audience stifling its yawns after the first 45 minutes, and the *loquaciousness* of a dinner guest can keep everyone else from getting a word in edgewise. Loquacious letters used to go on for pages, and a loquacious author might produce a 1,200-page novel. Lincoln's brief 269-word Gettysburg Address was delivered after a two-hour, 13,000-word speech by America's most famous orator, a windbag of *loquacity*.

loquacious 演讲者在最初四十五分钟后会让很多听众想忍住不要打哈欠。吃饭的客人的 *loquaciousness* 会让其他人没法说一句话。loquacious 书信以前会多达数页,loquacious 作者可能写出一千二百页的小说。林肯的《葛底斯堡演说》言简意赅,仅有二百六十九个单词,而这之前的演讲长达两个小时,一万三千个单词,演说者是美国最著名的演说家,说起话来没完没了,很是 *loquacity*(饶舌)。

Quizzes

A. Choose the closest definition:

1. sanction   a. pray   b. warn   c. trade   d. approve
2. soliloquy   a. love poem   b. monologue   c. lullaby   d. conversation
3. sanctimonious   a. hypocritical   b. holy   c. solemn   d. divine
4. sacrosanct   a. sacred   b. churchlike   c. Christian   d. priestly
5. loquacious   a. abundant   b. silent   c. talkative   d. informative
6. sanctuary   a. belief   b. holiness   c. cemetery   d. refuge
7. colloquial   a. slangy   b. disrespectful   c. conversational   d. uneducated
8. colloquium   a. field of study   b. university   c. college   d. scholarly discussion

B. Indicate whether the following pairs of words have the same or different meanings:

1. soliloquy / praise   same ____ / different ____

UNIT 24

2. sanction / dedicate   same ____ / different ____
3. loquacious / long-winded   same ____ / different ____
4. sacrosanct / heavenly   same ____ / different ____
5. colloquium / temple   same ____ / different ____
6. sanctuary / shelter   same ____ / different ____
7. colloquial / informal   same ____ / different ____
8. sanctimonious / passionate same ____ / different ____

VIR is Latin for "man." A *virtue* is a good quality—originally, the kind of quality an ideal man possessed. And *virtuous* behavior is morally excellent. All in all, the Romans seem to have believed that being a man was a good thing.

VIR 是拉丁语,意思是"男人"。一种 *virtue*(美德)就是一种美好的品质——最早是理想的男人拥有的品质。*virtuous* 行为从道德上说是好的。总之,罗马人似乎相信做男人是一件好事。

virility \və-'ri-lə-tē\   Energetic, vigorous manhood; masculinity. 活力;精力;阳刚之气

• For his entire life he believed that anyone who had been a Marine had established his virility beyond any doubt. 他一辈子都相信,当过海军陆战队员的人,毫无疑问已经成了真正的男人。

Luckily, there's no doubt about what virility is, since it's depicted on the covers of dozens of new romance novels every month! A masterful and dominating manner, a splendid bared chest, a full head of lustrous hair, and an array of stunning costumes seem to be what's required. (*Virile* traits often missing in these men are hair on the chest and any hint of future baldness.) High-school football provides a showplace for demonstrations of adolescent virility, and for years afterward virile high-school players can keep using football language in their business life: "get to the red zone," "Hail Mary pass," "move the ball," and on and on.

幸运的是,什么是 *virility* 是毫无疑问的,因为每个月都有几十本新的爱情小说,封面上画得很清楚。样子很强势、很专横,裸露的胸膛肌肉发达,一头光亮的头发,而且多种多样的光鲜的衣服似乎也是必需的。(这些男人的 *virile*[阳刚的]特点中通常缺少胸毛和将会秃头的蛛丝马迹。)高中橄榄球提供了展示青少年阳刚之气的机会,而且之后很多年,很有雄性气概的高中运动员还可以在商业生活中一直使用橄榄球语言:"get to the red zone"("到了进攻重点区")、"Hail Mary pass"("万福玛利亚传球")、"move the ball"("运球"),等等。

triumvirate \trī-'əm-və-rət\ (1) A commission or government of three. 三人委员会;三人领导小组 (2) A group or association of three. 三人组;三人协会

• A triumvirate slowly emerged as the inner circle of the White House, and the vice president wasn't among them. 一个三人领导小组慢慢出现了,成了白宫的内部圈子,但副总统不在其中。

The first triumvirate of the Roman Republic, which consisted of Julius Caesar,

Pompey, and Crassus, was simply an alliance or partnership, not a formal institution of the government. The alliance didn't last long, however, and Caesar eventually emerged with total power. This led to his assassination, after which a second triumvirate took over, with Octavian, Mark Antony, and Lepidus dividing the Roman world among themselves. But these *triumvirs* also soon turned on one another, with Octavian alone taking power; in time he would become Rome's first emperor.

第一个 triumvirate 出现在罗马共和国,由尤利乌斯·恺撒、庞培和克拉苏组成,只是一个联盟或者合作关系,不是什么正式的政府机构。可是,这一联盟没有存在多久,恺撒最终取得了绝对权力。这就导致其被人暗杀的结局,之后第二个 triumvirate 接手,屋大维、马克·安东尼和雷必达瓜分了罗马世界。但是,这些 triumvirs(三人领导成员)也很快就相互斗争了,结果屋大维一个人取得大权。最终,他成了罗马第一任皇帝。

virago \və-ˈrä-gō\   A loud, bad-tempered, overbearing woman. 泼妇;悍妇

• The staff called her a virago and other things behind her back, but everyone was respectful of her abilities. 全体成员都在背后叫她泼妇或者其他难听的字眼,但是谁都对其才能尊重有加。

The original Latin meaning of *virago* was "female warrior." But in later centuries the meaning shifted toward the negative. The most famous virago in English literature is the ferocious Kate in Shakespeare's *The Taming of the Shrew*. Some historical viragoes have also become famous. Agrippina poisoned her husband, the Emperor Claudius, so that her son Nero could take his place (but it was Nero himself who eventually had her assassinated). And Queen Eleanor of Aquitaine, a powerful virago of the 12th century, was imprisoned by her husband, King Henry II of England, after she encouraged their sons to rebel against him. Today some people are beginning to use *virago* admiringly again.

virago 在拉丁语中最初的意思是"女战士"。但是,在随后几个世纪,其意思发生了变化,有了否定的意味。英国文学中最有名的 virago(泼妇)就是莎士比亚戏剧《驯悍记》中的凯特。历史上有些 viragoes 也很有名。阿格里皮娜毒死了丈夫克劳迪亚斯皇帝,这样她儿子尼禄就可以取而代之(但是,尼禄最终让人把母亲暗杀了)。阿基坦的埃莉诺王后是 12 世纪很有权势的 virago。她被丈夫英国国王亨利二世投进了监狱,因为她鼓励几个儿子反叛国王。今天,有些人正开始以赞赏的方式使用 *virago* 一词。

virtuosity \ˌvər-chü-ˈä-sə-tē\   Great technical skill, especially in the practice of a fine art. 高超技艺;精湛演技

• Playing with the band, his virtuosity doesn't show through; you really have to hear him solo to appreciate him. 跟这个乐队演奏,他高超的技艺难以充分展示,你得听他单独演奏才能欣赏他。

Virtuosity is used particularly to describe musicians, but also often for writers, actors, dancers, and athletes. A *virtuoso* is a highly skilled performer, and a *virtuoso* performance is one that astonishes the audience by its feats. In ancient Greece the cities would hold male competitions in acrobatics, conjuring, public reciting, blowing the trumpet, and acting out scenes from Homer's epics, the winners of which would have been praised as *virtuous*, or "full of manly virtues."

virtuosity 尤其用来描述音乐家,但是也经常用于描述作家、演员、舞蹈家和运动员。一位 *virtuoso* 就是一位技术高超的表演者,而一个 *virtuoso* 表演是技艺高超、令人惊叹的表演。在古希腊,各个城市会举行男性比赛,有杂技比赛、变魔术比赛、背诵比赛、吹喇叭比赛、荷马史诗场景表演比赛,获胜者会得到表扬,被描述为 *virtuous*,即"富有男性美德"。

VAL

VAL has as its basic meaning "strength," from the Latin verb *valere*, meaning "to be worthy, healthy, or strong" and "to have power or influence." So *evaluating* a house involves determining how healthy it is. A *valid* license or credit card is one that's still in effect, and a valid proof is one that provides strong evidence.

VAL 基本意思是"力量",源自拉丁语动词 *valere*,意思是"值得尊敬的、健康的、强壮的",以及"有权力,有影响"。所以,*evaluating*(评价)一匹马(注:原文的 house 疑为 horse)包括确定其健康状况。一个 *valid* 执照或者信用卡仍然有效,一个 *valid* 证据能提供难以推翻的证明。

---

valor\ˈva-lər\ Personal bravery in the face of danger. 勇敢;勇气

● The gun duels of the Old West were invented by a novelist inspired by the valor of the knights in medieval tournaments. 美国西部的枪斗是一位小说家杜撰出来的,灵感来源于中世纪骑马比武的骑士们的勇气。

Valor in uniform is still rewarded by medals. Many American civic organizations award a Medal of Valor for physical courage, and the Air Force Medal of Honor displays the single word "Valor." The somewhat old-fashioned adjective *valorous* more often describes warriors of the past. But *valiant* is still in common use, though it less often describes military courage than other kinds of bravery or effort.

穿制服的人们的 valor(勇敢)仍然获得勋章。很多美国民间组织为勇气颁发 Medal of Valor(英勇勋章),空军荣誉勋章证明的就是一个词:"Valor"。*valorous* 这个有点古旧的形容词更多地用于描述过去的战士。但是 *valiant* 仍然普遍使用,虽然较少用于描述军人的勇气,而更多地用于其他类型的勇敢或者努力。

---

equivalent\i-ˈkwi-və-lənt\ (1) Equal in force, amount, value, area, or volume. 相等 (2) Similar or virtually identical in effect or function. 相似;几乎相同

● A square can be equivalent to a triangle in area, but not in shape. 正方形跟三角形可能面积相等,但形状不同。

Modern democracies have institutions and offices that are roughly *equivalent* to those found in others: the president of the United States has his British equivalent in the prime minister, for instance, and the U.S. Congress finds its equivalent in the British Parliament. The heavily armored knight on his great armored horse has been called the Middle Ages' equivalent of the army tank. In none of these examples are the two things identical to each other; they're simply very similar in their effect or purpose or nature, which is what *equivalence* usually implies.

当代民主国家有着与其他国家大致对应的机构和办公室:比如美国总统相当于英国首相,美国国会相当于英国议会。骑着披戴盔甲的骏马、身着沉重盔甲的骑士,被称为与坦克相当的中世纪重型武器。这些例子中,没有一对是完全相等的,它们只是在效果、目的或性质上很相似罢了,这就是 *equivalent* 通常所暗示的。

prevalent\\'pre-və-lənt\\ Widely accepted, favored, or practiced; widespread. 普遍接受的；普遍喜欢的；普遍实行的；普遍的

• On some campuses Frisbees seem to be more prevalent than schoolbooks, especially in the spring. 在某些校园，飞盘似乎比上课本更普遍，尤其是在春天。

Many diseases that were prevalent a century ago have been controlled by advances in medicine. Smallpox was prevalent on several continents for many centuries, and when Europeans brought it with them to the Americas, it killed more American Indians than the armed settlers did. But *prevalent* doesn't just describe diseases. One ideal of male or female beauty may be prevalent in a particular society and quite a different ideal in another. In the 1950s and 1960s, there was a prevalent notion that if you went swimming less than an hour after eating you might drown because of stomach cramps—which goes to show that not every prevalent idea is exactly true.

很多疾病一个世纪前很 prevalent（普遍），但是医学的发展使其得到了控制。天花在几个大陆普遍存在了几个世纪。当欧洲人将其带到美洲之后，因病而死的印第安人比殖民者使用武力杀死的更多。但是 *prevalent* 不仅仅用于描述疾病。某种男性美或女性美的标准可能在某一特定社会被普遍接受，但在另一社会却截然不同。在 20 世纪五六十年代，有一种 prevalent notion（普遍看法），认为如果你过饭不到一小时就去游泳，由于胃痉挛被淹死。这告诉我们，不是每个 prevalent idea（普遍看法）都完全正确。

validate\\'va-lə-ˌdāt\\ (1) To make legally valid; give official approval to. 使……有法律效力；批准 (2) To support or confirm the validity of. 确认……的有效性

• It will take many more research studies to validate a theory as far-reaching as this one. 要验证一个像这样影响深远的理论，还需要进行更多的研究。

Validating a pass might require getting an official stamp on it. Validating experimental data might require checking it against data from further experiments. An A on a test might validate your study methods. And you might go to a trusted friend to validate your decision to get rid of your boyfriend, buy a pet iguana, or sell everything and move to Las Vegas.

validating（批准）一个通行证，可能需要在上面盖章。validating（确认……的有效性）实验结果可能需要与进一步实验的结果对比检查。试卷上的 A 可能 validate（证明……有效）你的学习方法。你想甩了男朋友、买一条宠物鬣蜥或者卖掉所有东西搬到洛杉矶，可能会找一位最信赖的朋友 validate（证实……是正确的）你的决定。

Quizzes

A. Fill in each blank with the correct letter：

a. virago   e. valor
b. virtuosity   f. validate
c. triumvirate   g. prevalent
d. virility   h. equivalent

1. Some people think a man's _____ fades with age.
2. An election worker at the next table will _____ each voter's ID.
3. The orchestra will be performing with a solo violinist whose _____ has

already made her a star.

4. Colds and flu threaten to be unusually _____ this winter.

5. The ranch is owned by Mamie Peabody, a brawny _____ who sometimes competes in the men's events at the rodeo.

6. We may not be able to find an identical chair, but we'll find an _____ one.

7. The company is really run by a _____: Bailey, Sanchez, and Dr. Ross.

8. At a memorial ceremony, the slain guard who had tried to stop the gunman was honored for _____.

B. Match the word on the left to the correct definition on the right:

1. prevalent   a. courage
2. virago   b. masculinity
3. virtuosity   c. confirm
4. virility   d. strong woman
5. valor   e. skill
6. triumvirate   f. widespread
7. equivalent   g. three-person board
8. validate   h. similar in value

CRE/CRET

CRE/CRET comes from the Latin verb *crescere*, which means both "to come into being" and "to grow." So a *crescendo* in music occurs when the music is growing louder, and a *decrescendo* when it's growing softer.

CRE/CRET 源自拉丁语动词 *crescere*，意思是"形成，出现"和"生长"。所以，当音乐声音越来越大，就会出现音乐中的 *crescendo*（渐强），当音乐声音越来越小，就会出现 *decrescendo*（渐弱）。

crescent \ˈkre-sənt\ (1) The moon between the new moon and first quarter, and between the last quarter and the next new moon. 新月 (2) Anything shaped like the crescent moon. 新月形事物

• The symbol of Islam is a crescent moon with a star between the points, an astronomical impossibility. 伊斯兰教的象征符号是一弯新月，两端之间有一个星星，而这在天文学上是不可能的事情。

Crescent means basically "growing," since a crescent moon is in the process of "growing" to a full moon. A *crescent wrench*, with its open end (unlike the kind of wrench that has an almost circular end), can be found in almost any household. A *croissant*, or crescent pastry, is a breakfast staple. The curving region called the Fertile Crescent, which stretches from the Persian Gulf up through Iraq, across to Lebanon and Israel, and down into Egypt's Nile River valley, was the birthplace of civilization, where weaving, pottery, domesticated livestock, irrigation farming, and writing all first appeared.

crescent 的基本意思是"正在生长"，因为新月处于"正在生长"成满月的过程中。crescent wrench(可调月牙扳手)，顶端张开(与有着几乎是圆形顶端的扳手不同)，几乎家家都有。*croissant*，或者新月形面包，是早餐的基本食物。称为 Fertile Crescent(新月沃土)的那片弯弯的地区，从波斯湾穿过伊拉克延伸至黎巴嫩和以色列，再南下至埃及的尼罗河河谷，是文明的诞生地，是纺织、制陶、家畜、灌溉农业和文字出现的地方。

accretion\ə-ˈkrē-shən\ (1) Growth or enlargement by gradual buildup. 渐渐生长;渐渐增大 (2) A product of such buildup. 渐长的结果;渐增的结果

- The house and barn were linked by an accretion of outbuildings, each joined to the next. 房屋和谷仓因为附属建筑物渐渐扩大连在了一起，一个跟另一个连接了。

The slow accretion of scientific knowledge over many centuries has turned into an avalanche in our time. Any accretion of ice on a grounded jet will result in takeoff delays because of the danger it poses. The land area of the Mississippi Delta increases every year from the accretion of soil washed down the Mississippi River, though the accretions happen so slowly that it's difficult to detect any increase at all. Accretion is often used in scientific writing; its usual verb form, *accrue*, is more often used in financial contexts ("This figure doesn't count the accrued interest on the investments").

数个世纪以来，科学知识慢慢 accretion(增多)，在我们这个时代则激增了。停飞的喷气式飞机上结冰增多，会导致起飞延迟，因为冰构成了危险。密西西比三角洲的土地面积逐渐增加，原因是河流带来的泥土逐渐增多，虽然这一过程非常缓慢，根本看不出来任何增加。accretion 常常用于科学写作，其通常的动词形式是 *accrue*，更多地用于财政语境中("This figure doesn't count the accrued interest on the investment""这一数字不包括投资的应计利息")。

excrescence\ek-ˈskre-səns\ (1) A projection of growth, especially when abnormal. 赘生物;赘疣;瘤 (2) A disfiguring, unnecessary, or unwanted mark or part. 丑陋而多余的标记或部分

- The new warehouse squatted like some hideous excrescence on the landscape. 这座新仓库像一个丑陋的赘疣在那里破坏风景。

Warts and pimples are common excrescences that can usually be wiped out with medication; other excrescences such as cysts and tumors need to be removed surgically. Mushrooms are the excrescences of underground fungus networks. Some people consider slang words to be vulgar excrescences on the English language, but others consider slang the most colorful vocabulary of all.

瘤子和粉刺是常见的 excrescences(赘生物)，通常可以用药物除去;其他赘生物，比如胞囊和肿瘤，需要手术才能除去。蘑菇是地下真菌网络的赘生物。有些人认为俚俗词语是英语中粗俗的多余部分，但是其他人认为俚语是最有趣的词汇。

increment\ˈiŋ-krə-mənt\ (1) Something gained or added, especially as one of a series of regular additions or as a tiny increase in amount. 增长;增加 (2) The amount or extent of change, especially the positive or negative change in value of one or more variables. 正(或负)增量;正(或负)增额

- Her bank account has grown weekly by increments of $50 for the past two

• 580 •

UNIT 24

years. 她的银行存款过去两年每周增量为 50 美元。

Increment is used in many technical fields, but also nontechnically. *Incremental* increases in drug dosages are used for experimental purposes. Incremental tax increases are easier to swallow than sudden large increases. Incremental changes of any kind may be hard to notice, but can be very significant in the long run. Rome wasn't built in a day, but was instead built up by increments from a couple of villages in the 10th century B. C. to the capital of the Mediterranean world in the 1st century A. D.

increment 用于很多专业领域,但也用于专业领域之外。药物剂量的 incremental(渐进的,递进的)增加用于实验目的。incremental 税收增加比突然的大额增加更容易吸收。任何种类的 incremental 变化都很难觉察,但从长远来看则很突出。罗马不是一天建成的,而是由公元前 10 世纪的几个村庄逐渐扩建,到公元 1 世纪成了地中海世界的首都。

FUS comes from the Latin verb *fundere*, "to pour out" or "to melt." A *fuse* depends on melting metal to break an overloaded circuit. Nuclear *fusion* involves the "melting" together of light nuclei to form heavier nuclei, and fusion cuisine brings together the cooking of two or more cultures.

FUS 源自拉丁语动词 *fundere*,意思是"倒出"或"熔化"。Fuse(保险丝;熔断丝)依靠熔化金属来切断重负荷的电路。nuclear fusion(核融合,核聚变)就是质量轻的原子"融"在一起构成质量重的原子,而 fusion cuisine(融合式烹饪)将两个或多个文化的烹饪融合在一起。

transfusion \trans-ˈfyü-zhən\ (1) The process of transferring a fluid and especially blood into a blood vessel. 输入血管;输血 (2) Something transfused. 输入血管之物

• The transfusion gave her an immediate burst of energy, and her friends were astonished when they arrived at the hospital that afternoon. 这次输血立刻使她精力充沛。那天下午,朋友们到了医院都很吃惊。

When blood transfusions were first attempted by Europeans in the early 1600s, they were met with skepticism, since the established practice was to bleed patients, not *transfuse* them with blood. Some patients were transfused with animal blood, and so many died as a result that by 1700 transfusions had been widely outlawed. Not until 1900 were the major blood groups (A, B, AB, and O) recognized, making transfusions safe and effective.

17 世纪早期,当欧洲人首次尝试 blood transfusions(输血)时,他们遭遇了质疑,因为传统的做法是给病人放血,不是 transfuse(输入)血液。有些病人被输入了动物血液,结果很多人死了。于是,到 1700 年输血被普遍宣布为非法。直到 1900 年,人们识别出了主要的血型(A 型、B 型、AB 型和 O 型),从而使输血安全有效了。

effusive \i-ˈfyü-siv\ (1) Given to excessive display of feeling. 过分流露情感的 (2) Freely expressed. 自由表达的

• At the victory party she lavished effusive praise on all her supporters for almost half an hour.

Since to *effuse* is to "pour out," an effusive person makes a habit of pouring out emotions. Greeting someone *effusively* may include great hugs and wet kisses. Academy Award winners tend to become embarrassingly effusive once they've got the microphone. But at least *effusiveness* is generally an expression of positive rather than negative emotions.

由于 *effuse* 意思是"倒出"，一个 *effusive* 人习惯于流露出自己的情绪。向某人 *effusively* 问好可能包括热烈的拥抱和亲吻。学院奖获奖者往往一旦站在麦克风前，就会激情四射得令人尴尬。不过，至少 *effusiveness* 常常是正面情感而不是负面情感的流露。

profusion \prə-'fyü-zhən\ Great abundance. 大量；众多；充足

● In May the trees and flowers bloom with almost delirious profusion. 五月，树木和花草纷纷盛开，几乎让人欣喜若狂。

A profusion is literally a "pouring forth," so a profusion of gifts is a wealth or abundance of gifts. A *profusely* illustrated book is filled to overflowing with pictures. A bad social error should be followed by *profuse* apologies, and profound gratitude should be expressed with profuse thanks.

profusion 字面意思是"涌出"，所以 a profusion of 礼物就是大量的礼物。一本 *profusely* 插图的书，就是一本插图丰富的书。糟糕的社交错误之后应该是 *profuse*（大量的）道歉，而 *profound* 感激之情应该用千恩万谢来表达。

suffuse \sə-'fyüz\ To spread over or fill something, as if by fluid or light. 布满；充满；弥漫

● As the soft light of dawn suffused the landscape, they could hear the loons crying over the lake. 黎明时柔和的光线充满整个房间，他们可以听到湖上潜鸟的叫声

The odors of baking may suffuse a room, and so may the light of a sunset. A face may be suffused (that is, filled, but also probably flushed) with joy, or hope, or love. A novel may be suffused with Irish humor, and a room may be suffused with firelight. Scientists may even describe an insect's gray wings as being suffused with tinges of red.

烘烤糕点的香味 suffuse（弥漫）整个房间，落日的余晖也会充满房间。一个人的脸上可能 be *suffused* with 欢乐、希望或者爱（也就是充满了其中一种感情，但也可能会因为其中一种感情而满面红光）。一部小说可能 be suffused with（充满了）爱尔兰式的幽默，一个房间可能 be suffused with（充满了）火光。科学家甚至可能描述说，一只昆虫的翅膀 being suffused with（布满）淡淡的红色。

Quizzes

A. Choose the closest definition：

1. excrescence   a. disgust   b. outgrowth   c. extremity
   d. garbage
2. suffuse   a. overwhelm   b. flow
   c. spread through   d. inject
3. accretion   a. agreement   b. eruption   c. decision
   d. buildup

4. effusive	a. emotional	b. gradual	c. continual
d. general			
5. increment	a. entrance	b. slight increase	
c. construction	d. income		
6. transfusion	a. revision	b. change	c. transfer
d. adjustment			
7. crescent	a. semicircle	b. pastry	c. sickle shape
d. buildup			
8. profusion	a. distinction	b. abundance	c. addition
d. completion			

B. Indicate whether the following pairs of words have the same or different meanings:

1. effusive / gushy   same ____ / different ____
2. crescent / pinnacle   same ____ / different ____
3. transfusion / improvement   same ____ / different ____
4. excrescence / ugliness   same ____ / different ____
5. suffuse / fill   same ____ / different ____
6. increment / excess   same ____ / different ____
7. profusion / amount   same ____ / different ____
8. accretion / destruction   same ____ / different ____

Greek and Latin Borrowings 希腊语和拉丁语借词

apologia \ˌa-pə-ˈlō-jē-ə\   A defense, especially of one's own ideas, opinions, or actions. （为自己的看法、观点或者行动进行的）辩护；辩解

● His resignation speech was an eloquent apologia for his controversial actions as chairman. 他的辞职演说表达清晰，对自己作为主席时富有争议的行动进行了辩解。

An apologia and an *apology* usually aren't the same thing. An apology includes an admission of wrongdoing, but an apologia rarely *apologizes* in this sense, instead seeking to justify what was done. So, for example, in 1992 some of the books published for the 500th anniversary of Columbus's voyage were apologias explaining why European powers such as Spain acted as they did in the New World: because, for example, the Aztecs were a cruel people, practicing human sacrifice in grotesque ways (victims were skinned, and their skins were worn by the high priests), and Christianity hoped to reform them. Of course, the Spanish Inquisition was torturing and executing nonbelievers at the same time—but that would be the subject of other apologias.

一个 apologia 和一个 apology（道歉）通常是不一样的。Apology 包括承认做错了，但是 *apologia* 很少在这个意义上 *apologizes*（道歉），而是想方设法为所做的一切寻找正当理由。所以，比如在 1992 年，为纪念哥伦布航行五百周年而出版的书籍，有一些就是辩护性的，解释了西班牙这些欧洲强国在新世界的所作所为：比如因为阿兹特克人是残忍的民

族,以荒唐的方式实行人祭(受害者的皮剥下后,大祭司穿在身上),所以基督教希望改造他们。当然,西班牙宗教裁判所也在折磨、迫害不信仰基督教的人。

atrium \ˈā-trē-əm\ (1) An open rectangular patio around which a house is built. 天井 (2) A court with a skylight in a many-storied building. 中厅;中庭

- Best of all, their new home had a large atrium, where they could eat breakfast in the fresh air in spring and summer. 最妙的是,他们的新家有一个宽敞的天井,春夏两季可以在清新的空气中吃早餐。

In malls and grand office buildings today, the enclosed atrium, often with full-size trees growing in it and high indoor balconies with hanging vines, has become a common architectural feature. But the original atria (notice the unusual plural) were open to the sky and occupied the center of a house or villa in ancient Rome. The open Roman courtyard allowed air to circulate and light to enter, and even its plantings helped cool the house. Situating the cooking fireplace in the atrium was another way of keeping the house itself cool. Still today, houses around the Mediterranean Sea and in tropical Latin America often have internal courtyards. 今天,在购物中心和巨大的办公楼,封闭的 atrium(中厅)已经成为常见的建筑特色。里面通常有正常大小的树木和高高的室内阳台,阳台上是悬吊的藤蔓。但是,最早的 atria(注意其复数形式)在古罗马是朝向天空开放的,占据房屋或别墅的中心。罗马露天的院子让空气循环,让光线进入,连植物也有助于使房屋凉爽。将做饭的炉灶建在中厅,是使房屋保持凉爽的另一做法。今天,地中海周围和热带拉丁美洲的房屋仍然经常有内部院落。

oligarchy \ˈä-lə-ˌgär-kē\ A government in which power is in the hands of a small group. 寡头政府

- The population was shackled by an iron-willed oligarchy that dictated every aspect of their lives and ruthlessly crushed any hint of rebellion. 人们被铁石心肠的寡头政府牢牢束缚着,生活的方方面面都由其规定,只要有反叛的苗头,马上遭到无情镇压。

Oligarchy combines roots from the Greek words oligos, meaning "few," and archos, meaning "leader or ruler." In ancient Greece, an aristocracy was government by the "best" (in Greek, aristos) citizens. An oligarchy was a corrupted aristocracy, one in which a few evil men unjustly seized power and used it to further their own ends. Since at least 1542, oligarchy has been used in English to describe oppressive governments of the kind that serve the interests of a few very wealthy families. oligarchy 由两个希腊语词语的词根组合而成,一个是 oligos,意思是"少数",一个是 archos,意思是"领导者或统治者"。在古希腊,一个 aristocracy(贵族统治集团)就是由"最好的"(希腊语为 aristos)公民组成的统治集团。一个 oligarchy 就是腐败的 aristocracy(一群贵族),其中的少数邪恶之人以不正当手段取得权力,以此更好地实现自己的目的。至少从 1542 年以来,oligarchy 就在英语中用来描述仅为少数富人的利益服务的残暴政府。

encomium \en-ˈkō-mē-əm\ Glowing, enthusiastic praise, or an expression of such praise. 热情洋溢的赞扬;赞扬的话

- The surprise guest at the farewell party was the school's most famous graduate, who delivered a heartfelt encomium to the woman he called his favorite teacher of all. 告别晚会上,让人意想不到的客人就是学校最有名的毕业生。他发表了热情洋溢的讲话,衷心赞扬了那位他称为自己最喜欢的教师的女士。

Encomium comes straight from Latin. Mark Antony's encomium to the dead Caesar in Shakespeare's *Julius Caesar* ("Friends, Romans, countrymen, lend me your ears") is one of the most famous encomiums of all time, while Ben Jonson's encomium to the dead Shakespeare ("He was not of an age, but for all time") has also been widely read and discussed. The British poet laureate is expected to compose poetic encomiums to mark special events or to praise a person honored by the state. And any awards banquet is thick with encomiums, with each speaker trying to outdo the last in praise of those being honored.

encomium 直接源自拉丁语。在莎士比亚戏剧《尤利乌斯·恺撒》中,马克·安东尼对死去的恺撒的赞扬("Friends, Romans, countrymen, lend me your ears""朋友们、罗马公民们、同胞们,请听我讲")成了历代最有名的赞扬。而本·琼森对去世的莎士比亚的赞扬("He was not of an age, but for all time""他不属于一个时代,而是属于所有时代")也一直让人阅读、讨论。英国桂冠诗人应该写一首赞美诗纪念特殊事件,或者赞扬一位国家颁奖或者授予称号的人士。任何颁奖宴会都充满了赞扬,每位发言者在赞扬获奖者方面都力争超过上一位发言者。

neurosis \ nu̇-ˈrō-səs \ A mental and emotional disorder that is less severe than a psychosis and may involve various pains, anxieties, or phobias. 神经(官能)症;疼痛;忧虑;恐惧

● He has a neurosis about dirt, and is constantly washing his hands. 他对尘土有恐惧感,一直洗手。

A *neurosis* is a somewhat mild mental disorder; unexplained anxiety attacks, unreasonable fears, depression, and physical symptoms that are mentally caused are all examples of *neurotic* conditions. A superstitious person who compulsively knocks on wood or avoids anything with the number 13 might be suffering from a harmless neurosis. But a severe neurosis such as agoraphobia (see p. 632) can be very harmful, making a person a prisoner of his or her home. *Neurosis* is based on the Greek word for "nerve," since until quite recently neurotic behavior was often blamed on the nerves. Neurosis is usually contrasted with *psychosis*, which includes a considerably more serious group of conditions.

neurosis 是一种有些轻微的精神疾病,无法解释的阵阵担忧、不合理的害怕、抑郁以及精神引起的身体症状,都是 neurotic(神经质)状况的例子。一个迷信的人,如果不能自已地敲打木头或者避免任何与数字十三有关的事物,可能就患有无甚大碍的神经官能症。但是严重的神经官能症,比如广场恐惧症(见第632页)可能很有害,让人成为自己家的囚徒。Neurosis 以希腊语中指代"神经"的词语为基础,因为直到最近,神经官能症行为都被认为是由神经引起的。neurosis 通常与 psychosis(精神病)对比,后者包括严重程度高得多的一组疾病。

opprobrium \ ə-ˈprō-brē-əm \ (1) Something that brings disgrace. 带来耻辱的事物 (2) A public disgrace that results from conduct considered wrong or bad. 公开羞辱

● The writers of the New Testament hold the Pharisees up to opprobrium for their hypocrisy and hollow spirituality. 《新约》的作者们羞辱法利赛人,因为他们虚伪而且精神空虚。

Witches have long been the objects of *opprobrium*; in Europe in the 16th and

17th centuries, women thought to be witches were burned by the thousands. The *opprobrious* crime of treason could likewise result in the most hideous torture and execution. In *The Scarlet Letter*, the sin of adultery in Puritan times brought opprobrium on Hester Prynne. Today the country of Israel is the object of opprobrium in many countries, while the Palestinians suffer similar opprobrium in others. And mere smokers, or even overweight people, may sometimes feel themselves to be the objects of mild opprobrium. 女巫长期以来都是 opprobrium（公开羞辱）的目标。在 16、17 世纪的欧洲,成千上万的女性,因为被指认为女巫而被活活烧死。*opprobrious*（极为可耻的）的背叛行为同样会遭受可怕的折磨和迫害。在《红字》中,清教徒时代犯了通奸罪让海丝特•白兰遭受了公开羞辱。今天,以色列是很多国家羞辱的对象,而巴勒斯坦人在很多国家遭受了类似的羞辱。抽烟者,或者甚至是超重的人,有时候都可能觉得自己是人们委婉羞辱的对象。

referendum\ˌre-fə-ˈren-dəm\　(1) The referring of legislative measures to the voters for approval or rejection. 公民复决（投票）(2) A vote on such a measure. 对议案的投票

● The referendum on the tax needed for constructing the new hospital passed by seven votes. 为建造这所医院而征税的公民复决以七票优势通过。

Referendum is a Latin word, but its modern meaning only dates from the 19th century, when a new constitution adopted by Switzerland stated that the voters could vote directly on certain issues. Thus, a referendum is a measure that's *referred* (that is, sent on) to the people. Since the U.S. Constitution doesn't provide for referenda (notice the common plural form) at the national level, referenda tend to be on local and state issues. In most locales, a few questions usually appear on the ballot at election time, often involving such issues as new zoning ordinances, new taxes for schools, and new limits on spending. *referendum* 是拉丁语词语,但其当代的意思仅仅起源于 19 世纪。当时,瑞士采用的新宪法规定,投票人可以就某些问题直接投票。这样,一个 referendum 就是一个 *referred*（也就是"提交"）的议案。由于《美国宪法》没有规定可以进行全国范围的 refenda（注意这一常见的复数形式）,公民复决往往是当地或者州范围内的事情。在多数地点,选举时期通常会有几个问题出现在选票上,往往涉及新的分区法规、为建学校新设的税,以及对开支的新的限制。

ultimatum\ˌəl-tə-ˈmā-təm\　A final proposal, condition, or demand, especially one whose rejection will result in forceful action. 最后通牒

● The ultimatum to Iraq in 1991 demanding that it withdraw from Kuwait was ignored, and a U.S.-led invasion was the response. 1991 年向伊拉克发出的要求其从科威特撤军的最后通牒遭到忽视后,美国率领军队入侵了伊拉克。

An *ultimatum* is usually issued by a stronger power to a weaker one, since it wouldn't carry much weight if the one giving the ultimatum couldn't back up its threat. Near the end of World War II, the Allied powers issued an ultimatum to Japan: surrender completely or face the consequences. Japan rejected the ultimatum, and within days the U.S. had dropped atomic bombs on Hiroshima and Nagasaki, killing some 200,000 people.

ultimatum(最后通牒)往往是更强大的一方向较弱的一方发出的,因为如果没有足够的实力来实施威胁,最后通牒就没有威慑力。第二次世界大战临近结束时,盟国向日本发出最后通牒,要求其彻底投降,否则会面临后果。日本不予考虑,结果,美国在几天后向广岛和长崎投下了原子弹,使大约二十万人丧命。

Quizzes

Fill in each blank with the correct letter:

a. encomium
b. ultimatum
c. neurosis
d. atrium
e. apologia
f. oligarchy
g. referendum
h. opprobrium

1. His particular _____ was a fear of heights.
2. The country has a president, of course, but everyone knows he's just the front man for a shadowy _____.
3. The committee voted to submit the new zoning plan to the voters in a special _____.
4. The new office building was designed around a wide, sunlit _____ with a fountain and small trees.
5. His book is an _____ for his entire life, which may cause his enemies to rethink their opinion of him.
6. _____ has been heaped on the school board from angry parents on both sides of the issue.
7. When peace negotiations fell apart, an angry _____ was issued by the government.
8. Most of her speech was devoted to a glowing _____ to her staff members.

Review Quizzes

A. Complete the analogy:

1. church : temple :: sanctuary : _____
   a. destination   b. parish   c. destiny   d. refuge
2. relaxed : stiff :: colloquial : _____
   a. conversational   b. talkative   c. casual   d. formal
3. portion : segment :: increment : _____
   a. inroad   b. inflation   c. increase   d. instinct
4. reprimand : scolding :: encomium : _____
   a. warm drink   b. warm thanks   c. warm toast   d. warm praise
5. truce : treaty :: ultimatum : _____
   a. decision   b. negotiation   c. threat   d. attack

6. donate : contribute :: remand : _____
    a. pass over   b. send back   c. take on   d. give up
7. monarchy : king :: oligarchy : _____
    a. dictator   b. ruling group   c. emperor   d. totalitarian
8. cavity : hole :: excrescence : _____
    a. growth   b. deposit   c. residue   d. toad
9. rare : scarce :: prevalent : _____
    a. unique   b. commonplace   c. thick   d. preferred
10. evaporate : dry up :: inundate : _____
    a. flood   b. drain   c. wash   d. irrigate
11. order : demand :: commandeer : _____
    a. allow   b. seize   c. rule   d. lead
12. vamp : sexy :: virago : _____
    a. loud   b. attractive   c. powerful   d. elderly
13. generous : stingy :: effusive : _____
    a. emotional   b. thoughtful   c. restrained   d. passionate
14. release : restrain :: sanction : _____
    a. disapprove   b. request   c. train   d. decide
15. femininity : man :: virility : _____
    a. female   b. girl   c. woman   d. lady

B. Fill in each blank with the correct letter:

   a. referendum   i. apologia
   b. profusion   j. opprobrium
   c. crescent   k. transfusion
   d. validate   l. equivalent
   e. virtuosity   m. loquacious
   f. colloquium   n. sacrosanct
   g. redundancy   o. redound
   h. mandate

1. Although he was shy the first time he came to dinner, he's usually downright _____ these days.

2. Three new young staff members were hired this year, and they've given the whole place a real _____ of energy.

3. If our researchers receive the Nobel Prize this year, it will _____ to the university's credit for years to come.

4. The planning board submitted its proposal to the voters as a nonbinding _____.

5. My professor is participating in the _____, and we're all required to

attend.

6. Some politicians claim they have a _____ from the voters even when their margin of victory was actually small.

7. Under the new boss, no department here is _____ and almost any of them could be broken up tomorrow.

8. She was renowned for her _____ in the kitchen, whipping up delicious meals from any ingredients that came to hand.

9. The bower was hung with roses blooming in great _____.

10. At a scientific conference in July she delivered a convincing _____ for the unusual methods that had drawn so much criticism.

11. An endorsement from one of the major medical associations would help _____ the therapies we offer.

12. When a neo-Nazi group marched down Pennsylvania Avenue, it was greeted with loud _____ from egg-throwing anti-Nazi demonstrators.

13. The computer files contain a great deal of data _____ that isn't actually serving any purpose.

14. A speed of 100 kilometers per hour is _____ to about 60 miles per hour.

C. Match the definition on the left to the correct word on the right:

1. open courtyard
2. emotional disorder
3. spread over
4. accumulation
5. bravery
6. monologue
7. hypocritical
8. wavelike
9. required
10. three-person group

a. soliloquy
b. undulant
c. valor
d. triumvirate
e. suffuse
f. accretion
g. atrium
h. neurosis
i. sanctimonious
j. mandatory

UNIT 25

VERB comes from the Latin *verbum*, meaning "word." A *verb*—or action word—appears in some form in every complete sentence. To express something *verbally*—or to *verbalize* something—is to say it or write it.
VERB 一词源于拉丁语的 *verbum*，意思是"词"。动词（verb），或者说"行为词"（action word），以某种形式出现在每个完整的句子中。*verbally*（用词语）表达什么，或者说 *verbalize*（用词语表达）什么，就是将其说或者写出来。

verbose\vər-ˈbōs\ Using more words than are needed; wordy. 啰唆的，冗长的
• The writing style in government publications has often been both dry and verbose—a deadly combination. 政府出版物的写作风格通常枯燥而冗长——两个缺点相结合，真是要命。

Americans brought up on fast-paced TV shows and action films have lost any patience they once had for *verbosity*. So most American writing is brisk, and American speakers usually don't waste many words. But many of us love our own voices and opinions and don't realize we're being verbose until our listeners start stifling their yawns. And students still try to fill up the pages of their term papers with unneeded verbosity.
看电视节目和动作电影长大的美国人，已经根本没有以前那种忍受 *verbosity*（废话）的耐心了。因此，美国人写的东西大都轻快活泼，说话也通常没有太多废话。可是，我们很多人很喜欢自己的声音和看法，直到看到对方开始强忍哈欠了，才意识到自己 verbose（说个没完）。学生还在想办法用 verbosity（废话）填满学期论文。

proverb\ˈprä-ˌvərb\ A brief, often-repeated statement that expresses a general truth or common observation. 谚语
• "Waste not, want not" used to be a favorite proverb in many households. "勤俭节约，吃穿不缺"曾经是很多家庭最喜欢的谚语。

Proverbs probably appeared with the dawn of language. Sayings such as "A stitch in time saves nine," or "Pride goeth before a fall," or "Least said, soonest mended," or "To everything there is a season" are easily memorized nuggets of wisdom. But the convenient thing about proverbs is that there's often one for every point of view. For every "Look before you leap" there's a "He who hesitates is lost." "A fool and his money are soon parted" can be countered with "To make money you have to spend money." A cynic once observed, "Proverbs are invaluable treasures to dunces with good memories."

proverbs(谚语)很可能是跟语言同时出现的。"小洞不补,大洞吃苦",或者"骄兵必败",或者"少说少错",或者"凡事皆有定期",都是易读易记的智慧话语。不过,对谚语来说,有一个方便之处是,每一个观点都有一条谚语。对于每一条"三思而后行"来说,都有一条"迟疑失良机"。"傻瓜花钱快"可以用来反驳"要挣钱得花钱"。有个愤世嫉俗的人曾经说:"对记性不错的傻瓜来说,谚语是无价之宝。"

verbatim \vər-ˈbā-təm\ In the exact words; word for word. 一字不差地;逐字

• It turned out that the writer had lifted long passages verbatim from an earlier, forgotten biography of the statesman. 原来,这位作者一字不差地从这位政治家被人遗忘的早期传记中剽窃了大段大段的文字。

Verbatim comes directly from Latin into English with the same spelling and meaning. Memorizing famous speeches, poems, or literary passages is a good way to both train the memory and absorb the classic texts of our literature and culture. At one time the ability to recite verbatim the Gettysburg Address, the beginning of the Declaration of Independence, and great speeches from Shakespeare was the mark of a well-educated person. But when that language was quoted by a writer, he or she was always careful to put quotation marks around it and tell readers who the true author was.

verbatim 直接从拉丁语进入英语,拼写和意义相同。记住著名的演讲、诗歌或者文学片段,不但可以很好地锻炼记忆力,而且可以很好地从我们的文学和文化中吸收经典段落。能够一字不差地背诵《葛底斯堡演说》《独立宣言》开端部分以及莎士比亚戏剧作品中的伟大演讲,曾一度被认为是接受过良好教育的人的标志。不过,作家引用这些话时,总是小心谨慎,使用引号,告诉读者这些话实际上是谁写的。

verbiage \ˈvər-bē-ij\ An excess of words, often with little content; wordiness. 冗辞,赘语

• The agency's report was full of unnecessary verbiage, which someone should have edited out before the report was published. 该机构的报告废话连篇,出版前本应该有人将其删除。

Government reports are notorious for their unfortunate tendency toward empty *verbiage*, though part of the reason is simply that officials are anxious to be following all the rules. Legal documents are also generally full of verbiage, partly because lawyers want to be sure that every last possibility has been covered and no loopholes have been left. But writing that contains unneeded verbiage is often trying to disguise its lack of real substance or clarity of thought. And every writer, including government workers and lawyers, should be constantly on the lookout for opportunities to hit the Delete key.

政府报告有一种令人遗憾的倾向是出了名的,那就是 verbiage(废话连篇)。这其中部分原因是,官员急于遵守条条

框框。法律文件通常也是废话满篇,一定程度上是因为律师想要确保没有遗漏任何可能性,没有留下任何漏洞。可是,通篇废话的文字内容空洞或思维混乱,却常常企图遮丑。每一位作者,包括公务员和律师,应该始终注意,不要放过敲击删除键的机会。

SIMIL/SIMUL

SIMIL/SIMUL come from the Latin adjective *similis*, meaning "like, resembling, similar," and the verb *simulare*, "to make like." Two *similar* things resemble each other. Two *simultaneous* activities proceed at the same time. And a *facsimile*, such as you might receive from your *fax* machine, looks exactly the same as the original.

SIMIL/SIMUL 源自拉丁语形容词 *similis*,意思是"像,相似,类似",以及动词 *simulare*,意思是"使相似"。两个 *similar* 的事物具有相似之处。两个 *simultaneous* 的活动同时发生。*facsimile*,也就是你从自己的传真机收到的文件,与原件完全一样。

simile\ˈsi-mə-lē\ A figure of speech, introduced by *as* or *like*, that makes a point of comparison between two things different in all other respects. 明喻

• He particularly liked the simile he'd thought of for the last line of the song's chorus, "It felt like a bullet in his heart." 他尤其喜欢自己想出的那个用作这首歌副歌最后一行的比喻:"它感觉像是射入他心中的子弹。"

Fiction, poetry, and philosophy have been full of similes for centuries. In fact, the oldest literature known to us uses similes, along with their close relatives known as metaphors (see p. 501). This suggests that similes are an essential part of imaginative writing in all times and all cultures. When Tennyson, describing an eagle, writes "And like a thunderbolt he falls," he's using a simile, since the line makes a specific comparison. "The road was a ribbon of moonlight" could be called a metaphor, though "The road was like a ribbon of moonlight" would be a simile.

小说、诗歌和哲学几个世纪以来一直充满了 similes(明喻)。实际上,我们知道的最古老的文学就用明喻,也用暗喻这个明喻的近亲(见第501页)。这说明,明喻是各个时代、各种文化具有想象力作品的必要组成部分。当丁尼森描写一只鹰的时候,他写道"他像雷电一般扑了下来",就是在使用明喻,因为这行诗进行了具体的比较。"这路是一条月光丝带"可以称为暗喻,虽然"这条路像条丝带"是明喻。

assimilate\ə-ˈsi-mə-ˌlāt\ (1) To take in and thoroughly understand. 理解 (2) To cause to become part of a different society or culture. 同化

• One of the traditional strengths of American society has been its ability to assimilate one group of immigrants after another. 美国社会的一个传统优势,是其同化一批又一批移民的能力。

Assimilate comes from the Latin verb *assimulare*, "to make similar," and it originally applied to the process by which food is taken into the body and absorbed into the system. In a similar way, a fact can be taken into the mind, thoroughly digested, and absorbed into one's store of knowledge. A newcomer to a job or a subject must assimilate an often confusing mass of information; only after it's been thoroughly absorbed can the person make intelligent use of it. An immigrant family assimilates into its new culture by gradually adopting a new language and the habits of their new neighbors—a process that's always easier for the children than for the parents.

<small>*assimilate* 源自拉丁语动词 *assimulare*，意思是"使相似"。该词最初用于食物被摄入并被身体吸收这一过程。同样，事实可以被头脑摄入、消化，最终成为知识储备的一部分。某一工作或者学科的新手，必须理解常常混乱一团的信息。只有当信息被彻底消化，此人才能正确使用。一个移民家庭通过逐渐使用新语言、新邻居的新习惯，就会成为该文化的新成员。这一过程对孩子来说要比对父母来说更容易些。</small>

simulacrum \ˌsim-yə-ˈla-krəm\ A copy, especially a superficial likeness or imitation. 模拟物，仿制品，赝品

• As a boy he had filled his bedroom with model fighter jets, and these simulacra had kept his flying fantasies active for years. 小时候，他在卧室摆满了喷气式战斗机模型。这些模拟物让他飞翔的幻想活跃了多年。

In its original meaning, a simulacrum is simply a representation of something else; so an original oil painting, marble statue, or plastic figurine could all be simulacra (notice the plural form) in the old sense. But today the word usually means a copy that's meant to substitute for the real thing—and usually a cheap and inferior copy, a pale imitation of the original. So in old Persia a beautifully laid out garden was a simulacrum of paradise. Some countries' governments are mere simulacra of democracy, since the people in power always steal the elections by miscounting the votes. And a bad actor might do a simulacrum of grief on the stage that doesn't convince anyone.

<small>*simulacrum* 的原始意义是指事物的模本，所以一幅油画、一座大理石雕像或者一尊塑料小雕像都可以成为 simulacra（仿制品，注意这一复数形式）。不过，今天这一词语通常指代替真品的替代品，而且常常廉价、劣质，是真品的低劣模仿。所以，在古波斯，布局漂亮的花园是天堂的仿制品。一些国家的政府只是虚假的民主政府，因为大权在握者总是通过算错票数来赢得选举。演员演技拙劣，在台上假装悲伤，无法让任何人信服。</small>

simulate \ˈsim-yə-ˌlāt\ (1) To take on the appearance or effect of something, often in order to deceive. 假装；冒充；装作 (2) To make a realistic imitation of something, such as a physical environment. 模仿；仿造

• The armed services have made extensive use of video games to simulate the actual experience of warfare for their recruits. 武装部队大量使用电子游戏为新兵模拟真实的战争体验。

The zircon, that favorite of home shopping channels, simulates a diamond—more or less. A skilled furrier can dye lower-grade furs to simulate real mink. A skilled actress can simulate a range of emotions from absolute joy to crushing despair. And an apparatus that simulates the hazards of driving while intoxicated is likely to provide some very real benefits.

<small>锆石这一多个家庭购物频道的宠儿，有钻石的样子——几乎可以以假乱真。技术高明的批货商能将较低等级的皮货进行染色，仿造真正的貂皮。高明的女演员可以装出一系列的情感，从极大的欢乐到致命的绝望。能够模仿出醉驾种种危险的仪器，可能带来真正的好处。</small>

SIMIL/
SIMUL

Quizzes

A. Fill in each blank with the correct letter:

a. simulacrum
b. verbiage
c. simulate
d. verbatim
e. proverb
f. simile
g. verbose
h. assimilate

1. Please quote me _____ or don't "quote" me at all.
2. Most students can't _____ so much information all at once, so they approach it gradually.
3. He turned out to be a _____ old windbag, and I slept through the whole talk.
4. That restaurant doesn't offer real maple syrup, just an unconvincing _____.
5. She did her best to _____ pleasure at the news, but could barely manage a smile.
6. "Nothing ventured, nothing gained" was a favorite _____ of my grandmother's.
7. Unnecessary _____ usually gets in the way of clarity in writing.
8. "A day without sunshine is like a chicken without a bicycle" has to be the oddest _____ of all time.

B. Complete the analogy:

1. garbage : food :: verbiage : _____
   a. boxes   b. verbs   c. words   d. trash
2. create : invent :: assimilate : _____
   a. wring   b. absorb   c. camouflage   d. drench
3. frequently : often :: verbatim : _____
   a. later   b. closely   c. differently   d. exactly
4. painting : portrays :: simulacrum : _____
   a. imitates   b. shows   c. demonstrates   d. calculates
5. sound bite : quotation :: proverb : _____
   a. saying   b. sentence   c. introduction   d. phrase
6. inflate : expand :: simulate : _____
   a. reveal   b. entrap   c. devote   d. imitate
7. scarce : sparse :: verbose : _____
   a. poetic   b. wordy   c. fictional   d. musical
8. contrast : different :: simile : _____
   a. near   b. distant   c. alike   d. clear

UNIT 25

SCEND comes from the Latin verb *scandere*, "to climb." The staircase we *ascend* to our bedroom at night we will *descend* the next morning, since what goes up must come down.
SCEND 源自拉丁语动词 *scandere*(攀登)。我们夜里 *ascend*(上楼)走的那个楼梯,第二天早上会沿着它 *descend*(走下来),因为上升的必须下降。

transcend \tran-'send\ To rise above the limits of; overcome, surpass.
超越;克服

• His defeat in the election had been terribly hard on him, and it took two years before he finally felt he had transcended the bitterness it had produced. 竞选失败对他打击很大,两年后他才终于克服失败带来的痛苦。

Great leaders are expected to *transcend* the limitations of politics, especially during wartime and national crises. A great writer may transcend geographical boundaries to become internationally respected. And certain laws of human nature seem to transcend historical periods and hold true for all times and all places.
人们期待伟大的领袖能够 transcend(超越)政治的限制,尤其是在战争和民族危机期间。伟大的作家可能 transcend 地理界线,在国际上受到尊敬。人类本性的某些规律似乎能 transcend 历史时期,永远而且到处都有效。

condescend \ˌkän-di-'send\ (1) To stoop to a level of lesser importance or dignity. 屈尊;俯就 (2) To behave as if superior. 表现得高人一等

• Every so often my big brother would condescend to take me to a movie, but only when my parents made him. 我大哥有时会屈尊带我看电影,不过只是当我父母让他这么做了他才这样的。

Back when society was more rigidly structured, *condescend* didn't sound so negative. People of higher rank, power, or social position had to overlook certain established rules of behavior if they wished to have social dealings with people of lower status, but such *condescension* was usually gracious and courteous. In today's more classless society, the term implies a manner that may be slightly offensive. A poor relation is unlikely to be grateful to a wealthy and *condescending* relative who passes on her secondhand clothes, and employees at an office party may not be thrilled when the boss's wife condescends to mingle with them. Often the word is used rather unseriously, as when a friend comments that a snooty sales clerk condescended to wait on her after ignoring her for several minutes.
以前,当社会结构更为稳固时,*condescend*(屈尊)一词听起来并没有太多的贬义。职务更高、权力更大、社会地位更高者,如果希望与地位较低者交往,必须忽视某些既定的条条框框。不过,这样的 *condescension*(屈尊)通常是彬彬有礼的。今天,社会阶层不那么明显,这一词语暗含着略有侮辱性的言行。如果有钱的亲戚怀着优越感,将自己的二手衣服送人,穷亲戚不太可能心怀感激。在公司晚会上,如果老板的妻子摆出屈尊的样子走到员工中间,他们是不会欣喜若狂的。通常,人们使用这一词语时并不那么认真,比如当朋友说傲慢无礼的售货员对她忽视了几分钟才屈尊为她服务的时候。

descendant\di-ˈsen-dənt\ （1）One that has come down from another or from a common stock. 后裔；后代；子孙（2）One deriving directly from a forerunner or original. 派生物

• Though none of the great man's descendants ever came close to achieving what he had, most of them enjoyed very respectable careers. 这一伟人的后代没有一个取得这样的成就, 但大多数都从事着令人尊敬的职业。

Descendant is the opposite of *ancestor*. Your grandparents' descendants are those who are *descended* from them—your parents, your brothers and sisters, and any children that any of you may have. It's been claimed that every person on earth is a descendant of Muhammad, and of every historical person before him—Julius Caesar, the Buddha, etc.—who started a line of *descent*. (Some of us still find this hard to believe.) And not all descendants are human; every modern thesaurus, for example, could be called the descendant of the one devised by Peter Mark Roget in 1852. *descendant*(后代)是 *ancestor*(祖先)的反义词。你（外）祖父母的后代就是后面与其有亲缘关系的人——你的父母、你的兄弟姐妹以及你们当中任何人的孩子。据说, 地球上每个人都来源于穆罕默德以及他前面的每个历史人物——尤利乌斯·恺撒、佛陀, 等等。这些人是人类共同的祖先。(我们中一部分人还是觉得这令人难以置信。)不是所有的 descendants 都是人, 每一部分类词典都是彼得·马克·罗热 1852 年编纂的那部词典的后代。

ascendancy\ə-ˈsen-dən-sē\ Governing or controlling interest; domination. 支配；统治

• Under Augustus, Rome succeeded in establishing its ascendancy over the entire Mediterranean by 30 BC. 在奥古斯都领导下, 到公元前 30 年, 罗马成功取得了对整个地中海的统治权。

In the course of a year, the sun appears to pass through the twelve constellations of the zodiac in sequence, and all the planets also lie close to the solar path. The constellation and planet that are just rising, or *ascendant*, above the eastern horizon in the sun's path at the moment of a child's birth are said by astrologers to exercise a lifelong controlling influence over the child. This is the idea that lies at the heart of *ascendancy*, though the word today no longer hints at supernatural powers. 在一年当中, 太阳似乎依次穿过黄道带的十二个星座, 而且所有行星也位于太阳道很近的地方。据星象学家说当一个孩子出生那一刻, 正在东方地平线升起的, 或者 ascendant 的那个星座和那个行星, 离会对这个孩子的一生都有支配性影响。这就是 ascendancy 的核心观点, 虽然这一词语今天不再暗示超自然的力量。

ONYM comes from the Greek *onyma*, meaning "name, word." An *anonymous* donor or writer is one who isn't named. A *synonym* is a word with the same meaning as another word (see SYN, p. 710). And *homonyms* (see HOM/HOMO, p. 62) are words that look and sound alike but aren't actually related, such as *well* ("healthy") and *well* ("a deep hole with water in it").

ONYM 源自希腊语的 *onyma*("名字；词语")。Anonymous(匿名的)捐献者或作者就是没有说出名字的捐献者或作者。*synonym*(同义词)就是跟另一个词语意思相同的词语(见 SYN,第 710 页)。*homonyms*(见 HOM/HOMO,第 62 页)就是拼写和读音相同但实际上没有关联的词语,比如 *well*(健康)和 *well*(水井)。

antonym \ˈan-tə-ˌnim\ A word that means the opposite of some other word. 反义词

• There's no point in telling a three-year-old that *cat* isn't an antonym of *dog*, and *sun* isn't an antonym of *moon*. 告诉三岁的孩子 *cat*(猫)不是 *dog*(狗)的反义词,*sun*(太阳)不是 *moon*(月亮)的反义词,没什么意义。

Antonym includes the Greek prefix *ant-*, meaning "opposite" (see ANT/ANTI, p. 505). Antonyms are often thought of in pairs: *hot/ cold*, *up/down*, *wet/dry*, *buy/sell*, *failure/success*. But a word may have more than one antonym (*old/young*, *old/new*), especially when one of the words has synonyms (*small/large*, *small/big*, *little/big*), and a word may have many approximate antonyms (*adore/hate*, *adore/ detest*, *adore/loathe*). But although lots of words have synonyms, not so many have antonyms. What would be the antonym of *pink*? *weather*? *semipro*? *thirty*? *firefighter*? *wax*? *about*? *consider*?

antonym 一词含有希腊语前缀 *ant-*("相反")(见 ANT/ANTI,第 505 页)。antonyms(反义词)通常被认为是成对的: *hot*(热)/*cold*(冷)、*up*(向上)/*down*(向下)、*wet*(湿润)/*dry*(干燥)、*buy*(购买)/*sell*(销售)、*failure*(失败)/*success*(成功)。可是,一个词语可能会有不止一个反义词,比如 *old*(年老)/*young*(年轻)、*old*(旧)/*new*(新),尤其是当其中一个词语有同义词时,比如 *small*(小)/*large*(大)、*small*(小)/*big*(大)、*little*(小)/*big*(大),而且一个词语可能有很多近似反义词,比如 *adore*(爱)/*hate*(恨)、*adore*(爱)/*detest*(恨)、*adore*(爱)/*loathe*(恨)。可是,尽管很多词语都有同义词,有反义词的并没有那么多。*pink*(粉红)的反义词是什么呢? *weather*(天气)呢? *semipro*(半职业的)? *thirty*(三十)? *firefighter*(消防员)? *wax*(蜡)? *about*(关于)? *consider*(考虑)呢?

eponymous \i-ˈpä-nə-məs\ Of, relating to, or being the person for whom something is named. 与以其名命名某物之人有关的;以其名命名某物之人的

• Adjectives such as *Elizabethan*, *Victorian*, and *Edwardian* show how the names of certain British monarchs have become eponymous for particular time periods and styles. *Elizabethan*、*Victorian* 和 *Edwardian* 这样的形容词,表明某些英国君主的名字是如何用来命名特定时期或风格的。

Things as different as a bird, a river, and a drug may be named to honor someone. The Canadian city of Vancouver was named after the explorer George Vancouver; the diesel engine was named for its inventor, Rudolph Diesel; Alzheimer's disease was named after the physician Alois Alzheimer; and so on. Common eponymous terms include *Ohm's law*, *Parkinson's Law*, and the *Peter Principle*. And if the Beatles' famous "white album" actually has a name, it's usually called "The Beatles," which means that it's eponymous as well. Don't be surprised if *eponymous* turns out to be a hard word to use; lots of other people have discovered the same thing.

像鸟、河流和药物这些不同的事物,可能以某人的名字命名,以示敬意。加拿大城市 Vancouver(温哥华)是以探险家 George Vancouver(乔治·温哥华)的名字命名的;diesel(柴油机)是以发明家 Rudolph Diesel(鲁道夫·狄塞尔)的姓氏命

名的；Alzheimer's disease(阿尔茨海默病；老年性痴呆症)是以 Alois Alzheimer(阿洛伊斯·阿尔茨海默)医生的姓氏命名的，等等。常见的来源于人名的术语包括 Ohm's law(欧姆定律)、Parkinson's Law(帕金森定律)和 Peter Principle(彼得原理)。如果披头士乐队(the Beatles)著名的"白色唱片"真的有一个名字，通常就叫做"披头士"("The Beatles")，就是说，它也是以名字命名的。如果 *eponymous* 是个难词，不要吃惊；其他很多人也发现这一点了。

patronymic \ˌpa-trə-ˈni-mik\ Part of a personal name based on the name of one's father or one of his ancestors. (指人名的一部分)源自父亲(或男性祖先)名字的

• Reading Tolstoy's vast novel, it can be helpful to know that Helene Vasilievna's second name is a patronymic, and thus that her father is named Vasili. 要阅读托尔斯泰这部气势恢宏的小说，知道 Helene Vasilievna(瓦西里耶夫娜)名字的第二部分源自父亲的名字是很有益的，这样就知道她父亲名叫 Vasili(瓦西里)了。

A patronymic, or *patronym* (see also PATER/PATR, p. 468), is generally formed by adding a prefix or suffix to a name. Thus, a few centuries ago, the male patronymic of Patrick was Fitzpatrick ("Patrick's son"), that of Peter was Peterson or Petersen, that of Donald was MacDonald or McDonald, and that of Hernando was Hernández. Today, of course, each of these is an ordinary family name, or *surname*. In Russia, both a patronymic and a surname are still used; in the name Peter Ilyich Tchaikovsky, for example, Ilyich is a patronymic meaning "son of Ilya." *patronymic*，或者 *patronym*(从父名衍生的名字)(另见 PATER/PATR，第 468 页)通常通过给名字加前缀或后缀构成。这样，几个世纪前，从 Patrick(帕特里克)这一父名衍生的名字是 Fitzpatrick(菲茨帕特里克)("帕特里克的儿子")，从 Peter(彼得)这一父名衍生的名字是 Peterson 或者 Petersen(彼得森)，从 Donald(唐纳德)这一父名衍生出的名字是 MacDanold 或者 McDonald(麦克唐纳德)，从 Hernando(赫尔南多)这一父名衍生出的名字是 Hernández(赫尔南德斯)。当然了，今天，这些名字都是普通的 family name(姓氏)或者 surname(姓氏)。在俄罗斯，源自父名的名字和姓氏都仍在使用，比如 Peter Ilyich Tchaikovsky(彼得·伊里奇·柴可夫斯基)这个名字中 Ilyich(伊里奇)这个源自父名的名字意思是"son of Ilya"("伊里亚的儿子")。

pseudonym \ˈsü-də-ˌnim\ A name that someone (such as a writer) uses instead of his or her real name. 化名；笔名

• Hundreds of Hardy Boys, Nancy Drew, and Bobbsey Twins novels were churned out under such pseudonyms as Franklin W. Dixon, Carolyn Keene, and Laura Lee Hope. 成百上千的《哈迪男孩》《少女侦探》《鲍勃西双胞胎》小说，都是借助富兰克林·W.迪克森、卡洛琳·基恩和劳拉·霍普这几个笔名大量炮制出来的。

The Greek *pseudo-* is used in English to mean "false," or sometimes "resembling." A *pseudonym* is thus a false name, or alias. A writer's pseudonym is called a *pen name*, as in the case of Howard O'Brien (who usually writes as "Anne Rice" but sometimes under other names), and an actor's pseudonym is called a *stage name*, as in the case of Marion Morrison ("John Wayne"). A *cadre name* may be used for the sake of secrecy by a revolutionary plotter such as Vladimir Ulyanov ("Lenin") or Iosif Dzhugashvili ("Stalin"). And in many religious orders, members adopt *devotional names*, as Agnes Bojaxhiu did in 1931 ("Teresa," later known as "Mother Teresa"). 希腊语的 *pseudo-* 用在英语中，表示"虚假的"，有时也表示"相似的"。因此，*pseudonym* 就是假名。作家的假名叫做

ONYM

pen name(笔名),比如霍华德·奥布赖恩(Howard O'Brien)(通常用"安妮·赖斯"[Anne Rice]这一笔名写作,不过有时使用其他名字);演员的假名叫作"*stage name*"(艺名),比如 Marion Morrison(马里恩·莫里森)(艺名为 John Wayne[约翰·韦恩])。*Cadre name* 可以被策划革命的人为保密起见所使用,比如弗拉基米尔·乌里扬诺夫的化名("列宁"),或者约瑟夫·朱加什维利(Iosif Dzhugashvili)("斯大林")。在很多宗教派别中,成员都采用 *devotional name*(教名),就像艾格尼斯·波雅舒(Agnes Bojaxhiu)在 1931 年所做的那样("特蕾莎"Teresa,后来大家称其为"特蕾莎修女"["Mother Teresa"])。

Quizzes

A. Choose the closest definition:

1. ascendancy   a. growth   b. climb   c. dominance
   d. rank
2. eponymous   a. having several rulers
   b. written by three people   c. borrowed from literature
   d. taken from a name
3. descendant   a. offspring   b. ancestor   c. cousin
   d. forerunner
4. patronymic   a. client's name   b. name based on your father's
   c. last name   d. first name
5. transcend   a. exceed   b. astound   c. fulfill
   d. transform
6. antonym   a. technical name   b. third name
   c. word with opposite meaning   d. word with related meaning
7. condescend   a. stoop   b. remove   c. agree
   d. reject
8. pseudonym   a. alias   b. phony
   c. made-up word   d. honorary title

B. Fill in each blank with the correct letter:

a. condescend   e. transcend
b. antonym   f. eponymous
c. ascendancy   g. descendant
d. patronymic   h. pseudonym

1. He's one of the few people in the office who manages to _____ all the unpleasantness that goes on around here.
2. The best _____ for "popular" is "unpopular," not "shy."
3. The Democrats are in the at the _____ moment, but they may not be next year.
4. She'll remind you that she's a _____ of some fairly famous people, but she won't mention that the family also has some criminals in its past.
5. In a Russian family in which the father is named Fyodor, a boy's _____

would be Fyodorovich and a girl's would be Fyodorevna.

6. He was born Vlad Butsky, but he writes under _____ the Vance Bond.

7. She lives in a very glamorous world these days, and she would never _____ to show up at a family reunion.

8. The Restaurant Alain Savoy is the _____ establishment belonging to the great French chef.

SCRIB/SCRIP

SCRIB/SCRIP comes from the Latin verb *scribere*, "to write." *Scribble* is an old word meaning to write or draw carelessly. A written work that hasn't been published is a *manuscript*. And to *describe* is to picture something in words.
SCRIB/SCRIP 源自拉丁语动词 scribere("写")。scribble 是一个古老的词语,意思是粗心大意地写或者画。没有出版的亲笔作品叫做 manuscript(手稿)。describe 意思是用语言描绘事物。

conscription \ kən-ˈskrip-shən \   Enforced enlistment of persons, especially for military service; draft. 征募;征兵

• The first comprehensive system for nationwide conscription was instituted by France for the Napoleonic wars that followed the French Revolution. 第一个全面的国家范围的征募系统,是法国在大革命之后为拿破仑战争实行的。

With its *scrip-* root, *conscription* means basically writing someone's name on a list—a list that, unfortunately, a lot of people usually don't want to be on. Conscription has existed at least since ancient Egypt's Old Kingdom (27th century B.C.), though universal conscription has been rare throughout history. Forms of conscription were used by Prussia, Switzerland, Russia, and other European powers in the 17th and 18th centuries. In the U.S., conscription was first applied during the Civil War, by both the North and the South. In the North there were pockets of resistance, and the draft led to riots in several cities. The U.S. abandoned conscription at the end of the war and didn't revive it until World War I.
有了 *scrip-* 这一词根,*conscription* 的基本意思是在一个名单上写下某人的名字。不幸的是,很多人通常不想让自己的名字写在这个名单上。征兵这一做法至少从古埃及的古王国时期(公元前 27 世纪)就存在了,尽管普遍性的征兵在历史上很少存在。在 17 和 18 世纪,普鲁士、瑞士、俄罗斯及其他欧洲强国使用过不同形式的征兵。在美国,南方和北方在美国南北战争时第一次使用征兵制度。在北方,曾有少数人抵制这一做法,征兵在几个城市引发了暴动。美国南北战争结束时,美国放弃了这一做法,直到第一次世界大战才恢复这一做法。

circumscribe \ ˈsər-kəm-ˌskrib \   (1) To clearly limit the range or activity of something. 限制;约束 (2) To draw a line around or to surround with a boundary. 在……周围画线;用边界包围

• Some children do best when their freedom is clearly circumscribed and their activities are supervised. 当自由受到明确限制,或者行为受到监督时,一些孩子表现最好。

The prefix *circum-*, "around," is the key to *circumscribe*'s basic meaning. Thus, we could say that a boxing ring is circumscribed by ropes, just as the area for an archaeological dig may be. A governor's power is always circumscribed by a state's constitution. And a physician's assistant has a *circumscribed* role that doesn't include writing prescriptions.

前缀 *circum-*（在……周围）是 *circumscribe* 基本意义的关键。因此，我们可以说，拳击场 circumscribed（有绳子围着），就像考古发掘区域周围那样。州长的权力因为州宪法而 circumscribed（受到限制）。医生助手的职责是 circumscribed（受到限定的），不包括开药方。

inscription \in-'skrip-shən\ (1) Something permanently written, engraved, or printed, particularly on a building, coin, medal, or piece of currency. 碑文；铭刻；铭文；刻印文字 (2) The dedication of a book or work of art. 献词

• All U.S. coins bear the Latin inscription "E pluribus unum"— "From many, one." 美国所有钱币上都有拉丁语的刻印文字"E pluribus unum"——"合众为一"。

With its prefix *in-*, meaning "in" or "on," it's not surprising that an *inscription* is either written on or engraved into a surface. Inscriptions in the ancient world were always chiseled into stone, as inscriptions still may be today. The principal monument of the Vietnam memorial in Washington, D.C., for instance, is a black wall on which are *inscribed* the names of all the Americans who died during the war—each name in full, row upon seemingly endless row. But an inscription may also be a dedication, such as the words "For my wife" all by themselves on a page near the beginning of a book.

有了 *in-* 这一前缀（意思是"在……里面"或"在……上面"），inscription 要么是写在一个表面上，要么是刻在上面，也就不奇怪了。古代世界的 inscriptions 总是用凿子刻在石头上的，就跟现在一样。比如，华盛顿特区最主要的越战纪念碑是一面黑墙，上面 inscribed（刻着）战争期间阵亡的美国人的名字——每个都是全名，一行又一行，似乎没有尽头。但是，inscription 也可能是"献词"，比如书前面一页上的"For my wife"（"献给我的妻子"）这几个字。

proscribe \prō-'skrīb\ To forbid as harmful or unlawful; prohibit. 禁止

• Despite thousands of laws proscribing littering, many of America's streets and public spaces continue to be dumping grounds. 尽管有众多法令禁止乱扔垃圾，美国很多街道和公共空间仍然是垃圾倾倒场地。

The Latin prefix *pro-* sometimes meant "before," in the sense of "in front of" the people. So in ancient Rome *proscribere* meant to make public in writing the name of a person who was about to be executed, and whose property would be seized by the state. But the meaning of the English word soon shifted to mean simply "prohibit" instead. *Proscribe* today is actually often the opposite of the very similar *prescribe*, which means basically "require."

拉丁语前缀 *pro-* 原来有时候意思是"在……之前"，具体意思是"在（人们）面前"。所以，在古罗马，*proscribere* 意思是公布即将处决的人的名字，其财产将被国家没收。但是，这一英语单词的意思转变了，表示"禁止"。今天，*proscribe* 实际上常常是拼写非常相似的 *prescribe* 的反义词，后者的基本意思是"要求"。

SCRIB/
SCRIP

FALL comes from the Latin verb *fallere*, "to deceive." It's actually at the root of the word *false*, which we rarely use today to mean "deceptive," though that meaning does show up in older phrases: "Thou shalt not bear false witness against thy neighbor," for instance, or "A false-hearted lover will send you to your grave." *Fallere* is even at the root of *fail* and *fault*, though you might not guess it to look at them.

FALL 源自拉丁语动词 *fallere*（"欺骗"）。它实际上是 *false* 的意义所在。我们现在很少用这一词语来表示"具有欺骗性的"，虽然这一意思确实出现在较为古老的句子中，比如"Thou shalt not bear false witness against they neighbor"（汝不得作伪证陷害邻居）或者"A false-hearted lover will send you to your grave"（虚情假意的情人将把你送进坟墓）。*fallere* 甚至是 *fail* 和 *fault* 的根本意义所在，虽然你可能没有猜到，并将两者研究一番。

fallacy\ˈfa-lə-sē\ A wrong belief; a false or mistaken idea. 谬见；谬论；思维错误

• In her new article she exposes yet another fallacy at the heart of these economic arguments. 在最新一篇文章中，她揭示了这些经济论证核心的另一思维错误。

Philosophers are constantly using the word *fallacy*. For them, a fallacy is reasoning that comes to a conclusion without the evidence to support it. This may have to do with pure logic, with the assumptions that the argument is based on, or with the way words are used, especially if they don't keep exactly the same meaning throughout the argument. There are many classic fallacies that occur again and again through the centuries and everywhere in the world. You may have heard of such fallacies as the "ad hominem" fallacy, the "question-begging" fallacy, the "straw man" fallacy, the "slippery slope" fallacy, the "gambler's" fallacy, or the "red herring" fallacy. Look them up and see if you've ever been guilty of any of them.

哲学家不断使用 *fallacy* 一词。对他们来说，一个 fallacy 就是没有证据支持就得出结论的推理。这可能与纯逻辑有关，与作为辩论基础的假设有关，或者与词语使用的方式有关，尤其是如果它们在整个辩论过程中并不一直使用同一意思的话。有许多经典谬论多个世纪以来在世界各地反复出现。你可能听说过"诉诸感情"谬误、"乞题"谬误、"稻草人"谬误、"滑坡"谬误、"赌徒"谬误或者"转移话题"谬误。把它们查一查，看看你是否犯过其中一些谬误。

fallacious\fə-ˈlā-shəs\ Containing a mistake; not true or accurate. 有错误的；不真实的，不准确的

• Any policy that's based on a lot of fallacious assumptions is going to be a bad one. 只要以诸多错误假设为基础，任何政策都会很糟糕。

Fallacious is a formal and intellectual word. We rarely use it in casual speech; when we do, we risk sounding a bit full of ourselves and all-knowing. But it's used widely in writing, especially when one writer is arguing with another. And it's used to describe both errors in fact and errors in reasoning, including fallacies of the kind described in the previous entry.

fallacious 是一个正式的、富有知识气息的词语。我们在非正式口语中很少使用该词，使用该词的时候，可能让人觉得我们有点自高自大、无所不知。不过，这个词语在写作中使用广泛，尤其是作者跟另一个人争辩时。它还用来描述事

实错误和推理错误，包括前面描述的那种谬误。

fallibility \ˌfa-lə-ˈbi-lə-tē\ Capability of making mistakes or being wrong. 犯错误的可能；有错误的可能

• Doctors are concerned about the fallibility of these tests, which seem unable to detect the virus about 20% of the time. 医生们担心这些测试可能有错，因为大约百分之二十的情况下这些测试好像都不能发现病毒。

You'll find this word showing up in discussions of eyewitness testimony at crime scenes, of lie detectors, and of critical airplane parts. Some of us are most familiar with the fallibility of memory, especially when we remember something clearly that turns out never to have happened. Being fallible is part of being human, and sometimes the biggest errors are made by those who are thought of as the most brilliant of all.

你会发现，讨论目击者的犯罪现场证词、测谎仪以及飞机的关键部件时，会出现这个词语。我们一些人对记忆出错很熟悉，尤其是我们对某事记忆清晰但它原来从未发生时。fallible（出错）是人之常情，有时候，人们认为的最聪明的人却犯了最大的错误。

infallible \in-ˈfa-lə-bəl\ (1) Not capable of being wrong or making mistakes. 不会有错的；不会犯错误的 (2) Certain to work properly or succeed. 必然顺利的；定然成功的

• Two college friends of mine claimed to have an infallible system for beating the odds at roulette in Las Vegas. 我大学时代的两位朋友说，有个很保险的办法，在拉斯维加斯进行轮盘赌时，机会不大也能赌赢。

Watch out when you hear about infallible predictions, an infallible plan, an infallible cure, or even infallible lip gloss. Infallible isn't a claim that scientists, engineers, and doctors like to make, so you're probably getting better information when the word *not* comes first. You may have heard the phrase "papal infallibility," which refers to the official position of the Roman Catholic church, adopted in the 19th century, that certain solemn statements made by a Pope about faith or morals were not to be questioned. Popes since then have been careful not to make many of these statements.

当你听说 infallible（万无一失的）预计、infallible（万无一失的）计划、infallible（万无一失的）治疗方法或者 infallible（万无一失的）润唇膏时，要小心了。infallible 不是科学家、工程师和医生喜欢声称的，所以，当 *not*（不是）先出现时，你可能获取的信息更为可靠。你可能听到过"papal infallibility"（教皇不会犯错）这个说法，它指的是罗马天主教的官方立场，19世纪通过表决采纳，即教皇就信仰或道德所发表的声明不得受到质疑。

Quizzes

A. Fill in each blank with the correct letter:

a. proscribe   e. infallible
b. fallacious   f. circumscribe
c. inscription   g. fallacy

d. fallibility   h. conscription

1. The college feels a strong responsibility for ensuring students' safety, but at the same time it doesn't want to _____ student life too much.

2. At first glance the article's claims sounded interesting, but it wasn't hard to discover the basic _____ they were based on.

3. She already knew the _____ she wanted on her gravestone: "She done the best she could."

4. The _____ of these tests has been shown again and again, but some doctors keep using them.

5. The number of fistfights and accidents at the games had finally forced officials to _____ beer drinking completely.

6. Since 1973 there's been no military _____ in the U. S., but that doesn't mean the draft won't come back someday.

7. Saying that one cool summer disproves the whole idea of global warming is obviously _____ and no one really believes it.

8. In his teens he had read book after book about gambling strategies, all of which were claimed by their authors to be _____.

B. Match each word on the left with its correct definition on the right:

1. fallacy   a. prohibit
2. proscribe   b. error
3. fallibility   c. epitaph
4. conscription   d. unreliability
5. fallacious   e. wrong
6. circumscribe   f. limit
7. infallible   g. perfect
8. inscription   h. draft

SOLU

SOLU comes from the Latin verb *solvere*, "to loosen, free, release," and the root therefore may take the form *solv* as well. So to *solve* a problem means to find its *solution*, as if you were freeing up a logjam. And a *solvent* is a chemical that *dissolves* or "loosens up" oil or paint.

SOLU 源自拉丁语动词 *solvere*("使变松,使自由,释放"),因此词根也会以 *solv* 的形式出现。这样,要 *solve*(解决)一个问题,意思就是找到其 *solution*(解决方法),就好像你在解救堵塞河流的圆木,使其得到利用。*solvent* 是能够 *dissolve*(溶解)油或油漆的化学物质。

---

soluble \ säl-yə-bəl \ (1) Able to be dissolved in a liquid, especially water. 可以溶解(于水)的 (2) Able to be solved or explained. 可以解决的;可以解释的

• To an optimistic young principal, the problems of a school like this one might seem challenging but soluble. 对一位乐观的年轻校长来说,学校发生的这一问题可能看来很难,但并非不能解决。

Soluble looks like a word that should be confined to chemistry labs, though it's often used by nonchemists as well to describe substances that can be dissolved in liquids. On the other hand, the sense of *soluble* meaning "solvable" is also quite common. In this sense, *soluble*, like its opposite, *insoluble*, is usually paired with *problem*. If only all life's problems were soluble by stirring them in a container filled with water.

solute 看起来像是一个应该局限于化学实验室的词语,不过外行人也经常用来描述可以在液体中溶解的物质。另一方面,*soluble* "可以解决的;可以解释的"这个意思也很常见。在这个意思上,*soluble* 就像其反义词 *insoluble* 一样,通常与 *problem* (问题)搭配使用。如果生活中所有问题都可以在盛满水的容器中搅一搅就 soluble(解决了),那就好了。

absolution \ˌab-sə-ˈlü-shən\   The act of forgiving someone for their sins.
赦罪;赦免;解罪

• Every week she would kneel to confess her little sins and receive absolution from the priest. 她每周都跪下来,坦白自己的小小罪孽,并接受牧师赦罪。

Since the Latin *absolutus* meant "set free," it's easy to see how *absolution* came to mean "set free from sin." (And also easy to see why *absolute* means basically "pure"—that is, originally, "free of sin.") The verb for *absolution* is *absolve*. Just as a priest absolves believers of their sins, you may absolve your brother of blame for a household disaster, or you yourself may in time be absolved for that scrape on the car backing out of a parking space.

由于拉丁语 *absolutus* 一词意思是"释放",就很容易明白 *absolution* 如何有了"赦罪"的意思。(也很容易明白为什么 *absolute* 基本意思是"纯洁——也就是说,最初意思是"无罪"。)*absolution* 的动词形式是 *absolve*。就像牧师使信徒免于罪孽那样,你可以免去你弟弟在家里闯祸的责任,或者你从停车位倒车时刮坏了车,可能最终会得到原谅。

dissolution \ˌdi-sə-ˈlü-shən\   The act or process of breaking down or apart into basic components, as through disruption or decay. 解体;瓦解;分裂

• The dissolution of the U.S.S.R. was probably the most momentous event of the last quarter of the 20th century. 苏联解体可能是 20 世纪最后二十五年最重大的事件。

Dissolution is the noun form of *dissolve*, but it's a much less common word. Still, we refer to the fact that the dissolution of American marriages became far more common in the later 20th century. Or that when India won its independence in 1948, the dissolution of the once-global British empire was all but complete. Or that factors such as crime and drugs might be contributing to the dissolution of contemporary society's moral fabric. A *dissolute* person is someone in whom all restraint has dissolved, and who now indulges in behavior that shocks decent people.

dissolution 是 *dissolve* 的名词形式,不过远远不那么常用。但是,我们还是要提及这一事实:在 20 世纪晚期,美国人解除婚姻关系的现象很平常。或者,当印度在 1948 年赢得独立时,曾经覆盖全球的英帝国的解体几乎是彻底的。或者犯罪和毒品这样的因素可能正在促使当代社会道德结构的解体。一个 *dissolute* (放纵的;道德沦丧的)的人就是一个内

心所有限制都解体的人，而且这样的人沉溺于让正派人震惊的行为。

resolute \ˈre-zə-ˌlüt\ Marked by firm determination. 坚定的；坚决的

● After ten years of indecision, the Senate finally seems resolute about reaching an agreement. 犹豫不决了十年之后，参议院似乎终于有决心达成协议了。

Resolute comes from the same Latin verb as *resolved*, and the two words are often synonyms. So how did it get this meaning from the Latin? Essentially, when you resolve a question or problem, you come to a conclusion, and once you've reached a conclusion you can proceed to act. So in your New Year's *resolutions*, you resolve—or make up your mind—to do something. Unfortunately, New Year's resolutions aren't a good illustration of the meaning of *resolute*, since only about one in ten actually seems to succeed.

resolute 和 *resolved* 来自同一个拉丁语动词，两个词语常常同义。那么，它是如何从拉丁语获得这一意思的呢？从根本上说，解决问题了，你得出一个结论，一旦得出结论，就可以着手采取行动了。这样，在你的 New Year resolutions（新年决心）中，你 resolve 做某事，也就是下定决心做某事。不幸的是，新年计划不是解释 resolute 含义的最好办法，因为大约只有十分之一的决心可以实现。

HYDR

flows from the Greek word for "water." The "water" root can be found in the lovely flower called the *hydrangea*: its seed capsules resemble ancient Greek water vessels.

HYDR 源自拉丁语中表示"水"的那个词语。表示"水"的词根存在于 *hydrangea*（绣球花，一种漂亮的花）这一词语中：它的荚很像古希腊的水罐。

hydraulic \hī-ˈdrȯ-lik\ (1) Relating to water; operated, moved, or brought about by means of water. 跟水有关的；水驱动的；水引起的（2）Operated by the resistance or pressure of liquid forced through a small opening or tube. 液压驱动的

● Without any hydraulic engineers, the country is unlikely to build many dams or reservoirs on its own. 没有液压引擎，这个国家不太可能依靠自己的力量建造很多水坝。

By means of a *hydraulic* lift, the driver can lift the bed of a dump truck with the touch of a button. He might also repair the hydraulic steering, the hydraulic brake, or the hydraulic clutch—all of which, like the lift that holds everything up, take advantage of the way liquids act under pressure. Somewhat like a pulley or a lever, a hydraulic system magnifies the effect of moderate pressure exerted over a longer distance into powerful energy for a shorter distance.

利用 *hydraulic* life（液压升降机），摁一下按钮，司机就可以抬起倾斜车的底盘。他也可能修理液压转向机构、液压制动器，或者液压离合器。这些都跟什么都能举起的升降机一样，利用了压力之下液体的反应原理。液压系统有些像滑轮或者杠杆，能够增强通过较长距离施加的一般压力的效果，使其在较短距离内成为强大的力量。

dehydrate \dē-ˈhī-ˌdrāt\ (1) To remove water from. 使……脱水（2）To

deprive of energy and zest. 使……失去活力或热情

• The boy appeared at dusk staggering out of the desert, dangerously sunburned and dehydrated. 那个男孩黄昏时分出现了,蹒跚着走出沙漠,晒伤和脱水都很严重。

Dehydrating food is a good way to preserve it; raisins, which are dehydrated grapes, are a good example. Dehydration through industrial processes makes it possible to keep food even longer and store it in a smaller space. Freeze-drying produces food that only needs rehydration—that is, the addition of water—to restore its original consistency. Runners, cyclists, and hikers fearful of dehydration seem to be constantly hydrating themselves nowadays, sometimes even using a shoulder pack with a tube going straight into the mouth. Dehydrate can also be used for making something "dry" or "lifeless"; thus, a dull teacher can dehydrate American history, and an unimaginative staging can dehydrate a great Shakespeare play.

dehydrating(使……脱水)是保存食物的好办法,葡萄干,也就是 dehydrated(脱水的)葡萄,就是很好的例子。利用工业过程 dehydration(脱水)能让食物保存时间更长,而且占用空间较小。冷冻干燥的食物只需再水化,也就是增加水分,就可以恢复其黏稠度。目前,害怕脱水的跑步、骑车、远足的人,似乎不断 hydrating(吸收水分),有时候甚至背着双肩包,包上连着一根管子直接含在嘴里。dehydrate 也可以用来表示"使……乏味"或"使……缺乏生气",这样就可以说,一个笨蛋老师可以 dehydrate 美国历史,缺乏想象力的演出风格会 dehydrate 莎士比亚的伟大戏剧。

hydroelectric \ˌhī-drō-i-ˈlek-trik\ Having to do with the production of electricity by waterpower. 水力发电的

• A massive African hydroelectric project is creating the world's largest manmade lake, and is said to hold the key to the future for the country. 非洲一个庞大的水力发电项目正在产生世界上最大的人工湖,而且据说关乎该国的未来。

The prime component of most hydroelectric systems is a dam. A high dam funnels water downward at high pressure to spin turbines, which in turn drive generators to produce high-voltage electricity. Mountainous countries with rushing rivers can produce the most hydroelectricity. Though hydroelectricity comes from a clean and completely renewable energy source, dams disrupt natural systems in a way that disturbs environmentalists.

大多数 hydroelectric systems(水力发电系统)的主要部分是水坝。高大的水坝使水以很高的压力冲下,转动涡轮机,从而驱动发电机,产生高压电。有着湍急河流的多山国家,可以产生最多的 hydroelectricity(水电)。尽管水电来自干净的、完全可再生的能源,但水坝扰乱了自然体系,让环保主义者感到不安。

hydroponics \ˌhī-drō-ˈpä-niks\ The growing of plants in nutrient solutions, with or without supporting substances such as sand or gravel. 水培

• He had never thought hydroponics produced vegetables as tasty as those grown in soil, and the tomatoes seemed particularly disappointing. 他从没觉得水培生产的蔬菜跟土壤里种出的蔬菜一样好吃,而且西红柿尤其让人失望。

Hydroponics, also known as aquaculture or tank farming, began as a way of studying scientifically the mechanisms of plant nutrition. Hydroponically grown plants may have no solid material under them at all; instead, their roots often simply hang in water with a rich mix of nutrients dissolved in it. The principal advantage to hydroponics is the savings from reduced labor costs, since it's generally carried on in enclosed areas and the irrigation and fertilizing are done mechanically. Peppers, cucumbers, and various other vegetables are produced *hydroponically* in huge quantities.

*hydroponic*s 也叫 *aquaculture* 或者 *tank farming*,最初是对植物营养机制进行科学研究的方法。水培植物下面可能根本没有固体材料;相反,它们的根简直就是垂在水里,水里是融化的营养混合物。水培的主要优点是减少劳动力从而节约了资金,因为水培通常是在封闭区域进行的,灌溉和施肥是机械操作的。辣椒、黄瓜以及各种其他蔬菜都是 *hydroponically*(通过水培方式)大量生产的。

Quizzes

A. Complete the analogy:

1. freezing : melting :: dissolution : _____
   a. unification   b. separation   c. death   d. defiance
2. pneumatic : air :: hydraulic : _____
   a. solid   b. gas   c. liquid   d. evaporation
3. request : plea :: absolution : _____
   a. accusation   b. forgiveness   c. requirement   d. loss
4. sterility : bacteria :: hydroponics : _____
   a. water   b. soil   c. air   d. fire
5. determined : hesitant :: soluble : _____
   a. moist   b. dry   c. unexplainable   d. possible
6. nuclear : uranium :: hydroelectric : _____
   a. coal   b. petroleum   c. dynamics   d. water
7. puzzle : mystery :: resolution : _____
   a. determination   b. delay   c. detection   d. demand
8. drain : replenish :: dehydrate : _____
   a. find   b. dry out   c. rehydrate   d. add

B. Indicate whether the following pairs of words have the same or different meanings:

1. hydraulic / electric   same ____ / different ____
2. soluble / explainable   same ____ / different ____
3. dehydrate / dry   same ____ / different ____
4. dissolution / disintegration same ____ / different ____
5. hydroelectric / solar-powered same ____ / different ____
6. resolution / attitude   same ____ / different ____
7. hydroponics / waterworks   same ____ / different ____
8. absolution / forgiveness   same ____ / different ____

UNIT 25

Greek and Latin Borrowings 希腊语和拉丁语借词

aegis \ˈē-jəs\ (1) Something that protects or defends; shield. 保护物；防卫物；盾 (2) Sponsorship or guidance by an individual or organization. 赞助；指导

• The conference was held under the aegis of the World Affairs Council, which provided almost all of the funding. 这次会议是在世界事务委员会的赞助下举行的，委员会几乎提供了所需的全部资金。

The original *aegis* was a goatskin shield or breastplate, symbolizing majesty, that was worn by Zeus and his daughter Athena in Greek mythology. Athena's aegis bore the severed head of the monstrous Medusa. *Aegis* came to be used for any kind of invulnerable shield. But today we almost always use the word in the phrase "under the aegis of … ," which means "under the authority, sponsorship, or control of." 最早的 aegis 是希腊神话中一个山羊皮的盾或者胸铠，由宙斯和女儿雅典娜使用，代表着尊严。雅典娜的 aegis 上面有美杜莎被砍下的头。aegis 后来被用来指代任何坚固的盾。可是今天，这个词语几乎总是用于"under the aegis of..."这个短语中，意思是"由……授权/赞助/控制"。

charisma \ kə-ˈriz-mə \ (1) An extraordinary gift for leadership that attracts popular support and enthusiasm. 感召力；号召力 (2) A special ability to attract or charm; magnetism. 魅力；吸引力

• Many later leaders have envied the charisma of Napoleon Bonaparte, who many of his followers genuinely believed to be immortal. 拿破仑·波拿巴的很多追随者都发自内心地认为他是不朽人物，其感召力让后来的很多领袖人物都很羡慕。

Charisma is Greek for "gift," but its traditional meaning comes from Christian belief, where it originally referred to an extraordinary power—the gift of healing, the gift of tongues, or the gift of prophecy—bestowed on an individual by the Holy Spirit. The first nonreligious use of *charisma* didn't appear until the 20th century, when it was applied to that mysterious personal magnetism that a lucky few seem to possess, especially the magnetism with which a political leader can arouse great popular enthusiasm. When John Kennedy was elected president in 1960, its use by journalists popularized the term in the mass media. Since then, actors, rock stars, athletes, generals, and entrepreneurs have all been said to possess charisma. charisma 是希腊语，意思是"天赋"，但其传统意思来自基督教信仰，最初指圣灵赋予个人的非凡能力——治愈力、能说会道的能力或者预言能力。charisma 第一次与宗教无关的使用直到 20 世纪才出现，用来指少数幸运者似乎拥有的神秘的个人魅力，尤其是政治领袖能够激发普遍热情的魅力。约翰·F. 肯尼迪 1960 年当选总统时，新闻记者使这一词语在媒体中普遍使用。从此，演员、摇滚歌星、运动员、将军和企业家都被说成具有 charisma。

ego \ē-gō\ (1) A sense of confidence and satisfaction in oneself; self-esteem. 自信；自我满足；自尊 (2) An exaggerated sense of self-importance. 自大

• His raging ego was what his fellow lawyers remembered about him—his tantrums, his vanity, his snobbery, and all the rest of it. 有关他这个人，能让其他律师记住的，

就是他非常自高自大——爱发脾气、自负、自命清高,等等。

Ego is the Latin word for "I." So if a person seems to begin every sentence with "I," it's sometimes a sign of a big ego. It was the psychologist Sigmund Freud (well, actually his original translator) who put *ego* into the popular vocabulary, but what he meant by the word is complex, so only other psychologists really use it in the Freudian sense. The rest of us generally use *ego* simply to mean one's sense of self-worth, whether exaggerated or not. When used in the "exaggerated" sense, *ego* is almost the same thing as *conceit*. Meeting a superstar athlete without a trace of this kind of ego would be a most refreshing experience. But having a reasonable sense of your own worth is no sin. Life's little everyday victories are good—in fact, necessary—for a healthy ego.

ego 在拉丁语中表示"我"。所以,如果一个人每句话都以"我"开头,有时候这就是非常自负的表现。心理学家西格蒙德·弗洛伊德(实际上是他作品的第一个译者)使 *ego* 这个词语进入了大众词汇。不过,他用这个词语表示的意思比较复杂,所以,只有其他心理学家真正以弗洛伊德的意思使用该词。我们其余的人通常仅仅使用 *ego* 来表示自我价值感,不管是不是夸大了。使用"夸大"这一意思时,*ego* 与 *conceit*(自负)几乎同义。能遇到一个丝毫没有这种自负的超级明星,那几乎是令人耳目一新的体验。不过,有着合乎情理的自我价值感并非是什么罪孽。生活中日常的小小成绩对健康的自我成就感来说是有好处的,实际上也是必要的。

ethos \ˈē-ˌthäs\   The features, attitudes, moral code, or basic beliefs that define a person, a group, or an institution. (个人、团体、机构)的精神特质

• The company's ethos has always been an interesting blend of greed and generosity. 这家公司的风气一直是贪婪和慷慨的有趣结合。

Ethos means "custom" or "character" in Greek. As originally used by Aristotle, it referred to a man's character or personality, especially in its balance between passion and caution. Today *ethos* is used to refer to the practices or values that distinguish one person, organization, or society from others. So we often hear of the ethos of rugged individualism and self-sufficiency on the American frontier in the 19th century; and a critic might complain about, for example, the ethos of violence in the inner cities or the ethos of permissiveness in the suburbs.

ethos 在希腊语中的意思是"习俗"或"性格"。亚里士多德最早使用该词时是指一个人的性格,尤其是指激情和谨慎之间的平衡。今天,*ethos* 用来指将一个人、一个组织或者一个社会与众不同的做法或者价值观。所以,我们经常听说19世纪美国边疆的坚毅的个人主义和自给自足的精神特质。评论家可能抱怨内城的暴力特质或者郊区的纵容特质。

hubris \ˈhyü-brəs\   Unreasonable or unjustified pride or self-confidence. (过度的或者没有理由的)骄傲;自信

• Two hours later, the team's boastful pregame hubris bumped into the embarrassing reality of defeat. 两个小时后,这个队自吹自擂的赛前自信遭遇到了令人尴尬的失败。

To the Greeks, *hubris* referred to extreme pride, especially pride and ambition so great that they offend the gods and lead to one's downfall. Hubris was a character flaw often seen in the heroes of classical Greek tragedy, including Oedipus and Achilles. The familiar old saying "Pride goeth before a fall" is basically talking about hubris.

对希腊人来说，hubris 指极度的骄傲，尤其是惹得诸神生气、导致毁灭的骄傲和野心。hubris 是在希腊古典悲剧中的英雄（比如俄狄浦斯和阿喀琉斯）身上常常看到的性格缺陷。人们熟悉的谚语"骄者必败"基本上说的就是过度的自信。

id\\'id\\ The part of a person's unconscious mind that relates to basic needs and desires. 本我

• His own id often scared him, especially when a sudden violent impulse would well up out of nowhere. 他自己的本我常常让他害怕，尤其是在有了不知从何而来的强烈冲动时。

In Latin, *id* means simply "it." Sigmund Freud (and his translator) brought the word into the modern vocabulary as the name of what Freud believed to be one of the three basic elements of the human personality, the other two being the *ego* (see p. 609) and the *superego*. According to Freud, the id is the first of these to develop, and is the home of the body's basic instincts, particularly those involving sex and aggression. Since the id lacks logic, reason, or even organization, it can contain conflicting impulses. Primitive in nature, it wants to be satisfied immediately. Although its workings are completely unconscious, Freud believed that its contents could be revealed in works of art, in slips of the tongue ("Freudian slips"), and in one's dreams.

在拉丁语中，id 意思很简单，就是"它"。西格蒙德·弗洛伊德的作品（及其译者）将这一词语带进了当代词汇，用来命名弗洛伊德认为的人性中三个基本要素之一。其余两个是 ego（自我）（见第 609 页）和 superego（超我）。根据弗洛伊德的说法，本我是三者中首先发展出来的，是身体的基本本能（尤其是性和攻击性）的家园。由于本我缺少逻辑、理智或者甚至是条理性，它会有着相互冲突的冲动。它从本质上说是原始的，想要马上得到满足。虽然其工作原理完全是无意识的，弗洛伊德认为其内容可以在艺术品、口误（"Freudian slips"）和梦中展示出来。

libido\\lə-'bē-dō\\ （1）Sexual drive. 性欲 （2）In psychoanalytic theory, energy that is derived from primitive biological urges and is usu- ally goal-oriented. (源自原始的生理欲望、通常目标明确的)生理能量

• She would sit at home trying not to think about where his unmanageable libido had led him this time. 她会坐在家里，想要明白这一次他那无法控制的生理能量会将他引向何处。

The Latin word *libido*, meaning "desire, lust," was borrowed by Sigmund Freud as the name for a concept in his own theories. At first he defined *libido* to mean the instinctual energy associated with the sex drive. Later he broadened the word's meaning and began using it to mean the mental energy behind purposeful human activity of any kind; in other words, the libido (for which Freud also used the term *eros*, a Greek word meaning "sexual love") came to be regarded as the life instinct, which included sex along with all the other impulses we rely on to keep us alive. But those of us who aren't psychologists use the word simply as a synonym for "sex drive."

拉丁语 libido 一词意思是"欲望"，由西格蒙德·弗洛伊德借来用于命名其理论中一个概念。最初，他将 libido 界定为表示和性欲有关的本能的能量。后来，他扩大了该词的意思，开始用它表示任何一种有目的的人类活动背后的精神能量。换句话说，libido（弗洛伊德也用希腊语中意思是"性爱"的 eros 来表示）逐渐被认为是生命的本能，包括性以及其他

611

所有我们依赖其活下去的冲动。但是我们这些不是心理学家的人使用该词,也仅仅是将其作为"性欲"的同义词。

trauma\ˈtrȯ-mə\ （1）A serious injury to the body.（身体的）重伤（2）An abnormal psychological state caused by mental or emotional stress or physical injury. 创伤

• Fifteen years later, their adopted Cambodian daughter was still having nightmares in which she relived the trauma of those terrible years. 十五年后,他们收养的柬埔寨女儿仍然做噩梦,在梦中重新体验可怕的岁月留下的创伤。

Trauma is the Greek word for "wound." Although the Greeks used the term only for physical injuries, nowadays *trauma* is just as likely to refer to emotional wounds. We now know that a *traumatic* event can leave psychological symptoms long after any physical injuries have healed. The psychological reaction to emotional trauma now has an established name: *post-traumatic stress disorder*, or PTSD. It usually occurs after an extremely stressful event, such as wartime combat, a natural disaster, or sexual or physical abuse; its symptoms include depression, anxiety, flashbacks, and recurring nightmares.

trauma 在希腊语中表示"伤"。虽然希腊人仅仅用这一词语表示身体的伤害,但现在 trauma 同样可能指代情绪上的伤害。我们现在知道一件 traumatic（痛苦的）事情可以在任何身体伤害痊愈很长时间之后仍然留下心理症状。对情绪的创伤产生的心理反应有一个既定的名字:post-traumatic stress disorder（创伤后应激障碍）,或者 PTSD。它通常发生在令人极其紧张的事件之后,比如打仗、自然灾害或者性虐待或身体虐待,其症状包括抑郁、忧虑、闪回和反复做噩梦。

Quiz

Fill in each blank with the correct letter:

a. charisma　　　　　　　　e. ethos
b. libido　　　　　　　　　　f. trauma
c. aegis　　　　　　　　　　g. ego
d. id　　　　　　　　　　　　h. hubris

1. It seems like _____ to brag about a victory before it has been won.

2. It took her just a few weeks to recover from the physical _____, but the emotional scars were still with her years later.

3. He has such a massive _____ that no praise seems to satisfy him.

4. Those who enter the monastery don't lose their _____, just their opportunity to satisfy it.

5. She's going on a speaking tour through the Middle East under the _____ of the State Department.

6. Attracting and motivating such a terrific faculty required a principal of great personal _____.

7. The wildest of these underground comic books seem to be a pure expression of the teenage _____.

8. She joined the church because of its _____ of tolerance and social service.

Review Quizzes

A. Complete the analogy:

1. tag : label :: pseudonym : _____
   a. last name   b. title   c. maiden name   d. alias
2. drama : play :: trauma : _____
   a. wound   b. harm   c. mind   d. emotion
3. allow : prohibit :: proscribe : _____
   a. hesitate   b. stick   c. permit   d. lead
4. tune : melody :: proverb : _____
   a. poem   b. song   c. story   d. saying
5. extent : length :: simile : _____
   a. shape   b. contrast   c. kind   d. comparison
6. mob : crowd :: ego : _____
   a. self   b. other   c. friend   d. same
7. deceive : mislead :: simulate : _____
   a. increase   b. excite   c. grow   d. imitate
8. disease : cure :: dissolution : _____
   a. disintegration   b. unification   c. departure   d. solidity
9. baby : mother :: descendant : _____
   a. brother   b. offspring   c. child   d. ancestor
10. soak : drench :: dehydrate : _____
    a. liquidate   b. dry   c. dissolve   d. adjust

B. Fill in each blank with the correct letter:

a. transcend
b. libido
c. verbose
d. patronymic
e. circumscribe
f. absolution
g. simile
h. verbatim

i. id
j. condescend
k. hydroponics
l. ethos
m. proscribe
n. resolution
o. conscription

1. The doctor warned her that her _____ would be reduced while she was on the medication.

2. The use of _____ and greenhouses enables the floral industry to operate year-round.

3. He'd been very nervous about seeing her again, so when she smiled at him it felt like a kind of _____.

4. Stevenson was originally a _____ ("Steven's son"), which was later sometimes shortened to Stevens.

5. Military professionals often dislike _____ because most of the recruits don't want to be in the armed services.

6. He invites his wife's family to their place on holidays, but he would never _____ to go to their house instead.

7. Since the tape recorder wasn't turned on, there's no _____ record of the meeting.

8. The worst _____ in the song is the one that compares his beloved to a really solid six-cylinder engine.

9. Occasionally the Congress will try to _____ the president's power, but they usually end up deciding they'd rather not have the new responsibilities themselves.

10. All the states now _____ smoking inside public buildings.

11. She hates school, and she lacks the _____ to completeher high-school equivalency degree on her own.

12. These made-for-TV movies are made for very little money and almost never _____ the lowest level of acting and production.

13. In my afternoon class there's an extremely _____ guy whose "questions" sometimes go on for five minutes.

14. The _____ is completely primitive and reacts unthinkingly according to the pleasure-pain principle.

15. There's something very wrong with a company's _____ when the employees who get ahead are the ones who tell on their friends.

C. Match each word on the left to its correct definition on the right:

1. inscription   a. domination
2. verbiage   b. personal magnetism
3. dehydrate   c. prohibit
4. simulacrum   d. replica
5. soluble   e. protection
6. hubris   f. mistake
7. fallacy   g. dissolvable
8. dissolution   h. breakup
9. aegisi   i. excessive pride
10. hydraulic   j. involving liquid
11. ascendancy   k. absorb
12. proscribe   l. wordiness

13. assimilate
14. charisma
15. proverb

m. saying
n. dry
o. dedication

UNIT 26

MUR, from the Latin noun *murus*, meaning "wall," has produced a modest number of English words.

MUR 源自拉丁语名词 *murus*(墙壁)，已经产生了一些英语单词。

muralist\\ˈmyu̇r-ə-list\\ A painter of wall paintings. 壁画家

• She's enjoying her new career as a muralist, but it's terribly hard on her when she sees her works wrecked by vandals. 她喜欢作为壁画家的工作，不过看到自己的作品被人糟蹋时感到很不好受。

Any wall painting may be called a *mural*. Murals have been around since long before the framed painting. Scenic murals date back to at least 2000 B.C. on the island of Crete. Indoor murals for private homes were popular in ancient Greece and Rome, and many of those at Pompeii were preserved by the lava of Mt. Vesuvius. In the Renaissance the muralists Raphael and Michelangelo created great wall and ceiling paintings for the Catholic Church, and Leonardo da Vinci's *The Last Supper* became one of the most famous of all murals. Mural painting saw a great revival in Mexico beginning in the 1920s, when a group of muralists inspired by the Mexican Revolution, including Diego Rivera, J. C. Orozco, and D. A. Siqueiros, began taking their intensely political art to the public by creating giant wall paintings, sometimes on outdoor surfaces.

任何墙壁上的图画都叫做 *mural*。在框画出现之前很久就有壁画了。壁画可以追溯到至少公元前 2000 年前的克里特岛。私家室内壁画在古希腊和古罗马时期非常流行，庞贝城很多壁画被维苏威火山的岩浆保留下来了。文艺复兴期间，壁画家拉斐尔和米开朗琪罗为天主教堂创作了大幅壁画和天花板画。列奥纳多·达·芬奇的《最后的晚餐》成了所有壁画中最著名的作品。20 世纪 20 年，壁画在墨西哥再现辉煌。当时，一批壁画家从墨西哥革命中得到灵感，其中包括迭戈·里维拉、J. C. 奥罗斯科、D. A. 赛凯罗斯。他们创作了巨大的壁画(有时在户外的平面上)，开始向公众展示其富有政治气息的艺术。

intramural\\ˌin-trə-ˈmyu̇r-əl\\ Existing or occurring within the bounds

UNIT 26

of an institution, especially a school. 机构内部的；校内的

- At college he lacked the time to go out for sports in a serious way, but he did play intramural hockey all four years. 大学时代,他没时间好好出去运动,不过四年都在校内打曲棍球。

With its Latin prefix *intra-*, "within" (not to be confused with *inter-*, "between"), *intramural* means literally "within the walls." The word is usually used for sports played between teams made up only from students at one campus. Intramural athletics is often the most popular extracurricular activity at a college or university.

有了拉丁语前缀 *intra-*（在……之内）（不可与 *inter* 混淆,其意思是"在……之间"）, *intramural* 字面意思就是"在围墙之内"。该词通常用于来自同一校园的学生组成的两队之间的运动项目。校内体育运动常常是高校最受欢迎的课外运动。

extramural \ˌeks-trə-ˈmyu̇r-əl\ Existing outside or beyond the walls or boundaries of an organized unit such as a school or hospital. 机构之外的；校外的；医院之外的

- "Hospital Without Walls" is an extramural program that offers home healthcare services. "没有围墙的医院"是一个院外项目,提供家庭健康保健服务。

Extramural contains the Latin *extra-*, meaning "outside" or "beyond" (see EXTRA, p. 175). The walls in *extramural* are usually those of schools, colleges, and universities, and the word is often seen in phrases like "extramural activities" and "extramural competition," referring to things that involve the world beyond the campus. Some institutions use the term "extramural study" for what others call "distance learning"—that is, teaching and learning by means of Web connections to the classroom and to videos of lectures. Money that flows into universities to support research (from foundations, government institutes, etc.) is usually called "extramural income."

extramural 包含拉丁语前缀 *extra-*（"在……之外"或者"超过"）(见 EXTRA,第 175 页)。*extramural* 一词中的墙往往是学校、学院、大学的墙,而且该词常常出现在"extramural activities"（校外活动）和"extramural competition"（校外竞赛）之类的短语中,指的是涉及校园之外的事物。有些教育机构使用"extramural study"（校外学习）这一术语指代其他人所谓的"远程学习",就是通过教室和讲课视频的网络连接进行的教学活动。流入大学支持科研的资金（来自基金会、政府机构等）通常被称为"校外收入"。

immure \i-ˈmyu̇r\ To enclose within, or as if within, walls; imprison. 囚禁（在几堵墙壁内）；监禁；禁闭

MUR

- In Dumas's famous novel, the Count of Monte Cristo is in fact a sailor who had been unjustly immured in an island prison for 15 years before breaking out and taking his revenge. 在大仲马那部著名小说中,基督山伯爵实际上是个水手,越狱并复仇前,受到陷害,在一个岛上的监狱中囚禁了 15 年。

In Eastern European legend, whenever a large bridge or fort was completed, a young maiden would be *immured* in the stonework as a sacrifice. (It's not certain that such things were actually done.) In Poe's grim story "The Cask of

· 617 ·

Amontillado," a man achieves revenge on a fellow nobleman by chaining him to a cellar wall and bricking him up alive. At the end of Verdi's great opera *Aida*, Aida joins her lover so that they can die immured together. But real-life examples of *immurement* as a final punishment are somewhat harder to find.

在东欧传说中，只要修了一座大桥或者堡垒，一位姑娘就会 immured（被囚禁）在石头结构中作为祭品（还不知道是否真的有这种事）。在爱伦•坡《一桶白葡萄酒》这篇令人压抑的小说中，一位男性为了报仇，将另一个贵族用链子锁在酒窖的墙上，之后砌了砖墙，将其活活困在里面。在威尔第的《阿依达》这部伟大戏剧结尾处，阿依达主动与相爱的人囚禁在坟墓内，与其相伴至死。但是，在现实生活中，要发现以 *immurement*（囚禁在几堵墙壁内）作为最后惩罚的例子，更加困难一些。

POLIS/POLIT

POLIS/POLIT comes from the Greek word for "city." The ancient Greek city-states, such as Athens, Thebes, and Sparta, operated much like separate nations, so all their *politics* was local, like all their public *policy*—and even all their *police*!

POLIS/POLIT 源自希腊语表示"城市"的那个词语。古希腊城邦国家，比如雅典、底比斯和斯巴达，其运作很像不同的国家，所以它们的 *politics*（政治）是本地的，就像其所有公共 *policy*（政策）那样，甚至连所有的 *police*（警察）也是这样。

politic \ˈpä-lə-ˌtik\ (1) Cleverly tactful. 得体的；圆通的；明智的 (2) Wise in promoting a plan or plan of action. 善于推进（行动）计划的

• Anger is rarely a politic way to seek agreement, since it usually comes across as rude and self-righteous. 生气很少是达成一致意见的明智方式，因为它通常给人的印象是粗鲁和自以为是。

Politic behavior in class always requires a respectful attitude toward your teacher. It's never politic to ask for a raise when your boss is in a terrible mood. And once teenagers learn to drive, they quickly learn the politic way to ask for the car—that is, whatever gets the keys without upsetting the parents. As you can see, *politic* can be used for many situations that have nothing to do with public *politics*.

课堂上 politic（得体的）行为总是需要你对老师态度恭敬。老板情绪极差，你还要求加薪，永远都不是明智的。一旦十几岁的孩子学会开车，他们很快就学会借车的得体方式了，也就是不会让父母难过又能很快拿到钥匙的任何办法。你可以看到，*politic* 可以用于很多与公共 *politics*（政治）无关的情况。

politicize \pə-ˈli-tə-ˌsīz\ To give a political tone or character to. 使……具有政治特色或气氛

• By 1968 the Vietnam War had deeply politicized most of America's college campuses. 到1968年，越南战争已经使美国大学校园有了浓重的政治气氛。

Sexual harassment was once seen as a private matter, but in the 1980s and 1990s it became thoroughly *politicized*, with women loudly pressuring lawmakers to make it illegal. So, at the same time, the issue of sexual harassment politicized many women, who began to take an interest in political action because of it. In other words, we may speak of an issue becoming politicized, but also of a person or group becoming politicized.

性骚扰曾被视为私事,但在 20 世纪 80 和 90 年代,它变得彻底 politicized(具有政治特色了),女性大声疾呼,向立法人员施压,使其成为非法行为。所以,与此同时,性骚扰问题使很多女性具有政治特色,她们开始对政治行动感兴趣了。换句话说,我们可以说一个问题变得具有政治特色,但也可以说一个人或者一个群体具有政治特色。

acropolis \ə-ˈkrä-pə-ləs\ The high, fortified part of a city, especially an ancient Greek city. (古希腊都城的)卫城;城堡

• On the Athenian Acropolis, high above the rest of the city, stands the Parthenon, a temple to Athena. 雅典卫城高高耸立着帕台农神庙,是雅典娜的神庙。

The Greek root *acro-* means "high"; thus, an acropolis is basically a "high city." Ancient cities often grew up around a high point, in order that they could easily be defended. The Greeks and Romans usually included in their acropolises temples to the city's most important gods; so, for example, Athens built a great temple on its Acropolis to its protector goddess, Athena, from which the city took its name. Many later European cities cluster around a walled castle on a height, into which the population of the city and the surrounding area could retreat in case of attack, and even South American cities often contain a similar walled area on high ground.

希腊语词根 *acro-* 意思是"高",因此,卫城基本上就是一个"高城"。古代城市往往是在高高的地点附近发展起来的,这样它们就很容易得到保护。希腊人和罗马人通常会在他们的阿克罗波利斯神庙中供奉城市中最重要的神灵,例如,雅典在卫城上为她的守护女神雅典娜建造了一座巨大的神庙。许多后来的欧洲城市都集中在一个高墙上的城堡周围,城市和周围地区的人口在受到攻击时可以撤退到这个城堡里,甚至南美洲的城市在高处也经常有一个类似的卫城。

megalopolis \ˌme-gə-ˈlä-pə-ləs\ (1) A very large city. 大都市 (2) A thickly populated area that includes one or more cities with the surrounding suburbs. (包含一个或多个城市及其郊区的)人口稠密区

• With its rapid development, the southern coast of Florida around Miami quickly became a megalopolis. 由于发展迅速,迈阿密周围的佛罗里达南部海岸迅速成为人口稠密区。

A "large city" named Megalopolis was founded in Greece in 371 B.C. to help defend the region called Arcadia against the city-state of Sparta. Though a stadium seating 20,000 was built there, indicating the city's impressive size for its time, Megalopolis today has only about 5,000 people. Social scientists now identify 10 megalopolises in the U.S., each with more than 10 million people. The one on the eastern seaboard that stretches from Boston to Washington, D.C., where the densely populated cities seem to flow into each other all along the coast, is now home to over 50 million people. But it's easily surpassed by the Japanese megalopolis that includes Tokyo, with more than 80 million inhabitants.

公元前 371 年,古希腊建立了一个称为 Megalopolis 的"大城市",以帮助保卫叫作阿卡迪亚的地区,使其不受斯巴达城邦的侵犯。虽然这里建造了一个能容纳两万人的体育馆,说明了当时该城的巨大面积,但 Megalopolis 今天只有五千人。社会科学家目前在美国识别出了十个人口稠密区,每个都有一千万以上的人口。东海岸的人口稠密区从波士顿到华盛顿特区,这里人口稠密的城市似乎已经沿着海岸相互融入了,有五千万人口。但是,它很容易被日本那个人口稠密区超过,那里包括东京在内,居民多达八千万。

POLIS/POLIT

Quizzes

A. Fill in each blank with the correct letter:

a. muralist
b. politic
c. megalopolis
d. immure
e. extramural
f. acropolis
g. politicize
h. intramural

1. Chicago itself has fewer than 3 million inhabitants, but the _____ that includes Milwaukee and Madison has over 14 million.

2. Her fear of theft was so great that she actually intended to _____ all the gold and silver behind a brick wall in the basement, leaving clues to the location in her will.

3. He knew it was never _____ to mention his own children's achievements around his brother, whose oldest son was in prison.

4. They had hired a professional _____ to paint the walls of the staircase with a flowery landscape.

5. The city government buildings occupied an _____, high above the factories that lined the riverbank.

6. Women's softball was the most popular of the college's _____ sports.

7. Most voters thought it was unfortunate that the candidates had actually managed to _____ a traffic accident.

8. The government mental-health center in Washington, D.C., conducts its own research but also funds _____ research at universities across the country.

B. Match the word on the left with the correct definition on the right.

1. megalopolis
2. immure
3. intramural
4. politic
5. acropolis
6. politicize
7. muralist
8. extramural

a. within an institution
b. seal up
c. high part of a city
d. turn into a political issue
e. wall painter
f. huge urban area
g. shrewdly sensitive
h. outside an institution

NUMER comes from the Latin words meaning "number" and "to count." A *numeral* is the symbol that represents a number. *Numerous* means "many," and *innumerable* means "countless." *Numerical* superiority is superiority in numbers, and your numerical standing in a class is a ranking expressed as a number.

NUMER 源自拉丁语中意思是"数字"和"数数"的词语。*numeral*（数字代码）是代表数字的符号。*numerous* 意思是"很多"，*innumerable* 意思是"无数"。*numerical*（数字的，数量的）优势就是在数量上占有优势，而你在班上的数字排名是用数字表示的名次。

numerology \ ˌnü-mə-ˈrä-lə-jē \   The study of the occult significance of numbers. 数字命理学；数字占卜术

- Though he didn't believe in numerology as a mystical bond between numbers and living things, he never went out on Friday the 13th. 他不相信数字占卜术是数字和生物之间的神秘纽带，但他从不在13号的星期五出门。

As an element of astrology and fortune-telling, numerology has long been employed to predict future events. For many early Christians, 3 represented the Trinity, 6 represented earthly perfection, and 7 represented heavenly perfection; and still today, many of us like to group things into sets of 3 or 7, for no particular reason. Numerology has also been used to interpret personality; in particular, *numerologists* may assign numbers to each letter of a person's name and use the resulting figures, along with the person's date of birth, as a guide to his or her character.

作为占卜术和算命的一个元素，数字占卜术长期以来一直被用来预言未来。对很多早期基督徒来说，3代表三位一体，6代表尘世的完美，7代表天堂的完美。到了今天，我们很多人仍然喜欢把事物分成3个或者7个一组，但并没有什么特定的原因。数字占卜术还用来解释性格，尤其是 *numerologists*（数字占卜术士）可能会给某人名字的每个字母指派一个数字，利用得出的那些数字跟生日一起指导自己了解其性格。

alphanumeric \ ˌal-fə-nü-ˈmer-ik \   Having or using both letters and numbers. 有字母和数字的；利用字母和数字的

- Back in the 1950s, we always spoke our phone numbers in alphanumeric form, using the letters printed on the dial; for example, "TErrace 5-6642," instead of "835-6642." 早在20世纪50年代，人们总是使用印在拨号盘上的字母，以字母加数字的形式说电话号码；比如"TErrace5-6642"，而不是"835-6642"。

Alphanumeric passwords are much harder for a hacker to crack than plain alphabetic passwords, since the number of possible combinations is so much greater. License plates usually contain both letters and numbers, since, for a big state or country, the plate wouldn't be large enough to fit enough numbers for everyone. In computing, the standard alphanumeric codes, such as ASCII, may contain not only ordinary letters and numerals but also punctuation marks and math symbols.

与仅仅使用字母的密码相比，alphanumeric（字母加数字的）密码更难以被黑客破译，因为可能出现的组合数量要大得多。牌照通常既包含字母也包含数字，因为对一个大州或大国来说，牌照不至于大到为所有人放进足够多的数字。在计算机领域，标准的字母加数字代码，比如 ASCII，可能包含普通字母和数字，也有标点符号和数学符号。

enumerate \ i-ˈnü-mə-ˌrāt \   To specify one after another; list. 列举

- The thing he hated most was when she would start enumerating his faults out loud, while he would sit scowling into the newspaper trying to ignore her. 他最恨的事情，就是她大声地一一列出他的缺点，这种时候他会坐在那里怒视着报纸，想要当她不存在。

In a census year, the U.S. government attempts to *enumerate* every single citizen of the country—a task that, even in the modern era of technology, isn't truly possible. Medical tests often require the *enumeration* of bacteria, viruses, or other organisms to determine the progress of a disease or the effectiveness of a medication. Despite its *numer-* root, you don't have to use numbers when enumerating. For students of government and law, the "enumerated powers" are the specific responsibilities of the Congress, as listed in the U.S. Constitution; these are the only powers that Congress has, a fact that the Tenth Amendment makes even more clearly.

在人口统计的年份，美国政府努力 enumerate（列出）这个国家每个公民。这个任务，就是在当今技术时代，也不太可能。医疗测试经常需要 enumeration（列举）细菌、病菌或者其他微生物，以确定疾病的发展和药物的有效程度。虽然这个词语有 numer-这一词根，但列举时也不必使用数字。对于政治学和法学方面的学者来说，"enumerated powers"（国会的有限权力）指《美国宪法》列出的国会的那些权力。这些是国会仅有的权力，这一事实在"第十条修正案"中陈述得更加明确。

supernumerary \ˌsü-pər-ˈnü-mə-ˌrer-ē\ Exceeding the usual number. 过多的；额外的

● Whenever the workload for the city's courts and judges gets too large, supernumerary judges are called in to help. 每当该市的法庭和法官工作负担过重，就额外请一些法官前来协助。

Supernumerary starts off with the Latin prefix *super-*, "above" (see SUPER, p. 643). You may have heard of someone being born with supernumerary teeth, supernumerary fingers, or supernumerary toes. A supernumerary rainbow may show up as a faint line—red, green, or purple—just touching the main colored arc. *Supernumerary* is also a noun: A supernumerary is usually someone in a crowd scene onstage, otherwise known as an "extra" or a "spear-carrier."

supernumerary 起首部分是 super-（"超；超级"）这一前缀（见 SUPER，第 643 页）。你可能听说过有人生来就有超过正常数量的牙齿、手指或者脚拇指。supernumerary rainbow（多余虹）可能出现时只是隐隐约约的一条线——红色、绿色或者紫色的——刚好接触主要的彩色弧。*supernumerary* 也可用作名词，通常指舞台上多人场景中的一个人，也叫做"临时演员"或者"跑龙套的演员"。

KILO is the French version of the Greek word *chilioi*, meaning "thousand." France is also where the metric system originated, in the years following the French Revolution. So in English, *kilo-* shows up chiefly in metric-system units. Before the computer age, the most familiar *kilo-* words for English-speakers were probably *kilowatt*, meaning "1,000 watts," and *kilowatt-hour*, meaning the amount of energy equal to one kilowatt over the course of an hour.

KILO 是希腊语 chilioi（"千"）的法语说法。法国大革命之后，米制起源于法国。所以，在英语中，kilo-主要出现在米制单位中。在计算机时代之前，说英语的人最熟知的以 kilo-起首的词语可能是 kilowatt（千瓦），意思是"一千瓦"、kilowatt-hour(千瓦时)，意思是一小时内相当于一千瓦的能量。

kilobyte \ˈki-lə-ˌbīt\ A unit of computer information equal to 1,024 bytes. 千字节

• A 200-word paragraph in the simplest text format takes up about a kilobyte of storage space on your hard drive. 一个两百词的段落，以最简单的形式出现，在硬盘驱动器上大约占用一个千字节的储存空间。

Knowing the root *kilo*, you might think a kilobyte would be exactly 1,000 bytes. But actually a kilobyte represents the power of 2 that comes closest to 1,000：that is, 2^{10} (2 to the 10th power), or $2\times2\times2\times2\times2\times2\times2\times2\times2\times2$, or 1,024. Why 2? Because the capacity of memory chips is always based on powers of 2. Locations in electronic memory circuits are identified by binary numbers (numbers that use only the digits 0 and 1), so the number of addressable locations becomes a power of 2.

认识了 *kilo* 这一词根，你可能会认为一个千字节就是整整 1,000 个字节。实际上，一个千字节代表几乎等于 1,000 的 2 的次方：也就是 2^{10}（2 的 10 次方），或者 $2\times2\times2\times2\times2\times2\times2\times2\times2\times2$，或者 1,024。为什么是 2 呢？因为内存芯片的容量总是以 2 的次方为基础的。电子储存电路上的区是利用二进制数（只使用 0 和 1 的数）来确认的，所以可寻址区的数量就是 2 的次方。

kilometer \kə-ˈlä-mə-tər\ A unit of length equal to 1,000 meters. 千米；公里

• U. S. highway signs near the Canadian border often show distances in kilometers in addition to miles. 加拿大边境附近的美国公路标志，除了用英里标明距离外，也用公里。

A kilometer is equal to about 62/100 of a mile, and a mile is equal to about 1.61 kilometers. The U. S. has been slow to adopt metric measures, which are used almost everywhere else in the world. Though our car speedometers are often marked in both miles and kilometers, the U. S. and Great Britain are practically the only developed nations that still show miles rather than kilometers on their road signs. But even in the U. S., footraces are usually measured in meters or kilometers, like the Olympic races. Runners normally abbreviate *kilometer* to K："a 5K race"（3.1 miles），"the 10K run"（6.2 miles），and so on.

一 kilometer（公里）大约等于一英里的 62/100，而一英里大约等于 1.61 公里。美国迟迟不肯采用米制，而米制几乎在世界其他各地都在使用。虽然我们汽车的速度计经常标有英里也标有公里，但美国和英国几乎是仅有的在路标上使用英里而不是公里的发达国家。但是，即使在美国，竞走也通常使用米或公里来计量，就像奥运会的比赛那样。跑步的人常常将 *kilometer* 缩略为 K："5K 赛跑"(3.1 英里)，"跑步 10K"(6.2 英里)，等等。

kilohertz \ˈki-lə-ˌhərts\ A unit of frequency equal to 1,000 cycles per second. 千赫(兹)

• A drone aircraft nosedived and crashed after an onboard tape recorder turned out to be using a 10-kilohertz signal, the same frequency used by the aircraft's control system. 一架遥控无人驾驶飞机俯冲后坠毁，原来机上的磁带录音机使用了 10 千赫的信号，而该飞机控制系统使用的是同样的频率。

If your favorite AM radio station has a frequency of 680 *kilohertz* (kHz), that means the station's transmitter is oscillating (vibrating) at a rate of 680,000 cycles per second (i.e., 680,000 times a second). A related term is *megahertz* (MHz), meaning "*millions* of cycles per second." Shortwave radio operates between 5.9 and 26.1 MHz, and the FM radio band operates between 88 and 108 MHz. Garage-door openers work at about 40 MHz, baby monitors work at 49 MHz, and so on. The terms *hertz*, *kilohertz* and *megahertz* honor the great German physicist Heinrich Hertz, the first person to broadcast and receive radio waves.

如果你最爱的调频广播电台的频率是 680 千赫(kHz),这就意味着该电台的发射器正以每秒 680,000 周的速度波动(也就是每秒 680,000 次)。相关的术语是 megahertz(MHz)(兆赫),意思是"每秒数百万周"。短波广播在 5.9 和 26.1 兆赫之间运作,调频无线电波段在 88 至 108 兆赫之间运作。车库开门器以大约 40 兆赫的频率工作,婴儿监视器以 49 兆赫的频率工作,等等。Hertz、kilohertz 和 megahertz 这几个术语的产生,是为了纪念伟大的德国物理学家亨利希·赫兹。他是第一个进行无线电广播并收到无线电波的人。

kilogram \ˈki-lə-ˌgram\ A unit of weight equal to 1,000 grams. 千克;公斤

• The kilogram is the only base unit of measurement still defined by a physical object rather than a physical constant (such as the speed of light). 公斤是唯一仍然以物体而不是物理常数(比如光速)界定的基本计量单位。

The original concept of the *kilogram*, as the mass of a cubic decimeter of water (a bit more than a quart), was adopted as the base unit of mass by the new revolutionary government of France in 1793. In 1875, in the Treaty of the Meter, 17 countries, including the U.S., adopted the French kilogram as an international standard. In 1889 a new international standard for the kilogram, a metal bar made of platinum iridium, was agreed to; President Benjamin Harrison officially received the 1-kilogram cylinder for the U.S. in 1890. But no one uses that bar very often; for all practical purposes, a kilogram equals 2.2 pounds.

最初的公斤概念,作为一立方分米水的质量(比一夸特多一点),于 1793 年被法国新革命政府采用为质量的基本单位。1875 年,在《米制条约》中,包括美国在内的 17 个国家采用法国的公斤作为一个国际标准。1889 年,公斤的新国际标准,一个铂铱合金作的金属棒,得到了一致认可。1890 年,本杰明·哈里森总统代表美国正式接受了这个一公斤的圆筒。不过,没有谁经常使用这个金属棒;实际上,一公斤等于 2.2 磅。

Quizzes

A. Match each word on the left to its correct definition on the right:

1. kilobyte   a. 3/5 of a mile
2. enumerate   b. extra
3. supernumerary   c. measure of electronic capacity
4. kilogram   d. list
5. kilohertz   e. occult use of numbers
6. numerology   f. 1,000 vibrations per second
7. alphanumeric   g. 2.2 pounds

UNIT 26

8. kilometer   h. combining numbers and letters

B. Fill in each blank with the correct letter:

a. supernumerary   e. kilobyte
b. kilogram   f. kilometer
c. enumerate   g. alphanumeric
d. kilohertz   h. numerology

1. Every Tuesday there's a 5-_____ race along the river, which is short enough that 10-year-olds sometimes run it.

2. For his annual salary review, his boss always asks him to _____ the projects he completed during the previous year.

3. On a hard drive, a _____ is enough capacity for a few sentences of text, but for audio or video it's too small to even mention.

4. As a child, she had a couple of _____ teeth, which the dentist pulled when she was 8 years old.

5. The broadcast frequencies of FM stations are required to be 200 _____ apart so as not to interfere with each other.

6. When they first moved to Berlin, it took them a few days to get used to buying potatoes and oranges by the _____ rather than the pound.

7. She occasionally visited a local fortune-teller, who would use playing cards and _____ to predict her future.

8. The Web site uses six-character _____ passwords, of which there are enough for tens of millions of users.

MICRO

MICRO, from the Greek *mikros*, meaning "small," is a popular English prefix. A *microscope* lets the eye see *microscopic* objects, and libraries store the pages of old newspapers on *microfilm* at 1/400th of their original size. And we continue to attach *micro-* to lots of familiar words; most of us could figure out the meaning of *microbus* and *microquake* without ever having heard them before. Scientists often use *micro-* to mean "millionth"; thus, a *microsecond* is a millionth of a second, and a *micrometer* is a millionth of a meter.

MICRO 源自希腊语 mikros, 意思是"小", 是一个非常用的英语前缀。microscope(显微镜)可以让眼睛看到 microscopic (极其微小的)东西。图书馆在 microfilm(缩微胶卷)上存有一页一页的旧报纸, 大小只有原来的 1/400。我们还在把 micro- 加在很多熟悉的词语前, 大多数人即使没有听过 microbus 和 microquake, 也可以猜出意思。科学家经常用 micro- 表示"百万分之"; 这样, microsecond 就是百万分之一秒, micrometer 就是百万分之一米。

---

microbe\\'mī-ˌkrōb\\ An organism (such as a bacterium) of microscopic or less than microscopic size. 微生物(比如细菌)

• Vaccines reduce the risk of diseases by using dead or greatly weakened microbes to stimulate the immune system. 通过利用死亡的或者生命力大幅减弱的微生物来刺激免疫系统,疫苗可以减少疾病危险。

A hint of the Greek word *bios*, meaning "life," can be seen in *microbe*. Microbes, or *microorganisms*, include bacteria, protozoa, fungi, algae, amoebas, and slime molds. Many people think of microbes as simply the causes of disease, but every human is actually the host to billions of microbes, and most of them are essential to our life. Much research is now going into possible *microbial* sources of future energy; algae looks particularly promising, as do certain newly discovered or created microbes that can produce cellulose, to be turned into ethanol and other biofuels. 在 microbe 这一词语中,可以看到希腊语 bios 这一词语(意思是"生命")的一丝迹象。microbe(微生物),或者说 microorganims,包括细菌、单细胞生物、真菌、海藻、变形虫和黏菌。很多人以为微生物只会引发疾病,但每个人都是数十亿微生物的寄主,这些微生物大多数是我们的生命必不可少的。现在,科学家正进行大量研究,因为未来能源可能源自 microbial(微生物的)。海藻看起来最有希望,就像某些新发现或新创造的、可以产生纤维素的微生物那样,而纤维素可以变成乙醇和其他生物燃料。

microbiologist \ˌmī-krō-bī-ˈä-lə-jist\ A scientist who studies extremely small forms of life, such as bacteria and viruses. 微生物学家

• Food microbiologists study the tiny organisms that cause spoiling and foodborne illness. 食物微生物学家研究引起食物变质和食源性疾病的微小生物。

Since *microorganisms* are involved in almost every aspect of life on earth, *microbiologists* work across a broad range of subject areas. Some study only viruses, some only bacteria. A marine microbiologist studies the roles of microbial communities in the sea. A soil microbiologist might focus on the use and spread of nitrogen. Veterinary microbiologists might research bacteria that attack racehorses or diagnose anthrax in cows. And the government puts microbiologists to work studying whether microbes could adapt to life on the surface of Mars, and how to defend ourselves against the possibility of germ warfare. 由于微生物几乎涉及地球上所有生物的方方面面,微生物学家的工作覆盖诸多学科。有些只研究病毒,有些只研究细菌。海洋微生物学家研究海洋中微生物的作用。土壤微生物学家可能专注于氮的使用和分布。兽医微生物学家可能研究侵袭赛马的细菌或者为牛诊断炭疽。政府让微生物学家研究微生物是否可以适应火星表面的生活,以及如何使我们防卫可能发生的细菌战。

microbrew \ˈmī-krō-ˌbrü\ A beer made by a brewery that makes beer in small amounts. 微酿啤酒

• As a city of 75,000 people with eight breweries, it offers a greater variety of microbrews per capita than any other place in America. 这座人口七万五千人的城市有八家啤酒厂,平均为每人提供的微酿啤酒的种类超过美国其他任何地方。

Microbrews are usually beers or ales made with special malts and hops, unfiltered and unpasteurized, and thus distinctive in their aroma and flavor. Many microbreweries double as bar/restaurants, called *brewpubs*, where the gleaming vats may be visible behind a glass partition. "Craft brewing" and the opening of local brewpubs began in earnest in the U. S. in the 1980s. But not everyone is willing to pay extra for a beer, and lots of people are simply used to the blander taste of the best-selling beers, so by 2008 microbrews still only accounted for about 4% of all beer sold in the U. S.

微酿啤酒通常是利用特殊麦芽或啤酒花酿制的啤酒，未经过滤、未经高温消毒，因此有着独特的气味和味道。很多微酿啤酒厂兼作酒吧/餐厅，叫作 brewpubs（自酿啤酒酒吧），在那里可以看到玻璃隔板后闪闪发亮的酒缸。20 世纪 80 年代，"工艺酿造"和本地自酿啤酒酒吧的开业正式开始于美国。但是，不是谁都愿意多花钱喝一杯啤酒，很多人就习惯于味道更淡的畅销啤酒。于是，到 2008 年，微酿啤酒仍然只占有美国所销售啤酒量的百分之四。

microclimate \ˈmī-krō-ˌklī-mət\ The essentially uniform local climate of a small site or habitat. 小气候

● Temperature, light, wind speed, and moisture are the essential components of a microclimate. 温度、光、风速和湿度是小气候的基本组成部分。

The microclimate of an industrial park may be quite different from that of a nearby wooded park, since the plants absorb light and heat while asphalt parking lots and rooftops radiate them back into the air. A microclimate can offer a small growing area for crops that wouldn't do well in the wider region, so skilled gardeners take advantage of microclimates by carefully choosing and positioning their plants. San Francisco's hills, oceanfront, and bay shore, along with its alternating areas of concrete and greenery, make it a city of microclimates.

工业园的小气候与附近树木茂密的公园很不一样，因为植物吸收光和热，而沥青停车场和房顶将光和热反射到空气中。小气候可以为更大区域内生长不良的庄稼提供小面积的生长区域，因此，老练的园丁仔细选择和安置花木，以此利用小环境。旧金山的山丘、海滨、海湾沿岸以及相间的混凝土和绿色植物区域，使这座城市成了小气候城市。

MULTI comes from the Latin word *multus*, meaning "many." Thus, a *multicultural* society is one that includes people of several different countries, languages, and religions; a *multimedia* artwork uses two or more artistic media (dance, music, film, spoken text, etc.); and a *multitude* of complaints reaching your office would be a great many indeed.

MULTI

MULT 源自拉丁语 multus，意思是"多"。这样，multicultural（多文化的）社会就包括来自不同国家、不同地区、说不同语言的人。multimedia（多媒体的）艺术品使用两种或更多的艺术媒介（舞蹈、音乐、电影、口语文本，等等）；multitude（数量极大）的投诉一股脑儿到了你办公室，那就太多了。

multicellular \ˌməl-tē-ˈsel-yə-lər\ Consisting of many cells. 多细胞的

● Multicellular organisms—fungi, plants, and animals—have specialized cells that perform different functions. 多细胞生物——真菌、植物、动物——都有着专门发挥不同功能的细胞。

Multicellular organisms are distinguished from the very primitive single-celled organisms—bacteria, algae, amoebas, etc. Even sponges, simple as they are, have specialized cell types such as digestive cells. In complex multicellular organisms, only the surface cells can exchange substances with the external environment, so the organisms have developed transport systems such as the circulatory system, in which the blood brings gases and nutrients to the cells and removes waste products from them.

多细胞生物有别于原始的单细胞生物——细菌、藻类、变形虫，等等。即使是海绵，虽然简单，也有发挥不同作用的细胞类型，比如消化细胞。在复杂的多细胞生物体内，只有表皮细胞能与外界环境交换物质，所以生物进化出了运输系统，比如循环系统，血液将气体和营养输送到细胞中并从中除去废物。

multidisciplinary \ˌməl-tē-ˈdi-sə-plə-ˌner-ē\ Involving two or more subject areas. 多学科的

• Her favorite class was Opera, a multidisciplinary class taught jointly by a music professor and a literature professor. 她最喜欢的课是戏剧，这是一位音乐教授和文学教授合作授课的多学科课程。

A *discipline* is a field of study. So a multidisciplinary (or *interdisciplinary*) course is a team-taught course in which students are asked to understand a single subject as it's seen by two or more traditional disciplines. Multidisciplinary teaching can open students' eyes to different views of a subject that they had never considered before. A multidisciplinary panel discussion, on the other hand, presents views from scholars in different fields but may leave any merging of the information to the audience.

discipline 是一门学科。所以 *multidisciplinary*（或者 *interdisciplinary*）课程是团队授课的课程，要求学生理解一门传统上视为两门或多门学科的课程。多学科教学可以开阔学生眼界，使他们接触到对同一学科的不同看法，而这是他们以前未曾考虑过的。不过，多学科小组讨论虽然展示了不同领域学者的看法，但可能把这些信息的结合留给听众。

multifarious \ˌməl-tə-ˈfer-ē-əs\ Having or occurring in great variety; diverse. 多样的；多种的；各种各样的

• Natives put the coconut palm to multifarious uses: using the nuts for eating, the juice for drinking, the wood for building huts, the leaves for thatch, the fiber for mats, and the shells for utensils. 本地人以多种方式利用椰子树：椰子当食物，椰子汁当饮料，木头建造小屋，椰子缮屋顶，纤维编席子，椰子壳当器皿。

Multifarious is a rather grand word, probably not for everyday use, but when you want to emphasize great variety—such as the huge number of uses to which a state-of-the-art cell phone can be put—it can be effective. Dictionary fans are constantly amazed by the multifarious meanings of the word *set* (47 of them in one unabridged dictionary), and thesaurus lovers may marvel at the multifarious synonyms for *drunk*.

multifarious 是一个很大气的词语，可能不适合日常使用。但是，当你想要强调非常多样时，比如最先进的手机数量众多的用途，这个词是有效的。词典爱好者一直都惊奇于 *set* 这一词语多种多样的意思（非删节本词典中多达四十七个义项），类义词典爱好者可能对 *drunk* 各式各样的同义词感到吃惊。

multilateral \ˌməl-tē-ˈla-tə-rəl\ Involving more than two nations or parties. 多边的；涉及多个国家或多方的

• 628 •

UNIT 26

• A couple of times a year, representatives of the large industrial democracies meet for a round of multilateral trade negotiations. 重要的发达民主国家的代表,每年都会面几次,进行一轮商业谈判。

Since *lateral* means "side" (see LATER, p. 657), *multilateral* means basically "many-sided." The philosophy of *multilateralism* claims that the best solutions generally result when as many of the world's nations as possible are involved in discussions, and *multilateralists* often favor strengthening the United Nations. Today multilateralism can be seen at work in, for example, the World Health Organization, the World Trade Organization, and the International Criminal Court. But the U. S. doesn't always join the major multilateral organizations, instead often behaving as if a *unilateral* approach—that is, going it alone—was best for the interests of a powerful nation.

由于 lateral 意思是"边"(见 LATER,第 657 页), multilateral 的基本意思就是"多边的"。multilateralism(多边主义)哲学声称,世界上参与讨论的国家越多,越有可能产生最好的办法。multilateralists(多边主义者)通常更赞成加强联合国的力量。今天,我们可以看到多边主义在世界卫生组织、世界贸易组织和国际刑事法庭发挥作用。但是,美国并非总是加入主要的多边组织,而是经常让人觉得 unilateral(单边)的方法,也就是单独行动,最有利于强国的利益。

Quizzes

A. Fill in each blank with the correct letter:

a. multicellular
b. microbrew
c. microbe
d. multilateral
e. multidisciplinary
f. microbiologist
g. microclimate
h. multifarious

1. At the state fair their beer was judged Minnesota's best _____.
2. Researchers are interested in the role played in the disease by a _____ that no one had particularly noticed before.
3. The U. S. has been participating in _____ climate talks with the rest of the world's biggest polluters.
4. For a young _____ like herself, it seemed that the most interesting job possibilities lay in the study of viruses.
5. Arriving at college from his little high school, he was delighted but overwhelmed by the _____ course choices that were open to him.
6. Their 25-acre property, a bowl-shaped field surrounded by woods, had its own _____ which was perfect for certain fruit trees.
7. The subject of economics can often be approached in a _____ way, since it usually involves mathematics, sociology, political science, and other fields.
8. The smallest _____ organisms actually seem to have at least 1,000 cells, while the human body has trillions.

B. Choose the closest definition:

1. microbe   a. miniature ball   b. tiny organism
   c. infection   d. midget
2. multilateral   a. many-eyed   b. many-armed
   c. with many participants   d. many-angled
3. microclimate   a. short period of different weather
   b. weather in Micronesia   c. weather at the microscopic level
   d. special climate of a small area
4. multifarious   a. odd   b. varied   c. evil
   d. unusual
5. multicellular   a. bacterial   b. viral
   c. consisting of many cells   d. huge
6. microbrew   a. small serving of beer   b. half-cup of coffee
   c. beer from a small brewery   d. tea in a small container
7. multidisciplinary   a. punishment by several methods
   b. involving several subject areas   c. with many disciples
   d. punishment by different people
8. microbiologist   a. one who studies small insects
   b. small scientist   c. one who grows small plants
   d. one who studies bacteria and viruses

PAR, from the Latin, means "equal." Our English word *par* means an amount taken as an average or a standard, and especially the standard score for each hole on a golf course—which is why the phrase "par for the course" means "about as well as expected." We *compare* things to see if they're equal; similar things can be called *comparable*—that is, "equal with." And "on a par with" means "comparable to."
PAR 源自拉丁语,意思是"相等的"。我们的英语词语 par 意思是作为平均数量或标准的量,尤其是高尔夫球场上每个洞的标准分数——这就是短语"par for the course"意思是"跟预期的差不多"的原因。我们 compare(比较)事物,看他们是否相等;类似的事物可以说是 comparable(类似的),也就是"与……相等"。on a par with 意思是"与……类似"。

---

parity \\'per-ə-tē\ The state of being equal. 相等;平等;相同;对等

• That year the Canadian dollar reached parity with the U.S. dollar for the first time in three decades. 那一年,加元与美元三十年来第一次等值。

Parity has special meanings in such fields as physics, math, medicine, genetics, and marketing. Back when the Soviet Union and the U.S. were opposing superpowers, there was often talk of *parity* in nuclear weapons between the two sides. We sometimes hear about parity between mental and physical health in

630

insurance coverage, or parity in colleges' funding of men's and women's athletics. But parity may be most common in discussions of currencies. The *exchange rate* between two national currencies often changes every day, as each drifts higher or lower, and occasionally two similar currencies, such as the euro and the U.S. dollar, will achieve parity, but it rarely lasts long.

parity 在物理、数学、医学、遗传学和营销学领域有着特殊的意思。在苏联与美国两个超级大国对立的时代,人们经常谈论说双方之间的核武器势均力敌。我们有时会听说身体和精神健康之间的平衡,或者对大学男女生体育的资助金额相等。但是,*parity* 在对货币进行讨论时最常用。两个国家货币之间的汇率每天都在变化,一个升高,一个降低。有时,两种相似的货币,比如欧元和美元,会有汇率持平的时候,但不会持久。

disparity \ di-ˈsper-ə-tē \   A noticeable and often unfair difference between people or things. 差异

• He'd been noticing an increasing disparity between what the government was claiming and what he saw happening all around him. 他一直都注意到,政府声称的与他周围实际发生的之间差异越来越大。

Disparity contains the Latin *dis*, meaning "apart" or "non-" (see DIS, p. 64), so a disparity is a kind of "nonequality." The word is often used to describe a social or economic condition that's considered unfairly unequal: a racial disparity in hiring, a health disparity between the rich and the poor, an income disparity between men and women, and so on. Its adjective, *disparate* (accented on the first syllable), is often used to emphasize strong differences.

disparity 包含拉丁语 *dis* 一词,意思是"分开的"或者"非-"(见 DIS,第 64 页),所以,*disparity* 是一种"不平等"。这一词语经常用来描述不平等的社会或经济状况:雇佣方面的种族不平等,贫富之间的健康不均衡,男女之间收入不平等,等等。其形容词形式 *disparate*(重音在第一个音节)经常用来强调巨大的差异。

nonpareil \ ˌnän-pə-ˈrel \   Someone or something of unequaled excellence. 无与伦比的人或事物

• Critics seem to agree that this is the new nonpareil of video-game consoles, the one to beat. 评论家似乎一致认为这是一款无可匹敌的新游戏机。

American children learn this word (even if they can't pronounce it) as the name of the candies covered with white sugar pellets that they buy at the movie theater, and it's also the name of the pellets themselves. But the more general meaning is common too. *Nonpareil* is also an adjective. A famous boxing champion of the 1920s was known as Nonpareil Jack Dempsey, when he wasn't being called "the Manassa Mauler." Like its synonyms *paragon* and *peerless*, *nonpareil* is popular as a company and product name; it's also the name of a fruit, an almond, a bird, and a butterfly.

美国孩子学会这个词语(即使不会念)是因为它是一种糖果的名字。这种糖果在电影院可以买到,上面满是白色糖粒,它也是这种糖粒的名字。不过,该词更普遍的意思也很常见。*nonpareil* 也可作形容词。20 世纪 20 年代,一个著名的拳击冠军,人们不称他为"马纳沙大槌子"时,就称他为"无敌杰克·邓普西"。跟同义词 *paragon*(典范;完人)和 *peerless*(无可匹敌的;无与伦比的)一样,*nonpareil* 作为公司或产品名称是很常见的,它也是一种水果、一种杏仁儿、一种鸟和一种蝴蝶的名字。

subpar \\'səb-'pär\\ Below a usual or normal level. 低于正常水平的

• Because of a severe cold, her performance that evening had been subpar, but the audience seemed to love it anyway. 因为严重感冒,她那天晚上的表演没有发挥到正常水平,不过观众还是很喜欢。

Since *sub-* means "below" (see SUB, p. 491), almost anything that fails to measure up to a traditional standard may be called subpar. So you may hear of subpar ratings for a TV show, subpar care at a nursing home, subpar attendance at a concert, or subpar work by a contractor. If you played a subpar round of golf, though, you needed *more* strokes than you should have.

因为 *sub-* 意思是"低于"(SUB,第491页)几乎任何没有达到正常标准的事物都被称为 subpar。所以,你可能会听到电视节目收视率 subpar,养老院的照顾水平 subpar,音乐会出席率 subpar,承包商的工作 subpar。如果打了一场 subpar 高尔夫球,那就需要比对手少打几杆球。

PHOB

PHOB comes from the Greek noun *phobos*, "fear," and it shows up clearly in our noun *phobia*, meaning "unusual fear of a specific thing." Phobias vary greatly in seriousness and also in frequency. Most of us have experienced *claustrophobia* at some time, but few truly suffer from fear of the number 13, a condition known as *triskaidekaphobia*.

PHOB 源自希腊语 *phobos* 这一名词,意思是"恐惧"。这一词语很明显存在于 *phobia*,意思是"恐惧感"。恐惧感在程度和发生的频率上差异很大。我们大多数人都曾体验过 *claustrophobia*(幽闭恐惧),但是很少有人真正害怕13这个数字,这一恐惧感称为 *triskaidekaphobia*。

acrophobic \\ˌa-krə-'fō-bik\\ Fearful of heights. 恐高的

• She's so acrophobic that, whenever she can't avoid taking the route that includes the high bridge, she asks the police to drive her across. 她恐高很严重,每当不得不路过这座高桥时,总是让警察开车送她过去。

The Greek *akron* means "height" or "summit," and the *acro-* root can be seen in such words as *acrobat* and *Acropolis*. Almost everyone has some fear of heights, but an abnormal dread of high places, along with the vertigo (dizziness) that most *acrophobes* also experience, are common as well; in fact, *acrophobia* is one of the half-dozen most common recognized phobias. Acrophobia and *claustrophobia* both play a role in another well-known phobia: the fear of flying, itself often known as *aerophobia*.

希腊语 *akron* 一词意思是"高度"或者"顶峰",*acro-* 这一词缀存在于 *acrobat*(杂技演员)和 *Acropolis*(卫城)两个词语中。几乎每个人都有些恐高,但是,多数恐高症患者体验的对高处的不正常的恐惧,而且伴随着眩晕,也是常见的。实际上,*acrophobia*(恐高)是已经发现的六种常见恐惧症的一种。acrophobia(恐高)和 claustrophobia(幽闭恐惧)都在另一种常见的恐惧症中发挥作用:飞行恐惧,通常也称为 *aerophobia*。

agoraphobia \\ˌa-gə-rə-'fō-bē-ə\\ A fear of being in embarrassing or inescapable situations, especially in open or public places. 恐旷(症);公共场所恐惧(症)

- After barely surviving a terrible attack of agoraphobia in the middle of the Sonoran Desert, he finally agreed to start seeing a psychologist. 在索诺兰沙漠中心经历了一场严重的恐旷, 好不容易度过了之后, 他终于同意看心理医生了。

The *agora* was the marketplace in ancient Greece; thus, agoraphobia often involves fear of public places and crowds. But it also may involve fear of being in shops, or even fear of being in open spaces, or fear of traveling alone. It may also be a fear of experiencing some uncontrollable or embarrassing event (like fainting) in the presence of others with no help available. Agoraphobia can be hard to understand for those who don't suffer from it, especially because it can take so many different forms, but it is often a serious and socially crippling condition.

agora 是古希腊的市场, 因此, *agoraphobia* 就常常与害怕公共场所和人群有关。但是, 它也可能包括害怕置身商店, 甚至是害怕开阔空间, 或者害怕独自旅行。它也可能指害怕经历无法控制或者令人尴尬的事情 (比如昏倒), 跟其他人在一起, 却得不到帮助。agoraphobia 对没有此症的人来说很难理解, 尤其是因为它可以有多种不同的形式, 但它常常很严重, 让人难以正常社交。

xenophobe \ˈze-nə-ˌfōb\   One who has a fear or hatred of strangers or foreigners. 恐惧陌生人 (外国人) 的人; 仇恨陌生人 (外国人) 的人; 仇外者; 惧外者

- A Middle Easterner reading the U.S.'s visa restrictions might feel that the State Department was run by xenophobes. 读了美国对签证的限制条款, 中东人可能觉得国务院的人是一帮仇外者。

Xenophobe is partly based on the Greek noun *xenos*, meaning "stranger, guest, foreigner." Unlike other phobias, *xenophobia* isn't really considered an abnormal condition; instead, it's generally thought of as just serious narrow-mindedness, the kind of thinking that goes along with racism and extreme patriotism. In times of war, a government will often actually try to turn all its citizens into xenophobes.

xenophobe 这个词一部分源自希腊语名词 *xenos*, 意思是"陌生人, 客人, 外国人"。跟其他恐惧症不同的是, *xenophobia* 并没有被真正视为一种非正常状况; 相反, 它通常只被认为是严重的心胸狭隘, 是伴随种族主义和极端爱国主义的思维。在战争时期, 一个政府竟然常常将其公民变成仇外者。

arachnophobia \ə-ˌrak-nə-ˈfō-bē-ə\   Having a fear or dislike of spiders.
蜘蛛恐惧 (症)

- At 50, my sister still suffers from arachnophobia, and can't sleep in a room unless she knows it has no spiders. 我姐姐五十岁了, 还是害怕蜘蛛, 真到知道房间没有蜘蛛了才敢睡觉。

In Greek mythology, Arachne was a weaver of such skill that she dared to challenge the goddess Athena at her craft. When she won their competition by weaving a tapestry disrespectful to the gods, the enraged Athena tore it to shreds, and in despair Arachne hanged herself. Out of pity, Athena loosened the rope, which became a cobweb, and changed Arachne into a spider. Today, the spiders, scorpions, mites, and ticks all belong to the class known as arachnids. Arachnophobia is the most common of the animal phobias; but many people suffer from similar phobias regarding snakes (*ophidiophobia*), dogs (*cynophobia*), and mice and rats (*musophobia*).

在希腊神话中，*Arachne*(阿拉克尼)善于织布，水平很高，竟敢向雅典娜女神挑战。她比赛获胜了，但所织挂毯上的图案对众神极不恭敬，愤怒的雅典娜把挂毯撕成了碎片，阿拉克尼绝望之中上吊自杀。出于同情，雅典娜松开绳子，绳子变成了蛛网，雅典娜又将阿拉克尼变成了蜘蛛。今天，蜘蛛、蝎子、螨虫、扁虱都属于 *arachnids*(蛛形纲动物)。蜘蛛恐惧症是动物恐惧症中最常见的一种，但许多人对蛇(蛇恐惧症)、狗(恐犬症)和老鼠(恐鼠症)也有类似的恐惧症。

Quizzes

A. Fill in each blank with the correct letter:

a. acrophobic
b. parity
c. agoraphobia
d. disparity
e. xenophobe
f. nonpareil
g. arachnophobia
h. subpar

1. Customers kept complaining that the quality of the product was _____, so we eventually stopped selling it completely.

2. She still suffers from _____, even though she hasn't had spider nightmares for many years.

3. His _____ is so bad that he won't even accept an award at a ceremony.

4. She's concerned about the _____ between the performance on standardized tests and what she sees when she sits in on actual classes.

5. Immigration is almost the only thing he talks about these days, and he seems to have become a full-fledged _____.

6. For 25 years it has prided itself on being the _____ Japanese restaurant in the city.

7. He's so _____ that he had to stay in the car when we visited the Grand Canyon.

8. Since the 1970s women have been demanding _____ in pay with men, but they still lag well behind.

B. Match the definition on the left to the correct word on the right:

1. fear of spiders
2. gap
3. fear of open or public places
4. ideal
5. fearful of heights
6. equality
7. one fearful of foreigners
8. inferior

a. agoraphobia
b. xenophobe
c. nonpareil
d. acrophobic
e. subpar
f. parity
g. disparity
h. arachnophobia

UNIT 26

Medical Words 医学词语

HEM/HEMO comes from the Greek word for "blood" and is found at the beginning of many medical terms. By dropping the *h-*, the same word produced the suffix *-emia*, which likewise shows up in lots of "blood" words, including *anemia*, *leukemia* and *hyperglycemia*.
HEM/HEMO 源自希腊语表示"血"的词语,出现在很多医学术语的起首处。去掉 h-,这同一个词产生了后缀-emia,同样出现在很多跟血有关的词语中,包括 anemia(贫血)、leukemia(白血病)和 hyperglycemia(高血糖)。

hemorrhage \\'hem-rij\\ (1) A large loss of blood from a blood vessel. 大出血 (2) A rapid and uncontrollable loss or outflow. 大量失去;大量外流

● He arrived at the emergency room reporting headache, nausea, and drowsiness, and the doctor immediately suspected that he'd suffered a brain hemorrhage. 他赶到急诊室,说自己头痛、恶心、瞌睡,医生马上怀疑他有脑溢血。

A *hemorrhage* usually results from either a severe blow to the body or from medication being taken for something else. Though many hemorrhages aren't particularly serious, those that occur in the brain (cerebral hemorrhages) can be life-threatening. In older people, hemorrhages are often caused by blood-thinning medication taken to prevent heart attacks. A bruise (or *hematoma*) is a hemorrhage close enough to the surface of the skin to be visible. *Hemorrhage* is also a verb, which isn't always used to talk about actual blood; thus, we may hear that a business is hemorrhaging money, or that the U. S. has been hemorrhaging industrial jobs for decades. Be careful when writing *hemorrhage*; it's not an easy word to spell.

大出血一般是由于身体受到重击或者因另一种疾病服用了某种药物而导致的。虽然很多出血不是特别严重,但大脑中发生的出血(cerebral hemorrhage,脑溢血)可能危及生命。老年人大出血通常是由防止心脏病所服用的药物引起血管变细引起的。血肿(或称 hematoma)是接近皮肤表面可以看得到的出血。hemorrahage 也可作动词,并不总是用于谈论真正的出血;因此,我们可能会听说某公司正流失资金,或者美国的工业工作岗位几十年来一直在减少。写 hemorrhage 的时候要小心,这个词拼写起来不容易。

hematology \\ˌhē-mə-'tä-lə-jē\\ The study of blood and bloodforming organs. 血液学

● Her specialty in hematology let her work with patients of all ages and types, since blood problems may affect almost anyone. 她在血液学方面的专长使她能治疗各种年龄、各种类型的病人,因为任何人都可能出现血液问题。

Blood is basic to almost all the body's functions, and a blood test can reveal more about your physical condition than almost any other kind of examination, so hematology is an important medical specialty, with many separate subjects. Since blood cells are formed in the bone marrow, the bones are one important focus for *hematologists*. The coagulation, or thickening, of the blood is another important subject, since coagulation is what keeps us from bleeding to death from even small wounds. And there are dozens of serious blood diseases, including anemia (a lack of red blood cells) and leukemia (cancer involving a buildup of white blood cells).

血液几乎是身体所有功能都必需的,验血比其他几乎所有检查更能说明身体状况。所以,血液学是一个重要的医学专业,有很多独立的课题。由于血液细胞是在骨髓中形成的,骨头是 *hematologists*(血液学家)关注的重点。血液凝固是另一个重要课题,因为凝固使我们不至于因为小小的伤口而流血致死。严重的血液疾病有很多,包括贫血(缺少血红细胞)和白血病(与白细胞增多相关的癌症)。

hemophilia \ˌhē-mə-ˈfi-lē-ə\ A bleeding disorder caused by the blood's inability to coagulate. 血友病

• When he was a child, his hemophilia had kept him from joining the other kids in rough play at recess. 小时候,因患血友病,在课间休息时,他不能跟其他孩子一起激烈地玩耍。

The dreaded disease known as hemophilia is the result of an inherited gene, and almost always strikes boys rather than girls (though mothers may pass the gene to their sons). Since the blood lacks an ingredient that causes it to clot or coagulate when a blood vessel breaks, even a minor wound can cause a *hemophiliac* to bleed to death if not treated. Bleeding can be particularly dangerous when it's entirely internal, with no visible wound, since the person may not be aware it's happening. Queen Victoria transmitted the hemophilia gene to royal families all across Europe; the hemophilia of a young Russian prince played a part in the downfall of the Russian czars. Today, hemophiliacs take drugs that stop the bleeding by speeding coagulation, and hemophiliac life expectancies in developed countries are almost as long as the average.

令人恐惧的血友病是遗传基因导致的,几乎总是男孩而不是女孩患有这种疾病(虽然妈妈有可能把这种基因传给儿子)。血管破裂时,由于缺少一种使血液凝固的成分,如果不及时治疗,即使很小的伤口也会使 *hemophiliac*(血友病患者)流血致死。如果是体内流血,看不到伤口,就特别危险,因为患者可能意识不到正在流血。维多利亚女王将血友病基因传给了欧洲所有皇室,一个年轻的俄国王子的血友病在俄国沙皇倒台中发挥了一定作用。今天,血友病患者服用药物,通过加速凝固来止血。发达国家血友病患者的寿命几乎跟平均寿命一样长。

hemoglobin \ˈhē-mə-ˌglō-bən\ The element in blood that transports oxygen from the lungs to the body's tissues and transports carbon dioxide from the tissues back to the lungs. 血红蛋白

• Her doctor had noticed her low hemoglobin count and was insisting that she include more iron-rich vegetables in her diet. 医生注意到她的血红蛋白数量很少,坚持让她多吃富含铁质的蔬菜。

When filled with oxygen, the hemoglobin in your blood is bright red; returning to the lungs without its oxygen, it loses its brightness and becomes somewhat bluish. Hemoglobin levels can change from day to day, and may be affected by such factors as a lack of iron in the diet, a recent loss of blood, and being pregnant. When you give blood, a nurse first pricks your finger to test your hemoglobin level; a low hemoglobin count indicates anemia and may mean that you shouldn't give blood that day. Mild anemia is generally of little importance, but some types can be very serious.

充满氧气时,血液中的血红蛋白是鲜红的;回到肺部时没有了氧气,它就失去了鲜艳的颜色,变得有些发蓝。血红蛋白水平可以每天都不相同,可能影响它的因素有饮食中缺铁、近期失血、怀孕。献血时,护士先刺破你的手指,检测一下你的血红蛋白水平。血红蛋白水平低,说明患有贫血,可能意味着当天你不应该献血。轻微贫血一般来说无关紧要,但是有些类型会很严重。

ITIS

ITIS, a suffix found in both Greek and Latin, means "disease" or "inflammation." In *appendicitis* your appendix is swollen and painful, and in *tonsillitis* the same is true of your tonsils. With *laryngitis*, your throat and larynx may become so sore that it's difficult to talk. Some of us enjoy making up our own *-itis* words; high-school teachers, for example, long ago noticed that many of their seniors tended to lose all interest in schoolwork and start skipping classes, and labeled the condition *senioritis*.

ITIS 是希腊语和拉丁语中都有的一个后缀,意思是"疾病"或者"感染"。患有 appendicitis(阑尾炎)时,你的阑尾肿胀、疼痛;患有 tonsillitis(扁桃体炎)时,扁桃体也是这样。得了 laryngitis(喉炎)时,喉咙和喉可能会很疼,说话就会困难。我们有些人喜欢自己用-itis 造词,比如中学教师很久以前就注意到,很多毕业班学生往往失去了学习兴趣,开始逃课,就把这种情况称为 senioritis(高年级倦怠症)。

bursitis \bər-ˈsī-təs\ Inflammation of a lubricating sac (bursa), especially of the shoulder or elbow. 滑囊炎;黏液囊炎

● My barber developed bursitis after many years of lifting his arms all day. 我的理发师很多年都是整天抬着胳膊,就得了滑囊炎。

A *bursa* is a little pouch filled with fluid that sits between a tendon and a bone. When the fluid becomes infected by bacteria or irritated by too much movement, bursitis results. Throwing a baseball too many times at one session, for example, may inflame and irritate one of the *bursae* (notice the plural form) in the shoulder. Bursitis in another part of the body may be known by a traditional name such as "housemaid's knee," "soldier's heel," or "tennis elbow." Bursitis generally goes away after a few weeks of resting the affected area, and the pain can be treated with ice packs and aspirin.

bursa(滑囊)是一个小小的囊,充满了流体,位于腱和骨头之间。当流体受到细菌感染或者由于过多运动受到刺激时,就会出现滑囊炎。比如,在一场棒球赛中扔球次数太多,可能会使 bursae(滑囊;注意复数形式)之一发炎。身体另一部分的滑囊炎,传统上称为"女佣膝盖""士兵脚跟"或者"网球肘"。让感染区域休息几周,滑囊炎一般会消失。可以用冰袋和阿司匹林治疗滑囊炎引起的疼痛。

hepatitis \ˈhe-pə-ˈtī-təs\ Inflammation of the liver. 肝炎

● His skin now had a yellowish tinge, as did the whites of his eyes, and his doctor immediately recognized the signs of advanced hepatitis. 当时,他皮肤有些发黄,眼白也有些泛黄,于是医生马上就发现了严重肝炎的迹象。

The liver, the body's largest gland, performs many important tasks, but is also vulnerable to many illnesses. At least five types of hepatitis, labeled with the letters A-E, are caused by viruses. The most common are hepatitis A, acquired through contaminated food and water; hepatitis B, which usually travels via sexual activity or shared needles; and hepatitis C, generally passed through shared needles. Some other types, including alcoholic hepatitis (caused by drinking too much alcohol), aren't infectious. There are vaccines for types A and B, and drug treatments for A, B, and C, though the drugs aren't always effective.

肝脏是身体最大的腺体,执行很多重要任务,但也容易受到多种疾病的侵害。至少五种肝炎,分别用 A 到 E 五个字母标明,是病毒引起的。最常见的是甲型肝炎,一般通过受污染的食物和水传播;乙型肝炎一般通过性活动或者共用针头传播;丙型肝炎一般通过共用针头传播。其他类型的肝炎,包括酒精性肝炎(饮酒过量所致),没有传染性。甲型肝炎和乙型肝炎有疫苗,甲型肝炎、乙型肝炎和丙型肝炎有药物治疗,不过药物并非总是有效。

bronchitis \brän-ˈkī-təs\ Inflammation of the bronchial tubes. 支气管炎

• Before the smoking ban went into effect, three flight attendants had sued the airline, claiming secondhand smoke was to blame for their bronchitis. 实施禁烟以前,三位空乘人员控告航空公司,声称二手烟要为其支气管炎负责。

The *bronchial* tubes carry air into the tiny branches and smaller cells of the lungs. In bronchitis, the tubes become sore and you develop a deep cough. Bronchitis caused by bacteria can be treated with antibiotics, but there's no drug treatment for the more common kind caused by a virus. A bout of bronchitis may involve a couple of weeks of coughing (with no laughing allowed), weakness, and loss of energy and interest in doing things. Apart from that, bronchitis is rarely serious—at least if it doesn't progress to pneumonia.

bronchial tubes(支气管)将空气输送进 细微的支气管和更小的肺细胞中。患有支气管炎时,气管疼痛,人开始剧烈咳嗽。细菌引起的支气管炎可以用抗生素治疗,但是病毒引起的、更常见的类型就没法用药物治疗了。一场支气管炎可能让人咳嗽几周(不可能让你大笑),身体虚弱,没有精力和兴趣做事。除此以外,支气管炎很少会很严重,至少不会恶化成肺炎。

tendinitis \ˌten-də-ˈnī-təs\ A painful condition in which a tendon in the arm or leg becomes inflamed. 腱炎

• After years of tennis and bicycling, she now has tendinitis of both the elbow and the knee. 在她打网球、骑车子多年之后,她的胳膊肘和膝盖都患了腱炎。

Tendinitis is often seen in active, healthy people who do something that requires repeated motion, including golfers and tennis players (especially those with improper form), carpenters, and violinists. It's usually treated by keeping the joint from moving, by means of a splint, cast, or bandage. If not dealt with in time, tendinitis can turn into the more serious *tendinosis*, or tendon degeneration.

tendinitis(腱炎)常常发生在活跃、健康的人身上,包括网球运动员(尤其是动作不规范者)、木匠、小提琴手,他们做的事情需要做某种反复动作。腱炎的治疗方法通常是利用夹板、石膏或者绷带，让关节保持不动。如果不及时处理，腱炎可能恶化，成为更严重的 *tendinosis*(肌腱变性)。

Quiz

Fill in each blank with the correct letter：

a. hepatitis
b. hematology
c. bronchitis
d. hemophilia
e. bursitis
f. hemorrhage
g. hemoglobin
h. tendinitis

1. After a week of lifting boxes he got a case of _____, and they had to get movers in to finish the packing.

2. Blood samples get sent to the _____ department for analysis.

3. From the yellowness of her eyes, he suspected that it was a serious case of _____.

4. Soon after they start playing tennis and golf each spring, they both find they've developed _____ and have to give it up for a while.

5. He's a heavy smoker, and for several years he's been suffering from _____ several times a year.

6. Oxygen turns the _____ in the blood bright red; when the oxygen is removed, it becomes bluish.

7. The bleeding caused by the accident all seemed to be close to the surface, and there was no evidence of an internal _____.

8. The family had a history of _____, so she was naturally worried when her 3-year-old's wound kept bleeding for an hour.

Review Quizzes

A. Match the definition on the left to the correct word on the right：

1. one fearful of foreigners
2. list
3. wall up
4. 2.2 pounds
5. liver disease
6. varied
7. equality
8. lung inflammation
9. fear of spiders
10. inferior

a. immure
b. subpar
c. xenophobe
d. enumerate
e. arachnophobia
f. parity
g. bronchitis
h. kilogram
i. hepatitis
j. multifarious

B. Fill in each blank with the correct letter:

a. muralist
b. agoraphobia
c. multidisciplinary
d. nonpareil
e. supernumerary
f. kilometer
g. politicize
h. microclimate
i. intramural
j. disparity

1. By their careful planting on this south-facing hillside, they had created a _____ that was perfect for certain crops that no one else was able to grow.

2. Each year there seemed to be a larger _____ between their expected income and what they actually earned.

3. The college has had an _____ debating society for several years, but this year they've decided to challenge several nearby colleges in a debate competition.

4. Only six people could play on a side, so the _____ volleyball players had to wait five minutes before rotating into the game.

5. A _____ is more than half a mile but less than two-thirds of a mile.

6. The Congress has managed to _____ an issue that always used to be thought of as a private matter.

7. He has a good reputation as a _____ for the wall paintings he's done in public buildings.

8. Her _____ has gotten worse, and now she refuses to even leave the house.

9. She's a _____ classroom teacher—enthusiastic, knowledgeable, concerned, entertaining, funny, everything a teacher should be.

10. The journal is devoted to water, taking a _____ approach that involves chemistry, physics, biology, and environmental science.

C. Indicate whether the following pairs of terms have the same or different meanings:

1. immure / embrace   same ____ / different ____
2. subpar / below normal   same ____ / different ____
3. enumerate / solve   same ____ / different ____
4. acrophobic / fearful of heights   same ____ / different ____
5. supernumerary / extra   same ____ / different ____
6. hematology / liver medicine   same ____ / different ____
7. kilohertz / unit of frequency   same ____ / different ____
8. disparity / equality   same ____ / different ____
9. hemorrhage / blood circulation   same ____ / different ____
10. nonpareil / unlikely   same ____ / different ____

UNIT 27

NANO comes from the Greek *nanos*, meaning "dwarf." For a prefix meaning "small," English got by for centuries with the Greek *micro-*, and later *mini-* came to be used widely as well. But only recently, as a result of advances in scientific knowledge and technology, has there been a need for a prefix meaning "extremely small"—a need that's been filled by *nano-*, which today is being attached to all kinds of words, sometimes not very seriously (*nanoskirt*, *nanobrained*, etc.).

NANO源自希腊语nanos(侏儒)。曾有数个世纪,英语一直用源自希腊语的micro-这一前缀表示"小"。后来,mini-也得到了广泛使用。只是最近,由于科学知识和技术的进步,有必要使用一个表示"极其微小"的前缀,而满足这一需求的是nano-。今天,它正被附加于各种各样的词语,有时候并非很严肃(nanoskirt,nano-brained,等等)。

nanotechnology \ˌna-nō-tek-ˈnä-lə-jē\ The science of manipulating materials on an atomic or molecular scale, especially to build microscopic devices such as robots. 纳米技术

● Nanotechnology is now seen as contributing to numerous environmental solutions, from cleaning up hazardous waste sites to producing strong but lightweight materials for auto bodies. 现在,人们认为纳米技术有助于解决众多环境问题,从清洁有害危险废物现场到为车体制造坚固、轻量的材料。

Nanotechnology, or *nanotech* for short, deals with matter at a level that most of us find hard to imagine, since it involves objects with dimensions of 100 billionths of a meter (1/800th of the thickness of a human hair) or less. The chemical and physical properties of materials often change greatly at this scale. Nanotechnology is already being used in automobile tires, land-mine detectors, and computer disk drives. *Nanomedicine* is a particularly exciting field: Imagine particles the size of a blood cell that could be released into the bloodstream to form into tiny robots and attack cancer cells, or "machines" the size of a molecule that could actually repair the damaged interiors of individual cells.

nanotechnology，或者其缩略形式 nanotech，涉及的物质是我们多数人难以想象的，因为这些事物的尺寸只有一米的一千亿分之一（头发的八百分之一那么细）或者更微小。这样尺寸的材料，其物理性质常常变化很大。纳米技术已经用于车胎、地雷探测器、电脑磁盘驱动器。nanomedicine（纳米医学）是一个特别令人激动的领域；想象一下，血细胞那么大的颗粒，被释放进入血液，形成小小的机器人，攻击癌细胞；或者分子那么大的"机器"，竟然能够修复受损的细胞内部。

nanosecond \ˈna-nə-ˌse-kənd\ One billionth of a second. 十亿分之一秒

• When he finally asked if she would marry him, it took her about a nanosecond to say yes. 当他最终问她是否愿意跟他结婚时，她瞬间回答说愿意。

The nonserious use of *nanosecond* is probably much more common than the proper technical use. In measurement terms such as *nanosecond*, *nanogram*, and *nanometer*, *nano-* means "billionth"; in other kinds of words, its meaning isn't quite so precise. In computers, the speed of reading and writing to random access memory (RAM) is measured in nanoseconds. By comparison, the speed of reading or writing to a hard drive or a CD-ROM player, or for information to travel over the Internet, is measured in *milliseconds* (thousandths of a second), which are a million times longer than nanoseconds.

nanosecond 在不严肃语境下使用可能比恰当的、技术方面的使用更常见。在度量术语中，比如 nanosecond（十亿分之一秒）、nanogram（十亿分之一克）、nanometer（十亿分之一米），nano- 表示"十一分之一"；在其他词语中，其意思就不那么准确了。在计算机上，随机访问存储器储存读写的速度是按十亿分之一秒的速度计算的。相比之下，硬盘驱动器或者 CD-ROM 播放器是按毫秒（一秒的千分之一）计算的，这比十亿分之一秒长一百万倍。

nanostructure \ˈna-nə-ˌstrək-chər\ An arrangement, structure, or part of something of molecular dimensions. 纳米结构

• In the 1990s the physics department, which had been doing extensive research on microstructures, began to get deeply involved in nanostructures, including nanofoam, nanoflakes, and nanofibers. 20 世纪 90 年代，一直在对微结构进行广泛研究的物理系，开始深入研究纳米结构，包括纳米泡沫、纳米薄片和纳米纤维。

Two important types of *nanostructure* are *nanocrystals* (tiny crystals, often of semiconducting material) and *nanotubes* (tiny tubes, usually of pure carbon). Nanocrystals made from semiconductors change color depending on their size, and are being used for such tasks as detecting viruses in living cells. Nanotubes can conduct enormous amounts of electrical current, far more than metal wires. They are the basic material of tiny "paper" batteries, which can be rolled, folded, or cut while still producing power. Nanotubes are also now being used in materials for lightweight tennis rackets and golf clubs, and may soon enable the manufacture of TV screens no thicker than a film.

两种重要类型的纳米结构是 nanocrystals（纳米晶体，微小晶体，通常是半导体材料的）和 nanotubes（纳米管，微小的管子，通常是纯碳的）。半导体的纳米晶体根据尺寸不同会改变颜色，目前正用于发现细胞中的病菌之类的任务。纳米管可以传输大量的电流，远远胜过金属线。它们是微小的"纸"电池的基本材料，这些电池在产生能量时都可以被滚动、折叠或者切割。纳米管也正用于轻质网球拍和高尔夫球棒材料，可能很快就可以让人们生产厚度不超过胶片的电视屏幕。

nanoparticle\\'na-nə-ˌpär-ti-kəl\\ A tiny particle whose size is measured in billionths of a meter. 纳米粒

• Nanoparticles of iron are being used to clean up soil pollution, helping break down molecules of dangerous substances into simple compounds. 铁纳米粒正用于清除土壤污染,从而帮助分解危险物质的分子,使其成为简单的化合物。

Nanoparticles of a material usually have very different qualities from those that the material has at its ordinary scale, which is one reason why there's such excitement about the possibilities for how they might be used in future technologies. Many uses have already been developed. Aluminum nanoparticles added to rocket fuel can make the fuel burn twice as fast and release much more energy. Silicon nanoparticles are increasing the energy efficiency of solar cells by allowing the energy from ultraviolet light to be captured for the first time. Other nanoparticles are now helping prevent rust in metals, produce stronger batteries, enhance the diagnosis of cancer, and improve the filtering of water, and the number of other applications is growing fast. 一种材料的 nanoparticles(纳米粒)与其大小正常的粒子往往与有着差异很大的性质,因此,如何在未来的技术中使用纳米粒,其可能性令人激动。人们已经开发出纳米粒的多种用途了。加入火箭燃料的铝纳米粒可使其燃烧速度加快一倍,且释放出多得多的能量。硅纳米粒能使来自紫外线的能量第一时间被捕捉到,以此提高太阳电池的能量效率。其他纳米粒正帮助防止金属生锈,生产能量更多的电池,提高癌症的诊断率,改善水过滤,而且其他方面的应用也在飞速发展。

SUPER, a Latin prefix meaning "over, higher, more than," has become one of the most familiar prefixes in English, one of those prefixes that we use to create new words all the time: *supermodel*, *superpowerful*, *superjock*, *supersize*, *supersweet*—the list goes on and on. This all seems to have started in 1903 when the playwright B. Shaw translated the German word *übermensch*, Nietzsche's famous term for the person who rises to heroic heights through discipline and creative power, in the title of his play *Man and Superman*. The comic-book character with the same name wouldn't make his appearance for another 30 years. SUPER 这一拉丁语前缀意思是"超过,高于,多于"。它已成为英语中最为人熟知的前缀之一,是我们创造新词的前缀之一,这些新词有 *supermodel*(超模)、*superpowerful*(超强)、*superjock*(超级运动员)、*supersize*(超大的)、*supersweet*(超甜的),还可以一直列举下去。这似乎是从 1903 年开始的。当时,剧作家萧伯纳将德语单词 *übermesch* 译成了英语,这是尼采用在 *Man and Superman*(《人与超人》)这一剧作名称中的有名的词语,指通过自制力和创造力达到极高造诣的人。连环画人物超人直到三十年后才出现。

superfluous\\sù-ˈpər-flü-əs\\ Beyond what is needed; extra. 多余的;额外的

• My Freshman Comp professor removes all superfluous words from our essays, and usually ends up shortening mine by about 40 percent. 大一写作教授把我们作文中所有多余的词都删除了。结果,我的作文常常缩短百分之四十。

Since the Latin *fluere* means "to flow" (see FLU, p. 475), you can think of *superfluous* as describing a river with so much water that it's overflowing its banks. The word is used in all kinds of contexts. Superfluous characters in computer code may keep it from working. Most of the buttons on a remote control may strike us as superfluous, since we never use them. When a situation "speaks for itself," any comment may be superfluous. And whenever you yourself are feeling superfluous, as in a "Two's company, three's a crowd" situation, it's probably time to leave.

由于拉丁语 *fluere* 意思是"流"(见 FLU,第 475 页),你可以想到 *superfluous* 用来描绘一条河,水多得漫出了河岸。这个词语用在所有语境中。电脑密码字数太多可能使其不能使用。遥控器上多数按键都让我们觉得是多余的,因为从来都没用过。当某个情况"为自己说话"时,任何话都是多余的。每当你觉得自己是多余的,就像"两个是陪伴,三个人是一群"这种情况时,可能你就该走了。

insuperable \in-ˈsü-pə-rə-bəl\   Incapable of being solved or overcome. 无法解决的;无法克服的

• In learning to speak again after suffering a massive stroke, he had overcome what seemed like insuperable odds. 严重中风之后,他重新学说话时,克服了似乎是难以逾越的不利情况。

From its roots, the literal meaning of *insuperable* would be something like "un-get-overable"; *insurmountable* is a fairly exact synonym. *Insuperable* is used to describe obstacles, difficulties, barriers, obstructions, problems, and objections. Americans love stories of people who succeed in spite of terrible handicaps, whether as a result of physical limitations, prejudice, poverty, or lack of opportunity; such rugged spirits may be called *indomitable*, "incapable of being subdued."

从其词根看,*insuperable* 的字面意思大约是"*un-get-overable*"(不能克服的),*insurmountable* 是个很接近的同义词。*insuperable* 用来描述障碍、困难、阻碍、妨碍、问题、阻挠。美国人喜欢克服阻碍取得成功的故事,不管是身体的限制、偏见、贫穷还是缺少机遇;这种坚强的精神可以形容为"不屈不挠"。

supersede \sü-pər-ˈsēd\   To take the place of; to replace with something newer or more useful. 代替;取代

• The notorious decision in the Dred Scott case was superseded by the 14th Amendment to the Constitution, which stated that anyone born in the U.S. had all the rights of a citizen. 美国宪法第十四条修正案取代了德雷德·斯科特一案臭名昭著的判决,声明出生于美国的任何人都享有一切公民权利。

The Latin word *supersedere* means "sit on top of"—which is one way of taking someone else's place. Your boss may send around a memo that supersedes the memo she sent the day before (the one with all the errors in it). Every time the first-class postage rate goes up, the new stamps *supersede* the old ones. In science, a new theory often supersedes an older one; for example, the theory that a characteristic you acquire during your lifetime can be passed on biologically to your children (called *Lamarckism*) was superseded by Darwin's theory of evolution. Watch out when spelling this word; *supersede* is practically the only English word that ends in *sede*.

拉丁语 *supersedere* 一词意思是"坐在……顶部"——取代他人的一种方式。你的老板可能发送一份备忘录,以取代前一天发送的(上面有很多错误的那个)。每次只要第一类邮资上涨,新邮票就代替老邮票。在科学上,新理论常常取代旧理论。比如，你一生中培养的性格会遗传给孩子这一理论（叫做 Lamarckism，拉马克氏学说）被达尔文的进化论取代了。拼写这个词语时要小心，supersede 几乎是英语中唯一以 -sede 结尾的词语。

superlative\ˌsü-ˈpər-lə-tiv\ Supreme, excellent. 最好的

● The new restaurant turned out to be an elegant place, and we all agreed that the food and wine were superlative. 这家新开的餐厅很雅致，我们一致认为食物和酒很出色。

Superlative may sound high-flown when compared with a synonym like outstanding, but if your next paper comes back from your teacher with the comment "Superlative work!" at the top you probably won't complain. Since superlative means "best, greatest," it makes sense that superlative is also a term used in grammar for the highest degree of comparison. So for the adjective simple, for example, the comparative form is simpler and the superlative form is simplest; and for the adverb boldly, the comparative form is more boldly and the superlative is most boldly.

superlative 与 outstanding 之类的同义词相比，听起来可能高大上。不过，如果你的下一篇论文返回时，老师在最上面写了"Superlative work"（优秀），你不会抱怨的。由于 superlative 意思是"最好的"，它还用作表示最高级的语法术语，这是可以理解的。所以，举个例子，形容词 simple 的比较级是 simpler，最高级是 simplest；而副词 boldly，比较级是 more boldly，最高级是 most boldly。

Quizzes

A. Indicate whether the following pairs of terms have the same or different meanings:

1. superfluous / enormous　　　　same ____ / different ____
2. nanotechnology / computer science　same ____ / different ____
3. insuperable / impossible　　　　same ____ / different ____
4. nanosecond / million seconds　　same ____ / different ____
5. supersede / replace　　　　　　same ____ / different ____
6. nanoparticle / thousand particles　same ____ / different ____
7. superlative / outstanding　　　　same ____ / different ____
8. nanostructure / enclosed mall　　same ____ / different ____

B. Fill in each blank with the correct letter:

a. nanoparticle　　　　　　e. supersede
b. superlative　　　　　　　f. nanostructure
c. superfluous　　　　　　　g. insuperable
d. nanotechnology　　　　　h. nanosecond

1. Again and again she had overcome what seemed to be _____ odds.
2. Many scientists believe that _____ is the most exciting field in the physical sciences today, with possible uses in almost every aspect of life.
3. A _____ is something whose size is measured in billionths of a meter.
4. A lot of the language in these student essays is _____, since it just repeats

things that have already been said in different words.

5. Each picture illustrates a different _____ (a nanotube, a nanorod, a nanowire, etc.), each of which has its own set of important uses.

6. He raced down the hall and was back in about a _____ with the good news.

7. This new set of regulations will _____ the ones we've been working under for the last five years.

8. The movie had received _____ reviews, and we were looking forward to seeing it.

DE in Latin means "down, away." So a *descent* is a downward slope or climb, and a *decline* is a downward slide (of health, income, etc.). To *devalue* something is to take value away from it. And you might describe a *depressed* friend as "down."
DE 在拉丁语中意思是"向下,离开"。因此,*descent* 是向下的坡度或者攀登,*decline* 是一个向下的发展(指健康、收入等)。*devalue* 某物就是使其失去价值。你可以把一位 *depressed*(沮丧的)朋友形容为"*down*"(情绪低落)。

---

debase\di-ˈbās\ To lower the value or reputation of someone or something. 降低……的价值;毁坏……的名誉

● Every year she complains about how Christmas has been debased by commercialism. 每年她都抱怨说,圣诞节被商业主义搞得失去了宗教意义。

Debase is often used to talk about someone's lowered status or character. People are constantly blustering about the debased tastes of the ordinary American, and especially the debased music of America's youth. A commentator might observe that both candidates had managed to debase themselves by the end of a political campaign. *Debase* has a special meaning in economics: From time to time, governments find that they need to quietly debase their countries' currency by reducing the percentage of valuable metal in its coins; if they don't, the metal may become more valuable than the coin and people will begin melting the coins down and reselling the metal.

debase 经常用来谈论某人地位降低或者品质不如以前。人们总是生气地说普通美国人品味下降了,尤其是年轻人的音乐品质恶化了。评论家可能说两位候选人在政治运动结束时都毁了自己的声誉。*debase* 在经济学上有个特殊意思:政府有时发现需要减少硬币中贵重金属的百分比,以此降低本国货币价值;如果不这样的话,这种金属可能比硬币更值钱,人们就会熔化硬币,卖掉金属。

defamation\de-fə-ˈmā-shən\ The harming of someone's reputation by libel or slander. 污蔑;诽谤;中伤

● In a famous case in 1735, the newspaper publisher J. P. Zenger was found not guilty of defamation because everything he had printed about the plaintiff was true. 在1735年一桩有名的案件中,报纸出版商 J. P. 曾格被判没有诽谤罪,因为他印刷的关于原告的所有内容都是事实。

Harming someone's reputation in speech with falsehoods is known as *slander*, and doing the same thing in writing is known as *libel* (which sometimes includes speech as well). Any ordinary citizen who can claim to have suffered harm as a result of such *defamation* may sue. So why aren't politicians suing all the time? Because an exception is made for "public persons" (a category that includes most other celebrities as well), who must also prove that any such statement was made with "reckless disregard for the truth." And although, even by that standard, public persons are *defamed* all the time, most of them have decided that it's better to just grin and bear it.

用谎言口头毁坏某人的名誉称为 slander(口头诽谤)，用文字这么做，则称为 libel(诽谤)（有时也包括口头）。任何普通公民因为这样的诽谤而名誉受损都可以起诉。那么政治家为什么没有一直起诉呢？因为"公众人物"（这一类包括所有其他名人）可以例外，他们还要证明任何这样的说法"严重不符合事实"。即使按照这一标准，公众人物一直也都在遭受诽谤。尽管如此，他们大多数人还是决定一笑置之。

degenerative \di-ˈje-nə-rə-tiv\ Causing the body or part of the body to become weaker or less able to function as time passes. （身体或其一部分）变性的；退化的

• Alzheimer's is a degenerative disease of the brain, marked by the decline of mental and physical abilities. 阿尔茨海默病是一种大脑变性疾病，其标志是精神和身体能力下降。

Degenerative diseases—including cancer, glaucoma, Parkinson's, and diabetes, arthritis—are usually contrasted with infectious diseases (diseases caused by bacteria, viruses, fungi, and protozoa). However, many infectious diseases (Lyme disease, AIDS, etc.) can cause a body or body part to *degenerate*, and infective organisms play a part in some degenerative diseases. Some degen- erative diseases can be controlled; some can even be cured. But no one has yet discovered a way to reverse such degenerative conditions as multiple sclerosis, emphysema, or Alzheimer's.

变性疾病——包括癌症、青光眼、帕金森症、糖尿病和关节炎——通常与传染性疾病（由细菌、病毒、真菌、单细胞动物引起）进行对比。然而，很多传染性疾病（莱姆病、艾滋病，等等）可能使身体或身体的一部分 *degenerate*（变性；蜕化），而传染性微生物在某些变性疾病中发挥作用。有些变性疾病可以控制，有些甚至可以治愈。但是，尚无人发现使多发性硬化症、肺气肿或者阿尔茨海默病这样的变性疾病逆转的方法。

dejection \di-ˈjek-shən\ Sadness, depression, or lowness of spirits. 悲伤；沮丧；情绪低落

• Her friends were puzzled by her frequent periods of dejection, which seemed to occur with no obvious cause. 她时不时地情绪低落，似乎没有什么明显的理由，这让朋友们迷惑不解。

Based partly on the Latin *iacere*, "to throw" (see JECT, p. 33), *dejection* means literally "cast down"—that is, "downcast." Like *melancholy*, *gloom*, and even *sadness*, *dejection* seems to have been declining in use for many years; instead, we now seem to prefer *depression* (whose roots mean basically "a pressing down"). Since *depression* is also the word used by doctors, lots of people now assume that anyone depressed should be taking an antidepressant; if we went back to *dejected* and *dejection*, we might not be so quick to make that assumption. 拉丁语 *iacere* 意思是"扔"(见 JECT,第 33 页)。*dejection* 一定程度上以该词为基础,字面意思是"扔下"——也就是"情绪低落"。与 *melancholy*、*gloom* 甚至 *sadness* 相似的是,*dejection* 的使用似乎多年来也在减少;作为替代,我们现在似乎偏爱 *depression*(其词根的基本意思是"压下")。由于 *depression* 也是医生使用的词语,很多人现在认为任何人只要情绪低落,就应该服用抗抑郁药。如果我们重新开始使用 *dejected*(情绪低落的)和 *dejection*(情绪低落),可能就不会那么快地这样认为了。

NUL/NULL comes from the Latin word *nullus*, "none," which is itself a combination of *ne-* ("not") and *ullus* ("any"). Have you ever noticed how many of our negative words start with *n-*? Think of *no*, *not*, *never*, *nothing*, *none*, *no one*, *nowhere*, and the hundreds of *non-* words—just about all of which go back to the same Greek root. NUL/NULL 源自拉丁语 *nullus*,意思是"没有一个",其本身是 *ne*(非)和 *ullus*(任何)的结合。你有没有注意到过,我们很多表示否定的词语都以 *n-* 开头吗?想想 *no*、*not*、*never*、*nothing*、*none*、*no one*、*nowhere*,以及数百个以 *non-* 开头的词语,它们几乎每个都可以追溯到这同一个希腊语词根。

---

null\nəl\ (1) Having no legal power; invalid. 没有法律效力的;无效的 (2) Having no elements. 零的;等于零的

● If we can prove that you signed the contract because you were being physically threatened, it will automatically be declared null. 如果我们能够证明你是因为正受到人身威胁才在合同上签名的,它会自动被宣布无效。

Null is used mostly by lawyers, mathematicians, and computer programmers. In law, it usually occurs in the phrase "null and void"(which means about the same thing as *null* itself). When one of the parties that has signed a contract doesn't hold up his or her part of the deal—for example, if a contract states that a supplier must supply a million screws of a certain quality of steel, and it turns out the screws supplied were of inferior steel—the other company can refuse to pay anything, claiming the contract is null and void. In mathematics, *null* means "lacking any elements"; a *null set* is a set of figures that's actually empty. In computer programming, a *null* is a character that doesn't actually show up as a character, but instead may just be required to show that a series of digits or characters is finished. *null* 主要由律师、数学家和计算机程序员使用。在法律上,它通常用在 *null and void*(无法律效力的)这一短语中,意思几乎和 *null* 一样。当签合同的一方没有履行合同中自己一方的职责时——比如,如果合同中规定,某供应商必须提供一百万个用某种质量的钢材制造的螺丝钉,但结果该供应商提供了质量较差的钢材制造的螺丝钉——另一公司可拒绝付款,并声明合同无效。在数学上,*null* 意思是"没有任何元素的;零的",*null set*(零集;空集)就是实际上等于零的集。在计算机程序设计领域,一个 *null* 就是实际上并不作为一个符号出现的符号,但需要它来表明一系列数字或符号结束了。

nullity\ˈnə-lə-tē\ (1) Nothingness. 无;虚无 (2) A mere nothing. 不存在

● He couldn't believe she'd actually left him for that nullity—a guy with no style, no drive, no personality at all. 他无法相信,她竟然离开自己投奔那个什么都不是的家伙——一

个根本没有品位、没有干劲、没有人格的人。

Intellectuals may speak of a book or a film as a nullity, claiming it possesses nothing original enough to justify its existence. Legal scholars also use the word; a law passed by a legislature may be called a nullity if, for example, it's so obviously unconstitutional that it's going to be shot down by the courts in no time. And if you're in an unkind mood, you're also free to call a person a nullity, if you're not instead calling him a nobody, a nonentity, or a zero.

知识分子会说一本书或一部电影是个*nullity*,说它没有任何具有独创性的东西可以证明自己的存在。法律学者也使用该词。比如说,立法机构通过的一部法律,如果显然不符合宪法,将会很快被法庭拒绝,可以说是一个*nullity*。如果你情绪不佳,除了可以把一个人称为*nobody*,*nonentity* 或者 *zero* 之外,也可以把他叫做 *nullity*。

nullify \ˈnə-lə-ˌfī\ (1) To cancel legally. 取消;(2) To cause something to lose its value or to have no effect. 使……失去价值;废除,废止

- In soccer or water polo, a penalty can nullify a goal that has just been made. 在足球或水球运动中,如果被罚,可能使刚刚得到的一分无效。

A legislature may nullify a ban, a law, or a tax by simply passing a new law. Election results can be nullified if a court finds the voting process was improper, and a court ruling can be nullified by a higher court. Even the Supreme Court itself may have its decisions nullified by new laws passed by the Congress—though not if a decision is based on the Constitution. In the years leading up to the American Civil War, Southern states claimed the right to nullify any federal law (such as antislavery laws) that they believed to be unconstitutional, leading to the Nullification Crisis of 1832. Annul is a close synonym of nullify (with the same root), as are abrogate and invalidate.

立法机构仅仅通过一项新的法律就可以 nullify(取消)禁令、法律或者赋税。如果法庭发现投票过程不合规范,选举结果也可以 nullified(被宣布无效)。法院的裁决可以被更高级别的法院宣布无效。即使是美国最高法院,其裁决也可能因为国会通过的新法律而无效,除非其一裁决以宪法为基础。在美国南北战争前几年,南方各州要求有权废止他们认为不符合宪法的联邦法律(比如反对奴隶制度的法律),结果导致了 1832 年的 *Nullification* Crisis(废止联邦法律危机)。*annul* 是 *nullify* 的一个近义词(有着同一词根),*abrogate* 和 *invalidate* 也是。

annulment \ə-ˈnəl-mənt\ An official statement that something is no longer valid. 废除,废止

- He requested an annulment of the marriage from the Church, but his wife claimed that, after 15 years and two children, the idea of annulment was ridiculous. 他要求教会废除他和妻子的婚姻关系,但他的妻子声称,在他们共同生活了十五年,而且有两个孩子的情况下,这个想法很荒唐。

Annulment usually applies to marriage. In some states an annulment may be carried out by a court ("judicial annulment"), but annulment is generally practiced by a church ("ecclesiastic annulment"), and principally the Roman Catholic Church, which traditionally hasn't permitted divorce. The usual acceptable reason for annulment is a "failure to consummate" the marriage by having children. Unlike a marriage that ends in divorce, an annulled marriage is considered never to have existed. Other things can be annulled as well, including a contract (if one party fails to comply with its terms) or an election (if it wasn't carried out properly).

annulment 通常用于婚姻。在某些州,废除婚姻可以由法院来执行(这叫做"judicial annulmnet",即"司法废除"),但是,废除婚姻通常由教堂执行(这叫做"ecclesiastic annulment",即"教会废除"),主要是罗马天主教,因为它传统上不允许离婚。废除婚姻一般可以接受的理由是没有孩子而"未能使婚姻完满"。与以离婚告终的婚姻不同的是,废止的婚姻被认为从未存在。其他事物也可以废止,包括合同(如果一方未能遵守条款)或者选举(如果未能正确举行)。

Quizzes

A. Fill in each blank with the correct letter:

a. null   e. annulment
b. nullify   f. nullity
c. dejection   g. defamation
d. degenerative   h. debase

1. She's bringing suit against her former husband for _____, claiming that statements he had made to a reporter had caused her to lose her job.

2. If the judge's decision goes against the government, it will _____ a 10-year-old state law.

3. Her lawyer is going to argue that the first trial was a _____ because some of the jurors missed whole days of testimony.

4. Dogs often suffer from _____ joint diseases that get worse year by year.

5. His _____ after getting turned down by his top two colleges was so deep that he didn't smile for weeks.

6. We're claiming the contract is _____ and void because the other company failed to do what it had agreed to.

7. Her friends all told her that a star like her would just _____ herself by appearing in TV ads.

8. After five years and no children, she asked the church for an _____ of the marriage.

B. Match the definition on the left to the correct word on the right:

1. undo   a. annulment
2. weakening   b. defamation
3. nothingness   c. nullity
4. depression   d. debase
5. invalid   e. degenerative
6. cancellation   f. nullify
7. slander   g. dejection
8. disgrace   h. null

UNIT 27

ARM comes from the Latin *arma*, meaning "weapons, tools." The root is seen in such English words as *arms* (i.e., weapons), *armed*, and *army*. It has nothing to do with the limb that starts at your shoulder; the name for that kind of arm comes from the Latin word meaning "shoulder."

ARM 源自拉丁语 *arma*,意思是"武器,工具"。这一词根可在诸如 *arms*(武器)、*armed*(武装起来的)、*army*(军队)这些词语中见到。它与胳膊没有关系,那种 *arm* 来自拉丁语中表示"肩膀"的词语。

armada \är-ˈmä-də\ A large group of warships or boats. 舰队;船队

• The U.S. Navy hopes to build an electric armada, a new generation of ships driven by electric power. 美国海军希望建立一个电舰队,用电能驱动的新一代舰队。

A Spanish word that originally meant simply "armed," *armada* is now used in Spanish-speaking nations as the name of their national navies. In English, the word usually has historical overtones. The Great Armada of 1588 was a 120-ship fleet sent by Philip II of Spain in an attempt to invade Elizabethan England; it was defeated when British forces lit eight ships afire and sent them sailing into the Armada's midst, then blocked the passage to the south so that the remaining ships were forced to sail northward around Britain in order to return home, causing dozens more ships to be wrecked in the stormy northern seas. Today we sometimes use the word humorously for fleets of fishing boats, rowboats, or canoes.

armada 原来是西班牙语词,意思是"武装起来的",如今在西班牙语国家用作国家海军的名称。在英语中,这一词语常常具有历史含义。1588 年的 Great Armada(无敌舰队),是西班牙菲利普二世派遣的一百二十只船组成的舰队,企图入侵伊丽莎白一世统治下的英国。无敌舰队被击败了。英军点着八艘船,使其驶入无敌舰队中间,之后阻挡向南的航道,迫使其余船只向北航行,绕过不列颠岛回国,结果又有几十艘船在波涛汹涌的北海失事。今天,我们有时幽默地使用这一词语,指代一组渔船、划艇或者独木舟。

armistice \ˈär-mə-stəs\ An agreement to stop fighting a war; a truce. 停战协议

• Ambassadors from three neighboring countries were trying to arrange an armistice between the warring forces. 三个邻国的大使正努力安排交战国签署停战协议。

Just as the *solstice* is the time of year when the sun (Latin, *sol*) "stands still," an *armistice* is an agreement for armies to stop where they are and lay down their arms. The word is associated with the truce that marked the end of World War I on the Western Front, where the Allies had confronted Germany, in 1918. The day of the ceasefire, November 11th ("the eleventh day of the eleventh month"), was for many years called Armistice Day; today it's known as Veterans Day in the U.S. and as Remembrance Day in Canada and Australia.

正如 *solstice*(冬至;夏至)是一年中太阳(拉丁语中是 *sol*)"停下"的时间,armistice(停战协议)是停止打仗、放下武器的协议。该词与标志着第一次世界大战在西线结束的 *truce*(停战协议)有关。在西线,盟军 1918 年与德国对抗。停火的日子,也就是 11 月 11 日,有很多年被称为 Armistice Day(停战纪念日)。今天,这个日子在美国被称为 Veterans Day(退伍军人节),在加拿大和澳大利亚被称为 Remembrance Day(荣军纪念日)。

armory \ˈärm-rē\ A place where weapons are made or stored. 军械库

- The great military rifles known as the Springfield 30.06 and the M1 were developed at the Springfield Armory in Massachusetts. 被称为斯普林菲尔德 30.06 和 M1 的两种大号步枪,是在马萨诸塞州的斯普林菲尔德军械库研发出来的。

An *armory* has traditionally been a military storage compound where machine guns, rifles, pistols, ammunition, parts, and accessories are kept. In the U.S., National Guard and Reserve units often use armories as training headquarters in peacetime. Ever since George Washington established the country's first armory in Springfield in 1777, arsenals and armories of the Army Ordnance Corps have had a remarkable history of arms manufacture. armory(军械库)传统上一直是储存机枪、步枪、手枪、火药、部件和配件的仓库。在美国,和平时期,国民警卫队和预备役部队常常使用军械库作为训练总部。自从乔治·华盛顿于 1777 年在斯普林菲尔德建立该国第一个军械库以来,陆军军械部队的兵工厂和军械库一直有着辉煌的武器生产历史。

disarming \dis-ˈärm-iŋ\ Tending to remove any feelings of unfriendliness or distrust. 解除不信任感的;解除敌意的

- All of us at the meeting were charmed by the new manager's disarming openness and modesty. 新上任经理坦诚、谦虚,解除了我们所有参会人员的不信任感,我们都很喜欢他。

A defeated country is sometimes forced to *disarm* (give up its weapons), and research may be aimed at *disarming* a deadly virus (making it incapable of doing damage). But the meaning of the adjective *disarming* isn't quite so physical. If you say your nephew has a disarming smile, you mean that his smile's warmth and genuineness disarm the people he meets of any possible suspicion or criticism and of any verbal weapons they might have used against him. 战败国有时被迫 disarm(放下武装),研究工作可能旨在 disarming(使……失去伤害力)致命的病毒。但是,disarming 这一形容词的意思跟具体事物关系不大。如果你说自己的侄子有着 disarming smile,意思是说,他的微笑热情而真诚,使遇到他的人不再有任何怀疑或不赞同的想法,即使本来想对他使用语言武器,也会放弃使用的。

SURG comes from the Latin verb *surgere*, meaning "to rise, spring up." Our noun *surge* means "a sudden, large increase," and the verb *surge* means "to move with a surge." A *storm surge* occurs when violent storm winds at sea cause the water to pile up higher than normal sea level. A *surge protector* keeps a spike in electrical current from "frying" your computer when a lightning strike sends a sudden surge down the wires. SURG 源自拉丁语动词 *surgere*(抬起,弹起)。我们的名词 surge 的意思是"突然、大量增加",动词 surge 的意思是"涌动"。当海上剧烈的暴风使海水上升,高于正常海平面时,就发生 *storm surge*(风暴潮)。在雷击使电线中电流激增时,*surge protector*(浪涌电压保护器)使电脑不至于烧坏。

---

upsurge \ˈəp-ˌsərj\ A rapid or sudden increase or rise. 激增;飙升

- Almost forgotten for years, at 76 he was offered a colorful role in an odd little film, which brought an upsurge in interest in his career. 几乎被遗忘多年之后,76 岁的他时来运转,得以在一部怪异的电影短片中饰演一个有趣的角色,让人对他的演艺生涯兴趣激增。

An *upsurge* in drug use sometimes leads to an upsurge in crime. An upsurge of flu cases can be cause for alarm. And an upsurge of fury at overpaid CEOs might lead to new legislation to restrain high salaries. We seem to use *upsurge* more in negative contexts than in positive ones, but not always; we usually welcome an upsurge of consumer confidence, an upsurge in new-car sales, or an upsurge in the stock market.

吸毒量的 upsurge(激增),有时会导致犯罪率激增。流感病例激增,可能引起恐慌。对工资过高的总裁愤怒激增,可能产生新的立法,以限制高薪水。我们使用 *upsurge* 的语境,似乎否定的超过肯定的,不过也并非总是这样。我们通常欢迎顾客的信任激增、新车的销量激增,或者股市市值激增。

insurgency \in-ˈsər-jən-sē\ A usually violent attempt to take control of a government; a rebellion or uprising. 造反;起义;叛乱

• The Mexican press was fascinated by the armed insurgency's mysterious leader, who wore a mask and went by the name of Subcomandante Marcos. 墨西哥媒体对武装叛乱的神秘领袖很感兴趣。他带着面罩,自称副司令马科斯。

Insurgencies fall into the category of "irregular warfare," since an insurgency normally lacks the organization of a revolution, even though it has the same aims. Revolutions often begin within a country's armed forces, whereas insurgencies often arise in remote areas, where they gain strength slowly by winning the confidence of rural populations. An insurgency may be based on ethnic or religious identity, or its roots may be basically political or economic. Since insurgencies are rarely strong enough to face a national army headon, *insurgents* (often called *guerrillas*) tend to use such tactics as bombing, kidnapping, hostage taking, and hijacking.

insurgencies(叛乱)属于"非常规战争",因为它通常缺乏革命的系统性,尽管目标一样。革命常常开始于一个国家的武装部队内部,而叛乱常常发生在偏远地区,在那里通过赢得乡村人民的信任来积蓄力量。叛乱可能以种族或宗教认同为根据,或者其根本原因基本上跟政治或者经济有关。由于叛乱很少强大得足以正面抵抗国家军队,*insurgents*(叛乱分子,通常称为 *guerrillas*,游击队员)往往使用爆炸、绑架、抓人质和劫持等策略。

counterinsurgent \ˌkau̇n-tər-in-ˈsər-jənt\ A person taking military or political action against guerrillas or revolutionaries. 反叛乱人士

• Counterinsurgents who build trust with the local population will gradually begin to receive useful information. 与当地人们建立信任关系的反叛乱人士,通常会开始收到有用信息。

A *counterinsurgent* is, as you might guess, someone who combats an insurgency. *Counterinsurgency* efforts often attempt to win the "hearts and minds" of a population by hiring and paying local villagers, opening health clinics and schools, organizing sports programs, and providing agricultural assistance.

你可以猜到,一个 counterinsurgent(反叛乱人士)就是与叛乱作斗争的人。counterinsurgency(反叛乱)行动通常努力赢得人民的心,办法是雇佣当地村民并付给报酬、开办诊所和学校、组织体育活动、在农业上提供帮助。

resurgent \ri-ˈsər-jənt\ Rising again into life, activity, or prominence. 复苏的;

重新活跃的;复兴的
- The country had let down its guard over the summer, and in the fall a resurgent flu virus overwhelmed the public-health system, killing tens of thousands. 该国夏季期间放松了警惕,结果秋季时,恢复活力的流感病毒使公共卫生体系难以招架,数万人失去了生命。

Resurgent means literally a "rising again" (see RE, p. 682). We may speak of a resurgent baseball team, a resurgent steel industry, the *resurgence* of jogging, or a resurgence of violence in a war zone. *Resurgence* is particularly prominent in its Italian translation, *risorgimento*. In the 19th century, when the Italian peninsula consisted of a number of small independent states, a popular movement known as the Risorgimento managed to unify the peninsula and create the modern state of Italy in 1870. resurgent 字面意思是"再次升起"(见 RE,第 682 页)。我们可以说一个棒球队再次活跃起来,钢铁工业复兴了,跑步又流行起来,或者在战争地带暴力又一次猖獗起来。resurgence(resurgent 的名词形式)在其意大利语对应词 risorgimento 中特别显著。19 世纪,当意大利半岛由几个独立小国构成时,一场称为 Risorgimento(复兴运动)的人民运动成功统一了半岛,在 1870 年建立了现代国家。

Quizzes

A. Fill in each blank with the correct letter:

a. armistice
b. insurgency
c. armory
d. counterinsurgent
e. armada
f. upsurge
g. resurgent
h. disarming

1. The army was facing a large guerrilla _____ that had already taken over the fourth-largest city.

2. A cargo ship would suddenly be surrounded by an _____ of small pirate boats, against which it was impossible to defend itself.

3. The recent _____ in oil prices has alarmed investors, who worry that expensive oil will slow down the larger economy.

4. He's always had a _____ manner, and lots of people like him immediately because of his smile.

5. There seems to be a _____ interest in film musicals, after many years when none were being released at all.

6. The rebels were becoming stronger, and the country's army and police lacked the proper training to provide an effective _____ force.

7. The _____ that was signed that year had only prevented fighting for a few months.

8. Any _____ would have to be situated well away from the battlefront, since it would be a disaster if the enemy managed to seize it.

B. Indicate whether the following pairs of words have the same or different meanings:

1. armada / fleet   same ____ / different ____

2. disarming / trucelike   same ____ / different ____
3. upsurge / triumph   same ____ / different ____
4. counterinsurgent / guerrilla same ____ / different ____
5. armory / battleship   same ____ / different ____
6. resurgent / revived   same ____ / different ____
7. armistice / treaty   same ____ / different ____
8. insurgency / inflation   same ____ / different ____

STRAT comes from the Latin word *stratum*, meaning "spread" or "bed." *Strata*, a form of the same word, came to be used by the Romans to mean "paved road"—that is, *street*.
STRAT 源自拉丁语 stratum 一词,意思是"展开"或者"床"。strata 是该词的一种形式,被罗马人用来表示"铺好的路",也就是街道。

stratum \strā-təm\ (1) A layer of a substance, especially one of a series of layers. 层 (2) A level of society made up of people of the same rank or position. 阶层

• Alcohol and drug abuse are found in every stratum of society. 酗酒和吸毒现象存在于社会各阶层。

In geology, a stratum is a layer of rock or soil that is distinct from those above and below it. Rock and soil *strata* (notice the plural form) can be seen in road cuts, cliffs, quarries, riverbanks, and sand dunes, and in pieces of limestone, slate, and shale. Archaeologists digging in historical sites are careful to note the stratum where each artifact is found. Earth scientists divide the earth's atmosphere into strata, just as oceanographers divide the ocean's depths into strata. And for social scientists, a stratum is a group of people who are similar in some way, such as education, culture, or income.
在地质学上,stratum 指与上、下截然不同的岩层或者土层。岩石和土壤的 strata(层;注意复数形式)可见于路堑、峭壁、采石场、河岸、沙丘以及成块的石灰石、页岩和板岩。在历史遗迹挖掘的考古学家细心地注意每一个手工艺品被发现的土层。地球科学家将地球的大气分为层,就像海洋学家将海水分为层一样。对社会科学家来说,阶层就是在某方面(比如教育、文化、收入)类似的一群人。

stratification \ strā-tə-fə-ˈkā-shən \ The process or state of being formed, deposited, or arranged in layers. 分层;成层

• The stratification of the lake in summer keeps oxygen-rich cold water at the bottom, where coldwater fish such as trout take refuge. 湖泊在夏季的分层可使富含氧气的冷水处于底部,像鲑鱼这样的冷水鱼可以躲藏在那里。

If you look for it, you'll find stratification almost everywhere. On a tall rainforest tree, there may be different air plants clinging to it, different insects crawling on it, and different mammals making their homes at different levels. The earth beneath you may be *stratified* into several distinctive layers within the first 20 feet. If the wind you're feeling is moving at 10 miles per hour, at 30 feet above your head it may be 20 mph, and in the jet stream above that it may be 150 mph. If you climb a high mountain in Himalayas, you may begin in a lush, wet forest and end up in a windswept environment where not even lichen will grow.

如果你找一找的话,就会发现几乎到处都有 stratification(分层现象)。在高高的热带雨林树上,会有不同的气生植物附着在上面,不同的昆虫爬行其上,不同的哺乳动物在不同的层次上安家。你脚下的土壤,最上面二十英尺也 *stratified* (分)为明显不同的几层。如果你可以感到的风以十英里的时速移动,那么在你上空三十英尺,其时速则可能是二十英里,在更上面的喷流,时速可达一百五十英里。如果你攀登喜马拉雅山的一座高峰,就可能从茂盛、湿润的森林开始,最后到达一个狂风呼啸的环境,那里连地衣都不生长。

substrate \ˈsəb-ˌstrāt\ (1) An underlying layer. 下层 (2) The base on which an organism lives. (生物生长的)基础

● The soil is the substrate of most seed plants. 土壤是多数种子植物生长的基础。

With its Latin prefix *sub-*, "below" (see SUB, p. 491), *substrate* obviously refers to a layer under something else. Rock may serve as the substrate for the coral in a coral reef. Tiny wafers of silicon (or another semiconductor) serve as the substrate for computer chips. *Substrate* may also mean *subsoil*—that is, the layer under the topsoil, lacking in organic matter or humus. *Substrate* is part of the vocabulary of various other sciences, including chemistry and biology. But although it's mostly a scientific term, writers may also use it to mean simply "foundation"—for instance, when observing that reading is the substrate on which most other learning is based.

拉丁语前缀 *sub-* 意思是"在下面"(见 SUB,第 491 页),有了它,*substrate* 很明显指的是某物下面的一层。岩石可作为珊瑚礁中珊瑚的基础。微小的硅片(或者另一种半导体薄片)可作为电脑芯片的基础。*substrate* 也可表示 *subsoil*(底土),也就是表土下面的那层土,缺乏有机物质或者腐殖质。*substrate* 也是各种其他学科(包括化学和生物学)术语的一部分。但是虽然它多数时候是科学术语,作家也可能仅仅用它表示"基础",比如观察到阅读是其他大多数学问的基础时。

stratocumulus \ˌstrā-tō-ˈkyü-myə-ləs\ A low-lying cloud formation appearing as extensive and often dark horizontal layers, with tops rounded into large balls or rolls. 层积云

● A dark bank of stratocumulus clouds was moving in quickly, and in March that usually meant bad weather. 一大片黑色的层积云正飘过来,这在三月份意味着天气要恶化了。

When a cloud type forms a broad "layer" over the earth, the *strat-* root shows up in its scientific name. The type called simply *stratus* forms a low layer of gray extending over a large area. *Cirrostratus* ("curl layer") clouds form a high, thin layer often covering the entire sky (but without the wispy curls of ice crystals that give pure *cirrus* clouds their name). *Altostratus* ("high layer") clouds form a darkish gray mid-altitude layer. *Nimbostratus* ("rainstorm layer") clouds form a low, dark layer of gray cloud that usually produces light but continuous rain, snow, or sleet (but not violent storms of the kind that give pure *nimbus* clouds their name). *Cumulus* ("heap") is the familiar puffy fair-weather type of cloud; *stratocumulus* is its more wintry version, which spreads out in a fairly flat layer, much less "heaped up," and sometimes dense enough to cover almost the whole sky.

当某种类型的云在地面上空形成宽大的一层时，词根 strat- 就会出现在其科学学术语中。简单地被叫作 *stratus*(层云) 的这一类型的云，在低空形成灰色的一片，覆盖一片广大区域。*cirrostratus*(卷层云) 在高空形成薄薄的一层，常常布满整个天空(但没有卷层云获得其名称的一缕缕的冰晶)。*altostratus*(高层云) 在中海拔形成黑灰色的一层云。*nimbostratus*(雨层云) 形成低低的、深色的一层灰云，通常会产生少量但持续的雨、雪或者雨夹雪(但不是让 *nimbus*[雨云] 获得其名称的强烈暴风雨)。*cumulus*(积云) 是为人熟知的天气良好时松软洁白的云。*stratocumulus*(层积云) 是其更寒冷的类型，展开形成很平的一层，没有堆得那么高，有时候很密实，足以覆盖几乎整个天空。

LATER

LATER comes from the Latin adjective *lateralis*, meaning "side." The noun for "side" in Latin was *latus*, and the same word served as an adjective meaning "wide." The relationship between the two isn't hard to spot, since something wide extends far out to its sides. So lines of *latitude* extend east-west around the earth, in the dimension we tend to think of as its width (unlike lines of *longitude*, which extend north-south, in the dimension that, for some reason, we decided to think of as its "length").

LATER 源自拉丁语形容词 *lateralis*，意思是"边"。拉丁语中表示"边"的名词是 *latus*，这同一个词语也可用作形容词，表示"宽"。这两个词语之间的关系并不难以看出，因为宽的东西往两边延伸。所以 *lines of latitude*(纬线)绕着地球东西延伸，沿着我们倾向于认为是地球的宽度的维度延伸(*lines of longitude*[经线]是南北延伸的，由于某种原因，我们认为它是沿着地球的"长"这一维度延伸的)。

lateral \ˈla-tə-rəl\ Of or relating to the side. 侧面的；横向的

• Only in the lateral views did the X-rays reveal an suspiciouslooking shadow on the lung. 只有从侧面看，X 光片才显示出令人怀疑的肺部阴影。

Lateral shows up in all kinds of contexts. A lateral job change is one that keeps you at about the same job level and salary. A coach might have special drills to improve his players' lateral speed and agility. The British speak of "lateral thinking," thinking that grabs ideas that may not seem to be relevant but turn out to work well—what we might call "thinking outside the box." But we know *lateral* best from football. A lateral pass is a pass of the ball between teammates that usually goes to the side and slightly backward from the direction in which they're advancing; unlike a forward pass, a lateral may be made from any position, and any number may be made in a single play.

所有种类的语境中都会出现 lateral 这一词语。*lateral*(横向的)工作变换，工作的层次和薪水没有改变。教练可能进行特殊训练，显著改善运动员的侧向速度和能力。英国人会说到"横向思维"，这种思维能够捕捉到看似无关但会很有用的观点，也就是我们所谓的"盒子外面的思维"。但是，我们从橄榄球最能了解 *lateral*。侧向传球就是在前进的队员之间传球，通常传向一边或者稍稍往后。与前进传球不同的是，侧向传球可以从任何位置进行，一场球可以进行任何数量的侧向传球。

bilateral \bī-ˈla-tə-rəl\ Involving two groups or countries. 双边的

• Instead of working on a set of separate bilateral trade agreements, they propose bringing the countries of the region together to sign a single joint agreement. 他们没有致力于签署一系列双边贸易协定，而是建议该地区国家走到一起，签署一个联合协定。

Since the prefix *bi-* means "two" in Latin (see BI/BIN, p. 360), *bilateral* means essentially "two-sided." In the days when there were two superpowers, the U. S. and the Soviet Union regularly engaged in bilateral arms negotiations; such negotiations are much less common today. Sometimes *bilateral* refers to two sides of the same thing. A bilateral hip replacement, for instance, replaces both hip bones in the same operation. And *bilateral symmetry* (a term often used by biologists) refers to the fact that, in many organisms (such as humans), the left side is basically the mirror image of the right side. 由于前缀 *bi-* 在拉丁语中意思是 "二"（见 BI/BIN，第 360 页），*bilateral* 的意思基本上是 "双边的"。在两个超级大国存在的岁月，美国和苏联经常进行双边武器谈判，这样的谈判今天远远没有那么普遍。有时，*bilateral* 指同一事物的两个边。比如，双侧髋关节置换在同一手术中换去两个髋骨。*bilateral symmetry*（两侧对称，通常是生物学家使用的术语）指的是，在很多生物体内（比如人），左侧基本上是右侧的镜中影像。

collateral \kə-ˈla-tə-rəl\ (1) Associated but of secondary importance. 附属的；附带的 (2) Related but not in a direct or close way. 间接的

• Though the army referred to the civilian deaths as "collateral damage," since civilians weren't the intended targets, the incident aroused intense anger among the survivors. 虽然军方称平民死亡是 "附带伤害"，因为平民并非本来要攻击的目标，但该事件还是在幸存者中引起了极大的愤怒。

If an official talking about some policy refers to a *collateral issue*, he or she means something that may be affected but isn't central to the discussion. To an anthropologist, your cousin would be called a *collateral relative*, since he or she (unlike your grandmother, brother, or daughter) is "off to the side" of your direct line of descent. As a noun, *collateral* means something provided to a lender as a guarantee of repayment. So if you take out a loan or mortgage to buy a car or house, the loan agreement usually states that the car or house is collateral that goes to the lender if the sum isn't paid. 如果官员谈到某一政策时，说它是一个 collateral issue（附带问题），意思就是，虽然它可能会受到影响，但与讨论关系不大。对人类学家来说，你的表兄/弟/姐/妹可称为 collateral relative（旁系亲属），因为他或她跟你的祖母、哥哥/弟弟或者姐姐/妹妹不同，不是直系亲属。作为名词，*collateral* 指抵押物。所以，如果你借款或者取得抵押贷款来购车或购房，借款协议通常会说明，如果未能付款，车或者房就是给予借方的抵押物。

equilateral \ˌē-kwə-ˈla-tə-rəl\ Having all sides or faces equal. 等边的；等面的

• On her desk she kept an equilateral prism, through which every morning the sun would project the colors of the spectrum onto the far wall. 她桌子上放着一个等面棱镜。每天早上，阳光会把色谱中的颜色投射在较远那面墙上。

Since *equi-* means "equal" (see EQU, p. 120), the meaning of *equilateral* is easy to guess from its roots. The word is mostly used in geometry. The standard polygons (many-sided geometrical shapes)—the pentagon, hexagon, octagon, etc.—are assumed to be equilateral if we don't say otherwise; an equilateral rectangle has the special name *square*. But triangles are particularly important, and many triangles are not equal-sided. The standard polyhedrons (many-sided solids) are also equilateral. Most common is the cube, all of whose sides are square. The tetrahedron has four triangular sides and thus is a pyramid with a triangular base, unlike the pyramids of Egypt with their square bases.

因为 *equi* 的意思是"相等"(EQU, 第 120 页),*equilateral* 一词的意思从词根不难猜出。这一词语主要用于几何学。标准的多边形——五边形、六边形、八边形,等等,如果不另外说明,被认为是等边的。等边的方形有一个特殊的名字,叫正方形。但是,三角形尤其重要,很多三角形并不等边。标准的多面体(多边的立体图形)也是等边的。四面体有四个三边形的面,所以就是一个有着三角形底面的棱锥体,跟埃及的底面为正方形的金字塔不同。

Quizzes

A. Fill in each blank with the correct letter:

a. stratocumulus   e. substrate
b. equilateral   f. collateral
c. stratum   g. stratification
d. lateral   h. bilateral

1. His trainer is teaching him _____ weight lifts, in which you hold your arms out to the sides.

2. The Defense Department is headquartered in a huge building that forms an _____ pentagon.

3. It was a typical winter sky, covered in a gray layer of _____ clouds.

4. The coral may use any hard surface as its _____ , so artificial reefs have been created by sinking old ships.

5. The departure of the factory cost the community 150 jobs, and the _____ effects on the town's economy were severe.

6. In old mill towns you could actually see the social _____ , since the wealthy people lived on the high ground and the working class lived down below.

7. The two countries have been holding _____ talks, but the other countries in the region will be joining the process soon.

8. The _____ under the topsoil consisted of yellow lime mixed with gravel, and the one below that was of slatelike rock.

B. Indicate whether the following pairs of terms have the same or different meanings:

1. equilateral / equal-sided   same ____ / different ____
2. stratum / layer   same ____ / different ____

3. lateral / backward   same ____ / different ____
4. stratocumulus / puffy summer clouds   same ____ / different ____
5. bilateral / two-sided   same ____ / different ____
6. stratification / strategy   same ____ / different ____
7. collateral / many-sided   same ____ / different ____
8. substrate / topic   same ____ / different ____

TOM comes from the Greek root meaning "cut." Thus, the Latin word *anatomia*, from which we get *anatomy*, means "dissection"—that is cutting or separating the parts of an organism for detailed examination. In a *lobotomy*, the nerves linking a brain lobe to the rest of the brain are removed; even though lobotomies have hardly been performed in the last 50 years, the idea can still fill us with horror.

TOM 源自表示"切,割"的希腊语词根。因此,我们由其得来 *anotomy* 这一词语的拉丁语词 *anatomia*,意思就是"解剖",即切割或分开生物体各部分进行仔细检查。在 *lobotomy*(脑叶切除术)中,将脑叶和大脑其余部分连在一起的神经被切除。即使在过去至少五十年几乎没有进行过脑叶切除手术,这一想法也让我们感到恐惧。

appendectomy \ˌa-pən-ˈdek-tə-mē\ Surgical removal of the human appendix. 阑尾切除

• Appendectomy is an emergency procedure, since appendicitis can be fatal if its symptoms are ignored. 阑尾切除是急救手术,因为忽视其症状的话,阑尾炎可能会致命。

The *appendix* is a tiny tube attached to the large intestine that no longer has any real function. *Appendicitis*—inflammation and swelling of the appendix, usually as a result of bacterial infection—generally occurs between the ages of 10 and 19, and is the most common reason for emergency surgery in the U.S. today. Since the appendix has so little to do, *appendectomies* normally have no negative aftereffects at all. If appendicitis is ignored, bacteria may enter the blood and infect other parts of the body. *appendix*(阑尾)是附在大肠上的一根小管子,没有什么真正作用。*appendicitis*(阑尾炎),也就是阑尾发炎、肿大,通常是细菌感染的结果,一般发生在十岁到十九岁之间,在美国是紧急手术的最常见原因。由于阑尾很少有什么作用,阑尾切除手术正常情况下根本不会有不良后遗症。如果忽视了阑尾炎,细菌可能进入血液,感染身体其他部分。

gastrectomy \ga-ˈstrek-tə-mē\ Surgical removal of all or part of the stomach. 胃切除

• Gastrectomy is used to treat holes in the stomach wall, noncancerous tumors, and cancer, but is performed only when other treatments have been rejected. 胃切除用来治疗胃穿孔、良性肿瘤和癌症,但只有其他治疗被否决时才这么做。

Gastr- comes from the Greek word for "belly," and shows up in English in such words as *gastric* ("relating to the stomach") and *gastronomy* ("the cooking and eating of fine food"). Believe it or not, there are many people today who have had a gastrectomy and live without a stomach; some of them need to eat fairly steadily and carefully through the day, but many lead almost completely normal and even vigorous lives.

gastr 源自希腊语中表示"肚子"的那个词语,出现在英语单词 *gastric*(跟胃有关的)和 *gastronomy*(美食法)中。信不信由你,今天有很多人进行过胃切除,没有胃。这些人虽有的需要整天持续不断、小心翼翼地吃东西,但也有很多人则过着几乎是完全正常甚至是活跃的生活。

tonsillectomy \ˌtän-sə-ˈlek-tə-mē\   Surgical removal of the tonsils. 扁桃体切除

• His daughter's usual doctor thought antibiotics could cure her swollen tonsils, but a specialist recommended tonsillectomy. 通常给他女儿看病的医生认为,抗生素可以治疗她肿大的扁桃体,但有位专家建议切除。

The tonsils are the areas of tissue that you can see in the mirror on both sides of your throat (not to be confused with the uvula, which hangs down in the middle). Tonsillectomy, the most common surgery performed on children in the U. S., is intended to relieve *tonsillitis*, or inflammation of the tonsils (usually by strep or staph bacteria). But the fact is, tonsillitis can often be successfully treated with antibiotics, which means that surgery, including the week or two of pain and discomfort that follows it, is generally unnecessary.

tonsils(扁桃体)是可以照着镜子看到的,就在你喉咙两边(不要和小舌混淆了,小舌垂在中间)。扁桃体切除是美国孩子最常见的手术,目的是消除 *tonsillitis*(扁桃体炎,通常是链球菌或葡萄球菌引起的)。不过,实际上,扁桃体炎用抗生素通常是可以治好的,这就是说,手术,包括其后一两个星期的疼痛和不适,通常是不必要的。

mastectomy \ma-ˈstek-tə-mē\   Surgical removal of all or part of the breast. 乳房切除

• She has always dreaded being disfigured by mastectomy, but her talks with the surgeon have calmed her considerably. 她一直害怕乳房切除会让自己变丑,但是跟医生谈话之后平静了许多。

Breast cancer is the most common cancer among American women. Early cases can often be treated with drugs or with a small operation called a *lumpectomy* (because it removes a lump). Though a "simple mastectomy" is larger than a lumpectomy, it allows the breast to be reconstructed, using artificial implants or tissue from elsewhere on the body. But "radical mastectomy," which is required when the cancer is at an advanced stage, takes much of the chest muscle and makes reconstruction impossible.

乳腺癌是美国妇女最常见的癌症。早期病例的治疗通常利用药物或者叫做 *lumpectomy*(肿块切除,因为切除的是一个 lump,肿块)的小手术。虽然"简单的 mastectomy(乳房切除)"也比肿块切除规模要大,但它可以让乳房通过植入填充物或来自身体其他部分的组织得以修复。但是乳腺癌晚期所需要的"根治性乳房切除"会减少很多胸部肌肉,乳房就不可能修复了。

IATR, from the Greek *iatros*, "healer, physician," usually hides in the middle of words, where it isn't immediately noticed. A *pediatrician* treats children (see PED, p. 318). A *psychiatrist* is a physician who treats mental problems. (A psychologist, by contrast, doesn't have a medical degree and thus can't prescribe drugs.) And a *physiatrist* is a doctor who practices "physical medicine and rehabilitation," which may involve such things as testing various physical abilities, relieving pain through electric heat or massage, or training patients to exercise or to use an artificial limb. IATR 源自希腊语 *iatros*,意思是"治愈者,医生",通常隐藏在词语中间,不容易马上注意到。*pediatrician*(儿科医生)给儿童治病(见 PED,第 318 页),*psychiatrist*(精神病医生)治疗精神病(而心理学家没有医学学位,因此不能开药)。*physiatrist*(物理治疗医师)实施"物理药物治疗及和修复",这可能包括测试各种身体能力,利用电的热量和按摩来减轻疼痛,或者训练病人进行运动,或者使用人造肢体。

iatrogenic \ī-ˌa-trə-ˈje-nik\ Caused accidentally by medical treatment.
医疗引起的

● Most medical malpractice suits seek compensation for iatrogenic injury. 大多数医疗事故诉讼都要求为医疗伤害进行赔偿。

In the 21st century, patients with throat infections are no longer being bled to death by misguided doctors, like the unfortunate George Washington. But iatrogenic injury and death still remain serious risks. Because of a doctor's bad handwriting, a patient may be given the wrong powerful drug. The sheer number of drugs on the market has led to dangerous drug interactions, which often occur when one doctor doesn't know what another is doing. Too many patients go to the hospital for some common treatment and pick up an antibiotic-resistant staph infection. And let's not even think about those unlucky patients who wake up to find that the surgeon has removed the wrong foot. 在 21 世纪,有喉咙感染的病人不再被庸医放血致死,不会像倒霉的乔治·华盛顿那样了。但是,iatrogenic(医疗的)伤害和医疗死亡仍然很有可能。因为医生糟糕的笔迹,病人可能会使用错误的强效药。市场上药物的数量惊人,会导致药物相互作用,非常危险。一个医生不知道另一个医生在干什么,就会出现这种情况。太多病人去医院希望得到普通的治疗,却得了对抗生素有抵抗力的葡萄球菌感染。我们甚至不用想,有的病人很不幸,醒来后发现医生切除了不该切除的脚。

bariatric \ˌber-ē-ˈa-trik\ Relating to or specializing in the treatment of obesity. 治疗肥胖病的

● In the type of bariatric surgery called gastric bypass, part of the stomach is actually stapled off. 在称为胃绕道的肥胖病手术中,胃的一部分实际上被钉合了。

Baros means "weight" in Greek; so, for example, a *barometer* is an instrument that measures air pressure or weight. *Bariatric* describes the medical treatment of serious overweight—that is, obesity. Bariatric surgery is only employed when other methods of weight loss have been tried and failed. Though stapling the stomach may seem extreme, we now know that obesity greatly increases the risk of heart disease, diabetes, cancer, and stroke, so stomach surgery doesn't just help people look and feel better—it's a potential lifesaver.

baros 在希腊语中意思是"重量",所以,比如 barometer(气压计)这个词,指测量空气压力或空气重量的仪器。Bariatric(肥胖症学的)描述严重超重的治疗,也就是肥胖症的治疗。肥胖症手术只有当其他减肥方法失败了才能实施。尽管钉合人的胃看起来很极端,但我们知道,肥胖症大大增加罹患心脏病、糖尿病、癌症和中风的危险。所以,给胃做手术不仅仅有助于让人看起来而且感觉更好,它还可能救人一命。

geriatric \ˌjer-ē-ˈa-trik\ Of or relating to old people. 老年人的

• We guessed we were now in the hospital's geriatric wing, since all the patients seemed to be elderly. 我们当时猜到,我们正位于医院大楼的老年病侧翼,因为所有病人似乎年龄较大。

Since most medical care is devoted to those over 65, *geriatrics*, the medical treatment of the elderly, is a highly important specialty. The specific problems of the elderly include physical inactivity and instability, which result from weakness and loss of energy. Weakness of the eyes and ears plays a role, and weakening of the immune system often leads to more disease. All these conditions can be made worse by mental problems, such as declining intellectual activity, declining memory, and depression, which may prevent the patient from taking action to improve his or her condition. But the effects of aging can be greatly relieved by proper care. And the greatest improvement often results when the patient is persuaded to become more physically, mentally, and socially active.

由于大多数医疗护理都集中于六十五岁以上的老人,geriatrics 也就是为老人进行的治疗,是一个特别重要的专业。老年人的具体问题包括身体缺乏活动或者不稳定,原因是虚弱和缺少能量。眼睛和耳朵功能衰弱是一部分原因,免疫系统衰退常常导致更多疾病。所有这些状况会因为精神问题而恶化,比如智力活跃程度减弱、记忆力减弱及情绪低落,而这些会阻碍病人采取行动改善自己的状况。但是,衰老的不良影响可以通过正确的护理以减轻。当病人听从劝导,在身体、精神和社交方面更加活跃时,就会产生最好的效果。

podiatrist \pə-ˈdī-ə-trist\ A doctor who treats injuries and diseases of the foot. 足病医生

• Like most podiatrists, she spends a lot of time dealing with minor complaints like bunions, ankle sprains, arch pain, and hammertoes. 像大多数足病医生那样,她花很多时间治疗轻微伤病,比如拇囊肿、脚踝扭伤、脚弓疼痛、锤状脚趾。

Most foot problems result from the fact that human feet were never designed to walk on asphalt and concrete or even to wear shoes (all that cushioning we demand in our shoes may be doing us more harm than good). So today we have an entire medical specialty devoted to feet. In the U.S., a podiatrist is a doctor of *podiatric* medicine (D.P.M.), who is licensed to perform surgery. The root *pod-* comes from the Greek word for "foot" (compare PED, p. 83). But in England a foot doctor is often called a *chiropodist*, a term that dates from the time when the same specialist treated hands as well, since *chiro-* means "hand."

大多数脚部问题都源自这一事实：人类的双脚，从来就不是为了行走在沥青上、混凝土上的，甚至不是为了穿鞋子（我们要求的鞋子中的软垫可能对我们有害，而不是有益）。所以，今天我们有完整的一个专门针对脚的医学专业。在美国，足病医生是从事 *podiatric*（足病的）医学的医生（D. P. M.），他们获得许可实施手术。Pod- 这一词根源自希腊语中表示"脚"的词语（比较 PED，第 83 页）。但是，在英国，足病医生常常称为 *chiropodist*。这一术语源自同一专家也治疗手病的时代，因为 *chiro-* 意思是"手"。

Quiz

Fill in each blank with the correct letter：

a. iatrogenic   e. mastectomy
b. gastrectomy   f. podiatrist
c. appendectomy   g. tonsillectomy
d. bariatric   h. geriatric

1. Following his _____ surgery his weight dropped from 310 pounds to 220.

2. Because of the doctor's bad handwriting, the pharmacist had given her the wrong medicine, and she had sued, claiming her new condition was _____ in origin.

3. After her _____ the breast had been completely reconstructed.

4. He had undergone a _____ after tests had revealed tumors on the stomach wall.

5. After her last Kung Fu class she had a badly swollen foot, and her _____ was having some X-rays taken.

6. I myself had a _____ when I was 11, but my son's tonsils got better after a week of antibiotics.

7. With the growing elderly population, there's a crying need for more _____ specialists.

8. X-rays showed that the appendix was badly swollen, and they managed to schedule an _____ for that same afternoon.

Review Quizzes

A. Match the definition on the left to the correct word on the right：

1. layer   a. superlative
2. revived   b. equilateral
3. not in effect   c. lateral

UNIT 27

4. equal-sided
5. outstanding
6. doctor-caused
7. incidental
8. weapons depot
9. devalue
10. sidewise

d. stratum
e. armory
f. iatrogenic
g. null
h. resurgent
i. collateral
j. debase

B. Fill in each blank with the correct letter:

a. insurgency
b. bariatric
c. substrate
d. armistice
e. superfluous

f. supersede
g. nanotechnology
h. disarming
i. defamation
j. geriatric

1. After seven long years of war, the news of the _____ was greeted with tears of joy.

2. Amateurs can often grow mushrooms successfully on a _____ of sawdust, hay, or even coffee grounds.

3. _____ patients receive most of the country's medical care every year.

4. The government had beaten back a major _____ in the 1990s, but the rebels had regrouped and new fighting had begun.

5. The new version of the software will naturally _____ any previous versions, even if some users think it's not an improvement.

6. She had been making outrageous statements about him to the newspapers, and he finally sued for _____ of character.

7. The possible future medical uses of the tiny particles and structures employed in _____ seem to be limited only by scientists' imaginations.

8. The advice my doctors have been giving me about my condition has been _____, since I've known all these facts for years.

9. She had been prepared to find him terrifying, but his manner was so _____ that she relaxed almost immediately.

10. After years of failure at reducing, she was finally told by her doctor that _____ surgery was probably her best hope.

C. Indicate whether the following pairs of words have the same or different meanings:

1. insurgency / uprising   same ____ / different ____
2. degenerative / corrupt   same ____ / different ____
3. podiatrist / children's doctor   same ____ / different ____
4. annulment / undoing   same ____ / different ____

• 665 •

5. bilateral / two-sided   same ____ / different ____
6. geriatric / bacterial   same ____ / different ____
7. upsurge / increase   same ____ / different ____
8. dejection / sadness   same ____ / different ____
9. armada / fleet   same ____ / different ____
10. insuperable / excellent   same ____ / different ____

UNIT 28

MEDI

MEDI comes from the Latin *medius*, meaning "middle." Our word *medium* refers to something in a middle position. The *medieval* period of European history, also known as the Middle Ages, is the period between Greek and Roman antiquity and the "modern age." But why people around 1620 began to use the term "Middle Ages," because they regarded themselves as modern, is an interesting question.
MEDI 源自拉丁语 *medius*(中间)。我们的 *medium*(中等的,中号的)一词指处于中间位置的事物。欧洲的 *medieval*(中世纪的)时期,也叫 Middle Ages(中世纪),是古希腊和罗马时期和"现代"之间的时期。但是为什么1620年前后人们就开始使用"Middle Ages"一词,而当时他们应该认为自己是现代人,这是个有趣的问题。

---

median\ˈmē-dē-ən\ In the middle; especially, having a value that is in the middle of a series of values arranged from smallest to largest. 中间的;中间值的

• The city's west side is well-off but its east side isn't, so the city's median house prices are typical for the region. 这座城市西边富裕,东边则不然,所以该市不高不低的房价对该地区来说具有典型性。

People often use the word *average* without realizing that there are two common forms of average. Suppose you want to find the average net worth of a group of people—that is, the average value of everything they possess. To find one type of average, called the *mean*, you'd simply add up the total value of money and property of everyone in the group and divide it by the number of people. To find the other type, called the *median*, you'd identify the net worth of the person who is richer than half the people and poorer than the other half. So if Warren Buffett drove through a tiny village in India, the mean net worth of those in the village would suddenly rise to perhaps a billion dollars, but their median net worth would remain close to zero. Which figure would be more meaningful?
人们经常使用 *average*(平均的)一词,却没有意识到有两种常见形式的 average。假设你想发现某个群体的平均净

资产,也就是他们拥有的财产的平均价值。要发现一种类型的平均值(称为 mean),你会把这一群体每个人的金钱和财物的总价加起来。要发现另一种平均值(称为 median),你会去找比一半人富而比另一半人穷的那个人的净资产。所以,如果沃伦·巴菲特开车穿过印度一个小村庄,这个村庄的 mean 净资产就可能会猛增到十亿美元,但是他们的 median 净资产几乎仍然接近零。哪个数字更有意义呢?

mediate \\ˈmē-dē-ˌāt\\ (1) To work with opposing sides in an argument or dispute in order to get an agreement. 调停,调解;斡旋 (2) To achieve a settlement or agreement by working with the opposing sides. 促成(协议)

• He was the third person who had attempted to mediate the dispute between the firm and its striking workers, the first two having given up in despair. 他是第三个想在公司和罢工工人之间调解争端的人,前两个都放弃了。

Mediation is often used in disputes between companies and labor unions, and the government actually provides *mediators* for such disagreements. The mediator tries to bring the two sides to an agreement, but doesn't have the power to actually order such an agreement. Mediators also sometimes have a role in international disputes; when two neighboring countries claim exclusive fishing rights in the same ocean waters, for example, they may invite a trained mediator to help settle the argument. *Arbitration* is similar to mediation, but in arbitration both parties in a dispute agree to accept the arbitrator's decision.

mediation 常常用于公司和工会之间的争端,政府实际上经常为这样的纠纷提供 *mediators*(调解者)。调解者努力使双方达成协议。调解者有时候也在国际纠纷中发挥作用。比如,当两个邻国对同一片海域声明有独有的捕鱼权时,他们可能邀请一位训练有素的调停者帮助解决争端。*arbitration*(仲裁,公断)类似于调解,但是在仲裁中,有争议的双方同意接受仲裁者的决定。

intermediary \\ˌin-tər-ˈmē-dē-ˌer-ē\\ A person who works with opposing sides in a dispute in order to bring about an agreement. 中间人,调解人

• The divorce had been bitter, and the two now communicated only through an old friend who they both trusted as an intermediary. 这次离婚闹得很不愉快,双方只能通过一位他们相信可做调解人的老朋友进行沟通。

Since *inter-* means "between, among" (see INTER, p. 703), an *intermediary* is someone who moves back and forth in the middle area between two sides—a "go-between." *Mediator* (which shares the *medi-* root) is often a synonym, and so is *facilitator*; *broker* and *agent* are often others. Thus, a real-estate broker or agent shuttles between a house's buyer and seller, who may never even meet each other. Financial *intermediation* is what happens when you put money in a bank or investment firm, which then invests it in various companies; if you want, you can instead cut out the intermediary and invest the money directly in companies of your own choosing.

由于 *inter* 意思是"在……之间,在……中间"(见 INTER,第 703 页),*intermediary* 就是在双方之间的中间地带来回移动的人——一个"go-between"(中间人)。*mediator*(调停者,斡旋者)(也含有 *medi-* 这一词根)常常是同义词,*facilitator*(促成者)、*broker*(经纪人、掮客)和 *agent*(经纪人、代理人)常常也是它的同义词。这样,房地产 broker 或者 agent 在房屋买卖双方频繁往来,而双方可能从来不会见面。金融 *intermediation*(调停,调解)是在你把钱存入银行或者

投资公司而他们把钱投入各种各样公司时发生的事情，如果愿意，你则可以摆脱金融中介，直接把钱投入你自己选择的公司。

mediocrity \ˌmē-dē-ˈä-krə-tē\ The quality of being not very good. 平常；平庸

• He's the kind of person who can get depressed by the mediocrity of a dinner, or even a wine. 他是那种因为饭菜甚至葡萄酒质量一般就会情绪低落的人。

People interested in words always point out that *mediocrity* doesn't mean quite what its main root would indicate: Why doesn't it describe something that's right in the middle of the pack, exactly what you would expect? Instead the words *mediocrity* and *mediocre* always suggest disappointment. A mediocre play is one you wish you hadn't wasted an evening on, and the mediocre actor in it should probably find another profession. A person can even be called a mediocrity, though it isn't very nice and you'd never do it to his face.

对词语着迷的人总是说，mediocrity 的意思与其主要词根表示的不太一样：为什么它不像你所期待的那样描述中等水平的事物呢？相反，mediocrity 和 mediocre 却总是暗示失望。一个 mediocre（平庸的）戏剧是一个你希望没有浪费一晚上时间去看的戏剧，而戏中那个 mediocre（平庸的）演员应该换个工作。一个人甚至可以被称为 mediocrity（平庸之人），虽然这样称呼不太好，你也从没有当面这样做过。

OID

OID comes from the Greek word for "appearance" or "form." Since *aster* in ancient Greek meant "star," the small bodies orbiting between Mars and Jupiter that looked like stars through primitive telescopes were called *asteroids*. A *factoid* is a little bit of information that looks like a fact, whether it is or not. And some people these days will attach *-oid* to just about anything; you can probably figure out the meaning of *nutsoid*, *nerdoid*, and *freakazoid* without much help.

OID 源自表示"外貌"或"形状"的希腊词语。由于 aster 在古希腊语中意思是"星星"，那些在火星和金星之间运行的透过望远镜看着像星星的小天体，就被称为 asteroids（小行星）。factoid 是看起来像事实的一点信息，不管实际上是否如此。今天，有些人会把 -oid 加在几乎任何词语后。不需要多少帮助，你也可能猜得出来 nutsoid, nerdoid 和 freakazoid 的意思。

rhomboid \ˈräm-ˌbȯid\ In geometry, a shape with four sides where only the opposite sides and angles are equal. 长菱形

• The flimsy picture frame had been damaged en route, and its rectangular shape was now a rhomboid. 这个劣质的相框在路上就损坏了，长方形变成了长菱形。

Rhomboids, like triangles, may take various different shapes, but they always look like a lopsided diamond or rectangle. As both a noun and an adjective, *rhomboid* can be applied to anything with those shapes, such as certain muscles of the upper back when viewed from behind. Whenever you hear about rhomboid exercises, rhomboid strain, or rhomboid pain, it involves those muscles, which attach your shoulder blades to your spine and can be strained by carrying a heavy backpack, serving a tennis ball, or just slumping in your chair in front of a computer all day.

<small>rhomboids(长菱形),就像三角形一样,可能会有各种形状,但总是看起来像个歪到一边的菱形或者长方形。rhomboid 既是名词,又是形容词,可用于任何具有这些形状的事物,比如向后看时后背上部的某些肌肉。每当你听说 rhomboid exercises(菱形肌运动)、rhomboid strain(菱形肌扭伤)或者 rhomboid pain(菱形肌疼痛)时,就涉及这些肌肉。这些肌肉把你的肩胛骨固定在脊椎上,如果背着过重的背包、发网球或者整天弯腰坐在电脑前,它们就可能扭伤。</small>

deltoid \ˈdel-ˌtȯid\   A large muscle of the shoulder. 三角肌

• In Anatomy class she had learned about the deltoids, which her trainer at the gym just called "delts." <small>在结构学课堂上,她了解了 deltoids(三角肌),而教练在体操馆简单地将其称为 delts。</small>

The fourth letter of the Greek alphabet is *delta*, and a capital delta is triangle-shaped. In English, *delta* commonly means the sand deposits that form a huge triangle at the mouth of certain large rivers. *Deltoid* as an adjective means "having a triangular shape," and botanists often use the word to describe the shape of certain leaves. The triangular, swept-back wings seen on jet fighter aircraft are called *delta wings*. Your deltoid muscles—not far from your rhomboids—form a cap on your shoulders, and some gym trainers even treat *shoulder* and *deltoid* as synonyms. Can you guess the general shape of deltoids when seen from the side?

<small>希腊语第四个字母就是 delta,大写时是三角形的。在英语中,delta 通常指大河河口处形成的三角形的淤沙。deltoid 作为形容词,意思是"三角形的",植物学家经常用来描述某些叶子的形状。喷气式飞机上三角形的、向后倾斜的机翼称为 delta wings(三角翼)。你的三角肌——离菱形肌不远——构成肩膀的顶部,而且有的健身教练甚至把 shoulder(肩膀)和 deltoid(三角肌)作为同义词。你能猜出从侧面看时三角肌的大致形状吗?</small>

dendroid \ˈden-ˌdrȯid\   Resembling a tree in form. 树形的

• The reef was a fantastic jungle, its dendroid corals resembling luminous, poisonous trees in a landscape of bizarre beauty. <small>这珊瑚礁是个很漂亮的丛林。树形的珊瑚像奇异而美丽的风景中鲜艳、有毒的树。</small>

Dendrology is the study of trees, and those who do the studying are called *dendrologists*. So *dendroid* describes something that "branches" in all directions from a central "trunk" in an irregular way. The word is almost always used by biologists, who often speak of dendroid seaweeds, dendroid moss, and dendroid algae.

<small>dendrology(树木学)是研究树的学问,研究这种学问的人称为 dendrologists(树木学家)。所以 dendroid 描写从"干"向各个方向不规则"分岔"的事物。这个词语几乎总是被生物学家使用。他们经常说到 dendroid 海草、dendroid 苔藓、和 dendroid 海藻。</small>

humanoid \ˈhyü-mə-ˌnȯid\   Looking or acting like a human. (样子或行为)像人的

• We slowly learn that most of Dr. Bennell's friends have been replaced by humanoid substitutes that have emerged from pods. <small>我们慢慢了解到,本奈尔博士多数朋友已被从吊舱中出现的人形替代物取代了。</small>

A *humanoid* robot, sometimes called an *android*, is a robot that resembles a human. Accounts of the yeti, Sasquatch, and Bigfoot continue to fascinate us mainly because of their humanoid characteristics. The idea of creating a monstrous *humanoid*, such as the Jewish golem or Victor Frankenstein's creation, has intrigued us for centuries. "Humanoid Animation" is a standard for creating humanlike figures for video that lets the same figure be used in a variety of 3-D games—some of which have nothing but humanoids for characters.

humanoid robot(人形机器人)有时称为 *android*,是个像人的机器人。雪人、北美野人和大脚野人一直让我们着迷,主要是因为它们具有类似人的特点。创造一个巨大而丑陋的 *humanoid*(类人动物),比如犹太泥人或者维克多·弗兰肯斯坦造的怪物,这一想法几个世纪以来一直让我们着迷。"类人动画"是为电视创造类人角色的标准。这一标准让同一角色被用在各种 3-D 游戏中——其中一些游戏只有类人角色。

Quizzes

A. Fill in each blank with the correct letter:

a. mediocrity   e. intermediary
b. humanoid   f. dendroid
c. median   g. mediate
d. rhomboid   h. deltoid

1. Seen from up close, the mosses turn out to be _____, resembling a colony of tiny trees.

2. What he dislikes most about his body is his narrow shoulders, so the first thing he asked his trainer for was some good _____ exercises.

3. The school's wrestling team includes a couple of big guys, but the _____ weight is only about 160 pounds.

4. She'd been expecting a lot from the kids in the advanced-placement class, so she was dismayed by the _____ of the first papers they passed in.

5. If life is ever discovered on a distant planet, few scientists expect the life-forms to be _____, even if that's what sci-fi films always show.

6. The two kids are always fighting, and their father's main job is to _____ their disputes.

7. The antenna takes the shape of a _____, almost a diamond.

8. These illegal arms deals usually require an _____ who knows both languages and is trusted by both parties.

B. Indicate whether the following pairs of words have the same or different meanings:

1. mediate / exchange   same ____ / different ____
2. deltoid / shoulder muscle   same ____ / different ____
3. intermediary / agent   same ____ / different ____
4. dendroid / treelike   same ____ / different ____
5. mediocrity / ordinariness   same ____ / different ____
6. humanoid / manmade   same ____ / different ____

7. median / so-so   same _____ / different _____
8. rhomboid / shifting shape   same _____ / different _____

SCOP

SCOP, which usually appears in a suffix, comes from the Greek *skopein*, meaning "to look at." In English we have the simple noun *scope*, along with some other words it sometimes stands for: *telescope*, *microscope*, *periscope*, and so on. And have you ever used a *stereoscope*, a device your great-grandparents probably enjoyed, which lets you look through a viewer at two slightly different photographs of the same thing, one with each eye, to enjoy the illusion that you're seeing it in three dimensions?

SCOP 源自希腊语 *skopein*（看），通常以后缀的形式出现。在英语中，我们有相似的名词 *scope*，以及其他一些它有时可以代表的词语：*telescope*（望远镜）、*microscope*（显微镜）、*periscope*（潜望镜），等等。你是否用过 *stereoscope*（立体视镜）呢？这是你曾祖父母可能曾经喜欢过的器具，可以让你透过一个观看器，看到同一个事物两个稍有不同的照片，一只眼睛看到一个，以此享受以三维看到那个事物的错觉。

---

endoscope \ˈen-də-ˌskōp\ A lighted tubular medical instrument for viewing the interior or a hollow organ or body part that typically has one or more channels to permit passage of surgical instruments. 内窥镜；内腔镜

• Possible uses of the endoscope outside of medicine soon became apparent, and soon mechanics were using specially designed endoscopes to view the insides of jet engines. 在医学范围之外可能使用内窥镜，这很快就成为明显事实了，而且技师很快就在使用特别设计的内窥镜查看喷气式引擎的内部了。

The Greek prefix *endo-* means "within, inside," so around 1860 an early crude instrument for looking deep inside the body was named the endoscope. But modern *endoscopy* required the invention of the electric lightbulb and then fiber-optic cable, so the first modern endoscopes date only to 1967. An endoscope may be inserted through a natural passageway (for example, through the nose or down the esophagus) or through a tiny cut in the skin. A tiny camera with a light at the end of the cable sends back images onto a screen, and the surgeon uses special instruments that work through a tube alongside the cable. There are now specialized types of endoscopes for every part of the body, where they can take tissue samples, cut out small growths, or remove foreign objects.

希腊语前缀 *endo-* 意思是"在……之内，在……内部"，所以，在 1860 年前后，一个用来检查身体内部的原始、粗糙的仪器被命名为内腔镜。但是，现代 *endoscopy*（内窥镜检查）的使用在电灯泡和光纤电缆发明之后才成为可能，所以，第一个现代内窥镜只能追溯到 1967 年。内窥镜可以插入天然通道（比如鼻子或者食管），或者插入皮肤上微小的切口。一个电缆尽头带有灯的微小照相机将图像发回到屏幕上，医生使用与电缆并排的管子进行工作的特殊仪器。现在有专门类型的内窥镜，用于身体各部分，它们可以采集组织样本，切除微小的赘生物，或者除去异物。

arthroscopic \ˌär-thrə-ˈskä-pik\ Relating to a fiber-optic instrument that is inserted through an incision near a joint to examine the joint's interior. 关节镜的

• The day he scheduled the fourth arthroscopic operation on his knee was the day he decided to hang up his football cleats. 他安排第四次膝盖关节镜手术的日子,是他决定把足球防滑鞋挂起来的日子。

In Greek, *arthron* means "joint." *Arthritis* is a condition of swollen and painful joints, and *arthropods* are animals (including insects, arachnids, and crustaceans) that have a segmented body and jointed limbs. Arthroscopic surgery, or *arthroscopy*, has revolutionized the treatment of joint injuries. It's performed with an arthroscope, a specialized type of endoscope (see above). A tiny camera and a light are inserted through a small cut in the skin, and through another cut nearby a tiny surgical instrument, controlled through its own cable, is inserted. The surgeon then performs the operation, guided by the images sent back via the fiber-optic cable. Most patients walk out of the hospital on crutches the same day, though full recovery may take a couple of months. 在希腊语中,*arthron* 意思是"关节"。*arthritis*(关节炎)是关节肿大、疼痛这种状况,*arthropods*(节肢动物)是身体分成部分、肢体有关节的动物。*arthroscopic* surgery(关节镜手术),或称 *arthroscopy*,使关节损伤治疗发生了巨大变化。这种治疗用的是关节镜,一种特殊类型的内窥镜(见上文)。一个微小的照相机和灯通过皮肤上的小切口插入,从附近另一个切口插入一个通过自己的电缆控制的微小仪器。之后,医生开始手术,由通过光电缆发回的图像来指导。大多数病人当天就拄着拐杖走出医院了,虽然完全康复可能需要几个月时间。

laparoscopy \ˌla-pə-ˈräs-kə-pē\ Examination of the interior of the abdomen using a fiber-optic instrument inserted through a cut in the abdomen's wall. 腹腔镜检查

• The initial laparoscopy involves inserting the cable through a tiny cut and inflating the internal area with carbon dioxide so that a good-sized area will become visible. 第一次腹腔镜检查需要从一个小切口插入电缆,并用二氧化碳给内部区域充气,从而可以看到大片区域。

Since *laparo*- means "wall of the abdomen," a *laparoscope* is an endoscope designed especially to examine the abdomen. Common *laparoscopic* surgeries include removal of the gallbladder, appendix, or kidney, and removal of tumors from abdominal organs. Like the other endoscopic surgeries, *laparoscopy*, as compared to traditional surgery, reduces risk of bleeding, pain following the operation, patient recovery time, and length of hospital stays. 由于 *laparo* 意思是"腹腔壁",*laparoscope* 就是专门用来检查腹腔的内窥镜。普通的 *laparoscopic*(腹腔镜的)手术包括切除胆囊、阑尾或者肾脏,以及切除腹部器官的肿瘤。与其他内窥镜手术一样,laparoscropy(腹腔镜手术)与传统手术相比,可以减少流血的风险、术后疼痛、病人康复时间以及住院时间。

oscilloscope \ä-ˈsi-lə-ˌskōp\ An instrument that shows visual images of changing electrical current on a screen. 示波器

• An oscilloscope next to the bed was monitoring her vital signs, but otherwise it was hard for a visitor to be sure she was even alive. 床边一个示波器正监视她的生命体征,但除此

以外，探视的人很难肯定她甚至还活着。

In Latin *oscillare* means "to swing," and our word *oscillation* usually means "vibration" or "variation," especially in a changing flow of electricity. The *oscilloscope* basically draws a graph of an electrical signal. Since all kinds of physical phenomena can be converted into an electric voltage, oscilloscopes can be used to measure such things as sound, light, and heat. So an oscilloscope can analyze how one clarinet's sound is different from another's, or how one bulb's light differs from another's. Auto mechanics use oscilloscopes to measure engine vibrations; doctors use them to measure brain waves. Audio technicians use oscilloscopes to diagnose problems in audio equipment; TV and radio technicians use them to diagnose TV and radio problems. But oscilloscopes are most essential today to high-tech electronics experimentation.

在拉丁语中，*oscillare* 意思是"摇摆"，我们的单词 *oscillation* 通常的意思是"摇摆不定"或者"变化"，尤其是指在变化的电流之中。示波器基本用来画出电信号的示意图。由于所有种类的物理现象都可以转化成电压，示波器可用来测量诸如声、光、热之类的事物。所以，示波器可以分析一个单簧管的声音与另一个的声音如何不同，或者一个灯泡的光与另一个的光如何不同。机械技师使用示波器测量引擎的颤动，医生使用示波器测量脑波。音响师使用示波器诊断音频设备问题，电视和无线电技师用示波器诊断电视和无线电问题。但是，示波器在今天对高科技电子实验最重要。

TRANS

TRANS comes from Latin to indicate movement "through, across, or beyond" something. *Translation* carries a writer's meaning from one language to another. A television signal is sent or *transmitted* through the air (or a cable) to your set. When making your way through a city on public *transportation*, you may have to *transfer* from one bus or subway to another.

TRANS 源自拉丁语，表示"穿过或超过"某物。*translation*（翻译）将作家的意思从一种语言传入另一种语言。电视信号通过空气（或电缆）*transmitted*（被传送）到你的电视机。乘坐公共 *transportation*（交通工具）穿过城市时，你可能得从一辆车或地铁 *transfer*（转乘）另一辆。

transient \ˈtran-shē-ənt\ (1) Not lasting long; short-lived. 短暂的；转瞬即逝的 (2) Passing through a place and staying only briefly. 短暂居留的；暂住的

● It's a college town, so much of its population is transient. 这是一个大学城，很多人口都是流动人口。

A *transient* mood is one that passes quickly. A brief stopover in a town on your way to somewhere else is a transient visit. A summer job on a farm is transient work, lasting only as long as the growing season. You may occasionally experience a transient episode of dizziness or weakness, which vanishes without a trace. As a noun, *transient* means a person who passes through a place, staying only briefly. The hoboes and tramps of earlier years were some of our most colorful transients, known for hopping freight trains, panhandling on the street, and stealing homemade pies cooling on the windowsill.

transient 情绪转瞬即逝。前往某地的路上，在一个城镇中途停留不久，这是 transient 访问。夏天在一家农场干活，这是 transient 工作,持续时间只有生长季那么长。你可能偶尔体验 transient 眩晕或者虚弱,但它很快消失得无影无踪。作为名词,transient 指路过某地、短暂停留的人。早期的季节工人和流浪汉是最有趣的 transients,以登上货物列车、沿街乞讨、偷吃晾在窗台上的自制馅饼声名远扬。

transfiguration \ trans-ˌfi-gyə-ˈrā-shən \   A change in form or appearance; a glorifying spiritual change. 变形;(形状或外表)的变化;崇高

• Being in love caused a complete transfiguration of her personality. 恋爱使她性格彻底变化。

The Gospels relate that one day Jesus took three disciples up a mountain, where they witnessed his transfiguration into divine form: his face shone like the sun, his garments became brilliantly white, and a voice from heaven proclaimed that this was the son of God. Transfiguration was first used in English as the name of this biblical event, and the Feast of the Transfiguration remains the name of a holy day. So the word has always kept a somewhat religious—and almost always positive—tone. A face may be transfigured by joy, and an "ugly duckling" may be slowly transfigured into a radiant beauty. And as Harry Potter fans know, transfiguration is a subject long taught at the Hogwarts School by Minerva McGonagall.

《福音书》说,有一天,耶稣带着三个门徒上山,门徒目睹了耶稣变成了神的样子:他的脸像太阳一般发光,他的衣服白得发亮,一个声音从天空宣告说,这就是上帝的儿子。transfiguration(变容)在英语中首次使用就是作为这一事件的名称,Feast of the Transfiguration(主显圣容节)一直是这一神圣日子的名称。所以,这一词语一直保持着一些宗教的——而且总是正面的——气氛。一张脸可能因为快乐而改变,"丑小鸭"可能慢慢变成神采奕奕的美人。哈利·波特的粉丝都知道,变形是米勒娃·麦格在霍格沃茨学校长期教授的一个科目。

transponder \ tran-ˈspän-dər \   A radio or radar set that emits a radio signal after receiving such a signal. 转发器

• When a patient is admitted to an emergency room, an implanted transponder can relay important data about his or her medical history. 病人进入诊室之后,一个内置的转发器会转发其病史的重要信息。

This word was coined during World War II by simply joining pieces of the words transmitter and responder. Transponders are basic to modern aviation and communications satellites, and they're finding new uses in fields such as medicine as well. But they're now also part of everyday life. The "E-ZPass" that lets you drive right through turnpike tollbooths is a transponder, and the car you're driving may not even start unless it recognizes the signal from your personal key's transponder. In a big crowded foot race, you may carry a tiny transponder on your shoe that records when you cross both the starting line and the finish line.

这一词语是第二次世界大战期间将 transmitter 和 responder 两个词语各一部分连在一起造出来的。transponders(转发器)对现代航空和通信卫星来说必不可少,而且在诸如医学这样的领域也正找到新的用途。不过,它们现在也是日常生活的一部分。让你直接开过公路收费站的电子收费系统就是一个转发器,而且你驾驶的车,如果没有识别个人钥匙上转发器的信号,可能也发动不了。在人群拥挤的竞走比赛中,你可能在鞋子上携带一个微小的转发器,当你离开起跑线和穿过终点线时它都会进行记录。

• 675 •

transcendent \tran-ˈsen-dənt\ (1) Exceeding or rising above usual limits; supreme. 超常的；非凡的 (2) Beyond comprehension; beyond ordinary experience or material existence. 无法理解的；超验的

• Despite the chaos around her she remained calm, with a transcendent smile on her face. 周围一片混乱，但她仍保持平静，脸上是超脱的微笑。

The Latin verb *scandere* means "to climb," so *transcend* has the basic meaning of climbing so high that you cross some boundary. A transcendent experience is one that takes you out of yourself and convinces you of a larger life or existence; in this sense, it means something close to "spiritual." The American writers and thinkers known as the *Transcendentalists*, including Ralph Waldo Emerson and Henry David Thoreau, believed in the unity of all creation, the basic goodness of humankind, and the superiority of spiritual vision over mere logic. When we speak of the transcendent importance of an issue such as climate change, we may mean that everything else on earth actually depends on it.

拉丁语动词 *scandere* 意思是"攀登"，所以 *transcend* 的基本意思是攀登得如此之高，以至于可以穿过某种界限。*transcendent*（超凡的）经历就是让你超脱自己，使你相信有更伟大的生命或体验，在这个意义上，其意思接近 *spiritual*（精神的）。被称为 *Transcendentalists*（超验主义者）的美国作家和思想家，包括拉尔夫·沃尔多·爱默生和亨利·大卫·梭罗，相信所有创造物的统一、人类基本的善良以及精神远见高于纯粹逻辑。

Quizzes

A. Indicate whether the following pairs of words have the same or different meanings：

1. transient / temporary   same ____ / different ____
2. transcendent / sublime   same ____ / different ____
3. arthroscopic / insect-viewing   same ____ / different ____
4. oscilloscope / underwater viewer same ____ / different ____
5. transfiguration / transformation same ____ / different ____
6. endoscope / electron microscope same ____ / different ____
7. transponder / radio signaler   same ____ / different ____
8. laparoscopy / abdomen examination same ____ / different ____

B. Fill in each blank with the correct letter：

a. transcendent   e. transponder
b. oscilloscope   f. laparoscopy
c. transient   g. transfiguration
d. arthroscopic   h. endoscope

1. The mechanic always lets her watch the screen of the _____ as he tries to diagnose the sources of her engine's problems.

2. Painters are well aware of how _____ the color effects of the sunset are, and how the sky often looks completely different after five minutes.

3. With _____ surgery, knee operations now take only an hour or so, and the patient leaves the office on crutches soon afterward.

4. The community is surrounded by a high wall, and the gate opens only when signaled by a resident's _____.

5. Today there's a specialized type of _____ for looking inside practically every part of the body.

6. On the rare occasions when he conducts nowadays, the critics rave about his _____ performances of the great Mahler symphonies.

7. The _____ revealed a small stomach tumor, which appeared not to be cancerous.

8. Painters have tried to depict Jesus' _____ on the mountaintop, while realizing that it's probably impossible to do with mere paint.

PRO is an important prefix, with a couple of quite different broad meanings. In this section, we'll look at words in which *pro-* has the basic meaning "for" or "favoring." Everyone knows words like *pro-democracy* and *pro-American*, but other *pro-* words may not be quite so self-explanatory.

PRO 是一个重要的前缀,有两三个截然不同的宽泛意思。在这一部分,我们研究一下几个单词,其中的 *pro-* 都有着"为了"或者"偏爱"这一基本意思。每个人都认识 *pro-democracy* 和 *pro-American* 这两个单词,但是,其他含有 *pro-* 的单词不一定那么意思明确。

---

proactive\prō-ˈak-tiv\ Acting in anticipation of future problems, needs, or changes. 积极主动的;主动出击的

• Our president prides himself on being proactive, and is always imagining situations the company might be facing in three or four years. 我们的总裁以具有远见为骄傲,总是想象公司在未来三四年会面临什么情况。

People who tend to *react* to a problem only when it's gotten serious could be called *reactive* people. Until recently, *reactive* (in this sense) didn't really have an antonym. So *proactive* was coined to describe the kind of person who's always looking into the future in order to be prepared for anything. A good parent attempts to be proactive on behalf of his or her children, trying to imagine the problems they might be facing in a few months or years. A company's financial officers study the patterns of the company's earnings to make sure it won't risk running short of cash at any point in the next year or two. *Proactive* has only been around a few decades, and it can still sometimes sound like a fashionable buzzword.

问题严重了才 *react*(做出反应)的人,可以说是 *reactive*(有反应能力的)人。直到最近,*reactive*(在这个意思上)并没有真正的反义词。所以 *proactive* 被造出来以用来形容为了有备无患总是考虑未来的人。好的父母努力为自己的孩子想到未来,预见他们在未来几个月或者几年内可能面临的问题。一个公司的财政官员研究该公司的收益模式,以确保在未来一两年任何时候都不会有资金短缺的危险。*proactive* 才出现几年时间,有时候听起来仍然像是一个时髦的流行语。

pro bono \ˌprō-ˈbō-nō\ Being, involved in, or doing professional work, and especially legal work, donated for the public good. 无偿服务的；公益性的

• The law firm allows her to do several hours of pro bono work every week, and she devotes it to helping poor immigrant families. 这家律师事务所允许她每周做几个小时的公益性工作，她就借此帮助贫穷的移民家庭。

In Latin, *pro bono publico* means "for the public good"; in English we generally shorten the phrase to *pro bono*. Donating free legal help to those who need it has long been a practice of American law firms; the American Bar Association actually recommends that all lawyers donate 50 hours a year. Pro bono work is sometimes donated by nonlegal firms as well. For example, an advertising firm might produce a 60-second video for an environmental or educational organization, or a strategic-planning firm might prepare a start-up plan for a charity that funds shelters for battered women. 在拉丁语中，*pro bono publico* 意思是"为了公众的利益"；在英语中，我们通常将其缩略为 *pro bono*。为需要者提供免费法律帮助，这一直是美国律师事务所的一个做法，美国律师协会实际上建议所有律师每年免费工作五十小时。非法律性公司有时也无偿做些公益性工作。比如，一家广告公司可能为环境或者教育组织制作一个六十秒的录像，或者一个战略策划公司可能为资助受虐妇女收容所的慈善机构制定一个开工方案。

proponent \prə-ˈpō-nənt\ One who argues in favor of something; advocate. 倡导者；支持者；拥护者

• The new governor is a proponent of a longer school year, and he's gotten a lot of support from parents. 新一任州长支持延长学年，已经得到了很多家长的支持。

Proponent comes from the same Latin word as *propose*, so a proponent is someone who proposes something, or at least supports it by speaking and writing in favor of it. Thus, for example, proponents of casinos argue that they create jobs, whereas proponents of a casino ban—that is, casino *opponents*—argue that they're corrupting and they take money away from people who can't afford it. As a rule, just about anything important that gets proposed also gets *opposed*. *proponent* 与 *propose*（建议；提议）源自同一个拉丁语单词，所以 proponent 是 propose 某事或者至少通过语言和文字支持它的人。这样，比如支持建立赌场的人认为，这可以创造更多的工作岗位，而支持禁止赌场的人，也就是赌场 *opponents*（反对者）认为，赌场使人堕落腐化，吞掉赌不起的人的钱。通常，几乎任何得到提议的重要问题都会 *opposed*（受到反对）。

pro forma \prō-ˈfȯr-mə\ Done or existing as something that is required but that has little true meaning or importance. 流于形式的；摆样子的

• The letter she received from him after her husband's death struck her as pro forma, and she knew the old friendship between the two men had never really been repaired. 丈夫去世后，她收到了他的信，那信让她感觉只是做做样子。她知道这两个男人之间的友谊从没有真正恢复。

A lot of things are done for the sake of appearances. A teacher might get officially observed and evaluated every three years, even though everyone knows

UNIT 28

she's terrific and the whole thing is strictly *pro forma*. A critic might say that a orchestral conductor gave a pro forma performance, since his heart wasn't in it. A business owner might make a pro forma appearance at the funeral of a politician's mother, never having met her but maybe hoping for a favor from her son sometime in the future. In business, *pro forma* has some special meanings; a pro forma invoice, for example, will list all the items being sent but, unlike a true invoice, won't be an actual bill.

很多事情都是为了做做样子。一位教师即使谁都知道她工作很出色,可能也要每三年时间就接受一次正式观察和评价,这整件事情完全是 *pro forma*(流于形式)。一位评论家可能会说某个交响乐队指挥只是摆摆样子,因为他的心不在这上面。一位公司老板可能遵循惯例出席某个政治家母亲的葬礼,虽与逝者未曾谋面,但希望将来得到他儿子的帮助。在商业上,*pro forma* 有些特殊意思。比如,一个 *pro forma*(形式)发票会列出发送的所有货物,但与真正的发票不同的是,这不是真正的账单。

PRO, in its other broad meaning, means "before, in front of." So, for example, to *proceed* means "to move out in front"; to *progress* means to "to move forward"; and somebody *prominent* stands out, as if he or she were actually standing out in front of the crowd.

PRO 另一个宽泛的意思是"在……之前,在……前面"。所以,比如 *proceed* 这个词语,意思就是"在前面移动";*progress* 意思是"前进";*prominent*(杰出的)人很突出,好像他或她真的站在人群前面。

protrude \prō-ˈtrüd\   To jut out from the surrounding surface or context. 突出;鼓出

• As he leaned over, she noticed something protruding from under his jacket, and realized with a sickening feeling that he was armed. 他弯腰时,她注意到有个东西从他夹克衫下面突出来,于是感到不妙,意识到他携带武器了。

Since *trudere* means "to thrust" in Latin, *protrude* means basically "to thrust forward." If your neighbors' patio protrudes over your property boundary, you may want to discuss it with them. A *protruding* disc in your spine may have to be operated on sooner or later; superficial *protrusions*, such as corns or bunions, tend to be less serious than more deeply rooted ones.

由于 *trudere* 在拉丁语中意思是"冲",*protrude* 的基本意思就是"向前冲"。如果邻居家的露台延伸到了你的地产界限之内,你可能想跟他们谈谈这件事。你脊椎中一个 *protruding*(突出的)椎间盘可能迟早需要做手术;表面的 *protrusions*(突出物),比如鸡眼或者脚部肿块,往往不如扎根深处的那么严重。

prophylaxis \ˌprō-fə-ˈlak-səs\   Measures designed to preserve health and prevent the spread of disease. 疾病预防措施

• For rabies, prophylaxis in the form of vaccines for cats and dogs is much better than treating them after being bitten. 对狂犬病来说,采取给猫狗注射疫苗的预防措施,比被咬之后再治疗要好得多。

In Greek, *phylax* means "guard," so *prophylactic* measures guard against

• 679 •

disease by taking action ahead of time. Thus, for example, before the polio vaccine became available, *prophylaxis* against polio included avoiding crowds and public swimming pools. These days a well-known kind of *prophylactic* is used to prevent sexually transmitted diseases; but prophylactic measures only work when people use them.

在希腊语中，*phylax* 意思是"防卫"，所以，*prophylactic*（疾病预防的）措施通过提前采取行动预防疾病。因此，比如在出现小儿麻痹症疫苗之前，抵御小儿麻痹症的 prophylaxis（疾病预防措施）包括远离人群和公共游泳池。今天，一种有名的 *prophylactic*（预防药）被用来预防性病，但是疾病预防措施只有在人们使用时才有用。

promulgate\ˈprä-məl-ˌgāt\ (1) To proclaim or make public. 宣布；公布（2）To put (a law) into effect. 实施（法律）

• The country's new constitution was officially promulgated in a grand ceremony at the presidential palace. 该国在总统府举行盛大仪式，新宪法正式实施。

All laws need to be made public in some way so that citizens may know if they're in danger of breaking them. Since they can't be expected to go into effect until the population knows they exist, *promulgate* has the two meanings "proclaim" and "put into effect." In ancient Greece and Rome, when most people couldn't read, a new written law would actually be proclaimed in a public place; we've all seen such scenes in historical movies. But today *promulgation* of a law generally occurs simply by its being published in an official government publication and on a government Web site. New laws are also often reported in newspapers and on TV, though rarely in complete form.

所有宪法都要以某种方式公布出来，借此让公众知道自己是否有可能违法。只有当公众知道了法律的存在，法律才有可能实施，所以，*promulgate* 有两个意思"公布，宣布"和"实施"。在古希腊和古罗马，多数人不识字，新的成文法实际上要在公共场所进行宣布，我们在历史电影里都见过这种场面。但是今天，一项法律的 *promulgation*（实施），通常只要在政府的官方出版物和政府网址上出版就开始了。新的法律也经常在报纸或电视上进行报道，尽管很少以完整形式出现。

prologue\ˈprō-ˌlȯg\ (1) An introduction to a literary work. （文学作品的）序言 (2) An introductory event or development. 序幕

• The Boston Tea Party of 1773 turned out to be a prologue to the American Revolution. 1773 年的波士顿倾茶事件最后成了美国革命的序幕。

In ancient Greek drama, the *prologos* (a word that means basically "speaking before") was the opening portion of the play, before the entry of the all-important chorus. It might be spoken by a single actor, maybe playing a god, who would "set the scene" for the audience. Playwrights today instead often provide the same kind of "scene-setting" information through dialogue near the play's beginning; in movies, it may appear (as in the "Star Wars" series) in the form of actual written text. In a nonfiction book, the lead-in is now usually called a *preface* or *introduction*; novels rarely provide any introduction at all. Still, *prologue* remains a useful word for nonliterary purposes. The saying "The past is prologue" tells us that, in real life, almost everything can be a prologue to what follows it.

在古希腊戏剧中，*prologos*（这个词语基本意思是"在……之前说"）是极其重要的合唱队登台前的戏剧开幕部分。它可能是一个演员朗诵的，该演员可能演一个神，这个神会为观众看戏"做准备"。当今戏剧家却常常通过在戏剧即将正式开始前通过人物对话提供同样的"准备"信息；在电影中，它会以书面文本形式出现（比如《星球大战》通过人物对话）。在非小说书籍中，引子通常叫做 *preface*（前言）或者 *introduction*（引言）；小说很少提供什么引言。不过，*prologue* 对于非文学目的来说一直是个有用的词语。"过去的都是序幕"这一谚语告诉我们，在现实生活中，几乎一切都可能成为随后发生的事情的序幕。

Quizzes

A. Fill in each blank with the correct letter:

a. pro bono   e. pro forma
b. proponent   f. prologue
c. prophylaxis   g. proactive
d. promulgate   h. protrude

1. For the doctor, _____ requires the use of gloves and sometimes masks, and constant hand washing throughout the day.

2. The only part of being a lawyer that she really liked was her _____ work helping poor families with their housing problems.

3. Talk-show hosts were helping to _____ a made-up story about a scandal involving the First Lady.

4. He claims we're falling behind in education, which is why he's a _____ of a longer school year.

5. Economists worry that these scattered bank failures may turn out to be a _____ to a serious financial crisis.

6. He's gotten terribly thin, and the bones of his arms now _____ from under his skin.

7. Her apology was strictly _____, and didn't sound sincere at all.

8. The company has never spent much time thinking about its future, and it really needs to become more _____.

B. Match the definition on the left to the correct word on the right:

1. disease prevention   a. prophylaxis
2. formal   b. promulgate
3. introduction   c. prologue
4. broadcast   d. pro bono
5. backer   e. protrude
6. bulge   f. proponent
7. forward-looking   g. pro forma
8. unpaid   h. proactive

RE is a prefix which, like *pro-* (see PRO, p. 677), has more than one meaning. In this section, we'll focus on the meaning "again." We use *re-* words with this meaning every day—*redo*, *reheat*, *recheck*, *reread*, *resell*, *repaint*, etc.—and we feel free to make up new ones as needed. But in plenty of other *re-* words, the meaning isn't so obvious.

RE 这一前缀，就像 *pro-*（见 PRO，第 677 页）一样，有不止一个意思。在这一部分，我们关注"又"这一意思。我们每天使用 *re-* 起首的单词——*redo*, *reheat*, *recheck*, *reread*, *resell*, *repaint*, 等等，而且必要时我们还自由地创造新词。但是，在很多其他 *re-* 起首的单词中，"又"这一意思并不那么明显。

remorse \ri-ˈmȯrs\ A deep regret arising from a sense of guilt for past wrongs. 遗憾；懊悔

● Remorse for the accident that occurred that night seems to have altered the course of the senator's life. 参议员对那天晚上发生的事故深感懊悔，这似乎改变了他的生活。

In Latin, *mordere* means "to bite"; thus, *remorse* is something that "gnaws" at you over and over. In criminal court, judges are always looking for signs that a convicted felon is suffering remorse for his crime; if not, the judge may well lengthen his sentence or deny him parole after serving part of it. Remorse is stronger than mere regret; real remorse is the kind of thing that may last a lifetime.

在拉丁语中，*mordere* 意思是"咬"。这样，*remorse* 就是反复"咬"的东西。在刑事法庭上，法官总是寻找已定罪的重罪犯为自己的罪行感到懊悔的迹象。如果没有这一迹象，法官可能延长其刑期，或者在其服刑一段时间后拒绝给予假释。懊悔绝非仅仅是遗憾，真正的懊悔是那种持续一生的感觉。

reiterate \rē-ˈi-tə-ˌrāt\ To state or do over again or repeatedly. 重申；反复说；重做；反复做

● At the end of every class, Professor Lewis reiterates that we should get an early start on our term papers. 每次下课前，教授都再说一次，我们应该早些动手写学期论文。

In Latin, *iterum* means "again," so *reiterate* has the basic meaning of "repeat over and over." Our word *iteration* is used a lot by computer programmers today, often meaning a repeated response to program instructions that gets something closer to its final form, but also often meaning a new version of something, such as a program. But a *reiteration* is simply a repeat or several repeats.

在拉丁语中，*iterum* 意思是"又一次"，所以 *reiterate* 有"一再重复"这一基本意思。我们的 *iteration* 一词常常被计算机程序员使用，经常表示对使某物更加接近最终形式的程序指令反复作出的反应。但有时也指某事物的新版本，例如一个新程序。但是，*reiteration* 只是一次重复或者几次重复。

rejuvenate \ri-ˈjü-və-ˌnāt\ To make young or youthful again; to give new vigor to. 使……年轻；给……注入新活力

● He was in bad shape after his wife's death, but everyone says he's been rejuvenated by his remarriage. 妻子去世后，他身体状况很差。不过，大家说他再婚后他焕发青春了。

Juvenis, Latin for "young," can be seen in a word such as *juvenile*. *Rejuvenation* is something that can be carried out on a creaky old house, a clunker of a car, a sluggish career, a weak economy, or a company that's lost its edge, but *rejuvenate* and *rejuvenation* are probably used most often for talking about our physical selves. Ads for lotions promise skin rejuvenation; diet-book covers show rejuvenated (or maybe just young) models bursting with health. We still seem to be searching for that "Fuente de la Juventud" that Juan Ponce de León failed to discover five hundred years ago.

juvenis 在拉丁语中意思是"年轻",可以在 *juvenile*(少年的)这样的词语中看出其存在。*rejuvenation*(恢复青春活力)是可以在摇摇欲坠的老房子、破旧不堪的汽车、停滞不前的事业、衰弱的经济或者失去竞争力的公司身上实施的东西。但是,*rejuvenate* 和 *rejuvenation* 可能更多地用于我们自己的身体,比如承诺使皮肤恢复细嫩的护肤液、展示着青春焕发(或者本来就年轻的)活力四射的模特的饮食书籍封面。我们似乎还在寻找胡安·庞塞·德·莱昂五百年前未能发现的"青春泉"。

reconcile \ˈre-kən-ˌsīl\ （1）To make agree. 调和;使和谐一致 （2）To make friendly again. 使和解;使和好如初

● Now she has to reconcile her liking for her brother-in-law with the news that he was picked up for armed robbery last week. 她喜欢姐夫,现在却不得不接受姐夫上周因持械抢劫被捕的消息。

In Latin, *conciliare* means "to calm, soothe"; thus, *reconcile* means essentially "to calm again." Warring friends can often be reconciled by a nice note or apology. When you're faced with two things that don't square very well, you may have to reconcile them, the way a scientist might try to reconcile the differing results from two research projects. The U.S. House and Senate, in a process called *reconciliation*, try to produce one final bill from two different versions that they've passed separately. To reconcile yourself to something means to get used to it; thus, you may need to reconcile yourself to not getting to the beach next summer, or you may have reconciled yourself to the idea of your daughter in the Peace Corps marrying a Mongolian goat herder.

在拉丁语中,*conciliar* 意思是"使……平静,安慰";所以,*reconcile* 基本意思是"使……再次平静"。关系不和的朋友可以因为一封善意的书信或者道歉而和解。当你面临不太相符的两件事情时,你可能不得不进行协调,正如科学家努力协调两个研究项目的不同结果那样。美国众议院和参议院,在一个称为 *reconciliation* 的过程中,努力从他们分别通过的两个不同版本产生一个最终法案。reconcile 你自己和某事,意思是习惯它;因此,你可能需要接受明年夏天不能去海滩这件事,或者你可能已经接受你那加入维和部队的女儿和蒙古放山羊的人结婚这件事了。

RE, in its other main sense, means "back" or "backward." Since doing something again means going back to it, the two senses are actually related; still, the meaning of *re-* in most words is pretty clearly one or the other. So a *rebound* comes back at you; to *recall* means to "call back" a memory; and to *react* is to "act back" at someone else's action.

· 683 ·

RE 主要意思是"后"或者"向后"。由于重新做某事意味着回去了,所以这两个意思实际上是有联系的。很明显,*re* 的意思在大多数词语中要么是这个,要么是另一个。所以,一个 *rebound*(反弹球)又回到你身边;*recall*(回忆)意思是"召回"某个记忆;*react*(反映)是对另一个人的行为"做出回应"。

reciprocal \ ri-ˈsi-prə-kəl \ （1）Done, given, or felt equally by both sides. 互惠的;相互的 （2）Related to each other in such a way that one completes the other or is the equal of the other. 互补的;互等的

• They had done us a great favor, so as a reciprocal gesture we invited them for a weekend on the island. 他们帮了我们一个大忙,所以我们邀请他们去岛上度周末,算是一种互惠的表示吧。

In Latin, *reciprocus* means "returning the same way" or "alternating." So in a *reciprocating engine*, like the one in your car, the pistons move back and forth, and that motion is transformed into the rotary motion of the crankshaft. A *reciprocal* is a pair of numbers (such as 5/6 and 6/5) that can be multiplied to produce 1. *Reciprocity* (with the accent on the third syllable) between two nations means they agree to recognize certain things granted in one country as being valid in the other—for example, your driver's license.

在拉丁语中,*reciprocus* 意思是"以同样方式回报"或者"交替"。所以在 *reciprocating* engine(往复式发动机)中,比如你车上的那个,活塞来回移动,这一运动被转变成曲轴的旋转运动。*reciprocal* 是一对可以相乘后得出 1 的数字(比如 5/6 和 6/5)。两个国家之间的 *reciprocity*(重音在第三个音节)指他们同意将一个国家法律批准的事物在另一国家认可为有效,比如驾照。

rebut \ ri-ˈbət \ （1）To oppose by argument. 反驳;驳斥 （2）To prove to be wrong. 证明……是错误的

• The claims about receiving payoffs from builders were eventually rebutted by the mayor's office, but the damage had been done. 从建筑公司收受回报的说法,最终被市长办公室证明是错误的,不过造成的损失无法挽回了。

The *-but* in *rebut* once meant basically "butt," so *rebut*'s original meanings were "to drive or beat back" and "to attack with violent language." *Rebuttals* can still be rather violent, as anyone who has watched some heated moments in a presidential debate can testify. The word is often used by lawyers, since the lawyer for the accused or for the party being sued almost always tries to rebut the charges against his or her client; but it's also used in plenty of contexts outside the courtroom.

rebut 中的 *-but* 曾经的基本意思是"用头顶",所以 *rebut* 最初的意思是"赶走或击退"和"用激烈语言攻击"。*rebuttals*(反驳)仍然可以很激烈,任何看过总统辩论的人都可以证实这一点。这一词语律师经常使用,因为被告人或者被起诉方的律师几乎总是努力反驳对其委托人的指控;不过,法院以外的环境中也经常使用。

revoke \ ri-ˈvōk \ To officially cancel the power or effect of something (such as a law, order, or privilege). 取消;废除;使……无效

• His real-estate license had been revoked after his conviction for fraud three years earlier. 他三年前因欺骗罪被判有罪之后,他的房产经纪人执照被宣布无效。

Since *vocare* means "to call" in Latin (see VOC, p. 147), to revoke is to "call

UNIT 28

back." Your driver's license could be *revoked* after about three convictions for driving under the influence of alcohol; some people's licenses are even revoked for life. You could get your passport revoked if a judge thought you had violated the terms of your bail and suspected you might skip the country. And if you're out of prison on probation and violate the terms of probation, it will probably be revoked and you'll end up back in the slammer.

因为 *vocare* 在拉丁语中意思是"叫,喊"(见 VOC,第 147 页),*revoke* 意思就是"叫回"。在你酒驾三次被判有罪后,你的驾照就被收回了,有些人的驾照甚至被永久收回。如果法官认为你违反了保释的条件,而且怀疑你会悄悄离开该国,你的护照可能会被收回。如果你因为缓刑不用进监狱,但是违反了缓刑条件,缓刑可能被取消,你最终会回到监狱。

regress\ri-ˈgres\ To return to an earlier and usually worse or less developed condition or state. 倒退;退化

• In the years since she had left, the country seemed to have regressed badly, and its corruption and dire poverty had gotten much harder to ignore. 她离开后的那些年,该国似乎严重倒退了,腐败和贫穷更加难以忽视了。

As you might guess, *regress* is the opposite of *progress*. So if a disease regresses, that's generally a good thing, but in most other ways we prefer not to regress. If someone's mental state has been improving, we hope he or she won't start to regress; and when a nation's promising educational system begins to regress, that's a bad sign for the country's future. Economists often distinguish between a *progressive* tax and a *regressive* tax; in a progressive tax, the percentage that goes to taxes gets larger as the amount of money being taxed gets larger, while in a regressive tax the percentage gets smaller. (Rich people prefer regressive taxes.)

你可能会猜到,*regress* 是 *progress* 的反义词。所以,如果一种疾病退化了,这一般来说是好事,但在大多数其他方面,我们更愿意不要这样。如果某人的精神状态在改善,我们希望他或她不要退步;当一个国家很有希望的教育体制开始退步,对该国前途来说不是个好征兆。经济学家经常区别 *progressive*(累进)税和 *regressive*(累退)税。在累进税中,课税对象数额越大,税率越高,而在累退税中,税率降低。(富人更喜欢累退税。)

Quizzes

A. Fill in each blank with the correct letter:

a. remorse   e. reciprocal
b. rebut   f. regress
c. revoke   g. reconcile
d. reiterate   h. rejuvenate

1. State officials may _____ the factory's permit to release larger amounts of heated water into the river.

2. Her outburst at her daughter left her filled with _____ for days afterward.

3. These spas always promise to _____ your skin, and often your spirit as well.

• 685 •

4. She's trying to _____ the image she had of her friend with what she's recently learned about him.

5. The governor has been trying to _____ these new charges against him for days without success.

6. An American university may have a _____ arrangement with a European university, whereby each agrees to take the other's students for a year.

DERM

7. Sometimes our 15-year-old just seems to _____ and start acting the way he did when he was two years younger.

8. In almost every speech she tries to _____ the same few points, since she doesn't trust the voters to remember them otherwise.

B. Indicate whether the following pairs of words have the same or different meanings:

1. revoke / cancel   same ____ / different ____
2. regress / backslide   same ____ / different ____
3. remorse / regret   same ____ / different ____
4. rejuvenate / return   same ____ / different ____
5. reconcile / fight back   same ____ / different ____
6. rebut / send back   same ____ / different ____
7. reciprocal / mutual   same ____ / different ____
8. reiterate / modernize   same ____ / different ____

DERM

comes from the Greek *derma*, meaning "skin." For medical advice on a skin problem such as acne, we may go to a *dermatologist*, or skin specialist. When we get a shot, it's usually with a *hypodermic*, a needle that goes "under the skin" (see HYP/HYPO, p. 51). A *pachyderm* is a "thick-skinned" animal, which most of us just call an elephant.

DERM 源自希腊语 *derma*，意思是"皮肤"。要获得皮肤病（比如粉刺）方面的医学建议，我们去找 *dermatologist*（皮肤病专家）。我们打针时，通常使用 *hypodermic*（皮下注射器），也就是扎到"皮肤下"的针（见 HYP/HYPO，第 51 页）。*pachyderm* 是"厚皮"动物，我们大多数人称其为大象。

dermal \ˈdər-məl\ Relating to the skin and especially to the dermis. 皮肤的；真皮的

• The agency is always studying what can be done to prevent dermal exposure to chemicals in the workplace. 该机构一直研究如何在工作场所防止皮肤接触化学物质。

The word *dermal* often comes up nowadays in connection with cosmetic treatments. Dermal therapy usually means restoring moisture to dry, cracked skin. Dermal fillers such as collagen can be injected to fill in acne scars or reduce wrinkles. These have now been joined by treatments like Botox, which paralyzes facial dermal muscles, again in order to reduce wrinkles (since those dermal muscles are used to form expressions). A synonym for *dermal* is *cutaneous*.

现在，*dermal* 一词的出现常常跟美容有关。Dermal therapy（皮肤疗法）通常的意思是让干燥、龟裂的皮肤恢复水分。dermal fillers（皮肤填充剂），比如胶原蛋白，可以进行注射以填充粉刺瘢痕或者减少皱纹。除了这些，现在又有了保妥适这样的治疗方法，可以麻痹面部皮肤肌肉，还是为了减少皱纹（因为那些肌肉是用来形成表情的）。*dermal* 的一个同义词是 *cutaneous*。

epidermis \ˌe-pə-ˈdər-məs\ The outer layer of the skin. 表皮

- The epidermis is the body's first line of defense against infection, external injury, and environmental stresses. 表皮是身体预防感染、外伤和环境胁迫的第一道防线。

Epidermis includes the Greek prefix *epi-*, meaning "outer" (see EPI, p. 49); thus, the epidermis overlies the *dermis*, or inner layer of skin. The epidermis itself consists of four or five layers; the outermost layer is made of dead cells, which are being shed continuously. The epidermis acts as a physical barrier—a protective wrap over the body's surface, which, by preventing water loss, allows vertebrates to live on land.

epidermis 包括希腊语前缀 *epi-*，意思是"外表的"（见 EPI，第 49 页）；因此，表皮覆盖着真皮，也就是里面一层的皮肤。表皮本身由四到五层构成，最外面一层是死亡的细胞，一直脱落。表皮相当于一个物理障碍——身体表面一层护性的包裹材料，通过防止水分流失，让脊椎动物生活在陆地上。

taxidermist \ˈtak-sə-ˌdər-mist\ One who prepares, stuffs, and mounts the skins of dead animals. 动物标本剥制师

- The taxidermist suggested that the bobcat be displayed in the act of leaping fiercely toward the viewer. 这位动物标本剥制师建议，展示这只短尾猫时，让它处于向观看者猛扑的姿势。

Taxidermists are called on not only by sportsmen and collectors but by museums, movie studios, and advertisers. Taxidermists first remove the skin (with its fur, hair, or feathers), then create a plaster cast of the carcass with which to produce a "mannequin," on which they replace the skin. Producing trophies of lifelike quality that often recreate an exciting moment requires physical skill, attention to detail, and sometimes artistic talent.

请 taxidermists（动物标本剥制师）帮忙的，不但有运动员和收藏家，还有博物馆、电影制片厂和广告公司。他们首先剥皮（连带毛或者羽毛），之后做一个尸体的石膏模型，用来做一个"模特"，之后将皮套上。制造栩栩如生、常常再现激动人心时刻的战利品，需要的是身体技能、对细节的关注，有时候还有艺术天赋。

dermatitis \ˌdər-mə-ˈtī-təs\ Inflammation of the skin. 皮炎

- The only dermatitis she had ever suffered had been the result of playing in poison ivy when she was little. 她就得过一次皮炎，是因为小时候在气根毒藤中玩耍了。

Dermatitis usually appears as a rash, and may cause itching, blisters, swelling, and often scabbing and scaling. It often marks an allergic reaction of some kind. *Contact dermatitis* is caused by something (often a chemical) touching the skin. Atopic dermatitis usually affects the insides of the elbows, the backs of the knees, and the face; generally resulting from an inherited sensitivity, it's often triggered by inhaling something. Eczema, psoriasis, and dandruff are all forms of dermatitis. Even in the worst cases, dermatitis isn't infectious and doesn't produce serious health consequences.

dermatitis(皮炎)通常以皮疹的形式出现,可能引起瘙痒、水疱、肿胀,常常还有结痂和鳞屑脱落。它通常标志着出现了某种过敏反应。*contact dermatitis*(接触性皮炎)由皮肤接触某种东西(通常是化学物质)引起。*atopic dermatitis*(异位性皮炎)通常出现在肘部内侧、膝盖背部和脸部,这种皮炎一般产生于遗传性敏感,经常由吸入某物导致。湿疹、牛皮癣和头皮糠疹都是种种形式的皮炎。即使在最糟糕的情况下,皮炎也不具有传染性,不会产生严重的健康后果。

ENDO

ENDO comes from the Greek *endon*, meaning "within." In English it appears almost always in scientific terms, especially in biology. A nonscientific *endo-* word is *endogamy*, meaning marriage within a specific group as required by custom or law—one of the many customs that can be seen everywhere from the most remote tribes to the highest society in wealthy countries.

ENDO 源自希腊语 *endon*,意思是"在……内部"。在英语中,它几乎总是出现在科学术语中,尤其是生物学术语。一个与科学无关的 *endo-* 起首的词语是 *endogamy*(同族婚姻),意思是风俗或法律要求的某一特定群体内的婚姻。这是可以在各地看到的众多习俗之一,从最偏远的部落到发达国家最高层社会中都有。

endocrine \ˈen-də-krən\ (1) A hormone. 激素 (2) Any of several glands (such as the thyroid) that pour their secretions directly into the blood or lymph. 内分泌腺

● Since the endocrines are so vital to human life, affecting such things as cell growth and blood sugar, the chemicals known as endocrine disrupters can be destructive and even deadly. 激素对人类生命非常重要,会影响诸如细胞生长和血糖,因此,称为内分泌干扰物的化学物质可能具有破坏性,甚至是致命的。

The body's glands remove specific substances from the blood and alter them for rerelease into the blood or removal. Glands such as those that produce saliva and sweat secrete their products through tiny ducts or tubes on or near the body's surface. The glands without ducts, called the *endocrine* glands, instead secrete their products into the bloodstream; the *endo-* root indicates that the secretions are internal rather than on the surface. The endocrine system includes such glands as the pituitary (which controls growth, regulates the other endocrines, and performs many other tasks), the thyroid (another growth gland that also influences metabolism), the adrenals (which secrete adrenaline and steroids), the hypothalamus (which influences sleep and weight regulation), and the ovaries (which produce eggs). Endocrine problems are treated by *endocrinologists*.

人体的腺体从血液中转移某些特定物质,改变其性质,将其释放进入血液或者除去。那些产生唾液和汗液的腺体,通过身体表面或表面附近的微小管道分泌自己的物质。没有管道的腺体称为 *endocrine*(内分泌)腺体,则向血液中分泌自己的物质,*endo* 这一词根表明分泌物在内部而不在表面。内分泌系统包括下列腺体:垂体(控制生长、调节其他腺体、执行其他多种任务)、甲状腺(另外一个控制生长的腺体,还影响新陈代谢)、肾上腺(分泌肾上腺素和类固醇)、下丘脑(影响睡眠和体重调节)、卵巢(产生卵子)。内分泌问题由 *endocrinologists*(内分泌医生)来治疗。

endodontic \ˌen-də-ˈdän-tik\ Relating to a branch of dentistry that deals with the pulp of the teeth. 牙髓学的

• Her dentist told her the problem was endodontic and that she should see a specialist soon to prevent loss of the tooth. 牙科医生说,她的问题跟牙髓有关,应该尽快看专家,不要失去牙齿。

Endodontists, as you might expect from the endo- root, deal with the interior of the tooth. The tooth's enamel, on the outside, covers a thick layer called the dentin; this in turn surrounds the innermost part, called the pulp, a mass of soft tissue through which nerves and blood vessels run. When a tooth has been badly damaged by decay or cracking, producing a risk of dangerous infection of the pulp, a "root canal" procedure is performed by an endodontist. Try to avoid ever getting to know an endodontist; brush your teeth twice daily, floss before bedtime, and never let a cavity go unfilled for long.

endodontists(牙髓病医生),从 endo- 可能可以看出,是处理牙齿内部问题的医生。牙齿的釉质在外面,覆盖着称为 dentin(象牙质)这一厚厚的一层。象牙质则包围着最里面的部分,称为 pulp(牙髓),一种柔软的组织,其中分布有神经和血管。当牙齿因为腐蚀或断裂而严重受损,牙髓有可能受到感染时,牙髓病医生执行一个称为"牙根管填充手术"的程序。尽量避免结识牙髓病医生;每天刷牙两次,睡觉前用牙线剔牙,不要让牙洞留在那里很久都不填充。

endogenous \en-ˈdä-jə-nəs\ Developing or originating within a cell, organ, body, or system. 内源性的;内生的

• Vitamin D can be obtained from food and supplements, but it's also an endogenous vitamin, produced by the body when the skin is exposed to sunlight. 维生素D可以从食物和添加物中获取,但它也是内源性的,皮肤暴露在阳光下就可以产生。

When biologists need to make a distinction between things that are produced within a cell or organ and things that affect it from the outside, they use the terms endogenous and exogenous. It used to be thought, for instance, that mutations in cells always resulted from exogenous causes, until it was discovered that substances in the body, including those called oxidants, could cause them endogenously as well. "Circadian rhythms"—the regular cycles, roughly 24 hours in length, that plants, animals, and humans rely on to regulate their days—are endogenously generated and don't actually depend on the sun for their timing.

当生物学家需要区别细胞或器官内产生的物质和从外界影响它的物质时,他们使用 endogenous(内生的)和 exogenous(外生的)两个词。比如,以前人们认为,细胞内的变异总是由于 exogenous 原因,直到发现体内的物质,包括氧化剂,也可以 endogenously(从内部)引发变异。植物、动物和人类赖以调整自己日子的"昼夜节律"——有规律的周期,大约是二十四小时——是内部产生的,实际上不必依赖太阳来定时。

endorphin \en-ˈdȯr-fən\ Any of a group of proteins in the brain that are able to relieve pain. 内啡肽

• On the final stretch of her daily five-mile run, she could usually count on the endorphins kicking in, giving her that beautiful "runner's high." 她每天跑步五英里,快跑完全程时,内啡肽通常会开始生效,让她享受美好的"跑步者的愉悦感"。

The word *endorphin* was coined, back when the substances were discovered in the 1970s, by joining pieces of *endogenous* and *morphine*, morphine being a narcotic that closely resembles the endorphins and relieves pain in a similar way. Studies suggest that the pain-relieving practice called acupuncture (see p. 556) works by releasing endorphins. Endorphins also seem to play an important role in pregnancy. Though much remains to be learned about the endorphins, the general public seems ready to give them credit for any all-natural high.

endorphin 一词是20世纪70年代这些物质被发现时,用 *endogenous*(内生的)和 *morphine*(吗啡)各一部分造出来的。吗啡是一种很像内啡肽的镇静剂,镇痛方式相似。研究表明,叫作 acupuncture(针灸)(第556页)的这一镇痛法通过释放吗啡肽来发挥作用。吗啡肽在怀孕过程中似乎也起着重要作用。虽然对吗啡肽还有很多需要了解,大众似乎乐意将任何纯天然的快感都归功于它。

Quizzes

Fill in each blank with the correct letter:

a. taxidermist
b. endodontic
c. endogenous
d. dermatitis
e. endocrine
f. dermal
g. endorphin
h. epidermis

1. He had a mild form of _____ that occasionally produced a rash on his upper arms.

2. To get rid of wrinkles, you can have a _____ filler injected into parts of your face.

3. This _____ is released in large quantities during serious physical activity and seems to have important painkilling effects.

4. She has always had bad teeth, and now she's finally having _____ work done on the really rotten ones.

5. Low growth rate in teenagers is often an _____ problem that can be fixed with hormones.

6. The _____ keeps the body waterproof and provides a barrier against infection.

7. They had come across a dead eagle in perfect condition, and a _____ had done a beautiful job of mounting it for display.

8. Vitamin D is an _____ vitamin, but bodies seem to require sunlight to produce it.

Review Quizzes

A. Match the definition on the left to the correct word on the right:

1. go backward   a. transient

2. skin rash
3. brief
4. tree-shaped
5. internally produced
6. repeat
7. refresh
8. declare publicly
9. jut out
10. bring into agreement

b. dendroid
c. protrude
d. regress
e. reconcile
f. endogenous
g. reiterate
h. promulgate
i. dermatitis
j. rejuvenate

B. Fill in each blank with the correct letter:

a. pro forma
b. reciprocal
c. proponent
d. endodontic
e. revoke

f. pro bono
g. dermal
h. remorse
i. reconcile
j. rebut

1. When she tried to _____ the claims her opponent had made, the crowd broke out in jeers.

2. He has always been a _____ of women's issues, particularly government-funded day care.

3. In the past she's gotten _____ silicone injections to erase her facial wrinkles.

4. Most of the _____ work he's done has been for environmental groups that can't afford legal fees.

5. The application process was just _____, since they had already promised her the job.

6. _____ over the accident seems to be the main cause of his depression.

7. They haven't been able to _____ the results of the two studies, which came to very different conclusions.

8. The tooth had been aching for several weeks, but he was still surprised when his dentist told him it would require _____ work.

9. Expensive golf courses sometimes have _____ agreements that enable members to use courses in other cities for the same price.

10. Because of numerous violations, the city is threatening to _____ the nightclub's license to operate.

C. Indicate whether the following pairs of terms have the same or different meanings:

1. prophylaxis / support   same ____ / different ____
2. prologue / extension   same ____ / different ____
3. epidermis / outer skin   same ____ / different ____

• 691 •

4. endogenous / produced inside   same ____ / different ____
5. reiterate / restate   same ____ / different ____
6. endodontic / relating to tooth enamel   same ____ / different ____
7. proactive / anticipating   same ____ / different ____
8. rejuvenate / renew   same ____ / different ____
9. rebut / disprove   same ____ / different ____
10. dermal / skin-related   same ____ / different ____

UNIT 29

NECRO

NECRO comes from the Greek *nekros*, meaning "dead body," so it's not surprising that it shows up in some unappetizing places. A *necrophagous* insect, for instance, is one that feeds on dead bodies; when homicide investigators discover a corpse, they may use the insect evidence to figure out when the person died.
NECRO 源自希腊语 nekros，意思是"尸体"。因此，它出现在没有吸引力的地方并不让人吃惊。比如，necrophagous 昆虫是以死尸为食的昆虫；当凶杀调查人员发现尸体时，他们可能使用昆虫证据推测出死者的死亡时间。

necrosis \nə-ˈkrō-səs\ Death of living tissue, usually within a limited area. (有限范围的组织)坏死

• He had ignored the spider bite for several days, and his doctor was alarmed to see that serious necrosis had set in. 被蜘蛛咬了之后，他几天没管。医生发现组织开始严重坏死时，很是惊恐。

Cells die naturally after a period of time, but may also die as a result of injuries, infections, or cancer. Burns produce necrosis, and the bedsores suffered by nursing-home patients are a form of necrosis. The dreaded condition known as gangrene, in which the dying tissue turns black or green, is another form. When untreated, the dying cells release substances that lead to the death of surrounding cells, so untreated necrosis can lead to death. Treatment usually requires the removal of the *necrotic* tissue, and in severe cases can even involve amputating a limb.
细胞过一段时间会自然死亡，但也可能因为受伤、感染或者癌症而死亡。烧伤导致 necrosis（组织坏死），养老院的病人的褥疮也是一种形式的组织坏死。坏疽这一令人恐惧的疾病是另一种形式，死亡组织变黑或变绿。若不治疗，正在死亡的细胞会释放导致周围细胞死亡的物质。治疗通常需要切除 necrotic（坏死的）组织，情况严重时甚至需要切除肢体。

necromancer \ˈne-krə-ˌman-sər\ One who conjures the spirits of the dead in order to magically reveal the future or influence the course of events. 通灵者

NECRO

• Her specialty is communication with the dead, and she might once have been known as a necromancer, but her sign says simply "Psychic." 她的专长是与亡人交流,她曾经被当作通灵者,但她的招牌上只写着"有特异功能者"。

The practice of *necromancy* goes back as far as the ancient Assyrians and Babylonians and has continued through all the centuries since. In the Middle Ages it became associated with black magic; condemned by the church, it had to be practiced secretly. In Europe a *necromancer* might work in a remote graveyard at night, standing within a magical circle he had drawn to shield himself from the anger of the spirits. The grave of a person who had died suddenly or violently might be plundered for its body parts; the unused energy these were believed to contain made them valuable in the *necromantic* ceremony. But body parts aren't essential to necromancy, which is now practiced by channelers, mediums, and shamans, and even by groups of amateurs sitting around a Ouija board. *necromancy*(通灵)这一做法,可追溯到古代亚述人和巴比伦人时代,此后一直存在。在中世纪,通灵被人跟巫术联系起来了。它受到了教会的谴责,不得不秘密进行。在欧洲,*necromancer*(通灵者)可能夜里在遥远的墓地工作,站在自己画的有魔法的圆圈里,保护自己免遭愤怒的鬼魂的侵害。人突然死亡或者暴死后,可能有人为了其身体部位而盗墓,因为有人相信身体部位中没有使用的能量在 *necromantic*(通灵的)仪式中很有用。但是,这些部位对通灵来说并非必不可少。现在,灵媒、巫医和萨满教僧人都能通灵,连业余人士坐在灵应牌周围也能通灵。

necropolis\nə-ˈkrä-pə-ləs\ A cemetery, especially a large, elaborate cemetery of an ancient city. (尤指古代城市巨大、精致的)墓地

• On Sundays the downtown is like a necropolis, and he was always slightly disturbed by the complete absence of life among all those buildings. 星期天,商业区像个大墓地。楼房之间没有生命迹象,让他有些不安。

With its *-polis* ending, meaning "city" (see POLIS/POLIT, p. 618), a *necropolis* is a "city of the dead." Most of the famous necropolises of Egypt line the Nile River across from their cities. In ancient Greece and Rome, a necropolis would often line the road leading out of a city; in the 1940s a great Roman necropolis was discovered under the Vatican's St. Peter's Basilica. Some more recent cemeteries especially deserve the name necropolis because they resemble cities of aboveground tombs, a necessity in low-lying areas such as New Orleans where a high water table prevents underground burial. *-polis* 意思是"城市"(见 POLIS/POLIT,第618页),*necropolis* 就是"亡人的城市"。古埃及大多数著名的墓地排列在通往城外的路边。20世纪40年代,梵蒂冈的圣彼得大教堂下发现了一个古罗马大墓地。更近些时候发现的墓地尤其配得上 necropolis 这个名字,因为它们像地面坟墓构成的城市。这种坟墓是新奥尔良这样的低洼地区所必需的,因为高地下水位使地下埋葬无法进行。

necropsy\ˈne-ˌkräp-sē\ An autopsy, especially one performed on an animal. (尤指对动物进行的)尸检

• Daisy's sudden death was so mysterious that we paid for a necropsy, and it turned out she'd been a victim of lethal chemicals in our imported dog food. 黛西突然死

亡,太神秘了。我们花钱对其进行尸检,发现她死于狗粮中致命的化学物质。

Human autopsies are generally performed either to determine the cause of death or to observe the deadly effects of a disease for research or education purposes. Autopsies may be necessary when tracking an epidemic; they're also performed to discover whether a death might actually have resulted from murder, and if so, what evidence it might reveal that could help catch the murderer. Animal necropsies are actually more common than human autopsies, since a farmer with livestock is always concerned that whatever killed one animal not pose a threat to the others.

人类 autopsies(尸检)的目的通常是为了确定死因,或者为了研究或教育目的而观察某种疾病的致命影响。要跟踪传染病的发展,尸检可能是必要的。进行尸检也是为了发现死亡是否可能源于谋杀,如果是谋杀,这可能有助于抓住凶手。动物 necropsies(尸检)比人类 autopsies(尸检)更常见,因为养殖牲畜的农民总是担心,让一个动物死亡的东西可能对其他动物构成威胁。

PALEO

PALEO comes from the Greek *palaios*, meaning "ancient"—that is, "older than old." The prefix sometimes gets attached to very recognizable words; *paleobiology*, for instance, deals with the biology of fossil organisms, *paleogeography* is the study of geography in earlier geological eras, and *paleoecology* is the study of the relationship of plants and animals to their environment in those eras.

PALEO 源自希腊语 *paloios*,意思是"古老的",也就是"比老还要老"。这一前缀有时附着在很容易识别的词语上,比如 *paleobiology*(古生物学)的研究对象是化石动物的生理,*paleogeography*(古地理学)研究早期地理时代的地理,而 *paleoecology*(古生态学)研究早期地理时代动植物与其环境的关系。

Paleolithic \ˌpā-lē-ə-ˈli-thik\ Of or relating to the earliest period of the Stone Age, characterized by rough or chipped stone implements. 古石器时代的

• He raves about the health benefits of his Paleolithic diet, the kind that our pre-agricultural, hunting-and-gathering Stone Age ancestors would have eaten. 他兴致勃勃地谈论自己的古石器时代饮食的种种好处,这种饮食是农业社会前从事采集和狩猎的石器时代人类祖先享用的。

Since *lithos* means "stone" in Greek, the name Paleolithic was given to the older part of the Stone Age. The first known period of human culture, the Paleolithic actually covers almost all of human history, from the first use of stone tools around 2.5 million years ago until the invention of agriculture around 10,000 years ago. For almost all that time, humans used the very crudest of stone tools, produced by chipping away flakes of stone in order to make an edge for an ax or knife. Near the end of the period, animal bones and antlers were being used for tools, especially pointed tools, and sculpted figures and cave art were being produced. The Paleolithic gave way to the Mesolithic ("Middle Stone Age") period, with its tools made of polished stone, wood, and bone.

因为 *lithos* 在希腊语中意思是"石头",Paleolithic 就用来命名石器时代的更古老的阶段了。古石器时代是已知的人类文化的第一阶段,实际上涵盖几乎所有人类历史,从二百五十万年前使用石头工具直到一万年前发明农业。这一阶段

几乎所有时间，人类使用的都是粗糙的石头工具。这种工具是通过凿下石头碎片为斧头或刀具凿出刀刃而产生的。这一阶段快要结束时，人类也使用动物骨头和鹿角作为工具，尤其是尖锐的工具，这样就产生了雕刻和岩洞艺术。古石器时代让位于 Mesolithic（中石器的）时代，中石器时代的工具是打光的石头、木头和骨头。

paleography \ˌpā-lē-ˈä-grə-fē\ （1）The study of ancient writings and inscriptions. 古文字学（2）Ancient writings. 古文字

• For her thesis on Central American paleography, she spent a winter in Honduras studying rock inscriptions 30 miles upriver from the nearest town. 为了撰写中美洲古文字学论文，他在洪都拉斯待了一个冬天，研究了离最近一座城市三十英里的碑铭。

The world's oldest literature dates from about 4,000 years ago, from the land known as Sumer (now southern Iraq). Early writing took the form of pictographs, very simple pictures that first represented things or ideas and later came to represent actual words. The first actual alphabet, in which each character represents a sound, appeared in the same general region about 500 years later. But writing developed in very different ways in different parts of the world, and 1,000 years later, when Europeans first arrived in the New World, alphabetic writing still wasn't being used anywhere in the Americas. Decoding some ancient languages has proven to be a huge task for *paleographers*, and determining the age and the source of a piece of writing can pose major challenges.
世界最古老的文学可追溯至四千年前的苏美尔（今天的伊拉克南部）这片土地。早期作品使用的是象形文字。这是很简单的图画，先是指代事物或观点，之后逐渐代表具体的词语了。最早的字母表每个字母代表一个音，大约五百年后出现在大致同一地区。但是，文字在世界各地发展的方式区别很大。一千年后，当欧洲人最先到达新世界时，字母文字在美洲任何地方都尚未使用。对 *paleographer*（古文字学家）来说，破译古代语言已经证明是非常艰巨的任务，确定一篇文字的年代和来源非常困难。

paleontology \ˌpā-lē-ˌän-ˈtä-lə-jē\ A science dealing with the life of past geological periods as known from fossil remains. 古生物学

• Her obsession with dinosaurs as a child continued through her teens, and no one was surprised when she started graduate school in paleontology. 她童年时期就对恐龙非常着迷，青少年时期也一直如此。她上研究生时攻读古生物学，没一个人感到意外。

Until the 1820s, hardly anyone even suspected that dinosaurs had ever existed. In the years since, *paleontology* has sought to discover the entire history of life on earth, from the era of single-celled organisms up into the human era. *Paleontologists* continue to make remarkable discoveries, such as that a huge meteorite that fell in the Gulf of Mexico wiped out the dinosaurs—all except the birds, the only surviving dinosaurs. "Radiometric dating" can reveal the age (often tens of millions of years) of a rock or fossil or a tiny grain of pollen by measuring how much its radioactive elements have disintegrated. The study of molecules of DNA, RNA, and proteins has also become important for dating. Paleontologists often consult with geologists searching for oil, gas, and coal deposits, since all these "fossil fuels" were formed from plant and animal remains.

直到 19 世纪 20 年代,几乎没有人怀疑恐龙曾经存在过。此后,古生物学已经努力发现地球生命的整个历史了,从单细胞生物时代到人类时代。*paleontologists*(古生物学家)一直都有惊人的发现,比如落在墨西哥湾的一个巨大流星消灭了恐龙——除了鸟这种唯一幸存的恐龙。通过测量放射性元素分解的程度,同位素年龄测定可以发现岩石或者化石或者一粒微小的花粉的年龄。研究 DNA、RNA 和蛋白质构成的细胞,对年龄测定也很重要。古生物学家经常请教寻找石油、天然气和煤矿的地质学家,因为所有这些"化石燃料"都是动植物的遗体形成的。

Paleozoic \ˌpā-lē-ə-ˈzō-ik\ The era of geological history, ending about 248 million years ago, in which vertebrates and land plants first appeared. 古生代

• His geological specialty was the beginning of the Paleozoic, from which the earliest fish fossils date. 他的地理专长是古生代初期,最早的鱼化石就追溯到这个时期。

The Greek root *zo-* means "animal," so names such as Paleozoic were invented to refer to a period in the development of animal life. For geologists, the Paleozoic era is followed by the Mesozoic (*meso-* meaning "middle"), which is followed by the Cenozoic (*cen-* meaning "recent"). Eras are huge stretches of time; geolo-gists break eras down into smaller "periods" and "epochs." Thus, the Paleozoic ends with the Permian period, the Mesozoic ends with the Upper Cretaceous epoch, and the Cenozoic ends with the Holocene epoch—the epoch in which we are living. The Paleozoic era produced the first fish, the first land plants, the first insects, and the first amphibians and reptiles; the dinosaurs, birds, and mammals had to wait for the Mesozoic.

希腊语词根 *zo-* 意思是"动物",所以 Paleozoic 这样的名称被发明来指代动物生命发展的一个时期。对于地质学家来说,古生代之后是 Mesozoic(中生代;*meso-*意思是"中"),中生代之后是 Cenozoic(晚生代;*cen-* 意思是"最近")。era(代)是时间很长的阶段,地质学家将代分为较短的"period"(纪)和"epoch"(世)。因此,古生代和二叠纪同时结束,中生代和上白垩世同时结束,晚生代和人类生存的全新世同时结束。古生代产生了最早的鱼类、最早的陆地植物、最早的昆虫、最早的两栖类动物和爬行动物。恐龙、鸟类和哺乳动物得到中生代出现了。

Quizzes

A. Fill in each blank with the correct letter:

a. Paleolithic   e. paleography
b. necrosis   f. necromancer
c. Paleozoic   g. paleontology
d. necropsy   h. necropolis

1. The frostbite was bad and there was a chance of _____ setting in, so we had to work fast.

2. With his specialty in _____, he spent much of his time on the rivers of Peru looking for rocks with ancient carvings.

3. Grief-stricken parents would go to the village _____, who would try to contact their dead children.

4. They were certain the cat hadn't died of natural causes, and the _____

revealed that they were right.

5. The men's graves in this Iron Age _____ held numerous weapons.
6. The wall paintings date from the end of the _____, just before the beginning of settled farming villages.
7. Millions of kids are fascinated by dinosaurs, but not many will go on to study _____ in college.
8. Insects, reptiles, amphibians, and primitive fish inhabited the earth during the _____ era, but not mammals.

B. Indicate whether the following pairs of terms have the same or different meanings:

1. Paleozoic / of the period about 10,000 years ago   same ____ / different ____
2. necropsy / autopsy   same ____ / different ____
3. necromancer / gravedigger   same ____ / different ____
4. paleography / study of ancient writings   same ____ / different ____
5. Paleolithic / Old Stone Age   same ____ / different ____
6. necrosis / tissue death   same ____ / different ____
7. necropolis / cemetery   same ____ / different ____
8. paleontology / study of past geological periods   same ____ / different ____

CIRCU/CIRCUM

CIRCU/CIRCUM comes from the Latin *circus*, meaning "circle." So a *circus* is traditionally held under a round tent. A *circuit* can be a tour around an area or territory, or the complete path of an electric current. To *circumnavigate* means "to navigate around"— often around the world.

CIRCU/CIRCUM 源自拉丁语 *circus*, 意思是"圆圈"。所以 *circus* 传统上是在圆形帐篷下举行的。*circuit* 可以是绕着某一区域绕一周,或者是电流的整个路线。*circumnavigation* 的意思是"环绕……航行",通常是环绕世界。

circuitous \sər-ˈkyü-ə-təs\ (1) Having a circular or winding course. 圆形路线的;路线弯曲的 (2) Not forthright or direct in action. 间接的;拐弯抹角的

• She sometimes arrives at her conclusions by circuitous reasoning that her students can't even follow. 有时候,她利用迂回推理得出结论,结果学生们根本无法理解。

Circuitous is usually the opposite of *direct*, and it's generally used to describe either roads or explanations. Detours are usually circuitous, and a circuitous path, twisting and turning and cutting back on itself, is the kind of route you'd expect to find in the mountains. Lawyers often find themselves making circuitous arguments, which may get most circuitous when they're defending particularly undesirable clients.

circuitous 的反义词通常是 *direct*,而且常常用于描述道路或者解释。detours(绕行的路)通常是圆形的,曲折的小路弯弯曲曲、绕来绕去,又回到原点,是一种你在山里才能见到的路线。律师经常发现自己进行 circuitous arguments(迂回辩论),在为特别不喜欢的当事人辩护时最可能这样。

circumference \ sər-ˈkəm-frəns \ (1) The perimeter or boundary of a circle. 圆周长;圆周 (2) The outer boundary or surface of a shape or object. (物体或形状的)周界(或表面)

• To calculate the circumference of a circle, multiply its diameter by 3.1416. 要计算圆的周长,就用直径乘 3.1416。

Attempts have been made to measure the circumference of the earth since the time of Aristotle. The calculation that Columbus was relying on led him to think he could reach China by sailing west more quickly than by sailing east. But that measurement had calculated the earth's circumference as about a quarter too small, and the rest is history. Columbus wasn't the only one who got it wrong; many later attempts continued to produce different measurements for the earth's circumference—even though the Greeks had calculated it correctly way back in the 3rd century B.C. 从亚里士多德时代以来,人们就一直努力测量地球的 circumference(周长)。哥伦布依赖的计算法让他认为自己向西航行比向东航行可以更快到达中国。但是,那次测量计算的地球的周长少了大约十分之一,其余的就是历史了。哥伦布不是唯一出错的,后来很多次努力,还是为地球测出了不同的周长,尽管早在公元前 3 世纪希腊人已经测量正确了。

circumspect \ ˈsər-kəm-ˌspekt \ Careful to consider all circumstances and possible consequences; cautious. 小心谨慎的;考虑周密的;慎重的

• Her answer was careful and circumspect, and I couldn't help thinking she knew a lot more than she was telling. 她回答时小心翼翼,我不禁想,她知道的可能更多。

Since *spect-* comes from the Latin word for "look," *circumspect* basically means "looking around" yourself before you act. Being a doctor has traditionally called for a circumspect personality, which gives their patients confidence in them. Scholars are known for their *circumspection*, since there's nothing worse for scholars' reputations than mistakes in the books or articles they've written. Bankers once had a reputation for great circumspection, but the financial disaster of 2008 earned some bankers a very different kind of reputation. 由于 *spect-* 源自拉丁语中表示"看"的词语,*circumspect* 的基本意思就是"环视"周围之后再行动。行医传统上要求 circumspect personality(为人慎重),让病人产生信任感。学者以 *circumspection*(慎重)著称,因为没有什么比书和文章中的错误更能影响其声誉了。银行家曾以 circumspection(慎重)著称,但是 2008 年的金融灾难让其中一些人有了很不一样的声誉。

circumvent \ ˈsər-kəm-ˌvent \ (1) To make a circuit around. 绕过 (2) To manage to get around, especially by clever means. 规避;躲避

• We knew there was a traffic jam on the highway and circumvented it by using back roads. 我们知道公路上堵车,就走小路绕过去了。

In mythology, a person's attempts to circumvent fate are almost always doomed. In the *Iliad* we're told of how Achilles' mother, Thetis, hoping to circumvent the prophecy that her child would die in a war against Troy, disguised the boy as a woman. But clever Odysseus, recruiting for the Greek army, arrived disguised as a peddler, and among the jewels he displayed to the women of the household he laid a sword. The young Achilles, ignoring the jewelry, immediately seized the sword, thereby identifying himself for what he was. Today we more often hear of attempts to circumvent the law, or at least some requirements that we'd rather not have to deal with.

在神话中,一个人想 circumvent fate(逃避命运)的努力几乎总是注定要失败。在《伊利亚特》中,阿喀琉斯的母亲忒提斯希望逃脱儿子死于特洛伊战争的预言,就把他打扮成女性。但是聪明的奥德修斯在为希腊军队招募士兵时,装扮成小贩去找他。在向那家人的女性展示的珠宝中,他放了一把剑。年轻的阿喀琉斯没管那些珠宝,而是马上抓起了那把剑,这样就暴露了身份。今天,我们更多地听到有人想要 circumvent the law(规避法律),或至少规避一些我们宁可置之不理的规定。

MINI/MINU

come from Latin words meaning "small" and "least." So the *minimum* is the least, and a *minute* amount is almost nothing. And *mini-* is all too familiar as a prefix that we've been applying to all kinds of things since the 1950s: *minivan*, *miniskirt*, *mini-mart*, *minipark*, and the rest.

NINI/MINU 源自拉丁语中表示"小"和"最小"的词语。因此,*minimum* 就是最小的,*minute*(极小的)量就是几乎什么也没有。*Mini-* 作为前缀我们太熟悉了,从 20 世纪 50 年代就一直用于各种事物:*minivan*(小型面包车)、*miniskirt*(迷你裙,超短裙)、*mini-mart*(便利店)、*minipark*(小公园)等等。

minimalism \ˈmi-nə-mə-ˌli-zəm\
A style or technique (as in music, literature, or design) that is characterized by extreme spareness and simplicity. (音乐、文学、设计方面的)简约主义

• He'd never understood what anyone liked about minimalism, since minimalist stories always seemed to leave out any description of people's characters and motivation and rarely even described their surroundings. 他一直不明白简约主义有什么好的。简约主义的短篇小说似乎总是省去对人物性格和动机的描写,甚至极少描写环境。

In the 1960s, a few composers, including Philip Glass, Steve Reich, and John Adams, began writing music inspired by the music of India and Southeast Asia, often with a quick pulsing beat and chords that are repeated quickly over and over while small changes are slowly introduced. *Minimalist* art, which began appearing around the same time, tries to strip away all personal elements, often leaving only pure geometric forms; you may have seen the plain silver boxes of Donald Judd, or the straight neon tubes of Bruce Nauman. In literature, the stripped-down fiction of Samuel Beckett and Raymond Carver is often considered minimalist. But there's a real question whether these various types of minimalism should even be considered the same concept.

20 世纪 60 年代,几位作曲家,包括菲利普·格拉斯、史蒂夫·莱许和约翰·亚当斯,从印度和东南亚音乐中得到灵感,开始谱写音乐。这些音乐常常有着快速重复的飞快、强烈的节奏和弦,但是慢慢出现了微小的变化。*minimalist*(简约主义的)艺术几乎同时开始出现,它努力消除所有个人元素,常常只剩下纯粹的几何形状。你可能见过唐纳德·贾德的简朴的银盒子,或者布鲁斯·瑙曼的笔直的霓虹管子。在文学领域,塞缪尔·贝克特和雷蒙德·卡佛那仅仅保留基本元素的小说通常被认为是简约主义小说。但是,有个真正的问题,就是这各种类型的简约主义是否应该被认为是同一

概念。

minuscule \ˈmi-nəs-ˌkyül\ Very small. 极小的

• For someone who had been living on a minuscule budget since graduating from college, even the paycheck for a minimum-wage job felt like wealth to her. 她大学毕业后仅靠很少一点钱生活。对她来说，即使收入很低的一份工作的工资支票也感觉像一笔财富。

As a noun, *minuscule* means a style of ancient or medieval handwriting script with smaller letters than earlier scripts. There were actually several minuscules, but the most important was promoted from around A. D. 800 on by Charlemagne, who believed that any educated person in the Holy Roman Empire should be able to read the Latin written by anyone else. If you've ever looked at a medieval manuscript, you've probably seen minuscule script, along with socalled *majuscule* (for modern type, we would use the words *lowercase* and *capital* instead); even today most of us can read medieval minuscule and majuscule without too much trouble. Be careful about spelling *minuscule*; we tend to expect a word meaning "small" to begin with *mini-* rather than *minu-*.

作为名词，*minuscule*（小书写体）指古代或者中世纪的一种书写体，其字母比早期的书写体要小。实际上过去有几种小书写体，但是最重要的一种，由查理曼大帝从大约公元八百年推动了其发展。他认为，神圣罗马帝国任何接受过教育的人，都应该能够阅读其他任何人书写的拉丁语。如果你看过中世纪手稿，可能已经看到了小书写体以及所谓的 *majuscule*（大书写体）（对现代书写体来说，我们则会用 *lowercase*［小写字体］和 *capital*［大写字体］）。即使今天，大多数人阅读中世纪小书写体和大书写体，都不会太难。拼写 *minuscule* 要小心，我们倾向于希望意思是"小"的词语以 *mini-* 而不是 *minu-* 开头。

minutiae \mə-ˈnü-shē-ˌē\ Very small or minor details. 微小的细节；次要的细节

• She likes "thinking big," and gets annoyed when her job requires her to deal with what she considers minutiae. 她喜欢"做大事"，但工作需要处理她认为是细枝末节的东西，这让她不高兴。

As you might guess, this word comes straight from Latin. The Romans used it in its singular form, *minutia*, to mean "smallness," and in the plural to mean "trifles"; today we almost always use it in the plural with that same "trifles" meaning. Hardly anyone ever talks about minutiae except to dismiss their importance. So you may talk about the minutiae of daily life or the minutiae of a contract, or about getting bogged down or buried in minutiae at the office. Just don't forget that the devil is often in the details.

你可以猜到，这个词语直接来自拉丁语。罗马人用它的单数 *minutia* 表示"小"，用其复数表示"小事"。今天，我们几乎总是用它的复数，意思是一样的。几乎没有人谈论 *minutiae*，除非是要对其不屑一顾。所以，你可以谈论日常生活中的琐事或合同的细枝末节，或者谈论在办公室为芝麻蒜皮的小事所累。只是不要忘了，细节常常决定成败。

diminutive \də-ˈmi-nyə-tiv\ (1) Indicating small size. 指小的；昵称的；爱称的 (2) Very small. 微小的

• In German, Hänsel is a diminutive form of Hans (which is a diminutive form of Johannes), and Gretel is a diminutive form of Margaret. 在德语中，Hänsel 是 Hans 的昵称

形式（而 Hans 是 Johannes 的昵称形式），Gretel 是 Margaret 的昵称形式。

MINI/
MINU

Just as *diminish* means "to grow smaller," *diminutive* means "very small." When writing about language, *diminutive* as both an adjective and a noun refers to particular endings and the words made with them to indicate smallness. In English, such endings include *-et* and *-ette* (*piglet*, *dinette*, *cigarette*, *diskette*) as-well as *-ie* and *-y* (*doggy*, *bootie*, *Bobby*, *Debbie*). However, *diminutives* are more common in many other languages. Outside of language, *diminutive* is used for many things, including people ("She noticed a diminutive figure standing shyly by the door"), but often not very seriously ("We were served some rather diminutive rolls").

正如 *diminish* 意思是"变小"，*diminutive* 意思是"很小"。写到语言时，*diminutive* 作为形容词和名词都指特定的词尾，用这些词尾造的词表示"小"。在英语中，这样的词尾包括 *-et* 和 *-ette*（*piglet*、*dinette*、*cigarette*、*diskette*），以及 *-ie* 和 *-y*（*doggy*、*booties*、*Bobby*、*Debbie*）。不过，*diminutives*（指小词）在其他语言中更为常见。在语言之外，*diminutive* 用于很多事物，包括人（"She noticed a diminutive figure standing shyly by the door［她注意到一个小小的人儿羞涩地站在门边］"），不过常常不是那么严肃（"We were served some rather diminutive rolls［我们得到的是很小很小的面包］"）。

Quizzes

A. Fill in each blank with the correct letter：

a. circumference　　　　　　e. diminutive
b. minimalism　　　　　　　f. circumspect
c. circumvent　　　　　　　g. circuitous
d. minuscule　　　　　　　　h. minutiae

1. He enjoys working on actual cases, but he gets worn down by the flood of _____ involved in billing his clients.

2. She's a big fan of _____ in Web design, and Google's white home page has always been her ideal.

3. The banking industry generally works hard to _____ any laws that tend to restrict their ability to make profits.

4. Whenever we asked where his income came from, he would say something vague and _____ and treat it as a joke.

5. We finally found the house, but only after getting completely lost and taking an extremely _____ route.

6. She can't stand it when they start arguing over _____ differences while ignoring the really important issues.

7. People often comment on the contrast between his _____ physique and the enormous power he wields on Capitol Hill.

8. The race course runs the entire _____ of the lake twice, a total of ten miles.

B. Match the definition on the left to the correct word on the right：

1. cautious　　　　　　　　　　　　a. circumference

2. roundabout
3. rim
4. details
5. miniature
6. style of extreme simplicity
7. small
8. get around

b. circumvent
c. minuscule
d. minutiae
e. circumspect
f. diminutive
g. circuitous
h. minimalism

INTER comes straight from Latin. In English it has various meanings; all of them can be expressed broadly as "between," but they're still quite distinct: "moving between" (*intercity*), "communicating between" (*intercom*), "coming between" (*intercept*), and so on. No wonder so many English words begin with *inter-*.

INTER 直接来自拉丁语。在英语中,它有各种意思,都可以大致说是"在……之间",但意思还是很分明:"在……之间移动"(*intercity*)、"在……之间交流"(*intercom*)、"到……之间"(*intercept*),等等。难怪那么多英语单词以 *inter-* 开始。

intercede\ˌin-tər-ˈsēd\ (1) To act as a go-between between unfriendly parties. 调解;说和 (2) To beg or plead in behalf of another. 为……求情

● He had interceded for her with their boss on one important occasion, for which she was still grateful. 有一次,他为了一件重要事找老板替她求情,她为此仍心怀感激。

The Latin *cedere* means "to go," so "go between" is the most literal meaning of *intercede*. (The same *-cede* root can also be seen in such words as *precede* and *secede*.) If you've been blamed unfairly for something, a friend may intercede on your behalf with your coach or teacher. More often, it will be the coach or teacher who has to intercede in a student dispute. The *intercession* of foreign governments has sometimes prevented conflicts from becoming worse than they otherwise would have.

拉丁语 *cedere* 意思是"去",所以"go between"("做中间人")是 *intercede* 最基本的意思(也可以在 *precede* 和 *secede* 这样的词语中看到 *-cede* 这一词根)。如果被人错怪了,一位朋友可能会为你向教练或老师解释。更多情况下,是教练或老师不得不为两个学生之间的纠纷进行调解。外国政府的调停有时避免了可能恶化的冲突。

interstice\in-ˈtər-stəs\ A little space between two things; chink, crevice. 空隙;裂缝

● All the interstices between the rocks have been filled with new cement, and the wall should be fine for another hundred years. 岩石之间的空隙都用水泥填好了,这堵墙还会完好一百年。

People often speak of *interstices* in the physical sense (referring to the interstices in surfaces, for example, or microscopic interstices between particles in chemical compounds), but also often in a less literal way (the interstices in a movie's plot, in the economy, in what's covered by a complicated tax law, etc.). The pronunciation of *interstice* is slightly unusual; you might not guess that it's accented on the second syllable. This is also true in the plural *interstices*, which is used more often than the singular form; note also that in *interstices* the final *e* is usually pronounced long, so that it rhymes with *bees*.

人们经常说到物理意义上的 interstices(缝隙)(比如两个表面之间的缝隙,或者化学复合物颗粒之间的用显微镜才能看到的缝隙),但也经常使用其不那么平常的意思(影片情节的、经济学的、在一项复杂的税法所覆盖的范围内的缝隙,等等),interstice 发音有些不寻常,你可能没有猜到重音在第二个音节。其复数 interstices 的发音也是这样,只是使用得比单数形式频繁些。注意在 interstices 中,最后那个 e 通常发长音,所以它跟 bees 押韵。

interdict\in-tər-ˈdikt\ (1) To prohibit or forbid. 禁止 (2) To destroy, damage, or cut off (as an enemy line of supply) by firepower to stop or hamper an enemy. 破坏;毁坏;(用火力阻止或妨碍敌人以)切断(比如敌人的补给线)

• All weapons trade with the country had been interdicted by the NATO alliance, and ships were actually being stopped and searched before being allowed to dock. 跟该国所有的武器交易都遭到北约同盟禁止了,轮船竟然被截住、搜查,之后才允许进港。

Interdict and *interdiction* are used for very serious prohibitions—more serious than, say, a professor telling the class that texting is forbidden during lectures. During the Middle Ages and Renaissance, an *interdict* was a sentence imposed by the powerful Catholic Church forbidding a person or place, and sometimes even an entire country, from receiving church privileges or participating in church functions. *Interdict* now often means "cut off" in a physically forceful way as well; interdictions are usually targeted at either arms supplies or illegal drug shipments.

interdict 和 interdiction 都用于很严肃的禁止,要比教授告诉全班同学说上课期间禁止发短信更加严肃。在中世纪和文艺复兴时期,interdict 是强大的天主教会强加的禁令,禁止一个人或一个地方,有时甚至是一个国家,接受教会的特权或者参与教会的典礼。Interdict 现在常常也表示用很大的身体力量"切断"。interdictions(切断)的目标通常是武器供应或者毒品运输。

interpolate\in-ˈtər-pə-ˌlāt\ To put something between other things or parts, especially to put words into a piece of writing or a conversation. 插入,置入;(尤指在文字或谈话中)插入(字词)

• On page 6, she noticed that someone had interpolated a couple of sentences that completely altered the meaning of her original text. 她注意到,有人在第 6 页插入了几个句子,完全改变了她原文的意思。

The meaning of *interpolate* is often entirely innocent. An *interpolation* in a text may have been approved by everyone concerned, and an interpolation in conversation is usually just an interruption. But in its older meaning, interpolating usually meant tampering with a text secretly to change its apparent meaning. Legislators are sometimes enraged to discover what someone has quietly interpolated into their favorite bill at the last minute. And any contract always has to be read carefully to make sure the other lawyer didn't slip in an undesirable interpolation.

interpolate 的意思常常是完全没有恶意的。文本中的一个 *interpolation*（插入的字词）可能是经过每个相关人员同意的。但是在较早的意思中，interpolating 通常表示篡改文本以改变其明显的意思。立法者有时很生气地发现，有人最后一刻悄悄地在他们最爱的法案中插入了字词。任何一个合同都应该仔细阅读，确保对方律师没有偷偷插入不该有的字词。

SUR

SUR is actually a shortening of the Latin prefix *super-*, meaning "over, above" (see SUPER, p. 643), and has the same meaning. A *surface* is the face above or on the outside of something. A *surplus* is something above and beyond what is needed. And to *survey* a landscape is to look out over it. SUR 实际上是拉丁语前缀 *super-* 的缩略写法，意思是"多于，超过"（见 SUPER，第 643 页），而且意思一样。*surface*（表面）就是某物上面或者紧贴某物的一个面。*surplus*（多余物）就是超出需要以外的东西。*survey*（纵览）某一片区域就是放眼观望它。

surmount \sər-ˈmau̇nt\   To rise above; overcome. 高过；克服；解决

• The story of how he surmounted poverty and crippling physical ailments to achieve what he achieved is almost unbelievable. 他战胜贫穷、克服重病从而实现目标的故事，几乎令人难以置信。

Our verb *mount*, meaning "ascend, get up onto," comes from the same Latin root as *mountain*, and we keep those images in mind when using *surmount*, since climbing up or over a mountain is a symbol of achievement. The word almost always refers to human effort, and almost always in a positive way; thus, we speak of surmounting difficulties, surmounting problems, surmounting hurdles, surmounting handicaps—you get the idea. 动词 *mount* 的意思是"攀登，登上"，跟 *mountain* 源自同一拉丁语词根。我们使用 *surmount* 时，头脑中保留着那些形象，因为登山或者越过一座山是成就的象征。这个词语几乎总是指人类做出的努力，而且几乎总是具有肯定意义；这样，我们就会说到 *surmounting*（克服）困难、*surmounting*（解决）问题、*surmounting*（跨过）栏架、*surmounting*（越过）障碍——你明白了吧。

surcharge \ˈsər-ˌchärj\   An additional tax or charge. 增收的税；额外的收费

• Checking the bill, she discovered two surcharges that no one had warned her about. 查看账单后，她发现多收了两种费用，而这没人提前告诉她。

The Arab oil embargo of 1973 led airlines to add fuel surcharges to their passenger fares that were large enough to discourage air travel. *Surcharges* are usually added for special service. When you request a "rush job" from a service supplier, it will probably bring a surcharge along with it. A particularly difficult phone installation may carry a surcharge. An extra-large fine for a speeding offense after you've already had too many tickets could be called a surcharge. An added tax may be called a surcharge (or *surtax*) when it only affects people with incomes above a certain level. And if those low, low prices that show up in really big letters in ads for all kinds of services turn out to be misleading, it's probably because they don't include a bunch of surcharges that you won't find out about till later.

1973 年的阿拉伯石油禁运，使航空公司在乘客费用上增加了燃油费用，多到足以让人不愿再意乘坐飞机。 surcharges（额外的收费）通常是因为特殊服务而增加的。当你要求服务方"加快工作"时，可能会有附带费用。安装电话特别困难，或许会额外收费。在多次收到罚款单之后，因超速而被罚的一笔超大款项，可以称为额外罚款。当一笔税只影响收入高过某一水平的人的时候，增加的税可以称为增收税（或者 surtax）。如果所有的服务费用价格很低很低，在广告中以很大的字母出现来误导别人，那可能是因为许多额外费用没有被包含其中，而这些费用直到后来你才会发现。

surfeit \ˈsər-fət\ A supply that is more than enough; excess. 过量；过多

• Whenever he glanced into his daughter's room, he was always astonished at the utter surfeit of things—dolls, dollhouses, stuffed animals, cushions, games, posters, and clothing strewn everywhere. 无论什么时候往女儿房间瞥一眼，里面的东西都多得让他吃惊——玩偶、玩偶屋、填充的动物玩具、垫子、游戏机用具、海报、扔到处都是的衣服。

Book and film critics often use *surfeit* when complaining about how an author or director has given us too much of something. In our consumer society, we're always noticing a surfeit of one thing or another, such as breakfast cereals in the supermarket. Statistics are always indicating a surfeit of lawyers or doctors or accountants in some parts of the country and a lack of them in others. The death of a young star always results in a surfeit of articles and books about him or her. And a potluck supper usually results in a surfeit of food, which might leave you *surfeited*, or stuffed.

书籍和电影评论家经常使用 *surfeit* 一词，抱怨某个作家或导演给我们带来了太多某种东西。在这个消费社会，我们总是注意到，不是这个就是那个太多太多了，比如超市的谷类早餐食物。数据总是表明，这个国家有些地方有太多的律师、医生或者会计，而其他地方则又缺乏。一位年轻明星去世了，结果就会有太多关于他或她的文章和书籍。百乐餐常常有过多的食物，结果让你 *surfeited*（吃得过多）。

surreal \sə-ˈrēl\ Very strange or unusual; having the quality of a dream. 奇怪的；不寻常的；梦一般的

• In a surreal sequence, the main character gets a job on floor 7 1/2, which turns out to be only half as high as the other floors, so everyone must walk around stooped over. 在一个奇特的电影片段中，主要人物在 7 1/2 层楼找到了一份工作。原来，这层楼只有其他楼层一半那么高，所以每个人都得弯腰走动。

In 1924 a group of European poets, painters, and filmmakers founded a movement that they called *Surrealism*. Their central idea was that the unconscious mind (a concept Sigmund Freud had recently made famous) was the source of all imagination, and that art should try to express its contents. The unconscious, they believed, revealed itself most clearly in dreams. The *Surrealist* painters included René Magritte, Joan Miró, and Salvador Dalí, whose "limp watches" painting became the best-known Surrealist image of all. Since those years, we've used *surreal* to describe all kinds of situations that strike us as dreamlike. And even though the Surrealist movement ended long ago, surrealism now seems to be everywhere—not just in painting, literature, and movies but also in blogs, video games, and graphic novels.

1924 年，一群欧洲诗人、画家和制片人发起了一场运动，称为 *Surrealism*（超现实主义）。他们的中心观点是，人的无意识心理（在此前不久,西格蒙·弗洛伊德使这一概念出名了）是所有想象的来源,艺术应该努力表现其内容。他们相信,无意识在梦中最清晰展现自己。*Surrealist*（超现实主义的）画家包括雷尼·马格利特、胡安·米罗和萨尔瓦多·达利。达利的"软塌塌的钟表"的绘画成了超现实主义最有名的形象。那些年之后,我们一直使用 *surreal* 来描述各种让人感觉梦幻般的情况。虽然超现实主义运动很久以前就寿终正寝了,超现实主义现在却似乎无处不在——不仅仅存在于绘画、文学、电影中,也存在于博客、电子游戏和绘画小说中。

Quizzes

A. Fill in each blank with the correct letter：

a. surfeit
b. interdict
c. surcharge
d. interstice
e. interpolate
f. surreal
g. intercede
h. surmount

1. The door to the ruined barn was locked, but through an _____ in the wall I glimpsed an old tractor and several odd pieces of machinery.

2. Even though we know hardly any facts about the divorce, there's already been a _____ of talk on the radio about it.

3. The governor is calling for a _____ on all packaged snack foods with low nutritional value.

4. She would go on talking about her country by the hour, while I would occasionally _____ a comment to show that I was paying attention.

5. There was something _____ about gazing out from the deck of a luxurious cruise ship at the primitive huts lining the islands' shores.

6. The country's small coast guard hopes to _____ most of the arms at sea before they can reach the guerrilla fighters.

7. Only after I got the coach to _____ did the principal agree to change my suspension to probation.

8. When he was wheeled out to accept the award, most of the audience realized for the first time what terrible difficulties he had had to _____.

B. Match the word on the left to the correct definition on the right：

1. interdict   a. rise above
2. surcharge   b. block
3. surfeit   c. excess
4. intercede   d. chink
5. interpolate   e. dreamlike
6. surmount   f. extra fee
7. surreal   g. ask for mercy
8. interstice   h. stick in

CO is a Latin prefix that generally means "with, together," and we see it daily in such words as *costar*, *cofounder*, *co-owner*, and *coworker*. But many other *co-* words aren't quite so easy to understand when you first encounter them.

co 是一个拉丁语前缀，通常的意思是"和……一起，一起"。我们每天都可以看到他出现在 *costar*（合演；合演者）、*cofounder*（共同创办人）、*co-owner*（共有人）和 *coworker*（同事）之类的词语中。但是，很多其他 *co-* 起首的词语，第一次见到并不那么容易理解。

coalesce \ˌkō-ə-ˈles\ To come together to form one group or mass. 合作；联合；合并；结合

• Three local civic groups have recently coalesced to form a single organization, believing it will result in more effective campaigns. 三个当地民间团体最近合并成了一个机构，相信这个机构可以组织更有效的活动。

Social movements are often said to *coalesce* when groups with somewhat different interests realize how much they have in common. Some physicists believe that planets coalesced not from space rocks but from icy clouds of cosmic dust. Some people even study how languages coalesce—for example, the fairly new language Afrikaans, a mixture of Dutch and native languages spoken in South Africa, which only really solidified about 150 years ago.

通常，当利益稍有不同的团体意识到它们有很多共同之处时，社会运动就会 *coalesce*（结合在一起）。有些物理学家认为行星不是由太空岩石 *coalesced*（结合形成），而是由冰冷的云状宇宙尘结合形成的。有些人甚至研究语言是怎样 *coalesce*（结合）的。比如，相对比较新的南非荷兰语，是荷兰语跟南非人说的几种当地语言混合而成的，仅在一百五十年前才稳定下来。

cogeneration \ˌkō-ˌje-nə-ˈrā-shən\ The production of electricity using waste heat (as in steam) from an industrial process, or the use of steam from electric power generation as a source of heat. 热电联产；废热发电

• With its new cogeneration system, the company reports converting over 65% of the energy in natural gas to electricity, making this the most efficient power plant ever built. 有了新的热电联产系统，该公司报告说，可将天然气中能量的百分之六十五转变成电能，使其成为最有效的发电厂。

Cogeneration is basically the production of energy and usable heat (generally in the form of steam and hot water) in the same plant, usually by capturing heat that in older plants used to be simply wasted. It's one of the principal ways in which countries intend to reduce their greenhouse-gas emissions so as to slow climate change. Cogeneration plants are often small, and the fuels used in them are varied. Lumber mills, for instance, can operate their own cogeneration plants, feeding them with wood scraps and sawdust, and wastewater treatment plants generate gas that can likewise be used as a source of energy. Since it's hard to move heat long distances, cogeneration is most efficient when the heat can be used nearby. Though the general public today knows little about cogeneration, more and more of us will be benefiting from it in the coming years.

cogeneration(热电联产)从根本上说,是在同一工厂生产能量和可用的热量(通常的形式是蒸汽和热水),通常的方法是捕获以前在较老工厂浪费的热量。一些国家想要减少温室气体排放以延缓气候变化,这就是主要方法之一。热电联产工厂通常较小,使用的燃料多种多样。比如,锯木厂可以有自己的热电联产工厂,用木头碎片和锯木屑作为机器的燃料;废水处理厂产生的气体同样可用作能源的来源。由于热量难以运到远处,如果能在附近使用,热电联产是最有效的。虽然公众对热电联产知之甚少,我们越来越多的人将会在未来受益。

codependency \ˌkō-di-ˈpen-dən-sē\ A psychological condition or a relationship in which a person is controlled or manipulated by someone affected with a condition such as alcohol or drug addiction. (对伙伴的)极度依赖

• She never knew what codependency was until her daughter took up with a mean, abusive alcoholic and refused to leave him. 直到女儿结交了一个刻薄、粗野的酒鬼,而且拒绝离开他,她才知道什么是极度依赖。

Dependency on addictive substances has been known for centuries, but the concept of codependency got its name only as recently as 1979. For many of us, codependency isn't easy to understand; we may keep asking "Why doesn't she just leave him?" and find it hard to accept the answers we get. *Codependents* usually don't share their partners' addiction, but their lives tend to be taken over with the burden of caring for and protecting the spouse or partner. In recent years, people have started claiming that all kinds of conditions—anorexia, overeating, gambling, fear of intimacy, etc.—can result in codependency. Many experts think all of this has gone too far; still, almost everyone agrees that spouses of alcoholics and drug addicts face unique difficulties and should look for support and advice anywhere they can find it.

人们知道对易上瘾物质的 *dependency* (依赖)已经几个世纪了,但是,codependency(极度依赖)这一概念在1979年才有了名字。对我们很多人来说,极度依赖并不容易理解,我们可能老是会问"她为什么不离开他?"而且发现自己很难接受得到的答案。*codependents* (极度依赖者)通常并没有伙伴的瘾,但他们的生活往往为照顾和保护配偶或者伙伴所累。近些年,人们开始声言所有种类的疾病——厌食症、强迫性暴食、赌博成性、亲密恐惧症——都可能导致过度依赖。很多专家认为,所有这些都过度了;不过,几乎每个人都一致认为,酗酒者和吸毒者的配偶面临独特的困难,只要可能,应该寻求支持和建议。

cohesion \kō-ˈhē-zhən\ (1) The action or state of sticking together. 黏合;团结 (2) Molecular attraction by which the particles of a body are united throughout the mass. 内聚(性)

• The party's greatest strength was its cohesion and discipline, and on bill after bill that year not a single member voted with the other party. 该政党最大的长处是其团结和自律。那一年一个法案又一个法案,没有一个成员投票支持其他政党。

Cohesion is one of the noun forms of *cohere*; the others are *cohesiveness* and *coherence*, each of which has a slightly different meaning. *Coherence* is often used to describe a person's speech or writing. An *incoherent* talk or blog post is one that doesn't "hang together"; and if the police pick up someone who they describe as *incoherent*, it means he or she isn't making sense. But to describe a group or team that always sticks together, you would use *cohesive*, not *coherent*. And the words you'd use in Chemistry class to describe the way molecules hang together—for example, the way water forms into beads and drops—are *cohesion*, *cohesive*, and *cohesiveness*.

cohesion 是 cohere 的名词形式之一,其他形式是 cohesiveness(内聚;凝合)和 coherence(有条理;清楚易懂),每一个都有略微不同的意思。coherence 通常用来描述人的言语和文字。incoherent(无逻辑的;不连贯的)谈话或者博客帖子是不"连贯"的;如果警察抓住一个人,说他 incoherent,意思是他或她没法让人不明白。但是,要描述一个总是具有凝聚力的群体或者团队,你会用 cohesive,而不用 coherent。你在化学课上描述分子凝聚在一起,比如水形成水珠或者水滴,会使用的词语是 cohesion, cohesive 和 cohesiveness。

SYN

SYN is a Greek and Latin prefix meaning "together" or "at the same time." So "in *sync*" (short for "in *synchronization*") means "together in time." And a *synonym* is a word that can be considered together with another word since it has the same meaning.

SYN 是一个希腊语前缀,意思是"一起"或者"同时"。所以"insync"("in synchronization"的缩略写法)意思是"在时间上一起"。synonym 是一个能够跟另一词语同时考虑的词语,因为它们意思相同。

syntax \ˈsin-ˌtaks\ The way in which words are put together to form phrases, clauses, or sentences. 句法

• The president's critics complain about his odd and confusing syntax when he speaks in public. 批评总统的人抱怨说,他演讲时的句法奇怪而费解。

Syntax is basically about what word comes before and after another word; in other words, it's part of the larger subject of grammar. Syntax is often an issue in poetry, and it's usually discussed in connection with *diction*—that is, the poet's choice of words. So, for example, your English professor might point out the *syntactic* difference between "Whose woods these are I think I know" and "I think I know whose woods these are"; whereas if the discussion was about diction instead, the question might be about the choice of "woods" rather than "land," or "think" rather than "bet."

syntax(句法)涉及的基本上是什么词出现于另一词的前面或者后面,换句话说,它是语法的较大的处理对象。句法通常是诗歌中讨论的话题,常常与其共同被探讨的是 diction,也就是诗人的选词问题。所以,比如你的英语教授可能会指出下面这两个句子 syntactic(句法上的)差异:"Whose woods there are I think I know"和"I think I know whose woods these are"。而如果讨论的是选词,问题会是选择"woods"而不是"land",或者选择"think"而不是"bet"。

synthesize \ˈsin-thə-ˌsīz\ To make something by combining different things. 合成;综合

• From all the proposals put in front of us, we were asked to synthesize a plan that could get the support of the whole group. 我们被要求利用摆在面前的所有建议综合出一个计划,要能得到整个团体的支持。

Synthesize is a very common word in chemistry, since chemists are constantly synthesizing new compounds—that is, *synthetic* compounds—including drugs and industrial chemicals. It's also often used when talking about writing; nonfiction writers must often synthesize large amounts of material from many sources to produce a book—which represents a *synthesis* of the important materials. An electronic *synthesizer* creates new sounds (which may imitate the sounds of acoustic instruments) by generating different basic tones and then manipulating and merging them together with others.

synthesize 是化学领域很常见的词语，因为化学家一直都在合成新的化合物，也就是 synthetic（合成）化合物，包括药品和工业化学物质。它也常用于谈论写作时，非小说类作者必须经常综合来源很多的大量材料。通过产生不同的基本音调，之后将其与其他音调合并在一起，electronic synthesizer（电子合成器）创造新的声音（可以模仿声学仪器的声音）。

synergy \ˈsi-nər-jē\   The increased effectiveness that results when two or more people or businesses work together. 协同效应；协同增效作用

• With the first company's importance in print media and the second's success on the Web, everyone was convinced that the merger would result in an awesome synergy. 第一家公司在印刷媒体上很重要，第二家公司在网络上很成功。有了这些，大家深信，两家公司合并会产生令人惊叹的协同效应。

An old saying, "The whole is greater than the sum of its parts," expresses the basic meaning of *synergy*. The word is sometimes used in a purely physical sense, especially when talking about drugs; sometimes a "cocktail" of drugs may be more effective than the sum of the effectiveness of each of the separate drugs. But the word is best known in the world of business. The notion that, when the right two companies merge, they'll produce a profitable *synergy* seemed exciting in the 1990s, when *synergy* became a trendy buzzword (even though it's actually been around since the 17th century). The idea of synergy was one factor in what became a "merger mania"; unfortunately, business synergy often turned out to be harder to achieve than to imagine.

"整体大于部分之和"这一古老谚语表达了 synergy 的基本意思。该词有时用的是纯粹的物理意义，尤其是谈论药物时，有时药物的混合物的效力会超过每种药物的效力之和。但是这一词语在商业领域最为人熟知。当恰当的两家公司合并时，会产生有益的协同效应，这一观点在 20 世纪 90 年代似乎是很令人激动的。当时 synergy 一词成了一个时髦语（尽管 17 世纪以来它就存在了）。协同效应这一观点是"合并热"出现的一个因素；不幸的是，商业协同效应常常比想象的更加难以实现。

syndrome \ˈsin-ˌdrōm\   A group of signs and symptoms that occur together and characterize a particular abnormality or condition. 综合征；综合症状

• When there is no trembling—the most obvious symptom of Parkinson's disease—most doctors fail to recognize the Parkinson's syndrome. 作为帕金森病最典型的症状，颤抖消失时，大多数医生就会无法识别帕金森综合征。

Combining its two Greek roots, *syndrome* means basically "running together." So when diagnosing a condition or disease, doctors tend to look for a group of symptoms existing together. As long as a set of symptoms remains mysterious, it may be referred to as a specific syndrome. But if that name is used for a while, it may become the condition's permanent name, even after an underlying cause has been found. So today we have *Down syndrome*, *acquired immune deficiency syndrome*, *Asperger's syndrome*, *carpal tunnel syndrome*, *chronic fatigue syndrome*, *Tourette's syndrome*, *sick building syndrome*, and many more. And since mental conditions often turn out to have physical causes, *syndrome* is used in psychology as well as in medicine.

  syndrome 合并了两个希腊语词根,其基本意思是"一起跑"。所以,诊断某种疾病时,医生往往寻找同时存在的一组症状。只要一组症状难以理解,就可以将其称为某一特定综合征。但是,如果这一名字用了一段时间,即使隐藏的原因发现了,它也可能成为这一疾病的永久性名称。所以,今天我们有 Down syndrome(唐氏综合征)、acquired immune deficiency syndrome(获得性免疫缺陷综合征;艾滋病)、Asperger's syndrome(阿斯帕格综合征)、carpal tunnel syndrome(腕管综合征)、chronic fatigue syndrome(慢性疲劳综合征)、Tourette's syndrome(图雷特综合征)、sick building syndrome(病态建筑综合征)等等。由于精神疾病常常有身体原因,syndrome 用于医学,也用于心理学。

Quizzes

A. Fill in each blank with the correct letter:

a. cohesion   e. cogeneration
b. syntax   f. synthesize
c. syndrome   g. synergy
d. coalesce   h. codependency

1. The book manages to _____ a great deal of material that has rarely been discussed together.

2. When foreign students speak, they often employ _____ that seems odd in English but would be completely natural in their own language.

3. Paper mills are increasingly starting up _____ projects to turn their waste wood products into electricity and steam.

4. Team _____ is always a problem early in the football season, since the kids may not know each other or understand each other's strengths and weaknesses.

5. Spouses of alcoholics and drug addicts meet every week in the church basement to discuss the problems of _____.

6. Officials worry that these individual terrorist groups may be starting to _____ into one large network.

7. It wasn't obvious what kind of _____ could be achieved by merging an office-supplies company with a tractor manufacturer.

8. Doctors had become concerned about a _____ involving fever, mental confusion, and extreme weakness that had been appearing in dozens of local residents.

B. Indicate whether the following pairs have the same or different meanings:

1. syndrome / depression   same ____ / different ____

2. coalesce / combine   same ____ / different ____
3. cohesion / sticking together   same ____ / different ____
4. codependency / reliance on two parents   same ____ / different ____
5. synergy / combined action   same ____ / different ____
6. cogeneration / two-source power production   same ____ / different ____
7. syntax / sentence structure   same ____ / different ____
8. synthesize / create from several ingredients   same ____ / different ____

Words from Mythology and History 源自神话和历史的词语

Adonis \ə-ˈdä-nəs\ A very handsome young man. 美少年

• Conversation in the little clusters of girls suddenly stops whenever this Adonis—blond, muscular, with an athlete's gait—swaggers down the school corridor. 这个美少年金发碧眼、肌肉发达，走起路来像运动员一样。只要他沿着学校走廊大摇大摆地走过来，三五成群的女孩子突然就不说话了。

Adonis, like Narcissus (see p. 259), was a beautiful youth in Greek mythology. He was loved by both Aphrodite, goddess of love and beauty, and Persephone, goddess of the underworld. One day while hunting, he was killed by a wild boar. In answer to Aphrodite's pleas, Zeus allowed him to spend half the year with her and half in the underworld. Today a man called an Adonis probably has strikingly fine features, low body fat, rippling muscles—and a certain vain attitude of overconfidence. Adonises should beware; the boar that killed Adonis was sent by either the jealous Artemis (goddess of hunting) or the envious Ares (god of war).

Adonis(阿多尼斯)跟 Narcissus(那喀索斯)(见第259页)一样，是希腊神话中的英俊少年。爱神和美神阿芙洛狄忒和冥府王后珀耳塞福涅都爱着他。有一天打猎时，他被一头野猪咬死了。受到阿芙洛狄忒的请求，宙斯允许阿多尼斯每年有半年时间跟她在一起，半年时间在冥府。今天，人称阿多尼斯的人可能有着非常精美的五官、低脂率、凸起的肌肉，还有些过分自信。阿多尼斯们应该小心；咬死阿多尼斯的野猪，要么是心存嫉妒的阿特米斯(狩猎女神)派去的，要么是忌妒的阿瑞斯(战神)派去的。

amazon \ˈa-mə-ˌzän\ A tall, strong, often masculine woman. 高大健壮的女人

• I was greeted by the team's captain, a robust, broad-shouldered amazon who gripped my hand with crushing force. 队长是一个宽肩膀的健壮女人，问候时一下子抓住我的手，力气大得惊人。

In Greek mythology, an Amazon was a member of a race of women warriors. One of the famous labors of Heracles (Hercules) was to obtain the sash of the Amazon queen Hippolyta, and the hero Theseus married Hippolyta's sister. The Amazon River got its name when, in 1542, the first Europeans to descend the river were attacked by Indian warriors who, even at close range, they believed to be women. The mystery of these warriors continues to this day. However impressive a figure they cut, though, not every tall and strong woman today would take it as a compliment to be called an amazon.

在希腊神话中，Amazon(亚马孙战士)是一个女战士部落的成员。赫拉克勒斯(海格力斯)最著名的任务之一，是得到亚马孙女王希波吕忒的腰带。英雄忒休斯跟希波吕忒的妹妹结了婚。亚马孙河 1542 年得到了这个名字，当时，第一批欧洲人沿着河流前进，遭到了印第安战士的袭击。即使在很近的距离，欧洲人也以为这些印第安人是女性。这些战士直到今天仍是一个谜。但是，无论身材在人看来多么高大，今天不是每个高大健壮的女性都觉得被称为 amazon 是一种赞扬。

chimera \kī-ˈmir-ə\ An often grotesque creature of the imagination. （想象的）怪物

- This latest piece of legislation is a weird chimera, with sections devoted to agriculture, defense, welfare, law enforcement, and scientific research. 最近制定的法律是个怪物，其各部分涉及了农业、防卫、战争、执法和科研。

In Greek mythology, the Chimera was a fire-breathing she-monster with a lion's head, a goat's body, and a dragon's tail, which laid waste the countryside in southwestern Turkey. It was finally killed by the hero Bellerophon, whose flying horse, Pegasus, enabled him to attack from the air. Over time, *chimera* came to be used for any imaginary monster made up of strange and mismatched parts; today it's the name of several species of truly bizarre-looking fish. But more commonly a chimera is a fantasy, an illusion, a figment of the imagination, or a dream that will never come true.

在希腊神话中，the Chimera(喀迈拉)是个喷火的母怪物，有狮子的头、山羊的身体和龙的尾巴，在土耳其西南部造成了严重破坏。最后，柏勒洛丰将其杀死了，因为他的飞马帕格索斯让他能够从空中袭击喀迈拉。随着时间的推移，*chimera* 被用来指任何由奇怪的、毫不匹配的部分组成的想象中的怪物。今天，它是几种奇怪的鱼的名称。但是，chimera 更普遍地指幻想、错觉、虚构的事物，或者永远不会实现的梦想。

cornucopia \ˌkȯr-nə-ˈkō-pē-ə\ (1) A container shaped like a hollow horn full of fruits, vegetables, and ears of grain. 丰饶角 (2) An abundance of something desirable. 丰富；充足

- These books were a cornucopia of wonderful stories and poems, and as a child I spent countless hours with them. 这些书中有很多故事和诗歌，小时候我一看就是几个小时。

The Latin term *cornu copiae* meant "horn of plenty," and *cornucopia* and *horn of plenty* have both been used in English since the 16th century. Both terms refer to a hollow goat's horn, or a wicker basket shaped like one, overflowing with produce from the harvest. The cornucopia has been used as a decorative image to represent abundance since at least the 5th Century B. C., when it represented a gift given by the infant god Zeus to his beloved nurse: a broken goat's horn that would always magically be filled with whatever she wanted. In the U. S., cornucopias are often seen on altars, in store-window displays, and as table centerpieces, especially at harvesttime or Thanksgiving.

拉丁语 *cornucopiae* 意思是"丰饶角"，*cornucopia* 和 *horn of plenty* 从 16 世纪都一直使用，两者都指一个内空的山羊角或者柳条篮子，里面的农产品多得涌了出来。丰饶角用来作为点缀形象，代表丰足，从公元前 5 世纪就开始了。当时它代表幼年宙斯给他热爱的乳母的礼物：一个断掉的山羊角，里面总是神奇地充满了她想要的东西。在美国，丰饶角

通常出现在祭坛上、商店橱窗里，或作为桌子中央的装饰品，尤其是在收获时节或者感恩节。

Elysium \ i-ˈli-zhē-əm \ A place or condition of ideal happiness; paradise. 极乐世界；天堂

• They had named their estate Elysium, and as we gazed out over its fountains, ponds, and sweeping lawns we could see why. 他们把自家的庄园命名为天堂。当我们极目望去，看到的是喷泉、池塘和大片的草地时，也就明白为什么了。

This word came into Latin from the Greek *Elysion*. In classical mythology, *Elysium*, or the *Elysian fields*, was the home of the blessed after death, the final resting place of the souls of the heroic and the pure. So it's easy to see how the word came to mean any place or state of bliss or delight. When we try to picture heaven, many of us probably see a lovely park; the great boulevard of Paris was named for the beautiful park that originally bordered it: the Champs-Elysées, or Elysian Fields. 这一词语源自进入拉丁语的希腊语 Elysion。在古典神话中，*Elysium*，或者 *Elysian fields*（极乐世界），是神佑者死后的家园。所以，很容易明白该词为什么指代任何快乐的地方或快乐的状态。当我们想象天堂的样子时，很多人可能在脑海中看到的是一个可爱的花园。巴黎那条著名大道的名字就来自原来与其相邻的美丽公园：the *Champs-Elysées*（香榭丽舍），或者 Elysian Fields（极乐世界）。

epicure \ˈe-pi-ˌkyu̇r\ A person with cultivated taste, especially for food and drink; a gourmet. 鉴赏家；(尤指)美食家

• He reads trashy novels and watches junk on TV, but he has an epicure's love of fine cheeses and wines. 他读垃圾小说、看垃圾电视，却对优质奶酪和葡萄酒有着美食家的偏爱。

The Greek philosopher Epicurus was known for his original thinking about the nature of matter, but he's best remembered for his ideas about pleasure as the chief aim of life. By pleasure Epicurus chiefly meant the absence of pain and anxiety. However, over the years *Epicureanism* has come to mean a delight in fine sensual pleasures, and today an *epicure* is someone with refined taste, especially in food and wine. To display your own refined taste in language, you might try using *epicure* and *epicurean* in place of the overused *gourmet*. 希腊哲学家伊壁鸠鲁以其对事物本质那新奇的思考方式著称。不过，他最著名的却是其"快乐乃人生主要目标"的观点。快乐，在他看来主要指没有痛苦、没有忧虑。但是，这些年来，*Epicureanism*（享乐主义）已用来指对感官享受的喜爱，而且今天 epicure 指很有品位的人，尤其是在食物和酒方面的品位。要展示你在语言方面的品位，你可能会使用 *epicure* 和 *epicurean* 代替使用过滥的 *gourmet*。

exodus \ˈek-sə-dəs\ A situation in which many people leave a place at the same time. 大批离开

• The war led to a mass exodus of Iraq's Christians. 战争使伊拉克的基督教徒大批离去。

The second book of the Old Testament tells of the departure of Moses and the Israelites from Egypt and their difficult journey across the Sinai Desert to Mount Sinai, from which they would eventually complete their journey to their home in

Palestine. The book's original Hebrew name was Shemot, but it's known to English-speakers as Exodus, from the Greek *exodos*, "departure." Leon Uris chose the name *Exodus* for his powerful novel about the founding of Israel in the years after World War II, since the new state's postwar settlers had departed from many parts of the world for their new home in Palestine.

《圣经·旧约》中第二卷讲的内容是：摩西和以色列人离开埃及，克服困难穿过西奈沙漠到西奈山，从西奈山最终回到家乡巴勒斯坦。这一卷最初的希伯来语名称是 *Shemot*，但讲英语的人称其为 *Exodus*。*Exodus* 源自希腊语 *exodos*，意思是"离开"。里昂·乌里斯选择了 *Exodus* 作为其小说的名称。这部宏大的小说讲的是第二次世界大战后以色列建国的故事，因为这个新生国家的战后定居者已经从世界很多地方离开回到了巴勒斯坦的新家。

gorgon \ˈgȯr-gən\ An ugly, repulsive, or terrifying woman. 丑恶的女人

• The beautiful star disappeared into the makeup room and emerged two hours later transformed into a gorgon. 美丽的星星消失在化妆的房间，两小时后出现时，成了一个丑恶的女人。

The Gorgons were three monstrous sisters in Greek mythology, the most famous of whom was Medusa. They had snakes for hair, and anyone who looked directly at them was immediately turned to stone. Medusa herself was finally beheaded by the hero Perseus, who avoided looking straight at her by instead watching her reflection in his mirrorlike shield. Today the familiar types of jellyfish, with long snakelike tentacles descending from their headlike bodies, are known as medusas.

The Gorgons(戈耳工蛇发女)是希腊神话中的三个姐妹怪物，其中最有名的是美杜莎。她们的头发是毒蛇，谁正视她们都会马上变成石头。美杜莎最后被帕修斯砍掉了脑袋。这位英雄没有直接看她，而是从镜子一样的盾上看她的映像。今天，我们熟悉的几种水母，长长的、蛇一样的触须从长得像脑袋的身体上垂下来，称为 *medusas*(水螅水母)。

Quiz

Fill in each blank with the correct letter:

a. epicure   e. gorgon
b. Elysium   f. exodus
c. Adonis   g. chimera
d. amazon   h. cornucopia

1. Her boss was a _____ who terrorized the office.
2. As he aged he began to think the CIA was watching him, and even though it was just a _____ it caused him a lot of anxiety.
3. She spoke about her country place as an _____ where they could spend their lives surrounded by beauty.
4. He's a serious _____, and you have to be brave to invite him over for dinner.
5. When the economy is good, a job fair can be a _____ of employment opportunities.
6. Her departure from the company led to an _____ of other employees.
7. To everyone's surprise, he ended up marrying a robust, outdoorsy _____

UNIT 29

an inch taller than he was.

8. Everyone thought her new boyfriend was an _____, and she liked watching girls' heads turn as they walked around campus together.

Review Quizzes

A. Choose the closest definition:

1. circumspect   a. lazy   b. all-seeing   c. careful
   d. winding
2. surmount   a. increase   b. overcome   c. look through
   d. reject
3. interdict   a. scold   b. allow   c. cut off
   d. intrude
4. diminutive   a. little   b. cozy   c. detailed
   d. comfortable
5. surreal   a. excessive   b. artistic   c. secret
   d. dreamlike
6. circuitous   a. circular   b. electrical   c. roundabout
   d. circulating
7. surfeit   a. surplus   b. waves   c. conclusion
   d. topic
8. coalesce   a. begin   b. merge   c. cooperate
   d. end
9. interstice   a. filling   b. gap   c. layer
   d. village
10. minutiae   a. particles   b. leftovers   c. moments
    d. trivia

B. Fill in each blank with the correct letter:

a. cogeneration   f. surcharge
b. paleontology   g. circumvent
c. codependency   h. minimalism
d. syntax   i. interdict
e. Paleolithic   j. cohesion

1. He knew his daughter wasn't alcoholic, but he worried about the _____ he'd been noticing between her and her husband.

2. From the odd _____ of the sentences, she guessed that the writer didn't know English that well.

3. After going on a fossil dig in Africa in junior year, he decided to pursue

· 717 ·

graduate work in _____.

4. The college's new _____ system will use natural gas to produce both electricity and heat.

5. To help balance its budget, the city is now considering adding a _____ to all speeding tickets.

6. We found some chipped-stone arrowheads and took them to a local professor, who identified them as products of the _____ period.

7. More agents will be needed to _____ the drugs being carried north to Panama from Colombia.

8. Some people worry about the _____ of the European Union, especially as the number of member nations grows and national interests begin to shift.

9. Some outside hackers have managed to _____ the country's Internet censorship by clever electronic means.

10. The critics call her novels good examples of _____, since she barely describes people or scenes at all and the action is never really explained.

C. Indicate whether the following pairs of words have the same or different meanings:

1. minuscule / empty   same ____ / different ____
2. interpolate / fill up   same ____ / different ____
3. circumference / spiral   same ____ / different ____
4. intercede / invade   same ____ / different ____
5. synthesize / perform   same ____ / different ____
6. necropolis / graveyard   same ____ / different ____
7. syndrome / group of symptoms   same ____ / different ____
8. circumspect / visible from afar   same ____ / different ____
9. necrosis / black magic   same ____ / different ____
10. coalesce / come together   same ____ / different ____

UNIT 30

TOXI comes from the Greek and Latin words for "poison," something the Greeks and Romans knew a good deal about. Socrates died by taking a solution of poison hemlock, a flowering plant much like wild carrot that now also grows in the U. S. Rome's enemy Mithridates, king of Pontus, was obsessed with poisons, experimented with them on prisoners, and tried to make himself immune to them by eating tiny amounts of them daily. Nero's mother Agrippina poisoned several of her son's rivals to power—and probably did the same to her own husband, the emperor Claudius.

TOXI 源自希腊语和拉丁语中表示"毒"的词语。希腊人和罗马人对毒相当了解。苏格拉底喝下毒芹溶液而死。毒芹是一种开花植物,很像今天美国生长的野胡萝卜。罗马的敌人、本都王国的国王米特里达梯对毒药很着迷,他在犯人身上做实验,还想通过每天服用微量毒药,使自己对毒药产生免疫力。尼禄的母亲阿格里皮娜,毒死了几个与自己儿子争夺权力的对手,可能也毒死了自己的丈夫克劳迪亚斯皇帝。

toxin \ˈtäk-sən\   A substance produced by a living organism (such as bacteria) that is highly poisonous to other organisms. 毒素

• Humans eat rhubarb stems without ill effects, while cattle may die from eating the leaves, which seem to contain two different toxins. 人类食用大黄的茎没什么不良反应,而牛食用了大黄的叶子则可能死亡。两者似乎含有两种不同的毒素。

Long before chemists started creating poisons from scratch, humans were employing natural toxins for killing weeds and insects. For centuries South American tribes have used the toxin curare, extracted from a native vine, to tip their arrows. The garden flower called wolfsbane or monkshood is the source of aconite, an extremely potent toxin. The common flower known as jimsonweed contains the deadly poison scopolamine. And the castor-oil plant yields the almost unbelievably poisonous toxin called ricin. Today we hear health advisers of all kinds talk about ridding the body of toxins; but they're usually pretty vague about which ones they mean, and most of these "toxins" wouldn't be called that by biologists.

在药剂师创造毒药很久之前,人类就在使用自然 toxins(毒素)除草杀虫了。几个世纪以来,南美部落在箭头上涂抹毒素箭毒,该毒是从当地一种藤蔓中提炼的。名为附子草或舟形乌头的园中花卉,是提炼附子这一剧毒的来源。曼陀罗这一常见花卉含有东莨菪碱(làng dàng jiǎn)这一致命毒药。蓖麻能产生毒性几乎令人难以置信的蓖麻毒素。今天,我们听到各类健康顾问谈到给身体排毒;但是他们通常很不明确是哪些毒素,而且这些"毒素"大多数并不被生物学家称为毒素。

toxicity \ täk-ˈsi-sə-tē \   The state of being poisonous; the degree to which something is poisonous. 有毒;毒性

• Though they had tested the drug on animals, they suspected the only way to measure its toxicity for humans was by studying accidental human exposures. 他们虽然在动物身上测试了这种药,但是怀疑要测量它对人的毒性,只能研究偶然的人类中毒案例。

Toxicity is often a relative thing; in the words of a famous old saying, "The dose makes the poison." Thus, it's possible to die from drinking too much water, and lives have been saved by tiny doses of arsenic. Even though botulinum toxin is the most *toxic* substance known, it's the basic ingredient in Botox, which is injected into the face to get rid of wrinkles. With some poisons, mere skin contact can be lethal; others are lethal when breathed into the lungs in microscopic amounts. To determine if a chemical will be officially called a poison, researchers often use the "LD50" test: If 50 milligrams of the substance for every kilogram of an animal's body weight results in the death of 50% of test animals, the chemical is a poison. But there are problems with such tests, and toxicity remains a very individual concept.

toxicity(毒性)是相对的,用一句著名的古老谚语说:"剂量决定毒性。"这样,喝水太多也可能丧命,微小剂量的砒霜也救过命。即使肉毒素是已知最 *toxic*(有毒的)物质,它却是注射进脸部用以除皱的保妥适注射液的基本成分。有些毒药,仅仅皮肤接触都可能是致命的;其他毒药,吸入微量是致命的。要确定某一化学物质是否可以正式称为毒药,研究人员经常使用"LD50"测试;如果动物身体每千克体重有 50 毫克该物质能让 50% 的被试动物死掉,这种化学物质就是毒药。不过,这种测试是有问题的,毒性仍然是个很独特的概念。

toxicology \ ˌtäk-si-ˈkä-lə-jē \   A science that deals with poisons and their effect. 毒理学

• At medical school he had specialized in toxicology, hoping eventually to find work in a crime laboratory. 他在医学院专修毒理学,希望最后在犯罪实验室找到工作。

Even though most of us are aware of toxicology primarily from crime shows on TV, *toxicologists* actually do most of their work in other fields. Many are employed by drug companies, others by chemical companies. Many work for the government, making sure the public is being kept safe from environmental poisons in the water, soil, and air, as well as unhealthy substances in our food and drugs. These issues often have to do with quantity; questions about how much of some substance should be considered dangerous, whether in the air or in a soft drink, may be left to toxicologists. But occasionally a toxicology task may be more exciting: for instance, discovering that what looked like an ordinary heart attack was actually brought on by a hypodermic injection of a paralyzing muscle relaxant.

虽然大多数人是从电视上的犯罪节目知道了 *toxicity*（毒理学）的，但 *toxicologists*（毒理学家）的大部分工作是在其他领域进行的。很多人在制药公司工作，其他人在化学公司工作。很多人为政府工作，确保公众安全避开水、土壤和空气中的环境毒物，以及食物和药品中的不健康物质。这些问题常常与量有关。某种物质多少才可以认定为有毒，不管是在空气中还是在软饮料中，应该留给毒理学家。但是，偶尔会有一个毒理学任务更加令人激动，比如发现看似普通的心脏病发作，实际上是皮下注射令人瘫痪的肌松剂引发的。

neurotoxin \ˌnu̇r-ō-ˈtäk-sən\ A poisonous protein that acts on the nervous system. 神经毒素

● From her blurred vision, slurred speech, and muscle weakness, doctors realized she had encountered a neurotoxin, and they suspected botulism. 她视线模糊、话语不清、肌肉虚弱，医生意识到她遭遇了神经毒素，怀疑是肉毒中毒。

The nervous system is almost all-powerful in the body: all five senses depend on it, as do breathing, digestion, and the heart. So it's an obvious target for poisons, and *neurotoxins* have developed as weapons in many animals, including snakes, bees, and spiders. Some wasps use a neurotoxin to paralyze their prey so that it can be stored alive to be eaten later. Snake venom is often *neurotoxic* (as in cobras and coral snakes, for example), though it may instead be *hemotoxic* (as in rattlesnakes and coppermouths), operating on the circulatory system. Artificial neurotoxins, called *nerve agents*, have been developed by scientists as means of chemical warfare; luckily, few have ever been used.

神经系统在体内几乎具有无上权力，所有五种官能都要依靠它，就像呼吸、消化和心脏那样。所以，它是毒物的明显目标。neurotoxins（神经毒素）在很多动物体内都发展成了武器，包括蛇、蜜蜂和蜘蛛。有些马蜂利用神经毒素使猎物瘫痪，这样可以将其储存起来以后食用。蛇毒常常是 *neurotoxic*（毒害神经的）（比如就像眼镜蛇毒和珊瑚蛇毒那样），虽然它也可能是 *hemotoxic*（毒害血液的）（像响尾蛇毒和铜嘴蛇毒那样），对循环系统产生作用。人造神经毒素称为 *nerve agents*（神经毒气），作为化学战争的手段已经被科学家开发出来了；幸运的是，很少人使用过。

TEN/TENU comes from the Latin *tenuis*, meaning "thin." So to *extend* something is to stretch it, and lots of things get thin when they're stretched. The *ten-* root is even seen in *pretend*, which once meant to stretch something out above or in front; that something came to be a claim that you were something that you actually weren't.

TEN/TENU 源自拉丁语 *tenuis*，意思是"薄"。所以要 *extend* 什么东西，就是伸展它，很多东西伸展了就会变薄。词根 *ten-* 可以在 *pretend*（假装）中看到。这个词语曾经的意思是将某物在上面或前面伸展，这一"某物"后来成了一个声称，说自己是什么，但实际上却不是。

---

tenuous \ˈten-yə-wəs\ Having little substance or strength; flimsy, weak. 实质性内容很少的；弱的；容易损坏的

● It's a rather tenuous theory, and the evidence supporting it has been questioned by several researchers. 那个理论很大程度上是站不住脚的，支持它的证据已经遭到几个研究人员的质疑。

Something tenuous has been stretched thin and might break at any time. A person with a tenuous hold on his sanity should be watched carefully. If a business is only *tenuously* surviving, it will probably go bankrupt in the next recession. If there seems to be only a tenuous connection between two crimes, it means the investigators have more work to do.

tenuous 东西已经被伸展得很薄了,随时可能断裂。难以控制自己理智的人应该受到仔细监视。如果一家公司只能 *tenuously*(勉强)生存,下次经济不景气时,它可能就破产了。如果两次犯罪之间只有 tenuous(微弱的)联系,那就意味着调查人员有更多的工作要做了。

attenuated \ə-'ten-yə-ˌwā-təd\ Thinned or weakened. 薄的;细的;减弱的

• The smallpox shot is an injection of the virus in an attenuated form too weak to produce an actual case of smallpox. 这一针天花注射的是减弱毒性的病毒,不会真的引起天花。

A friendship can become *attenuated* if neither person bothers to keep in touch. Radio waves can become attenuated by the shape of the landscape, by foliage, by atmospheric conditions, and simply by distance. Factory workers and rock musicians often use noiseattenuating ear plugs to save their hearing. To *attenuate* something isn't to stop it, just to tone it down.

如果两个朋友都不屑于联系对方,友谊就变得 attenuated(淡薄)了。无线电波会因为地形、枝叶、大气条件和距离而减弱。工厂的工人和摇滚歌手经常用减弱噪声的耳塞保护听力。要 attenuate 什么东西,不是让它停下,而只是将其减弱。

extenuating \ik-'sten-yə-ˌwā-tiŋ\ Partially excusing or justifying. 情有可原的;可减轻罪行的

• A good college rarely accepts someone who has dropped out of high school twice, but in his case there were extenuating circumstances, including the death of both parents. 一所好大学很少会录取高中时期两次辍学的学生,但就他而言,有一些可以理解的情况,包括父母双亡。

Extenuating is almost always used today before "circumstances." *Extenuating circumstances* are an important concept in the law. If you steal to feed your children, you're naturally less guilty than someone who steals just to get richer; if you kill someone in selfdefense, that's obviously an extenuating circumstance that makes your act different from murder. Juries will usually consider extenuating circumstances (even when they're instructed not to), and most judges will listen carefully to an argument about extenuating circumstances as well. And they work outside of the courtroom as well; if you miss your daughter's performance in the middle-school pageant, she may forgive you if it was because you had to race Tigger to the vet's emergency room.

extenuating 在今天几乎总是用在"circumstances"(情节)前面。extenuating circumstances(可减轻罪行的情节)是法律上的一个重要概念。如果你盗窃的目的是喂养孩子,罪行自然会比为了发财而盗窃的人轻一些;如果为了自卫而杀死某人,这显然是可减轻罪行的情节,使你的行为与谋杀有所不同。陪审团通常会考虑可减轻罪行的情节(即使被指示不要这样做),而且大多数法官也会倾听关于可减轻罪行情节的辩论。这些情节在法庭之外也是有用的;如果你错过了女儿的中学选美比赛,而这是因为你不得不赶紧把跳跳虎送往兽医的急诊室,她可能会原谅你。

UNIT 30

distended \ di-ˈsten-dəd \ Stretched or bulging out in all directions; swelled. 肿胀的;浮肿的

• All the children's bellies were distended, undoubtedly because of inadequate nutrition or parasites. 所有孩子的肚子都是肿胀的,毫无疑问是因为营养不良或者寄生虫。

Before giving you a shot, the nurse may wrap a rubber tube around your upper arm to *distend* the veins. When the heart isn't pumping properly, the skin of the feet and ankles may become distended. A doctor who notices that an internal organ has become distended will always want to find out the cause. As you can see, *distended* tends to be a medical term.

给你打针前,护士可能在你上臂缠一根橡胶管子,来 *distend*(使……膨胀)血管。心脏跳动不规律,双脚和脚腕的皮肤都会浮肿。医生注意到内部器官肿胀了,总是想要找出原因。你可以看到,*distended* 往往是医学术语。

Quizzes

A. Fill in each blank with the correct letter:

a. attenuated   e. distended
b. toxicity   f. neurotoxin
c. extenuating   g. tenuous
d. toxicology   h. toxin

1. Guidebooks warn against the _____ of the water hemlock, the deadliest plant in North America.

2. The dog we used to have bit everyone, and only my mother ever tried to come up with _____ circumstances for his behavior.

3. We used to play with our cousins a lot in our childhood, but all those old friendships have become _____ over the years.

4. He was now yelling, his face red and his veins _____, and I feared he might have a heart attack.

5. Sarin, a manmade _____ 500 times more powerful than cyanide, was outlawed by treaty in 1993.

6. The university offers a graduate degree in environmental _____, which deals with chemical and biological threats to public health.

7. Everyone knows that the ceasefire is _____ and would collapse if one armed soldier decided to go on a rampage.

8. Ricin, a _____ that comes from the castor bean, can be lethal if an amount the size of a grain of sand is inhaled.

B. Match the definition on the left with the correct word on the right:

1. flimsy   a. toxicity
2. nerve poison   b. distended
3. study of poisons   c. attenuated

4. bulging
5. plant-based poison
6. poisonousness
7. weakened
8. justifying

d. extenuating
e. toxin
f. tenuous
g. neurotoxin
h. toxicology

TECHNI/TECHNO

TECHNI/TECHNO comes from the Greek *techne*, meaning "art, craft, skill," and shows up in dozens of English words. Some, such as *technical*, *technology*, and *technique*, have long been familiar. Others, such as *techno-thriller*, were only coined in the current computer age, which has also seen the new cut-down terms *techno* (for *techno-pop*, the electronic dance music) and *tech* (for *technician* or *technology*).

TECHNI/TECHNO 源自希腊语 techne，意思是"艺术，工艺，技术"，出现在很多英语词语中。有些词语，比如 technical、technology 和 technique，人们一直都很熟悉。其他词语，比如 techno-thriller，是在目前这个计算机时代造出来的。这个时代也出现了缩略的新词 techno（techno-pop 的缩略语，指电子舞曲）和 tech（technician 或 technology 的缩略语）。

technocrat \ˈtek-nə-ˌkrat\ A scientist or technical expert with power in politics or industry. 技术官僚；技术专家官员

• The new president, a great fan of science, had surrounded himself with an impressive team of technocrats. 这位新任总统是个科学迷，周围聚集的技术官僚数量惊人。

In 1919 W. H. Smyth coined the term *technocracy* to mean basically "management of society by technical experts." Technocracy grew into a movement during the Great Depression of the 1930s, when politicians and financial institutions were being blamed for the economic disaster, and fans of technocracy claimed that letting technical experts manage the country would be a great improvement. (They also suggested that dollars could be replaced by "energy certificates" representing energy units called *ergs*.) Today *technocrat* and *technocratic* are still popular words for experts with a highly rational and scientific approach to public policy issues. But these experts aren't always the best politicians, and when a terrific technological solution to a problem is opposed by a powerful group or industry, lawmakers find it easier to just ignore it.

1919 年，W. H. 史密斯创造了 technocracy 一词，基本上是指"技术专家管理社会"。技术专家政治在 20 世纪 30 年代的大萧条时代成了一场运动。当时，政治家和金融机构因为这次经济灾难遭到了指责。技术爱好者声称，让技术专家管理国家会是很大的进步。（他们还说，美元可以用代表能源单位 ergs〔尔格〕的"能源证书"来代替。）今天，对于那些对公共政策问题有着高度合理和科学处理方法的专家来说，technocrat 和 technocratic 仍然是很受欢迎的词语。但是，这些专家并不总是最好的政治家。当一个出色的解决问题的技术方法遭到实力很强的群体或行业反对时，立法人员发现对它置之不理更容易些。

technophobe \ˈtek-nə-ˌfōb\ One who fears or dislikes advanced technology or

complex devices and especially computers. 先进技术恐惧者；(尤指)电脑恐惧者

• The new employee was a middle-aged technophobe, who seemed startled every time a new page popped up on her computer screen. 这位新雇员是个中年人,害怕先进技术,每次电脑屏幕上跳出新的网页,都会大吃一惊。

The condition known as *technophobia* got its name around 1965 (though its synonym *Luddite* had been around for a long time), and since then we've been flooded with electronic gadgetry. But even today few people actually understand any electrical technology more complicated than a lightbulb, so there's still plenty of technophobia around. And it isn't limited to computer users. The explosion of the atomic bomb made *technophobes* out of millions of people; and since human-caused climate change has been a result of technology, it's not surprising that it too has produced a *technophobic* response. But if technology turns out to be part of a solution rnaybe that will change.

technophobia(新技术恐惧症)这种疾病 1965 年左右有了这个名字(虽然当时其同义词 *Luddite* 已存在很久了)。从此以后,电子机器让我们应接不暇。但是,即使今天也很少有人对哪个电气技术的了解超过对灯泡的了解,所以先进技术恐惧症仍普遍存在。这也不只局限于电脑使用者。原子弹爆炸使无数人成了先进技术恐惧者；由于人类引起的气候变化是技术造成的,它引发了 *technophobic*(先进技术恐惧症的)反应也不稀奇。但是,如果技术能解决部分上述问题,也许这会有所变化。

technophile \ˈtek-nə-ˌfīl\ One who loves technology. 技术迷

• Back in my day, the high-school technophiles subscribed to *Popular Mechanics*, built ham radios, and were always taking apart the engines of their clunkers. 在我那个年代,中学技术迷都订阅《大众机械学》,制造业余无线电,还总是拆开老爷车的发动机。

The word *technophile* came along soon after *technophobe*, which seemed to need an antonym. Its own synonyms include *geek*, *gearhead*, and *propeller-head* (for the characters in 1950s comic books who wore propeller beanies to indicate that they were sci-fi fans). Even before American inventors began amazing the world with their "Yankee ingenuity" in the 19th century, most Americans could be described as technology lovers. Today, American *technophilia* may be seen most vividly when a new version of a popular video game sells millions of copies to young buyers on the day of its release.

technophile 一词在 *technophobe* 之后不久就出现了,因为后者似乎需要反义词。前者的同义词包括 *geek*,*gear-head* 和 *propeller-head*(用来指代 20 世纪 50 年代的连环画人物,他们戴着螺旋桨无檐小便帽,表明自己是科幻迷)。即使是在 19 世纪美国发明家以其"美国佬的聪明"让世人吃惊之前,多数美国人都可以称为技术爱好者。今天,美国人的 *technophilia*(技术迷)最生动的表现是,某一流行电子游戏新版本发行当天,可以卖给年轻人数百万份。

pyrotechnic \ˌpī-rə-ˈtek-nik\ Of or relating to fireworks. 焰火的;出色的;引起轰动的

• Her astonishing, pyrotechnic performance in the concerto left the audience dazed. 她在这一协奏曲中令人吃惊的出色表现令观众眩晕。

You've read about funeral *pyres*, and you may even have survived a *pyromaniac* ("insane fire-starting") stage in your youth, so you might have guessed that *pyr* means "fire" in Greek. *Pyrotechnic* refers literally to fireworks, but always seems to be used for something else—something just as exciting, explosive, dazzling, sparkling, or brilliant. The performances of sports stars and dancers are often described as *pyrotechnic*, and a critic may describe the *pyrotechnics* of a rock guitarist's licks or a film's camerawork. A pyrotechnic performance is always impressive, but the word occasionally suggests something more like "flashy" or "flamboyant."

你读到过葬礼 *pyres*(柴堆),甚至在年轻时安全度过了 *pyromaniac*(放火狂)阶段,所以,你可能已经猜到 *pyr* 在希腊语中意思是"火"。*pyrotechnic* 字面意思指焰火,但似乎总是用在其他事物上——同样激动人心的、引起强烈情绪的、令人目眩的、出色的或者巧妙的事物。体育明星和舞蹈演员的表演常被描述为 pyrotechnic,评论家可能描述摇滚吉他手的小过门或者电影摄影风格的 *pyrotechnics*(技能展示)。pyrotechnic 表演总是令人赞叹,但这个词有时暗示某物更像是"炫耀技巧的"或者"卖弄的"。

LONG

LONG comes from Latin *longus*, which, as you might guess, means "long." The English word *long* shows up in many compound terms such as *long-suffering* ("patiently enduring lasting offense or hardship") and *long-winded* ("boringly long in speaking or writing"), but the *long-* root also sometimes shows up less obviously. To *prolong* something is to lengthen it, for example, and a *chaise longue* (not *lounge*!) is "a long reclining chair."

LONG 源自拉丁语 *longus*。你可以猜到,它意思是"长的"。英语单词 *long* 出现在很多复合词中,比如 *long-suffering*("长期忍受的")和 *long-winded*("冗长枯燥的")。但是,*long-* 这一词根有时不那么明显。比如,*prolong* 某物,意思是将其延长,*chaise longue*(不是 lounge!)是"长靠椅"。

longitude \ˈlän-jə-ˌtüd\ Distance measured by degrees or time east or west from the prime meridian. 经度

• Checking the longitude, she was surprised to see that the tip of South America is actually east of New York City. 查看经度之后,她吃惊地看到,南美洲顶端居然在纽约市以东。

The imaginary (but very important) lines of longitude run from the North Pole to the South Pole. Each is identified by the number of degrees it lies east or west of the so-called prime meridian in Greenwich, England (part of London). A circle is divided into 360°; so, for example, the longitude of the Egyptian city of Cairo is about 31°E—that is, about 31° east of London. The "long" sense of the root may be easier to see in some uses of the adjective *longitudinal*: A longitudinal study is a research study that follows its subjects over many long years, and a longitudinal engine is one that drives a crankshaft that runs lengthwise under a vehicle (as in rear-wheel-drive cars) rather than crosswise.

想象的(但却是很重要的)lines of longitude(经线)从北极延伸到南极。每一条线都用它在英格兰(英国的一部分)的格林尼治的本初子午线以东或以西的度数来标明。一圈经度被分为 360 度,所以,比如埃及城市开罗的经度大约是东经 31 度,也就是在伦敦以东大约 31 度的地方。这一词根的"长"这一意思在 *longitudinal*(经度的)这一形容词的某些用法中比较容易看出：longitudinal(纵向的)研究指跟踪研究对象多年的研究，而 longitudinal(纵置式的)发动机驱动交通工具下面的纵向而不是横向的曲柄轴。

elongate \i-ˈlȯṅ-ˌgāt\ (1) To extend the length of; stretch. 延长；伸长 (2) To grow in length. 变长

• When mammals gained the ability to fly, it wasn't by means of feathered wings; instead, over thousands of years the digits of their "hands" elongated and a web formed between them. 哺乳动物获得了飞行能力，靠的不是长满羽毛的翅膀，而是经过数千年之后，"手指"变长而且它们之间形成了蹼。

Elongate is often found in scientific writing, but the adjective *elongated* is more common, and frequently used to describe body parts in discussions of anatomy. This was even the case when the superhero Elongated Man made his appearance back in 1960. But some other characters with the same powers—Plastic Man, Elastic Lad, and Mr. Fantastic—ended up having longer careers. *elongate* 常常存在于科学文本中，但是其形容词 *elongated*(细长的)更为常见，频繁在解剖学文章中用来描述身体部位。当超级英雄伸缩人 20 世纪 60 年代出现时，就更是如此了。但是有着同样能力的一些其他角色，比如塑胶人、伸缩少年和神奇先生，结果都有更长的生命力。

longueur \lȯṅ-ˈgər\ A dull and boring portion, as of a book. (书籍等的)乏味的部分

• She tells me the book is extremely rewarding, in spite of some longueurs during which she occasionally drops off to sleep. 她告诉我，虽然这本书有些部分很无聊，她有时会睡着，但读了还是很有收获的。

Longueur comes straight from French, a language based on Latin. When we borrow a foreign word, it's usually because English doesn't have a really good synonym, which is the case here. *Longueur* is used mostly when talking about books, but also when describing lectures and speeches. Like certain other French words, *longueur* tends to be used mainly by critics and professors—but lots of us who aren't either could find plenty of use for it too. *longueur* 直接来自法语这种以拉丁语为基础的语言。我们借用外来语时，通常是因为英语没有真正好的同义词，这里就是这种情况。*longueur* 多数情况下用于谈论书籍，但也用于描述讲课和演讲。像某些其他法语单词那样，*longueur* 往往主要是评论家和大学教师使用的，不过我们中很多不属于这两者的人也可以经常使用。

oblong \ˈä-ˌblȯṅ\ Longer in one direction than in the other. 长的；长方形的

• Their apartment was awkwardly oblong, with a long skinny hall running past the cramped rooms. 他们的公寓很长很别扭，沿着细长的走廊是狭小的房间。

Oblong is a general but useful term for describing the shape of things such as leaves. There's no such thing as an oblong circle, since a stretched circle has to be called an oval, and any rectangle that isn't square is oblong, at least if it's lying on its side (such rectangles can actually be called *oblongs*). Pills are generally oblong rather than round, to slide down the throat more easily. An oblong table will often fit a living space better than a square or round one with the same area. And people are always buried in oblong boxes.

oblong 是个意思宽泛但常用的词语，用来描述诸如叶子这些事物的形状。没有长圆这种东西，因为圆拉长了叫做椭圆形，任何不是正方形的有直角的平行四边形都是长方形，至少如果它平放时是这样（这种有直角的平行四边形实际上叫作 *oblongs*）。药片通常是长的，而不是圆的，这样沿着喉咙滑下去会更容易。在同一生活空间，长方形桌子常常比正方形和圆形的更合适。人总是埋葬在长方形的箱子里。

Quizzes

A. Indicate whether the following pairs of words have the same or different meaning：

1. technophobe / computer genius   same ____ / different ____
2. longueur / boring passage   same ____ / different ____
3. pyrotechnic / spectacular   same ____ / different ____
4. oblong / unnatural   same ____ / different ____
5. technocrat / mechanic   same ____ / different ____
6. elongate / stretch   same ____ / different ____
7. longitude / lines parallel to the equator   same ____ / different ____
8. technophile / technology hater   same ____ / different ____

B. Fill in each blank with the correct letter：

a. technocrat   e. oblong
b. longitude   f. technophobe
c. technophile   g. longueur
d. elongate   h. pyrotechnic

1. By following a few basic tips, you can _____ your laptop battery's life by a month or more.

2. Even the Greeks knew how to calculate latitude from the sun and stars, but no one managed to measure _____ accurately until the 18th century.

3. All through high school and college, computer jocks like him were called nerds or geeks, but he always preferred to be described as a _____.

4. The talk was just one _____ after another, and she finally got up and tiptoed out of the lecture hall.

5. The shields used by Celtic warriors were _____ rather than round, and thus able to protect much of the body.

6. As governor, he had the reputation of being a _____, convinced that much of the state's problems could be solved by using proper technology and data.

7. The debate between these two remarkable minds was a _____ display of brilliant argument and slashing wit.

8. My father is making a real effort to master e-mail, but my mother is a genuine _____ who just wishes the computer would go away.

IDIO comes from the Greek *idios*, meaning "one's own" or "private." In Latin this root led to the word *idiota*, meaning "ignorant person"— that is, a person who doesn't take in knowledge from outside himself. And that led to a familiar English word that gets used too often, usually to describe people who aren't ignorant at all. IDIO 源自希腊语 *idios*("自己的"或者"私人的")。在拉丁语中,这一词根产生了 *idiota*,意思是"无知的人",也就是一个不从自身以外吸收知识的人。这就产生了一个使用过多的为人熟知的英语词语,通常用来描述根本就不无知的人。

idiom\ˈi-dē-əm\ An expression that cannot be understood from the meanings of its separate words but must be learned as a whole. 习语

• As a teacher of foreign students, you can't use idioms like "Beats me!" and "Don't jump the gun" in class unless you want to confuse everyone. 作为外国学生的教师,你不能在课堂使用"Beats me"和"Don't jump the gun"这样的习语,除非你想让大家一头雾水。

If you had never heard someone say "We're on the same page," would you have understood that they weren't talking about a book? And the first time someone said he'd "ride shotgun," did you wonder where the gun was? A modern English-speaker knows thousands of *idioms*, and uses many every day. Idioms can be completely ordinary ("first off," "the other day," "make a point of," "What's up?") or more colorful ("asleep at the wheel," "bite the bullet," "knuckle sandwich"). A particular type of idiom, called a *phrasal verb*, consists of a verb followed by an adverb or preposition (or sometimes both); in *make over*, *make out*, and *make up*, for instance, notice how the meanings have nothing to do with the usual meanings of *over*, *out*, and *up*. 如果你从未听到过谁说"We are on the same page",你会明白这根本不是在说一本书吗?某人第一次说他"ride shotgun",你有没有想知道枪在哪里?当代说英语的人知道成千上万的习语,每天也使用很多。习语可以非常普通("first off""the other day""make a point of""What's up?")或者很有趣("asleep at the wheel""bite the bullet""knuckle sandwich")。有一种特殊类型的习语叫做 *phrasal verb*(短语动词),由一个动词和一个副词或者介词构成(或者有时候两者都有);比如在 *make over*,*make out* 和 *make up* 中,请注意习语的意义与 *over*,*out*,*up* 的通常意思毫无关系。

idiomatic\ˌi-dē-ə-ˈma-tik\ In a manner conforming to the particular forms of a language. 地道的;符合某一语言形式的

• The instructions for assembling the TV probably sounded fine in the original Chinese but weren't exactly written in idiomatic English. 组装电视的说明书,汉语原文本来可能听起来不错,但不是用地道的英语写的。

The speech and writing of a native-born English-speaker may seem crude, uneducated, and illiterate, but will almost always be *idiomatic*—that is, a native speaker always sounds like a native speaker. For a language learner, speaking and writing *idiomatically* in another language is the greatest challenge. Even highly educated foreign learners—professors, scientists, doctors, etc.—rarely succeed in mastering the kind of idiomatic English spoken by an American 7th-grader.

英语国家出生的人，其口语和文字或许看似粗俗、缺乏教育、不够通顺，但几乎总是 *idiomatic*（地道的），也就是说，本族语者总是听着像本族语者。对语言学习者来说，要用另一种语言 *idiomatically*（地道地）说或写，是最大的挑战。即使接受过极好教育的外语学习者，比如大学教师、科学家、医生等等，也很少能掌握美国七年级学生那种地道的英语。

idiosyncrasy \ ˌi-dē-ə-ˈsiŋ-krə-sē \ An individual peculiarity of a person's behavior or thinking. （行为、思维的）个人怪异之处；怪异行为；怪异思维

• Mr. Kempthorne, whose idiosyncrasies are well known to most of us, has recently begun walking around town talking to two ferrets he carries on his shoulders. 肯普索恩先生的怪异之处，我们多数人都很熟悉。他最近开始在城里闲逛，边走边跟肩上两只雪貂说话。

Idiosyncrasies are almost always regarded as harmless. So, for example, filling your house with guns and Nazi posters might be called something stronger than *idiosyncratic*. But if you always arrange your Gummi candies in table form by color and type, then eat them in a special order starting with the pterodactyls (purple ones must die first!), you might qualify. Harmless though your strange habits might be, they may not be the kind of thing you'd tell people about; most Americans are careful to hide their idiosyncrasies, since our culture doesn't seem to value odd behavior. The British, however, are generally fond of their eccentrics, and English villages seem to be filled with them. By the way, few words are harder to spell than *idiosyncrasy*—be careful.

idiosyncrasies（个人的怪异之处）几乎总被认为是没什么害处的。所以，比如你在房子填满了枪支和纳粹的海报，或许可以被认为比 *idiosyncratic*（怪异的）更严重。但是，如果你按照颜色和类型，把橡皮软糖以一览表的形式列出来，之后按照特殊顺序吃，先从翼手龙开始（紫色的必须先死！），那就合格了。你的怪习惯也许没什么害处，它们也许不是你要告诉别人的内容。多数美国人都很小心地隐藏自己的怪异之处，因为我们的文化似乎不重视奇怪的行为。而英国人呢，普遍喜欢怪人，他们的村庄似乎满是这种人。顺便告知一声，很少有词语的拼法比 *idiosyncrasy* 更难——小心。

idiopathic \ ˌi-dē-ə-ˈpa-thik \ Arising spontaneously or from an obscure or unknown cause. 自然发生的；原因不明的

• After her doctor hemmed and hawed and finally described her condition as "idiopathic," she realized she needed a second opinion. 医生支支吾吾了半天，最后说她的病"来源不明"。她觉得需要另找医生了。

Words with the *-pathy* suffix generally name a disease or condition (see PATH, p. 226), so you might think *idiopathic* should describe a disease or condition that's unique to an individual. But the word is actually generally used to describe any medical condition that no one has yet figured out. Most facial tics are called idiopathic by doctors, since no cause can be found. Other well-known conditions, including chronic fatigue syndrome, irritable bowel syndrome, and fibromyalgia, still perplex the medical community. And even though doctors expect that the causes of all of them will eventually be found, and that those causes will turn out to be the same for hundreds of thousands of people, the conditions are still called idiopathic.

带有 *-pathy* 这一后缀的词语通常指代疾病（见 PATH，第 226 页），所以，你可能认为 *idiopath*（特发病）应该描述某

• 730 •

人特有的疾病。但是，这个词语实际上通常用来描述无人明白的疾病。大多数面部抽搐被医生描述为原因不明，因为发现不了原因。其他众所周知的疾病，包括慢性疲劳综合征、过敏性肠综合征和纤维性肌痛，仍然使医学界迷惑不解。虽然医生期待所有这些疾病的原因最终能够真相大白，而且这些原因对千千万万人来说是一样的，但这些疾病仍然是原因不明。

AER/AERO comes from the Greek word for "air." The *aerospace* industry manufactures vehicles that travel through the atmosphere and beyond into space. *Aerodynamic* designs move through the air with maximum speed. And *aerophobia* is the technical name for what we usually just call fear of flying.
AER/AERO 源自希腊语中表示"空气"的词语。aerospace（航天的；太空的）工业生产穿过大气、进入太空的交通工具。aerodynamic（空气动力学的）设计以最大速度穿越空气。aerophobia（高空恐惧症）是通常所谓的飞行恐惧的专业名称。

aerial \ˈer-ē-əl\ (1) Performed in the air. 空中表演的 (2) Performed using an airplane. 飞机表演的

• They're doing an aerial survey of the whale population, which involves scanning the ocean's surface from an airplane. 他们在对鲸鱼的数量进行航测，这需要从飞机上查看海洋表面。

Shakespeare himself may have coined this word, in *Othello*, and later he gave the name Ariel to the famous air-spirit character in *The Tempest*. An *aerialist* is an acrobat who performs high above the audience. In painting, *aerial perspective* is the way an artist creates the illusion that a mountain or city is far away (something that early painters only slowly learned how to do), usually by making it slightly misty and bluish gray—as if seen through miles of air. An *aerial work platform*, or "cherry picker," supports a worker at a high elevation on the end of a crane. And *aerial* itself can be used as a noun, meaning a TV antenna, a forward pass in football, or a high-flying stunt performed by a skateboarder or snowboarder.
莎士比亚本人可能在《奥赛罗》中造了这个词，后来把 Ariel（阿里尔）这个名字给了《暴风雨》中那个著名的空中精灵。aerialist（高空杂技演员）是在观众头上的高空中表演的杂技演员。在绘画艺术中，aerial perspective（空中透视）指画家创造山或者城市在远方这一错觉的方式（这是早期画家慢慢才学会的），通常的方法是使其有些雾蒙蒙的、烟灰色的，好像是透过几英里的空气看到的。aerial work platform（高空作业平台），或称"车载升降台"，支撑着工人在高空的起重机顶端工作。aerial 一词本身可用作名词，意思是电视天线、足球的向前传球，或者滑板运动员或滑雪运动员表演的高飞特技。

aerate \ˈer-ˌāt\ To supply with air or oxygen. 提供空气；提供氧气

• The garden soil was well aerated, since they had recently plowed in all the compost and manure and even added a box of earthworms. 花园的土壤透气性很好，因为它们最近把混合肥料、粪肥都翻进土壤了，甚至还加了一盒子蚯蚓。

Faucet *aerators* and aerating showerheads can be easily installed by homeowners to cut water (and especially hot water) use by as much as 50%. A lawn aerator removes little plugs of soil in order to let air deep into the soil, greatly improving the quality of soil that may have gotten too compacted. And a pond aerator, such as a fountain, is a necessity for an ornamental pond with no stream feeding it, since oxygen in the water is necessary to prevent the growth of algae and allow fish to live.

房主很容易安装水龙头 *aerators*(起泡器)和充气喷头,以减少高达百分之五十的用水量(尤其是热水使用量)。草坪打孔器除去小块土壤让空气进入土壤深处,从而大大改善板结土壤的质量。池塘增氧工具,比如喷泉,是没有水流入的观赏水池所必需的,因为需要水中的氧气阻止藻类生长,使鱼类活下去。

aerobic \ ˌer-ˈō-bik \ (1) Living or occurring only in the presence of oxygen. 需氧的 (2) Involving or increasing oxygen consumption. 有氧的

● Trainers measure a person's aerobic capacity by means of the VO_2 max ("maximum volume of oxygen") test. 教练员利用最大摄氧量测试来测量人的有氧能力。

Aerobic exercise is exercise that takes an extended amount of time— usually ten minutes or more—but is usually performed at only moderate intensity. Running, swimming, bicycling, and cross-country skiing are classic aerobic exercises. In 1968 a best-selling book called *Aerobics* introduced a system of exercise for increasing the body's ability to take in and use oxygen, and today aerobics classes, often mimicking such outdoor exercise as running and bicycling, take place every afternoon in thousands of gyms and YMCAs across the country. Aerobic exercise particularly strengthens the heart and lungs, but usually has many other good effects as well. Aerobic bacteria, which need oxygen to live, are essential for breaking down living matter so that it returns to the soil. They include the famous intestinal *E. coli*, as well as the staph and strep bacteria that can make a visit to the hospital risky.

aerobic exercise(有氧运动)是持续时间较长的运动——通常是十分钟或者更长——但通常只是一般的强度。跑步、游泳、骑自行车和越野滑雪都是典型的有氧运动。1968 年,一本叫做 *Aerobics*(《有氧健身运动》)的畅销书,介绍了一套运动,以提高身体吸入和使用氧气的能力。今天的有氧健身运动课,经常模仿跑步和骑自行车这样的室外运动,每天下午在全国成千上万的健身房和基督教青年会进行。有氧运动特别能强心健肺,但通常也有很多其他好处。需氧细菌需要氧气来生存,对于分解有机物使其回归土壤来说是必要的。它们包括众所周知的大肠杆菌以及葡萄球菌和链球菌。通常因后两者去医院的话,是有危险的。

anaerobic \ ˌa-nə-ˈrō-bik \ (1) Living or occurring in the absence of oxygen. 厌氧的 (2) Relating to activity in which the body works temporarily with inadequate oxygen. 无氧的

● He's never run a mile in his life, and everything he does at the gym is anaerobic. 他从来没有跑过一英里,在健身馆的活动都是无氧的。

In Greek, the prefix *a-* or *an-* means "not" or "without," and *bios* means "life." Anaerobic sports and exercise, such as gymnastics, weight lifting, and sprinting, are of high intensity but short duration, so they don't involve much oxygen intake. Anaerobic exercise triggers a different type of cell activity from aerobic exercise. As a result, it doesn't do much for your heart and lungs and it doesn't burn off fat; what it does do is build muscle. Anaerobic bacteria are bacteria that live without oxygen. They're responsible for several nasty conditions, including tetanus, gangrene, botulism, and food poisoning. They often live in deep wounds, so a bad dog bite—or, even worse, a human bite—can be dangerous, since the mouth is full of anaerobic bacteria. But most anaerobic bacteria are harmless, and many are essential to our lives.

在希腊语中，前缀 *a-* 或者 *an-* 意思是"非"或者"没有"，*bios-* 意思是"生命"。anaerobic sports and exercise（无氧体育运动），比如体操、举重、短跑，都是强度高但时间短，所以它们不需要大量吸入氧气。无氧运动引发了一种与有氧运动不同类型的细胞活动。因此，它对你心和肺没有多少作用，也不燃烧很多脂肪；它能做的是增大肌肉。厌氧细菌的生存不需要氧气。它们是几种严重疾病的罪魁祸首，包括破伤风、坏疽、肉毒中毒、食物中毒。它们经常生活在很深的伤口，所以严重的狗咬伤——或者，更糟糕的是，人咬伤——可能很危险，因为伤口满是厌氧细菌。但是，大多数厌氧细菌是无害的，很多是我们生命必需的。

Quizzes

A. Fill in each blank with the correct letter:

a. idiomatic
b. aerate
c. anaerobic
d. idiopathic
e. aerial
f. idiom
g. idiosyncrasy
h. aerobic

1. My Italian friend sometimes says "According to me" when the _____ way of saying it would be "In my opinion."

2. One famous _____ of the great pianist was playing his instrument while wearing fingerless gloves.

3. When she suspected that a patient was just imagining his symptoms, she'd tell him the illness was unusual and _____ and give him some harmless drug.

4. Since oxygen improves the taste of most red wines, wine lovers will usually _____ a newly opened bottle for a few minutes before drinking.

5. _____ photos of the earthquake's destruction showed dramatically how it had cut straight through the city.

6. Most of us say things like "tongue in cheek" or "pound the pavement" without even knowing what an _____ is.

7. She goes running four times a week, and on the other days she does _____ workouts at the gym.

8. The only _____ exercise he gets is biking, but he goes so slowly that it hardly even counts.

B. Indicate whether the following pairs of words have the same or different meanings:

1. idiosyncrasy / quirk   same ____ / different ____
2. aerobic / involving oxygen   same ____ / different ____
3. idiomatic / foreign   same ____ / different ____
4. aerate / supply with air   same ____ / different ____
5. idiom / stupidity   same ____ / different ____

6. aerial / performed in the air   same _____ / different _____
7. anaerobic / inflated   same _____ / different _____
8. idiopathic / of unknown cause   same _____ / different _____

CAD comes from the Latin verb *cadere*, "to fall." Thus, a *cascade* is usually a waterfall, but sometimes a flood of something else that seems to pour on top of you: a cascade of new problems, a cascade of honors, and so on.

CAD源自拉丁语动词 *cadere*，意思是"落下，倒下"。这样，*cascade* 通常是指瀑布，但有时是指仿佛泼在你头上的其他东西：大量的新问题、大量的荣誉等等。

CAD

cadaver \kə-ˈda-vər\   A dead body, especially one that is to be dissected; a corpse. 死尸；尸体

• The cadaver she was given to work on, from the Manhattan morgue, was that of an unclaimed homeless woman. 让她处理的是一具无人认领的无家可归的妇女的尸体，是从曼哈顿停尸房送来的。

Since a corpse is a body that has "fallen down dead," the root *cad-* seems at home here. For most of us, *cadaver* has an impersonal sound, and indeed the word is often used for a body whose identity isn't important: most medical students probably don't spend much time wondering who they're dissecting. Someone with *cadaverous* features looks like a corpse before he or she is dead.

由于尸体是"倒下死掉"的身体，词根 *cad-* 在这里很得其所。对多数人来说，*cadaver* 听起来没有人情味，而实际上他也经常指身份并不重要的尸体：多数医学院学生可能不会花很多时间琢磨他们正在解剖的是谁。有着 *cadaverous*（像尸体的；憔悴的）五官的人死前看上去像尸体。

decadent \ˈde-kə-dənt\   Marked by decay or decline, especially in morals. 衰退的；衰弱的；堕落的

• The French empire may have been at its most decadent just before the French Revolution. 在法国革命前，法帝国可能处在最堕落的时候。

To be decadent is to be in the process of *decay*, so a powerful nation may be said to be in a decadent stage if its power is fading. But the word is more often used to speak of moral decay. Ever since the Roman empire, we've tended to link Rome's fall to the moral decay of its ruling class, who indulged in extreme luxuries and unwholesome pleasures while providing the public with cruel spectacles such as the slaughter of the gladiators. But not everyone agrees on what moral *decadence* looks like (or even how it might have hastened the fall of Rome), though most people think it involves too many sensual pleasures—as, for instance, among the French and English poets and artists of the 1880s and 1890s called the Decadents. These days, for some reason, people have decided *decadent* is the way to describe rich chocolate cakes.

to be decadent(衰退)的就是处于 *decay*(衰退)这一过程,所以一个强大的国家,如果权力在削弱,可以说是处于衰弱阶段。但是这个词语更多时候用于道德沦丧。自从罗马帝国时期,我们就常常将罗马的灭亡与统治阶级道德沦丧联系起来。统治阶级沉溺于极度奢华和不健康的快乐,给公众提供的是杀死角斗士这样的残忍场面。但是,不是每个人都对道德 decadence(堕落)是什么样子有着一致看法(甚至是它如何加速罗马灭亡),尽管多数人都认为它涉及太多的感官之乐,比如就像人称颓废派艺术家的 19 世纪八九十年代的法、英诗人和画家沉溺的那种快乐一样。今天,由于某种原因,人们认为 decadent 可用于描述油腻的巧克力糕饼。

cadence\ˈkā-dᵊns\ (1) The close of a musical phrase, especially one that moves to a harmonic point of rest. (乐句的)收束;静止 (2) The rhythmic flow of sound in language. (语言的)抑扬顿挫

● As the piano came to a cadence, the singer ascended to a beautiful high note, which she held for several seconds until the piano came in again in a new key. 随着轻声演奏的乐句的收束,歌手的声音上升至美丽的高音,持续了几秒,直到音乐又以新调开始响起。

Most of us hear the ending of a piece of music as a fall to a rest- ing place, even if the melody ends on a high note. And that's the way endings were being heard way back in the 16th century, when *cadence* first began to be used in English for musical endings. Most cadences are harmonic "formulas" (standard harmonic patterns that we've all heard thousands of times) and we don't expect them to be original; so whether you're consciously aware of it or not, a *cadential* passage is usually quite recognizable. When *cadence* means "speech rhythm," its *cad-* root refers to the way the accents "fall."

我们多数人听到音乐结束,感觉就像什么东西落在了休息的地方,即使这一旋律以高音结束也是这样。16 世纪,人们就是这样听到音乐的结尾的。当时,cadence 刚开始在英语中指音乐的结尾部分。大多数收束都是和声的"公式"(我们都已听过千万次的标准和声模式),我们不期待它们很有新意;所以不管你是否有意识地注意到了它,cadential(华彩段的)段落通常都很容易识别。cadence 意思是"讲话节奏"时,cad- 这一词根指的是重音"落下"的方式。

cadenza\kə-ˈden-zə\ A virtuosic flourish or extended passage by a soloist, often improvised, that occurs shortly before the end of a piece or movement. 华彩段

● Each of her arias was greeted with greater applause, but it was the brilliant improvised cadenza of her final number that brought down the house. 她每首咏叹调都赢得了更加热烈的掌声,不过,最后一首即兴演唱的华彩段博得了满堂喝彩。

A concerto is a large piece for an instrumental soloist (usually playing piano or violin) and orchestra. Concertos are often extremely demanding for the soloist, but the most difficult part of all may be the *cadenza*, when the orchestra drops out completely, leaving the soloist to dazzle the audience with a set of flourishes, often completely original, right before a movement ends. Cadenzas are also heard in many vocal arias, especially those of the 18th century. The word, borrowed from Italian, originally meant "cadence"; thus, the cadenza, even if it lasts for a couple of minutes, is essentially a decoration of the final important harmonic cadence of the piece.

concerto(协奏曲)是供独奏者(通常是演奏钢琴或者小提琴)和管弦乐队演奏的很长的曲子。它们通常对独奏者有

着很高的要求,但是最难的部分可能是华彩段,即管弦乐队完全退出,让独奏者在乐章结束前,用一系列往往是完全独创的装饰乐句倾倒听众。能让我们听到华彩段的还有很多咏叹调,尤其是18世纪的那些。该词借自意大利语,最初意思是"收束";因此,华彩段虽然能持续几分钟,但基本上只是乐曲最后的重要和声终止的点缀。

TRIB

TRIB comes from the Latin *tribuere*, meaning "to give" or "to pay." So a group that *distributes* food passes it out to those in need, and when you *contribute* to the group you give your money or energy to it.

TRIB 源自拉丁语 tribuere("给"或"致")。所以,distribute(分发)食物的人把它给那些需要食物的人;当你向这一群体 contribute(捐赠)时,你把钱或者能源给他们。

tribute\ˈtri-ˌbyüt\ (1) Something (such as a gift or speech) that is given or performed to show appreciation, respect, or affection. 致敬之物;感恩之物;挚爱之物 (2) Something that proves the good quality or effectiveness of something. (质量或效力的)体现;展示

• Near the end of his speech, he paid tribute to the two pioneers in the field who were in the audience. 演讲快要结束前,他向听众中间两位本领域的先驱者致敬。

Tribute originally took the form of things given from a weaker group to the dominant power of a region—a bit like the "protection money" the Mafia gets from small businesses after making them offers they can't refuse, though the older form of tribute actually did buy the weaker group some protection from enemy forces. Tribute could come in the form of valuables, cattle, or even produce, and might include the loan of warriors to strengthen the ruler's army. But when we "pay tribute" today, it's generally in the form of praise. And when we say, for instance, that a successful school "is a tribute to" the vision of its founder, we mean that its success is itself a form of praise for the person who founded it. And a "tribute band" is a rock group intended to honor a great band of the past.

tribute 最初的形式是较弱群体给某地区主宰者的物品,有些像黑手党向小生意人提供他们不能拒绝的东西之后,从他们那里得到的"保护费"一样。不过,较为古老的 tribute 形式的确让较弱一方得到了一定程度的保护,免受敌军的侵害。tribute 可以是贵重物品、牛甚至农产品,可能包括出借士兵以增强统治者的军队力量。可是,我们今天"pay tribute"(致敬)时,通常是以赞颂的形式。比如当我们说一所成功的学校是建校者远见卓识的 tribute(体现,展示)时,意思是说,学校的成功本身对建校者就是一种赞扬。"tribute band"(翻唱乐队)是对过去一支伟大的乐队致敬的摇滚乐队。

tributary\ˈtri-byə-ˌter-ē\ A stream flowing into a larger stream or a lake. 支流;进贡者;进贡国

• The entire expedition had perished of fever attempting to reach the source of one of the Amazon's great tributaries. 探险队想要到达亚马孙河一个支流的发源地,结果全部死于热病。

A tributary was originally a person or state that owed tribute to a more powerful person or state. Ancient China, for instance, had dozens of tributary states, and the emperor would receive elephants from Siam or young girls from Korea as tribute.

UNIT 30

Just as a smaller power gave some of its wealth to a larger power, a small river contributes its waters to a larger one. A tributary can be a tiny stream, but some are immense rivers. The Missouri River, for example, could be called a tributary to the Mississippi, even though it's about 2,500 miles long and receives hundreds of tributaries itself.

tributary 原先指向更强的人或国家进献贡品的人或者国家。比如,古代中国有很多 *tributary* 国家,皇帝会从暹罗得到大象,或者从朝鲜得到美女。就像较弱国家会给较强国家一些财富那样,小河将其河流献给较大河流。支流可以是潺潺小溪,但有些却是大河。比如密苏里河,虽然长达两千五百英里,也有数百条自己的支流,却可称为密西西比河的支流。

attribute \ə-'tri-ˌbyüt\ (1) To explain by indicating a cause. 把……归因于;认为……是由于 (2) To regard as likely to be a quality of a person or thing. 认为……可能是某人或某物的品质

TRIB

• He attributed his long life to a good sense of humor and a glass of wine with lunch and dinner every day. 他认为自己长寿的原因是有幽默感,而且每天午饭和晚饭各来一杯葡萄酒。

Attribute means something rather similar to "pay tribute." So, for example, an award winner who pays tribute to an inspiring professor is, in a sense, attributing her success to the professor. Though if you attribute your fear of dogs to an incident in your childhood, you're not exactly praising the nasty dog that bit you way back when. The second sense of *attribute* is slightly different: If you attribute bad motives to a politician, it means you think he or she is doing things for the wrong reasons (even if you don't have any proof). When *attribute* is accented on its first syllable, it's being used as a noun, usually as a synonym for *quality*. So, for instance, you may believe that an even temper is an attribute of the best presidents, or that cheerfulness is your spouse's best attribute.

attribute 的意思很像"pay tribute"。所以,比如一位向善于鼓励的教授致敬的获奖者,在一定程度上就是将她本人的成功归因于这位教授。不过如果你将自己怕狗归因于童年时代发生的一件事,你却不是在赞扬当时咬你的那只恶狗。(译者注:原文的 when 应该是 then。)attribute 第二个意思稍有不同:如果你认为一个警察动机不良,意思就是你认为他或她做事的理由是错误的(即使你没有任何证据)。当 attribute 的重音在第一个音节时,它用作名词,通常是 *quality* 的同义词。所以,比如你可能认为平和的脾气是合格总裁的品质之一,或者积极乐观是你配偶的最好品质。

retribution \ˌre-trə-'byü-shən\ Something given in payment for a wrong; punishment. 报应;惩罚

• The victims' families have been clamoring for retribution, sometimes even interrupting the trial proceedings. 受害者家人已经开始大声要求惩罚了,有时甚至打断审判程序。

With its prefix *re*, meaning "back," *retribution* means literally "payback." And indeed we usually use it when talking about personal revenge, whether it's retribution for an insult in a high-school corridor or retribution for a guerrilla attack on a government building. But retribution isn't always so personal: God takes "divine retribution" on humans several times in the Old Testament, especially in the great Flood that wipes out almost the entire human race. And retribution for criminal acts, usually in the form of a prison sentence, is taken by the state, not the victims.

有了表示"回"的 *re* 这一前缀，*retribution* 字面意思就是"回报"。谈论报私仇时，不管是为了高中时走廊里遭到侮辱，还是游击队攻打政府大楼，我们确实都经常使用这一词语。但是，retribution 并不总是那么私人的事情：在《圣经·旧约》中，上帝几次对人类进行"divine retribution"（"神的惩罚"），尤其是那次大洪水，几乎毁灭整个人类。对犯罪行为的惩罚（通常的形式是坐牢）由国家而不是受害者来执行。

Quizzes

A. Indicate whether the following pairs have the same or different meanings:

1. cadence / musical ending   same ____ / different ____
2. attribute / donate   same ____ / different ____
3. decadent / morally declining   same ____ / different ____
4. tributary / small lake   same ____ / different ____
5. cadaver / bodily organ   same ____ / different ____
6. tribute / praise   same ____ / different ____
7. cadenza / side table   same ____ / different ____
8. retribution / revenge   same ____ / different ____

B. Fill in each blank with the correct letter:

a. tributary   e. attribute
b. retribution   f. cadaver
c. cadenza   g. decadent
d. cadence   h. tribute

1. The soloist's _____ was breathtaking, and the audience burst into applause as he played his final notes.

2. The insult had left her seething, and within minutes she had begun planning her terrible _____.

3. As _____ to his huge achievements, the university announced that it would be naming the new science building for him.

4. It was a major _____ to the Amazon, but until 1960 no one but the native Indians had ever attempted to reach its source.

5. Every time it seemed as if the piece was reaching its final _____, the harmony would shift and the music would continue.

6. Her roommate's family struck her as _____, with the younger generation spending its huge allowances on expensive and unhealthy pleasures.

7. In those days grave robbers would dig up a _____ at night after the burial and deliver it to the medical school.

8. He wants to _____ his success entirely to his own brains and energy, forgetting that not everyone is born with $30 million to play with.

UNIT 30

Words from Mythology and History 源自神话和历史的词语

halcyon \ˈhal-sē-ən\ （1）Calm and peaceful. 平静的；宁静的（2）Happy and successful. 成功而快乐的

• She looks back fondly on those halcyon childhood days when she and her sisters seemed to inhabit a magical world where it was always summer. 她亲切地回顾快乐的童年时期,那时她和姐妹们似乎住在一个神奇的世界,那里永远都是夏天。

For the Greeks, the halcyon was a bird (probably the kingfisher) that was believed to nest on the Mediterranean Sea around the beginning of winter, and had the power to quiet the rough December waters around Sicily for about two weeks—the "halcyon days." Thus the adjective *halcyon* came to mean calm and serene. Today people especially use it to describe a golden time in their past.

对希腊人来说,halcyon 是一只鸟(可能是翠鸟吧),据说初冬时节在地中海上筑巢,能够让十二月份西西里岛周围汹涌的海水平静两周,即"halcyon days"(平静的日子)。这样,形容词 halcyon 后来表示平静。今天,人们尤其使用该词描绘过去的黄金时期。

meander \mē-ˈan-dər\ （1）To follow a winding course. 蜿蜒；曲折（2）To wander slowly without a specific purpose or direction. 闲逛

• A little-used trail meanders through the mountains, crossed by cowpaths onto which hikers often stray and get lost. 一条鲜有人走的小路在山间蜿蜒,只有远足者常常走失迷路的牛径与其交叉。

Now and then, geography contributes an ordinary word to the language. The Greek word *maiandros* came from the Maiandros River (now the Menderes River) in western Turkey, which rises in the mountains and flows 240 miles into the Aegean Sea. *Meandering* is a natural tendency especially in slow-moving rivers on flat ground with fine-grained sand, and the Maiandros was well known for its many windings and wanderings. Roads and trails, like rivers, can be said to meander, but so can relaxed music, lazy writing, and idle thoughts.

有时,地理会给语言贡献一个普通词语。希腊语词语 maiandros 源自土耳其西部的 *Maiandros River*(现在的曼德列斯河)。这条河发源于山区,长达二百四十英里,注入爱琴海。蜿蜒尤其是细沙平地上流速很慢的河流的自然趋势,而曼德列斯河就以其蜿蜒曲折著称。大小道路,就像河流一样,可以用 meander 来描述,轻松的音乐、懒散的文字、琐碎的想法也一样。

oedipal \ˈe-də-pəl\ Relating to an intense emotional relationship with one's mother and conflict with one's father. 恋母情结的

• Already on her first visit she sensed a tense oedipal situation, with her boyfriend and his father barely getting through dinner without coming to blows. 第一次拜访,她就感受到一种紧张的恋母情形,男友和父亲席间几乎动手打起来。

In Greek mythology, the king of Thebes, in response to a dreadful prophecy, abandoned his infant son Oedipus, who was then brought up by shepherds. Grown to manhood, Oedipus slew his father almost accidentally, not recognizing him, and then married his mother. When the shameful truth was discovered, the mother committed suicide and Oedipus blinded himself and went into exile. The psychiatrist Sigmund Freud invented the term *Oedipus complex* to mean a sexual desire that a child normally feels toward the parent of the opposite sex, along with jealous feelings toward the parent of the same sex. In Freud's theory (not accepted by everyone today), lingering oedipal feelings are an essential source of adult personality disorder, and can result in choosing a spouse who closely resembles your father or mother.

在希腊神话中，底比斯国王听到一个可怕的预言，就将出生不久的儿子俄狄浦斯抛弃了，但牧羊人将其养大。长大后，俄狄浦斯不认识父亲，几乎是偶然杀死了他，之后跟母亲结婚了。当这一可耻行为真相大白后，母亲自杀，俄狄浦斯弄瞎自己的双眼，过起了流亡生活。精神病学家弗洛伊德创造了 *Oedipus complex*（恋母情结）这一术语，用来指孩子对异性父母正常情况下怀有的性欲望，以及对同性父母怀有的嫉妒感。在弗洛伊德的理论中（今天并非所有人接受），迟迟不去的恋母感是成年人的人格障碍的基本来源，可能的结果是选择一个很像父亲或者母亲的配偶。

ostracize \ˈäs-trə-ˌsīz\   To exclude someone from a group by common consent. 排挤

● Back in the 1950s she had been ostracized by her fellow countryclub members for her radical political beliefs. 20世纪50年代，她政治观点激进，被乡村俱乐部同事排挤出去了。

In the ancient democracy of Athens, citizens were permitted to vote once a year to exile anyone who they thought might pose a problem to the city-state. The man with the most votes was banished for ten years, even if no one had ever made a single charge against him. Voting was done on *ostraka*—bits of broken pottery, the Greek equivalent of scrap paper—and the process was known as *ostrakizein*. Today the most common kind of *ostracism* is exclusion from a social group. It can be especially painful in school: no more sleepovers, no more party invitations, just lots of whispering behind your back.

在古老的民主国家雅典，公民有权利一年投票一次，放逐任何可能对城邦国家构成威胁的公民。票数最多的那个人，即使没有任何人指控过他，也会被驱逐出去十年之久。投票用的是 *ostraka*——陶器碎片，相当于希腊人的纸片——投票过程称为 *ostrakizein*。今天，最常见的 *ostracism*（排挤）方式是将人从某个社交团体中排除出去。在学校这尤其令人痛苦：再没有聚会、再没有聚会邀请，只有许许多多的背后中伤。

paean \ˈpē-ən\   (1) A song of joy, praise, tribute, or triumph. 欢乐之歌；赞歌；颂歌；凯歌 (2) A work that praises or honors its subject. 赞颂作品

● At his retirement party, the beloved president was treated to paeans from friends and employees to his years at the head of the company. 在退休晚会上，朋友和雇员都赞颂大家热爱的总裁带领全公司奋斗的岁月。

Originally in ancient Greece, a *paian* was a choral hymn to Apollo as the god of healing. More generally, it could be a hymn of thanksgiving, as when, in Homer's *Iliad*, the followers of Achilles sing a *paean* on the death of his enemy Hector. Paeans could be sung at banquets, at public funerals, to armies departing for battle and fleets leaving the harbor, and in celebrations of military victories.

最初在古希腊，*paian* 是献给作为康复之神的阿波罗的合唱颂歌。在更加广泛意义上，它可以是感恩的颂歌，比如在荷马史诗《伊利亚特》中，阿喀琉斯的追随者在其杀死敌人赫克托尔时演唱了颂歌。颂歌可以在宴会、公开葬礼上演唱，唱给奔赴战场的军队和离开港口的舰队，以及庆祝军事胜利。

philippic \fə-ˈli-pik\ A speech full of bitter condemnation; a tirade. 谴责演讲

• Every few days he launches another philippic against teenagers: their ridiculous clothes, their abominable manners, their ghastly music. 每过几天，他就要对青少年们谴责一番：他们荒唐可笑的服装、令人厌恶的习惯、让人讨厌的音乐。

In 351-350 B.C., the great Greek orator Demosthenes delivered a series of speeches against King Philip II of Macedon, the so-called *philippikoi logoi* ("speeches regarding Philip"). Three centuries later, in 44-43 B.C., the great Roman orator Cicero delivered a series of speeches against Mark Antony, which soon became known as the *philippica* or *orationes philippicae*, since they were modeled on Demosthenes' attacks. Splendid though both men's speeches were, Demosthenes was eventually exiled by the Macedonians, and Cicero was executed at Mark Antony's orders.

公元前351—前350年，希腊伟大的演说家狄摩西尼发表了一系列演说，谴责马其顿国王菲利普二世，即所谓的 *philippikoi logoi*（"关于菲利普的系列演讲"）。三个世纪之后，在公元前44—前43年，伟大的罗马演说家西塞罗发表了一系列演说，以谴责马克·安东尼。这些演说很快成了著名的 *philippica* 或者 *orationes philippicae*，因为这些演说模仿了狄摩西尼的攻击演说。虽然两个人的演说很精彩，但狄摩西尼最终被马其顿人流放了，西塞罗被人按照马克·安东尼的命令处死了。

satyr \ˈsā-tər\ A man with a strong desire for many women. 性欲极强的男人

• Still drinking and womanizing at the age of 70, he likes to think of himself as a satyr rather than an old goat. 他七十岁了，仍然喝酒、玩女人，喜欢自认为是性欲旺盛而不是老不正经。

Satyrs, the minor forest gods of Greek mythology, had the face, torso, and arms of a man, the ears and tail of a goat, and two goatlike legs. Fond of the pleasures associated with Dionysus (or Bacchus), the god of wine, they were full of playful and sometimes violent energies, and spent much of their time chasing the beautiful nature spirits known as nymphs. Satyrs show up over and over in ancient art. The Greek god Pan, with his reed pipes and mischievous delight in life, had the appearance and character of a satyr but greater powers. Notice how *satyr* is pronounced; it's quite different from *satire*.

Satyrs（萨提尔）是希腊神话中次要的森林神，有着男人的脸、躯干和胳膊，山羊的耳朵和尾巴，两条像山羊的腿。他们喜欢享受与酒神狄奥尼索斯（或者巴克斯）有关的乐趣。他们精力旺盛，很顽皮，有时很粗暴，喜欢追逐称为仙女的自然精灵。萨提尔频繁出现在古代艺术作品中。希腊神话中的潘，拿着芦苇排箫，顽皮而喜欢享受生活。他有着萨提尔的外貌和性格，但是本领更强。注意 *satyr* 的发音，它与 *satire* 发音差别很大。

zealot \ˈze-lət\ A fanatical supporter. 狂热的支持者

• My girlfriend's father is a religious zealot, so I always find excuses not to have dinner at their house. 我女友的爸爸是个宗教狂热分子,所以我总是找理由不在她家吃饭。

In the 1st century A. D., a fanatical sect arose in Judaea to oppose the Roman domination of Palestine. Known as the Zealots, they fought their most famous battle at the great fortress of Masada, where 1,000 defenders took their own lives just as the Romans were about to storm the fort. Over the years, *zealot* came to mean anyone who is passionately devoted to a cause. The adjective *zealous* may describe someone who's merely dedicated and energetic ("a zealous investigator," "zealous about combating inflation," etc.). But *zealot* (like its synonym *fanatic*) and *zealotry* (like its synonym *fanaticism*) are used disapprovingly—even while Jews everywhere still honor the memory of those who died at Masada.

公元1世纪,一个狂热的宗派在犹大出现了,反对罗马人统治巴勒斯坦。他们被称为吉拉德人,在马萨达的大堡垒打了最有名的一场战斗。就在罗马人即将突袭堡垒时,一千名守卫士兵自杀。多年过去了,*zealot* 逐渐用来指代任何热情献身于某一事业的人。形容词 *zealous* 可用来形容只是具有献身精神、充满活力的人("a zealous investigator" "zealous about combating inflation"等)。但是,*zealot*(就像其同义词 *fanatic* 一样)和 *zealotry*(就像其同义词 *fanaticism* 一样)使用时表示不赞同。即使在各地犹太人仍然怀念在马萨达战死的那些勇士时,人们仍这样使用。

Quiz

Fill in each blank with the correct letter:

a. paean   e. satyr
b. philippic   f. zealot
c. halcyon   g. oedipal
d. meander   h. ostracize

1. In those _____ summers, he and his cousins spent every day sailing and swimming in the blue Wisconsin lakes.

2. His most famous speech was a _____ on the Vietnam War delivered on the floor of the Senate in 1967.

3. At her 40th birthday party, her best friend delivered a glowing _____ that left her in tears.

4. Meeting him again after five years, she was dismayed to discover that he'd become a religious _____ who could talk about no other subject.

5. Though he hasn't been convicted of anything yet, it's obvious that the community is going to _____ him.

6. She describes her uncle as a _____, who behaves outrageously around every young woman he meets at a party.

7. The paths _____ through the lovely woods, curving back on themselves in long loops.

8. When psychologists refer to _____ behavior, they may think of a four-year-old boy competing with his father for his mother's attention.

UNIT 30

Review Quizzes

A. Choose the closest definition:

1. cadaver   a. patient   b. skeleton   c. zombie   d. corpse
2. longueur   a. couch   b. distance   c. boring section   d. length
3. retribution   a. gift   b. revenge   c. response   d. duplication
4. pyrotechnic   a. dazzling   b. fire-starting   c. boiling   d. passionate
5. elongate   a. continue   b. smooth over   c. close off   d. lengthen
6. distended   a. overturned   b. expired   c. swollen   d. finished
7. tenuous   a. weak   b. sturdy   c. contained   d. stubborn
8. zealot   a. spokesman   b. leader   c. joker   d. fanatic
9. neurotoxin   a. brain wave   b. nerve poison   c. brain virus   d. antidepressant
10. aerate   a. fly   b. inflate   c. supply with oxygen   d. glide

B. Fill in each blank with the correct letter:

a. technophobe   f. idiom
b. idiopathic   g. anaerobic
c. cadence   h. extenuating
d. oedipal   i. decadent
e. technocrat   j. attenuated

1. The _____ virus should be incapable of actually causing disease.

2. A piece of music that doesn't end with a firm _____ leaves most audiences tense and unsatisfied.

3. When you use an _____ like "losing your edge" or "dressed to kill" in class, your foreign students are just going to be puzzled.

4. She does a lot of _____ muscle training, but just running for the bus will leave her panting.

5. Getting a _____ like him to start using a cell phone would be a major

achievement.

6. The patient's account of her symptoms was so sketchy that for now her condition is just being called _____.

7. His fiancée looks just like his mother, and we joke with him that he's never gotten through his _____ period.

8. The mayor is a _____ who thinks all the city's problems can be fixed by technology _____ and rational management.

9. The scene in the hip downtown nightclubs just seemed _____ and unhealthy to her.

10. If you're caught stealing a flat-screen TV, the fact that you can't afford to buy one doesn't count as an _____ circumstance.

C. Indicate whether the following pairs have the same or different meanings:

1. cadenza / solo section   same ____ / different ____
2. idiosyncrasy / oddity   same ____ / different ____
3. halcyon / delightful   same ____ / different ____
4. toxin / vitamin   same ____ / different ____
5. tribute / praise   same ____ / different ____
6. ostracize / shun   same ____ / different ____
7. meander / wind   same ____ / different ____
8. aerial / lively   same ____ / different ____
9. toxicity / poisonousness   same ____ / different ____
10. technophile / apparatus   same ____ / different ____

ANSWERS

UNIT 1

p. 4
A 1. c 2. c 3. a 4. b
5. c 6. a 7. a 8. b
p. 5
B 1. d 2. c 3. b 4. b
5. d 6. d 7. d 8. a
p. 9
A 1. d 2. g 3. f 4. c
5. h 6. e 7. b 8. a
B 1. e 2. a 3. f 4. d
5. c 6. h 7. b 8. g
p. 13
A 1. S 2. D 3. D
4. D 5. D 6. S 7. S
8. D
B 1. e 2. a 3. b 4. f
5. d 6. h 7. g 8. c
p. 17
A 1. d 2. f 3. c 4. h
5. b 6. a 7. e 8. g
B 1. f 2. a 3. g 4. b
5. c 6. h 7. d 8. e
p. 21
1. d 2. b 3. a 4. c
5. b 6. d 7. a 8. c
p. 21
A 1. e 2. d 3. k
4. b 5. h 6. l 7. f 8. j
9. a 10. c 11. n 12. g
13. m 14. i

p. 22
B 1. d 2. a 3. c 4. c
5. b 6. b 7. d 8. b
9. c 10. c 11. c 12. a
p. 23
C 1. f 2. c 3. e 4. d
5. h 6. g 7. j 8. a 9. b
10. i

UNIT 2

p. 28
A 1. d 2. a 3. e 4. f
5. b 6. c 7. g 8. h
B 1. f 2. g 3. h 4. b
5. a 6. c 7. e 8. d
p. 32
A 1. h 2. g 3. d 4. a
5. b 6. f 7. e 8. c
B 1. f 2. d 3. b 4. g
5. h 6. c 7. e 8. a
p. 36
A 1. d 2. c 3. d 4. d
5. d 6. c 7. b 8. a
B 1. d 2. e 3. h 4. f
5. g 6. a 7. c 8. b
p. 40
A 1. b 2. c 3. e 4. a
5. g 6. h 7. d 8. f
B 1. h 2. d 3. a 4. f
5. e 6. b 7. g 8. c
p. 44
1. a, c 2. d, b 3. b, a
4. c, b 5. c, a 6. a, b

7. c, a 8. d, a
p. 45
A 1. b 2. b 3. b 4. d
5. d 6. c 7. c 8. c 9. a
10. d
B 1. c 2. f 3. e 4. a
5. i 6. d 7. b 8. g 9. j
10. h
C 1. f 2. h 3. c 4. i
5. d 6. e 7. j 8. b 9. g
10. a

UNIT 3

p. 51
A 1. b 2. c 3. f 4. d
5. e 6. a 7. g 8. h
B 1. c 2. f 3. e 4. h
5. a 6. d 7. b 8. g
p. 56
A 1. b 2. d 3. b 4. b
5. d 6. c 7. b 8. a
B 1. D 2. D 3. S
4. D 5. D 6. S 7. D
8. D
p. 61
A 1. a 2. g 3. f 4. d
5. c 6. b 7. h 8. e
B 1. D 2. S 3. S
4. D 5. S 6. D 7. S
8. S
p. 65
A 1. d 2. b 3. b 4. d
5. c 6. d 7. a 8. d

p. 66
B 1. d 2. g 3. h 4. a
5. f 6. e 7. b 8. c
p. 69
1. c 2. b 3. a 4. c 5. a
6. a 7. b 8. d
p. 70
A 1. b 2. b 3. a 4. d
5. d 6. d 7. b 8. d
B 1. m 2. j 3. c 4. l
5. f 6. i 7. e 8. g 9. d
10. k 11. b 12. n 13. h
14. a 15. o
p. 71
C 1. S 2. D 3. S
4. S 5. D 6. S 7. S
8. D 9. D 10. D 11. D
12. D 13. D 14. S 15. D

UNIT 4

p. 77
A 1. S 2. D 3. S
4. S 5. D 6. S 7. D
8. S
B 1. f 2. g 3. b 4. h
5. e 6. c 7. d
p. 81
A 1. h 2. b 3. a 4. c
5. g 6. e 7. f 8. d
B 1. a 2. c 3. h 4. g
5. f 6. b 7. e 8. d
p. 85
A 1. c 2. b 3. e 4. f

5. g 6. h 7. a 8. d
B 1. h 2. a 3. c 4. b
5. g 6. f 7. d 8. e
p. 89
A 1. c 2. b 3. b 4. c
5. d 6. b 7. a 8. a
p. 90
B 1. b 2. d 3. c 4. a
5. d 6. d 7. a 8. d
p. 94
1. b 2. c 3. f 4. a 5. d
6. e 7. h 8. g
p. 94
A 1. b 2. b 3. b 4. d
5. b 6. a 7. c 8. b 9. b
10. c
p. 95
B 1. D 2. D 3. S 4. S
5. S 6. D 7. S 8. D
9. S 10. S
C 1. b 2. d 3. d 4. a
5. a 6. c 7. c 8. b

UNIT 5

p. 99
A 1. a 2. c 3. c 4. b
5. d 6. c 7. b 8. d
p. 100
B 1. D 2. D 3. S 4. S
5. S 6. D 7. S 8. D
p. 104
A 1. d 2. g 3. c 4. b
5. a 6. e 7. h 8. f
B 1. f 2. e 3. d 4. a
5. h 6. g 7. b 8. c
p. 108
A 1. c 2. b 3. d 4. c
5. d 6. b 7. c 8. a
B 1. D 2. S 3. D 4. D
5. D 6. S 7. S 8. D
p. 112
A 1. a 2. g 3. c 4. e
5. f 6. d 7. h 8. b
p. 113

B 1. c 2. e 3. f 4. g
5. a 6. h 7. b 8. d
p. 116
1. h 2. f 3. d 4. e 5. b
6. g 7. a 8. c
p. 117
A 1. d 2. b 3. c 4. b
5. c 6. d 7. b 8. a 9. a
10. d
B 1. g 2. i 3. a 4. o
5. b 6. n 7. m 8. k
9. c 10. c 11. f 12. d
13. h 14. j 15. l
p. 118
C 1. S 2. S 3. S 4. S
5. D 6. D 7. D 8. S
9. D 10. D 11. D 12. D
13. S 14. D 15. D

UNIT 6

p. 123
A 1. D 2. D 3. S 4. D
5. D 6. S 7. D 8. D
p. 124
B 1. g 2. b 3. c 4. a
5. e 6. f 7. d 8. h
p. 128
A 1. d 2. f 3. h 4. b
5. e 6. a 7. g 8. c
B 1. b 2. c 3. d 4. a
5. b 6. a 7. d 8. b
p. 132
A 1. S 2. D 3. S 4. S
5. D 6. D 7. D 8. S
B 1. b 2. e 3. c 4. h
5. g 6. a 7. f 8. d
p. 136
A 1. c 2. b 3. d 4. c
5. d 6. a 7. c 8. b
B 1. f 2. c 3. e 4. b
5. d 6. a 7. h 8. g
p. 140
1. c 2. c 3. b 4. a 5. a
6. b 7. c 8. a

p. 141
A 1. g 2. a 3. j 4. c
5. i 6. b 7. d 8. e 9. h
10. f
B 1. a 2. b 3. c 4. b
5. a 6. d
C 1. e 2. j 3. a 4. i
5. f 6. h 7. c 8. b 9. d
10. g

UNIT 7

p. 147
A 1. b 2. d 3. g 4. f
5. c 6. h 7. a 8. e
B 1. c 2. e 3. f 4. g
5. a 6. g 7. d 8. h
p. 151
A 1. c 2. a 3. a 4. b
5. a 6. a 7. d 8. b
B 1. D 2. D 3. D 4. S
5. D 6. S 7. D 8. D
p. 155
A 1. a 2. e 3. b 4. f
5. c 6. g 7. d 8. h
B 1. d 2. c 3. c 4. a
5. b 6. b 7. d 8. a
p. 160
A 1. S 2. D 3. D 4. D
5. D 6. S 7. D 8. D
p. 161
B 1. c 2. f 3. d 4. a
5. e 6. g 7. h 8. b
p. 164
1. a 2. d 3. c 4. h 5. f
6. g 7. b 8. e
p. 165
A 1. d, a 2. d, b
3. a, b 4. b, c 5. c, a
6. a, b 7. d, c 8. c, a
9. d 10. a, c 11. c, a
12. b, c
B 1. c 2. a 3. a 4. b
5. c 6. a 7. a 8. a 9. d

10. a 11. b 12. b
13. c 14. a 15. c
p. 166
C 1. i 2. f 3. c 4. h
5. e 6. j 7. g 8. a 9. b
10. d

UNIT 8

p. 172
A 1. d 2. b 3. d 4. a
5. c 6. d 7. b 8. c
B 1. f 2. b 3. e 4. a
5. g 6. c 7. h 8. d
p. 177
A 1. a 2. g 3. b 4. h
5. e 6. c 7. d 8. b
B 1. D 2. S 3. D
4. S 5. S 6. D 7. S 8. D
p. 181
A 1. d 2. a 3. c 4. f
5. g 6. b 7. e 8. h
p. 182
B 1. b 2. f 3. d 4. c
5. g 6. h 7. a 8. e
p. 186
A 1. d 2. a 3. b 4. b
5. c 6. b 7. d 8. b
B 1. e 2. d 3. g 4. h
5. c 6. f 7. a 8. b
p. 191
1. g 2. f 3. e 4. d 5. a
6. h 7. b 8. c
p. 191
A 1. j 2. e 3. c 4. f
5. h 6. b 7. a 8. d
9. g 10. i
p. 192
B 1. D 2. S 3. S 4. D
5. S 6. S 7. D 8. S
9. S 10. D 11. D 12. D
13. S 14. S 15. D 16. D
17. D 18. S 19. D 20. S
C 1. h 2. g 3. i 4. b
5. a 6. f 7. d 8. j 9. c

746

ANSWERS

10. e

UNIT 9

p. 197

A 1. a 2. g 3. f 4. b
5. c 6. e 7. h 8. d

p. 198

B 1. a 2. b 3. c 4. d
5. d 6. b 7. d 8. b

p. 202

A 1. b 2. b 3. b 4. a
5. b 6. b 7. a 8. d
B 1. d 2. c 3. e 4. f
5. g 6. h 7. a 8. b

p. 206

A 1. b 2. a 3. b 4. a
5. a 6. c 7. b 8. c

p. 207

B 1. S 2. D 3. S 4. D
5. S 6. D 7. S 8. D

p. 210

A 1. h 2. c 3. g 4. d
5. e 6. b 7. f 8. a

p. 211

B 1. g 2. f 3. b 4. c
5. h 6. a 7. e 8. d

p. 214

1. c 2. b 3. b 4. b 5. c
6. d 7. b 8. c

p. 215

A 1. a 2. d 3. c 4. b
5. a 6. d 7. c 8. a 9. a
10. c
B 1. d 2. g 3. a 4. b
5. j 6. e 7. c 8. i 9. h
10. f

p. 216

C 1. a 2. h 3. i 4. b
5. e 6. d 7. g 8. c 9. j
10. f

UNIT 10

p. 221

A 1. S 2. S 3. D 4. D
5. S 6. D 7. D 8. D
B 1. d 2. c 3. d 4. b
5. a 6. b 7. d 8. d

p. 225

A 1. c 2. c 3. d 4. c
5. b 6. a 7. b 8. d
B 1. f 2. h 3. g 4. e
5. d 6. a 7. c 8. b

p. 229

A 1. a 2. g 3. c 4. f
5. b 6. h 7. e 8. d

p. 230

B 1. c 2. a 3. d 4. c
5. b 6. c 7. a 8. b

p. 234

A 1. d 2. d 3. a 4. a
5. d 6. b 7. a 8. d
B 1. c 2. d 3. h 4. a
5. b 6. e 7. g 8. f

p. 238

1. e 2. b 3. d 4. c 5. g
6. f 7. a 8. h

p. 238

A 1. D 2. S 3. D 4. S
5. D 6. D 7. S 8. D
9. S 10. D 11. S 12. D
13. S 14. S 15. D 16. D
17. S 18. D 19. D 20. S

p. 239

B 1. d 2. a 3. d 4. b
5. a 6. a 7. d 8. a
9. d 10. a

p. 240

C 1. c 2. e 3. a 4. d
5. f 6. b 7. h 8. g

UNIT 11

p. 244

A 1. b 2. a 3. a 4. b
5. c 6. b 7. a 8. d

p. 245

B 1. D 2. D 3. D 4. D
5. D 6. D 7. D 8. D

p. 248

A 1. a 2. g 3. b 4. h
5. e 6. c 7. d 8. f

p. 249

B 1. c 2. d 3. b 4. c
5. a 6. a 7. b 8. d

p. 253

A 1. d 2. b 3. a 4. d
5. c 6. a 7. c 8. a
B 1. b 2. e 3. h 4. a
5. f 6. g 7. d 8. c

p. 257

A 1. a 2. d 3. e 4. b
5. h 6. c 7. f 8. g
B 1. S 2. D 3. S 4. S
5. D 6. S 7. D 8. D

p. 261

1. a 2. g 3. f 4. d 5. c
6. e 7. b 8. h

p. 262

A 1. d 2. a 3. c 4. d
5. d 6. b 7. d 8. d
9. a 10. b 11. c 12. c
13. a 14. c 15. d
B 1. D 2. D 3. D
4. S 5. D 6. S 7. S
8. S 9. D 10. S

p. 263

C 1. f 2. b 3. e 4. g
5. i 6. j 7. l 8. h 9. a
10. d 11. k 12. c

UNIT 12

p. 267

A 1. f 2. c 3. g 4. d
5. e 6. a 7. b 8. h

p. 268

B 1. f 2. h 3. g 4. c
5. b 6. e 7. a 8. d

p. 273

A 1. a 2. g 3. c 4. b
5. f 6. d 7. e 8. h
B 1. c 2. f 3. h 4. e
5. d 6. g 7. a 8. b

p. 278

A 1. b 2. b 3. c 4. b
5. c 6. d 7. a 8. d
B 1. a 2. f 3. d 4. b
5. g 6. c 7. h 8. e

p. 283

A 1. b 2. c 3. a 4. b
5. c 6. b 7. d 8. c
B 1. S 2. D 3. S
4. D 5. D 6. S D 8. D

p. 286

1. a 2. f 3. b 4. g 5. e
6. h 7. d 8. c

p. 287

A 1. b 2. b 3. d 4. a
5. c 6. a 7. d 8. a
9. d 10. c 11. b 12. d
13. b 14. d 15. a 16. b

p. 288

B 1. f 2. b 3. g 4. j
5. d 6. e 7. i 8. a 9. h
10. c
C 1. h 2. j 3. g 4. a
5. i 6. c 7. d 8. f 9. e
10. b

UNIT 13

p. 293

A 1. b 2. d 3. c 4. b
5. c 6. c 7. b 8. a
B 1. g 2. h 3. b 4. f
5. a 6. e 7. d 8. c

p. 297

A 1. c 2. b 3. f 4. g
5. a 6. h 7. e 8. d

p. 298

B 1. D 2. D 3. D 4. S
5. D 6. S 7. S 8. S

p. 302

A 1. g 2. b 3. a 4. c
5. e 6. h 7. d 8. f

p. 303

B 1. e 2. f 3. a 4. c
5. b 6. g 7. h 8. d

p. 306

• 747 •

ANSWERS

A 1. e 2. a 3. b 4. g
5. c 6. h 7. f 8. d
p. 307
B 1. a 2. b 3. d 4. d
5. b 6. c 7. a 8. b
p. 311
1. D 2. S 3. D 4. D
5. D 6. S 7. D 8. S
p. 311
A 1. g 2. h 3. c 4. m
5. j 6. e 7. k 8. i 9. a
10. b 11. n 12. f 13. d
14. l 15. o
p. 312
B 1. c 2. a 3. d 4. a
5. b 6. c 7. d 8. a
9. d 10. b
p. 313
C 1. c 2. b 3. d 4. d
5. a 6. c 7. b 8. c
9. b 10. d

UNIT 14

p. 318
A 1. d 2. g 3. a 4. e
5. f 6. b 7. h 8. c
p. 322
B 1. g 2. a 3. d 4. c
5. h 6. f 7. e 8. b
p. 322
A 1. S 2. D 3. S 4. D
5. D 6. D 7. S 8. S
p. 323
B 1. d 2. a 3. f 4. c
5. e 6. h 7. g 8. b
p. 327
A 1. f 2. g 3. b 4. a
5. d 6. e 7. h 8. c
p. 328
B 1. c 2. b 3. h 4. g
5. d 6. f 7. a 8. e
p. 332
A 1. a 2. a 3. c 4. c
5. d 6. c 7. b 8. b
B 1. D 2. S 3. S 4. D

5. D 6. D D 8. S
p. 337
1. b 2. h 3. g 4. c
5. e 6. a 7. f 8. d
p. 337
A 1. a 2. c 3. b 4. d
5. d 6. b 7. b 8. d 9. c
10. b 11. a 12. d
p. 338
B 1. a 2. b 3. h 4. i
5. d 6. e 7. f 8. c 9. g
10. j
C 1. D 2. S 3. D 4. D
5. S 6. S 7. S 8. S
9. S 10. S

UNIT 15

p. 344
A 1. b 2. d 3. d 4. b
5. b 6. a 7. b 8. b
B 1. h 2. c 3. f 4. b
5. e 6. a 7. d 8. g
p. 348
A 1. d 2. e 3. h 4. a
5. c 6. b 7. f 8. g
p. 349
B 1. d 2. g 3. f 4. e
5. a 6. h 7. b 8. c
p. 353
A 1. S 2. D 3. S 4. S
5. S 6. S 7. S 8. D
B 1. d 2. f 3. e 4. h
5. c 6. g 7. a 8. b
p. 357
A 1. c 2. b 3. c 4. c
5. b 6. a 7. c 8. c
p. 358
B 1. c 2. e 3. f 4. g
5. h 6. d 7. b 8. a
p. 362
1. h 2. e 3. a 4. d 5. f
6. g 7. b 8. c
p. 362
A 1. q 2. f 3. h 4. o

5. m 6. k 7. d 8. n
9. r 10. l 11. p 12. c
13. e 14. s 15. b 16. a
17. i 18. t 19. g 20. j
p. 364
B 1. d, c 2. b, c 3. b,
d 4. b, a 5. b, c 6. a,
d 7. d, a 8. c, d 9. c,
a 10. b, a
C 1. a 2. b 3. a 4. b
5. c 6. a 7. d 8. b
9. d 10. c

UNIT 16

p. 369
A 1. c 2. e 3. h 4. b
5. g 6. f 7. d 8. a
p. 370
B 1. e 2. d 3. f 4. b
5. h 6. g 7. c 8. a
p. 374
A 1. b 2. a 3. d 4. b
5. b 6. c 7. c 8. b
B 1. c 2. d 3. c 4. b
5. d 6. a 7. c 8. a
p. 379
A 1. a 2. e 3. c 4. b
5. f 6. g 7. h 8. d
B 1. f 2. c 3. e 4. h
5. d 6. g 7. b 8. a
p. 384
A 1. b 2. d 3. c 4. a
5. b 6. c 7. d 8. b
B 1. c 2. g 3. h 4. f
5. d 6. e 7. b 8. a
p. 388
1. b 2. c 3. c 4. c
5. b 6. c 7. d 8. b
p. 389
A 1. j 2. g 3. i 4. d
5. o 6. a 7. h 8. m
9. n 10. e 11. c 12. l
13. k 14. b 15. f
p. 390

B 1. c 2. c 3. b 4. c
5. b 6. b 7. c 8. d
9. d 10. a
C 1. i 2. d 3. f 4. j
5. g 6. b 7. h 8. a
9. e 10. c

UNIT 17

p. 395
A 1. a 2. g 3. f 4. e
5. b 6. c 7. h 8. d
p. 396
B 1. D 2. S 3. D 4. D
5. D 6. S 7. D 8. S
p. 400
A 1. c 2. b 3. c 4. b
5. d 6. b 7. a 8. c
B 1. c 2. d 3. f 4. e
5. g 6. h 7. b 8. a
p. 404
A 1. f 2. c 3. b 4. h
5. d 6. a 7. e 8. g
B 1. D 2. S 3. D
4. D 5. S 6. D 7. D
8. S
p. 408
A 1. b 2. a 3. c 4. d
5. c 6. b 7. d 8. a
B 1. c 2. e 3. f 4. a
5. d 6. g 7. h 8. b
p. 412
1. f 2. g 3. e 4. b 5.
6. c 7. h 8. d
p. 413
A 1. a, c 2. d, b
3. b, d 4. d, a 5. c, a
6. d, b 7. b, c 8. b, a
9. d, b 10. c, a
B 1. c 2. i 3. k 4. o
5. a 6. t 7. s 8. l 9. n
10. j 11. f 12. g 13. b
14. e 15. h 16. d 17. m
18. r 19. p 20. q
p. 414

ANSWERS

C 1. g 2. i 3. d 4. a
5. c 6. f 7. b 8. h 9. j
10. e

UNIT 18

p. 419
A 1. d 2. f 3. b 4. h
5. g 6. a 7. e 8. c
p. 420
B 1. d 2. e 3. a 4. g
5. h 6. f 7. c 8. b
p. 424
A 1. a 2. c 3. b 4. a
5. c 6. a 7. d 8. b
p. 425
B 1. D 2. S 3. D 4. D
5. D 6. S 7. D 8. D
p. 429
A 1. b 2. c 3. d 4. b
5. c 6. b 7. d 8. a
B 1. h 2. b 3. f 4. g
5. c 6. e 7. a 8. d
p. 433
A 1. S 2. D 3. S 4. D
5. D 6. S 7. S 8. S
B 1. f 2. e 3. h 4. b
5. c 6. d 7. a 8. g
p. 438
1. f 2. g 3. d 4. e 5. a
6. h 7. c 8. b
p. 438
A 1. d 2. b 3. d 4. c
5. d 6. c 7. b 8. c 9. c
10. a
p. 439
B 1. k 2. d 3. i 4. f
5. l 6. e 7. o 8. b 9. m
10. a 11. h 12. c 13. j
14. g 15. n
p. 440
C 1. c 2. a 3. d 4. c
5. c 6. a 7. c 8. d 9. c
10. b 11. d 12. a 13. a
14. d 15. b

UNIT 19

p. 445
A 1. f 2. g 3. c 4. d
5. e 6. b 7. h 8. a
B 1. S 2. D 3. S 4. S
5. S 6. S 7. D 8. D
p. 449
A 1. a 2. b 3. a 4. d
5. c 6. a 7. b 8. d
p. 450
B 1. a 2. b 3. c 4. b
5. c 6. d 7. b 8. b
p. 454
A 1. d 2. f 3. b 4. a
5. g 6. h 7. e 8. c
p. 455
B 1. c 2. d 3. g 4. a
5. f 6. b 7. h 8. e
p. 459
A 1. c 2. a 3. d 4. b
5. a 6. c 7. d 8. b
B 1. S 2. D 3. D
4. D 5. S 6. D 7. D
8. S
p. 463
1. d 2. e 3. h 4. g
5. c 6. b 7. a 8. f
p. 464
A 1. a 2. a 3. d 4. c
5. d 6. d 7. c 8. d
9. a 10. d
B 1. f 2. k 3. d 4. l
5. g 6. n 7. i 8. m
9. b 10. j 11. h 12. c
13. o 14. e 15. a
p. 465
C 1. D 2. S 3. D
4. D 5. D 6. D 7. S
8. S 9. D 10. S

UNIT 20

p. 470
A 1. d 2. f 3. b 4. a

5. e 6. c 7. g 8. h
p. 471
B 1. c 2. e 3. d 4. a
5. h 6. g 7. f 8. b
p. 474
A 1. b 2. c 3. c 4. b
5. d 6. a 7. b 8. c
p. 475
B 1. h 2. g 3. c 4. e
5. f 6. d 7. a 8. b
p. 479
A 1. a 2. b 3. b 4. b
5. c 6. a 7. d 8. c
B 1. D 2. S 3. D 4. S
5. S 6. D 7. S 8. S
p. 483
A 1. e 2. f 3. g 4. a
5. b 6. c 7. d 8. h
B 1. h 2. g 3. f 4. e
5. d 6. c 7. b 8. a
p. 487
1. f 2. b 3. h 4. d 5. a
6. g 7. c 8. e
p. 488
A 1. b 2. d 3. c 4. d
5. d 6. c 7. c 8. d
9. a 10. d
B 1. b 2. b 3. c 4. a
5. c 6. c 7. a 8. d
9. b 10. c 11. c 12. b
13. b 14. d 15. d
C 1. k 2. l 3. g 4. o
5. m 6. h 7. d 8. a
9. j 10. e 11. i 12. f
13. n 14. b 15. c

UNIT 21

p. 495
A 1. d 2. h 3. g 4. f
5. e 6. c 7. b 8. a
B 1. f 2. g 3. a 4. e
5. h 6. b 7. c 8. d
p. 499

A 1. b 2. a 3. d 4. d
5. c 6. b 7. b 8. c
p. 500
B 1. a 2. c 3. e 4. f
5. b 6. d 7. g 8. h
p. 505
A 1. h 2. b 3. a 4. g
5. f 6. e 7. c 8. d
B 1. d 2. e 3. c 4. f
5. h 6. a 7. b 8. g
p. 509
A 1. c 2. d 3. b 4. b
5. d 6. c 7. c 8. c
p. 510
B 1. S 2. S 3. D 4. D
5. S 6. D 7. S 8. D
p. 513
1. f 2. c 3. b 4. a 5. e
6. h 7. d 8. g
p. 514
A 1. d 2. b 3. c 4. b
5. c 6. a 7. d 8. c 9. c
10. d
B 1. g 2. a 3. b 4. o
5. m 6. i 7. c 8. j 9. k
10. e 11. f 12. d 13. n
14. h 15. l
p. 515
C 1. a 2. a 3. d 4. a
5. b 6. c 7. b 8. d
9. a 10. c 11. a 12. a
13. d 14. d 15. c

UNIT 22

p. 521
A 1. S 2. D 3. D 4. S
5. D 6. S 7. D 8. D
B 1. h 2. a 3. g 4. e
5. d 6. b 7. c 8. f
p. 526
A 1. d 2. c 3. c 4. d
5. a 6. b 7. b 8. d
B 1. D 2. S 3. S 4. S
5. D 6. D 7. S 8. D

p. 530
A 1. f 2. g 3. h 4. a 5. b 6. d 7. c 8. e
B 1. c 2. a 3. b 4. b 5. b 6. b 7. a 8. d

p. 534
A 1. c 2. c 3. b 4. d 5. d 6. b 7. c 8. c

p. 535
B 1. D 2. D 3. S 4. S 5. S 6. S 7. S 8. S

p. 539
1. h 2. f 3. b 4. g 5. e 6. c 7. d 8. a

p. 539
A 1. a 2. c 3. d 4. d 5. d 6. d 7. b 8. b 9. c 10. a

p. 540
B 1. h 2. i 3. j 4. g 5. f 6. e 7. o 8. n 9. m 10. l 11. k 12. a 13. b 14. c 15. d

p. 541
C 1. d 2. a 3. b 4. b 5. b 6. c 7. b 8. c 9. c 10. b 11. c 12. b 13. c 14. c 15. d

UNIT 23

p. 546
A 1. d 2. f 3. g 4. c 5. e 6. a 7. b 8. h
B 1. d 2. e 3. f 4. a 5. h 6. c 7. b 8. g

p. 550
A 1. b 2. c 3. c 4. a 5. c 6. d 7. d 8. b
B 1. S 2. S 3. D 4. D 5. S 6. S 7. D 8. D

p. 554
A 1. f 2. g 3. h 4. b 5. c 6. e 7. a 8. d

p. 555

B 1. f 2. e 3. g 4. h 5. a 6. d 7. c 8. b

p. 559
A 1. b 2. c 3. a 4. d 5. b 6. b 7. c 8. d
B 1. D 2. D 3. S 4. S 5. D 6. S 7. D 8. D

p. 562
1. f 2. b 3. h 4. c 5. e 6. g 7. a 8. d

p. 563
A 1. c 2. d 3. b 4. d 5. a 6. d 7. a 8. d
B 1. g 2. l 3. d 4. i 5. b 6. m 7. j 8. c 9. a 10. f 11. o 12. e 13. k 14. h 15. n

p. 564
C 1. a 2. b 3. d 4. b 5. d 6. b 7. a 8. d 9. c 10. d 11. b 12. b 13. c 14. d 15. c

UNIT 24

p. 569
A 1. h 2. b 3. c 4. g 5. a 6. e 7. f 8. d

p. 570
B 1. d 2. g 3. e 4. c 5. h 6. a 7. b 8. f

p. 574
A 1. d 2. b 3. a 4. a 5. c 6. d 7. c 8. d
B 1. D 2. D 3. S 4. D 5. D 6. S 7. S 8. D

p. 578
A 1. d 2. f 3. b 4. g 5. a 6. h 7. c 8. e

p. 579
B 1. f 2. d 3. e 4. b 5. a 6. g 7. h 8. c

p. 582
A 1. b 2. c 3. d 4. a 5. b 6. c 7. c 8. b

p. 583
B 1. S 2. D 3. D 4. D 5. S 6. D 7. D 8. D

p. 587
1. c 2. f 3. g 4. d 5. e 6. h 7. b 8. a

p. 587
A 1. d 2. d 3. c 4. d 5. c 6. b 7. b 8. a 9. b 10. a 11. b 12. c 13. c 14. a 15. c

p. 588
B 1. m 2. k 3. o 4. a 5. f 6. h 7. n 8. e 9. b 10. i 11. d 12. j 13. g 14. l

p. 589
C 1. g 2. h 3. e 4. f 5. c 6. a 7. i 8. b 9. j 10. d

UNIT 25

p. 594
A 1. d 2. h 3. g 4. a 5. c 6. e 7. b 8. f
B 1. c 2. b 3. d 4. c 5. a 6. d 7. b 8. c

p. 599
A 1. c 2. d 3. a 4. b 5. a 6. c 7. a 8. a
B 1. e 2. b 3. c 4. g 5. d 6. h 7. a 8. f

p. 603
A 1. f 2. g 3. c 4. d 5. a 6. h 7. b 8. e
B 1. b 2. a 3. d 4. h 5. e 6. f 7. g 8. c

p. 608
A 1. a 2. c 3. b 4. b 5. c 6. d 7. a 8. c
B 1. D 2. S 3. S 4. S 5. D 6. D 7. D 8. S

p. 612
1. h 2. f 3. g 4. b 5. c 6. a 7. d 8. e

p. 613
A 1. d 2. a 3. c 4. c 5. d 6. a 7. d 8. b 9. d 10. b
B 1. b 2. k 3. f 4. c 5. o 6. j 7. h 8. g 9. e 10. m 11. n 12. a 13. c 14. i 15. l

p. 614
C 1. o 2. l 3. n 4. c 5. g 6. i 7. f 8. h 9. b 10. j 11. a 12. c 13. k 14. b 15. m

UNIT 26

p. 620
A 1. c 2. d 3. b 4. a 5. f 6. h 7. g 8. e
B 1. f 2. b 3. a 4. g 5. c 6. d 7. e 8. h

p. 624
A 1. c 2. d 3. b 4. a 5. f 6. e 7. h 8. a

p. 625
B 1. f 2. c 3. e 4. c 5. d 6. b 7. h 8. g

p. 629
A 1. b 2. c 3. d 4. f 5. h 6. g 7. e 8. a

p. 630
B 1. b 2. c 3. d 4. b 5. c 6. c 7. b 8. b

p. 634
A 1. h 2. g 3. c 4. b 5. e 6. f 7. a 8. b
B 1. h 2. g 3. a 4. c 5. d 6. f 7. b 8. e

p. 639
1. e 2. b 3. a 4. h 5. c 6. g 7. f 8. d

p. 639

ANSWERS

A 1. c 2. d 3. a 4. h
5. i 6. j 7. f 8. g 9. e
10. b
B 1. h 2. j 3. i 4. e
5. f 6. g 7. a 8. b
9. d 10. c
p. 640
C 1. D 2. S 3. D
4. S 5. S 6. D 7. S
8. D 9. D 10. D

UNIT 27

p. 645
A 1. D 2. D 3. S 4. D
5. S 6. D 7. S 8. D
B 1. g 2. d 3. a 4. c
5. f 6. h 7. e 8. b
p. 650
A 1. g 2. b 3. f 4. d
5. c 6. a 7. h 8. e
B 1. f 2. e 3. c 4. g
5. h 6. a 7. b 8. d
p. 654
A 1. b 2. e 3. f 4. h
5. g 6. d 7. a 8. c
B 1. S 2. D 3. D 4. D
5. D 6. S 7. S 8. D
p. 659
A 1. d 2. b 3. a 4. e
5. f 6. g 7. h 8. c
B 1. S 2. S 3. D 4. D
5. S 6. D 7. D 8. D
p. 664
1. d 2. a 3. e 4. b 5. f
6. g 7. h 8. c
p. 664
A 1. d 2. h 3. g 4. b
5. a 6. f 7. i 8. e 9. j
10. c
p. 665

B 1. d 2. c 3. j 4. a
5. f 6. i 7. g 8. e 9. h
10. b
C 1. S 2. D 3. D 4. S
5. S 6. D 7. S 8. S
9. S 10. D

UNIT 28

p. 671
A 1. f 2. h 3. c 4. a
5. b 6. g 7. d 8. e
B 1. D 2. S 3. S 4. S
5. S 6. D 7. D 8. D
p. 676
A 1. S 2. S 3. D 4. D
5. S 6. D 7. S 8. S
B 1. b 2. c 3. d 4. e
5. h 6. a 7. f 8. g
p. 681
A 1. c 2. a 3. d 4. b
5. f 6. h 7. e 8. g
B 1. a 2. g 3. c 4. b
5. f 6. e 7. h 8. d
p. 685
A 1. c 2. a 3. h 4. g
5. b 6. e 7. f 8. d
p. 686
B 1. S 2. S 3. S 4. D
5. D 6. D 7. S 8. D
p. 690
1. d 2. f 3. g 4. b
5. e 6. h 7. a 8. c
p. 690
A 1. d 2. i 3. a 4. b
5. f 6. g 7. j 8. h 9. c
10. e
p. 691
B 1. j 2. c 3. g 4. f
5. a 6. h 7. i 8. d 9. b

10. e
C 1. D 2. D 3. S 4. S
5. S 6. D 7. S 8. S
9. S 10. S

UNIT 29

p. 697
A 1. b 2. e 3. f 4. d
5. h 6. a 7. g 8. c
p. 698
B 1. D 2. S 3. D 4. S
5. S 6. S 7. S 8. S
p. 702
A 1. h 2. b 3. c 4. f
5. g 6. d 7. e 8. a
B 1. e 2. g 3. a 4. d
5. c 6. h 7. f 8. b
p. 707
A 1. d 2. a 3. c 4. e
5. f 6. b 7. g 8. h
B 1. b 2. f 3. c 4. g
5. h 6. a 7. e 8. d
p. 712
A 1. f 2. b 3. e 4. a
5. h 6. d 7. g 8. c
B 1. D 2. S 3. S 4. D
5. S 6. S 7. S 8. S
p. 716
1. e 2. g 3. b 4. a
5. h 6. f 7. d 8. c
p. 717
A 1. c 2. b 3. c 4. a
5. d 6. c 7. a 8. b
9. b 10. d
B 1. c 2. d 3. b 4. a
5. f 6. e 7. i 8. j 9. g
10. h
p. 718
C 1. D 2. D 3. D 4. D

5. D 6. S 7. S 8. D
9. D 10. S

UNIT 30

p. 723
A 1. b 2. c 3. a 4. e
5. f 6. d 7. g 8. h
B 1. f 2. g 3. h 4. b
5. e 6. a 7. c 8. d
p. 728
A 1. D 2. S 3. S 4. D
5. D 6. S 7. D 8. D
B 1. d 2. b 3. c 4. g
5. e 6. a 7. h 8. f
p. 733
A 1. a 2. g 3. d 4. b
5. e 6. f 7. c 8. h
B 1. S 2. S 3. D
4. S 5. D 6. S 7. D
8. S
p. 738
A 1. S 2. D 3. S 4. D
5. D 6. S 7. D 8. S
B 1. c 2. b 3. h 4. a
5. d 6. g 7. f 8. e
p. 742
1. c 2. b 3. a 4. f 5. h
6. e 7. d 8. g
p. 743
A 1. d 2. c 3. b 4. a
5. d 6. c 7. a 8. d
9. b 10. c
B 1. j 2. c 3. f 4. g
5. a 6. b 7. d 8. e 9. i
10. h
p. 744
C 1. S 2. S 3. S 4. D
5. S 6. S 7. S 8. D
9. S 10. D

INDEX

AB/ABS, 316
aberrant, 133
abjure, 432
abnegation, 457
abscond, 316
absolution, 605
abstemious, 316
abstraction, 317
abstruse, 317
accede, 135
acclamation, 551
accord, 290
accretion, 580
acculturation, 276
ACER/ACR, 517
acerbic, 517
Achilles' heel, 161
acme, 535
acquisitive, 123
acrid, 517
acrimony, 518
acrophobic, 632
acropolis, 619
acupuncture, 556
adequacy, 120
adherent, 194
ad hoc, 66
ad hominem, 67
adjunct, 203
Adonis, 713
adumbrate, 264
advocate, 148
aegis, 609
aeolian harp, 187
AER/AERO, 731
aerate, 731
aerial, 731
aerobic, 732
aerodynamics, 423
affidavit, 79
affluence, 476
a fortiori, 113
aggravate, 15
aggregate, 473
agnostic, 296
agoraphobia, 632
alleviate, 15
alphanumeric, 621
alter ego, 67
AM, 3
amazon, 713
AMBI, 47
ambient, 47
ambiguous, 47
ambit, 48
ambivalent, 48
ambrosia, 559
amicable, 3
amorous, 4
amorphous, 349
amortize, 183
anachronism, 383
anaerobic, 732
Anglophile, 456
ANIM, 392
animated, 392
animosity, 393
ANN/ENN, 396
annuity, 396
annulment, 649
ANT/ANTI, 505
antagonist, 506
ANTE, 102
antebellum, 5
antecedent, 103
antechamber, 102
antedate, 103
anterior, 103
ANTHROP, 418
anthropoid, 418
anthropology, 418
anthropomorphic, 349
antigen, 506
antipathy, 506
antithesis, 507
antonym, 597
apathetic, 226
apiary, 307
Apollonian, 41
apologia, 583
a posteriori, 113
apotheosis, 268
append, 171
appendage, 171
appendectomy, 660
apprehend, 477
approbation, 11
appropriate, 525
a priori, 114
AQU, 232
aquaculture, 232
aquamarine, 224
aquanaut, 232
aqueduct, 233
aquifer, 233
aquiline, 283
arachnid, 211
arachnophobia, 633
arcadia, 161
aristocrat, 553
ARM, 651
armistice, 651
armada, 651
armory, 652
ART, 300
artful, 300
arthroscopic, 672
artifact, 301

INDEX

artifice, 301
artisan, 302
ascendancy, 596
asinine, 284
aspect, 145
assimilate, 592
atheistic, 269
atrium, 584
atrophy, 184
attenuated, 722
attribute, 737
AUD, 129
audition, 130
auditor, 129
auditory, 129
Augean stable, 137
AUT/AUTO, 546
autism, 548
autocratic, 553
autoimmune, 547
automaton, 547
autonomy, 547
aver, 247
avert, 347
bacchanalian, 41
bariatric, 662
BELL, 5
bellicose, 6
belligerence, 6
BENE, 1
benediction, 1
benefactor, 2
beneficiary, 2
benevolence, 2
BI/BIN, 360
biennial, 361
bilateral, 658
binary, 361
BIO, 441

biodegradable, 442
bioluminescent, 256
bionic, 441
biopsy, 441
biosphere, 345
bipartisan, 360
bipartite, 204
bipolar, 361
bona fide, 114
bon vivant, 529
bovine, 284
British thermal unit, 55
bronchitis, 638
bureaucrat, 553
bursitis, 637
cacophony, 151
CAD, 734
cadaver, 734
cadence, 735
cadenza, 735
calligraphy, 298
calliope, 211
calypso, 90
canine, 284
CANT, 241
cantata, 241
cantilever, 16
cantor, 242
caper, 308
CAPIT, 416
capitalism, 416
capitulate, 417
carcinogenic, 444
cardiology, 220
CARN, 75
carnage, 75
carnal, 75

carnivorous, 73
carpe diem, 115
Cassandra, 162
CATA, 97
cataclysm, 98
catacomb, 98
catalyst, 98
catatonic, 99
catharsis, 536
caveat emptor, 115
CED, 134
cede, 134
CENT, 461
centenary, 462
centigrade, 462
centimeter, 462
CENTR/CENTER, 368
centrifugal, 196
centurion, 463
CEPT, 29
cereal, 235
charisma, 609
chimera, 714
choreography, 299
CHRON, 382
chronic, 382
chronology, 382
cicerone, 18
CIRCU/CIRCUM, 698
circuitous, 698
circumference, 699
circumscribe, 600
circumspect, 699
circumvent, 699
CIS, 305
CLAM/CLAIM,

551
clamor, 551
CLUS, 533
CO, 708
coalesce, 708
codependency, 709
codex, 405
CODI/CODE, 405
codicil, 405
codify, 406
coeval, 398
cogeneration, 708
cognitive, 296
cohere, 194
cohesion, 709
collateral, 658
colloquial, 573
colloquium, 572
colossus, 536
commandeer, 567
commute, 448
compel, 209
complement, 125
comport, 169
comprehend, 478
compunction, 556
concede, 135
concise, 305
concord, 290
concurrent, 82
condescend, 595
conducive, 37
configuration, 394
confine, 30
confluence, 476
conform, 352
congregation, 473
conjecture, 33
conjunct, 204

• 753 •

conscientious, 200
conscription, 600
consequential, 39
constrict, 520
construe, 523
contemporary, 381
context, 542
contort, 527
CONTRA, 507
contraband, 507
contraindication, 508
contrarian, 509
contravene, 508
converter, 347
convoluted, 252
CORD, 290
cordial, 291
cornucopia, 714
CORP, 400
corporal, 401
corporeal, 400
corpulent, 401
corpus delicti, 115
COSM, 198
cosmology, 199
cosmopolitan, 200
cosmos, 198
counterinsurgent, 653
CRAC/CRAT, 552
CRE/CRET, 579
CRED, 77
credence, 77
credible, 78
credo, 79
credulity, 79
crescent, 579

CRIM, 10
criminology, 10
CRIT, 430
criterion, 430
critique, 430
Croesus, 137
cross-cultural, 276
CRYPT, 314
crypt, 314
cryptic, 315
cryptography, 315
CULP, 292
culpable, 292
CULT, 275
CUR, 152
curative, 152
curator, 152
CURR/CURS, 82
curriculum vitae, 116
cursory, 82
cyclopean, 162
cynosure, 187
DE, 646
debase, 646
DEC, 459
decadent, 734
decalogue, 460
decapitate, 417
decathlon, 460
decibel, 460
decimate, 461
declaim, 552
decode, 406
deconstruction, 522
decriminalize, 10
deduction, 37
de facto, 67

defamation, 646
definitive, 31
deflect, 86
defunct, 446
degenerative, 647
degrade, 425
dehydrate, 606
dejection, 647
de jure, 433
delegation, 472
delphic, 41
deltoid, 670
DEM/DEMO, 279
demagogue, 280
demographic, 279
demotic, 280
dendroid, 670
deplete, 125
deportment, 169
DERM, 686
dermal, 686
dermatitis, 687
descant, 242
descendant, 596
desensitize, 157
detritus, 537
devolve, 251
DI/DUP, 358
dichotomy, 358
DICT, 294
diction, 294
dictum, 295
diffident, 80
diminutive, 701
dimorphic, 359
Dionysian, 42
dipsomaniac, 24
directive, 108
DIS, 64

disarming, 652
discordant, 291
discredit, 64
discursive, 82
disjunction, 203
dislodge, 65
disorient, 64
disparity, 631
dispiriting, 246
disrepute, 217
dissolution, 605
dissonant, 131
dissuade, 64
distemper, 481
distended, 723
divert, 346
divest, 266
DOC/DOCT, 354
docent, 354
doctrinaire, 355
doctrine, 354
dogma, 560
DOM, 370
domination, 372
domineering, 371
dominion, 370
draconian, 162
dragon's teeth, 138
dryad, 212
DUC/DUCT, 37
duplex, 359
duplicity, 360
DYNAM, 422
dynamic, 422
dynamo, 423
DYS, 110
dysfunctional, 447
dyslexia, 112

dyspeptic, 112
dysplasia, 112
dystopia, 111
dystrophy, 185
eccentric, 368
ectopic, 366
edict, 294
effigy, 394
effluent, 476
effusive, 581
ego, 609
egocentric, 369
egomaniac, 25
egregious, 473
elevation, 16
elongate, 727
elucidate, 180
Elysium, 715
emissary, 208
empathy, 227
enamored, 3
encomium, 584
encrypt, 314
encyclopedic, 320
endemic, 279
ENDO, 688
endocrine, 688
endodontic, 689
endogenous, 689
endorphin, 689
endoscope, 672
entropy, 321
enumerate, 621
envisage, 144
EPI, 49
epicenter, 368
epicure, 715
epidermis, 687
epilogue, 49

epiphyte, 49
epitaph, 50
epithet, 50
eponymous, 597
EQU, 120
equable, 120
equestrian, 308
equilateral, 658
equilibrium, 121
equinox, 121
equivalent, 577
equivocate, 148
ERR, 133
errant, 133
erratic, 134
erroneous, 134
ethnocentric, 369
ethos, 610
EU, 109
eugenic, 109
eulogy, 110
euphemism, 109
euphoria, 110
eureka, 560
eutrophication, 185
EV, 398
evolution, 252
ex post facto, 68
exacerbate, 518
excise, 305
exclusive, 533
excrescence, 580
exculpate, 292
exodus, 715
expatriate, 469
expel, 209
expropriate, 525
expurgate, 482

extemporaneous, 381
extenuating, 722
extort, 527
EXTRA, 175
extradite, 175
extramural, 617
extraneous, 176
extrapolate, 175
extrasensory, 157
extrovert, 176
exurban, 274
FAC, 254
facile, 254
facilitate, 255
factor, 254
factotum, 254
FALL, 602
fallacious, 602
fallacy, 602
fallibility, 603
fauna, 212
feline, 285
FID, 79
fiduciary, 80
FIG, 393
figment, 395
figurative, 394
FIN, 30
finite, 31
FLECT, 86
flora, 213
FLU, 475
FORM, 351
formality, 352
format, 351
formative, 352
FORT, 303
forte, 304

fortification, 304
fortify, 303
fortitude, 364
FRACT, 450
fractal, 451
fractious, 450
FUG, 195
fugue, 196
FUNCT, 446
functionary, 446
FUS, 581
gastrectomy, 660
GEN, 443
generator, 443
genesis, 443
genre, 444
genuflect, 87
GEO, 342
geocentric, 342
geophysics, 342
geostationary, 343
geothermal, 343
geriatric, 663
GNI/GNO, 296
gorgon, 716
GRAD, 425
gradation, 425
gradient, 426
GRAPH, 298
GRAT, 548
gratify, 549
gratis, 560
gratuitous, 549
gratuity, 549
GRAV, 14
grave, 14
gravitas, 14
gravitate, 15
GREG, 472

habeas corpus, 511
Hades, 138
hagiography, 299
halcyon, 739
hector, 18
hedonism, 19
heliotrope, 321
HEM/
HEMO, 635
hematocrit, 431
hematology, 635
HEMI/SEMI, 486
hemiplegia, 487
hemisphere, 346
hemoglobin, 636
hemophilia, 636
hemorrhage, 635
hepatitis, 637
HER, 194
herbivorous, 73
herculean, 213
hoi polloi, 537
HOL/HOLO, 375
holistic, 375
holocaust, 377
Holocene, 376
hologram, 376
HOM/HOMO, 62
homogeneous, 62
homogenize, 63
homologous, 63
homonym, 62
horticulture, 277
hubris, 610
humanoid, 670
HYDR, 606
hydraulic, 606
hydrodynamic, 424
hydroelectric, 607

hydroponics, 607
HYP/HYPO, 51
HYPER 493
hyperactive, 493
hyperbole, 493
hypercritical, 431
hyperkinetic, 421
hypertension, 494
hypertext, 543
hypertrophy, 184
hyperventilate, 494
hypochondriac, 52
hypoglycemia, 52
hypothermia, 53
hypothetical, 53
IATR, 662
iatrogenic, 662
ICON, 270
icon, 270
iconic, 271
iconoclast, 271
iconography, 272
id, 611
ideology, 219
IDIO, 729
idiom, 729
idiomatic, 729
idiopathic, 730
idiosyncrasy, 730
ignominious, 467
immure, 617
immutable, 448
impartial, 205
impediment, 84
impel, 209
impetus, 562
implacable, 545
impose, 328
impotent, 557

impunity, 228
impute, 218
in memoriam, 510
inanimate, 393
inaudible, 130
incantation, 241
incarnate, 76
incisive, 306
incognito, 297
incoherent, 195
incorporate, 402
increment, 580
incriminate, 11
inculpate, 292
indeterminate, 340
indoctrinate, 355
induce, 38
infallible, 603
infinitesimal, 32
inflection, 87
infraction, 451
infrastructure, 522
ingratiate, 550
inherent, 195
innovation, 326
inquisition, 122
inscription, 601
insectivorous, 74
insignia, 407
instrumental, 523
insuperable, 644
insurgency, 653
intemperate, 480
INTER, 703
intercede, 703
intercept, 29
interdict, 704
interject, 33
intermediary, 668

interminable, 341
interpolate, 704
interregnum, 427
interstice, 703
interurban, 275
intractable, 36
intramural, 616
intuition, 356
inundate, 568
investiture, 266
iridescent, 258
irrevocable, 148
ITIS, 637
JECT, 33
jovial, 42
JUNCT, 203
juncture, 203
Junoesque, 235
JUR, 432
jurisdiction, 295
jurisprudence, 432
juxtapose, 329
KILO, 622
kilobyte, 623
kilogram, 624
kilohertz, 623
kilometer, 623
KINE, 420
kinescope, 421
kinesiology, 420
kleptomania, 24
kudos, 537
laconic, 188
laparoscopy, 673
LATER, 657
lateral, 657
LEGA, 471
legacy, 471
legate, 471

leonine, 285
lethargic, 139
LEV, 15
levity, 16
libido, 611
LINGU, 242
lingua franca, 243
linguine, 244
linguistics, 243
lithograph, 300
LOG, 218
LONG, 726
longevity, 398
longitude, 726
longueur, 727
LOQU, 572
loquacious, 574
LUC, 179
lucid, 180
lucubration, 180
LUM, 255
lumen, 255
luminary, 257
luminous, 256
lupine, 309
lycanthropy, 419
magnanimous, 392
magnum opus, 510
MAL, 96
malevolent, 96
malfunction, 446
malicious, 96
malign, 97
malnourished, 97
MAND, 566
mandate, 566
mandatory, 566
MANIA, 24
MAR, 223

marina, 223
mariner, 224
maritime, 225
martial, 235
mastectomy, 661
maternity, 230
MATR/MATER, 230
matriarch, 231
matrilineal, 231
matrix, 231
mausoleum, 258
mea culpa, 293
meander, 739
MEDI, 667
median, 667
mediate, 668
medieval, 399
mediocrity, 669
megalomaniac, 25
megalopolis, 619
mellifluous, 477
memento mori, 511
mentor, 259
mercurial, 43
META, 500
metadata, 501
metamorphosis, 350
metaphorical, 501
metaphysics, 502
meter, 126
methodology, 219
metonymy, 502
METR/METER, 126
metric, 126
MICRO, 625

microbe, 625
microbiologist, 626
microbrew, 626
microclimate, 627
microcosm, 199
Midas touch, 139
MILL, 484
millefleur, 484
millenarianism, 484
millennium, 397
millipede, 485
millisecond, 485
MINI/MINU, 700
minimalism, 700
minuscule, 701
minutiae, 701
MIS, 207
misanthropic, 419
misnomer, 467
mission, 207
missionary, 207
mnemonic, 188
modus operandi, 68
modus vivendi, 69
MONO, 333
monoculture, 333
monogamous, 333
monolithic, 334
monotheism, 334
MOR/MORT, 182
moribund, 183
MORPH, 349
morphology, 350
mortality, 182
mortify, 183
MULTI, 627
multicellular, 627

multidisciplinary, 628
multifarious, 628
multilateral, 628
multilingual, 243
MUR, 616
muralist, 616
muse, 258
MUT, 447
myrmidon, 163
NANO, 641
nanoparticle, 643
nanosecond, 642
nanostructure, 642
nanotechnology, 641
narcissism, 259
NECRO, 693
necromancer, 693
necropolis, 694
necropsy, 694
necrosis, 693
NEG, 457
negligent, 457
negligible, 458
nemesis, 163
NEO, 323
neoclassic, 323
neoconservative, 324
Neolithic, 324
neonatal, 325
nescience, 201
nestor, 19
neurosis, 585
neurotoxin, 721
NOM, 466
nomenclature, 467
nominal, 466

nonpareil, 631
non sequitur, 39
NOV, 325
novel, 326
novice, 326
NUL/NULL, 648
null, 648
nullify, 649
nullity, 648
NUMER, 620
numerology, 621
oblong, 727
occlusion, 533
odometer, 127
odyssey, 91
oedipal, 739
oenophile, 455
OID, 669
oligarchy, 584
Olympian, 43
OMNI, 372
omnibus, 373
omnipotent, 373
omniscient, 374
omnivore, 372
onus, 538
ONYM, 596
opprobrium, 585
opus, 561
ornithologist, 309
ORTHO, 105
orthodontics, 105
orthodox, 105
orthography, 106
orthopedics, 106
oscilloscope, 673
ostracize, 740
ovine, 309
PAC, 7

pace, 8
pacifist, 7
pacify, 7
pact, 8
paean, 740
PALEO, 695
paleography, 696
Paleolithic, 695
paleontology, 696
Paleozoic, 697
palladium, 91
PAN, 173
panacea, 173
pandemonium, 173
Pandora's box, 213
panoply, 174
pantheism, 174
pantheon, 269
PAR, 630
PARA, 497
paralegal, 498
paramedic, 498
paramilitary, 499
paramour, 4
paraphrase, 497
parity, 630
PART, 204
parterre, 222
participle, 205
partisan, 206
PATER/
PATR, 468
paternalistic, 470
PATH, 226
pathos, 226
patriarchy, 469
patrician, 468
patronymic, 598
PED, 83

PED, 318
pedagogy, 319
pedant, 319
pedestrian, 84
pediatrician, 319
pedigree, 84
PEL, 209
PEN/PUN, 228
penal, 228
penance, 229
PEND, 170
pendant, 170
Penelope, 92
PENT, 434
pentameter, 435
Pentateuch, 435
pentathlon, 434
Pentecostal, 435
penumbra, 265
per se, 561
PER, 503
perceptible, 30
percolate, 503
perennial, 397
perfidy, 80
PERI, 153
perimeter, 154
periodontal, 154
peripatetic, 154
peripheral, 155
perjury, 432
permeate, 504
permutation, 448
perquisite, 122
persevere, 504
perspective, 146
perturb, 250
pervade, 503
PHIL, 455

philanthropy, 456
philatelist, 456
philippic, 741
PHOB, 632
PHON, 149
phonetic, 150
phonics, 149
PHOT, 177
photoelectric, 178
photon, 178
photosynthesis, 179
photovoltaic, 178
physiology, 219
PLAC, 544
placate, 544
placebo, 544
placidity, 545
platonic, 189
PLE/PLEN, 124
plenary, 124
plenipotentiary, 558
plutocracy, 554
podiatrist, 663
POLIS/
POLIT, 618
politic, 618
politicize, 618
POLY, 57
polyglot, 57
polygraph, 58
polymer, 58
polyp, 57
polyphonic, 150
POPUL, 281
populace, 281
populist, 281
populous, 282

porcine, 285
PORT, 168
portage, 168
portfolio, 168
POS, 328
POST, 87
posterior, 88
posthumous, 88
postmodern, 88
postmortem, 89
POT, 557
potentate, 558
potential, 557
PRE, 495
precedent, 135
precision, 306
preclude, 496
precocious, 491
precursor, 83
predispose, 496
predominant, 371
PREHEND/
PREHENS, 477
prehensile, 477
prerequisite, 497
prescient, 201
prevalent, 578
PRIM, 59
primal, 59
primate, 60
primer, 60
primeval, 399
primordial, 60
PRO, 677
PRO, 679
proactive, 677
PROB, 11
probate, 12
probity, 12

pro bono, 677
proclaim, 552
procrustean, 92
procure, 153
pro forma, 678
profusion, 582
prognosis, 297
projection, 33
prologue, 680
Promethean, 236
promulgate, 680
PROP/
PROPRI, 523
prophylaxis, 679
proponent, 678
proprietary, 524
propriety, 524
proscribe, 601
prospect, 145
prospectus, 146
PROT/
PROTO, 100
protagonist, 100
protean, 92
protocol, 101
protoplasm, 101
prototype, 102
protracted, 35
protrude, 679
proverb, 590
pseudonym, 598
PSYCH, 26
psyche, 26
psychedelic, 26
psychosomatic, 27
psychotherapist, 27
psychotropic, 322
PUNC, 555

punctilious, 555
punctual, 555
punitive, 229
PURG, 481
purgative, 482
purgatory, 482
purge, 481
PUT, 217
putative, 218
pyrotechnic, 725
Pyrrhic
victory, 139
QUADR/
QUART, 409
quadrant, 409
quadrille, 410
quadriplegic, 410
quadruped, 83
quartile, 410
quid pro quo, 68
quincentennial, 436
QUINT, 436
quintessential, 436
quintet, 437
quintile, 437
QUIS, 122
RE, 682
RE, 683
rebellion, 6
rebut, 684
recapitulate, 417
reception, 29
reciprocal, 684
recluse, 534
reconcile, 683
recrimination, 11
RECT, 106

rectify, 107
rectilinear, 107
rectitude, 107
redound, 569
redundancy, 569
referendum 586
reflective, 86
refraction, 452
refuge, 196
REG, 427
regalia, 428
regency, 428
regimen, 427
regress, 685
reincarnation, 76
reiterate, 682
rejuvenate, 682
relegate, 472
remand, 567
remorse, 682
renege, 458
repel, 210
replete, 125
reprehensible, 478
reprobate, 13
reputed, 217
requisition, 123
resolute, 606
resonance, 131
respirator, 246
restrictive, 519
resurgent, 653
retract, 35
retribution, 737
RETRO, 377
retroactive, 377
retrofit, 378
retrograde, 426
retrogress, 378

retrospective, 378
revert, 348
revivify, 529
revoke, 684
rhomboid, 669
rigor mortis, 512
sacrosanct, 571
SANCT, 570
sanctimonious, 571
sanction, 570
sanctuary, 572
sapphic, 189
satyr, 741
SCEND, 595
SCI, 200
SCOP, 672
SCRIB/
SCRIP, 600
Scylla and Charybdis, 214
seclusion, 534
seduction, 38
segregate, 474
semicolon, 486
semiconductor, 487
semitone, 486
SENS, 156
sensor, 156
sensuous, 158
SEQU, 38
sequential, 38
serpentine, 310
SERV, 531
serviceable, 531
servile, 531
servitude, 532
sibyl, 93
SIGN, 407

signatory, 407
signet, 408
signify, 407
simian, 310
SIMIL/
SIMUL, 592
simile, 592
simulacrum, 593
simulate, 593
sinecure, 153
sine qua non, 512
siren, 93
Sisyphean, 236
Socratic, 190
solecism, 190
soliloquy, 573
SOLU, 604
soluble, 604
SON, 130
sonic, 130
SOPH, 158
sophisticated, 159
sophistry, 158
sophomoric, 159
spartan, 19
SPECT, 145
SPHER, 345
spherical, 345
SPIR, 245
spirited, 245
stentorian, 20
stigma, 538
stoic, 20
STRAT, 655
stratification, 655
stratocumulus, 656
stratosphere, 345
stratum, 655
STRICT, 518

stricture, 519
STRU/STRUCT, 521
stygian, 140
SUB, 491
subconscious, 491
subculture, 277
subjugate, 491
subliminal, 492
subpar, 632
subsequent, 39
subservient, 532
substrate, 656
subterfuge, 197
subterranean, 222
subtext, 543
subversion, 492
suffuse, 582
SUPER, 643
superannuated, 396
superfluous, 643
superimpose, 330
superlative, 645
supernova, 327
supernumerary, 622
supersede, 644
SUR, 705
surcharge, 705
surfeit, 706
SURG, 652
surmount, 705
surreal, 706
susceptible, 30
suspend, 171
sybaritic, 20
symbiosis, 442
SYN, 710

synchronous, 383
syndrome, 711
synergy, 711
syntax, 710
synthesize, 710
tabula rasa, 512
tachometer, 127
tact, 402
tactile, 403
TANG/
TACT, 402
tangential, 403
tangible, 403
tantalize, 260
taxidermist, 687
TECHNI/
TECHNO, 724
technocrat, 724
technophile, 725
technophobe, 724
TELE, 452
telecommute, 454
telegenic, 452
telekinesis, 422
telemetry, 453
teleological, 453
telepathic, 227
TEMPER, 479
temper, 480
temperance, 480
TEMPOR, 380
temporal, 380
temporize, 381
TEN, 330
TEN/TENU, 721
tenable, 331
tenacious, 331
tendinitis, 638
tenet, 331

INDEX

tenuous, 721
tenure, 330
TERM/TERMIN, 340
terminal, 340
terminus, 341
TERR, 221
terra incognita, 513
terrarium, 222
terrestrial, 223
TETR, 411
tetracycline, 411
tetrahedron, 411
tetralogy, 411
tetrapod, 412
TEXT, 542
textual, 542
THE/THEO, 268
theocracy, 270
theosophy, 160
THERM/THERMO, 54
thermal, 54
thermodynamics, 54
thermonuclear, 55
thesis, 562
thespian, 260
titanic, 237
TOM, 660
tonsillectomy, 661
TOP, 366
topical, 366
topography, 367
TORT, 526
tort, 527
tortuous, 528
TOXI, 719
toxicity, 720
toxicology, 720
toxin, 719
TRACT, 34
traction, 34
trajectory, 34
TRANS, 674
transcend, 595
transcendent, 675
transfiguration, 675
transfusion, 581
transient, 674
translucent, 181
transmission, 208
transmute, 449
transpire, 246
transponder, 675
transpose, 329
transvestite, 266
trauma, 612
travesty, 267
TRI, 385
triad, 385
TRIB, 736
tributary, 736
tribute, 736
triceratops, 386
trident, 386
trilogy, 385
trimester, 386
trinity, 387
triptych, 387
Triton, 237
triumvirate, 575
trivial, 388
Trojan horse, 164
TROP, 320
TROPH, 184
tropism, 320
tuition, 356
TURB, 249
turbid, 250
turbine, 250
turbulent, 251
TUT/TUI, 356
tutelage, 357
tutorial, 356
ultimatum, 586
ultrasonic, 132
umber, 264
UMBR, 264
umbrage, 265
unconscionable, 201
UND, 568
undulant, 568
UNI, 335
unicameral, 335
unilateral, 335
unison, 336
unitarian, 336
upsurge, 652
URB, 273
urbane, 274
urbanization, 275
utopian, 367
VAL, 577
validate, 578
valor, 577
vasoconstrictor, 520
venereal, 44
VER, 247
veracity, 248
VERB, 590
verbatim, 591
verbiage, 591
verbose, 590
verify, 247
verisimilitude, 247
VERT, 346
VEST, 266
VIR, 575
virago, 576
virility, 575
virtuosity, 576
VIS, 143
vis-à-vis, 143
visionary, 144
vista, 143
VIV, 528
vivacious, 528
vivisection, 530
VOC, 147
vociferous, 149
VOLU/VOLV, 251
voluble, 251
VOR, 73
voracious, 74
vox populi, 282
vulcanize, 237
vulpine, 286
xenophobe, 633
zealot, 741
zephyr, 261

《韦氏英汉双解扩词手册》词根、词族

思维导图

本思维导图为辅助读者进行词汇记忆的简图，与正文并非完全一致。

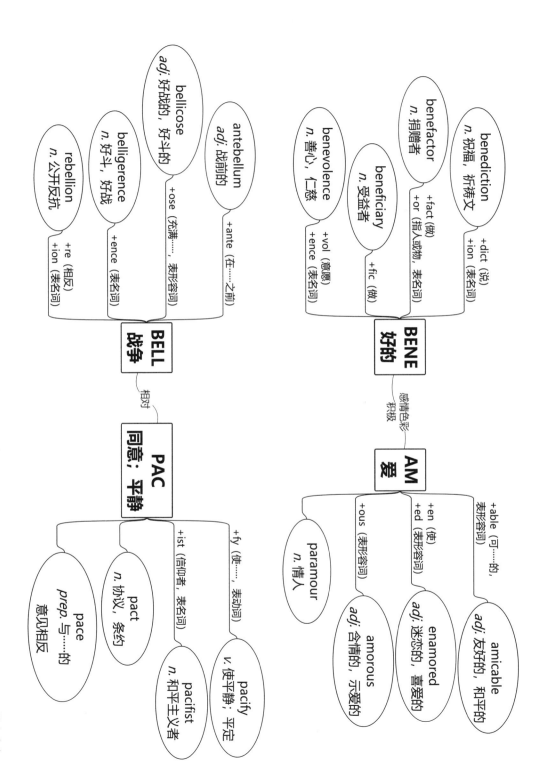

Unit 1-1

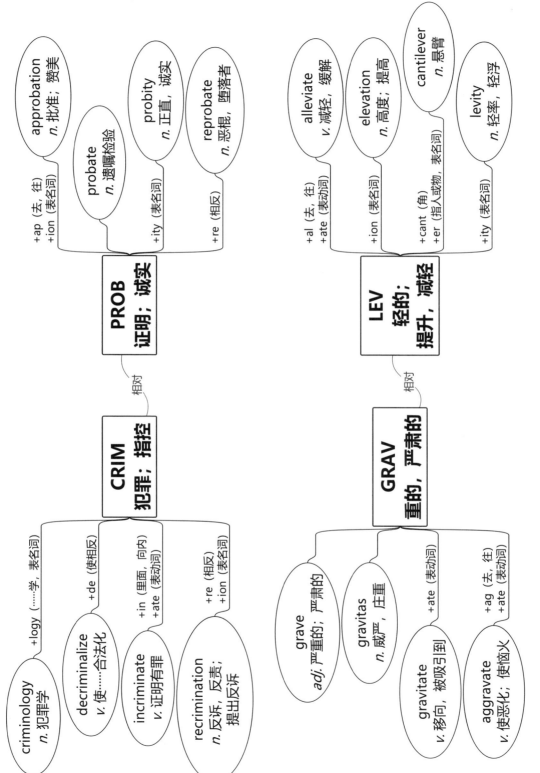

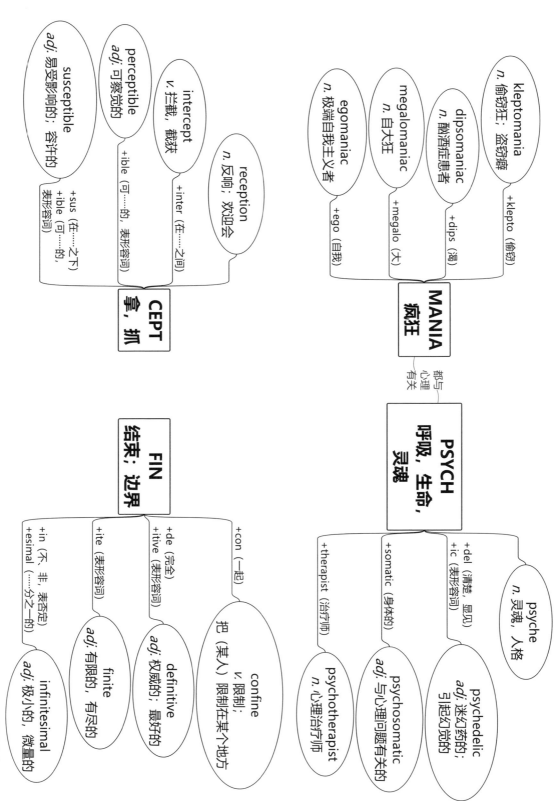

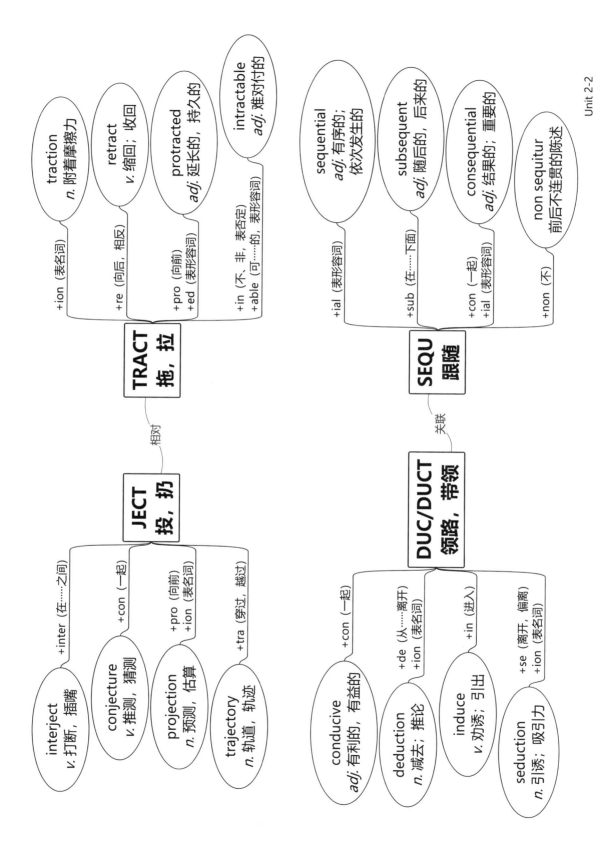

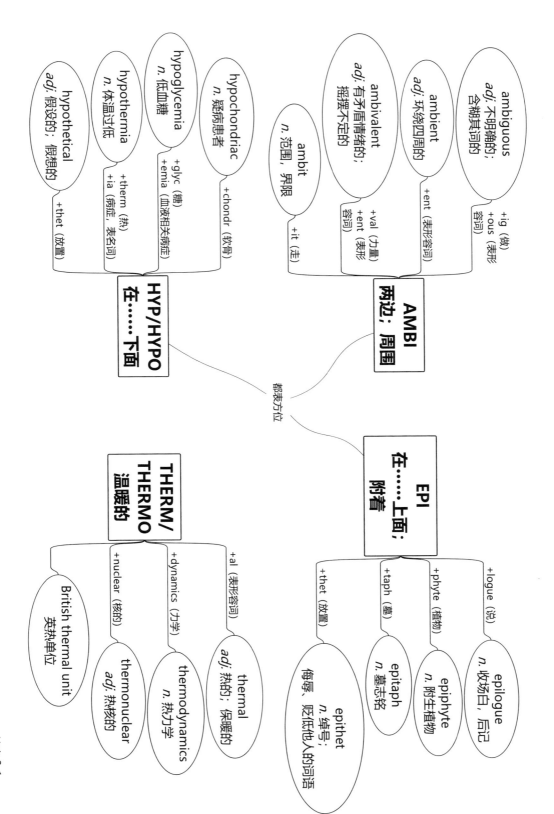

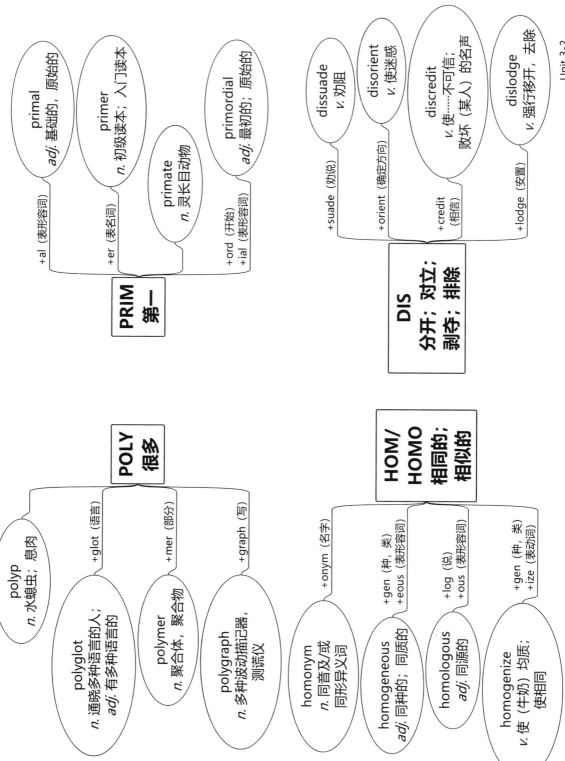

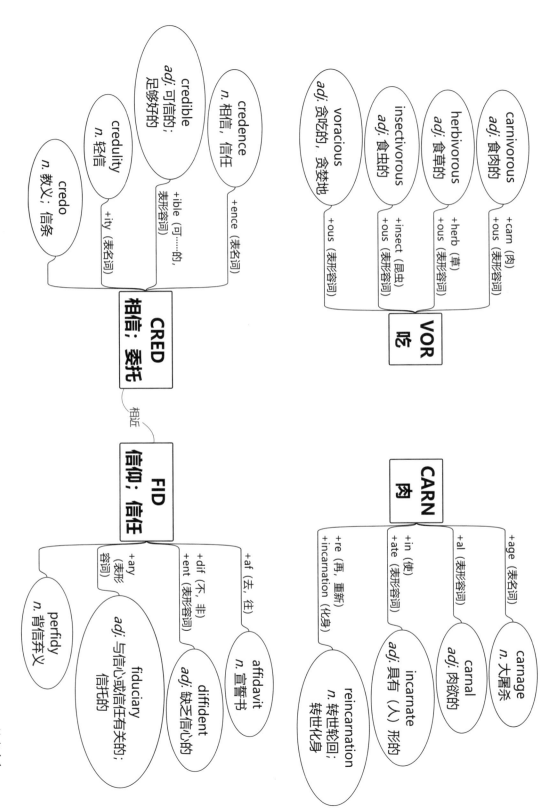

CURR/CURS 跑

- concurrent *adj.* 同时发生的 — +con (一起) +ent (表形容词)
- cursory *adj.* 仓促的, 匆忙的 — +ory (表形容词)
- discursive *adj.* 东拉西扯的 — +dis (分开) +ive (表形容词)
- precursor *n.* 先驱, 先兆 — +pre (在……之前) +or (表名词)

与足部有关

PED 脚

- quadruped *n.* 四足动物 — +quadr (四)
- pedigree *n.* 血统, 家谱
- impediment *n.* 妨碍, 障碍 — +im (里面, 向内) +ment (表名词)
- pedestrian *adj.* 平常的, 普通的

FLECT 使弯曲

- deflect *v.* 转向, 偏离 — +de (离开)
- reflective *adj.* 反射的; 沉思的 — +re (相反) +ive (表形容词)
- genuflect *v.* 行屈膝礼 — +genu (膝盖)
- inflection *n.* 抑扬变化; 屈折变化 — +in (里面, 向内) +ion (表名词)

POST 在……之后

- posterior *adj.* 后部的 *n.* 后部 — +ior (较……的)
- posthumous *adj.* 死后出版的; 死后的 — +hum (土地) +ous (表形容词)
- postmodern *adj.* 后现代的 — +modern (现代的)
- postmortem *adj.* 死后的; 事后的 — +mort (死亡)

Unit 4-2

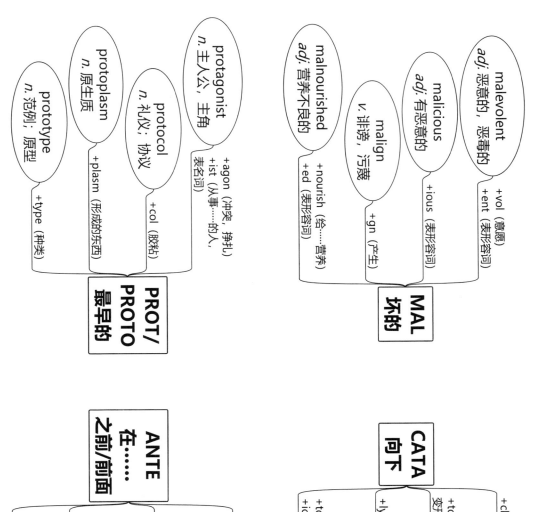
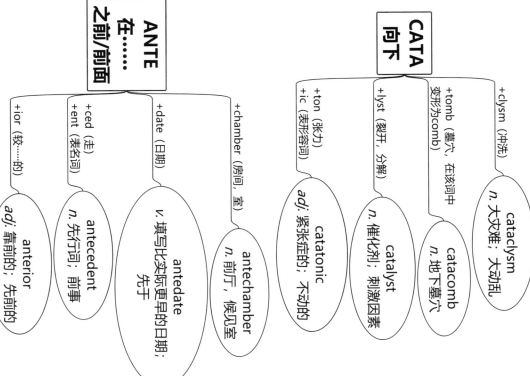

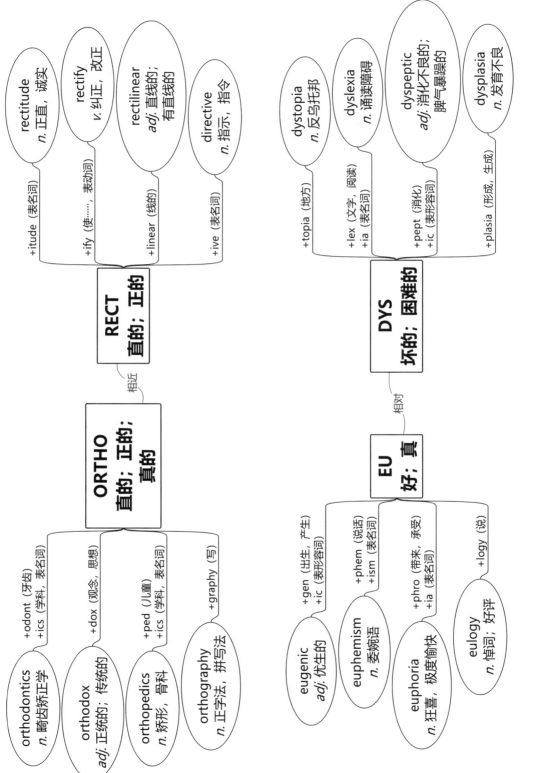

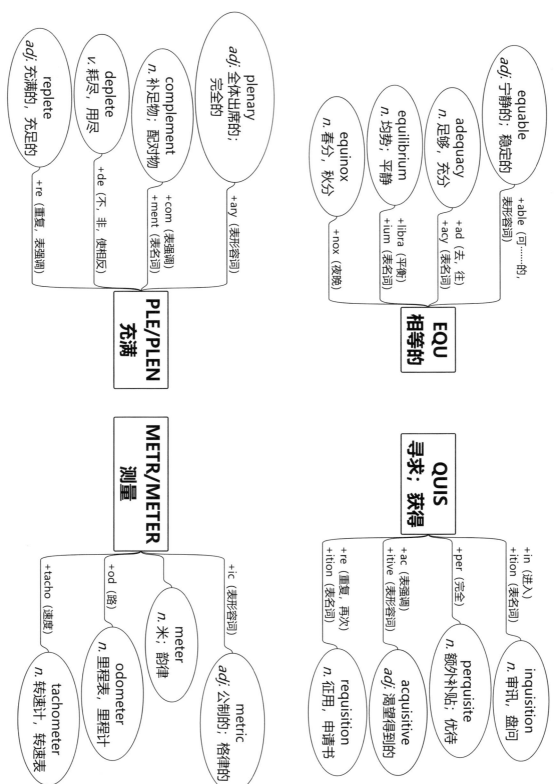

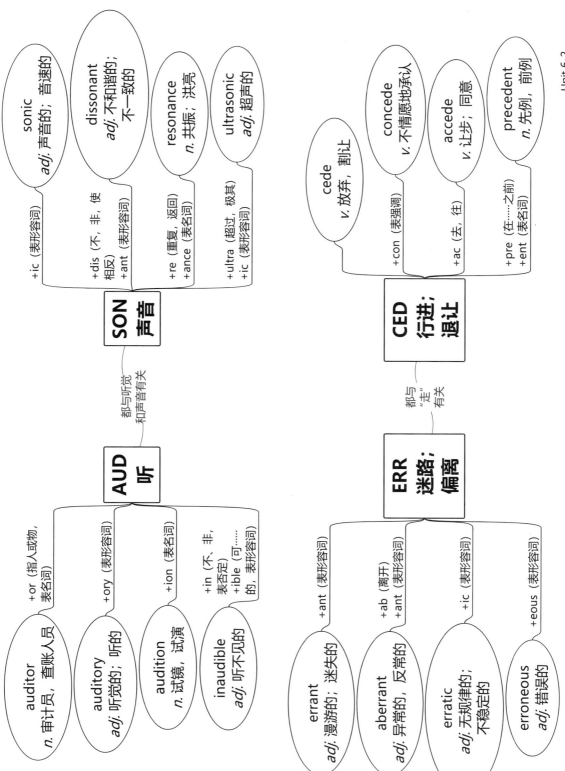

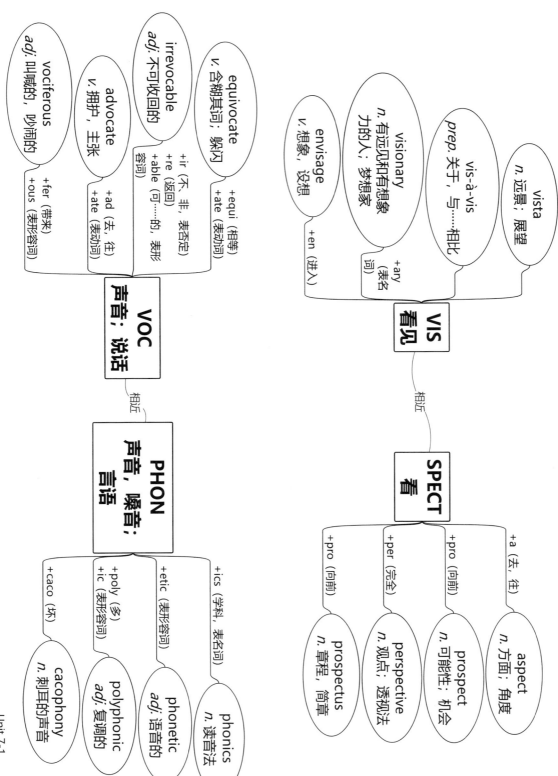

Unit 7-1

PERI 周围

- **perimeter** *n.* 周边, 周长 — +meter (测量)
- **periodontal** *adj.* 牙周的 — +odont (牙齿) +al (表形容词)
- **peripatetic** *adj.* 漫步的; 巡游的 — patein (走, 希腊语) +etic (表形容词)
- **peripheral** *adj.* 外围的; 次要的 — +pher (带来) +al (表形容词)

SOPH 聪明, 智慧

- **sophistry** *n.* 诡辩 — +istry (学科, 表名词)
- **sophisticated** *adj.* 老于世故的; 非常复杂的 — +ed (表形容词)
- **sophomoric** *adj.* 一知半解的 — +mor (笨) +ic (表形容词)
- **theosophy** *n.* 通神学, 神智学 — +theo (神)

CUR 关心, 照料

- **curative** *adj.* 治疗的 — +ative (表形容词)
- **curator** *n.* 馆长, 负责人 — +ator (人或物, 表名词)
- **procure** *v.* 取得, 获得 — +pro (代表)
- **sinecure** *n.* 闲职, 挂名职位 — +sine (无, 没有)

SENS 感觉

- **sensor** *n.* 传感器 — +or (指人或物)
- **desensitize** *v.* 使不敏感, 使脱敏 — +de (不, 非, 使相反) +ize (表动词)
- **extrasensory** *adj.* 超感觉的 — +extra (以外, 超过) +ory (表形容词)
- **sensuous** *adj.* 美好感觉的; 感觉的 — +uous (表形容词)

Unit 7-2

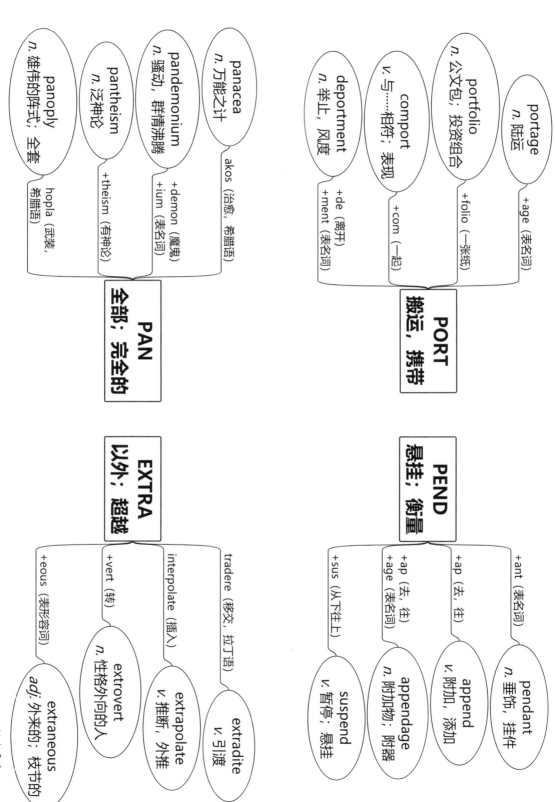

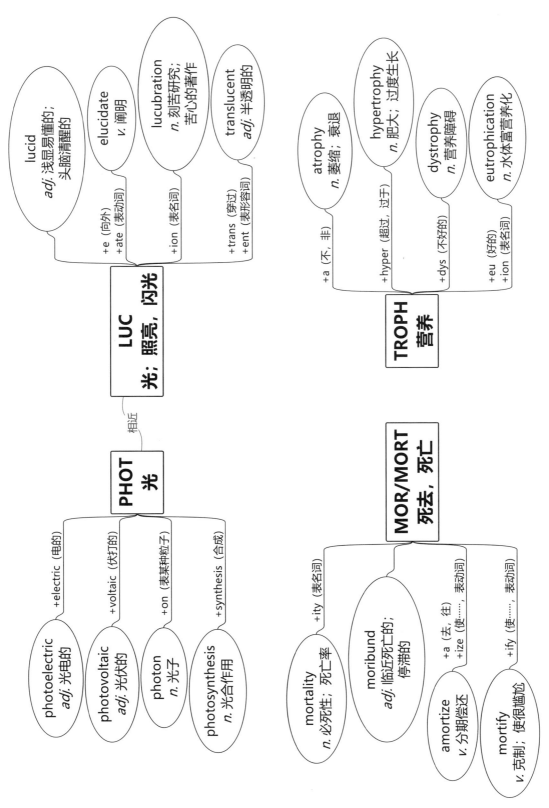

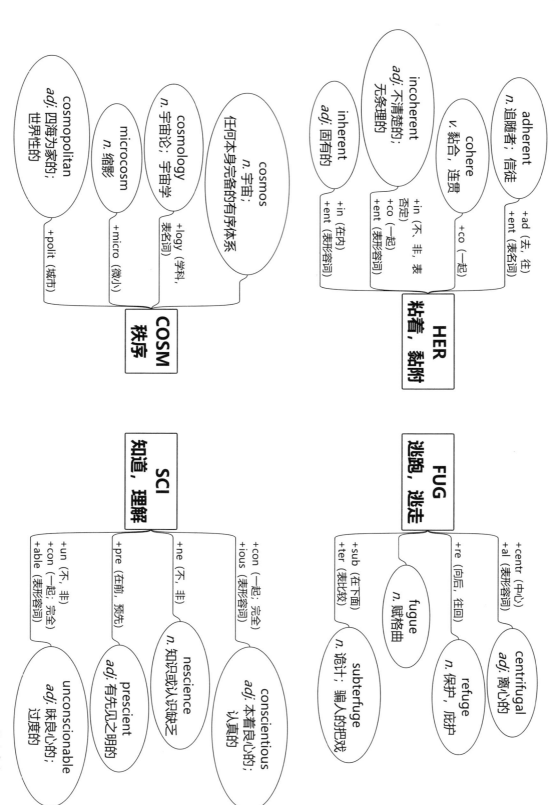

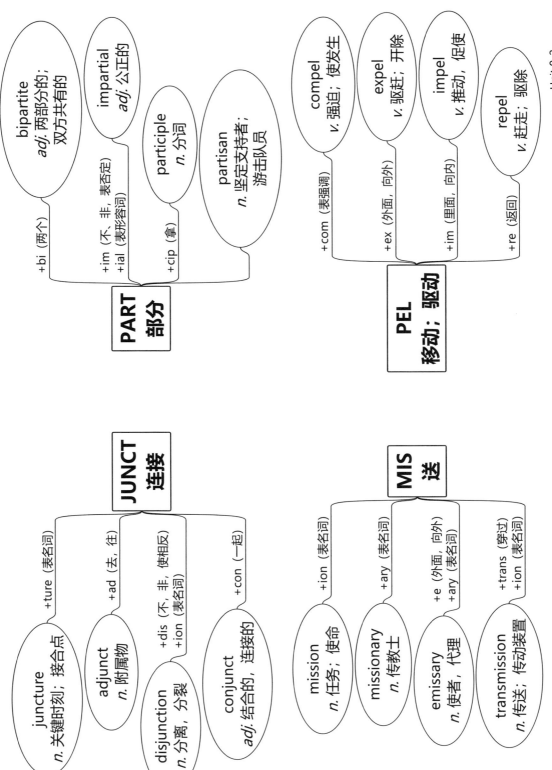

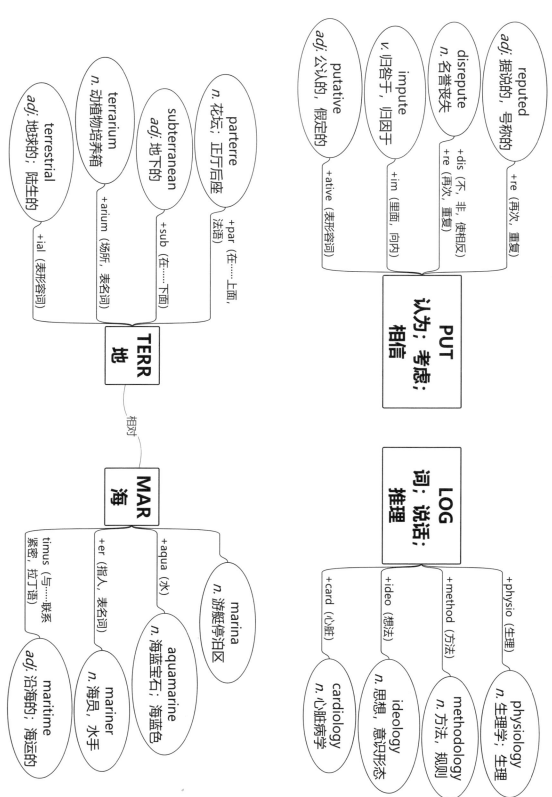

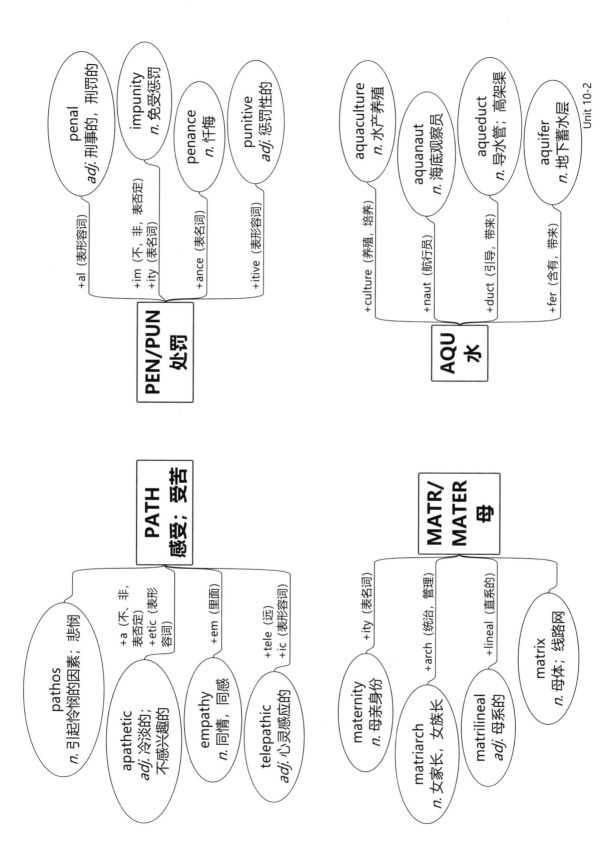

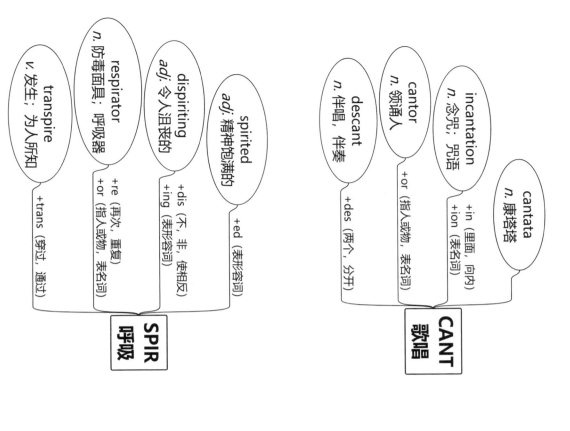
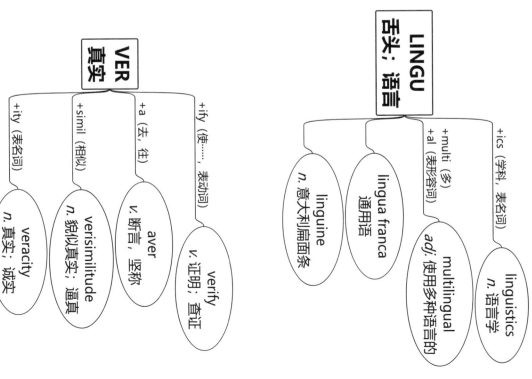

VOLU/VOLV 滚动，缠绕，转身，转动

- **voluble** *adj.* 滔滔不绝的 (+able 可……的，表形容词)
- **devolve** *v.* 移交；退化 (+de 向下)
- **evolution** *n.* 进化，演变 (+e 外面，向外；+ion 表名词)
- **convoluted** *adj.* 盘绕的；错综复杂的 (+con 一起；+ed 表形容词)

LUM 光

- **lumen** *n.* 流明
- **luminous** *adj.* 发光的；照亮的 (+ous 表形容词)
- **bioluminescent** *adj.* 生物发光的 (+bio 生物，生命；+escent 表形容词)
- **luminary** *n.* 名人，杰出人物 (+ary 人或场所，表名词)

TURB 引起混乱；人群；混乱

- **turbid** *adj.* 浑浊的；不清的
- **perturb** *v.* 使不安，使担心 (+per 完全)
- **turbine** *n.* 涡轮机，汽轮机
- **turbulent** *adj.* 汹涌的；骚乱的 (+ent 表形容词)

FAC 做

- **factor** *n.* 因素，成分 (+or 表名词)
- **factotum** *n.* 事务总管 (+totum 所有，拉丁语)
- **facile** *adj.* 容易得到的；肤浅的 (+ile 表形容词)
- **facilitate** *v.* 使更容易，促进 (+ate 表动词)

Unit 11-2

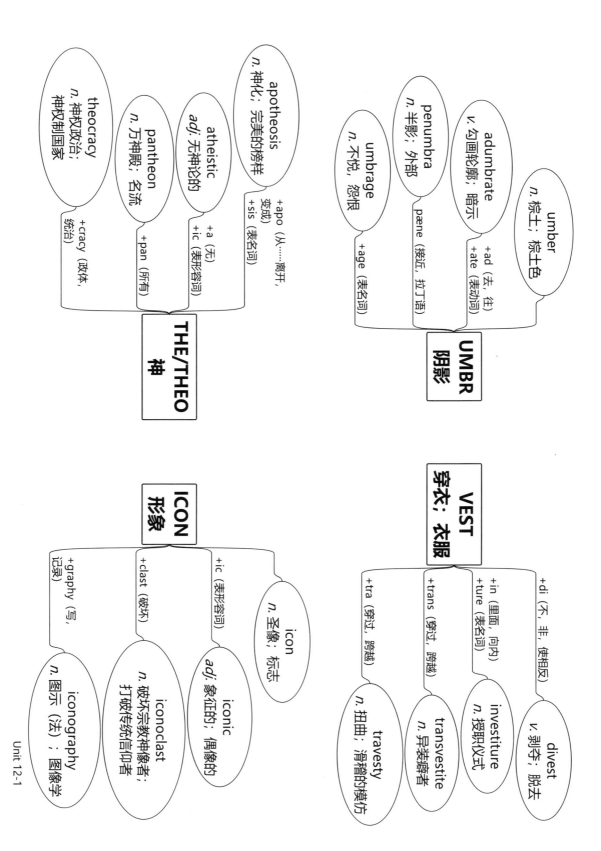

URB 城市

- urbane *adj.* 温文尔雅的
- +ex (在……外面) → exurban *adj.* 城市远郊的
- +inter (在……之间) → interurban *adj.* 城际的, 市际的
- +ation (表名词) → urbanization *n.* 城市化

CULT 照料

- +ac (去, 往) +ion (表名词) → acculturation *n.* 文化适应; 文化移入
- +cross (跨越) +al (表形容词) → cross-cultural *adj.* 跨文化的
- +horti (花园) → horticulture *n.* 园艺学
- +sub (亚于, 在……下面) → subculture *n.* 亚文化群

DEM/DEMO 人民

- +graph (写, 记录) +ic (表形容词) → demographic *adj.* 人口学的
- +en (在……里面) +ic (表形容词) → endemic *adj.* 某地特有的; 某职业、地区或环境特有的
- +agogue (领导) → demagogue *n.* 蛊惑民心的政客
- +ic (表形容词) → demotic *adj.* 大众化的, 通俗的

POPUL 人民

（与 DEM/DEMO 相近）

- +ist (信仰者, 表名词) → populist *n.* 平民主义者
- +ace (表名词) → populace *n.* 民众; 人口
- +ous (表形容词) → populous *adj.* 人口稠密的
- +vox (声音) → vox populi 公众舆论

Unit 12-2

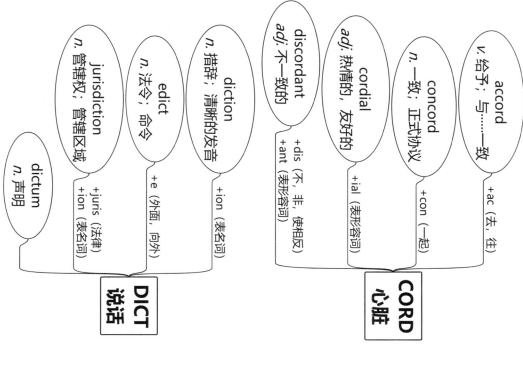
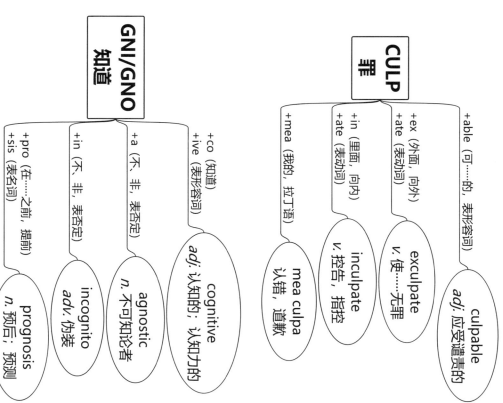

Unit 13-1

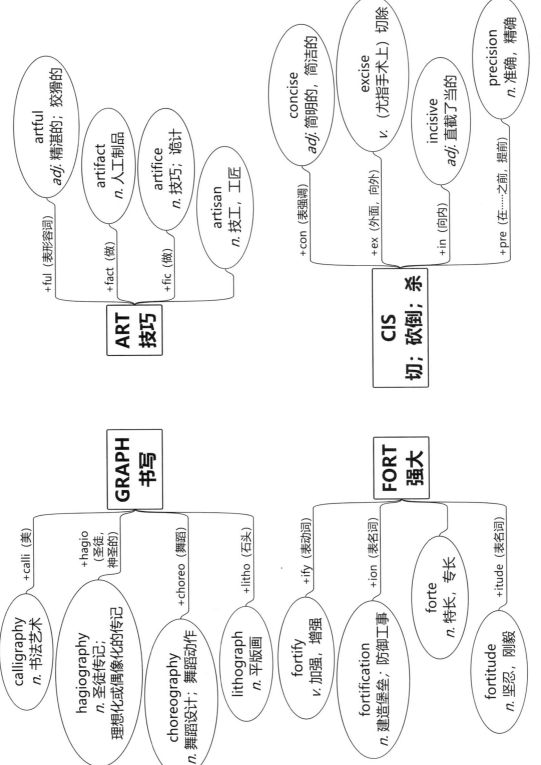

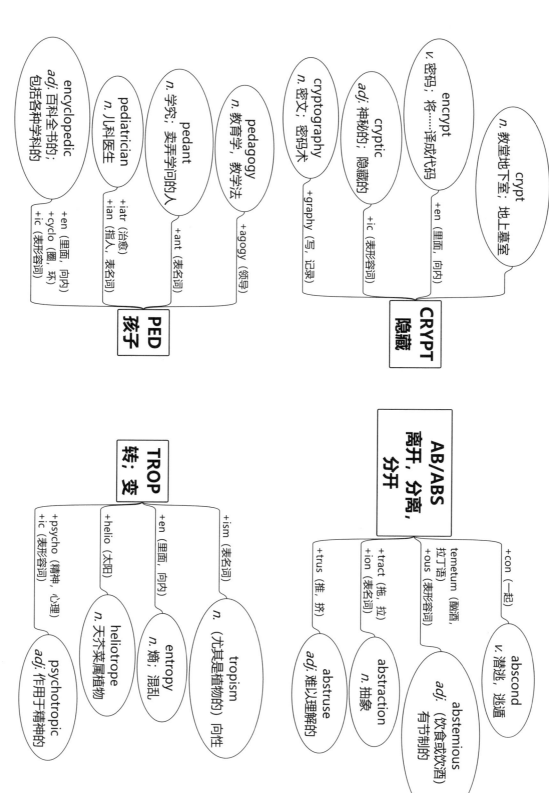

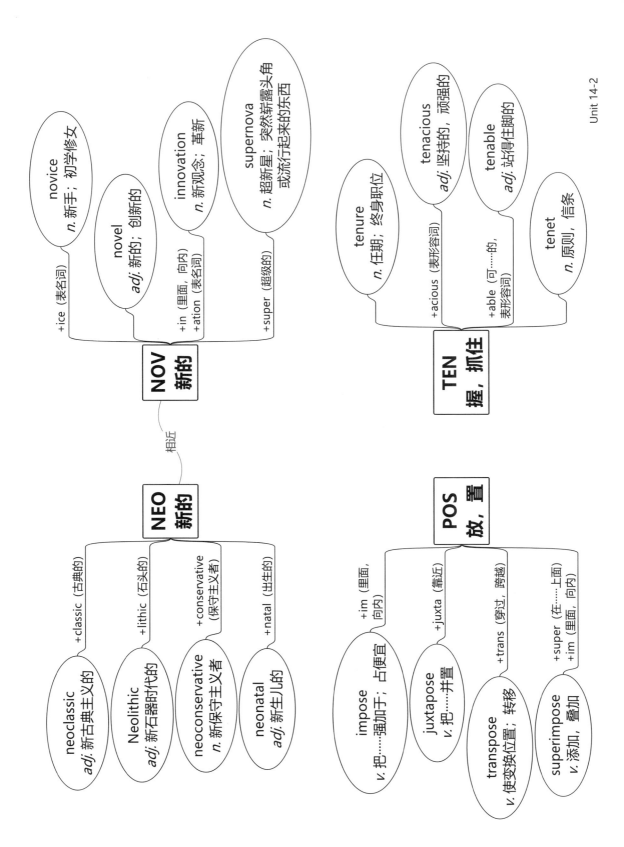

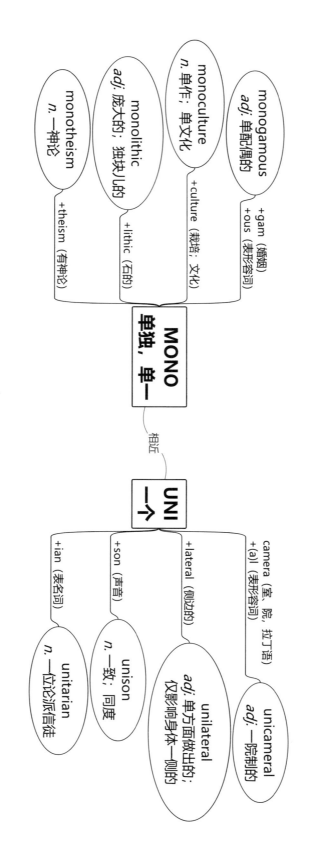

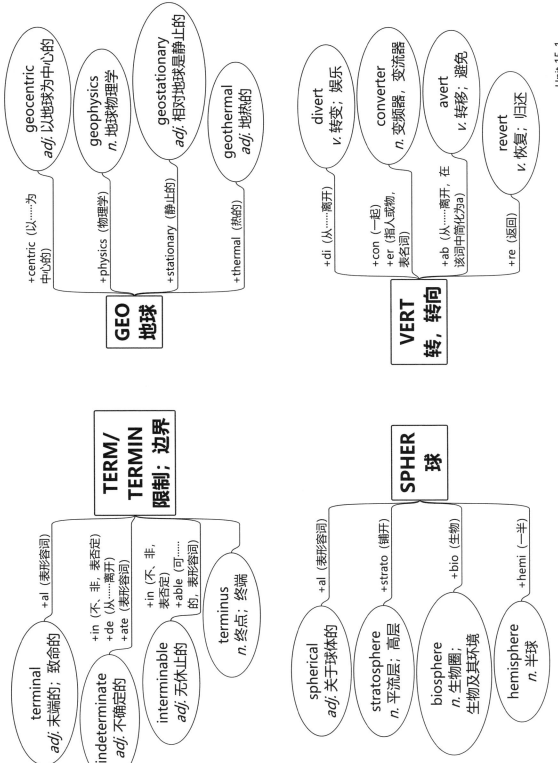

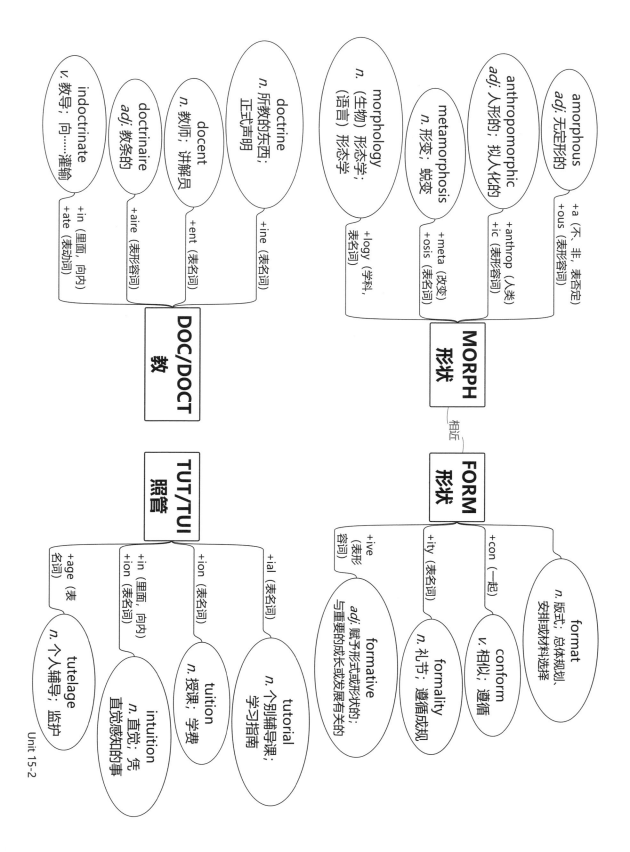

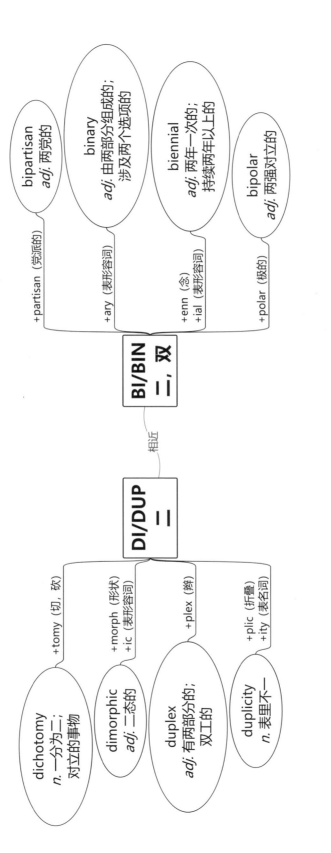

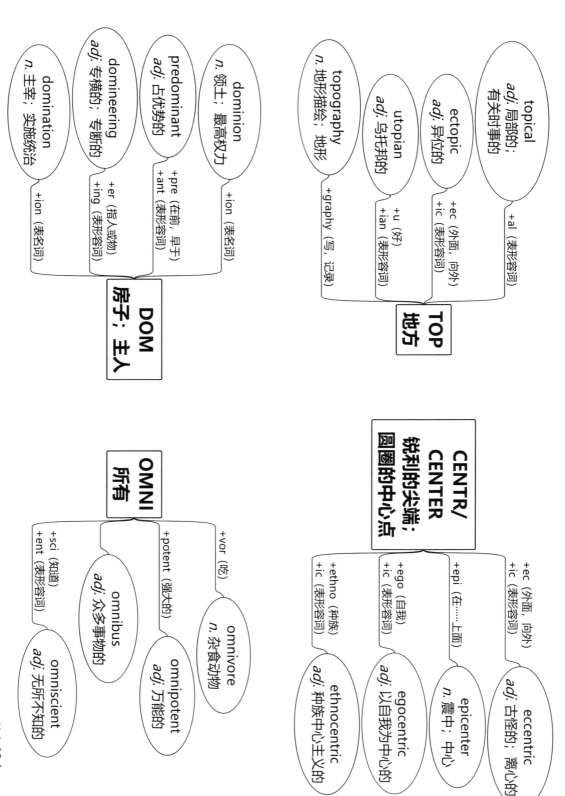

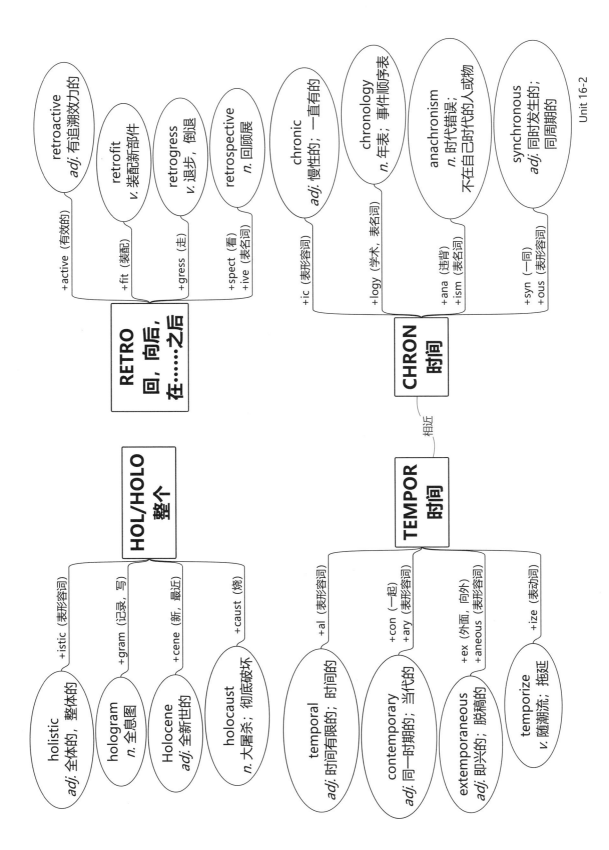

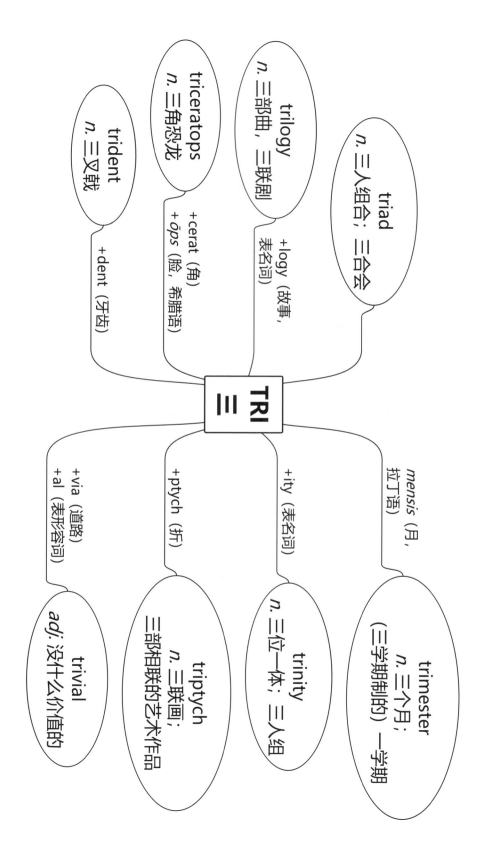

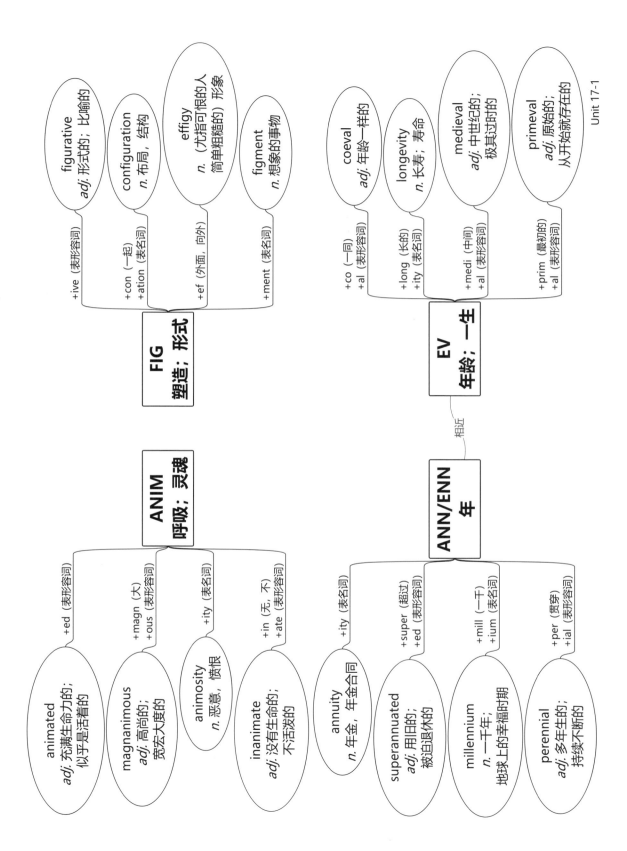

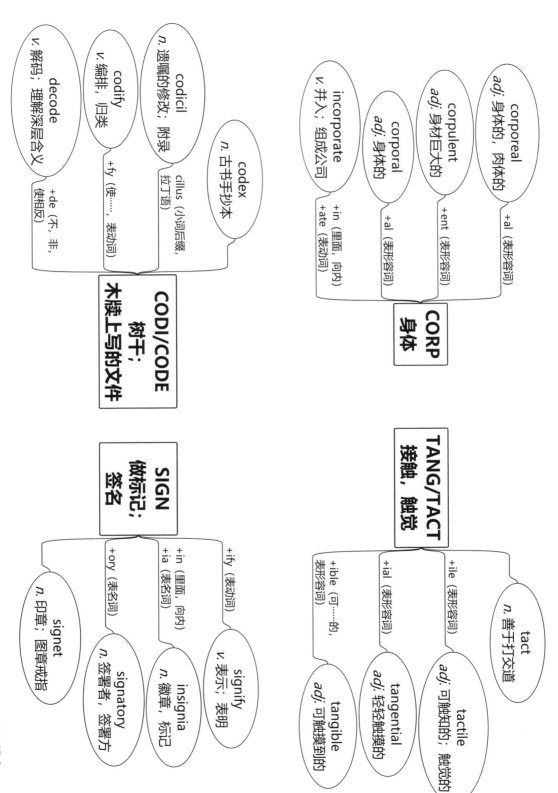

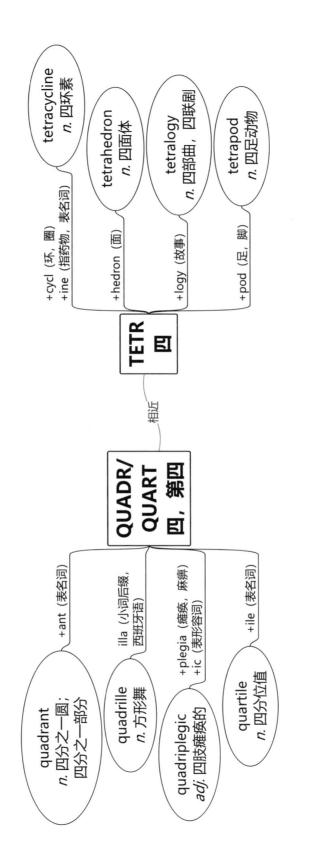

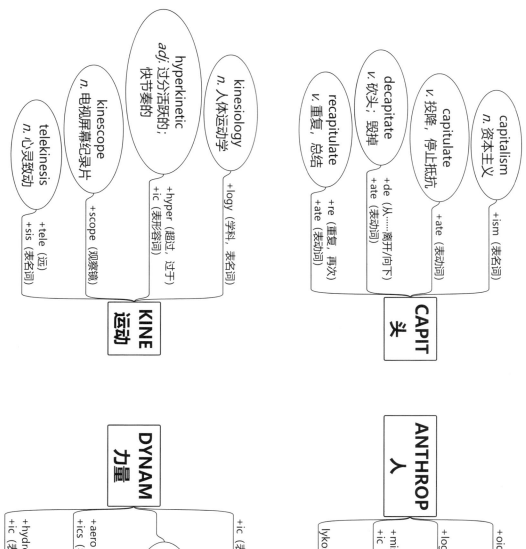
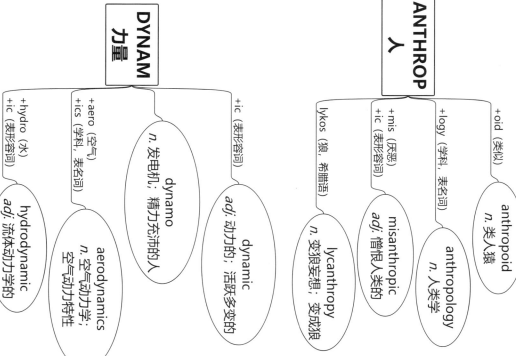

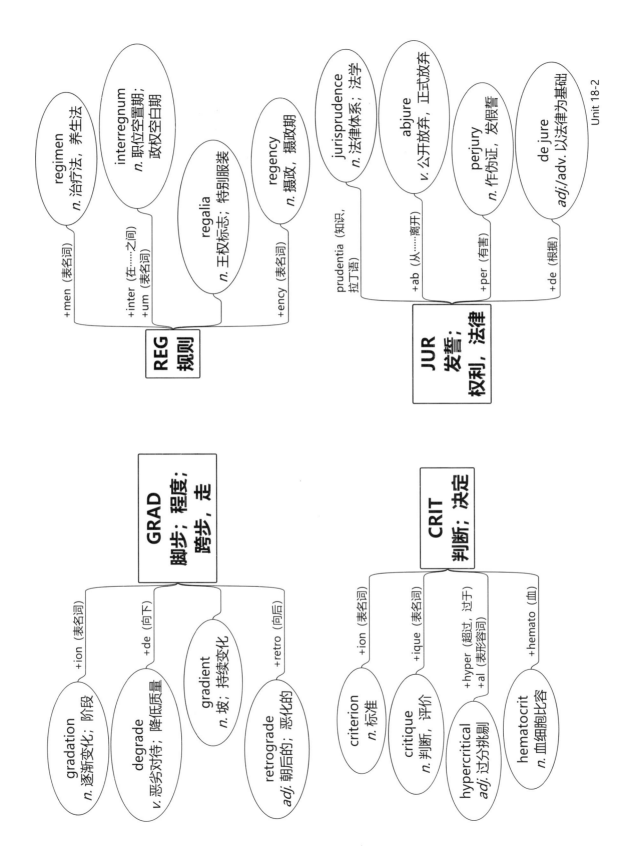

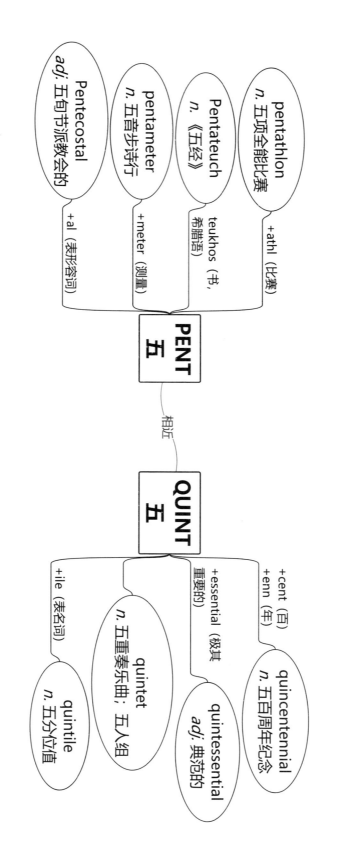

Unit 18-3

GEN 生

- **genesis** *n.* 起源，开端 (+sis 表名词)
- **generator** *n.* 发电机 (+or 指人或物，表名词)
- **genre** *n.* 种类，体裁
- **carcinogenic** *adj.* 致癌的 (+carcino 癌症, +ic 表形容词)

BIO 生命

关联

- **bionic** *adj.* 更加强大的 (+ic 表形容词)
- **biopsy** *n.* 活组织检查 (+opsy 检查)
- **biodegradable** *adj.* 可生物降解的 (+degradable 可降解的)
- **symbiosis** *n.* 共生；合作关系 (+sym 一起, +sis 表名词)

MUT 变化

- **commute** *v.* 替换；通勤 (+com 表强调)
- **immutable** *adj.* 不能变化的 (+im 不、非，表否定; +able 可……的，表形容词)
- **permutation** *n.* 顺序的变化 (+per 完全，彻底; +ion 表名词)
- **transmute** *v.* 变化；经历变化 (+trans 穿过，越过)

FUNCT 进行，做

- **functionary** *n.* 履行某一职责的人；官员 (+ary 表名词)
- **malfunction** *n.* 失灵，出现故障 (+mal 坏, +ion 表名词)
- **defunct** *adj.* 已灭绝的 (+de 不、非，使相反)
- **dysfunctional** *adj.* 难以处理正常社会关系的；运转不正常的 (+dys 坏，失常, +al 表形容词)

Unit 19-1

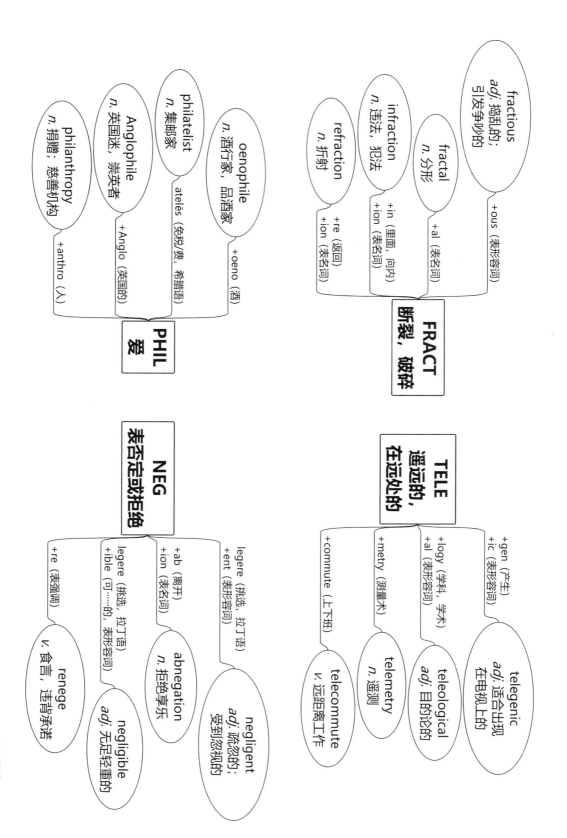

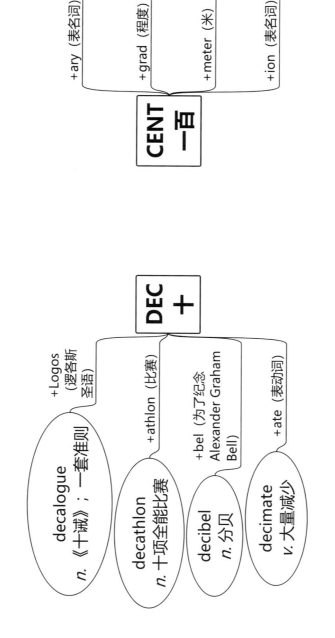

Unit 19-3

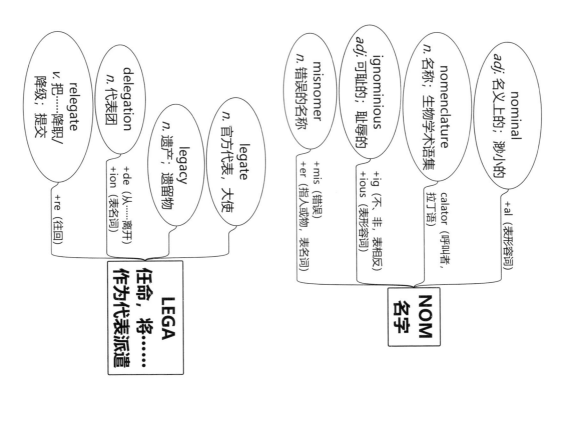
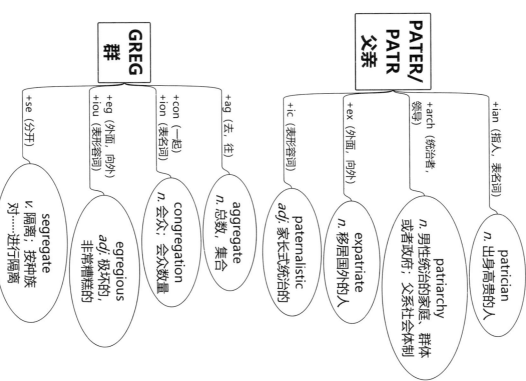

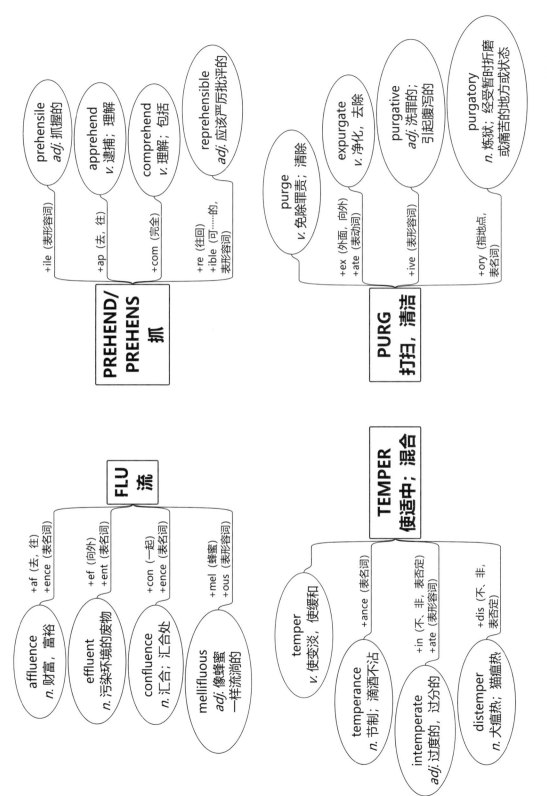

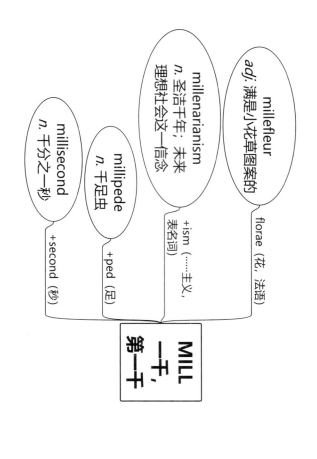
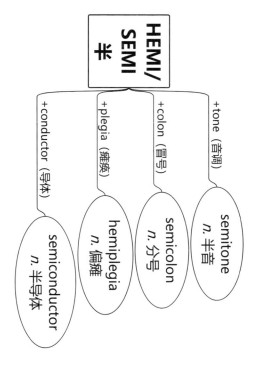

HYPER 在……上面/较远的一边

- +active (活跃的) → hyperactive *adj.* 极度活跃的
- +bole (扔) → hyperbole *n.* 夸张
- +tension (紧张) → hypertension *n.* 高血压
- +ventilate (换气) → hyperventilate *v.* 强力呼吸

PARA 在……旁边；与……有密切关系

- +phrase (表述) → paraphrase *v.* 复述
- +legal (法律的) → paralegal *adj.* 律师助理的
- +medic (医生) → paramedic *n.* 医务辅助人员
- +military (军队的) → paramilitary *adj.* 辅助军事的

SUB 在……下面

- +conscious (意识到的) → subconscious *adj.* 下意识的
- jugus (轭, 拉丁语) → subjugate *v.* 征服, 控制
- +liminal (阈限的) → subliminal *adj.* 下意识的
- +vers (转, 变) +ion (表名词) → subversion *n.* 颠覆；削弱

PRE 在……之前/前面

- +clud (关闭) → preclude *v.* 使……不可能
- coquere (熟, 拉丁语) → precocious *adj.* 早熟的
- +dispose (使倾向于) → predispose *v.* 提前影响以产生某一特定印象；使……更可能染上某种疾病或身体状况
- +requisite (必需的事物) → prerequisite *n.* 前提, 前提条件

相对 (HYPER ↔ SUB)
都与方位有关

Unit 21-1

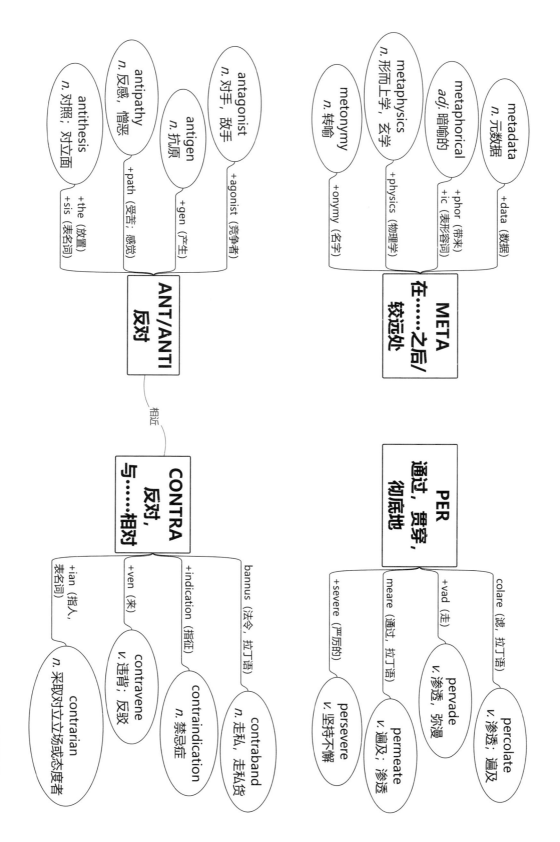

ACER/ACR 浓烈的；酸的

- acerbic *adj.* 尖刻的，辛辣的 — +ic (表形容词)
- acrid *adj.* 尖刻的；辛辣的
- acrimony *n.* 尖刻；辛辣 — +mony (表名词)
- exacerbate *v.* 使恶化，使加重 — +ex (完全) +ate (使……，表动词)

STRICT 拉紧，绑起来，捆好

- stricture *n.* 限制；批评 — +ure (表名词)
- restrictive *adj.* 限制的；限制使用的 — +re (往回) +ive (表形容词)
- constrict *v.* 收紧；限制 — +con (一起)
- vasoconstrictor *n.* 血管收缩神经药 — +vaso (血管)

STRU/STRUCT 放在一起，建筑，安排

- deconstruction *n.* 解构 — +de (不，非，使相反) +ion (表名词)
- infrastructure *n.* 基础；基础设施 — +infra (在……下面) +ure (表名词)
- construe *v.* 解释；理解 — +con (一起)
- instrumental *adj.* 发挥重要作用的；乐器的 — +in (在……上) +al (表形容词)

PROP/PROPRI 自己的

- proprietary *adj.* 所有人的；由私人经营的 — +ary (表形容词)
- propriety *n.* 适当；举止得当 — +ety (表名词)
- appropriate *v.* 独占；专用 — +ap (去，往) +ate (表动词)
- expropriate *v.* 剥夺；据为己有 — +ex (离开) +ate (表动词)

Unit 22-1

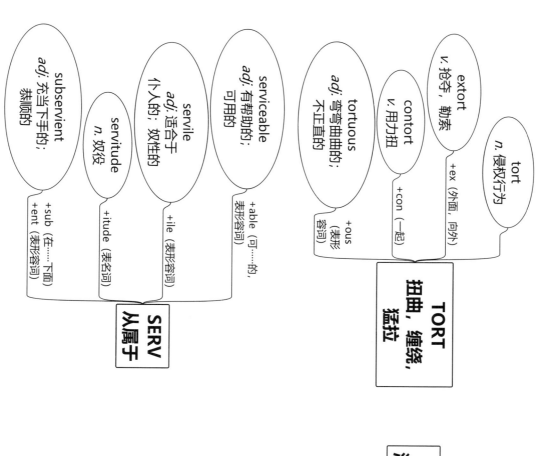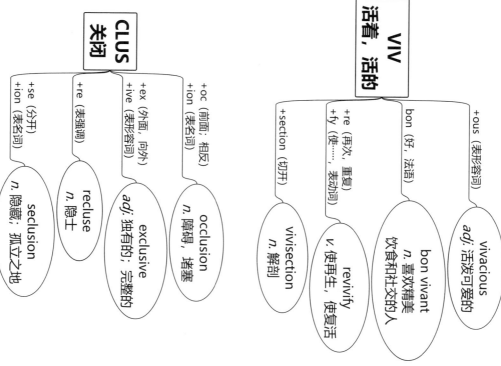

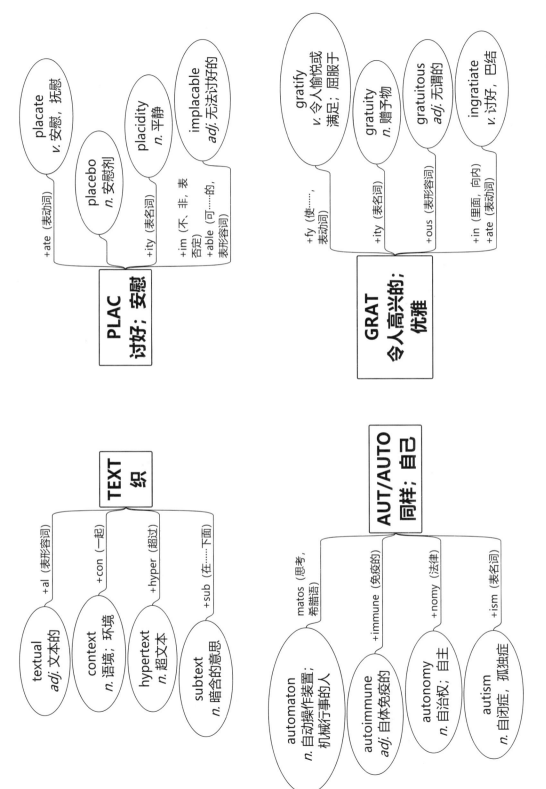

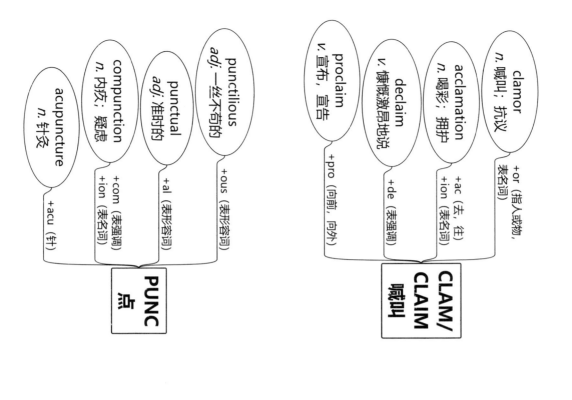
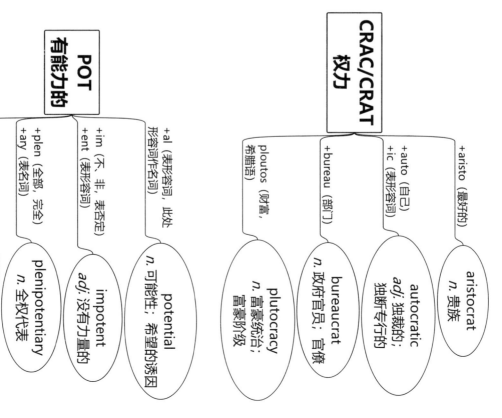

MAND 委托；命令

- mandate + dat (给予) → **mandate** *n.* 正式命令；授权
- mandatory + dat (给予) + ory (表形容词) → **mandatory** *adj.* 要求的，强制的
- commandeer + com (表强调) → **commandeer** *v.* 强征，征用
- remand + re (往回) → **remand** *v.* 发回原审法院重审；还押候审

UND 波浪；往上涌

- undulant + ant (表形容词) → **undulant** *adj.* 波浪般起伏的；波浪形的
- inundate + in (在……上) + ate (表动词) → **inundate** *v.* 淹没；使……难以承受
- redound + re (往回) → **redound** *v.* 起作用；反弹
- redundancy + re (重复) + ancy (表名词) → **redundancy** *n.* 多余；不必要的重复

SANCT 神圣的

- sanction + ion (表名词) → **sanction** *n.* 批准，准许
- sanctimonious + ous (表形容词) → **sanctimonious** *adj.* 假装圣洁的
- sacrosanct + sacro (神圣) → **sacrosanct** *adj.* 极具神圣的；仿佛神圣不容置疑或干扰的
- sanctuary + ary (指地点，表名词) → **sanctuary** *n.* 圣所；庇护所

LOQU 谈话

- colloquium + col (一起) + ium (表名词) → **colloquium** *n.* 学术研讨会
- soliloquy + soli (独自) → **soliloquy** *n.* 独白
- colloquial + col (一起) + al (表形容词) → **colloquial** *adj.* 谈话风格的
- loquacious + ous (表形容词) → **loquacious** *adj.* 善于言谈的

Unit 24-1

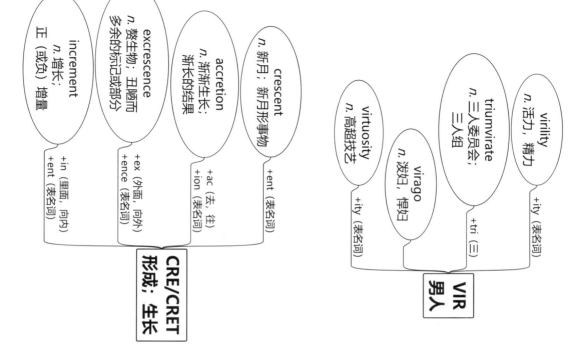
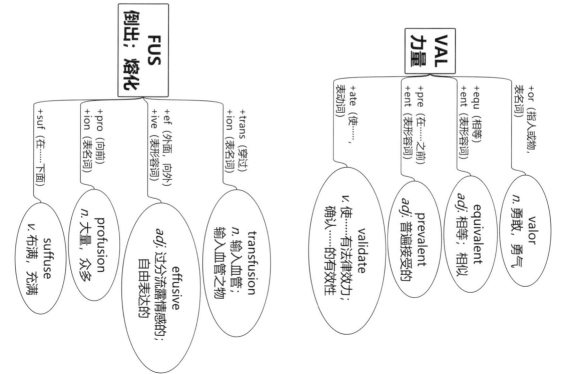

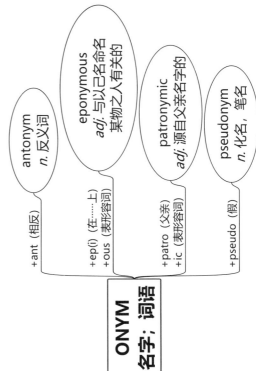
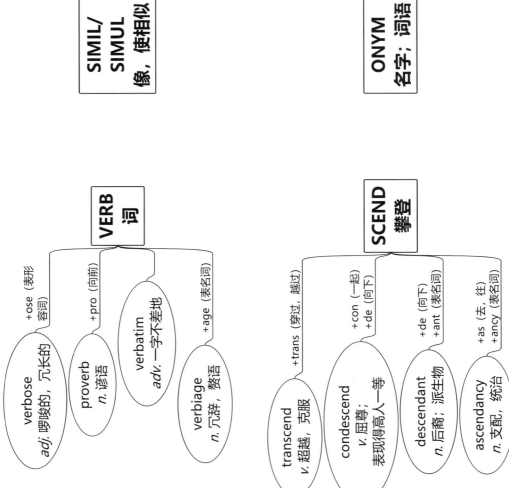

Unit 25-1

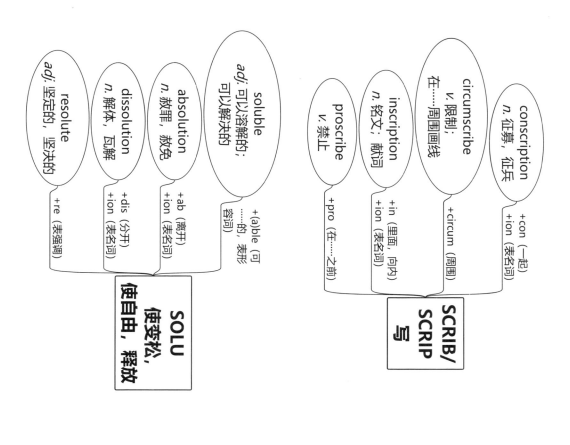
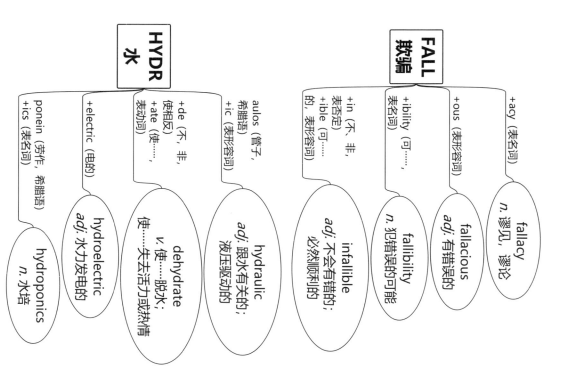

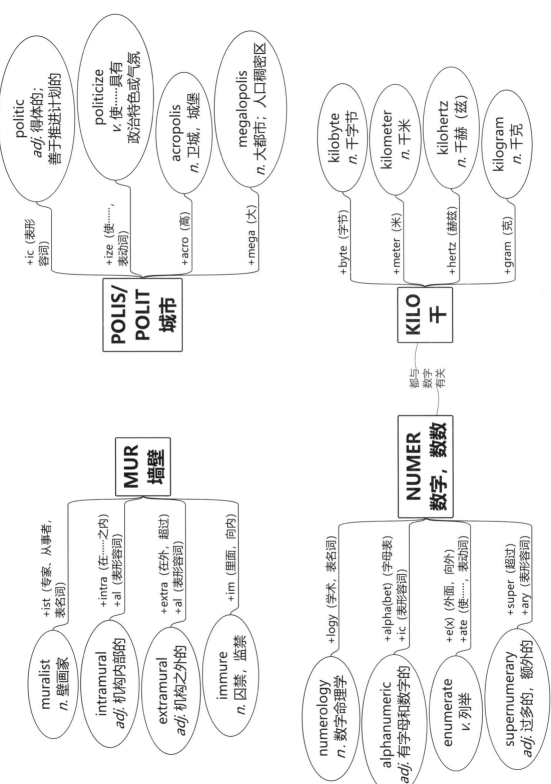

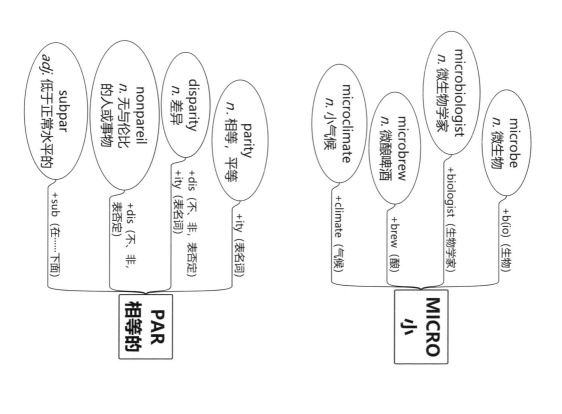
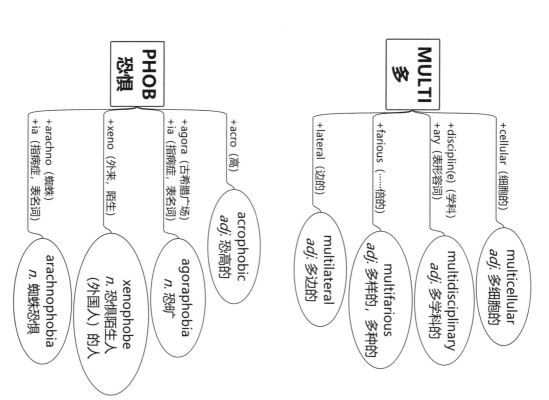

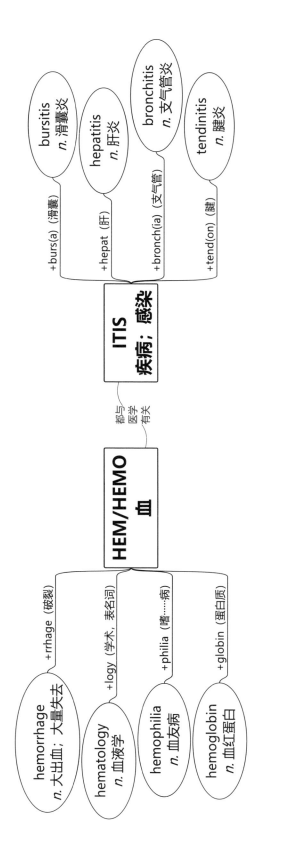

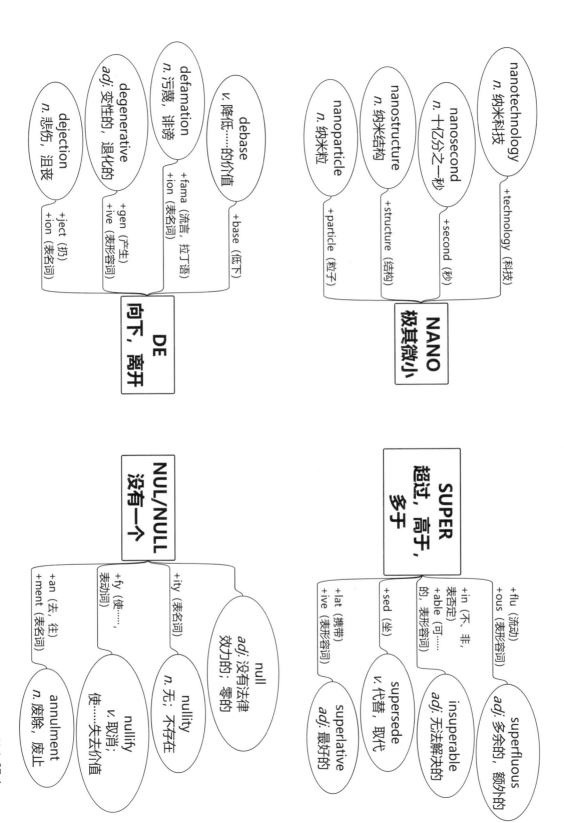

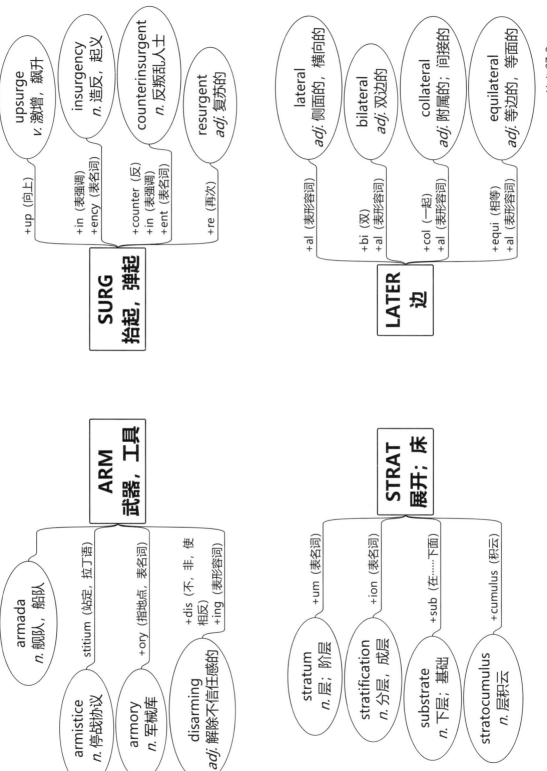

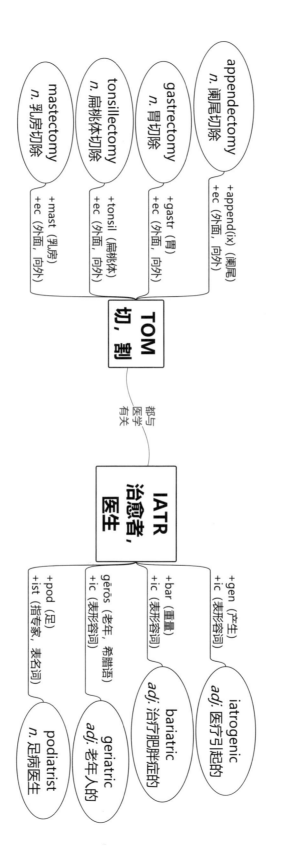

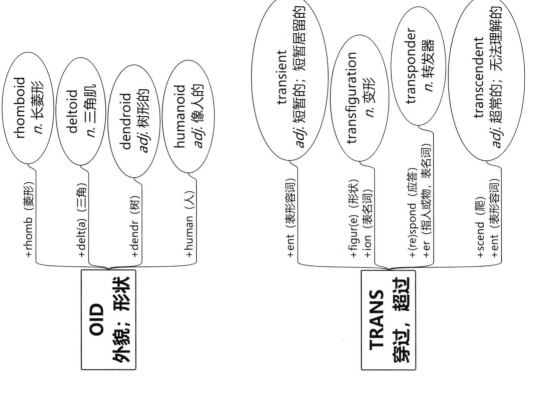

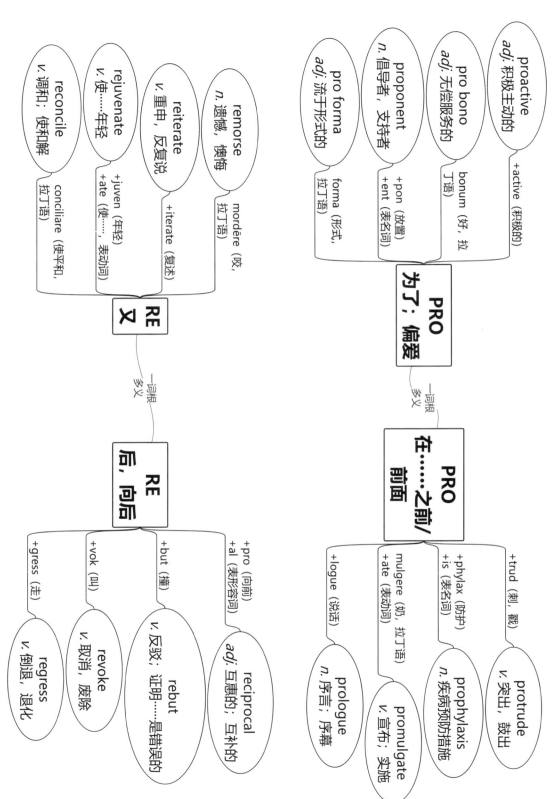

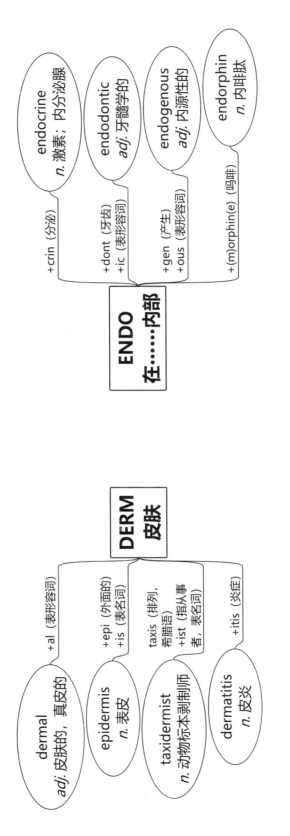

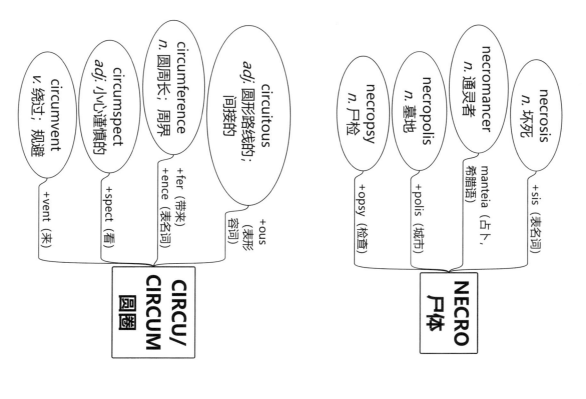
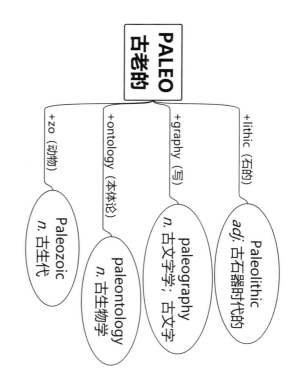
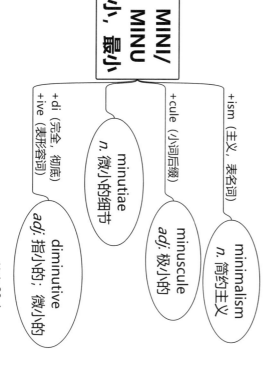

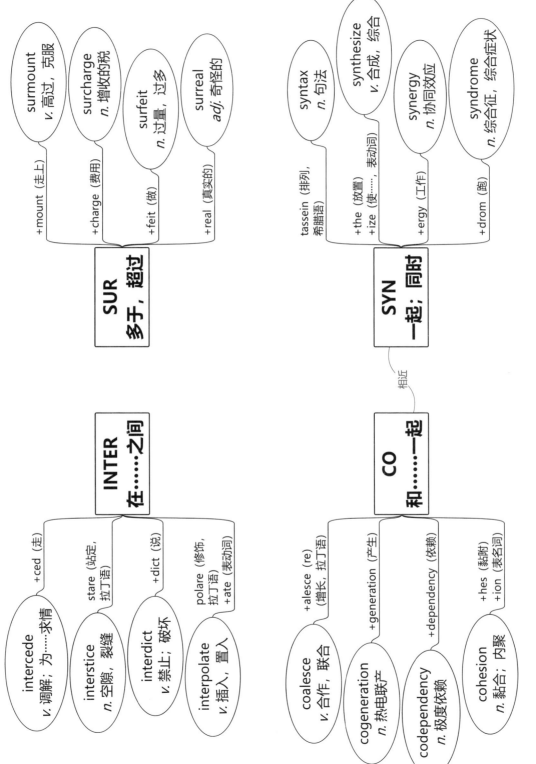

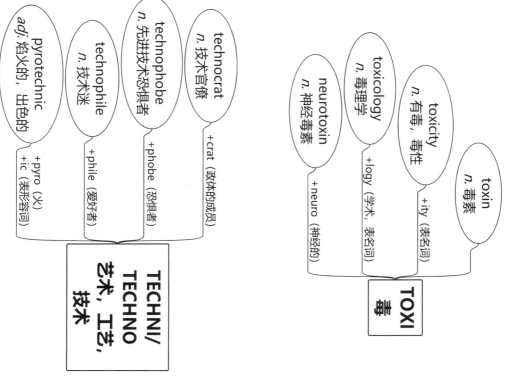
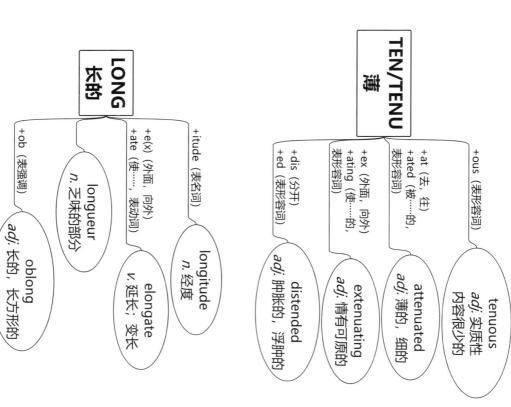

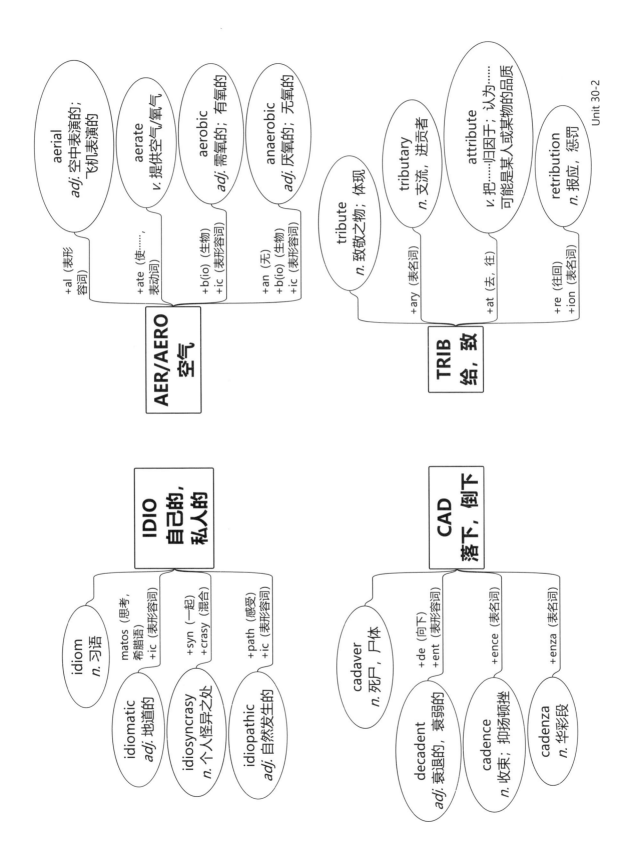

（贈品）